AF863667

Rapid Java™ Application Development Using Sun™ ONE Studio 4

Y. Daniel Liang
School of Computing
Armstrong Atlantic State University

An Alan R. Apt Book

Prentice Hall

Prentice Hall
Upper Saddle River, New Jersey 07458
http://www.prenhall.com

Library of Congress Cataloging-in-Publication Data

Liang, Y. Daniel.
Rapid Java application development using Sun ONE Studio 4 / Y. Daniel Liang.
p. cm.
ISBN 0-13-047378-2
1. Java (computer program language) 2. Application
software--Development. I. Title.
QA76.73J38 L533 2003
005.2--dc21 2002012891

Vice President and Editorial Director, ECS: *Marcia J. Horton*
Publisher: *Alan R. Apt*
Associate Editor: *Toni D. Holm*
Editorial Assistant: *Patrick Lindner*
Vice President and Director of Production and Manufacturing, ESM: *David W. Riccardi*
Executive Managing Editor: *Vince O'Brien*
Assistant Managing Editor: *Camille Trentacoste*
Production Editor: *Patty Donovan*
Director of Creative Services: *Paul Belfanti*
Creative Director: *Carole Anson*
Art Director: *Heather Scott*
Cover Designer: *Geoffrey Cassar*
Art Editor: *Xiaohong Zhu*
Manufacturing Manager: *Trudy Pisciotti*
Manufacturing Buyer: *Lynda Castillo*
Senior Marketing Manager: *Pamela Shaffer*
Marketing Assistant: *Barrie Reinhold*

Pearson Education, Inc.
Upper Saddle River, New Jersey

The author and publisher of this book have used their best efforts in preparing this book. These efforts include the development, research, and testing of the theories and programs to determine their effectiveness. The author and publisher make no warranty of any kind, expressed or implied, with regard to these programs or the documentation contained in this book. The author and publisher shall not be liable in any event for incidental or consequential damages in connection with, or arising out of, the furnishing, performance, or use of these programs.

Printed in the United States of America
10 9 8 7 6 5 4 3 2 1

ISBN 0-13-047378-2

Pearson Education Ltd., *London*
Pearson Education Australia Pty. Ltd., *Sydney*
Pearson Education Singapore, Pte. Ltd.
Pearson Education North Asia Ltd., *Hong Kong*
Pearson Education Canada, Inc., *Toronto*
Pearson Educacíon de Mexico, S.A. de C.V.
Pearson Education—Japan, *Tokyo*
Pearson Education Malaysia, Pte. Ltd.
Pearson Education, *Upper Saddle River, New Jersey*

To Samantha, Michael, and Michelle

PREFACE

When I began writing my first introductory Java text in the summer of 1996, only a few schools were teaching Java. Today, Java has become the programming language of choice for many schools. The incorporation of Java into the computer science curriculum has increased the need for an advanced Java text. This book covers the advanced Java features that are needed to support upper-level CS courses, such as software engineering, graphical user interface design, database programming, and distributed programming. It can be used as a text for advanced Java programming or as a supplement for upper-level CS courses. In addition, it is perfectly suitable for Java programmers who want to learn rapid application development techniques using *Sun ONE Studio 4* (formerly known as *Forte 4*).

In this book I introduce the concepts of JavaBeans, bean event models, model-view control, developing customized components, Swing components, creating custom layout managers, bean persistence, bound properties and constraint properties, bean introspection and customization, Java database programming, and enterprise programming using servlets, JSP, and remote method invocations. The promotion of rapid Java application development is the main thread of the book, however. Rapid application development, or RAD, is a software-development technology for developing programs efficiently and effectively. This technology has been successfully implemented in Visual Basic, Delphi, Power Builder, Oracle Developer 2000, and many other program-development tools. Using a RAD tool, projects can be developed quickly and efficiently with minimum coding. Projects developed using RAD are easy to modify and easy to maintain. The key elements in a RAD tool are the software components, such as buttons, labels, combo boxes, lists, check boxes, radio buttons, and menus. These components can be visually manipulated and tailored during design time in order to develop customized programs.

One of the central issues in software development is how to reuse programs effectively. Java is an object-oriented programming language that provides great flexibility, modularity, clarity, and reusability through method abstraction, class abstraction, and class inheritance. A Java program can be viewed as a collection of cooperating objects that are created during runtime. The JavaBeans technology is a significant extension and enhancement of the Java language that makes it possible for programmers to rapidly build applications by assembling objects and testing them during design time, thus making reuse of the software more productive.

To facilitate developing and managing Java programs, the book is aided by Sun ONE Studio, one of the best Java tools. Sun ONE Studio rapidly simplifies Java program development for maximum productivity. It provides a fully scalable, distributed, and cross-platform architecture for building reusable components. Sun ONE Studio provides a tightly integrated development environment that lets you visually design user interface and rapidly build applications using the Form Editor. Sun ONE Studio's Bean Pattern wizard makes it point-and-click easy to create JavaBeans components. Sun ONE Studio also contains many intelligent wizards that can be conveniently used to generate source code automatically.

Throughout the book there are numerous examples with step-by-step instructions that will guide you in creating reusable components and using them to assemble large practical applications. It is assumed that you are familiar with the basics of Java programming, including creating graphical user interfaces using Swing, exception handling, internationalization, multithreads, IO streams, and the Java Collections framework. These topics are covered in *Introduction to Java Programming with Sun ONE Studio 4* (Prentice Hall, 2002).

One of the major considerations in choosing Sun ONE Studio to teach rapid Java application development is the clarity of the generated source code. The source code generated by Sun ONE Studio Form Editor, and various wizards does not contain any proprietary code. Thus, the generated source code is easy to read and to maintain. With Sun ONE Studio, students can not only develop Java programs more productively, but can also learn advanced Java programming more effectively by following the source code.

Most of the examples in this book are Java applets. A main method is provided for each applet to enable it to run standalone. However, for the sake of brevity, the main method is not listed in source code in the text.

Note

Sun ONE Studio 4 Community Edition is sufficient for every chapter except Chapter 16, "Remote Method Invocation." Sun ONE Studio 4 CE does not support RMI. You have to use Sun ONE Studio 4 Enterprise Edition for this chapter.

Note

Sun ONE Studio is the new brand name for Forte. Forte is still a better known name. For convenience, this book will use Forte and Sun ONE Studio interchangeably.

Pedagogical Features of This Book

The philosophy of this book is "teaching by example and learning by doing." Basic features are explained by example so that you can learn by doing. The book uses the following elements to get the most out of the material:

- **Objectives** list what students learn from the chapter. This helps them to determine whether they have met the objectives after completing the chapter.
- **Introduction** opens the discussion with a brief overview of what to expect from the chapter.
- **Examples**, carefully chosen and presented in an easy-to-follow style, teach programming concepts. Each example is described, and includes the source code, a sample run, and an example review. The source code of the examples is contained in the companion CD-ROM. Almost all of the examples can run in two modes: standalone application or applets. Each program is complete and ready to be compiled and executed. The sample run of the program is captured from

the screen to give students a live presentation of the example. Reading these examples is much like entering and running them on a computer.

- **Chapter Summary** reviews the important subjects that students should understand and remember. It also helps students to reinforce the key concepts they have learned in the chapter.
- **Review Questions** help students to track their progress and evaluate their learning.
- **Programming Exercises** at the end of each chapter provide students opportunities to apply the skills on their own. The trick of learning programming is practice, practice, and practice. To that end, this book provides a large number of exercises.
- **Notes**, **Tips**, and **Cautions** are inserted throughout the text to offer students valuable advice and insight on important aspects of program development.

NOTE
Provides additional information on the subject and reinforces important concepts.

TIP
Teaches good programming style and practice.

CAUTION
Helps students steer away from the pitfalls of programming errors.

The Organization of This Book

Java is a comprehensive and powerful language with many evolving features. There is plenty of room for an advanced Java text. This book is centered on rapid Java application development. It is divided into five parts that, taken together, form a comprehensive course on rapid Java application development.

The early chapters introduce JavaBeans, which are the basis of rapid Java application development. Subsequent chapters apply RAD techniques to build comprehensive, robust, and useful GUI applications, database and client/server applications, Java servlets and JavaServer pages, and distributed applications, with step-by-step instructions.

Part I: Introduction to Forte and JavaBeans

The first part of the book begins with an introduction to Sun ONE Studio, presents the concept of JavaBeans, discusses the bean event model, introduces the model-view architectures, and teaches developing and using beans in rapid Java application development.

Chapter 1, "Getting Started with Forte," gives an overview of Forte's integrated development environment. You will learn how to develop Java programs with a variety of Forte wizards for creating projects, applications, applets, and classes, and how to compile and run programs.

Chapter 2, "Introduction to JavaBeans," introduces the concept of JavaBeans. This chapter explains the relationship between JavaBeans and Java RAD builder tools, and shows you how to write simple JavaBeans and visually manipulate the beans in Forte.

Chapter 3, "Bean Events," covers the Java event delegation model, inner classes, and anonymous inner classes. You will learn how to develop source beans and listener beans and how to associate the listener beans with the source beans in Forte.

Chapter 4, "Developing and Using Components," discusses the differences between developing beans and using beans in rapid Java application development. This chapter introduces the model-view architecture. You will learn how to use the Bean Pattern wizard to create properties and events, and the Package wizard to deploy applications and applets.

Part II: Rapid Application Development with Swing Components

The book's second part covers Swing components and their use in rapid Java application development. You will learn how to use a variety of Swing components to develop Java projects using Forte.

Chapter 5, "Swing Components," introduces the concept of Swing components and discusses the differences between lightweight components and heavyweight components. You will learn how to use various Swing components in rapid application development.

Chapter 6, "Containers and Layout Managers," introduces Swing containers and layout managers, examines the structure of Swing containers, and studies the layout managers provided in Forte. You will learn how to create custom layout managers and install them in Forte. The components `JTabbedPane` and `JSplitPane` are also covered in this chapter.

Chapter 7, "Menus, Toolbars, and Dialogs," introduces menus, popup menus, toolbars, `JOptionPane` dialogs, custom dialogs, `JColorChooser`, and `JFileChooser`. This chapter also teaches you how to use the Menu designer to visually design menus and popup menus.

Chapter 8, "Advanced Swing Components," shows how to use several advanced Swing components, such as `JList`, `JComboBox`, `JTable`, and `JTree`, in rapid application development. You will learn various data models, selection models, renderers, and editors for supporting these advanced components.

Part III: Bean Persistence, Introspection, and Customization

This part introduces the JavaBeans API. You will learn how to develop persistent beans, use bound and constraint properties, and create bean property editors.

Chapter 9, "Bean Persistence and Versioning," introduces object serialization, which is a built-in Java mechanism for persistently storing and restoring beans. You will learn how to use Sun's Beanbox, a tool for testing beans that can be used to verify bean persistence. You will also learn how to customize serialization and bean versioning.

Chapter 10, "Bound and Constraint Properties," introduces bound and constraint properties. A *bound property* of a component is one for which a property notification service is provided when the property changes. A *constraint property* allows the listener component to verify the property change to determine whether to accept or reject it. These properties are useful for creating custom property editors. They can be used to simplify the model-view components.

Chapter 11, "Bean Introspection and Customization," takes an in-depth look at how builder tools learn bean information through introspection. You will learn how to create and deploy custom editors.

Part IV: Java Database Programming

This part of the book is devoted to developing database projects using Java. You will learn the Java database programming interface, handle database metadata, and create and process SQL statements.

Chapter 12, "Introduction to Java Database Programming," begins with an overview of the JDBC interface for accessing relational databases from Java. A thorough introduction to the four types of JDBC drivers is presented through examples of the use of MS Access, Oracle, and JDataStore.

Chapter 13, "Advanced Java Database Programming," gives a comprehensive treatment of obtaining database metadata, and processing statements, prepared statements, and callable statements. You will also learn how to manipulate scrollable result sets.

Part V: Enterprise Java Programming

The book's final part introduces enterprise Java programming with Java servlets, JavaServer pages, and remote method invocation.

Chapter 14, "Servlets," introduces the technique of creating dynamic HTML contents using Java servlets. You will learn how to write server-side Java programs to access databases. You will also learn the techniques for session tracking.

Chapter 15, "JavaServer Pages," introduces the technique of creating JavaServer pages. You will learn JSP constructs, predefined variables, and directives. You will also learn how to use JavaBeans in JSP.

Chapter 16, "Remote Method Invocations," introduces remote method invocation, a technology that provides a framework for building distributed Java systems. You will learn how to use it to create useful distributed applications.

Prerequisites and Chapter Dependency Chart

The book has been used as a text for advanced Java programming and rapid Java application development and as a supplement for software engineering, graphical user interface design, database and client/server programming, distributed systems and network programming, and Web application development. Instructors have used this book in many creative ways. Here is a recommended sequence.

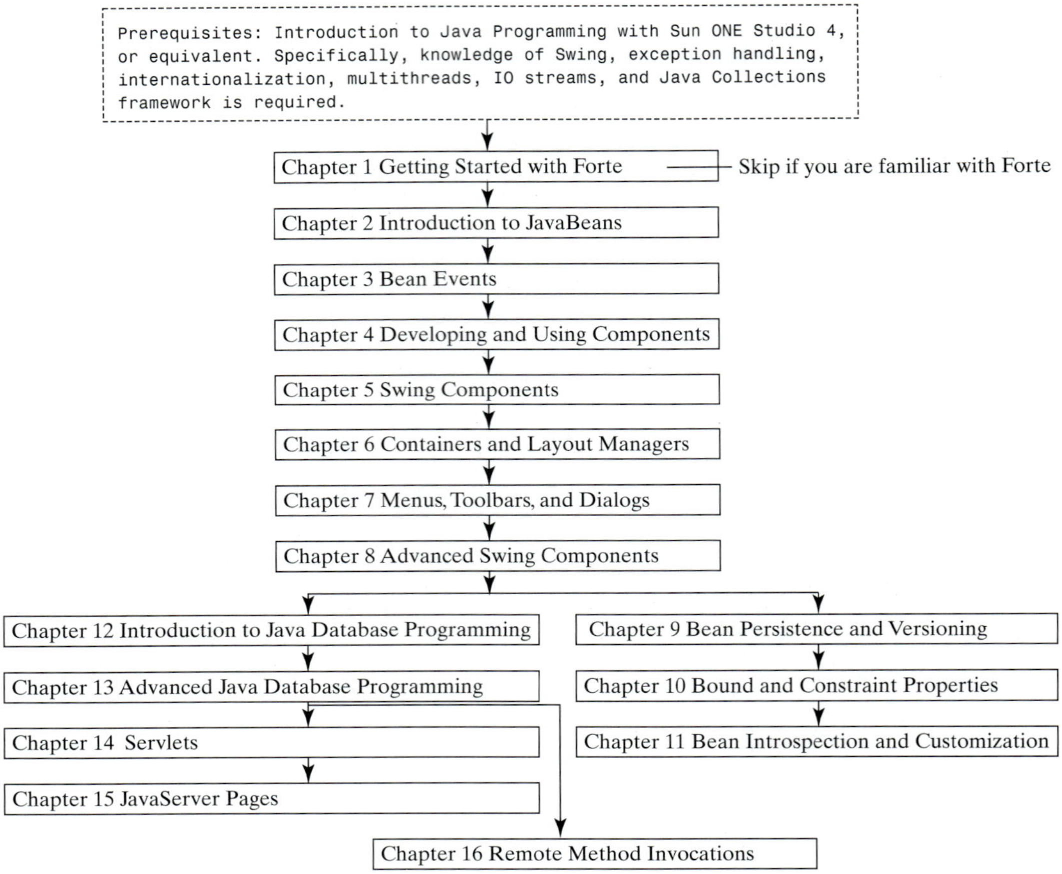

About the Author

Y. Daniel Liang is the author and editor of the Prentice Hall Liang Java Series. He has taught more than sixty Java courses to university students and corporate employees.

Dr. Liang is currently a Yamacraw professor of software engineering in the Department of Computer Science at Armstrong Atlantic State University, Savannah, Georgia. He can be reached at liangjava@yahoo.com.

Acknowledgments

I am grateful to the readers of my Java Series, both students and instructors, who offered comments, suggestions, bug reports, and praise. Their enthusiastic support contributed to the success of these books.

My students and colleagues at Armstrong Atlantic State University have been great supporters of this ongoing project. I would like to thank Ray Greenlaw for his support of incorporating Java into the CS curriculum, and for his tireless efforts to build a first-class undergraduate computer science program.

This edition has benefited from the previous editions of all my Java books. I would like to acknowledge the following people who contributed to the previous editions: Greg Geller, Ben Page, Michael Willig, Russell Minnich, Balaram Nair, Ben Stonebraker, Michael Sunderman, and Russell R. Colegrove.

For this edition, I would like to thank Alan Apt, Toni Holm, Patrick Lindner, Xiaohong Zhu, Jake Warde, and their colleagues at Prentice-Hall for organizing and managing this project, and Patty Donovan, Robert Milch, Dana Smith, and their colleagues at Pine Tree Composition for producing the book.

As always, I am indebted to my wife, Samantha, for love, support, and encouragement.

Supplements to the Book

Student CD-ROM

The student CD-ROM comes with the book. Its contents are listed below:

- Java™ 2 Software Development Kit Standard Edition Version 1.4.0 for Windows and Linux (Intel x86)
- Sun™ ONE Studio 4, Community Edition (formerly Forte™ for Java™ 4, Community Edition) for Windows and Linux
- Source code for the examples in the book

Companion Web Site for the Book

The companion Web site for the book can be accessed from **www.prenhall.com/liang/radft.html**. The Web site contains the following resources:

- Answers to review questions
- Java Programming Style and Documentation Guidelines
- Errata
- Useful Links
- FAQs

Instructor Resources

The Instructor's Resource CD-ROM is available for instructors using this book. It contains the following resource:

- Microsoft PowerPoint slides for lectures
- Solutions to all exercises. Students will have access to the solutions to the even-numbered exercises in the book's CD-ROM.

To obtain the Instructor's Resource CD-ROM, contact your Prentice Hall sales representative.

CONTENTS AT A GLANCE

TABLE OF CONTENTS

PART I

Introduction to Forte and JavaBeans

You have heard a lot about Java and its rapid application development capability. You are anxious to start rapid Java development. The first part of the book is a stepping stone that will prepare you to embark on the journey of rapid Java application development using Forte. You will begin to learn Forte, the concept of JavaBeans, and the bean event model, and how to develop and use beans in rapid Java application development.

CHAPTER 1

Getting Started with Forte

Objectives

- To get a quick start on Forte.
- To become familiar with the Forte IDE.
- To create and manage projects.
- To create classes, applications, and applets using the various template wizards.
- To learn how to use the Forte Form Editor to create user interfaces.
- To create and install Javadoc documents in Forte.
- To customize Forte environments.
- To get online help from Forte.

1.1 Introduction

Forte for Java is a powerful, extensible, integrated development environment (IDE) for developing Java programs. Since it is based on the NetBeans technology, which is an open-source, modular IDE, written in the Java language, Forte can run on any platform with a Java Virtual Machine.

Forte for Java is available in three editions: Forte for Java Community Edition, Forte for Java Enterprise Edition, and Forte for Java Mobile Edition.

- The Community Edition is ideal for beginners to learn the basics of Java programming. The Community Edition is free and included in the companion CD-ROM. This book teaches Java programming with the latest version, Forte Community Edition 4.0.
- The Enterprise Edition contains all the components in Community Edition, plus support for J2EE.
- The Mobile Edition is for developing applications for mobile devices.

Note
Forte 4 CE is sufficient for all the chapters except Chapter 16, "Remote Method Invocation." Forte 4 CE does not support RMI. You have to use Forte 4 Enterprise Edition for this chapter.

1.2 Getting Started with Forte

Let us assume that you have successfully installed Forte on your machine. Start Forte from Windows, Linux, or Solaris. The Forte main window appears, as shown in Figure 1.1.

Figure 1.1 *The Forte main window is the command center for the IDE.*

Note
To install Forte from the Student CD-ROM, please refer to Installing Forte at **www.prenhall.com/liang/radft.html**. I recommend that you follow this document when installing Forte so that your Forte IDE will match the screen shots in the book.

Note
The screen shots in this book are from Forte Community Edition. If you use Forte Enterprise Edition, your screen may look slightly different.

The Forte main window contains menus, toolbars, and four workspace tabs (Editing, GUI Editing, Running, and Debugging).

1.2.1 The Main Menu

The main menu is similar to that of other Windows applications and provides most of the commands you need to use Forte, including those for creating, editing, compiling, running, and debugging programs. The menu items are enabled and disabled in response to the current context.

1.2.2 The Toolbar

The toolbar provides buttons for several frequently used commands on the menu bar. The toolbars are enabled and disabled in response to the current context. Clicking a toolbar is faster than using the menu bar. For many commands, you also can use function keys or keyboard shortcuts. For example, you can save a file in three ways:

- Select *File, Save* from the menu bar.
- Click the "save" toolbar button ().
- Use the keyboard shortcut Ctrl+S.

TIP

You can display a label, known as *ToolTip*, for a toolbar button by pointing the mouse to the button without clicking.

1.2.3 Workspaces

A workspace is a collection of top-level windows that are pertinent to performing certain types of operations, such as debugging or editing. The workspace windows can be displayed from the workspace tabs or from the View menu.

1.2.4 Creating a Project

When you use Forte for the first time, a default project is opened. A project in Forte holds the information about the project, such as program files and IDE environment settings. You can use the default project or create your own project. For convenience, a new project will be created to hold all the examples in the book. Here are the steps in creating this project:

1. Choose *Project, Project Manager* to display the Project Manager, as shown in Figure 1.2.
2. Click *New* to display the Create New Project dialog box, as shown in Figure 1.3.

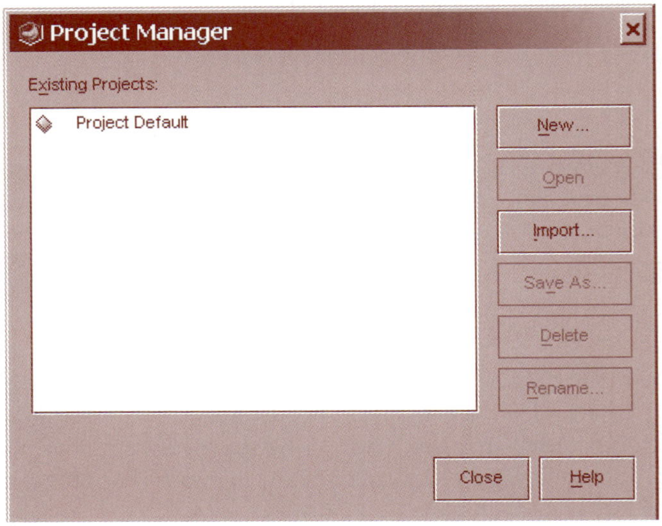

Figure 1.2 *You may create a new project, open or delete an existing project, rename a project, or import a project.*

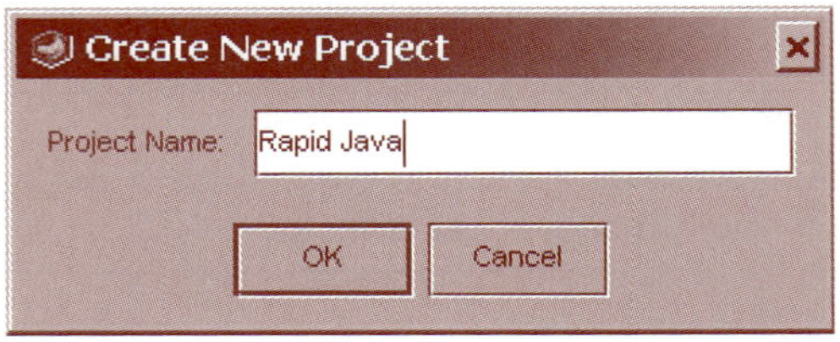

Figure 1.3 *You need to enter a new project name in the Create New Project dialog box.*

3. Type `RadBook` in the Project Name field and click *OK* to create the new project. The Explorer window is displayed, as shown in Figure 1.4. If it is not shown, choose *View*, *Explorer* from the main window.

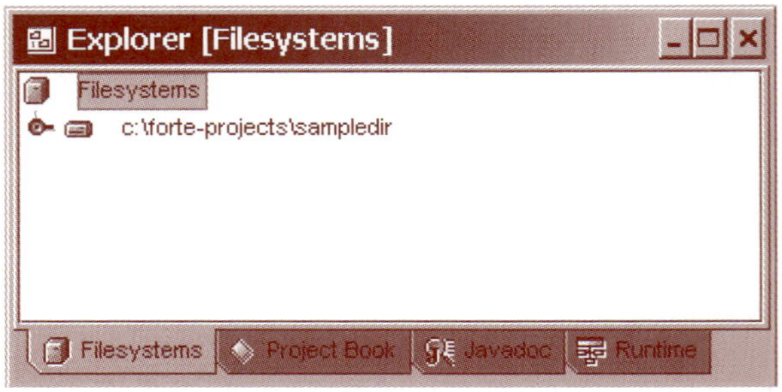

Figure 1.4 *The Explorer window lets you explore the packages, files, and objects in the project.*

Note
Figures 1.2 and 1.4 may look different on your screen if you have installed Forte differently.

The Explorer provides a tree view of packages, files, and other objects and provides a starting point for programming. You can browse files there or monitor running processes and debugging.

The Explorer has four tabs: Filesystems, Project, Javadoc, and Runtime. The *Filesystems* tab displays any file hierarchies you have mounted (and chosen to display) in the IDE.

Note
The use of the Project, Javadoc, and Runtime tabs will be introduced later. Forte is a powerful and sophisticated tool. You will learn many of its features throughout the book.

1.2.5 File Systems

By default, **c:\forte-projects\sampledir** is mounted in the project, as shown in Figure 1.4. You can unmount it as follows: (Skip this step if c:\forte-projects\sampledir is not mounted in your project.)

1. Select *c:\forte-projects\sampledir* in the Explorer and right-click the mouse button to display a context menu, as shown in Figure 1.5.

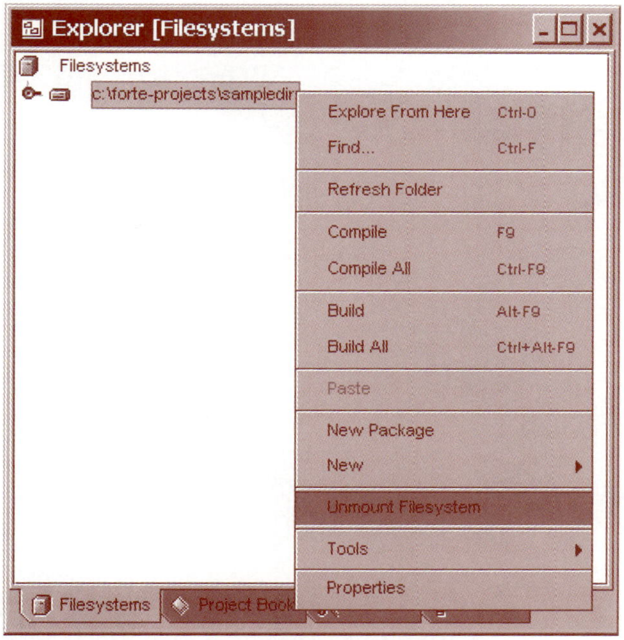

Figure 1.5 *You can unmount a directory from the context menu of the directory in the Explorer.*

2. Choose *Unmount Filesystem* in the context menu.

TIP

Many items in various windows in Forte have an associated context-sensitive popup menu. You can display a context menu by pointing to the item in the window and right-clicking the mouse button.

For convenience, I will create a new file system in **c:\radft** to hold all the examples in the book. Here are the steps to create it:

1. Right-click Filesystems to display a context menu, as shown in Figure 1.6. Choose *Mount*, *Local Directory* to display the New Wizard—Local Directory dialog box, as shown in Figure 1.7.

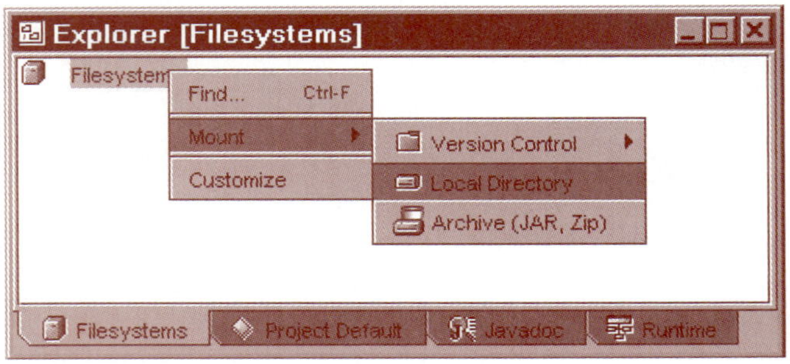

Figure 1.6 *You can mount a file system from the context menu of the Filesystems node in the Explorer.*

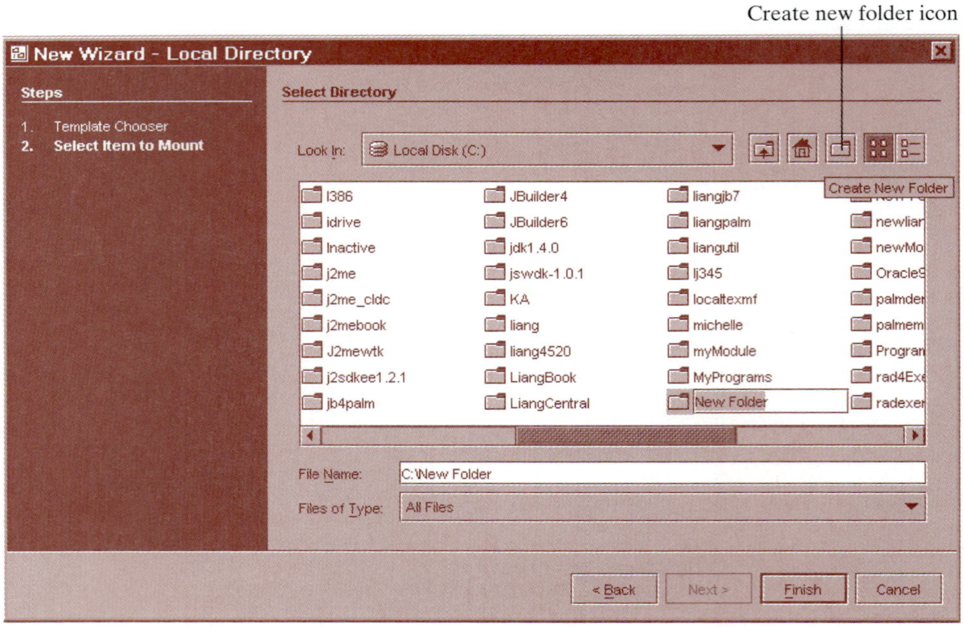

Figure 1.7 *You can create a new directory from the New Wizard—Local Directory dialog box.*

2. You may create a new directory from the operating system or within the New Wizard—Local Directory dialog box. To create it from the New Wizard—Local Directory dialog box, click the Create New Folder icon, as shown in Figure 1.7. This action creates a new folder named **New Folder**, as shown in Figure 1.7. Right-click on this item and rename it **radft**, as shown in Figure 1.8.

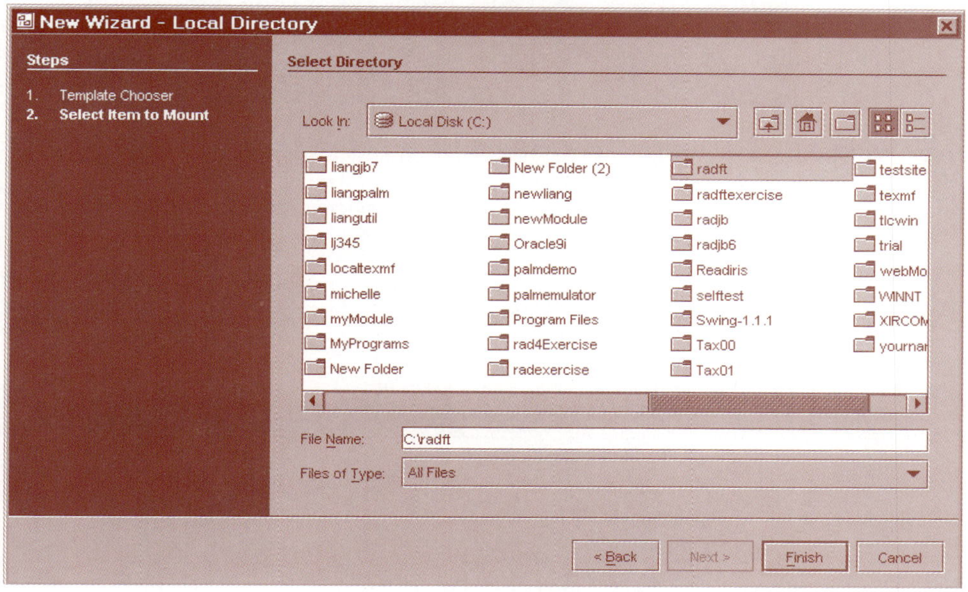

Figure 1.8 *You can mount an existing directory from the New Wizard—Local Directory dialog box.*

3. To mount the **c:\radft** folder, type `radft` in the File name field and click Mount, as shown in Figure 1.8.

TIP

You can work with objects in the Explorer using commands found on their contextual menus (displayed by right-clicking on the node) as well as on the menus in the main window.

1.2.6 Creating Packages and Files

All the examples in this book are grouped into packages, and the packages are placed under **c:\radft**. Here are the steps in creating a package named introdemo:

1. Right-click the *c:\radft* node in the Explorer to display a context menu. Choose *New*, *Java Package* to display the New Wizard—Java Package dialog box, as shown in Figure 1.9.

2. Type `introdemo` in the Name field and click *Yes* to add the package.

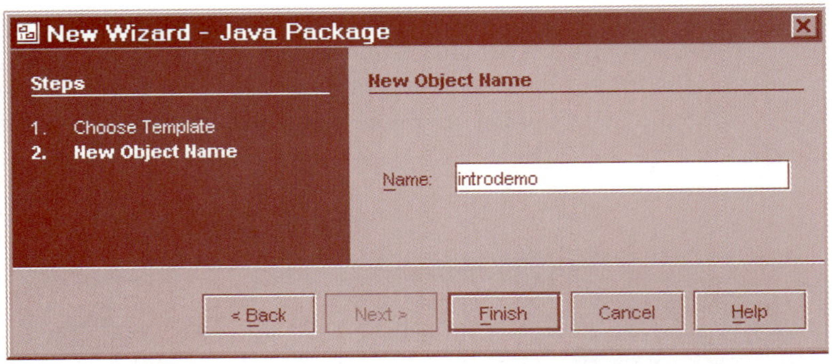

Figure 1.9 *You can create a new package using the Package wizard.*

Now you can create a simple program in package introdemo to display the message Welcome to Java:

1. Right-click *introdemo* in the Explorer to display a context menu. Choose *New*, *Classes*, *Class* (see Figure 1.10) to display the Class wizard, as shown in Figure 1.11.

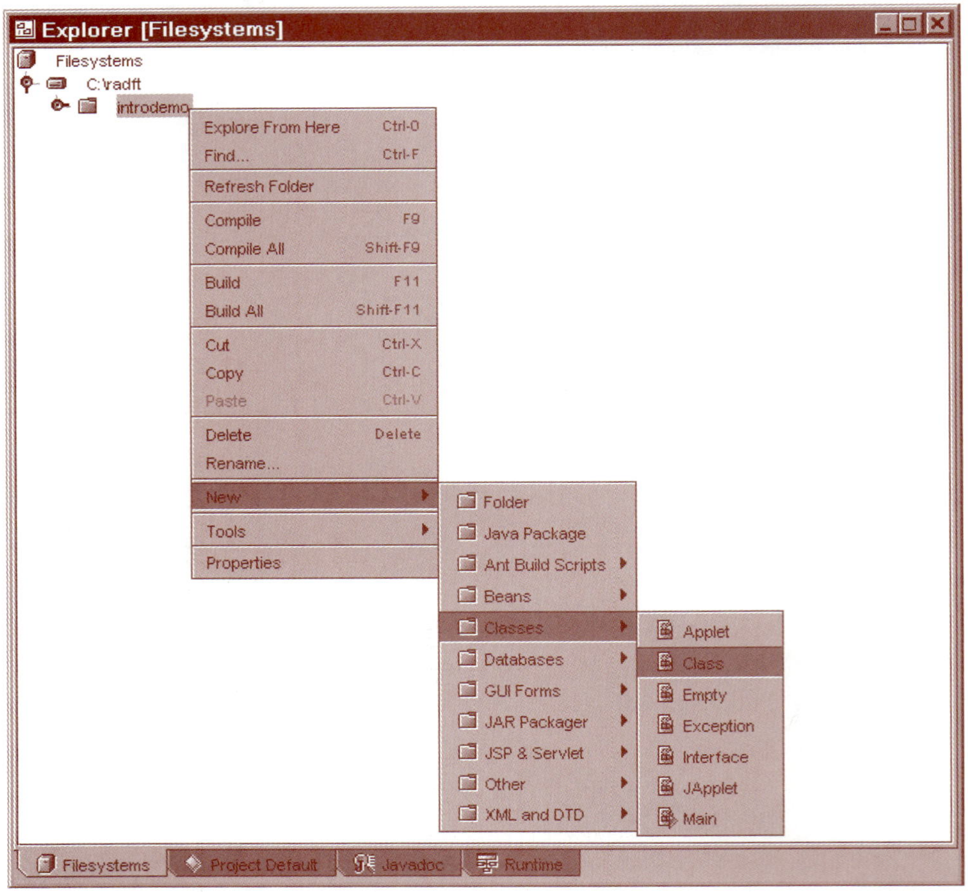

Figure 1.10 *You can create classes from the Explorer.*

Figure 1.11 *The Class wizard can be used to create a new class template.*

2. Type `Welcome` in the Name field and click *Finish* to create a template for Java class. Welcome now appears in the Explorer, and its source code is displayed in the Source Editor, as shown in Figure 1.12.

Figure 1.12 *A template for the Welcome class was created.*

3. Type the source code for the Welcome class in the Source Editor, as shown in Figure 1.13.

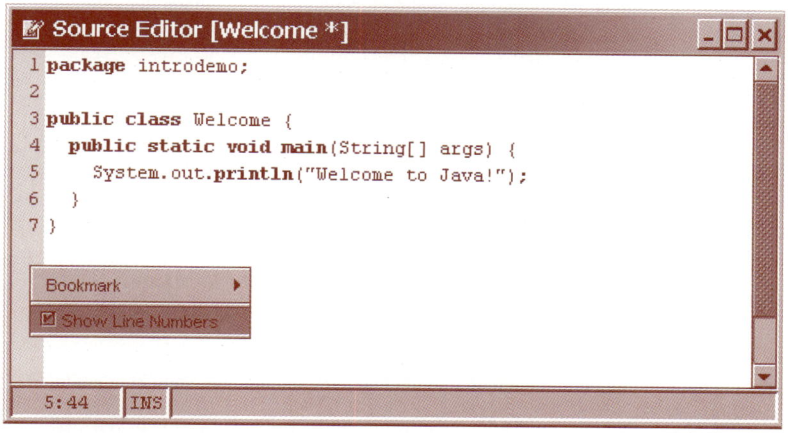

Figure 1.13 *The Source Editor window enables you to edit Java source code.*

Tip

To display line numbers in the Source Editor, right-click on the left margin in the Source Editor to display a context menu and check Show Line Numbers, as shown in Figure 1.13.

Note

You may also choose *New*, *Classes*, *Main* in the context menu of the node introdemo to create a class with a main method.

Note

As you type, the code completion assistance may automatically come up to give you suggestions for completing the code. For instance, when you type a dot (.) after System and pause for a second, Forte displays a popup menu with suggestions on how to complete the code, as shown in Figure 1.14. You can then select the appropriate item from the menu to complete the code.

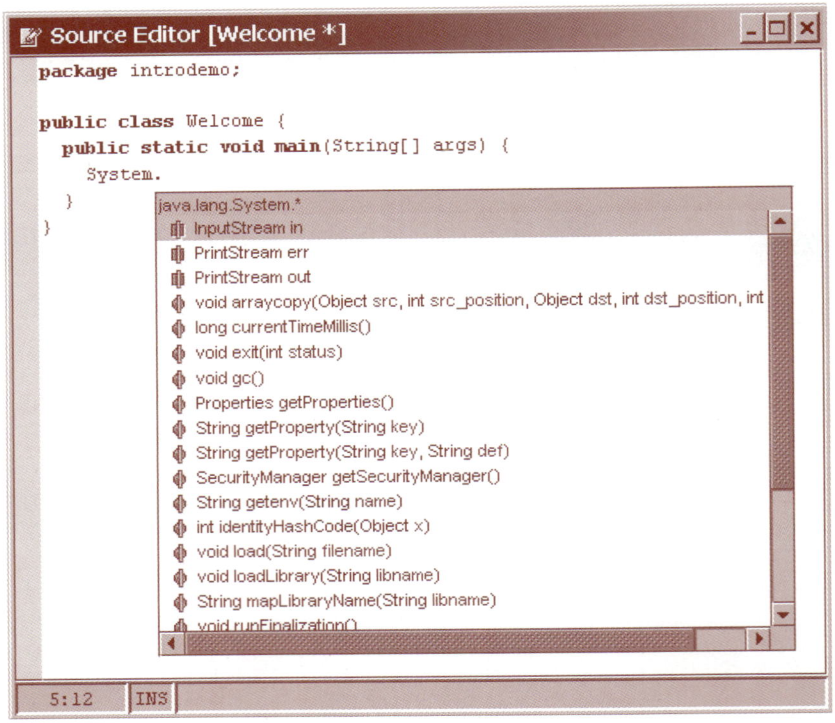

Figure 1.14 *The Code Completion popup menu is automatically displayed to help you complete the code.*

1.2.7 Compiling and Running a Java Program

To compile Welcome.java, use one of the following methods. (Be sure that the node Welcome.java is selected in the Explorer.)

- Choose *Build*, *Compile*, or press F9.
- Right-click *Welcome.java* to display a context menu and choose *Compile*.
- Click the *Build* toolbar button ( ).
- Right-click in the Source Editor for *Welcome.java* and choose *Compile*. The compilation status is displayed in the Output window, as shown in Figure 1.15. If there are no syntax errors, the bytecode file Welcome.class is generated.

Figure 1.15 *The compilation status is displayed in the Output window.*

Note

When you compile the file, it will be automatically saved.

Note

The icon for Java source code is . A Java source code may have an additional icon , which indicates that the file is not compiled. If the class has a main method, the icon is after the class is compiled.

Tip

You can find the descriptions of the node icons in the Explorer from Forte Help. Choose *Help*, *Contents* from the main window, and select *Core IDE Help*, *Filesystems and Objects*, *Managing Objects in the IDE*, *Node Icons* in the Explorer to display the descriptions for the icons, as shown in Figure 1.16.

Note

The package in Java corresponds to the directory in the file system. **introdemo** is also a directory under **radft**. The bytecode for the class Welcome is stored in the directory **introdemo**. The file structures for the examples in this book are shown in Figure 1.17. Welcome.java~ is the backup file for Welcome.java.

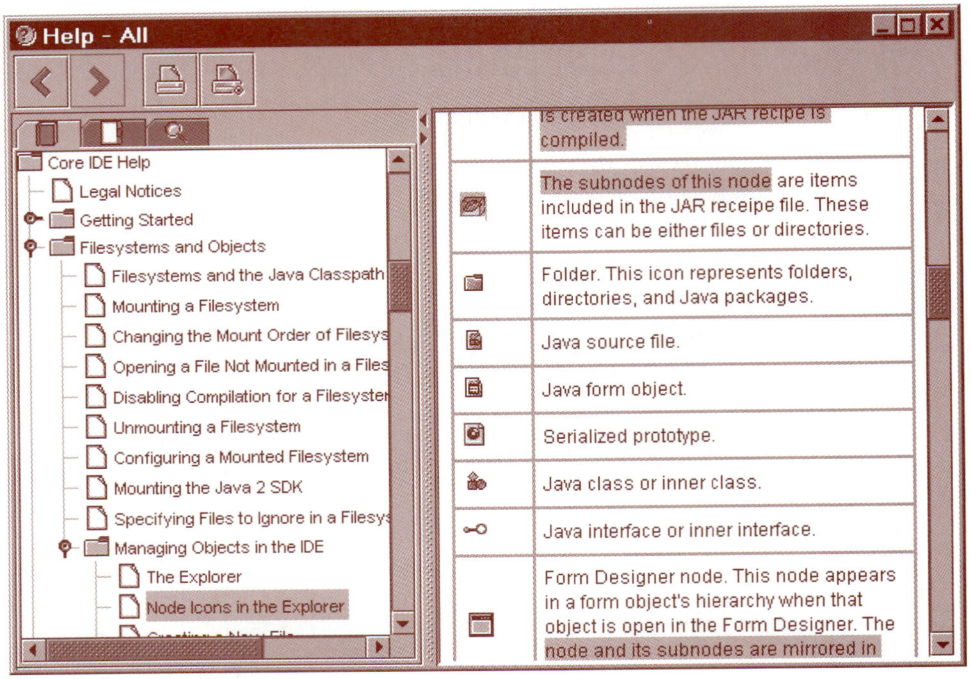

Figure 1.16 *You can find descriptions of node icons in the Explorer from Forte Help.*

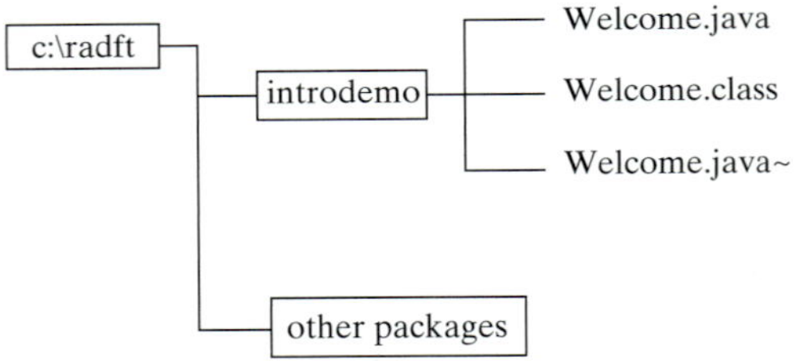

Figure 1.17 *Welcome.java and Welcome.class are placed in c:\radft\introdemo.*

1.2.8 Executing a Java Application

To run Welcome.class, use one of the following methods. (Be sure that Welcome.java is selected in the Explorer.)

- Choose *Build*, *Execute*, or press F6.
- Right-click *Welcome.java* to display a context menu and choose *Execute*.
- Click the *Execute* toolbar button (▷).
- Right-click in the Source Editor for *Welcome.java* and choose *Execute*.

When this program executes, Forte displays the output in the Output window, as shown in Figure 1.18.

Figure 1.18 *The execution result is shown in the Output window.*

NOTE
The Execute command invokes the Compile command if the program is not compiled or was modified after the last compilation.

TIP
If the Output window is not displayed, choose *View, Output Window* to display it.

1.3 Creating Java Applets

Forte provides a wizard for generating class templates that you can use to speed up your development of applications, applets, beans, dialogs, and so forth. You used this wizard to create the `Welcome` class in the preceding section. This section shows you how to create Java applets using the wizard. You will write an applet that adds two integers and displays the sum (see Figure 1.19).

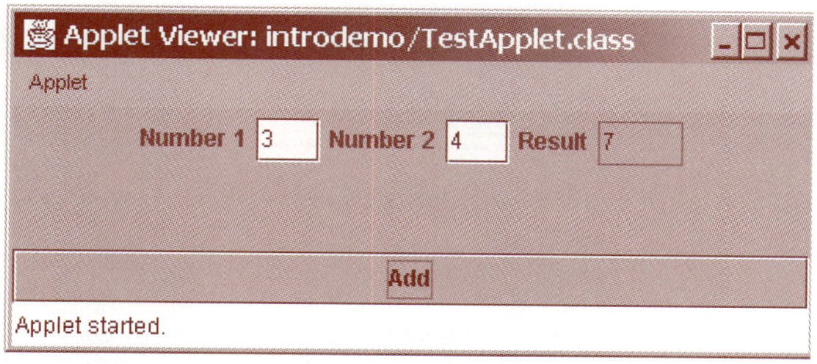

Figure 1.19 *The program adds the numbers from Number 1 and Number 2 and displays the result.*

Here are the steps to complete the project:

1. In the context menu of the introdemo node in the Explorer, choose *New, Classes, JApplet* (see Figure 1.20) to display the Swing applet wizard, as shown in Figure 1.21.

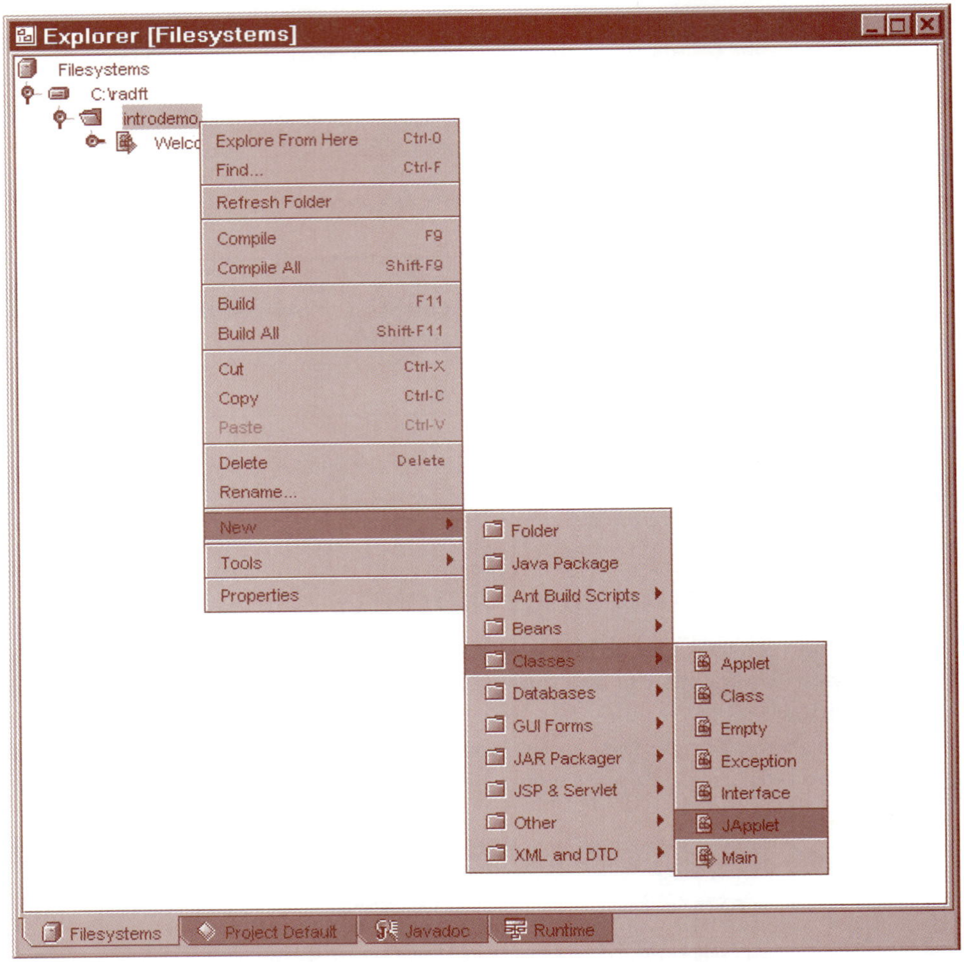

Figure 1.20 *You can start the Swing Applet wizard from the context menu of the package in the Explorer.*

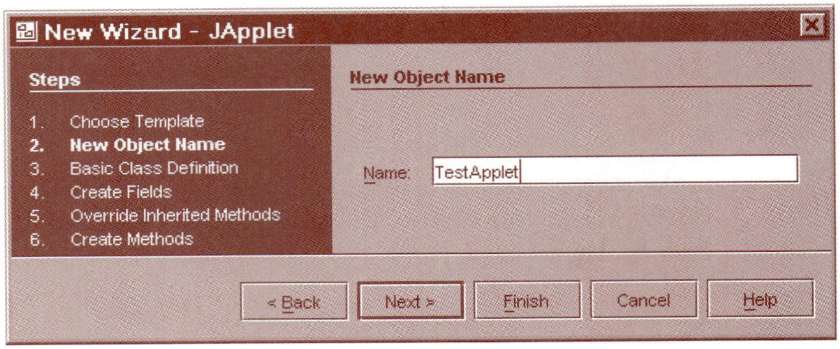

Figure 1.21 *You can create an applet using the Swing applet wizard.*

2. Enter `TestApplet` in the Name field and click *Finish* to create the template for the applet.

3. Type the code as shown in listing 1.1 in the Source Editor for TestApplet.java.

NOTE

The code that you manually typed is highlighted in the listing throughout the book. Coding style adopted in this book is summarized at **www.cs.armstrong.edu/liang/radft/codingstyle.html**.

```java
package introdemo;

import java.awt.*;
import java.awt.event.*;
import java.applet.*;
import javax.swing.*;

public class TestApplet extends JApplet implements ActionListener {
  // Declare three text fields
  private JTextField jtfNum1, jtfNum2, jtfResult;

  // Declare Add button
  private JButton jbtAdd;

  /** Initialize the applet */
  public void init() {
    this.setSize(new Dimension(400,300));

    // Place labels and text fields in a panel
    JPanel p1 = new JPanel();
    p1.setLayout(new FlowLayout());
    p1.add(new JLabel("Number 1"));
    p1.add(jtfNum1 = new JTextField(3));
    p1.add(new JLabel("Number 2"));
    p1.add(jtfNum2 = new JTextField(3));
    p1.add(new JLabel("Result"));
    p1.add(jtfResult = new JTextField(4));
    jtfResult.setEditable(false);  // Set it noneditable

    // Add the panel and the Add button in the frame
    this.getContentPane().add(p1, BorderLayout.CENTER);
    this.getContentPane().add(jbtAdd = new JButton("Add"),
      BorderLayout.SOUTH);

    // Register listener
    jbtAdd.addActionListener(this);
  }

  /** Handle add button action */
  public void actionPerformed(ActionEvent e) {
    int num1 =
      (Integer.valueOf(jtfNum1.getText().trim())).intValue();
    int num2 =
      (Integer.valueOf(jtfNum2.getText().trim())).intValue();
    int result = num1 + num2;

    // Display result
    jtfResult.setText(String.valueOf(result));
  }
}
```

Listing 1.1 *TestApplet.java*

4. In the context menu for the TestApplet node in the Explorer, choose *Execute* to run this applet. Forte automatically generates an HTML file for this applet, as shown in Figure 1.22. The applet is now displayed in the applet viewer, as shown in Figure 1.19.

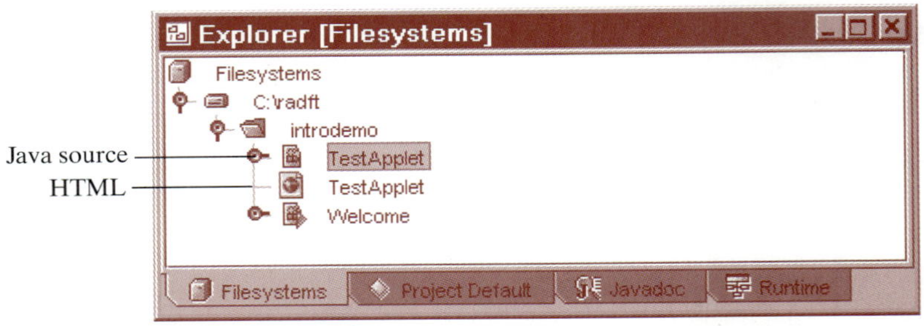

Figure 1.22 *The HTML file for the applet is automatically created upon first-time execution of the applet.*

Note
The applet can be viewed from Netscape 6 or Internet Explorer 6. To view applets from other browsers, such as IE 5.0 and Netscape 4.7, you have to use the Java Plug-In. Please see supplements for information on Java Plug-In, at **www.prenhall.com/liang/radft.html**.

1.3.1 Enabling Applets to Run Standalone

You can always run an applet standalone by providing a main method in the applet. For instance, you can add the following method in the `TestApplet` class to enable `TestApplet` to run standalone.

```
/** Main method */
  public static void main(String[] args) {
    TestApplet applet = new TestApplet();
    JFrame frame = new JFrame();
    frame.setDefaultCloseOperation(JFrame.EXIT_ON_CLOSE);
    frame.setTitle("TestApplet");
    frame.getContentPane().add(applet, BorderLayout.CENTER);
    applet.init();
    frame.setSize(400,320);
    Dimension d = Toolkit.getDefaultToolkit().getScreenSize();
    frame.setLocation((d.width - frame.getSize().width) / 2,
      (d.height - frame.getSize().height) / 2);
    frame.setVisible(true);
  }
```

To run TestApplet standalone from Forte, follow the steps below:

1. Choose *Properties* from the context menu of TestApplet in the Explorer to display the Properties dialog box for TestApplet, as shown in Figure 1.23.

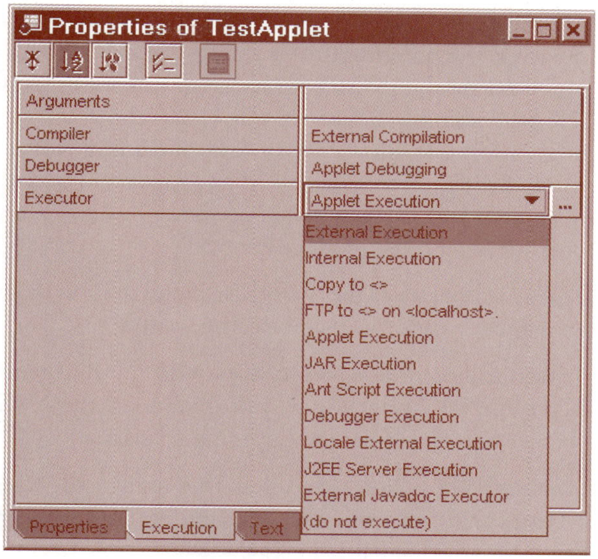

Figure 1.23 *You need to set External Execution for the Executor in order to run the applet standalone from Forte.*

2. Select External Execution in the Executor field from the Execution tab in the dialog box.

3. In the context menu for the TestApplet node in the Explorer, choose *Execute* to run this applet standalone, as shown in Figure 1.24.

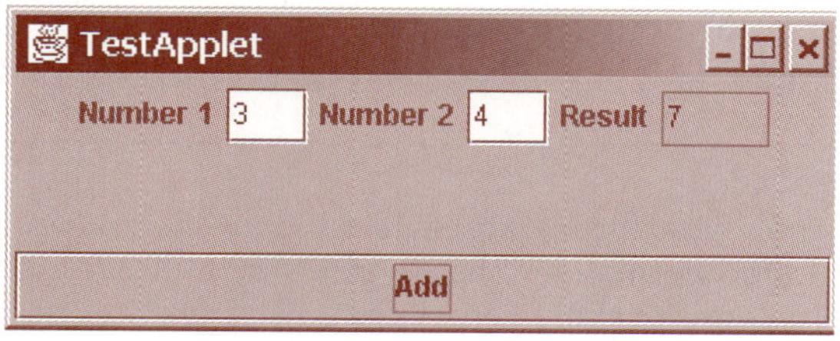

Figure 1.24 *The* `TestApplet` *class runs standalone from the main method.*

1.4 Designing User Interfaces Using the Form Editor

Forte provides the Form Editor for visually designing and programming Java classes. This enables you to quickly and easily assemble the elements of a user interface (UI) for a Java application or applet. You can construct the UI with various building blocks chosen from the component palette that contains such components as buttons, text areas, lists, dialogs, and menus. Then you set the values of the component properties and attach event-handler code to the component events, telling the program how to respond to UI events.

Forte's Form Editor makes programming in Java easier and more productive. No tools, however, can accomplish everything you need. You have to modify the program produced by the tools. Thus, it is imperative to know the basic concept of Java GUI programming before starting to use the visual tools. This book assumes that you have a basic knowledge of Java, including creating graphical user interfaces using Swing, exception handling, internationalization, multithreads, IO streams, and the Java Collections framework. Now you can use the Form Editor to make programming more productive.

This section demonstrates the use of visual design tools to create the same program that you manually coded in the preceding section.

Forte's Form Editor is designed to work with the class templates created from the wizards. To use the Form Editor, you should use the AWT Forms wizard or the Swing Forms wizard to create AWT or Swing classes.

You wrote the code to create the UI in TestApplet.java. Now you will learn how to use the Form Editor to create the user interface in TestUIApplet.java. The steps to complete the example are listed below:

1. In the context menu for the introdemo package in the Explorer, choose *New, GUI Forms, JApplet* (see Figure 1.25) to display the JApplet Form wizard, as shown in Figure 1.26.
2. Type `TestUIApplet` in the Name field and click Finish to create the form, as shown in Figure 1.26. You will see the Form Editor window displayed in Figure 1.27. (If the form is not displayed, click the GUI Editing workspace tab in the main window.) This window presents the design-time view of the form. If it is not shown, click the GUI Editing tab in the Workspace tabs section of the main window. The generated source code is shown in Figure 1.28.

NOTE

The GUI Form wizard generates a .java file for the source code and a .form file to store form information. The .form file is an XML text file. Whenever you change the form from the Form Editor, Forte updates the .java file and .form file. Forte uses the information in the .form file to reconstruct the form at design time. The .form file is not used at runtime.

NOTE

The Form Editor contains the component palette, form pane, form tree, and component inspector. The *component palette* contains numerous components grouped in seven tabs. These components are used for rapid Java application development. The *form pane* contains the GUI form. The *form tree* enables you to browse the components in the form in a hierarchic tree. The component inspector enables you to view and edit the properties of the component selected in the form.

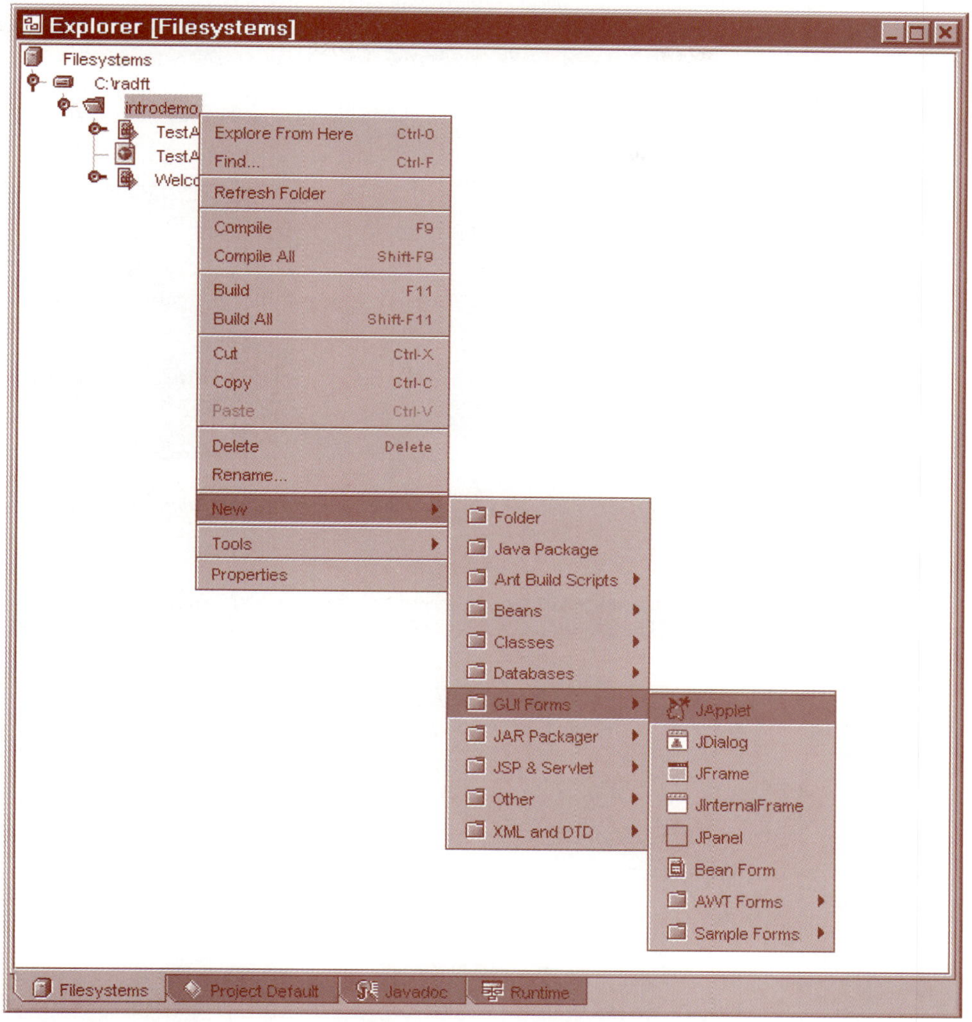

Figure 1.25 *You have to use the appropriate form wizards to create the templates for visual designing.*

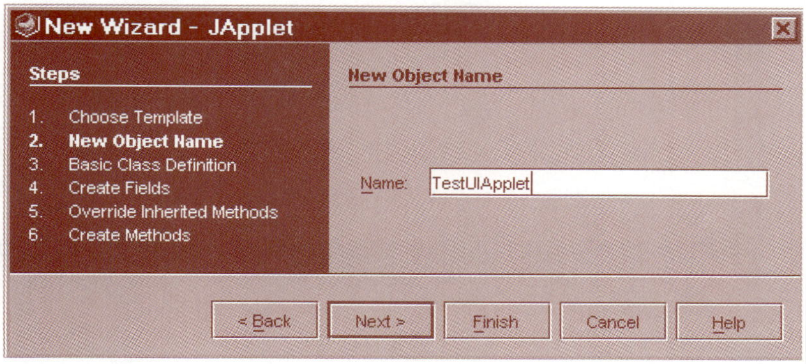

Figure 1.26 *The JApplet Form wizard enables you to create a Swing form for applet.*

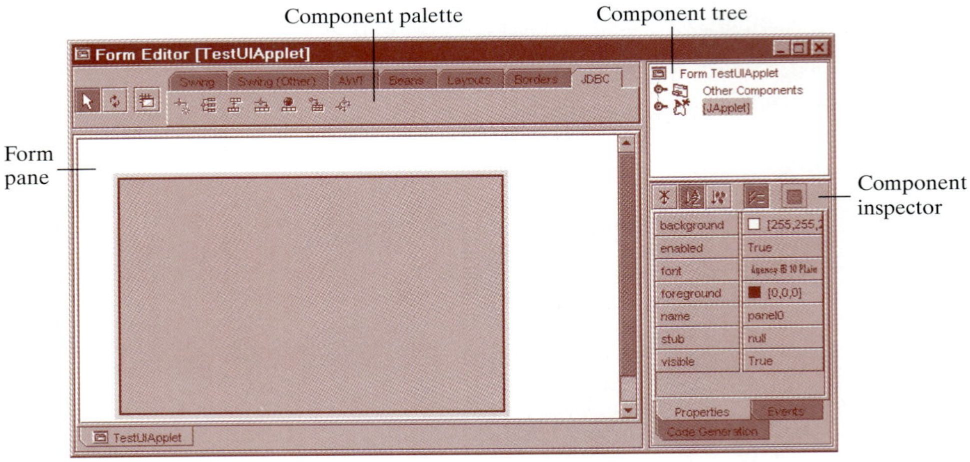

Figure 1.27 *The Form Editor enables you to create user interfaces using components from the component palette.*

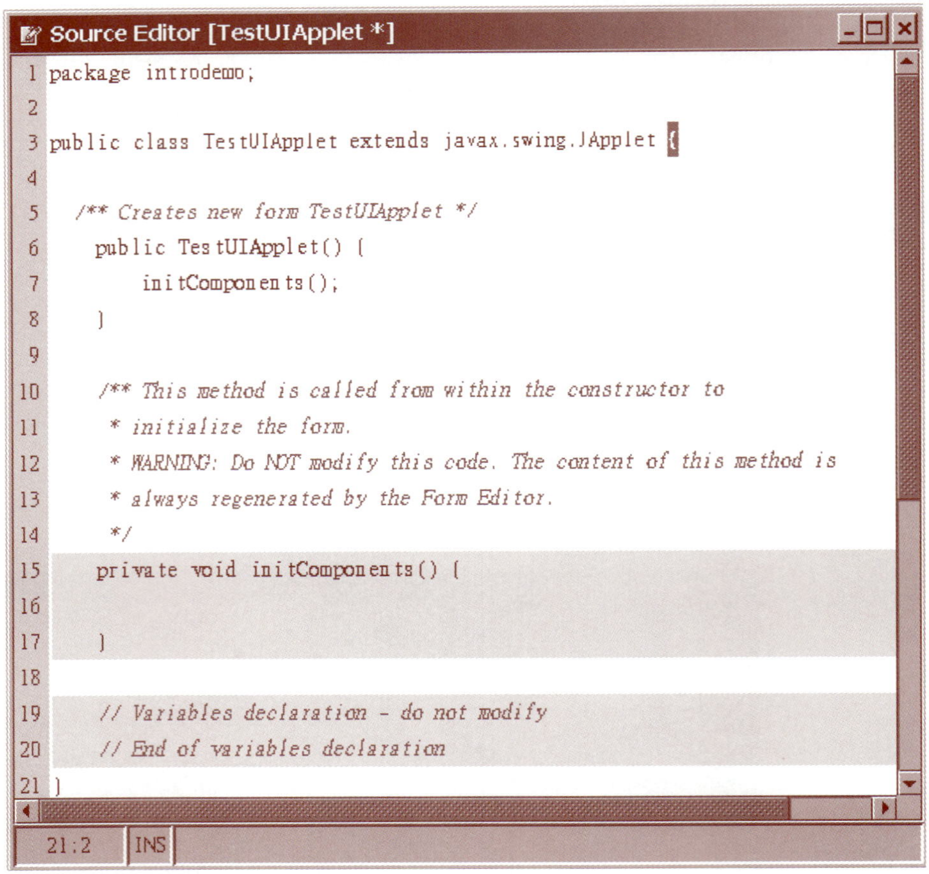

Figure 1.28 *Forte creates a form template for the applet.*

3. Start to create the user interface. Click the `JButton` icon in the component palette (this icon is the second in the Swing tab). Drop it to the south of the form, as shown in Figure 1.29. This action causes Forte to create an instance of `JButton` named `jButton1` and place it in the south of the applet's content pane. You can view the components in the form in the component inspector. You can view and modify the properties, events, layout, and code in the content pane. The Properties tab displays frequently used properties for the component, and the Other Properties tab displays other properties. Figure 1.29 displays the frequently used properties for `jButton1`, and Figure 1.30 displays other properties.

Figure 1.29 *An instance of* `javax.swing.JButton` *was added in the south of the applet's content pane.*

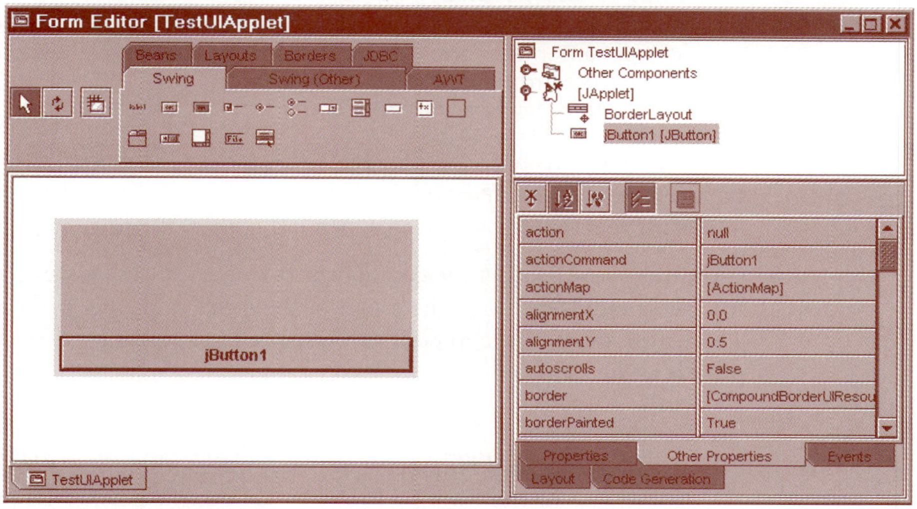

Figure 1.30 *The Other Properties tab displays less frequently used properties for the selected component in the form.*

TIP

If `jButton1` is not in the north of the applet, you can set it in the Layout tab of the content pane for `jButton1` in the component inspector, as shown in Figure 1.31.

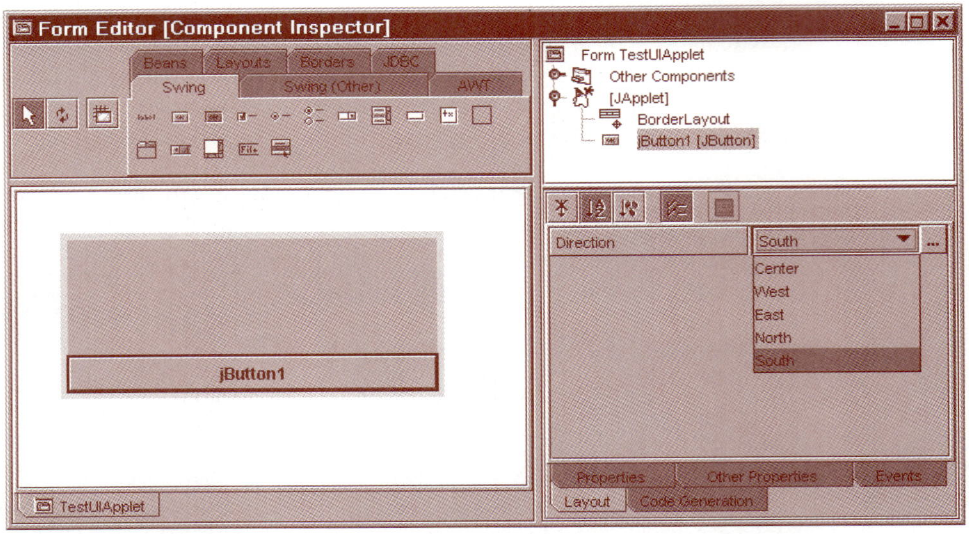

Figure 1.31 *You can set the direction of component in a container of the* `BorderLayout`.

NOTE

As you create components and modify their properties, the source code is generated and modified. The source code generated by Forte in the `initComponents` method cannot be modified in the Source Editor.

TIP

To delete a component in the form, choose *Delete* from the context menu of the component in the form window or the form tree.

4. In the component inspector for `jButton1`, set the `text` property to Add. In the context menu for `jButton1` in the component inspector, choose *Rename* to rename `jButton1` to `jbtAdd`, as shown in Figure 1.32.

5. Click the `JPanel` icon in the component palette (this icon is the eleventh in the Swing tab). Drop it to the center of the form, as shown in Figure 1.33. This action causes Forte to create an instance of `JPanel` named `jPanel1` and place it in the center of the applet's content pane.

6. Create labels and text fields in `jPanel1`.

   6.1. To create the label Number 1 in `jPanel1`, click the `JLabel1` icon, which is the first in the Swing tab of the component palette. Drop it into

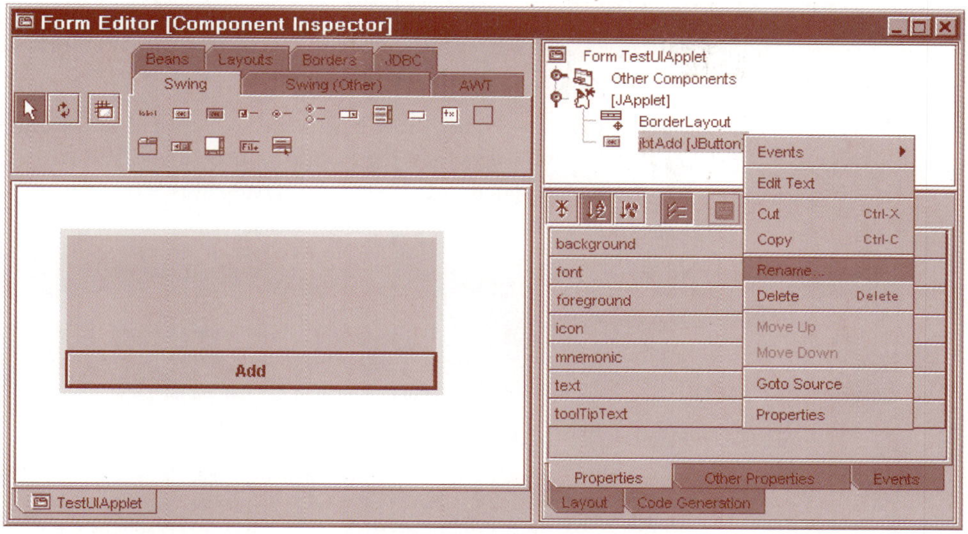

Figure 1.32 *You can rename an object in the form.*

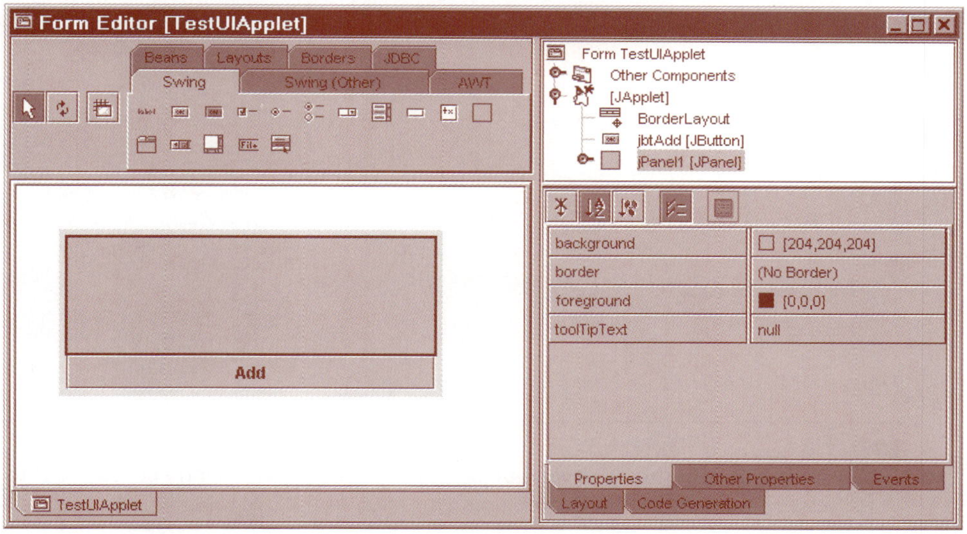

Figure 1.33 *An instance of JPanel is dropped to the form.*

`jPanel1` in the form. This action creates a label named `jLabel1` in `jPanel1`. In the component inspector for `jLabel1`, set the `text` property to Number 1. In the context menu for `jLabel1` in the form tree, choose *Rename* to rename `jLabel1` to `jlblNum1`.

6.2. To place a text field in `jPanel1`, click the `JTextField` icon, which is the ninth in the Swing page of the component palette, and drop it into `jPanel1` after the label Number 1. This action creates a `JTextField` named `jTextField1` in `jPanel1`. In the component inspector for `jTextField1`, set the `column` property to 4 and the `text` property to empty, and rename the object `jtfNum1`.

6.3. Similarly, you can create a label Number 2, a text field for Number 2, a label Result, and a text field for Result in `jPanel1`, as shown in Figure 1.34. Name the labels `jlblNum2` and `jlblResult` and the text fields `jtfNum2` and `jtfResult`.

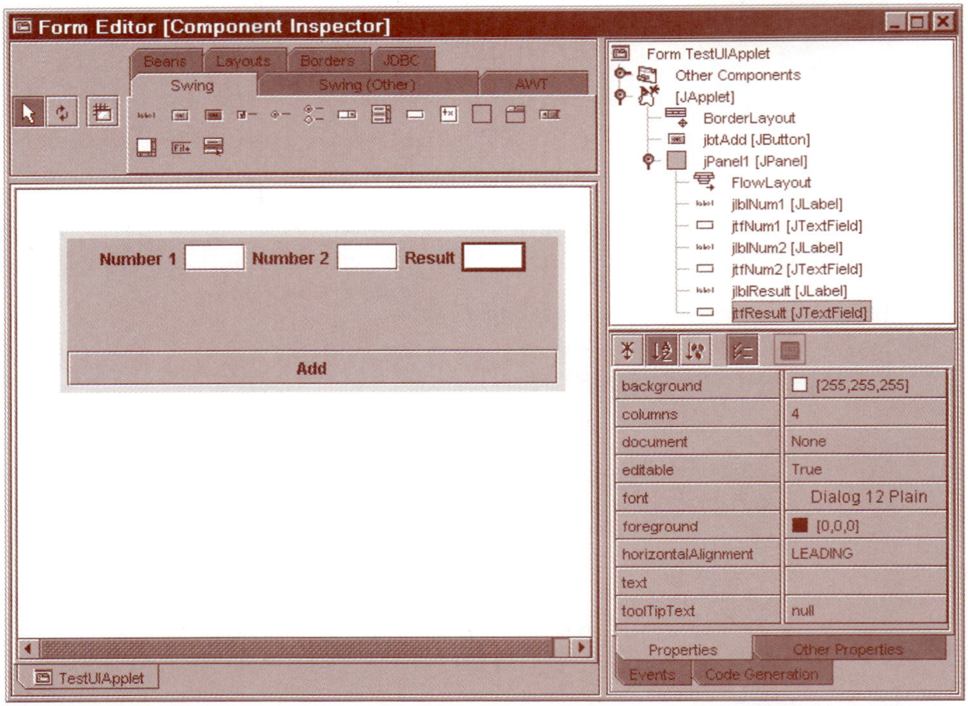

Figure 1.34 *The labels and text fields were added to* `jPanel1`.

TIP

For safety, you should save your work frequently by choosing *File, Save All* to save all the files before proceeding.

TIP

Forte also allows you to change the attributes of the layout manager from the component inspector. For instance, if you want to change the attributes in the `FlowLayout` manager in `jPanel1`, select the `FlowLayout` node in the component tree, as shown in Figure 1.35. You can now view and modify the properties `alignment`, `horizontalGap`, and `verticalGap`. You can also change the layout for a container in the component tree. To do so, choose *Set Layout* from the context menu of the layout manager in the component tree, as shown in Figure 1.36.

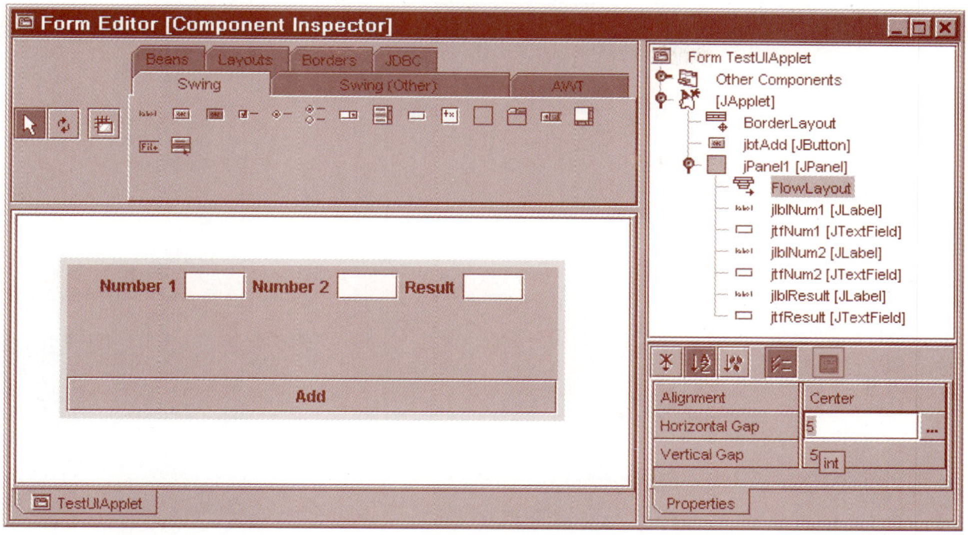

Figure 1.35 *You can use the component inspector to change the attributes of a layout manager.*

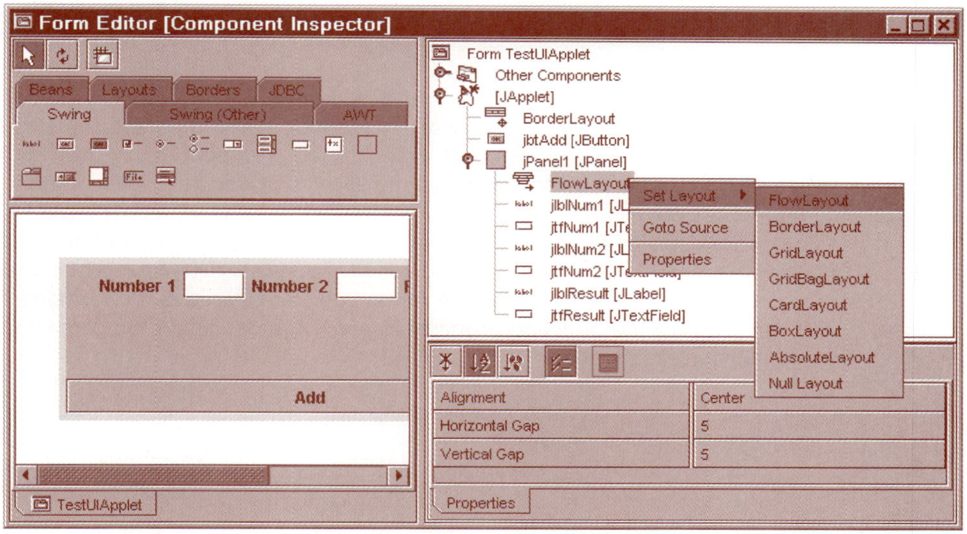

Figure 1.36 *You can change the layout manager from the context menu of the layout manager node in the component tree.*

TIP

If you double-click a visual component in the component tree, the component becomes the top-level component in the form pane. For instance, if you double-click `jPanel1` in the component tree, `jPanel1` becomes the top-level component in the form pane, as shown in Figure 1.37. If you double-click the TestUIApplet node in the component tree, TestUIApplet becomes the top-level component in the form pane.

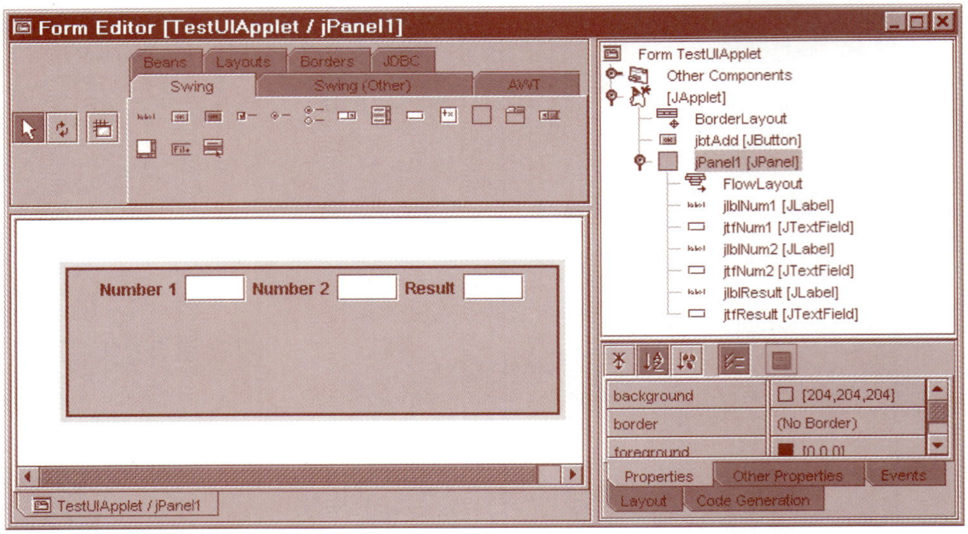

Figure 1.37 *Double-clicking* `jPanel1` *in the component tree causes* `jPanel1` *to become the top-level component in the form pane.*

TIP

To add components into a container of `BorderLayout`, first add the components to the four sides (East, West, North, and South), and then add the component to the center. This makes it easy to place components in the right position. If you add a component to the center first and then add another component to the container, the other component may be wrongly placed inside the centered component. Another way to circumvent this problem is to first set the layout of the component to `AbsoluteLayout`, then change the layout back to `BorderLayout` after all the components are placed in the container. You can then set the direction property for each component in the container to an appropriate direction.

7. Now that you have created the user interface, you are ready to implement the code for handling the Add button action. Use one of the following two approaches to generate the even handling code:

   - Double-click the Add button in the form.
   - In the Events page of for `jbtAdd` in the component inspector, choose *jbtAddActionPerformed* in the value field of `actionPerformed` and press Enter.

   Either of the above actions will cause Forte to generate the following code:

   ➤ A listener was created and registered with `jbtAdd` using the anonymous adapter, as follows.

```
jbtAdd.addActionListener(new java.awt.event.ActionListener() {
  public void actionPerformed(java.awt.event.ActionEvent evt) {
    jbtAddActionPerformed(evt);
  }
});
```

- ➤ The method `jbtAddActionPerformed` for handling the action event is created. You need to fill in the code to carry out the actual action.

8. Implement `jbtAddActionPerformed` using the same code as in the `actionPerformed` method in TestApplet.java in the preceding section. The complete code for TestUIApplet.java is shown in Listing 1.2.

```
package introdemo;

public class TestUIApplet extends javax.swing.JApplet {
  /** Creates new form TestUIApplet */
  public TestUIApplet() {
    initComponents();
  }

  /** This method is called from within the constructor to
   * initialize the form.
   * WARNING: Do NOT modify this code. The content of this method is
   * always regenerated by the Form Editor.
   */
  private void initComponents() {
    jbtAdd = new javax.swing.JButton();
    jPanel1 = new javax.swing.JPanel();
    jlblNum1 = new javax.swing.JLabel();
    jtfNum1 = new javax.swing.JTextField();
    jlbNum2 = new javax.swing.JLabel();
    jTextField2 = new javax.swing.JTextField();
    jLabel3 = new javax.swing.JLabel();
    jTextField3 = new javax.swing.JTextField();

    jbtAdd.setText("Add");
    jbtAdd.addActionListener(new java.awt.event.ActionListener() {
      public void actionPerformed(java.awt.event.ActionEvent evt) {
        jbtAddActionPerformed(evt);
      }
    });

    getContentPane().add(jbtAdd, java.awt.BorderLayout.SOUTH);
    jPanel1.setLayout(new java.awt.FlowLayout(
      java.awt.FlowLayout.CENTER, 10, 5));

    jlblNum1.setText("Number 1");
    jPanel1.add(jlblNum1);
    jtfNum1.setColumns(4);
    jPanel1.add(jtfNum1);
    jlbNum2.setText("Number 2");
    jPanel1.add(jlbNum2);
    jTextField2.setColumns(4);
    jPanel1.add(jTextField2);
    jLabel3.setText("Result");
    jPanel1.add(jLabel3);
    jTextField3.setColumns(5);
    jPanel1.add(jTextField3);
    getContentPane().add(jPanel1, java.awt.BorderLayout.CENTER);
  }

  private void jbtAddActionPerformed(
    java.awt.event.ActionEvent evt) {
    int num1 =
      (Integer.valueOf(jtfNum1.getText().trim())).intValue();
    int num2 =
      (Integer.valueOf(jtfNum2.getText().trim())).intValue();
```

Listing 1.2 *TestUIApplet.java*

```
56      int result = num1 + num2;
57
58      // Display result
59      jtfResult.setText(String.valueOf(result));
60    }
61
62    // Variables declaration - do not modify
63    private javax.swing.JButton jbtAdd;
64    private javax.swing.JPanel jPanel1;
65    private javax.swing.JLabel jlblNum1;
66    private javax.swing.JTextField jtfNum1;
67    private javax.swing.JLabel jlbNum2;
68    private javax.swing.JTextField jtfNum2;
69    private javax.swing.JLabel jlblResult;
70    private javax.swing.JTextField jtfResult;
71    // End of variables declaration
72 }
```

Listing 1.2 *continued*

All the code in TestUIApplet.java was automatically generated except the body of the `jbtAddActionPerformed` method. The content of the `initComponents` method is generated and modified by the Form Editor. You cannot change it manually. The Form Editor enables you to rapidly develop Java programs with minimum coding. All the components in the component palette are JavaBeans components. JavaBeans provides the foundations for rapid application development in Java. The rest of the book is centered on creating JavaBeans components and using the beans in rapid application development.

NOTE

The Swing applet generated in Forte contains a default constructor that invokes the `initComponents` method (Lines 6–9). When the applet is started from the applet viewer or Web browser, an instance of the applet is created using the default constructor, so the `initComponents` method is invoked too. The applet does not contain the `init` method. The `init` method is needed if you want to pass parameters from an HTML to the applet.

TIP

If the Form Editor is not displayed, click the GUI Editing workspace tab in the main window.

1.4.1 Enabling TestUIApplet to Run Standalone

To enable TestUIApplet to run standalone, add the following main method:

```
/** Main method */
  public static void main(String[] args) {
    TestUIApplet applet = new TestUIApplet();
    JFrame frame = new JFrame();
    frame.setDefaultCloseOperation(javax.swing.JFrame.EXIT_ON_CLOSE);
    frame.setTitle("TestUIApplet");
    frame.getContentPane().add(applet, java.awt.BorderLayout.CENTER);
    frame.setSize(400,320);
    java.awt.Dimension d =
      java.awt.Toolkit.getDefaultToolkit().getScreenSize();
```

```
    frame.setLocation((d.width - frame.getSize().width) / 2,
      (d.height - frame.getSize().height) / 2);
    frame.setVisible(true);
  }
```

To run it standalone from Forte, set the Executor field to External Execution in the Properties dialog box of TestUIApplet, as shown in Figure 1.23.

NOTE
Most of the examples in the book will be Java applets with a main method, so you can run the programs either as applets or applications. For brevity, the main method will not be listed in the book, but it will be included in each applet in the student CD-ROM. Some of the screen shots are for the applets that run standalone.

1.5 Customizing Forte IDE Options

Forte allows you to customize your development environment by changing the IDE options. You can create, delete, and change toolbars, menus, and workspaces. You can add an object to the component palette and then use that object in visual design. You can look at files in the Source Editor side-by-side instead of in separate tabbed panes, and you can change the Source Editor's keyboard shortcut assignments.

To set the IDE options, choose *Tools*, *Options* to display the Options dialog box, as shown in Figure 1.38. The dialog box is a split pane, with the navigation pane on the left and the content pane on the right.

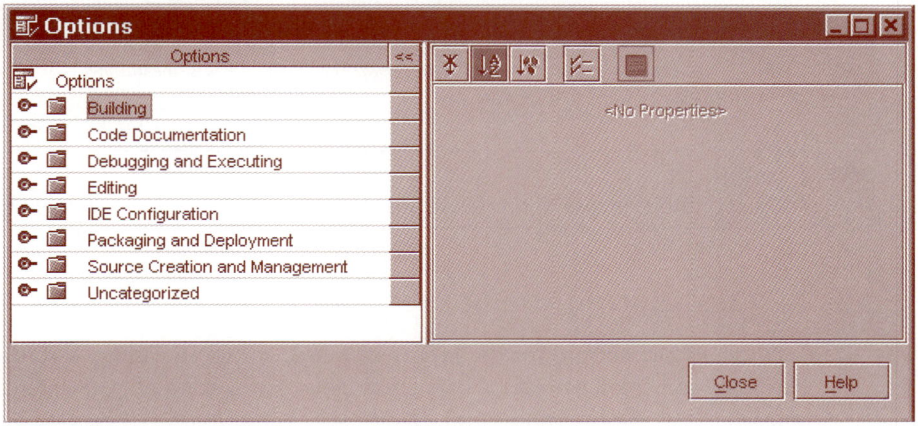

Figure 1.38 *The Options dialog box enables you to set the options for Forte IDE.*

The navigation pane contains a list of options in a hierarchical tree. When you choose an option in the list, its content (if any) is displayed in the content pane. Each option in the navigation pane has its own context menu that provides commands for customizing the options. For example, to add a new toolbar, choose *IDE Configuration*, *Look and Feel*, and right-click on Toolbar to display a context menu. Choose *Add, Toolbar* from the context menu to add a new toolbar, as shown in Figure 1.39. You can delete or rename a toolbar button from the toolbar's context menu, as shown in Figure 1.40.

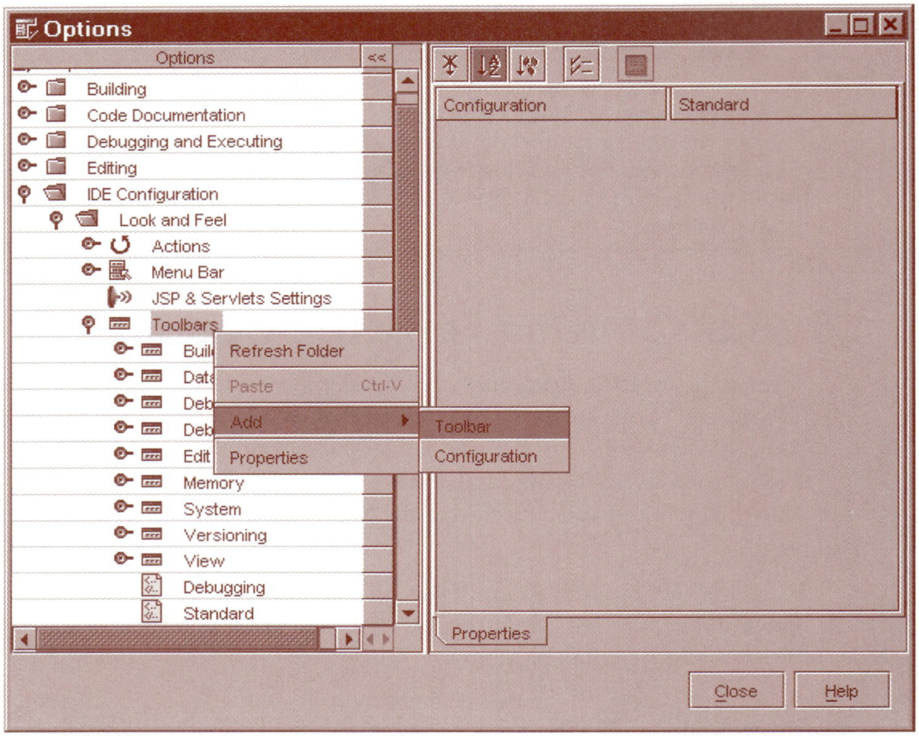

Figure 1.39 *You can add a new toolbar button from the Forte Options window.*

Caution

For novice users, please don't delete any default toolbar buttons and menus.

1.5.1 Configuring the Source Editor

You can set the options for the Java source code editor, including keyboard shortcuts, font and color settings, abbreviation tables, formatting of generated code, and appearance of the insertion point. To do so, choose *Editing, Editor Settings, Java Editor* in the Options window, as shown in Figure 1.41.

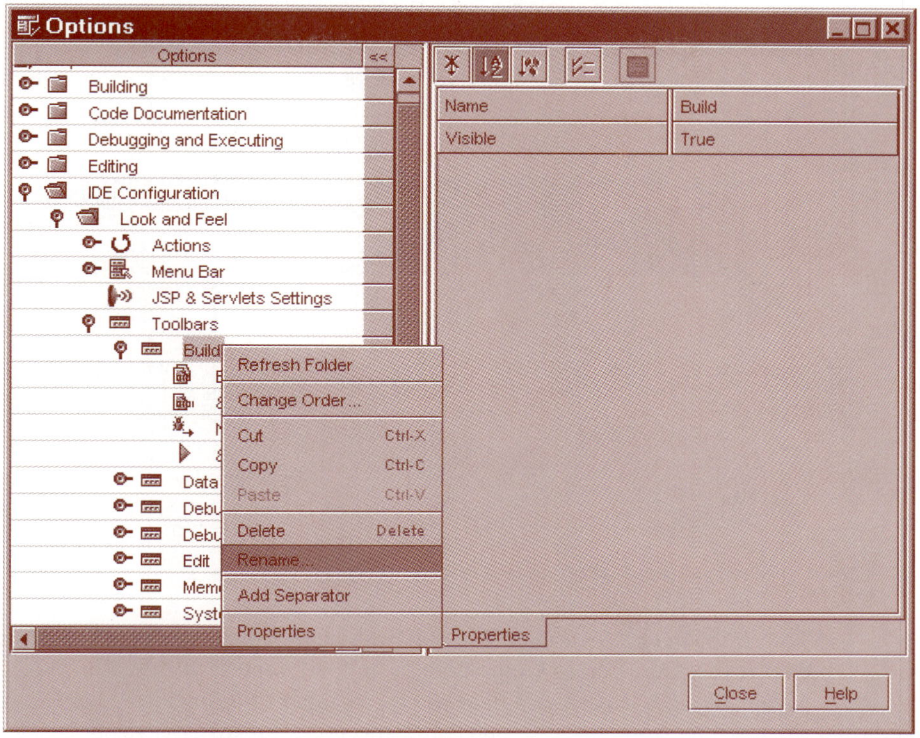

Figure 1.40 *You can delete or rename a toolbar button.*

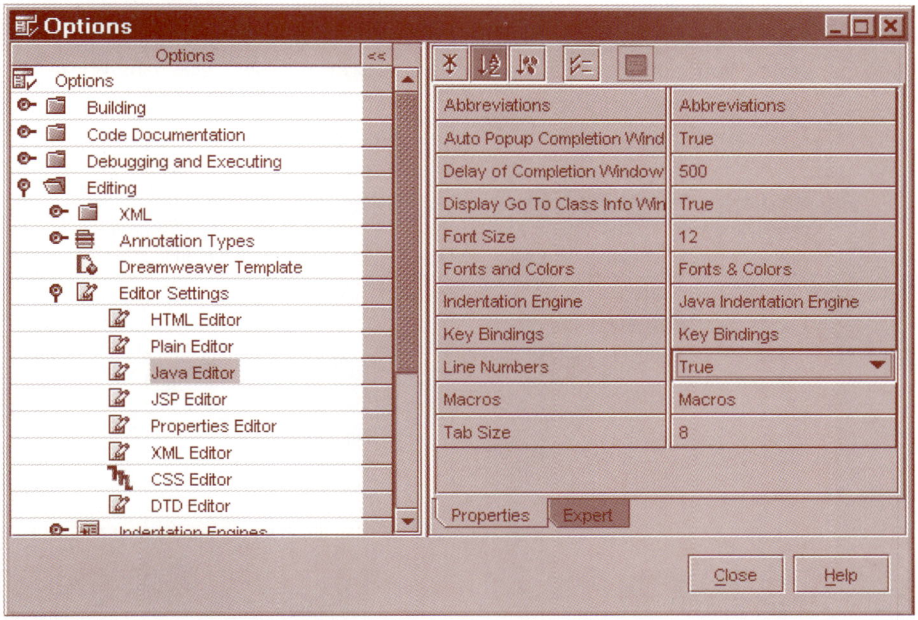

Figure 1.41 *The Java Editor Options enables you to set the options for editing Java source code.*

The *Abbreviations* field lets you specify abbreviations for terms that you want the editor to expand automatically to avoid repetitive typing. Click the ellipsis button to edit abbreviations, as shown in Figure 1.42. To use an abbreviation in the Source Editor, type it and press CTRL+L to expand it.

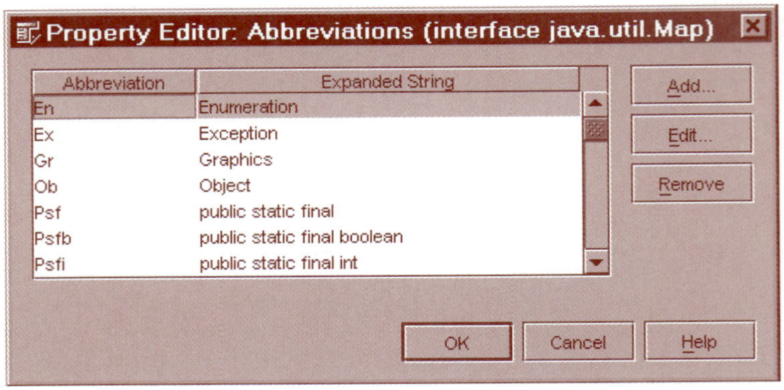

Figure 1.42 *You can use abbreviations to speed up typing.*

The *Auto Popup Completion Window* field enables or disables the code completion box. If the Auto Popup Completion Window property is true, the *Delay of Completion Window Auto Popup* field sets the number of milliseconds between the time when typing stops and the code completion box is displayed.

The *Font Size* and *Fonts and Colors* fields enable you to specify a font size, name, type, and color.

The *Indentation Engine* field lets you invoke the Indentation Engine window, in which you can set the properties for indentation, as shown in Figure 1.43. This property editor can also be accessed by choosing *Editing, Indentation Engines, Java Indentation Engine* from the Options window, as shown in Figure 1.44.

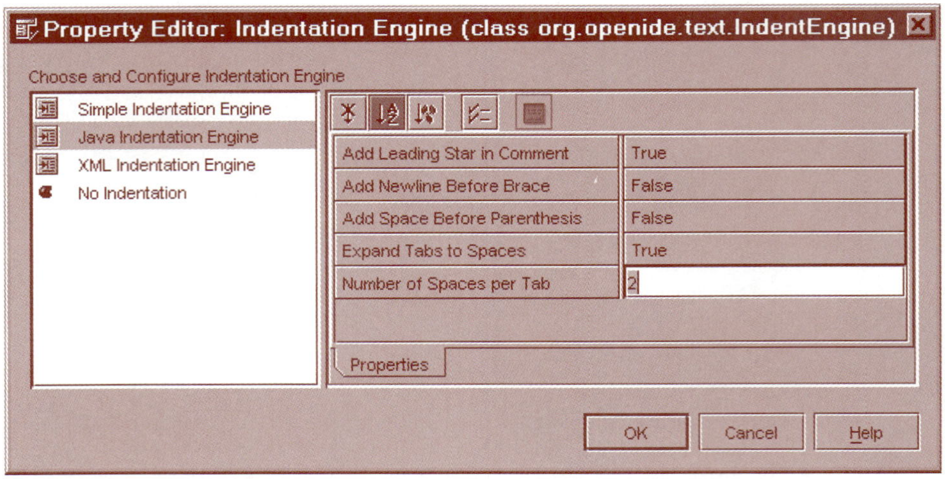

Figure 1.43 *You can set indentation properties for the Source Editor.*

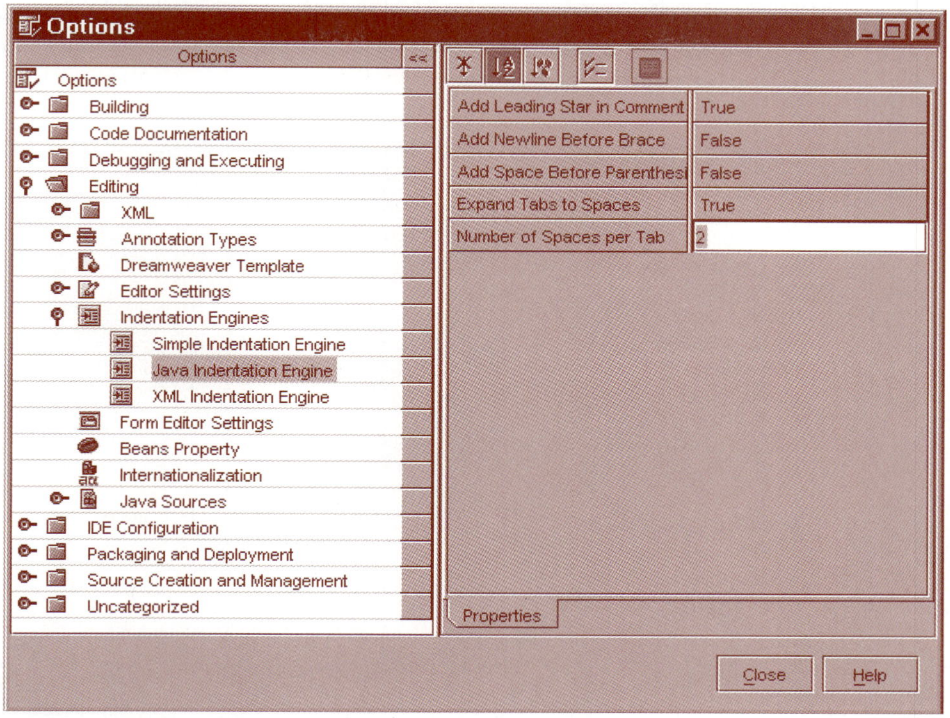

Figure 1.44 *You can edit the properties in the Java Indentation Engine.*

Note

The tab spaces are set to 2 for the source code in the book. You can reformat the code using the Reformat Code command from the context menu in the Source Editor. However, the code that is automatically generated by Forte's Form Editor cannot be reformatted.

The *Key Bindings* field enables you to edit, add, and remove keystroke shortcuts.

The *Line Numbers* field lets you enable or disable line numbers in the editor.

The *Macros* field enables you to edit, add, and remove Source Editor macros.

The *Tab Size* field sets the number of spaces inserted per tab character (`\t`) when a file is imported. This is set as 8 by default for compliance with many other applications. Note that this field is different from the *Number of Spaces per Tab* field in the Indentation Engine. The *Number of Spaces per Tab* field specifies tab settings for text that is typed, generated, or formatted in the Source Editor.

1.5.2 Configuring the Print Settings

You can set the options for printing in the Print Setting node, as shown in Figure 1.45. This node has seven subnodes: Java Editor, HTML Editor, Property Editor, XML Editor, JSP Editor, Plain Editor, and DTD Editor. The Print Setting node specifies general print properties. Each subnode lets you specify additional properties pertaining to the subnode. For example, you can specify print fonts and colors and whether to print line numbers for Java Editors, as shown in Figure 1.46.

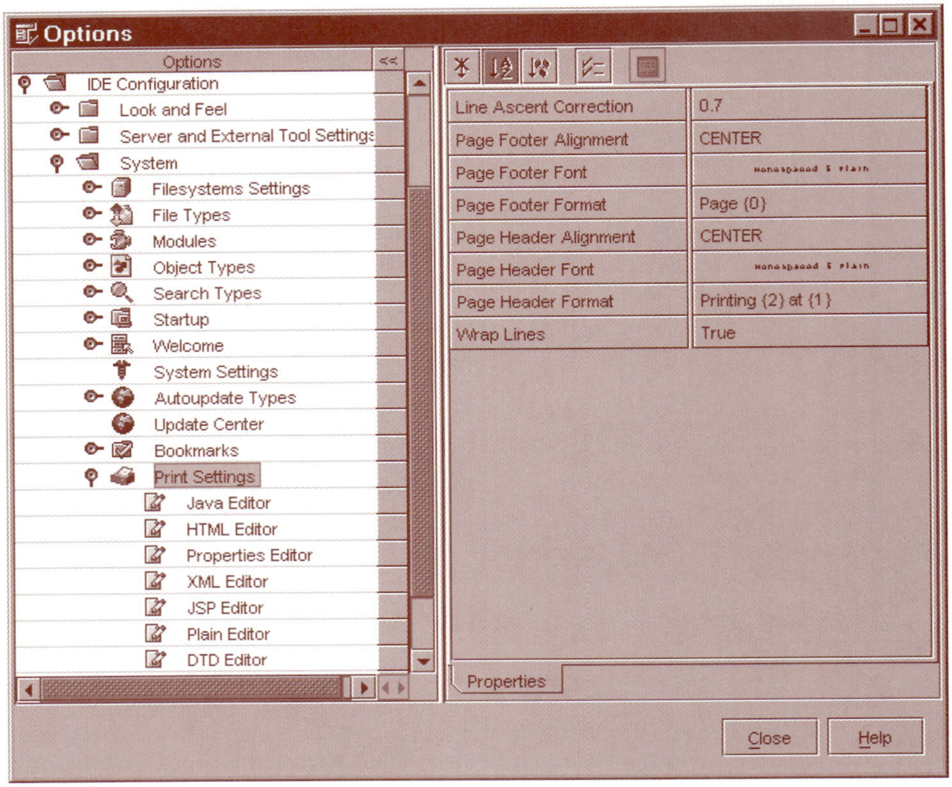

Figure 1.45 *The Print Setting enables you to set the options for printing.*

1.6 Forte Menu Commands

The main menu contains commands similar to those of other windows applications. In this section, you will learn how to use the commands in the File, Edit, View, Project, and Build menus. For information on the Debug menu, refer to Debugging in Forte at **www.prenhall.com/liang/radft.html**.

1.6.1 The File Commands

The File menu (see Figure 1.47) contains the commands for creating new templates, for mounting and unmounting file systems, for opening, saving, and printing files, and for exiting Forte.

Note

The Delete command is not in the File menu. To delete a file system or a file, use the context menu of a file system or a file in the Explorer window.

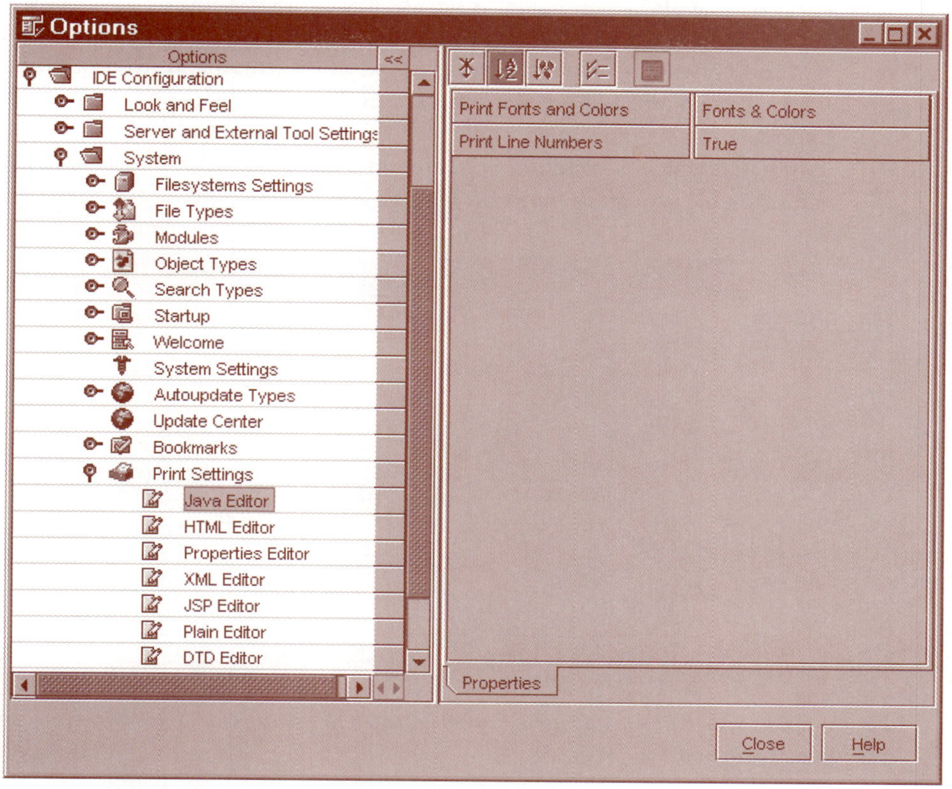

Figure 1.46 *You can set additional print options for individual editors.*

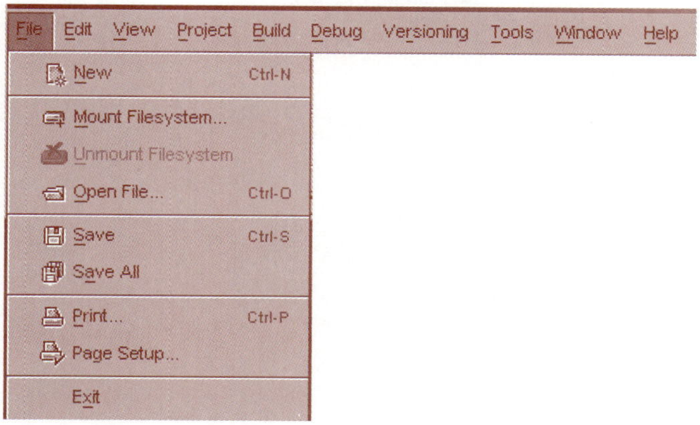

Figure 1.47 *The File menu contains commands for handling files.*

1.6.2 The Edit Commands

The Edit menu contains the standard windows commands Undo, Redo, Cut, Copy, Paste, and Delete for editing text, and Find, Replace, and Goto for finding and replacing text, as shown in Figure 1.48. It also contains the Search Filesystems command, which is useful for searching files based on text, object, type, or date in the entire file system, as shown in Figure 1.49.

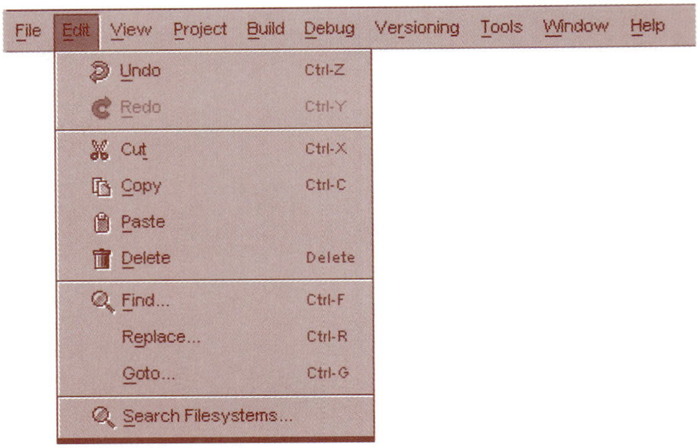

Figure 1.48 *The Edit menu contains commands for editing source code, and for searching and replacing text in the source file.*

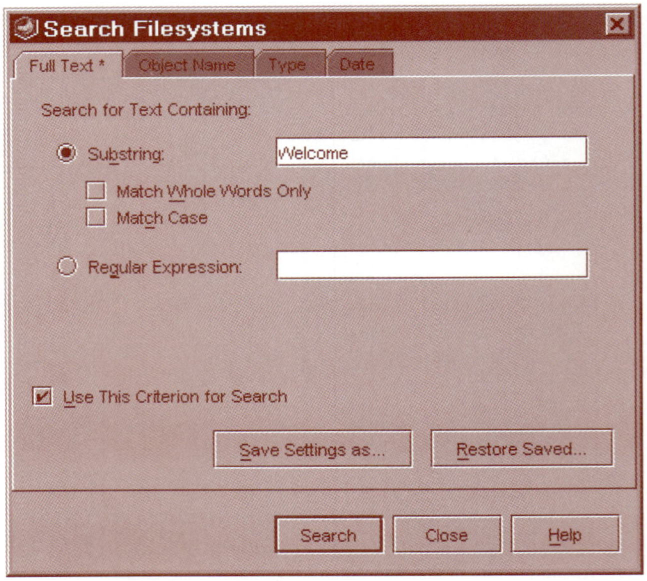

Figure 1.49 *You can search files based on text, object, type, or date in a file system.*

The Search Filesystems window contains four tabs: Full Text, Object Name, Type, and Date. The *Full Text* tab enables you to search for a text in a file. For example, if you type `Welcome` in the Regular Expression field, and click Search, you will see the result displayed in the Search Results dialog box, as shown in Figure 1.50.

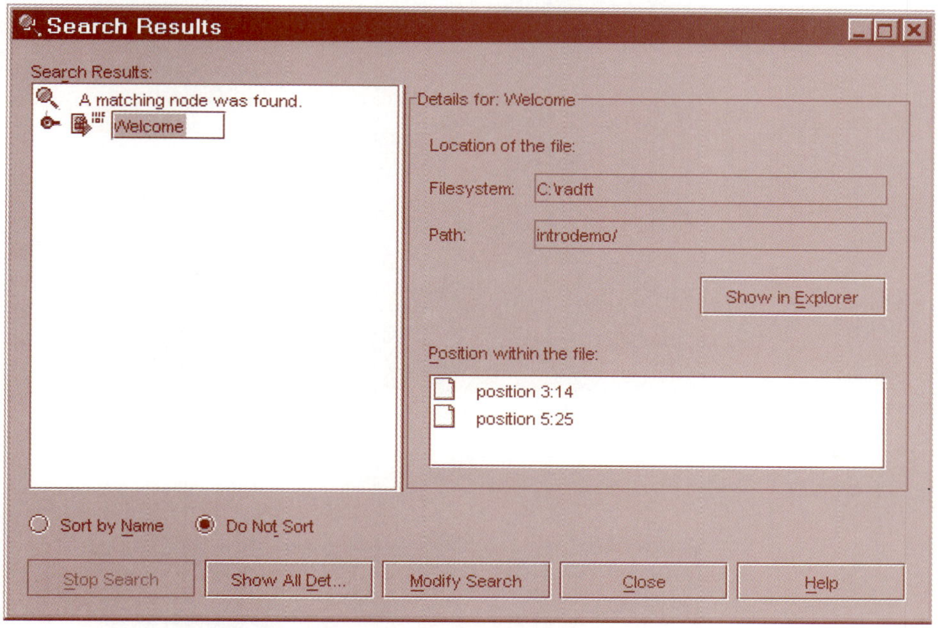

Figure 1.50 *The search results are displayed in the Search Results window.*

The *Object Name* tab enables you to search for files whose names match a text partially or completely, as shown in Figure 1.51. The *Type* tab enables you to search files for a specified type, such as Java source code, as shown in Figure 1.52. The *Date* tab enables you to search files based on their modification date, such as within two days, as shown in Figure 1.53.

1.6.3 The View Commands

The View menu (see Figure 1.54) contains the commands for displaying various windows. The *Explore From Here* command displays an Explorer for a selected package. For example, to browse the introdemo package, select it in the Explorer and click Explorer From Here in the View menu. The new Explorer is shown in Figure 1.55. The Web Browser command displays a Web browser in Forte. The *Javadoc Index Search* command displays a window that enables you to search in the Javadoc documents, as shown in Figure 1.56. The Javadoc documents to be searched must be created and mounted in Forte. For more information, see *Creating, Mounting, and Viewing Javadoc Documents* in **www.prenhall.com/liang/radft.html**.

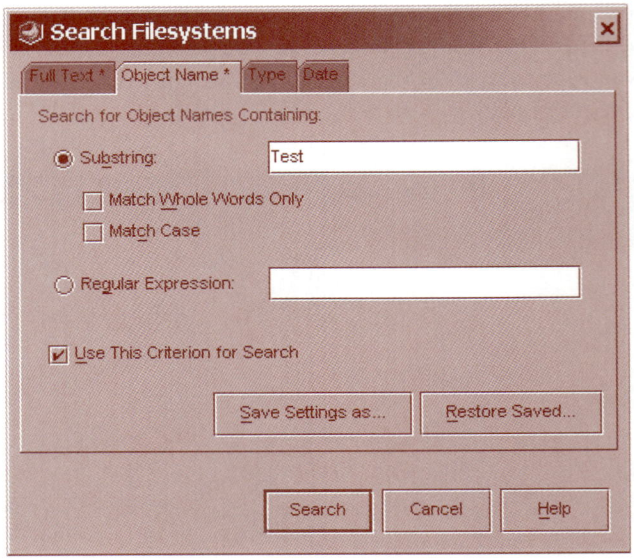

Figure 1.51 *You can search files whose names match a text partially or completely.*

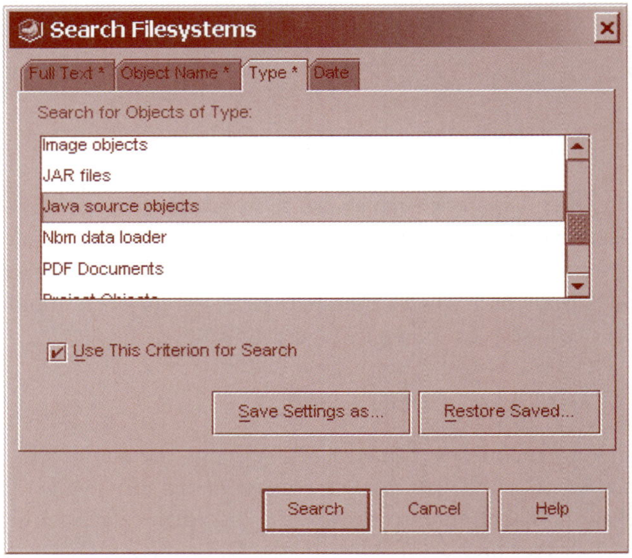

Figure 1.52 *You can search files for a specified type.*

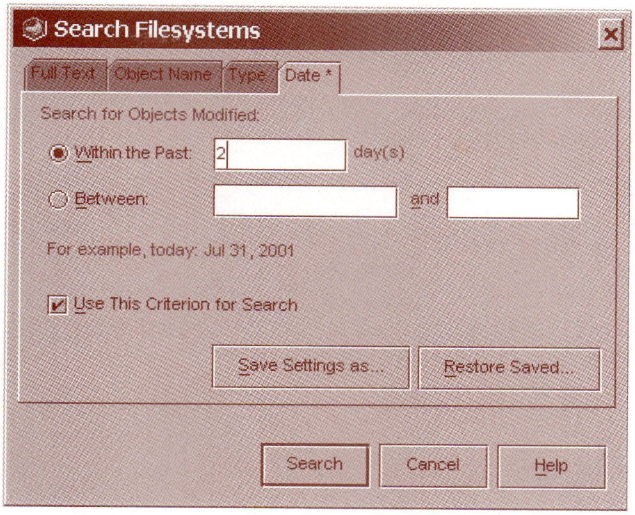

Figure 1.53 *You can search files based on their modification date.*

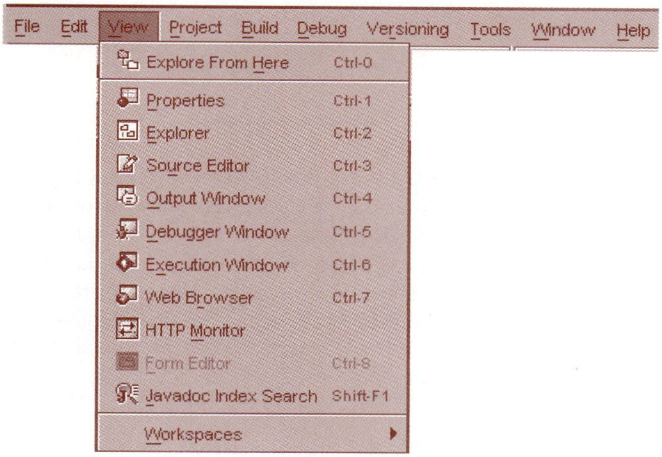

Figure 1.54 *The View menu contains commands to display various windows in Forte.*

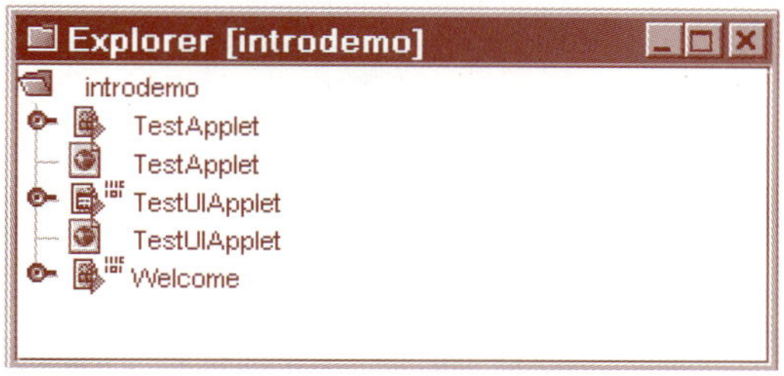

Figure 1.55 *The Explorer From Here command enables you to explore a package.*

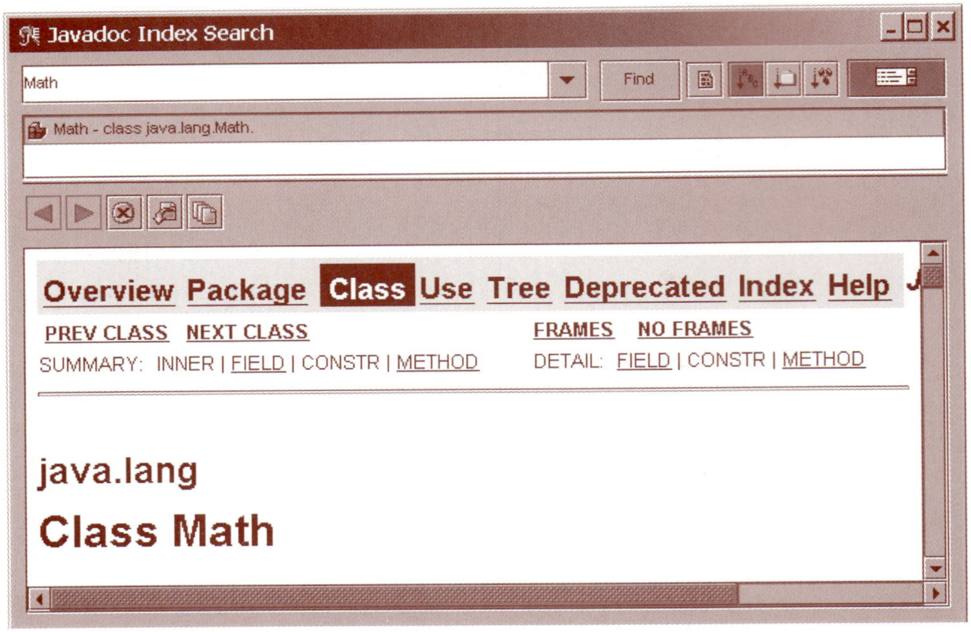

Figure 1.56 *The Javadoc Index Search window enables you to search Javadoc documents.*

TIP

If the Javadoc documents for the Java API are installed in your Forte IDE, you can also show the documents of a class or a method from its context menu in the Source Editor by choosing *Show Javadoc*. For example, you can display the documents for the `JApplet` class by choosing *Show Javadoc* in the context menu for JApplet in the Source Editor, as shown in Figure 1.57. The documents are displayed in the Forte Web browser, as shown in Figure 1.58.

TIP

You can change a default Web browser from the Setup wizard by choosing *Tools*, *Setup Wizard* as shown in Figure 1.59.

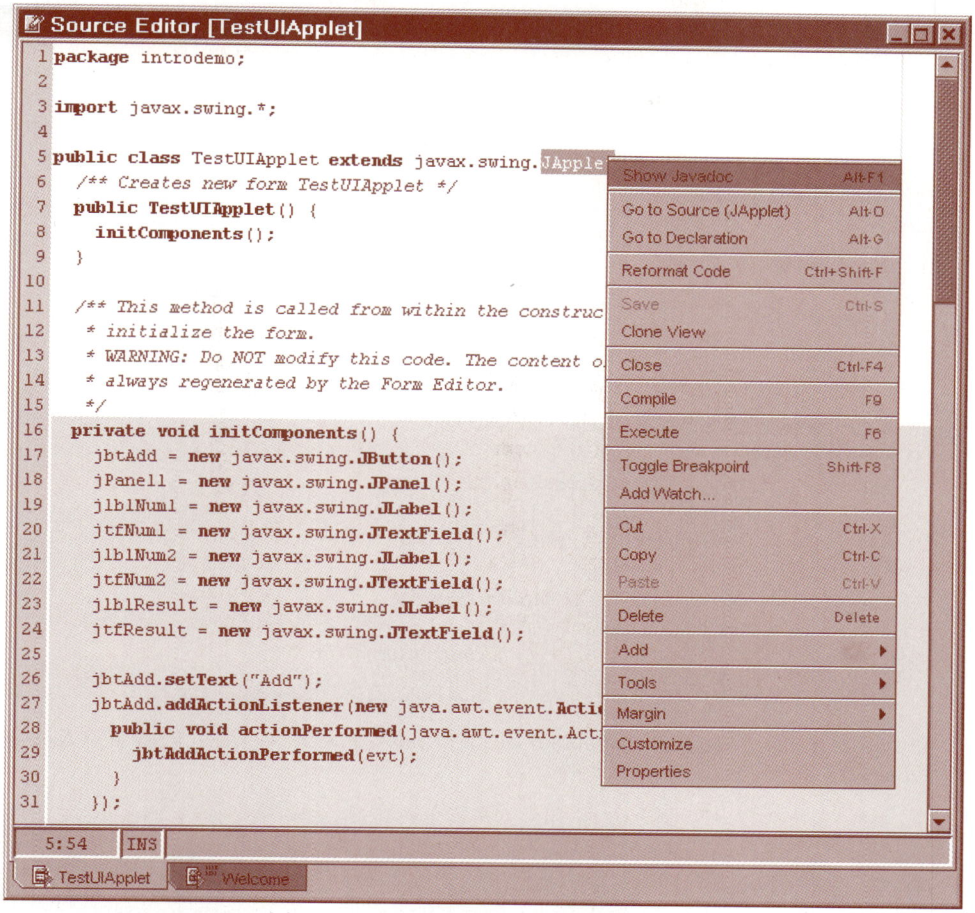

Figure 1.57 *You can show Javadoc documents for a class and method by choosing Show Javadoc from the context menu of the class or method.*

1.6.4 The Project Commands

The Project menu (see Figure 1.60) contains the commands for managing, compiling, building, executing, and debugging projects. It also contains the commands for importing projects that were developed in other IDEs.

The *Project Manager* command displays the Project Manager window, as shown in Figure 1.2. The *Compile Project* command compiles all the files in a project that have been changed or have not been compiled. The *Build Project* command compiles all the files of the current project and the files they are dependent on regardless of whether they were previously compiled. The *Set Project Main Class* specifies a main class to run from the Execute Project command.

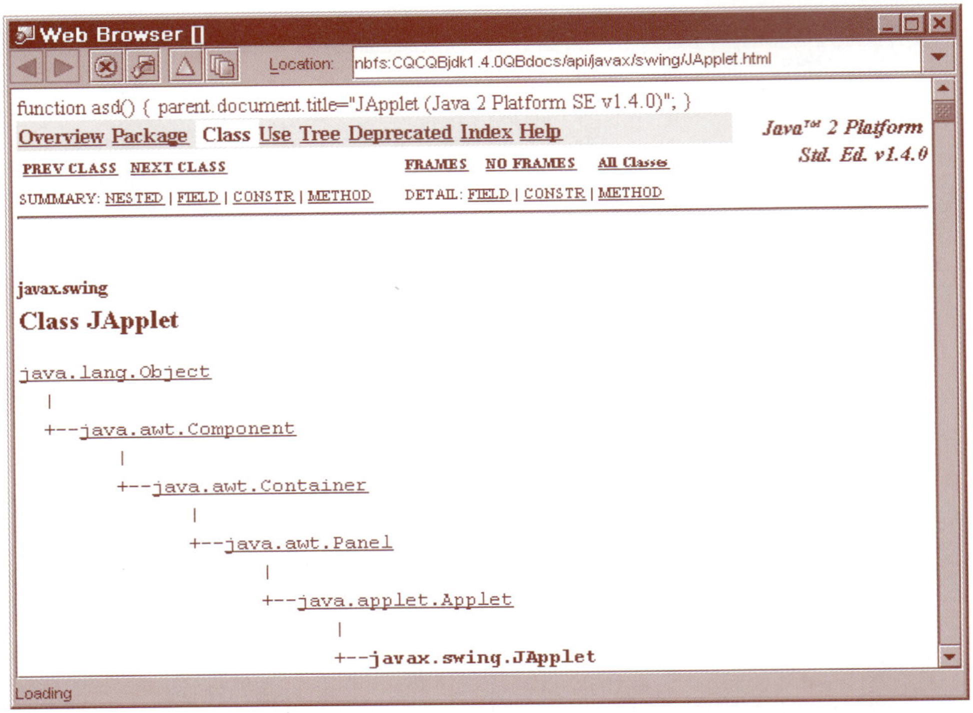

Figure 1.58 *The Javadoc documents for a class and method are displayed in the Web Browser window.*

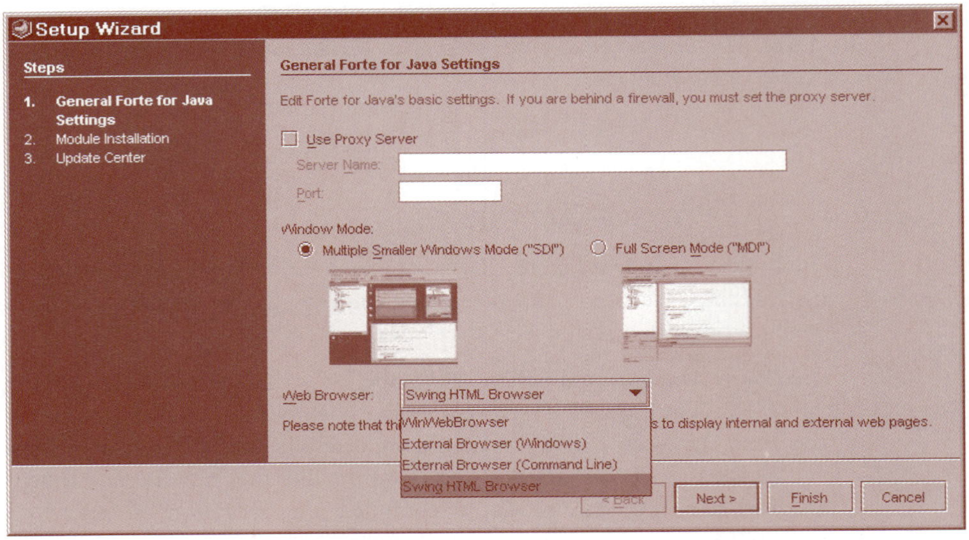

Figure 1.59 *The Setup wizard enables you to change the default Web browser.*

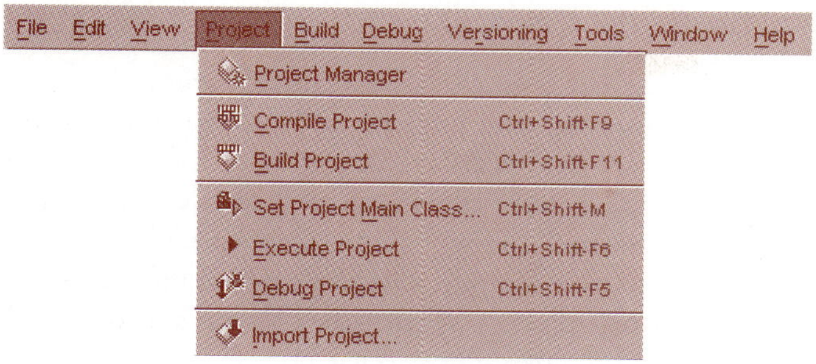

Figure 1.60 *The Project menu contains the commands for managing and processing projects.*

Note

Forte 3 has a Settings command in the Project menu to display the Project Settings window for setting project properties. This command does not exist in Forte 4. To set project settings, choose *Tools*, *Options*. For example, you can set a default executor for your project in the Default Executor field of the Java Sources, as shown in Figure 1.61. You can choose *External Execution* to run your application outside Forte, or Internal Execution to run your application inside Forte. Running it internally is faster than running it externally, but if it crashes, the Forte IDE might be crashed. By default, applications are run externally. When you create an applet using Forte's wizards, the Executor is set to Applet Execution.

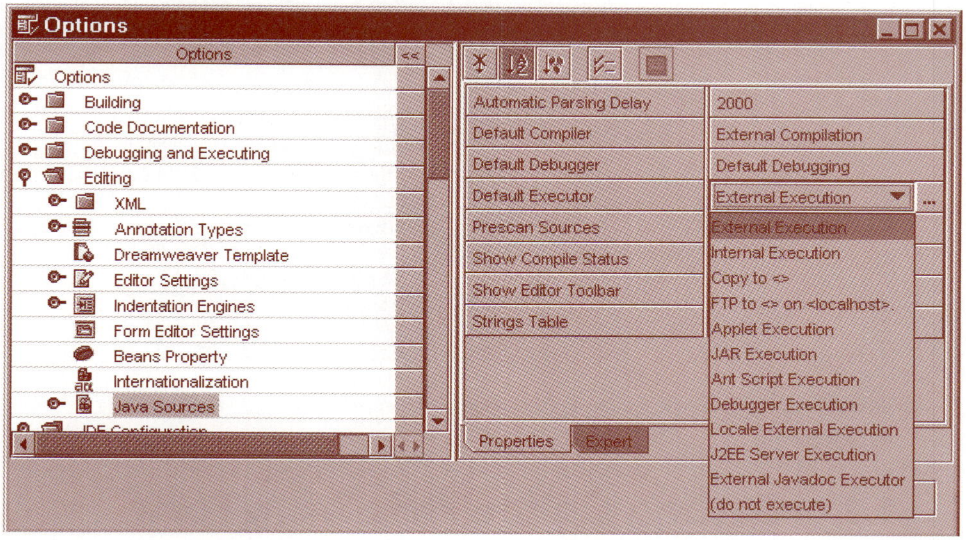

Figure 1.61 *The Options window enables you to set various properties for the project.*

1.6.5 The Build Commands

The Build menu (see Figure 1.62) contains the commands for compiling, building, cleaning, and running your programs. The *Compile* command compiles whichever selected file(s) are new or have changed since the last compile. The *Compile All* command compiles all the files in the selected folder that are new or have changed. The *Build* command compiles the selected files regardless of whether they have changed since the last compile. The *Build All* command compiles all the files in the selected folder regardless of whether they have changed since the last compile. The *Clean* command removes the selected class in the Explorer. The *Clean All* command removes all the classes in the selected folder in the Explorer. The *Stop Compile* command stops the compile currently in progress. The *Next Error* command scrolls the Source Editor to the line that contains the next compile error. The *Previous Error* command scrolls the Source Editor to the line that contains the previous compile error. The *Set Arguments* command opens a dialog box in which you specify command-line arguments to pass to a program's main method when you run the program. The Execute command runs the selected program.

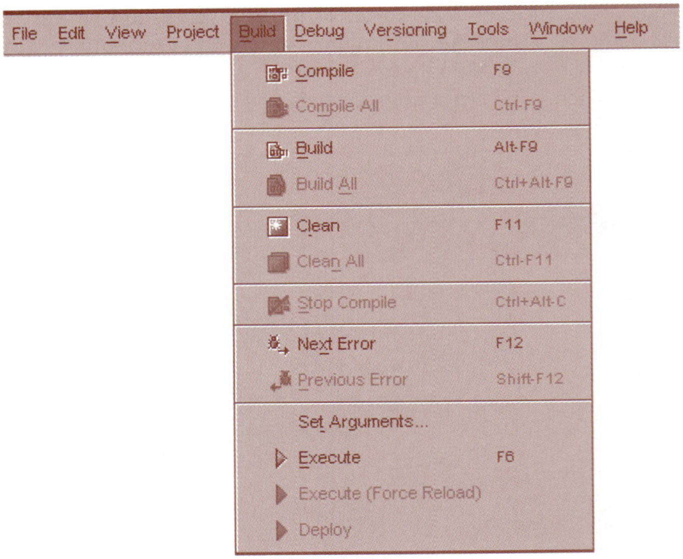

Figure 1.62 *The Build menu contains the commands for compiling, building, cleaning, and running programs.*

1.7 Getting Online Help from Forte

Forte provides a large number of documents online, giving you a great deal of information on a variety of topics pertaining to the use of Forte.

To access online help, choose *Help*, *Contents* to display Forte Help, as shown in Figure 1.63.

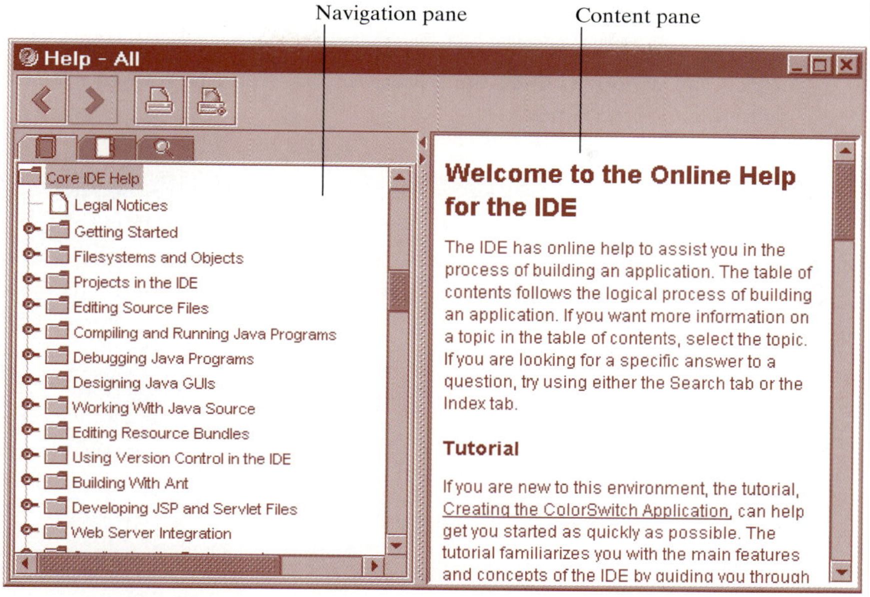

Figure 1.63 *All help documents are displayed in Forte Help.*

Forte Help behaves like a Web browser and contains the toolbar buttons, navigation pane, and content pane. The toolbar buttons contain four buttons: **Previous**, **Next**, **Print**, and **Print Setup**. The Previous and Next buttons are for going to the previous and next topic in the history list. The Print button prints the document in the content pane. The Print Setup button enables you to set up the print layout.

The navigation pane contains three tabs: **Contents**, **Index,** and **Search**. The Contents tab displays available documents. The table of contents of the document is displayed in a tree-like list in the navigation pane. To view a given topic, select the node in the tree associated with the topic. Forte Help displays the document for the topic in the content pane.

The Index tab shows the index entries for the current document. The Search tab shows the combined index entries for all the available documents in Forte.

1.8 Using a Multiple Document Interface (Optional)

You can use single document interface (SDI) or multiple document interface (MDI) for Forte IDE. The *single document interface* uses a primary main window with a set of supplementary windows for Explorer, Source Editor, Output, and so on. You can also switch to a multiple document interface (MDI) that confines all supplementary windows inside the main window. To set up a new interface, choose *Tools, Setup Wizard* to display the Setup wizard, as shown in Figure 1.64. To use the MDI interface, select Full Screen Mode ("MDI") from the Window mode section. Click Finish to switch to the new interface, as shown in Figure 1.65. You can also use the commands in the Windows menu from the main window to attach the windows, dock the windows, and create new single frames, multi-tab frames, and split frames.

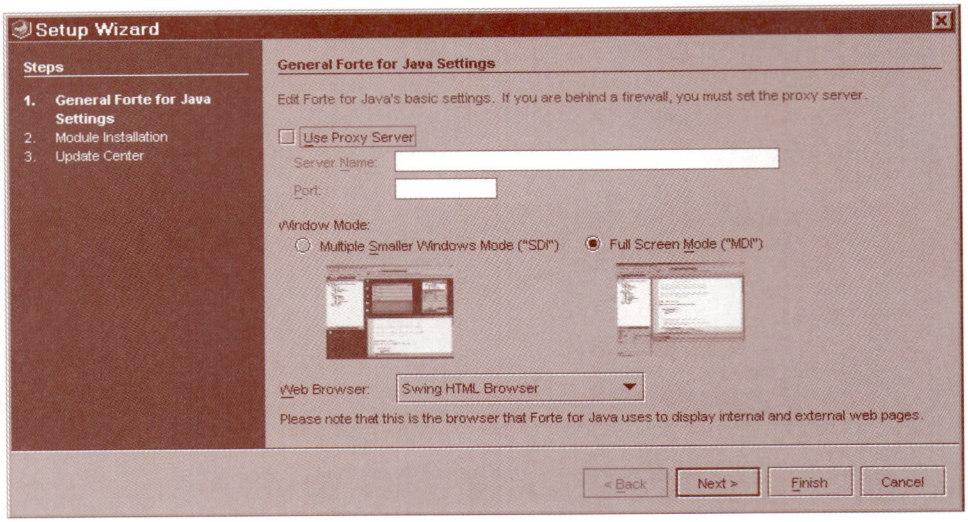

Figure 1.64 *You can set up a new IDE interface from the Setup wizard.*

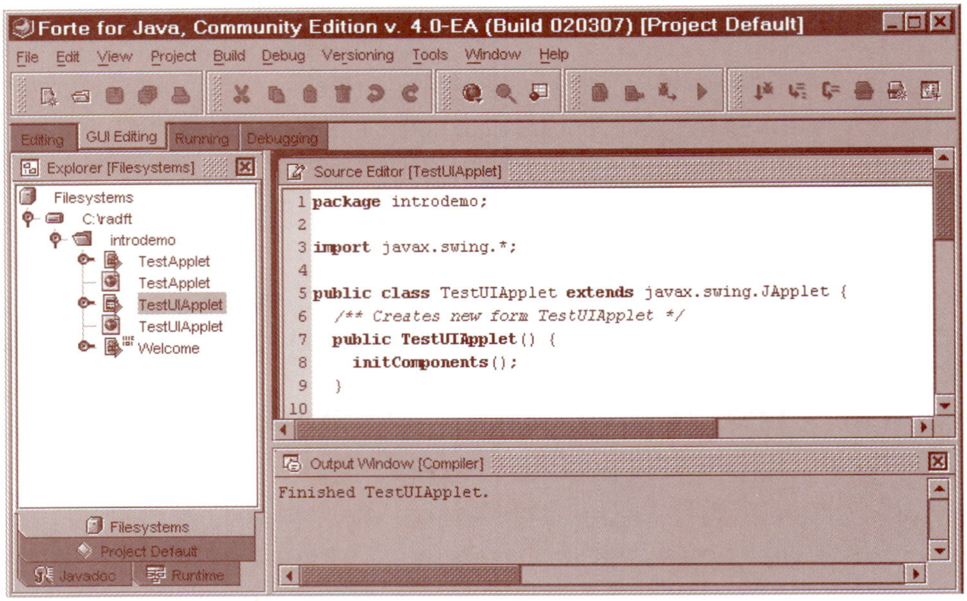

Figure 1.65 *You can use MDI interface in Forte, which contains multiple documents in a single window.*

Chapter Summary

This chapter gave you a quick start on the use of Forte to develop Java programs. You learned how to mount file systems, and to create packages and programs. You learned how to use the wizards to create various types of classes. You learned how to use the Form Editor for creating user interfaces and generating event-handling code with minimum coding. You also learned how to customize project properties by using the commands in the File, Edit, View, Project, and Build menus.

Review Questions

1.1 How do you create and delete a Java project in Forte?

1.2 How do you mount and unmount a file system in Forte?

1.3 How do you create, delete, and rename a package in Forte?

1.4 How do you create, delete, and rename a class and an applet in Forte?

1.5 How do you compile a Java program in Forte?

1.6 How do you run a Java application in Forte?

1.7 How do you run a Java applet in Forte? How do you set the Executor to run an applet standalone?

1.8 Where is the .class file stored after successful compilation in Forte?

1.9 How do you rename a file and delete a file in Forte?

1.10 How do you set the indentation, font, and color in the Source Editor?

1.11 How do you add and remove a toolbar button?

1.12 How do you set the options for printing?

1.13 Describe the commands in the File, Edit, View, Project, and Build menus in Forte.

1.14 How do you turn off the Code Completion popup window?

1.15 How do you display Javadoc documents for a class or a method from the Source Editor?

Programming Exercises

Note
All the exercises in this book are mounted in c:\radftexercise.

1.1 Use the JFrame Form wizard to create a form that converts a Celsius temperature to a Fahrenheit temperature with the following requirements:

a. Create a package named exercise1_1.

b. Create a form named `Exercise1_1` in the exercise1_1 package.

c. Use the Form Editor to create the user interface, as shown in Figure 1.66. Implement the code that converts the temperature when the Convert button is clicked and displays the resulting Fahrenheit temperature.

The formula for converting Celsius to Fahrenheit is as follows:

fahrenheit = (9.0 / 5.0) * celsius + 32.0;

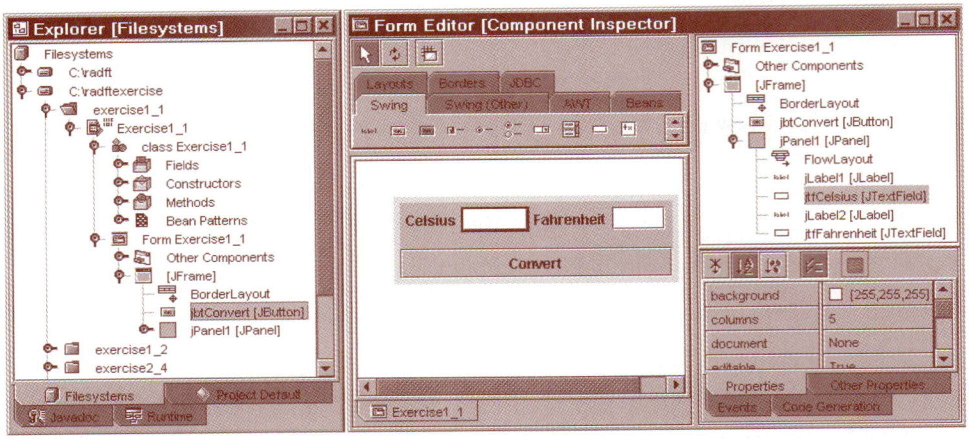

Figure 1.66 *The user enters a temperature in Celsius and clicks the Convert button to display the corresponding temperature in Fahrenheit.*

1.2 Use the JApplet Form wizard to create an applet that converts a Celsius temperature to a Fahrenheit temperature with the following requirements:

a. Create a package file named exercise1_2 under the c:\radftexercise file system.

b. Create a form named `Exercise1_2` in the exercise1_2 package.

c. Use the Form Editor to create the same user interface as in the preceding exercise. Implement the code that converts the temperature when the Convert button is clicked and displays the resulting Fahrenheit temperature.

CHAPTER 2

INTRODUCTION TO JAVABEANS

Objectives

- To know what a JavaBeans component is.
- To discover the similarities and differences between beans and regular objects.
- To learn how to create JavaBeans components in Forte and install them in the component palette.
- To understand JavaBeans properties and naming patterns.
- To become familiar with JavaBeans property types.
- To know how to use the component inspector in Forte.

2.1 Introduction

JavaBeans technology is a significant extension and enhancement of the Java language. This technology enables programmers to rapidly build applications by assembling objects and testing them during design time. It is the foundation for the Java builder tools that support rapid Java application development.

JavaBeans are 100% pure Java programs. They are simple to develop and easy to use. JavaBeans are a special kind of Java class. If you know Java, you may have already developed JavaBeans. In fact, all the AWT and Swing user interface classes are JavaBeans components. With JavaBeans, you can create new applications by connecting various off-the-shelf software components using a builder tool, such as Forte, with minimum coding. The JavaBeans technology ushers in a new era of component computing. An application can be viewed as a framework consisting of various software components that can be added, removed, or customized, as needed.

This chapter introduces the concept of JavaBeans and the relationship between JavaBeans and Java RAD builder tools. You will begin to write simple JavaBeans and use them in Forte.

2.2 Beans and Objects

JavaBeans is a software component architecture that extends the power of the Java language to enable well-formed objects to be manipulated visually in a builder tool like Forte during design time. Such well-formed objects are referred to as *Java beans* or simply *beans*. The classes that define the beans, referred to as *JavaBeans components* or *bean components*, or simply *components*, must conform to the JavaBeans component model with the following requirements:

- A bean must be a public class.
- A bean component must have a public default constructor (one that takes no arguments), although it can have other constructors if needed. For example, a bean named `MyBean` must either have a constructor with the signature

  ```
  public MyBean();
  ```

  or have no constructor if its superclass has a default constructor.
- A bean component must implement the `Serializable` interface to ensure a persistent state. JavaBeans can be used in a wide variety of tools, such as Lotus, Delphi, MS Visual Basic, and MS Word. Bean persistence may be required when JavaBeans are used in other tools. Some tools need to save the beans and restore them later. Bean persistence ensures that the tools can reconstruct the properties and behaviors of the bean to the state in which it was saved. Persistence and serialization will be further discussed in Chapter 9, "Bean Persistence and Versioning."
- A bean component usually has properties with public accessor methods that enable them to be seen and updated visually by a builder tool. To enable the

properties to be manipulated, the accessor methods must conform to the naming patterns or be specified explicitly, using the `BeanInfo` interface. According to the accessor method naming pattern, the method must be named `get<PropertyName>()` for getting the property value and `set<PropertyName>()` for setting the property value. The naming patterns of properties and their accessor methods will be discussed in detail in Section 2.5, "Bean Properties." The `BeanInfo` interface will be introduced in Chapter 11, "Bean Introspection and Customization."

- A bean component may have events with public registration methods that enable it to add and remove listeners. If the bean plays a role as the source of events, it must provide registration methods. This will be discussed in depth in Chapter 3, "Bean Events."

The first three requirements must be observed by all beans, and therefore are referred to as *minimum JavaBeans component requirements*. The last two requirements are dependent on implementations. It is possible to write a bean without accessor methods and event registration methods.

A JavaBeans component is a special kind of Java class. The relationship of a JavaBeans component and a Java class is illustrated in Figure 2.1.

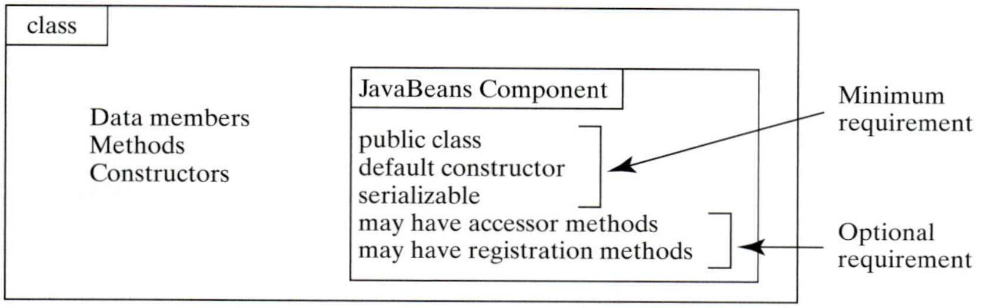

Figure 2.1 *A JavaBeans component is a serializable public class with a default constructor.*

Example 2.1 Writing a Simple JavaBeans Component

In this example, you will learn how to write a simple Java bean component named `MessagePanel` that displays a message on the panel. The UML diagram of this class is shown in Figure 2.2. The UML Graphical Notations are summarized in the book's companion Web site.

To see the development in action, follow these steps:

1. Choose *New, Java Package* in the context menu of **c:\radft** in the Explorer to display the Package wizard to create a new package named `messagepaneldemo`.

continued

Example 2.1 continued

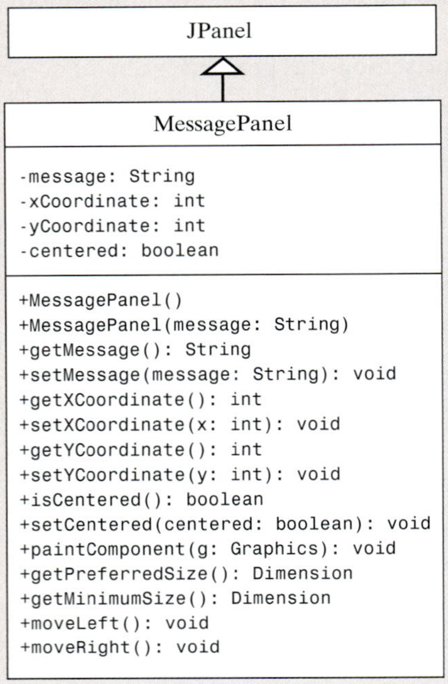

Figure 2.2 *The* `MessagePanel` *class extends* `JPanel` *to display a message.*

2. Choose *New*, *Classes*, *Class* in the context menu of messagepaneldemo to display the Class wizard, as shown in Figure 2.3.

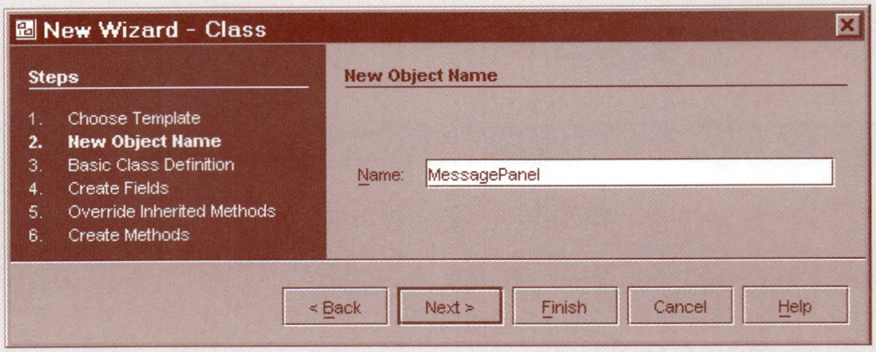

Figure 2.3 *You can create a new Java class using the Class wizard.*

3. Type `MessagePanel` in the Name field and click *Next* to display the Basic Class Definition panel, as shown in Figure 2.4.

4. Enter `javax.swing.JPanel` in the Superclass field and click *Finish* to generate the `MessagePanel` class.

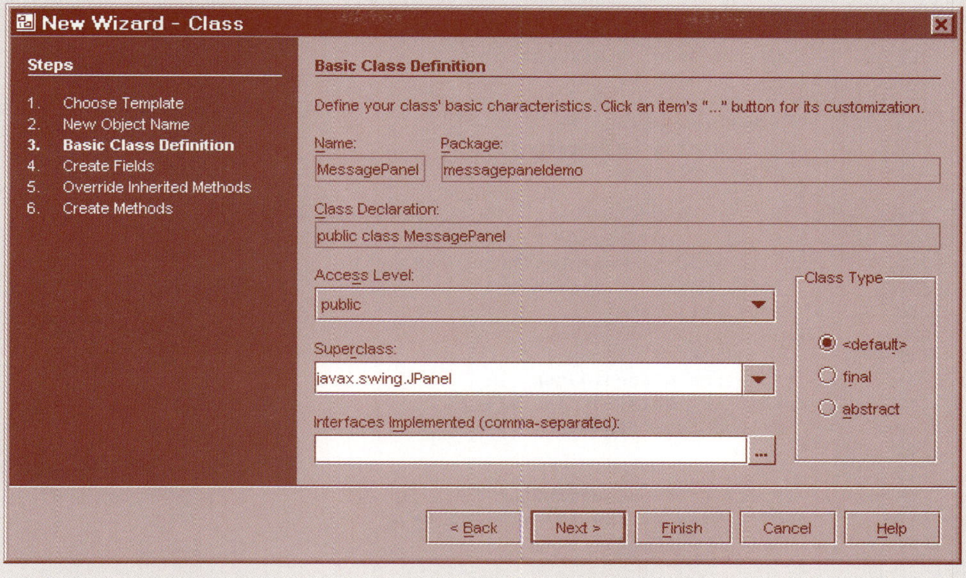

Figure 2.4 *The Class wizard generates a Java class template.*

5. Complete the code for `MessagePanel`, as shown in Listing 2.1. The structural information of the `MessagePanel` class can be displayed in the Explorer, as shown in Figure 2.5.

```
package messagepaneldemo;

import java.awt.Font;
import java.awt.FontMetrics;
import java.awt.Dimension;
import java.awt.Graphics;

public class MessagePanel extends javax.swing.JPanel {
  /** The message to be displayed */
  private String message = "Welcome to Java";

  /** The x coordinate where the message is displayed */
  private int xCoordinate = 20;

  /** The y coordinate where the message is displayed */
  private int yCoordinate = 20;

  /** Indicate whether the message is displayed in the center */
  private boolean centered;

  /** Default constructor */
  public MessagePanel() {
  }

  /** Constructor with a message parameter */
  public MessagePanel(String message) {
```

Listing 2.1 *MessagePanel.java*

continued

Example 2.1 continued

```
      this.message = message;
    }

    /** Return message */
    public String getMessage() {
      return message;
    }

    /** Set a new message */
    public void setMessage(String message) {
      this.message = message;
      repaint();
    }

    /** Return xCoordinator */
    public int getXCoordinate() {
      return xCoordinate;
    }

    /** Set a new xCoordinator */
    public void setXCoordinate(int x) {
      this.xCoordinate = x;
    }

    /** Return yCoordinator */
    public int getYCoordinate() {
      return yCoordinate;
    }

    /** Set a new yCoordinator */
    public void setYCoordinate(int y) {
      this.yCoordinate = y;
    }

    /** Return centered */
    public boolean isCentered() {
      return centered;
    }

    /** Set a new centered */
    public void setCentered(boolean centered) {
      this.centered = centered;
    }

    /** Paint the message */
    public void paintComponent(Graphics g) {
      super.paintComponent(g);

      if (centered) {
        // Get font metrics for the current font
        FontMetrics fm = g.getFontMetrics();

        // Find the center location to display
        int w = fm.stringWidth(message);  // Get the string width
        // Get the string height, from top to the baseline
        int h = fm.getAscent();
        xCoordinate = getWidth() / 2 - w / 2;
        yCoordinate = getHeight() / 2 + h / 2;
      }

```

Listing 2.1 *continued*

```
87        g.drawString(message, xCoordinate, yCoordinate);
88      }
89
90      /** Override get method for preferredSize */
91      public Dimension getPreferredSize() {
92        return new Dimension(200, 100);
93      }
94
95      /** Override get method for minimumSize */
96      public Dimension getMinimumSize() {
97        return new Dimension(200, 100);
98      }
99
100     /** Move the message in the panel to the left */
101     public void moveLeft() {
102       if (getXCoordinate() > 10) {
103         // Shift the message to the left
104         setXCoordinate(getXCoordinate()-10);
105         repaint();
106       }
107     }
108
109     /** Move the message in the panel to the right */
110     public void moveRight() {
111       if (getXCoordinate() < getSize().width - 20) {
112         // Shift the message to the right
113         setXCoordinate(getXCoordinate() + 10);
114         repaint();
115       }
116     }
117   }
```

Listing 2.1 *continued*

Example Review

Since `javax.awt.Component` implements `Serializable`, and `MessagePanel` is a subclass of `JPanel`, which is a subclass of `Component`, `MessagePanel` is serializable.

The `MessagePanel` class is a public class with a default constructor, `MessagePanel()`. Since `MessagePanel` is a serializable public class with a default constructor, it is a JavaBeans component.

The `MessagePanel` class has the properties `message`, `xCoordinate`, `yCoordinate`, and `centered`. The `getMessage()`, `getXCoordinate()`, `getYCoordinate()`, and `isCentered()` methods read the `message`, `xCoordinate`, `yCoordinate`, and `centered` properties, respectively; and the `setMessage`, `setXCoordinate`, `setYCoordinate`, and `setCentered` methods update these properties. The message is painted on the panel starting at the position specified by the coordinates `xCoordinate` and `yCoordinate`.

The `getPreferredSize()` (Lines 91–93) and `getMinimumSize()` (Lines 96–98) methods are overridden to specify the `preferredSize` and `minimumSize` properties for instances of `MessagePanel`. The `MessagePanel` class also contains two methods, `moveLeft()`(Lines 101–107) and `moveRight()` (Lines 110–116), for moving the message to the left and to the right on the panel.

continued

Example 2.1 continued

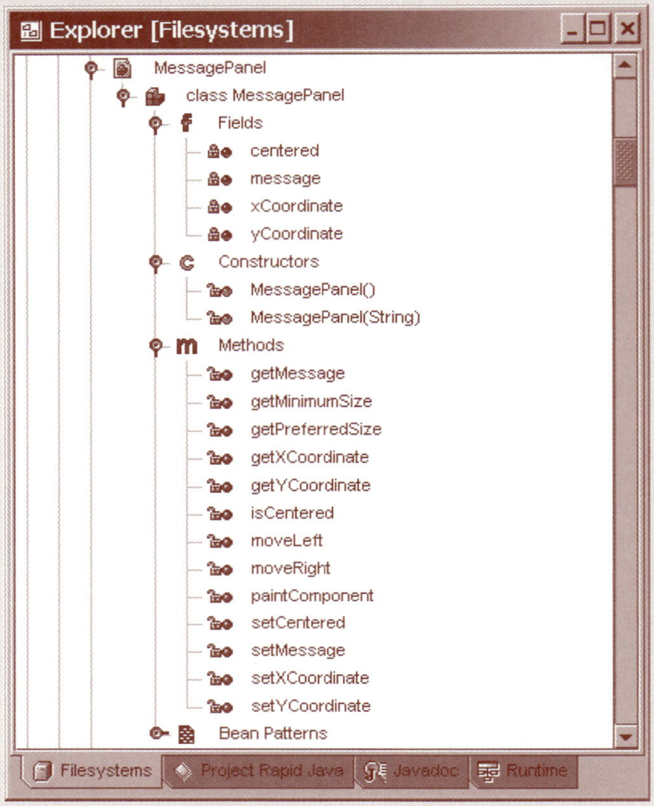

Figure 2.5 *The structural information of a class can be displayed in the Explorer.*

CAUTION

The `MessagePanel` class uses the properties `xCoordinate` and `yCoordinate` to specify the position of the message displayed on the panel. Do not use property names `x` and `y`, because they are already defined in the `Component` class to specify the position of the component in the parent's coordinate system.

NOTE

You wrote the code for declaring the properties and their accessor methods in this example. In Chapter 4, "Developing and Using Components," you will learn to use Forte's Bean Pattern wizard to automatically generate the code.

2.3 JavaBeans and Java Builder Tools

Since a JavaBeans component is a Java class, it can be used wherever a class is applicable. You can create a JavaBeans component, access its properties, and invoke its methods in a scripting environment, just as you use regular classes. Nevertheless, JavaBeans components are specially designed for use in a builder tool that enables the bean user to visually manipulate the beans during design time. The builder tool may be a Java IDE such as Forte or JBuilder, a non-Java IDE such as Microsoft Visual Basic or Borland Delphi, a Web page builder such as Microsoft FrontPage, or even a word processor such as Microsoft Word.

A builder tool can discover the contents (properties, methods, and events) and expose them to the bean user for visual manipulation during design time. The contents are presented on a user interface, referred to in Forte as a *component inspector*, or simply *inspector*, on which the user can update property values and register events of the bean. The JavaBeans architecture provides a core API to enable builder tools to find out what is inside the beans. The process of discovering and analyzing a bean, referred to as *bean introspection*, will be covered in Chapter 11, "Bean Introspection and Customization."

A builder tool usually has an internal component, referred to as a *reflector*, which is responsible for communication between the bean and the component inspector during design time. The reflector analyzes the bean and presents its properties and events on the component inspector. When the bean user modifies the properties, the reflector applies the changes to the bean by invoking the set method of the properties. The relationship of component inspector, reflector, and bean is illustrated in Figure 2.6.

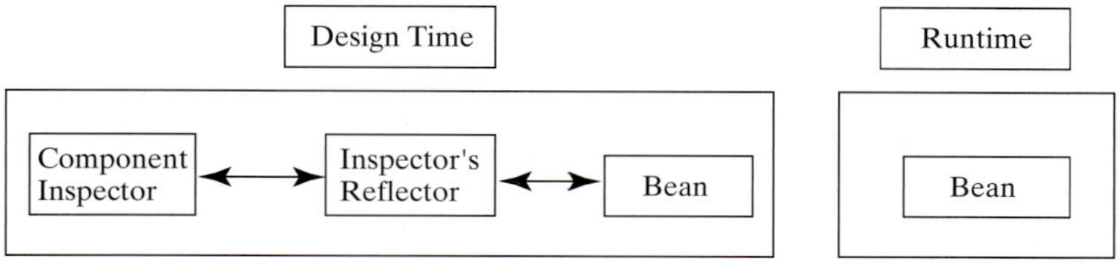

Figure 2.6 *During design time, the user interacts with the inspector, and the reflector controls the execution of the bean. During runtime, the bean runs just like a regular object.*

NOTE
The component inspector and the reflector are used during design time and play no role at runtime.

If the bean follows the naming patterns for properties and events, the reflector will automatically recognize and present it on the component inspector. If not, you have to provide a bean information class that implements the `BeanInfo` interface to describe the properties and events of the bean to the reflector in order for the inspector to reveal the properties and events to the user. How to write such a description class will be introduced in Chapter 11, "Bean Introspection and Customization."

2.4 Using JavaBeans in Forte

One of the major applications of JavaBeans is for rapid application development, or RAD, a powerful feature used in software development tools for visual programming. RAD allows you to select a component and drop it to a desired location. The click-and-drop capability enables you to write programs with little or no coding, thereby greatly improving software reusability, productivity and maintainability.

RAD in Forte is completely based on JavaBeans, and each RAD component in Forte is a bean accessible from the component palette. In this section, you will learn how to add a bean to the component palette and utilize it in the applications, using the example of the `MessagePanel` bean presented in Example 2.1.

2.4.1 Adding a Bean to the Component Palette

All the user-interface classes in AWT and Swing are beans. Some of them, such as `JButton`, `JCheckBox`, `JComboBox`, `JLabel`, `JList`, `JRadioButton`, `JTextArea`, `JTextField`, `JMenuBar`, `JPopupMenu`, `JScrollbar`, `JPanel`, and `JScrollPanel`, are already added into the Swing page and Swing (Other) page in the component palette. This book uses Swing components to create graphical user interfaces. The necessary basic knowledge of Swing components is covered in my *Introduction to Java Programming with Sun ONE Studio 4*. Advanced features of Swing components will be covered in Part II, "Rapid Application Development with Swing Components."

Suppose you want to use the `MessagePanel` bean to create Forte forms. First you must add it to the component palette following the steps below.

1. (Optional) Create a new tab in the component palette named RadBook:
   - 1.1 Choose *Tools, Options* to display the Options dialog, as shown in Figure 2.7.
   - 1.2 In the context menu of the component palette node, choose *Add Palette Category* to display the New Palette Category dialog box (Figure 2.8), enter `RadBook` in the New Category Name field, and click *OK* to create a new category named RadBook.
   - 1.3 If RadBook is not in the desired order in the component palette, you can change its order by choosing an appropriate command (Move Up or Move Down) in the context menu of the RadBook node, as shown in Figure 2.9.
2. In the context menu of MessagePanel in the Explorer, choose *Tools, Add to component palette* (Figure 2.10) to display the Palette Category dialog box, as shown in Figure 2.11. Choose *RadBook* and click *OK* to add MessagePanel in the component palette. You will see MessagePanel appearing in the component palette in the Form Editor, as shown in Figure 2.12.

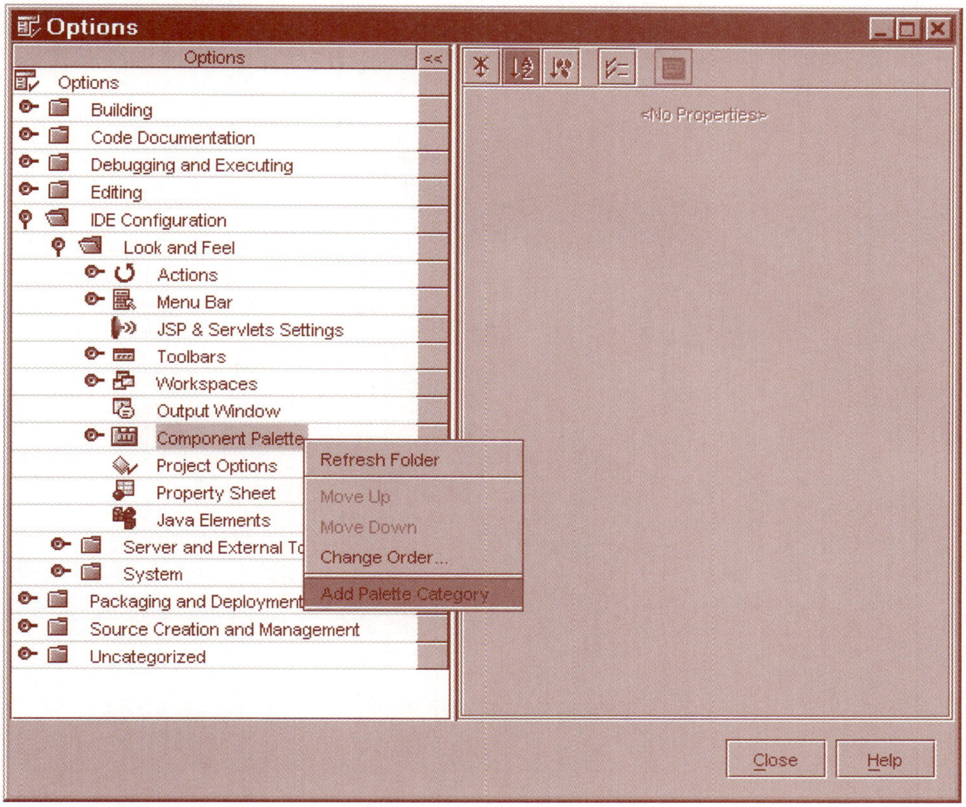

Figure 2.7 *You can create a new category in the component palette in the Options dialog box.*

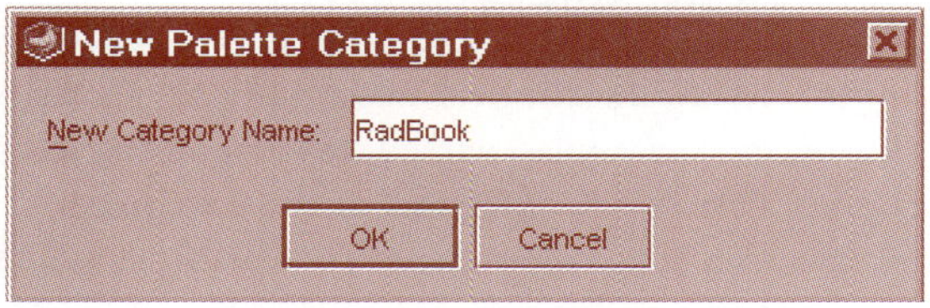

Figure 2.8 *You can add a new category in the component palette.*

TIP

To remove a component from the component palette, right-click the component to display its context menu and choose *Delete*.

TIP

By default, the components in the component palette appear in alphabetical order of the component's full name. For example, if you have two components named `messagedemo.MessagePanel` and `clockdemo.Clock`, `clockdemo.Clock` appears before `messagedemo.MessagePanel` in the component palette.

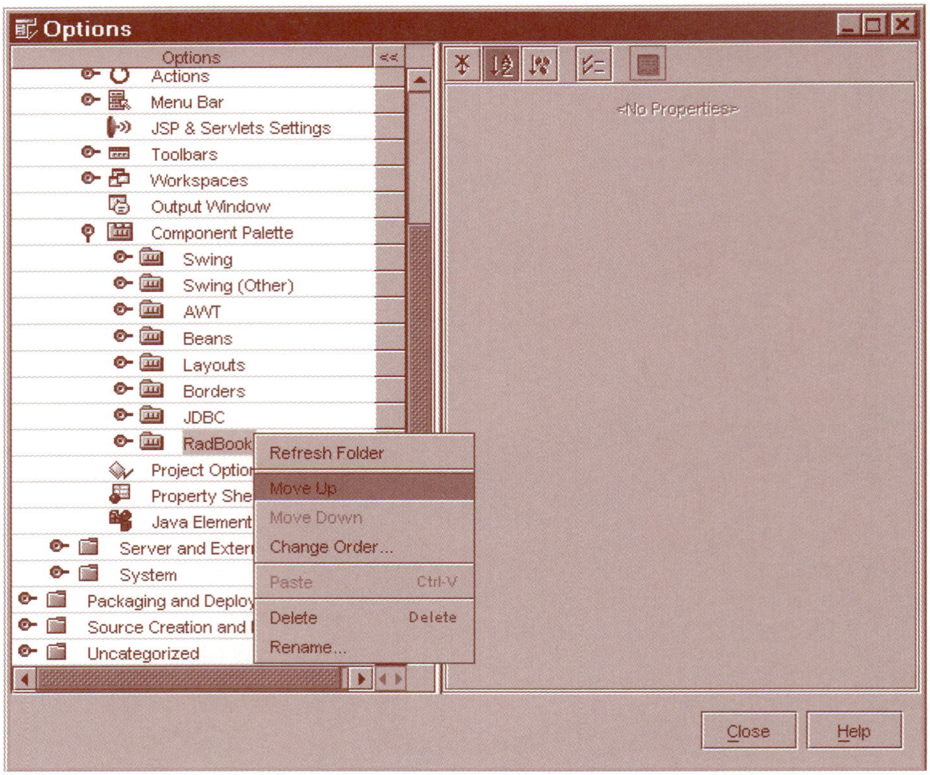

Figure 2.9 *You can move a category tab up or down from the context menu of the category tab in the Options dialog box.*

2.4.2 Using Beans in Forte

You are now ready to test the `MessagePanel` bean you just added to the component palette. Create a new applet named `TestMessagePanel` using the Swing JApplet form wizard. Click *TestMessagePanel* in the Explorer to display its form. `TestMessagePanel` itself is a bean component. You can visually inspect and update its properties through the Form Editor, as shown in Figure 2.12. If the Form Editor is not displayed, choose *View, Form Editor* to display it.

To add a `MessagePanel` bean, click the MessagePanel icon in the component palette and drop it to the center of the form, as shown in Figure 2.13.

Forte generates a bean named `messagePanel1`. You can change the bean's properties, including its name, from the component inspector. The properties `message`, `xCoordinate`, `yCoordinate`, and `centered` are defined in `MessagePanel`, and all the other properties are defined in the superclasses of `MessagePanel`. Type `Welcome to JavaBeans` in the `message` property and press the Enter key to let the change take effect. You will see "Welcome to JavaBeans" displayed on the panel. You don't need to run the program to see the changes. The changes can be verified instantaneously, since the bean is live during design time.

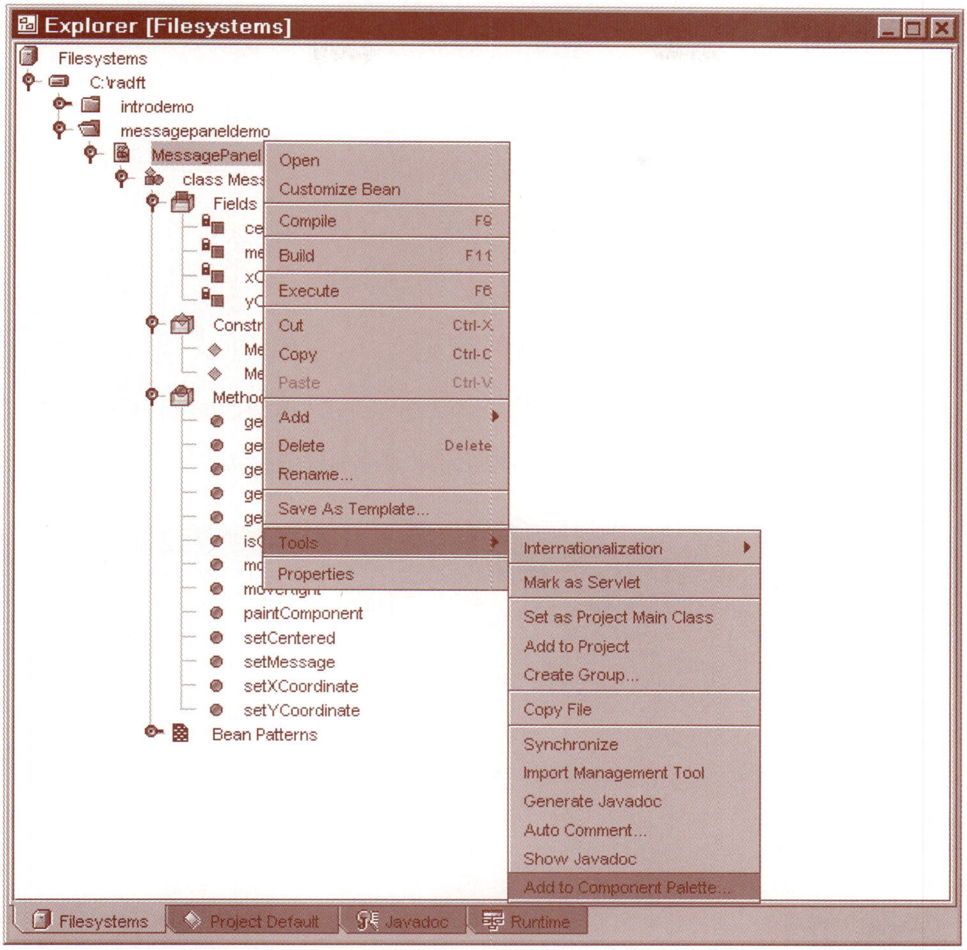

Figure 2.10 *The Palette Properties dialog box lets you add beans to the component palette.*

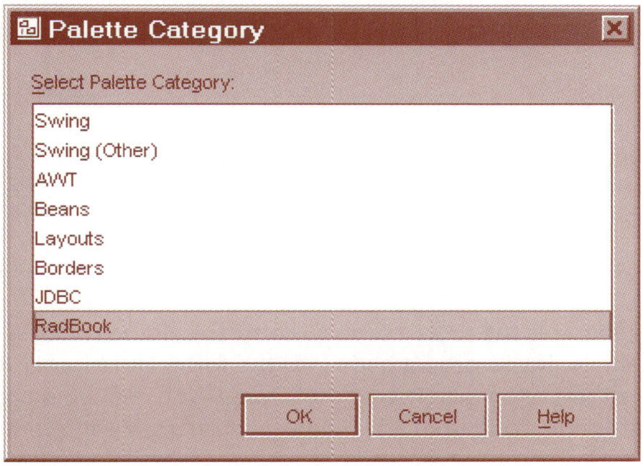

Figure 2.11 *The Palette Category dialog box lets you choose a category for the bean to be added to the component palette.*

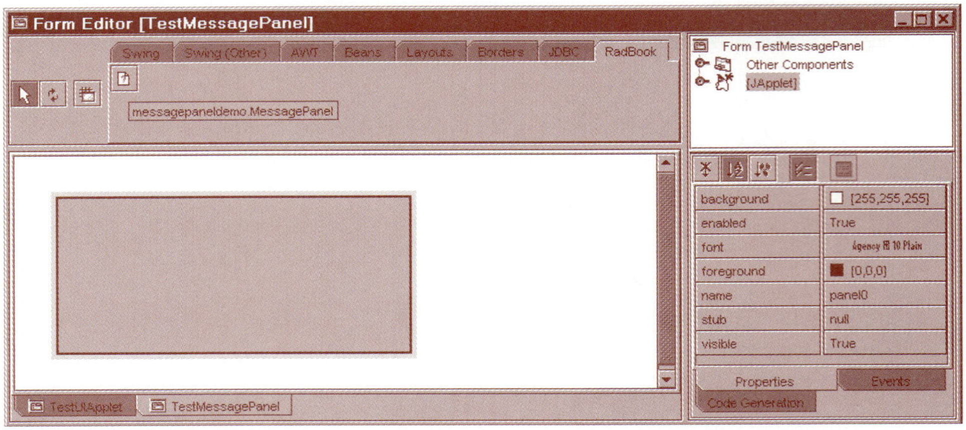

Figure 2.12 *You can now use MessagePanel from the component palette.*

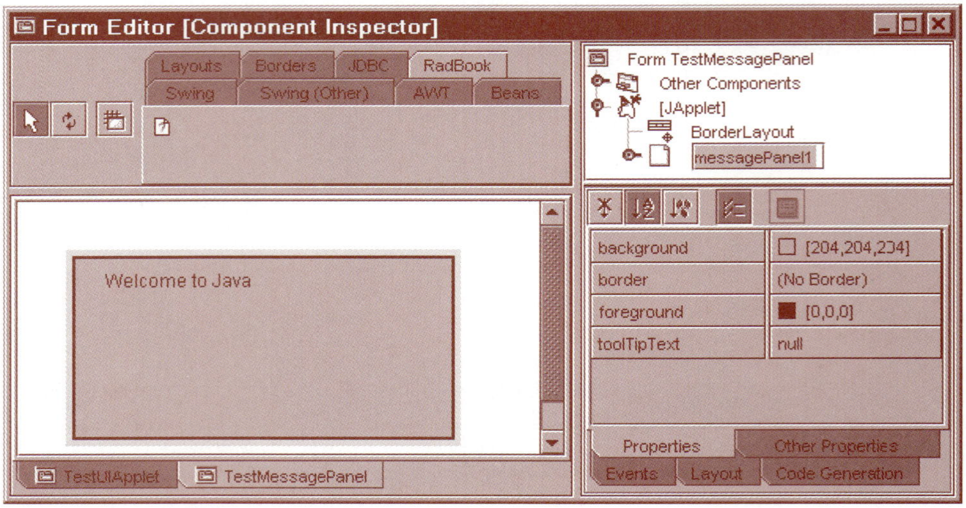

Figure 2.13 *A* `MessagePanel` *bean is placed inside* `TestMessagePanel`.

Tip

To rename or delete a bean, select the bean in the component inspector or in the form, and choose *Rename* or *Delete* from its context menu.

Note

Forte generates the source code to carry out all the changes made in the form. For example, if you drop a bean into the form, Forte generates the code to declare and create an instance of the bean; if you change a property value, Forte generates the code that invokes the property's set method to update the value.

Note
When a nondefault value is assigned to the property from the inspector, the set method is created in the source code for the change. When a default value is assigned to the property, the set method is deleted from the source code, so that the default value can take effect.

Note
If the bean component is modified, you may have to restart Forte for the change to take effect in the component inspector.

You have learned how to create a simple bean component, install it in the component palette, and manipulate it in the form. Below, you will see an example that uses the `MessagePanel` bean in a project with other beans.

Example 2.2 Moving a Message on a Panel

This example involves a `MessagePanel` bean and two `JButton` beans. The `MessagePanel` bean displays a message and two `JButton` beans for moving the message to the left and right, respectively. A sample run of the program is shown in Figure 2.14.

Figure 2.14 *You can use the buttons to move the message to the left and the right.*

Here are the steps to complete the example.

1. Create a new Java applet form named `MoveMessage` in the messagepaneldemo package.
2. Drop a `MessagePanel` from the component palette to the center of the applet to create an instance of `MessagePanel`, named `messagePanel1`.
3. Drop `JPanel` from the Swing page in the component palette to the south of the applet to create an instance of `JPanel`, named `jPanel1`. `jPanel1` may appear very small now, but its size will change after buttons are added to the panel.

continued

Example 2.2 continued

TIP

If you find it difficult to place this panel in the south side of the applet, change the layout of the applet to `AbsoluteLayout` first, as shown in Figure 2.15. Enlarge the applet in the form and place the panel to the applet. Reset the layout back to `BorderLayout` and reset the Direction field for the component in the applet in the Layout tab of the component, as shown in Figure 2.16.

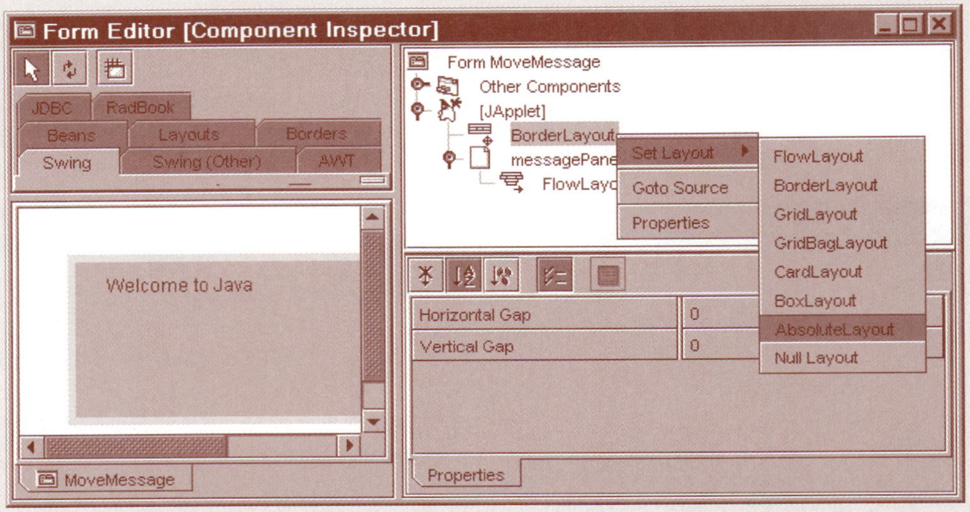

Figure 2.15 *You may change the layout of the applet.*

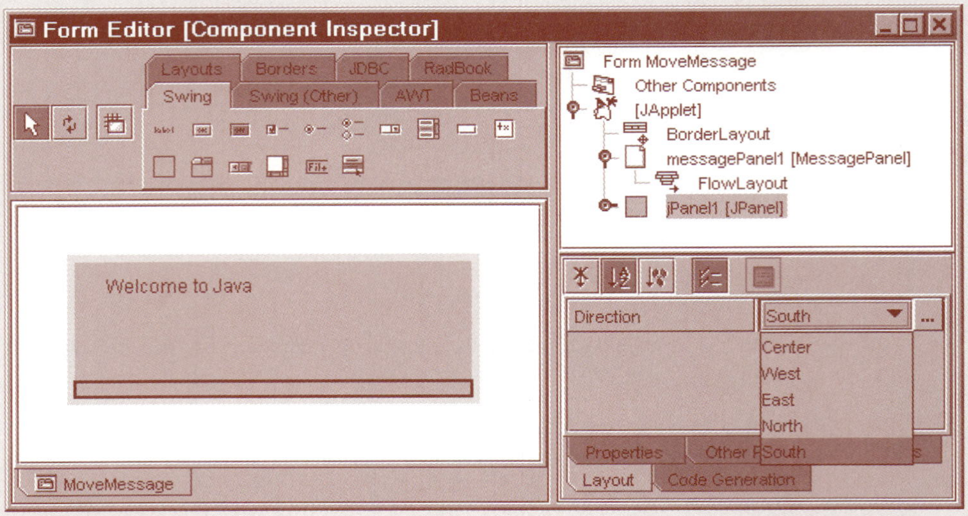

Figure 2.16 *You may set the direction of the component in the applet from the Layout tab of the component.*

4. Drop a `JButton` from the Swing page of the component palette to `jPanel1` twice to create `jButton1` and `jButton2`. In the component inspector, change their names to `jbtLeft` and `jbtRight`, and change their `text` properties to <= and =>, respectively.

5. Double-click the <= button in the form to generate the handler for the `jbtLeft` button. Implement the handler `jbtLeftActionPerformed(ActionEvent e)` to move the message to the left, as shown in Listing 2.2 (Line 44).

6. Double-click the => button in the form to generate the handler for the `jbtRight` button. Implement the handler `jbtRightActionPerformed(ActionEvent e)` to move the message to the right, as shown in Listing 2.2 (Line 39).

```
1    package messagepaneldemo;
2
3    public class MoveMessage extends javax.swing.JApplet {
4      /** Creates new form MoveMessage */
5      public MoveMessage() {
6        initComponents();
7      }
8
9      private void initComponents() {
10       messagePanel1 = new messagepaneldemo.MessagePanel();
11       jPanel1 = new javax.swing.JPanel();
12       jbtLeft = new javax.swing.JButton();
13       jbtRight = new javax.swing.JButton();
14
15       getContentPane().add(messagePanel1,
16         java.awt.BorderLayout.CENTER);
17
18       jbtLeft.setText("<=");
19       jbtLeft.addActionListener(new java.awt.event.ActionListener() {
20         public void actionPerformed(java.awt.event.ActionEvent evt) {
21           jbtLeftActionPerformed(evt);
22         }
23       });
24
25       jPanel1.add(jbtLeft);
26
27       jbtRight.setText("=>");
28       jbtRight.addActionListener(new java.awt.event.ActionListener() {
29         public void actionPerformed(java.awt.event.ActionEvent evt) {
30           jbtRightActionPerformed(evt);
31         }
32       });
33       jPanel1.add(jbtRight);
34       getContentPane().add(jPanel1, java.awt.BorderLayout.SOUTH);
35     }
36
37     private void jbtRightActionPerformed(
38       java.awt.event.ActionEvent evt) {
39       messagePanel1.moveRight();
40     }
41
```

Listing 2.2 *MoveMessage.java*

continued

Example 2.2 continued

```
    private void jbtLeftActionPerformed(
      java.awt.event.ActionEvent evt) {
      messagePanel1.moveLeft();
    }

    // Variables declaration - do not modify
    private messagepaneldemo.MessagePanel messagePanel1;
    private javax.swing.JPanel jPanel1;
    private javax.swing.JButton jbtLeft;
    private javax.swing.JButton jbtRight;
    // End of variables declaration
  }
```

Listing 2.2 *continued*

Example Review

When the <= button is clicked, the messagePanel1's moveLeft() method is invoked to move the message to the left if there is room for the move. When the => button is clicked, the messagePanel1's moveRight() method is invoked to move the message to the right if there is room for the move.

During design time, you can set properties for each bean and generate handlers for bean events. You cannot test how beans interact with one another, however. For example, you cannot see the effect of clicking a button at design time. You will only see it at runtime.

2.5 Bean Properties

Properties are discrete, named attributes of a Java bean that can affect its appearance or behavior. They are often data fields of a bean. For example, the MessagePanel component has a property named message that represents the message to be displayed on the panel. Private data fields are often used to hide specific implementations from the user and prevent the user from accidentally corrupting the properties. Accessor methods are provided instead to let the user read and write the properties. To enable properties to be accessed from a builder tool, either the signatures of the accessor methods must conform to the accessor method naming pattern or the properties and their accessor methods have to be explicitly specified using a custom BeanInfo class.

2.5.1 Property-Naming Patterns

The bean property naming pattern is a mechanism of the JavaBeans component model that simplifies the bean developer's task of presenting properties for inspection in a builder tool. A property can be a primitive data type or an object type. The property type dictates the signature of the accessor methods and determines how the user edits the property in the component inspector.

In general, the get method is named get<PropertyName>(), which takes no parameters and returns an object of a type identical to the property type. For example,

```
public String getMessage() { }

public int getXCoordinate() { }

public int getYCoordinate() { }
```

For a property of `boolean` type, the get method should be named `is<PropertyName>()`, which returns a `boolean` value. For example,

```
public boolean isCentered() { }
```

The set method should be named `set<PropertyName>()`, which takes a single parameter identical to the property type and returns `void`. For example,

```
public void setMessage(String s) { }

public void setXCoordinate(int x) { }

public void setYCoordinate(int y) { }

public void setCentered(boolean centered) { }
```

NOTE

A property may be read-only with a get method but no set method, or write-only with a set method but no get method. However, Forte cannot expose the property in the component inspector unless its get and set methods are both provided in the component.

2.5.2 Properties and Data Fields

Properties describe the state of the bean. Naturally, data fields are used to store properties. However, a bean property is not necessarily a data field. For example, you may create a new property named `messageLength` that represents the number of the characters in `message`. The get method for the property may be defined as follows:

```
public int getMessageLength() {
  return message.length();
}
```

To enable the property to be seen in the Forte's component inspector window, both the get and set methods must be provided. Since the `messageLength` property has no set method, you would not see it in the component inspector. To be able to see it, you must provide a set method with a dummy parameter that does nothing, as shown below:

```
public void setMessageLength(int dummy) { }
```

NOTE

You may have multiple get and set methods, but there must be one get or set method with a signature conforming to the accessor method patterns. Any other methods are for programmatic use, and are not available to the visual designer.

2.5.3 Property Types

Properties can have any data type, including primitive data types, arrays, and objects. JavaBeans classifies properties into four types: *simple*, *indexed*, *bound,* and *constraint.*

A *simple property* represents a single value of primitive data types or object types. A pair of get and set methods defines the simple property. The get method is constructed as `get<Property>` or `is<Property>` for `boolean` values. The set method is constructed as `set<Property>`.

An *indexed property,* or array property, represents an array of elements. The property supports getting and setting the entire array at once. Some builder tools may also support getting and setting individual elements. Forte provides a built-in editor for arrays of strings. The signatures of the accessor methods are:

```
public PropertyType[] get<Property>() { }

public void set<Property>(PropertyType[] a) { }
```

JavaBeans provides support for bound and constraint properties. A *bound property* of a component is one for which a notification service is provided when the property changes. The components interested in the property receive the notification and perform operations in response to the property change. These components are related through the bound property. Sometimes, when a property change occurs, the listener component for the bound property may wish to validate the change and reject it if it is inappropriate. Such a property is referred to as *constraint property*. These properties will be introduced in Chapter 10, "Bound and Constraint Properties."

2.6 Property Editors

The inspector uses property editors to update property values. Forte provides standard editors for the properties of primitive data types, array of strings, and several commonly used object types, such as `Color` and `Font`. The standard editors can be classified into *simple editor*, *array editor*, *choice-menu editor,* and *object editor* according to their appearance in the inspector.

- A *simple editor* edits a single value, such as a number, a character, or a string. The user edits the value of the property directly in the component inspector. The property editors for `message`, `xCoordinate`, and `yCoordinate` in the `MessagePanel` component are all examples of simple editors.
- An *array editor* edits an array of elements. The elements may be of any data type. The inspector has no built-in support for editing array properties except for arrays of strings. The component developer may provide a property editor for manipulating the array property.
- A *choice-menu editor* edits the value as numbers, characters, or strings, with all possible values enumerated in a choice menu. A `boolean` property is of the

enumerated type with the values True and False, which is built into Forte. The component developer has to provide a property editor for any other choice-menu editor.

- An *object editor* edits an instance of the object. Properties of the object type must have their own property editors, except for several standard Java classes, such as `Color` and `Font`, whose editors are predefined in Forte.

The editors of array properties and object properties appear in the inspector with an ellipsis (. . .) at the right of the value when the property is selected. The user clicks the ellipsis to bring up the property editor.

The following example demonstrates the use of Forte's built-in property editors to manipulate array properties, enumerated type properties, and object properties. In Chapter 11, "Bean Introspection and Customization," you will learn how to write your own property editors.

Example 2.3 Using Editors for Array, Enumerated, and Object Properties

This example creates a bean to display a single message or a composite message. The composite message is constructed from an array of strings. The bean uses a `boolean` property, `displayed`, to turn the display on or off, and another `boolean` property, `showingSingleMessage`, to determine whether a single message or a composite message is shown on the panel when `displayed` is true. The new component is shown in Figure 2.17.

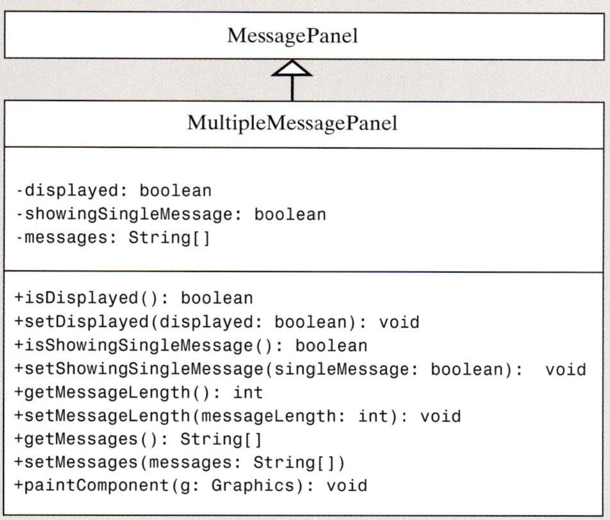

Figure 2.17 *The* `MultipleMessagePanel` *extends* `MessagePanel` *to display multiple messages.*

continued

Example 2.3 continued

Follow the steps below to complete the example.

1. Create a new class for the `MultipleMessagePanel` component that extends `messagepaneldemo.MessagePanel`. Complete `MultipleMessagePanel`, as shown in Listing 2.3. Compile it and install it in the component palette.

2. Create an applet form named `TestMultipleMessagePanel`. Click `MultipleMessagePanel` in the component palette and drop it into the form for `TestMultipleMessagePanel` to create `multipleMessagePanel1`. The Form Editor for the project is shown in Figure 2.18.

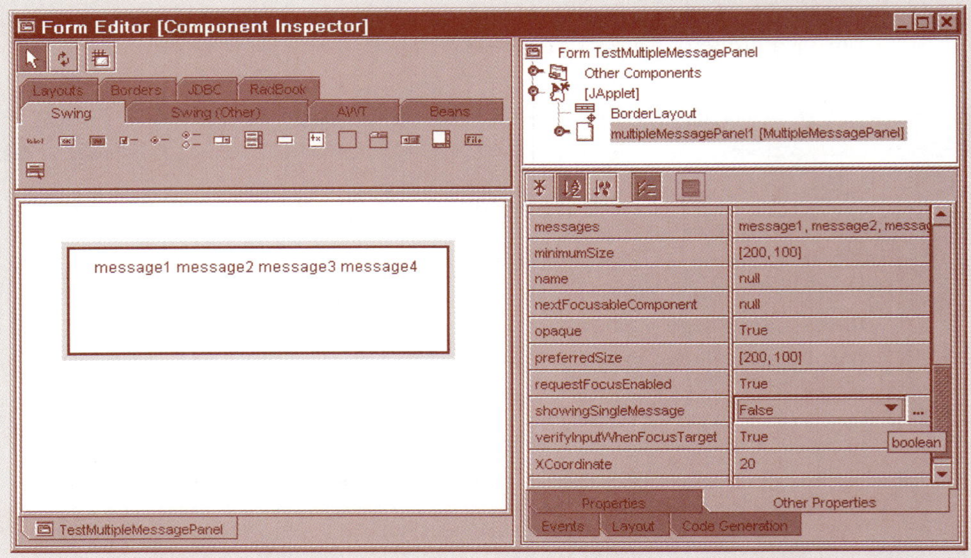

Figure 2.18 *A* `MultipleMessagePanel` *bean is placed into the applet.*

```
package messagepaneldemo;

import java.awt.*;

public class MultipleMessagePanel extends MessagePanel {
  private String[] messages =
    {"message1", "message2", "message3", "message4"};
  private boolean displayed = true;
  private boolean showingSingleMessage = false;

  public MultipleMessagePanel() {
  }

  public boolean isDisplayed() {
    return displayed;
  }

```

Listing 2.3 *MultipleMessagePanel.java*

```
  public void setDisplayed(boolean displayed) {
    this.displayed = displayed;
  }

  public int getMessageLength() {
    return getMessage().length();
  }

  public void setMessageLength(int dummy) {
  }

  public boolean isShowingSingleMessage() {
    return showingSingleMessage;
  }

  public void setShowingSingleMessage(boolean b) {
    this.showingSingleMessage = b;
  }

  public String[] getMessages() {
    return messages;
  }

  public void setMessages(String[] messages) {
    System.arraycopy(messages, 0, this.messages, 0, messages.length);
    repaint();
  }

  public void paintComponent(Graphics g) {
    // Clear the panel
    g.clearRect(0, 0, getSize().width, getSize().height);

    // Things to display
    String thingsToDisplay = new String();

    if (displayed) {
      if (showingSingleMessage)
        thingsToDisplay = getMessage();
      else {
        for (int i=0; i<messages.length; i++)
          thingsToDisplay += messages[i] + " ";
      }
    }

    if (isCentered()) {
      // Get font metrics for the font
      FontMetrics fm = g.getFontMetrics(getFont());

      // Find the center location to display
      int w = fm.stringWidth(thingsToDisplay); // Get the width
      int h = fm.getAscent(); // Get the string height
      setXCoordinate((getSize().width-w)/2);
      setYCoordinate((getSize().height+h)/2);
    }

    g.drawString(thingsToDisplay,
      getXCoordinate(), getYCoordinate());
  }
}
```

Listing 2.3 *continued*

continued

Example 2.3 continued

Example Review

The `MultipleMessagePanel` class extends the `MessagePanel` class created in Example 2.1.

The `showingSingleMessage` is a `boolean` property that determines whether a single message or a composite message is displayed. By default, it is false, indicating that a composite message is displayed. If you change the property to True in the component inspector and double-click `multipleMessagePanel1`, you would see a single message, "Welcome to Java," displayed. The `boolean` property is an enumerated type with two values, True and False, for selection in a choice menu. Double-clicking `multipleMessagePanel1` in the component tree causes the `paintComponent` method to be executed. When you set the `showingSingleMessage` property, the `paintComponent` method is not invoked.

The `messageLength` property represents the number of characters in `message`. It is worth noting that it is not a data field in the `MultipleMessagePanel` component. The set method of the property does nothing, and its presence in the component is for the property to be read during design time, since Forte requires both get and set methods to be present for the property to be shown in the inspector.

The `messages` property is an array property, consisting of four strings with initial values, "message1," "message2," "message3," and "message4." The strings in the array are separated by commas, as shown in the component inspector in Figure 2.19. Click the ellipsis to bring up the property editor shown in Figure

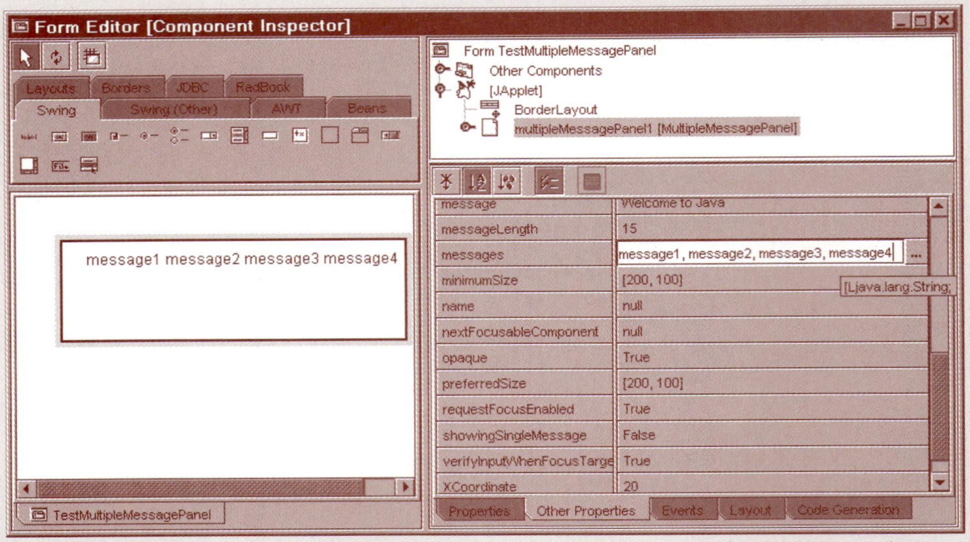

Figure 2.19 *You may edit an array of strings from the component inspector using a standard editor in Forte.*

2.20. Change the strings to "Welcome," "to," Java," "!!!"; and click OK to finish editing. You will see "Welcome to Java!!!" displayed on the panel, if the `showingSingleMessage` property is false.

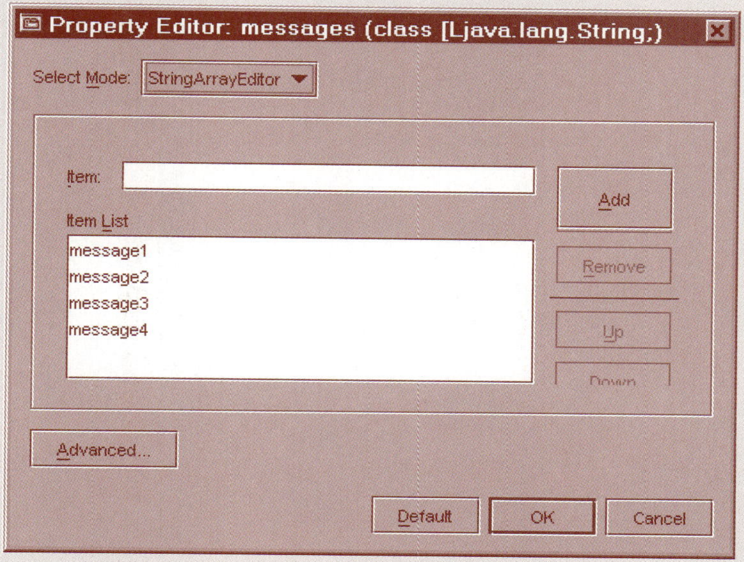

Figure 2.20 *Forte has a built-in property editor for manipulating an array of strings.*

Note

There is a bug in Forte that prevents you from editing the strings. To circumvent it, remove the string you want to edit, and add a new string.

The `background`, `foreground`, and `font` are the object properties. They are defined in `java.awt.Component` and inherited by `MultipleMessagePanel`. Forte provides built-in editors for the `Color` class and the `Font` class. For example, you can click the ellipsis on the `font` property to bring up the font property editor, as shown in Figure 2.21.

This class can be improved to display the multiple messages on different lines. See Exercise 2.5.

continued

Example 2.3 continued

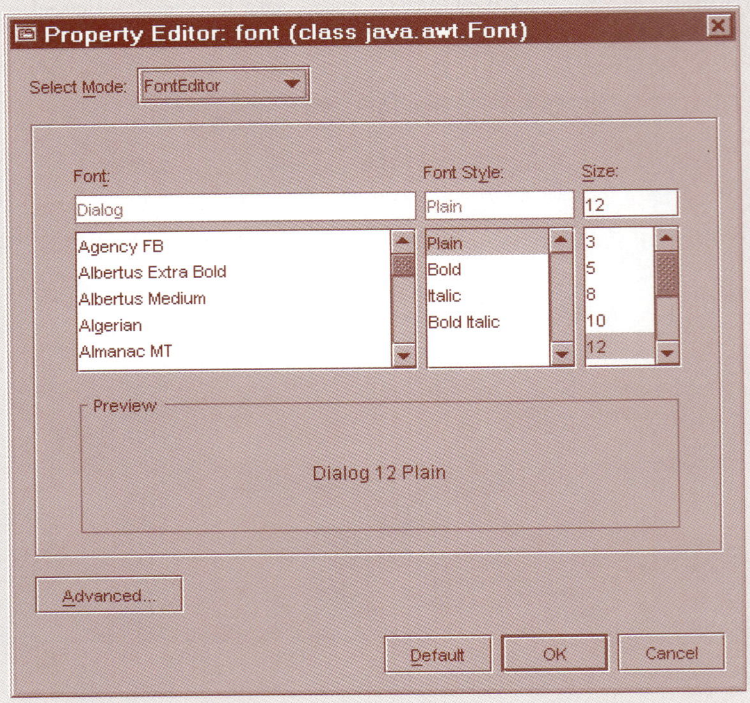

Figure 2.21 *The* `Font` *class property editor lets you choose desired type, style, and size for the font.*

Chapter Summary

In this chapter, you learned that a JavaBeans component is simply a Java class that is public and serializable and has a public default constructor. Beans are especially useful in builder tools that enable programmers to visually manipulate them through the component inspector during design time. You learned how to write simple beans, install beans in the component palette in Forte, and update bean properties during runtime.

Review Questions

2.1 What are the minimum requirements for a bean component? Is a bean component a Java class? Is a Java class a bean component?

2.2 How do you install a bean component into the component palette in Forte?

2.3 How do you display the component inspector?

2.4 How do you name a get method for a non-boolean property? How do you name a get method for a boolean property? How do you name a set method for a property?

2.5 List the types of properties.

2.6 Is a property always a data field of the class?

2.7 Some Java builder tools can work with read-only properties. Can Forte display read-only properties in the inspector?

2.8 If a superclass is not a bean component, can a subclass be a bean component?

2.9 Is a bean component always a GUI component?

Programming Exercises

2.1 Add a button labeled Up and a button labeled Down in Example 2.2 to move the message upward and downward, as shown in Figure 2.22.

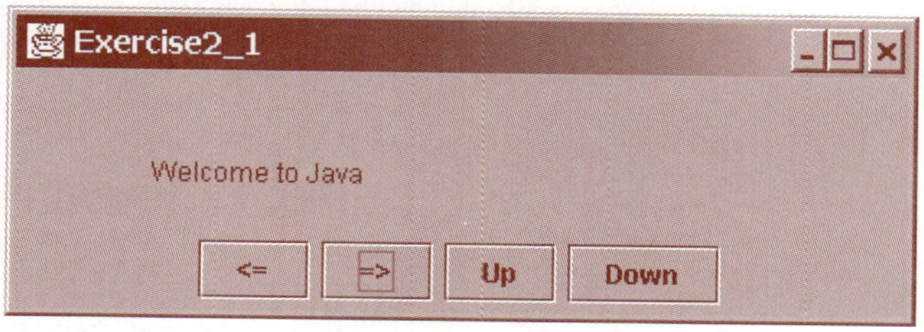

Figure 2.22 *You can move the message up and down as well as left and right.*

2.2 Create a bean component named `Circle` that displays a circle in the center of the panel. The `Circle` component has a property named `radius` that determines the size of the circle, and it also contains a method for computing the area of the circle. Install the component in the component palette and use it to create an applet that enables the user to set the radius and displays the area of the circle. A sample run of the applet is shown in Figure 2.23.

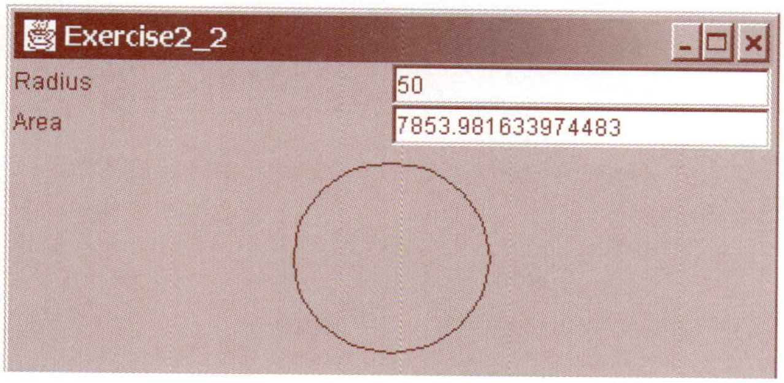

Figure 2.23 *You can set the radius of the circle and display its area.*

2.3 Create a bean component named `MessageControl` that controls how a message is displayed. The message can blink or move from right to left circularly, or both at the same time. The properties of `MessageControl` are as follows:

- **`message`** is a string for the message to be displayed.
- **`blinking`** is a `boolean` value indicating whether the message should blink.
- **`moving`** is a `boolean` value indicating whether the message moves.

2.4 Create a bean component named `ImageControl` that displays an image for a specified image file. The properties of `ImageControl` are as follows:

- **`imageFilename`** is the name of the file containing the image.
- **`stretched`** is a `boolean` value indicating whether the image is stretched to fill the entire view area.
- Use the Form Editor to create an applet with two objects of `ImageControl` placed in its content pane of the `GridLayout`, as shown in Figure 2.24.

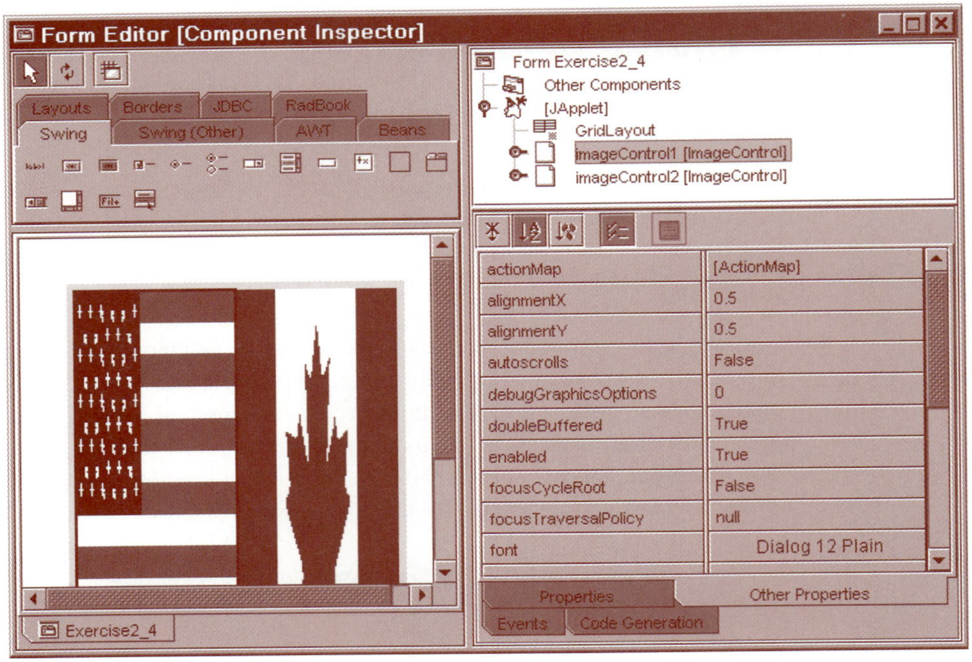

Figure 2.24 *The* `ImageControl` *component is used to display an image.*

2.5 Modify the `MultipleMessagePanel` class in Example 2.3 to display each message on a separate line. Add the property `vgap` to indicate the vertical gap between the lines. The messages are centered if the `centered` property is true, as shown in Figure 2.25.

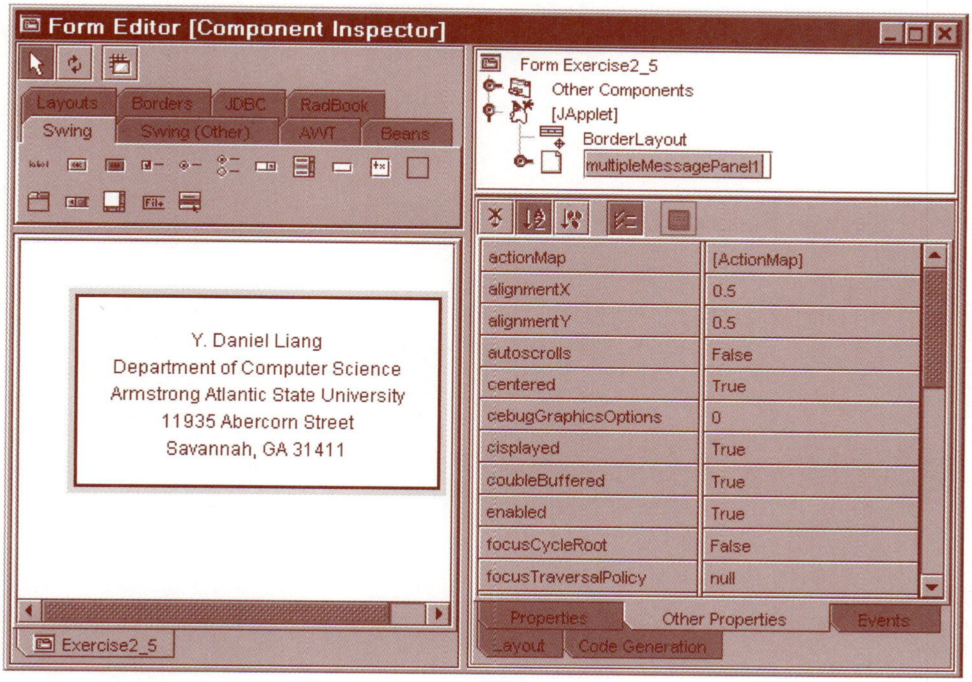

Figure 2.25 *Multiple messages are displayed on different lines.*

CHAPTER 3

Bean Events

Objectives

- To review the Java event delegation model.
- To create a new event class and listener interface.
- To develop source components using new event sets or existing event sets.
- To make source components from scratch or from existing components.
- To implement listener components.
- To become familiar with adapters, inner classes, and anonymous classes.
- To learn how to hook up source components with listener components in Forte.

3.1 Introduction

A bean may communicate with other beans. The Java event delegation model provides the foundation for beans to send, receive, and handle events. When something happens to a bean, such as a mouse click on a `javax.swing.JButton` bean, an event object is created that encapsulates information pertaining to the event. The bean passes the event object to the interested beans for the event to be processed.

Events are typically generated by Java GUI components, such as `javax.swing.JButton`, but are not limited to GUI components. This chapter introduces the development of beans that can generate events and beans that listen for events. You will learn how to create custom events and link beans via events in Forte.

3.2 Java Event Model

The Java event model consists of the following four types of classes. Their interrelationship is illustrated in Figure 3.1.

- The event object
- The event source
- The event listener interface
- The event listener

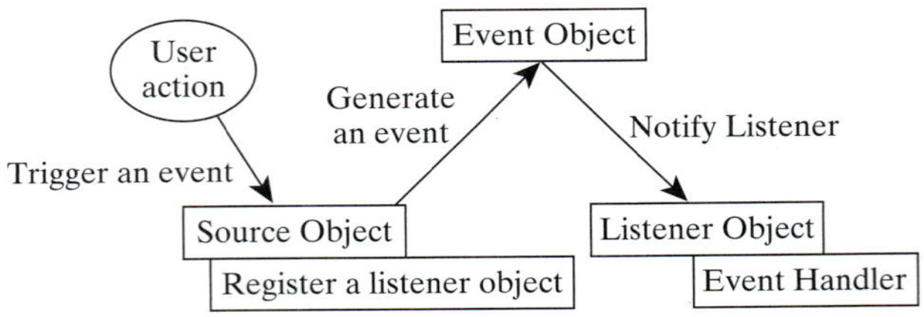

Figure 3.1 *An event is triggered by user or system actions on a source object, and the source object "fires" the event and invokes the handler of the listener object to process the event.*

An *event* is a signal to the program that something has happened. It can be generated by external user actions, such as mouse movements, mouse button clicks, and keystrokes, or by the operating system, such as a timer. An *event object* contains the information that describes the event. A *source object* is where the event originates. When an event occurs on a source object, an event object is created. An object interested in the event receives the event. Such an object is called a *listener*. Not all objects can receive events. To become a listener, an object must be registered as a listener by the source object. The source object maintains a list of listeners and notifies all the registered listeners by invoking the event-handling method implemented on the listener object. The handlers are defined in the class known as the *event listener interface*. Each class of an event object has a corresponding event listener interface.

NOTE
The Java event model is referred to as a *delegation-based model* because the source object delegates the event to the listeners for processing.

3.2.1 Event Objects

The Java event model is essential to Java GUI programming. Each GUI component is associated with one or more events, as shown in Figure 3.2.

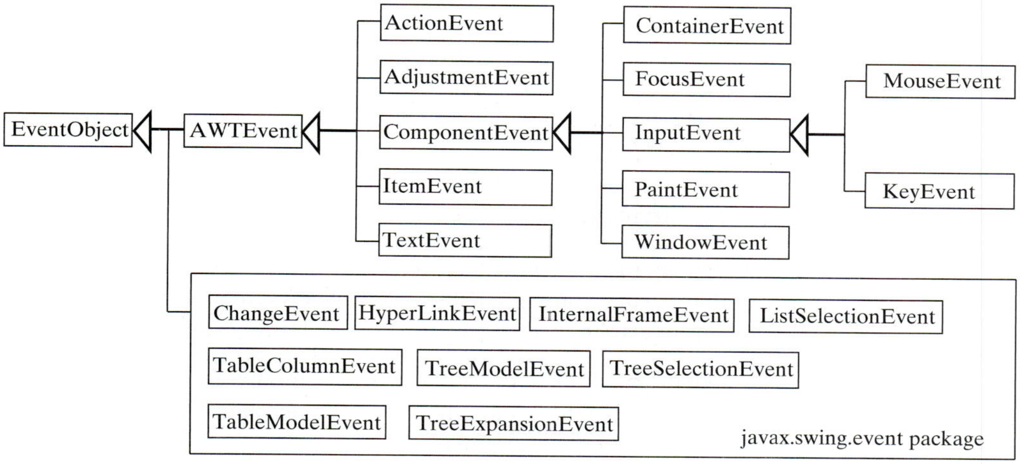

Figure 3.2 *The* `java.util.EventObject` *class is the root of all Java event classes.*

The event classes introduced in JDK 1.1 are grouped in the `java.awt.event` package. These classes were originally designed for AWT components, but many Swing components generate these events. The events in the `javax.swing.event` package are only applicable to Swing components.

The event class contains whatever data values and methods are pertinent to the particular event type. For example, the `KeyEvent` class describes the data values related to a key event and contains the methods, such as `getKeyChar()`, for retrieving the key associated with the event.

All the event classes extend `EventObject`. Below, in Section 3.3 "Creating Custom Event Sets and Source Components," you will learn how to create custom event classes by extending `EventObject`.

3.2.2 Source Components

The component on which an event is generated is referred to as an *event source*. Every Java AWT and Swing user interface component is an *event source*. For example, `JButton` is an event source because it generates a `java.awt.event.ActionEvent` when a button object is clicked.

The source component contains the code that detects an external or internal action that triggers the event. Upon detecting the action, the source should fire an event to the listeners by invoking the event handler defined by the listeners. The source component must also contain methods for registering and deregistering listeners.

3.2.3 Event Listener Interface

Every event class is associated with an event listener interface that defines one or more methods referred to as *handlers*. The handlers are implemented by the listener components. The source component invokes the listeners' handlers when an event is detected.

Since an event class and its listener interface are coexistent, they are often referred to as an *event set* or *event pair*. The event listener interface must be named as *X*Listener for the *X*Event. For example, the listener interface for `ActionEvent` is `ActionListener`.

3.2.4 Listener Components

A listener component for an event must implement the event listener interface. The object of the listener component cannot receive event notifications from a source component unless the object is registered as a listener of the source.

A listener component may implement any number of listener interfaces to listen to several types of events. A source component may register many listeners. A source component may register itself as a listener.

Here is an example that creates a source object and two listener objects, and registers the listeners with the source object.

```
import javax.swing.*;
import java.awt.event.*;

public class Test {
  public static void main(String[] args) {
    JFrame frame = new JFrame("Test");
    // Create a source object
    JButton jbt = new JButton("OK");
    frame.getContentPane().add(jbt);
    frame.setSize(200, 200);
    frame.setVisible(true);

    // Create listeners
    MyListener listener1 = new MyListener();
    YourListener listener2 = new YourListener();

    // Register listeners
    jbt.addActionListener(listener1);
    jbt.addActionListener(listener2);
  }
}

/** MyListener class */
class MyListener implements ActionListener {
  public void actionPerformed(ActionEvent e) {
```

```
      System.out.println("I will process it!");
    }
  }

  /** YourListener class*/
  class YourListener implements ActionListener {
    public void actionPerformed(ActionEvent e) {
      System.out.println("You will process it!");
    }
  }
```

3.2.5 Review of the *JButton* Component

To learn how to create custom event sets and your own source components, let us take a look at the `JButton` component and its associated event set and listener component.

TIP

You can find the source code of a class in the Java 2 API from src.zip in JDK 1.4 installation directory.

A `JButton` instance can fire an `ActionEvent`. `java.awt.event.ActionEvent` extends `java.awt.AWTEvent`, which extends `java.util.EventObject`. `ActionEvent` contains two constructors:

```
public ActionEvent(Object source, int id, String command)
public ActionEvent(Object source, int id, String command,
  int modifiers)
```

These constructors can be used by source components to create event objects.

A listener of `ActionEvent` must implement the `ActionListener` interface. `java.awt.event.ActionListener` extends `java.util.EventListener`. `ActionListener` simply contains the `actionPerformed` method, which must be implemented by the listener component that responds to `ActionEvent`.

The `JButton` is a subclass of `AbstractButton`. The `fireActionPerformed` method defined in `AbstractButton` is invoked when a `JButton` object is clicked. This method invokes the registered listener's `actionPerformed` handler.

The `AbstractButton` class also provides the `addActionListener` and `removeActionListener` methods for registering listeners. These registration methods are defined as follows:

```
public synchronized void addActionListener(ActionListener l)
public synchronized void removeActionListener(ActionListener l)
```

As shown in Figure 3.3, a listener component implements the `ActionListener` interface and provides the actual code for handling the event in the `actionPerformed` method. The application class creates an instance of `JButton` and an instance of the listener component, and registers the listener with the source. When an `Action-`

`Event` occurs on a button, the button object invokes the listener's `actionPerformed` method to deal with the event.

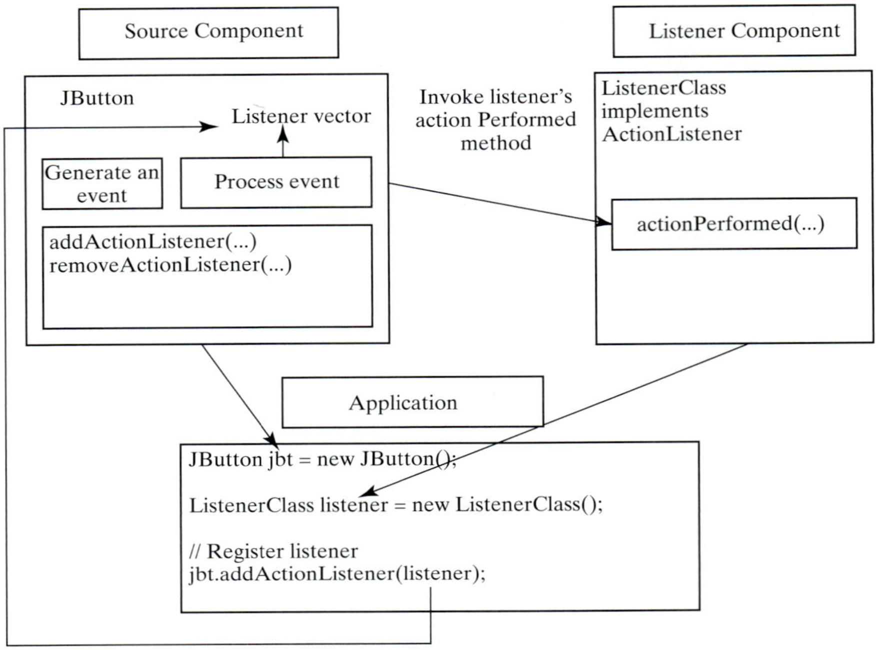

Figure 3.3 *The source component invokes the listener's handler to process the events.*

3.3 Creating Custom Event Sets and Source Components

You have already used event sets and event source components in Java GUI programming, since certain event sets and source components are provided as part of the Java API. In this section, you will learn how to create custom event sets and develop your own source components. By developing your own event sets and source components, you will gain a better understanding of the Java event model.

A custom event class must extend `java.util.EventObject` or a subclass of `java.util.EventObject`. Additionally, you need to provide data members and methods to describe and process the event.

A custom event listener interface must always extend `java.util.EventListener`. You need to define the signature of the handlers for the event. The listener interface should be named <*Event*>Listener for a builder tool to recognize it during design time.

A source component must have the appropriate registration methods for adding and removing listeners. To enable a builder tool to recognize events, the registration methods must conform to the registration method naming patterns. Events can be unicasted (only one object is notified of the event) or multicasted (each object in a list of listeners is notified of the event). The naming pattern for adding a unicast listener is

```
public void add<Event>Listener(<Event>Listener l) throws
  TooManyListenersException;
```

The naming pattern for adding a multicast listener is the same, except that it does not throw the `TooManyListenersException`.

```
public void add<Event>Listener(<Event>Listener l)
```

The naming pattern for removing a listener (either unicast or multicast) is:

```
public void remove<Event>Listener(<Event>Listener l)
```

A source component contains the code that creates an event object and passes it to the listening components by calling a method in the listener's event listener interface. You may use a standard Java event class like `ActionEvent` to create event objects or may define your own event classes if necessary.

Example 3.1 Creating a Custom Event Set and a Source Component

This example creates a custom event set named `TickEvent` and `TickListener` for describing tick events, and develops a source component that generates a tick event at every specified time interval in milliseconds. The event class shown in Listing 3.1 contains the information on tick count and tick interval.

```
package eventdemo;

public class TickEvent extends java.util.EventObject {
  /** tickCount counts the number of ticks for the event */
  private long tickCount;

  /** tickInterval is the interval between ticks in milliseconds */
  private long tickInterval;

  /** Construct a TickEvent */
  public TickEvent(Object o) {
    super(o);
  }

  /** Return tickCount */
  public long getTickCount() {
    return tickCount;
  }

  /** Set a new tickCount */
  public void setTickCount(long tickCount) {
    this.tickCount = tickCount;
  }

  /** Return tickInterval */
  public long getTickInterval() {
```

Listing 3.1 *TickEvent.java*

continued

Example 3.1 continued

```
      return tickInterval;
    }

    /** Set a new tickInterval */
    public void setTickInterval(long milliseconds) {
      tickInterval = milliseconds;
    }
  }
```

Listing 3.1 *continued*

An event listener interface must be defined for each new event class. The listener interface for `TickEvent` presented in Listing 3.2 contains a method, `handleTick`, that will be implemented by the listeners of `TickEvent`.

```
package eventdemo;

import eventdemo.TickEvent;

public interface TickListener extends java.util.EventListener {
  /** Handle a TickEvent, to be implemented by a listener */
  public void handleTick(TickEvent e);
}
```

Listing 3.2 *TickListener.java*

The source component is responsible for registering listeners, generating events, and notifying listeners by invoking the methods defined in the listeners' interfaces. The `Tick` component presented in Listing 3.3 is capable of registering multiple listeners, generating a `TickEvent` object at every specified time interval, and notifying the listeners by invoking their `handleTick` methods.

```
package eventdemo;

import eventdemo.*;
import java.util.Vector;

public class Tick implements java.io.Serializable, Runnable {
  /** A thread to control tick */
  protected Thread thread = null;

  /** Whether the thread is suspended */
  private boolean suspended = true;

  /** Store Tick listeners in a vector */
  private Vector tickListenerList;

  /** Tick event e */
  private TickEvent e;

  /** Tick count and Tick interval */
  private long tickCount = 0;
  private long tickInterval = 1000;

  /** Default constructor */
  public Tick() {
    // Create a TickEvent
```

Listing 3.3 *Tick.java*

```
    e = new TickEvent(this);

    // Create and start the thread
    thread = new Thread(this);
    thread.start();
  }

  /** Return tickInterval */
  public long getTickInterval() {
    return tickInterval;
  }

  /** Set a tickInterval */
  public void setTickInterval(long interval) {
    tickInterval = interval;
  }

  /** Run the thread */
  public void run() {
    while (true) {
      try {
        Thread.sleep(tickInterval);
        synchronized (this) {
          while (suspended)
            wait();
        }
      }
      catch (InterruptedException ex) {  }

      // Adjust Tick count and interval
      e.setTickCount(tickCount++);
      e.setTickInterval(tickInterval);

      // Fire TickEvent
      processEvent(e);
    }
  }

  /** Resume the thread */
  public synchronized void resume() {
    if (suspended) {
      suspended = false;
      notify();
    }
  }

  /** Suspend the thread */
  public synchronized void suspend() {
    suspended = true;
  }

  /** Register a tick event listener */
  public synchronized void addTickListener(TickListener l) {
    Vector v = tickListenerList == null ?
      new Vector(2) : (Vector)tickListenerList.clone();
    if (!v.contains(l)) {
      v.addElement(l);
      tickListenerList = v;
    }
  }

```

Listing 3.3 *continued*

continued

Example 3.1 continued

```
87    /** Remove a tick event listener */
88    public synchronized void removeTickListener(TickListener l) {
89      if (tickListenerList != null && tickListenerList.contains(l)) {
90        tickListenerList.removeElement(l);
91      }
92    }
93
94    /** Fire TickEvent */
95    public void processEvent(TickEvent e) {
96      Vector v;
97
98      synchronized (this) {
99        v = (Vector)tickListenerList.clone();
100     }
101
102     for (int i = 0; i < v.size(); i++) {
103       TickListener listener = (TickListener)v.elementAt(i);
104       listener.handleTick(e);
105     }
106   }
107 }
```

Listing 3.3 *continued*

Follow the steps below to complete the project:

1. Create a new package named eventdemo, and create an applet named `TestTick` using the Swing JApplet form wizard. Create classes for `TickEvent`, `TickListener`, and `Tick` in the project, compile the classes, and install the `Tick` component into the component palette. See Section 2.4.2, "Using Beans in Forte," for installing a JavaBeans component to the component palette in Forte.

2. Click `Tick` from the component palette and drop it in the form for `TestTick`, as shown in Figure 3.4. Since `Tick` is not a UI component, it is not seen in the form, but in the component inspector you can see a bean named `tick1` whose properties and event handler can be visually manipulated in the component inspector. The component inspector in Figure 3.4 shows the bean property. To reveal the bean event handlers, choose the Event tab at the bottom of the component inspector, as shown in Figure 3.5. In Section 3.7, "Using Adapters in Forte," you will learn how to link the source component with the listeners by implementing the handlers using Forte's Form Editor.

Example Review

The `Tick` class is a JavaBeans component, but `TickEvent` and `TickListener` are not JavaBeans components. Therefore, `Tick` can be installed in the component palette, but not `TickEvent` and `TickListener`.

The `suspend()` (Lines 73–75) and `resume()`(Lines 65–70) methods defined in the `Tick` class are for suspending and resuming ticking. Their implementation is

Figure 3.4 *You can add a non-UI JavaBeans component into the form and manipulate its properties and event handlers from the component inspector.*

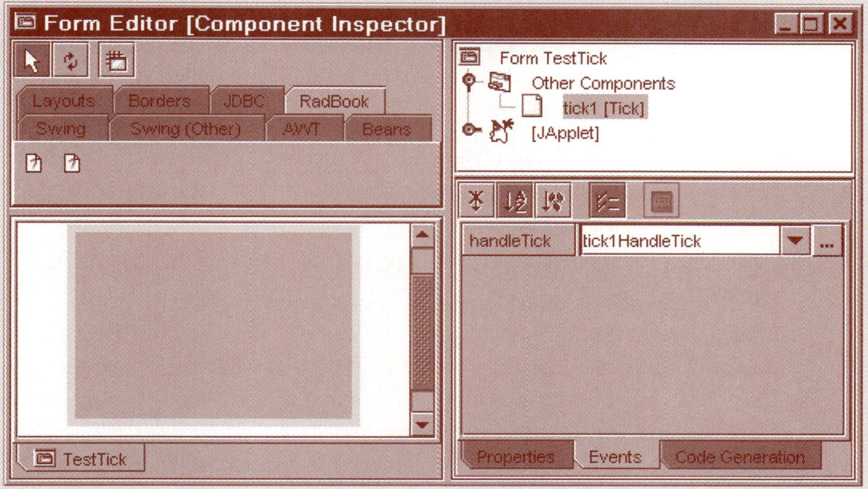

Figure 3.5 *The* `handleTick` *handler is shown in the component inspector, where you can link the source component to a listener in Forte.*

compatible with Java 2. The `suspend()` and `resume()` methods defined in the `Thread` class in Java 1 are deprecated because they are known to be deadlock-prone. They are replaced by the new implementation in the `Tick` class. In the implementation for the `run()` method (Lines 44–62), the `wait()` method is used, along with a `boolean` variable, to indicate whether a thread is suspended.

continued

Example 3.1 continued

`TickEvent` is a new event class. Most of the time you don't need to create your own event classes unless you want to encapsulate information not available in the existing event classes, as in the case of the `TickEvent` class that contains tick count and tick interval. In this case, you need to write an event set that includes the event class and its listener interface.

Since the source component `Tick` is designed for multiple listeners, a `java.util.Vector` instance called `tickListenerList` is used to hold all the listeners for the source component. The data type of the elements in the vector is `Object`. To add a listener `listener` to the `tickListenerList` vector, use

```
tickListenerList.addElement(listener);
```

To remove a listener, `listener`, from `tickListenerList`, use

```
tickListenerList.removeElement(listener);
```

The `addTickListener` method does not add the listener twice if it is already in the list. The `removeTickListener` method removes a listener if it is in the list. `tickListenerList` is an instance of `Vector`, which is like a flexible array that can grow or shrink dynamically. Initially, `tickListenerList` is new `Vector(2)`, which implies that the capacity of the vector is 2, but the capacity can be changed dynamically. If more than two listeners are added to `tickListenerList`, the vector size will be automatically increased.

The `addTickListener` and `removeTickListener` methods are synchronized to prevent data corruption on `tickListenerList` when attempting to register multiple listeners concurrently.

The `processEvent` method is invoked at every `tickInterval` in milliseconds. This notifies the listeners in the `tickListenerList` vector by calling each listener's `handleTick` method to process the event. It is possible that a new listener may be added or an existing listener may be removed when `processEvent` is running. To avoid corruption on `tickListenerList`, a clone `v` of `tickListenerList` is created for use to notify listeners. To avoid corruption when creating the clone, all the methods of the object are synchronized, as follows:

```
synchronized (this) {
  v = (Vector)tickListenerList.clone();
}
```

The `Tick` component is created from scratch. If you build a new component that extends a component capable of generating events, the new component inherits the ability to generate the same type of events. For example, the `MessagePanel` component is derived from `javax.swing.JPanel`, which is a subclass of `java.awt.Component`. The `MessagePanel` component can detect and generate a number of events, such as key and mouse events. You don't need to write the code to generate these events and register listeners for them, since the code is already given in the superclass. However, you still need to write the code to make your component capable of firing events not supported in the superclass.

NOTE

Instead of using `Vector`, you can use `java.util.ArrayList` to store listeners. You can also use `javax.swing.EventListenerList` to store listeners. Using `EventListenerList` is preferred, since it provides the support for synchronization and is efficient in the case of no listeners. In Chapter 4, "Developing and Using Components," you will learn how to use Forte's Bean Pattern wizard to generate the code for registering and deregistering events and for processing events using `EventListenerList`.

3.4 Creating Listener Components

If a component is to be a listener for an event, it must implement the event listener interface and be registered with a source object. For example, to listen for `TickEvent`, the listener component must implement `TickListener`, and must be registered with an instance of a source component, such as `Tick`.

A builder tool can help to automate the process of creating a listener and registering it with a source. For example, in Forte, the code can be generated by selecting and pressing the event handler in the component inspector. To understand how Forte generates listeners, let us first look at the following example, which creates a listener manually.

Example 3.2 Writing a Listener Component Manually

In this example, a hand-coded class named `ShowTick` is given to display the tick count and tick interval when a tick event occurs. `ShowTick` is a subclass of `JFrame`. The display is shown in a `MessagePanel` bean placed in `ShowTick`. The `MessagePanel` component was presented in Example 2.1. A `Tick` bean is used to generate tick events. The `ShowTick` class is the listener for tick events. Figure 3.6 shows the relationship among these classes.

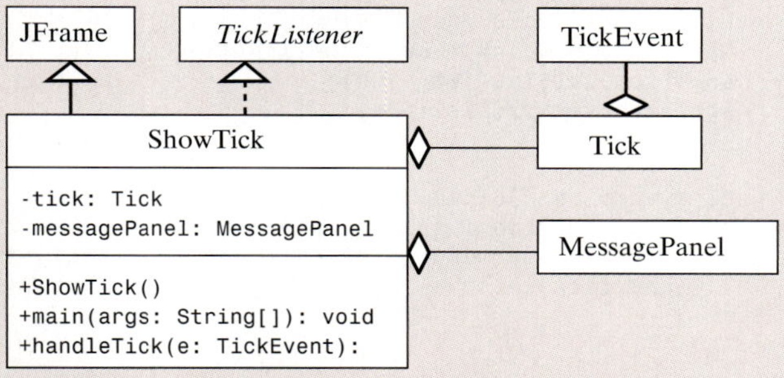

Figure 3.6 *The* `ShowTick` *class uses* `Tick` *and* `MessagePanel` *to control and display a message.*

continued

Example 3.2 continued

Follow the steps below to complete the example:

1. Create a class named `ShowTick` in package eventdemo that extends `JFrame` and implements `TickListener` interface using the Interface wizard.

2. Complete the code as shown in Listing 3.4. A sample run of the program is shown in Figure 3.7.

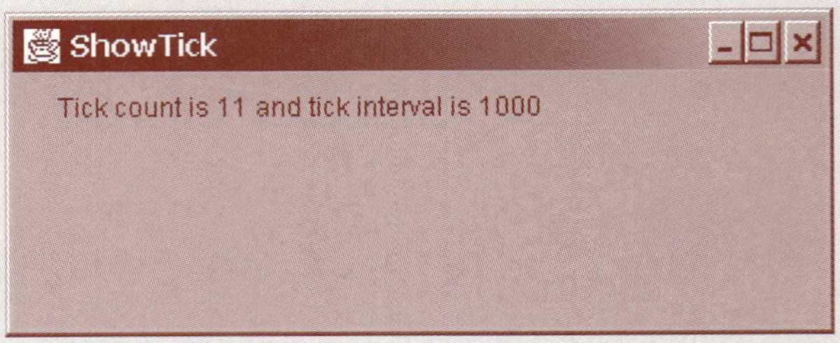

Figure 3.7 *The tick count is updated every 1 second.*

```
package eventdemo;

import javax.swing.*;
import messagepaneldemo.MessagePanel;
import java.awt.*;

public class ShowTick extends JFrame implements TickListener {
  private Tick tick1 = new Tick();
  private MessagePanel messagePanel = new MessagePanel();

  /** Default constructor */
  public ShowTick() {
    tick1.start();

    // Place the message canvas to the frame
    this.getContentPane().setLayout(new BorderLayout());
    this.getContentPane().add(messagePanel);
    setTitle("ShowTick");

    // Register listener
    tick1.addTickListener(this);
  }

  /** Main method */
  public static void main(String[] args) {
    ShowTick showTick = new ShowTick();
    showTick.setSize(100, 100);
    showTick.setVisible(true);
  }

  public void handleTick(TickEvent e) {
    // TODO: implement this eventdemo.TickListener method;
    messagePanel.setMessage("Tick count is " + e.getTickCount() +
      " and tick interval is " + e.getTickInterval());
  }
}
```

Listing 3.4 *ShowTick.java*

Example Review

The program starts from the main method (Lines 25–29), which creates an instance of `ShowTick` and displays the frame on the screen.

To make `ShowTick` a listener for `Tick`, `ShowTick` implements `TickListener` and provides the code for handling tick events in the `handleTick` method. You should also register the listener by invoking `Tick`'s add listener method, as follows (Line 21):

```
tick1.addTickListener(this);
```

When an event occurs in `tick1`, the `processEvent` method in the `Tick` class is invoked to notify the listener `ShowTick` by invoking its `handleTick` method. The flow of the event processing from the source to the listener is shown in Figure 3.8.

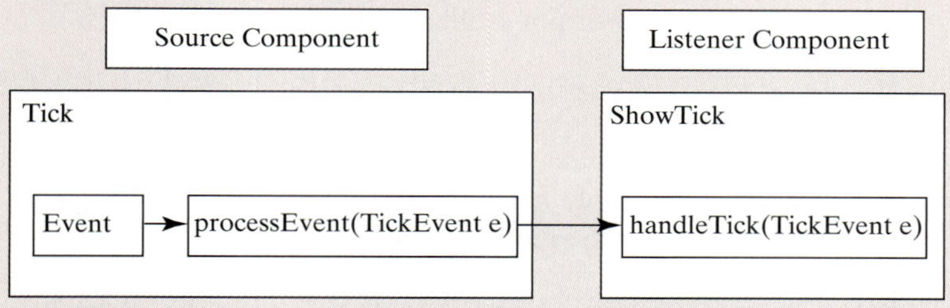

Figure 3.8 *When a Tick event occurs, the* `processEvent` *method is invoked, which invokes the* `handleTick` *method defined in the listener's interface and implemented in the listener.*

3.5 Event Adapters

The Java event model shown in Figure 3.1 is flexible, allowing modifications and variations. One useful variation of the model is the addition of adapters, as shown in Figure 3.9. When an event occurs, the source object notifies the adapter. The adapter then delegates the handling of the event to the real listener object, which is referred to as a *target*.

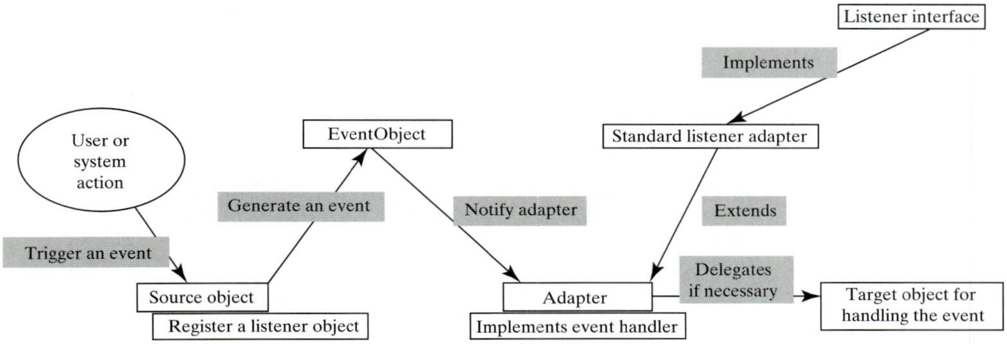

Figure 3.9 *The adapter listens for events and delegates handling to the actual listener (target).*

The adapter is a service object that provides a level of indirection between the source and the target. It is registered as a listener for the source event. Instead of passing the event object to the target, the source passes the event object to the adapter and lets it delegate to the target handler.

At first glance, the advantages of using adapters are not apparent. Adapters seem to make things more complex, but they are valuable in many situations. Here are some examples:

- If you need to hook a source to an existing bean that cannot be modified or extended, you can use an adapter as a listener to the source and register it with the source. When an event occurs, the source notifies the adapter, which then invokes the methods in the target.
- You can use an adapter to place all the event notifications from the source in a queue to allow the source object to resume execution without blocking. This is particularly useful in a distributed environment where the target object may be busy or not available when the event occurs.
- You can create a generic adapter to listen for all types of events from all sources, then deliver them to one or multiple targets. This generic adapter can be used as a filter for the events before they are delegated out to the targets. You can apply all kinds of business rules and logic to the delivery of events and sort the events by priority.

Here is an example (see Listing 3.5) of rewriting ShowTick.java using an event adapter. The code related to the adapter is highlighted.

```
package eventdemo;

import java.awt.*;
import messagepaneldemo.*;

public class ShowTickWithAdapter extends javax.swing.JApplet {
  Tick tick1 = new Tick();
  MessagePanel messagePanel1 = new MessagePanel();

  /** Component initialization */
  public void init() {
    this.setSize(new Dimension(400,300));
    tick1.start();
    tick1.addTickListener(new ShowTickWithAdapter_TickAdapter(this));
    this.getContentPane().add(messagePanel1, BorderLayout.CENTER);
  }

  void tick1HandleTick(TickEvent e) {
    messagePanel1.setMessage("Tick count is " + e.getTickCount() +
      " and tick interval is " + e.getTickInterval());
  }
}

/** Adapter class */
class ShowTickWithAdapter_TickAdapter
  implements eventdemo.TickListener {
  ShowTickWithAdapter adaptee;

```

```
  ShowTickWithAdapter_TickAdapter(ShowTickWithAdapter adaptee) {
    this.adaptee = adaptee;
  }

  public void handleTick(TickEvent e) {
    adaptee.tick1HandleTick(e);
  }
}
```

Listing 3.5 *ShowTickWithAdapter.java.*

The listener adapter (`ShowTickWithAdapter_TickAdapter`) serves as an intermediary class interposed between an event source and the real listener, as shown in Figure 3.10 for the `TickEvent`. The adapter plays the role of pairing a source event with a listener. When a `TickEvent` occurs, the `processEvent` method in the event source invokes the `handleTick` method in the adapter, which then invokes the real handler `tick1HandleTick` in the target component.

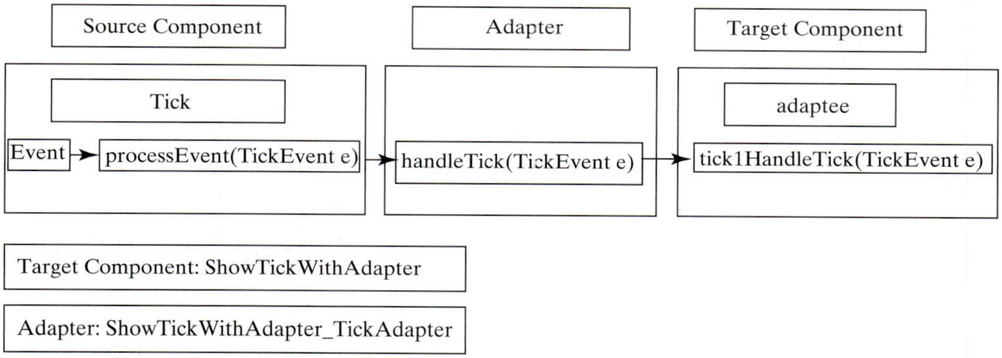

Figure 3.10 *When a* `TickEvent` *occurs, the* `processEvent` *method is invoked, which invokes the* `handleTick` *method in the adapter, which in turn invokes the real handler,* `handleTick`.

The adapter shown in Listing 3.5 is known as a *standard adapter*. It can be simplified using inner classes.

3.6 Inner Classes and Anonymous Inner Classes

An *inner class* is a class defined within the scope of another class. Here is an example (see Listing 3.6) of rewriting ShowTickAdapter.java using inner classes. The code related to inner classes is highlighted.

```
package eventdemo;

import java.awt.*;
import messagepaneldemo.*;

public class ShowTickWithInnerClass extends javax.swing.JApplet {
  Tick tick1 = new Tick();
  MessagePanel messagePanel1 = new MessagePanel();

```

```
  /** Component initialization */
  public void init() {
    this.setSize(new Dimension(400,300));
    tick1.start();
    tick1.addTickListener(new ShowTickWithAdapter_TickAdapter());
    this.getContentPane().add(messagePanel1, BorderLayout.CENTER);
  }

  void tick1HandleTick(TickEvent e) {
    messagePanel1.setMessage("Tick count is " + e.getTickCount() +
      " and tick interval is " + e.getTickInterval());
  }

  /** Inner class */
  class ShowTickWithAdapter_TickAdapter
    implements eventdemo.TickListener {
    public void handleTick(TickEvent e) {
      tick1HandleTick(e);
    }
  }
}
```

Listing 3.6 *ShowTickWithInnerClass.java.*

The adapters are simplified inside `ShowTickWithInnerClass` using inner classes. Inner classes are just like any regular classes with the following features:

- An inner class can reference the data and methods defined in its parent class so that you do not need to pass the reference of the parent class to the constructor of the inner class. Therefore, the constructors of the adapters are eliminated and the `handleTick` method invokes `tick1HandleTick`, which is defined in `ShowTickWithInnerClass`.
- Inner classes make programs simple and concise. As you can see, the new class is shorter and leaner.
- An inner class is only for supporting the work of its containing outer class, and is compiled into a class named `OutClassName$InnerClassName.class`. For example, the inner class `ShowTickWithInnerClass_TickAdapter` in `ShowTickWithInnerClass` is compiled into

  ```
  ShowTickWithInnerClass$ShowTickWithInnerClass_TickAdapter.class.
  ```

- An inner class can be declared `public`, `protected`, or `private` subject to the same visibility rules applied to a member of the class.
- An inner class can be declared `static`. A `static` inner class can be accessed using the outer class name. A static inner class cannot access nonstatic members of the outer class.
- Objects of an inner class are often created in the outer class. But you can also create an object of an inner class from another class. If the inner class is nonstatic, you must first create an instance of the outer class, then use the following syntax to create an object for the inner class:

  ```
  OuterClass.InnerClass innerObject = outerObject.new InnerClass();
  ```

- If the inner class is static, use the following syntax to create an object for the inner class:

```
OuterClass.InnerClass innerObject = new OuterClass.InnerClass();
```

The inner class can be further shortened by using an anonymous inner class. An *anonymous inner class* is an inner class without a name. An anonymous inner class combines declaring an inner class and creating an instance of the class in one step. An anonymous inner class is declared as shown here:

```
new SuperClassName() [or InterfaceName()] {
  // Implement or override methods in superclass or interface

  // Other methods if necessary
}
```

Since an anonymous inner class is a special kind of inner class, it is treated like an inner class in many ways. In addition, an anonymous inner class has the following features:

- An anonymous inner class must always extend a superclass or implement an interface, but it cannot have an explicit `extends` or `implements` clause.
- An anonymous inner class must implement all abstract methods in the superclass and in the interface.
- An anonymous inner class always uses the default constructor from its superclass to create an instance. If an anonymous inner class implements an interface, the default constructor is `Object()`.

Here is an example (see Listing 3.7) of rewriting ShowTickWithInnerClass.java using anonymous inner classes. The code related to anonymous inner classes is highlighted.

```
package eventdemo;

import java.awt.*;
import java.applet.*;
import javax.swing.*;
import messagepaneldemo.*;

public class ShowTickWithAnonymousAdapter extends JApplet {
  MessagePanel messagePanel1 = new MessagePanel();
  Tick tick1 = new Tick();

  /** Component initialization */
  public void init() {
    this.setSize(new Dimension(400,300));
    tick1.start();

    // Anonymous inner class adapter
    tick1.addTickListener(new eventdemo.TickListener() {
      public void handleTick(TickEvent e) {
        tick1HandleTick(e);
      }
    });
    this.getContentPane().add(messagePanel1, BorderLayout.CENTER);
  }

```

```
    void tick1HandleTick(TickEvent e) {
      messagePanel1.setMessage("Tick count is " + e.getTickCount() +
        " and tick interval is " + e.getTickInterval());
    }
  }
```

Listing 3.7 *ShowTickWithAnonymousAdapter.java*

3.7 Using Adapters in Forte

A builder tool such as Forte uses adapters to delegate handling events to the target objects. For example, suppose a target object is a listener for two buttons named Ok and Cancel, respectively. Forte generates an adapter for the Ok button and an adapter for the Cancel button, as shown in Figure 3.11. The target object contains a method (say `okActionPerformed(. . .)`) for handling the Ok button and a separate method (say `cancelActionPerformed(. . .)`) for handling the Cancel button. When you click on the Ok button, it fires the `ActionEvent` to the Ok adapter, which then delegates the event to `okActionPerformed(. . .)`.

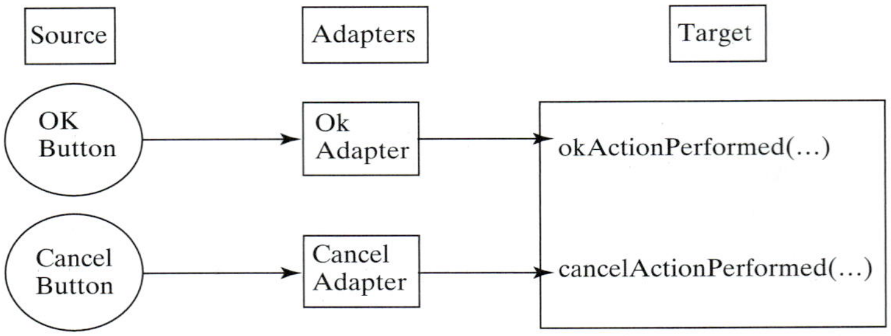

Figure 3.11 *Forte uses adapters to hook up source components with listeners.*

Forte greatly simplifies the task of creating listeners. It automatically registers listeners and provides an empty method for the user to fill in the code for handling the event. In the following example, you will learn how to use Forte's Form Editor to link source components and listeners via anonymous adapters.

Example 3.3 Creating a Listener Component Using Forte

This example uses Forte's Form Editor to develop the same program as in Example 3.2. Additionally, the program stops the tick when the mouse is pressed, and the tick resumes when the mouse is released. Suppose that the `MessagePanel` and `Tick` components are already placed in the component palette. To see the development in action, follow these steps:

1. In the eventdemo package, create an applet named `ShowTickForm` using the Swing JApplet form wizard.

2. Drop a `MessagePanel` component to the center of the applet to create `messagePanel1`. Set its `background` to Cyan and `yCoordinate` to 30 in the component inspector.

3. Drop a `Tick` component to the frame. You will see `tick1` in the component tree under the Other Components node.

4. With `tick1` selected in the component tree, switch to the Events page of the component inspector. Select the `handleTick` event and press Enter in its value field. The following code is automatically generated.

   ➤ The following line was added into the `initComponents()` method to register the listener for `TickEvent`.

```
tick1.addTickListener(new eventdemo.TickListener() {
  public void handleTick(eventdemo.TickEvent evt) {
    tick1HandleTick(evt);
  }
});
```

   ➤ An empty handler method is created for you to fill in the code for handling the `TickEvent`.

```
private void tick1HandleTick(TickEvent evt) {
}
```

5. Fill in the following code in the method `tick1HandleTick` to handle the tick event.

```
private void tick1HandleTick(TickEvent evt) {
  messagePanel1.setMessage("Tick count is " + evt.getTickCount() +
    " and tick interval is " + evt.getTickInterval());
}
```

6. To generate the code for handling the `mousePressed` events, press enter in the value field of `mousePressed` in the Events page of the component inspector for `messagePanel1`. The code shown below is automatically generated.

   ➤ The following line is added into the `initComponents` method to register the listener for `MouseEvent`.

```
messagePanel1.addMouseListener(new java.awt.event.MouseAdapter() {
  public void mousePressed(java.awt.event.MouseEvent evt) {
    messagePanel1MousePressed(evt);
  }
});
```

   ➤ An empty handler method was created for you to fill in the code for handling the `mousePressed` event.

```
private void messagePanel1MousePressed(MouseEvent evt) {
}
```

7. Fill in the following code in the method `messagePanel1MousePressed` to suspend the tick when the mouse is pressed.

```
private void messagePanel1MousePressed(MouseEvent evt) {
  tick1.stop();
}
```

continued

Example 3.3 continued

8. To generate the code for handling the `mouseReleased` event, press Enter in the value field of `mouseReleased` in the Events page for `messagePanel1`. Since the adapter for the `MouseEvent` has already been created and is registered with the source as a `MouseEvent` listener, this code will not be regenerated. Instead the following code was generated.

   - A handler for the `mouseReleased` event was added to the anonymous adapter.

   ```
   public void mouseReleased(MouseEvent evt) {
     adaptee.messagePanel1MouseReleased(evt);
   }
   ```

   - An empty handler method was created for you to fill in the code for handling the `mouseReleased` event.

   ```
   private void messagePanel1MouseReleased(MouseEvent evt) {
   }
   ```

9. Fill in the following code in the method `messagePanel1MouseReleased` to resume the tick when the mouse is pressed.

   ```
   private void messagePanel1MouseReleased(MouseEvent evt) {
     tick1.start();
   }
   ```

10. Add `tick1.start()` in the constructor to start the tick, as shown in Listing 3.8.

11. The ShowTickForm.java code generated by Forte is shown in Listing 3.8. Run ShowTickForm.java to test the program with mouse pressed to stop tick and mouse released to resume tick.

```
package eventdemo;

public class ShowTickForm extends javax.swing.JApplet {
  /** Creates new form ShowTickForm */
  public ShowTickForm() {
    initComponents();
    tick1.start();
  }

  private void initComponents() {
    tick1 = new eventdemo.Tick();
    messagePanel1 = new messagepaneldemo.MessagePanel();

    tick1.addTickListener(new eventdemo.TickListener() {
      public void handleTick(eventdemo.TickEvent evt) {
        tick1HandleTick(evt);
      }
    });

    messagePanel1.setBackground(java.awt.Color.cyan);
    messagePanel1.setYCoordinate(30);
    messagePanel1.addMouseListener(
      new java.awt.event.MouseAdapter() {
```

Listing 3.8 *ShowTickForm.java*

```
24            public void mousePressed(java.awt.event.MouseEvent evt) {
25              messagePanel1MousePressed(evt);
26            }
27            public void mouseReleased(java.awt.event.MouseEvent evt) {
28              messagePanel1MouseReleased(evt);
29            }
30          });
31
32          getContentPane().add(messagePanel1,
33            java.awt.BorderLayout.CENTER);
34        }
35
36        private void messagePanel1MouseReleased(
37          java.awt.event.MouseEvent evt) {
38          tick1.start();
39        }
40
41        private void messagePanel1MousePressed(
42          java.awt.event.MouseEvent evt) {
43          tick1.stop();
44        }
45
46        private void tick1HandleTick(eventdemo.TickEvent evt) {
47          messagePanel1.setMessage("Tick count is " + evt.getTickCount() +
48            " and tick interval is " + evt.getTickInterval());
49        }
50
51        // Variables declaration - do not modify
52        private eventdemo.Tick tick1;
53        private messagepaneldemo.MessagePanel messagePanel1;
54        // End of variables declaration
55      }
```

Listing 3.8 *continued*

Example Review

The `Tick` component can generate `TickEvent`. `MessagePanel` can generate `MouseEvent`, since `MessagePanel` is a subclass of `java.awt.Component` and the `Component` class can generate `MouseEvent`.

When a `MouseEvent` occurs, the `processMouseEvent` method in the event source invokes one of the five mouse events (`mousePressed`, `mouseReleased`, `mouseClicked`, `mouseEntered`, and `mouseExited`), as shown in Figure 3.12. Which of the five events is processed depends on the event ID. For the detailed code of the `processMouseEvent` method, please refer to `java.awt.Component`. Since you are only interested in the `mousePressed` and `mouseReleased` events, these two handlers are provided in the adapter. When one of these two handlers is invoked in the adapter, the corresponding real handler in the target component is invoked.

The anonymous adapter for the `TickEvent` implements the `TickListener` interface (Lines 14–18), and the adapter for the `MouseEvent` extends the `MouseAdapter` convenience listener adapter class (Lines 22–30). A *convenience listener adapter* is a support class that provides default implementations for all the methods in the listener interface. The default implementation is usually an empty body. Java provides convenience listener adapters for all the AWT listener inter

continued

Example 3.3 continued

faces except the `ActionListener`. A convenience listener adapter is named *X*Adapter for *X*Listener. For example, `MouseAdapter` is a standard listener adapter for `MouseListener`.

A listener interface may contain many methods for handling various types of actions of an event. For example, `MouseListener` contains the methods `mouseClicked`, `mousePressed`, `mouseReleased`, `mouseEntered`, and `mouseExited`. The convenience listener adapter is convenient because a listener class may simply extend the adapter and implement only the method for the intended type of action instead of all the methods of the listener interface.

Forte creates adapters by extending the listener interface's convenience adapter class, if the convenience adapter exists.

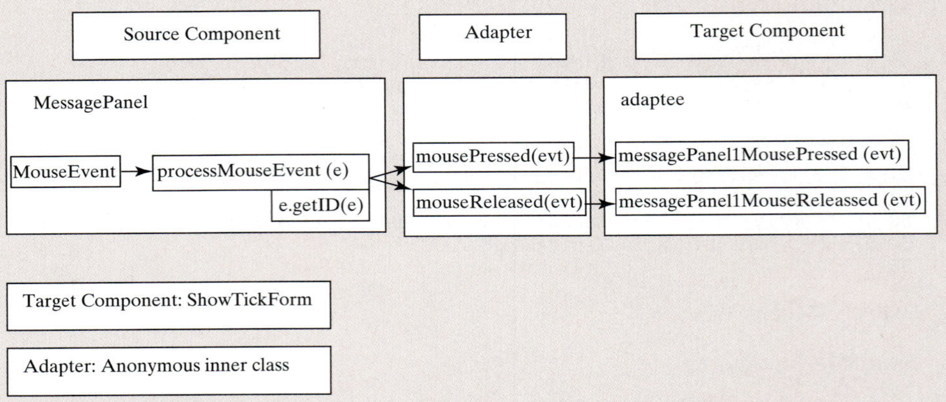

Figure 3.12 *When a* `MouseEvent` *occurs, the* `processMouseEvent` *method is invoked, which invokes the* `mousePressed` *method or* `mouseReleased` *method in the adapter, and then the real handler,* `messagePanel1MousePressed` *or* `messagePanel1MouseReleased`.

TIP
To delete an existing event handler, highlight the entire value field of the event handler in the Events page, press the Delete key, and then press the Enter key. Forte automatically deletes the adapter class and the registration method from the source code. The associated event-handling method is also deleted.

3.8 Working with Existing Event Sets

You created `TickEvent` and `TickListener` in Section 3.3, "Creating Custom Event Sets and Source Components." Most of the time you will not need to create event sets from scratch, since you will be able to use existing event sets. For example, suppose you don't need the tick count and tick interval contained in a tick event. There is no need to create a `TickEvent` class; instead you can use `java.awt.ActionEvent` and let the `Tick` class generate an `ActionEvent` instance when a tick event occurs.

Example 3.4 Developing a Source Component Using Existing Event Sets

This example presents a new component that generates an `ActionEvent` when a tick event occurs. The new source component named `TickUsingActionEvent` is created as shown in Listing 3.9. The code related to generating and handling the action event is in italic. The class `ShowTickUsingActionEvent` is created to test `TickUsingActionEvent`. Their relationship is shown in Figure 3.13.

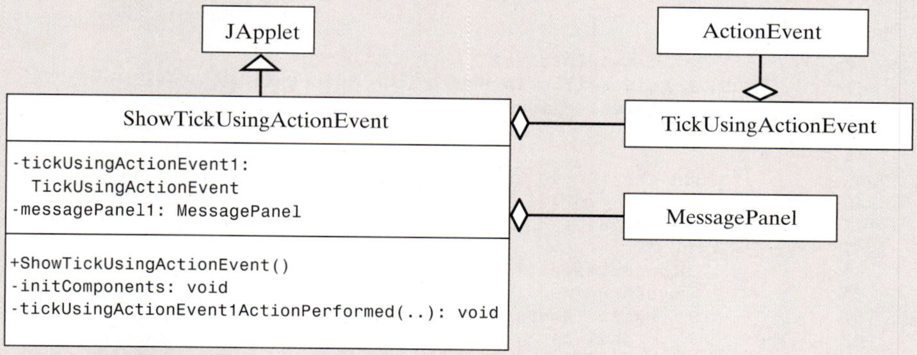

Figure 3.13 *The* `ShowTickUsingActionEvent` *class uses* `Tick` *and* `MessagePanel` *to control and display a message.*

```
package eventdemo;

import java.util.*;
import java.awt.event.*;

public class TickUsingActionEvent
  implements java.io.Serializable, Runnable {
  /** A thread to control tick */
  protected Thread thread = null;

  /** Whether the thread is suspended */
  private boolean suspended = true;

  /** Store Tick listeners in a vector */
  private Vector tickListenerList;

  /** tickCount */
  private long tickCount = 0;

  /** tickInterval */
  private long tickInterval = 1000;

  /** Default constructor */
  public TickUsingActionEvent() {
    // Create and start the thread
    thread = new Thread(this);
    thread.start();
  }

```

Listing 3.9 *TickUsingActionEvent.java*

continued

Example 3.4 continued

```
    /** Return tickInterval */
    public long getTickInterval() {
      return tickInterval;
    }

    /** Return tickCount */
    public long getTickCount() {
      return tickCount;
    }

    /** Set a tickInterval */
    public void setTickInterval(long interval) {
      tickInterval = interval;
    }

    /** Run the thread */
    public void run() {
      while (true) {
        try {
          Thread.sleep(tickInterval);
          synchronized (this) {
            while (suspended)
              wait();
          }
        }
        catch (InterruptedException ex) {  }

        // Increase the tick count
        tickCount++;

        // Fire ActionEvent
        processEvent(new ActionEvent(this,
          ActionEvent.ACTION_PERFORMED, null));
      }
    }

    /** Resume the thread */
    public synchronized void start() {
      if (suspended) {
        suspended = false;
        notify();
      }
    }

    /** Suspend the thread */
    public synchronized void stop() {
      suspended = true;
    }

    /** Register an action event listener */
    public synchronized void addActionListener(ActionListener l) {
      Vector v = tickListenerList == null ?
        new Vector(2) : (Vector)tickListenerList.clone();
      if (!v.contains(l)) {
        v.addElement(l);
        tickListenerList = v;
      }
    }
```

Listing 3.9 *continued*

```
  /** Remove an action event listener */
  public synchronized void removeActionListener(ActionListener l) {
    if (tickListenerList != null && tickListenerList.contains(l)) {
      tickListenerList.removeElement(l);
    }
  }

  /** Fire TickEvent */
  public void processEvent(ActionEvent e) {
    Vector v;

    synchronized (this) {
      v = (Vector)tickListenerList.clone();
    }

    for (int i = 0; i < v.size(); i++) {
      ActionListener listener = (ActionListener)v.elementAt(i);
      listener.actionPerformed(e);
    }
  }
}
```

Listing 3.9 *continued*

Follow the steps below to complete the example.

1. In the eventdemo package, create `ShowTickUsingActionEvent` using the Swing JApplet form wizard.
2. Create `TickUsingActionEvent` as shown in Listing 3.9, compile, and place it in the component palette.
3. Drop a `MessagePanel` component into the center of the applet to create `messagePanel1`. Change `messagePanel1`'s background to Cyan and `yCoordinate` to 30 in the inspector.
4. Drop the `TickUsingActionEvent` component on the applet. You will see `tickUsingActionEvent1` created in the component tree under the node Other Components.
5. Add `tickUsingActionEvent1.start()` in the constructor to start the tick, as shown in Listing 3.10 (Line 7).
6. With `tickUsingActionEvent1` selected in the component inspector, switch to the Events tab. Select the `actionPerformed` event and press Enter in its value. Forte generates the adapter and an empty event-handling method, `tickUsingActionEvent1ActionPerformed`. Fill in the following code in this method:

```
void tickUsingActionEvent1ActionPerformed(ActionEvent evt) {
  messagePanel1.setMessage("Tick count is " +
    tickUsingActionEvent1.getTickCount() +
    " and tick interval is "
    + tickUsingActionEvent1.getTickInterval());
}
```

continued

Example 3.4 continued

TIP

The adapter for `ActionEvent` of a source object can be generated by double-clicking the object in the form. This is quicker than generating the adapter from the inspector.

```
package eventdemo;

public class ShowTickUsingActionEvent extends javax.swing.JApplet {
  /** Creates new form ShowTickUsingActionEvent */
  public ShowTickUsingActionEvent() {
    initComponents();
    tickUsingActionEvent1.start();
  }

  private void initComponents() {
    tickUsingActionEvent1 = new eventdemo.TickUsingActionEvent();
    messagePanel1 = new messagepaneldemo.MessagePanel();

    tickUsingActionEvent1.addActionListener(
      new java.awt.event.ActionListener() {
      public void actionPerformed(java.awt.event.ActionEvent evt) {
        tickUsingActionEvent1ActionPerformed(evt);
      }
    });

    messagePanel1.setBackground(java.awt.Color.cyan);
    messagePanel1.setYCoordinate(30);
    getContentPane().add(messagePanel1,
      java.awt.BorderLayout.CENTER);
  }

  private void tickUsingActionEvent1ActionPerformed(
    java.awt.event.ActionEvent evt) {
    messagePanel1.setMessage("Tick count is " +
      tickUsingActionEvent1.getTickCount() + " and tick interval is "
      +tickUsingActionEvent1.getTickInterval());
  }

  // Variables declaration - do not modify
  private eventdemo.TickUsingActionEvent tickUsingActionEvent1;
  private messagepaneldemo.MessagePanel messagePanel1;
  // End of variables declaration
}
```

Listing 3.10 *ShowTickUsingActionEvent.java*

Example Review

`TickUsingActionEvent` is very similar to the `Tick` component presented in Example 3.1 except that it utilizes `ActionEvent` to generate events and register listeners. Invoking the following constructor (Lines 61–62) generates an `ActionEvent`.

```
new ActionEvent(this, ActionEvent.ACTION_PERFORMED, null);
```

The listener interface for ActionEvent is an ActionListener that contains a handler actionPerformed for the listener to implement. The registration methods addActionListener and removeActionListener are defined in the component for adding and removing listeners.

The TickEvent class contains the methods getTickCount() and getTickInterval(), but the ActionEvent class does not contain these methods. Therefore, when processing an event using the actionPerformed(ActionEvent e) handler, you cannot get tick count or tick interval from e. To enable the listener to obtain tick count and tick interval, getTickCount() and getTickInterval() are defined in the TickUsingActionEvent class. Since tickUsingActionEvent1 is an instance of TickUsingActionEvent, you can get tick count and tick interval from tickUsingActionEvent1.

Chapter Summary

This chapter took you inside the Java delegation model and showed you the basics on event sets, source components, and listener components. The event delegation model separates the tasks of generating events from handling events, thus making it possible to develop source components and listener components independently. Adapters are used to listen for events and delegate them to the right components for handling them. You learned how to hook a listener with a source using standard adapters and anonymous inner class adapters.

You learned how to create a custom event like TickEvent by extending java.util.EventObject and an event listener interface like TickListner by extending java.util.EventListener. You can use custom event sets to create a source component like Tick and Java-provided event sets to create a source component like TickUsingActionEvent.

Review Questions

3.1 If an event class is named *X*Event, what should you name its associated listener interface? If an event listener interface is named *X*Listener, what should you name the registration methods in the source component?

3.2 Is an event class a subclass of java.util.EventObject? Is an event listener interface a subinterface of java.util.EventListener?

3.3 Show the code that generates and fires the event in the Tick component in Listing 3.3.

3.4 How do you register events for multicasting or for unicasting?

3.5 How are the listeners notified of the events?

3.6 What are the benefits of adapters?

3.7 What is a convenience adapter? What are the benefits of convenience adapters?

3.8 How do you create an instance of `ActionEvent`?

3.9 What code does Forte generate for handling a button-click action?

3.10 The `new` operator cannot be used to create an instance of an interface. Why does Forte generate the anonymous adapter using `new TickListener()` in Line 18 in Listing 3.7?

Programming Exercises

3.1 The `MessagePanel` class in Example 2.1 is a subclass of `JPanel`; it can fire a `MouseEvent`, `KeyEvent`, and `ComponentEvent`, but not an `ActionEvent`. Modify the `MessagePanel` class so that it can fire an `ActionEvent` when an instance of the `MessagePanel` class is clicked. Name the new class `MessagePanelWithActionEvent`. Test it with a Java applet that displays the current time in a message panel whenever the message panel is clicked, as shown in Figure 3.14.

Figure 3.14 *The current time is displayed whenever you click on the message panel.*

3.2 Develop a project that meets the following requirements:

- Create a source component named `MemoryWatch` for monitoring memory. The component generates a `MemoryEvent` when the free memory space exceeds a specified `highLimit` or is below a specified `lowLimit`. The `highLimit` and `lowLimit` are customizable properties in `MemoryWatch`.
- Create an event set named `MemoryEvent` and `MemoryListener`. The `MemoryEvent` simply extends `java.util.EventObject` and contains two methods, `freeMemory` and `totalMemory`, which return the free memory and total memory of the system. The `MemoryListener` interface contains two handlers, `sufficientMemory` and `insufficientMemory`. The `sufficientMemory` method is invoked when the free memory space exceeds the specified high limit, and `insufficientMemory` is invoked when the free memory space is lower than the specified low limit.

- Develop a listener component that displays free memory, total memory, and whether the memory is sufficient or insufficient when a `MemoryEvent` occurs. Make the listener an applet with a main method to run standalone.

3.3 Create a class named `Hurricane` with properties `name` and `category` and its accessor methods. The `Hurricane` component generates an `ActionEvent` whenever its `category` property is changed. Write a listener that displays the hurricane category. If the category is 2 or greater, a message "Hurricane Warning!!!" is displayed, as shown in Figure 3.15.

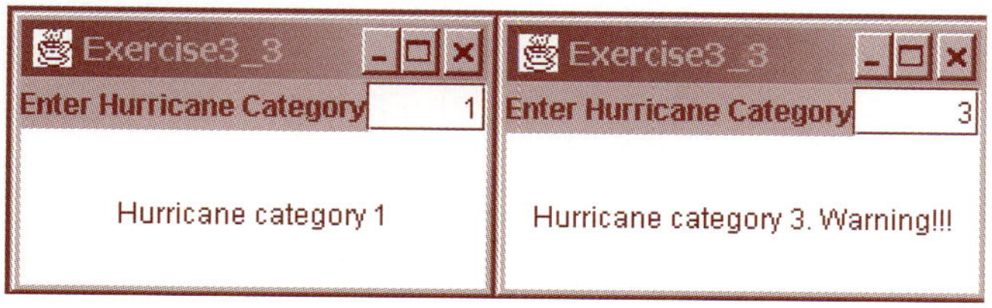

Figure 3.15 *Whenever the hurricane category is changed, an appropriate message is displayed in the message panel.*

CHAPTER 4

Developing and Using Components

Objectives

- To understand the differences between writing components and using components.
- To become familiar with the component-development process.
- To know component design guidelines.
- To use the model-view approach to separate data and logic from the presentation of data.
- To understand the application-development process.
- To learn how to package and deploy applications and applets.

4.1 Introduction

You developed the components `MessagePanel` and `MultipleMessagePanel` in Chapter 2, "Introduction to JavaBeans," and the components `Tick` and `TickUsingActionEvent` in Chapter 3, "Bean Events." From these examples, you learned the techniques of writing components. These techniques are not new. Developing JavaBeans components is nothing more than writing Java classes that follow some fairly strict naming conventions for accessor methods and event registration methods. There are, however, differences between developing components and using components. This chapter explores these differences, and, through comprehensive examples, introduces the process of developing components and using them in rapid Java application development. You will learn how to use Forte's Bean Pattern wizard to create bean properties and bean events, and how to develop components using the model-view approach. You will also learn how to package and deploy Java projects.

4.2 Developing Components versus Using Components

Throughout the book, you will develop JavaBeans components and use them to build projects. Sometimes, you will play the role of both component writer and component user. It is important to note the differences between developing components and using components.

From a user's perspective, a component consists of properties, methods, and events. The user may use a component to create beans in a builder tool or in scripting programming. The user creates a bean and customizes its behavior by changing properties and writing code to carry out responses to events.

From a writer's perspective, a component is designed for use in a visual environment where the component properties and events are exposed during design time. In order to expose the properties and events of the component in a builder tool, the component writer must follow property and event design patterns.

There are three major differences between developing components and using components.

- A component is a black box to the component user. The user manipulates the component through public accessor methods and events without knowing the implementation of the component. However, the component writer knows all the details of the component if the component is created from scratch. If the component is derived from a superclass, the writer has access to all the public and protected data fields and methods of the superclass.
- Components are usually designed for use by many different customers. To make your components useful in a wide range of applications, they should provide a variety of ways for customization through properties, methods, and events.

- Components are designed for reuse. Users can incorporate components in many different combinations, orders, and environments. Therefore, you should design a component that imposes no restrictions on what or when the user can do with it, design the properties to ensure that the user can set them in any order and with any combination of values, and design events and methods to function independently of their order of occurrence at runtime.

4.3 Component Design Guidelines

A JavaBeans component is a special type of Java class. The guidelines for designing classes apply to designing components.

4.3.1 General Guidelines

A class should describe a single entity or a set of similar operations. You can use a class for students, for example, but do not combine students and staff in the same class, because students and staff have different operations. Since the `Math` class provides mathematical operations, it is natural to group mathematical methods in one class. A single entity with too many responsibilities can be broken into several classes to separate responsibilities. The `String` class, `StringBuffer` class, and `StringTokenizer` class all deal with strings, for example, but have different responsibilities.

Provide a public default constructor and override the `equals` method and the `toString` method defined in the `Object` class whenever possible.

Follow standard Java programming style and naming conventions. Choose informative names for classes, data fields, and methods. Always place the data declaration before the constructor, and place constructors before methods. Always provide a constructor and initialize variables to avoid programming errors.

4.3.2 Using the Modifiers *public, protected, private*, and *static*

Each class can present two contracts—one for the users of the class and one for the extenders of the class. Make the fields *`private`* and the accessor methods *`public`* if they are intended for the users of the class. Make the fields or method *`protected`* if they are intended for extenders of the class. The contract for the extenders encompasses the contract for the users. The extended class may increase the visibility of an instance method from `protected` to `public`, or change its implementation, but you should never change the implementation in a way that violates that contract.

A class should use the *`private`* modifier to hide its data from direct access by users. You can use get methods and set methods to provide users with access to the private data, but only to private data you want the user to see or to modify. A class should also hide methods not intended for users.

A property that is shared by all the instances of the class should be declared as a static property.

4.3.3 Using Inheritance or Composition

In general, the difference between inheritance and composition is the difference between the *is-a* relationship and the *has-a* relationship. For example, an apple is a fruit; thus, you would use inheritance to model the relationship between the classes `Apple` and `Fruit`. A person has a name; thus, you would use composition to model the relationship between the classes `Person` and `Name`. Sometimes, the choice between inheritance and composition is not obvious. For example, you can use inheritance to model the relationship between the classes `Circle` and `Cylinder`. One could argue that a cylinder consists of circles; thus, you might use composition to define the `Cylinder` class, as follows:

```
public class Cylinder {
  private Circle circle;

  /** Constructors */

  /** Methods */
}
```

Both designs are fine. Which one is preferred? If polymorphism is desirable, use the inheritance design. If you don't care about polymorphism, the composition design gives more flexibility because the classes are less dependent using composition than using inheritance.

4.3.4 Using Interfaces or Abstract Classes

Both interfaces and abstract classes can be used to generalize common features. How do you decide whether to use an interface or a class? In general, a *strong is-a relationship* that clearly describes a parent-child relationship should be modeled using classes. For example, since an orange is a fruit, their relationship should be modeled using class inheritance. A *weak is-a relationship*, also known as an *is-kind-of relationship*, indicates that an object possesses a certain property. A weak is-a relationship can be modeled using interfaces. For example, all strings are comparable, so the `String` class implements the `Comparable` interface. A circle or a rectangle is a geometric object, for example, so `Circle` can be designed as a subclass of `GeometricObject`. Circles are different and comparable based on their radius, for example, so `Circle` can implement the `Comparable` interface.

Interfaces are more flexible than abstract classes, because a subclass can extend only one superclass but implement any number of interfaces. However, interfaces cannot contain concrete methods. You can combine the virtues of interfaces and abstract classes by creating an interface with a companion abstract class that implements the interface. So you can use the interface or its companion class, whichever is more convenient.

4.4 Component-Development Process

As in the development of any software, developing JavaBeans components requires an engineering approach that involves the following steps:

1. Understand the requirements of the component and determine what functions it requires.

2. Design the properties, methods, and events to support the functions required by the component.

3. Based on the requirements, decide whether to create a UI component or a non-UI component. A UI component must extend `java.awt.Component` or its subclass. A non-UI component can extend any appropriate class. A UI component can have drawings on it and can become part of the user interface of the application. A non-UI component is invisible on the Form Editor, but generally provides encapsulated functionality to interact with the UI components. The `MessagePanel` component in Example 2.1, "Writing a Simple JavaBeans Component," is a UI component, but the `Tick` component in Example 3.1, "Creating a Custom Event Set and a Source Component," is a non-UI component.

4. Create properties. Choose the names for properties to follow the JavaBeans property-naming convention. Decide whether to use the default property editor or a customized property editor. Creating a customized property editor will be introduced in Chapter 11, "Bean Introspection and Customization."

5. Create the customized events your component needs by writing their event classes and event listener interfaces.

6. Implement the code that generates and fires events. Implement event registration methods and choose the names according to the naming conventions.

7. Implement public methods. Component methods encapsulate the behavior of the component. They are standard Java methods that can be called from other components. Unlike accessor methods, component methods cannot change the behavior of the bean during design time. Component methods are available only at runtime.

8. Create a `BeanInfo` class for the component to customize the exposure of the bean's properties and events, if necessary. Creating a component's `BeanInfo` class will be introduced in Chapter 11, "Bean Introspection and Customization."

9. Compile, install the component in the component palette, and test the component.

NOTE

The development process is cyclic. If the requirements are changed, you will have to redevelop or modify the component following the development process.

Examples 4.1 and 4.2 demonstrate how to create beans with a variety of properties. Example 4.3 demonstrates how to create beans with events. In Chapter 11, "Bean Introspection and Customization," you will learn how to use the BeanInfo designer and the property editor designer to generate `BeanInfo` classes and custom property editors.

Example 4.1 Creating an Image Viewer

This example creates an image viewer that displays an image in a component. This bean allows the user to customize an image viewer through the following properties:

- **`image`** is the image in the image viewer.
- **`imageFilename`** is the file name of the image.
- **`stretched`** is a `boolean` value indicating whether the image is stretched.
- **`xCoordinate`** is the x-Coordinate of the upper-left corner of the image in the component.
- **`yCoordinate`** is the y-Coordinate of the upper-left corner of the image in the component.

The properties of an `ImageViewer` bean are shown in the component inspector.

Figure 4.1 *When using the* `ImageViewer` *bean, you can customize it to suit your needs with a variety of properties provided by the component.*

This example demonstrates how to use Forte's Bean Pattern wizard to create the properties. Here are the steps in creating the component:

1. Create a new package named imageviewerdemo and create a Java class named `ImageViewer` that extends `java.awt.Component` using the Class wizard.

2. Expand the ImageViewer node under the imageviewerdemo package node. Expand the class node for ImageViewer to display Fields, Constructors, Methods, and Bean Patterns, as shown in Figure 4.2. In the context menu of Bean Patterns, choose *Add*, *Property* to display the New Property Pattern dialog box, as shown in Figure 4.3.

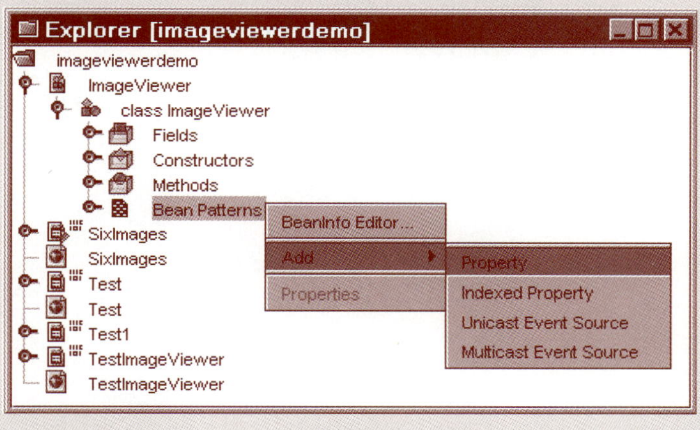

Figure 4.2 *You can start the Bean Pattern wizard from the Bean Patterns node in a class in the Explorer.*

3. Type `image` in the Name field and `java.awt.Image` in the Type field. Check the options Generate Field, Generate Return Statement, and Generate Set Statement. Click *OK* to generate the `image` property and its accessor methods. You can similarly generate the properties `imageFilename`, `stretched`, `image`, `xCoordinate`, and `yCoordinate` and their accessor methods.

4. Modify the default implementation for the set methods of these properties to repaint the component, as shown in Listing 4.1 (Lines 80, 96, 111, 126, 141).

5. Override the `paint` method to draw the image in the component, as shown in Listing 4.1 (Lines 59–66).

TIP
You can delete a property and its accessor methods by choosing *Delete* from the context menu of the property under the Bean Patterns node, as shown in Figure 4.4.

continued

Example 4.1 continued

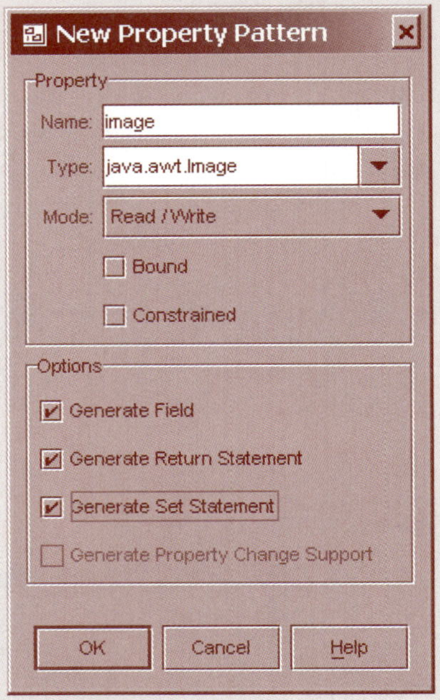

Figure 4.3 *You can use the New Property Pattern dialog box to generate properties and accessor methods automatically.*

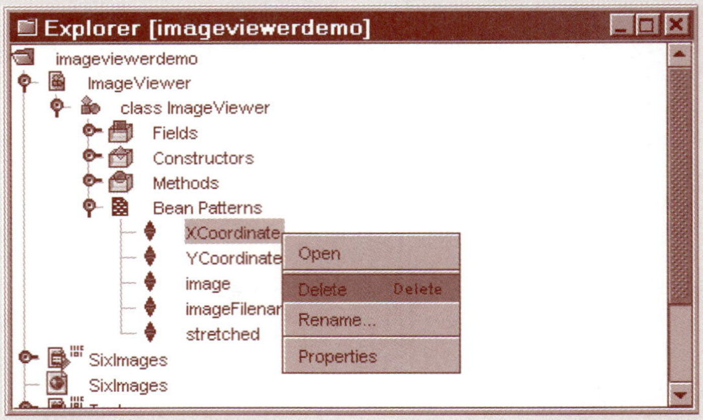

Figure 4.4 *You can delete a property and its accessor methods in the Bean Pattern wizard.*

TIP

I recommend providing default values for properties for the following three reasons:

- A default value gives the user an example of the property value.

- Some builder tools will not display a property unless a default value is provided for it.
- Using default values helps avoid runtime errors. For example, when using a property of object type, a null pointer exception would occur if the property were not initialized.

```
package imageviewerdemo;

import java.awt.*;
import java.net.URL;
import java.awt.image.ImageProducer;
import javax.swing.*;

public class ImageViewer extends Component {
  /** Holds value of property image. */
  private java.awt.Image image;

  /** Holds value of property imageFilename. */
  private String imageFilename = " ";

  /** Holds value of property stretched. */
  private boolean stretched = true;

  /** Holds value of property xCoordinate. */
  private int xCoordinate;

  /** Holds value of property yCoordinate. */
  private int yCoordinate;

  public ImageViewer() {
  }

  public ImageViewer(Image image) {
    this.image = image;
    repaint();
  }

  /**Create an image icon from an image file through the resource
   * of the object.
   */
  public static ImageIcon createImageIcon(String imageFilename,
    Object object) {
    try {
      URL url = object.getClass().getResource(imageFilename);
      return new ImageIcon(url);
    }
    catch (Exception ex) {
    }

    return null;
  }

  /**Create an image from an image file through the resource
   * of the object.
   */
```

Listing 4.1 *ImageViewer.java*

continued

Example 4.1 continued

```
    public static Image createImage(String imageFilename,
      Object object) {
      ImageIcon imageIcon = createImageIcon(imageFilename, object);
      if (imageIcon != null)
        return imageIcon.getImage();
      else
        return null;
    }

    public void paint(Graphics g) {
      if (image != null)
        if (isStretched())
          g.drawImage(image, xCoordinate, yCoordinate,
            getSize().width, getSize().height, this);
        else
          g.drawImage(image, xCoordinate, yCoordinate, this);
    }

    /** Getter for property image.
     * @return Value of property image.
     */
    public java.awt.Image getImage() {
      return image;
    }

    /** Setter for property image.
     * @param image New value of property image.
     */
    public void setImage(java.awt.Image image) {
      this.image = image;
      repaint();
    }

    /** Getter for property imageFilename.
     * @return Value of property imageFilename.
     */
    public String getImageFilename() {
      return imageFilename;
    }

    /** Setter for property imageFilename.
     * @param imageFilename New value of property imageFilename.
     */
    public void setImageFilename(String imageFilename) {
      this.imageFilename = imageFilename;
      image = createImage(imageFilename, this);
      repaint();
    }

    /** Getter for property stretched.
     * @return Value of property stretched.
     */
    public boolean isStretched() {
      return stretched;
    }

    /** Setter for property stretched.
     * @param stretched New value of property stretched.
     */
```

Listing 4.1 *continued*

```
    public void setStretched(boolean stretched) {
      this.stretched = stretched;
      repaint();
    }

    /** Getter for property xCoordinate.
     * @return Value of property xCoordinate.
     */
    public int getXCoordinate() {
      return xCoordinate;
    }

    /** Setter for property xCoordinate.
     * @param xCoordinate New value of property xCoordinate.
     */
    public void setXCoordinate(int xCoordinate) {
      this.xCoordinate = xCoordinate;
      repaint();
    }

    /** Getter for property yCoordinate.
     * @return Value of property yCoordinate.
     */
    public int getYCoordinate() {
      return yCoordinate;
    }

    /** Setter for property yCoordinate.
     * @param yCoordinate New value of property yCoordinate.
     */
    public void setYCoordinate(int yCoordinate) {
      this.yCoordinate = yCoordinate;
      repaint();
    }
  }
```

Listing 4.1 *continued*

To test the component, compile ImageViewer.java and install it in the component palette. You may simply drop the bean on the Form Editor, change its properties from the component inspector, and see how the bean responds to the changes. Below you will use it to display six images in an applet.

Note

Due to a bug in Forte, the images are not displayed in the Form Editor when they are set in the image viewer initially. You will see the image after restarting Forte.

---

1. Create a new applet named `SixImages` in the imageviewerdemo package using the Forte Swing JApplet form wizard. Set `layout` of the applet to `GridLayout` with `rows` set to 2, `hgap` set to 5, and `vgap` set to 5, so as to have three images in one row and three in the other row, with a 5-pixel gap horizontally and vertically.

continued

Example 4.1 continued

2. Drop `ImageViewer` six times to the applet. Set the imageFilename properties to /image/us.gif, /image/ca.gif, /image/india.gif, /image/china.gif, /image/uk.gif, and /image/norway.gif, as shown in Figure 4.5. The generated source code for SixImages.java is shown in Listing 4.2.

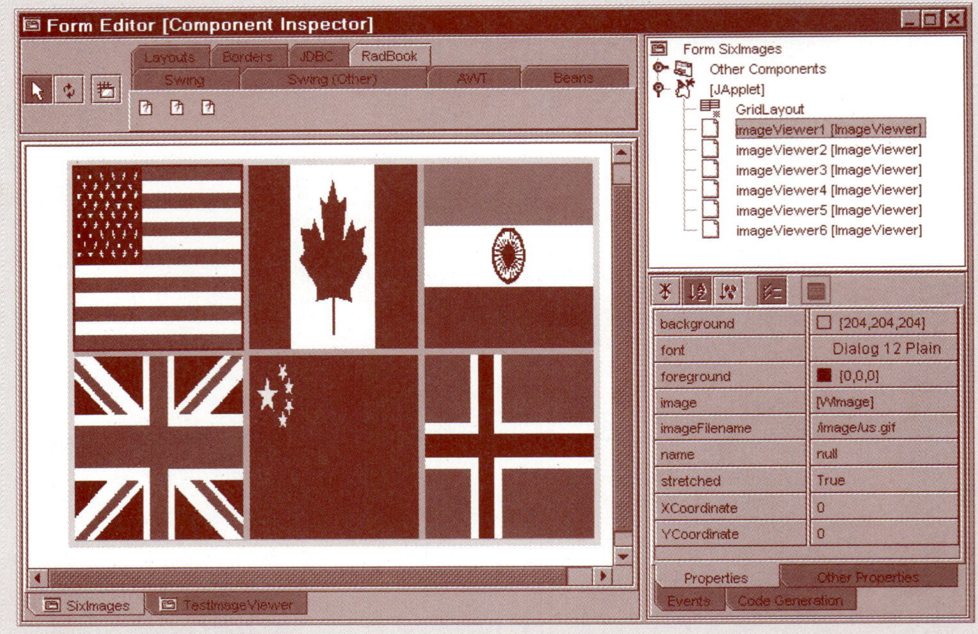

Figure 4.5 *Six instances of* `ImageViewer` *were added in the applet.*

```java
package imageviewerdemo;

import javax.swing.*;
import java.awt.*;

public class SixImages extends javax.swing.JApplet {
  /** Creates new form SixImages */
  public SixImages() {
    initComponents();
  }

  /** This method is called from within the constructor to
   * initialize the form.
   * WARNING: Do NOT modify this code. The content of this method is
   * always regenerated by the Form Editor.
   */
  private void initComponents() {
    imageViewer1 = new imageviewerdemo.ImageViewer();
    imageViewer2 = new imageviewerdemo.ImageViewer();
    imageViewer3 = new imageviewerdemo.ImageViewer();
    imageViewer4 = new imageviewerdemo.ImageViewer();
```

Listing 4.2 *SixImages.java*

```
      imageViewer5 = new imageviewerdemo.ImageViewer();
      imageViewer6 = new imageviewerdemo.ImageViewer();
      getContentPane().setLayout(new java.awt.GridLayout(2, 0, 5, 5));

      imageViewer1.setImageFilename("/image/us.gif");
      getContentPane().add(imageViewer1);
      imageViewer2.setImageFilename("/image/ca.gif");
      getContentPane().add(imageViewer2);
      imageViewer3.setImageFilename("/image/india.gif");
      getContentPane().add(imageViewer3);
      imageViewer4.setImageFilename("/image/uk.gif");
      getContentPane().add(imageViewer4);
      imageViewer5.setImageFilename("/image/china.gif");
      getContentPane().add(imageViewer5);
      imageViewer6.setImageFilename("/image/norway.gif");
      getContentPane().add(imageViewer6);
    }

    // Variables declaration - do not modify
    private imageviewerdemo.ImageViewer imageViewer1;
    private imageviewerdemo.ImageViewer imageViewer2;
    private imageviewerdemo.ImageViewer imageViewer3;
    private imageviewerdemo.ImageViewer imageViewer4;
    private imageviewerdemo.ImageViewer imageViewer5;
    private imageviewerdemo.ImageViewer imageViewer6;
    // End of variables declaration
  }
```

Listing 4.2 *continued*

Example Review

The `Component` class is the root of all Java graphical user interface components. Since `ImageViewer` extends `java.awt.Component`, it can be used with both AWT components and Swing components.

The `ImageViewer` class provides two static methods, `createImageIcon` (Lines 35–45) and `createImage` (Lines 50–57). The `createImageIcon(imageFilename, object)` method returns an `ImageIcon` from the image file name through the resource of the object. The `createImage(imageFilename, object)` method returns an `Image` instance from the image file through the resource of the object.

The image icon is created using `new ImageIcon(url)` (Line 39) in the `createImageIcon` method, where `url` is obtained using the `getResource` method in a `Class` instance of the object. You may create an image icon directly from the absolute path of the image file, as follows:

```
new ImageIcon("c:\\radft\\imageviewerdemo\\someimage.gif");
```

This approach is simple, but it works only with standalone applications. To load images in Java applets, you have to obtain the URL of the image and load the image through it. This approach works for both Java applications and applets.

The `createImage` method invokes the `createImageIcon` method to create an image icon and then returns the image from the image icon using the `getImage` method.

continued

Example 4.1 continued

The `imageFilename` property enables you to set a filename for the image. The `setImageFilename` method sets the `imageFilename` and creates the image for the file.

The `ImageViewer` component also provides the `image` property. You can set the image directly using the `setImage` method. This is convenient if your program knows the image but not the filename for the image. This is a good example of a JavaBeans component that provides many ways to use the bean. You can use the `imageFilename` property or the image property to set the image for `ImageViewer`, whichever is convenient.

Note

The `createImageIcon` method and `createImage` method could have been eliminated and combined with the `setImageFilename` method. The purpose of creating these two static methods is for use by other programs. You can now use these two methods as well as other methods to create image icons and images.

Note

To paint a non-Swing component, you need to override the `paint` method in the `Component` class. To paint a Swing component, you need to override the `paintComponent` method in the `JComponent` class.

Note

You can use images in the Swing components, such as `JLabel` and `JButton`, but the images are not stretchable and image filenames cannot be used directly with these components. The `ImageViewer` component provides better support for displaying images.

Tip

If `ImageViewer` instances are not placed in the right order inside the content pane of the applet, you can drag and move them in the Form Editor.

Note

Java currently supports three image formats: GIF (Graphics Interchange Format), JPEG (Joint Photographic Experts Group), and PNG (Portable Network Graphics). The image filenames for these types end with .gif, .jpg, and .png respectively. If you have a bitmap file or image files in other formats, you can use image-processing utilities to convert them into GIF, JPEG, or PNG format for use in Java. GIF uses a lossless compression algorithm, but JPEG uses a lossy compression algorithm. GIF file size is larger than JPEG. The PNG format was designed to replace GIF. PNG uses a lossless compression algorithm that creates images that are usually a bit smaller than their GIF counterparts.

NOTE
File names are not case-sensitive on Windows, but are case-sensitive on Unix. To enable your programs to run on all platforms, I recommend that you name all the image files consistently.

Example 4.2 Creating a Clock Component

This example creates a useful bean for displaying an analog clock. This bean allows the user to customize a clock through the following properties:

- **`secondHandColor`** is the color of the second hand.
- **`minuteHandColor`** is the color of the minute hand.
- **`hourHandColor`** is the color of the hour hand.
- **`headerColor`** is the color of header. Header is an optional title for the clock, displayed above the analog clock.
- **`header`** is the contents of the header (a string).
- **`showingHeader`** is a `boolean` value indicating whether the header is displayed.
- **`digitalDateTimeColor`** is the color of the optional digital time, displayed below the analog clock.
- **`showingDigitalDateTime`** is a `boolean` value indicating whether the digital time is displayed.
- **`dateStyle`** is an `int` value representing four formats for displaying date. The values are `DateFormat.FULL` (0), `DateFormat.LONG` (1), `DateFormat.MEDIUM` (2), and `DateFormat.SHORT` (3).
- **`timeStyle`** is an `int` value representing four formats for displaying time. The values are `DateFormat.FULL` (0), `DateFormat.LONG` (1), `DateFormat.MEDIUM` (2), and `DateFormat.SHORT` (3).
- **`usingTimeZoneID`** is a `boolean` value indicating whether the `timeZoneID` property is used to set the `timeZoneOffset` property.
- **`timeZoneID`** is a string representing a valid time zone. All the time zone IDs can be obtained in `TimeZone.getAvailableIDs()`.

continued

Example 4.2 continued

- **`timeZoneOffset`** is an `int` value representing a time zone offset from GMT. The valid values are between -12 and 12.
- **`running`** is a boolean value indicating whether the clock is running.

Figure 4.6 shows the properties of a `Clock` bean in the component inspector.

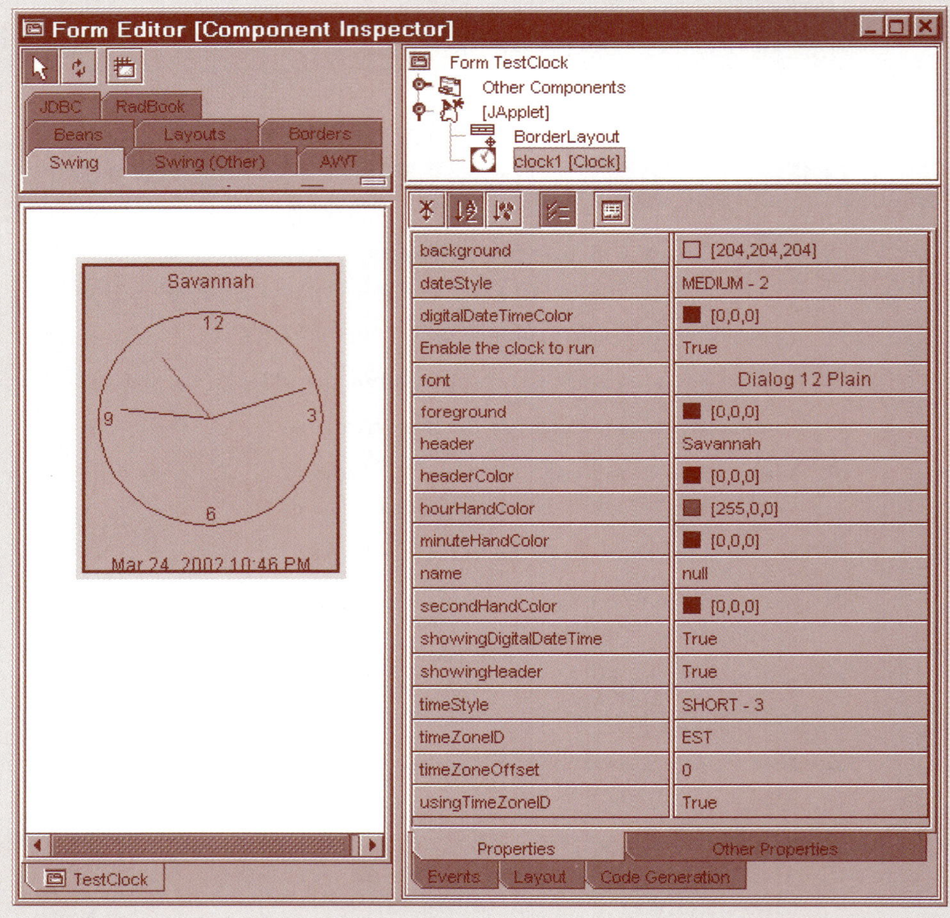

Figure 4.6 *When using the* `Clock` *bean, you can customize it to suit your needs with a variety of properties provided by the component.*

The `Clock` component also provides two public methods, `start()` and `stop()`, to let the component user start and stop the clock. Here are the steps in creating the component:

1. Create a new package named clockdemo, and create a Java class named `Clock` that extends `java.awt.Component` using the Class wizard.

2. Use the Bean Pattern wizard to create the properties and their accessor methods.

3. Modify the default implementation for the `setRunning` method and set the default values of the properties, as shown in Listing 4.3 (Lines 278–281).

4. Implement the `java.lang.Runnable` interface and declare an instance of `Thread`, named `thread`, for running the clock and drawing it.

5. Override the `paint` method to paint the clock every second, as shown in Listing 4.3 (Lines 68–143).

6. Create public methods `start()` (Lines 160–165) and `stop()` (Lines 168–172) for starting and stopping the clock, as shown in Listing 4.3.

```
1    package clockdemo;
2
3    import java.awt.*;
4    import javax.swing.*;
5    import java.lang.Runnable;
6    import java.util.*;
7    import java.text.*;
8    import java.io.*;
9
10   public class Clock extends Component implements Runnable {
11     // Create a thread to control clock running
12     protected transient Thread thread = null;
13
14     /** Create TimeZone */
15     protected TimeZone tz = TimeZone.getDefault();
16
17     /** Holds value of property secondHandColor. */
18     private java.awt.Color secondHandColor = Color.black;
19
20     /** Holds value of property minuteHandColor. */
21     private java.awt.Color minuteHandColor = Color.black;
22
23     /** Holds value of property hourHandColor. */
24     private java.awt.Color hourHandColor = Color.red;
25
26     /** Holds value of property headerColor. */
27     private java.awt.Color headerColor = Color.black;
28
29     /** Holds value of property header. */
30     private String header = "Savannah";
31
32     /** Holds value of property showingHeader. */
33     private boolean showingHeader = true;
34
35     /** Holds value of property digitalDateTimeColor. */
36     private java.awt.Color digitalDateTimeColor = Color.black;
37
38     /** Holds value of property showingDigitalDateTime. */
39     private boolean showingDigitalDateTime = true;
40
41     /** Holds value of property dateStyle:
42      * DateStyle 0-FULL, 1-LONG, 2-MEDIUM, 3-SHORT
43      */
44     private int dateStyle = 3;
```

Listing 4.3 *Clock.java*

continued

Example 4.2 continued

```

  /** Holds value of property timeStyle:
   * 0-FULL, 1-LONG, 2-MEDIUM, 3-SHORT
   */
  private int timeStyle = 3;

  /** Holds value of property usingTimeZoneID. */
  private boolean usingTimeZoneID = true;

  /** Holds value of property timeZoneID. */
  private String timeZoneID = "EST";

  /** Holds value of property running. */
  private boolean running;

  /** Holds value of property timeZoneOffset. */
  private int timeZoneOffset;

  public Clock() {
    // Start clock
    setRunning(true);
  }

  /** Display the clock*/
  public void paint(Graphics g) {
    int clockRadius =
      (int)Math.min(getWidth(), getHeight() * 0.7 * 0.5);
    int xCenter = (getWidth())/2;
    int yCenter = (getHeight())/2;

    // Draw circle
    g.setColor(Color.black);
    g.drawOval(xCenter - clockRadius, yCenter - clockRadius,
      2*clockRadius, 2*clockRadius);
    g.drawString("12", xCenter - 5, yCenter - clockRadius + 12);
    g.drawString("9", xCenter - clockRadius + 3, yCenter + 5);
    g.drawString("3", xCenter + clockRadius - 10, yCenter + 3);
    g.drawString("6", xCenter - 3, yCenter + clockRadius - 3);

    if (usingTimeZoneID)
      tz = TimeZone.getTimeZone(timeZoneID);
    else
      tz.setRawOffset(timeZoneOffset * 1000 * 3600);

    // Get current time using GregorianCalendar
    GregorianCalendar cal = new GregorianCalendar(tz);

    // Draw second hand
    int s = (int)cal.get(GregorianCalendar.SECOND);
    int sLength = (int)(clockRadius * 0.9);
    int secondx =
      (int)(xCenter + sLength * Math.sin(s * (2 * Math.PI / 60)));
    int secondy =
      (int)(yCenter - sLength * Math.cos(s * (2 * Math.PI / 60)));
    g.setColor(secondHandColor);
    g.drawLine(xCenter, yCenter, secondx, secondy);

```

Listing 4.3 *continued*

```
    // Draw minute hand
    int m = (int)cal.get(GregorianCalendar.MINUTE);
    int mLength = (int)(clockRadius * 0.8);
    int minutex =
      (int)(xCenter + mLength * Math.sin(m * (2 * Math.PI / 60)));
    int minutey =
      (int)(yCenter - mLength * Math.cos(m * (2 * Math.PI / 60)));
    g.setColor(minuteHandColor);
    g.drawLine(xCenter, yCenter, minutex, minutey);

    // Draw hour hand
    int h = (int)cal.get(GregorianCalendar.HOUR_OF_DAY);
    int hLength = (int)(clockRadius * 0.7);
    int hourx = (int)(xCenter + hLength *
      Math.sin((h + m / 60.0) * (2 * Math.PI / 12)));
    int houry = (int)(yCenter - hLength *
      Math.cos((h + m / 60.0) * (2 * Math.PI / 12)));
    g.setColor(hourHandColor);
    g.drawLine(xCenter, yCenter, hourx, houry);

    if (showingHeader) {
      // Display header
      FontMetrics fm = g.getFontMetrics();
      g.setColor(headerColor);
      g.drawString(header, (getWidth() -
        fm.stringWidth(header)) / 2, (yCenter - clockRadius) / 2);
    }

    if (showingDigitalDateTime) {
      // Set display format in specified style, locale and timezone
      DateFormat myFormat = DateFormat.getDateTimeInstance
        (dateStyle, timeStyle, getLocale());
      myFormat.setTimeZone(tz);

      // Display time
      String today = myFormat.format(cal.getTime());
      FontMetrics fm = g.getFontMetrics();
      g.setColor(digitalDateTimeColor);
      g.drawString(today, (getWidth() -
        fm.stringWidth(today)) / 2, yCenter + clockRadius + 30);
    }
  }

  /** Run the clock */
  public void run() {
    //TODO: implement this java.lang.Runnable method;
    while (true) {
      if (thread == null) return;

      try {
        thread.sleep(1000);
      }
      catch (InterruptedException e) {}
      repaint();
    }
  }

```

Listing 4.3 *continued*

continued

Example 4.2 continued

```
      /** Start the clock */
      public void start() {
        if (thread == null) {
          thread = new Thread(this);
          thread.start();
        }
      }

      /** Stop the clock */
      public void stop() {
        if (thread != null) {
          thread = null;
        }
      }

      public java.awt.Color getSecondHandColor() {
        return secondHandColor;
      }

      public void setSecondHandColor(java.awt.Color secondHandColor) {
        this.secondHandColor = secondHandColor;
      }

      public java.awt.Color getMinuteHandColor() {
        return minuteHandColor;
      }

      public void setMinuteHandColor(java.awt.Color minuteHandColor) {
        this.minuteHandColor = minuteHandColor;
      }

      public java.awt.Color getHourHandColor() {
        return hourHandColor;
      }

      public void setHourHandColor(java.awt.Color hourHandColor) {
        this.hourHandColor = hourHandColor;
      }

      public java.awt.Color getHeaderColor() {
        return headerColor;
      }

      public void setHeaderColor(java.awt.Color headerColor) {
        this.headerColor = headerColor;
      }

      public String getHeader() {
        return header;
      }

      public void setHeader(String header) {
        this.header = header;
      }

      public boolean isShowingHeader() {
        return showingHeader;
      }

```

Listing 4.3 *continued*

```
    public void setShowingHeader(boolean showingHeader) {
      this.showingHeader = showingHeader;
    }

    public java.awt.Color getDigitalDateTimeColor() {
      return digitalDateTimeColor;
    }

    public void setDigitalDateTimeColor(
      java.awt.Color digitalDateTimeColor) {
      this.digitalDateTimeColor = digitalDateTimeColor;
    }

    public boolean isShowingDigitalDateTime() {
      return showingDigitalDateTime;
    }

    public void setShowingDigitalDateTime(
      boolean showingDigitalDateTime) {
      this.showingDigitalDateTime = showingDigitalDateTime;
    }

    public int getDateStyle() {
      return dateStyle;
    }

    public void setDateStyle(int dateStyle) {
      this.dateStyle = dateStyle;
    }

    public int getTimeStyle() {
      return timeStyle;
    }

    public void setTimeStyle(int timeStyle) {
      this.timeStyle = timeStyle;
    }

    public boolean isUsingTimeZoneID() {
      return usingTimeZoneID;
    }

    public void setUsingTimeZoneID(boolean usingTimeZoneID) {
      this.usingTimeZoneID = usingTimeZoneID;
    }

    public String getTimeZoneID() {
      return timeZoneID;
    }

    public void setTimeZoneID(String timeZoneID) {
      this.timeZoneID = timeZoneID;
    }

    public boolean isRunning() {
      return running;
    }

```

Listing 4.3 *continued*

continued

Example 4.2 continued

```
    public void setRunning(boolean running) {
      this.running = running;
      if (running)
        start();
      else
        stop();
    }

    public int getTimeZoneOffset() {
      return timeZoneOffset;
    }

    public void setTimeZoneOffset(int timeZoneOffset) {
      this.timeZoneOffset = timeZoneOffset;
    }

    /** Set the preferred size for the clock */
    public Dimension getPreferredSize() {
      return new Dimension(200, 200);
    }
  }
```

Listing 4.3 *continued*

To test the component, compile Clock.java and install it in the component palette. You simply drop the bean on the Form Editor, change its properties from the component inspector, and see how the bean responds to the changes. Below you will use it to develop a program that shows a set of clocks for displaying the time in London, Paris, Savannah, Chicago, Denver, and San Francisco.

Here are the steps to complete the project.

1. Create a new applet named `SixClocks` in the clockdemo package using the Forte Swing JApplet form wizard. Set `layout` of the applet to `GridLayout`. In the component inspector of `gridLayout1`, set `rows` to 2, `hgap` to 10, and `vgap` to 10, so as to have three clocks in one row and three in the other row, with a 10-pixel gap horizontally and vertically.

2. Add six clocks to the applet. Set the appropriate header and time zone ID for each clock. The generated source code for SixClocks.java is shown in Listing 4.4. Figure 4.7 contains a sample run of the program.

```
package clockdemo;

public class SixClocks extends javax.swing.JApplet {
  /** Creates new form SixClocks */
  public SixClocks() {
    initComponents();
  }

  private void initComponents() {
    clock1 = new clockdemo.Clock();
    clock2 = new clockdemo.Clock();
    clock3 = new clockdemo.Clock();
    clock4 = new clockdemo.Clock();
```

Listing 4.4 *SixClocks.java*

```
      clock5 = new clockdemo.Clock();
      clock6 = new clockdemo.Clock();
      getContentPane().setLayout(
       new java.awt.GridLayout(2, 3, 10, 10));
      clock1.setTimeZoneID("GMT");
      clock1.setHeader("London");
      getContentPane().add(clock1);
      clock2.setTimeZoneID("Europe/Paris");
      clock2.setHeader("Paris");
      getContentPane().add(clock2);
      getContentPane().add(clock3);
      clock4.setTimeZoneID("CST");
      clock4.setHeader("Chicago");
      getContentPane().add(clock4);
      clock5.setTimeZoneID("MST");
      clock5.setHeader("Denver");
      getContentPane().add(clock5);
      clock6.setTimeZoneID("PST");
      clock6.setHeader("San Francisco");
      getContentPane().add(clock6);

     }

     // Variables declaration - do not modify
     private clockdemo.Clock clock1;
     private clockdemo.Clock clock2;
     private clockdemo.Clock clock3;
     private clockdemo.Clock clock4;
     private clockdemo.Clock clock5;
     private clockdemo.Clock clock6;
     // End of variables declaration
    }
```

Listing 4.4 *continued*

Example Review

In the `Clock` component, `thread` is an instance of `Thread`. Since it cannot be serialized, the `transient` modifier was used to mark it so that `thread` is not stored when a `Clock` object is stored. If `transient` were not used, this example would work fine, because no objects are stored during design time in Forte. However, it might be erroneous if used in another development tool. To ensure portability, make your beans serializable by marking `transient` on all nonserializable data fields. More discussion of the `transient` keyword and bean serialization will be presented in Chapter 9, "Bean Persistence and Versioning."

Since the `Thread thread` is `protected` rather than `private`, `thread` can be referenced in a subclass of `Clock` in Example 9.4, "Making the Clock Component Persistent," and Example 9.5, "Using the `Externalizable` Interface."

A variety of properties are provided in `Clock` to make the bean versatile and useful. For instance, you can set the clock using the time zone ID or using the offset to the GMT time, whichever is convenient.

continued

Example 4.2 continued

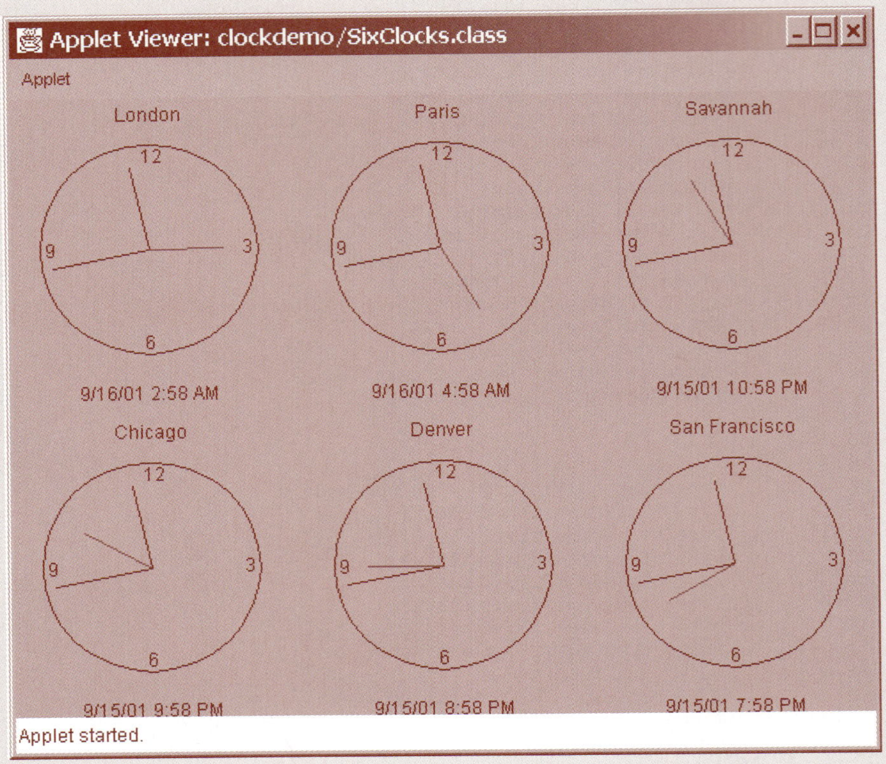

Figure 4.7 *The Clock bean is used to develop a set of six clocks.*

Note

The `timeZoneOffset` value is automatically adjusted when `timeZoneID` is changed. However, the reverse is not true. A time zone may have several IDs. For instance, IET (Indiana Eastern Time) and CST (Central Standard Time) are the same during the summer, and IET and EST (Eastern Standard Time) are the same during the winter. Therefore, when you set the `time-ZoneOffset` property, the `timezoneID` property cannot be automatically adjusted.

4.5 Creating a Component with Events

In the preceding example you created a `Clock` component. Now your customers want to have an alarm clock. In this section, you will learn how to use Forte's Bean Pattern wizard to develop a new clock component that fires an `ActionEvent` for the alarm.

Example 4.3 Creating an Alarm Clock

This example creates an alarm clock, named `ClockWithAlarm`, which extends the `Clock` component built in Example 4.2. This component contains two new properties:

- **`alarmDate`** is a string consisting of year, month, and day, separated by commas. For example, 1998,5,13 represents the year 1998, month 5, and day 13.
- **`alarmTime`** is a string consisting of hour, minute, and second, separated by commas. For example, 10,45,2 represents 10 hours, 45 minutes, and 2 seconds.

When the clock time matches the alarm time, `ClockWithAlarm` fires an `ActionEvent`.

Follow the steps below to create the `ClockWithAlarm` component.

1. In the clockdemo package, create a new class, `ClockWithAlarm`, that extends `Clock` using the Class wizard.
2. In the context menu of the Bean Patterns node, choose *Add, Multicast Event Source* (see Figure 4.8) to display the New Multicast Event Set dialog box, as shown in Figure 4.9. Select *java.awt.event.ActionListener* in the Type field, select *Generate EvenListenerList Implementation* and check *Generate Event Firing Methods*, as shown in Figure 4.9. Click *OK* to generate the code for registering and deregistering events and for firing the events, as shown in italic in Listing 4.5. You can choose `ArrayList` implementation or `EventListenerList` implementation to hold the listener. `EventListenerList` is preferred because it provides the support for synchronization and is efficient in the case of no listeners.
3. Add properties `alarmDate` and `alarmTime` using the Bean Pattern wizard's New Property Pattern dialog box.
4. Initialize `alarmTime` and `alarmDate` in the `ClockWithAlarm` constructor, and override the `run()` method to run the clock and fire an `ActionEvent` when the clock matches the alarm time so as to notify the listeners of the event, as shown in Listing 4.5.

```
package clockdemo;

import java.awt.*;
import java.util.*;
import java.awt.event.*;

public class ClockWithAlarm extends Clock {
  /** Utility field used by event firing mechanism. */
  private javax.swing.event.EventListenerList listenerList =  null;

```

Listing 4.5 *ClockWithAlarm.java*

continued

Example 4.3 continued

```
  /** Holds value of property alarmDate. */
  private String alarmDate;

  /** Holds value of property alarmTime. */
  private String alarmTime;

  public ClockWithAlarm() {
    super();

    // Get initial date and time
    GregorianCalendar cal = new GregorianCalendar(tz);

    // Initialize alarm date, which consists of current
    // year, month, and date, separated by commas.
    alarmDate = cal.get(cal.YEAR) + "," + cal.get(cal.MONTH)
      + "," + cal.get(cal.DATE);

    // Initialize alarm time, which consists of current
    // hour, minute, and second, separated by commas.
    alarmTime = cal.get(cal.HOUR) + "," + cal.get(cal.MINUTE)
      + "," + cal.get(cal.SECOND);
  }

  public void run() {
    while (true) {
      try {
        thread.sleep(1000);
      }
      catch (InterruptedException e) {}
      repaint();

      // Fire tick event if the current time matches alarm time
      GregorianCalendar rightNow = new GregorianCalendar(tz);
      String rightNowDate = rightNow.get(rightNow.YEAR)
        + "," +  rightNow.get(rightNow.MONTH) + "," +
        rightNow.get(rightNow.DATE);
      String rightNowTime = rightNow.get(rightNow.HOUR)
        + "," +  rightNow.get(rightNow.MINUTE) + "," +
        rightNow.get(rightNow.SECOND);
      if (rightNowDate.equals(alarmDate)
        && rightNowTime.equals(alarmTime))
        fireActionListenerActionPerformed(new ActionEvent
          (this, ActionEvent.ACTION_PERFORMED, null));
    }
  }

  /** Registers ActionListener to receive events.
   * @param listener The listener to register.
   */
  public synchronized void addActionListener(
    java.awt.event.ActionListener listener) {
    if (listenerList == null ) {
      listenerList = new javax.swing.event.EventListenerList();
    }
    listenerList.add(java.awt.event.ActionListener.class, listener);
  }

  /** Removes ActionListener from the list of listeners.
   * @param listener The listener to remove.
   */
```

Listing 4.5 *continued*

```
      public synchronized void removeActionListener(
        java.awt.event.ActionListener listener) {
        listenerList.remove(
          java.awt.event.ActionListener.class, listener);
      }

      /** Notifies all registered listeners about the event.
       *
       * @param e The event to be fired
       */
      private void fireActionListenerActionPerformed(
        java.awt.event.ActionEvent event) {
        if (listenerList == null) return;
        Object[] listeners = listenerList.getListenerList();
        for (int i = listeners.length - 2; i >= 0; i -= 2) {
          if (listeners[i]==java.awt.event.ActionListener.class) {
            ((java.awt.event.ActionListener)listeners[i + 1]).
              actionPerformed(event);
          }
        }
      }

      /** Getter for property alarmDate.
       * @return Value of property alarmDate.
       */
      public String getAlarmDate() {
        return alarmDate;
      }

      /** Setter for property alarmDate.
       * @param alarmDate New value of property alarmDate.
       */
      public void setAlarmDate(String alarmDate) {
        this.alarmDate = alarmDate;
      }

      /** Getter for property alarmTime.
       * @return Value of property alarmTime.
       */
      public String getAlarmTime() {
        return alarmTime;
      }

      /** Setter for property alarmTime.
       * @param alarmTime New value of property alarmTime.
       */
      public void setAlarmTime(String alarmTime) {
        this.alarmTime = alarmTime;
      }
    }
```

Listing 4.5 *continued*

Tip

You can delete the code for the event by choosing *Delete* from the context menu of the event under the Bean Patterns node, as shown in Figure 4.10.

continued

Example 4.3 continued

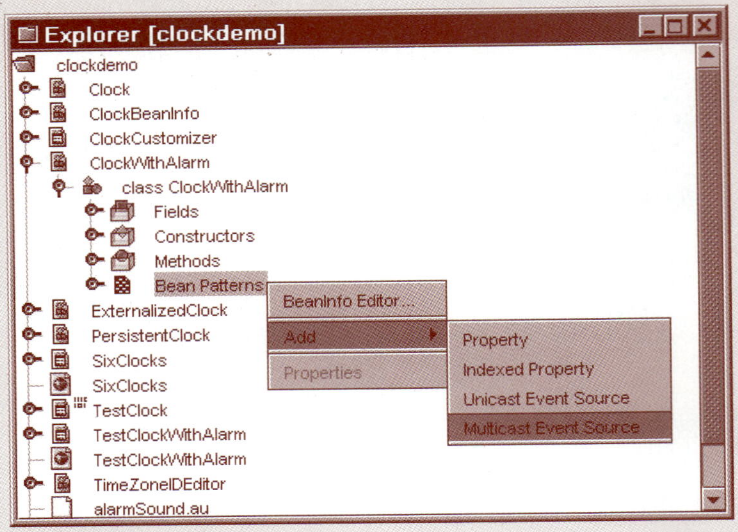

Figure 4.8 *You can use the Bean Pattern wizard to generate the code for event registration methods and for firing events.*

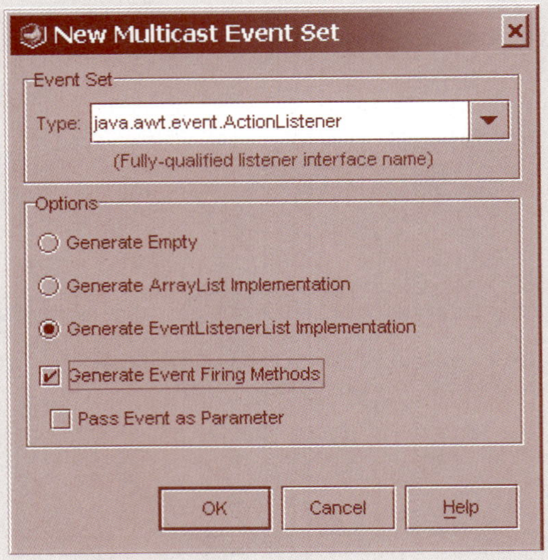

Figure 4.9 *The New Multicast Event Set dialog box enables you to generate the code for event registration methods and for firing events.*

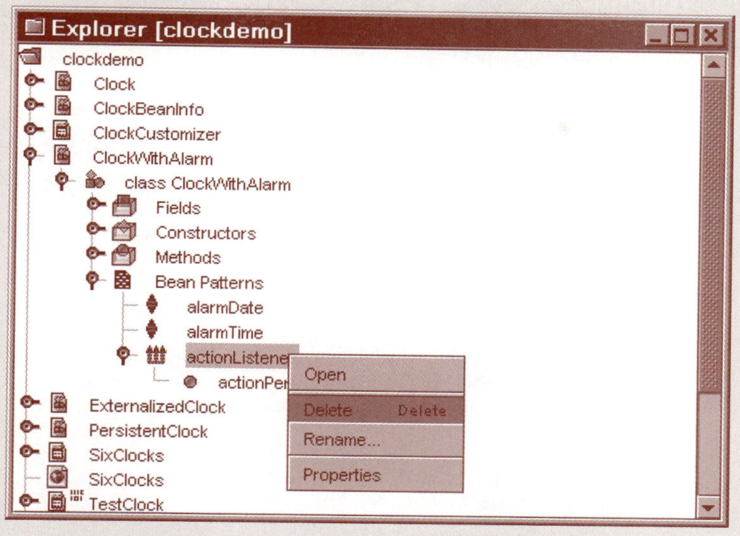

Figure 4.10 *You can delete the code for an event in the Bean Pattern wizard.*

To test the `ClockWithAlarm` component, follow the steps below to create an applet that makes a sound when the clock alarms.

1. Compile `ClockWithAlarm` and install it in the component palette. Create an applet named `TestClockWithAlarm` using the Forte Swing JApplet form wizard.
2. Set the `layout` to `BorderLayout` for the applet. Drop a `ClockWithAlarm` to the applet to create `clockWithAlarm1`, and set its `alarmDate` and `alarmTime` to a later time, as shown in Figure 4.11.
3. Double-click `clockWithAlarm1` in the Form Editor to generate the handler for handling the alarm event.
4. Declare an `AudioClip` instance named `alarmSound` for playing sound file alarmSound.au, create the audio clip in the `jbInit()` method, and complete the `clockWithAlarm1_actionPerformed` handler to play the audio clip, as shown in Listing 4.6.

```
package clockdemo;

import java.applet.*;
import java.net.*;

public class TestClockWithAlarm extends javax.swing.JApplet {
  /** Declare alarmSound */
  AudioClip alarmSound;

```

Listing 4.6 *TestClockWithAlarm.java*

continued

Example 4.3 continued

```
    public TestClockWithAlarm() {
      initComponents();

      // Get the URL for the file name
      URL url = this.getClass().getResource("alarmSound.au");

      // Get the audio clip
      alarmSound = Applet.newAudioClip(url);
    }

    private void initComponents() {
      clockWithAlarm1 = new clockdemo.ClockWithAlarm();
      clockWithAlarm1.addActionListener(
        new java.awt.event.ActionListener() {
        public void actionPerformed(java.awt.event.ActionEvent evt) {
          clockWithAlarm1ActionPerformed(evt);
        }
      });
      getContentPane().add(clockWithAlarm1,
        java.awt.BorderLayout.CENTER);
    }

    private void clockWithAlarm1ActionPerformed(
      java.awt.event.ActionEvent evt) {
      alarmSound.play();
    }

    // Variables declaration - do not modify
    private clockdemo.ClockWithAlarm clockWithAlarm1;
    // End of variables declaration
  }
```

Listing 4.6 *continued*

Example Review

When designing a component, you may have two conflicting objectives. On the one hand, you want the bean to be simple, so that it will not intimidate an inexperienced user; on the other hand, you want the bean to be comprehensive, so that it will meet the needs of a variety of customers in various applications. The only way to resolve the conflict is to make several versions of the component available, and let users choose whichever one suits their needs. As in the case of the clock, if you don't need the alarm function, you could simply choose `Clock` rather than `ClockWithAlarm`.

`ClockWithAlarm` extends `Clock` with the capability of firing an `ActionEvent` when the clock time matches the alarm time. The `run()` method is overridden to repaint the clock every second and check to see whether the current time matches the alarm time. When they match, an `ActionEvent` is fired.

The test program makes a sound for the alarm. It declares and creates an `AudioClip` instance, `alarmSound`, for alarmSound.au, in the `ClockWithAlarm` class. It plays the `alarmSound` when the current time matches the specified alarm time.

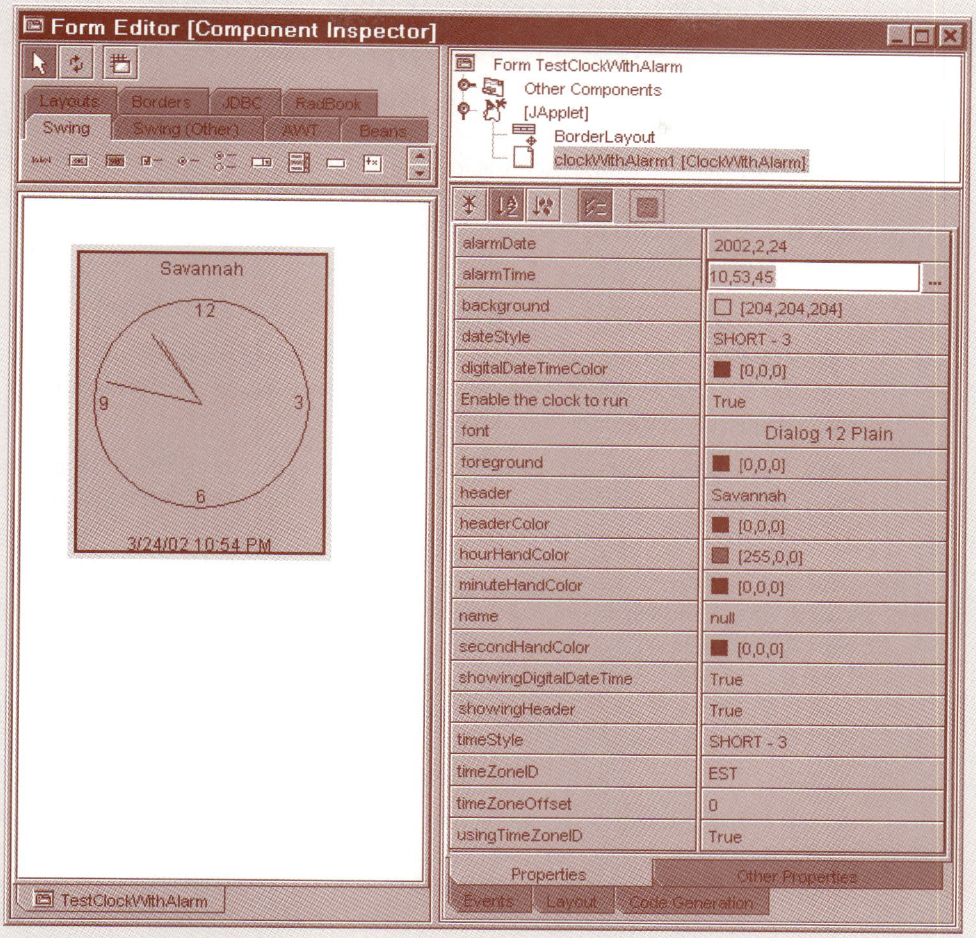

Figure 4.11 `alarmDate` *and* `alarmTime` *are the two new properties in the* `ClockWithAlarm` *component.*

The test program can run as an applet as well as an application. The `newAudioClip(url)` method is a new static method in the `Applet` class in Java 2 for creating an `AudioClip` in an applet or in an application.

There is an annoying problem in this example. When the alarm starts, the clock pauses. The clock resumes only after the audio clip finishes playing. To fix this problem, play the audio clip on a separate thread, as suggested in Exercise 4.3.

Note

When entering `alarmDate` and `alarmTime`, you must follow the pattern. Do not pad zeros before the number. For example, use 4 rather than 04 for number 4.

4.6 Developing Components Using the Model-View Approach

The model-view approach is a way of developing components by separating data storage and handling from the visual representation of the data. The component for storing and handling data, known as a *model*, contains the actual contents of the component. The component for presenting the data, known as a *view*, handles all essential component behaviors. It is the view that comes to mind when you think of the component. It does all the displaying of the components.

Separating a component into a model and a view has two major benefits:

- It makes multiple views possible so that data can be shared through the same model. For example, a model storing student names can simultaneously be displayed in a combo box or in a list box.
- It simplifies the task of writing complex applications and makes system maintenance easier. Changes can be made to the view without affecting the model, and vice versa.

A model contains data, whereas a view makes the data visible. Once a view is associated with a model, it immediately displays updates to the model. This ensures that all the views of the model display the same data consistently. To achieve consistency and synchronize the model with its dependent views, the model should notify the views when there is a change in a property in the model that is used in the view. In response to a change notification, the view is responsible for redisplaying the viewing area affected by the property change.

A view is responsible for presenting data. It can also be used as an interface to interact with the user and accept user input, as shown in Figure 4.12. Sometimes it is helpful to further separate user interaction from display, using a component known as a *controller*. A controller is the means by which the user interacts with the application. A controller accepts input from the user and instructs the model and view to perform actions based on that input, as shown in Figure 4.13. In effect, the controller is responsible for mapping end-user action to application response. For example, if the user clicks the mouse button or chooses a menu item, the controller is responsible for determining how the application should respond. For this reason, the model-view approach is also known as the *model-view-controller architecture*. Whether to separate the controller from the view depends on whether the view and the controller are tightly intertwined or loosely connected. If there is a good deal of communication between the two, it makes sense to combine them. If they don't have to be used together, separating them makes these components more scalable and maintainable.

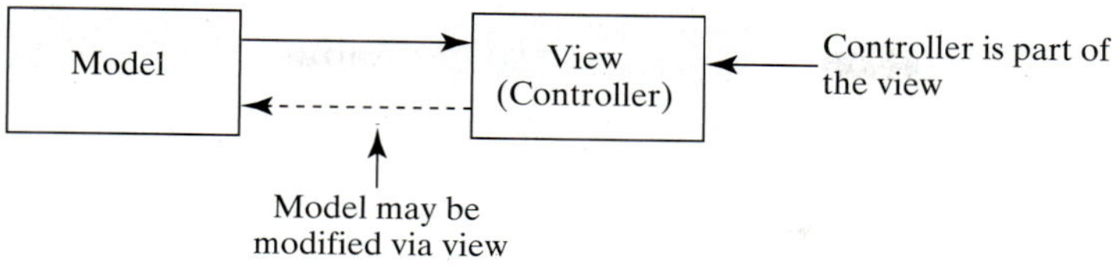

Figure 4.12 *The view can display data as well as interact with the user.*

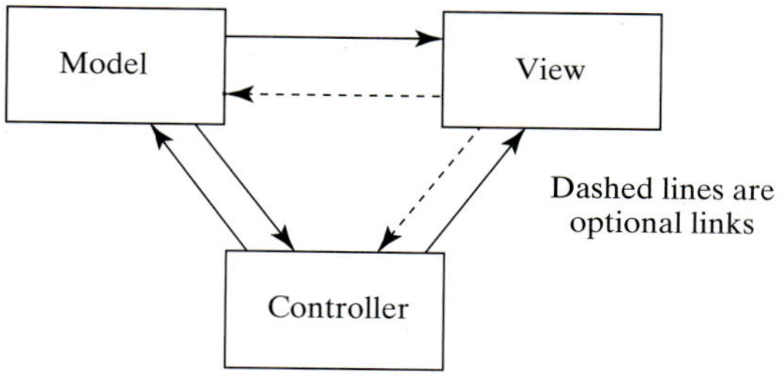

Figure 4.13 *The controller is separated from the view to facilitate interaction with the user.*

Prior to JDK 1.1, you would create a model by extending the `java.util.Observable` class, and would create a view by implementing the `java.util.Observer` interface. `Observable` and `Observer` were introduced in JDK 1.0, and their use is not consistent with the JDK 1.1 event model. With the arrival of the new Java event delegation model, using `Observable` and `Observer` is obsolete. The JDK event delegation model provides a superior architecture for supporting model-view component development. The model can be implemented as a source with appropriate event and event listener registration methods. The view can be implemented as a listener. Thus, if data are changed in the model, the view will be notified. To enable the selection of the model during design time in a builder tool, simply add the model as a property in the view. You can easily create a property for each kind of model in the view with the event delegation model, but this task would be difficult with the Observable/Observer architecture.

Example 4.4 Developing Model-View Components

This example demonstrates the development of components using the model-view approach with the event delegation model. The example creates a model named `CircleModel`, and its two dependent views, named `CircleView` and `CircleEditor`. `CircleView` draws a circle according to the properties of the circle and enables changes that increase or decrease the circle's radius by a left mouse click or a right mouse click. `CircleEditor` displays all the circle properties and enables editing of the `radius` property in a text field. An applet is created to host the instances of `CircleModel`, `CircleView`, and `CircleEditor` and test the interaction among them. The relationship of these classes is shown in Figure 4.14. A sample run of the applet is shown in Figure 4.15.

continued

Example 4.4 continued

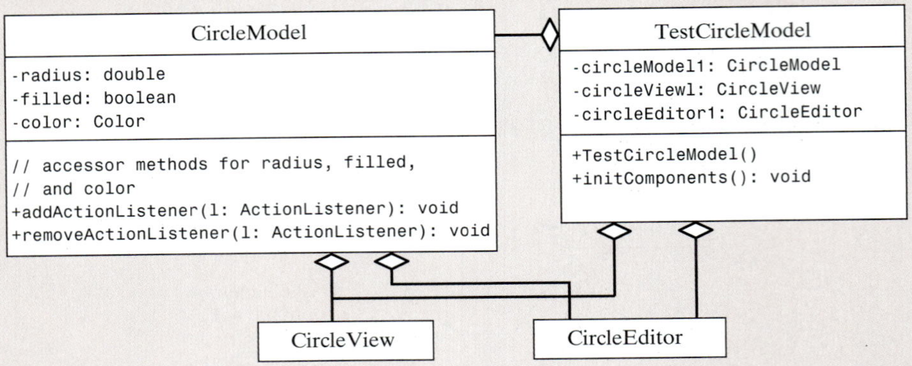

Figure 4.14 *The* `CircleModel` *class contains data. The* `CircleView` *and* `CircleEditor` *classes display and control data.* `TestCircleModel` *is a test class for these components.*

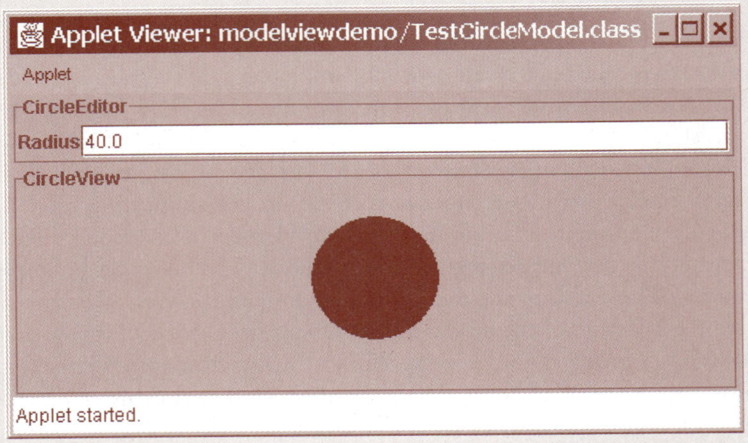

Figure 4.15 *A* `CircleEditor` *is shown in the north, and a* `CircleView` *is shown in the center of the applet. A* `CircleModel` *is shared by both* `CircleEditor` *and* `CircleView`.

The `CircleModel` contains the following properties:

- **`radius`** is the radius of the circle.
- **`filled`** is a boolean value indicating whether the circle is filled with a color.
- **`color`** is the color used to fill in the circle.

When a property value is changed, the `CircleModel` generates an `ActionEvent` and notifies its views of the associated change. Here are the steps in creating `CircleModel`:

1. Create a package named modelviewdemo. Use the Class wizard to create a template for CircleModel.java.

2. Use the Bean Pattern wizard to create the properties `radius`, `filled`, and `color`.

3. Use the Bean Pattern wizard to generate the code for firing and registering `ActionEvent`.

4. Modify the `setRadius`, `setFilled`, and `setColor` methods to invoke the `fireActionPerformed` method upon a property change, as shown in Listing 4.7.

```
package modelviewdemo;

import java.awt.event.*;
import java.util.*;

public class CircleModel {
  /** Holds value of property radius. */
  private double radius = 20;

  /** Holds value of property filled. */
  private boolean filled;

  /** Holds value of property color. */
  private java.awt.Color color;

  /** Utility field used by event firing mechanism. */
  private javax.swing.event.EventListenerList listenerList =  null;

  public CircleModel() {
  }

  public double getRadius() {
    return radius;
  }

  public void setRadius(double radius) {
    this.radius = radius;

    // Notify the listener for the change on radius
    fireActionListenerActionPerformed(
      new ActionEvent(this, ActionEvent.ACTION_PERFORMED, "radius"));
  }

  public boolean isFilled() {
    return filled;
  }

  public void setFilled(boolean filled) {
    this.filled = filled;

    // Notify the listener for the change on filled
    fireActionListenerActionPerformed(
      new ActionEvent(this, ActionEvent.ACTION_PERFORMED, "filled"));
  }

```

Listing 4.7 *CircleModel.java*

continued

Example 4.4 continued

```
    public java.awt.Color getColor() {
      return color;
    }

    public void setColor(java.awt.Color color) {
      this.color = color;

      // Notify the listener for the change on color
      fireActionListenerActionPerformed(
        new ActionEvent(this, ActionEvent.ACTION_PERFORMED, "color"));
    }

    public synchronized void addActionListener(
      java.awt.event.ActionListener listener) {
      if (listenerList == null ) {
        listenerList = new javax.swing.event.EventListenerList();
      }
      listenerList.add(java.awt.event.ActionListener.class, listener);
    }

    public synchronized void removeActionListener(
      java.awt.event.ActionListener listener) {
      listenerList.remove(
        java.awt.event.ActionListener.class, listener);
    }

    private void fireActionListenerActionPerformed(
      java.awt.event.ActionEvent event) {
      if (listenerList == null) return;
      Object[] listeners = listenerList.getListenerList();
      for (int i = listeners.length - 2; i >= 0; i -= 2) {
        if (listeners[i] == java.awt.event.ActionListener.class) {
          ((java.awt.event.ActionListener)listeners[i + 1]).
            actionPerformed(event);
        }
      }
    }
  }
```

Listing 4.7 *continued*

Follow the steps below to create the `CircleView` component.

1. Create `CircleView` using the Forte Swing JPanel form wizard.
2. Use the Bean Pattern wizard to create a property named `model` with type `CircleModel`. Modify the `setModel` method to set the new model and register the view with the model, as shown in Listing 4.8 (Line 38–48).
3. Implement the `ActionListener` for `CircleView`, and implement the `actionPerformed` method to add the `repaint()` method to repaint the circle upon receiving a property-change notification from the model. Implement the `paintComponent` method to paint the circle in the center of the panel.
4. Press Enter in the value field of the `mouseClicked` handler to generate the code for handling mouse-clicked events. Implement the `mouseClicked`

method to handle the right-button click for increasing radius and the left-button click for decreasing radius, as shown in Listing 4.8 (Lines 75–82).

```
1  package modelviewdemo;
2
3  import java.awt.*;
4  import java.awt.event.*;
5
6  public class CircleView extends javax.swing.JPanel
7    implements ActionListener {
8    private modelviewdemo.CircleModel model;
9
10   /** Creates new form CircleView */
11   public CircleView() {
12     initComponents();
13   }
14
15   private void initComponents() {
16     setLayout(new java.awt.BorderLayout());
17     addMouseListener(new java.awt.event.MouseAdapter() {
18       public void mouseClicked(java.awt.event.MouseEvent evt) {
19         formMouseClicked(evt);
20       }
21     });
22   }
23
24   private void formMouseClicked(java.awt.event.MouseEvent evt) {
25     if (model == null) return;
26
27     if (evt.isMetaDown())
28       model.setRadius(model.getRadius() - 5);
29     else
30       model.setRadius(model.getRadius() + 5);
31   }
32
33   public void actionPerformed(
34     java.awt.event.ActionEvent actionEvent) {
35     repaint();
36   }
37
38   /** Set a model */
39   public void setModel(modelviewdemo.CircleModel newModel) {
40     model = newModel;
41
42     if (model != null) {
43       // Register the view as listener for the model
44       model.addActionListener(this);
45     }
46
47     repaint();
48   }
49
50   public modelviewdemo.CircleModel getModel() {
51     return model;
52   }
53
54   public void paintComponent(Graphics g) {
55     super.paintComponent(g);
56
```

Listing 4.8 *CircleView.java*

continued

Example 4.4 continued

```
      if (model == null) return;

      g.setColor(model.getColor());

      int xCenter = getWidth() / 2;
      int yCenter = getHeight() / 2;
      int radius = (int)model.getRadius();

      if (model.isFilled()) {
        g.fillOval(xCenter - radius, yCenter - radius,
          2 * radius, 2 * radius);
      }
      else {
        g.drawOval(xCenter - radius, yCenter - radius,
          2 * radius, 2 * radius);
      }
    }

    void this_mouseClicked(MouseEvent e) {
      if (model == null) return;

      if (e.isMetaDown())
        model.setRadius(model.getRadius() - 5);
      else
        model.setRadius(model.getRadius() + 5);
    }

    // Variables declaration - do not modify
    // End of variables declaration
  }
```

Listing 4.8 *continued*

Follow the steps below to create the `CircleEditor` component.

1. Create `CircleEditor` using the Forte Swing JPanel form wizard.
2. Drop a `JLabel` to the west of `CircleEditor`, and change the text of the label to Radius. Drop a `JTextField` to the center of `CircleEditor` and rename it `jtfRadius`.
3. Use the Bean Pattern wizard to create a property named `model` with type `CircleModel`. Modify the `setModel` method to set the new model and register the view with the model as shown in Listing 4.9 (Line 41–48).
4. Implement the `ActionListener` for `CircleView`, and implement the `actionPerformed` method to set the radius from the model (Lines 34–39).
5. To enable `CircleEditor` to edit the radius in the `jtfRadius` text field, switch to the Form Editor and double-click `jtfRadius` to generate `jtfRadius_actionPerformed` method and its associated event adapter. Implement `jtfRadiusActionPerformed` to set a new radius in the model, as shown in Listing 4.9 (Lines 28–32).

```
package modelviewdemo;

import java.awt.event.*;

public class CircleEditor extends javax.swing.JPanel
  implements ActionListener {
  private modelviewdemo.CircleModel model;

  /** Creates new form CircleEditor */
  public CircleEditor() {
    initComponents();
  }

  private void initComponents() {
    jLabel1 = new javax.swing.JLabel();
    jtfRadius = new javax.swing.JTextField();
    setLayout(new java.awt.BorderLayout());
    jLabel1.setText("Radius");
    add(jLabel1, java.awt.BorderLayout.WEST);
    jtfRadius.addActionListener(new java.awt.event.ActionListener() {
      public void actionPerformed(java.awt.event.ActionEvent evt) {
        jtfRadiusActionPerformed(evt);
      }
    });
    add(jtfRadius, java.awt.BorderLayout.CENTER);
  }

  private void jtfRadiusActionPerformed(
    java.awt.event.ActionEvent evt) {
    model.setRadius(
      new Double(jtfRadius.getText()).doubleValue());
  }

  public void actionPerformed(ActionEvent e) {
    if (model != null)
      if (e.getActionCommand().equals("radius"))
        jtfRadius.setText(
          new Double(model.getRadius()).toString());
  }

  public void setModel(modelviewdemo.CircleModel newModel) {
    model = newModel;

    if (model != null) {
      // Register the view as listener for the model
      model.addActionListener(this);
    }
  }

  public modelviewdemo.CircleModel getModel() {
    return model;
  }

  // Variables declaration - do not modify
  private javax.swing.JLabel jLabel1;
  private javax.swing.JTextField jtfRadius;
  // End of variables declaration
}
```

Listing 4.9 *CircleEditor.java*

continued

Example 4.4 continued

After creating a model and two views, you are ready to put them together in an applet. Here are the steps in creating this applet:

1. Create an applet named `TestCircleModel` using the Forte Swing JApplet form wizard.

2. Install `CircleModel`, `CircleView`, and `CircleEditor` to the component palette. In the Form Editor for TestCircleModel.java, drop a `CircleEditor` to the north of the applet to create `circleEditor1`, and drop a `CircleView` to the center of the applet to create `circleView1`. Drop a `CircleModel` to create `circleModel1`. Since `circleModel1` is a nonvisual component, it appears under the Other Components node in the component tree, as shown in Figure 4.16.

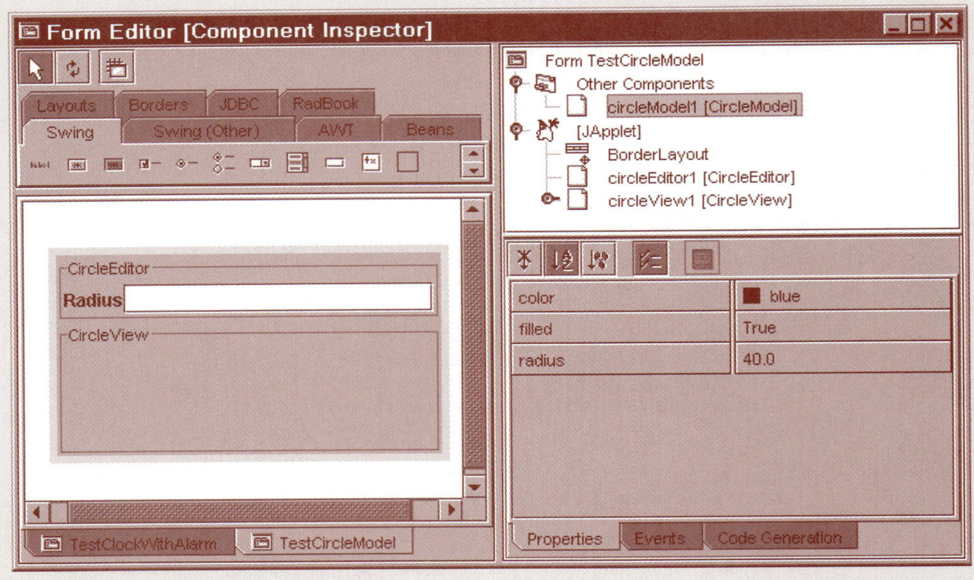

Figure 4.16 *The instances of* `CircleModel`, `CircleEditor`, *and* `CircleView` *were added to the applet.*

3. Click the ellipsis button in the `model` property of `circleEditor1` to display the CircleModel property editor, as shown in Figure 4.17. Check the User Code radio button and enter `circleMode1` as the code. Click *OK*. Forte generates `circleEditor1.setModel(circleModel1)` in the `initComponents` method, as shown in Listing 4.9 (Line 18). Similarly, set `circleModel1` to the model property for `circleView1`.

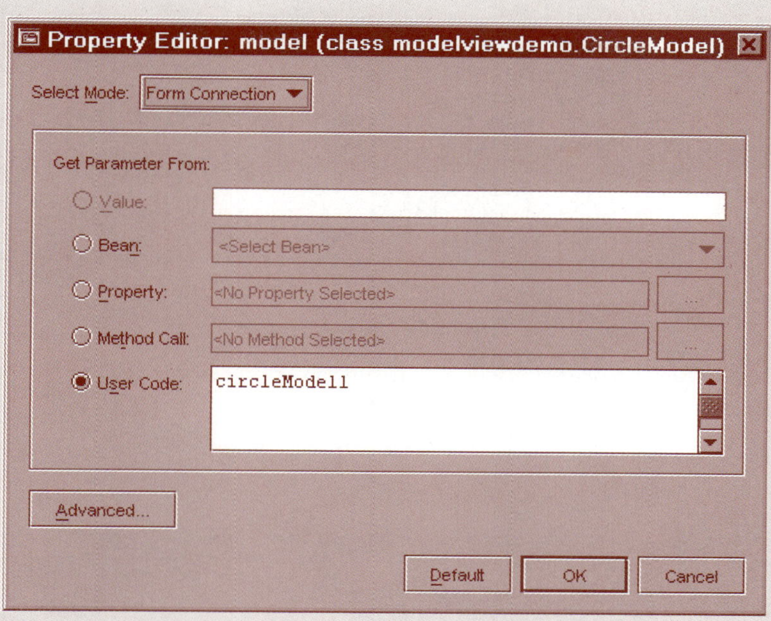

Figure 4.17 *You can associate a model in the property editor for the object.*

4. Click the ellipsis button in the `border` property of `circleEditor1` to display the border property editor, as shown in Figure 4.18. Select `TitledBorder` in the Available Borders section and set CircleEditor in the *Title* field. Similarly, create a border title named CircleView for `circleView1`.

5. In the inspector for `circleModel1`, change `radius` to 40, `color` to Blue, and `filled` to True. The code for `TestCircleModel` is shown in Listing 4.10.

Note

Due to a bug in Forte, the circle is not displayed in the form.

```
package modelviewdemo;

public class TestCircleModel extends javax.swing.JApplet {
  /** Creates new form TestCircleModel */
  public TestCircleModel() {
    initComponents();
  }

  private void initComponents() {
    circleModel1 = new modelviewdemo.CircleModel();
    circleEditor1 = new modelviewdemo.CircleEditor();
    circleView1 = new modelviewdemo.CircleView();
    circleModel1.setRadius(40.0);
    circleModel1.setColor(java.awt.Color.blue);
```

Listing 4.10 *TestCircleModel.java*

continued

Example 4.4 continued

```
      circleModel1.setFilled(true);
      circleEditor1.setBorder(
        new javax.swing.border.TitledBorder("CircleEditor"));
      circleEditor1.setModel(circleModel1);
      getContentPane().add(circleEditor1, java.awt.BorderLayout.NORTH);
      circleView1.setBorder(
        new javax.swing.border.TitledBorder("CircleView"));
      circleView1.setModel(circleModel1);
      getContentPane().add(circleView1, java.awt.BorderLayout.CENTER);
     }

     // Variables declaration - do not modify
     private modelviewdemo.CircleModel circleModel1;
     private modelviewdemo.CircleEditor circleEditor1;
     private modelviewdemo.CircleView circleView1;
     // End of variables declaration
    }
```

Listing 4.10 *continued*

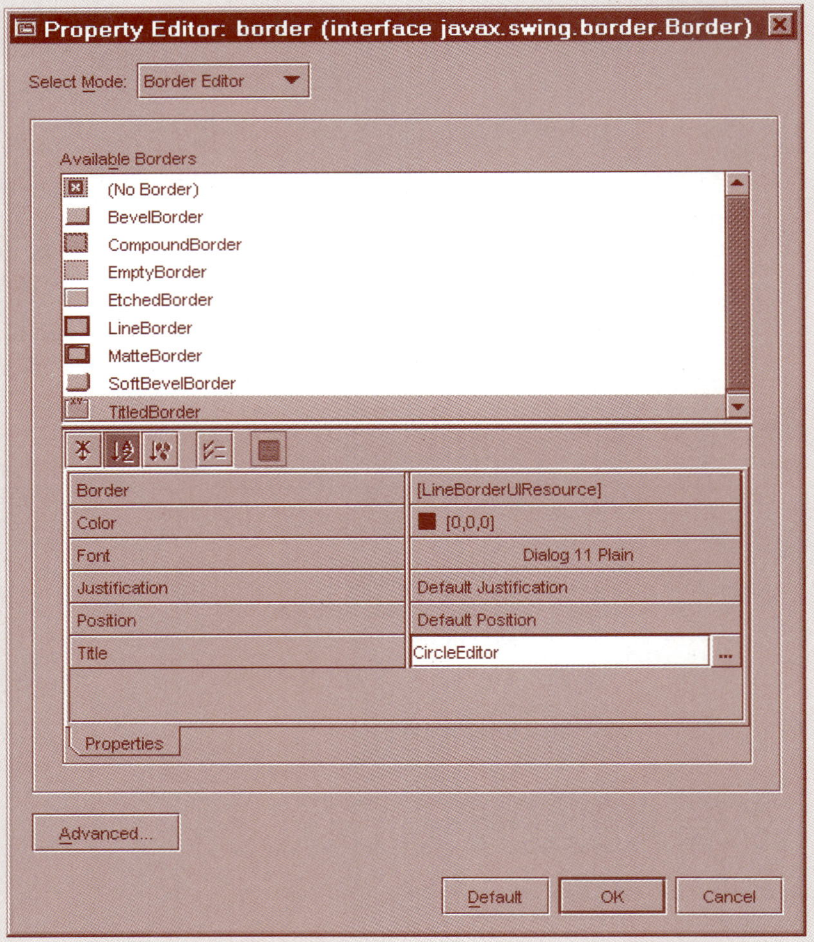

Figure 4.18 *You can set border title using the border property editor.*

Example Review

The model stores and handles data, and the view is responsible for presenting data. The fundamental issue in the model-view approach is to ensure consistency between the views and the model. Any change in the model should be notified to the dependent views, and all the views should display the same data consistently. You can change the radius either by entering a value in the radius text field in `circleEditor1` or by clicking the left or right mouse button to increase or decrease it in `circleView1`. Both views will display the same radius at the same time.

The methods `setRadius`, `setFilled`, and `setColor` in `CircleModel` invoke the `fireActionPerformed` method to notify listeners of any change in the properties. The `setModel` method in `CircleView` and `CircleEditor` set a new model and registered the view with the model by invoking the model's `addActionListener` method. This is the preferred approach for implementing the view. It simplifies the use of the model-view components. If registration were not done in the `setModel` method, you would have to attach the view to the model in `TestCircle`.

There is no definitive definition for a controller. You may well consider `CircleEditor` as a controller that accepts user input for the `CircleModel` and `CircleView`.

4.7 Rapid Application Development Process

Rapid application development, or RAD, is a software development technology introduced in the 1980s by researchers at the Xerox Palo Alto Research Lab. This technology for developing programs efficiently and effectively has been successfully implemented in program development tools like Visual Basic, Delphi, Power Builder, and Oracle Developer 2000, among many others. Using a RAD tool, projects can be developed quickly and efficiently with minimum coding. Projects developed using RAD are easy to modify and easy to maintain. The key elements in a Java RAD tool are the JavaBeans components. These components can be visually manipulated and tailored during design time in order to develop customized programs.

The application development process is similar to the component development process in many ways. Developing a software project is an engineering process. Software products, no matter how large or how small, have the same developmental phases: requirement specification, analysis, design, implementation, testing, deployment, and maintenance, as shown in Figure 4.19.

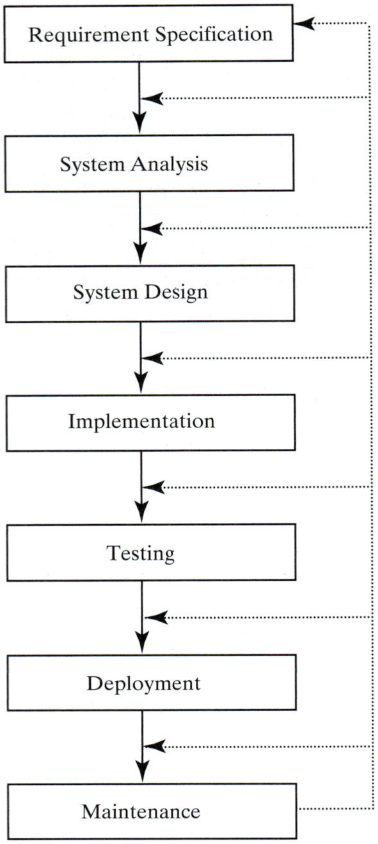

Figure 4.19 *Developing a project involves requirements specification, system analysis, system design, implementation, testing, deployment, and maintenance.*

Requirement specification is a formal process that seeks to understand the problem and document in detail what the proposed system or project needs to do. This phase involves close interaction between users and designers. Most of the examples in this book are simple, and their requirements are clearly stated. In the real world, however, problems are not well defined. You need to study a problem carefully to identify its requirements.

System analysis seeks to analyze the business process in terms of data flow, and to identify the system's input and output.

System design is the process of designing the system's components. This phase involves the use of many levels of abstraction to decompose the problem into manageable components and design algorithms for each of them.

Implementation is the process of translating the system design into programs. Programs are written for each component and then put to work together. This phase requires the use of a specific programming language.

Testing ensures that the code meets the requirement specification and weeds out bugs. An independent team of software engineers not involved in design and implementation of the project usually conducts such testing.

Deployment makes the project available for use. For a Java applet, this means installing it on a Web server. For a Java application, install it on the client's computer. For a Java servlet or a server page, install it with a Web server that has a servlet engine. The project usually consists of many classes. An effective approach for deployment is to package all the classes into a Java archive file, which is introduced in Section 4.8, "Packaging and Deploying Java Projects in Forte."

Maintenance is concerned with changing and improving the product. A software product must continue to perform and improve in a changing environment. This requires periodic upgrades of the product to fix newly discovered bugs and to incorporate changes.

The development phases are cyclic. You can use a CASE (Computer Aided Software Engineering) tool to aid software development. Requirement specification, analysis, and design are usually taught in a software engineering course. This chapter focuses on creating a project using rapid application development.

When writing a project using a RAD tool, you should first carefully plan the project before implementing it. The major part of the planning involves designing the user interface. You may draw a sketch of the screens that shows all the beans you plan to use. Indicate the layout for the containers, and identify all the objects with appropriate names.

The implementation is a two-step process that involves creating user interfaces and writing code. To create a user interface, click-and-drop the bean components, such as buttons, labels, combo boxes, lists, and text fields, from the component palette to the Form Editor, and set the beans properties in the inspector.

After the user interface is created, you will add event handlers and write the code to carry out the actions for the associated events.

The following example illustrates the process for rapid Java application development.

Example 4.5 Developing a Mortgage Calculator

This example creates a mortgage calculator for computing mortgage payments, as shown in Figure 4.20. The mortgage calculator lets the user enter loan amount, interest rate, and years; when the user clicks the Compute button, monthly payment and total payment are displayed.

continued

Example 4.5 continued

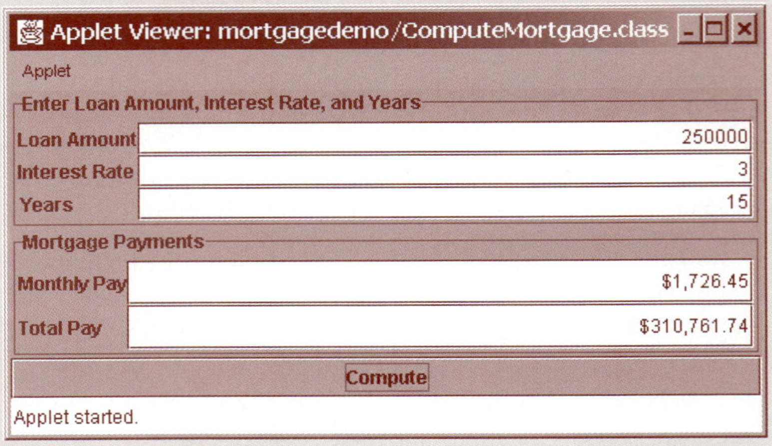

Figure 4.20 *The mortgage calculator gets input on loan amount, annual interest rate, and loan period in number of years, and computes monthly payment and total payment.*

Here are the steps to follow in completing the project:

1. It is often helpful to draw a sketch of a complex user interface, as shown in Figure 4.21.

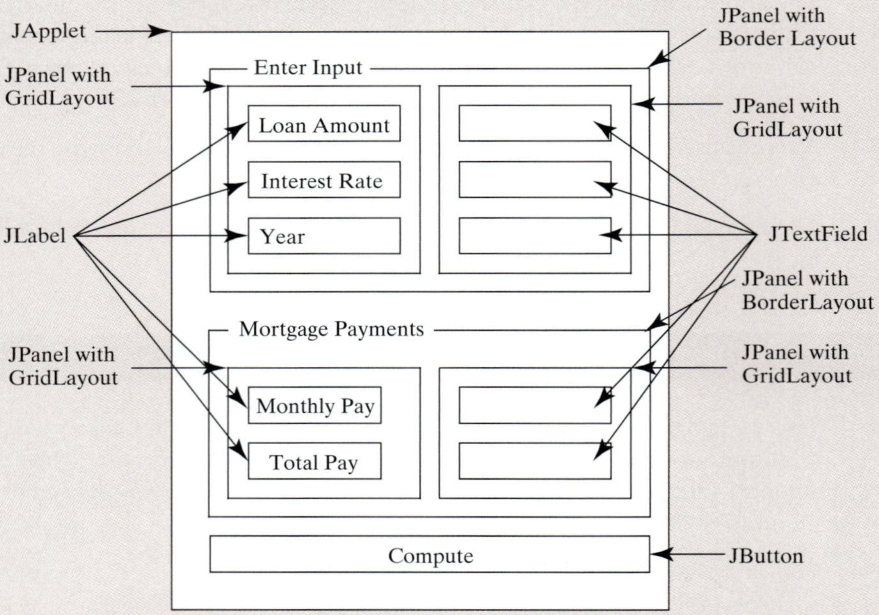

Figure 4.21 *The labels, text fields, borders, and a button are placed in the applet.*

2. Create a new package named mortgagedemo, and create an applet named `ComputeMortgage` using the Swing JApplet form wizard.
3. Drop a `JPanel` to the north of the applet to create `jpInput`, drop a `JButton` to the south of the applet to create `jbtCompute` with text Compute, and drop a `JPanel` to the center of the applet to create `jpResults`. Set the border titles of `jpInput` and `jpResults` to "Enter Loan Amount, Interest Rate, and Years" and "Mortgage Payments," respectively.
4. Set the `layout` of `jpInput` to `BorderLayout`. Drop a `JPanel` to the west of `jpInput` to create `jpInputLabels`, and drop a `JPanel` to the center of `jpInput` to create `jpInputTextFields`.
5. Set the `layout` of `jpInputLabels` to `GridLayout` with three rows, and drop three labels with texts "Loan Amount," "Interest Rate," and "Years." Set the `layout` of `jpInputTextFields` to `GridLayout` with three rows, and drop three text fields to create `jtfLoanAmount`, `jtfInterestRate`, and `jtfYears`.
6. Set the `layout` of `jpResults` to `BorderLayout`. Drop a `JPanel` to the west of `jpResults` to create `jpResultLabels`, and drop a `JPanel` to the center of `jpResults` to create `jpResultTextFields`. Set the horizontal alignment for all text fields to RIGHT.
7. Set the `layout` of `jpResultLabels` to `GridLayout` with two rows, and drop two labels with the texts "Monthly Pay" and "Total Pay." Set the `layout` of `jpResultTextFields` to `GridLayout` with two rows, and drop two text fields to create `jtfMonthlyPay` and `jtfTotalPay`.
8. Double-click `jbtCompute` to generate the handler `jbtComputeActionPerformed` for handling the button event. Fill in the code in this handler to read the input, compute, and display monthly payment and total payment. The code can be found in Listing 4.11.

```
package mortgagedemo;

import java.text.*;

public class ComputeMortgage extends javax.swing.JApplet {
  /** Creates new form ComputeMortgage */
  public ComputeMortgage() {
    initComponents();
  }

  private void initComponents() {
    jpInput = new javax.swing.JPanel();
    jpInputLabels = new javax.swing.JPanel();
    jLabel1 = new javax.swing.JLabel();
    jLabel2 = new javax.swing.JLabel();
    jLabel3 = new javax.swing.JLabel();
    jpInputTextFields = new javax.swing.JPanel();
```

Listing 4.11 *MortgageApplet.java.*

continued

Example 4.5 continued

```
        jtfLoanAmount = new javax.swing.JTextField();
        jtfInterestRate = new javax.swing.JTextField();
        jtfYears = new javax.swing.JTextField();
        jbtCompute = new javax.swing.JButton();
        jpResults = new javax.swing.JPanel();
        jpResultLabels = new javax.swing.JPanel();
        jLabel4 = new javax.swing.JLabel();
        jLabel5 = new javax.swing.JLabel();
        jpResultTextFields = new javax.swing.JPanel();
        jtfMonthlyPay = new javax.swing.JTextField();
        jtfTotalPay = new javax.swing.JTextField();
        jpInput.setLayout(new java.awt.BorderLayout());
        jpInput.setBorder(new javax.swing.border.TitledBorder(
          "Enter Loan Amount, Interest Rate, and Years"));
        jpInputLabels.setLayout(new java.awt.GridLayout(3, 0));
        jLabel1.setText("Loan Amount");
        jpInputLabels.add(jLabel1);
        jLabel2.setText("Interest Rate");
        jpInputLabels.add(jLabel2);
        jLabel3.setText("Years");
        jpInputLabels.add(jLabel3);
        jpInput.add(jpInputLabels, java.awt.BorderLayout.WEST);
        jpInputTextFields.setLayout(new java.awt.GridLayout(3, 0));
        jtfLoanAmount.setHorizontalAlignment(
          javax.swing.JTextField.RIGHT);
        jpInputTextFields.add(jtfLoanAmount);
        jtfInterestRate.setHorizontalAlignment(
          javax.swing.JTextField.RIGHT);
        jpInputTextFields.add(jtfInterestRate);
        jtfYears.setHorizontalAlignment(javax.swing.JTextField.RIGHT);
        jpInputTextFields.add(jtfYears);
        jpInput.add(jpInputTextFields, java.awt.BorderLayout.CENTER);
        getContentPane().add(jpInput, java.awt.BorderLayout.NORTH);
        jbtCompute.setText("Compute");
        jbtCompute.addActionListener(
          new java.awt.event.ActionListener() {
          public void actionPerformed(java.awt.event.ActionEvent evt) {
            jbtComputeActionPerformed(evt);
          }
        });
        getContentPane().add(jbtCompute, java.awt.BorderLayout.SOUTH);
        jpResults.setLayout(new java.awt.BorderLayout());
        jpResults.setBorder(new javax.swing.border.TitledBorder(
          "Mortgage Payments"));
        jpResultLabels.setLayout(new java.awt.GridLayout(2, 0));
        jLabel4.setText("Monthly Pay");
        jpResultLabels.add(jLabel4);
        jLabel5.setText("Total Pay");
        jpResultLabels.add(jLabel5);
        jpResults.add(jpResultLabels, java.awt.BorderLayout.WEST);
        jpResultTextFields.setLayout(new java.awt.GridLayout(2, 0));
        jtfMonthlyPay.setHorizontalAlignment(
          javax.swing.JTextField.RIGHT);
        jpResultTextFields.add(jtfMonthlyPay);
        jtfTotalPay.setHorizontalAlignment(javax.swing.JTextField.RIGHT);
        jpResultTextFields.add(jtfTotalPay);
        jpResults.add(jpResultTextFields, java.awt.BorderLayout.CENTER);
        getContentPane().add(jpResults, java.awt.BorderLayout.CENTER);
    }

```

Listing 4.11 *continued*

```
78      private void jbtComputeActionPerformed(
79        java.awt.event.ActionEvent evt) {
80        // Retrieve input from user
81        double loan = new Double(jtfLoanAmount.getText()).doubleValue();
82        double interestRate =
83          new Double(jtfInterestRate.getText()).doubleValue() / 1200;
84        int year = new Integer(jtfYears.getText()).intValue();
85
86        // Calculate payment
87        double monthlyPay = loan * interestRate / (1 - (Math.pow(1 /
88          (1 + interestRate), year * 12)));
89        double totalPay = monthlyPay * year * 12;
90
91        // Display results in currency format
92        NumberFormat nf = NumberFormat.getCurrencyInstance(getLocale());
93        jtfMonthlyPay.setText(nf.format(monthlyPay));
94        jtfTotalPay.setText(nf.format(totalPay));
95      }
96
97      // Variables declaration - do not modify
98      private javax.swing.JPanel jpInput;
99      private javax.swing.JPanel jpInputLabels;
100     private javax.swing.JLabel jLabel1;
101     private javax.swing.JLabel jLabel2;
102     private javax.swing.JLabel jLabel3;
103     private javax.swing.JPanel jpInputTextFields;
104     private javax.swing.JTextField jtfLoanAmount;
105     private javax.swing.JTextField jtfInterestRate;
106     private javax.swing.JTextField jtfYears;
107     private javax.swing.JButton jbtCompute;
108     private javax.swing.JPanel jpResults;
109     private javax.swing.JPanel jpResultLabels;
110     private javax.swing.JLabel jLabel4;
111     private javax.swing.JLabel jLabel5;
112     private javax.swing.JPanel jpResultTextFields;
113     private javax.swing.JTextField jtfMonthlyPay;
114     private javax.swing.JTextField jtfTotalPay;
115     // End of variables declaration
116   }
```

Listing 4.11 *continued*

Example Review

This example uses many panels to group components in order to achieve the desired layout. Creating UI interfaces using Java is more complex than using Visual Basic or Delphi, mainly because Java has a variety of layout styles. However, VB and Delphi use the fixed-position layout. Chapter 6, "Containers and Layout Managers," presents a thorough discussion of Java layout managers.

The program displays monthly payment and total payment in a locale-sensitive format. An instance, named `nf`, of `NumberFormat` is created to format the number in the applet's locale (Line 92). The `format` method in `nf` is used to format the number into a locale-sensitive string. For more information on number formatting, please refer to Chapter 14, "Internationalization," in my *Introduction to Java Programming with Sun ONE Studio 4*.

continued

Example 4.5 continued

You created the user interface with labels, text fields, and a button. The default name for an object is *xi*, where *x* stands for the name of the bean, and *i* is an integer indicating that it is the *i*th object created for the same type of bean. There are five text fields named `jTextField1`, `jTextField2`, `jTextField3`, `jTextField4`, and `jTextField5`. For better identification, these names were changed to `jftLoanAmount`, `jftInterestRate`, `jftYears`, `jftMonthlyPay`, and `jftTotalPay`.

TIP

I recommend replacing the default names of multiple objects of the same type with more descriptive names to help identify them. It is not necessary to rename the objects, however, if they are not used in handwritten code. For example, the five text fields are used in the handwritten code; thus renaming them makes referencing easier. But since the five labels are not referenced in the code, it is not necessary to rename them.

4.8 Packaging and Deploying Java Projects in Forte

Your project may consist of many classes and supporting files, such as image files and audio files. All of these files have to be provided to the end-users if your programs are to run on their side. For convenience, Java supports an archive file that can group all the project files in a compressed file.

The Java archive file format (JAR) is based on the popular ZIP file format. JAR can be used as a general archiving tool, but transporting Java applications, applets, and their requisite components (.class files, images, and sounds) in a single file was the primary motivation for its development.

This single file can be deployed on an end-user's machine as an application. It also can be downloaded to a browser in a single HTTP transaction, so that it is not necessary to open a new connection for each piece. This greatly simplifies application deployment and improves the speed with which an applet can be loaded onto a Web page and begin functioning. The JAR format also supports compression, which reduces the size of the file and improves download time still further. Additionally, individual entries in a JAR file can be digitally signed by the applet author to authenticate their origin.

You can create an archive file using the JDK **jar** command or the Forte Archive wizard. The following command creates an archive file named mortgage.jar for the classes ComputeMortgage.class and ComputeMortgage$1.class:

```
jar -cf mortgage.jar ComputeMortgage.class ComputeMortgage$1.class
```

The **-c** option is for creating a new archive file, and the **-f** option specifies the archive file's name.

NOTE
ComputeMortgage.java is compiled into ComputeMortgage.class and ComputeMortgage$1.class. ComputeMortgage$1.class is for the anonymous inner class in ComputeMortgage.java.

4.8.1 Creating JAR Files in Forte

To create a JAR file in Forte, you must first create a JAR content file. The JAR content file stores information about your JAR file, which you can later modify and use to create a new JAR file.

4.8.1.1 Creating JAR Content Files

Here are the steps in creating a JAR content file for the ComputeMortgage class in Example 4.4.

1. In the context menu of the mortgagedemo node in the Explorer, choose *New, Java Packager, Jar Recipe* to display the JAR Recipe wizard, as shown in Figure 4.22.

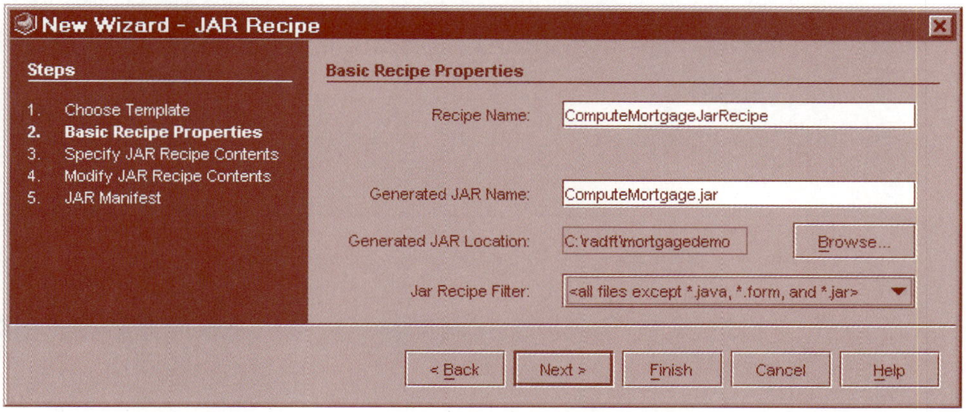

Figure 4.22 *You can create a JAR recipe using the Jar Recipe wizard.*

2. Type `ComputeMortgageJarRecipe` in the Recipe Name field, ComputeMortgage.jar in the Generated JAR Name field, and click *Next* to display the Specify Recipe Contents panel, as shown in Figure 4.23.

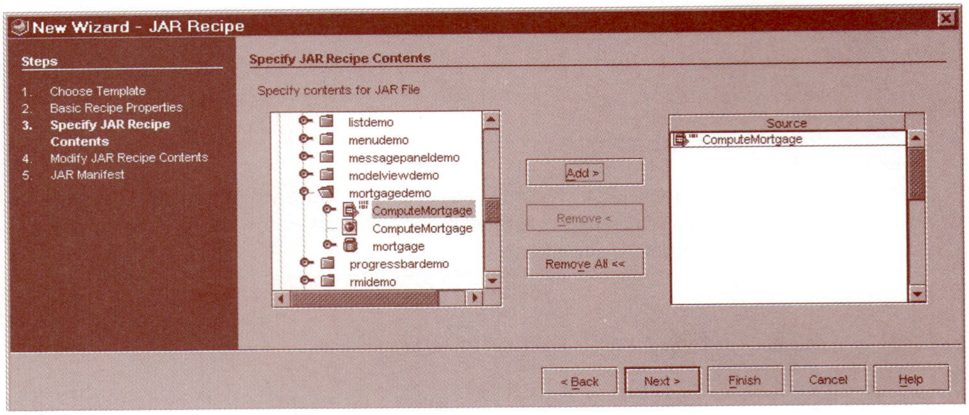

Figure 4.23 *You can add class files and other resource files to the JAR content.*

3. Choose *ComputeMortgage* and add it to the Source pane. Click *Next* to display the Modify JAR Recipe Contents panel, as shown in Figure 4.24. Click *Next* to display the JAR Manifest panel, as shown in Figure 4.25.

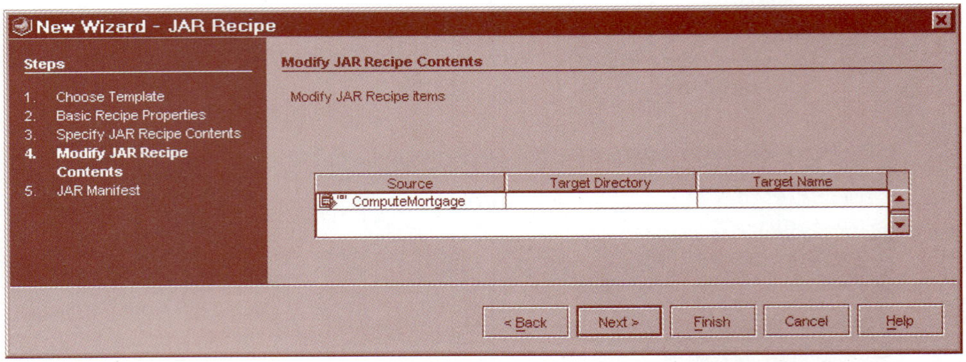

Figure 4.24 *You can modify JAR Recipe Contents in the wizard.*

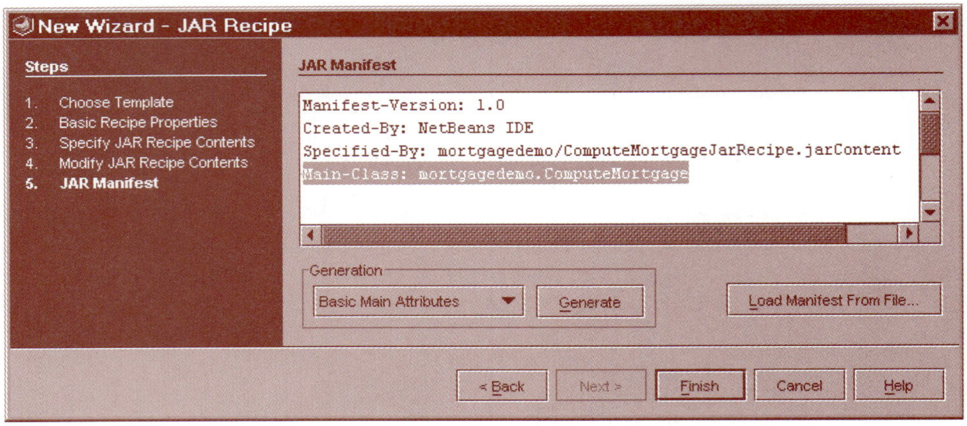

Figure 4.25 *You can generate and modify a manifest file in the JAR Manifest panel.*

4. In the Generation section of the JAR Manifest panel, choose *Basic Main Attributes* and click the *Generate* button to generate the manifest information. Add the following line to specify a main class so you can run the class from the JAR standalone. (Note ComputeMortgage has the main method, but it is omitted in the listing.)

```
Main-Class: mortgagedemo.ComputeMortgage
```

5. Click *Finish* to generate the JAR content file. A filesystem node for the JAR content file with the icon (▣) appears in the Explorer, as shown in Figure 4.26. Since you specified ComputeMortgageJarRecipe as the RecipeName in Figure 4.22, the label for this node is ComputeMortgageJarRecipe.

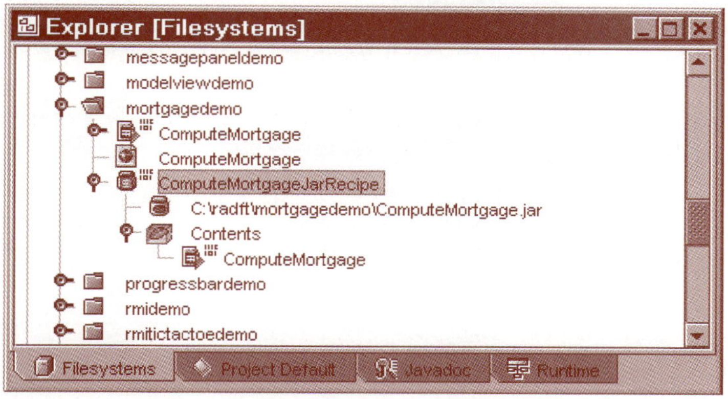

Figure 4.26 *The ComputeMortgageJarRecipe node appears in the Explorer.*

NOTE
If you show the directory in **c:\radft**\mortgagedemo, you will see the file ComputeMortgageJarRecipe.jarContent. This file describes the contents of the JAR file to be created.

4.8.2 Generating JAR Files

To generate the actual JAR specified by the content file, choose *Compile* from the context menu of the JAR Recipe file node (ComputeMortgageJarRecipe) in the Explorer. A JAR file named ComputeMortgage.jar is now created. To modify the JAR file, you have to modify the JAR content file and recompile the JAR content file. To modify the JAR content file, choose the *JAR content* file node in the Explorer, and choose *Properties* to display the Properties window, as shown in Figure 4.27. Click the ellipsis button in the Manifest field to display the property editor for the manifest file, as shown in Figure 4.28.

NOTE
If your Java source code is changed, you need to update the .jar file. You can do this by choosing *Compile* in the context menu of the JAR recipe file node in the Explorer.

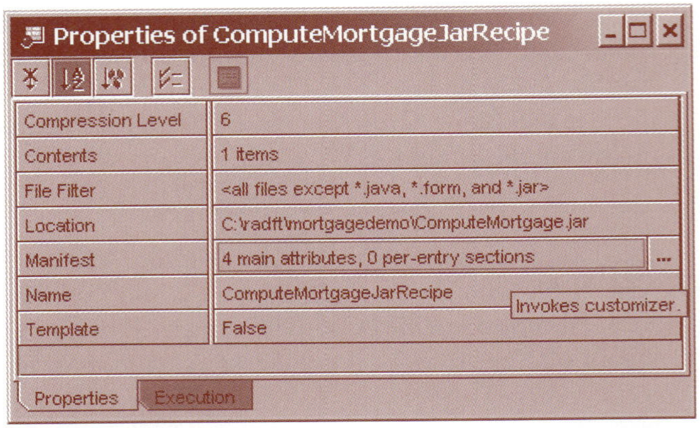

Figure 4.27 *You can modify the JAR recipe file in the Properties window for the recipe file.*

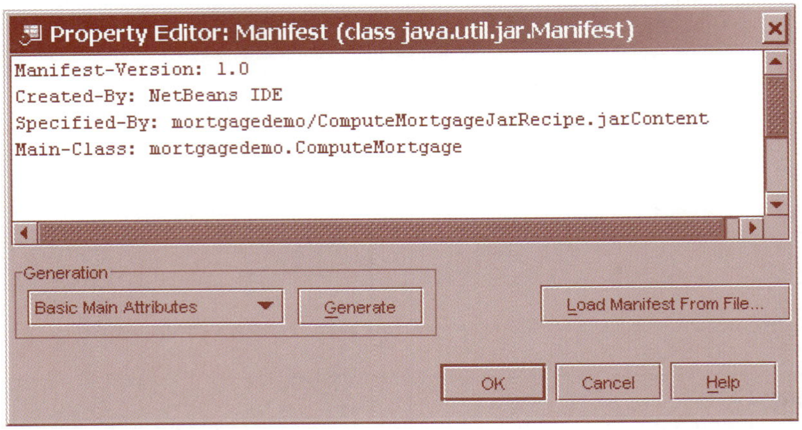

Figure 4.28 *You can modify the manifest file in the Manifest property editor.*

4.8.3 Running Archived Projects

The JAR file packages all the class files and dependent resource files into one compressed file that can be distributed to the end-user. If the project is a Java application, the user should have a Java Runtime Environment already installed. If it is not installed, the user can download Java Runtime Environment (JRE) from JavaSoft at **java.sun.com/** and install it.

Note

The Java Runtime Environment is the minimum standard Java platform for running Java programs. It contains the Java interpreter, Java core classes, and supporting files. The JRE does not contain any of the development tools (such as Applet Viewer or javac) or classes that pertain only to a development environment. The JRE is a subset of JDK.

4.8.3.1 Running Archived Files from Java Applications

You can run a JAR file if a main class is specified in the manifest. To run it from Forte, simply choose *Execute* from the context menu of the JAR content node in the Explorer. You can also run it from the DOS prompt using the java command with the –jar option, as follows:

```
java -jar ComputeMortgage.jar
```

NOTE

You can create an icon on the Windows Desktop to enable the end-user to run the program by double-clicking on it. To learn how to do this, see **www.prenhall.com/liang/radft.html**.

4.8.3.2 Running Archived Files from Java Applets

To run `ComputeMortgage` as an applet from the JAR file, you need to include an ARCHIVE attribute in the HTML file. The ARCHIVE attribute specifies the archive file that contains the applet. For example, shown below is how you would modify the HTML file for running `ComputeMortgage`:

```
<applet
  codebase=..
  code="mortgagedemo/ComputeMortgage.class"
  archive  = "ComputeMortgage.jar"
  width   = 400
  height   = 300
>
</applet>
```

Chapter Summary

This chapter introduced the process of developing bean components and developing applications using beans, component design guidelines, the model-view approach, and the rapid application development process. You learned the difference between a bean developer and a bean user, and learned how to apply the bean development process to create bean components `ImageView`, `Clock`, and `AlarmClock`. You learned how to develop components using the model-view approach. You learned how to rapidly develop Java projects using the `ComputeMortgage` example. Finally, you learned how to package and deploy Java projects in Forte.

Review Questions

4.1 Describe the differences between developing beans and using beans.

4.2 Describe the component development process.

4.3 How do you set a border title?

4.4 How do you set a model from the model property editor?

4.5 What is the model-view approach? What are advantages of developing components using the model-view approach? How do you implement the model and the view so that they are synchronized when a property is changed?

4.6 Describe the project development process.

4.7 Describe the steps in developing projects using RAD.

4.8 Describe the preinstalled components in Forte's component palette.

4.9 How do you package a Java project in Forte? How do you execute an application from an archive, and how do you specify an applet in an archive file?

4.10 How do you mount a JAR file to the file system?

Programming Exercises

4.1 Use the `Clock` component to develop an applet, as shown in Figure 4.29, which can display the time in London, New York, Savannah, Chicago, Denver, and San Francisco.

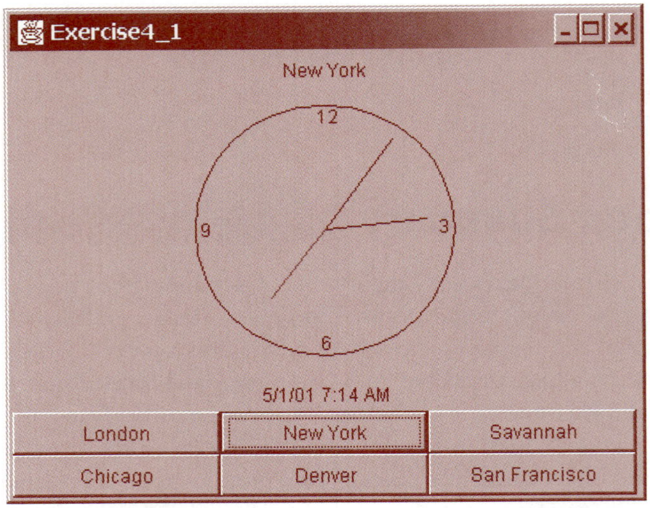

Figure 4.29 *The applet displays the clock for one of the six cities.*

4.2 Create a program that displays three clocks in a group. Each clock has individual Resume and Suspend control buttons. You can also resume or suspend all the clocks by using group control Resume All and Suspend All buttons, as shown in Figure 4.30.

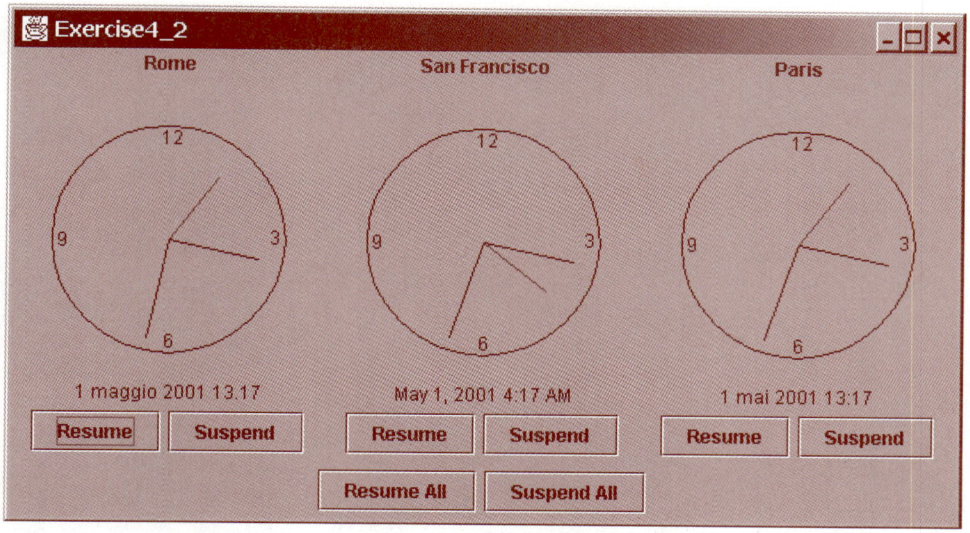

Figure 4.30 *Three clocks run independently with individual control and group control.*

4.3 Modify TestClockWithAlarm in Example 4.3 to play the alarm audio clip on a separate thread, so as to avoid interfering with repainting the clock.

4.4 Develop a model, named `Rectangle`, for describing rectangles. `Rectangle` contains the properties `width`, `height`, `color`, and `filled` and the methods `findArea` and `findPerimeter` for computing the area and the perimeter of the rectangle. Develop a view that displays the rectangle as a figure, and develop another view like a component inspector that displays all the properties of the rectangle. Assemble these components in a test program.

4.5 Create a model, named `Student`, for storing student information, including ssn, lastName, firstName, mi, streetAddress, city, state, phone, and imageFileName (for photo). Develop the following three views for `Student`:

- A panel that is similar to a component inspector to display the student's information and enable editing properties.
- A panel that displays a mailing label.
- A component (like an ID card) that contains the photo and other essential information on the card.

4.6 Create a project that meets the following requirements:

- Develop a `CalendarPanel` component with the properties `month` and `year`, as shown in Figure 4.31.
- Use the bean to create a program that displays the calendar based on the specified locale, as shown in Figure 4.32. The user can specify a locale from a combo box that consists of a list of all the available locales supported by the system.

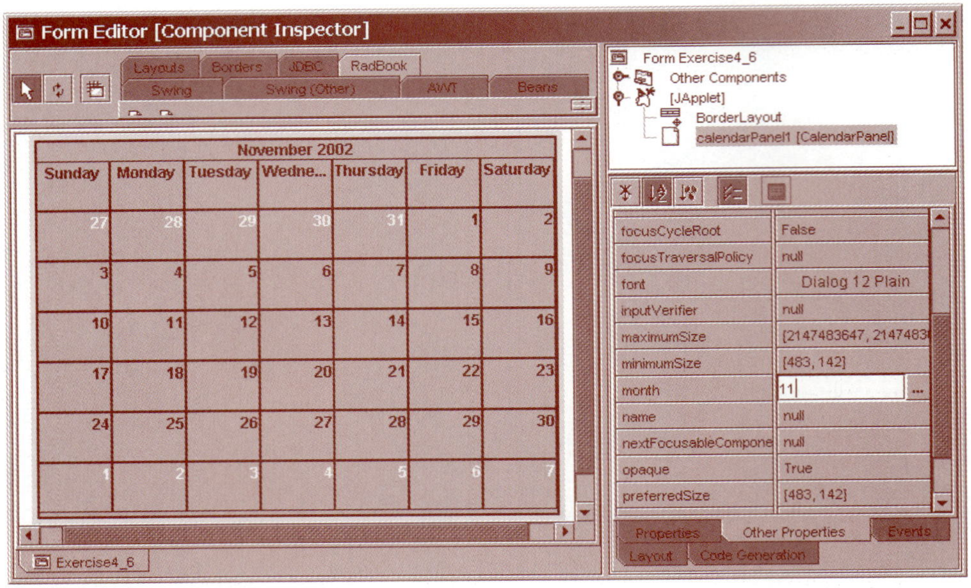

Figure 4.31 *An instance of* `CalendarPanel` *is shown in the Form Editor.*

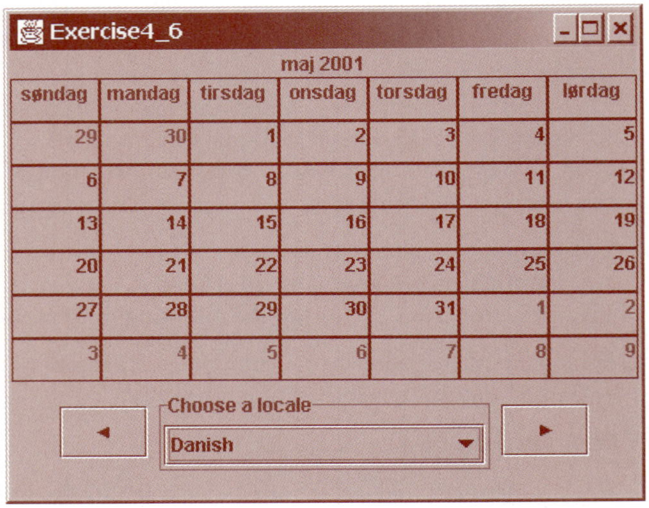

Figure 4.32 *The calendar applet displays the calendar with the Danish locale.*

4.7 Create a project that meets the following requirements:

- Develop a `Fan` bean that displays a fan with the properties `running`, `speed`, and `reversed`.
- Use the bean to create a program that displays and controls the fan, as shown in Figure 4.33.

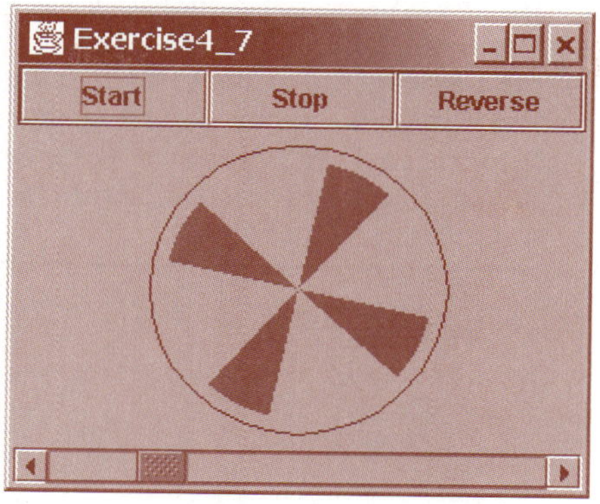

Figure 4.33 *The program simulates a running fan.*

4.8 Create a model that holds the data in an array of double elements, named `data`, and the names for the data in an array of strings, named `dataName`. For example, the enrollment data {200, 40, 50, 100, 40} stored in the array `data` are for {"CS", "Math", "Chem", "Biol", "Phys"} in the array `dataName`. These two properties have their respective get methods, but not individual set methods. Both properties are set together in the `setChartData(String[] newDataName, double[] newData)` method so that they can be displayed properly. Create a view named `PieChart` to present the data in a pie chart, and create a view named `BarChart` to present the data in a bar chart, as shown in Figure 4.34. In Exercise 8.10, you will create a controller that enables the user to insert, delete, and update data interactively using a table.

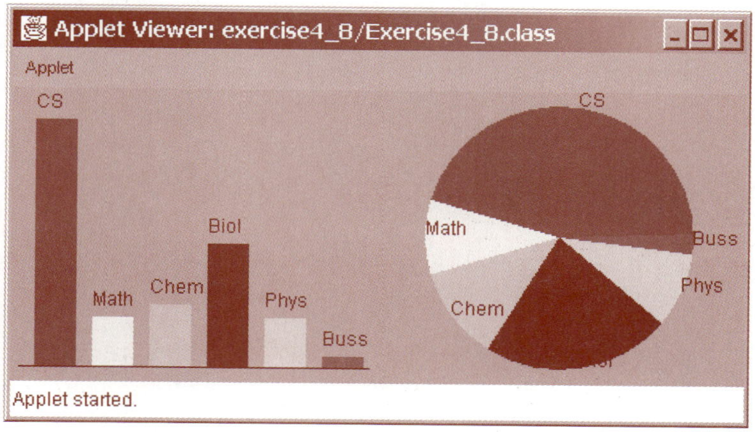

Figure 4.34 *The two views,* `PieChart` *and* `BarChart`*, receive data from the* `ChartModel`.

HINT

Each pie represents a percentage of the total data. Color the pie using the colors from an array named colors, which is `{Color.red, Color.yellow, Color.green, Color.blue, Color.cyan, Color.magenta, Color.orange, Color.pink, Color.darkGray}`. Use `colors[i%colors.length]` for the *i*th pie. Use black color to display the data names.

PART II

Rapid Application Development with Swing Components

Swing components are the essential elements in creating graphical user interfaces. This part of the book covers Swing components and uses them in rapid Java application development. You will learn how to use a variety of Swing components to develop Java projects with Forte.

CHAPTER 5

Swing Components

Objectives

- To know the differences between Swing components and AWT components.
- To understand Swing model-view architecture.
- To become familiar with the basic features of `JComponent`.
- To create projects using the Swing components `JButton`, `JRadioButton`, `JToggleButton`, `JCheckBox`, `JLabel`, `JTextField`, `JTextArea`, `JEditorPane`, `JScrollPane`, `JScrollBar`, `JSlider`, and `JProgressBar`.

5.1 Introduction

When Java was introduced, the GUI components were bundled in a library known as *Abstract Window Toolkit,* or *AWT*. For each platform on which Java runs, the AWT components are automatically mapped to the platform-specific components through their respective agents, known as *peers*. AWT is fine for developing simple GUI applications, but it is inadequate for developing comprehensive GUI applications. Besides, AWT is prone to platform-specific bugs, because its peer-based approach relies heavily on the underlying platform. With the release of JDK 1.2, the AWT user interface components were replaced by a more robust and versatile set of classes known as *Swing components*. Swing components are painted directly on canvases using Java code, except for components that are subclasses of `java.awt.Window` or `java.awt.Panel`, which must be drawn using native GUI on a specific platform. Swing components are less dependent on the target platform and use fewer native GUI resources. For this reason, Swing components are referred to as *lightweight components,* and AWT components are referred to as *heavyweight components*. Although AWT components are still supported in Java 2, I recommend that you learn to program with Swing components, because the AWT user interface components will eventually fade away. That is why this book uses Swing components exclusively.

Java provides a rich set of classes to help you build graphical user interfaces. You can use various GUI-building classes, such as frames, panels, labels, buttons, text fields, text areas, combo boxes, check boxes, radio buttons, menus, scroll bars, scroll panes, and tabbed panes, to construct user interfaces. This chapter introduces the basic Swing components. You will learn how to use them in rapid application development.

5.2 Lightweight Component Framework

Swing components are lightweight. To understand what a lightweight component is, it is necessary to review the design of the AWT components.

AWT provides a platform-independent interface to develop visual programs and graphical user interfaces. For each platform on which Java runs, the AWT components are automatically mapped to the platform-specific components. These platform-specific mappings, called *peers*, are defined in `java.awt.peer` package. The user interface components (`java.awt.Button`, `java.awt.Canvas`, `java.awt.Label`, `java.awt.Window`, `java.awt.Panel`, etc.) all have their supporting peers, named *X*Peer for component *X*. For example, the button peer is named `ButtonPeer`. Since the peers enable the user applications to be consistent with other applications running on the same platform, a Java user interface on Windows has the same look-and-feel as other Windows applications.

Peer architecture has the obvious advantage of simultaneously preserving the look-and-feel of each platform on which Java runs and maintaining a platform-independent API that can be used on all platforms. This architecture has two drawbacks, however.

- The peer architecture consumes a lot of resources. To create a new GUI class, you must subclass `java.awt.Canvas` or `java.awt.Panel`. Components that extend these classes have their own native windows. These native windows, the peers, exist along with the components you are creating. In essence, creating one component using this peer model consumes the resources of two. For this reason, the component with an underlying peer is referred to as *heavyweight.*
- The native windows are also opaque (nontransparent). This means that a window onscreen covers any other windows behind it; you can't "see through" such windows.

To alleviate these problems, Swing components with no native peer were introduced. These components are completely implemented in Java without an underlying native peer. Because they don't require native data structures or peer classes, they are indeed "lighter" in their consumption of resources. For this reason, they are referred to as *lightweight.*

Lightweight components extend `java.awt.Component` and `java.awt.Container` classes instead. As a result, these components no longer have native windows associated with them. Also, lightweight components need not be opaque. They can have transparent parts if their paint methods do not render the components.

Caution

Do not mix AWT peer components with Swing components. Mixing them may cause problems. This book only uses Swing components.

5.3 The Swing Model-View Architecture

In Chapter 4, "Developing and Using Components," you learned how to use the model-view approach in developing models and views that separate data storage and handling from the visual representation of the data. The model-view approach is the backbone of the Swing architecture. Swing user interface components are implemented using a variation of the classic model-view approach known as *Swing Model-View Architecture.*

A Swing user interface component usually consists of the following objects:

- A component, such as `JButton`, which extends `JComponent`.
- A UI delegate, such as `BasicButtonUI`, which is responsible for displaying the component.
- A model, such as `ButtonModel`, which maintains a component's data.

Swing components delegate visual presentation to their respective UI delegates. A UI delegate plays the role of the controller in the classic model-view architecture. Programmers use Swing components to create user interfaces. Components indirectly create their UI delegates. The UI delegates work behind the scenes to paint the components whenever the models change. The UI delegates can be plugged into a component when the components are constructed. The major benefit of delegating painting to the UI delegates is for implementing pluggable look-and-feel, which is introduced in the next section.

Each UI delegate listens for the model change. The change listeners are implemented as inner classes for most of the UI delegates. A few listeners, such as `ButtonUIListener`, are implemented as separate classes, because `ButtonUIListener` is shared by `JButton`, `JToggleButton`, `JCheckBox`, and `JRadioButton`.

The models for most components are implemented by interfaces whose names end with `Model`. For example, the model for button component is `ButtonModel`; its default implementation is `DefaultButtonModel`. For convenience, most Swing components contain some properties of their models, and these properties can be modified directly from the component without knowing the existence of the model. For example, the properties `actionCommand` and `mnemonic` are defined in both `DefaultButtonModel` and `JButton`. Some Swing models even contain properties that are not stored in the model, but are used by the UI delegate for painting the component. In any case, all the data are synchronized behind the scenes. For instance, when one of its properties changes, the component notifies the model, and the model sends the change to the UI delegate. The UI delegate then repaints the component.

Most Swing user interface components have a property named `model` that enables programmers to access and manipulate the model through the component. When you create a Swing user interface component, a default model is assigned to the `model` property. For simple components like `JButton`, `JToggleButton`, `JCheckBox`, `JRadioButton`, `JTextField`, and `JTextArea`, you need not be concerned about the models. For advanced components like `JList`, `JComboBox`, `JTable`, and `JTree`, you have to work with the models directly and access the components through the models.

5.4 Pluggable Look-and-Feel

Lightweight components consume fewer resources and can be transparent, but they lack the AWT's platform-specific look-and-feel advantage. To address this problem, a new pluggable look-and-feel feature was introduced in Java.

The pluggable look-and-feel feature lets you design a single set of GUI components that automatically has the look-and-feel of any OS platform. The implementation of this feature is independent of the underlying native GUI, yet it can imitate the native behavior of the native GUI.

Currently, Java supports the following three look-and-feel styles:

- Metal
- Motif
- Windows

JavaSoft provides an example that demonstrates these three styles. To run this example, in the context menu of the FileSystems node in the Explorer, choose *Mount, Archive* to mount c:\j2sdk1.4.0\demo\jfc\SimpleExample.jar. Expand the SimpleExample.jar node in the Explorer. Run SimpleExample, as shown in Figure 5.1.

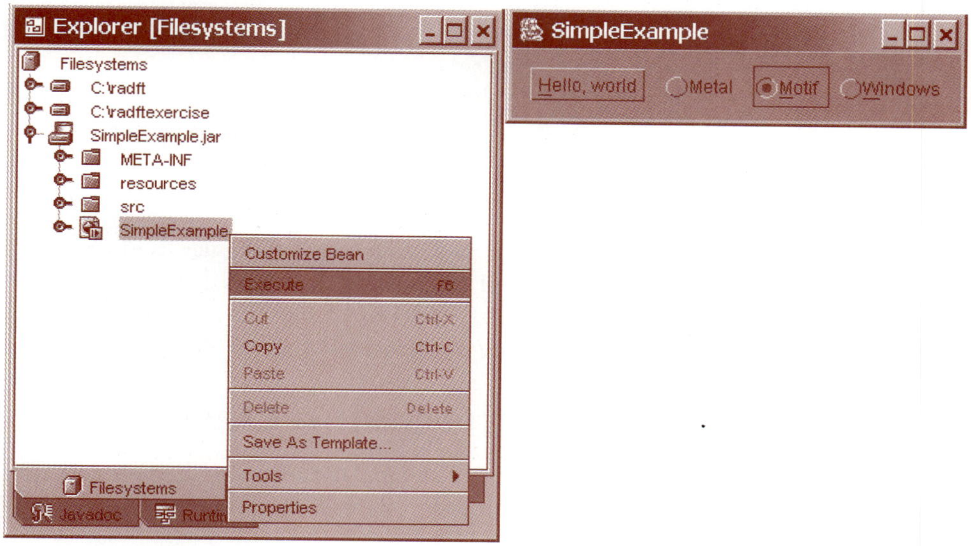

Figure 5.1 *The SimpleExample demonstrates three look-and-feel styles.*

Tip

You can also run it from the DOS prompt by changing the directory to c:\j2sdk1.4.0\demo\jfc\SimpleExample and typing the following command at the DOS prompt:

```
java -jar SimpleExample.jar
```

The Metal style, also known as the *Java style*, gives you a consistent look regardless of operating systems. The Windows style is currently only available on Windows due to Windows copyright restrictions. The Motif style is used on Unix operating systems.

The `javax.swing.UIManager` class manages the look-and-feel of the user interface. You can use one of the following three methods to set the look-and-feel for Metal, Motif, or Windows:

```
UIManager.setLookAndFeel
  (UIManager.getCrossPlatformLookAndFeelClassName());
UIManager.setLookAndFeel
  (new javax.swing.plaf.motif.MotifLookAndFeel());
UIManager.setLookAndFeel
  (new javax.swing.plaf.windows.WindowsLookAndFeel());
```

The `setLookAndFeel` method throws `UnsupportedLookAndFeelException`, so you have to put the method inside a `try/catch` block for it to compile. To ensure that the setting takes effect, the `setLookAndFeel` method should be executed before any of the components are instantiated. Thus, you need to place the code in the beginning of the `main` method for applications and in the beginning of the `init` method for applets. Alternatively, you can put the code in an anonymous static block, as shown below:

```
static {
  try {
    // Get system default look-and-feel
    UIManager.setLookAndFeel(
      UIManager.getSystemLookAndFeelClassName());
    //UIManager.setLookAndFeel
    //   (UIManager.getCrossPlatformLookAndFeelClassName());
  }
  catch (Exception e) {}
}
```

The anonymous static block is always executed when the class is instantiated. Static initialization blocks are executed when the class is loaded. For more information on static initialization blocks, please refer to Chapter 8, "Class Inheritance and Interfaces," in *Introduction to Java Programming with Sun ONE Studio 4*.

5.5 Overview of the Swing Classes

The Swing classes are extensions of and enhancements to the Java API. There are more than 250 Swing classes grouped in the following packages:

- **`javax.swing`** contains the lightweight user interface components, including pure Java implementation of the standard AWT components, such as `JButton` for `java.awt.Button`, `JLabel` for `java.awt.Label`, and `JPanel` for `java.awt.Panel`, plus a rich set of advanced components, such as `JProgressBar`, `JTree`, and `JTable`.
- **`javax.swing.border`** contains classes that describe the borders of the Swing components. You can use the border styles, such as `BevelBorder`, `SoftBevelBorder`, `EtchedBorder`, `LineBorder`, `TitledBorder`, and `MatteBorder`, to create a (decorated or plain) area around the edge of a component with optional titles.
- **`javax.swing.event`** contains the event sets (the event classes and their listeners) for Swing components. Swing components use the event sets in the `java.awt.event` package as well as in the `javax.swing.event` package.
- **`javax.swing.text`** contains the classes for viewing and editing text.
- **`javax.swing.text.html`** contains the `HTMLEditorKit` class, which provides a default implementation of HTML editing functionality. The primary goal here is to be small but flexible. It is not intended to be a full-fledged HTML implementation, but it meets modest needs, with the idea that more substantial needs can be met with alternative implementations.
- **`javax.swing.text.html.parser`** contains the parser classes for HTML files.

- **`javax.swing.text.rtf`** contains the `RTFEditorKit` class, which provides a default implementation of RTF editing functionality.
- **`javax.swing.undo`** contains the classes for supporting the cut, copy, and paste operations.
- **`javax.accessibility`** provides the support for developers to make products that are compatible with Assistive Technologies (for alternative interfaces like Braille). All of the Swing components implement interface `Accessible`, which is the main interface for the accessibility package.
- **`javax.swing.table`** contains the classes for supporting `JTable`. `JTable` is a user interface component that presents data in a two-dimensional table format.
- **`javax.swing.tree`** contains the classes for supporting `JTree`. `JTree` is a user interface component that presents a set of hierarchical data as an outline.
- **`javax.swing.colorchooser`** contains support classes and interfaces for the `javax.swing.JColorChooser` component.
- **`javax.swing.filechooser`** contains support classes and interfaces for the `javax.swing.JFileChooser` component.
- **`javax.swing.plaf`** contains one interface and many abstract classes that Swing uses to provide its pluggable look-and-feel capabilities.
- **`javax.swing.plaf.basic`** provides user interface objects built according to the basic look-and-feel.
- **`javax.swing.plaf.metal`** provides user interface objects built according to the Metal look-and-feel.

Figures 5.2 and 5.3 illustrate the hierarchical relationships of Swing classes using the UML graphical notations. An open triangle pointing to the superclass is used to denote the inheritance relationship between the two classes involved. A filled diamond is attached to the composed class to denote the composition relationship, and a hollow diamond is attached to the aggregated class to denote the aggregation relationship. Abstract class names, interface names, and abstract methods are italicized. Dashed lines and open triangles are used to point to the interface. For more information, see UML Graphical Notations at the book's companion Web site.

5.6 The *JComponent* Class

The Swing components preinstalled in the Swing page and the Swing(Other) page in the component palette all extend `javax.swing.JComponent` or a subclass of `JComponent`. `JComponent` is derived from `java.awt.Container`. `JComponent` provides the following basic features of Swing components:

- A pluggable look-and-feel feature that can be specified by the programmer or (optionally) selected by the user at runtime.

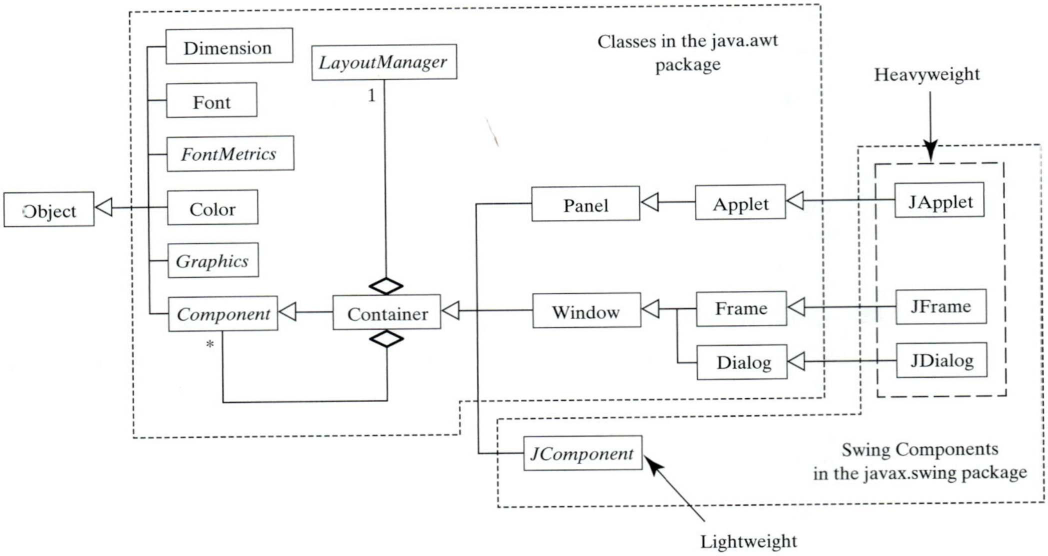

Figure 5.2 *Java graphics programming utilizes the classes shown in this hierarchical diagram.*

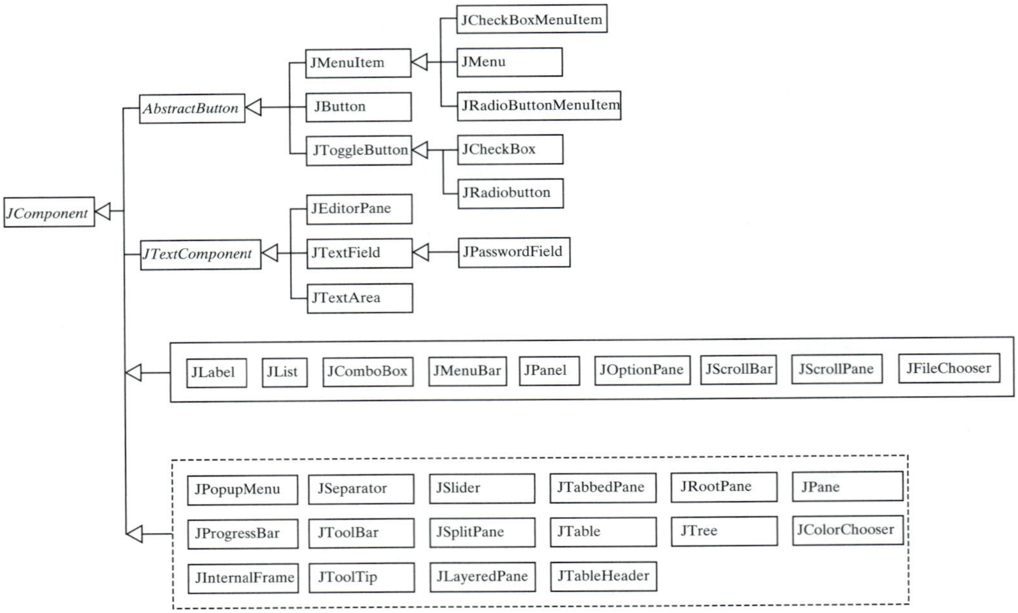

Figure 5.3 *The* `JComponent` *and its subclasses are the basic elements for building graphical user interfaces.*

- Comprehensive keystroke handling that works with nested components.
- Action objects for single-point control of program actions initiated by multiple components.
- Support for accessibility. Accessibility involves magnifying fonts for sight-impaired users or displaying captions associated with sounds for hearing-impaired users.
- Support for international localization. Each swing component has a `locale` property that encapsulates information about a specific locale. A locale determines how locale-sensitive information like date, time, and number is displayed, and how locale-sensitive operations like sorting strings are performed. Swing components can also display Unicode characters.

5.6.1 Keystroke Handling

The `JComponent` architecture makes it easy to handle keyboard events in nested components. You can register interest in a particular combination of keystrokes by creating a `KeyStroke` object and registering it with the component. When you register the keystroke combination and its associated action, you also specify one of the following conditions to determine when the action is initiated:

- The component has the focus.
- A child or grandchild of the component has the focus.

You can use this capability to define global actions for a composite component. For example, a tree control could act on the Plus key to expand all the elements in the tree, as long as any component in the tree has the focus.

The window in which the component is located has the focus. In other words, if the component is a child or grandchild of a window, and any component in the window has the focus, then the component receives the event. You can use this capability to direct the keystroke combination Alt+C to the Cancel button in a dialog, for example, as long as any component in the dialog has the focus.

An example of keystroke handling is given in Example 7.1, "Using Menu Designer."

5.6.2 Action Objects

Action-interface objects provide a single point of control for program actions. For example, a toolbar icon and a menu item can reference the same action object. When the action object is disabled, the GUI items that reference it are automatically disabled. The `Action` interface extends `java.awt.event.ActionListener`, specifying an `enabled` property as well as properties for text descriptions and graphic icons.

An example of using action objects is given in Example 7.4, "Using Actions."

5.6.3 *JComponent* Properties

Since `JComponent` is the root for all Swing GUI components, all the properties of `JComponent` are inherited by the other Swing GUI components, and thus it is important to understand the properties.

- **`alignmentX`** is the preferred horizontal alignment of the component, which specifies how the component would like to be aligned relative to other components along the x-axis. The value should be a number between 0 and 1, where 0 represents alignment along the origin, 1 is aligned the farthest away from the origin, 0.5 is centered, etc. This property is used with the `BoxLayout`, which is introduced in Chapter 6, "Containers and Layout Managers."
- **`alignmentY`** is the preferred vertical alignment of the component, which specifies how the component would like to be aligned relative to other components along the y-axis. The value should be a number between 0 and 1, where 0 represents alignment along the origin, 1 is aligned the farthest away from the origin, 0.5 is centered, etc. This property is used with the `BoxLayout`.
- **`autoscrolls`** is a `boolean` property that enables automatic scrolling in a list, table, or tree when the user is dragging the mouse. By default, it is `false`.
- **`background`** is the background color of the component.
- **`border`** specifies a border of the component with an optional title. Many types of border styles are available, and they can be combined to create compound borders.
- **`debugGraphicsOption`** allows you to set slow-motion graphics rendering, so that you can see what is being displayed on screen and whether or not it is being overwritten. This feature is useful in debugging.
- **`doubleBuffered`** specifies whether the component is painted using double-buffering. This is a technique for reducing flickering. In AWT programming, you have to manually implement this technique in the program. With Swing, this capability is automatically supported if the `doubleBuffered` property is set to `true`. By default, it is `true`.
- **`enabled`** determines whether the component is enabled. An enabled component can respond to user input and generate events. By default, `enabled` is true.
- **`font`** is the font used to display text on the component.
- **`foreground`** is the foreground color of the component.
- **`layout`** specifies a layout manager in the component. Although this property is available to all subclasses of `JComponent`, it is used when the component is a container, such as `JPanel`. You could use a `JButton` to contain other components, but it would be better to use `JPanel`.

- **maximumSize** specifies the maximum size the component needs so that the layout manager won't waste space giving it to a component that does not need it. For instance, `BorderLayout` could limit the center component's size to its maximum size, and then either give the space to edge components or limit the size of the outer window when resized.
- **minimumSize** specifies the minimum size for the component to be useful. For most Swing components, `minimumSize` is the same as `preferredSize`. Layout managers generally respect `minimumSize` rather than `preferredSize`.
- **preferredSize** indicates the ideal size at which the component will look best. This property may or may not be considered by some layout managers, depending on their rules. For example, a component uses its preferred size in a container with a `FlowLayout` manager, but its preferred size may be ignored if it is placed in a container with a `GridLayout` manager.
- **nextFocusableComponent** specifies the next focusable component or null if the focus manager should choose the next focusable component automatically.
- **requestFocusEnabled** determines whether the receiving component can obtain the focus by calling the `requestFocus()` method. The default value is true.
- **opaque** specifies whether the component is opaque. By default it is true.
- **toolTipText** is the text displayed when the mouse points on the component without clicking. This text is generally used to give the user a tip about the function of the component.
- **visible** is a `boolean` value indicating whether the component is visible.
- **size** is the size of the component displayed. This property's type is `java.awt.Dimension`.

NOTE

The background, enabled, font, foreground, maximumSize, minimumSize, and preferredSize properties are defined in java.awt.Component; the alignmentX, alignmentY, and layout properties are defined in java.awt.Container.

NOTE

The subclasses of `JComponent` may change the default values of the properties initialized in `JComponent`. For example, the default value for `doubleBuffered` property in `JButton` is false.

5.7 Simple Swing Components

This section demonstrates how to use simple Swing components: `JButton`, `JToggleButton`, `JCheckBox`, `JRadioButton`, `Border`, `JLabel`, `JScrollPane`, `JTextField`, `JTextArea`, `JEditorPane`, `JScrollBar`, `JSlider`, and `JProgressBar`.

5.7.1 Simple Swing Components

Swing comes with a variety of samples that demonstrate various aspects of the Swing components. By far the most interesting of all the samples is the SwingSet example, which is an excellent demonstration of many important and useful features of Swing components. To run the example, mount c:\j2sdk1.4.0\demo\jfc\SwingSet2\SwingSet2.jar in the FileSystems in the Explorer, and run SwingSet2. A sample run of the example is shown in Figure 5.4.

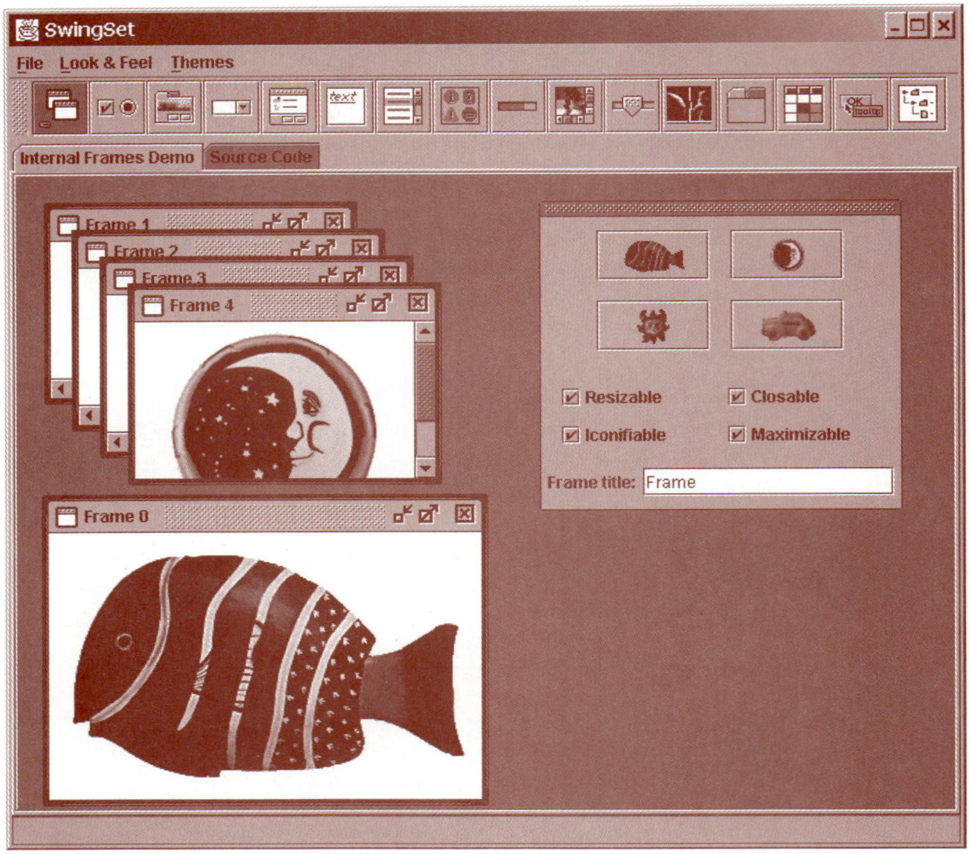

Figure 5.4 *SwingSet is a comprehensive example that demonstrates many interesting features of the Swing components.*

5.7.2 JButton

`JButton` is the Swing version of a button component. You can have a text on the button, an image icon on the button, or both a text and an image icon at the same time. You can have a pressed icon, which appears when the button is pressed. You can have a rollover icon, which appears when the mouse points to the button without clicking. Figure 5.5 shows buttons in the SwingSet demo.

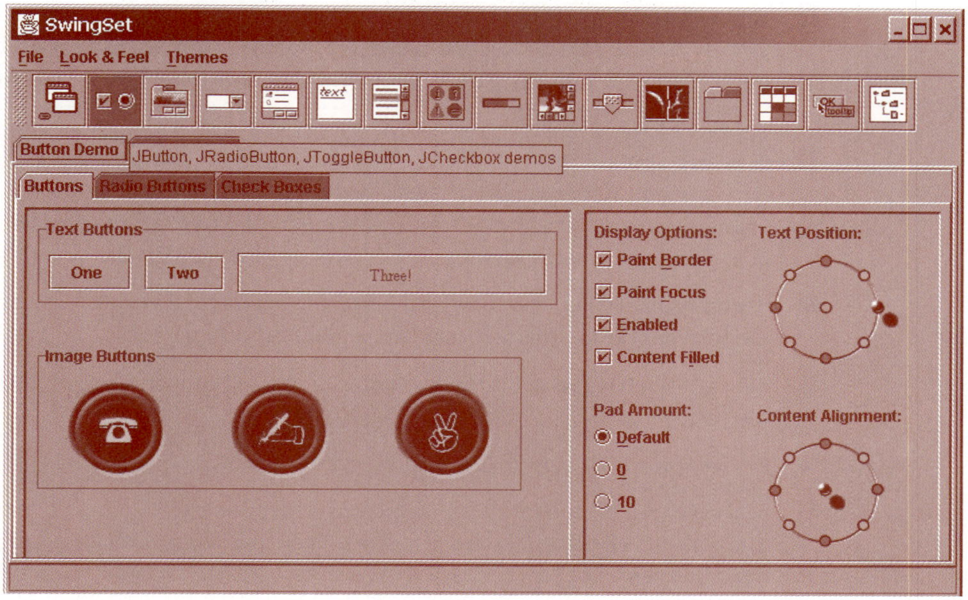

Figure 5.5 *The SwingSet demo demonstrates the features of* `JButton`.

`JButton` is a subclass of `AbstractButton`, which defines the common behaviors for `JButton`, `JToggleButton`, `JCheckBox`, and `JRadioButton`. All the properties of `JButton` are defined in its superclass, such as `JComponent` and `AbstractButton`.

The following properties are defined in the `AbstractButton` class.

- **`text`** is the label on the button. You can set a label using the `setText` method.
- **`horizontalAlignment`** is one of the three values (`SwingConstants.LEFT`, `SwingConstants.CENTER`, `SwingConstants.RIGHT`) that specify how the text is placed horizontally on a button. The default horizontal alignment is `SwingConstants.CENTER`.
- **`horizontalTextPosition`** is one of the five values (`SwingConstants.LEFT`, `SwingConstants.CENTER`, `SwingConstants.RIGHT`, `SwingConstants.LEADING`, `SwingConstants.TRAILLING`) that specify the horizontal position of the text relative to the icon. The default horizontal text position is `SwingConstants.RIGHT`.
- **`verticalAlignment`** is one of the three values (`SwingConstants.TOP`, `SwingConstants.CENTER`, `SwingConstants.BOTTOM`) that specify how the label is placed vertically on a button. The default vertical alignment is `SwingConstants.CENTER`.
- **`verticalTextPosition`** is one of the three values (`SwingConstants.TOP`, `SwingConstants.CENTER`, `SwingConstants.BOTTOM`) that specify the vertical position of the text relative to the icon. The default vertical text position is `SwingConstants.CENTER`.

- **actionCommand** specifies an action command string associated with the button. By default, the action command is the same as the button text. The action command string is passed to the `ActionEvent` when an `ActionEvent` is generated on the button.
- **mnemonic** specifies a shortcut key. You can select the button by pressing the ALT key and the mnemonic key at the same time. The mnemonic is underlined. As shown in Figure 5.5, B is the mnemonic for the Paint Border check box. You can check or uncheck the option by pressing Alt+B.
- **disabledIcon** is the icon displayed when the button is disabled. You can set a disabled icon using the `setDisableIcon` method.
- **icon** is the image icon on the button. You can set an icon using the `setIcon` method.
- **pressedIcon** is an icon that is displayed when a button is pressed.
- **rolloverIcon** is an icon that is displayed when the mouse points to the button without clicking. To see a rollover icon, the `rolloverEnabled` property must be `true`.
- **rolloverEnabled** determines whether rollover is enabled. By default, it is `true`. When you set a rollover icon in the component inspector, the `rolloverEnabled` property is automatically set to `true`.
- **borderPainted** determines whether the button border is painted. By default, it is true.
- **contentAreaFilled** determines whether the button should paint the content area or leave it transparent. By default, the content area is painted.
- **focusPainted** determines whether a focus indicator is painted when a button has the focus. By default, it is true.
- **margin** is the space between the button's border and its content. The margin property type is `java.awt.Insets`. An `Insets` object is a representation of the borders of a container. It specifies the space that a container must leave at each of its edges. The space can be a border, a blank space, or a title.
- **model** is the model that a button represents. Rarely used with buttons.
- **selected** has no meaning in `JButton` but is used in `JRadioButton`, `JCheckBox`, and `JToggleButton`.
- **selectedIcon** has no meaning in `JButton` but is used in `JRadioButton`, `JCheckBox`, and `JToggleButton`.

Buttons can generate many types of events, but often you will use `ActionEvent` to respond to button-click action. Most of the events are inherited from `JButton`'s superclass.

Note

Forte provides an Icon property editor that enables you to set an icon at design time, as shown in Figure 5.6. To display this property editor, click the ellipsis button in the value field of a property of the `Icon` type. You may choose image source types URL, File, or Classpath. The URL type enables you to specify an image through a URL. The File type specifies a local file with absolute path. The Classpath type enables you to specify a file with a relative class path. The classpath is preferred because it works for both applications and applets. All the image icons are created using the classpath option in this book unless specified otherwise.

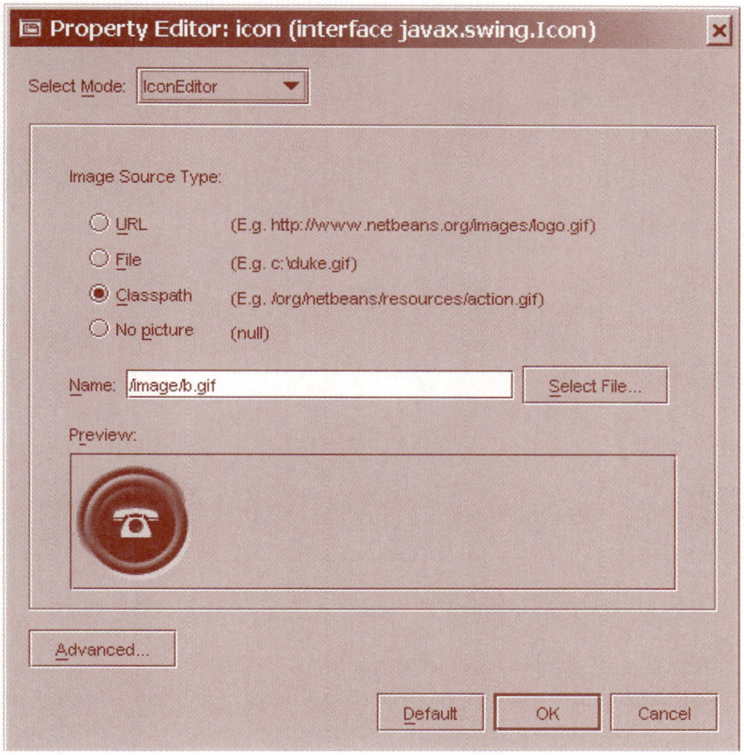

Figure 5.6 *The icon property editor enables you to set an icon at design time.*

5.7.3 JToggleButton

Toggle buttons are buttons that have two states: *selected* and *deselected.* `JToggleButton` is a subclass of `AbstractButton` and a superclass of `JRadioButton` and `JCheckBox`. `JToggleButton` provides an implementation of a two-state button, which is the basis for `JRadioButton` and `JCheckBox`.

All the properties of the `JToggleButton` class are inherited from its superclass. These properties are the same as the properties of `JButton`. `JToggleButton` can fire all the events that can be generated by a `JButton` object. Whenever a button is clicked, an `ActionEvent` and an `ItemEvent` are generated.

`JRadioButton` and `JCheckBox` are subclasses of `JToggleButton`. These two classes are often used instead of the `JToggleButton` class.

5.7.4 JCheckBox

A check box is a component that enables the user to toggle a choice on or off, like a light switch. Check boxes are usually displayed in a group and allow multiple selections. Figure 5.7 shows the use of `JCheckBox` in the SwingSet demo.

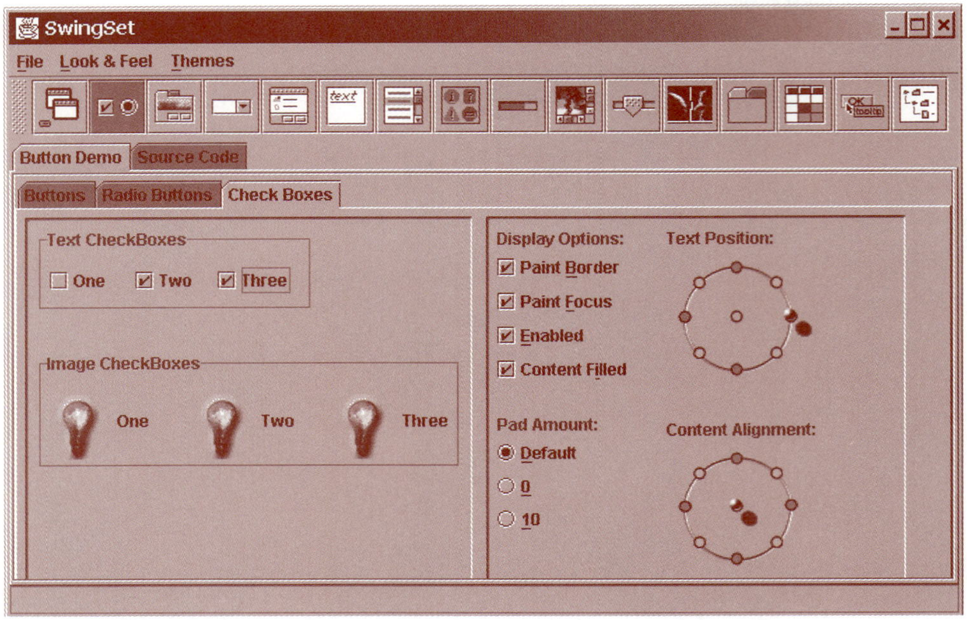

Figure 5.7 *The SwingSet demo demonstrates the features of* `JCheckBox`.

`JCheckBox` is a subclass of `JToggleButton`. All the properties of `JCheckBox` are inherited from its superclasses. These properties are the same as the properties in `JToggleButton`, but the default values may be different. By default, `borderPainted` is `false` for a `JCheckBox` object. If an image icon is used, the image icon replaces the check box indicator.

`JCheckBox` can fire all the events that can be generated by its superclass. Whenever a check box is checked or unchecked, an `ActionEvent` and an `ItemEvent` are generated.

5.7.5 JRadioButton

Radio buttons, also known as *option buttons,* are often used to choose one item exclusively from a list of choices. In appearance they are similar to check boxes. A check box displays a square that is either checked or blank, and a radio button displays a circle that is either filled (if selected) or blank (if not selected). Figure 5.8 demonstrates the use of `JRadioButton` in the SwingSet demo.

`JRadioButton` is a subclass of `JToggleButton`. All the properties of `JRadioButton` are inherited from its superclasses. These properties are the same as the properties in

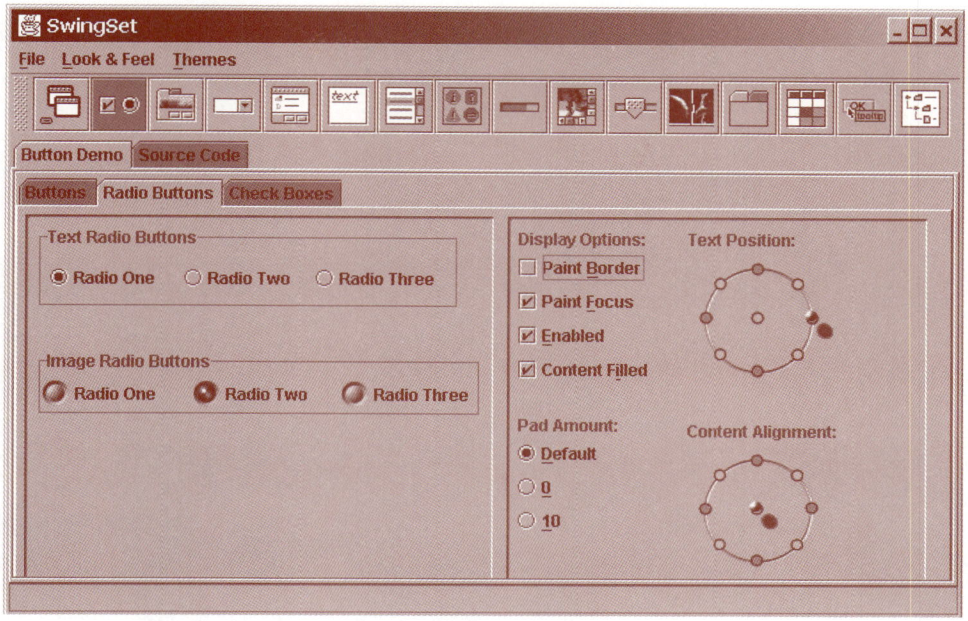

Figure 5.8 *The SwingSet demo demonstrates the features of* `JRadioButton`.

`JToggleButton`, but the default values may be different. By default, `borderPainted` is `false` for a `JRadioButton` object. If an image icon is used, the image icon replaces the radio button indicator.

`JRadioButton` can fire all the events that can be generated by its superclass. Whenever a radio button is checked or unchecked, an `ActionEvent` and an `ItemEvent` are generated.

`JRadioButton` has the `buttonGroup` property. To group radio buttons, set the `buttonGroup` property of these radio buttons to the same instance of `ButtonGroup`. In Forte, you can drop the `ButtonGroup` icon from the Swing tab in the component palette to create an instance of `ButtonGroup`. This instance automatically appears as a selection item in the value field for an instance of `JRadionButton`, as shown in Figure 5.9.

5.7.6 Border

Border, one of the interesting and useful new Swing components features, renders a border around the edges of a Swing component. The `BevelBorder`, `SoftBevelBorder`, `EtchedBorder`, `LineBorder`, `TitledBorder`, and `MatteBorder` classes are used to create specific border styles. You can use `EmptyBorder` to create a plain border, and `CompoundBorder` to nest multiple border objects, creating a single, combined border.

To create a titled border, use the following statement:

```
Border titledBorder = new TitledBorder("A Title");
```

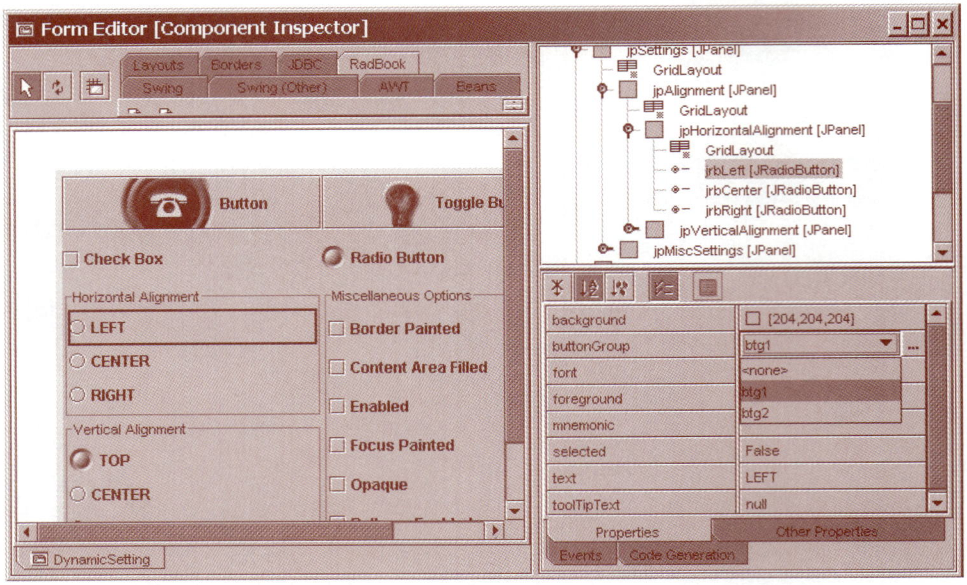

Figure 5.9 *An instance of* `ButtonGroup` *appears as a selection item in the value field of a* `JRadioButton` *object.*

`Border` is the interface for all types of borders. `TitledBorder` is an implementation of `Border` with a title. You can create a desired titled border using the following properties:

- **`title`** is the title of the border.
- **`titleColor`** is the color of the title.
- **`titleFont`** is the font of the title.
- **`titleJustification`** specifies `Border.LEFT`, `Border.CENTER`, or `Border.RIGHT` for left, center, or right title justification.
- **`titlePosition`** is one of the six values (`Border.ABOVE_TOP`, `Border.TOP`, `Border.BELOW_TOP`, `Border.ABOVE_BOTTOM`, `Border.BOTTOM`, `Border.BELOW_BOTTOM`) that specify the title position above the border line, on the border line, or below the border line.
- **`border`** is the property in `TitledBorder` for building composite borders.

The other types of borders can be created using the following classes:

- **`BevelBorder`** creates a border with a 3-D look that can be lowered or raised. To construct a `BevelBorder`, use the following constructor, which creates a `BevelBorder` with the specified `bevelType` (`BevelBorder.LOWERED` or `BevelBorder.BevelBorder`):

```
public BevelBorder(int bevelType)
```

- **EtchedBorder** creates an etched border which can either be etched-in or etched-out. You can use its default constructor to construct an EtchedBorder with lowered border. EtchedBorder has a property etchType with values LOWERED or RAISED.

- **LineBorder** creates a line border of arbitrary thickness in a single color. To create a LineBorder, use the following constructor:

```
public LineBorder(Color c, int thickness)
```

- **MatteBorder** creates a matte-like border padded with icon images. To create a MatteBorder, use the following constructor:

```
public MatteBorder(Icon tileIcon)
```

- **EmptyBorder** creates a border with border space but no drawings. To create an EmptyBorder, use the following constructor:

```
public EmptyBorder(int top, int left, int bottom, int right)
```

NOTE

All the border classes and interfaces are grouped in the javax.swing.border package.

Swing also provides the javax.swing.BorderFactory class, which contains static methods for creating borders. Some of the static methods are:

```
public static TitledBorder createTitledBorder(String title)

public static Border createLoweredBevelBorder()

public static Border createRaisedBevelBorder()

public static Border createLineBorder(Color color)

public static Border createLineBorder(Color color, int thickness)

public static Border createEtchedBorder()

public static Border createEtchedBorder(
  Color highlight, Color shadow)

public static Border createEmptyBorder()

public static Border createEmptyBorder(
  int top, int left, int bottom, int right)

public static MatteBorder createMatteBorder(
  int top, int left, int bottom, int right, Color color)

public static MatteBorder createMatteBorder(
  int top, int left, int bottom, int right, Icon tileIcon)

public static Border createCompoundBorder(
  Border outsideBorder, Border insideBorder)
```

For example, to create an etched border, simply use the following statement:

```
Border border = BorderFactory.createEtchedBorder();
```

`Border` instances can be shared. Rather than create a new border object using one of the border classes, you can create a shared instance of the common border types. You can also create a custom border class that inherits `AbstractBorder`.

Note

Forte provides a border property editor that enables you to set the border without coding, as shown in Figure 5.10. Each Swing component has the `border` property. To display the editor, click the ellipsis in the value field of the `border` property in the component tree.

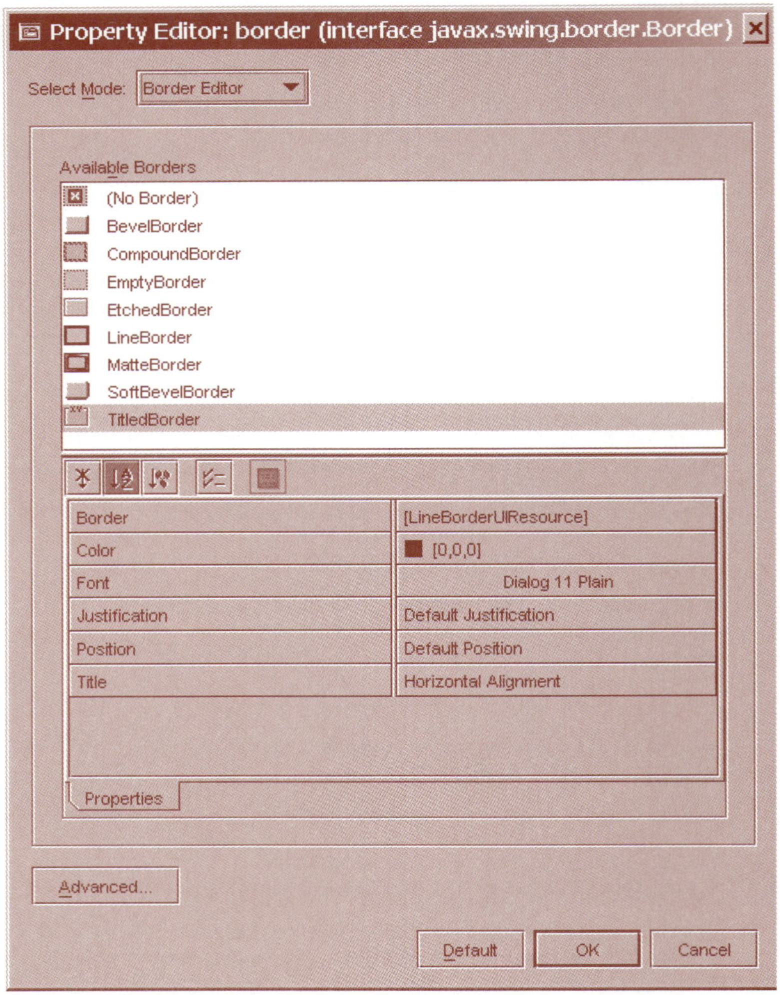

Figure 5.10 *The property editor enables you to set borders without coding.*

Tip

To delete the border, choose *No Border* in the border property editor.

TIP

Another way to set borders is to click a border icon in the Borders tab in the component palette and drop it to a Swing lightweight component in the form. The `border` property of the Swing component will change in response to the selected border.

Example 5.1 Using `JButton`, `JToggleButton`, `JCheckBox`, `JRadioButton`, and borders

This example demonstrates the use of `JButton`, `JToggleButton`, `JCheckBox`, `JRadioButton`, and borders. A sample run of the example is shown in Figure 5.11. The program enables you to dynamically set the properties of `JButton`, `JToggleButton`, `JCheckBox`, and `JRadioButton` at runtime.

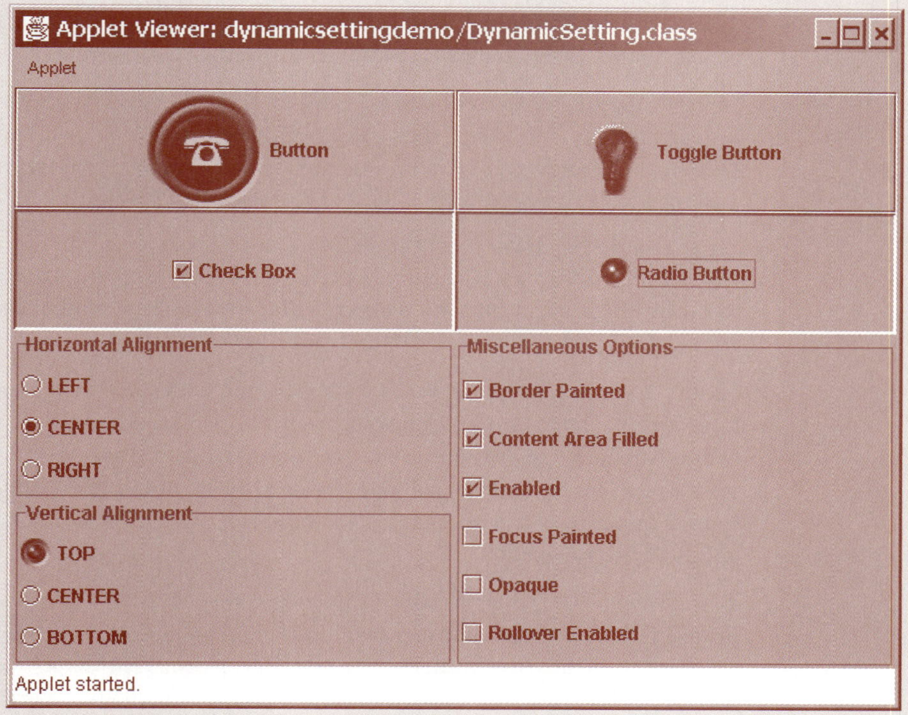

Figure 5.11 *You can set the properties of the button, toggle button, check box, and radio button dynamically.*

Here are the steps to complete the project:

1. Create a new package named dynamicsettingsdemo and an applet named DynamicSetting.java, using the Forte Swing JApplet form wizard.

continued

Example 5.1 continued

2. Drop a `JPanel` into the south of the applet and rename it `jpSettings`, and drop a `JPanel` into the center of the applet and rename it `jpButtons`.

3. Set the `layout` property of `jpButtons` to `GridLayout`, and set the `row` and `column` of the `GridLayout` to 2. Drop a `JButton`, a `JToggleButton`, a `JCheckBox`, and a `JRadioButton` into `jpButtons`, and rename them `jbt`, `jtb`, `jchk`, and `jrb`. Set their texts to Button, Toggle Button, Check Box, and Radio Button, and `tooltip` to appropriate strings.

4. Set the layout of `jpSettings` to `GridLayout`. Drop a `JPanel` twice into `jpSettings` to create two panels, and rename them `jpAlignment`, and `jpMiscSettings`.

5. Set the layout of `jpAlignment` to `GridLayout`, and set the row of the `GridLayout` to 2. Drop a `JPanel` twice into `jpAlignment` to create two panels named `jpHorizontalAlignment` and `jpVerticalAlignment`.

6. Set the `layout` of `jpHorizontalAlignment` to `GridLayout` with the `row` property set to 3. Drop a `JRadioButton` three times into `jpHorizontalAlignment` to create three radio buttons named `jrbLeft`, `jrbCenter`, and `jrbRight` with text set to LEFT, CENTER, and RIGHT.

7. Set the `layout` of `jpVerticalAlignment` to `GridLayout` with the `row` property set to 3. Drop a `JRadioButton` three times into `jpVerticalAlignment` to create three radio buttons named `jrbTop`, `jrbVCenter`, and `jrbBottom` with text set to TOP, CENTER, and BOTTOM.

8. Set the `layout` of `jpMiscSettings` to `GridLayout` with the `row` property set to 6. Drop a `JCheckBox` six times into `jpMiscSettings` to create six check boxes named `jchkBorderPainted`, `jchkContentAreaFilled`, `jchkEnabled`, `jchkFocusPainted`, `jchkOpaque`, and `jchkRolloverEnabled` with text set to Border Painted, Content Area Filled, Enabled, Focus Painted, Opaque, and Rollover Enabled.

9. To set the borders, click the ellipsis button in the value field of the `border` property for `jpHorizontalAlignment`, `jpVerticalAlignment`, and `jpMiscSettings` to display the border property editor. Select *TitledBorder* and set their titles to "Horizontal Alignment," "Vertical Alignment," and "Miscellaneous Options."

10. Set properties `icon`, `pressedIcon`, `rolloverIcon`, `rolloverSelectedIcon`, and `selectedIcon` for `jbt`, `jtb`, `jrb`, and `jrbTop` using the icon property editor. Note that the `rolloverSelectedIcon` property and the `selectedIcon` property are not applicable for `jtb`. So don't set them.

11. Drop a `ButtonGroup` twice to the form to create `btg1` and `btg2`. Set the `buttonGroup` property of `jrbLeft`, `jrbCenter`, and `jrbRight` to `btg1` and set the `buttonGroup` property of `jrbTop`, `jrbVCenter`, and `jrbBottom` to `btg2`.

12. Generate action events for the radio buttons in the `jpHorizontalAlignment` panel, in the `jpVerticalAlignment` panel, and in the `jpMiscSettings` panel, and implement these handlers for setting the properties of the buttons in the `jpButtons` panel, as shown in Listing 5.1 (Lines 193–291).

```
1   package dynamicsettingdemo;
2
3   public class DynamicSetting extends javax.swing.JApplet {
4     /** Creates new form DynamicSetting */
5     public DynamicSetting() {
6       initComponents();
7     }
8
9     private void initComponents() {
10      btg1 = new javax.swing.ButtonGroup();
11      btg2 = new javax.swing.ButtonGroup();
12      jpSettings = new javax.swing.JPanel();
13      jpAlignment = new javax.swing.JPanel();
14      jpHorizontalAlignment = new javax.swing.JPanel();
15      jrbLeft = new javax.swing.JRadioButton();
16      jrbCenter = new javax.swing.JRadioButton();
17      jrbRight = new javax.swing.JRadioButton();
18      jpVerticalAlignment = new javax.swing.JPanel();
19      jrbTop = new javax.swing.JRadioButton();
20      jrbVCenter = new javax.swing.JRadioButton();
21      jrbBottom = new javax.swing.JRadioButton();
22      jpMiscSettings = new javax.swing.JPanel();
23      jchkBorderPainted = new javax.swing.JCheckBox();
24      jchkContentAreaFilled = new javax.swing.JCheckBox();
25      jchkEnabled = new javax.swing.JCheckBox();
26      jchkFocusPainted = new javax.swing.JCheckBox();
27      jchkOpaque = new javax.swing.JCheckBox();
28      jchkRolloverEnabled = new javax.swing.JCheckBox();
29      jpButtons = new javax.swing.JPanel();
30      jbt = new javax.swing.JButton();
31      jtb = new javax.swing.JToggleButton();
32      jchk = new javax.swing.JCheckBox();
33      jrb = new javax.swing.JRadioButton();
34      jpSettings.setLayout(new java.awt.GridLayout(1, 0));
35      jpAlignment.setLayout(new java.awt.GridLayout(2, 0));
36      jpHorizontalAlignment.setLayout(new java.awt.GridLayout(3, 0));
37      jpHorizontalAlignment.setBorder(
38        new javax.swing.border.TitledBorder("Horizontal Alignment"));
39      jrbLeft.setText("LEFT");
40      btg1.add(jrbLeft);
41      jrbLeft.addActionListener(new java.awt.event.ActionListener() {
42        public void actionPerformed(java.awt.event.ActionEvent evt) {
43          jrbLeftActionPerformed(evt);
44        }
45      });
46      jpHorizontalAlignment.add(jrbLeft);
47      jrbCenter.setText("CENTER");
48      btg1.add(jrbCenter);
49      jrbCenter.addActionListener(new java.awt.event.ActionListener() {
50        public void actionPerformed(java.awt.event.ActionEvent evt) {
51          jrbCenterActionPerformed(evt);
52        }
53      });
```

Listing 5.1 *DynamicSetting.java*

continued

Example 5.1 continued

```
        jpHorizontalAlignment.add(jrbCenter);
        jrbRight.setText("RIGHT");
        btg1.add(jrbRight);
        jrbRight.addActionListener(new java.awt.event.ActionListener() {
          public void actionPerformed(java.awt.event.ActionEvent evt) {
            jrbRightActionPerformed(evt);
          }
        });
        jpHorizontalAlignment.add(jrbRight);
        jpAlignment.add(jpHorizontalAlignment);
        jpVerticalAlignment.setLayout(new java.awt.GridLayout(3, 0));
        jpVerticalAlignment.setBorder(
          new javax.swing.border.TitledBorder("Vertical Alignment"));
        jrbTop.setText("TOP");
        btg2.add(jrbTop);
        jrbTop.setRolloverIcon(new javax.swing.ImageIcon(getClass().
          getResource("/image/rbr.gif")));
        jrbTop.setIcon(new javax.swing.ImageIcon(getClass().
          getResource("/image/rb.gif")));
        jrbTop.setPressedIcon(new javax.swing.ImageIcon(getClass().
          getResource("/image/rbp.gif")));
        jrbTop.setSelectedIcon(new javax.swing.ImageIcon(
          getClass().getResource("/image/rbs.gif")));
        jrbTop.setRolloverSelectedIcon(new javax.swing.ImageIcon(
          getClass().getResource("/image/rbrs.gif")));
        jrbTop.addActionListener(new java.awt.event.ActionListener() {
          public void actionPerformed(java.awt.event.ActionEvent evt) {
            jrbTopActionPerformed(evt);
          }
        });
        jpVerticalAlignment.add(jrbTop);
        jrbVCenter.setText("CENTER");
        btg2.add(jrbVCenter);
        jrbVCenter.addActionListener(
          new java.awt.event.ActionListener() {
          public void actionPerformed(java.awt.event.ActionEvent evt) {
            jrbVCenterActionPerformed(evt);
          }
        });
        jpVerticalAlignment.add(jrbVCenter);
        jrbBottom.setText("BOTTOM");
        btg2.add(jrbBottom);
        jrbBottom.addActionListener(new java.awt.event.ActionListener() {
          public void actionPerformed(java.awt.event.ActionEvent evt) {
            jrbBottomActionPerformed(evt);
          }
        });
        jpVerticalAlignment.add(jrbBottom);
        jpAlignment.add(jpVerticalAlignment);
        jpSettings.add(jpAlignment);
        jpMiscSettings.setLayout(new java.awt.GridLayout(6, 0));
        jpMiscSettings.setBorder(
          new javax.swing.border.TitledBorder("Miscellaneous Options"));
        jchkBorderPainted.setText("Border Painted");
        jchkBorderPainted.addActionListener(
          new java.awt.event.ActionListener() {
          public void actionPerformed(java.awt.event.ActionEvent evt) {
            jchkBorderPaintedActionPerformed(evt);
          }
        });
```

Listing 5.1 *continued*

```
jpMiscSettings.add(jchkBorderPainted);
jchkContentAreaFilled.setText("Content Area Filled");
jchkContentAreaFilled.addActionListener(
  new java.awt.event.ActionListener() {
  public void actionPerformed(java.awt.event.ActionEvent evt) {
    jchkContentAreaFilledActionPerformed(evt);
  }
});
jpMiscSettings.add(jchkContentAreaFilled);
jchkEnabled.setText("Enabled");
jchkEnabled.addActionListener(
  new java.awt.event.ActionListener() {
  public void actionPerformed(java.awt.event.ActionEvent evt) {
    jchkEnabledActionPerformed(evt);
  }
});
jpMiscSettings.add(jchkEnabled);
jchkFocusPainted.setText("Focus Painted");
jchkFocusPainted.addActionListener(
  new java.awt.event.ActionListener() {
  public void actionPerformed(java.awt.event.ActionEvent evt) {
    jchkFocusPaintedActionPerformed(evt);
  }
});
jpMiscSettings.add(jchkFocusPainted);
jchkOpaque.setText("Opaque");
jchkOpaque.addActionListener(
  new java.awt.event.ActionListener() {
  public void actionPerformed(java.awt.event.ActionEvent evt) {
    jchkOpaqueActionPerformed(evt);
  }
});
jpMiscSettings.add(jchkOpaque);
jchkRolloverEnabled.setText("Rollover Enabled");
jchkRolloverEnabled.addActionListener(
  new java.awt.event.ActionListener() {
  public void actionPerformed(java.awt.event.ActionEvent evt) {
    jchkRolloverEnabledActionPerformed(evt);
  }
});
jpMiscSettings.add(jchkRolloverEnabled);
jpSettings.add(jpMiscSettings);
getContentPane().add(jpSettings, java.awt.BorderLayout.SOUTH);
jpButtons.setLayout(new java.awt.GridLayout(2, 0));
jbt.setIcon(new javax.swing.ImageIcon(getClass().
  getResource("/image/b.gif")));
jbt.setText("Button");
jbt.setRolloverIcon(new javax.swing.ImageIcon(getClass().
  getResource("/image/br.gif")));
jbt.setPressedIcon(new javax.swing.ImageIcon(getClass().
  getResource("/image/bp.gif")));
jpButtons.add(jbt);
jtb.setIcon(new javax.swing.ImageIcon(getClass().
  getResource("/image/tb.gif")));
jtb.setText("Toggle Button");
jtb.setRolloverIcon(new javax.swing.ImageIcon(getClass().
  getResource("/image/tbr.gif")));
jtb.setSelectedIcon(new javax.swing.ImageIcon(getClass().
  getResource("/image/tbs.gif")));
```

Listing 5.1 *continued*

continued

Example 5.1 continued

```
        jtb.setRolloverSelectedIcon(new javax.swing.ImageIcon(
          getClass().getResource("/image/tbrs.gif")));
        jpButtons.add(jtb);
        jchk.setText("Check Box");
        jpButtons.add(jchk);
        jrb.setText("Radio Button");
        jrb.setRolloverIcon(new javax.swing.ImageIcon(getClass().
          getResource("/image/rbr.gif")));
        jrb.setIcon(new javax.swing.ImageIcon(getClass().
          getResource("/image/rb.gif")));
        jrb.setPressedIcon(new javax.swing.ImageIcon(getClass().
          getResource("/image/rbp.gif")));
        jrb.setSelectedIcon(new javax.swing.ImageIcon(getClass().
          getResource("/image/rbs.gif")));
        jrb.setRolloverSelectedIcon(new javax.swing.ImageIcon(
          getClass().getResource("/image/rbrs.gif")));
        jpButtons.add(jrb);
        getContentPane().add(jpButtons, java.awt.BorderLayout.CENTER);
      }

      private void jchkRolloverEnabledActionPerformed(
        java.awt.event.ActionEvent evt) {
        jbt.setRolloverEnabled(jchkRolloverEnabled.isSelected());
        jtb.setRolloverEnabled(jchkRolloverEnabled.isSelected());
        jchk.setRolloverEnabled(jchkRolloverEnabled.isSelected());
        jrb.setRolloverEnabled(jchkRolloverEnabled.isSelected());
      }

      private void jchkOpaqueActionPerformed(
        java.awt.event.ActionEvent evt) {
        jbt.setOpaque(jchkOpaque.isSelected());
        jtb.setOpaque(jchkOpaque.isSelected());
        jchk.setOpaque(jchkOpaque.isSelected());
        jrb.setOpaque(jchkOpaque.isSelected());
      }

      private void jchkFocusPaintedActionPerformed(
        java.awt.event.ActionEvent evt) {
        jbt.setFocusPainted(jchkFocusPainted.isSelected());
        jtb.setFocusPainted(jchkFocusPainted.isSelected());
        jchk.setFocusPainted(jchkFocusPainted.isSelected());
        jrb.setFocusPainted(jchkFocusPainted.isSelected());
      }

      private void jchkEnabledActionPerformed(
        java.awt.event.ActionEvent evt) {
        jbt.setEnabled(jchkEnabled.isSelected());
        jtb.setEnabled(jchkEnabled.isSelected());
        jchk.setEnabled(jchkEnabled.isSelected());
        jrb.setEnabled(jchkEnabled.isSelected());
      }

      private void jchkContentAreaFilledActionPerformed(
        java.awt.event.ActionEvent evt) {
        jbt.setContentAreaFilled(jchkContentAreaFilled.isSelected());
        jtb.setContentAreaFilled(jchkContentAreaFilled.isSelected());
        jchk.setContentAreaFilled(jchkContentAreaFilled.isSelected());
        jrb.setContentAreaFilled(jchkContentAreaFilled.isSelected());
      }
```

Listing 5.1 *continued*

```

  private void jchkBorderPaintedActionPerformed(
    java.awt.event.ActionEvent evt) {
    jbt.setBorderPainted(jchkBorderPainted.isSelected());
    jtb.setBorderPainted(jchkBorderPainted.isSelected());
    jchk.setBorderPainted(jchkBorderPainted.isSelected());
    jrb.setBorderPainted(jchkBorderPainted.isSelected());
  }

  private void jrbBottomActionPerformed(
    java.awt.event.ActionEvent evt) {
    if (jrbBottom.isSelected())
      setVerticalAlignment(javax.swing.SwingConstants.BOTTOM);
  }

  private void jrbVCenterActionPerformed(
    java.awt.event.ActionEvent evt) {
    if (jrbVCenter.isSelected())
      setVerticalAlignment(javax.swing.SwingConstants.CENTER);
  }

  private void jrbTopActionPerformed(
    java.awt.event.ActionEvent evt) {
    if (jrbTop.isSelected())
      setVerticalAlignment(javax.swing.SwingConstants.TOP);
  }

  private void jrbRightActionPerformed(
    java.awt.event.ActionEvent evt) {
    if (jrbRight.isSelected())
      setHorizontalAlignment(javax.swing.SwingConstants.RIGHT);
  }

  private void jrbCenterActionPerformed(
    java.awt.event.ActionEvent evt) {
    if (jrbCenter.isSelected())
      setHorizontalAlignment(javax.swing.SwingConstants.CENTER);
  }

  private void jrbLeftActionPerformed(
    java.awt.event.ActionEvent evt) {
    if (jrbLeft.isSelected())
      setHorizontalAlignment(javax.swing.SwingConstants.LEFT);
  }

  /** Set horizontal alignment */
  private void setHorizontalAlignment(int alignment) {
    jbt.setHorizontalAlignment(alignment);
    jtb.setHorizontalAlignment(alignment);
    jchk.setHorizontalAlignment(alignment);
    jrb.setHorizontalAlignment(alignment);
  }

  /** Set vertical alignment */
  private void setVerticalAlignment(int alignment) {
    jbt.setVerticalAlignment(alignment);
    jtb.setVerticalAlignment(alignment);
    jchk.setVerticalAlignment(alignment);
    jrb.setVerticalAlignment(alignment);
  }

```

Listing 5.1 *continued*

continued

Example 5.1 continued

```
    // Variables declaration - do not modify
    private javax.swing.ButtonGroup btg1;
    private javax.swing.ButtonGroup btg2;
    private javax.swing.JPanel jpSettings;
    private javax.swing.JPanel jpAlignment;
    private javax.swing.JPanel jpHorizontalAlignment;
    private javax.swing.JRadioButton jrbLeft;
    private javax.swing.JRadioButton jrbCenter;
    private javax.swing.JRadioButton jrbRight;
    private javax.swing.JPanel jpVerticalAlignment;
    private javax.swing.JRadioButton jrbTop;
    private javax.swing.JRadioButton jrbVCenter;
    private javax.swing.JRadioButton jrbBottom;
    private javax.swing.JPanel jpMiscSettings;
    private javax.swing.JCheckBox jchkBorderPainted;
    private javax.swing.JCheckBox jchkContentAreaFilled;
    private javax.swing.JCheckBox jchkEnabled;
    private javax.swing.JCheckBox jchkFocusPainted;
    private javax.swing.JCheckBox jchkOpaque;
    private javax.swing.JCheckBox jchkRolloverEnabled;
    private javax.swing.JPanel jpButtons;
    private javax.swing.JButton jbt;
    private javax.swing.JToggleButton jtb;
    private javax.swing.JCheckBox jchk;
    private javax.swing.JRadioButton jrb;
    // End of variables declaration
}
```

Listing 5.1 *continued*

Example Review

Each button has an icon, a pressed icon, a rollover icon, a rollover selected icon, and a selected icon. When you point the mouse to the button, the rollover icon is displayed if the Rollover Enabled option box is checked. When you press the button, the pressed icon is displayed. When you roll over a selected toggle button, radio button, and check box button, the rollover-selected icon is displayed.

Using the radio buttons in the Horizontal Alignment and Vertical Alignment panels, you can set the horizontal alignment and vertical alignment of the icon and the button.

By default, the border of `JButton` and `JToggleButton` is painted and the border of `JCheckBox` and `JRadioButton` is not painted. You can use the `borderPainted` property to specify a border. When an icon is associated with `JCheckBox` or `JRadioButton`, the check box or the radio button is replaced by the icon.

The program contains over 300 lines of code, but Forte generates most of the code automatically. The code is easy to read and easy to maintain. This example and many other examples in this book demonstrate the power of rapid Java application development.

TIP

The icons and borders can be shared. You can modify this program to share icons and borders among different components. See Exercise 5.5.

5.7.7 JLabel

`JLabel` is a Swing implementation of a `java.awt.Label`. A `JLabel` object can display text, an image, or both.

`JLabel` inherits all the properties from `JComponent` and has many properties used in `JButton`, such as `text`, `icon`, `horizontalAlignment`, and `verticalAlignment`. Setting the vertical and horizontal alignments specifies the label's location. By default, labels are vertically centered in their display area, text-only labels are left-aligned, and image-only labels are horizontally centered. You can also specify the position of the text relative to the image. By default, the text is to the right of the image, with the text and image vertically aligned.

5.7.8 JScrollPane

`JScrollPane` is a component that supports *automatically* scrolling without coding. You can add a Swing component to a scroll pane. The scroll pane takes care of scrolling.

A scroll pane can be viewed as a specialized container with a view port for displaying the contained component. In addition to horizontal and vertical scroll bars, a `JScrollPane` can have a column header, a row header, and corners, as shown in Figure 5.12.

The view port is an instance of `JViewport` through which a scrollable component is displayed. Adding a component to the scroll pane actually places it in the scroll pane's view port.

The following properties of `JScrollPane` are often useful:

- **`horizontalScrollBarPolicy`** determines when the horizontal scrollbar appears in the scroll pane. This property can be one of the three values: `JScrollPane.HORIZONTAL_SCROLLBAR_AS_NEEDED`, `JScrollPane.HORIZONTAL_SCROLLBAR_NEVER`, and `JScrollPane.HORIZONTAL_SCROLLBAR_ALWAYS`. The default value is `JScrollPane.HORIZONTAL_SCROLLBAR_AS_NEEDED`.
- **`verticalScrollBarPolicy`** determines when the vertical scrollbar appears in the scroll pane. This property can be one of the three values: `JScrollPane.VERTICAL_SCROLLBAR_AS_NEEDED`, `JScrollPane.VERTICAL_SCROLLBAR_NEVER`, and `JScrollPane.VERTICAL_SCROLLBAR_ALWAYS`. The default value is `JScrollPane.VERTICAL_SCROLLBAR_AS_NEEDED`.
- **`viewportView`** specifies the component to be viewed in the view port.
- **`viewportBorder`** specifies a border around the view port in the scroll pane.
- **`rowHeaderView`** specifies the row-header view component to be used in the scroll pane.
- **`columnHeaderView`** specifies the column-header view component to be used in the scroll pane.

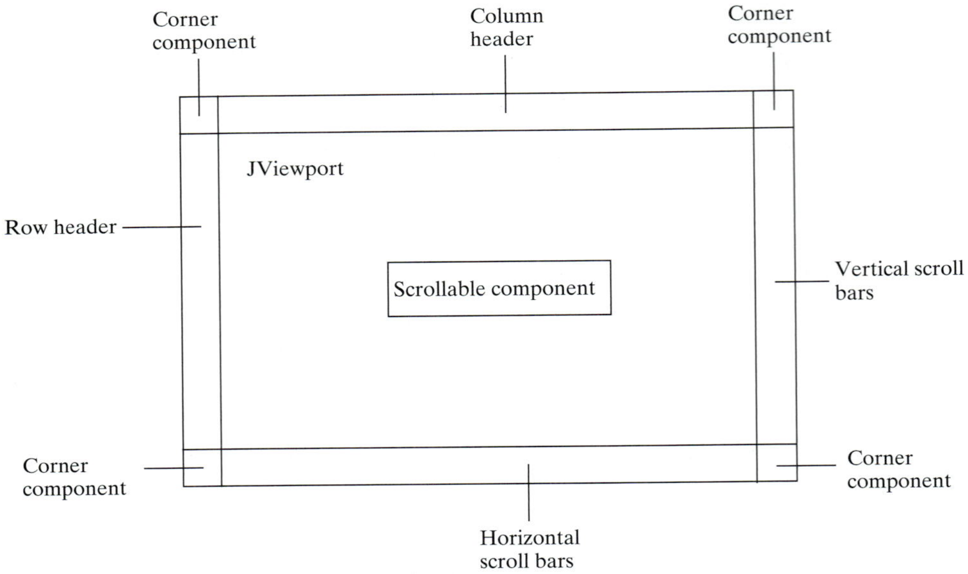

Figure 5.12 *A* `JScrollPane` *has a view port, optional horizontal and vertical bars, optional column and row headers, and optional corners.*

To set a corner component, use the following method:

```
public void setCorner(String key, Component corner)
```

Legal values for the `key` parameter are the following:

- `JScrollPane.LOWER_LEFT_CORNER`
- `JScrollPane.LOWER_RIGHT_CORNER`
- `JScrollPane.UPPER_LEFT_CORNER`
- `JScrollPane.UPPER_RIGHT_CORNER`

Example 5.2 Using Labels and Scroll Panes

This example uses a scroll pane to browse large maps. The program lets the user choose a map from a radio button and displays the map in the scroll pane, as shown in Figure 5.13.

Here are the steps to complete the example:

1. Create a new package named displaymapdemo and an applet named `DisplayMap` using the Forte Swing JApplet form wizard.

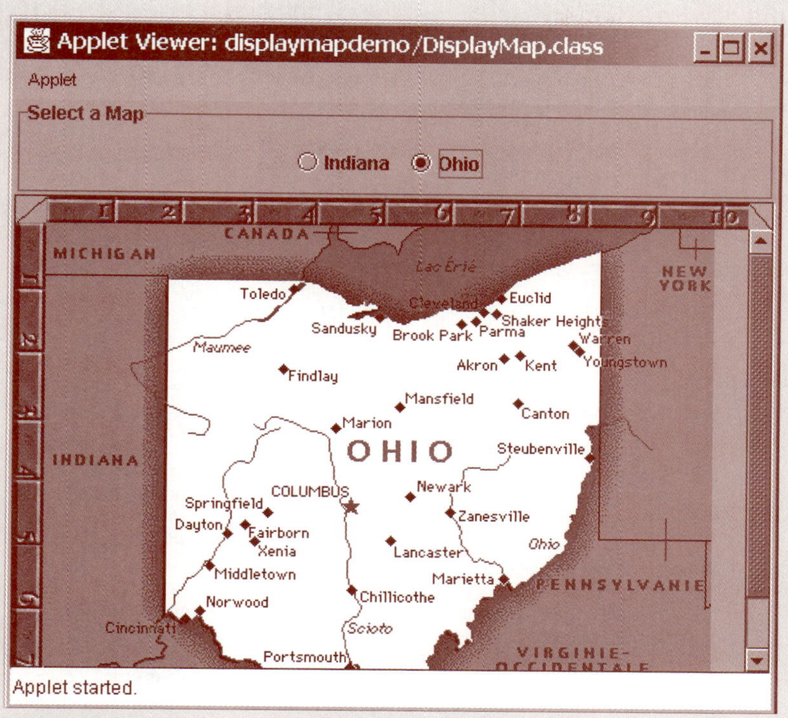

Figure 5.13 *You can choose a map from a radio button and display it in a scroll pane.*

2. Create a class named `CornerPanel` for displaying scroll pane corners, as shown in Listing 5.3. This class extends `JPanel` and draws simple lines on a panel for decorating the scroll pane corners.

3. In the form window for `DisplayMap`, drop a `JPanel` to the north of the applet, and rename it `jpSelection`. Drop a `JScrollPane` to the center of the applet, and rename it `jspMap`. Set the title to the border of `jpSelection` to "Select a Map."

4. Drop a `JRadioButton` twice into `jpSelection` to create `jrbMap1` and `jrbMap2`. Set the `text` property of these two radio buttons "Indiana" and "Ohio." Drop a `ButtonGroup` into the form to create `buttonGroup1`. Set the `buttonGroup` property of `jrbMap1` and `jrbMap2` to `buttonGroup1`.

5. Drop a `JLabel` to `jspMap` and rename it `jlblMap` with no text.

6. Declare and create two image icons named `map1` and `map2` for two image maps using the static `createImageIcon` method in the `ImageViewer` class. Set row header, column header, and corner header in the constructor, as shown in Listing 5.2 (Lines 16–18).

7. Generate action-event handlers for the two radio buttons, and implement the handlers for map selections, as shown in Listing 5.2 (Lines 70–78).

continued

Example 5.2 continued

```
// DisplayMap.java: Display maps in a label placed in a scroll pane
package displaymapdemo;

import imageviewerdemo.ImageViewer;
import javax.swing.*;

public class DisplayMap extends javax.swing.JApplet {
  javax.swing.ImageIcon map1;
  javax.swing.ImageIcon map2;

  /** Creates new form DisplayMap */
  public DisplayMap() {
    initComponents();

    // Load images
    map1 = ImageViewer.createImageIcon(
      "/image/indianaMap.gif", this);
    map2 = ImageViewer.createImageIcon("/image/ohioMap.gif", this);
    javax.swing.ImageIcon hRuler = ImageViewer.createImageIcon(
      "/image/horizontalRuler.gif", this);
    javax.swing.ImageIcon vRuler = ImageViewer.createImageIcon(
      "/image/verticalRuler.gif", this);

    // Set row header, column header and corner header
    jspMap.setColumnHeaderView(new JLabel(hRuler));
    jspMap.setRowHeaderView(new JLabel(vRuler));
    jspMap.setCorner(JScrollPane.UPPER_LEFT_CORNER,
      new CornerPanel(JScrollPane.UPPER_LEFT_CORNER));
    jspMap.setCorner(ScrollPaneConstants.UPPER_RIGHT_CORNER,
      new CornerPanel(JScrollPane.UPPER_RIGHT_CORNER));
    jspMap.setCorner(JScrollPane.LOWER_RIGHT_CORNER,
      new CornerPanel(JScrollPane.LOWER_RIGHT_CORNER));
    jspMap.setCorner(JScrollPane.LOWER_LEFT_CORNER,
      new CornerPanel(JScrollPane.LOWER_LEFT_CORNER));

    // Set initial image icon
    jlblMap.setIcon(map1);
  }

  private void initComponents() {
    buttonGroup1 = new javax.swing.ButtonGroup();
    jpSelection = new javax.swing.JPanel();
    jrbMap1 = new javax.swing.JRadioButton();
    jrbMap2 = new javax.swing.JRadioButton();
    jspMap = new javax.swing.JScrollPane();
    jlblMap = new javax.swing.JLabel();
    jpSelection.setBorder(
      new javax.swing.border.TitledBorder("Select a Map"));
    jrbMap1.setText("Indiana");
    buttonGroup1.add(jrbMap1);
    jrbMap1.addActionListener(new java.awt.event.ActionListener() {
      public void actionPerformed(java.awt.event.ActionEvent evt) {
        jrbMap1ActionPerformed(evt);
      }
    });
    jpSelection.add(jrbMap1);
    jrbMap2.setText("Ohio");
    buttonGroup1.add(jrbMap2);
```

Listing 5.2 *DisplayMap.java*

```
    jrbMap2.addActionListener(new java.awt.event.ActionListener() {
      public void actionPerformed(java.awt.event.ActionEvent evt) {
        jrbMap2ActionPerformed(evt);
      }
    });
    jpSelection.add(jrbMap2);
    getContentPane().add(jpSelection, java.awt.BorderLayout.NORTH);
    jspMap.setViewportView(jlblMap);
    getContentPane().add(jspMap, java.awt.BorderLayout.CENTER);
  }

  private void jrbMap2ActionPerformed(
    java.awt.event.ActionEvent evt) {
    if (jrbMap2.isSelected()) jlblMap.setIcon(map2);
  }

  private void jrbMap1ActionPerformed(
    java.awt.event.ActionEvent evt) {
    if (jrbMap1.isSelected()) jlblMap.setIcon(map1);
  }

  // Variables declaration - do not modify
  private javax.swing.ButtonGroup buttonGroup1;
  private javax.swing.JPanel jpSelection;
  private javax.swing.JRadioButton jrbMap1;
  private javax.swing.JRadioButton jrbMap2;
  private javax.swing.JScrollPane jspMap;
  private javax.swing.JLabel jlblMap;
  // End of variables declaration
}
```

Listing 5.2 *continued*

```
// CornerPanel.java: A panel displaying a line used for scroll
// pane corner
package displaymapdemo;

import javax.swing.*;
import java.awt.*;

public class CornerPanel extends JPanel
  implements ScrollPaneConstants {
  /** Line location */
  private String location;

  /** Construct a corner panel */
  public CornerPanel(String location) {
    this.location = location;
  }

  /** Draw a line depending on the location */
  public void paintComponent(Graphics g) {
    super.paintComponents(g);

    if (location == "UPPER_LEFT_CORNER")
      g.drawLine(0, getSize().height, getSize().width, 0);
    else if (location == "UPPER_RIGHT_CORNER")
      g.drawLine(0, 0, getSize().width, getSize().height);
```

Listing 5.3 *CornerPanel.java*

continued

Example 5.2 continued

```
26        else if (location == "LOWER_RIGHT_CORNER")
27          g.drawLine(0, getSize().height, getSize().width, 0);
28        else if (location == "LOWER_LEFT_CORNER")
29          g.drawLine(0, 0, getSize().width, getSize().height);
30      }
31    }
```

Listing 5.3 *continued*

Example Review

`JLabel` can be used to display images as well as text. The program displays an image map in a label, and places the label in the scroll pane. You cannot directly place an image into a scroll pane, because an image is not a component.

The scroll pane holds a label in its view port. Choosing a radio button causes an image icon to be set in the label and displayed in the view port. The scroll pane has a row header, column header, and corners. The row header, column header, and corners can be any components. The program places a label with a horizontal-ruler image as the row header (Line 25), and another label with a vertical ruler as the column header (Line 26). The corners are instances of `CornerPanel` (Lines 27–34). The `CornerPanel` class is a subclass of `JPanel`, which draws simple lines on the panel.

5.7.9 JTextField

`JTextField` is a Swing implementation of `java.awt.TextField` that allows the editing of a single line of text. The `setEchoChar` and `getEchoChar` methods in `TextField` are not provided in `JTextField` in order to avoid a new implementation of a pluggable look-and-feel inadvertently exposing password characters. To provide password-like services, a separate class, `JPasswordField`, extends `JTextField` to provide this service with an independently pluggable look-and-feel.

`JTextField` has capabilities not found in `TextField`. For example, the horizontal alignment of `JTextField` can be set to be left-justified, centered, or right-justified if the required size of the field text is smaller than the size allocated to it. This is determined by the `horizontalAlignment` property. The default is to be left-justified.

In addition to properties like `text` and `horizontalAlignment`, `JTextField` has the following useful properties:

- **`actionCommand`** specifies an action command string associated with the text. By default, the action command is the same as the text. The action command string is passed to the `ActionEvent` when an `ActionEvent` is generated on the button.
- **`editable`** is a `boolean` property indicating whether the text field can be edited by the user.
- **`columns`** specifies the width of the text field.

`JTextField` can fire `ActionEvent` and `ItemEvent`, among many other events. Pressing Enter in a text field triggers the `ActionEvent`. Changing contents in a text field triggers the `TextEvent`.

5.7.10 JTextArea

`JTextArea` is a Swing implementation of `java.awt.TextArea`, a multi-line area that displays plain text. `JTextArea` and `JTextField` are subclasses of `JTextComponent`. In addition to properties like `text`, `editable`, and `columns` shared with `JTextField`, `JTextArea` has the following properties

- **`lineWrap`** is a `boolean` property indicating whether the line in the text area is automatically wrapped.
- **`wrapStyleWord`** is a `boolean` property indicating whether the line is wrapped on word or character. The default value is false, which indicates that the line is wrapped on character boundaries.
- **`rows`** specifies the number of lines in the text area.
- **`lineCount`** specifies the number of lines in the text.
- **`tabSize`** specifies the number of characters inserted when the Tab key is pressed.

You can use the following methods to insert, append, and replace text:

- `public void insert(String s, int pos)`

  This inserts string s in the specified position in the text area.

- `public void append(String s)`

  This appends string `s` to the end of the text.

- `public void replaceRange(String s, int start, int end)`

  This replaces partial texts in the range from position `start` to position `end` with string `s`.

`JTextArea` does not handle scrolling, but you can create a `JScrollPane` object to hold an instance of `JTextArea` and let the scroll pane handle scrolling for `JTextArea`.

5.7.11 JEditorPane

Swing provides a new component named `javax.swing.JEditorPane` that can be used to display HTML files. `JEditorPane` is a subclass of `JTextArea`. Thus it inherits all the behavior and properties from `JTextArea`. Additionally, it is capable of rendering an HTML file with a given URL, as shown in Figure 5.14.

The `JEditorPane` class has a `page` property that can be used to specify a URL for the HTML file. The signature of the `setPage` method is as follows:

```
public void setPage(URL url) IOException
```

`JEditorPane` generates `javax.swing.event.HyperlinkEvent` when a hyperlink in the editor pane is clicked. Through this event, you can get the URL of the hyperlink and display the content again, using the `setPage(url)` method.

Figure 5.14 `JEditorPane` *is demonstrated in the SwingSet example.*

Example 5.3 Using JEditorPane

This example creates a simple Web browser to render HTML files. The program lets the user enter an HTML file in a text field and press the Enter key to display the HTML file in an editor pane, as shown in Figure 5.15.

Here are the steps to complete the project:

1. Create a new package named viewhtmldemo and an applet named ViewHTML using the Forte Swing JApplet form wizard.

2. Drop a `JPanel` to the north of the applet and rename it `jpURL`. Drop a `JScrollPane` to the center of the applet, and drop a `JEditorPane` from the Swing (Other) tab to the scroll pane and rename it `jep`.

3. Set the `layout` of `jpURL` to `BorderLayout`. Drop a `JLabel` to the west of `jpURL` and set its text to URL. Drop a `JTextField` to the center of `jpURL` and rename it `jtfURL`.

4. Generate an action-event handler for the text field, and implement the handler for displaying the URL in the editor pane, as shown in Listing 5.4 (Lines 49–58).

5. Generate a hyperlinkUpdate event handler for the editor pane, and implement it to display the content of the hyperlink in the editor pane, as shown in Listing 5.4 (Lines 39–44).

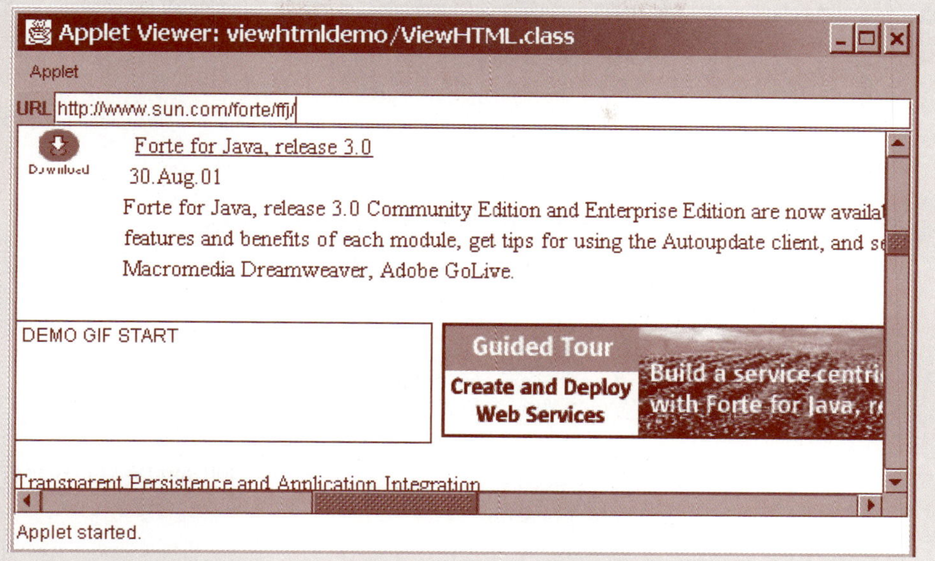

Figure 5.15 *You can specify a URL in the text field and display the HTML file in an editor pane.*

```
// ViewHTML.java: Display HTML file in JEditorPane
package viewhtmldemo;

public class ViewHTML extends javax.swing.JApplet {
  /** Creates new form ViewHTML */
  public ViewHTML() {
    initComponents();
  }

  private void initComponents() {
    jpURL = new javax.swing.JPanel();
    jLabel1 = new javax.swing.JLabel();
    jtfURL = new javax.swing.JTextField();
    jScrollPane1 = new javax.swing.JScrollPane();
    jep = new javax.swing.JEditorPane();
    jpURL.setLayout(new java.awt.BorderLayout());
    jLabel1.setText("URL");
    jpURL.add(jLabel1, java.awt.BorderLayout.WEST);
    jtfURL.addActionListener(new java.awt.event.ActionListener() {
      public void actionPerformed(java.awt.event.ActionEvent evt) {
        jtfURLActionPerformed(evt);
      }
    });
    jpURL.add(jtfURL, java.awt.BorderLayout.CENTER);
    getContentPane().add(jpURL, java.awt.BorderLayout.NORTH);
    jep.addHyperlinkListener(
      new javax.swing.event.HyperlinkListener() {
      public void hyperlinkUpdate(
        javax.swing.event.HyperlinkEvent evt) {
        jepHyperlinkUpdate(evt);
      }
    });
```

Listing 5.4 *ViewHTML.java*

continued

Example 5.3 continued

```
      jScrollPane1.setViewportView(jep);
      getContentPane().add(jScrollPane1, java.awt.BorderLayout.CENTER);
    }

    private void jepHyperlinkUpdate(
      javax.swing.event.HyperlinkEvent evt) {
      try {
        jep.setPage(evt.getURL());
      }
      catch (java.io.IOException ex) {
        ex.printStackTrace();
      }
    }

    private void jtfURLActionPerformed(
      java.awt.event.ActionEvent evt) {
      try {
        // Get the URL of the HTML file
        java.net.URL url = new java.net.URL(jtfURL.getText().trim());

        // Display the HTML file
        jep.setPage(url);
      }
      catch (java.io.IOException ex) {
        ex.printStackTrace();
      }
    }

    // Variables declaration - do not modify
    private javax.swing.JPanel jpURL;
    private javax.swing.JLabel jLabel1;
    private javax.swing.JTextField jtfURL;
    private javax.swing.JScrollPane jScrollPane1;
    private javax.swing.JEditorPane jep;
    // End of variables declaration
  }
```

Listing 5.4 *continued*

Example Review

In this example, a simple Web browser is created using the `JEditorPane` class. `JEditorPane` is capable of displaying files in the HTML format or in the RTF format. To enable scrolling, the editor pane is placed inside a scroll pane.

The user enters a URL of the HTML file in the text field and presses the Enter key to fire an action event to display the URL in the editor pane. To display the URL in the editor pane, simply set the URL in the `page` property of the editor pane.

The editor pane does not have all the functions of a commercial Web browser, but it is convenient for displaying HTML files, including embedded images.

This program cannot view a local HTML file. To view a remote HTML file, you have to enter a URL beginning with http://. In Exercise 5.6, you will modify the program so that it can also view an HTML file from the local host and accept URLs beginning with either http:// or www.

5.7.12 JScrollBar

You used scroll panes to view large contents with automatic scrolling. In many cases, a scroll pane is simple, convenient, and sufficient to provide scrolling functions, but occasionally you need to use scroll bars to manually control scrolling. A *scroll bar* is a control that enables the user to select from a range of values. A scroll bar appears in two styles, *horizontal* and *vertical*, as shown in Figure 5.16.

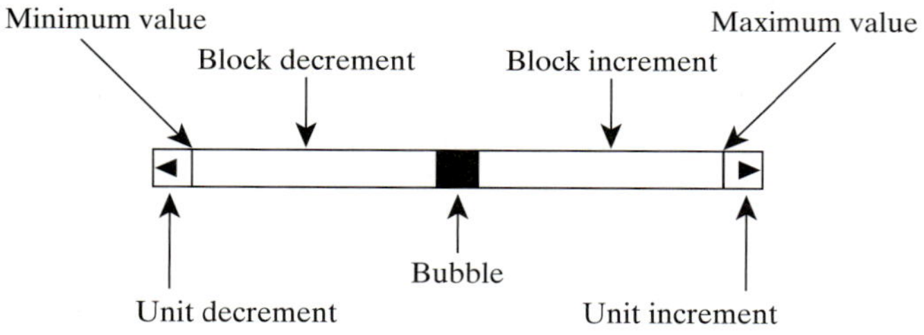

Figure 5.16 *A scroll bar represents a range of values graphically.*

`JScrollBar` has the following properties.

- **`orientation`** specifies horizontal or vertical style, with 0 for horizontal and 1 for vertical.
- **`maximum`** specifies the maximum value the scroll bar represents when the bubble reaches to the right end of the scroll bar for horizontal style or to the bottom of the scroll bar for vertical style.
- **`minimum`** specifies the minimum value the scroll bar represents when the bubble reaches to the left end of the scroll bar for horizontal style or to the top of the scroll bar for vertical style.
- **`visibleAmount`** specifies the relative width of the scroll bar's bubble. The actual width appearing on the screen is determined by the maximum value and the value of `visibleAmount`.
- **`value`** is the current value of the scroll bar. Normally, a program should change a scroll bar's value by calling the `setValue` method. The `setValue` method simultaneously and synchronously sets the minimum, maximum, visible amount, and value properties of a scroll bar, so that they are mutually consistent.
- **`blockIncrement`** is the value that is added (subtracted) when the user activates the block increment (decrement) area of the scroll bar, as shown in Figure 5.16. The `blockIncrement` property, which is new in JDK 1.1, supersedes the `pageIncrement` property used in JDK 1.02.
- **`unitIncrement`** is the value that is added (subtracted) when the user activates the unit increment (decrement) area of the scroll bar, as shown in Figure 5.16. The `unitIncrement` property, which is new in JDK 1.1, supersedes the `lineIncrement` property used in JDK 1.02.

NOTE

The actual width of the scroll bar's track is `maximum+visibleAmount`. When the scroll bar is set to its maximum value, the left side of the bubble is at `maximum`, and the right side is at `maximum+visibleAmount`.

Normally, the user changes the value of the scroll bar by making a gesture with the mouse. For example, the user can drag the scroll bar's bubble up and down or click in the scroll bar's unit increment or block increment area. Keyboard gestures can also be mapped to the scroll bar. By convention, the Page Up and Page Down keys are equivalent to clicking in the scroll bar's block increment and block decrement areas.

When the user changes the value of the scroll bar, the scroll bar generates an instance of `AdjustmentEvent` that is passed to any registered listeners. Any object that wishes to be notified of changes to the scroll bar's value should implement the `adjustmentValueChanged` method in the `AdjustmentListener` interface defined in the package `java.awt.event`.

5.7.13 JSlider

`JSlider` is similar to `JScrollBar` in the sense that both can be used to represent a range of values, but `JSlider` has more properties than `JScrollBar` and can appear in many forms and styles, as shown in Figure 5.17.

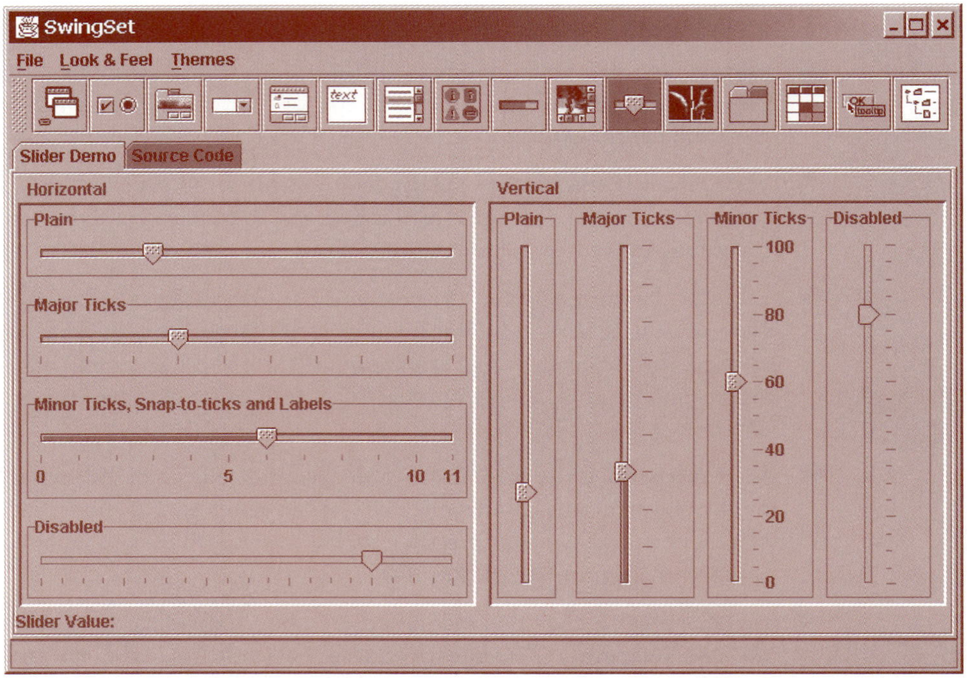

Figure 5.17 *The SwingSet demo demonstrates the features of* `JSlider`.

`JSlider` lets the user graphically select a value by sliding a knob within a bounded interval. The slider can show both major tick marks and minor tick marks between them. The number of pixels between the tick marks is controlled with `setMajorTickSpacing` and `setMinorTickSpacing`. Sliders can be displayed horizontally or vertically, with or without ticks, and with or without labels.

The following properties are defined in the `JSlider` class.

- **`extend`** is the size of the range covered by the knob. The default value is 0.
- **`inverted`** is a `boolean` value. If `true`, indicating values increase from right to left or from bottom to top. If `false`, indicating values increase from left to right or from top to bottom. The default value is `false`.
- **`maximum`** is the maximum value the slider represents. The default value is 100.
- **`minimum`** is the minimum value the slider represents. The default value is 0.
- **`majorTickSpacing`** is the number of units between major ticks. The default value is 0.
- **`minorTickSpacing`** is the number of units between minor ticks. The default value is 0.
- **`orientation`** is the orientation of the slider, either `HORIZONTAL` or `VERTICAL`. The default value is `HORIZONTAL`.
- **`paintLabels`** is a `boolean` value indicating whether the labels are painted at tick marks. The default value is false, which indicates that the labels are not painted.
- **`paintTicks`** is a `boolean` value indicating whether the tick marks are painted. The default value is `false`, which indicates that the tick marks are not painted.
- **`paintTrack`** is a `boolean` value indicating whether the track is painted. The default value is true, which indicates that the track is painted.
- **`value`** is the current value of the slider. The default value is 50.
- **`valueIsAdjusting`** is a `boolean` value indicating whether the knob is being dragged. The default value is `false`.

When the user changes the value of the slider, the slider generates an instance of `javax.swing.event.ChangeEvent` that is passed to any registered listeners. Any object that wishes to be notified of changes to the slider's value should implement the `stateChanged` method in the `ChangeListener` interface defined in the package `javax.swing.event`.

Example 5.4 Using Sliders

This example uses three sliders to specify the red, green, and blue components of a color and set the color as the background color for a panel, as shown in Figure 5.18.

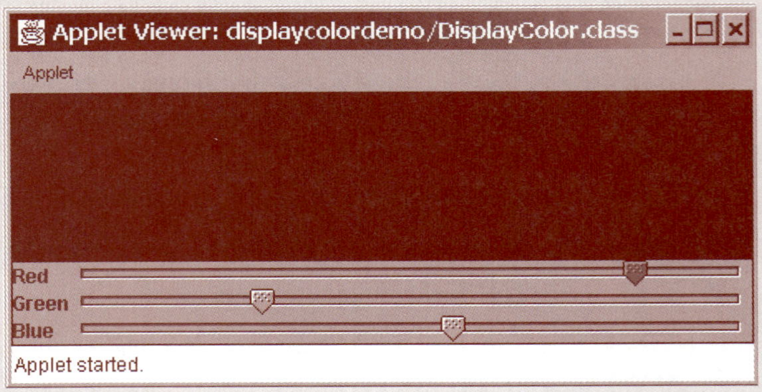

Figure 5.18 *The background color of the panel changes as you adjust the scroll bars.*

Here are the steps to complete the project:

1. Create a new package named displaycolordemo and a new applet named DisplayColor using the Forte Swing JApplet form wizard.

2. Drop a `JPanel` to the south of the applet and rename it `jpSelections`. Drop a `JPanel` to the center of the applet and rename it `jpColor`.

3. Set the `layout` of `jpSelections` to `BorderLayout`. Drop a `JPanel` to the west of `jpSelections` and rename it `jpLabels`, and drop a `JPanel` to the Center of `jpSelections` and rename it `jpSliders`. Set the `border` property of `jpSelections` to a line border.

4. Set the `layout` of `jpLabels` to `GridLayout` and set the `row` property of the `GridLayout` to 3. Drop a `JLabel` three times into `jpLabels`, and set the `text` of the labels to Red, Green, and Blue.

5. Set the `layout` of `jpSliders` to `GridLayout`, and set the `row` property of the `GridLayout` to 3. Drop a `JSlider` three times and rename them `jslRed`, `jslGreen`, and `jslBlue`. Set their maximum property to 128.

6. Declare variables `redValue`, `greenValue`, and `blueValue` for representing the red, green, and blue components of the color. Generate adjustment-event handlers for the sliders, and implement them to adjust these variables and update the background color in the panel `jpColor`, as shown in Listing 5.5 (Lines 66–87).

```
// DisplayColor.java: Use scroll bars to select colors and
// display colors in a panel
package displaycolordemo;

public class DisplayColor extends javax.swing.JApplet {
  // Declare color component values
  int redValue, greenValue, blueValue;
  java.awt.Color color;

  /** Creates new form DisplayColor */
  public DisplayColor() {
    initComponents();
  }

  private void initComponents() {
    jpSelections = new javax.swing.JPanel();
    jpLabels = new javax.swing.JPanel();
    jLabel1 = new javax.swing.JLabel();
    jLabel2 = new javax.swing.JLabel();
    jLabel3 = new javax.swing.JLabel();
    jpSliders = new javax.swing.JPanel();
    jslRed = new javax.swing.JSlider();
    jslGreen = new javax.swing.JSlider();
    jslBlue = new javax.swing.JSlider();
    jpColor = new javax.swing.JPanel();
    jpSelections.setLayout(new java.awt.BorderLayout());
    jpSelections.setBorder(
      new javax.swing.border.LineBorder(java.awt.Color.black));
    jpLabels.setLayout(new java.awt.GridLayout(3, 0));
    jLabel1.setText("Red");
    jpLabels.add(jLabel1);
    jLabel2.setText("Green");
    jpLabels.add(jLabel2);
    jLabel3.setText("Blue");
    jpLabels.add(jLabel3);
    jpSelections.add(jpLabels, java.awt.BorderLayout.WEST);
    jpSliders.setLayout(new java.awt.GridLayout(3, 0));
    jslRed.setMaximum(128);
    jslRed.addChangeListener(new javax.swing.event.ChangeListener() {
      public void stateChanged(javax.swing.event.ChangeEvent evt) {
        jslRedStateChanged(evt);
      }
    });
    jpSliders.add(jslRed);
    jslGreen.setMaximum(128);
    jslGreen.addChangeListener(
      new javax.swing.event.ChangeListener() {
      public void stateChanged(javax.swing.event.ChangeEvent evt) {
        jslGreenStateChanged(evt);
      }
    });
    jpSliders.add(jslGreen);
    jslBlue.setMaximum(128);
    jslBlue.addChangeListener(
      new javax.swing.event.ChangeListener() {
      public void stateChanged(javax.swing.event.ChangeEvent evt) {
        jslBlueStateChanged(evt);
      }
    });
```

Listing 5.5 *DisplayColor.java*

continued

Example 5.4 continued

```
      jpSliders.add(jslBlue);
      jpSelections.add(jpSliders, java.awt.BorderLayout.CENTER);
      getContentPane().add(jpSelections, java.awt.BorderLayout.SOUTH);
      getContentPane().add(jpColor, java.awt.BorderLayout.CENTER);
    }

    private void jslBlueStateChanged(
      javax.swing.event.ChangeEvent evt) {
      blueValue = jslBlue.getValue();
      updateColor();
    }

    private void jslGreenStateChanged(
      javax.swing.event.ChangeEvent evt) {
      greenValue = jslGreen.getValue();
      updateColor();
    }

    private void jslRedStateChanged(
      javax.swing.event.ChangeEvent evt) {
      redValue = jslRed.getValue();
      updateColor();
    }

    void updateColor() {
      color = new java.awt.Color(redValue, greenValue, blueValue);
      jpColor.setBackground(color);
    }

    // Variables declaration - do not modify
    private javax.swing.JPanel jpSelections;
    private javax.swing.JPanel jpLabels;
    private javax.swing.JLabel jLabel1;
    private javax.swing.JLabel jLabel2;
    private javax.swing.JLabel jLabel3;
    private javax.swing.JPanel jpSliders;
    private javax.swing.JSlider jslRed;
    private javax.swing.JSlider jslGreen;
    private javax.swing.JSlider jslBlue;
    private javax.swing.JPanel jpColor;
    // End of variables declaration
  }
```

Listing 5.5 *continued*

Example Review

The color of the panel above the sliders changes as you adjust the sliders. The colors are determined by the values represented in the sliders. Since the red, green, and blue component values range from 0 to 128, the maximum values of the sliders are set at 128.

Whenever the user adjusts a slider, a `ChangeEvent` is fired. The event handler obtains the current value of the color and updates the background color of the panel.

5.7.14 JProgressBar

`JProgressBar` is a component that displays a value graphically within a bounded interval. A progress bar is typically used to show the percentage of completion of a lengthy operation; it comprises a rectangular bar that is "filled in" from left to right horizontally or from bottom to top vertically as the operation is performed. It provides the user with feedback on the progress of the operation. For example, when a file is being read, it alerts the user to the progress of the operation, thereby keeping the user attentive.

You can choose the ProgressBar toolbar to see the demo for using `JProgressBar` in the SwingDemo project, as shown in Figure 5.19.

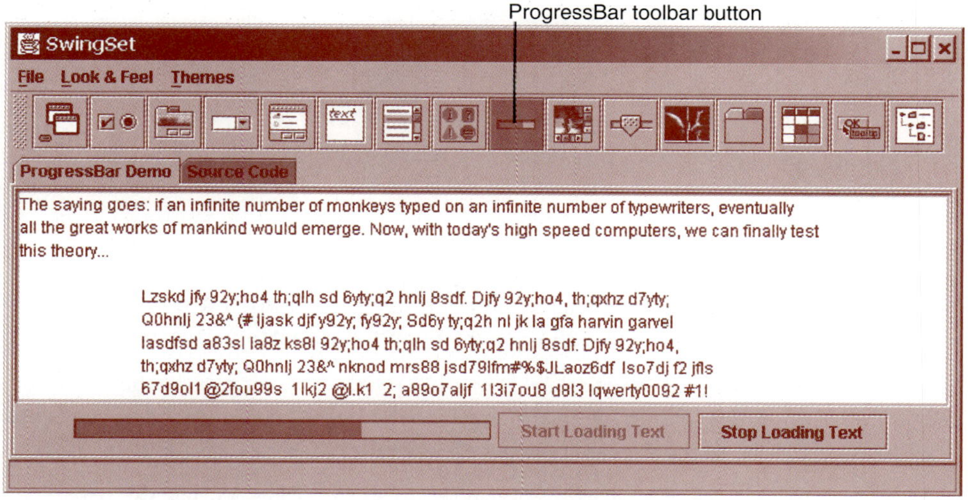

Figure 5.19 *The ProgressBar Demo demonstrates the features of* `JProgressBar`.

When the SwingSet demo starts, a progress bar displays the loading status of all the panels. The progress bar can be displayed horizontally or vertically, as determined by its `orientation` property. The `minimum`, `value`, and `maximum` properties determine the minimum, current, and maximum length on the progress bar.

Example 5.5 Using the Progress Bar

This example creates a program that lets you copy files. A progress bar is used to show the progress of the copying operation, as shown in Figure 5.20.

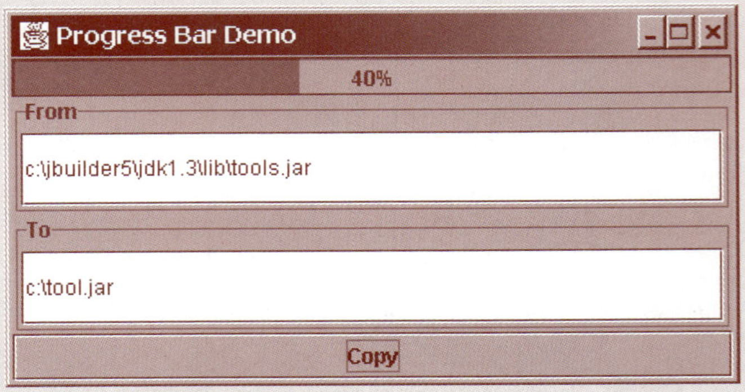

Figure 5.20 *The user enters the files in the text fields and clicks the Copy button to start copying files.*

Here are the steps to complete the project.

1. Create a new package named progressbardemo and use the Forte Swing JFrame form wizard to create an application named `TestProgressBar`.
2. Drop a `JProgressBar` from the Swing (Other) tab to the north of the frame, a `JButton` to the south of the frame, and a `JPanel` to the center of the frame. Rename the generated objects `jpb`, `jbtCopy`, and `jpFiles`.
3. Set the `stringPainted` property of `jpb` to True, so that the percentage of completion will be displayed in the progress bar.
4. Set the `layout` of `jpFiles` to `GridLayout` with two rows. Drop a `JPanel` twice into `jpFiles` to create `jpFromFile` and `jpToFile`. Set the border with the title "From" for `jpFromFile` and the border with the title "To" for `jpToFile`.
5. Set the layout of `jpFromFile` and `jpToFile` to `BorderLayout`. Drop a `JTextField` to the center of `jpFromFile` and the center of `jpToFile` to create `jtfFrom` and `jtfTo`.
6. Generate and implement the code for handling the Copy button, as shown in Listing 5.6 (Lines 49–51).
7. Create a thread class for copying files and updating the progress bar.

```
1   package progressbardemo;
2
3   import java.io.*;
4
```

Listing 5.6 *TestProgressBar.java*

```
public class TestProgressBar extends javax.swing.JFrame {
  /** Creates new form TestProgressBar */
  public TestProgressBar() {
    initComponents();
    setTitle("Progress Bar Demo");
  }

  private void initComponents() {
    jpb = new javax.swing.JProgressBar();
    jbtCopy = new javax.swing.JButton();
    jpFiles = new javax.swing.JPanel();
    jpFromFile = new javax.swing.JPanel();
    jtfFrom = new javax.swing.JTextField();
    jpToFile = new javax.swing.JPanel();
    jtfTo = new javax.swing.JTextField();
    addWindowListener(new java.awt.event.WindowAdapter() {
      public void windowClosing(java.awt.event.WindowEvent evt) {
        exitForm(evt);
      }
    });
    jpb.setStringPainted(true);
    jbtCopy.setText("Copy");
    jbtCopy.addActionListener(new java.awt.event.ActionListener() {
      public void actionPerformed(java.awt.event.ActionEvent evt) {
        jbtCopyActionPerformed(evt);
      }
    });
    getContentPane().add(jbtCopy, java.awt.BorderLayout.SOUTH);
    jpFiles.setLayout(new java.awt.GridLayout(2, 0));
    jpFromFile.setLayout(new java.awt.BorderLayout());
    jpFromFile.setBorder(
      new javax.swing.border.TitledBorder("From"));
    jpFromFile.add(jtfFrom, java.awt.BorderLayout.CENTER);
    jpFiles.add(jpFromFile);
    jpToFile.setLayout(new java.awt.BorderLayout());
    jpToFile.setBorder(new javax.swing.border.TitledBorder("To"));
    jpToFile.add(jtfTo, java.awt.BorderLayout.CENTER);
    jpFiles.add(jpToFile);
    getContentPane().add(jpFiles, java.awt.BorderLayout.CENTER);
    pack();
  }

  private void jbtCopyActionPerformed(
    java.awt.event.ActionEvent evt) {
    // Create a thread for copying files
    CopyFileThread thread = new CopyFileThread(this);
    thread.start();
  }

  /** Exit the Application */
  private void exitForm(java.awt.event.WindowEvent evt) {
    System.exit(0);
  }

  /**
   * @param args the command line arguments
   */
  public static void main(String args[]) {
    new TestProgressBar().show();
  }

```

Listing 5.6 *continued*

continued

Example 5.5 continued

```
    // Copy file and update progress bar in a separate thread
    class CopyFileThread extends Thread {
      int currentValue;
      Runnable updateProgressBar;
      TestProgressBar applet;

      public CopyFileThread(final TestProgressBar applet) {
        this.applet = applet;

        updateProgressBar = new Runnable() {
          public void run() {
            javax.swing.JProgressBar jpb = applet.jpb;
            jpb.setValue(currentValue);
          }
        };
      }

      public void run() {
        java.io.BufferedInputStream in = null;
        java.io.BufferedOutputStream out = null;
        try  {
          // Create file input stream
          java.io.File inFile = new java.io.File(applet.jtfFrom.
              getText().trim());
          in = new BufferedInputStream(new FileInputStream(inFile));

          // Create file output stream
          java.io.File outFile = new File(applet.jtfTo.getText());
          out =  new BufferedOutputStream(new FileOutputStream(out-
              File));

          // Get total bytes in the file
          long totalBytes = in.available();

          // Start progress meter bar
          applet.jpb.setValue(0);
          applet.jpb.setMaximum(100);

          int r;
          long bytesRead = 0;
          byte[] b = new byte[512];
          while ((r = in.read(b, 0, b.length)) != -1) {
            out.write(b, 0, r);
            bytesRead += r;
            currentValue = (int)(bytesRead*100/totalBytes);

            // Update the progress bar
            javax.swing.SwingUtilities.invokeLater(updateProgressBar);
          }
        }
        catch (FileNotFoundException ex) {
          ex.printStackTrace();
        }
        catch (IOException ex) {
          ex.printStackTrace();
        }
        finally {
```

Listing 5.6 *continued*

```
123             try {
124               if (in != null) in.close();
125               if (out != null) out.close();
126             }
127             catch (Exception ex) {}
128           }
129         }
130       }
131
132       // Variables declaration - do not modify
133       private javax.swing.JProgressBar jpb;
134       private javax.swing.JButton jbtCopy;
135       private javax.swing.JPanel jpFiles;
136       private javax.swing.JPanel jpFromFile;
137       private javax.swing.JTextField jtfFrom;
138       private javax.swing.JPanel jpToFile;
139       private javax.swing.JTextField jtfTo;
130       // End of variables declaration
141     }
```

Listing 5.6 *continued*

Example Review

The class `CopyFileThread` is a subclass of `Thread`. This class is for copying a file on a separate thread. Swing components are not *thread-safe*, meaning that they can only be accessed from the event dispatch thread once they are displayed. The event dispatch thread is the thread that invokes callback methods like `update` and `paint` as well as the event handlers in the event listener interface. Occasionally, you need to update GUI components from a nonstandard event, as in this case, where the progress bar is repainted in the thread that copies files. To ensure that the progress bar is updated in the event dispatch thread, you need to use the `SwingUtilities`'s `invokeLater` method to invoke the thread for updating the progress bar, as shown in the italicized code in the `CopyFileThread` class in Listing 5.6 (Line 113).

The object `updateProgessBar` is an instance of `Runnable`, which is created using an anonymous inner class. This object is responsible for updating the progress bar, which must run from the event dispatch thread.

Chapter Summary

Swing lightweight components are written in Java, without platform-specific code. This facilitates a customizable look-and-feel without relying on the native windowing system, and simplifies the deployment of applications. Swing also supports a pluggable look-and-feel architecture. Thanks to this feature, users can switch the look-and-feel of an application or an applet without restarting it and without the developer having to subclass the entire component set.

This chapter introduced the basic features of Swing components. You learned how to create projects using the components `JButton`, `JRadioButton`, `JToggleButton`, `JCheckBox`, `Border`, `JLabel`, `JScrollPane`, `JTextField`, `JTextArea`, `JEditorPane`, `JSlider`, and `JProgressBar` in Forte.

Review Questions

5.1 Why are the AWT user interface components considered heavyweight? Why are the Swing user interface components considered lightweight?

5.2 Describe the Swing model-view architecture.

5.3 How do you specify a particular look-and-feel in Java programs?

5.4 Can you preview a particular look-and-feel in Forte?

5.5 Describe the properties of `JComponent`.

5.6 Describe the properties of `AbstractButton`.

5.7 How do you create a scrollable text area?

5.8 How do you display an HTML page in a `JEditorPane`?

5.9 Describe the similarities and differences between `JScrollPane` and `JScrollBar`.

5.10 Describe the similarities and differences between `JScrollBar` and `JSlider`.

5.11 Why is it necessary to use the `invokeLater` method in Example 5.5?

5.12 What is the property that displays the percentage of work completed in `JProgressBar`?

5.13 Suppose you want to display four identical buttons in a panel of grid layout. You create one button and add this button four times into the panel. Can you see four buttons displayed in the panel?

Programming Exercises

5.1 Develop a program to set the horizontal alignment and column size properties of a text field dynamically, as shown in Figure 5.21.

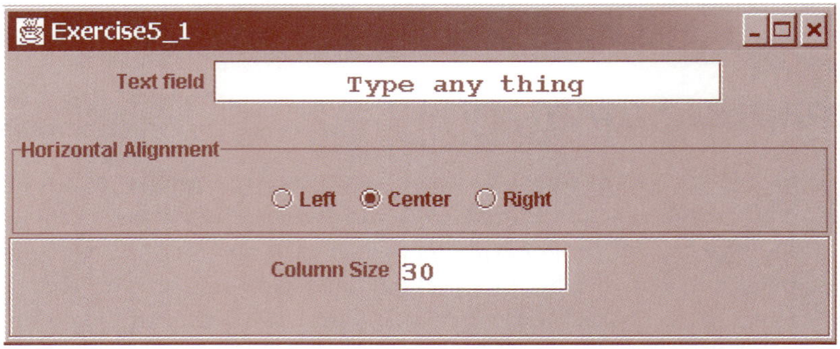

Figure 5.21 *You can set the horizontal alignment and column size properties of a text field dynamically.*

5.2 Create a program that demonstrates the wrapping styles of the text area. The program uses a check box to indicate whether the text area is wrapped. In the case where the text area is wrapped, you need to specify whether it is wrapped by characters or by words, as shown in Figure 5.22.

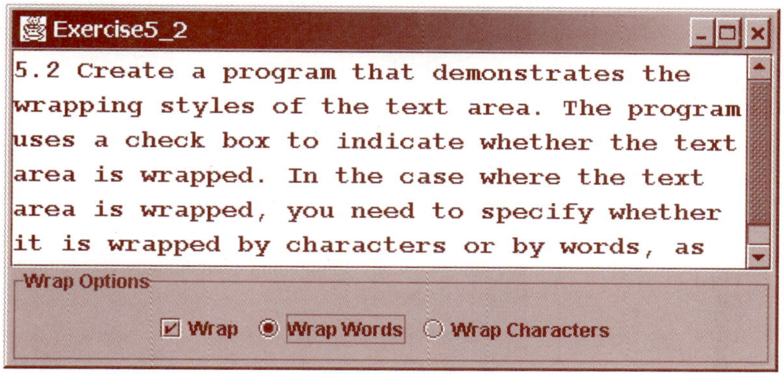

Figure 5.22 *You can set the options to wrap a text area by characters or by words dynamically.*

5.3 Modify Example 5.4 and use `JScrollBar` to select colors instead of using `JSlider`.

5.4 Create a program that displays an instance of `JProgressBar` and sets its value property randomly every 500 milliseconds infinitely.

5.5 Modify Example 5.1 to set the icons for the radio buttons in Horizontal Alignment section, as shown in Figure 5.23. The icons are the same as used by the radio buttons in the Vertical Alignment section. Create a composite matte border of red color that is 2 pixels thick. Share this border among four buttons in the top panel. The top panel shares the same border.

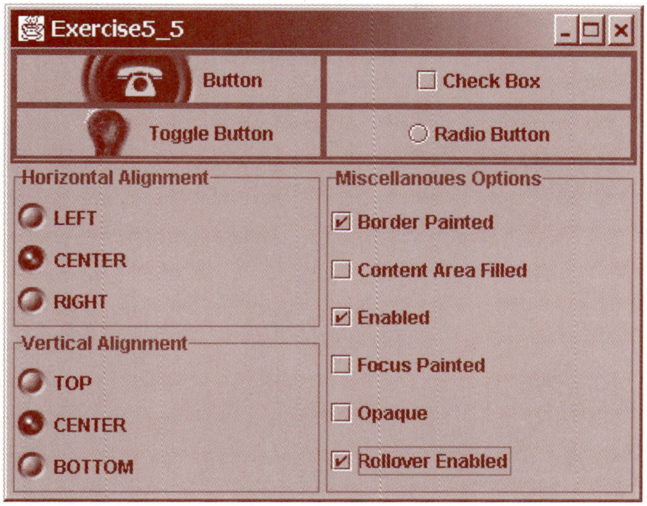

Figure 5.23 *The icons and borders can be shared.*

5.6 Modify Example 5.3, "Using `JEditorPane`," as follows:

- It accepts an HTML file from a local host. Assume that a local HTML filename begins neither with http:// nor with www.
- It accepts a remote HTML file. A remote HTML filename begins with either http:// or www.

CHAPTER 6

CONTAINERS AND LAYOUT MANAGERS

Objectives

- To know the structures of the Swing container.
- To understand how a layout manager works in Java.
- To examine the layout managers provided in Forte.
- To learn how to create custom layout managers.
- To use `JTabbedPane` to create tabbed panes.
- To use `JSplitPane` to create split panes.

6.1 Introduction

If you have used a Windows-based RAD tool like Visual Basic, you know that it is easier to create user interfaces with Visual Basic than with a Java RAD tool like Forte. This is mainly because the components are placed in absolute positions and sizes in Visual Basic, whereas they are placed in containers using a variety of layout managers in Java. Absolute positions and sizes are fine if the application is developed and deployed on the same platform, but what looks fine on a development system may not look right on a deployment system on a different platform. To solve this problem, Java provides a set of layout managers that place components in containers in a way that is independent of fonts, screen resolutions, and platform differences.

A *container* is an object that holds and groups components. A *layout manager* is a special object used to place components in a container. Containers and layout managers play a crucial role in creating user interfaces. This chapter presents a conceptual overview of containers, reviews the layout managers in Java, and introduces the new layout managers provided by Forte. You will also learn how to create your own layout manager.

6.2 About Containers

User interface components like `JButton` cannot be displayed without being placed in a container. A container is a component that is capable of containing other components. You do not display a user interface component; you place it in a container, and the container displays the components it contains.

The base class for all containers is `java.awt.Container`, which is a subclass of `java.awt.Component`. The `Container` class has the following essential functions:

- It adds and removes components using various `add` and `remove` methods.
- It maintains a `layout` property for specifying a layout manager that is used to lay out components in the container. Every container has a default layout manager.
- It provides registration methods for the `java.awt.event.ContainerEvent`.

In AWT programming, the `java.awt.Frame` class is used as a top-level container for Java applications, the `java.awt.Applet` class is used for all Java applets, and `java.awt.Dialog` is used for dialog windows. These classes do not work properly with Swing lightweight components. Special versions of `Frame`, `Applet`, and `Dialog` named `JFrame`, `JApplet`, and `JDialog` have been developed to accommodate Swing components. `JFrame` is a subclass of `Frame`, `JApplet` is a subclass of `Applet`, and `JDialog` is a subclass of `Dialog`. `JFrame` and `JApplet` inherit all the functions of their heavyweight counterparts, but they have a more complex internal structure with several layered panes, as shown in Figure 6.1.

`javax.swing.JRootPane` is a lightweight container used behind the scenes by Swing's top-level containers, such as `JFrame`, `JApplet`, and `JDialog`.

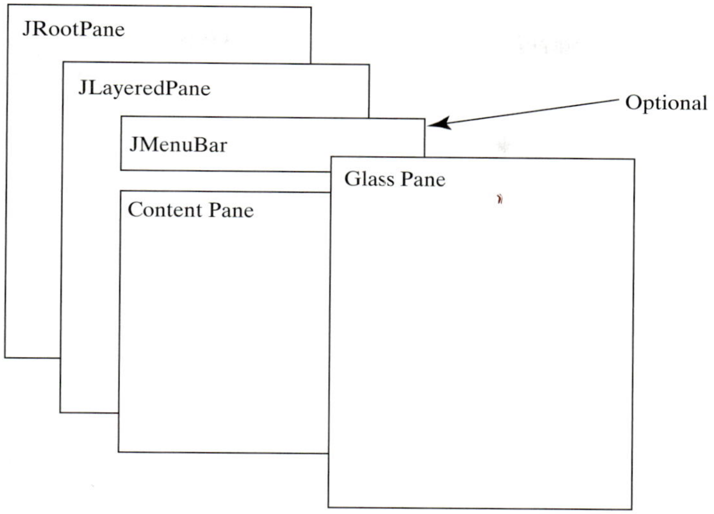

Figure 6.1 *Swing top-level containers use layers of panes to group lightweight components and make them work properly.*

`javax.swing.JLayeredPane` is a container that manages the optional menu bar and the content pane. The content pane is an instance of `Container` with default `BorderLayout`. This is the container where the user interface components are added. To obtain the content pane in a `JFrame` or in a `JApplet`, use the `getContentPane()` method. The glass pane floats on top of everything. `javax.swing.JGlassPane` is a hidden pane by default. If you make the glass pane visible, then it's like a sheet of glass over all the other parts of the root pane. It's completely transparent unless you implement the glass pane's paint method so that it does something, and it intercepts input events for the root pane. In general, `JRootPane`, `JLayeredPane`, and `JGlassPane` are not used directly.

Now let us review the three most frequently used Swing containers: `JFrame`, `JApplet`, and `JPanel`.

6.2.1 JFrame

`JFrame`, a Swing version of `Frame`, is a top-level container for Java graphics applications. Like `Frame`, `JFrame` is displayed as a standalone window with a title bar and a border. The following properties are often useful in `JFrame`.

- **`layout`** is inherited from `Frame`, but is not used in `JFrame` because the components are not directly placed in the frame; instead they are placed in the content pane. In Forte, this property is associated with the content pane of the frame. When you set a new layout, Forte sets the layout in the content pane of `JFrame`. This property value appears below the Other Components node under the frame in the component inspector.
- **`contentPane`** is the content pane of the frame.

- **`iconImage`** is the image that represents the frame. This image replaces the default Java image on the frame's title bar and is also displayed when the frame is minimized. This property type is `Image`. You can get an image using the `ImageIcon` class, as follows:

  ```
  Image image = (new ImageIcon(filename)).getImage();
  ```

- **`jMenuBar`** is the optional menu bar for the frame.
- **`resizable`** is a `boolean` value indicating whether the frame is resizable. The default value is `true`.
- **`title`** specifies the title of the frame.

Note
All the above properties are inherited from `Frame` except `contentPane` and `jMenuBar`. The `contentPane` and `jMenuBar` properties do not appear in the property editor. Forte takes care of them automatically when a component or a menu bar is added to the form.

Note
`JFrame` is a top-level container. You can also create internal frames using the `JInternalFrame` class. Creating internal frames is presented in the companion Web site at **www.prenhall.com/liang/radft.html**.

6.2.2 JApplet

`JApplet` is a Swing version of `Applet`. Since it is a subclass of `Applet`, it has all the functions required by the Web browser. Here are the four essential methods defined in `Applet`:

```
// Called by the browser when the Web page containing
// this applet is initially loaded
public void init()

// Called by the browser after the init() method and
// every time the Web page is visited.
public void start()

// Called by the browser when the page containing this
// applet becomes inactive.
public void stop()

// Called by the browser when the Web browser exits.
public void destroy()
```

Additionally, `JApplet` has the `contentPane` and `jMenuBar` properties, among others. As with `JFrame`, you do not place components directly into `JApplet`; instead you place them into the content pane of the applet. The `Applet` class cannot have the menu bar, but the `JApplet` class allows you to set the menu bar using the `setJMenuBar` method.

NOTE
To use the Swing components in an applet, the applet must extend `JApplet` or a subclass of `JApplet` instead of `Applet`. To use the Swing components in an application, the application must extend `JFrame` or a subclass of `JFrame`.

NOTE
When an applet is loaded, the Web browser creates an instance of the applet by invoking the applet's default constructor. So the constructor is invoked before the init method.

6.2.3 JPanel

Panels act as smaller containers for grouping user interface components. `javax.swing.JPanel` is different from `JFrame` and `JApplet`. First, `JPanel` is not a top-level container; it must be placed inside another container, and it can be placed inside another `JPanel`. Second, since `JPanel` is a subclass of `JComponent`, it is a lightweight component, but `JFrame` and `JApplet` are heavyweight components.

`JPanel` is a Swing version of `Panel`, but it is not a subclass of `Panel`. Nevertheless, you can use `JPanel` the same way you use `Panel`. As a subclass of `JComponent`, `JPanel` can take advantage of `JComponent`, such as double buffering and borders. You should draw figures on `JPanel` rather than `JFrame` or `JApplet`, because `JPanel` supports double buffering, which is the technique for eliminating flickers.

6.3 Layout Managers

Every container has a layout manager that is responsible for arranging its components. The container's `setLayout` method can be used to set a layout manager. Certain types of containers have default layout managers. For instance, the content pane of `JFrame` or `JApplet` uses `BorderLayout`, and `JPanel` uses `FlowLayout`.

A container's `layout` property appears in the inspector for the container, as shown in Figure 6.2. You can specify a layout manager for a container by selecting one from a list of available layout managers. Forte automatically updates the container's call to `setLayout`.

The layout manager places the components in accordance with its own rules and property settings, and with the constraints associated with each component.

Every layout manager has its own specific set of rules. For example, the `FlowLayout` manager places components in rows from left to right and starts a new row when the previous row is filled. The `BorderLayout` manager places components in the north, south, east, west, or center of the container. The `GridLayout` manager places components in a grid of cells in rows and columns from left to right in order.

Some layout managers have properties that can affect the sizing and location of the components in the container. For example, `BorderLayout` has properties called `hgap`

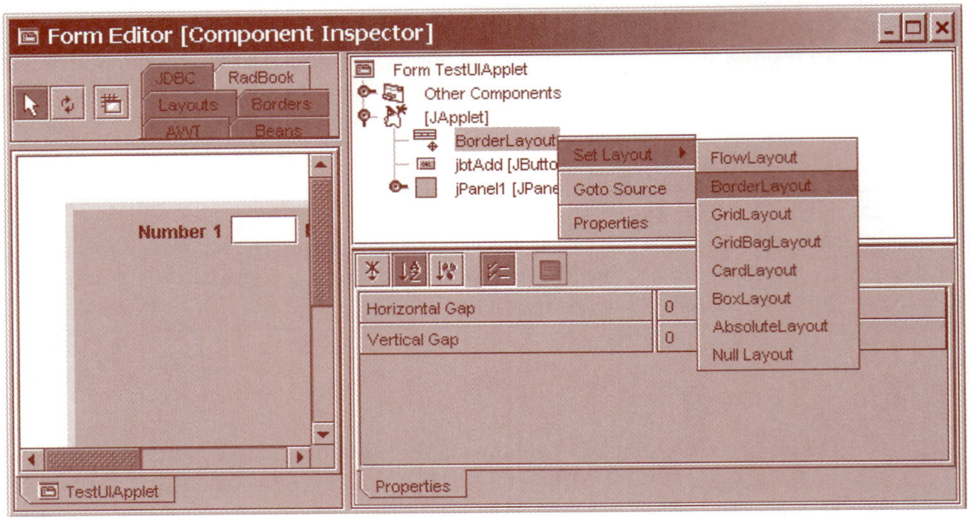

Figure 6.2 *Every container has a* `layout` *property. You can choose a layout from a drop-down list of layout managers in Forte.*

(horizontal gap) and `vgap` (vertical gap) that determine the distance between components horizontally and vertically. `FlowLayout` has properties that can be used to specify the alignment (left, center, right) of the components and properties for specifying the horizontal or vertical gap between the components. `GridLayout` has properties that can be used to specify the horizontal or vertical gap between columns and rows and the properties for specifying the number of rows and columns. These properties can be viewed and edited in the inspector when the layout manager is selected in the component tree. As shown in Figure 6.2, the layout manager is displayed as an item in the component tree just below the container to which it is attached.

The size of a component in a container is determined by many factors, such as:

- The type of layout manager used by the container.
- The layout constraints associated with each component.
- The size of the container.
- Certain properties common to all components (such as `preferredSize`, `minimumSize`, `maximumSize`, `alignmentX`, and `alignmentY`).

The `preferredSize` property indicates the ideal size at which the component looks best. Depending on the rules of the particular layout manager, this property may or may not be considered. For example, the preferred size of a component is used in a container with a `FlowLayout` manager, but ignored if it is placed in a container with a `BorderLayout` manager.

The `minimumSize` property specifies the minimum size at which the component is useful. For most GUI components, `minimumSize` is the same as `preferredSize`. Layout managers generally respect `minimumSize` more than `preferredSize`.

The `maximumSize` property specifies the maximum size needed by a component, so that the layout manager won't wastefully give space to a component that does not need it. For instance, `BorderLayout` limits the center component's size to its maximum size and gives the space to edge components.

The `alignmentX` property specifies how the component would like to be aligned relative to other components along the x-axis. This value should be a number between 0 and 1, where 0 represents alignment along the origin, 1 is aligned the farthest away from the origin, 0.5 is centered, etc.

The `alignmentY` property specifies how the component would like to be aligned relative to other components along the y-axis. The value should be a number between 0 and 1, where 0 represents alignment along the origin, 1 is aligned the farthest away from the origin, 0.5 is centered, etc.

6.4 Working with Layout Managers

Java provides a variety of layout managers. In addition, you can create custom layout managers. `BorderLayout`, `FlowLayout`, `GridLayout`, `CardLayout`, `GridBagLayout`, and `Null` were introduced with Java AWT. `BoxLayout` and `OverlayLayout` were introduced in Swing. `AbsoluteLayout` is a custom layout manager provided by Forte.

6.4.1 *BorderLayout*

`BorderLayout` arranges and resizes its components to fit in five regions: North, South, East, West, and Center. The components are laid out according to their preferred sizes and constraints. The North and South components may be stretched horizontally; the East and West components may be stretched vertically; the Center component may stretch both horizontally and vertically to fill any space left over.

By default, `BorderLayout` puts no gap between the components in the container. However, you can specify the horizontal gap (`hgap`) and the vertical gap (`hgap`) in the inspector.

`BorderLayout` is ideal for docking components to one or more edges of a container, and for filling up the center of the container with a component. Use `BorderLayout` if you want a single component to occupy the entire container.

6.4.2 *FlowLayout*

`FlowLayout` arranges components according to their `preferredSize` in a left-to-right flow, much like lines of text in a paragraph.

You can choose how to place components in the rows by specifying an alignment justification of left, right, or center on the `alignment` property in the inspector for the layout manager. You can also specify the size of the horizontal or vertical gap between the components, using the `hgap` and `vgap` properties. By default, the gap is 5 pixels.

6.4.3 *GridLayout*

`GridLayout` arranges components in a rectangular grid of cells. The container is divided into equal-sized rectangles, and one component is placed in each rectangle. `GridLayout` expands each component to fill the entire cell.

You can specify the number of columns and rows in the grid; one of these can be zero, but at least one must be nonzero. For example, if you specify four columns and zero rows, `GridLayout` creates a grid with four columns and a variant number of rows depending on the number of components that are added to the container. You can also specify the gap between rows and columns. By default, the gap is 0.

`GridLayout` is ideal when you want the components in a container to be the same size. In Example 4.2, "Creating a Clock Component," you put six clocks in an applet, using `GridLayout` to ensure that all the clocks were the same size.

6.4.4 *CardLayout*

`CardLayout` places components in the container as cards. Only one card is visible at a time, and the container acts as a stack of cards. The ordering of cards is determined by the container's own internal ordering of its component objects. `CardLayout` defines a set of methods that allow an application to flip through the cards sequentially or to show a specified card directly.

You can specify the size of the horizontal and vertical gap surrounding a stack of components in a `CardLayout` manager.

`CardLayout` is ideal when you need to manage two or more panels that have to share the same display area. In many situations, `CardLayout` can be replaced by `JTabbedPane`, which is introduced later in this chapter.

6.4.5 *GridBagLayout*

`GridBagLayout` is the most flexible and the most complex. It is similar to `GridLayout` in the sense that both layout managers arrange components in a grid. However, in `GridBagLayout` the components can vary in size and can be added in any order.

`GridBagLayout` uses a dynamic rectangular grid of cells, with each component occupying one or more cells called its *display area.* Each component managed by a `GridBagLayout` manager is associated with a `GridBagConstraints` instance that specifies how the component is laid out within its display area. How a `GridBagLayout` places a set of components depends on each component's `GridBagConstraints` and minimum size, as well as the preferred size of the component's container.

To use `GridBagLayout` effectively, you must customize one or more of its components' `GridBagConstraints`. You customize a `GridBagConstraints` object by setting one or more of its instance variables:

- **`gridx`** and **`gridy`** specify the cell at the upper left of the component's display area, where the upper-left-most cell has address `gridx=0, gridy=0`. Note that gridx specifies the column in which the component will be placed, and gridy specifies the row in which the component will be placed.

- **gridwidth** and **gridheight** specify the number of cells in a row (for gridwidth) or column (for gridheight) in the component's display area. The default value is 1.
- **weightx** and **weighty** specify the extra space to allocate the component horizontally and vertically when the window is resized. Unless you specify a weight for at least one component in a row (weightx) and column (weighty), all the components clump together in the center of their container. This is because when the weight is zero (the default), the GridBagLayout puts any extra space between its grid of cells and the edges of the container.
- **fill** specifies how the component should be resized if its viewing area is larger than its current size. Valid values are GridBagConstraints.NONE (the default), GridBagConstraints.HORIZONTAL (make the component wide enough to fill its display area horizontally, but don't change its height), GridBagConstraints.VERTICAL (make the component tall enough to fill its display area vertically, but don't change its width), and GridBagConstraints.BOTH (make the component fill its display area entirely).
- **anchor** specifies where the component is placed in the area when it does not fill in the entire area. Valid values are GridBagConstraints.CENTER (the default), GridBagConstraints.NORTH, GridBagConstraints.NORTHEAST, GridBagConstraints.EAST, GridBagConstraints.SOUTHEAST, GridBagConstraints.SOUTH, GridBagConstraints.SOUTHWEST, GridBagConstraints.WEST, and GridBagConstraints.NORTHWEST.
- **insets** specifies the minimum amount of external space (padding) in pixels between the component and the edges of its display area.

The fill and anchor parameters deal with how to fill and place the component when the viewing area is larger than the requested area. The fill and anchor parameters are class variables, while gridx, gridy, width, height, weightx, and weighty are instance variables.

GridBagLayout is a complex layout manager that many people find difficult to use. Forte greatly simplifies the use of GridBagLayout with a property editor. The GridBagLayout property editor enables you to edit all the GridBagConstraints values, as shown in Figure 6.3. To open the editor, right-click the GridBagLayout manager in the component tree and choose *Customize*.

TIP

While GridBagLayout can accommodate a complex grid, it behaves more predictably if you organize your components into smaller panels, nested inside the GridBagLayout container. These nested panels can use other layouts and can contain additional panels if necessary.

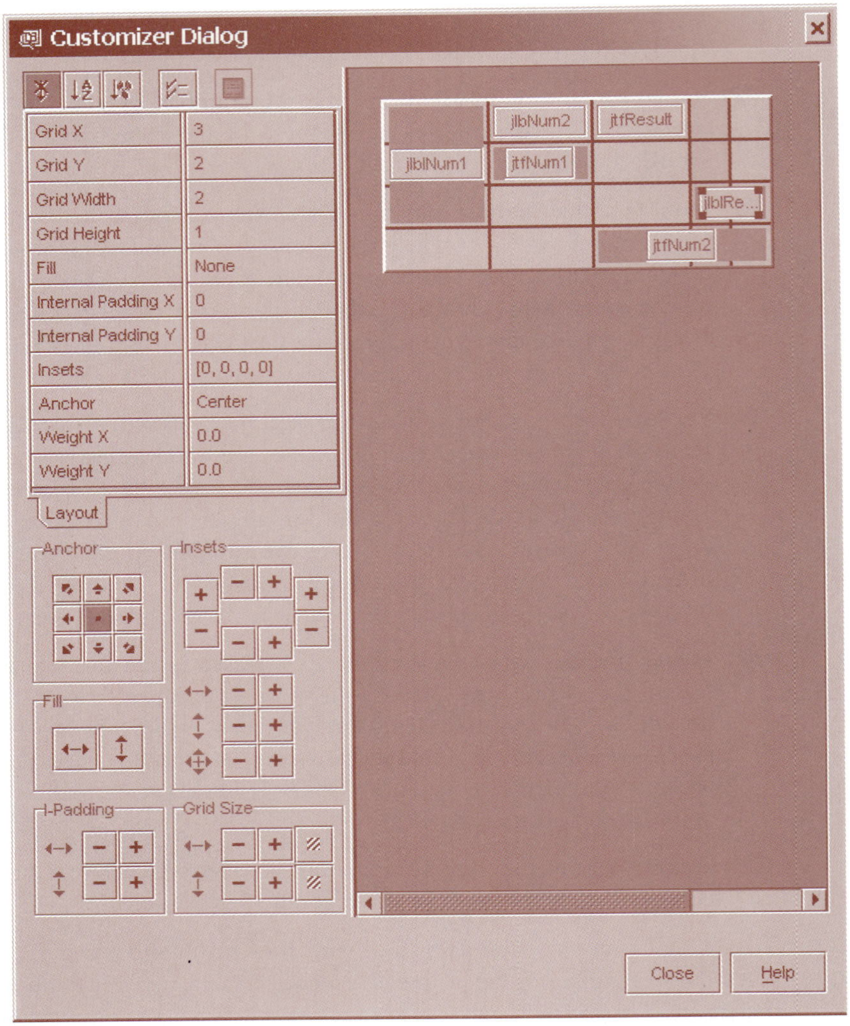

Figure 6.3 *The* `GridBagLayout` *property editor lets you edit all the properties of a component's constraints.*

6.4.6 *Null*

Null means that no layout manager is assigned to the container. The components in the container are arranged in absolute positions and sizes. It is easy to use, but lacks portability, because when you resize a container, the components do not reposition or resize. You should avoid using null layout for cross-platform projects.

Note

If you choose null layout, no layout manager will be displayed in the component tree.

6.4.7 *BoxLayout*

`BoxLayout` is a Swing layout manager that arranges components in a row or a column. The `JToolBar` component to be introduced in Chapter 7, "Menus, Toolbars, and Dialogs," uses `BoxLayout`. You can use `BoxLayout` in any container, but it is simpler to use the `Box` class, which is a container of `BoxLayout`. To create a `Box` container, use one of the following two static methods:

```
Box box1 = Box.createHorizontalBox();
Box box2 = Box.createVerticalBox();
```

The former creates a box that contains components horizontally, and the latter creates a box that contains components vertically.

You can add components to a box programmatically in the same way that you add them to the containers of `FlowLayout` or `GridLayout` using the `add` method, as follows:

```
box1.add(new JButton("A Button"));
```

You can drop components to a box in the same way that you drop components to a container. The components are laid left to right in a horizontal box, and top to bottom in a vertical box.

`BoxLayout` is similar to `GridLayout`, but `BoxLayout` has many unique features.

First, `BoxLayout` respects a component's preferred size, maximum size, and minimum size. If the total preferred size of all the components in the box is less than the box size, then the components are expanded up to their maximum size. If the total preferred size of all the components in the box is greater than the box size, then the components are shrunk down to their minimum size. If the components do not fit at their minimum width, some of them will not be shown. In the `GridLayout`, the container is divided into cells of equal size, and the components are fit in regardless of their preferred maximum or minimum size.

Second, unlike other layout managers, `BoxLayout` considers the component's `alignmentX` or `alignmentY` property. The `alignmentX` property is used to place the component in a vertical box layout, and the `alignmentY` property is used to place it in a horizontal box layout.

Third, `BoxLayout` does not have gaps between the components, but you can use fillers to separate components. A filler is an invisible component. There are three kinds of fillers: struts, rigid areas, and glues.

A *strut* simply adds some space between components. The static method `createHorizontalStrut()` in the `Box` class is used to create a horizontal strut, and the static method `createVerticalStrut()` to create a vertical strut. For example, the following code adds a vertical strut of 8 pixels between two buttons in a vertical box.

```
box2.add(new JButton("Button 1"));
box2.add(Box.createVerticalStrut(8));
box2.add(new JButton("Button 2"));
```

A *rigid area* is a two-dimensional space that can be created using the static method `createRigidArea(dimension)` in the `Box` class. For example, the following code adds a rigid area 10 pixels wide and 20 pixels high into a box.

```
box2.add(Box.createRigidArea(new Dimension(10, 20));
```

A *glue* separates components as much as possible. For example, by adding a glue between two components in a horizontal box, you place one component at the left end and the other at the right end. A glue can be created using the `Box.createGlue()` method.

6.4.8 AbsoluteLayout

Like the `Null` layout manager, `AbsoluteLayout` arranges components in absolute positions and sizes. `AbsoluteLayout` is the same as `Null` Layout, except that `AbsoluteLayout` uses a layout manager and `Null` Layout means that no layout manager is used at all.

An advantage of using the `AbsoluteLayout` manager instead of `Null` Layout is that you don't need to programmatically set the size of the container component in order to keep it from initially displaying at the minimum size.

`AbsoluteLayout` is not recommended for production applications. The fixed locations and sizes of components do not change when the environment changes. Therefore, significant distortions in appearance can occur when such an application is run on a different platform or when using a different look-and-feel. Nevertheless, `AbsoluteLayout` is very useful for prototyping UI design. You can use `AbsoluteLayout` to design complex UI with multiple, nested panels, then convert the design using portable layout managers. It is especially convenient to use `AbsoluteLayout` for prototyping designs involving `GridBagLayout`. This can speed up your design work. Forte intelligently converts the layout to `GridBagLayout`.

CAUTION

Save the source code before converting from one layout to the other, because sometimes the conversion distorts the UI design and makes it unusable.

TIP

When prototyping with `AbsoluteLayout`, use `AbsoluteLayout` for all the nested containers. When converting the design, start from the inner containers.

The following example demonstrates the use of a variety of Swing containers and layout managers to create projects in Forte.

Example 6.1 Choosing Colors

This example creates a project that selects a standard color from a combo box or selects any color by specifying an RGB value or an HSB value. A sample run of the project is shown in Figure 6.4.

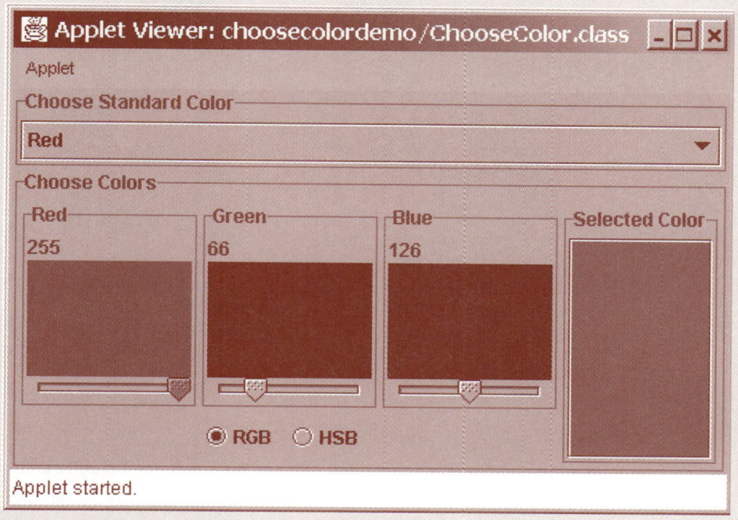

Figure 6.4 *You can choose a standard color from the combo box or choose any color by specifying either RGB or HSB values.*

The three color-selection panels titled Red, Green, and Blue in the Choose Color panel have similar functions. This makes it ideal to create a bean component for modeling these panels. Let the bean component be named `ColorPanel`. This component generates an `ActionEvent` to notify listeners whenever the color value changes in the panel. The UML diagram of this component is shown in Figure 6.5.

Here are the steps in creating `ColorPanel`.

1. Create a new package named choosecolordemo and create a new JavaBean named `ColorPanel` that extends `JPanel` using the Forte Swing JPanel form wizard.

2. Use the Bean Pattern wizard to create the properties `colorValue` (an `int` value) and `title` (a string for the title on the border of the panel) with accessor methods.

3. Use the Bean Pattern wizard to create the Action event. The Action event is needed to notify the listeners that a new color has been selected, as shown in Listing 6.1.

continued

Example 6.1 continued

```
ColorPanel
-----------------------------------------------
-colorType: String
-colorValue: int
-buttonType: String
-actionListeners: Vector
-jblColorValue: JLabel
-jslColor: Jslider
-jtfColor: JTextField
-----------------------------------------------
+getColorType(): String
+setColorType(newColorType: String): String
+getColorValue(): int
+getTitle(): String
+setTitle(newTitle: String): void
+addActionListener(1: ActionListener): void
+removeActionListener(l: ActionListener): void
+fireActionPerformed(e: ActionEvent): void
+jslColorStateChanged(evt: ChangeEvent):void
+switchButton(buttonType: String): void
```

Figure 6.5 *The ColorPanel class can be used to set a value for a single color (red, green, or blue).*

4. Set the `layout` of the panel to `BorderLayout`. Drop a `JLabel` to the North, a `JSlider` to the South, and a `JTextField` to the Center of the panel. Rename these components `jlblColorValue`, `jslColor`, and `jtfColor`. The UI layout of `ColorPanel` is shown in Figure 6.6.

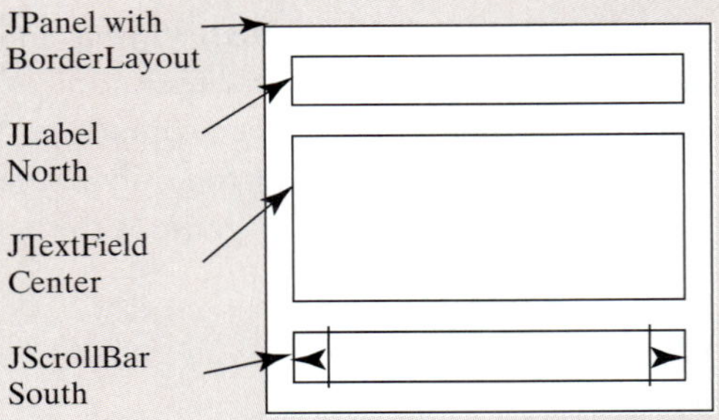

Figure 6.6 *The* `ColorPanel` *consists of a* `JSlider` *for selecting values, a* `JTextField` *for showing the color, and a* `JLabel` *for displaying the value.*

5. In the Events tab of `jslColor` in the component inspector, press Enter in the value field of `stateChanged` to generate the code for handling the adjustment value change of the slider. Fill in the code, as shown in Listing 6.1 (Lines 44–54).

6. Create a variable named `buttonType` to indicate whether RGB radio button or HSB radio button is selected. Code the `switchButton` method to

switch to either the RGB mode or the HSB mode, as shown in Listing 6.1 (Lines 61–71).

7. Install `ColorPanel` in the component palette for use in the `ChooseColor` class.

```
1   package choosecolordemo;
2
3   import java.awt.event.*;
4   import java.awt.*;
5   import java.util.*;
6   import javax.swing.border.*;
7
8   public class ColorPanel extends javax.swing.JPanel {
9     private String buttonType = "RGB";
10
11    /** Holds value of property colorType. */
12    private String colorType = "Red";
13
14    /** Holds value of property currentValue. */
15    private int colorValue = 0;
16
17    /** Utility field used by event firing mechanism. */
18    private javax.swing.event.EventListenerList listenerList =  null;
19
20    /** Creates new form ColorPanel */
21    public ColorPanel() {
22      initComponents();
23    }
24
25    private void initComponents() {
26      jlblColorValue = new javax.swing.JLabel();
27      jslColor = new javax.swing.JSlider();
28      jtfColor = new javax.swing.JTextArea();
29      setLayout(new java.awt.BorderLayout());
30      jlblColorValue.setText("jLabel1");
31      add(jlblColorValue, java.awt.BorderLayout.NORTH);
32      jslColor.addChangeListener(
33        new javax.swing.event.ChangeListener() {
34        public void stateChanged(javax.swing.event.ChangeEvent evt) {
35          jslColorStateChanged(evt);
36        }
37      });
38      add(jslColor, java.awt.BorderLayout.SOUTH);
39      add(jtfColor, java.awt.BorderLayout.CENTER);
40    }
41
42    private void jslColorStateChanged(
43      javax.swing.event.ChangeEvent evt) {
44      colorValue = jslColor.getValue();
45      jlblColorValue.setText(colorValue+"");
46
47      if (buttonType.equals("RGB")) {
48        if (colorType.equals("Red"))
49          jtfColor.setBackground(new Color(colorValue, 0, 0));
50        else if (colorType.equals("Green"))
51          jtfColor.setBackground(new Color(0, colorValue, 0));
52        else if (colorType.equals("Blue"))
```

Listing 6.1 *ColorPanel.java*

continued

Example 6.1 continued

```
        jtfColor.setBackground(new Color(0, 0, colorValue));
      jtfColor.repaint();
    }

    fireActionListenerActionPerformed(
      new ActionEvent(this, ActionEvent.ACTION_PERFORMED, null));
  }

  public void switchButton(String buttonType) {
    if (buttonType.equals("RGB"))
      jslColor.setMaximum(255);
    else if (buttonType.equals("HSB"))
      jslColor.setMaximum(100);
    jtfColor.setBackground(Color.white);
    jtfColor.repaint();
    jslColor.setValue(0);
    this.repaint();
    this.buttonType = buttonType;
  }

  public String getColorType() {
    return colorType;
  }

  public void setColorType(String colorType) {
    this.colorType = colorType;
  }

  public int getColorValue() {
    return colorValue;
  }

  public void setColorValue(int colorValue) {
    this.colorValue = colorValue;
  }

  public String getTitle() {
    return ((TitledBorder)this.getBorder()).getTitle();
  }

  public void setTitle(String title) {
    this.setBorder(new TitledBorder(title));
  }

  public synchronized void addActionListener(
    java.awt.event.ActionListener listener) {
    if (listenerList == null ) {
      listenerList = new javax.swing.event.EventListenerList();
    }
    listenerList.add(java.awt.event.ActionListener.class, listener);
  }

  public synchronized void removeActionListener(
    java.awt.event.ActionListener listener) {
    listenerList.remove(
      java.awt.event.ActionListener.class, listener);
  }

```

Listing 6.1 *continued*

```
    private void fireActionListenerActionPerformed(
      java.awt.event.ActionEvent event) {
      if (listenerList == null) return;
      Object[] listeners = listenerList.getListenerList();
      for (int i = listeners.length - 2; i >= 0; i -= 2) {
        if (listeners[i] == java.awt.event.ActionListener.class) {
          ((java.awt.event.ActionListener)listeners[i + 1]).
            actionPerformed(event);
        }
      }
    }

    // Variables declaration - do not modify
    private javax.swing.JLabel jlblColorValue;
    private javax.swing.JSlider jslColor;
    private javax.swing.JTextArea jtfColor;
    // End of variables declaration
  }
```

Listing 6.1 *continued*

NOTE

`title` is not declared as a data field in the class. But `title` is a JavaBeans property. Recall that a bean property is not necessarily a data field (see Section 2.5.2, "Properties and Data Fields" in Chapter 2, "Introduction to JavaBeans.")

Let us turn our attention to the main part of this example for creating the `ChooseColor` class.

1. Use the Forte Swing JApplet form wizard to create the `ChooseColor` class. Create the UI interface as shown in Figure 6.7.

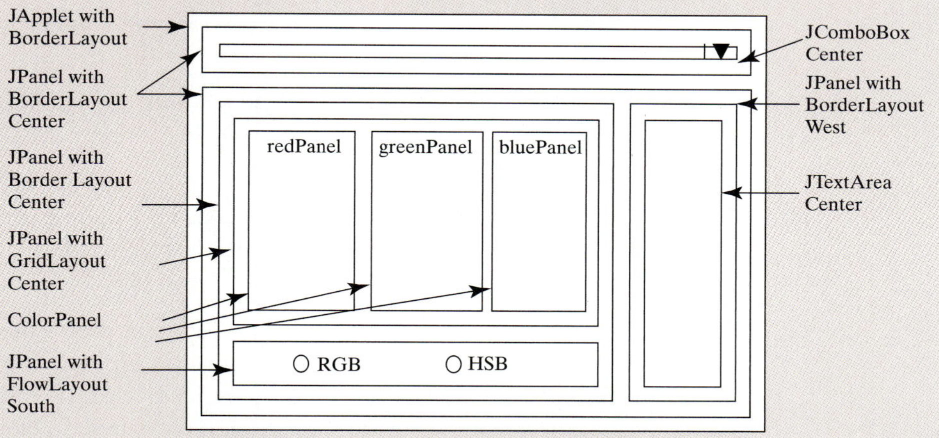

Figure 6.7 *The user interface employs nested panels to group the components in order to achieve the desired layout.*

continued

Example 6.1 continued

2. Drop a `JPanel` to the north of the applet and rename it `jpStandardColor`. Set the `layout` of `jpStandardColor` to `BorderLayout`; drop a `JComboBox` to the center of `jpStandardColor` and rename it `jcboStandardColor`. Drop a `JPanel` to the center of the applet and rename it `jpSelection`.

3. Set the `layout` of `jpSelection` to `BorderLayout`. Drop a `JPanel` to the east of `jpSelection` and a `JPanel` to the center of `jpSelection`, and rename them `jpSelectedColor` and `jpSelectColor`.

4. Set the `layout` of `jpSelectedColor` to `BorderLayout`, and the width (the first argument) of the `preferredSize` property to 100. Drop a `JTextArea` to the center of `jpSelectedColor` and rename it `jtaSelectedColor`.

5. Set the `layout` of `jpSelectColor` to `BorderLayout`. Drop a `JPanel` to the south of `jpSelectColor` and a `JPanel` to the center of `jpSelectColor`. Rename them `jpRadioButtons` and `JpColors`.

6. Set the `layout` of `jpColors` to `GridLayout` and drop a `ColorPanel` to `jpColors` three times to create `redPanel`, `greenPanel`, and `bluePanel`. Set the title properties of these three panels to "Red," "Green," and "Blue," respectively.

7. Drop a `JRadioButtons` into `jpRadioButtons` to create `jrbRGB`, and set its `text` to `RGB`. Drop a `JRadioButton` into `jpRadioButtons` to create `jrbHSB`, and set its text to `HSB`. Drop a `ButtonGroup` and name it `btg`. Set the `buttonGroup` property of `jrbRGB` and `jrbHSB` to `btg`. Set the `selected` property of `jrbRGB` to True.

8. Set a border with the title "Choose Standard Color" in `jpStandardColor`, a border with the title "Choose Colors" in `jpSelection`, and a border with the title "Selected Color" in `jpSelectedColor`.

9. Add items "Red," "Green," "Blue," and "Yellow" into the combo box `jcboStandardColor` in the constructor, as shown in Listing 6.2 (Lines 11–14).

10. Double-click `jcboStandardColor` to generate the code for handling combo item selection. Implement the handler to display the selected color in `jtaSelectedColor`, as shown in Listing 6.2 (Lines 106–114).

11. In the Events tab of `redPanel` in the component inspector, press Enter in the value field of `actionPerformed` to generate the code for handling the color value change action. This action is generated when the color value changes. Implement the handler to display the selected color in `jtaSelectedColor`, as shown in Listing 6.2 (Lines 127–130). Similarly, create the code for handling actions from `greenPanel` and `bluePanel`.

12. Double-click on `jrbRGB` to generate the code for handling the radio button switch. Implement the handler to switch the RGB mode for selecting

colors, as shown in Listing 6.2 (Lines 137–140). Similarly, generate and implement the code for handling the HSB radio button.

```
1     package choosecolordemo;
2
3     import java.awt.*;
4
5     public class ChooseColor extends javax.swing.JApplet {
6       /** Creates new form ChooseColor */
7       public ChooseColor() {
8         initComponents();
9
10        // Intialize combo box
11        jcboStandardColor.addItem("Red");
12        jcboStandardColor.addItem("Green");
13        jcboStandardColor.addItem("Blue");
14        jcboStandardColor.addItem("Yellow");
15
16        // Set RGB radio button by default
17        switchButton("RGB");
18      }
19
20      private void initComponents() {
21        btg = new javax.swing.ButtonGroup();
22        jpStandardColor = new javax.swing.JPanel();
23        jcboStandardColor = new javax.swing.JComboBox();
24        jpSelection = new javax.swing.JPanel();
25        jpSelectedColor = new javax.swing.JPanel();
26        jtaSelectedColor = new javax.swing.JTextField();
27        jpSelectColor = new javax.swing.JPanel();
28        jpRadioButtons = new javax.swing.JPanel();
29        jrbRGB = new javax.swing.JRadioButton();
30        jrbHSB = new javax.swing.JRadioButton();
31        jpColors = new javax.swing.JPanel();
32        redPanel = new choosecolordemo.ColorPanel();
33        greenPanel = new choosecolordemo.ColorPanel();
34        bluePanel = new choosecolordemo.ColorPanel();
35        jpStandardColor.setLayout(new java.awt.BorderLayout());
36        jpStandardColor.setBorder(new javax.swing.border.TitledBorder
37          ("Choose Standard Color"));
38        jcboStandardColor.addActionListener(
39          new java.awt.event.ActionListener() {
40          public void actionPerformed(java.awt.event.ActionEvent evt) {
41            jcboStandardColorActionPerformed(evt);
42          }
43        });
44        jpStandardColor.add(jcboStandardColor,
45          java.awt.BorderLayout.CENTER);
46        getContentPane().add(jpStandardColor,
47          java.awt.BorderLayout.NORTH);
48        jpSelection.setLayout(new java.awt.BorderLayout());
49        jpSelection.setBorder(
50          new javax.swing.border.TitledBorder("Choose Colors"));
51        jpSelectedColor.setLayout(new java.awt.BorderLayout());
52        jpSelectedColor.setBorder(
53          new javax.swing.border.TitledBorder("Selected Color"));
54        jpSelectedColor.setPreferredSize(
55          new java.awt.Dimension(100, 0));
56        jpSelectedColor.add(jtaSelectedColor,
57          java.awt.BorderLayout.CENTER);
```

Listing 6.2 *ChooseColor.java*

continued

Example 6.1 continued

```
      jpSelection.add(jpSelectedColor, java.awt.BorderLayout.EAST);
      jpSelectColor.setLayout(new java.awt.BorderLayout());
      jrbRGB.setSelected(true);
      jrbRGB.setText("RGB");
      btg.add(jrbRGB);
      jrbRGB.addActionListener(new java.awt.event.ActionListener() {
        public void actionPerformed(java.awt.event.ActionEvent evt) {
          jrbRGBActionPerformed(evt);
        }
      });
      jpRadioButtons.add(jrbRGB);
      jrbHSB.setText("HSB");
      btg.add(jrbHSB);
      jrbHSB.addActionListener(new java.awt.event.ActionListener() {
        public void actionPerformed(java.awt.event.ActionEvent evt) {
          jrbHSBActionPerformed(evt);
        }
      });
      jpRadioButtons.add(jrbHSB);
      jpSelectColor.add(jpRadioButtons, java.awt.BorderLayout.SOUTH);
      jpColors.setLayout(new java.awt.GridLayout(1, 3));
      redPanel.addActionListener(new java.awt.event.ActionListener() {
        public void actionPerformed(java.awt.event.ActionEvent evt) {
          redPanelActionPerformed(evt);
        }
      });
      jpColors.add(redPanel);
      greenPanel.addActionListener(
        new java.awt.event.ActionListener() {
        public void actionPerformed(java.awt.event.ActionEvent evt) {
          greenPanelActionPerformed(evt);
        }
      });
      jpColors.add(greenPanel);
      bluePanel.addActionListener(
        new java.awt.event.ActionListener() {
        public void actionPerformed(java.awt.event.ActionEvent evt) {
          bluePanelActionPerformed(evt);
        }
      });
      jpColors.add(bluePanel);
      jpSelectColor.add(jpColors, java.awt.BorderLayout.CENTER);
      jpSelection.add(jpSelectColor, java.awt.BorderLayout.CENTER);
      getContentPane().add(jpSelection, java.awt.BorderLayout.CENTER);
    }

    private void jcboStandardColorActionPerformed(
      java.awt.event.ActionEvent evt) {
      String s = (String)jcboStandardColor.getSelectedItem();
      if (s.equals("Red"))
        jtaSelectedColor.setBackground(Color.red);
      else if (s.equals("Green"))
        jtaSelectedColor.setBackground(Color.green);
      else if (s.equals("Blue"))
        jtaSelectedColor.setBackground(Color.blue);
      else if (s.equals("Yellow"))
        jtaSelectedColor.setBackground(Color.yellow);
    }

```

Listing 6.2 *continued*

```
  private void bluePanelActionPerformed(
    java.awt.event.ActionEvent evt) {
    showSelectedColor();
  }

  private void greenPanelActionPerformed(
    java.awt.event.ActionEvent evt) {
    showSelectedColor();
  }

  private void redPanelActionPerformed(
    java.awt.event.ActionEvent evt) {
    showSelectedColor();
  }

  private void jrbHSBActionPerformed(
    java.awt.event.ActionEvent evt) {
    switchButton("HSB");
  }

  private void jrbRGBActionPerformed(
    java.awt.event.ActionEvent evt) {
    switchButton("RGB");
  }

  /** Switch to RGB or HSB for selecting colors */
  private void switchButton(String radioButtonName) {
    if (radioButtonName.equals("RGB")) {
      redPanel.setTitle("Red");
      redPanel.setToolTipText("Specify red component of the color");
      greenPanel.setTitle("Green");
      greenPanel.setToolTipText(
        "Specify green component of the color");
      bluePanel.setTitle("Blue");
      bluePanel.setToolTipText(
        "Specify blue component of the color");
    }
    else {
      redPanel.setTitle("Hue");
      redPanel.setToolTipText("Specify hue of the color");
      greenPanel.setTitle("Saturation");
      greenPanel.setToolTipText("Specify saturation of the color");
      bluePanel.setTitle("Brightness");
      bluePanel.setToolTipText("Specify brightness of the color");
    }

    redPanel.switchButton(radioButtonName);
    greenPanel.switchButton(radioButtonName);
    bluePanel.switchButton(radioButtonName);
  }

  /** Get selected colors and display it in the text area */
  private void showSelectedColor() {
    if (jrbRGB.isSelected()) {
      Color c = new Color(redPanel.getColorValue(),
        greenPanel.getColorValue(),
      bluePanel.getColorValue());
      jtaSelectedColor.setBackground(c);
    }
```

Listing 6.2 *continued*

continued

Example 6.1 continued

```
          else {
            Color c = Color.getHSBColor(redPanel.getColorValue(),
              greenPanel.getColorValue(),
            bluePanel.getColorValue());
            jtaSelectedColor.setBackground(c);
          }
        }

        // Variables declaration - do not modify
        private javax.swing.ButtonGroup btg;
        private javax.swing.JPanel jpStandardColor;
        private javax.swing.JComboBox jcboStandardColor;
        private javax.swing.JPanel jpSelection;
        private javax.swing.JPanel jpSelectedColor;
        private javax.swing.JTextField jtaSelectedColor;
        private javax.swing.JPanel jpSelectColor;
        private javax.swing.JPanel jpRadioButtons;
        private javax.swing.JRadioButton jrbRGB;
        private javax.swing.JRadioButton jrbHSB;
        private javax.swing.JPanel jpColors;
        private choosecolordemo.ColorPanel redPanel;
        private choosecolordemo.ColorPanel greenPanel;
        private choosecolordemo.ColorPanel bluePanel;
        // End of variables declaration
      }
```

Listing 6.2 *continued*

Example Review

You can choose a color either by using the slider to specify the red, green, and blue components of the color or by selecting a standard color from the combo box. The selected color is displayed as the background of the text area. This program does not synchronize the color selected in the combo box with the color displayed in the `jpColors` panel. You can fix the problem by adding a set method for the `colorValue` property in the `ColorPanel` class and setting the red, green, and blue components in the `redPanel`, `greenPanel`, and `bluePanel` to match the selected color in the combo box. See Exercise 6.4 for more details.

This is a quite sophisticated project with pages of source code, but the amount of the code you hand-wrote is very small. Most of the code was generated automatically by Forte. Once again, this demonstrates that you can develop powerful programs in Java using Forte with minimal coding.

Tip

You can nest panels within other panels to gain more control over the placement of components. Each panel may use a different layout manager to achieve the desired look.

6.5 How Does a Layout Manager Lay Out Components?

A container's `setLayout` method specifies a layout manager for the container. The layout manager is responsible for laying out the components and displaying them in a desired location with an appropriate size. Many introductory Java texts state that once a layout manager is selected for a container, it works dutifully behind the scenes to place the components in the right place and automatically display them in the right size. This statement is true, but it does not explain how a layout manager works and interacts with the components. This section will help you understand the nuts and bolts of layout managers so that you can create your own custom layout managers in the next section, "Creating Custom Layout Managers."

Every layout manager must directly or indirectly implement the `LayoutManager` interface. For instance, `FlowLayout` directly implements `LayoutManager`, and `BorderLayout` implements `LayoutManager2`, which implements `LayoutManager`. The `LayoutManager` interface provides the following methods for laying out components in a container:

- `public void addLayoutComponent(String name, Component comp)`

  Adds the specified component with the specified name to the container.

- `public void layoutContainer(Container parent)`

  Lays out the components in the specified container. In this method, you should provide concrete instructions that specify where the components are to be placed.

- `public Dimension minimumLayoutSize(Container parent)`

  Calculates the minimum size dimensions for the specified panel, given the components in the specified parent container.

- `public Dimension preferredLayoutSize(Container parent)`

  Calculates the preferred size dimensions for the specified panel, given the components in the specified parent container.

- `public void removeLayoutComponent(Component comp)`

  Removes the specified component from the layout.

These methods in `LayoutManager` are invoked by the methods in the `java.awt.Container` class through the layout manager in the container. `Container` contains a property named `layout` (an instance of `LayoutManager`) and the methods for adding and removing components from the container. There are five overloading `add` methods defined in `Container` for adding components with various options. The `remove` method removes a component from the container. The `add` method invokes `addImpl`, which then invokes the `addLayoutComponent` method defined in the `LayoutManager` interface. The `layoutContainer` method in the `LayoutManager` interface is indirectly invoked by `validate` through several calls. The `remove` method invokes `removeLayoutComponent` in `LayoutManager`. The `validate` method is invoked to refresh the container after the components it contains have been added to or modified. The relationship of `Container` and `LayoutManager` is shown in Figure 6.8.

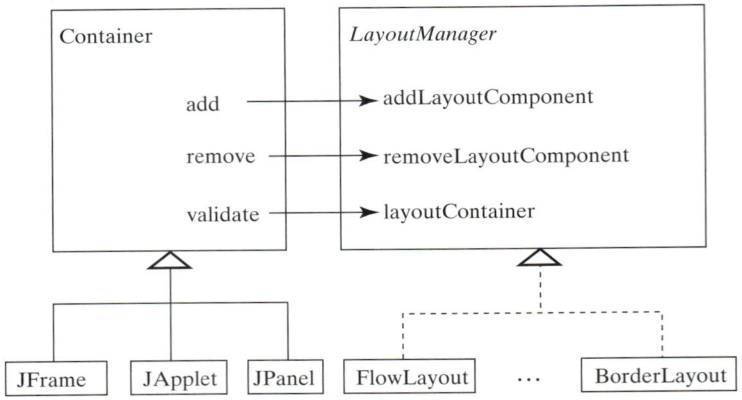

Figure 6.8 *The* `add`, `remove`, *and* `validate` *methods in* `Container` *invoke the methods defined in the* `LayoutManager` *interface.*

6.6 Creating Custom Layout Managers

In addition to the layout managers provided in Java, you can create your own layout managers. In the current version of Forte, you cannot use custom layout managers in the Form Editor, but this feature will be supported in the future release.

A custom layout manager can be created by simply implementing the `LayoutManager` interface. In the following example, you will learn how to create a custom layout manager.

Example 6.2 Creating a Custom Layout Manager

This example creates a layout manager named `DiagonalLayout` that places the components in a diagonal. To test `DiagonalLayout`, the example creates an applet with radio buttons named "FlowLayout," "GridLayout," and "DiagonalLayout," as shown in Figure 6.9. You can dynamically select one of these three layouts in the panel.

The `DiagonalLayout` class is similar to `FlowLayout`. `DiagonalLayout` arranges components along a diagonal using each component's natural `preferredSize`. It contains three constraints: `gap`, `lastFill`, and `majorDiagonal`.

- **`gap`** specifies the gap between the components.
- **`lastFill`** is a `boolean` value that specifies whether the last component in the container is stretched to fill the rest of the space.
- **`majorDiagonal`** is a `boolean` value that specifies whether components are placed along the major diagonal or the subdiagonal.

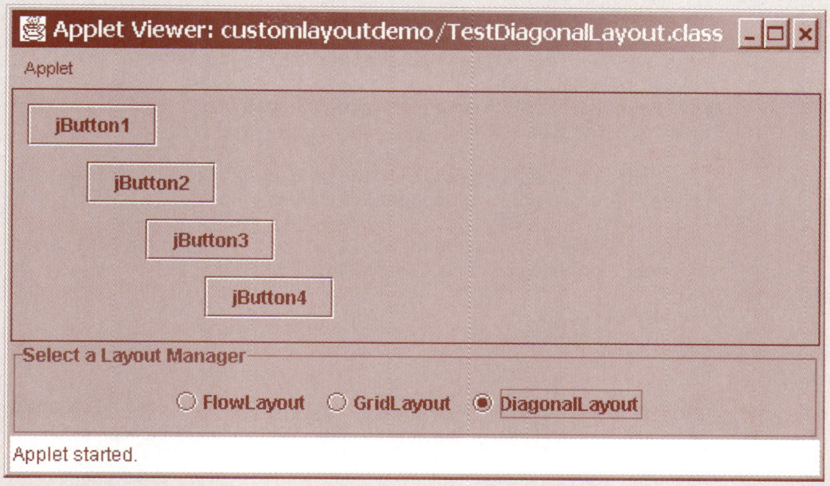

Figure 6.9 *The* `DiagonalLayout` *manager places the components in a diagonal in the container.*

Here are the steps to complete the project.

1. Create a new package named customlayoutdemo and a JavaBeans component named `DiagonalLayout` using the Class wizard. The source code for `DiagonalLayout` is shown in Listing 6.3.
2. Create an applet named `TestDiagonalLayout` using the Forte Swing JApplet form wizard. Drop a `JPanel` to the south of the applet to create `jPanel1`, and drop a `JPanel` to the center of the applet to create `jPanel2`. Set the titled border for `jPanel1` with title "Select a Layout Manager." Set the line border for `jPanel2`.
3. Add four buttons into `jPanel2`. Add three radio buttons to `jPanel1` and rename them `jrbFlowLayout`, `jrbGridLayout`, and `jrbDiagonalLayout`. Set their `text` property to FlowLayout, GridLayout, and DiagnoalLayout. Set the `selected` property of `jrbDiagonalLayout` to True. Drop a `ButtonGroup` into the form to create `buttonGroup1`, and set the `buttonGroup` property of the three radio buttons to `buttonGroup1`.
4. Write the code to declare and create an instance of `FlowLayout` named `flowLayout`, an instance of `GridLayout` named `gridLayout` with two rows and two columns, and an instance of `DiagonalLayout` named `diagonalLayout`.
5. Generate the action event handlers for the three radio buttons and implement them, as shown in Listing 6.4 (Lines 73–89).

```
package customlayoutdemo;

import java.awt.*;

```

Listing 6.3 *DiagonalLayout.java*

continued

Example 6.2 continued

```
public class DiagonalLayout implements LayoutManager,
  java.io.Serializable {
  /** Vertical gap between the components */
  private int gap = 10;

  /** True if components are placed along the major diagonal */
  private boolean majorDiagonal = true;

  /*True if the last component is stretched to fill the space */
  private boolean lastFill = false;

  /** Constructor */
  public DiagonalLayout() {
  }

  public void addLayoutComponent(String name, Component comp) {
    //TODO: implement this java.awt.LayoutManager method;
  }

  public void removeLayoutComponent(Component comp) {
    //TODO: implement this java.awt.LayoutManager method;
  }

  public Dimension preferredLayoutSize(Container parent) {
    //TODO: implement this java.awt.LayoutManager method;
    return minimumLayoutSize(parent);
  }

  public Dimension minimumLayoutSize(Container parent) {
    //TODO: implement this java.awt.LayoutManager method;
    return new Dimension(0, 0);
  }

  public void layoutContainer(Container parent) {
    //TODO: implement this java.awt.LayoutManager method;
    int numberOfComponents = parent.getComponentCount();

    Insets insets = parent.getInsets();
    int w = parent.getSize().width - insets.left - insets.right;
    int h = parent.getSize().height - insets.bottom - insets.top;

    if (majorDiagonal) {
      int x = 10, y = 10;

      for (int j = 0; j < numberOfComponents; j++) {
        Component c = parent.getComponent(j);
        Dimension d = c.getPreferredSize();

        if (c.isVisible())
          if (lastFill && (j == numberOfComponents - 1))
            c.setBounds(x, y, w - x, h - y);
          else
            c.setBounds(x, y, d.width, d.height);
        x += d.height + gap;
        y += d.height + gap;
      }
    }
    else { // It is subdiagonal
      int x = w - 10, y = 10;

```

Listing 6.3 *continued*

```
      for (int j = 0; j < numberOfComponents; j++) {
        Component c = parent.getComponent(j);
        Dimension d = c.getPreferredSize();

        if (c.isVisible())
          if (lastFill & (j == numberOfComponents - 1))
            c.setBounds(0, y, x, h - y);
          else
            c.setBounds(x  d.width, y, d.width, d.height);

        x -= (d.height + gap);
        y += d.height + gap;
      }
    }
  }

  public int getGap() {
    return gap;
  }

  public void setGap(int gap) {
    this.gap = gap;
  }

  public void setMajorDiagonal(boolean newMajorDiagonal) {
    majorDiagonal = newMajorDiagonal;
  }

  public boolean isMajorDiagonal() {
    return majorDiagonal;
  }

  public void setLastFill(boolean newLastFill) {
    lastFill = newLastFill;
  }

  public boolean isLastFill() {
    return lastFill;
  }
}
```

Listing 6.3 *continued*

```
package customlayoutdemo;

import java.awt.*;

public class TestDiagonalLayout extends javax.swing.JApplet {
  private FlowLayout flowLayout = new FlowLayout();
  private GridLayout gridLayout = new GridLayout(2, 2);
  private DiagonalLayout diagonalLayout = new DiagonalLayout();

  /** Creates new form TestDiagonalLayout */
  public TestDiagonalLayout() {
    initComponents();

    // Set default layout in jPanel2
    jPanel2.setLayout(diagonalLayout);
  }

```

Listing 6.4 *TestDiagonalLayout.java*

continued

Example 6.2 continued

```
    private void initComponents() {
      buttonGroup1 = new javax.swing.ButtonGroup();
      jPanel1 = new javax.swing.JPanel();
      jrbFlowLayout = new javax.swing.JRadioButton();
      jrbGridLayout = new javax.swing.JRadioButton();
      jrbDiagonalLayout = new javax.swing.JRadioButton();
      jPanel2 = new javax.swing.JPanel();
      jButton1 = new javax.swing.JButton();
      jButton2 = new javax.swing.JButton();
      jButton3 = new javax.swing.JButton();
      jButton4 = new javax.swing.JButton();
      jPanel1.setBorder(new javax.swing.border.TitledBorder(
        "Select a Layout Manager"));
      jrbFlowLayout.setText("FlowLayout");
      buttonGroup1.add(jrbFlowLayout);
      jrbFlowLayout.addActionListener(
        new java.awt.event.ActionListener() {
        public void actionPerformed(java.awt.event.ActionEvent evt) {
          jrbFlowLayoutActionPerformed(evt);
        }
      });
      jPanel1.add(jrbFlowLayout);
      jrbGridLayout.setText("GridLayout");
      buttonGroup1.add(jrbGridLayout);
      jrbGridLayout.addActionListener(
        new java.awt.event.ActionListener() {
        public void actionPerformed(java.awt.event.ActionEvent evt) {
          jrbGridLayoutActionPerformed(evt);
        }
      });
      jPanel1.add(jrbGridLayout);
      jrbDiagonalLayout.setSelected(true);
      jrbDiagonalLayout.setText("DiagonalLayout");
      buttonGroup1.add(jrbDiagonalLayout);
      jrbDiagonalLayout.addActionListener(
        new java.awt.event.ActionListener() {
        public void actionPerformed(java.awt.event.ActionEvent evt) {
          jrbDiagonalLayoutActionPerformed(evt);
        }
      });
      jPanel1.add(jrbDiagonalLayout);
      getContentPane().add(jPanel1, java.awt.BorderLayout.SOUTH);
      jPanel2.setBorder(new javax.swing.border.LineBorder(
        java.awt.Color.black));
      jButton1.setText("jButton1");
      jPanel2.add(jButton1);
      jButton2.setText("jButton2");
      jPanel2.add(jButton2);
      jButton3.setText("jButton3");
      jPanel2.add(jButton3);
      jButton4.setText("jButton4");
      jPanel2.add(jButton4);
      getContentPane().add(jPanel2, java.awt.BorderLayout.CENTER);
    }

    private void jrbDiagonalLayoutActionPerformed(
      java.awt.event.ActionEvent evt) {
      jPanel2.setLayout(diagonalLayout);
      jPanel2.validate();
    }

```

Listing 6.4 *continued*

```
79          private void jrbGridLayoutActionPerformed(
80            java.awt.event.ActionEvent evt) {
81            jPanel2.setLayout(gridLayout);
82            jPanel2.validate();
83          }
84
85          private void jrbFlowLayoutActionPerformed(
86            java.awt.event.ActionEvent evt) {
87            jPanel2.setLayout(flowLayout);
88            jPanel2.validate();
89          }
90
91          // Variables declaration - do not modify
92          private javax.swing.ButtonGroup buttonGroup1;
93          private javax.swing.JPanel jPanel1;
94          private javax.swing.JRadioButton jrbFlowLayout;
95          private javax.swing.JRadioButton jrbGridLayout;
96          private javax.swing.JRadioButton jrbDiagonalLayout;
97          private javax.swing.JPanel jPanel2;
98          private javax.swing.JButton jButton1;
99          private javax.swing.JButton jButton2;
100         private javax.swing.JButton jButton3;
101         private javax.swing.JButton jButton4;
102         // End of variables declaration
103     }
```

Listing 6.4 *continued*

Example Review

The standard layout managers in the Java API and the Forte custom `AbsoluteLayout` manager are incorporated so that they can be set automatically in the Form Editor. The `DiagonalLayout` manager can be used programmatically, just like other layout manger in Java, but it cannot be installed in Forte in the current edition.

The `DiagonalLayout` manager is a JavaBeans component that implements the `LayoutManger` and `Serializable` interfaces. The `Insets` class describes the size of the borders of a container. It contains the variables `left`, `right`, `bottom`, and `top`, which correspond to the measurements for the *left border, right border, top border,* and *bottom border.*

The `Dimension` class used in `DiagonalLayout` encapsulates the width and height of a component in a single object. The class is associated with certain properties of components. Several methods defined by the `Component` class and the `LayoutManager` interface return a `Dimension` object.

The `TestDiagonalLayout` class enables you to dynamically set the layout in `jPanel2`. When you select a new layout, the layout manager is set in `jPanel2`, and the validate method is invoked (Lines 76, 82, 88), which in turn invokes the `layoutContainer` method in the `LayoutManager` interface to display the components in the container.

6.7 JTabbedPane

`JTabbedPane` is a useful Swing container that provides a set of mutually exclusive tabs for accessing multiple components. Usually you place the panels inside a `JTabbedPane` and associate a tab with each panel. `JTabbedPane` is easy to use, since the selection of the panel is handled automatically by clicking the corresponding tab. You can switch between a group of panels by clicking on a tab with a given title and/or icon.

`JTabbedPane` has the following useful properties:

- **`selectedComponent`** is the component that is currently selected.
- **`selectedIndex`** is the index of the currently selected tab.
- **`tabPlacement`** is the location of the tabs. Valid values are `JTabbedPane.TOP`, `JTabbedPane.LEFT`, `JTabbedPane.BOTTOM`, and `JTabbedPane.RIGHT`.

The following methods in the `JTabbedPane` class are often useful:

- `public void setIconAt(int index, Icon icon)`

  Sets the icon at the tab with the specified index.

- `public int getTabCount()`

  Returns the number of tabs in the tabbed pane.

- `public void setTitleAt(int index, Icon icon)`

  Sets the title at the tab with the specified index.

Example 6.3 Using JTabbedPane

This example uses a tabbed pane with four tabs to display four types of figures: Square, Rectangle, Circle, and Oval. You can select a figure to display by clicking the corresponding tab, as shown in Figure 6.10.

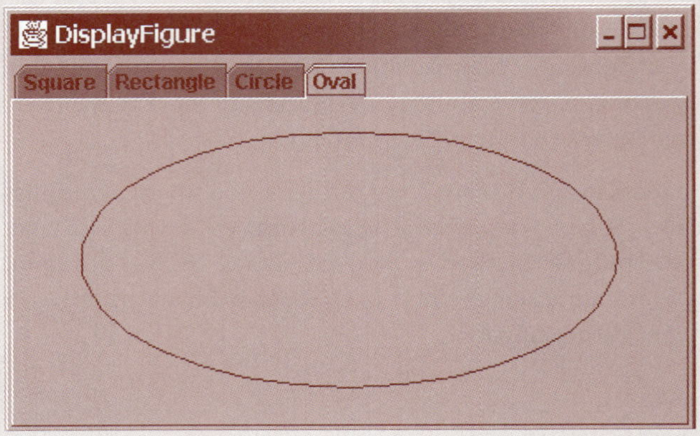

Figure 6.10 *The tabbed pane lets you automatically select figure panels with tabs.*

The example first creates the `FigurePanel` to display a figure in the panel. The class contains the property `figureType` of the `int` type to specify a figure type. Here are the steps to complete the project.

1. Create a new package named displayfiguredemo, and create a JavaBean component named `FigurePanel` that extends `JPanel` using the Class wizard. The source code for `FigurePanel` is shown in Listing 6.5. Install it into the component palette.
2. Create a new Java applet named `DisplayFigure` using the Forte Swing JApplet form wizard. Drop a `JTabbedPane` from the Swing tab in the component palette and rename it `jtpFigures`.
3. Drop a `FigurePanel` four times to `jtpFigures` and rename them `squarePanel`, `rectanglePanel`, `circlePanel`, and `ovalPanel`. Set the `figureType` property to 1 for `squarePanel`, 2 for `rectanglePanel`, 3 for `circlePanel`, and 4 for `ovalPanel`.
4. In the Layout tab of `squarePanel` in the component inspector, set Tab Title to Square. Similarly, set the Tab Title for `rectanglePanel`, `circlePanel`, and `ovalPanel` to Rectangle, Circle, and Oval. The source code for `DisplayFigure` is shown in Listing 6.6.

```
package displayfiguredemo;

import java.awt.*;
import javax.swing.JPanel;

public class FigurePanel extends JPanel {
  private int figureType = 1;

  // Define constants
  public static final int SQUARE = 1;
  public static final int RECTANGLE = 2;
  public static final int CIRCLE = 3;
  public static final int OVAL = 4;

  /** Constructor */
  public FigurePanel() {
  }

  /** Draw a figure on the panel */
  public void paintComponent(Graphics g) {
    super.paintComponent(g);

    // Get the appropriate size for the figure
    int width = getSize().width;
    int height = getSize().height;
    int side = (int)(0.80*Math.min(width, height));

    switch (figureType) {
      case SQUARE: // Display a square
        g.drawRect((width-side)/2, (height-side)/2, side, side);
        break;
      case RECTANGLE: // Display a rectangle
```

Listing 6.5 *FigurePanel.java*

continued

Example 6.3 continued

```
          g.drawRect((int)(0.1*width), (int)(0.1*height),
            (int)(0.8*width), (int)(0.8*height));
          break;
        case CIRCLE: // Display a circle
          g.drawOval((width-side)/2, (height-side)/2, side, side);
          break;
        case OVAL: // Display an oval
          g.drawOval((int)(0.1*width), (int)(0.1*height),
            (int)(0.8*width), (int)(0.8*height));
          break;
      }
    }

    /** Setter figureType */
    public void setFigureType(int newFigureType) {
      figureType = newFigureType;
    }

    /** Return figureType */
    public int getFigureType() {
      return figureType;
    }

    /** Specify preferred size */
    public Dimension getPreferredSize() {
      return new Dimension(80, 80);
    }
  }
```

Listing 6.5 *continued*

```
  package displayfiguredemo;

  import java.awt.*;
  import java.awt.event.*;
  import java.applet.*;
  import javax.swing.*;

  public class DisplayFigure extends JApplet {
    boolean isStandalone = false;
    JTabbedPane jtpFigures = new JTabbedPane();
    FigurePanel squarePanel = new FigurePanel();
    FigurePanel rectanglePanel = new FigurePanel();
    FigurePanel circlePanel = new FigurePanel();
    FigurePanel ovalPanel = new FigurePanel();

    /** Initialize the applet */
    public void init() {
      try {
        jbInit();
      }
      catch(Exception e) {
        e.printStackTrace();
      }
    }

    /** Component initialization */
    private void jbInit() throws Exception {
      this.setSize(new Dimension(400,300));
```

Listing 6.6 *DisplayFigure.java*

```
            squarePanel.setFigureType(FigurePanel.SQUARE);
            rectanglePanel.setFigureType(FigurePanel.RECTANGLE);
            circlePanel.setFigureType(FigurePanel.CIRCLE);
            ovalPanel.setFigureType(FigurePanel.OVAL);
            this.getContentPane().add(jtpFigures, BorderLayout.CENTER);
            jtpFigures.add(squarePanel, "Square");
            jtpFigures.add(rectanglePanel, "Rectangle");
            jtpFigures.add(circlePanel, "Circle");
            jtpFigures.add(ovalPanel, "Oval");
        }
    }
```

Listing 6.6 *continued*

Example Review

The program creates a tabbed pane to hold four panels, each of which displays a figure. A panel is associated with a tab. Tabs are titled Square, Rectangle, Circle, and Oval, which can be set in the Tab Title field of the Layout tab in the component inspector for the component inside the tabbed pane.

By default, the tabs are placed at the top of the tabbed pane. You can select a different placement using the `tabPlacement` property.

6.8 JSplitPane

`JSplitPane` is a convenient Swing container that contains two components with a separate bar known as a *divider*. The bar can divide the container horizontally or vertically, and can be dragged to change the amount of space occupied by each component.

`JSplitPane` has the following useful properties:

- **`bottomComponent`** is the component to the left or below the divider.
- **`continousLayout`** is a `boolean` value indicating whether the components in the split pane are continuously resized and repainted as the bar moves. By default, it is `false`.
- **`dividerLocation`** is an `int` value that specifies the location of the divider from the top or left edge of the split pane in pixels.
- **`dividerSize`** is the size of the divider in pixels.
- **`lastDividerLocation`** is the previous location of the divider.
- **`leftComponent`** is the component to the left of or above the divider.
- **`oneTouchExpandable`** is a `boolean` property with the default value `false`. If the property is true, the divider has an expanding and contracting look, so that it can expand and contract with one touch.
- **`orientation`** specifies whether the container is divided horizontally or vertically. The possible values are `JSplitPane.HORIZONTAL_SPILT` and `JSplitPane.VERTICAL_SPLIT`. The default value is `JSplitPane.HORIZONTAL_SPILT`, which divides the container into a left part and a right part.

- **`rightComponent`** is the same as `bottomComponent`.
- **`topComponent`** is the same as `leftComponent`.

You can also set the divider location as a percentage of `JSplitPane`'s size using the following method:

```
public void setDividerLocation(double proportionalLocation)
```

where `proportionalLocation` is a value between 0.0 and 1.0.

Example 6.4 Using JSplitPane

This example demonstrates the use of split panes. The user is able to select a layout manager dynamically and use it to show buttons in a panel. The usage of the layout manager is displayed in an instance of `JEditorPane` at the same time. A sample run of the program is shown in Figure 6.11.

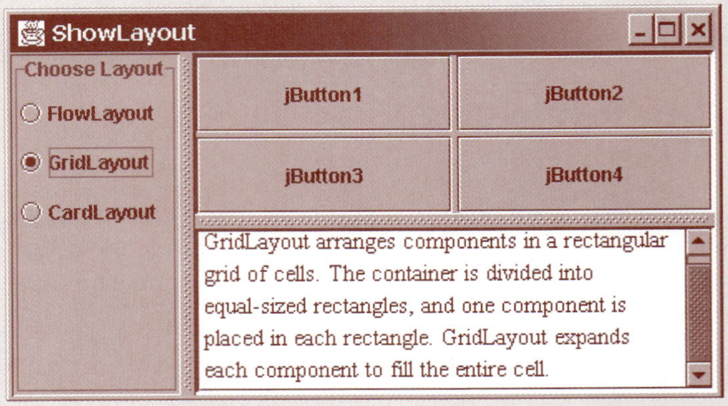

Figure 6.11 *The split pane lets you adjust the component size in the split panes.*

Here are the steps to complete the project:

1. Create a new package named splitpanedemo and a Java applet named ShowLayout using the Forte Swing JApplet form wizard.

2. Drop a `JSplitPane` from the Swing (Other) tab in the component palette to create `jSplitPane1`. Drop a `JPanel` to the left part of `jSplitPane1` to create `jpChooseLayout`, and drop a `JSplitPane` to the right part of `jSplitPane1` to create `jSplitPane2`.

3. Set the `orientation` of `jSplitPane2` to `VERTICAL_SPLIT`. Drop a `JPanel` to the top part of `jSplitPane2` to create `jpComponents`, and drop a `JScrollPane` to the bottom part of `jSplitPane2` to create `jScrollPane1`.

4. Drop a `JButton` four times to `jpComponents` to create `jButton1`, `jButton2`, `jButton3`, and `jButton4`.

5. Set the layout of `jpChooseLayout` to `GridLayout` with three rows. Drop a `JRadionButton` three times to `jpChooseLayout` to create `jrbFlowLayout`, `jrbGridLayout`, and `jrbCardLayout`, and set the `text` of radio buttons to `FlowLayout`, `GridLayout`, and `CardLayout`. Drop a `ButtonGroup` to create `btg`. Set the `buttonGroup` property of these three radio buttons to `btg`.
6. Drop a `JEditorPane` from the Swing (Other) tab to `jScrollPane1` to create `jEditorPane1`. Set the `editable` property of `jEditorPane1` to false.
7. Generate handlers for three radio buttons, and implement the handlers, as shown in Listing 6.7 (Lines 93–112). Set the `selected` property to True for `jrbGridLayout` to make the radio button for `GridLayout` as default (Line 25).

```
1   package splitpanedemo;
2
3   import java.awt.*;
4   import java.net.*;
5
6   public class ShowLayout extends javax.swing.JApplet {
7     // Create layout managers
8     FlowLayout flowLayout = new FlowLayout();
9     GridLayout gridLayout = new GridLayout(2, 2, 3, 3);
10    CardLayout cardLayout = new CardLayout();
11
12    // Get the url for HTML files
13    URL urlFlowLayoutHTML =
14      this.getClass().getResource("FlowLayout.html");
15    URL urlGridLayoutHTML =
16      this.getClass().getResource("GridLayout.html");
17    URL urlCardLayoutHTML =
18      this.getClass().getResource("CardLayout.html");
19
20    /** Creates new form ShowLayout */
21    public ShowLayout() {
22      initComponents();
23
24      // Set GridLayout as default
25      jpComponents.setLayout(gridLayout);
26      jpComponents.validate();
27      displayHTML(urlGridLayoutHTML);
28    }
29
30    private void initComponents() {
31      btg = new javax.swing.ButtonGroup();
32      jSplitPane1 = new javax.swing.JSplitPane();
33      jpChooseLayout = new javax.swing.JPanel();
34      jrbFlowLayout = new javax.swing.JRadioButton();
35      jrbGridLayout = new javax.swing.JRadioButton();
36      jrbCardLayout = new javax.swing.JRadioButton();
37      jSplitPane2 = new javax.swing.JSplitPane();
38      jpComponents = new javax.swing.JPanel();
39      jButton1 = new javax.swing.JButton();
40      jButton2 = new javax.swing.JButton();
41      jButton3 = new javax.swing.JButton();
42      jButton4 = new javax.swing.JButton();
43      jScrollPane1 = new javax.swing.JScrollPane();
44      jEditorPane1 = new javax.swing.JEditorPane();
```

Listing 6.7 *ShowLayout.java*

continued

Example 6.4 continued

```
    jpChooseLayout.setLayout(new java.awt.GridLayout(3, 0));
    jrbFlowLayout.setText("FlowLayout");
    btg.add(jrbFlowLayout);
    jrbFlowLayout.addActionListener(
      new java.awt.event.ActionListener() {
      public void actionPerformed(java.awt.event.ActionEvent evt) {
        jrbFlowLayoutActionPerformed(evt);
      }
    });
    jpChooseLayout.add(jrbFlowLayout);
    jrbGridLayout.setSelected(true);
    jrbGridLayout.setText("GridLayout");
    btg.add(jrbGridLayout);
    jrbGridLayout.addActionListener(
      new java.awt.event.ActionListener() {
      public void actionPerformed(java.awt.event.ActionEvent evt) {
        jrbGridLayoutActionPerformed(evt);
      }
    });
    jpChooseLayout.add(jrbGridLayout);
    jrbCardLayout.setText("CardLayout");
    btg.add(jrbCardLayout);
    jrbCardLayout.addActionListener(
      new java.awt.event.ActionListener() {
      public void actionPerformed(java.awt.event.ActionEvent evt) {
        jrbCardLayoutActionPerformed(evt);
      }
    });
    jpChooseLayout.add(jrbCardLayout);
    jSplitPane1.setLeftComponent(jpChooseLayout);
    jSplitPane2.setOrientation(
      javax.swing.JSplitPane.VERTICAL_SPLIT);
    jButton1.setText("jButton1");
    jpComponents.add(jButton1);
    jButton2.setText("jButton2");
    jpComponents.add(jButton2);
    jButton3.setText("jButton3");
    jpComponents.add(jButton3);
    jButton4.setText("jButton4");
    jpComponents.add(jButton4);
    jSplitPane2.setLeftComponent(jpComponents);
    jEditorPane1.setEditable(false);
    jScrollPane1.setViewportView(jEditorPane1);
    jSplitPane2.setRightComponent(jScrollPane1);
    jSplitPane1.setRightComponent(jSplitPane2);
    getContentPane().add(jSplitPane1, java.awt.BorderLayout.CENTER);
  }

  private void jrbCardLayoutActionPerformed(
    java.awt.event.ActionEvent evt) {
    jpComponents.setLayout(cardLayout);
    jpComponents.validate();
    displayHTML(urlCardLayoutHTML);
  }

  private void jrbGridLayoutActionPerformed(
    java.awt.event.ActionEvent evt) {
    jpComponents.setLayout(gridLayout);
```

Listing 6.7 *continued*

```
103       jpComponents.validate();
104       displayHTML(urlGridLayoutHTML);
105     }
106
107     private void jrbFlowLayoutActionPerformed(
108       java.awt.event.ActionEvent evt) {
109       jpComponents.setLayout(flowLayout);
110       jpComponents.validate();
111       displayHTML(urlFlowLayoutHTML);
112     }
113
114     /** Display an HTML file in EditorPane */
115     void displayHTML(java.net.URL url) {
116       try {
117         // Render the HTML file
118         jEditorPane1.setPage(url);
119       }
120       catch (java.io.IOException ex) {
121         System.out.println(ex);
122       }
123     }
124
125     // Variables declaration - do not modify
126     private javax.swing.ButtonGroup btg;
127     private javax.swing.JSplitPane jSplitPane1;
128     private javax.swing.JPanel jpChooseLayout;
129     private javax.swing.JRadioButton jrbFlowLayout;
130     private javax.swing.JRadioButton jrbGridLayout;
131     private javax.swing.JRadioButton jrbCardLayout;
132     private javax.swing.JSplitPane jSplitPane2;
133     private javax.swing.JPanel jpComponents;
134     private javax.swing.JButton jButton1;
135     private javax.swing.JButton jButton2;
136     private javax.swing.JButton jButton3;
137     private javax.swing.JButton jButton4;
138     private javax.swing.JScrollPane jScrollPane1;
139     private javax.swing.JEditorPane jEditorPane1;
140     // End of variables declaration
141   }
```

Listing 6.7 *continued*

Example Review

Split panes can be embedded. Adding a split pane to an existing split results in three split panes. The program creates two split panes to hold a panel for radio buttons, a panel for buttons, and a scroll pane.

The radio buttons are used to select layout managers. A selected layout manager is used in the panel for laying out the buttons. The scroll pane contains a `JEditorPane` for displaying the HTML file that describes the selected layout manager.

The HTML files are preloaded using the `getResource` method in the `Class` class (Lines 12–18). The `displayHTML` method (Lines 114–123) is invoked by the radio button handler for displaying a specified HTML file in the `JEditorPane`.

Chapter Summary

A Java container is an object that holds and groups user interface components. A *layout manager* is a special object used to manage how the components in the container are displayed. Java provides a set of layout managers that you can use to intelligently place components that are independent of fonts, screen resolutions, and platform. This chapter discussed Swing containers and reviewed the layout managers provided in Forte. You learned how to use two useful Swing containers, `JTabbedPane` and `JSplitPane`. You also learned how to create custom layout managers.

Review Questions

6.1 How does the layout in Java differ from the ones in Visual Basic and Delphi?

6.2 Are the following statements correct?

- Each layout has a set of properties applied to all the components in the container.
- The constraints property is associated with a component.

6.3 Describe the various preinstalled layout managers in Forte.

6.4 When should `AbsoluteLayout` be used?

6.5 How do you use `JTabbedPane` and `JSplitPane`? Can you specify a layout manager in these two containers?

Programming Exercises

6.1 Create a program that enables the user to set the properties of a `FlowLayout` manager dynamically, as shown in Figure 6.12. The `FlowLayout` manager is used to place fifteen components in a panel. You can set the `alignment`, `hgap`, and `vgap` properties of the `FlowLayout` dynamically.

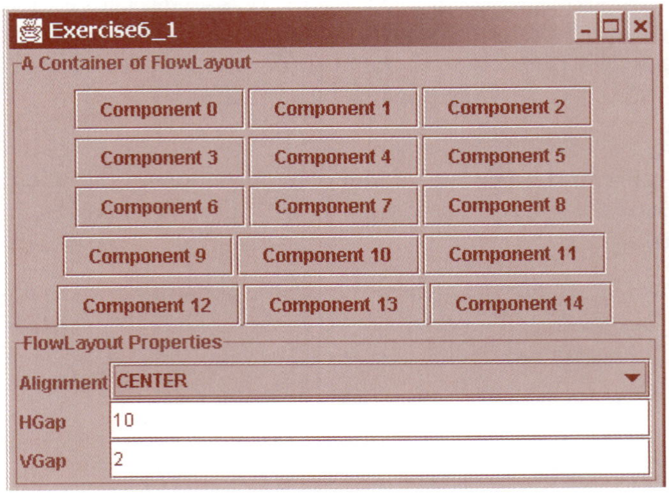

Figure 6.12 *The program enables you to set the properties of a* `FlowLayout` *manager dynamically.*

6.2 Create a program that enables the user to set the properties of a `GridLayout` manager dynamically, as shown in Figure 6.13. The `GridLayout` manager is used to place fifteen components in a panel. You can set the `rows`, `columns`, `hgap`, and `vgap` properties of the `GridLayout` dynamically.

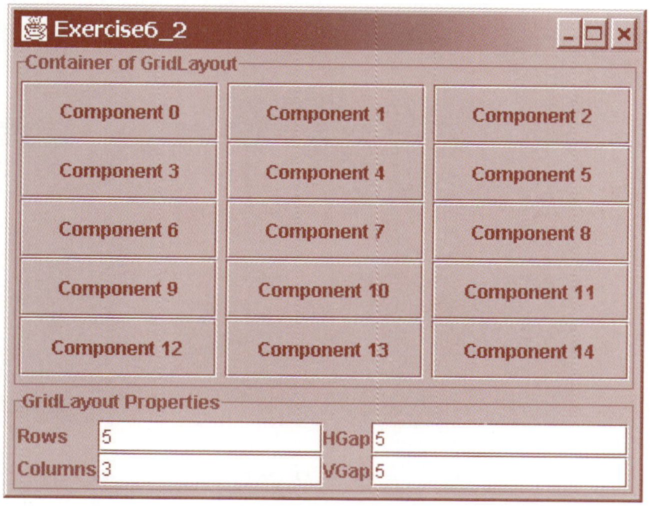

Figure 6.13 *The program enables you to set the properties of a* `GridLayout` *manager dynamically.*

6.3 Create a program that enables the user to set the properties of a `BorderLayout` manager dynamically, as shown in Figure 6.14. The `BorderLayout` manager is used to place five components in a panel. You can set the `hgap` and `vgap` properties of the `BorderLayout` dynamically.

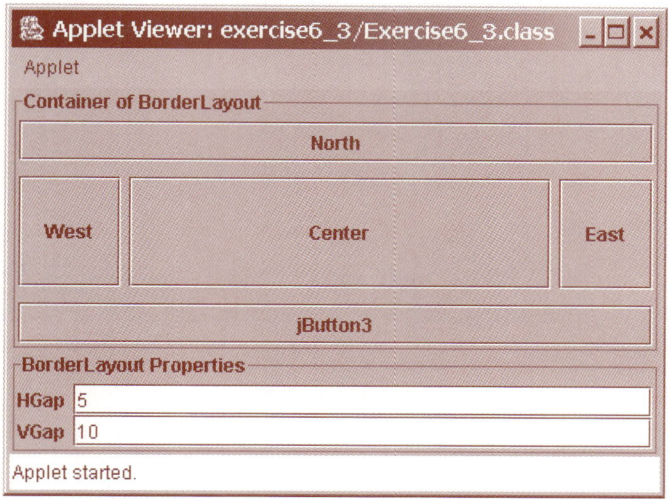

Figure 6.14 *The program enables you to set the properties of a* `BorderLayout` *manager dynamically.*

6.4 Modify Example 6.1 to set the red, green, and blue components in the `redPanel`, `greenPanel`, and `bluePanel` to match the selected colors in the combo box.

6.5 Create a program that displays four figures in split panes, as shown in Figure 6.15. Use the `FigurePanel` class defined in Example 6.3. to display figures.

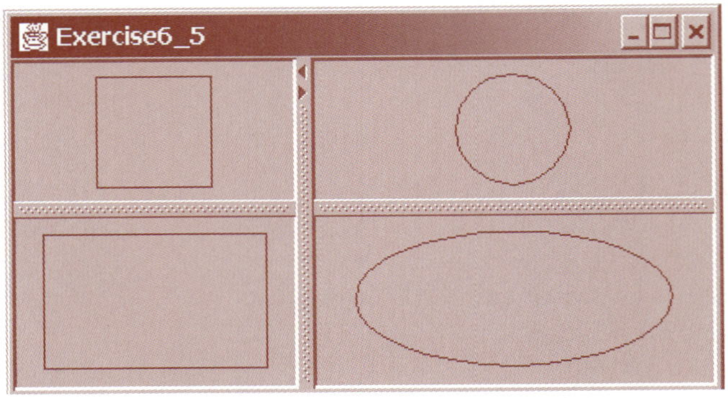

Figure 6.15 *Four figures are displayed in split panes.*

6.6 Modify Example 6.3 to add a panel of radio buttons for specifying the tab placement of the tabbed pane, as shown in Figure 6.16.

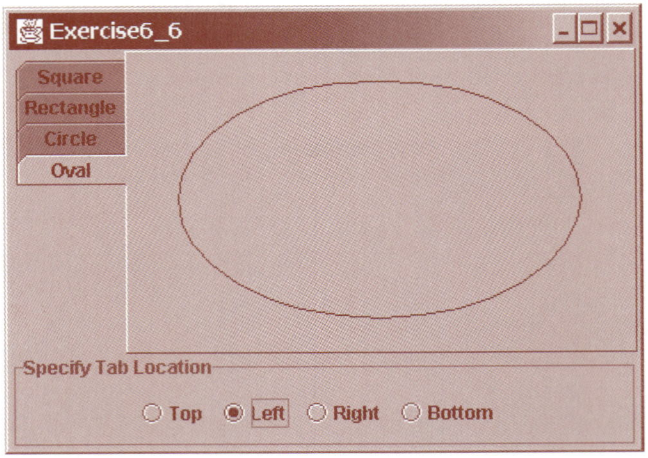

Figure 6.16 *The radio buttons let you choose the tab placement of the tabbed pane.*

6.7 Create a program that enables the user to set the properties of a split pane dynamically, as shown in Figure 6.17.

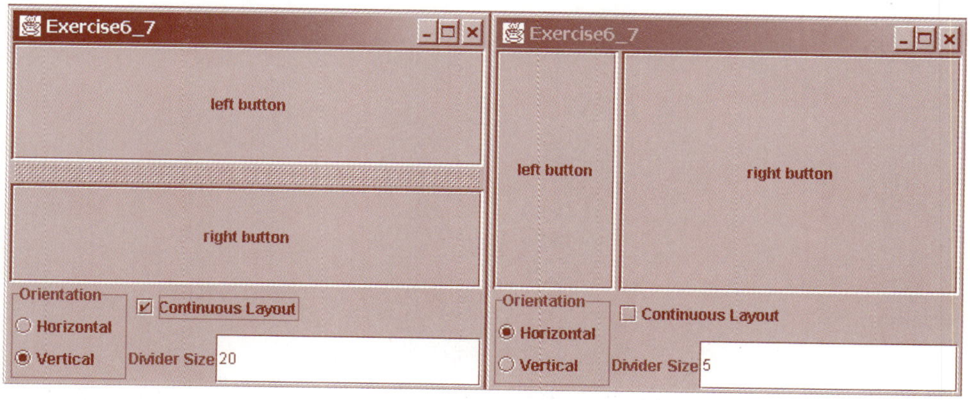

Figure 6.17 *The program enables you to set the properties of a split pane dynamically.*

6.8 Rewrite Example 6.1, "Choosing Colors" using the `GridBagLayout`.

CHAPTER 7

MENUS, TOOLBARS, AND DIALOGS

Objectives

- To learn the menu components `JMenuBar`, `JMenu`, `JPopupMenu`, `JMenuItem`, `JCheckBoxMenuItem`, and `JRadioButtonMenuItem`.
- To create menus and popup menus using the Menu designer.
- To use `JToolBar` to create tool bars.
- To use the `Action` objects to centralize the code for processing action.
- To create standard dialogs using the `JOptionPane` class.
- To extend the `JDialog` class to create custom dialogs.
- To select colors using `JColorChooser`.
- To use `JFileChooser` to display Open and Save File dialogs.

7.1 Introduction

In the preceding two chapters, you learned how to use Swing components, containers, and layout managers. This chapter introduces menus, popup menus, tool bars, and dialogs. Using these components effectively can greatly boost your programming productivity.

7.2 Menus

Menus make selection easier and are widely used in Windows applications. Java provides five classes, `JMenuBar`, `JMenu`, `JMenuItem`, `JCheckBoxMenuItem`, and `JRadioButtonMenuItem`, to implement menus.

`JMenuBar`, the top-level menu component, is used to hold the menus. Menus consist of *menu items* that the user can select (or toggle on or off). Menu items can be an instance of `JMenuItem`, `JCheckBoxMenuItem`, or `JRadioButtonMenuItem`.

The sequence of implementing menus in Java is as follows:

1. Create a menu bar and associate it with a frame or an applet.

```
JFrame frame = new JFrame();
frame.setSize(300, 200);
frame.setVisible(true);
JMenuBar jmb = new JMenuBar();
frame.setJMenuBar(jmb);  // Attach a menu bar to a frame or an applet
```

   This code creates a frame and a menu bar, and sets the menu bar in the frame.

Note

A menu bar cannot be added to an AWT applet, but it can be added to a Swing JApplet.

---

2. Create menus.

   You can use the following constructor to create a menu:

```
public JMenu(String label)
```

   The following is an example of creating menus:

```
JMenu fileMenu = new JMenu("File");
JMenu helpMenu = new JMenu("Help");
jmb.add(fileMenu); //Add menu to menu bar
jmb.add(helpMenu);
```

   This creates two menus labeled `File` and `Help`, as shown in Figure 7.1. The menus will not be seen until they are added to `JMenuBar`.

3. Create menu items and add them to menus.

```
fileMenu.add(new JMenuItem("New"));
fileMenu.add(new JMenuItem("Open"));
fileMenu.addSeparator();
```

Figure 7.1 *The menu bar appears below the title bar on the frame.*

```
fileMenu.add(new JMenuItem("Print"));
fileMenu.addSeparator();
fileMenu.add(new JMenuItem("Exit"));
```

This code adds the menu items New, Open, a separator bar, Print, another separator bar, and Exit in this order into the File menu, as shown in Figure 7.2.

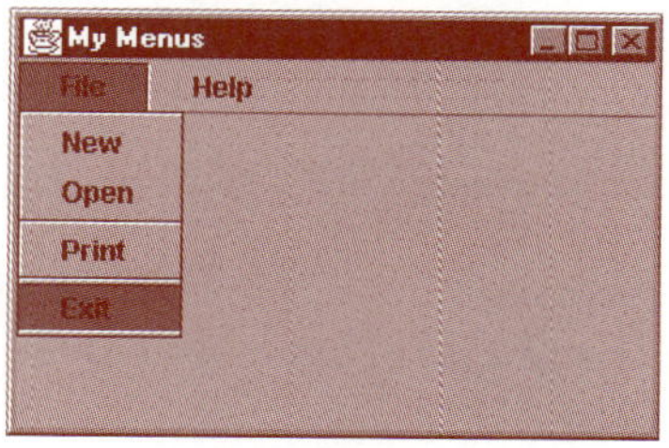

Figure 7.2 *Clicking a menu on the menu bar reveals the items under the menu.*

The `addSeparator()` method adds a separate bar in the menu.

You can also embed menus inside menus so that the embedded menus become submenus. Here is an example:

```
JMenu softwareHelpSubMenu = new JMenu("Software");
JMenu hardwareHelpSubMenu = new JMenu("Hardware");
helpMenu.add(softwareHelpSubMenu);
helpMenu.add(hardwareHelpSubMenu);
softwareHelpSubMenu.add(new JMenuItem("Unix"));
softwareHelpSubMenu.add(new JMenuItem("NT"));
softwareHelpSubMenu.add(new JMenuItem("Win95"));
```

This code adds two submenus, `softwareHelpMenu` and `hardwareHelpMenu`, in `helpMenu`. The menu items `Unix`, `NT`, and `Win95` are added into `softwareHelpMenu` (see Figure 7.3).

You can also add a `JCheckBoxMenuItem` to a `JMenu`. `JCheckBoxMenuItem` is a subclass of `JMenuItem` that adds a `boolean` state to the `JMenuItem`, and displays a check when its state is `true`. You can click the menu item to turn it on and off. For example, the following statement adds the check box menu item `Check it` (see Figure 7.4).

```
helpMenu.add(new JCheckBoxMenuItem("Check it"));
```

You can also add radio buttons in a menu using the `JRadioButtonMenuItem` class. This is often useful when you have a group of mutually exclusive

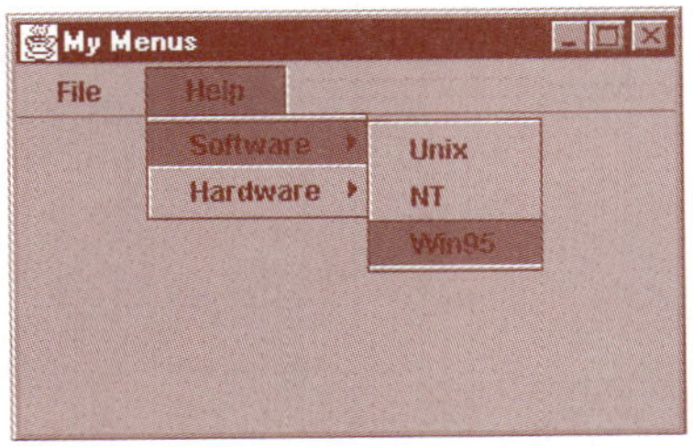

Figure 7.3 *Clicking a menu item reveals the secondary items under the menu item.*

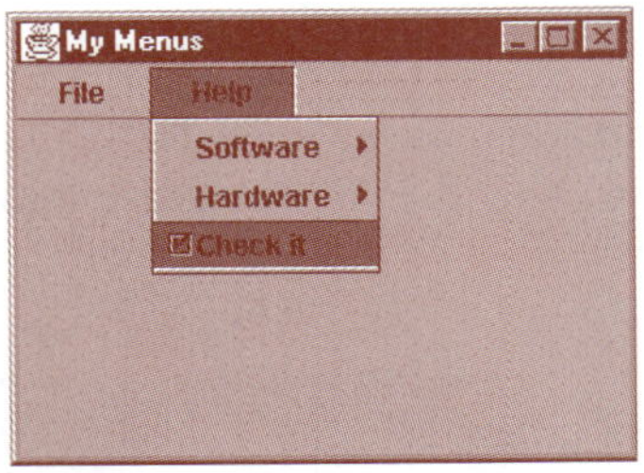

Figure 7.4 *A check box menu item, just like a check box, lets you check or uncheck a menu item.*

choices in the menu. For example, the following statements add a submenu named Color and a set of radio buttons for choosing a color (see Figure 7.5).

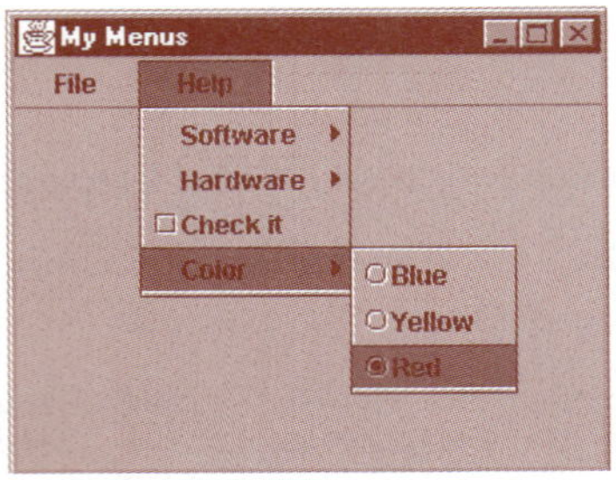

Figure 7.5 *You can use* `JRadioButtonMenuItem` *to choose a mutually exclusive menu choice.*

```
JMenu colorHelpSubMenu = new JMenu("Color");
helpMenu.add(colorHelpSubMenu);

JRadioButtonMenuItem jrbmiBlue, jrbmiYellow, jrbmiRed;
colorHelpSubMenu.add(jrbmiBlue =
  new JRadioButtonMenuItem("Blue"));
colorHelpSubMenu.add(jrbmiYellow =
  new JRadioButtonMenuItem("Yellow"));
colorHelpSubMenu.add(jrbmiRed = new JRadioButtonMenuItem("Red"));

ButtonGroup btg = new ButtonGroup();
btg.add(jrbmiBlue);
btg.add(jrbmiYellow);
btg.add(jrbmiRed);
```

4. The menu items generate `ActionEvent`. Your program must implement the `actionPerformed` handler to respond to the menu selection. An example is shown below.

```
public void actionPerformed(ActionEvent e) {
  String actionCommand = e.getActionCommand();

  // Make sure the source is JMenuItem
  if (e.getSource() instanceof JMenuItem)
    if ("New".equals(actionCommand))
      respondToNew();
}
```

This code executes the method `respondToNew()` when the menu item labeled New is selected.

7.3 Image Icons, Keyboard Mnemonics, and Keyboard Accelerators

The menu components `JMenu`, `JMenuItem`, `JCheckBoxMenuItem`, and `JRadioButton-MenuItem` have `icon` and `mnemonic` properties. For example, you can set icons for the New and Open menu items and set keyboard mnemonics for File, Help, New, and Open using the code shown below:

```
JMenuItem jmiNew, jmiOpen;
fileMenu.add(jmiNew = new JMenuItem("New"));
fileMenu.add(jmiOpen = new JMenuItem("Open"));
jmiNew.setIcon(new ImageIcon("/image/new.gif"));
jmiOpen.setIcon(new ImageIcon("/image/open.gif"));
helpMenu.setMnemonic('H');
fileMenu.setMnemonic('F');
jmiNew.setMnemonic('N');
jmiOpen.setMnemonic('O');
```

The new icons and mnemonics are shown in Figure 7.6. You can also use `JMenu-Item` constructors like the following to construct and set an icon or a mnemonic in one statement.

```
public JMenuItem(String label, Icon icon);

public JMenuItem(String label, int mnemonic);
```

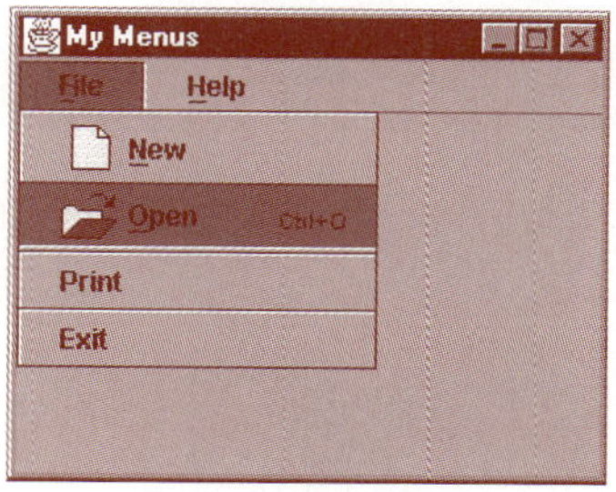

Figure 7.6 *You can set image icons, keyboard mnemonics, and keyboard accelerators in menus.*

To select a menu, press the ALT key and the mnemonic key. For example, press ALT+F to select the File menu. You can then press ALT+O to select the Open menu item. Keyboard mnemonics are useful, but they only let you select menu items from the currently open menu. Key accelerators, however, let you select a menu item directly by pressing the CTRL key and the accelerator key. For example, you can attach the accelerator key CTRL+O to the Open menu item using the following code:

```
jmiOpen.setAccelerator(KeyStroke.getKeyStroke
  (KeyEvent.VK_O, ActionEvent.CTRL_MASK));
```

The `setAccelerator()` method takes an object of the `KeyStroke` class. The static method `getKeyStoke()` in the `KeyStroke` class creates an instance of the keystroke. `VK_O` is a constant representing the O key, and `CTRL_MASK` is a constant indicating that the CTRL key is associated with the keystroke.

7.4 Designing Menus in Forte

This section demonstrates how to create menus in Forte's Form Editor with simple examples.

Example 7.1 Using Menu Designer

This example demonstrates how to create the menus shown in Figure 7.6 using Forte's Form Editor. You will learn how to add and remove menus, menu items, separator bars, submenus, check box menus, and radio button menus.

Here are the steps to complete the project.

1. Create a new package named menudemo and create an applet named `TestMenuDesigner` using the Forte Swing JApplet form wizard.

2. Drop a `JMenuBar` in the Swing tab to the form. This action causes Forte to create `jMenuBar1`, a `jMenu1` (an instance of `JMenu`), and add `jMenu1` into `jMenuBar1`, as shown in Figure 7.7.

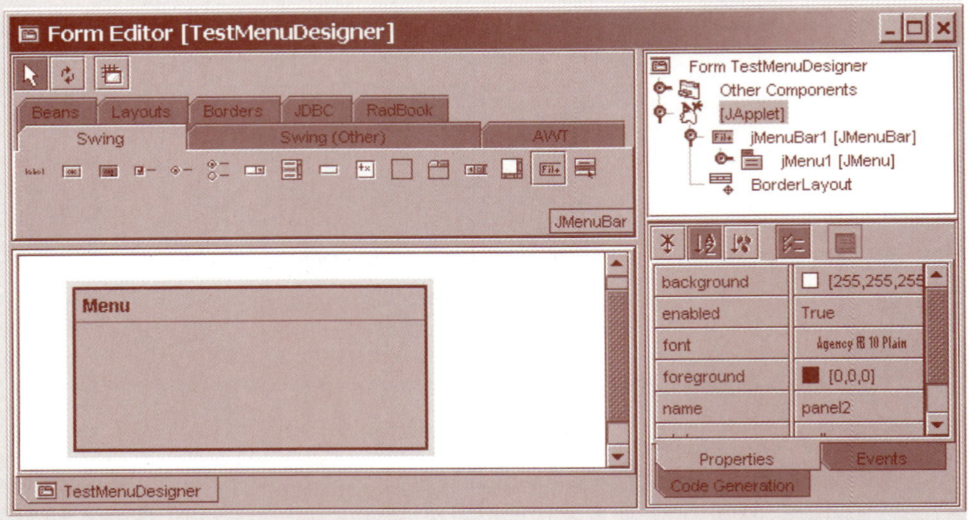

Figure 7.7 *You can visually add and remove menus, menu items, separator bars, submenus, check box menus, and radio button menus.*

NOTE

I recommend that you drop `JMenuBar` to the form before any other components. If `JMenuBar` is dropped to a form that is already filled with a container such as `JPanel` in the center, it is likely an instance of `JMenuBar` will appear in the Other Components node in the component tree. In this case, the menu bar is not attached to the form. You have to manually set the menu bar in the form using the `setJMenuBar` method.

3. You are going to create a new menu named File and add four menu items named New, Open, Print, and Exit into the File menu. Add a separator bar between Open and Print, and another separator between Print and Exit, as follows:

   3.1. Set the `text` property of `jMenu1` to File.

   3.2. In the context menu of `jMenu1`, choose *Add, JMenuItem* to create a menu item named `jMenuItem1`, as shown in Figure 7.8. Set its `text` property to New and its `icon` property to /image/new.gif using the Icon property editor. Set its mnemonic property to 78, which is the ASCII code for 'N'.

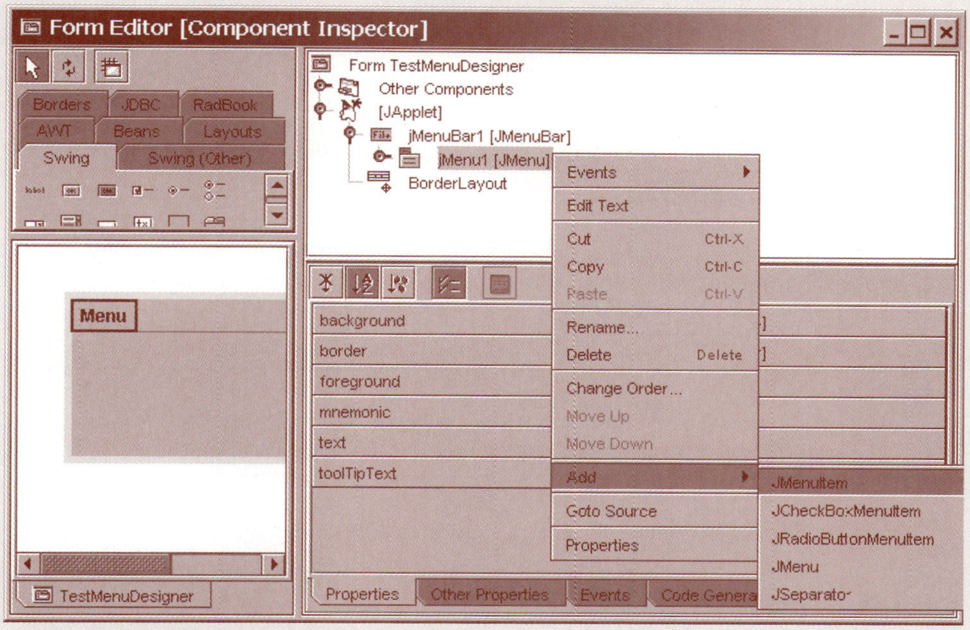

Figure 7.8 *You can add a menu item into a menu from the menu's context menu in the component tree.*

   3.3. Create a menu item with text Open under the File menu and set its icon property with /image/open.gif. Set its mnemonic property to 79, which is the ASCII code for 'O'. In the accelerator property editor, as shown in Figure 7.9, check the ctrl checkbox, and choose

continued

Example 7.1 continued

VK_O in the Virtual key combo box. This action generates an accelerate key for O.

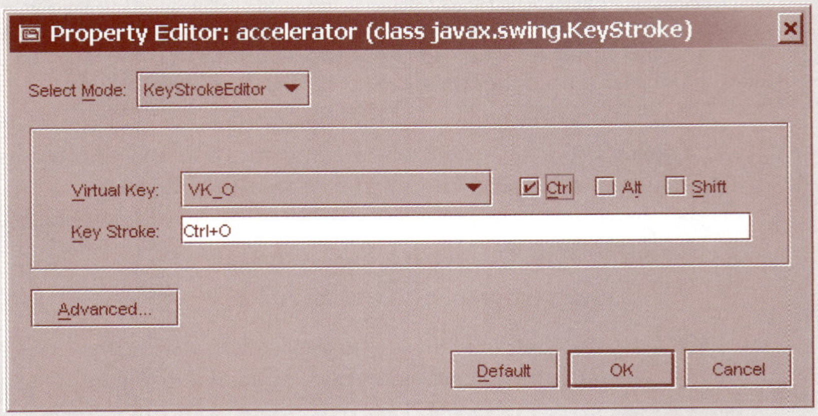

Figure 7.9 *You can create an accelerate keystroke from the accelerate property editor.*

3.4. In the context menu of `jMenu1`, choose *Add, JSeparator* to create a separator.

3.5. Create a menu item under the File menu with text Print. Create a separator. Create a menu item with the text Exit.

3.6. Rename the menu items to `jmiNew`, `jmiOpen`, `jmiPrint`, and `jmiExit`.

Tip

You can reorder the menu items in a menu by choosing the Move Up and Move Down commands from a menu item's context menu in the component tree.

Note

When you drop the first menu item into the form, Forte automatically inserts the statement `setJMenuBar(jMenuBar1)` in the `initComponents` method.

---

4. You are going to create a new menu with the text Help after the File menu and create submenus, check box menu items, and radio button menu items under Help, as follows:

4.1. In the context menu for `jMenuBar1`, choose *New JMenu* to create `jMenu2`.

4.2. In the context menu for `jMenu2`, choose *Add, JMenu* to create `jMenu3` with text Software and rename it `softwareHelpSubMenu`. In the context menu of `softwareHelpSubMenu`, choose *Add, JMenuItem* to create a new menu item and rename it `jmiUnix` with the text Unix. Create two additional menu items under `softwareHelpSubMenu` and set their text property to NT and Win95.

4.3. In the context menu for `jMenu2`, choose *Add, JMenu* to create a new menu with the text Hardware and rename it `hardwareHelpSubMenu`.

4.4. In the context menu for `jMenu2`, choose *Add, JCheckBoxMenuItem* to create a check box menu item with the text Check it.

4.5. In the context menu for `jMenu2`, choose *Add, JMenu* to create a new menu with the text Color and rename it `colorHelpSubMenu`. In the context menu for `colorHelpSubMenu`, choose *Add, JRadioButton-MenuItem* to create a new radio button menu item named `jrbmiBlue`. Set its `text` property to Blue. Similarly create two additional radio button menu items named `jrbmiYellow` and `jrbmiRed` with the texts Yellow and Red. Drop a `ButtonGroup` to the form to create `buttonGroup1`. Set the `buttonGroup` property of the three radio buttons to `buttonGroup1`. The structural relationship of the menu components is shown in Figure 7.10.

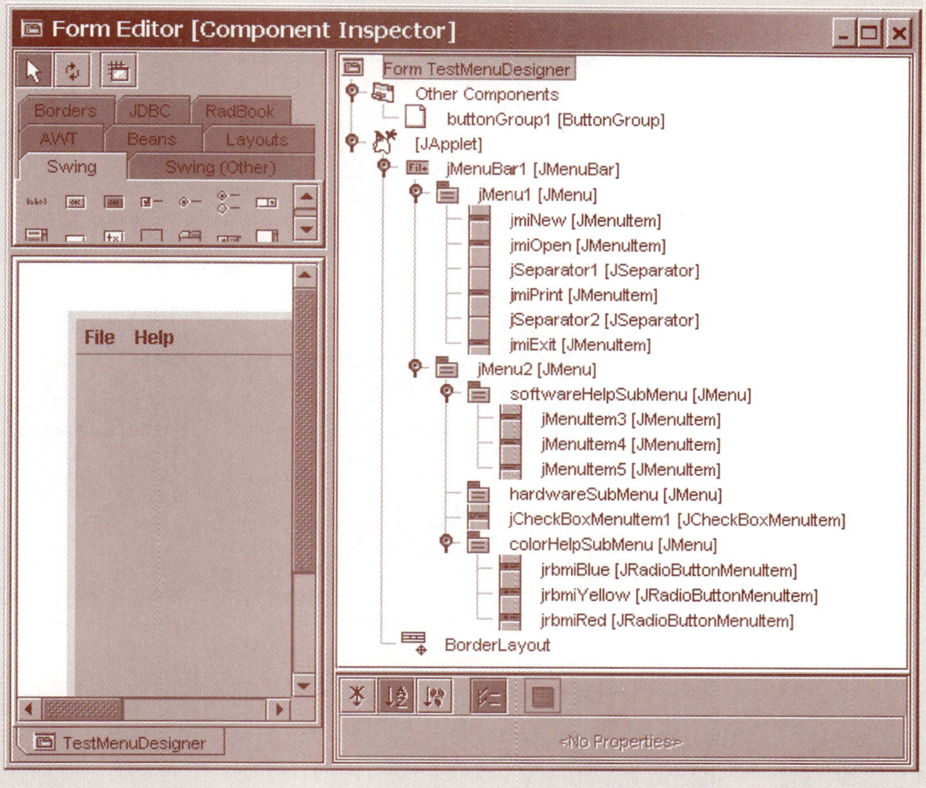

Figure 7.10 *All the menu components are shown in the component tree.*

continued

Example 7.1 continued

5. Double-click the Exit menu item from the form to generate the code for handling the Exit menu item. Add the code to terminate the program in the handler, as shown in Listing 7.1 (Line 91). You have to add a main method to run it as an application to test the Exit command.

```
1   package menudemo;
2
3   public class TestMenuDesigner extends javax.swing.JApplet {
4     /** Creates new form TestMenuDesigner */
5     public TestMenuDesigner() {
6       initComponents();
7     }
8
9     private void initComponents() {
10      jMenuBar1 = new javax.swing.JMenuBar();
11      jMenu1 = new javax.swing.JMenu();
12      jmiNew = new javax.swing.JMenuItem();
13      jmiOpen = new javax.swing.JMenuItem();
14      jSeparator1 = new javax.swing.JSeparator();
15      jmiPrint = new javax.swing.JMenuItem();
16      jSeparator2 = new javax.swing.JSeparator();
17      jmiExit = new javax.swing.JMenuItem();
18      jMenu2 = new javax.swing.JMenu();
19      softwareHelpSubMenu = new javax.swing.JMenu();
20      jMenuItem3 = new javax.swing.JMenuItem();
21      jMenuItem4 = new javax.swing.JMenuItem();
22      jMenuItem5 = new javax.swing.JMenuItem();
23      hardwareSubMenu = new javax.swing.JMenu();
24      jCheckBoxMenuItem1 = new javax.swing.JCheckBoxMenuItem();
25      colorHelpSubMenu = new javax.swing.JMenu();
26      jrbmiBlue = new javax.swing.JRadioButtonMenuItem();
27      jrbmiYellow = new javax.swing.JRadioButtonMenuItem();
28      jrbmiRed = new javax.swing.JRadioButtonMenuItem();
29      buttonGroup1 = new javax.swing.ButtonGroup();
30      jMenu1.setText("File");
31      jmiNew.setMnemonic(78);
32      jmiNew.setText("New");
33      jmiNew.setIcon(new javax.swing.ImageIcon(getClass().
34        getResource("/image/new.gif")));
35      jMenu1.add(jmiNew);
36      jmiOpen.setAccelerator(javax.swing.KeyStroke.getKeyStroke(
37        java.awt.event.KeyEvent.VK_O,
38        java.awt.event.InputEvent.CTRL_MASK));
39      jmiOpen.setText("Open");
40      jmiOpen.setIcon(new javax.swing.ImageIcon(getClass().
41        getResource("/image/open.gif")));
42      jmiOpen.addActionListener(new java.awt.event.ActionListener() {
43        public void actionPerformed(java.awt.event.ActionEvent evt) {
44          jmiOpenActionPerformed(evt);
45        }
46      });
47      jMenu1.add(jmiOpen);
48      jMenu1.add(jSeparator1);
49      jmiPrint.setMnemonic(80);
50      jmiPrint.setText("Print");
51      jMenu1.add(jmiPrint);
52      jMenu1.add(jSeparator2);
```

Listing 7.1 *TestMenuDesigner.java*

```
        jmiExit.setText("Exit");
        jmiExit.addActionListener(new java.awt.event.ActionListener() {
          public void actionPerformed(java.awt.event.ActionEvent evt) {
            jmiExitActionPerformed(evt);
          }
        });
        jMenu1.add(jmiExit);
        jMenuBar1.add(jMenu1);
        jMenu2.setText("Help");
        softwareHelpSubMenu.setText("Software");
        jMenuItem3.setText("Unix");
        softwareHelpSubMenu.add(jMenuItem3);
        jMenuItem4.setText("NT");
        softwareHelpSubMenu.add(jMenuItem4);
        jMenuItem5.setText("Win95");
        softwareHelpSubMenu.add(jMenuItem5);
        jMenu2.add(softwareHelpSubMenu);
        hardwareSubMenu.setText("Hardware");
        jMenu2.add(hardwareSubMenu);
        jCheckBoxMenuItem1.setText("CheckBox");
        jMenu2.add(jCheckBoxMenuItem1);
        colorHelpSubMenu.setText("Menu");
        jrbmiBlue.setText("RadioButton");
        buttonGroup1.add(jrbmiBlue);
        colorHelpSubMenu.add(jrbmiBlue);
        jrbmiYellow.setText("RadioButton");
        buttonGroup1.add(jrbmiYellow);
        colorHelpSubMenu.add(jrbmiYellow);
        jrbmiRed.setText("RadioButton");
        buttonGroup1.add(jrbmiRed);
        colorHelpSubMenu.add(jrbmiRed);
        jMenu2.add(colorHelpSubMenu);
        jMenuBar1.add(jMenu2);
        setJMenuBar(jMenuBar1);
    }

    private void jmiExitActionPerformed(
      java.awt.event.ActionEvent evt) {
      System.exit(0);
    }

    // Variables declaration - do not modify
    private javax.swing.JMenuBar jMenuBar1;
    private javax.swing.JMenu jMenu1;
    private javax.swing.JMenuItem jmiNew;
    private javax.swing.JMenuItem jmiOpen;
    private javax.swing.JSeparator jSeparator1;
    private javax.swing.JMenuItem jmiPrint;
    private javax.swing.JSeparator jSeparator2;
    private javax.swing.JMenuItem jmiExit;
    private javax.swing.JMenu jMenu2;
    private javax.swing.JMenu softwareHelpSubMenu;
    private javax.swing.JMenuItem jMenuItem3;
    private javax.swing.JMenuItem jMenuItem4;
    private javax.swing.JMenuItem jMenuItem5;
    private javax.swing.JMenu hardwareSubMenu;
    private javax.swing.JCheckBoxMenuItem jCheckBoxMenuItem1;
    private javax.swing.JMenu colorHelpSubMenu;
```

Listing 7.1 *continued*

continued

Example 7.1 continued

```
    private javax.swing.JRadioButtonMenuItem jrbmiBlue;
    private javax.swing.JRadioButtonMenuItem jrbmiYellow;
    private javax.swing.JRadioButtonMenuItem jrbmiRed;
    private javax.swing.ButtonGroup buttonGroup1;
    // End of variables declaration
}
```

Listing 7.1 *continued*

Example Review

All the code in this program is created automatically except the code for handling the Exit command. Forte IDE maintains everything in sync as you work. As you edit menu items in the component tree, all changes are reflected immediately in the form and in the source code.

The program exits when you click the Exit menu item. The Exit command is ignored if the applet runs from a Web browser.

NOTE
The menu bar is usually attached to the window using the `setJMenuBar` method. However, like any other component, it can be placed in a container. For instance, you can place a menu bar in the south of the container with `BorderLayout`.

7.5 Popup Menus

A popup menu, also known as *a context menu*, is like a regular menu, but does not have a menu bar and can float anywhere on the screen. Creating a popup menu is similar to creating a regular menu in Forte's Form Editor.

A regular menu is always attached to a menu bar using the `setJMenuBar` method, but a popup menu is associated with a parent component and is displayed using the `show` method in the `JPopupMenu` class. You specify the parent component and the location of the popup menu, using the coordinate system of the parent like this:

```
popupMenu.show(component, x, y);
```

The popup menu usually contains the commands for an object. Customarily, you display a popup menu by pointing to the object and clicking a certain mouse button, the so-called *popup trigger*. Popup triggers are system-dependent. In Windows, the popup menu is displayed when the right mouse button is released. In Motif, the popup menu is displayed when the third mouse button is pressed and held down.

Example 7.2 Using Popup Menus

This example demonstrates how to create popup menus using Forte's Form Editor. The program creates a text area in a scroll pane. The popup menu is displayed when the mouse pointed to the text area triggers the popup menu, as shown in Figure 7.11.

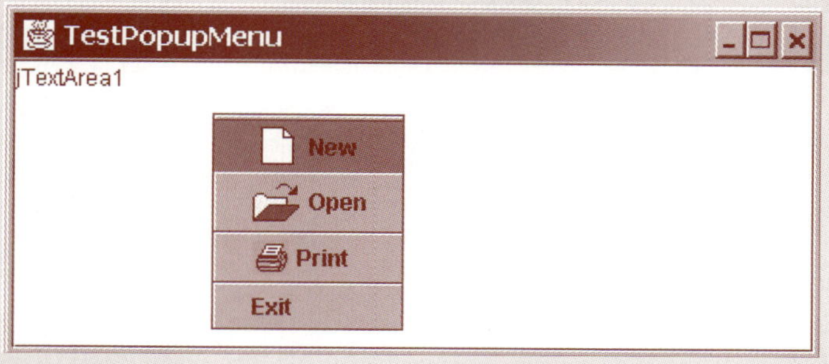

Figure 7.11 *A popup menu is displayed when the popup trigger is issued on the text area.*

Here are the steps to complete the project.

1. In package menudemo, create an applet named `TestPopupMenu` using the Forte Swing JApplet form wizard.
2. Drop a `JScrollPane` to the center of the applet, and drop a `JTextArea` into the scroll pane to create `jTextArea1`.
3. Drop a `JPopupMenu` from the Swing page to the applet. This action causes Forte to create `jPopupMenu1`, as shown in Figure 7.12.
4. In the context menu of `jPopupMenu1`, choose *Add, JMenuItem* to create a new menu item. Name it `jmiNew`. Set its `text` property to New and its icon to `/image/new.gif` using the icon property editor.
5. In the context menu of `jPopupMenu1`, choose *Add, JMenuItem* to create a new menu item. Name it `jmiOpen`. Set its `text` property to Open and its icon to /image/open.gif.
6. In the context menu of `jPopupMenu1`, choose *Add, JSeparator* to create a separator.
7. In the context menu of `jPopupMenu1`, choose *Add, JMenuItem* to create a new menu item. Name it `jmiPrint`. Set its `text` property to Print and its `icon` to /image/print.gif.
8. In the context menu of `jPopupMenu1`, choose *Add, Separator* to create a separator.
9. In the context menu of `jPopupMenu1`, choose *Add, JMenuItem* to create a new menu item. Name it `jmiExit`. Set its `text` property to Exit.

continued

Example 7.2 continued

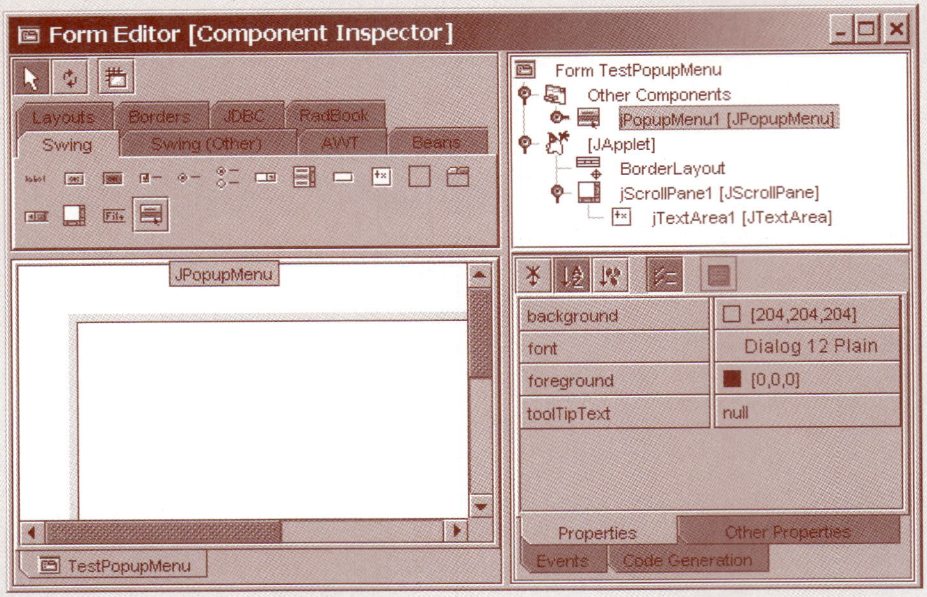

Figure 7.12 *You can design popup menus in the Component Inspector.*

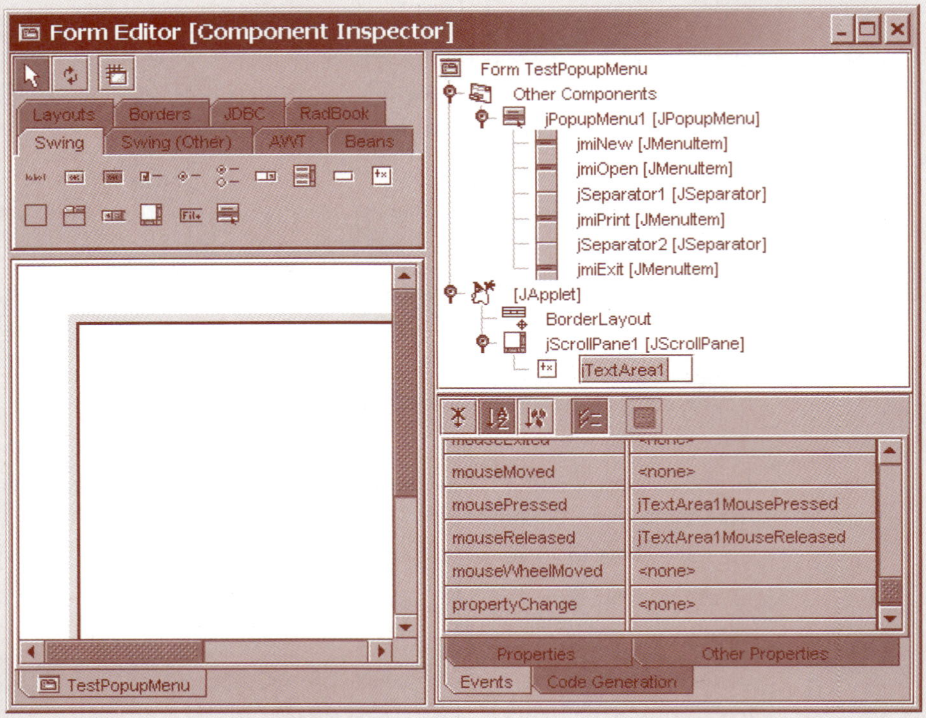

Figure 7.13 *The components for the popup menu are shown in the component tree.*

10. In the Events tab of `jmiExit` in the component inspector, press Enter in the value field of `actionPerformed` to generate the handler for the Exit command. Implement it as shown in Listing 7.2 (Lines 68–71).

11. In the Events tab of `jTextArea1`, double-click the value field of `mousePressed` and `mouseReleased` to generate the code for displaying the popup menu, as shown in Listing 7.2 (Lines 52–66). The structural relationship of these menu components is shown in Figure 7.13.

```
1   package menudemo;
2
3   public class TestPopupMenu extends javax.swing.JApplet {
4     /** Creates new form TestPopupMenu */
5     public TestPopupMenu() {
6       initComponents();
7     }
8
9     private void initComponents() {
10      jPopupMenu1 = new javax.swing.JPopupMenu();
11      jmiNew = new javax.swing.JMenuItem();
12      jmiOpen = new javax.swing.JMenuItem();
13      jSeparator1 = new javax.swing.JSeparator();
14      jmiPrint = new javax.swing.JMenuItem();
15      jSeparator2 = new javax.swing.JSeparator();
16      jmiExit = new javax.swing.JMenuItem();
17      jScrollPane1 = new javax.swing.JScrollPane();
18      jTextArea1 = new javax.swing.JTextArea();
19      jmiNew.setText("New");
20      jmiNew.setIcon(new javax.swing.ImageIcon(getClass().
21        getResource("/image/new.gif")));
22      jPopupMenu1.add(jmiNew);
23      jmiOpen.setText("Open");
24      jmiOpen.setIcon(new javax.swing.ImageIcon(getClass().
25        getResource("/image/open.gif")));
26      jPopupMenu1.add(jmiOpen);
27      jPopupMenu1.add(jSeparator1);
28      jmiPrint.setIcon(new javax.swing.ImageIcon(getClass().
29        getResource("/image/print.gif")));
30      jmiPrint.setLabel("Print");
31      jPopupMenu1.add(jmiPrint);
32      jPopupMenu1.add(jSeparator2);
33      jmiExit.setText("Exit");
34      jmiExit.addActionListener(new java.awt.event.ActionListener() {
35        public void actionPerformed(java.awt.event.ActionEvent evt) {
36          jmiExitActionPerformed(evt);
37        }
38      });
39      jPopupMenu1.add(jmiExit);
40      jTextArea1.addMouseListener(new java.awt.event.MouseAdapter() {
41        public void mousePressed(java.awt.event.MouseEvent evt) {
42          jTextArea1MousePressed(evt);
43        }
44        public void mouseReleased(java.awt.event.MouseEvent evt) {
45          jTextArea1MouseReleased(evt);
46        }
47      });
```

Listing 7.2 *TestPopupMenu.java*

continued

Example 7.2 continued

```
      jScrollPane1.setViewportView(jTextArea1);
      getContentPane().add(jScrollPane1, java.awt.BorderLayout.CENTER);
    }

    private void jTextArea1MouseReleased(
      java.awt.event.MouseEvent evt) {
      showPopup(evt);
    }

    private void jTextArea1MousePressed(
      java.awt.event.MouseEvent evt) {
      showPopup(evt);
    }

    /**Display popup menu when triggered*/
    private void showPopup(java.awt.event.MouseEvent evt) {
      if (evt.isPopupTrigger())
        jPopupMenu1.show(evt.getComponent(), evt.getX(), evt.getY());
    }

    private void jmiExitActionPerformed(
      java.awt.event.ActionEvent evt) {
      System.exit(0);
    }

    // Variables declaration - do not modify
    private javax.swing.JPopupMenu jPopupMenu1;
    private javax.swing.JMenuItem jmiNew;
    private javax.swing.JMenuItem jmiOpen;
    private javax.swing.JSeparator jSeparator1;
    private javax.swing.JMenuItem jmiPrint;
    private javax.swing.JSeparator jSeparator2;
    private javax.swing.JMenuItem jmiExit;
    private javax.swing.JScrollPane jScrollPane1;
    private javax.swing.JTextArea jTextArea1;
    // End of variables declaration
  }
```

Listing 7.2 *continued*

Example Review

The process of creating popup menus is similar to the process for creating regular menus. To create a popup menu, drop a `JPopupMenu` from the component palette to the form to create an instance of `JPopupMenu`. This instance appears in the Other Components node in the component tree. You can create menu items, radio button menu items, check box menu items, and separators from the context menu of the popup menu in the component tree.

To show a popup menu, the applet uses the `show` method by specifying the parent component and the location for the popup menu. The `show` method is invoked when the popup menu is triggered by a particular mouse click on the text area. Popup triggers are system-dependent. This program implements the `mouseReleased` handler for displaying the popup menu in the Windows and the `mousePressed` handler for displaying the popup menu in the Motif.

7.6 Tool Bars

In user interfaces, a *toolbar* is often used to hold commands that also appear in the menus. Frequently used commands are placed in a toolbar for quick access. Clicking a command in the toolbar is faster than choosing it from the menu.

Swing provides the `JToolBar` class as the container to hold tool bar components. `JToolBar` uses `BoxLayout` to manage components. The components usually appear as icons. Since icons are not components, they cannot be placed into a tool bar directly. Instead you may place buttons into the tool bar and set the icons on the buttons. An instance of `JToolBar` is like a regular container. Often it is placed in the north, west, or east of a container of `BorderLayout`.

The following properties in the `JToolBar` class are often useful:

- **`orientation`** specifies whether the items in the tool bar appear horizontally or vertically. The possible values are `JToolBar.HORIZONTAL` and `JToolBar.VERTICAL`. The default value is `JToolBar.HORIZONTAL`.
- **`floatable`** is a `boolean` value that specifies whether the tool bar can be floated. By default, the tool bar is floatable.

Example 7.3 Creating Tool Bars

This example demonstrates how to create a tool bar for the commands New, Open, and Print, as shown in Figure 7.14.

Figure 7.14 *The tool bar contains the icons representing the commands New, Open, and Print.*

Here are the steps to complete the example:

1. Create a new package named toolbardemo and an applet named `TestToolBar` using the Forte Swing JApplet form wizard.
2. Drop a `JToolBar` from the Swing (Other) tab in the component palette into the north of the applet to create `jToolBar1`.
3. Drop a `JButton` three times into `jToolBar1` and name the buttons `jbtNew`, `jbtOpen`, and `jbtPrint`, as shown in Figure 7.15.

continued

Example 7.3 continued

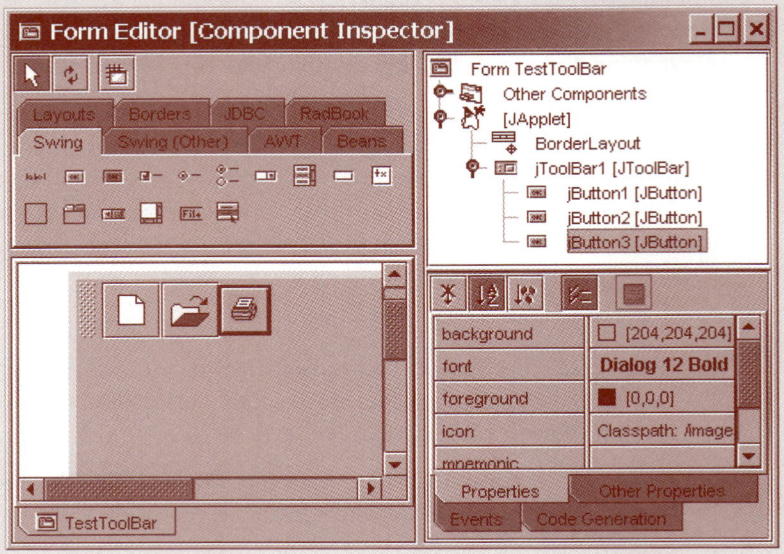

Figure 7.15 *The buttons are added to the tool bar, and the icons are set on the buttons.*

4. Set the `icon` properties of the three buttons to /image/new.gif, /image/open.gif, and /image/print.gif, set their `toolTip` properties to New, Open, and Print, and set empty in their `text` properties.

5. The Print toolbar button appears too small. Increase its size by setting the `margin` property to [2, 2, 4, 4]. The generated source code is shown in Listing 7.3.

```
package toolbardemo;

public class TestToolBar extends javax.swing.JApplet {
  /** Creates new form TestToolBar */
  public TestToolBar() {
    initComponents();
  }

  private void initComponents() {
    jToolBar1 = new javax.swing.JToolBar();
    jButton1 = new javax.swing.JButton();
    jButton2 = new javax.swing.JButton();
    jButton3 = new javax.swing.JButton();
    jButton1.setIcon(new javax.swing.ImageIcon(getClass().
      getResource("/image/new.gif")));
    jButton1.setToolTipText("New");
    jToolBar1.add(jButton1);
    jButton2.setIcon(new javax.swing.ImageIcon(getClass().
      getResource("/image/open.gif")));
    jButton2.setToolTipText("Open");
    jToolBar1.add(jButton2);
    jButton3.setIcon(new javax.swing.ImageIcon(getClass().
```

Listing 7.3 *TestToolBar.java*

```
          getResource("/image/print.gif")));
        jButton3.setToolTipText("Print");
        jButton3.setMargin(new java.awt.Insets(2, 2, 4, 4));
        jToolBar1.add(jButton3);
        getContentPane().add(jToolBar1, java.awt.BorderLayout.NORTH);
      }

      // Variables declaration - do not modify
      private javax.swing.JToolBar jToolBar1;
      private javax.swing.JButton jButton1;
      private javax.swing.JButton jButton2;
      private javax.swing.JButton jButton3;
      // End of variables declaration
    }
```

Listing 7.3 *continued*

Example Review

The tool bar is a container with `BoxLayout`. The layout is fixed and cannot be changed. Using the `orientation` property, you can specify whether components in the tool bar are organized horizontally or vertically.

By default, the tool bar is floatable, and a floatable controller is displayed in front of its components. You can drag the floatable controller to move the tool bar to different locations of the window or can show the tool bar in a separate window, as shown in Figure 7.16.

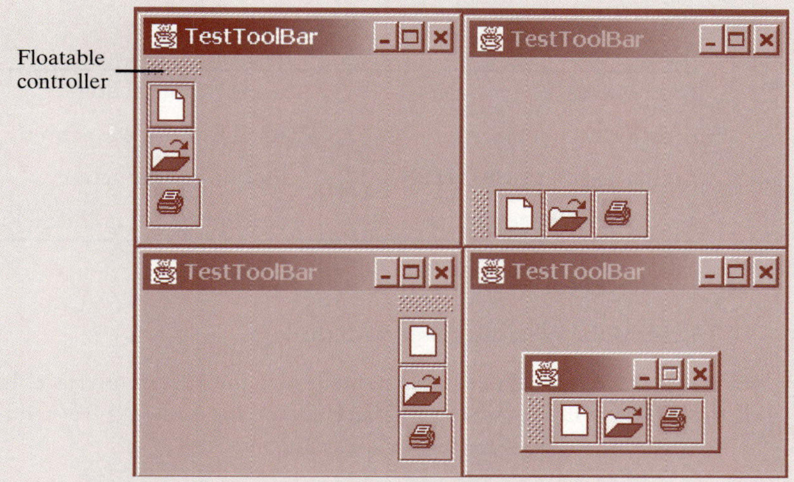

Figure 7.16 *The toolbar buttons are floatable.*

7.7 Processing Actions Using the *Action* Interface

Often menus and tool bars contain some common actions. For example, you can save a file by choosing *File*, *Save*, or by clicking the save button in the tool bar. Swing provides the `Action` interface, which can be used to create action objects for processing actions. Using `Action` objects, common action processing can be centralized and separated from the other application code.

The `Action` interface is a subinterface of `ActionListener`. Additionally, it defines several methods for retrieving and setting the associated action value, for checking whether the action is enabled, and for enabling and disabling the action. These methods are:

- `public boolean isEnabled()`

  Returns true if action is enabled.

- `public void setEnabled(boolean newValue)`

  Enables or disables the action.

- `public void putValue(String key, Object value)`

  Associates a key/value pair with the action. The key can be any string, but four names have predefined meanings:

Name	*Value*
`Action.NAME`	A name for the action
`Action.SMALL_ICON`	A small icon for the action
`Action.SHORT_DESCRIPTION`	A tool tip for the action
`Action.LONG_DESCRIPTION`	A description for online help

- `public Object getValue(String key)`

  Returns the value associated with the key.

`AbstractAction` is a default implementation of the `Action` interface. It implements all the methods in the `Action` interface except the `actionPerformed` method. The constructors of `AbstractionAction` are as follows:

- `public AbstractAction()`

  Defines an `Action` object with a default description string and default icon.

- `public AbstractAction(String name)`

  Defines an `Action` object with the specified description string and a default icon.

- `public AbstractAction(String name, Icon icon)`

  Defines an `Action` object with the specified description string and the specified icon.

Since `AbstractAction` is an abstract class, you cannot create an instance using its constructor. However, you can create a concrete subclass of `AbstractAction` and implement the `actionPerformed` method. This subclass can be defined as an anonymous inner class. For example, the following code creates an `Action` object for terminating the program.

```
Action exitAction = new AbstractAction("Exit") {
  public void actionPerformed(ActionEvent e) {
    System.exit(0);
  }
};
```

Certain containers, such as `JMenu` and `JToolBar`, know how to add an `Action` object. When an `Action` object is added to such a container, the container automatically creates an appropriate component for the `Action` object, and registers a listener with the `Action` object. Here is an example of adding an `Action` object to a menu and a tool bar:

```
jMenu.add(exitAction);
jToolBar.add(exitAction);
```

`Action` objects can also be used to respond to keystrokes. To associate actions with keystrokes, you need to create an instance of the `KeyStroke` class using the static `getKeyStroke` method, as follows:

```
KeyStroke exitKey =
  KeyStroke.getKeyStroke(KeyEvent.VK_E, KeyEvent.CTRL_MASK);
```

You can now associate an action with the keystroke by registering it with an instance of `JComponent`. For example, the following code associates `exitAction` with `exitKey`, and registers this action with `jPanel1`.

```
jPanel1.registerKeyboardAction
   (exitAction, exitKey, JComponent.WHEN_IN_FOCUSED_WINDOW);
```

The `registerKeyboardAction(ActionListener anAction, KeyStroke aKeyStroke, int aCondition)` method is defined in the `JComponent` class. The argument `aCondition` indicates under what condition the action should be invoked. Three possible values for the condition are `WHEN_FOCUSED`, `WHEN_IN_FOCUSED_WINDOW`, and `WHEN_ANCESTOR_OF_FOCUSED_COMPONENT`. Keystrokes are delivered to the component that has focus. Actions are invoked when keystrokes are detected in the focused component, in the focus window, or in the focused ancestor component under these conditions.

Example 7.4 Using Actions

This example demonstrates how to process actions using the `Action` interface. The program creates three menu items, Left, Center, and Right, three tool bar buttons, Left, Center, and Right, and three regular buttons, Left, Center, and Right, as shown in Figure 7.17. The actions of these components are processed through common action handlers.

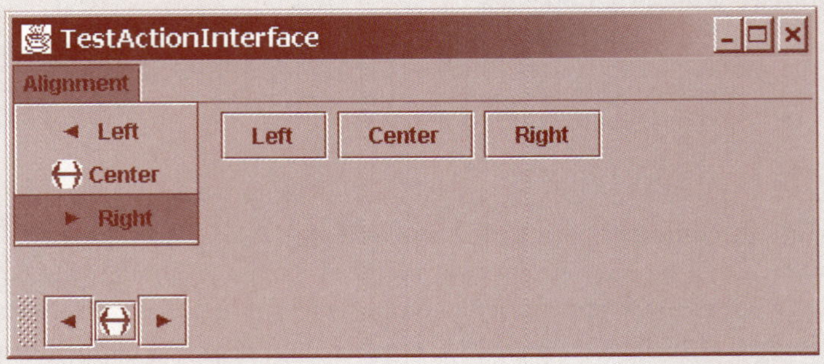

Figure 7.17 *Left, Center, and Right appear in the menu, in the toolbar, and in regular buttons.*

Here are the steps to complete the example:

1. Create a new package named actiondemo and an applet named `TestActionInterface` using the Swing JApplet form wizard.
2. Drop a `JToolBar` from the Swing (Other) tab into the north of the applet to create `jToolBar1`.
3. Drop a `JPanel` to the center of the applet. Drop `JButton` three times into the panel and name the buttons `jbtLeft`, `jbtCenter`, and `jbtRight`.
4. Drop a `JMenuBar` to the applet to create `jMenuBar1`. Create a menu named `jmenuAlignment` with text Alignment.
5. Write the code for an inner class `MyAction` that extends `AbstractAction`, as shown in Listing 7.4 (Lines 81–93).
6. Write the code to create image icons (Lines 12–18). Write the code to create `leftAction`, `centerAction`, and `rightAction` (Lines 20–23). Write the code to process keystrokes for the actions, as shown in Listing 7.4 (Lines 43–57).

```
1    package actiondemo;
2
3    import java.awt.*;
4    import java.awt.event.*;
5    import java.applet.*;
6    import javax.swing.*;
7    import imageviewerdemo.ImageViewer;
8
```

Listing 7.4 *TestActionInterface.java*

```
public class TestActionInterface extends javax.swing.JApplet {
  /** Creates new form TestActionInterface */
  public TestActionInterface() {
    initComponents();

    // Create image icons
    ImageIcon leftImageIcon = ImageViewer.createImageIcon(
      "/image/left.gif", this);
    ImageIcon centerImageIcon = ImageViewer.createImageIcon(
      "/image/center.gif", this);
    ImageIcon rightImageIcon = ImageViewer.createImageIcon(
      "/image/right.gif", this);

    // Create actions
    Action leftAction = new MyAction("Left", leftImageIcon);
    Action centerAction = new MyAction("Center", centerImageIcon);
    Action rightAction = new MyAction("Right", rightImageIcon);

    // Add actions to the toolbar
    jToolBar1.add(leftAction);
    jToolBar1.add(centerAction);
    jToolBar1.add(rightAction);

    // Add actions to the buttons
    jbtLeft.addActionListener(leftAction);
    jbtCenter.addActionListener(centerAction);
    jbtRight.addActionListener(rightAction);

    // Add actions to the menu
    jmenuAlignment.add(leftAction);
    jmenuAlignment.add(centerAction);
    jmenuAlignment.add(rightAction);

    // Set menu bar to the applet
    setJMenuBar(jMenuBar1);

    // Create KeyStroke instances
    KeyStroke leftKey =
      KeyStroke.getKeyStroke(KeyEvent.VK_L, KeyEvent.CTRL_MASK);
    KeyStroke centerKey =
      KeyStroke.getKeyStroke(KeyEvent.VK_C, KeyEvent.CTRL_MASK);
    KeyStroke rightKey =
      KeyStroke.getKeyStroke(KeyEvent.VK_R, KeyEvent.CTRL_MASK);

    // Register keystrokes
    jPanel1.registerKeyboardAction
      (leftAction, leftKey, JComponent.WHEN_IN_FOCUSED_WINDOW);
    jPanel1.registerKeyboardAction
      (centerAction, centerKey, JComponent.WHEN_IN_FOCUSED_WINDOW);
    jPanel1.registerKeyboardAction
      (rightAction, rightKey, JComponent.WHEN_IN_FOCUSED_WINDOW);
  }

  private void initComponents() {
    jMenuBar1 = new javax.swing.JMenuBar();
    jmenuAlignment = new javax.swing.JMenu();
    jToolBar1 = new javax.swing.JToolBar();
    jPanel1 = new javax.swing.JPanel();
    jbtLeft = new javax.swing.JButton();
    jbtCenter = new javax.swing.JButton();
```

Listing 7.4 *continued*

continued

Example 7.4 continued

```
67        jbtRight = new javax.swing.JButton();
68        jmenuAlignment.setText("Alighnment");
69        jMenuBar1.add(jmenuAlignment);
70        getContentPane().add(jToolBar1, java.awt.BorderLayout.NORTH);
71        jbtLeft.setText("Left");
72        jPanel1.add(jbtLeft);
73        jbtCenter.setText("Center");
74        jPanel1.add(jbtCenter);
75        jbtRight.setText("Right");
76        jPanel1.add(jbtRight);
77        getContentPane().add(jPanel1, java.awt.BorderLayout.CENTER);
78        setJMenuBar(jMenuBar1);
79      }
80
81      private class MyAction extends AbstractAction {
82        String name;
83
84        MyAction(String name, Icon icon) {
85          super(name, icon);
86          putValue(Action.SHORT_DESCRIPTION, name);
87          this.name = name;
88        }
89
90        public void actionPerformed(ActionEvent e) {
91          System.out.println("It is " + name);
92        }
93      }
94
95      // Variables declaration - do not modify
96      private javax.swing.JMenuBar jMenuBar1;
97      private javax.swing.JMenu jmenuAlignment;
98      private javax.swing.JToolBar jToolBar1;
99      private javax.swing.JPanel jPanel1;
100     private javax.swing.JButton jbtLeft;
101     private javax.swing.JButton jbtCenter;
102     private javax.swing.JButton jbtRight;
103     // End of variables declaration
104   }
```

Listing 7.4 *continued*

Example Review

The inner class `MyAction` extends `AbstractAction` with a constructor to construct an action with a name and an icon (Lines 84–88). It implements the `actionPerformed` method to display the action to the console (Lines 90–92).

Three actions, `leftAction`, `centerAction`, and `rightAction`, were created from the `MyAction` class (Lines 20–23). Each action has a name and an associated icon. The actions are for the menu items and the toolbar button. The menu and toolbar know how to add these objects. The tool tip is effective in the toolbar, but is ignored (not displayed) in the menu.

Since `Action` is a subinterface of `ActionListener`, `leftAction` is an instance of `ActionListener`. Therefore, to associate actions with the regular buttons, you can use the `addActionListener` method, such as `jbtLeft.addActionListener(leftAction)` (Lines 30–33).

7.8 JOptionPane Dialogs

A *dialog box* is normally used as a temporary window to receive additional information from the user or to provide notification that some event has occurred. Java provides the `JOptionPane` class, which can be used to create standard dialogs. You can also build custom dialogs by extending the `JDialog` class.

The `JOptionPane` class can be used to create four kinds of standard dialogs:

- *Message dialog* shows a message and waits for the user to click OK.
- *Confirmation dialog* shows a question and asks for confirmation, such as OK and Cancel.
- *Input dialog* shows a question and gets the user's input from a text field, combo box, or list.
- *Option dialog* shows a question and gets the user's answer from a set of options.

These dialogs are created using the static methods `showXxxDialog` and generally appear as shown in Figure 7.18.

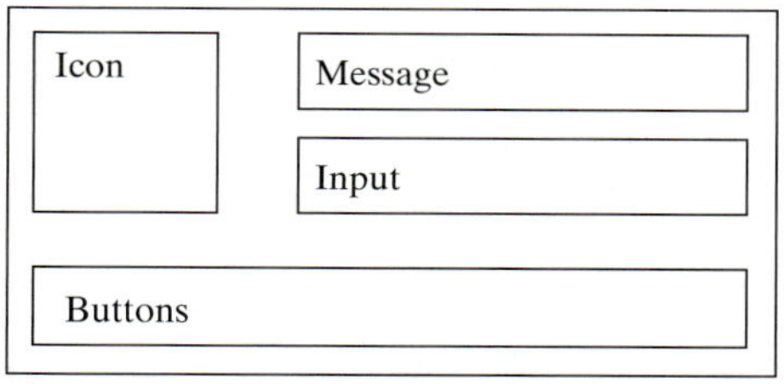

Figure 7.18 *A standard dialog can display an icon, a message, an input, and option buttons.*

For example, you can use the following method to create a message dialog box, as shown in Figure 7.19.

```
JOptionPane.showMessageDialog(this, "SSN not found",
  "For Your Information", JOptionPane.INFORMATION_MESSAGE);
```

Figure 7.19 *The Message dialog displays a message and waits for the user to click OK.*

7.8.1 Message Dialogs

A *message dialog* box displays a message to alert the user and waits for the user to click the OK button to close the dialog. The methods for creating message dialogs are shown below:

```
public static void showMessageDialog(Component parentComponent,
                                     Object message)

public static void showMessageDialog(Component parentComponent,
                                     Object message,
                                     String title,
                                     int messageType)

public static void showMessageDialog(Component parentComponent,
                                     Object message,
                                     String title,
                                     int messageType,
                                     Icon icon)
```

The `parentComponent` can be any component. The `message` is an object, but often a string is used. These two parameters must always be specified. The `title` is a string displayed in the title bar of the dialog with default value "Message."

The `messageType` is one of the following constants:

- `JOptionPane.ERROR_MESSAGE`
- `JOptionPane.INFORMATION_MESSAGE`
- `JOptionPane.PLAIN_MESSAGE`
- `JOptionPane.WARNING_MESSAGE`
- `JOptionPane.QUESTION_MESSAGE`

By default, `messageType` is `JOptionPane.INFORMATION_MESSAGE`. Each type has an associated icon except the `PLAIN_MESSAGE` type, as shown in Figure 7.20. You can also supply your own icon in the `icon` parameter.

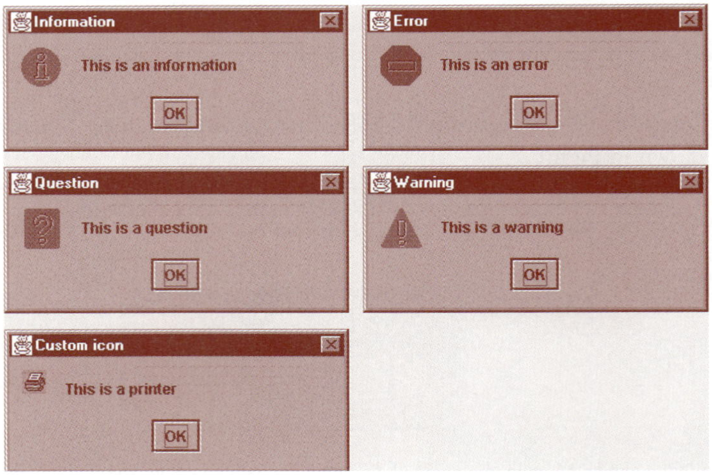

Figure 7.20 *There are five types of message dialog boxes.*

The `message` parameter is an object. If it is a GUI component, the component is displayed. If it is a non-GUI component, the string representation of the object is displayed. For example, the following statement displays a clock in a message dialog, as shown in Figure 7.21.

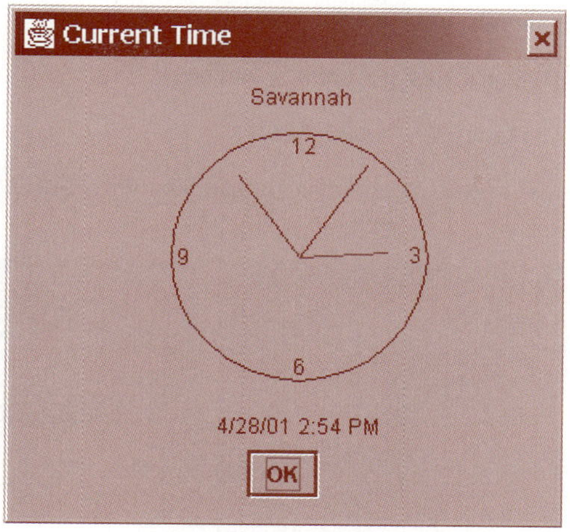

Figure 7.21 *A clock is displayed in a message dialog.*

```
JOptionPane.showMessageDialog(this, new Clock(),
  "Current Time", JOptionPane.PLAIN_MESSAGE);
```

7.8.2 Confirmation Dialogs

A message dialog box displays a message and waits for the user to click the OK button to dismiss the dialog. The message dialog does not return any value. A *confirmation dialog* asks a question and requires the user to respond with an appropriate button. The confirmation dialog returns a value that corresponds to a selected button.

The methods for creating confirmation dialogs are as follows:

```
public static int showConfirmDialog(Component parentComponent,
                                    Object message)

public static int showConfirmDialog(Component parentComponent,
                                    Object message,
                                    String title,
                                    int optionType)

public static int showConfirmDialog(Component parentComponent,
                                    Object message,
                                    String title,
                                    int optionType,
                                    int messageType)

public static int showConfirmDialog(Component parentComponent,
                                    Object message,
                                    String title,
                                    int optionType,
                                    int messageType,
                                    Icon icon)
```

The parameters `parentComponent`, `message`, `title`, `icon`, and `messageType` are the same as in the `showMessageDialog` method. The default value for `title` is "Select an Option" and for `messageType` is `QUESTION_MESSAGE`. The `optionType` determines which buttons are displayed in the dialog. The possible values are as follows:

- `JOptionPane.YES_NO_OPTION`
- `JOptionPane.YES_NO_CANCEL_OPTION`
- `JOptionPane.OK_CANCEL_OPTION`

Figure 7.22 shows the confirmation dialogs with these options.

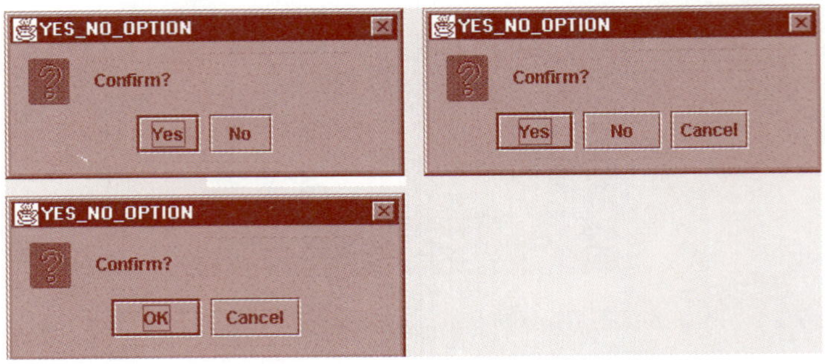

Figure 7.22 *The confirmation dialog displays a question and three types of option buttons, and requires responses from the user.*

The `showConfirmDialog` method returns one of the following `int` values corresponding to the selected option.

- `JOptionPane.YES_OPTION`
- `JOptionPane.NO_OPTION`
- `JOptionPane.CANCEL_OPTION`
- `JOptionPane.OK_OPTION`
- `JOptionPane.CLOSED_OPTION`

These options correspond to the button that was activated, except for the `CLOSED_OPTION`, which implies that the dialog box is closed without buttons activated.

7.8.3 Input Dialogs

An *input dialog* box is used to receive input from the user. The input can be entered from a text field or selected from a combo box or a list. Selectable values can be specified in an array, and a particular value can be designated as the initial selected value. If no selectable value is specified when an input dialog is created, a text field is used for entering input. If fewer than twenty selection values are specified, a combo box is displayed in the input dialog. If twenty or more selection values are specified, a list is used in the input dialog.

The methods for creating input dialogs are shown below:

```
public static String showInputDialog(Object message)

public static String showInputDialog(Component parentComponent,
                                     Object message)
```

```
public static String showInputDialog(Component parentComponent,
                                     Object message,
                                     String title,
                                     int messageType)

public static Object showInputDialog(Component parentComponent,
                                     Object message,
                                     String title,
                                     int messageType,
                                     Icon icon,
                                     Object[] selectionValues,
                                     Object initialSelectionValue)
```

The first three methods listed above use text field for input, as shown in Figure 7.23. The last method listed above specifies an array of `Object` type as selection values in addition to an object that is specified as an initial selection. The first three methods return a `String` that is entered from the text field in the input dialog. The last method returns an `Object` selected from a combo box or a list. The input dialog displays a combo box if there are fewer than twenty selection values, as shown in Figure 7.24; it displays a list if there are twenty or more selection values, as shown in Figure 7.25.

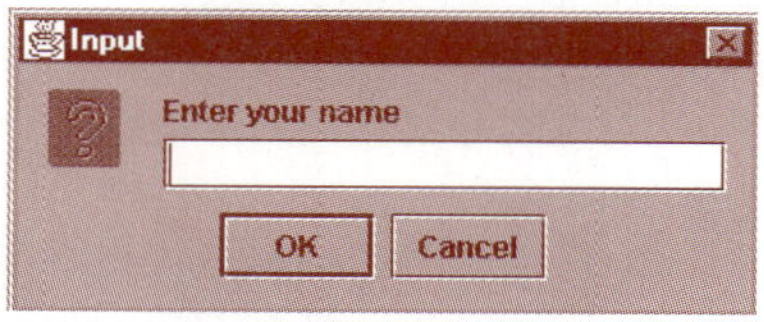

Figure 7.23 *When creating an input dialog without specifying selection values, the input dialog displays a text field for data entry.*

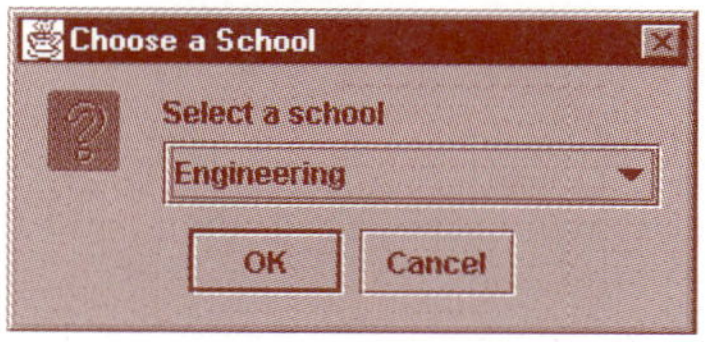

Figure 7.24 *When creating an input dialog with selection values, the input dialog displays a combo box if there are fewer than twenty selection values.*

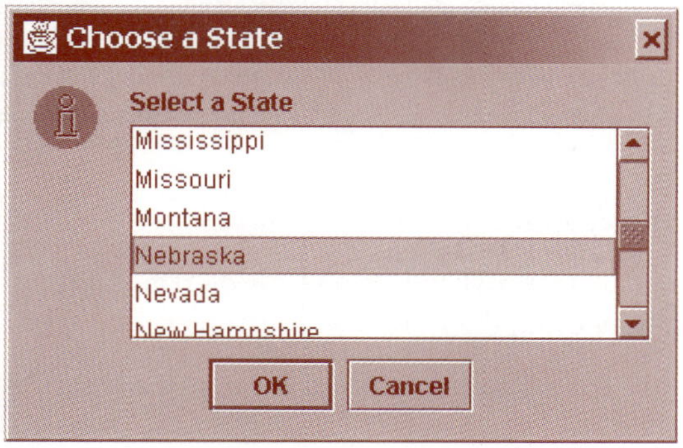

Figure 7.25 *When creating an input dialog with selection values, the input dialog displays a list if there are twenty or more selection values.*

Note
The `showInputDialog` method does not have the `optionType` parameter. The buttons for input dialog are not configurable. The OK and Cancel buttons are always used.

7.8.4 Option Dialogs

An *option dialog* allows you to create custom buttons. You can create an option dialog using the following method:

```
public static int showOptionDialog(Component parentComponent,
                                   Object message,
                                   String title,
                                   int optionType,
                                   int messageType,
                                   Icon icon,
                                   Object[] options,
                                   Object intialValue)
```

The buttons are specified using the `options` parameter. The `intialValue` parameter allows you to specify a button to receive initial focus. The `showOptionDialog` method returns an `int` value indicating the button that was activated. For example, here is the code that creates an option dialog, as shown in Figure 7.26.

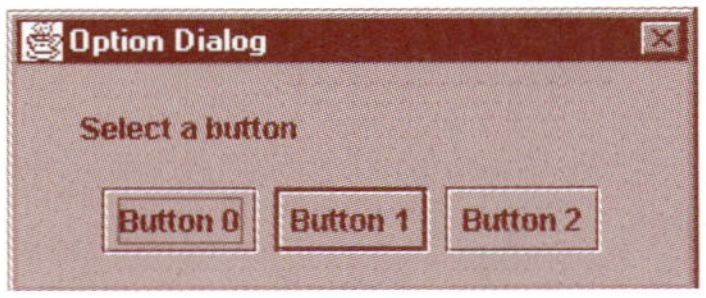

Figure 7.26 *The option dialog displays the custom buttons.*

```
int value =
  JOptionPane.showOptionDialog(this, "Select a button",
    "Option Dialog", JOptionPane.DEFAULT_OPTION,
    JOptionPane.PLAIN_MESSAGE, null,
     new Object[]{"Button 0", "Button 1", "Button 2"}, "Button 1");
```

Example 7.5 Creating Standard Dialogs

This example demonstrates how to create message dialogs, confirmation dialogs, input dialogs, and option dialogs. The example uses menus to display the dialogs, as shown in Figure 7.27.

Here are the steps to complete the project:

1. Create a new package named dialogdemo and an applet named `TestOptionPane` using the Forte Swing JApplet form wizard.

2. Drop a `JLabel` to the south of the applet to create `jlblStatus`.

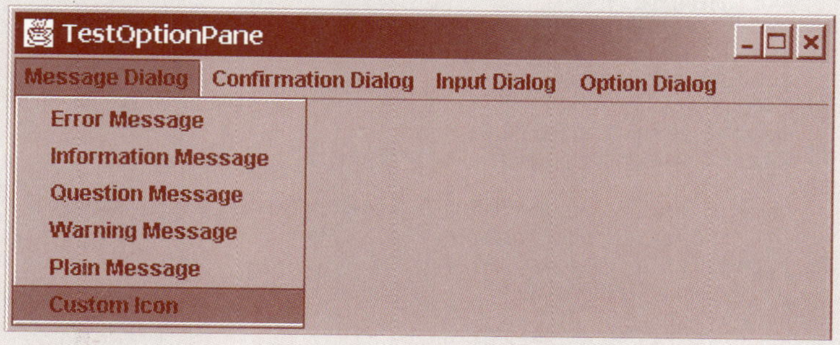

Figure 7.27 *You can display a dialog box by clicking a menu item.*

3. Drop a `JMenuBar` to the applet to create `jMenuBar1`. Add menus Message Dialog, Confirmation Dialog, Input Dialog, and Option Dialog, and their appropriate menu items.

4. Generate and implement the handlers for the menu items to display dialog boxes. The structural relationship of the components in this example is shown in Figure 7.28. The source code is shown in Listing 7.5.

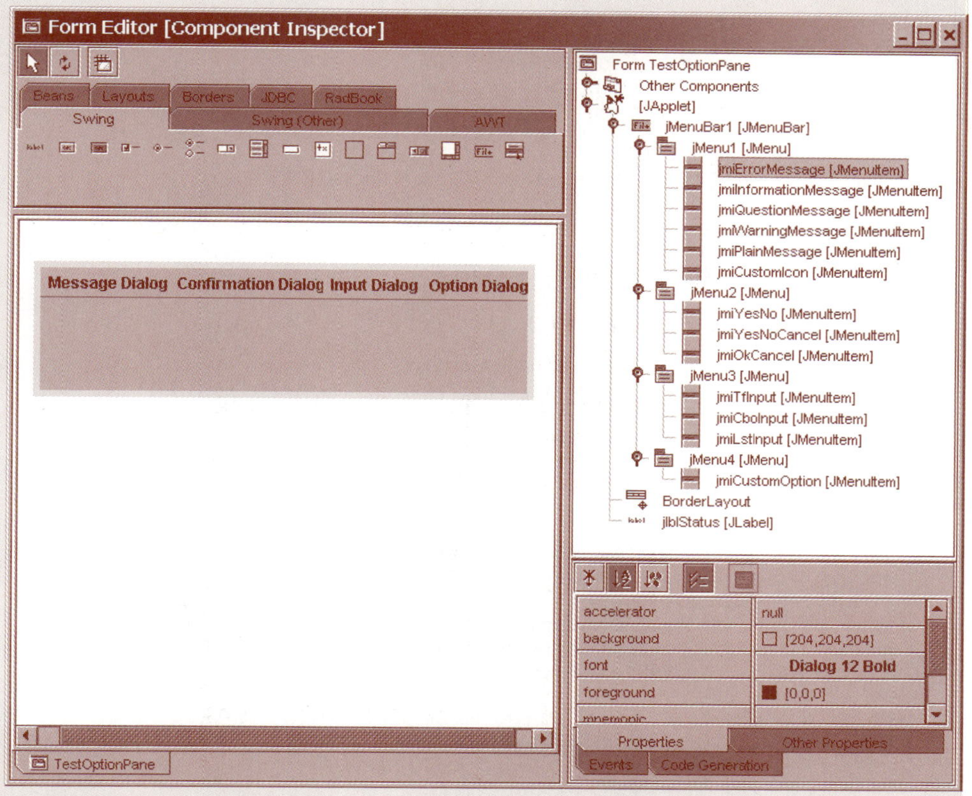

Figure 7.28 *Various menu items are created in the form to demonstrate dialog boxes.*

continued

Example 7.5 continued

```
package dialogdemo;

import javax.swing.*;
import imageviewerdemo.ImageViewer;

public class TestOptionPane extends javax.swing.JApplet {
  /** Creates new form TestOptionPane */
  public TestOptionPane() {
      initComponents();
  }

  private void initComponents() {
    jMenuBar1 = new javax.swing.JMenuBar();
    jMenu1 = new javax.swing.JMenu();
    jmiErrorMessage = new javax.swing.JMenuItem();
    jmiInformationMessage = new javax.swing.JMenuItem();
    jmiQuestionMessage = new javax.swing.JMenuItem();
    jmiWarningMessage = new javax.swing.JMenuItem();
    jmiPlainMessage = new javax.swing.JMenuItem();
    jmiCustomIcon = new javax.swing.JMenuItem();
    jMenu2 = new javax.swing.JMenu();
    jmiYesNo = new javax.swing.JMenuItem();
    jmiYesNoCancel = new javax.swing.JMenuItem();
    jmiOkCancel = new javax.swing.JMenuItem();
    jMenu3 = new javax.swing.JMenu();
    jmiTfInput = new javax.swing.JMenuItem();
    jmiCboInput = new javax.swing.JMenuItem();
    jmiLstInput = new javax.swing.JMenuItem();
    jMenu4 = new javax.swing.JMenu();
    jmiCustomOption = new javax.swing.JMenuItem();
    jlblStatus = new javax.swing.JLabel();
    jMenu1.setText("Message Dialog");
    jmiErrorMessage.setText("Error Message");
    jmiErrorMessage.addActionListener(
      new java.awt.event.ActionListener() {
      public void actionPerformed(java.awt.event.ActionEvent evt) {
        jmiErrorMessageActionPerformed(evt);
      }
    });

    jMenu1.add(jmiErrorMessage);
    jmiInformationMessage.setText("Information Message");
    jmiInformationMessage.addActionListener(
      new java.awt.event.ActionListener() {
      public void actionPerformed(java.awt.event.ActionEvent evt) {
        jmiInformationMessageActionPerformed(evt);
      }
    });
    jMenu1.add(jmiInformationMessage);
    jmiQuestionMessage.setText("Question Message");
    jmiQuestionMessage.addActionListener(
      new java.awt.event.ActionListener() {
      public void actionPerformed(java.awt.event.ActionEvent evt) {
        jmiQuestionMessageActionPerformed(evt);
      }
    });
    jMenu1.add(jmiQuestionMessage);
```

Listing 7.5 *TestOptionPane.java*

```
    jmiWarningMessage.setText("Warning Message");
    jmiWarningMessage.addActionListener(
      new java.awt.event.ActionListener() {
      public void actionPerformed(java.awt.event.ActionEvent evt) {
        jmiWarningMessageActionPerformed(evt);
      }
    });
    jMenu1.add(jmiWarningMessage);
    jmiPlainMessage.setText("Plain Message");
    jmiPlainMessage.addActionListener(
      new java.awt.event.ActionListener() {
      public void actionPerformed(java.awt.event.ActionEvent evt) {
        jmiPlainMessageActionPerformed(evt);
      }
    });
    jMenu1.add(jmiPlainMessage);
    jmiCustomIcon.setText("Custom Icon");
    jmiCustomIcon.addActionListener(
      new java.awt.event.ActionListener() {
      public void actionPerformed(java.awt.event.ActionEvent evt) {
        jmiCustomIconActionPerformed(evt);
      }
    });
    jMenu1.add(jmiCustomIcon);
    jMenuBar1.add(jMenu1);
    jMenu2.setText("Confirmation Dialog");
    jmiYesNo.setText("YES_NO_OPTION");
    jmiYesNo.addActionListener(new java.awt.event.ActionListener() {
      public void actionPerformed(java.awt.event.ActionEvent evt) {
        jmiYesNoActionPerformed(evt);
      }
    });
    jMenu2.add(jmiYesNo);
    jmiYesNoCancel.setText("YES_NO_CANCEL_OPTION");
    jmiYesNoCancel.addActionListener(
      new java.awt.event.ActionListener() {
      public void actionPerformed(java.awt.event.ActionEvent evt) {
        jmiYesNoCancelActionPerformed(evt);
      }
    });
    jMenu2.add(jmiYesNoCancel);
    jmiOkCancel.setText("OK_CANCEL_OPTION");
    jmiOkCancel.addActionListener(
      new java.awt.event.ActionListener() {
      public void actionPerformed(java.awt.event.ActionEvent evt) {
        jmiOkCancelActionPerformed(evt);
      }
    });

    jMenu2.add(jmiOkCancel);
    jMenuBar1.add(jMenu2);
    jMenu3.setText("Input Dialog");
    jmiTfInput.setText("TextField Input");
    jmiTfInput.addActionListener(
      new java.awt.event.ActionListener() {
      public void actionPerformed(java.awt.event.ActionEvent evt) {
        jmiTfInputActionPerformed(evt);
      }
    });
```

Listing 7.5 *continued*

continued

Example 7.5 continued

```
      jMenu3.add(jmiTfInput);
      jmiCboInput.setText("ComboBox Input");
      jmiCboInput.addActionListener(
        new java.awt.event.ActionListener() {
        public void actionPerformed(java.awt.event.ActionEvent evt) {
          jmiCboInputActionPerformed(evt);
        }
      });
      jMenu3.add(jmiCboInput);
      jmiLstInput.setText("List Input");
      jmiLstInput.addActionListener(
        new java.awt.event.ActionListener() {
        public void actionPerformed(java.awt.event.ActionEvent evt) {
          jmiLstInputActionPerformed(evt);
        }
      });
      jMenu3.add(jmiLstInput);
      jMenuBar1.add(jMenu3);
      jMenu4.setText("Option Dialog");
      jmiCustomOption.setText("Custom Option");
      jmiCustomOption.addActionListener(
        new java.awt.event.ActionListener() {
        public void actionPerformed(java.awt.event.ActionEvent evt) {
          jmiCustomOptionActionPerformed(evt);
        }
      });
      jMenu4.add(jmiCustomOption);
      jMenuBar1.add(jMenu4);
      getContentPane().add(jlblStatus, java.awt.BorderLayout.SOUTH);
      setJMenuBar(jMenuBar1);
    }

    private void jmiOkCancelActionPerformed(
      java.awt.event.ActionEvent evt) {
      int selectedOption =
        JOptionPane.showConfirmDialog(this, "Confirm?",
          "YES_NO_OPTION", JOptionPane.OK_CANCEL_OPTION,
          JOptionPane.QUESTION_MESSAGE);
      jlblStatus.setText("Option " + selectedOption + " selected");
    }

    private void jmiYesNoCancelActionPerformed(
      java.awt.event.ActionEvent evt) {
      int selectedOption =
        JOptionPane.showConfirmDialog(this, "Confirm?",
          "YES_NO_OPTION", JOptionPane.YES_NO_CANCEL_OPTION,
          JOptionPane.QUESTION_MESSAGE);
      jlblStatus.setText("Option " + selectedOption + " selected");
    }

    private void jmiYesNoActionPerformed(
      java.awt.event.ActionEvent evt) {
      int selectedOption =
        JOptionPane.showConfirmDialog(this, "Confirm?",
          "YES_NO_OPTION", JOptionPane.YES_NO_OPTION,
          JOptionPane.QUESTION_MESSAGE);
      jlblStatus.setText("Option " + selectedOption + " selected");
    }

```

Listing 7.5 *continued*

```
  private void jmiCustomOptionActionPerformed(
    java.awt.event.ActionEvent evt) {
    int value =
      JOptionPane.showOptionDialog(this, "Select a button",
        "Option Dialog", JOptionPane.DEFAULT_OPTION,
        JOptionPane.PLAIN_MESSAGE, null,
        new Object[]{"Button 0", "Button 1", "Button 2"},
        "Button 1");
    jlblStatus.setText("Value is " + value);
  }

  private void jmiLstInputActionPerformed(
    java.awt.event.ActionEvent evt) {
    Object input =
      JOptionPane.showInputDialog(this, "Select an item",
        "Choose a State", JOptionPane.QUESTION_MESSAGE, null,
        new String[]{"Item 1", "Item 2", "Item 3", "Item 4",
          "Item 5", "Item 6", "Item 7", "Item 8", "Item 9",
          "Item 10", "Item 11", "Item 12", "Item 13", "Item 14",
          "Item 15", "Item 16", "Item 17", "Item 18", "Item 19",
          "Item 20"},
        "Item 5");
    jlblStatus.setText("Input is " + input);
  }

  private void jmiCboInputActionPerformed(
    java.awt.event.ActionEvent evt) {
    Object input =
      JOptionPane.showInputDialog(this, "Select a school",
        "Choose a School", JOptionPane.QUESTION_MESSAGE, null,
        new String[]{"Arts and Science", "Engineering", "Education"},
        "Engineering");
    jlblStatus.setText("Input is " + input);
  }

  private void jmiTfInputActionPerformed(
    java.awt.event.ActionEvent evt) {
    String input =
      JOptionPane.showInputDialog(this, "Enter your name");
    jlblStatus.setText("Input is " + input);
  }

  private void jmiCustomIconActionPerformed(
    java.awt.event.ActionEvent evt) {
    JOptionPane.showMessageDialog(this, "This is a printer",
      "Custom icon", JOptionPane.INFORMATION_MESSAGE,
      ImageViewer.createImageIcon("/image/print.gif", this));
  }

  private void jmiPlainMessageActionPerformed(
    java.awt.event.ActionEvent evt) {
    JOptionPane.showMessageDialog(this, new clockdemo.Clock(),
      "Current Time", JOptionPane.PLAIN_MESSAGE);
  }

  private void jmiWarningMessageActionPerformed(
    java.awt.event.ActionEvent evt) {
    JOptionPane.showMessageDialog(this, "This is a warning",
      "Warning", JOptionPane.WARNING_MESSAGE);
  }

```

Listing 7.5 *continued*

continued

Example 7.5 continued

```
    private void jmiQuestionMessageActionPerformed(
      java.awt.event.ActionEvent evt) {
      JOptionPane.showMessageDialog(this, "This is a question",
        "Question", JOptionPane.QUESTION_MESSAGE);
    }

    private void jmiInformationMessageActionPerformed(
      java.awt.event.ActionEvent evt) {
      JOptionPane.showMessageDialog(this, "This is an information",
        "Information", JOptionPane.INFORMATION_MESSAGE);
    }

    private void jmiErrorMessageActionPerformed(
      java.awt.event.ActionEvent evt) {
      JOptionPane.showMessageDialog(this, "This is an error",
        "Error", JOptionPane.ERROR_MESSAGE);
    }

    // Variables declaration - do not modify
    private javax.swing.JMenuBar jMenuBar1;
    private javax.swing.JMenu jMenu1;
    private javax.swing.JMenuItem jmiErrorMessage;
    private javax.swing.JMenuItem jmiInformationMessage;
    private javax.swing.JMenuItem jmiQuestionMessage;
    private javax.swing.JMenuItem jmiWarningMessage;
    private javax.swing.JMenuItem jmiPlainMessage;
    private javax.swing.JMenuItem jmiCustomIcon;
    private javax.swing.JMenu jMenu2;
    private javax.swing.JMenuItem jmiYesNo;
    private javax.swing.JMenuItem jmiYesNoCancel;
    private javax.swing.JMenuItem jmiOkCancel;
    private javax.swing.JMenu jMenu3;
    private javax.swing.JMenuItem jmiTfInput;
    private javax.swing.JMenuItem jmiCboInput;
    private javax.swing.JMenuItem jmiLstInput;
    private javax.swing.JMenu jMenu4;
    private javax.swing.JMenuItem jmiCustomOption;
    private javax.swing.JLabel jlblStatus;
    // End of variables declaration
  }
```

Listing 7.5 *continued*

Example Review

There are four types of standard dialog boxes: Message, Confirmation, Input, and Option. Use the message dialog if you want to display a message to the user. Use the confirmation dialog if you want the user to confirm the question. Use the input dialog if you want input from the user. Use the option dialog if you want custom buttons in the dialog.

The standard dialogs can be easily created using the methods `showMessageDialog`, `showConfirmDialog`, `showInputDialog`, and `showOptionDialog`. These methods use the parameters `parentComponent`, `message`, `title`, `optionType`, `messageType`, `options`, and `initialValue`. The `message` is usually a string, but it can be a GUI component. The `optionType` specifies the buttons. The message dialog has a fixed OK button, and the input dialog has two fixed buttons, OK and Cancel. Therefore, the `optionType` parameter is not used in the message and input dialogs.

7.9 Creating Custom Dialogs

Standard dialogs are sufficient in most cases. Occasionally, you need to create custom dialogs. In Swing, the `JDialog` class can be extended to create custom dialogs.

`JDialog` is a subclass of `java.awt.Dialog` fitted with an instance of `JRootPane`. As with `JFrame`, components are added to the `contentPane` of `JDialog`. Creating a custom dialog usually involves laying out user interface components in the dialog, adding buttons for dismissing the dialog, and installing listeners that respond to button actions.

The standard dialog is *modal*, which means that no other window can be accessed before the dialog is dismissed. However, the custom dialogs derived from `JDialog` are not modal by default. To make a dialog modal, set its `modal` property to `true`. To display an instance of `JDialog`, set its `visible` property to `true`.

Example 7.6 Creating Custom Dialogs

This example demonstrates how to create custom dialogs using the Forte Swing JDialog form wizard. The example creates a button. When you click the button, a dialog for selecting colors is displayed, as shown in Figure 7.29.

Figure 7.29 *The custom dialog allows you to choose a color for the button's foreground.*

The color dialog can be created as follows:

1. In the context menu of the dialogdemo package, choose *New, Swing Forms, JDialog* to create a Forte Swing JDialog form named ColorDialog.
2. Drop a `JPanel` to the south of the form to create `jpButtons`, and set its layout to `FlowLayout`. Drop a `JButton` twice into `jpButtons` to create `jbtOK` and `jbtCancel` with text OK and Cancel.
3. Drop a `JPanel` to the center of the form to create `jpColor`, and set its layout to `BorderLayout`.

continued

Example 7.6 continued

4. Drop a `JPanel` to the south of `jpColor` to create `jpSelectColor`, and a `JPanel` to the center of `jpColor` to create `jpSelectedColor`. Set the `layout` of `jpSelectColor` to `BorderLayout`. Set the border with title "Select Color" for `jpSelectColor`.

5. Drop a `JPanel` to the west of `jpSelectColor` to create `jpLabels`. Drop a `JPanel` to the center of `jpSelectColor` to create `jpSliders`.

6. Set the `layout` of `jpLabels` and `jpSlider` to `GridLayout` with three rows. Drop three labels to `jpLabels` with text Red, Green, and Blue. Drop three sliders to `jpSlider`. Rename them `jslRed`, `jslGreen`, and `jslBlue`. Set the `maximum` property of the sliders to 128.

7. Declare a variable named `color` of the `java.awt.Color` type for the currently selected color (Line 8). Declare variables named `redValue`, `greenValue`, and `blueValue` for the currently selected red, green, and blue colors (Line 7).

8. Generate and implement the handlers for handling the `stateChanged` event in the sliders (Lines 105–123). Generate and implement the handlers for handling the action event in the buttons, as shown in Listing 7.6 (Lines 125–129, 135–137).

```
1   package dialogdemo;
2
3   import java.awt.Color;
4
5   public class ColorDialog extends javax.swing.JDialog {
6     // Declare color component values and selected color
7     private int redValue, greenValue, blueValue;
8     private java.awt.Color color = null;
9
10    /** Default constructor */
11    public ColorDialog() {
12      this(null, true);
13    }
14
15    /** Creates new form ColorDialog */
16    public ColorDialog(java.awt.Frame parent, boolean modal) {
17      super(parent, modal);
18      setTitle("Choose Color");
19      initComponents();
20    }
21
22    /**  Return color */
23    public Color getColor() {
24      return color;
25    }
26
27    private void initComponents() {
28      jpButtons = new javax.swing.JPanel();
29      jbtOK = new javax.swing.JButton();
30      jbtCancel = new javax.swing.JButton();
31      jpColor = new javax.swing.JPanel();
32      jpSelectColor = new javax.swing.JPanel();
```

Listing 7.6 *ColorDialog.java*

```
        jpLabels = new javax.swing.JPanel();
        jLabel1 = new javax.swing.JLabel();
        jLabel2 = new javax.swing.JLabel();
        jLabel3 = new javax.swing.JLabel();
        jpSliders = new javax.swing.JPanel();
        jslRed = new javax.swing.JSlider();
        jslGreen = new javax.swing.JSlider();
        jslBlue = new javax.swing.JSlider();
        jpSelectedColor = new javax.swing.JPanel();
        addWindowListener(new java.awt.event.WindowAdapter() {
          public void windowClosing(java.awt.event.WindowEvent evt) {
            closeDialog(evt);
          }
        });
        jbtOK.setText("OK");
        jbtOK.addActionListener(new java.awt.event.ActionListener() {
          public void actionPerformed(java.awt.event.ActionEvent evt) {
            jbtOKActionPerformed(evt);
          }
        });
        jpButtons.add(jbtOK);
        jbtCancel.setText("Cancel");
        jbtCancel.addActionListener(new java.awt.event.ActionListener() {
          public void actionPerformed(java.awt.event.ActionEvent evt) {
            jbtCancelActionPerformed(evt);
          }
        });
        jpButtons.add(jbtCancel);
        getContentPane().add(jpButtons, java.awt.BorderLayout.SOUTH);
        jpColor.setLayout(new java.awt.BorderLayout());
        jpSelectColor.setLayout(new java.awt.BorderLayout());
        jpSelectColor.setBorder(
          new javax.swing.border.TitledBorder("Select Color"));
        jpLabels.setLayout(new java.awt.GridLayout(3, 0));
        jLabel1.setText("Red");
        jpLabels.add(jLabel1);
        jLabel2.setText("Green");
        jpLabels.add(jLabel2);
        jLabel3.setText("Blue");
        jpLabels.add(jLabel3);
        jpSelectColor.add(jpLabels, java.awt.BorderLayout.WEST);
        jpSliders.setLayout(new java.awt.GridLayout(3, 0));
        jslRed.setMaximum(128);
        jslRed.addChangeListener(new javax.swing.event.ChangeListener() {
          public void stateChanged(javax.swing.event.ChangeEvent evt) {
            jslRedStateChanged(evt);
          }
        });
        jpSliders.add(jslRed);
        jslGreen.setMaximum(128);
        jslGreen.addChangeListener(
          new javax.swing.event.ChangeListener() {
          public void stateChanged(javax.swing.event.ChangeEvent evt) {
            jslGreenStateChanged(evt);
          }
        });
        jpSliders.add(jslGreen);
        jslBlue.setMaximum(128);
        jslBlue.addChangeListener(
          new javax.swing.event.ChangeListener() {
```

Listing 7.6 *continued*

continued

Example 7.6 continued

```
      public void stateChanged(javax.swing.event.ChangeEvent evt) {
        jslBlueStateChanged(evt);
      }
    });
    jpSliders.add(jslBlue);
    jpSelectColor.add(jpSliders, java.awt.BorderLayout.CENTER);
    jpColor.add(jpSelectColor, java.awt.BorderLayout.SOUTH);
    jpColor.add(jpSelectedColor, java.awt.BorderLayout.CENTER);
    getContentPane().add(jpColor, java.awt.BorderLayout.CENTER);
    pack();
  }

  private void jslBlueStateChanged(
    javax.swing.event.ChangeEvent evt) {
    blueValue = jslBlue.getValue();
    color = new Color(redValue, greenValue, blueValue);
    jpSelectedColor.setBackground(color);
  }

  private void jslGreenStateChanged(
    javax.swing.event.ChangeEvent evt) {
    greenValue = jslGreen.getValue();
    color = new Color(redValue, greenValue, blueValue);
    jpSelectedColor.setBackground(color);
  }

  private void jslRedStateChanged(
    javax.swing.event.ChangeEvent evt) {
    redValue = jslRed.getValue();
    color = new Color(redValue, greenValue, blueValue);
    jpSelectedColor.setBackground(color);
  }

  private void jbtCancelActionPerformed(
    java.awt.event.ActionEvent evt) {
    color = null;
    setVisible(false);
  }

  public java.awt.Dimension getPreferredSize() {
    return new java.awt.Dimension(200, 200);
  }

  private void jbtOKActionPerformed(java.awt.event.ActionEvent evt) {
    setVisible(false);
  }

  // Variables declaration - do not modify
  private javax.swing.JPanel jpButtons;
  private javax.swing.JButton jbtOK;
  private javax.swing.JButton jbtCancel;
  private javax.swing.JPanel jpColor;
  private javax.swing.JPanel jpSelectColor;
  private javax.swing.JPanel jpLabels;
  private javax.swing.JLabel jLabel1;
  private javax.swing.JLabel jLabel2;
  private javax.swing.JLabel jLabel3;
  private javax.swing.JPanel jpSliders;
  private javax.swing.JSlider jslRed;
  private javax.swing.JSlider jslGreen;
```

Listing 7.6 *continued*

```
    private javax.swing.JSlider jslBlue;
    private javax.swing.JPanel jpSelectedColor;
    // End of variables declaration
}
```

Listing 7.6 *continued*

Now you create a test class to use the color dialog, as follows:

1. Reopen the dialogdemo package and create an applet named `TestCustomDialog` using the Forte Swing JApplet form wizard.
2. Set the `layout` of the applet to `FlowLayout`. Drop a `JButton` in the applet to create `jbtChangeColor`. Set the `text` of the button to "Change Button Text Color."
3. Declare and create an instance of `ColorDialog`.
4. Generate and implement the handler for the button to show the dialog. Change the color of the button text using the selected color from the dialog box, as shown in Figure 7.29. Listing 7.7 gives the source code for `TestCustomDialog`.

NOTE

If you install `ColorDialog` to the component palette and drop to the form, Forte will report an exception. You cannot drop an instance of `JFrame`, `JApplet`, or `JDialog` into the form in the current edition of Forte.

```
package dialogdemo;

public class TestCustomDialog extends javax.swing.JApplet {
  ColorDialog colorDialog1 = new ColorDialog();

  /** Creates new form TestCustomDialog */
  public TestCustomDialog() {
    initComponents();
  }

  private void initComponents() {
    jbtChangeColor = new javax.swing.JButton();
    getContentPane().setLayout(new java.awt.FlowLayout());
    jbtChangeColor.setText("Change Button Text Color");
    jbtChangeColor.addActionListener(
      new java.awt.event.ActionListener() {
      public void actionPerformed(java.awt.event.ActionEvent evt) {
        jbtChangeColorActionPerformed(evt);
      }
    });
    getContentPane().add(jbtChangeColor);
  }

  private void jbtChangeColorActionPerformed(
    java.awt.event.ActionEvent evt) {
    colorDialog1.setVisible(true);

```

Listing 7.7 *TestCustomDialog.java*

continued

Example 7.6 continued

```
        if (colorDialog1.getColor() != null)
          jbtChangeColor.setForeground(colorDialog1.getColor());
      }

      // Variables declaration - do not modify
      private javax.swing.JButton jbtChangeColor;
      // End of variables declaration
    }
```

Listing 7.7 *TestCustomDialog.java*

Example Review

The custom dialog box allows the user to use the sliders to select colors. The selected color is stored in the `color` variable. When the user clicks the Cancel button, color becomes `null`, which implies that no selection has been made.

The dialog box is displayed when the user clicks the "Change Button Text Color" button and is closed when the OK button or the Cancel button is clicked.

TIP

Not setting the dialog modal when needed is a common mistake. In this example, the dialog is set modal (Line 12 in Listing 7.6). If the dialog is not modal, all the statements in the "Change Button Text Color" button handler are executed before the color is selected from the dialog box.

7.10 JColorChooser

You created a color dialog in the preceding example. This dialog is a subclass of `JDialog`, which is a subclass of `java.awt.Dialog`. Therefore, it cannot be added to a container as a component. Color dialogs are commonly used in GUI programming. Swing provides a convenient and versatile color dialog named `javax.swing.JColorChooser`. Like `JOptionPane`, `JColorChooser` is a lightweight component inherited from `JComponent`. It can be added to any container. Figure 7.30 shows a `JColorChooser` in an applet.

Often an instance of `JColorChooser` is added to a dialog window to display a color dialog. To display color chooser in a dialog box, use `JColorChooser`'s static `showDialog` method:

```
public static Color showDialog(Component parentComponent,
                               String title,
                               Color initialColor)
```

This method creates an instance of `JDialog` with three buttons, OK, Cancel, and Reset, to hold a `JColorChooser` object, as shown in Figure 7.31. The method displays a modal dialog. If the user clicks the OK button, the method dismisses the

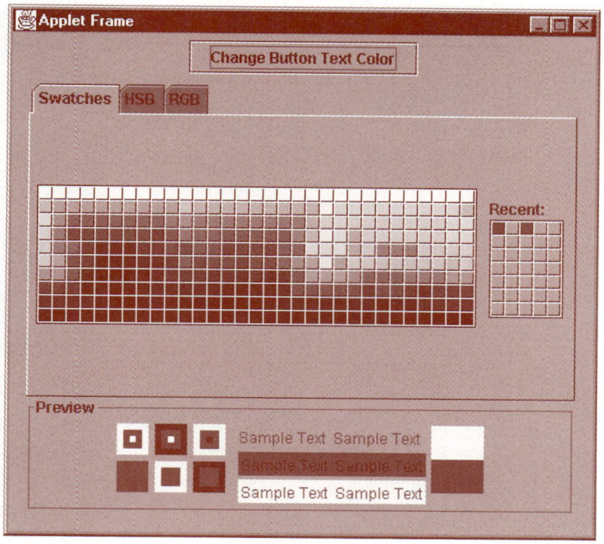

Figure 7.30 *An instance of* `JColorChooser` *is displayed in an applet.*

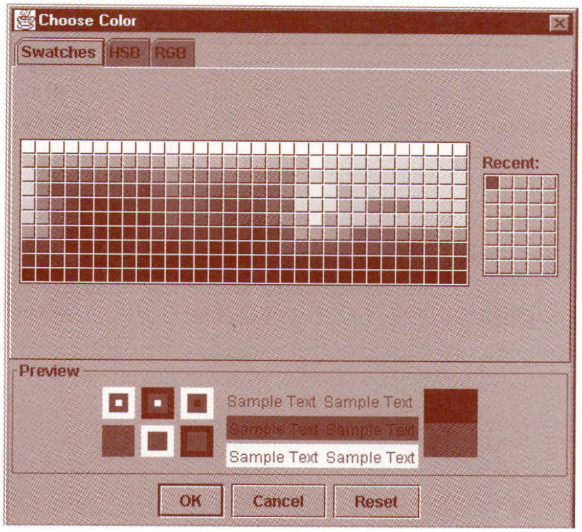

Figure 7.31 *An instance of* `JColorChooser` *is displayed in a dialog box with the OK, Cancel, and Reset buttons.*

dialog and returns the selected color. If the user clicks the Cancel button or closes the dialog, the method dismisses the dialog and returns null.

`JColorChooser` consists of a tabbed pane and a color preview panel. The tabbed pane has three tabs for choosing colors using Swatches, HSB, and RGB, as shown in Figure 7.32. The preview panel shows the effect of the selected color.

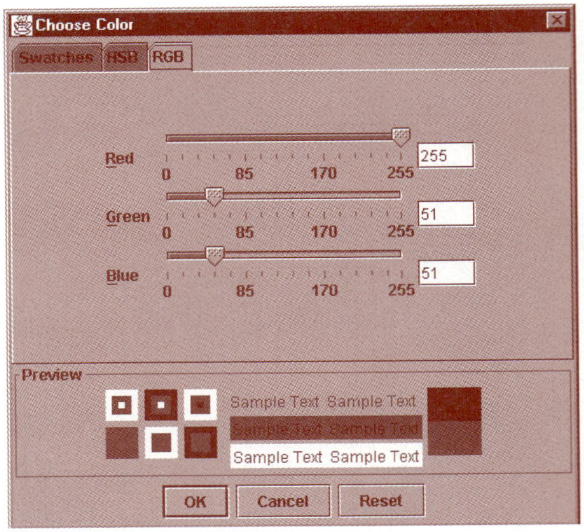

Figure 7.32 *The* `JColorChooser` *class contains a tabbed pane with three tabs for selecting colors using Swatches, HSB, and RGB.*

NOTE

`JColorChooser` is very flexible. It allows you to replace the tabbed pane or the color preview panel with custom components. The default tabbed pane and the color preview panel are sufficient. You rarely need to use custom components.

7.11 JFileChooser

Swing provides the `javax.swing.JFileChooser` class that displays a dialog box from which the user can navigate through the file system and select files for loading or saving, as shown in Figure 7.33.

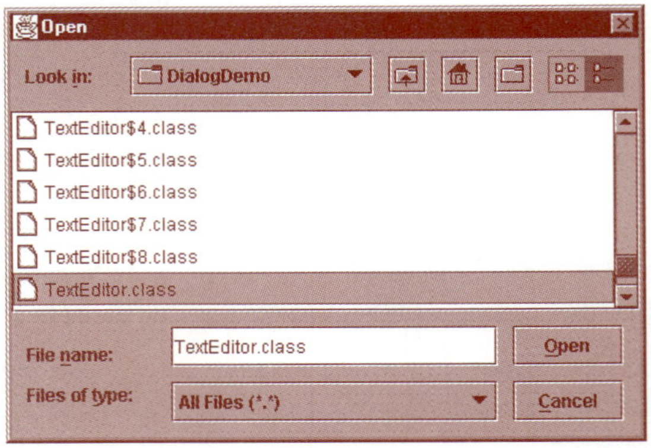

Figure 7.33 *The Swing* `JFileChooser` *shows files and directories, and enables the user to navigate through the file system visually.*

Like `JColorChooser`, `JFileChooser` is a lightweight component inherited from `JComponent`. It can be added to any container if desired, but often you create an instance of `JFileChooser` and display it standalone.

`JFileChooser` is a subclass of `JComponent`. There are several ways to construct a file dialog box. The simplest is to use `JFileChooser`'s default constructor.

The file dialog box can appear in two types: open and save. The *open type* is for opening a file, and the *save type* is for storing a file. To create an open file dialog, use the following method:

```
public int showOpenDialog(Component parent)
```

This method creates a dialog box that contains an instance of `JFileChooser` for opening a file. The method returns an `int` value, either `APPROVE_OPTION` or `CANCEL_OPTION`, which indicates whether the OK button or the Cancel button was clicked.

Similarly, you can use the following method to create a dialog for saving files.

```
public int showSaveDialog(Component parent)
```

The file dialog box created with the `showOpenDialog` or `showSaveDialog` is modal. The `JFileChooser` class has the properties inherited from `JComponent`. It also has the following useful properties:

- **`dialogType`** specifies the type of this dialog. Use `OPEN_DIALOG` when you want to bring up a file chooser that the user can use to open a file. Likewise, use `SAVE_DIALOG` to let the user choose a file for saving.
- **`dialogTitle`** is the string that is displayed in the title bar of the dialog box.
- **`currentDirectory`** is the current directory of the file. The type of this property is `java.io.File`. If you want the current directory to be used, use `setCurrentDirectory(new File("."))`.
- **`selectedFile`** is the file you have selected. You can use `getSelectedFile()` to return the selected file from the dialog box. The type of this property is `java.io.File`. If you have a default file name that you expect to use, use `setSelectedFile(new File(filename))`.
- **`selectedFiles`** is a list of the files selected if the file chooser is set to allow multi-selection. The type of this property is `File[]`.
- **`multiSelectionEnabled`** is a `boolean` value indicating whether multiple files can be selected. By default, it is `false`.

Example 7.7 Creating a Text Editor

This example uses Swing menus, tool bar, file chooser, and color chooser to create a simple text editor, as shown in Figure 7.34, which allows the user to open and save text files, clear text, and change the color and font of the text.

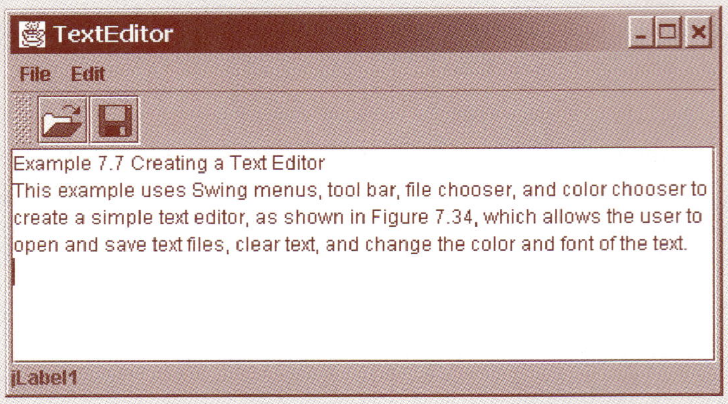

Figure 7.34 *The editor enables you to open and save text files from the File menu or from the tool bar, and to change the color and font of the text from the Edit menu.*

Follow the steps below to complete the project.

1. In the dialogdemo package, create an applet named `TextEditor` using the Forte Swing JApplet form wizard.
2. Drop a `JToolBar` to the north of the applet to create `jToolBar1`. Drop a `JButton` twice to `jToolBar1` to create `jbtOpen` and `jbtSave`. Drop a `JLabel` to the south of the applet to create `jlblStatus`.
3. Drop a `JScrollPane` to the center of the applet, and drop a `JTextArea` to the scroll pane to create `jta`.
4. Drop a `JMenuBar` to the applet to create `jMenuBar1`. Add the menus File and Edit. In the File menu, add the menu items Open, Save, Clear, separator, and Exit. In the Edit menu, add the menu items Foreground Color and Background Color. Rename the menu items `jmiOpen`, `jmiSave`, `jmiClear`, `jmiExit`, `jmiForeground`, and `jmiBackground`.
5. Declare and create an instance of `JFileChooser` named `jFileChooser1` (Line 9).
6. Declare and create image icons named `openImageIcon` and `saveImageIcon` (Lines 15–19). Write the code to set the `icon` property of `jtbOpen` and `jmiOpen` to `openImageIcon` (Lines 21–22), and the `icon` property of `jtbSave` and `jmiSave` to `saveImageIcon` (Lines 23–24).
7. Generate the action event handlers for buttons and menu items. Implement the handlers, as shown in Listing 7.8 (Lines 116–168).

```
package dialogdemo;

import java.io.*;
import java.awt.*;
import javax.swing.*;
import imageviewerdemo.ImageViewer;

public class TextEditor extends javax.swing.JApplet {
  JFileChooser jFileChooser1 = new JFileChooser();

  /** Creates new form TextEditor */
  public TextEditor() {
    initComponents();

    // Declare and create image icons
    ImageIcon openImageIcon = ImageViewer.createImageIcon(
      "/image/open.gif", this);
    ImageIcon saveImageIcon = ImageViewer.createImageIcon(
      "/image/save.gif", this);

    jmiOpen.setIcon(openImageIcon);
    jbtOpen.setIcon(openImageIcon);
    jmiSave.setIcon(saveImageIcon);
    jbtSave.setIcon(saveImageIcon);

    // Set current directory
    jFileChooser1.setCurrentDirectory(new File("."));
  }

  private void initComponents() {
    jMenuBar1 = new javax.swing.JMenuBar();
    jMenu1 = new javax.swing.JMenu();
    jmiOpen = new javax.swing.JMenuItem();
    jmiSave = new javax.swing.JMenuItem();
    jmiClear = new javax.swing.JMenuItem();
    jSeparator1 = new javax.swing.JSeparator();
    jmiExit = new javax.swing.JMenuItem();
    jMenu2 = new javax.swing.JMenu();
    jmiForeground = new javax.swing.JMenuItem();
    jmiBackground = new javax.swing.JMenuItem();
    jToolBar1 = new javax.swing.JToolBar();
    jbtOpen = new javax.swing.JButton();
    jbtSave = new javax.swing.JButton();
    jlblStatus = new javax.swing.JLabel();
    jScrollPane1 = new javax.swing.JScrollPane();
    jta = new javax.swing.JTextArea();
    jMenu1.setText("File");
    jmiOpen.setText("Open");
    jmiOpen.addActionListener(new java.awt.event.ActionListener() {
      public void actionPerformed(java.awt.event.ActionEvent evt) {
        jmiOpenActionPerformed(evt);
      }
    });
    jMenu1.add(jmiOpen);
    jmiSave.setText("Save");
    jmiSave.addActionListener(new java.awt.event.ActionListener() {
      public void actionPerformed(java.awt.event.ActionEvent evt) {
        jmiSaveActionPerformed(evt);
      }
    });
```

Listing 7.8 *TextEditor.java*

continued

Example 7.7 continued

```
        jMenu1.add(jmiSave);
        jmiClear.setText("Clear");
        jmiClear.addActionListener(new java.awt.event.ActionListener() {
          public void actionPerformed(java.awt.event.ActionEvent evt) {
            jmiClearActionPerformed(evt);
          }
        });
        jMenu1.add(jmiClear);
        jMenu1.add(jSeparator1);
        jmiExit.setText("Exit");
        jmiExit.addActionListener(new java.awt.event.ActionListener() {
          public void actionPerformed(java.awt.event.ActionEvent evt) {
            jmiExitActionPerformed(evt);
          }
        });
        jMenu1.add(jmiExit);
        jMenuBar1.add(jMenu1);
        jMenu2.setText("Edit");
        jmiForeground.setText("Foreground");
        jmiForeground.addActionListener(
          new java.awt.event.ActionListener() {
          public void actionPerformed(java.awt.event.ActionEvent evt) {
            jmiForegroundActionPerformed(evt);
          }
        });
        jMenu2.add(jmiForeground);
        jmiBackground.setText("Background");
        jmiBackground.addActionListener(
          new java.awt.event.ActionListener() {
          public void actionPerformed(java.awt.event.ActionEvent evt) {
            jmiBackgroundActionPerformed(evt);
          }
        });
        jMenu2.add(jmiBackground);
        jMenuBar1.add(jMenu2);
        jbtOpen.addActionListener(new java.awt.event.ActionListener() {
          public void actionPerformed(java.awt.event.ActionEvent evt) {
            jbtOpenActionPerformed(evt);
          }
        });
        jToolBar1.add(jbtOpen);
        jbtSave.addActionListener(new java.awt.event.ActionListener() {
          public void actionPerformed(java.awt.event.ActionEvent evt) {
            jbtSaveActionPerformed(evt);
          }
        });
        jToolBar1.add(jbtSave);
        getContentPane().add(jToolBar1, java.awt.BorderLayout.NORTH);
        jlblStatus.setText("jLabel1");
        getContentPane().add(jlblStatus, java.awt.BorderLayout.SOUTH);
        jScrollPane1.setViewportView(jta);
        getContentPane().add(jScrollPane1, java.awt.BorderLayout.CENTER);
        setJMenuBar(jMenuBar1);
      }

      private void jbtSaveActionPerformed(
        java.awt.event.ActionEvent evt) {
        save();
      }

```

Listing 7.8 *continued*

```
  private void jbtOpenActionPerformed(
    java.awt.event.ActionEvent evt) {
    open();
  }

  private void jmiBackgroundActionPerformed(
    java.awt.event.ActionEvent evt) {
    Color selectedColor =
      JColorChooser.showDialog(this, "Choose Background Color",
        jta.getForeground());

    if (selectedColor != null)
      jta.setBackground(selectedColor);
  }

  private void jmiForegroundActionPerformed(
    java.awt.event.ActionEvent evt) {
    Color selectedColor =
      JColorChooser.showDialog(this, "Choose Foreground Color",
        jta.getForeground());

    if (selectedColor != null)
      jta.setForeground(selectedColor);
  }

  private void jmiExitActionPerformed(
    java.awt.event.ActionEvent evt) {
    System.exit(0);
  }

  private void jmiClearActionPerformed(
    java.awt.event.ActionEvent evt) {
    jta.setText(null);
  }

  private void jmiSaveActionPerformed(
    java.awt.event.ActionEvent evt) {
    save();
  }

  private void jmiOpenActionPerformed(
    java.awt.event.ActionEvent evt) {
    open();
  }

  /** Open file */
  private void open() {
    if (jFileChooser1.showOpenDialog(this) ==
      JFileChooser.APPROVE_OPTION) {
      open(jFileChooser1.getSelectedFile());
    }
  }

  /** Open file with the specified File instance */
  private void open(File file) {
    try {
      // Read from the specified file and store it in jta
      BufferedInputStream in = new BufferedInputStream(
```

Listing 7.8 *TextEditor.java*

continued

Example 7.7 continued

```
          new FileInputStream(file));
        byte[] b = new byte[in.available()];
        in.read(b, 0, b.length);
        jta.append(new String(b, 0, b.length));
        in.close();

        // Display the status of the Open file operation in jlblStatus
        jlblStatus.setText(file.getName() + " Opened");
      }
      catch (IOException ex) {
        jlblStatus.setText("Error opening " + file.getName());
      }
    }

    /** Save file */
    private void save() {
      if (jFileChooser1.showSaveDialog(this) ==
      JFileChooser.APPROVE_OPTION) {
        save(jFileChooser1.getSelectedFile());
      }
    }

    /** Save file with specified File instance */
    private void save(File file) {
      try {
        // Write the text in jta to the specified file
        BufferedOutputStream out = new BufferedOutputStream(
        new FileOutputStream(file));
        byte[] b = (jta.getText()).getBytes();
        out.write(b, 0, b.length);
        out.close();

        // Display the status of the save file operation in jlblStatus
        jlblStatus.setText(file.getName()  + " Saved ");
      }
      catch (IOException ex) {
        jlblStatus.setText("Error saving " + file.getName());
      }
    }

    public static void main(String[] args) {
      TextEditor applet = new TextEditor();
      JFrame frame = new JFrame();
      frame.setDefaultCloseOperation(javax.swing.JFrame.EXIT_ON_CLOSE);
      frame.setTitle("TextEditor");
      frame.getContentPane().add(applet, java.awt.BorderLayout.CENTER);
      frame.setSize(400,320);
      java.awt.Dimension d =
      java.awt.Toolkit.getDefaultToolkit().getScreenSize();
      frame.setLocation((d.width - frame.getSize().width) / 2,
      (d.height - frame.getSize().height) / 2);
      frame.setVisible(true);
    }

    // Variables declaration - do not modify
    private javax.swing.JMenuBar jMenuBar1;
    private javax.swing.JMenu jMenu1;
    private javax.swing.JMenuItem jmiOpen;
```

Listing 7.8 *continued*

```
238      private javax.swing.JMenuItem jmiSave;
239      private javax.swing.JMenuItem jmiClear;
240      private javax.swing.JSeparator jSeparator1;
241      private javax.swing.JMenuItem jmiExit;
242      private javax.swing.JMenu jMenu2;
243      private javax.swing.JMenuItem jmiForeground;
244      private javax.swing.JMenuItem jmiBackground;
245      private javax.swing.JToolBar jToolBar1;
246      private javax.swing.JButton jbtOpen;
247      private javax.swing.JButton jbtSave;
248      private javax.swing.JLabel jlblStatus;
249      private javax.swing.JScrollPane jScrollPane1;
250      private javax.swing.JTextArea jta;
251      // End of variables declaration
252    }
```

Listing 7.8 *continued*

Example Review

The program creates the File and Edit menus. The File menu contains the menu commands Open for loading a file, Save for saving a file, Clear for clearing the text editor, and Exit for terminating the program. The Edit menu contains the menu commands Foreground Color and Background Color for setting foreground color and background color in the text. The Open and Save menu commands can also be accessed from the tool bar. The status of executing Open and Save is displayed in the status label.

An instance `jFileChooser1` of `JFileChooser` is created for displaying the file dialog box to open and save files. The `setCurrentDirectory(new File("."))` method (Line 27) is used to set the current directory to the directory where the class is stored.

The `open` method (Line 164) is invoked when the user clicks the Open menu command. The `showOpenDialog` method (Line 169) displays an Open dialog box, as shown in Figure 7.33. Upon receiving the selected file, the method `open(file)` (Line 171) is invoked to load the file to the text area using a `BufferedInputStream` wrapped on a `FileInputStream`.

The `save` method (Line 159) is invoked when the user clicks the Save menu command. The `showSaveDialog` method (Line 195) displays a Save dialog box. Upon receiving the selected file, the method `save(file)` (Line 197) is invoked to save the contents from the text area to the file using a `BufferedOutputStream` wrapped on a `FileOutputStream`.

The color dialog is displayed using the static method `showDialog` (Line 130, 140) of `JColorChooser`. Thus you don't need to create an instance of `JFileChooser`. The `showDialog` method returns the selected color if the OK button is clicked after a color is selected.

Icons can be set from the component inspector, but the example handtyped the code to create image icons and set the icons in the menu items and in the buttons. This has the benefit of allowing different components to share the same icons.

continued

Example 7.7 continued

You have to run the program standalone as an application. If you tried to run it as an applet, a security exception would occur. The exception can be circumvented by editing the security permission. See Java Security from the companion Web site for more information.

NOTE
If you drop a `JFileChooser` to the form, it will become a component inside a container in the form. Future editions of Forte may allow you to drop it to the Other Components node so that it does not have to be a visual component in the form.

Chapter Summary

You learned how to create menus visually using Forte's Form Editor and how to create tool bars using `JToolBar`. You learned how to display standard dialogs using `JOptionPane`, how to create custom dialog by directly extending the `JDialog` class, and how to use `JColorChooser` and `JFileChooser` for selecting colors and files.

Review Questions

7.1 How do you create a menu bar in Forte?

7.2 How do you create a submenu? How do you create a check box menu item? How do you create a radio button menu item?

7.3 What would cause an instance of `JMenuBar` to appear under the Other Components node in the component tree?

7.4 How do you create a popup menu in Forte? How do you show a popup menu? Describe a popup trigger.

7.5 Describe the standard dialog boxes created using the `JOptionPane` class.

7.6 How do you create a message dialog? What are the message types? What is the button in the message dialog?

7.7 How do you create a confirmation dialog? What are the button option types?

7.8 How do you create an input dialog with a text field for entering input? How do you create a combo box dialog for selecting values as input? How do you create a list dialog for selecting values as input?

7.9 How do you show an instance of `JDialog`? Is a standard dialog box created using the static methods in `JOptionPane` modal? Is an instance of `JDialog` modal?

7.10 How do you display an instance of `JColorChooser`? Is an instance of `JColorChooser` modal? How do you obtain the selected color?

7.11 How do you display an instance of `JFileChooser`? Is an instance of `JFileChooser` modal? How do you obtain the selected file?

Programming Exercises

7.1 Write a program that calculates the future value of an investment at a given interest rate for a specified number of years. The formula for the calculation is as follows:

$$\text{futureValue} = \text{investmentAmount} * (1 + \text{monthlyInterestRate})^{\text{years}*12}$$

Use text fields for interest rate, investment amount, and years. Display the future amount in a text field when the user clicks the Calculate button or chooses Calculate from the Operation menu (see Figure 7.35). Show a message dialog box when the user clicks the About menu item from the Help menu.

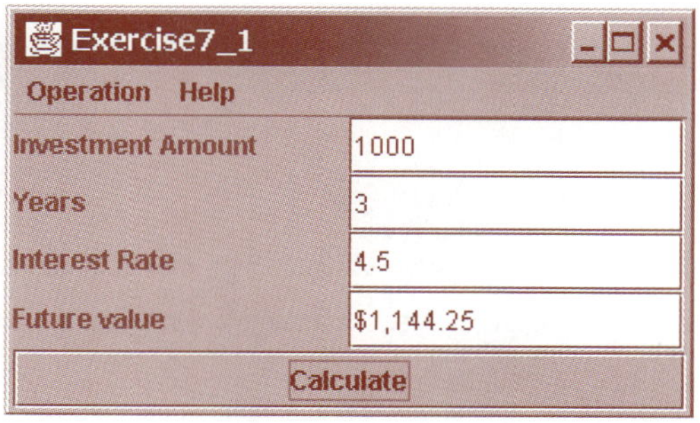

Figure 7.35 *The user enters the investment amount, years, and interest rate to compute future value.*

7.2 Write a program that emulates a paint utility. Your program should enable the user to choose options and draw shapes or get characters from the keyboard based on the selected options (see Figure 7.36). The options are displayed in a tool bar. To draw a line, the user first clicks the line icon in the tool bar and then uses the mouse to draw a line in the same way you would draw using Microsoft Paint.

Figure 7.36 *This exercise produces a prototype drawing utility that enables you to draw lines, rectangles, ovals, and characters.*

7.3 Forte displays a dialog for choosing fonts when you click the `font` property in the inspector, as shown in Figure 7.37. Create this dialog as an exercise.

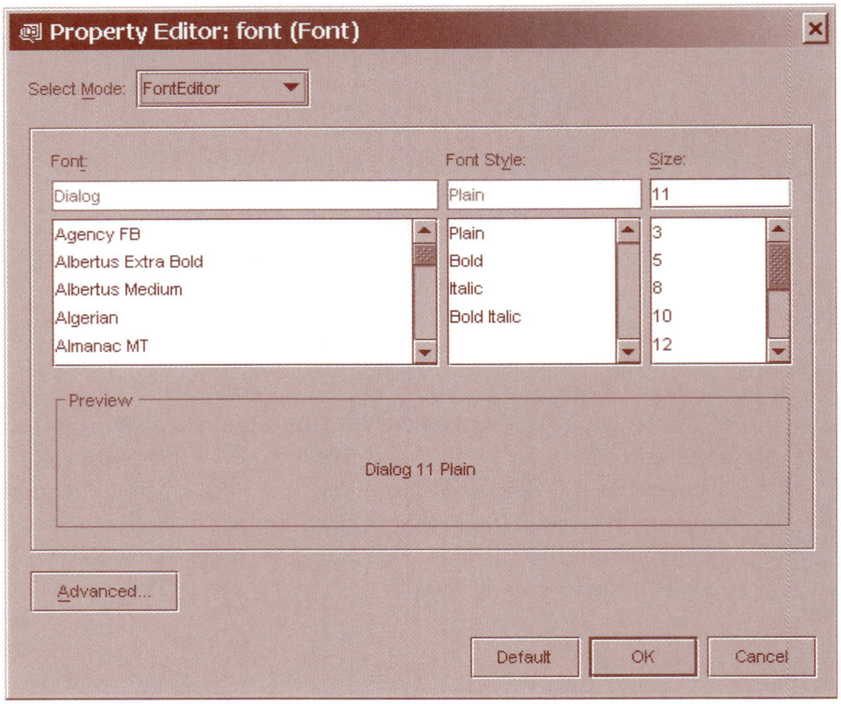

Figure 7.37 *The font dialog box allows you to choose a font by specifying font name, font style, and font size.*

CHAPTER 8

ADVANCED SWING COMPONENTS

Objectives

- To use `JList` to select single or multiple items in a list.
- To use `JComboBox` to select a single item from a combo box.
- To use `JTable` to display and process tables.
- To use `JTree` to display data in a tree hierarchy.
- To learn how to create custom renderers for `JList`, `JComboBox`, `JTable`, and `JTree`.
- To learn how to create custom editors for `JComboBox`, `JTable`, and `JTree`.

8.1 Introduction

In the preceding three chapters, you learned how to use Swing components, containers, layout managers, menus, tool bars, and dialog boxes. This chapter will show you how to work with some of the complex Swing components. You will learn how to use `JList`, `JComboBox`, `JTable`, and `JTree` to create advanced graphical user interfaces.

8.2 JList

A *list* is a component that enables you to choose one or more items. It is useful in limiting a range of choices and avoids the cumbersome validation of data input. `JList` is the Swing version of a list. Functionally it is similar to a set of check boxes or radio buttons, but the selectable items are placed in a list and are chosen by clicking on the items themselves. Figure 8.1 shows an example of `JList`.

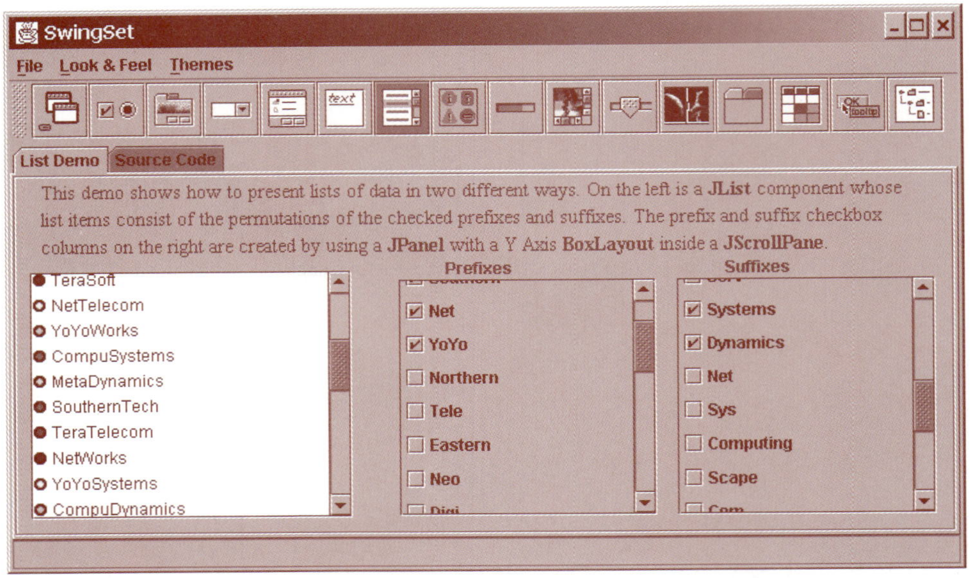

Figure 8.1 *SwingSet demonstrates the features of* `JList`.

`JList` doesn't support scrolling directly. To create a scrollable list, you need to create a `JScrollPane` and add an instance of `JList` to it. An instance of `JList` can be created using its default constructor or one of these three constructors:

- `public JList(ListModel dataModel)`
- `public JList(Object[] listData)`
- `public JList(Vector listData)`

If you have a list of a fixed number of string items, an instance of `JList` can easily be created, as follows:

```
String[] listData = {"Item 1", "Item 2", "Item 3"};
JList jlst = new JList(listData);
```

`JList` supports three selection modes: single selection, single-interval selection, and multiple-interval selection. *Single selection* allows only one item to be selected. *Single-interval selection* allows multiple selections, but the selected items must be contiguous. *Multiple-interval selection* is the most flexible, because it allows selections of any items.

`JList` has the following useful properties:

- **`cellRenderer`** is an object used to render the cells in a list. By default, an instance of `DefaultListCellRenderer` is used to display items in a list that can display strings or icons. Using custom cell renderer is introduced in Section 8.2.3, "List Cell Renderers."
- **`listData`** is a write-only property used to set an array or a vector of objects for a list.
- **`fixedCellHeight`** specifies the height of a list cell. All the cells in a list have the same height. If this property is not specified, the tallest item in the list dictates the cell height for all the cells.
- **`fixedCellWidth`** specifies the width of a list cell. All the cells in a list have the same width. If this property is not specified, the widest item in the list dictates the cell width for all the cells.
- **`model`** is an object that maintains the data for the list. List models must be used explicitly when adding or deleting items in a list. List models are introduced in Section 8.2.1, "List Models."
- **`prototypeCellValue`** is an object whose cell size dictates the cell size of a list.
- **`selectedIndex`** is an `int` value indicating the index of a selected item in a list.
- **`selectedIndices`** is an array of `int` values representing the indices of the selected items in a list.
- **`selectedValue`** is the first selected value in a list.
- **`selectedValues`** is an array of objects representing selected values in a list. This property is read-only.
- **`selectionBackground`** is the background color for selected cells.
- **`selectionForeground`** is the foreground color for selected cells.
- **`selectionMode`** is one of the three values (`SINGLE_SELECTION`, `SINGLE_INTERVAL_SELECTION`, `MULTIPLE_INTERVAL_SELECTION`) that indicate whether single items, single-interval items, or multiple-interval items can be selected.
- **`selectionModel`** is an object that tracks list selection. List-selection models are rarely used explicitly. They are discussed in Section 8.2.2, "List-Selection Models."

- **`visibleRowCount`** is the preferred number of rows in a list that can be displayed without a scroll bar. The default value is 8.

`JList` generates `javax.swing.event.ListSelectionEvent` to notify the listeners of the selections. The listener must implement the `valueChanged` handler to process the event.

Example 8.1 Simple List Demo

This example creates a list of a fixed number of items displayed as strings. The example allows you to set a selection mode dynamically from a combo box, as shown in Figure 8.2. When you select one or more items, their values are displayed in a status label below the list.

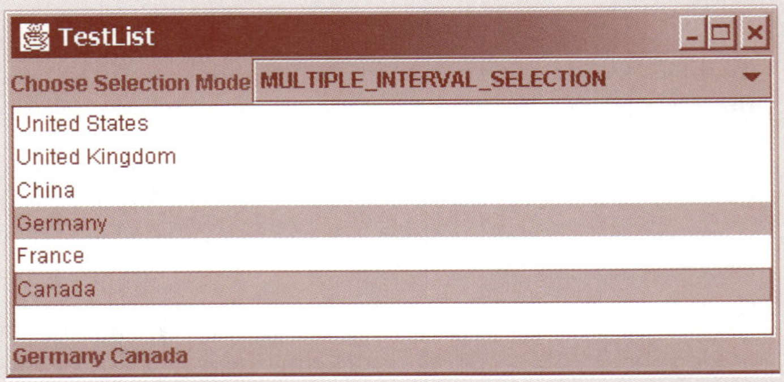

Figure 8.2 *You can choose single selection, single-interval selection, or multiple-interval selection in a list.*

Here are the steps to complete the project:

1. Create a new package named listdemo and a new applet named TestList using the Forte Swing JApplet form wizard.
2. Drop a `JPanel` to the north of the applet to create `jpSelectionMode`. Drop a `JLabel` to the south of the applet to create `jlblStatus`. Drop a `JScrollPane` to the center of the applet, and drop a `JList` to the scroll pane to create `jList1`.
3. Set `layout` of `jpSelectionMode` to `BorderLayout`. Drop a `JLabel` to the west of `jpSelectionMode` and a `JComboBox` to the center of `jpSelectionMode`. Rename the combo box `jcboSelectionMode`, and set the text of the label to "Choose Selection Mode."
4. Create an array of strings named `countries` for the names of several countries (Line 7–8 in Listing 8.1). Add countries to the list using the following method (Line 14 in Listing 8.1):

```
jList1.setListData(countries);
```

5. Add three items “SINGLE_SELECTION,” “SINGLE_INTERVAL_SELECTION,” and “MULTIPLE_INTERVAL_SELECTION” to the combo box using the `addItem` method (Lines 17–19).

6. Generate the `ActionEvent` handler for the combo box, and implement it to set a selection mode for the list (Lines 69–79).

7. Generate the `ListSelectionEvent` handler for the list, and implement it to display the selected items in the label (Lines 69–79).

```
1   package listdemo;
2
3   import javax.swing.*;
4
5   public class TestList extends javax.swing.JApplet {
6     // Create an array of strings for country names
7     String[] countries = {"United States", "United Kingdom", "China",
8       "Germany", "France", "Canada"};
9
10    /** Creates new form TestList */
11    public TestList() {
12      initComponents();
13
14      jList1.setListData(countries);
15
16      // Add selection modes to the combo box
17      jcboSelectionMode.addItem("SINGLE_SELECTION");
18      jcboSelectionMode.addItem("SINGLE_INTERVAL_SELECTION");
19      jcboSelectionMode.addItem("MULTIPLE_INTERVAL_SELECTION");
20    }
21
22    private void initComponents() {
23      jpSelectionMode = new javax.swing.JPanel();
24      jLabel2 = new javax.swing.JLabel();
25      jcboSelectionMode = new javax.swing.JComboBox();
26      jScrollPane1 = new javax.swing.JScrollPane();
27      jList1 = new javax.swing.JList();
28      jlblStatus = new javax.swing.JLabel();
29      jpSelectionMode.setLayout(new java.awt.BorderLayout());
30      jLabel2.setText("Choose Selection Mode");
31      jpSelectionMode.add(jLabel2, java.awt.BorderLayout.WEST);
32      jcboSelectionMode.addActionListener(
33        new java.awt.event.ActionListener() {
34        public void actionPerformed(java.awt.event.ActionEvent evt) {
35          jcboSelectionModeActionPerformed(evt);
36        }
37      });
38      jpSelectionMode.add(jcboSelectionMode,
39        java.awt.BorderLayout.CENTER);
40      getContentPane().add(jpSelectionMode,
41        java.awt.BorderLayout.NORTH);
42      jList1.addListSelectionListener(
43        new javax.swing.event.ListSelectionListener() {
44        public void valueChanged(
45          javax.swing.event.ListSelectionEvent evt) {
46          jList1ValueChanged(evt);
47        }
48      });
```

Listing 8.1 *TestList.java*

continued

Example 8.1 continued

```
        jScrollPane1.setViewportView(jList1);
        getContentPane().add(jScrollPane1, java.awt.BorderLayout.CENTER);
        getContentPane().add(jlblStatus, java.awt.BorderLayout.SOUTH);
    }

    private void jList1ValueChanged(
        javax.swing.event.ListSelectionEvent evt) {
        int[] indices = jList1.getSelectedIndices();
        Object[] selectedItems = jList1.getSelectedValues();
        String display = "";

        for (int i = 0; i < indices.length; i++) {
          display += (String)selectedItems[i] + " ";
        }

        jlblStatus.setText(display);
    }

    private void jcboSelectionModeActionPerformed(
        java.awt.event.ActionEvent evt) {
        String selectedMode =
        (String)jcboSelectionMode.getSelectedItem();

        if (selectedMode.equals("SINGLE_SELECTION"))
          jList1.setSelectionMode(ListSelectionModel.SINGLE_SELECTION);
        else if (selectedMode.equals("SINGLE_INTERVAL_SELECTION"))
          jList1.setSelectionMode(
          ListSelectionModel.SINGLE_INTERVAL_SELECTION);
        if (selectedMode.equals("MULTIPLE_INTERVAL_SELECTION"))
          jList1.setSelectionMode(
          ListSelectionModel.MULTIPLE_INTERVAL_SELECTION);
    }

    // Variables declaration - do not modify
    private javax.swing.JPanel jpSelectionMode;
    private javax.swing.JLabel jLabel2;
    private javax.swing.JComboBox jcboSelectionMode;
    private javax.swing.JScrollPane jScrollPane1;
    private javax.swing.JList jList1;
    private javax.swing.JLabel jlblStatus;
    // End of variables declaration
}
```

Listing 8.1 *continued*

Example Review

The program creates an array of strings and sets the array as `listData` in the list. The list is placed in a scroll pane so that you can scroll it when the number of items in the list exceeds the viewing area.

When the user selects an item in the list, the `valueChanged` handler is executed, which gets the selected items and displays all the items in the label.

The example enables you to specify selection mode from a combo box. When you choose SINGLE_SELECTION, only one item can be selected at a given time. When you choose SINGLE_INTERVAL_SELECTION, multiple consecutive items can be selected all together by holding down the SHIFT key. When you choose MULTIPLE_INTERVAL_SELECTION, you can choose any number of items anywhere in the list by holding down the CTRL key.

8.2.1 List Models

The preceding example constructs a list with a fixed set of strings. If you want to add new items to the list or delete existing items, you have to use a list model. This section introduces list models.

The `JList` class delegates the responsibilities of storing and maintaining data to its data model. The `JList` class itself does not have methods for adding or removing items from the list. These methods are supported in the list model.

All list models implement the `ListModel` interface, which defines the registration methods for `ListDataEvent`. The instances of `ListDataListener` are notified when the items in the list are modified. `ListModel` also defines the methods `getSize` and `getElementAt`. The `getSize` method returns the length of the list, and the `getElementAt` method returns the element at the specified index.

`AbstractListModel` implements the `ListModel` and `Serializable` interfaces. `AbstractListModel` implements the registration methods in the `ListModel`, but does not implement the `getSize` and `getElementAt` methods.

`DefaultListModel` extends `AbstractListModel` and implements the two methods `getSize` and `getElementAt`, which are not implemented by `AbstractListModel`. The relationship among `ListModel`, `AbstractListModel`, and `DefaultListModel` is shown in Figure 8.3.

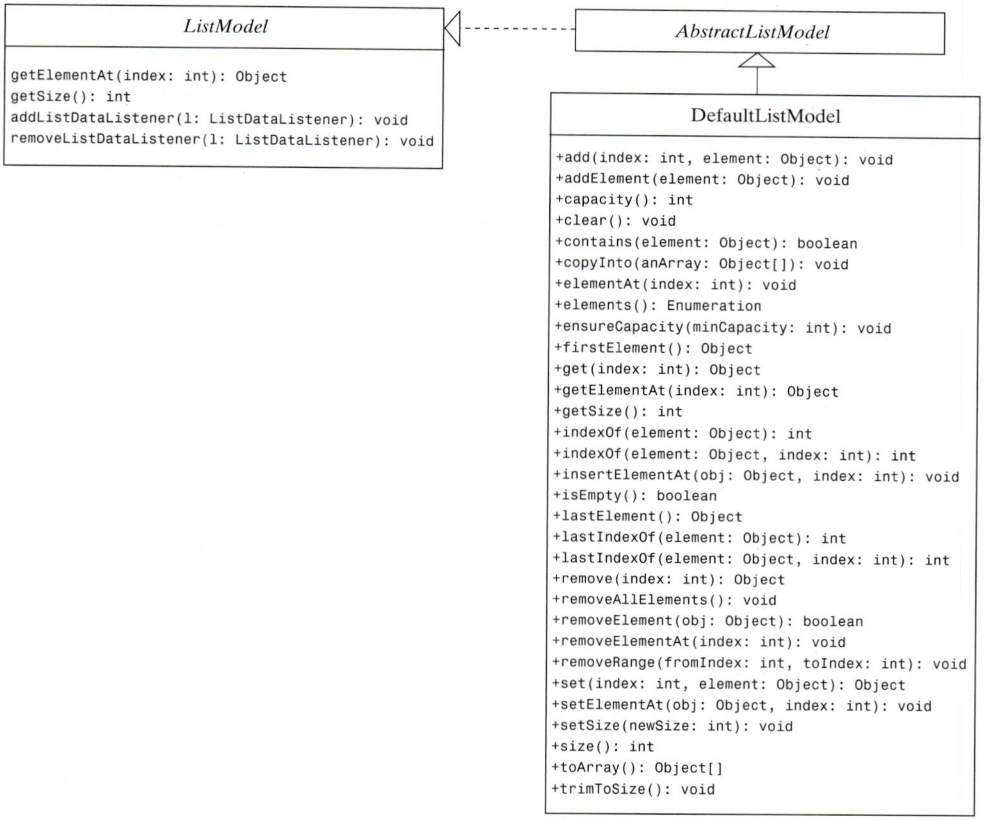

Figure 8.3 `DefaultListModel` *is a concrete implementation of* `ListModel`.

The methods in `DefaultListModel` are similar to those in the `java.util.Vector` class. You use the `add` method to insert an element to the list, the `remove` method to remove an element from the list, the `clear` method to clear the list, the `getSize` method to return the number of elements in the list, and the `getElementAt` method to retrieve an element. In fact, the `DefaultListModel` stores data in an instance of `Vector`, which is essentially a resizable array. Swing components were developed before the Java Collections Framework. In future implementations, `Vector` may be replaced by `java.util.ArrayList`.

Example 8.2 List Model Demo

This example creates a list using a list model and allows the user to add and delete items in the list. A sample run of the program is shown in Figure 8.4.

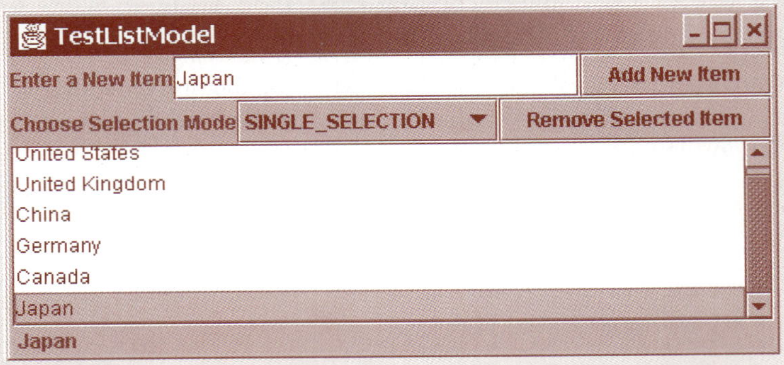

Figure 8.4 *You can add elements and remove elements in a list using list models.*

Here are the steps to complete the project:

1. In the listdemo package, create a new applet named TestListModel using the Forte Swing JApplet form wizard.
2. Drop a `JPanel` to the north of the applet to create `jpSettings`. Drop a `JLabel` to the south of the applet to create `jlblStatus`. Drop a `JScroll-Pane` to the center of the applet, and drop a `JList` to the scroll pane to create `jList1`.
3. Set `layout` of `jpSettings` to `BorderLayout`, and drop a `JPanel` to the north of `jpSettings` and a `JPanel` to the south of `jpSettings` to create `jpAdd` and `jpRemove`. Set `layout` of `jpAdd` and `jpRemove` to `BorderLayout`. Drop a `JLabel` labeled "Enter a New Item," a `JTextField`, and a `JButton` with text "Add New Item" to the east, center, and west of `jpAdd`, and rename the text field and button `jtfNewItem` and `jbtAdd`. Drop a `JLabel` labeled "Choose Selection Mode," a `JComboBox`, and a `JButton` with text "Remove Selected Item" to the east, center, and west of `jpRemove`, and rename the combo box and button `jcboSelectionMode` and `jbtRemove`.

4. Create an instance of `DefaultListModel` named `listModel`, and add items to the model using `listModel.addElement(item)`, as shown in Listing 8.2 (Lines 13–19). Add three items "SINGLE_SELECTION," SINGLE_INTERVAL_SELECTION," and "MULTIPLE_INTERVAL_SELECTION" to the combo box `jcboSelectionMode` (Lines 21–24).

5. Write the code to set the `model` property of `jList1` to `listModel` (Line 27 in Listing 8.2).

6. Generate the `ActionEvent` handlers for the combo box, the Add New Item button, and the Remove Selected Item button, and implement these handlers for setting a selection mode, adding a new element, and deleting elements in the list (Lines 100–127).

7. Generate the `ListSelectionEvent` handler for the list and implement it to display the selected items in the label (Lines 87–98).

```
1    package listdemo;
2
3    import javax.swing.*;
4
5    public class TestListModel extends javax.swing.JApplet {
6      // Create a list model
7      DefaultListModel listModel = new DefaultListModel();
8
9      /** Creates new form TestListModel */
10     public TestListModel() {
11       initComponents();
12
13       // Add items to the list model
14       listModel.addElement("United States");
15       listModel.addElement("United Kingdom");
16       listModel.addElement("China");
17       listModel.addElement("Germany");
18       listModel.addElement("France");
19       listModel.addElement("Canada");
20
21       // Add selection modes to the combo box
22       jcboSelectionMode.addItem("SINGLE_SELECTION");
23       jcboSelectionMode.addItem("SINGLE_INTERVAL_SELECTION");
24       jcboSelectionMode.addItem("MULTIPLE_INTERVAL_SELECTION");
25
26       // Set list model to the list
27       jList1.setModel(listModel);
28     }
29
30     private void initComponents() {
31       jpSettings = new javax.swing.JPanel();
32       jpAdd = new javax.swing.JPanel();
33       jLabel2 = new javax.swing.JLabel();
34       jtfNewItem = new javax.swing.JTextField();
35       jbtAdd = new javax.swing.JButton();
36       jpRemove = new javax.swing.JPanel();
37       jLabel3 = new javax.swing.JLabel();
38       jcboSelectionMode = new javax.swing.JComboBox();
```

Listing 8.2 *TestListModel.java*

continued

Example 8.2 continued

```
        jbtRemove = new javax.swing.JButton();
        jlblStatus = new javax.swing.JLabel();
        jScrollPane1 = new javax.swing.JScrollPane();
        jList1 = new javax.swing.JList();
        jpSettings.setLayout(new java.awt.BorderLayout());
        jpAdd.setLayout(new java.awt.BorderLayout());
        jLabel2.setText("Enter a New Item");
        jpAdd.add(jLabel2, java.awt.BorderLayout.WEST);
        jpAdd.add(jtfNewItem, java.awt.BorderLayout.CENTER);
        jbtAdd.setText("Add New Item");
        jbtAdd.addActionListener(new java.awt.event.ActionListener() {
          public void actionPerformed(java.awt.event.ActionEvent evt) {
            jbtAddActionPerformed(evt);
          }
        });
        jpAdd.add(jbtAdd, java.awt.BorderLayout.EAST);
        jpSettings.add(jpAdd, java.awt.BorderLayout.NORTH);
        jpRemove.setLayout(new java.awt.BorderLayout());
        jLabel3.setText("Choose Selection Mode");
        jpRemove.add(jLabel3, java.awt.BorderLayout.WEST);
        jcboSelectionMode.addActionListener(
          new java.awt.event.ActionListener() {
          public void actionPerformed(java.awt.event.ActionEvent evt) {
            jcboSelectionModeActionPerformed(evt);
          }
        });
        jpRemove.add(jcboSelectionMode, java.awt.BorderLayout.CENTER);
        jbtRemove.setText("Remove Selected Item");
        jbtRemove.addActionListener(new java.awt.event.ActionListener() {
          public void actionPerformed(java.awt.event.ActionEvent evt) {
            jbtRemoveActionPerformed(evt);
          }
        });
        jpRemove.add(jbtRemove, java.awt.BorderLayout.EAST);
        jpSettings.add(jpRemove, java.awt.BorderLayout.SOUTH);
        getContentPane().add(jpSettings, java.awt.BorderLayout.NORTH);
        getContentPane().add(jlblStatus, java.awt.BorderLayout.SOUTH);
        jList1.addListSelectionListener(
          new javax.swing.event.ListSelectionListener() {
          public void valueChanged(
            javax.swing.event.ListSelectionEvent evt) {
            jList1ValueChanged(evt);
          }
        });
        jScrollPane1.setViewportView(jList1);
        getContentPane().add(jScrollPane1, java.awt.BorderLayout.CENTER);
      }

      private void jList1ValueChanged(
        javax.swing.event.ListSelectionEvent evt) {
        int[] indices = jList1.getSelectedIndices();
        Object[] selectedItems = jList1.getSelectedValues();
        String display = "";

        for (int i = 0; i < indices.length; i++) {
          display += " " + (String)selectedItems[i];
        }

```

Listing 8.2 *continued*

```
      jlblStatus.setText(display);
    }

    private void jcboSelectionModeActionPerformed(
      java.awt.event.ActionEvent evt) {
      String selectedMode =
      (String)jcboSelectionMode.getSelectedItem();

      if (selectedMode.equals("SINGLE_SELECTION"))
        jList1.setSelectionMode(ListSelectionModel.SINGLE_SELECTION);
      else if (selectedMode.equals("SINGLE_INTERVAL_SELECTION"))
        jList1.setSelectionMode(
        ListSelectionModel.SINGLE_INTERVAL_SELECTION);
      if (selectedMode.equals("MULTIPLE_INTERVAL_SELECTION"))
        jList1.setSelectionMode(
        ListSelectionModel.MULTIPLE_INTERVAL_SELECTION);
    }

    private void jbtRemoveActionPerformed(
      java.awt.event.ActionEvent evt) {
      int selectedIndices[] = jList1.getSelectedIndices();

      for (int i=0; i<selectedIndices.length; i++) {
        listModel.removeElementAt(selectedIndices[i] - i);
      }
    }

    private void jbtAddActionPerformed(
      java.awt.event.ActionEvent evt) {
      listModel.addElement(jtfNewItem.getText());
    }

    // Variables declaration - do not modify
    private javax.swing.JPanel jpSettings;
    private javax.swing.JPanel jpAdd;
    private javax.swing.JLabel jLabel2;
    private javax.swing.JTextField jtfNewItem;
    private javax.swing.JButton jbtAdd;
    private javax.swing.JPanel jpRemove;
    private javax.swing.JLabel jLabel3;
    private javax.swing.JComboBox jcboSelectionMode;
    private javax.swing.JButton jbtRemove;
    private javax.swing.JLabel jlblStatus;
    private javax.swing.JScrollPane jScrollPane1;
    private javax.swing.JList jList1;
    // End of variables declaration
  }
```

Listing 8.2 *continued*

Example Review

The program creates `listModel`, which is an instance of `DefaultListModel`, and uses it to manipulate data in the list. The model enables you to add and remove items in the list,

To add an element, the user enters the new element in the text field, and clicks the Add New Item button to add the element to the model. The model notifies the list's UI delegate to display the new element in the list.

continued

Example 8.2 continued

To remove elements, the user specifies a selection mode, selects the elements, and clicks the Remove Selected Item to remove the item(s) from the model. The `getSelectedIndices()` method returns the indices of all selected items in strict order. Whenever an item is removed from the list, the indices of the items are immediately rearranged. Thus, the current index of the *i*th item to remove is `selectedIndices[i] - i`, as shown in Listing 8.2 (Line 120).

8.2.2 List-Selection Models

Unlike most Swing components, `JList` has two models: a list model and a list-selection model. *List models* handle data management, and *list-selection models* deal with data selection. A list-selection model must implement the `ListModelSelection` interface, which defines constants for three selection modes (`SINGLE_SELECTION`, `SINGLE_INTERVAL_SELECTION`, and `MULTIPLE_INTERVAL_SELECTION`), and registration methods for `ListSectionListener`. It also defines the methods for adding and removing selection intervals, and the access methods for the properties, such as `selectionMode`, `anchorSelectionIndex`, `leadSelectionIndex`, and `valueIsAdjusting`.

By default, an instance of `JList` uses `DefaultListSelectionModel`, which is a concrete implementation of `ListSelectionModel`. Usually, you do not need to provide a custom list-selection model, because the `DefaultListSelectionModel` class is sufficient in most cases. Unlike the list data model, you do not need to access the list-selection model directly, because most of the methods you need from the list-selection model are also defined in `Jlist`.

8.2.3 List Cell Renderers

The preceding example displays items as strings in a list. `JList` is very flexible and versatile, and it can be used to display images and drawings in addition to simple text. This section introduces list cell renderers for displaying graphics.

In addition to delegating data storage and processing to list models, `JList` delegates the rendering of the list cells to list cell renderers. All list cell renderers implement the `ListCellRenderer` interface, which defines a single method, `getListCellRendererComponent`, as follows:

```
public Component getListCellRendererComponent
  (JList list, Object value, int index, boolean isSelected,
   boolean cellHasFocus)
```

This method is passed with a list, the value associated with the cell, the index of the value, and information regarding whether the value is selected and the cell has the focus. The component returned from the method is painted on the cell in the list.

By default, `JList` uses `DefaultListCellRenderer` to render its cells. The `DefaultListCellRenderer` class implements `ListCellRenderer`, extends `JLabel`, and can display either a string or an icon, but not both in the same cell. You can create a custom renderer by implementing `ListCellRenderer`.

Example 8.3 List Cell Renderer Demo

This example creates a list of countries and displays the country flags and country names in the list, as shown in Figure 8.5. When a country is selected in the list, its flag is displayed in a panel next to the list.

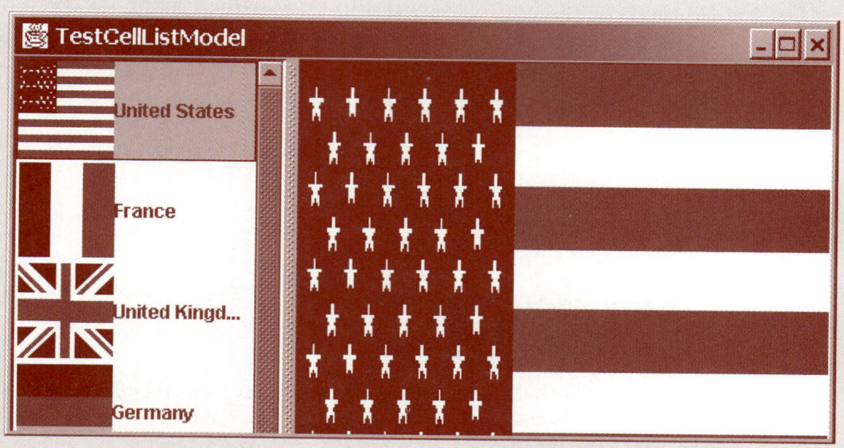

Figure 8.5 *The image and the text are displayed in the list cell.*

The program requires a custom list cell renderer to display an image and a text in the same cell. Often you need to create a new list model that provides additional information for rendering the cell. In this example, each item has an image and a label, which should be stored in the list model for use by the list cell renderer as well as by the users of the list. The new list model named `MyListModel` is given in Listing 8.3.

```
package listdemo;

import javax.swing.*;
import java.awt.*;

public class MyListModel extends DefaultListModel {
  public MyListModel(String[] name, Image[] image) {
    for (int i = 0; i < name.length; i++) {
      addElement(new Object[] {name[i], image[i]});
    }
  }

  /** Override the getName method in DefaultListModel */
  public String getName(Object value) {
    Object[] array = (Object[])value;
    return (String)array[0];
  }

  /** Override the getImage method in DefaultListModel */
  public Image getImage(Object value) {
    Object[] array = (Object[])value;
    return (Image)array[1];
  }
}
```

Listing 8.3 *MyListModel.java*

Example 8.3 continued

The `MyListModel` class extends `DefaultListModel` and is constructed with an array of country names and country flag images. Each pair consisting of a country name and a country flag image is stored as an array object in the list model. The `getName(value)` method returns the country name for the specified object value, and the `getImage(value)` method returns the country flag image for the specified object value. These two methods are used by the list cell renderer to obtain the name and image of the value of the cell.

The custom list cell renderer that displays the image and the name is given in Listing 8.4.

```
package listdemo;

import java.awt.*;
import javax.swing.*;
import javax.swing.border.*;
import imageviewerdemo.ImageViewer;

public class MyListCellRenderer implements ListCellRenderer {
  JPanel listCellPanel = new JPanel();
  ImageViewer imageViewer = new ImageViewer();
  JLabel jlbl = new JLabel(" ", JLabel.LEFT);
  Border lineBorder =
    BorderFactory.createLineBorder(Color.black, 1);
  Border emptyBorder =
    BorderFactory.createEmptyBorder(2, 2, 2, 2);

  public MyListCellRenderer() {
    listCellPanel.setOpaque(true);
    jlbl.setPreferredSize(new Dimension(100, 60));
    listCellPanel.setLayout(new BorderLayout());
    listCellPanel.add(imageViewer, BorderLayout.CENTER);
    listCellPanel.add(jlbl, BorderLayout.EAST);
  }

  /** Implement this method in ListCellRenderer */
  public Component getListCellRendererComponent
    (JList list, Object value, int index, boolean isSelected,
      boolean cellHasFocus) {
    MyListModel listModel =
      (MyListModel)list.getModel();
    String country = listModel.getName(value);
    Image image = listModel.getImage(value);
    jlbl.setText(country);
    imageViewer.setImage(image);

    if (isSelected) {
      listCellPanel.setForeground(list.getSelectionForeground());
      listCellPanel.setBackground(list.getSelectionBackground());
    }
    else {
      listCellPanel.setForeground(list.getForeground());
      listCellPanel.setBackground(list.getBackground());
    }

```

Listing 8.4 *MyListCellRenderer.java*

```
      if (cellHasFocus)
        listCellPanel.setBorder(lineBorder);
      else
        listCellPanel.setBorder(emptyBorder);

      return listCellPanel;
    }
  }
```

Listing 8.4 *continued*

The `MyListCellRenderer` class implements the `getListCellRendererComponent` method in the `ListCellRenderer` interface. The `getListCellRendererComponent` method obtains the name and image of the cell value through the list model. It then displays the image in an image panel and the name in a label. The image panel and the label are placed in a panel (`listCellPanel`) that is the returned component of the `getListCellRendererComponent` method.

The `ImageViewer` class for displaying an image was presented in Example 4.1, "Creating an Image Viewer."

Finally, let us construct the main program that utilizes the custom list model and custom list cell renderer in a list. Here are the steps to complete the project:

1. In the listdemo package, create a new applet named TestListCellRenderer using the Forte Swing JApplet form wizard.

2. Drop a `JSplitPanel` to the center of the applet. Drop a `JScrollPane` to the left part of the split pane and a `JList` to the scroll pane to create `jList1`. Drop an `ImageViewer` to the right part of the split pane to create `imageViewer1`.

3. Write the code to create images for the flags of several countries, as shown in Listing 8.5 (Lines 18–36). Create an instance of `MyListModel` named `listModel` (Line 9) and set the `model` property of `jList1` to this instance (Line 48). Create an instance of `MyListCellRenderer` (Line 12) and set the `cellRenderer` property of `jList1` to this instance (Line 51).

4. Generate the `ListSelectionEvent` handler (`valueChanged` for the list, and implement it to display the selected flag in `imageViewer1` (Lines 73–77).

```
1    package listdemo;
2
3    import javax.swing.*;
4    import java.awt.*;
5    import imageviewerdemo.ImageViewer;
6
7    public class TestListCellRenderer extends javax.swing.JApplet {
8      // Create a list model
9      MyListModel listModel;
10
```

Listing 8.5 *TestListCellRenderer.java*

continued

Example 8.3 continued

```
    // Create a list cell renderer
    ListCellRenderer myListCellRenderer = new MyListCellRenderer();

    /** Creates new form TestListCellRenderer */
    public TestListCellRenderer() {
      initComponents();

      // Create images
      Image imageUS = ImageViewer.createImage(
        "/image/us.gif", this);
      Image imageFrance = ImageViewer.createImage(
        "/image/fr.gif", this);
      Image imageUK = ImageViewer.createImage(
        "/image/uk.gif", this);
      Image imageGermany = ImageViewer.createImage(
        "/image/germany.gif", this);
      Image imageIndia = ImageViewer.createImage(
        "/image/india.gif", this);
      Image imageNorway = ImageViewer.createImage(
        "/image/norway.gif", this);
      Image imageChina = ImageViewer.createImage(
        "/image/china.gif", this);
      Image imageCanada = ImageViewer.createImage(
        "/image/ca.gif", this);
      Image imageDenmark = ImageViewer.createImage(
        "/image/denmark.gif", this);

      // Create a list model
      listModel = new MyListModel(
      new String[]
      {"United States", "France", "United Kingdom", "Germany",
       "India", "Norway", "China", "Canada", "Denmark"},
       new Image[]
       {imageUS, imageFrance, imageUK, imageGermany, imageIndia,
        imageNorway, imageChina, imageCanada, imageDenmark});

      // Set list model
      jList1.setModel(listModel);

      // Set list cell renderer
      jList1.setCellRenderer(myListCellRenderer);
    }

    private void initComponents() {
      jSplitPane1 = new javax.swing.JSplitPane();
      jScrollPane1 = new javax.swing.JScrollPane();
      jList1 = new javax.swing.JList();
      imageViewer1 = new guipropertyeditordemo.ImageViewer();
      jList1.addListSelectionListener(
        new javax.swing.event.ListSelectionListener() {
        public void valueChanged(
          javax.swing.event.ListSelectionEvent evt) {
          jList1ValueChanged(evt);
        }
      });
      jScrollPane1.setViewportView(jList1);
      jSplitPane1.setLeftComponent(jScrollPane1);
```

Listing 8.5 *continued*

```
        jSplitPane1.setRightComponent(imageViewer1);
        getContentPane().add(jSplitPane1, java.awt.BorderLayout.CENTER);
      }

      private void jList1ValueChanged(
        javax.swing.event.ListSelectionEvent evt) {
        Image image = listModel.getImage(jList1.getSelectedValue());
        imageViewer1.setImage(image);
      }

      // Variables declaration - do not modify
      private javax.swing.JSplitPane jSplitPane1;
      private javax.swing.JScrollPane jScrollPane1;
      private javax.swing.JList jList1;
      private guipropertyeditordemo.ImageViewer imageViewer1;
      // End of variables declaration
    }
```

Listing 8.5 *continued*

Example Review

The example uses four classes: `MyListModel`, `MyListCellRenderer`, `ImageViewer`, and `TestListCellRenderer`. The `MyListModel` class is responsible for storing data that include image and text for the list. The `MyListCellRenderer` class is responsible for rendering the cell with image and text. The `ImageViewer` class displays an image in the panel. The `TestListCellRenderer` class tests the list with the custom list cell renderer.

When you choose a country in the list, the list selection event handler is invoked. This handler obtains the list model for the list, uses it to retrieve the country's flag image, and displays the image in the image panel on the right side of the split pane.

The `getListCellRendererComponent` method in `MyListCellRenderer` is passed with the parameters `list`, `value`, `index`, `isSelected`, and `isFocused`. The `list` is used to obtain the list model. The `value` determines the image and name of the country displayed in the cell. If the cell is selected, the background and foreground of the cell are set to the list's selection background and foreground. If the cell is focused, the cell's border is set to the line border; otherwise, it is set to the empty border. The empty border serves as a divider between the cells.

Note

The images may not be displayed immediately, because it takes time to load them. You can use image tracker techniques to ensure that the images are loaded before they are displayed. Tracking loading images is introduced in Chapter 16, "Multimedia," in my *Introduction to Java Programming with Sun ONE Studio 4*.

continued

Example 8.3 continued

> **TIP**
> The label's preferred size is set to 100 by 60 in the `MyListCellRenderer` class, so it will be limited to 100 by 60 and the rest of the space in the cell renderer is allocated to the image.

8.3 JComboBox

A *combo box* is a component similar to a list. Both combo box and list are used for selecting items from a list. A combo box allows the user to select one item at a time, while a list permits multiple selections. A combo box displays a drop-down list contained in a popup menu when the combo box is clicked. The selected item can be edited in the cell as if it were a text field.

The constructors of `JComboBox` are similar to those of `JList`. An instance of `JComboBox` can be created using its default constructor or one of the following three constructors:

- `public JComboBox(ComboBoxModel model)`
- `public JComboBox(Object[] objectArray)`
- `public JComboBox(Vector vector)`

The following properties of `JComboBox` are often useful:

- **`actionCommand`** is an action command string associated with `JComboBox`.
- **`editable`** is a `boolean` value indicating whether the combo box can be edited. The default value is `false`.
- **`itemCount`** counts the number of items in the combo box. This property is read-only.
- **`maximumRowCount`** specifies the maximum number of rows that can be seen without scrolling. The default value is 8.
- **`model`** is an object that maintains the data for the list. Combo box models must be used explicitly to add or delete items in a combo box.
- **`popupVisible`** is a `boolean` value indicating whether the popup menu that contains the list is displayed. The default value is `false`, which means that the user has to click the combo box to display the popup menu.
- **`renderer`** is an instance of the class that implements the `ListCellRenderer` interface. The renderer is responsible for rendering the cell in the combo box.
- **`selectedIndex`** is the index of the selected item in the combo box.
- **`selectedItem`** is the current selected object in the combo box.

Like `JList`, the `JComboBox` class delegates the responsibilities of storing and maintaining data to its data model. All combo box models implement the

ComboBoxModel interface, which extends the ListModel interface and defines the getSelectedItem and setSelectedItem methods for retrieving and setting a selected item. The methods for adding and removing items are defined in the MutableComboBoxModel interface, which extends ComboBoxModel.

When an instance of JComboBox is created without explicitly specifying a model, an instance of DefaultComboBoxModel is used. The DefaultComboBoxModel class extends AbstractListModel and implements MutableComboBoxModel. Recall that the DefaultListModel class also extends AbstractListModel. So DefaultComboBoxModel and DefaultListModel share many common methods.

Unlike JList, the JComboBox class has methods for adding or removing items from the list. The following methods are useful in operating a JComboBox object:

- `public void addItem(Object item)`

  Adds the item of any object into the combo box.

- `public Object getItemAt(int index)`

  Returns an item from the combo box at the specified index.

- `public void removeItem(Object anObject)`

  Removes an item from the item list.

- `public void removeAllItems()`

  Removes all items from the item list.

Combo boxes render cells exactly like lists, because the combo box items are displayed in a list contained in a popup menu.

JComboBox can generate ActionEvent and ItemEvent, among many other events. Whenever a new item is selected, JComboBox generates ItemEvent twice, once for deselecting the previously selected item, and the other for selecting the currently selected item. JComboBox generates an ActionEvent after generating ItemEvent.

Example 8.4 Combo Box Demo

This example creates a combo box that contains a list of countries and displays the country flags and country names in the list cell, as shown in Figure 8.6. When a country is selected in the list, its flag is displayed in a panel below the combo box.

This example is similar to Example 8.3. A custom data model named MyComboBoxModel is created to store data (flag image and country name), as shown in Listing 8.6. A custom cell renderer, named MyComboBoxRenderer, is created to render the cells, as shown in Listing 8.7. These two classes are almost identical to the data model and list renderer in Example 8.3, except for the following differences:

continued

Example 8.4 continued

Figure 8.6 *The image and the text are displayed in the list cell of a combo box.*

- `MyComboBoxModel` extends `DefaultComboBoxModel`, but `MyListModel` extends `DefaultListModel`.
- The data model obtained from the `list` parameter in the `getListCellRendererComponent` method is casted to `MyComboBoxModel`, while the data model in `MyListCellRenderer` is casted to `MyListModel`.

```
package comboboxdemo;

import javax.swing.*;
import java.awt.*;

public class MyComboBoxModel extends DefaultComboBoxModel {
  public MyComboBoxModel(String[] name, Image[] image) {
    for (int i = 0; i < name.length; i++) {
      addElement(new Object[] {name[i], image[i]});
    }
  }

  /** Override this method in DefaultComoboBoxModel */
  public String getName(Object value) {
    Object[] array = (Object[])value;
    return (String)array[0];
  }

  /** Override this method in DefaultComoboBoxModel */
  public Image getImage(Object value) {
    Object[] array = (Object[])value;
    return (Image)array[1];
  }
}
```

Listing 8.6 *MyComboBoxModel.java*

```
package comboboxdemo;

import java.awt.*;
import javax.swing.*;
import javax.swing.border.*;
import imageviewerdemo.ImageViewer;

public class MyComboBoxRenderer implements ListCellRenderer {
  JPanel listCellPanel = new JPanel();
  ImageViewer imageViewer = new ImageViewer();
  JLabel jlbl = new JLabel(" ", JLabel.LEFT);
  Border lineBorder =
    BorderFactory.createLineBorder(Color.black, 1);
  Border emptyBorder =
    BorderFactory.createEmptyBorder(2, 2, 2, 2);

  public MyComboBoxRenderer() {
    jlbl.setPreferredSize(new Dimension(100, 60));
    listCellPanel.setLayout(new BorderLayout());
    listCellPanel.add(imageViewer, BorderLayout.CENTER);
    listCellPanel.add(jlbl, BorderLayout.EAST);
  }

  /** Override this method in ListCellRenderer */
  public Component getListCellRendererComponent
    (JList list, Object value, int index, boolean isSelected,
     boolean cellHasFocus) {
    MyComboBoxModel listModel =
      (MyComboBoxModel)list.getModel();
    String country = listModel.getName(value);
    Image image = listModel.getImage(value);
    jlbl.setText(country);
    imageViewer.setImage(image);

    if (isSelected) {
      listCellPanel.setForeground(list.getSelectionForeground());
      listCellPanel.setBackground(list.getSelectionBackground());
    }
    else {
      listCellPanel.setForeground(list.getForeground());
      listCellPanel.setBackground(list.getBackground());
    }

    if (cellHasFocus)
      listCellPanel.setBorder(lineBorder);
    else
      listCellPanel.setBorder(emptyBorder);

    return listCellPanel;
  }
}
```

Listing 8.7 *continued*

Let us construct the main program that utilizes the custom combo box model and custom combo box cell renderer in a combo box. Here are the steps to complete the project:

continued

Example 8.4 continued

1. Create a new package named `comboboxdemo`, and create a new applet named `TestComboBox` using the Forte Swing JApplet form wizard.

2. Drop a `JComboBox` to the north of the applet to create `jcboCountries`. Drop an `ImageViewer` to the center of the applet to create `imageViewer1`.

3. Write the code to create images for the flags of several countries, as shown in Listing 8.8 (Lines 16–34). Create an instance of `MyComboBoxModel` named `comboBoxModel` (Lines 37–44), and set the `model` property of `jcboCountries` to this instance (Line 47). Create an instance of `MyComboBoxRenderer` (Line 10), and set the `renderer` property of `jcboCountries` to this instance (Line 50).

4. Generate the `ActionEvent` handler for the combo box, and implement it to display the selected flag in `imageViewer1` (Lines 67–72).

```
1   package comboboxdemo;
2
3   import java.awt.*;
4   import imageviewerdemo.ImageViewer;
5
6   public class TestComboBox extends javax.swing.JApplet {
7     MyComboBoxModel comboBoxModel;
8
9     // Create a list cell renderer
10    MyComboBoxRenderer myComboBoxRenderer = new MyComboBoxRenderer();
11
12    /** Creates new form TestComboBox */
13    public TestComboBox() {
14      initComponents();
15
16      // Create images
17      Image imageUS = ImageViewer.createImage(
18        "/image/us.gif", this);
19      Image imageFrance = ImageViewer.createImage(
20        "/image/fr.gif", this);
21      Image imageUK = ImageViewer.createImage(
22        "/image/uk.gif", this);
23      Image imageGermany = ImageViewer.createImage(
24        "/image/germany.gif", this);
25      Image imageIndia = ImageViewer.createImage(
26        "/image/india.gif", this);
27      Image imageNorway = ImageViewer.createImage(
28        "/image/norway.gif", this);
29      Image imageChina = ImageViewer.createImage(
30        "/image/china.gif", this);
31      Image imageCanada = ImageViewer.createImage(
32        "/image/ca.gif", this);
33      Image imageDenmark = ImageViewer.createImage(
34        "/image/denmark.gif", this);
35
36      // Create a list model
37      comboBoxModel = new MyComboBoxModel(
38      new String[]
39      {"United States", "France",
```

Listing 8.8 *TestComboBox.java*

```
          "United Kingdom", "Germany",
          "India", "Norway", "China", "Canada", "Denmark"},
          new Image[]
          {imageUS, imageFrance, imageUK, imageGermany, imageIndia,
           imageNorway, imageChina, imageCanada, imageDenmark});

        // Set list model
        jcboCountries.setModel(comboBoxModel);

        // Set list cell renderer
        jcboCountries.setRenderer(myComboBoxRenderer);
      }

      private void initComponents() {
        jcboCountries = new javax.swing.JComboBox();
        imageViewer1 = new guipropertyeditordemo.ImageViewer();

        jcboCountries.addActionListener(
          new java.awt.event.ActionListener() {
          public void actionPerformed(java.awt.event.ActionEvent evt) {
            jcboCountriesActionPerformed(evt);
          }
        });
        getContentPane().add(jcboCountries, java.awt.BorderLayout.NORTH);
        getContentPane().add(imageViewer1, java.awt.BorderLayout.CENTER);
      }

      private void jcboCountriesActionPerformed(
        java.awt.event.ActionEvent evt) {
        Image image = comboBoxModel.getImage(
          jcboCountries.getSelectedItem());
        imageViewer1.setImage(image);
      }

      // Variables declaration - do not modify
      private javax.swing.JComboBox jcboCountries;
      private guipropertyeditordemo.ImageViewer imageViewer1;
      // End of variables declaration
    }
```

Listing 8.8 *continued*

Example Review

If you don't need to provide custom methods in the data model, you can simply use the `DefaultComboBoxModel`, which is used by all the combo boxes if no data model is explicitly specified. In fact, you don't need the combo box data model as much as you need the list data model for `JList`, because `JComboBox` directly supports the methods for adding and removing items in the combo box, but `JList` does not contain those methods.

Each combo box has a default cell renderer that displays a string or an icon, but not both at the same time. To display a combination of images, drawings, and text, you need to create a custom renderer.

continued

Example 8.4 continued

This example creates a custom data model to hold country names and flag images, and to provide the methods for getting names and images. The methods are used in the custom renderer for displaying images and names in cells in the combo box. The combo box renderer is the same as the list box renderer. They all implement the `ListCellRenderer` interface. In fact, a combo box cell is displayed in a list contained in a popup menu. You can modify Examples 8.3 and 8.4 so that they share the same renderer (See Exercise 8.9).

8.3.1 Editing Combo Boxes

Unlike lists, combo boxes can be edited. By default, a combo box is not editable. To make a combo box editable, set its `editable` property to `true`. Editing only affects the current item and does not change the contents of the list. Editing changes are lost after another item in the combo box is selected. To make changes permanent, you have to implement the `ActionEvent` handler to replace the current item with the modified item.

Example 8.5 Editing in a Combo Box

This example creates a simple Web browser to render HTML files. The program lets the user enter a URL in a combo box and save it. When the user presses the Enter key after entering the URL or selects an existing URL from the combo box, the HTML file is displayed in an editor pane, as shown in Figure 8.7.

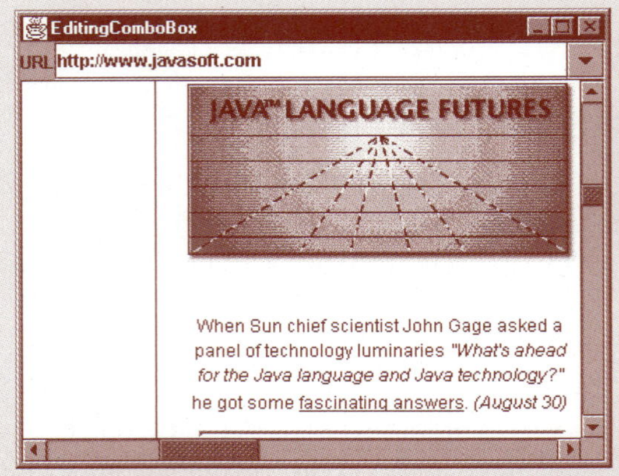

Figure 8.7 *You can enter a URL in the combo box and display the HTML file in an editor pane.*

Here are the steps to complete the project:

1. In the comboboxdemo package, create a new applet named `EditingComboBox` using the Forte Swing JApplet wizard.

2. Drop a `JPanel` to the north of the applet to create `jpURL`. Drop a `JScrollPane` to the center of the applet, and drop a `JEditorPane` to the scroll pane and rename it `jep`.

3. Set `layout` of `jpURL` to `BorderLayout`. Drop a `JLabel` labeled URL to the west of `jpURL`, and drop a `JComboBox` to the center of `jpURL` to create `jcboURL`. Set `editable` of `jcboURL` to True.

3. Generate an `ActionEvent` handler for `jcboURL`, implement the handler to display the contents at URL in the editor pane, and add the URL to the combo box, as shown in Listing 8.9 (Lines 49–60).

4. Generate a hyperlink event handler for the editor pane, and implement it to display the content of the hyperlink in the editor pane, as shown in Listing 8.9 (Lines 40–47).

```
1   package comboboxdemo;
2
3   import java.io.IOException;
4   import java.net.URL;
5
6   public class EditingComboBox extends javax.swing.JApplet {
7     /** Creates new form EditingComboBox */
8     public EditingComboBox() {
9       initComponents();
10    }
11
12    private void initComponents() {
13      jpURL = new javax.swing.JPanel();
14      jLabel1 = new javax.swing.JLabel();
15      jcboURL = new javax.swing.JComboBox();
16      jScrollPane1 = new javax.swing.JScrollPane();
17      jep = new javax.swing.JEditorPane();
18      jpURL.setLayout(new java.awt.BorderLayout());
19      jLabel1.setText("URL");
20      jpURL.add(jLabel1, java.awt.BorderLayout.WEST);
21      jcboURL.setEditable(true);
22      jcboURL.addActionListener(new java.awt.event.ActionListener() {
23        public void actionPerformed(java.awt.event.ActionEvent evt) {
24          jcboURLActionPerformed(evt);
25        }
26      });
27      jpURL.add(jcboURL, java.awt.BorderLayout.CENTER);
28      getContentPane().add(jpURL, java.awt.BorderLayout.NORTH);
29      jep.addHyperlinkListener(
30        new javax.swing.event.HyperlinkListener() {
31        public void hyperlinkUpdate(
32          javax.swing.event.HyperlinkEvent evt) {
33          jepHyperlinkUpdate(evt);
34        }
35      });
36      jScrollPane1.setViewportView(jep);
37      getContentPane().add(jScrollPane1, java.awt.BorderLayout.CENTER);
38    }
39
```

Listing 8.9 *EditingComboBox.java*

continued

Example 8.5 Editing in a Combo Box

```
    private void jepHyperlinkUpdate(
      javax.swing.event.HyperlinkEvent evt) {
      try {
        jep.setPage(evt.getURL());
      }
      catch (IOException ex) {
        System.out.println(ex);
      }
    }

    private void jcboURLActionPerformed(
      java.awt.event.ActionEvent evt) {
      jcboURL.addItem(jcboURL.getSelectedItem());

      try {
        // Display the HTML file
        jep.setPage(new URL((String)(jcboURL.getSelectedItem())));
      }
      catch (IOException ex) {
        System.out.println(ex);
      }
    }

    // Variables declaration - do not modify
    private javax.swing.JPanel jpURL;
    private javax.swing.JLabel jLabel1;
    private javax.swing.JComboBox jcboURL;
    private javax.swing.JScrollPane jScrollPane1;
    private javax.swing.JEditorPane jep;
    // End of variables declaration
  }
```

Listing 8.9 *continued*

Example Review

To enable editing, the `editable` property of the combo box must be `true`. By default, `editable` is `false`.

The user enters a URL of the HTML file in the combo box and presses the Enter key to fire an `ActionEvent`. The `ActionEvent` handler stores the URL and displays the URL in the editor pane. You can also select a URL from the combo box.

8.4 JTable

`JTable` is a Swing component that displays data in rows and columns in a two-dimensional grid. Figure 8.8 shows the Swing table in the SwingSet demo.

`JTable` doesn't directly support scrolling. To create a scrollable table, you need to create a `JScrollPane` and add an instance of `JTable` to the scroll pane. If a table is not placed in a scroll pane, its column header will not be visible, because the column header is placed in the header of the view port of a scroll pane.

`JTable` has three different models: a table model, a column model, and a list-selection model. The *table model* is for storing and processing data. The *column*

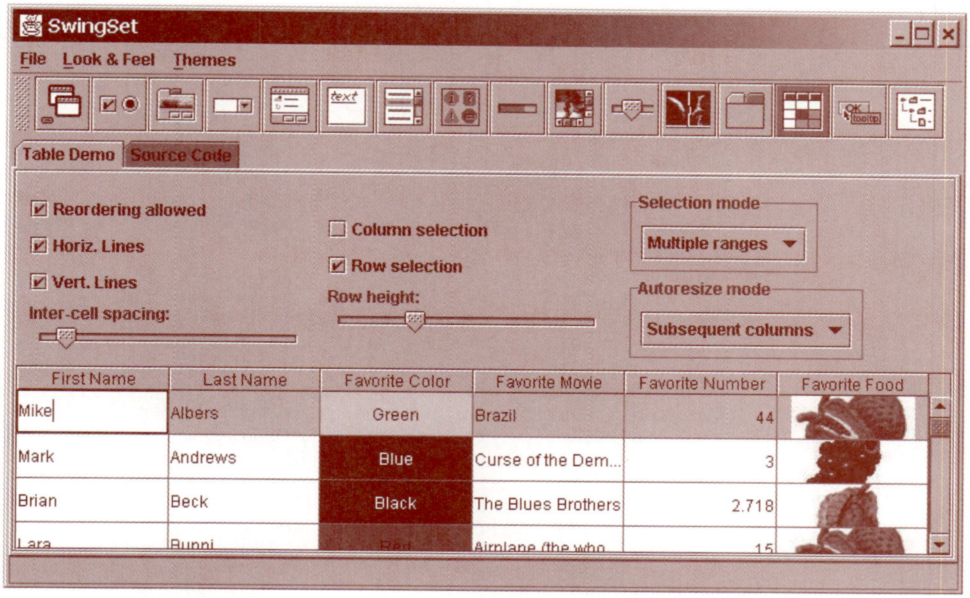

Figure 8.8 *The SwingSet demo demonstrates the features of* `JTable`.

model deals with column management. The *list-selection model* is the same as the one used by `JList` for selecting rows, columns, and cells in a table.

Like `JList` and `JComboBox`, `JTable` has renderers and editors. `JTable` has many features that make it possible to customize its rendering and editing. `JTable` also provides many convenient, easy-to-use renderers and editors.

There are seven constructors in the `JTable` class. The builder tool always uses the default constructor to create an instance of `JTable`. The constructor shown below constructs a table from a two-dimensional array representing data and an array representing column names:

```
public JTable(Object[][] rowData, Object[] columnNames)
```

For instance, the following statements construct a table, as shown in Figure 8.9.

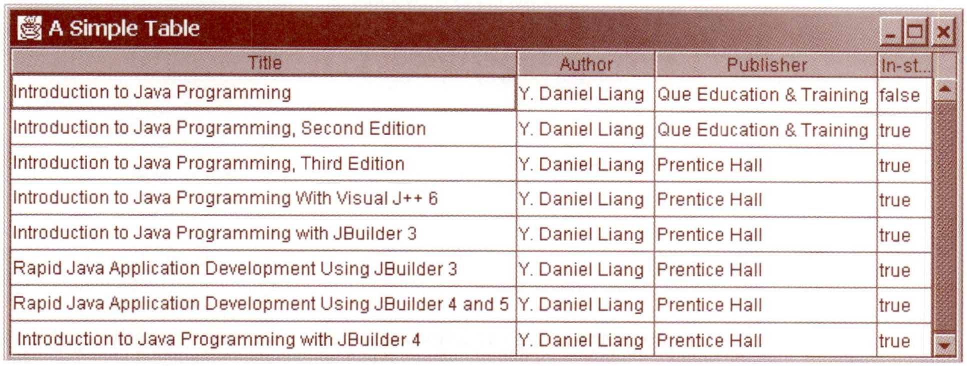

Title	Author	Publisher	In-st...
Introduction to Java Programming	Y. Daniel Liang	Que Education & Training	false
Introduction to Java Programming, Second Edition	Y. Daniel Liang	Que Education & Training	true
Introduction to Java Programming, Third Edition	Y. Daniel Liang	Prentice Hall	true
Introduction to Java Programming With Visual J++ 6	Y. Daniel Liang	Prentice Hall	true
Introduction to Java Programming with JBuilder 3	Y. Daniel Liang	Prentice Hall	true
Rapid Java Application Development Using JBuilder 3	Y. Daniel Liang	Prentice Hall	true
Rapid Java Application Development Using JBuilder 4 and 5	Y. Daniel Liang	Prentice Hall	true
Introduction to Java Programming with JBuilder 4	Y. Daniel Liang	Prentice Hall	true

Figure 8.9 *You can construct a simple table using the* `JTable` *constructor.*

```
// Create table column names
String[] columnNames =
  {"Title", "Author", "Publisher", "In-stock"};

// Create table data
Object[][] data = {
  {"Introduction to Java Programming", "Y. Daniel Liang",
   "Que Education & Training", new Boolean(false)},
  {"Introduction to Java Programming, Second Edition",
   "Y. Daniel Liang", "Que Education & Training",
   new Boolean(true)},
  {"Introduction to Java Programming, Third Edition",
   "Y. Daniel Liang", "Prentice Hall", new Boolean(true)},
  {"Introduction to Java Programming With Visual J++ 6",
   "Y. Daniel Liang", "Prentice Hall", new Boolean(true)},
  {"Introduction to Java Programming with JBuilder 3",
   "Y. Daniel Liang", "Prentice Hall", new Boolean(true)},
  {"Rapid Java Application Development Using JBuilder 3",
   "Y. Daniel Liang", "Prentice Hall", new Boolean(true)},
  {"Rapid Java Application Development Using JBuilder 4 and 5",
   "Y. Daniel Liang", "Prentice Hall", new Boolean(true)},
  {" Introduction to Java Programming with JBuilder 4",
   "Y. Daniel Liang", "Prentice Hall", new Boolean(true)},
};

// Create a table
JTable jTable1 = new JTable(data, columnNames);
```

NOTE

JTable has many supporting classes. For convenience, all the table classes except JTable are grouped in the javax.swing.table package.

8.4.1 JTable Properties

JTable is a powerful control with a variety of properties and methods that provide many ways to customize tables. The following properties are often used:

- **autoCreateColumnsFromModel** is a boolean value indicating whether the columns are created in the table. The default value is true.
- **autoResizingMode** specifies how columns are resized (you can resize table columns but not rows). Possible values are:

```
JTable.AUTO_RESIZE_OFF
JTable.AUTO_RESIZE_LAST_COLUMN
JTable.AUTO_RESIZE_SUBSEQUENT_COLUMNS
JTable.AUTO_RESIZE_NEXT_COLUMN
JTable.AUTO_RESIZE_ALL_COLUMNS
```

  The default mode is JTable.AUTO_RESIZE_SUBSEQUENT_ COLUMNS.

- **cellSelectionEnabled** is a boolean value specifying whether individual cells can be selected.
- **columnModel** is an object that maintains the table column data. Table column models are introduced in Section 8.4.3, "Table Column Models."
- **columnSelectionAllowed** is a boolean value specifying whether column selection is allowed.

- **defaultEditor** is the default editor for table cells. `JTable` provides a set of default editors that can be overridden, if desired. The editors are introduced in Section 8.4.5, "Table Renderers and Editors."
- **defaultRenderer** is the default renderer for table cells. `JTable` provides a set of default renderers that can be overridden, if desired. The renderers are introduced in Section 8.4.5, "Table Renderers and Editors."
- **editingColumn** is the column of the cell that is currently being edited.
- **editingRow** is the row of the cell that is currently being edited.
- **gridColor** is the color used to draw grid lines. The default color is `Color.gray`.
- **intercellSpacing** is a dimension that represents the horizontal and vertical margins between cells. The default spacing is (1, 1), which provides room to draw the grid.
- **model** is an object that maintains the table data. Table models are introduced in Section 8.4.2, "Table Models."
- **rowHeight** specifies the row height of the table. The default value is 16 pixels.
- **rowMargin** specifies the vertical margin between rows. It is equivalent to `getIntercellSpacing().height`.
- **rowCount** counts the number of rows in a table.
- **rowSelectionAllowed** is a `boolean` value specifying whether the rows can be selected.
- **selectionBackground** is the background color of selected cells.
- **selectionForeground** is the foreground color of selected cells.
- **selectionMode** specifies how table cells can be selected. This property is write-only. The possible values are:

```
ListSelectionModel.SINGLE_SELECTION
ListSelectionModel.SINGLE_INTERVAL_SELECTION
ListSelectionModel.MULTIPLE_INTERVAL_SELECTION
```

- **selectionModel** is an object that tracks the selection of table cells. The table-selection model is the same as the list-selection model.
- **showGrid** is a `boolean` value indicating whether the grid lines are displayed. The default value is `true`.
- **showHorizontalGrid** is a `boolean` value indicating whether the horizontal grid lines are displayed. The default value is `true`.
- **showVerticalGrid** is a `boolean` value indicating whether the vertical grid lines are displayed. The default value is `true`.
- **tableHeader** is an instance of `JTableHeader` that is displayed in the header of the view port in a scroll pane. Table header is usually specified as an array of strings in the table model.

Example 8.6 Testing Table Properties

This example demonstrates the use of several `JTable` properties. The example creates a table and allows the user to choose an Auto Resize Mode, specify the row height and margin, and indicate whether the grid is shown. A sample run of the program is shown in Figure 8.10.

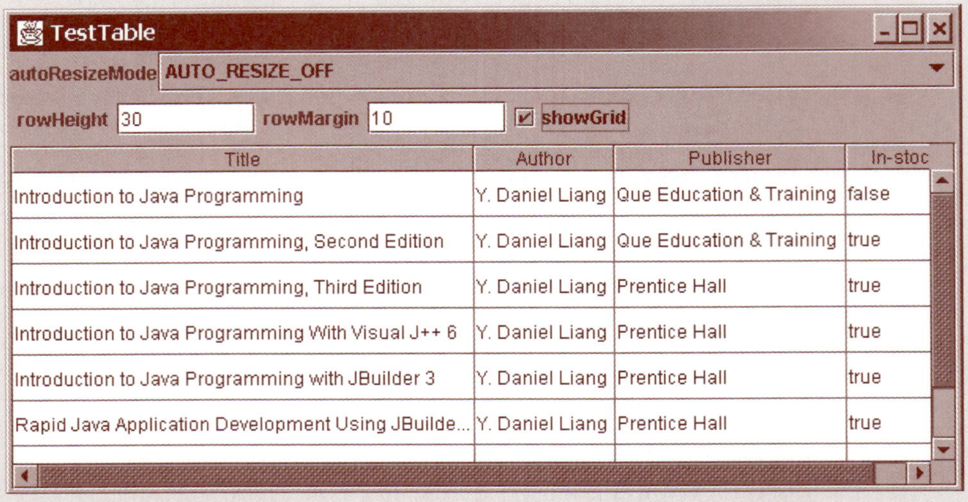

Figure 8.10 *You can specify an auto-resizing mode, the table's row height and row margin, and whether to show the grid in the table.*

Here are the steps to complete the project:

1. Create a new package named tabledemo and create a new applet named `TestTable` using the Forte Swing JApplet form wizard.
2. Drop a `JPanel` to north of the applet to create `jpProperties`. Drop a `JScrollPane` to the center of the applet, and drop a `JTable` from the Swing (Other) tab to the scroll pane to create `jTable1`.
3. Set `layout` of `jpProperties` to `BorderLayout`. Drop a `JPanel` to the north of `jpProperties` to create `jpAutoResizeMode`. Drop a `JPanel` to the south of `jpProperties` to create `jpRowGrid`.
4. Set `layout` of `jpAutoResizingMode` to `BorderLayout`. Drop a `JLabel` labeled autoResizeMode to the west of `jpAutoResizingMode`, and drop a `JComboBox` to the center of `jpAutoResizingMode` to create `jcboAutoResizingMode`.
5. Set `layout` of `jpRowGrid` to `FlowLayout` with left alignment. Drop a `JLabel`, a `JTextField`, a `JLabel`, a `JTextField`, and a `JCheckBox` to `jpRowGrid`. Set `text` of the labels to rowHeight and rowMargin. Rename the text fields to `jtfRowHeight` and `jtfRowMargin`. Rename the check box `jchkShowGrid`. Set `text` of `jchkShowGrid` to showGrid.

6. Declare and create table data and column header, as shown in Listing 8.10 (Lines 6–15). Add five auto-resizing modes to the combo box (Lines 21–26).

7. Click the ellipsis button in the `model` field of `jTable1` (see Figure 8.11) to display the `TableModel` property editor, as shown in Figure 8.12. You can create a table using the property editor. For convenience, all the examples in this chapter write the code to create table data and column names. When you drop a `JTable` into the form, an instance of `JTable` is created along with a sample table model. Click the Default button in the `TableModel` property editor to remove the sample model so that you can use your handcoded data and column names for the table. As shown in Figure 8.13, the sample table data model is gone.

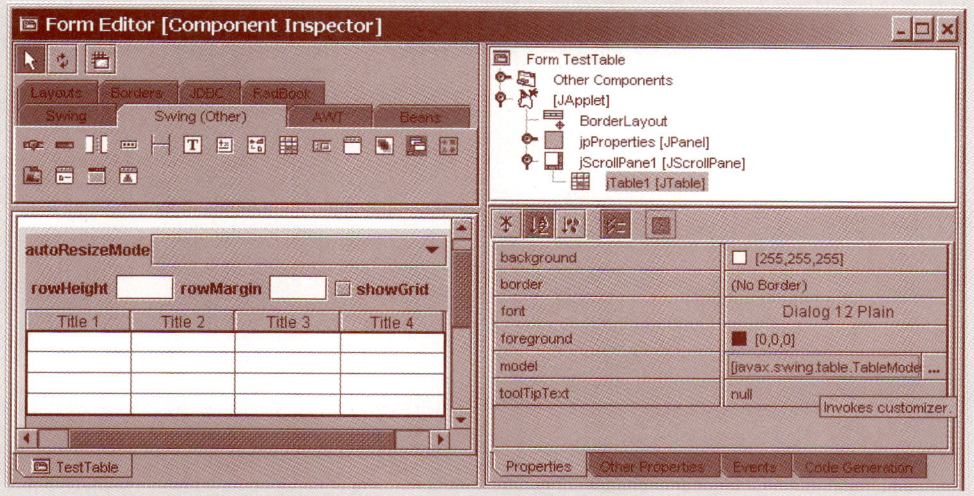

Figure 8.11 *Forte provides a sample table model with a* `JTable` *instance.*

8. In the Code Generation tab of `jTable1` in the component inspector, type `new JTable(data, columnNames);` in the Custom Creation Code to create an instance of `JTable`, as shown in Figure 8.14. This action generates the statement `jTable1 = new JTable(data, columnNames);` in the `initComponents` method, as shown in Line 41 in Listing 8.10.

9. Generate and implement the code for handling combo box selection, obtaining and using values in the text fields, and checking and unchecking the showGrid check box (Lines 91–126).

continued

Example 8.6 continued

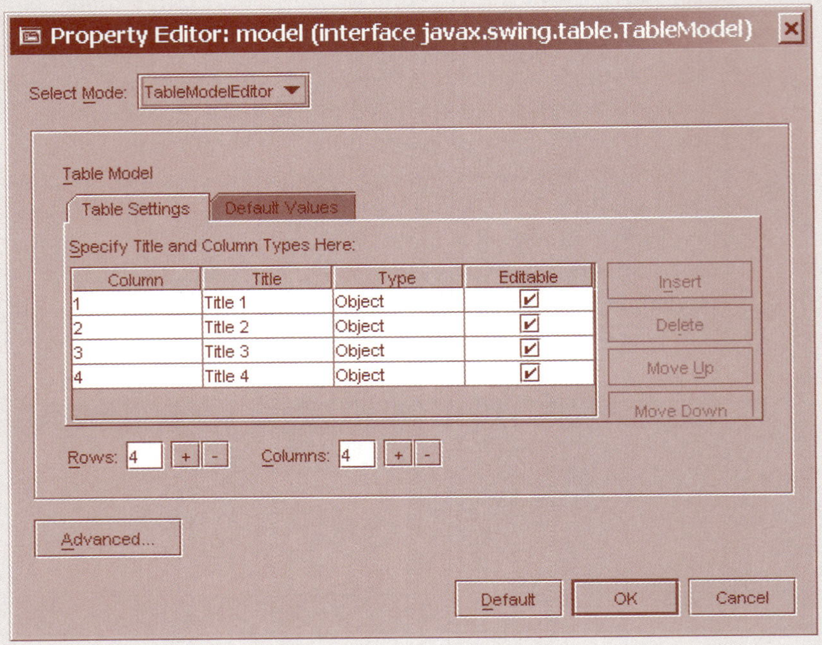

Figure 8.12 *You can create table columns and data using the TableModel property editor.*

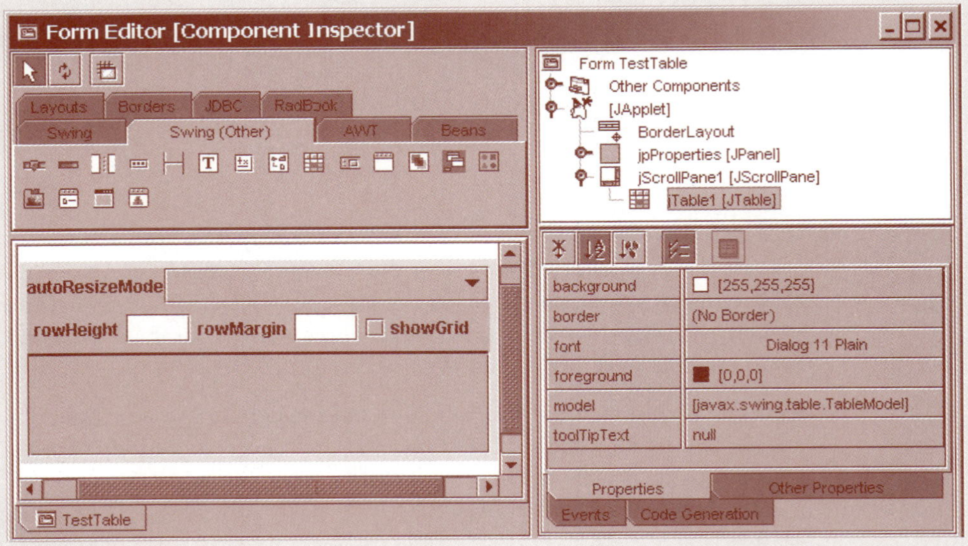

Figure 8.13 *The sample data model is removed when you press the Default button in the TableModel editor.*

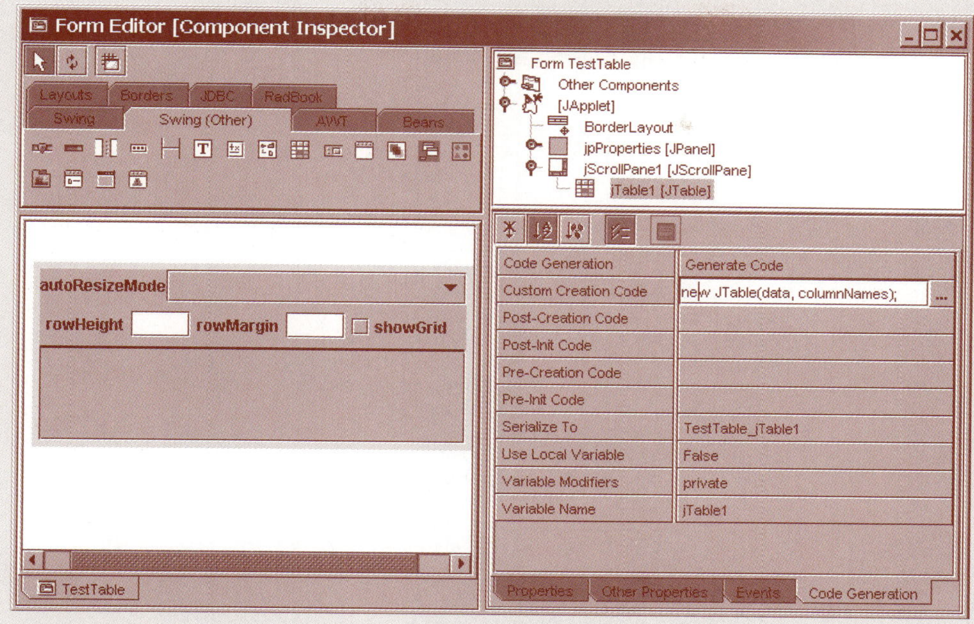

Figure 8.14 *You can provide custom code to generate objects in Forte's Form Editor.*

```
package tabledemo;

import javax.swing.*;

public class TestTable extends javax.swing.JApplet {
  // Create table column names
  String[] columnNames =
  {"Title", "Author", "Publisher", "In-stock"};

  // Create table data
  Object[][] data = {
    {"Introduction to Java Programming", "Y. Daniel Liang",
     "Que Education & Training", new Boolean(false)},
    // Omitted for brevity
  };

  /** Creates new form TestTable */
  public TestTable() {
    initComponents();

    // Add auto resize modes to jcboAutoResizingMode
    jcboAutoResizingMode.addItem("AUTO_RESIZE_OFF");
    jcboAutoResizingMode.addItem("AUTO_RESIZE_LAST_COLUMN");
    jcboAutoResizingMode.addItem("AUTO_RESIZE_SUBSEQUENT_COLUMNS");
    jcboAutoResizingMode.addItem("AUTO_RESIZE_NEXT_COLUMN");
    jcboAutoResizingMode.addItem("AUTO_RESIZE_ALL_COLUMNS");
  }

```

Listing 8.10 *TestTable.java*

continued

Example 8.6 continued

```
  private void initComponents() {
    jpProperties = new javax.swing.JPanel();
    jpAutoResizeMode = new javax.swing.JPanel();
    jLabel1 = new javax.swing.JLabel();
    jcboAutoResizingMode = new javax.swing.JComboBox();
    jpRowGrid = new javax.swing.JPanel();
    jLabel2 = new javax.swing.JLabel();
    jtfRowHeight = new javax.swing.JTextField();
    jLabel3 = new javax.swing.JLabel();
    jtfRowMargin = new javax.swing.JTextField();
    jchkShowGrid = new javax.swing.JCheckBox();
    jScrollPane1 = new javax.swing.JScrollPane();
    jTable1 = new javax.swing.JTable(data, columnNames);
    jpProperties.setLayout(new java.awt.BorderLayout());
    jpAutoResizeMode.setLayout(new java.awt.BorderLayout());
    jLabel1.setText("autoResizeMode");
    jpAutoResizeMode.add(jLabel1, java.awt.BorderLayout.WEST);
    jcboAutoResizingMode.addActionListener(
      new java.awt.event.ActionListener() {
      public void actionPerformed(java.awt.event.ActionEvent evt) {
        jcboAutoResizingModeActionPerformed(evt);
      }
    });
    jpAutoResizeMode.add(
      jcboAutoResizingMode, java.awt.BorderLayout.CENTER);
    jpProperties.add(jpAutoResizeMode, java.awt.BorderLayout.NORTH);
    jpRowGrid.setLayout(
      new java.awt.FlowLayout(java.awt.FlowLayout.LEFT));
    jLabel2.setText("rowHeight");
    jpRowGrid.add(jLabel2);
    jtfRowHeight.setColumns(4);
    jtfRowHeight.addActionListener(
      new java.awt.event.ActionListener() {
      public void actionPerformed(java.awt.event.ActionEvent evt) {
        jtfRowHeightActionPerformed(evt);
      }
    });
    jpRowGrid.add(jtfRowHeight);
    jLabel3.setText("rowMargin");
    jpRowGrid.add(jLabel3);
    jtfRowMargin.setColumns(4);
    jtfRowMargin.addActionListener(
      new java.awt.event.ActionListener() {
      public void actionPerformed(java.awt.event.ActionEvent evt) {
        jtfRowMarginActionPerformed(evt);
      }
    });
    jpRowGrid.add(jtfRowMargin);
    jchkShowGrid.setText("showGrid");
    jchkShowGrid.addActionListener(
      new java.awt.event.ActionListener() {
      public void actionPerformed(java.awt.event.ActionEvent evt) {
        jchkShowGridActionPerformed(evt);
      }
    });
    jpRowGrid.add(jchkShowGrid);
    jpProperties.add(jpRowGrid, java.awt.BorderLayout.SOUTH);
```

Listing 8.10 *continued*

```
    getContentPane().add(jpProperties, java.awt.BorderLayout.NORTH);
    jScrollPane1.setViewportView(jTable1);
    getContentPane().add(jScrollPane1, java.awt.BorderLayout.CENTER);
  }

  private void jchkShowGridActionPerformed(
    java.awt.event.ActionEvent evt) {
    jTable1.setShowGrid(jchkShowGrid.isSelected());
  }

  private void jtfRowMarginActionPerformed(
    java.awt.event.ActionEvent evt) {
    int rowMargin = new Integer(
    jtfRowMargin.getText().trim()).intValue();
    jTable1.setRowMargin(rowMargin);
  }

  private void jtfRowHeightActionPerformed(
    java.awt.event.ActionEvent evt) {
    int rowHeight = new Integer(
    jtfRowHeight.getText().trim()).intValue();
    jTable1.setRowHeight(rowHeight);
  }

  private void jcboAutoResizingModeActionPerformed(
    java.awt.event.ActionEvent evt) {
    String selectedItem =
    (String)jcboAutoResizingMode.getSelectedItem();

    if (selectedItem.equals("AUTO_RESIZE_OFF"))
      jTable1.setAutoResizeMode(JTable.AUTO_RESIZE_OFF);
    else if (selectedItem.equals("AUTO_RESIZE_LAST_COLUMN"))
      jTable1.setAutoResizeMode(JTable.AUTO_RESIZE_LAST_COLUMN);
    else if (selectedItem.equals("AUTO_RESIZE_SUBSEQUENT_COLUMNS"))
      jTable1.setAutoResizeMode(
      JTable.AUTO_RESIZE_SUBSEQUENT_COLUMNS);
    else if (selectedItem.equals("AUTO_RESIZE_NEXT_COLUMN"))
      jTable1.setAutoResizeMode(JTable.AUTO_RESIZE_NEXT_COLUMN);
    else if (selectedItem.equals("AUTO_RESIZE_ALL_COLUMNS"))
      jTable1.setAutoResizeMode(JTable.AUTO_RESIZE_ALL_COLUMNS);
  }

  // Variables declaration - do not modify
  private javax.swing.JPanel jpProperties;
  private javax.swing.JPanel jpAutoResizeMode;
  private javax.swing.JLabel jLabel1;
  private javax.swing.JComboBox jcboAutoResizingMode;
  private javax.swing.JPanel jpRowGrid;
  private javax.swing.JLabel jLabel2;
  private javax.swing.JTextField jtfRowHeight;
  private javax.swing.JLabel jLabel3;
  private javax.swing.JTextField jtfRowMargin;
  private javax.swing.JCheckBox jchkShowGrid;
  private javax.swing.JScrollPane jScrollPane1;
  private javax.swing.JTable jTable1;
  // End of variables declaration
}
```

Listing 8.10 *continued*

continued

Example 8.6 continued

Example Review

Initially, each column in the table occupies the same width (75 pixels). You can resize the columns but not the rows. There are five options for resizing columns: `AUTO_RESIZE_OFF`, `AUTO_RESIZE_LAST_COLUMN`, `AUTO_RESIZE_SUBSEQUENT_COLUMNS`, `AUTO_RESIZE_NEXT_COLUMN`, and `AUTO_RESIZE_ALL_COLUMNS`. With `AUTO_RESIZE_OFF`, resizing a column does not affect the widths of the other columns. With `AUTO_RESIZE_LAST_COLUMN`, resizing a column affects the width of the last column. With `AUTO_RESIZE_SUBSEQUENT_COLUMNS`, resizing a column affects the widths of all the subsequent columns. With `AUTO_RESIZE_NEXT_COLUMN`, resizing a column affects the widths of the next columns. With `AUTO_RESIZE_ALL_COLUMNS`, resizing a column affects the widths of all the columns.

`rowHeight` and `rowMargin` are properties in the `JTable` class. To set the width and margin for columns, you need to use the `TableColumn` class and the table's column model, which are introduced in Sections 8.4.3 and 8.4.4, "Table Column Models" and "The `TableColumn` Class."

`JTable` does not provide methods for manipulating data, such as adding or removing rows and columns. Those methods are defined in the table models and table column models.

TIP

You can use the Code Generation tab of an object in the component inspector to provide custom creation code, post-creation code, pre-creation code, and pre-init code for the object. The custom creation code replaces the default constructor. The post-creation code is inserted after the object is created. The pre-creation code is inserted before the object is created. The pre-init code is inserted before any property for the object is set.

8.4.2 Table Models

Like `JList` and `JComboBox`, `JTable` delegates data storing and processing to its table data model. A table data model must implement the `TableModel` interface, which defines the methods for registering table model listeners, manipulating cells, and obtaining row count, column count, column class, and column name.

The `AbstractTableModel` class provides default implementations for most of the methods in `TableModel`. It takes care of the management of listeners and provides some conveniences for generating `TableModelEvents` and dispatching them to the listeners. To create a concrete `TableModel`, you simply extend `AbstractTableModel` and implement at least the following three methods:

- `public int getRowCount()`
- `public int getColumnCount()`
- `public Object getValueAt(int row, int column)`

The `DefaultTableModel` class extends `AbstractTableModel` and implements these three methods. Additionally, `DefaultTableModel` provides concrete storage for data. The data are stored in a vector. The elements in the vector are arrays of objects, each of which represents an individual cell value.

The following methods in `DefaultTableModel` for accessing and modifying data are often useful:

```
// For processing cells
public Object getValueAt(int row, int column)
public void setValueAt(Object value, int row, int column)
public boolean isCellEditable(int row, int column)

// For processing columns
public void addColumn(Object columnName)
public void addColumn(Object columnName, Object[] columnData)
public void addColumn(Object columnName, Vector columnData)
public int getColumnCount()
public Class getColumnClass(int column)
public String getColumnName()

// For processing rows
public void addRow(Object[] rowData)
public void addRow(Vector rowData)
public int getRowCount()
public void insertRow(int index, Object[] rowData)
public void insertRow(int index, Vector rowData)
public void moveRow(int startIndex, int endIndex, int toIndex)
```

An instance of `DefaultTableModel` can be constructed using these constructors:

```
public DefaultTableModel()
public DefaultTableModel(int numRows, int numColumns)
public DefaultTableModel(Object[] columnNames, int numRows)
public DefaultTableModel(Object[][] data, object[] columnNames)
public DefaultTableModel(Vector columnNames, int numRows)
public DefaultTableModel(Vector data, Vector columnNames)
```

8.4.3 Table Column Models

Table column models manage columns in a table. They can be used to select, add, move, and remove table columns. A table column model must implement the `TableColumnModel` interface, which defines the methods for registering table column model listeners, and for accessing and manipulating columns.

The `DefaultTableColumnModel` class is a concrete implementation of `TableColumnModel`. The `DefaultTableColumnModel` class stores its columns in a vector and contains an instance of `ListSelectionModel` for selecting columns.

The following methods in `DefaultColumnModel` for manipulating and selecting columns are often useful:

```
// For manipulating columns
public void addColumn(TableColumn tableColumn)
public void removeTableColumn(TableColumn tableColumn)
public void moveColumn(int fromIndex, int toIndex)
public int getColumnMargin()
public void setColumnMargin(int newMargin)
public TableColumn getColumn(int columnIndex)
public int getColumnCount()
```

```
public int getColumnIndex(Object columnIdentifier)
public Enumeration getColumns()
public int getTotalColumnWidth()

// For selecting columns
public boolean getColumnSelectionAllowed()
public void setColumnSelectionAllowed(boolean flag)
public int getSelectedColumnCount()
public int getSelectedColumns()
public ListSelectionModel getSelectionModel()
public void setSelectionModel(ListSelectionModel newModel)
```

8.4.4 The *TableColumn* Class

The column model deals with all the columns in a table. The `TableColumn` class is used to represent an individual column in the table. An instance of `TableColumn` for a specified column can be obtained using the `getColumn(index)` method in `TableColumnModel` or the `getColumn(columnIdentifier)` method in `JTable`.

The following methods in `TableColumn` are used for manipulating column width and specifying cell renderer, cell editor, and header renderer:

```
// Column width, max width, min width, and preferred width
public int getWidth()
public void setWidth(int width)
public int getMaxWidth()
public void setMaxWidth(int maxWidth)
public int getMinWidth()
public void setMinWidth(int minWidth)
public int getPreferredWidth()
public void setPreferredWidth(int minWidth)

// Resizes the column to fit the width of its header cell
public void sizeWidthToFit()

// Renderers and editors for the cells in the column
public TableCellEditor getCellEditor()
public void setCellEditor(TableCellEditor anEditor)
public TableCellRenderer getCellRenderer()
public void setCellRenderer(TableCellRenderer aRenderer)
public TableCellRenderer getHeaderRenderer()
public void setHeaderRenderer(TableCellRenderer aRenderer)
```

Example 8.7 Using Table Models

This example demonstrates the use of table models, table column models, list-selection models, and the `TableColumn` class. The program allows the user to choose selection mode and selection type, to add or remove rows and columns, and to save table to a file, as shown in Figure 8.15.

Here are the steps to complete the project:

1. In the tabledemo package, create a new applet named `TestDefaultTableModels` using the Forte Swing JApplet form wizard.

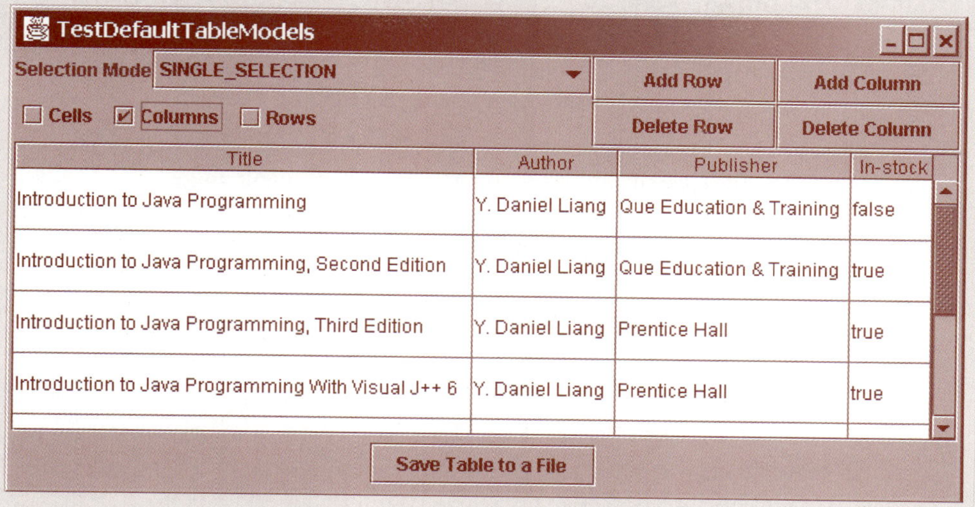

Figure 8.15 *You can add or remove rows and columns in a table.*

2. Drop a `JPanel` to north of the applet to create `jpOperations`. Drop a `JPanel` to the south of the applet to create `jpSaveToFile`. Drop a `JScroll-Pane` to the center of the applet, and drop a `JTable` to the scroll pane to create `jTable1`.

3. Set `layout` of `jpOperations` to `BorderLayout`. Drop a `JPanel` to the east of `jpOperations` to create `jpAddRemove`. Drop a `JPanel` to the center of `jpOperations` to create `jpSelections`.

4. Set `layout` of `jpSelections` to `BorderLayout`. Drop a `JPanel` to the north of `jpSelections` to create `jpSelectionMode`, and drop a `JPanel` to the south of `jpSelections` to create `jpSelectionType`.

5. Set `layout` of `jpSelectionMode` to `BorderLayout`. Drop a `JLabel` labeled "Selection Mode" to the west of `jpSelectionMode`, and drop a `JComboBox` to the center of `jpSelectionMode` to create `jcboSelectionMode`.

6. Set `layout` of `jpSelectionType` to `FlowLayout` with left alignment. Drop a `JCheckBox` three times into `jpSelectionType` to create `jchkCells`, `jchkColumns`, and `jchkRows`.

7. Set `layout` of `jpAddRemove` to `GridLayout` with two rows and two columns. Drop a `JButton` four times to create `jbtAddRow`, `jbtAddColumn`, `jbtDeleteRow`, and `jbtDeleteColumn`.

8. Drop a `JButton` to `jpSaveToFile` to create `jbtSaveToFile`. Set the button's text to "Save Table to a File."

9. Write the code to create `jFileChooser1`, an instance of `JFileChooser`, as shown in Figure 8.15 (Line 25).

continued

Example 8.7 continued

10. Create an instance, named `tableModel`, of `DefaultTableModel` with table data and column, as shown in Listing 8.11 (Lines 21–22).

11. In the TableModel property editor for the model property of `jTable1`, click the Default button to remove the sample table model. In the Code Generation tab of `jTable1`, type `new javax.swing.JTable(tableModel);` in the Custom Creation Code field to create a `JTable` instance with the specified table model.

12. Generate the `ActionEvent` handlers for combo box, check boxes, and buttons, and implement the handlers for choosing a selection mode, choosing selection types, adding or removing rows and columns, and saving the current contents of the table to a file (Lines 143–236).

13. Add a main method to run it as application to circumvent security restrictions on applets. The main method is omitted in the listing.

```
1  package tabledemo;
2
3  import java.util.*;
4  import java.io.*;
5  import javax.swing.table.*;
6  import javax.swing.*;
7
8  public class TestDefaultTableModels extends javax.swing.JApplet {
9    // Create table column names
10   String[] columnNames =
11   {"Title", "Author", "Publisher", "In-stock"};
12
13   // Create table data
14   Object[][] data = {
15     {"Introduction to Java Programming", "Y. Daniel Liang",
16      "Que Education & Training", new Boolean(false)},
17     // Omitted for brevity
18   };
19
20   // Create table model
21   DefaultTableModel tableModel =
22     new DefaultTableModel(data, columnNames);
23
24   // Create a file chooser
25   JFileChooser jFileChooser1 = new JFileChooser();
26
27   /** Creates new form TestDefaultTableModels */
27   public TestDefaultTableModels() {
28     initComponents();
29
30     // Add selection modes to jcboSelectionMode
31     jcboSelectionMode.addItem("SINGLE_SELECTION");
32     jcboSelectionMode.addItem("SINGLE_INTERVAL_SELECTION");
33     jcboSelectionMode.addItem("MULTIPLE_INTERVAL_SELECTION");
34   }
35
```

Listing 8.11 *TestDefaultTableModels.java*

```
      private void initComponents() {
        jpOperations = new javax.swing.JPanel();
        jpAddRemove = new javax.swing.JPanel();
        jbtAddRow = new javax.swing.JButton();
        jbtAddColumn = new javax.swing.JButton();
        jbtDeleteRow = new javax.swing.JButton();
        jbtDeleteColumn = new javax.swing.JButton();
        jpSelections = new javax.swing.JPanel();
        jpSelectionMode = new javax.swing.JPanel();
        jLabel1 = new javax.swing.JLabel();
        jcboSelectionMode = new javax.swing.JComboBox();
        jpSelectionType = new javax.swing.JPanel();
        jchkCells = new javax.swing.JCheckBox();
        jchkColumns = new javax.swing.JCheckBox();
        jchkRows = new javax.swing.JCheckBox();
        jScrollPane1 = new javax.swing.JScrollPane();
        jTable1 = new javax.swing.JTable(tableModel);
        jpSaveToFile = new javax.swing.JPanel();
        jbtSaveToFile = new javax.swing.JButton();
        jpOperations.setLayout(new java.awt.BorderLayout());
        jpAddRemove.setLayout(new java.awt.GridLayout(2, 2));
        jbtAddRow.setText("Add Row");
        jbtAddRow.addActionListener(new java.awt.event.ActionListener() {
          public void actionPerformed(java.awt.event.ActionEvent evt) {
            jbtAddRowActionPerformed(evt);
          }
        });
        jpAddRemove.add(jbtAddRow);
        jbtAddColumn.setText("Add Column");
        jbtAddColumn.addActionListener(
          new java.awt.event.ActionListener() {
          public void actionPerformed(java.awt.event.ActionEvent evt) {
            jbtAddColumnActionPerformed(evt);
          }
        });
        jpAddRemove.add(jbtAddColumn);
        jbtDeleteRow.setText("Delete Row");
        jbtDeleteRow.addActionListener(
          new java.awt.event.ActionListener() {
          public void actionPerformed(java.awt.event.ActionEvent evt) {
            jbtDeleteRowActionPerformed(evt);
          }
        });
        jpAddRemove.add(jbtDeleteRow);
        jbtDeleteColumn.setText("Delete Column");
        jbtDeleteColumn.addActionListener(
          new java.awt.event.ActionListener() {
          public void actionPerformed(java.awt.event.ActionEvent evt) {
            jbtDeleteColumnActionPerformed(evt);
          }
        });
        jpAddRemove.add(jbtDeleteColumn);
        jpOperations.add(jpAddRemove, java.awt.BorderLayout.EAST);
        jpSelections.setLayout(new java.awt.BorderLayout());
        jpSelectionMode.setLayout(new java.awt.BorderLayout());
        jLabel1.setText("Selection Mode");
        jpSelectionMode.add(jLabel1, java.awt.BorderLayout.WEST);
```

Listing 8.11 *continued*

continued

Example 8.7 continued

```
      jcboSelectionMode.addActionListener(
        new java.awt.event.ActionListener() {
        public void actionPerformed(java.awt.event.ActionEvent evt) {
          jcboSelectionModeActionPerformed(evt);
        }
      });
      jpSelectionMode.add(jcboSelectionMode,
        java.awt.BorderLayout.CENTER);
      jpSelections.add(jpSelectionMode, java.awt.BorderLayout.NORTH);
      jpSelectionType.setLayout(
        new java.awt.FlowLayout(java.awt.FlowLayout.LEFT));
      jchkCells.setText("Cells");
      jchkCells.addActionListener(
        new java.awt.event.ActionListener() {
        public void actionPerformed(java.awt.event.ActionEvent evt) {
          jchkCellsActionPerformed(evt);
        }
      });
      jpSelectionType.add(jchkCells);
      jchkColumns.setText("Columns");
      jchkColumns.addActionListener(
        new java.awt.event.ActionListener() {
        public void actionPerformed(java.awt.event.ActionEvent evt) {
          jchkColumnsActionPerformed(evt);
        }
      });
      jpSelectionType.add(jchkColumns);
      jchkRows.setText("Rows");
      jchkRows.addActionListener(new java.awt.event.ActionListener() {
        public void actionPerformed(java.awt.event.ActionEvent evt) {
          jchkRowsActionPerformed(evt);
        }
      });
      jpSelectionType.add(jchkRows);
      jpSelections.add(jpSelectionType, java.awt.BorderLayout.SOUTH);
      jpOperations.add(jpSelections, java.awt.BorderLayout.CENTER);
      getContentPane().add(jpOperations, java.awt.BorderLayout.NORTH);
      jScrollPane1.setViewportView(jTable1);
      getContentPane().add(jScrollPane1, java.awt.BorderLayout.CENTER);
      jbtSaveToFile.setText("Save Table to a File");
      jbtSaveToFile.addActionListener(
        new java.awt.event.ActionListener() {
        public void actionPerformed(java.awt.event.ActionEvent evt) {
          jbtSaveToFileActionPerformed(evt);
        }
      });
      jpSaveToFile.add(jbtSaveToFile);
      getContentPane().add(jpSaveToFile, java.awt.BorderLayout.SOUTH);
    }

    private void jbtDeleteColumnActionPerformed(
      java.awt.event.ActionEvent evt) {
      DefaultTableColumnModel tableColumnModel =
        (DefaultTableColumnModel)jTable1.getColumnModel();
      int selectedColumn = jTable1.getSelectedColumn();
      tableColumnModel.removeColumn(
      tableColumnModel.getColumn(selectedColumn));
    }

```

Listing 8.11 *continued*

```
  private void jbtDeleteRowActionPerformed(
    java.awt.event.ActionEvent evt) {
    tableModel.removeRow(jTable1.getSelectedRow());
  }

  private void jbtAddColumnActionPerformed(
    java.awt.event.ActionEvent evt) {
    tableModel.addColumn(new String("New Column"),
      new Object[] {"1", "2", "3", "4", "5", "6", "7"});
  }

  private void jbtAddRowActionPerformed(
    java.awt.event.ActionEvent evt) {
    tableModel.addRow(new Object[]{
      " ", " ", " ", new Boolean(false)});
  }

  private void jchkRowsActionPerformed(
    java.awt.event.ActionEvent evt) {
    jTable1.setRowSelectionAllowed(
    jchkRows.isSelected());
  }

  private void jchkColumnsActionPerformed(
    java.awt.event.ActionEvent evt) {
    jTable1.setColumnSelectionAllowed(
    jchkColumns.isSelected());
  }

  private void jchkCellsActionPerformed(
    java.awt.event.ActionEvent evt) {
    jTable1.setCellSelectionEnabled(
    jchkCells.isSelected());
  }

  private void jcboSelectionModeActionPerformed(
    java.awt.event.ActionEvent evt) {
    String selectedItem =
    (String)jcboSelectionMode.getSelectedItem();

    if (selectedItem.equals("SINGLE_SELECTION"))
      jTable1.setSelectionMode(ListSelectionModel.SINGLE_SELECTION);
    else if (selectedItem.equals("SINGLE_INTERVAL_SELECTION"))
      jTable1.setSelectionMode(
      ListSelectionModel.SINGLE_INTERVAL_SELECTION);
    else if (selectedItem.equals("MULTIPLE_INTERVAL_SELECTION"))
      jTable1.setSelectionMode(
      ListSelectionModel.MULTIPLE_INTERVAL_SELECTION);
  }

  private void jbtSaveToFileActionPerformed(
    java.awt.event.ActionEvent evt) {
    if (jFileChooser1.showSaveDialog(this) ==
    JFileChooser.APPROVE_OPTION) {
      save(jFileChooser1.getSelectedFile());
    }
  }

  /** Save file with specified File instance */
  private void save(File file) {
    try {
      // Write table to the specified file
```

Listing 8.11 *continued*

continued

Example 8.7 continued

```
            BufferedWriter out = new BufferedWriter(new FileWriter(file));
            String header = "";

            // Write header to the file
            for (int i = 0; i < jTable1.getColumnCount(); i++)
              header += jTable1.getColumnName(i) + '\t';s
            out.write(header);
            out.newLine();

            // Write rows to the file
            for (int i = 0; i < jTable1.getRowCount(); i++) {
              for (int j = 0; j < jTable1.getColumnCount(); j++) {
                out.write(jTable1.getValueAt(i, j).toString() + '\t');
              }
              out.newLine();
            }

            out.close();
          }
          catch (IOException ex) {
            ex.printStackTrace();
          }
        }

        // Variables declaration - do not modify
        private javax.swing.JPanel jpOperations;
        private javax.swing.JPanel jpAddRemove;
        private javax.swing.JButton jbtAddRow;
        private javax.swing.JButton jbtAddColumn;
        private javax.swing.JButton jbtDeleteRow;
        private javax.swing.JButton jbtDeleteColumn;
        private javax.swing.JPanel jpSelections;
        private javax.swing.JPanel jpSelectionMode;
        private javax.swing.JLabel jLabel1;
        private javax.swing.JComboBox jcboSelectionMode;
        private javax.swing.JPanel jpSelectionType;
        private javax.swing.JCheckBox jchkCells;
        private javax.swing.JCheckBox jchkColumns;
        private javax.swing.JCheckBox jchkRows;
        private javax.swing.JScrollPane jScrollPane1;
        private javax.swing.JTable jTable1;
        private javax.swing.JPanel jpSaveToFile;
        private javax.swing.JButton jbtSaveToFile;
        // End of variables declaration
      }
```

Listing 8.11 *continued*

Example Review

The table-selection mode is the same as the list-selection mode. You can choose to select a single object, objects in a single interval, or objects in multiple intervals. The objects can be cells, columns, or rows. The selectable object types can be specified using the following `JTable` `boolean` properties:

- cellSelectionAllowed
- `columnSelectionAllowed`
- rowSelectionAllowed

When you click the Add Row button, a new row is appended to the table. When you click the Add Column button, a new column entitled "New Column" is appended to the table. To delete a row, first select a row, then click the Delete Row button. To delete a column, first select a column, then click the Delete Column button. The program only deletes one row or one column at a time, but you can modify the handlers to enable the deletion of multiple rows and columns.

When you click the Save Table to a File button, a file save dialog box is displayed. You can choose or specify a filename, then click OK to save the current contents of the table to a file.

Some of the methods defined in the table model and the table column model are also defined in the `JTable` class for convenience. For instance, the `getColumnCount()` method is defined in `JTable`, `TableModel`, and `TableColumnModel`, the `addColumn` method defined in the column model is also defined in the table model, and the `getColumn()` method defined in the column model is also defined in the `JTable` class.

NOTE

Due to a bug, `TableModel` and `TableColumnModel` are not synchronized. If you add or delete a column from `TableColumnModel`, the change is not effected in `TableModel`. However, the change does take place in `JTable`. Always use the methods from `JTable` as much as possible. For example, to get a column count, use the `getColumnCount` method from the `JTable` class instead of from the `TableColumnModel` class. Therefore, in the `save` method in this example, `jTable1.getColumnCount()` (Line 218) was used instead of `tableModel.getColumnCount()`.

8.4.5 Table Renderers and Editors

Table cells are painted by cell renderers. By default, a cell object's string representation is displayed and the string can be edited as it was in a text field. `JTable` maintains a set of predefined renderers and editors, listed in Table 8.1, which can be specified to replace default string renderers and editors.

TABLE 8.1 Predefined renderers and editors for tables

Class	*Renderer*	*Editor*
`Object`	`JLabel` (left aligned)	`JTextField`
`Date`	`JLabel` (right aligned)	`JTextField`
`Number`	`JLabel` (right aligned)	`JTextField`
`ImageIcon`	`JLabel` (center aligned)	
`Boolean`	`JCheckBox` (center aligned)	`JCheckBox` (center aligned)

The predefined renderers and editors are automatically located and loaded to match the class return from the `getColumnClass()` method in the table model. To use a predefined renderer or editor for a class other than `String`, you need to create your own table model by extending a subclass of `TableModel`. In your table model class, you need to override the `getColumnClass()` method to return the class of the column, as follows:

```
public Class getColumnClass(int column) {
  return getValueAt(0, column).getClass();
}
```

Example 8.8 Using Predefined Table Renderers and Editors

This example demonstrates the use of predefined table renderers and editors for `boolean` values, dates, and image icons, as shown in Figure 8.16.

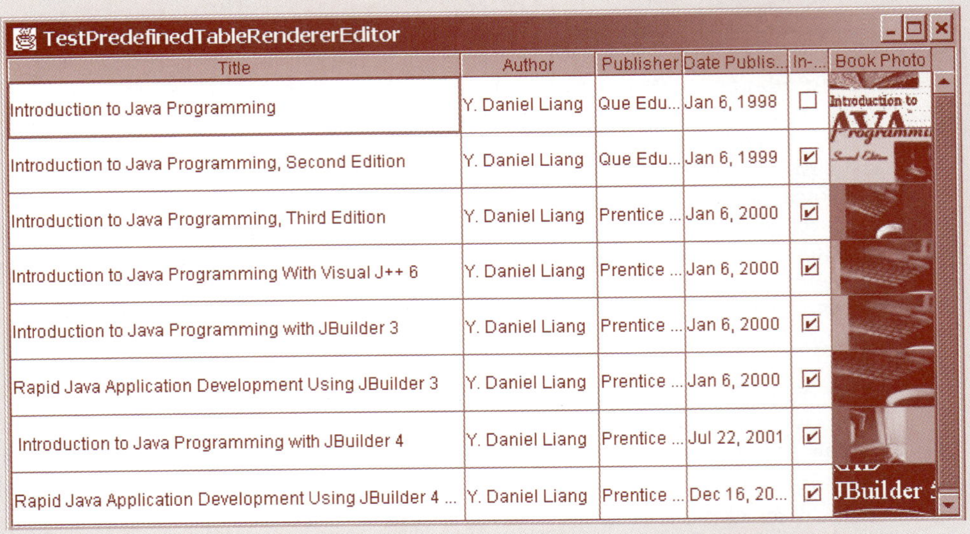

Figure 8.16 `JTable` *uses predefined renderers and editors for* `boolean` *values, dates, and image icons.*

Here are the steps to complete the project:

1. In the tabledemo package, create a new class named `MyTableModel` that extends `DefaultTableModel`, as shown in Listing 8.12. Create a new applet named `TestPredefinedTableRendererEditor` using the Forte Swing JApplet form wizard.

2. Drop a `JScrollPane` to the center of the applet, and drop a `JTable` to the scroll pane to create `jTable1`. Set its `rowHeight` property to 40.

3. Create an instance, named `tableModel`, of `MyTableModel` with table data and column, as shown in Listing 8.13 (Line 29). Create image icons, table column names, and data (Lines 9–26).

4. In the TableModel property editor of the model property for `jTable1`, click the Default button to remove the sample table model for `jTable1`.

5. In the Code Generation tab for `jTable1` in the component inspector, type `new javax.swing.JTable(tableModel);` in the Custom Creation Code field to create an instance of `JTable` with the specified data and column names.

```
package tabledemo;

import javax.swing.*;
import javax.swing.table.*;
import java.util.*;

public class MyTableModel extends DefaultTableModel {
  // Default constructor
  public MyTableModel() {
 }

  public MyTableModel(Object[][] data, Object[] columnNames) {
    super(data, columnNames);
  }

  /** Override this method to return a class for the column */
  public Class getColumnClass(int column) {
    return getValueAt(0, column).getClass();
  }

  /** Override this method to return true if cell is editable */
  public boolean isCellEditable(int row, int column) {
    Class columnClass = getColumnClass(column);
    return columnClass != ImageIcon.class &&
      columnClass != Date.class;
  }
}
```

Listing 8.12 *MyTableModel.java*

```
1    package tabledemo;
2
3    import imageviewerdemo.ImageViewer;
4    import javax.swing.*;
5    import java.util.*;
6
7    public class TestPredefinedTableRendererEditor
8      extends javax.swing.JApplet {
9      // Create images
10     ImageIcon intro1eImageIcon = ImageViewer.createImageIcon(
11       "/image/intro1e.gif", this);
12     // Create image icons, omitted for brevity
13
14     // Create table column names
```

Listing 8.13 *TestPredefinedTableRendererEditor.java*

continued

Example 8.8 continued

```
    String[] columnNames =
      {"Title", "Author", "Publisher", "Date Published", "In-stock",
       "Book Cover"};

    // Create table data
    Object[][] data = {
      {"Introduction to Java Programming", "Y. Daniel Liang",
       "Que Eduction & Training",
       new GregorianCalendar(1998, 1-1, 6).getTime(),
       new Boolean(false), intro1eImageIcon},
    // Omitted for brevity
    };

    // Create table model
    MyTableModel tableModel = new MyTableModel(data, columnNames);

    /** Creates new form TestPredefinedTableRendererEditor */
    public TestPredefinedTableRendererEditor() {
      initComponents();
    }

    private void initComponents() {
      jScrollPane1 = new javax.swing.JScrollPane();
      jTable1 = new javax.swing.JTable(tableModel);
      jTable1.setRowHeight(40);
      jScrollPane1.setViewportView(jTable1);
      getContentPane().add(jScrollPane1, java.awt.BorderLayout.CENTER);
    }

    // Variables declaration - do not modify
    private javax.swing.JScrollPane jScrollPane1;
    private javax.swing.JTable jTable1;
    // End of variables declaration
  }
```

Listing 8.13 *continued*

Example Review

The example creates two classes: `MyTableModel` and `TestPredefinedTableRendererEditor`. `MyTableModel` is an extension of `DefaultTableModel`. The purpose of `MyTableModel` is to override the default implementation of the `getColumnClass()` method to return the class of the column, so that an appropriate predefined `JTable` can be used for the column. By default, `getColumnClass()` returns `Object.class`.

`MyTableModel` also overrides the `isCellEditable()` method. By default, `isCellEditable()` returns `true`. You can override it to prohibit editing of a cell. This example does not allow the user to edit image icons and dates. For a cell to be editable, both `isCellEditable()` in the table model and `isEditing` in `JTable` class must be `true`.

The `TestPredefinedTableRendererEditor` class creates a table model using `MyTableModel`. `JTable` assigns a predefined cell renderer and a predefined editor to the cell, whose class is specified in the `getColumnClass()` method in `MyTableModel`.

8.4.6 Custom Table Renderers and Editors

Predefined renderers and editors are convenient and easy to use, but their functions are limited. The predefined image icon renderer displays the image icon in a label. The image icon cannot be scaled. If you want the whole image to fit in a cell, you need to create a custom renderer.

A custom renderer can be created by extending the `DefaultTableCellRenderer`, which is a default implementation for the `TableCellRender` interface. The custom renderer must override the `getTableCellRendererComponent()` to return a component for rendering the table cell.

The `getTableCellRendererComponent()` is defined as follows:

```
public Component getTableCellRendererComponent
  (JTable table, Object value, boolean isSelected,
   boolean isFocused, int row, int column)
```

This method signature is very similar to the `getListCellRendererComponent()` method used to create custom list cell renderers. Their implementations are similar too. The following class, `MyImageCellRenderer`, shown in Listing 8.14, creates a renderer for displaying image icons in a panel.

```
package tabledemo;

import javax.swing.*;
import javax.swing.table.*;
import imageviewerdemo.ImageViewer;
import java.awt.*;

public class MyImageCellRenderer extends DefaultTableCellRenderer {
  /** Override this method in DefaultTableCellRenderer */
  public Component getTableCellRendererComponent
    (JTable table, Object value, boolean isSelected,
     boolean isFocused, int row, int column) {
    Image image = ((ImageIcon)value).getImage();
    ImageViewer imageViewer = new ImageViewer(image);
    return imageViewer;
  }
}
```

Listing 8.14 *MyImageCellRenderer.java*

You can also create a custom editor. `JTable` provides the `DefaultCellEditor` class, which can be used to edit a cell in a text field, a check box, or a combo box. To use it, simply create a text field, a check box, or a combo box, and pass it to `DefaultCellEditor`'s constructor to create an editor.

Example 8.9 Using Custom Table Renderers and Editors

This example demonstrates the use of custom table renderers to display image icons and the use of a custom combo editor to edit items. A sample run of the program is shown in Figure 8.17

continued

Example 8.9 continued

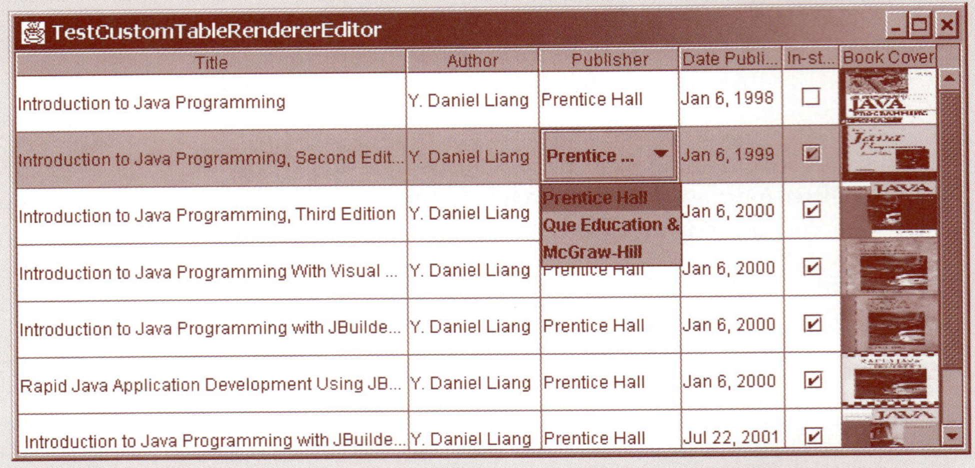

Figure 8.17 *A custom renderer displays a scaled image, and a custom editor edits the Publisher column using a combo box.*

Here are the steps to complete the project:

1. In the tabledemo package, create a new class named `MyImageCellRenderer` that extends `DefaultTableCellRenderer`, as shown in Listing 8.14. Create a new applet named `TestCustomTableRendererEditor` using the Forte Swing JApplet form wizard.

2. Drop a `JScrollPane` to the center of the applet, and drop a `JTable` to the scroll pane to create `jTable1`.

3. Create an instance, named `tableModel`, of `MyTableModel` with table data and column names, as shown in Listing 8.15 (Line 30).

4. In the TableModel property editor of the model property for `jTable1`, click the Default button to remove the sample table model for `jTable1`.

5. In the Code Generation tab for `jTable1` in the component inspector, type `new javax.swing.JTable(tableModel);` in the Custom Creation Code field to create an instance of `JTable` with the specified data and column names.

6. Create an instance of `MyImageCellRenderer` and set it as the cell renderer for the Book Cover column, as shown in Listing 8.15 (Line 38).

7. Create an instance of `JComboBox` and add three publisher names, as shown in Listing 8.15 (Lines 41–44). Pass the combo box to the constructor of `DefaultCellEditor` to create a custom editor and set it as the cell editor for the Publisher column (Lines 48–49).

```
package tabledemo;

import imageviewerdemo.ImageViewer;
import javax.swing.*;
import javax.swing.table.*;
import java.util.*;

public class TestCustomTableRendererEditor
  extends javax.swing.JApplet {
  // Create images
  ImageIcon intro1eImageIcon = ImageViewer.createImageIcon(
    "/image/intro1e.gif", this);
  // Create other images omitted for brevity

  // Create table column names
  String[] columnNames =
    {"Title", "Author", "Publisher", "Date Published", "In-stock",
     "Book Cover"};

  // Create table data
  Object[][] data = {
   {"Introduction to Java Programming", "Y. Daniel Liang",
    "Que Eduction & Training",
    new GregorianCalendar(1998, 1-1, 6).getTime(),
    new Boolean(false), intro1eImageIcon},
    // Omitted for brevity
  };

  // Create table model
  MyTableModel tableModel = new MyTableModel(data, columnNames);

  /** Creates new form TestCustomTableRendererEditor */
  public TestCustomTableRendererEditor() {
    initComponents();

    // Set custom renderer for displaying images
    TableColumn bookCover = jTable1.getColumn("Book Cover");
    bookCover.setCellRenderer(new MyImageCellRenderer());

    // Create a combo box for publishers
    JComboBox jcboPublishers = new JComboBox();
    jcboPublishers.addItem("Prentice Hall");
    jcboPublishers.addItem("Que Education & Training");
    jcboPublishers.addItem("McGraw-Hill");

    // Set combo box as the editor for the publisher column
    TableColumn publisherColumn = jTable1.getColumn("Publisher");
    publisherColumn.setCellEditor(
      new DefaultCellEditor(jcboPublishers));
  }

  private void initComponents() {
    jScrollPane1 = new javax.swing.JScrollPane();
    jTable1 = new javax.swing.JTable(tableModel)
    jScrollPane1.setViewportView(jTable1);
    getContentPane().add(jScrollPane1, java.awt.BorderLayout.CENTER);
  }

```

Listing 8.15 *TestCustomTableRendererEditor.java*

continued

Example 8.9 continued

```
    // Variables declaration - do not modify
    private javax.swing.JScrollPane jScrollPane1;
    private javax.swing.JTable jTable1;
    // End of variables declaration
}
```

Listing 8.15 *continued*

Example Review

This example uses the same table model (`MyTableModel`) that was created in the preceding example. By default, image icons are displayed using the predefined image icon renderer. To use `MyImageCellRenderer` to display the image, you have to explicitly specify the `MyImageCellRenderer` renderer for the Book Cover column. Likewise, you have to explicitly specify the combo box editor for the Publisher column; otherwise the default editor would be used.

When you edit a cell in the Publisher column, a combo box of three items is displayed. When you select an item from the box, it is displayed in the cell. You did not write the code for handling selections. The selections are handled by the `DefaultCellEditor` class.

When you resize the Book Cover column, the image is resized to fit into the whole cell. With the predefined image renderer, you can only see part of the image if the cell is smaller than the image.

8.4.7 Table Events

Table events are fired by table models, table column models, and table-selection models whenever changes are made to these models. The `JTable` class does not fire table events. Table models fire `TableModelEvent` when table data are changed. Table column models fire `TableColumnModelEvent` when columns are added, removed, or moved, or when the column selection changes. Table-selection models fire `ListSelectionEvent` when the selection changes.

To listen for these events, a listener must be registered with an appropriate model and implement the correct listener interface. The following example demonstrates how to use these events.

Example 8.10 Using Table Events

This example demonstrates handling table events. The program displays messages on a label when a row or a column is selected, when a cell is edited, or when a column is removed. Figure 8.18 is a sample run of the example.

Here are the steps to complete the project:

1. In the tabledemo package, create a new applet named TestTableEvents using the Forte JApplet form wizard.

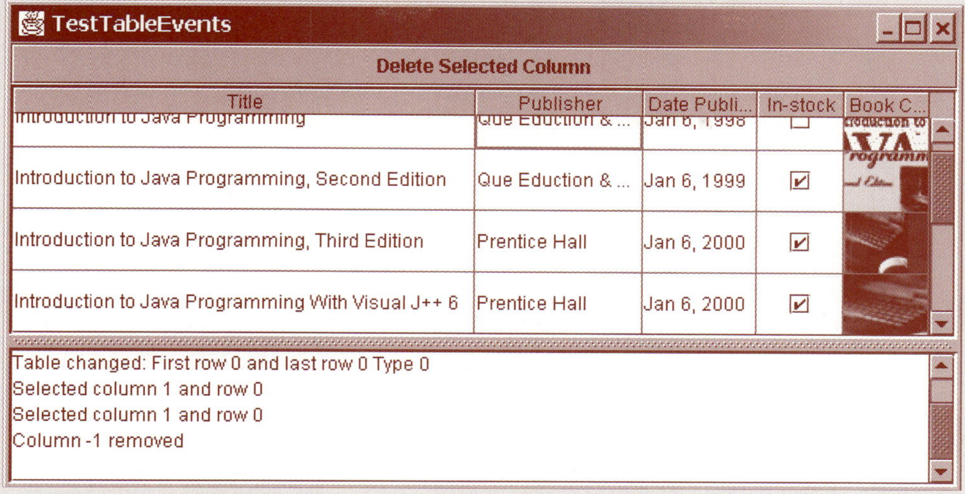

Figure 8.18 *Table event handlers display table events on a text area.*

2. Drop a `JButton` to the north of the applet to create `jbtDeleteColumn`. Drop a `JSplitPane` to the center of the applet and set its `orientation` to `VERTICAL`. Drop a `JScrollPane` to the top of the split pane, and drop a `JTable` to the scroll pane to create `jTable1`. Drop a `JScrollPane` to the bottom of the split pane, and drop a `JTextArea` to the scroll pane to create `jtaMessage`.

3. Install `MyTableModel` into the component palette and drop it into the form to create `myTableModel1` under the Other Components node in the component tree. In the Code Generation tab of `myTableModel1`, type `new MyTableModel(data, columnNames);` in the Custom Creation Code field to create an instance of `MyTableModel` with specified `data` and `columnNames`.

4. In the `TableModel` property editor of the model property for `jTable1`, click the Default button to remove the sample table model for `jTable1`.

5. In the Code Generation tab for `jTable1` in the component inspector, type `new javax.swing.JTable(myTableModel1);` in the Custom Creation Code field to create an instance of `JTable` with the specified data and column names.

6. Create an instance named `tableColumnModel` obtained from `jTable1.getColumnModel()` (Line 36). Create an instance named `selectionModel` obtained from `jTable1.getSelectionModel()` (Line 39).

7. In the Events page of `myTableModel1`, press Enter in the value field of `tableChanged` to generate the handler for table model changed event. Implement the handler to display the changes in the text area, as shown in Listing 8.16.

continued

Example 8.10 continued

8. Write the code to register the listener for `tableColumnModel` (Lines 47–60) and handle the `columnRemoved` event (Lines 122–125), as shown in Listing 8.16.

9. Write the code to register the listener for `selectionModel` (Lines 41–46) and handle for the `valueChanged` event (Lines 128–132), as shown in Listing 8.16.

10. Double-click the Delete Selected Column button to generate a handler for button action. Implement the handler to delete the currently selected column (Lines 107–112), as shown in Listing 8.16.

```
1   package tabledemo;
2
3   import javax.swing.table.*;
4   import javax.swing.event.*;
4   import javax.swing.*;
5   import java.util.*;
6   import imageviewerdemo.ImageViewer;
7
8   public class TestTableEvents extends javax.swing.JApplet {
9     // Table column model
10    TableColumnModel tableColumnModel;
11
12    // Create images
13    ImageIcon intro1eImageIcon = ImageViewer.createImageIcon(
14    "/image/intro1e.gif", this);
15    // Create other images, omitted for brevity
16
17    // Create table column names
18    String[] columnNames =
19      {"Title", "Author", "Publisher", "Date Published", "In-stock",
20       "Book Cover"};
21
22    // Create table data
23    Object[][] data = {
24      {"Introduction to Java Programming", "Y. Daniel Liang",
25       "Que Eduction & Training",
26       new GregorianCalendar(1998, 1-1, 6).getTime(),
27       new Boolean(false), intro1eImageIcon},
28       // Omitted for brevity
29    };
30
31    /** Creates new form TestTableEvents */
32    public TestTableEvents() {
33     initComponents();
34
35     // Create table column model
36     tableColumnModel = jTable1.getColumnModel();
37
38     // Create table selection model
39     ListSelectionModel selectionModel = jTable1.getSelectionModel();
40
```

Listing 8.16 *TestTableEvents.java*

```
      selectionModel.addListSelectionListener(
      new javax.swing.event.ListSelectionListener() {
        public void valueChanged(ListSelectionEvent e) {
          selectionModel_valueChanged(e);
        }
      });
      tableColumnModel.addColumnModelListener(
      new javax.swing.event.TableColumnModelListener() {
        public void columnAdded(TableColumnModelEvent e) {
        }
        public void columnMarginChanged(ChangeEvent e) {
        }
        public void columnMoved(TableColumnModelEvent e) {
        }
        public void columnRemoved(TableColumnModelEvent e) {

        }
        public void columnSelectionChanged(ListSelectionEvent e) {
        }
      });
    }

    private void initComponents() {
      myTableModel1 = new MyTableModel(data, columnNames);
      jbtDeleteColumn = new javax.swing.JButton();
      jSplitPane1 = new javax.swing.JSplitPane();
      jScrollPane1 = new javax.swing.JScrollPane();
      jTable1 = new javax.swing.JTable(myTableModel1);
      jScrollPane2 = new javax.swing.JScrollPane();
      jtaMessage = new javax.swing.JTextArea();
      myTableModel1.addTableModelListener(
        new javax.swing.event.TableModelListener() {
       public void tableChanged(
        javax.swing.event.TableModelEvent evt) {
         myTableModel1TableChanged(evt);
       }
      });
      jbtDeleteColumn.setText("Delete Selected Column");
      jbtDeleteColumn.addActionListener(
        new java.awt.event.ActionListener() {
       public void actionPerformed(java.awt.event.ActionEvent evt) {
         jbtDeleteColumnActionPerformed(evt);
       }
      });
      getContentPane().add(jbtDeleteColumn,
        java.awt.BorderLayout.NORTH);
      jSplitPane1.setOrientation(
        javax.swing.JSplitPane.VERTICAL_SPLIT);
      jTable1.setRowHeight(40);

      jScrollPane1.setViewportView(jTable1);
      jSplitPane1.setLeftComponent(jScrollPane1);
      jScrollPane2.setViewportView(jtaMessage);
      jSplitPane1.setRightComponent(jScrollPane2);
      getContentPane().add(jSplitPane1, java.awt.BorderLayout.CENTER);
    }

    private void jbtDeleteColumnActionPerformed(
      java.awt.event.ActionEvent evt) {
      int selectedColumn = jTable1.getSelectedColumn();
```

Listing 8.16 *continued*

continued

Example 8.10 continued

```
      tableColumnModel.removeColumn(
        tableColumnModel.getColumn(selectedColumn));
    }

    private void myTableModel1TableChanged(
      javax.swing.event.TableModelEvent evt) {
      jtaMessage.append("Table changed: First row " + evt.getFirstRow()
        + " and last row " + evt.getLastRow() + " Type " +
        evt.getType() + '\n');
    }

    /** Handle column removed event */
    void tableColumnModel_columnRemoved(TableColumnModelEvent e) {
      jtaMessage.append("Column " + jTable1.getSelectedColumn() +
        " removed " + '\n');
    }

    /** Handle selection events */
    void selectionModel_valueChanged(ListSelectionEvent e) {
      jtaMessage.append("Selected column " +
      jTable1.getSelectedColumn() + " and row " +
      jTable1.getSelectedRow() + '\n');
    }

    // Variables declaration - do not modify
    private tabledemo.MyTableModel myTableModel1;
    private javax.swing.JButton jbtDeleteColumn;
    private javax.swing.JSplitPane jSplitPane1;
    private javax.swing.JScrollPane jScrollPane1;
    private javax.swing.JTable jTable1;
    private javax.swing.JScrollPane jScrollPane2;
    private javax.swing.JTextArea jtaMessage;
    // End of variables declaration
  }
```

Listing 8.16 *continued*

Example Review

This example creates a table model for the table. To make it visible in the component inspector, you installed `MyTableModel` to the component palette and dropped it to the form. The default constructor was added in Lines 9–10 in Listing 8.12 so that you can use MyTableModel as a JavaBeans component.

The table column model and selection model are obtained from the table. You wrote the code manually to register listeners and handle the events.

When a row or a column is selected, a `ListSelectionEvent` is fired by `selectionModel`, which invokes the handler to display the selected row and column in the text area. When the content or structure of the table is changed, a `TableModelEvent` is fired by `tableModel`, which invokes the handler to display the last row, last column, and event type in the text area. When a column is deleted by clicking the Delete Selected Column button, a `ColumnModelEvent` is fired by `tableColumnModel`, which invokes the handler to display the index of the deleted column.

8.5 JTree

`JTree` is a Swing component that displays data in a treelike hierarchy. Figure 8.19 shows the Swing tree in the SwingSet demo.

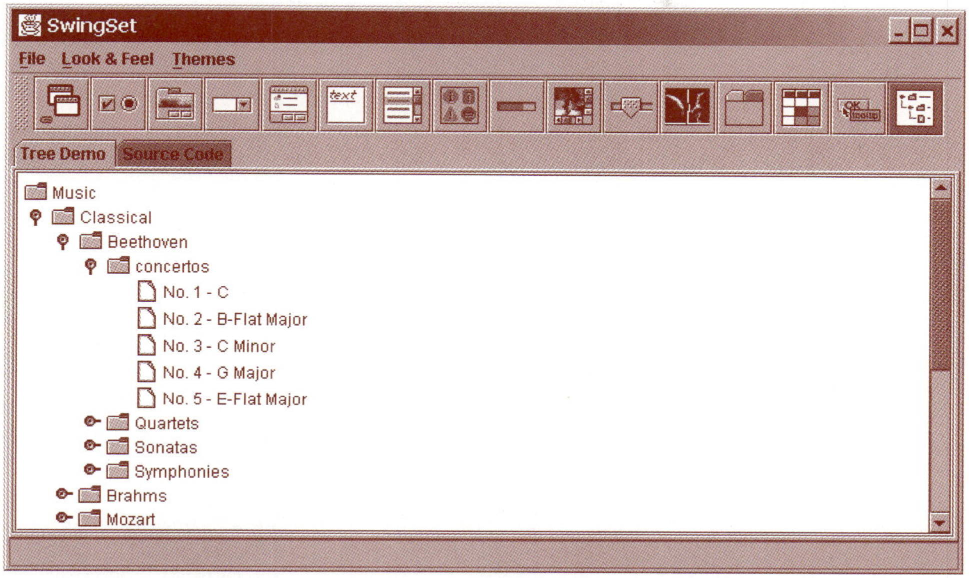

Figure 8.19 *The SwingSet demo demonstrates the features of* `JTree`.

All the nodes displayed in the tree are in the form of a hierarchical indexed list. The tree can be used to navigate structured data with hierarchical relationships. The Forte Explorer window is an example of displaying items as nodes in a treelike structure. A node can have child nodes. A node is called a *leaf* if it has no children; a node with no parent is called the *root* of its tree. A tree may consist of many subtrees, each node acting as the root for its own subtree.

A nonleaf node can be expanded or collapsed by double-clicking on the node or on the node's handle in front of the node. The handle usually has a visible sign to indicate whether the node is expanded or collapsed. For example, on Windows, the + symbol indicates that the node is collapsed, and the – symbol, that it is expanded.

Like `JTable`, `JTree` is a very complex component with many supporting interfaces and classes. `JTree` is in the `javax.swing` package, but its supporting classes are all included in the `javax.swing.tree` package. These supporting classes are `DefaultMutableTreeNode`, `DefaultTreeModel`, `TreeSelectionModel`, `DefaultTreeCellEditor`, `DefaultTreeCellRenderer`, and `TreePath`.

While `JTree` displays the tree, the data representation of the tree is handled by the `DefaultMutableTreeNode` class, which provides operations for creating nodes, for examining and modifying a node's parent and children, and also for examining the tree to which the node belongs. While the `DefaultMutableTreeNode` represents a node, the `DefaultTreeModel` represents the entire tree. Unlike the `ListModel` or `TableModel`, the tree model does not directly store or manage tree data. Tree data are stored and managed by the `DefaultMutableTreeNode` class. To create a tree model, you first create an instance of `DefaultMutableTreeNode` to represent the root of the tree, and then create an instance of `DefaultTreeModel` fitted with the root.

The `TreeSelectionModel` class handles tree node selection. The `DefaultTreeCell-Renderer` class provides a default tree node renderer that can display a label and/or an icon in a node. The `DefaultTreeCellEditor` can be used to edit the cells in a text field. The `TreePath` class is a support class that represents a set of nodes in a path.

`JTree` has the following useful properties:

- **`cellEditor`** is an object used to edit the cell in a tree node. By default, an instance of `DefaultCellEditor` is used to edit the cells in a text field. Using custom tree cell renderer is introduced in Section 8.5.3, "Tree Node Rendering and Editing."
- **`cellRenderer`** is an object used to render the cells in a tree node. By default, an instance of `DefaultTreeCellRenderer` is used to display nodes in a tree that can display strings or icons. Using custom tree cell renderer is introduced in Section 8.5.3, "Tree Node Rendering and Editing."
- **`editable`** is a `boolean` value indicating whether the cell is editable. The default value is `false`.
- **`model`** is an instance of `TreeModel`.
- **`rootVisible`** is a `boolean` value indicating whether the root is displayed in the tree. The default value is `true`.
- **`rowHeight`** specifies the height of the row for the node displayed in the tree. The default height is 16 pixels.
- **`selectionModel`** is an instance of `TreeSelectionModel`.

8.5.1 Creating Trees

`JTree` doesn't directly support scrolling. To create a scrollable tree, you need to create a `JScrollPane` and add an instance of `JTree` to the scroll pane.

There are several constructors that can be used to create a `JTree`. You can create a `JTree` with an array of objects, a vector, or a hash table. The builder tool always uses the default constructor to create an instance of `JTree` with a default tree model. The default tree is shown in Figure 8.20, because the default tree model is defined in the `getDefaultTreeModel` method of the `JTree` class, as follows:

```
// Excerpted from JTree.java
protected static TreeModel getDefaultTreeModel() {
  DefaultMutableTreeNode root = new DefaultMutableTreeNode("JTree");
  DefaultMutableTreeNode parent;
```

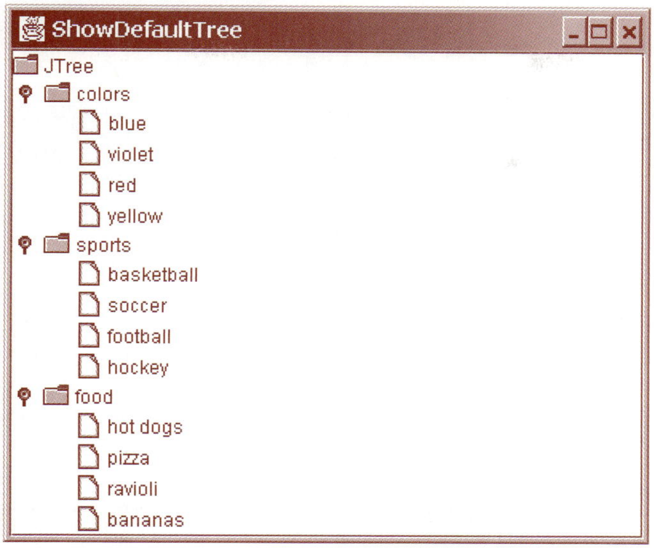

Figure 8.20 *The default tree constructed with the default constructor of* `JTree` *displays sample data.*

```
    parent = new DefaultMutableTreeNode("colors");
    root.add(parent);
    parent.add(new DefaultMutableTreeNode("blue"));
    parent.add(new DefaultMutableTreeNode("violet"));
    parent.add(new DefaultMutableTreeNode("red"));
    parent.add(new DefaultMutableTreeNode("yellow"));

    parent = new DefaultMutableTreeNode("sports");
    root.add(parent);
    parent.add(new DefaultMutableTreeNode("basketball"));
    parent.add(new DefaultMutableTreeNode("soccer"));

    // Omitted for brevity

    return new DefaultTreeModel(root);
  }
```

As demonstrated in the following example, a custom tree model can be created in the same way as the default model.

Example 8.11 Creating Custom Trees

This example creates a tree that displays the table of contents of this book, as shown in Figure 8.21.

Here are the steps to complete the example:

1. Create a new package named treedemo and an applet named `TestTree` using the Forte Swing JApplet form wizard.
2. Drop a `JScrollPane` to the center of the applet, and drop a `JTree` from the Swing (Other) tab to the scroll pane to create `jTree1`.

continued

Example 8.11 Creating Custom Trees

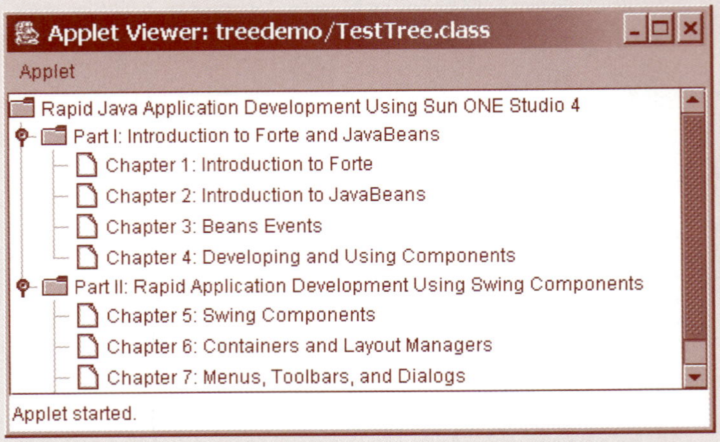

Figure 8.21 *The table of contents of this book is displayed in a tree.*

3. Create a method named `createTreeModel()` to create a tree model, as shown in Listing 8.17. Declare and create an instance of `TreeModel` named `treeModel` (Line 11). Set the `model` property of `jTree1` to `treeModel` (Line 12).

```
1   package treedemo;
2
3   import javax.swing.tree.*;
4
5   public class TestTree extends javax.swing.JApplet {
6     /** Creates new form TestTree */
7     public TestTree() {
8       initComponents();
9
10      // Create a tree model and set the tree model in jTree1
11      DefaultTreeModel treeModel = createTreeModel();
12      jTree1.setModel(treeModel); // Set this value manually
13    }
14
15    private void initComponents() {
16      jScrollPane1 = new javax.swing.JScrollPane();
17      jTree1 = new javax.swing.JTree();
18      jScrollPane1.setViewportView(jTree1);
19      getContentPane().add(jScrollPane1, java.awt.BorderLayout.CENTER);
20    }
21
22    /** Create a tree model */
23    private DefaultTreeModel createTreeModel() {
24      DefaultMutableTreeNode root = new DefaultMutableTreeNode
25      ("Rapid Java Application Development Using Sun ONE Studio 4");
26
27      DefaultMutableTreeNode parent = new DefaultMutableTreeNode
28        ("Part I: Introduction to Forte and JavaBeans");
29      root.add(parent);
30
31      parent.add(new DefaultMutableTreeNode
32        ("Chapter 1: Introduction to Forte"));
33      parent.add(new DefaultMutableTreeNode
34        ("Chapter 2: Introduction to JavaBeans"));
```

Listing 8.17 *TestTree.java*

```
        parent.add(new DefaultMutableTreeNode
          ("Chapter 3: Beans Events"));
        parent.add(new DefaultMutableTreeNode
          ("Chapter 4: Developing and Using Components"));

        parent = new DefaultMutableTreeNode("Part II: Rapid Application "
          + "Development Using Swing Components");
        root.add(parent);

        parent.add(new DefaultMutableTreeNode
          ("Chapter 5: Swing Components"));
        parent.add(new DefaultMutableTreeNode
          ("Chapter 6: Containers and Layout Managers"));
        parent.add(new DefaultMutableTreeNode
          ("Chapter 7: Menus, Toolbars, and Dialogs"));
        parent.add(new DefaultMutableTreeNode
          ("Chapter 8: Advanced Swing Components"));

        // Omitted for brevity
        return new DefaultTreeModel(root);
    }

    // Variables declaration - do not modify
    private javax.swing.JScrollPane jScrollPane1;
    private javax.swing.JTree jTree1;
    // End of variables declaration
}
```

Listing 8.17 *continued*

Example Review

The example creates a tree for the table of contents of this book. Each node is created using the `DefaultMutableTreeNode` class. The `createTreeModel()` method returns a `TreeModel` fitted with the root of the tree.

When you drop a `JTree` to the form, the default tree model is used. Thus you see the sample data created in the default model. Once you set the `model` property with the new model, the new data replace the sample data.

8.5.2 Processing Tree Nodes

Swing uses the `TreeNode` interface to model a single node. The `MutableTreeNode` interface extends `TreeNode`. The `DefaultMutableTreeNode` class is an implementation of `MutableTreeNode`. The `DefaultMutableTreeNode` class stores data for a node and provides methods for tree traversal in various orders or for following the path between two nodes. Breadth-first traversal, depth-first traversal, postorder traversal, and preorder traversal are supported. These traversals are often used in algorithm design and are popular topics in courses on data structures.

The following methods in `DefaultMutableTreeNode` are often useful:

```
// The useful methods in DefaultMutableTreeNode
public TreeNode getParent() // Return the parent node
public Enumeration children() // Get all children
public boolean isLeaf() // is the node a leaf
```

```
public Enumeration breadthFirstEnumeration()
public Enumeration depthFirstEnumeration()
public Enumeration preorderEnumeration()
public Enumeration postOrderEnumeration()
```

The last four methods create and return an enumeration that traverses the subtree rooted at this node in breadth-first order, depth-first order, preorder, or postorder, respectively. The code shown below displays the nodes in breadth-first traversal order:

```
Enumeration bf = root.breadthFirstEnumeration();
while (bf.hasMoreElements()) {
  System.out.print(bf.nextElement().toString());
}
```

Swing uses the `TreePath` class to represent a path between an ancestor and a descendant in a tree. Instances of `TreePath` are often instantiated by Swing classes. For instance, the `getLeadSelectionPath()` method in the `TreeSelectionModel` returns the path from the root to the selected node. There are many ways to extract the nodes from a tree path. Often you use the `getLastPathComponent()` method to obtain the last node in the path, and then the `getParent()` method to get all the nodes in the path upward through the link.

The selection of tree nodes is defined in the `TreeSelectionModel` interface. The `DefaultTreeSelectionModel` class is an implementation of the `TreeSelectionModel`, which maintains an array of `TreePath` objects representing the current selection. The last `TreePath` selected, called the *lead path*, can be obtained using the `getLeadSelectionPath()` method. To obtain all the selection paths, use the `getSelectionPaths()` method, which returns an array of tree paths.

`TreeSelectionModel` supports three selection modes: contiguous selection, discontiguous selection, and single selection. *Single selection* allows only one item to be selected. *Contiguous selection* allows multiple selections, but the selected items must be contiguous. *Discontigous selection* is the most flexible; it allows any item to be selected at a given time. The default tree selection mode is discontiguous. To set a selection mode, use the `setSelectionMode()` method in `TreeSelectionModel`. The constants for the three modes are:

- `CONTIGUOUS_TREE_SELECTION`
- `DISCONTIGUOUS_TREE_SELECTION`
- `SINGLE_TREE_SELECTION`

The `TreeModel` interface defines operations for inserting or removing tree nodes. The `DefaultTreeModel` class is a concrete implementation of `TreeModel`. To insert or remove a node, use the following methods:

```
public void insertNodeInto(MutableTreeNode newNode,
                           MutablTreeNode parent,
                           int index)

public void removeNodeFromParent(MutableTreeNode theNode)
```

Example 8.12 Adding and Removing Nodes

This example uses the classes `DefaultMutableTreeNode`, `TreePath`, `DefaultTreeSelectionModel`, and `DefaultTreeModel`. The example enables the user to add or remove nodes from a tree, as shown in Figure 8.22.

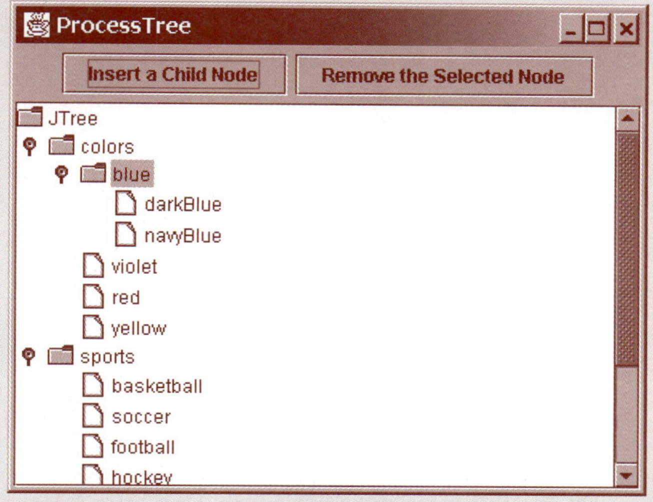

Figure 8.22 *You can add or remove nodes dynamically in a tree.*

Here are the steps to complete the example:

1. In the treedemo package, create an applet named `ProcessTree` using the Forte Swing JApplet form wizard.

2. Drop a `JPanel` to create `jpButtons`, and add two buttons named `jbtAdd` and `jbtRemove` into `jpButtons`. Drop a `JScrollPane` to the center of the applet, and drop a `JTree` to the scroll pane to create `jTree1`.

3. Declare and obtain the tree model and the selection model from `jTree1` using the `getModel()` and `getSelectionModel()` methods. Set the selection mode to single selection.

4. Generate and implement the code for handling `jbtAdd` and `jtbRemove`, as shown in Listing 8.18.

```
package treedemo;

import javax.swing.tree.*;
import javax.swing.*;

public class ProcessTree extends javax.swing.JApplet {
  // Declare selection model
  TreeSelectionModel selectionModel;

```

Listing 8.18 *ProcessTree.java*

continued

Example 8.12 Adding and Removing Nodes

```
  // Declare tree model
  DefaultTreeModel treeModel;

  /** Creates new form ProcessTree */
  public ProcessTree() {
    initComponents();

    // Get selection model
    selectionModel = jTree1.getSelectionModel();

    // Get tree model
    treeModel = (DefaultTreeModel)jTree1.getModel();

    // Set single selection
    selectionModel.setSelectionMode(
    TreeSelectionModel.SINGLE_TREE_SELECTION);
  }

  private void initComponents() {
    jpButtons = new javax.swing.JPanel();
    jbtAdd = new javax.swing.JButton();
    jbtRemove = new javax.swing.JButton();
    jScrollPane1 = new javax.swing.JScrollPane();
    jTree1 = new javax.swing.JTree();

    jbtAdd.setText("Insert a Child Node");
    jbtAdd.addActionListener(new java.awt.event.ActionListener() {
      public void actionPerformed(java.awt.event.ActionEvent evt) {
        jbtAddActionPerformed(evt);
      }
    });
    jpButtons.add(jbtAdd);
    jbtRemove.setText("Remove a Child Node");
    jbtRemove.addActionListener(new java.awt.event.ActionListener() {
      public void actionPerformed(java.awt.event.ActionEvent evt) {
        jbtRemoveActionPerformed(evt);
      }
    });
    jpButtons.add(jbtRemove);
    getContentPane().add(jpButtons, java.awt.BorderLayout.NORTH);
    jScrollPane1.setViewportView(jTree1);
    getContentPane().add(jScrollPane1, java.awt.BorderLayout.CENTER);
  }

  private void jbtRemoveActionPerformed(
    java.awt.event.ActionEvent evt) {
    // Get the selection path
    TreePath path = selectionModel.getLeadSelectionPath();

    // Get the last node in the path
    DefaultMutableTreeNode treeNode =
      (DefaultMutableTreeNode)path.getLastPathComponent();

    if (treeNode == treeModel.getRoot()) {
      JOptionPane.showMessageDialog(this, "Cannot remove the root");
    }
```

Listing 8.18 *continued*

```
66          else
67            // Remove the selected node
68            treeModel.removeNodeFromParent(treeNode);
69        }
70
71        private void jbtAddActionPerformed(
72          java.awt.event.ActionEvent evt) {
73          // Get the selection path
74          TreePath path = selectionModel.getLeadSelectionPath();
75
76          // Get the last node in the path
77          DefaultMutableTreeNode treeNode =
78            (DefaultMutableTreeNode)path.getLastPathComponent();
79
80          // Enter a new node
81          String nodeName = JOptionPane.showInputDialog(
82            this, "Enter a name for this new node", "Add a Child",
83            JOptionPane.QUESTION_MESSAGE);
84
85          // Insert the new node as a child of treeNode
86          treeModel.insertNodeInto(new DefaultMutableTreeNode(nodeName),
87          treeNode, treeNode.getChildCount());
88        }
89
90        // Variables declaration - do not modify
91        private javax.swing.JPanel jpButtons;
92        private javax.swing.JButton jbtAdd;
93        private javax.swing.JButton jbtRemove;
94        private javax.swing.JScrollPane jScrollPane1;
95        private javax.swing.JTree jTree1;
96        // End of variables declaration
97      }
```

Listing 8.18 *continued*

Example Review

The example creates a tree using the default constructor. The `getModel()` method (Line 21) returns the tree model, and the `getSelectionModel()` method (Line 18) obtains the tree selection model. The methods for inserting and removing nodes are provided in the tree model, and the tree selection model can be used to find the selected path using the `getLeadSelectionPath()` method. The selected node is the last node in the lead path, which can be found using the `getLastPathComponent()` method.

To insert a node, first select a parent in the tree, then click the Insert a Child Node button, which displays an input dialog box to receive the new node name. The new node is added as a child of the selected node.

To remove a node, first select the node in the tree, then click the Remove the Selected Node button. If you attempt to remove the root, a message dialog is displayed to alert you that the root cannot be removed.

8.5.3 Tree Node Rendering and Editing

Like all the advanced Swing components, `JTree` delegates node rendering to a renderer. The `DefaultTreeCellRenderer` interface defines how cells are rendered, which is implemented by the `DefaultTreeCellRenderer` class. The `DefaultTreeCellRenderer` class maintains three icon properties named `leafIcon`, `openIcon`, and `closedIcon` for leaf nodes, expanded nodes, and collapsed nodes. It also provides colors for text and background. The following code sets new leaf, open and closed icons, and new background selection color in the tree.

```
DefaultTreeCellRenderer renderer =
  (DefaultTreeCellRenderer)jTree1.getCellRenderer();
renderer.setLeafIcon(leafImageIcon);
renderer.setOpenIcon(openImageIcon);
renderer.setClosedIcon(closedImageIcon);
renderer.setBackgroundSelectionColor(Color.red);
```

NOTE
The default leaf, open icon, and closed icon are dependent on the look-and-feel. For instance, on Windows look-and-feel, the open icon is -, and the closed icon is +.

`JTree` comes with a default cell editor. If `JTree`'s `editable` property is `true`, the default editor activates a text field for editing when the node is clicked three times. By default, this property is set to `false`. To create a custom editor, you need to extend the `DefaultCellEditor` class, which is the same class you used in table cell editing. You can use a text field, a check box, or a combo box, and pass it to `DefaultCellEditor`'s constructor to create an editor. The following code uses a combo box for editing colors. The combo box editor is shown in Figure 8.23.

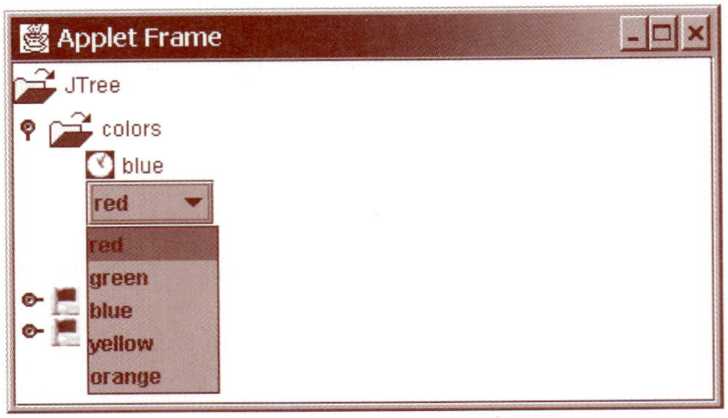

Figure 8.23 *You can supply a custom editor for editing tree nodes.*

```
// Customize editor
JComboBox jcboColor = new JComboBox();
jcboColor.addItem("red");
jcboColor.addItem("green");
jcboColor.addItem("blue");
```

```
jcboColor.addItem("yellow");
jcboColor.addItem("orange");

jTree1.setCellEditor(new DefaultCellEditor(jcboColor));
jTree1.setEditable(true);
```

There are two annoying problems with the editor created in the preceding code. First, it is activated with just one mouse click. Second, it overlaps the node's icon, as shown in Figure 8.23. The first problem can be fixed by creating a subclass of `DefaultCellEditor` that overrides the `isCellEditable()` method, which returns true if the mouse click count is 3. The second problem can be fixed by using the `DefaultTreeCellEditor`, as shown below. The new editor is shown in Figure 8.24.

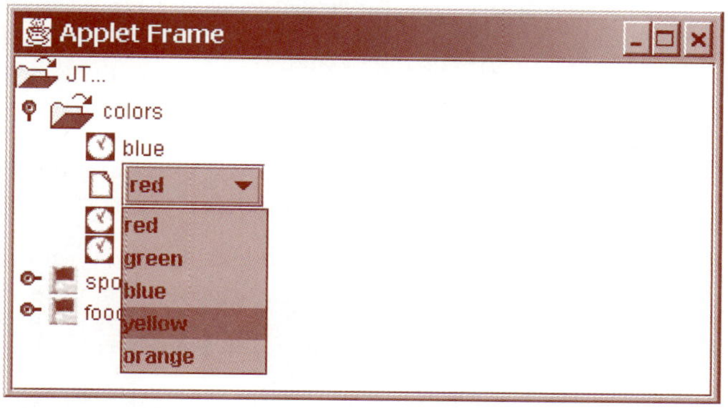

Figure 8.24 *The* `DefaultTreeCellEditor` *displays an editor that does not overlap a node's icon.*

```
jTree1.setCellEditor
  (new DefaultTreeCellEditor(jTree1,
    new DefaultTreeCellRenderer(),
    new DefaultCellEditor(jcboColor)));
```

8.5.4 Tree Events

`JTree` can fire `TreeSelectionEvent` and `TreeExpansionEvent`, among many other events. Whenever a new node is selected, `JTree` fires a `TreeSelectionEvent`. Whenever a node is expanded or collapsed, `JTree` fires a `TreeExpansionEvent`. To handle the tree selection event, a listener must implement the `TreeSelectionListener` interface, which contains a single handler named `valueChanged` method. `TreeExpansionListener` contains two handlers named `treeCollapsed` and `treeExpanded` for handling node expansion or node closing.

The following code displays a selected node:

```
void jTree1_valueChanged(TreeSelectionEvent e) {
  TreePath path = e.getNewLeadSelectionPath();
  TreeNode treeNode = (TreeNode)path.getLastPathComponent();
  System.out.println("The selected node is " + treeNode.toString());
}
```

Chapter Summary

This chapter introduced four advanced Swing components: `JList`, `JComboBox`, `JTable`, and `JTree`. You learned how to use their data models to store and process data, and how to use selection models to handle data selection, renderer classes to display views, and the editor class to edit cells in these components.

Review Questions

8.1 Does `JList` have a method, such as `addItem`, for adding an item to a list? How do you add items to a list? Can `JList` display icons and custom GUI objects in a list? Can a list item be edited? How do you initialize data in a list? How do you specify the maximum number of visible rows in a list without scrolling? How do you specify the height of a list cell? How do you specify the horizontal margin of list cells?

8.2 How do you create a list model? How do you add items to a list model? How do you remove items from a list model?

8.3 What are the three list-selection modes? Can you set the selection modes directly in an instance of `JList`? How do you obtain the selected item(s)?

8.4 How do you create a custom list cell renderer?

8.5 What is the handler for handling the `ListSelectionEvent`?

8.6 Can multiple items be selected from a combo box? Can a combo box item be edited? How do you specify the maximum number of visible rows in a combo box without scrolling? Can you specify the height of a combo box cell using a method in `JComboBox`? How do you obtain the selected item in a combo box?

8.7 How do you add or remove items from a combo box?

8.8 Why is the cell renderer for a combo box the same as the renderer for a list?

8.9 How do you initialize a table? Can you specify the maximum number of visible rows in a table without scrolling? How do you specify the height of a table cell? How do you specify the horizontal margin of table cells?

8.10 How do you modify table contents? How do you add or remove a row? How do you add or remove a column?

8.11 What is auto-resizing of a table column? How many types of auto-resizing are available?

8.12 What are the properties that show grids, horizontal grids, and vertical grids? What are the properties that specify the table row height, vertical margin, and horizontal margin?

8.13 What are the default table renderers and editors? How do you create a custom table cell renderer and editor?

8.14 How do you create a tree? How do you specify the row height of a tree node? How do you obtain the default tree model and tree selection model from an instance of `JTree`?

8.15 How do you initialize data in a tree using `TreeModel`? How do you add a child to an instance of `DefaultMutableTreeNode`?

8.16 How do you add or remove a node from a tree?

8.17 How do you obtain a selected tree node?

Programming Exercises

8.1 Create a program that shows a list of geometrical shapes along with a label in an instance of `JList`, as shown in Figure 8.25. Display the selected figure in a panel when selecting a figure from the list. The figures are represented in the `FigurePanel` class in Example 7.3, "Using `JTabbedPane`."

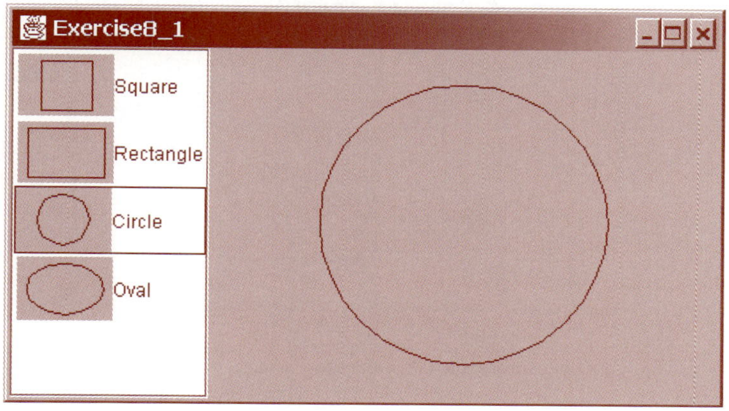

Figure 8.25 *The list displays geometrical shapes and their names.*

8.2 Create a program that shows a list of geometrical shapes along with a label in a combo box, as shown in Figure 8.26. This exercise may share the list cell renderer with the preceding exercise.

8.3 Create a table for student records. Each record consists of name, birthday, class status, in-state, and a photo, as shown in Figure 8.27. The name is of the `String` type; birthday is of the `Date` type; class status is one of the following five values: Freshman, Sophomore, Junior, Senior, and Graduate; in-state is a `boolean` value indicating whether the student is a resident of the state; and photo is an image icon. The program enables the user to add, remove, or edit a record. Use the default editors for name, birthday, and in-state. Supply a combo box as custom editor for class status.

Figure 8.26 *The combo box contains a list of geometrical shapes and the shape names.*

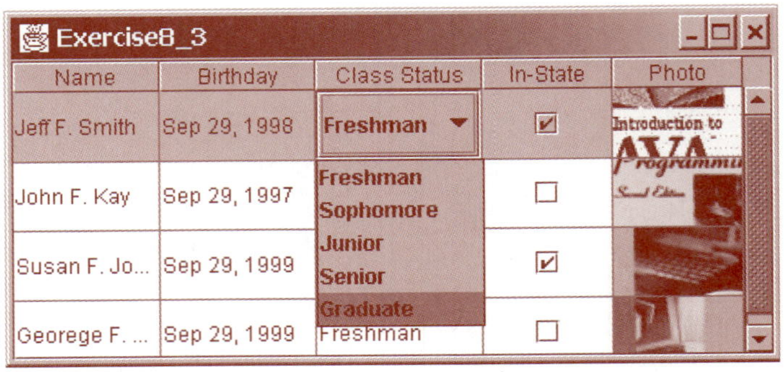

Figure 8.27 *The table displays student records and supports add, remove, and edit operations.*

8.4 Modify Example 8.11 as follows:

- Run it in the look-and-feel of Motif, Metal, or Windows.
- Display the nodes in breadth-first order, depth-first order, preorder, and postorder.
- Set custom icons for leaf, open, and closed nodes, and create custom editors for choosing colors in a combo box.
- Display a paragraph in a text area for each node in the tree, as shown in Figure 8.28.

8.5 Suppose a table is stored in a text file. The first line in the file is the header, and the remaining lines correspond to rows in the table. The elements are separated by the Tab characters. Write a program to display the table using the `JTable` component.

8.6 Modify Example 8.10, "Using Table Events," to delete a row or a column by pressing the DELETE key.

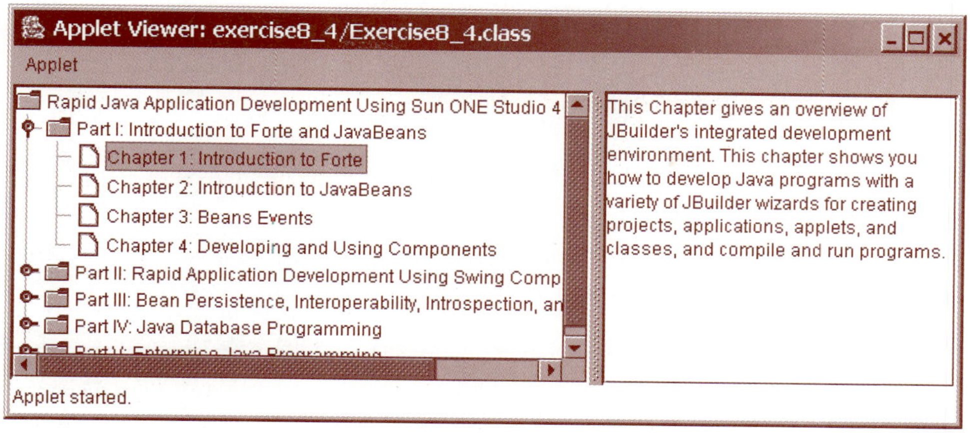

Figure 8.28 *The content of the node is displayed in a text area when a node is clicked.*

8.7 Modify Example 8.12, "Adding and Removing Nodes," to add a new child node by pressing the INSERT key, and delete a node by pressing the DELETE key.

8.8 Create a custom tree node renderer that uses a combo box to choose colors, as shown in Figure 8.24. Display the combo box upon three consecutive mouse clicks on the node.

8.9 Modify Example 8.3, "List Cell Renderer Demo," and Example 8.4, "Combo Box Demo," to share the same renderer class:

- Create an interface named `ImageModel`, as follows:

```
public interface ImageModel {
  public String getName(Object value);
  public Image getImage(Object value);
}
```

- Modify `MyListModel` to implement the `ImageModel` interface.
- Modify `MyComboBoxModel` to implement the `ImageModel` interface.
- Modify `MyListCellRenderer` to replace `MyListModel` by `ImageModel`.
- You should be able to run `TestListCellRenderer` with no changes.
- In the `TestComboBox` class, change any reference to `MyComboBoxRenderer` to `MyListCellRenderer`. Now `TestComboBox` and `TestListCellRenderer` share the same renderer.

8.10 In Exercise 4.8, you created a chart model (`ChartModel`) and two views (`PieChart` and `BarChart`). Create a controller that enables the user to modify the data, as shown in Figure 8.29. You will see the changes take effect in the pie chart view and bar chart view. Your exercise consists of the following classes:

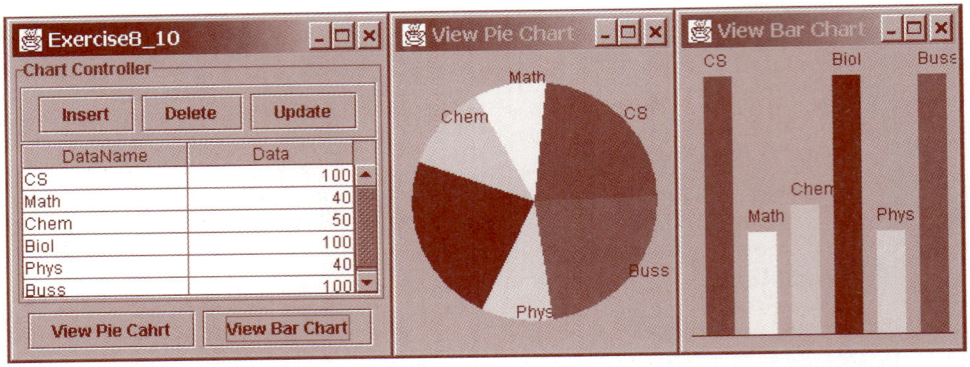

Figure 8.29 *You can modify the data in the controller. The views are synchronized with the controller.*

- The controller named `ChartController`. This class uses a table to display data. You can modify the data in the table. Click the Insert button to insert a new row above the selected row in the table, click the Delete button to delete the selected row in the table, and click the Update button to update the changes you made in the table.
- The class `MyTableModel`. This class extends `DefaultTableModel` to override the `getColumnClass` method so that you can use the `JTable`'s default editor for numerical values.
- The classes `ChartModel`, `PieChart`, and `BarChart` from Exercise 4.8.
- The main class Exercise8_10. This class creates a user interface with a controller, and two buttons, View Pie Chart and View Bar Chart. Click the View Pie Chart button to pop up a frame to display a pie chart, and click the View Bar Chart button to pop up a frame to display a bar chart.

PART III

Bean Persistence, Introspection, and Customization

This part of the book introduces JavaBeans API. You will learn how to develop persistent beans, use beans in other tools, implement bound and constraint properties, and create bean property editors.

CHAPTER 9

BEAN PERSISTENCE AND VERSIONING

Objectives

- To understand the concept of bean persistence.
- To know object serialization and use it to store and restore beans persistently.
- To use the `Beans.instantiate(. . .)` method to load serialized beans.
- To become familiar with Sun's BeanBox and use it to test bean persistence.
- To customize object serialization.
- To use bean versioning to make beans of different versions compatible.

9.1 Introduction

Forte does not store beans during design time. Changes in properties from the inspector are stored in the source code and `.form` files. The `.form` file is an XML file that stores properties for the form. The Form Editor reconstructs the user interface by parsing the XML file. However, other tools, such as Sun's Beanbox, IBM Visual Age for Java, and MS Visual Basic, need to store the beans and then restore them later during design time. Bean persistence ensures that these tools can correctly reconstruct the properties of the bean to the state when it was saved.

This chapter introduces object serialization, which is a built-in Java mechanism that stores and restores beans persistently. You will learn Sun's Beanbox, a tool for testing beans, which can be used to verify bean persistence. You will also learn how to customize serialization and use bean versioning to handle different versions of beans.

9.2 Object Serialization and Deserialization

In order to be persistent, a bean has to implement the `java.io.Serializable` interface. The `Serializable` interface is a marker interface. It has no methods, so you don't need to add additional code in your class that implements `Serializable`. Implementing this interface enables the Java serialization mechanism to automate the process of storing the object.

To appreciate this automation feature and understand how an object is stored, consider what you need to do in order to store an object without using this feature. Suppose you want to store an object of the `MessagePanel` class in Example 2.1 "Writing a Simple Java Bean." To do this you need to store all the current values of the properties in a `MessagePanel` object. The properties defined in `MessagePanel` are `message` (`String`), `centered` (`boolean`), `xCoordinate` (`int`), and `yCoordinate` (`int`). Since `MessagePanel` is a subclass of `JPanel`, the property values of `JPanel` have to be stored as well as the properties of all the superclasses of `JPanel`. If a property is of an object type, storing it requires storing all the property values inside this object. As you can see, this is a very tedious process. Fortunately you don't have to go through this process with Java. Since JDK 1.1, Java has provided a built-in mechanism that automates the process of writing objects. This process is referred to as *object serialization*. In contrast, the process of reading objects is referred to as *object deserialization*.

To store and restore an object, you need to use the `ObjectOutputStream` class for storing objects and the `ObjectInputStream` class for restoring objects. These two classes are built upon several other classes. Figure 9.1 shows the hierarchic relationship of these related classes.

`ObjectOutputStream` implements `ObjectOutput`, which inherits `DataOutput`. `DataOutput` provides methods for writing Java primitive-type values. `ObjectOutput` extends `DataOutput` to include output of objects, arrays, and strings. An `ObjectOutputStream` writes Java primitive-type values and objects to an `OutputStream`. Persis-

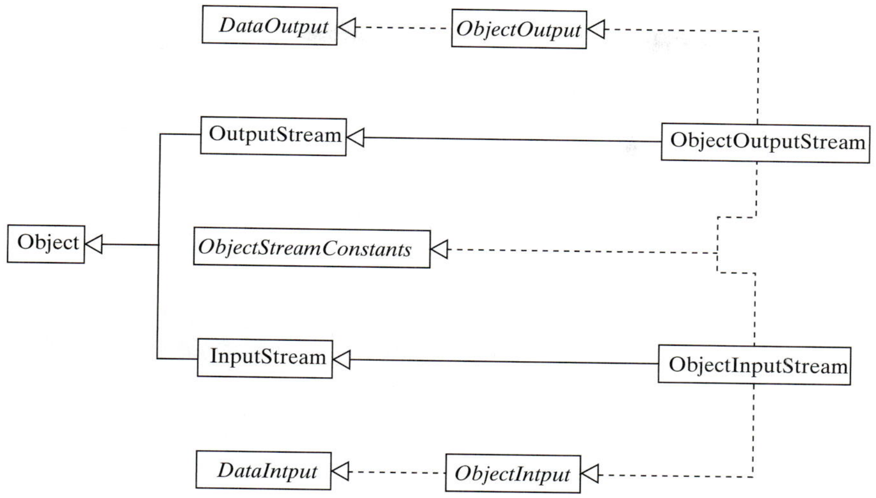

Figure 9.1 `ObjectOutputStream` *extends* `OutputStream` *and implements* `ObjectOutput` *and* `ObjectStreamConstants`. `ObjectInputStream` *extends* `InputStream` *and implements* `ObjectInput` *and* `ObjectStreamConstants`.

tent storage can be accomplished using a file for the stream. The format of the output is platform-independent. The `OutputStream` can also be a network socket stream.

`ObjectInputStream` is the inverse of `ObjectOutputStream`. `ObjectInputStream` implements `ObjectInput`, which inherits `DataInput`. `DataInput` provides methods for reading primitive-type values. `ObjectInput` extends `DataInput` to include input of objects, arrays, and strings. An `ObjectInputStream` reads the data previously written using an `ObjectOutputStream` with a file stream and a network socket stream.

Only objects whose class implements the `java.io.Serializable` interface can use `ObjectOutputStream` and `ObjectInputStream`. The `writeObject` method is used to write an object to the `ObjectOutputStream`, and `readObject` is used to read an object from the `ObjectInputStream`. Attempting to store an object that does not support the `Serializable` interface would cause `java.io.NotSerializableException`.

When a serializable object is stored, the class of the object is encoded; this includes the class name and the signature of the class, the values of the object's fields and arrays, and any other objects referenced from the initial object. When a primitive-type value is stored, appropriate methods, such as `writeInt`, `writeBoolean` in the `DataOutput` interface, are used. Multiple objects or primitives can be written to the stream. The objects must be read back from the corresponding `ObjectInputstream` with the same types and in the same order as they were written. Java's safe casting should be used to get the desired type. For instance, when reading an object of the `MessagePanel` class, the object should be cast to `MessagePanel`.

Here is an example of creating an `ObjectOutputStream` and storing an object `messagePanel1` of `MessagePanel` and an `int` value to the file named beans.dat.

```
ObjectOutputStream out = new ObjectOutputStream(
  new FileOutputStream("beans.dat"));
out.writeObject(messagePanel1);
out.writeInt(5);
```

The corresponding code to restore the object and the `int` value is as follows:

```
ObjectInputStream in = new ObjectInputStream(
  new FileInputStream("beans.dat"));
MessagePanel c = (MessagePanel)in.readObject();
int x = in.readInt();
```

Example 9.1 Testing Object Serialization

This example creates a program to manipulate `MessagePanel`, as shown in Figure 9.2. You will use radio buttons to set the background color, and two buttons, <= and =>, to move the message to left and right. The Store button is provided to save a `MessagePanel` object, and the Restore button is used to reload the saved `MessagePanel` object.

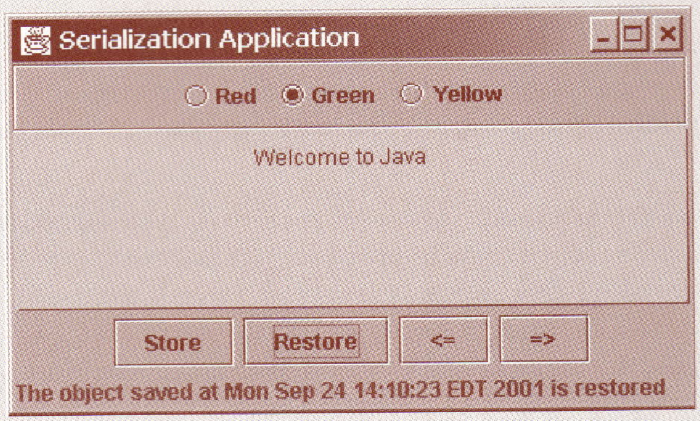

Figure 9.2 *You can use the Store button to save the* `MessagePanel` *object shown in the middle of the window, and the Restore button to reload the saved object later.*

Follow the steps below to complete the project.

1. Create a new package named serializationdemo and create a new frame named SerializationApplication using the Forte Swing JFrame form wizard.
2. Drop a `JLabel` to the south of the frame to create `jlblStatus`. Drop a `JPanel` to the center of the frame to create `jpSerialization`. Set the layout of `jpSerialization` to `BorderLayout`. Drop a `JPanel` to the north of `jpSerialization` to create `jpRadioButtons`, drop a `JPanel` to the south of `jpSerialization` to create `jpButtons`, and drop a `MessagePanel` in the center of `jpSerialization` to create `messagePanel1`.
3. Set the `border` property of `jpRadioButtons` and `jpButtons` to `EtchedBorder`, and `messagePanel1` to `SoftBevelBorder`.

4. Drop a `JRadioButton` three times to `jpRadioButtons` to create `jrbRed`, `jrbGreen`, and `jrbYellow` with their `text` properties set to Red, Green, and Yellow. Drop a `ButtonGroup` into the form to create `buttonGroup1`. Set the `buttonGroup` properties of these radio buttons to `buttonGroup1`.

5. Drop a `JButton` four times to `jpButtons` to create `jbtStore`, `jbtRestore`, `jbtLeft`, and `jbtRight` with `text` properties set to Store, Restore, <=, and =>.

6. Generate and implement the code for handling the radio buttons and buttons, as shown in Listing 9.1 (Lines 102–163).

```
1   package serializationdemo;
2
3  import messagepaneldemo.MessagePanel;
4  import java.io.*;
5  import java.util.Date;
6  import java.awt.*;
7
8  public class SerializationApplication extends javax.swing.JFrame {
9    /** Creates new form SerializationApplication */
10   public SerializationApplication() {
11     initComponents();
12   }
13
14   private void initComponents() {
15     buttonGroup1 = new javax.swing.ButtonGroup();
16     jlblStatus = new javax.swing.JLabel();
17     jpSerialization = new javax.swing.JPanel();
18     jpRadioButtons = new javax.swing.JPanel();
19     jrbRed = new javax.swing.JRadioButton();
20     jrbGreen = new javax.swing.JRadioButton();
21     jrbYellow = new javax.swing.JRadioButton();
22     jpButtons = new javax.swing.JPanel();
23     jbtStore = new javax.swing.JButton();
24     jbtRestore = new javax.swing.JButton();
25     jbrLeft = new javax.swing.JButton();
26     jbtRight = new javax.swing.JButton();
27     messagePanel1 = new messagepaneldemo.MessagePanel();
28     setTitle("Serialization Application");
29     addWindowListener(new java.awt.event.WindowAdapter() {
30       public void windowClosing(java.awt.event.WindowEvent evt) {
31         exitForm(evt);
32       }
33     });
34     jlblStatus.setText("jLabel1");
35     getContentPane().add(jlblStatus, java.awt.BorderLayout.SOUTH);
36     jpSerialization.setLayout(new java.awt.BorderLayout());
37     jpRadioButtons.setBorder(new javax.swing.border.EtchedBorder());
38     jrbRed.setText("Red");
39     buttonGroup1.add(jrbRed);
40     jrbRed.addActionListener(new java.awt.event.ActionListener() {
41       public void actionPerformed(java.awt.event.ActionEvent evt) {
42         jrbRedActionPerformed(evt);
43       }
44     });
```

Listing 9.1 *SerializationApplication.java*

continued

Example 9.1 continued

```
      jpRadioButtons.add(jrbRed);
      jrbGreen.setText("Green");
      buttonGroup1.add(jrbGreen);
      jrbGreen.addActionListener(new java.awt.event.ActionListener() {
        public void actionPerformed(java.awt.event.ActionEvent evt) {
          jrbGreenActionPerformed(evt);
        }
      });
      jpRadioButtons.add(jrbGreen);
      jrbYellow.setText("Yellow");
      buttonGroup1.add(jrbYellow);
      jrbYellow.addActionListener(new java.awt.event.ActionListener() {
        public void actionPerformed(java.awt.event.ActionEvent evt) {
          jrbYellowActionPerformed(evt);
        }
      });
      jpRadioButtons.add(jrbYellow);
      jpSerialization.add(jpRadioButtons, java.awt.BorderLayout.NORTH);
      jbtStore.setText("Store");
      jbtStore.addActionListener(
        new java.awt.event.ActionListener() {
        public void actionPerformed(java.awt.event.ActionEvent evt) {
          jbtStoreActionPerformed(evt);
        }
      });
      jpButtons.add(jbtStore);
      jbtRestore.setText("Restore");
      jbtRestore.addActionListener(
        new java.awt.event.ActionListener() {
        public void actionPerformed(java.awt.event.ActionEvent evt) {
          jbtRestoreActionPerformed(evt);
        }
      });
      jpButtons.add(jbtRestore);
      jbrLeft.setText("<=");
      jbrLeft.addActionListener(new java.awt.event.ActionListener() {
        public void actionPerformed(java.awt.event.ActionEvent evt) {
          jbrLeftActionPerformed(evt);
        }
      });
      jpButtons.add(jbrLeft);
      jbtRight.setText("=>");
      jbtRight.addActionListener(new java.awt.event.ActionListener() {
        public void actionPerformed(java.awt.event.ActionEvent evt) {
          jbtRightActionPerformed(evt);
        }
      });
      jpButtons.add(jbtRight);
      jpSerialization.add(jpButtons, java.awt.BorderLayout.SOUTH);
      messagePanel1.setBorder(new javax.swing.border.SoftBevelBorder(
        javax.swing.border.BevelBorder.RAISED));
      jpSerialization.add(messagePanel1, java.awt.BorderLayout.CENTER);
      getContentPane().add(jpSerialization,
        java.awt.BorderLayout.CENTER);
      pack();
    }

```

Listing 9.1 *continued*

```
    private void jbtRightActionPerformed(
      java.awt.event.ActionEvent evt) {
      messagePanel1.moveRight();
    }

    private void jbrLeftActionPerformed(
      java.awt.event.ActionEvent evt) {
      messagePanel1.moveLeft();
    }

    private void jbtRestoreActionPerformed(
      java.awt.event.ActionEvent evt) {
      try {
        ObjectInputStream in =
        new ObjectInputStream(new FileInputStream("beans.dat"));
        MessagePanel c = (MessagePanel)in.readObject();
        Date d = (Date)in.readObject();
        jpSerialization.remove(messagePanel1);
        messagePanel1 = c;
        jpSerialization.add(messagePanel1, BorderLayout.CENTER);
        jpSerialization.repaint();
        in.close();
        jlblStatus.setText("The object saved at " + d.toString()
          + " is restored");
      }
      catch (IOException ex1) {
        System.out.println(ex1);
      }
      catch (ClassNotFoundException ex2) {
        System.out.println(ex2);
      }
    }

    private void jbtStoreActionPerformed(
      java.awt.event.ActionEvent evt) {
      try {
        ObjectOutputStream out =
        new ObjectOutputStream(new FileOutputStream("beans.dat"));
        out.writeObject(messagePanel1);
        out.writeObject(new Date());
        out.close();
        jlblStatus.setText("The object is stored in beans.dat");
      }
      catch (IOException ex) {
        System.out.println(ex);
      }
    }

    private void jrbYellowActionPerformed(
      java.awt.event.ActionEvent evt) {
      messagePanel1.setBackground(Color.yellow);
    }

    private void jrbGreenActionPerformed(
      java.awt.event.ActionEvent evt) {
      messagePanel1.setBackground(Color.green);
    }

```

Listing 9.1 *continued*

continued

Example 9.1 continued

```
160     private void jrbRedActionPerformed(
161       java.awt.event.ActionEvent evt) {
162       messagePanel1.setBackground(Color.red);
163     }
164
165     /** Exit the Application */
166     private void exitForm(java.awt.event.WindowEvent evt) {
167       System.exit(0);
168     }
169
170     /**
171      * @param args the command line arguments
172      */
173     public static void main(String args[]) {
174       new SerializationApplication().show();
175     }
176
177     // Variables declaration - do not modify
178     private javax.swing.ButtonGroup buttonGroup1;
179     private javax.swing.JLabel jlblStatus;
180     private javax.swing.JPanel jpSerialization;
181     private javax.swing.JPanel jpRadioButtons;
182     private javax.swing.JRadioButton jrbRed;
183     private javax.swing.JRadioButton jrbGreen;
184     private javax.swing.JRadioButton jrbYellow;
185     private javax.swing.JPanel jpButtons;
186     private javax.swing.JButton jbtStore;
187     private javax.swing.JButton jbtRestore;
188     private javax.swing.JButton jbrLeft;
189     private javax.swing.JButton jbtRight;
190     private messagepaneldemo.MessagePanel messagePanel1;
191     // End of variables declaration
192   }
```

Listing 9.1 *continued*

Example Review

When you click the Store button, the current state of the `messagePanel1` and the current time (`new Date()`) are saved to file beans.dat using `ObjectOutputStream` (Lines 140–141). When you click the Restore button, these objects are read back from the same file. They must be read back in the same order as they were stored. Explicit type casting must be used to ensure that the objects read are of the right type.

In the handler for the Restore button, `messagePanel1` was removed from `jpSerialization`, and then a new `messagePanel1` was created and added to `jpSerialization`. This is necessary to ensure that the newly restored `messagePanel1` is used in the windows, not the old copy.

Like many Java classes, `java.awt.Component` and `java.util.Date` implement `java.io.Serializable`, so the objects of these classes or their subclasses can be stored using object streams.

9.2.1 The *transient* Keyword

By default, all the nonstatic properties of a serialized object are written to the object stream. However, not all the nonstatic properties can be serialized. For example, since the `java.awt.Thread` class does not implement `Serializable`, a `Thread` object cannot be serialized. The `transient` keyword should be used to mark a nonserializable property, as shown in Example 4.2, "Creating a `Clock` Component," so that it is not stored during serialization of the object that contains the property.

The `transient` keyword can also be used to mark a property not to be stored for security reasons. Since the state of the object is stored in a stream of bytes using a file stream or a network socket stream, the stream could be modified to result in a change in the actual value of the property. To see how easy it would be to tamper with the data, just modify beans.dat using a Hex editor like Hex Workshop, which is a shareware product available from Break Point Software at **www.bpsoft.com**. Suppose you change the word Java to C++ in beans.dat, as shown in Figure 9.3. `Welcome to C++` is displayed on the panel when the Restore button is clicked, as shown in Figure 9.4.

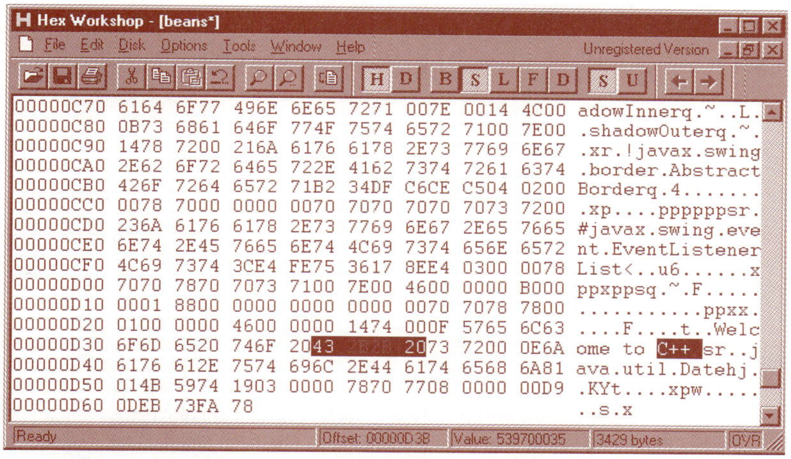

Figure 9.3 *You can use Hex Workshop to modify the beans.dat file.*

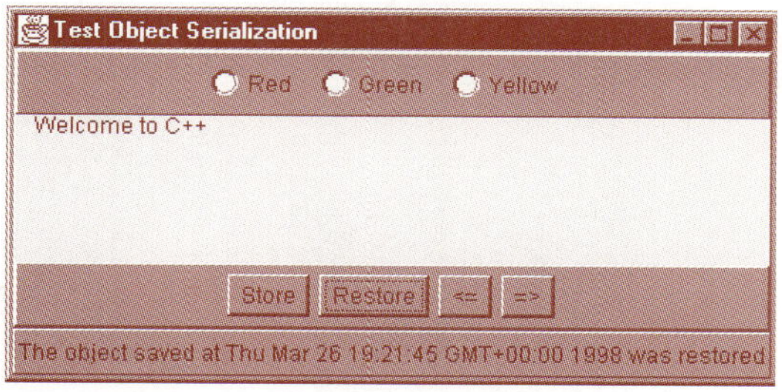

Figure 9.4 *The contents of beans.dat are restored. The modified message* `Welcome to C++` *is displayed.*

9.3 Instantiating Serialized Beans

A serialized bean can be directly loaded to a program without using the `new` operator. This important advance in component-based software deployment makes it possible to provide different versions of the bean without changing the application. Suppose your application requires a `Clock` bean; you can ship it to London with a serialized Clock bean tailored for British users, and to Paris with a different serialized `Clock` bean tailored for French users.

The static method `instantiate` in the `java.beans.Beans` class is designed to dynamically load the serialized bean.

```
public static Object instantiate(ClassLoader cls, String beanName)
  throws IOException, ClassNotFoundException
```

The first argument is a class loader. If it is `null`, the system class loader is used. The second argument is the name of the bean. This method searches for the bean with the specified name and a .ser file extension. If not found, an attempt is made to find a class file with the specified name. If this attempt fails, a `ClassNotFoundException` is thrown. The `instantiate` method may also throw `IOException` if the serialized bean file is corrupted.

It is not difficult to write a program to store a bean, but the simplest way to serialize a bean is to use the bean customizer in Forte. Here are the steps for serializing a `MessagePanel` bean.

1. In the context menu of `MessagePanel` in the Explorer, choose *Customize Bean* to display the Customize Bean, as shown in Figure 9.5. The Customize Bean has two windows: one displays the bean, and the other displays properties of the bean.

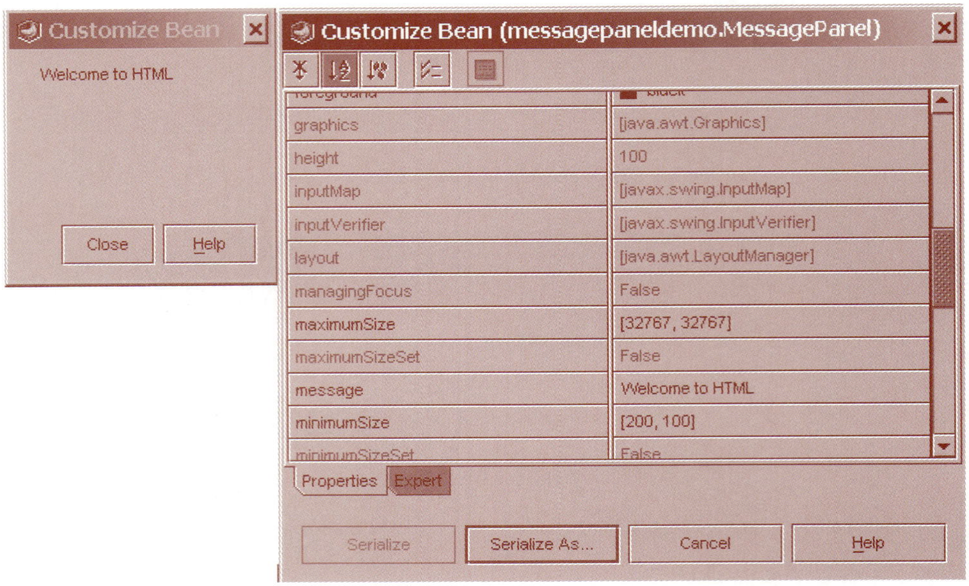

Figure 9.5 *You can customize a bean and save it in a file by choosing Serialize As in the Customize Bean window.*

2. Change the `message` property to "Welcome to HTML."
3. Click Serialize As to display the Serialize As dialog, as shown in Figure 9.6. Type a file name and press OK to save the bean.

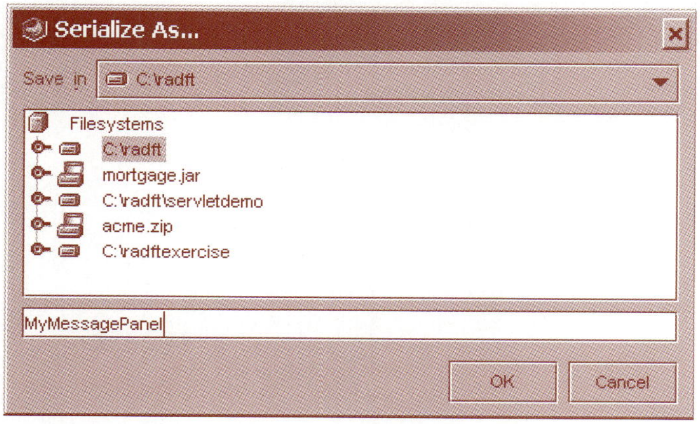

Figure 9.6 *The bean is saved to a file with a .ser extension.*

Example 9.2 Instantiating Beans

This example demonstrates how to create code with serialized beans using the `Beans.instantiate` method. You will create a program that displays a square, rectangle, circle, and oval, as shown in Figure 9.7.

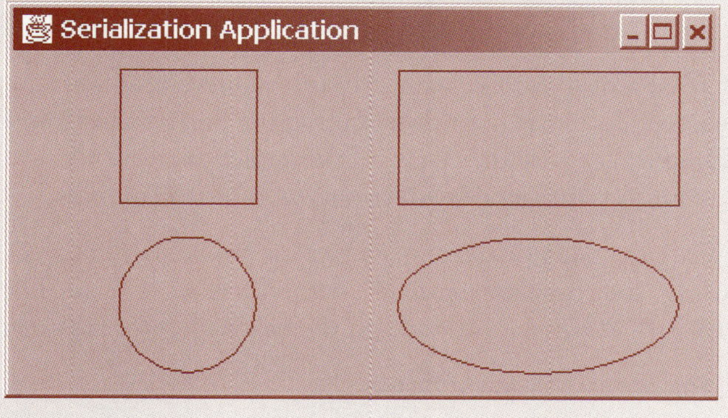

Figure 9.7 *Four figures are displayed in the form.*

Follow the steps below to complete the project.

1. In the context menu of FigurePanel under the displayfiguredemo in the Explorer, choose Customize Bean to display the Customize Bean windows for the `FigurePanel` class, as shown in Figure 9.8. The FigurePanel class was introduced in Example 6.3, "Using JTabbedPane."

continued

Example 9.2 continued

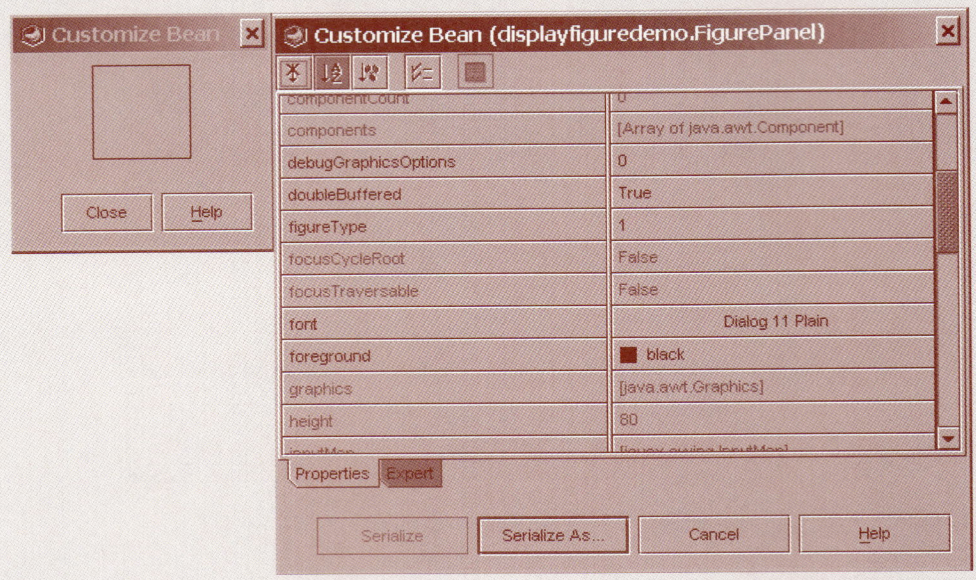

Figure 9.8 *Use the Customize Bean dialog box to save the beans as Square, Rectangle, Circle, and Oval.*

2. Set the `figureType` property to 1 and save the bean as Square. Set the `figureType` property to 2 and save the bean as Rectangle. Set the `figureType` property to 3 and save the bean as Circle. Set the `figureType` property to 4 and save the bean as Oval. All the beans are saved in **c:\radft**.

3. Create a new package named beaninstantiationdemo, and create an applet named TestBeanInstantiation using the Forte Swing JApplet form wizard. Drop a `JPanel` to the center of the applet to create `jPanel1`. Set the panel's layout to GridLayout with two rows and two columns.

4. Write the code to create instances for Square, Rectangle, Circle, and Oval using the Beans.instantiate method, as shown in Listing 9.2 (Lines 13–20). Write the code to add the beans to `jPanel1` (Lines 22–26).

```
1    package beaninstantiationdemo;
2
3    import java.beans.*;
4    import displayfiguredemo.FigurePanel;
5
6    public class TestBeanInstantiation extends javax.swing.JFrame {
7      /** Creates new form TestBeanInstantiation */
8      public TestBeanInstantiation() {
9        initComponents();
10
```

Listing 9.2 *TestBeanInstantiation.java*

```
11        // Create beans
12        try {
13          FigurePanel square = (FigurePanel)Beans.instantiate(
14            getClass().getClassLoader(), "Square");
15          FigurePanel rectangle = (FigurePanel)Beans.instantiate(
16            getClass().getClassLoader(), "Rectangle");
17          FigurePanel circle = (FigurePanel)Beans.instantiate(
18            getClass().getClassLoader(), "Circle");
19          FigurePanel oval = (FigurePanel)Beans.instantiate(
20            getClass().getClassLoader(), "Oval");
21
22          // Add beans to the form
23          jPanel1.add(square);
24          jPanel1.add(rectangle);
25          jPanel1.add(circle);
26          jPanel1.add(oval);
27        }
28        catch (Exception ex) {
29          ex.printStackTrace();
30        }
31      }
32
33      private void initComponents() {
34        jPanel1 = new javax.swing.JPanel();
35        setTitle("Serialization Application");
36        addWindowListener(new java.awt.event.WindowAdapter() {
37          public void windowClosing(java.awt.event.WindowEvent evt) {
38            exitForm(evt);
39          }
40        });
41        jPanel1.setLayout(new java.awt.GridLayout(2, 2));
42        getContentPane().add(jPanel1, java.awt.BorderLayout.CENTER);
43        pack();
44      }
45
46      /** Exit the Application */
47      private void exitForm(java.awt.event.WindowEvent evt) {
48        System.exit(0);
49      }
50
51      public static void main(String args[]) {
52        new TestBeanInstantiation().show();
53      }
54
55      // Variables declaration - do not modify
56      private javax.swing.JPanel jPanel1;
57      // End of variables declaration
58    }
```

Listing 9.2 *continued*

Example Review

The `getClass()` method (Line 14) defined in the `Object` class returns the runtime class of the object. The `getClassLoader()` method (Line 14) determines the class loader for the class. This class loader is used to load the classes in the files: Square.ser, Rectangle.ser, Circle.ser, and Oval.ser.

Since the `instantiate` method returns the `Object` type, the casting to `FigurePanel` is necessary for the program to compile.

9.4 The BeanBox (Optional)

You want to know whether the components can be used in a variety of tools after they are developed. JavaSoft provides a BeanBox for testing bean properties, events, and persistence, and for demonstrating the use of beans. The BeanBox utility is compressed in a file named bdk1_1-win.exe, which can be obtained from `http://www.javasoft.com/beans/software/bdk_download.html`.

TIP

Double-click bdk1_1-win.exe in the windows to install the BeanBox. In the Choose Install Folder dialog of the BDK installation, choose c:\BDK1.1 instead of c:\Programs Files\BDK1.1, as shown in Figure 9.9. Installing into a directory path that contains spaces may cause problems for environment variables used by the various tools that come with JDK.

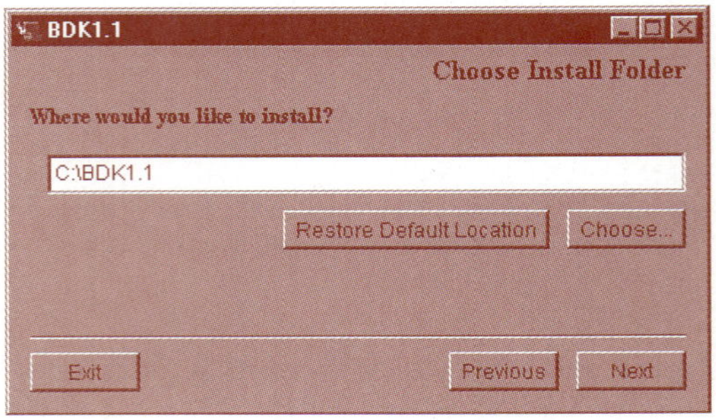

Figure 9.9 *You should install BDK in a directory path without spaces.*

After a successful installation, you can start to run BeanBox from the DOS prompt by the **run** command at the beanbox directory. The beanbox directory is under the BDK1.1 directory. When the BeanBox starts, you first see a message box indicating that the BeanBox is analyzing the packages and loading the beans. The beans are packaged in the .jar archive files stored in the **jars** directory. Several .jar files are installed by default in this directory, and the beans in these .jar files are analyzed and loaded during startup. If you want your beans to be loaded when the BeanBox starts, place their .jar files in this directory.

NOTE

Running the BeanBox requires that the JDK bin directory be in the DOS environment path. To set the path, type the following command:

```
set path=%path%;c:\j2sdk.1.4.0\bin
```

After the BeanBox is started, you will see four separate windows entitled ToolBox, BeanBox, Properties, and Method Tracer, as shown in Figure 9.10. The ToolBox consists of all the beans available for use by the BeanBox. The BeanBox window is where you test and manipulate beans installed in the ToolBox window. The Prop-

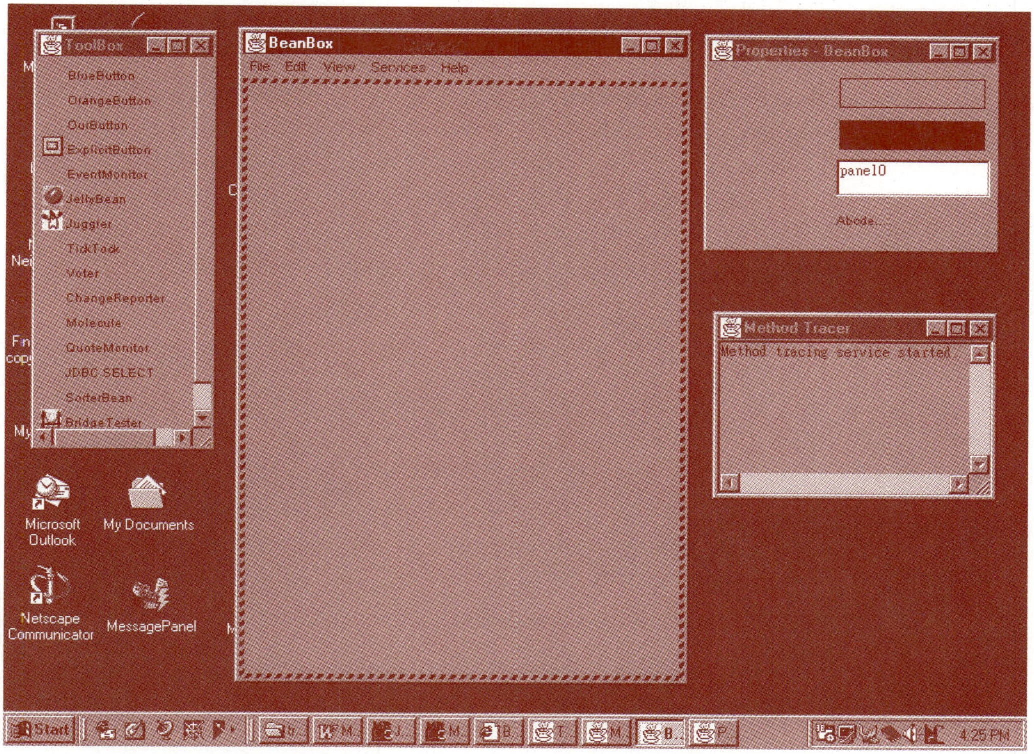

Figure 9.10 *The BeanBox consists of four independent windows entitled ToolBox, BeanBox, Properties, and Method Tracer.*

erty window enables you to set or modify bean properties. The Method Tracer traces the methods in the bean.

By default, the ToolBox contains sixteen beans. Some beans have associated icons appearing on the left of the bean name. You will learn how to specify bean icons in Chapter 11, "Bean Introspection and Customization." A new bean can be added to the ToolBox by placing its .jar file in the jars directory or by choosing File, LoadJar from the menu. The BeanBox can be used to test bean properties, events, and persistence, and it can also be used to create applets from the beans. Here is an example of using the BeanBox to create an applet for controlling clocks.

Example 9.3 Using BeanBox

This example installs a `Clock` component to ToolBox and uses the BeanBox to assemble an applet with a Start button and a Stop button to control the clock in the BeanBox. Recall that the `Clock` bean was created in Example 4.2, "Creating a Clock Component." Here are the steps to complete the project.

continued

Example 9.3 continued

1. The BeanBox requires the beans to be packaged in a JAR file with an appropriate manifest file that describes the beans. You can create the JAR file from Forte, as introduced in Section 4.8, "Packaging and Deploying Java Projects in Forte." Alternatively, you can create it from the DOS prompt. Here are the steps to create a JAR file for the `Clock` component:

   a. Create a text file named temp.mf, as follows:

```
Manifest-Version: 1.0
Name: ClockDemo/Clock.class
Java-Bean: True
```

Note
You need to leave a blank line after Java-Bean: True.

   b. Change directory to **c:\radft** and type the following command to generate the archive file Clock.jar.

```
jar -cfm Clock.jar temp.mf clockdemo\Clock.class
```

2. Start BeanBox. Choose *File, LoadJar* to load the `Clock` bean into the ToolBox from C:\radft\Clock.jar.

3. Select the `Clock` bean in the ToolBox. The cursor becomes a crosshair upon selected. Drop it in the BeanBox, as shown in Figure 9.11. With the bean selected in the BeanBox (a hatched border indicates that the bean has been selected), you can move it to the desired location or resize it to

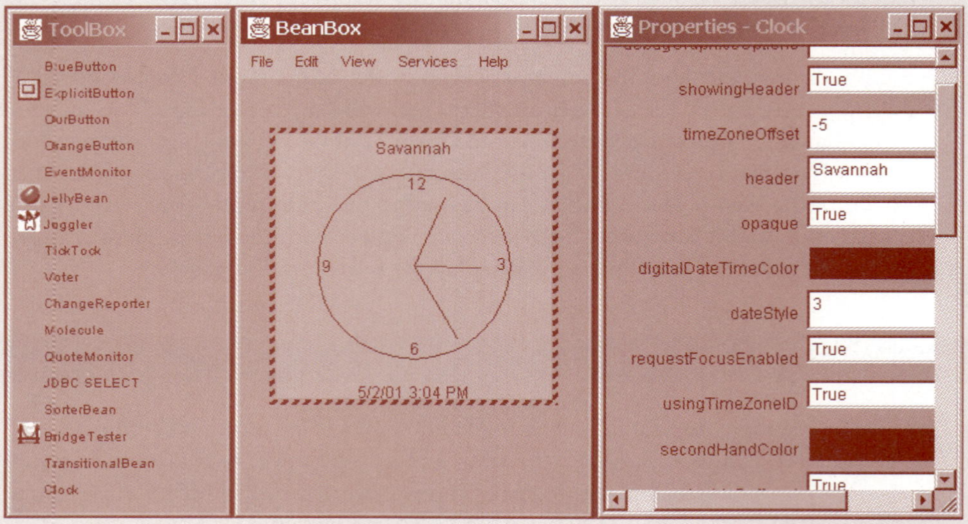

Figure 9.11 *A* `Clock` *bean is created in the BeanBox with its* `hourHandColor` *set to red, and* `showingHeader` *set to True.*

the preferred size. With the `Clock` bean selected in the BeanBox, set `showingHeader` to True and `hourHandColor` to red in the Properties window.

TIP

If you accidentally select a bean other than the `Clock` bean in the ToolBox, you have to remove it from the BeanBox by choosing *Edit, Cut* to delete it.

NOTE

A property will not be shown in the Property window if it has no default value explicitly specified in the bean component. For example, if the default header "Savannah" were not given in the `Clock` class, the property `header` would not be shown in the Properties window.

---

4. Select `OurButton` from the ToolBox, drop it to the BeanBox, and set its label to Start in the Properties window. Repeat the same operation to create another button labeled Stop.
5. Now you are ready to hook up the Start button to the `start()` method, and the Stop button to the `stop()` method, in the `Clock` bean. With the Start button selected, choose *Edit, Events, mouse, mouseClicked,* as shown in Figure 9.12. You will see a red line originating from the Start button, as shown in Figure 9.13. Click on the `Clock` bean to hook up the button with the bean. You will see a list of methods in Figure 9.14. Select

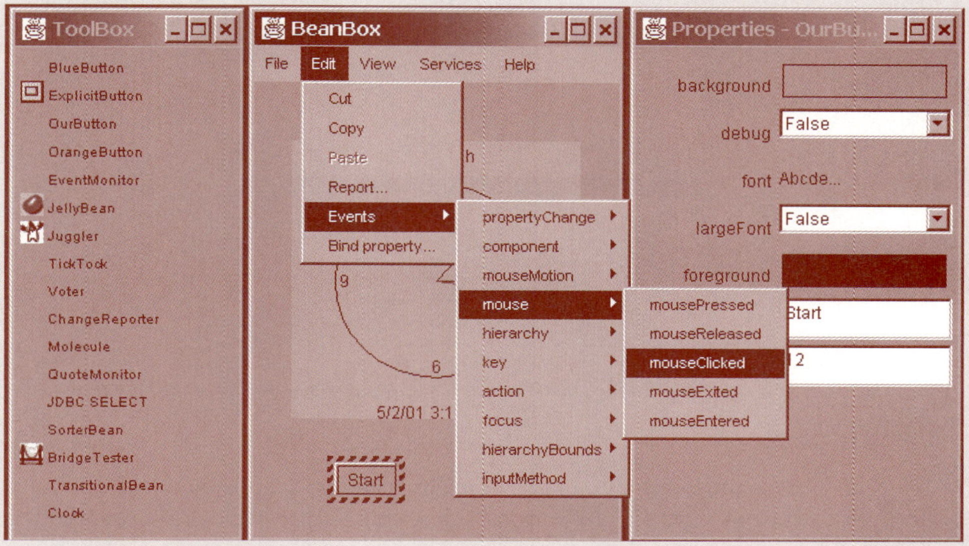

Figure 9.12 *With the Start button selected, you can implement mouse-click events on the button.*

continued

Example 9.3 continued

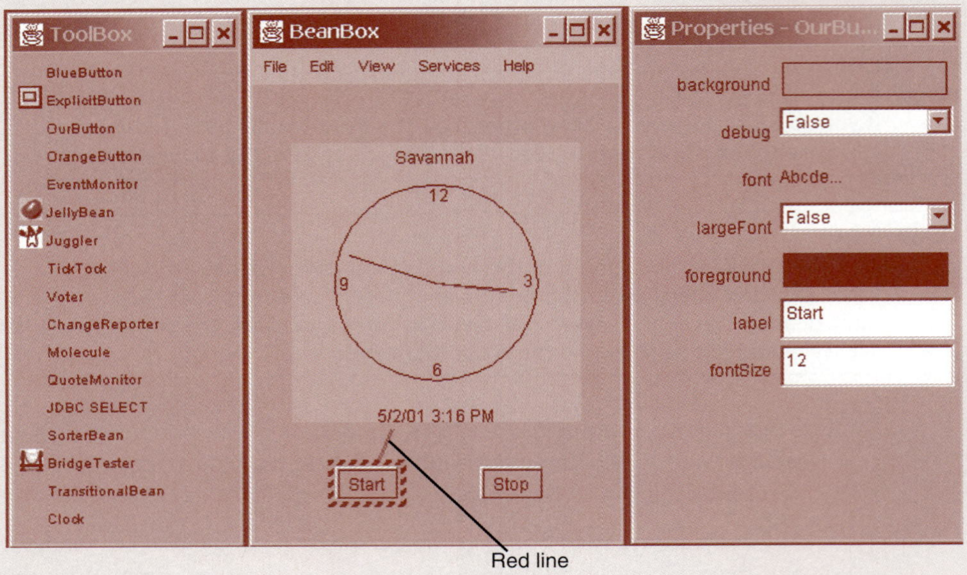

Figure 9.13 *The red line originating from the Start button indicates that the Start button is the source of the event.*

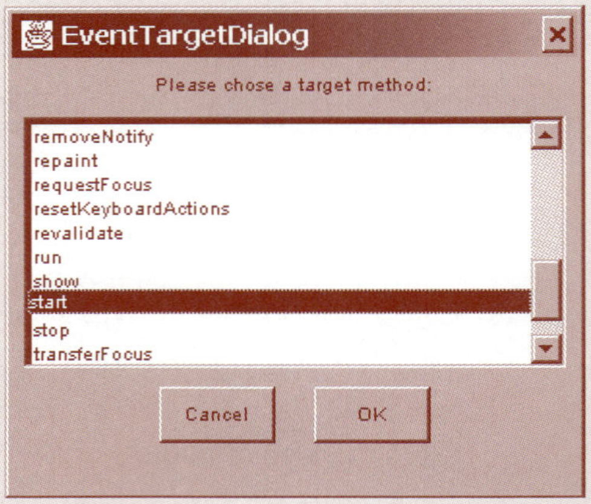

Figure 9.14 *The EventTargetDialog allows you to choose a method on the target for handling the source object event.*

start and press OK to let BeanBox generate adapters and other needed code to carry out the button-click action. Similarly, hook the Stop button to the `stop()` method in the `Clock` bean.

6. By now you have created two buttons and associated the button-press action to the `start()` and `stop()` methods in the `Clock` bean. To put all the

9.5 Customizing Serialization

A serialized bean is not guaranteed to be persistent. If you save a clock bean in the BeanBox and then reload it, you will notice that the clock is not ticking. Obviously the clock is not restored to the correct running state. This is because the thread that controls the clock is not restarted after being restored. To make the `Clock` bean persistent, you need to recreate the thread and start it after the bean is loaded. The bean is saved using the `writeObject` method and loaded to the BeanBox using the `readObject` method by Java's built-in serialization system. You can implement these methods to add customized operations to preserve bean persistence. In the case of the `Clock` bean, you can add code to stop the clock before saving bean properties and add code to create and start the thread after the properties are restored, as will be demonstrated in Example 9.4.

The `writeObject` and `readObject` methods you will implement must have the exact signatures shown below.

```
private void writeObject(java.io.ObjectOutputStream out)
  throws IOException

private void readObject(java.io.ObjectInputStream in)
  throws IOException, ClassNotFoundException
```

The `writeObject` method is responsible for saving the state of the object. The default mechanism for saving the object's fields can be invoked by calling `out.defaultWriteObject(. . .)`. The `readObject()` method is responsible for restoring the state of the object by reading the data stored by the `writeObject` method. The default mechanism for restoring the object can be invoked by calling `in.defaultReadObject()`, which restores the fields that were written using the `out.defaultWriteObject(. . .)` method.

Example 9.4 Making the `Clock` Component Persistent

This example implements the `writeObject` and `readObject` methods to add additional operations to make the `Clock` bean persistent. The new `Clock` component named `PersistentClock` is presented in Listing 9.3.

```
package clockdemo;

import java.io.*;

public class PersistentClock extends Clock {
  /** Restore clock to the persistent state */
  private void readObject(ObjectInputStream in)
    throws IOException, ClassNotFoundException {
    in.defaultReadObject();
    thread = new Thread(this);
    thread.start();
  }

```

Listing 9.3 *PersistentClock.java*

continued

Example 9.4 Making the `Clock` Component Persistent

```
    /** Store clock */
    private void writeObject(ObjectOutputStream out)
      throws IOException {
      thread = null;
      out.defaultWriteObject();
    }
  }
```

Listing 9.3 *continued*

Example Review

You have to use the exact signatures for the `readObject` and `writeObject` methods. It is often thought, erroneously, that these two methods are defined in the `Serializable` interface. In fact, however, they are unique methods in the Java serialization mechanism, which are invoked when an object of the class is serialized or deserialized.

The default `readObject` and `writeObject` methods are usually sufficient to maintain bean persistence. Customizing serialization is needed when the bean contains nonserializable data, such as a thread, that needs to be restored, as in the case of the `Clock` bean.

The `Serializable` interface provides a valuable mechanism for automating the process of storing and restoring the state of a bean. You can define your own mechanism to store and restore object data by implementing the `Externalizable` interface. This interface is a subinterface of `Serializable` and has two public methods, `writeExternal` and `readExternal`, with the following signatures:

```
public void writeExternal(ObjectOutput out) throws IOException

public void readExternal(ObjectInput in)
  throws IOException, ClassNotFoundException
```

Example 9.5 Using the `Externalizable` Interface

This example uses the `Externalizable` interface to store and restore a `Clock` bean. The new `Clock` component, named `ExternalizedClock`, is presented in Listing 9.4.

```
package clockdemo;

import java.awt.*;
import java.io.*;

public class ExternalizedClock extends PersistentClock
  implements Externalizable {
  /** Restore clock */
```

Listing 9.4 *ExternalizedClock.java*

```
  public void readExternal(ObjectInput in)
    throws IOException, ClassNotFoundException {
    setShowingDigitalDateTime(in.readBoolean());
    setTimeZoneID(in.readUTF());
    setSecondHandColor((Color)in.readObject());
    setMinuteHandColor((Color)in.readObject());
    setHourHandColor((Color)in.readObject());
    setDigitalDateTimeColor((Color)in.readObject());
    setRunning(in.readBoolean());
    thread = new Thread(this);
    thread.start();
  }

  /** Store clock */
  public void writeExternal(ObjectOutput out) throws IOException {
    thread = null;
    out.writeBoolean(isShowingDigitalDateTime());
    out.writeUTF(getTimeZoneID());
    out.writeObject(getSecondHandColor());
    out.writeObject(getMinuteHandColor());
    out.writeObject(getHourHandColor());
    out.writeObject(getDigitalDateTimeColor());
    out.writeBoolean(isRunning());
  }
}
```

Listing 9.4 *continued*

Example Review

When a bean of the component that implements `Externalizable` is stored in a builder tool like BeanBox, the builder tool invokes the bean's `writeExternal()` method. The builder tool invokes the `readExternal()` method to restore the bean. These methods are fully responsible for storing and restoring object data. You have total control over what data are stored (including the data defined in the superclass).

Note

The `readObject` and `writeObject` methods are private and use `InputObjectStream` and `OutputObjectStream`, but the `readExternal` and `writeExternal` methods are public, and read and write data using `InputObject` and `OutputObject`.

9.6 Bean Versioning

The bean components you have developed are subject to upgrade and modification. For example, you may add a new property named `showing` in `messagepaneldemo.MessagePanel` to control whether the message is shown. If you have stored a `MessagePanel` bean in the beans.dat file using `serializationdemo.SerializationApplication` with the old version of `MessagePanel`, you cannot restore the bean from the file using the new `MessagePanel`, as shown in Figure 9.18. The error message shown in Figure 9.19 would appear in the DOS window when you attempt to

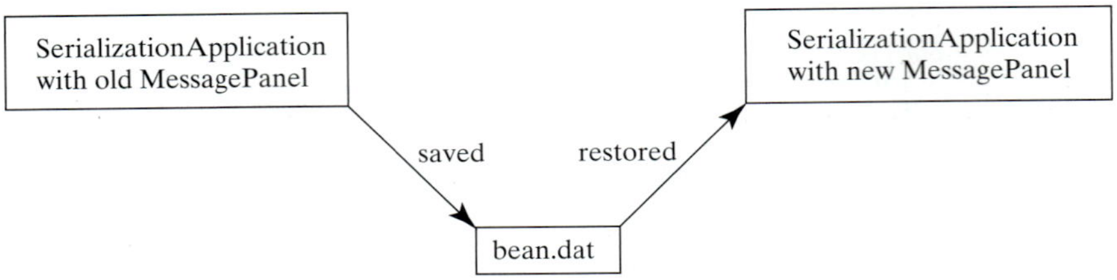

Figure 9.18 *The beans saved in beans.dat cannot be restored with the new* `MessagePanel` *unless you use bean versioning.*

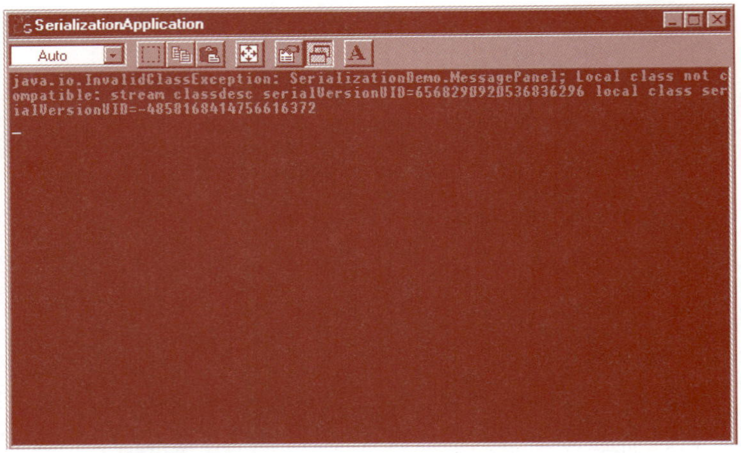

Figure 9.19 *The* `InvalidClassException` *indicates that a different version of class is used.*

read the old file using `serializationdemo.SerializationApplication` with the new bean.

The bean was stored in the old version, but the program that reads the bean uses a new version. This difference is detected by the Java runtime system. Java assigns every class a unique ID, known as the *serialVersionUID*, which is determined by the contents of the class, including package name, class name, interface name, data fields, and methods defined in the class. When a bean is saved, its ID is saved. When the bean is restored, its ID is compared with the current bean ID. The Java runtime system refuses to restore the saved bean if its ID differs from the current bean ID. However, a class can indicate that it is compatible with an old version of itself by specifying the ID of the old version in the new class, which forces the Java runtime system to assign the new bean the specified ID. For this to occur, you must first find the ID of the old class. JDK contains a command-line utility `serialver` to let you find the ID of a class. For example, the command

```
serialver messagepaneldemo.MessagePanel
```

gets the ID of the class, as shown in Figure 9.20. If you type the command **serialver -show**, a graphic dialog box is displayed, as shown in Figure 9.21.

Figure 9.20 *The* `serialver` *command finds the ID of the class.*

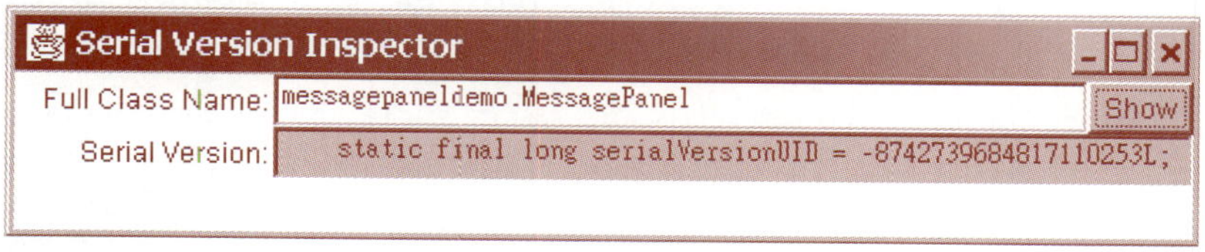

Figure 9.21 *The graphic version of the* `serialver` *command finds the ID of the class.*

To specify that the new class is compatible with its old version, add the old class's ID as a static final long constant named `serialVersionUID` in the new class, so that the new class uses the same ID as its old version. For example, to make the new `MessagePanel` compatible with its old version, add the following statement in the new `MessagePanel`:

```
static final long serialVersionUID = -8742739684817110253L;
```

With this declaration, the new program can read beans saved with the old version, and the old program can read beans saved with the new version, because the beans of both versions have the same ID. If two beans differ only in the methods, then reading the objects poses no problem. However, if the beans differ in data fields, special handling is needed to convert the stream object to the current version. Consider the following cases.

- If two fields have the same name but different types, the `InvalidClassException` is thrown with the message, indicating that the two data types are incompatible.
- If the object in the stream has a data field that is not present in the current version, these data are ignored.
- If the current version has data that are not in the object in the stream, they are set to their default values when restored. For example, the data are null for objects, `false` for `boolean` type, and zero for numbers.

Example 9.6 Testing Bean Versioning

This example uses bean versioning to restore old files using new classes. You will add a new field `showing` to `MessagePanel` to control whether the message is shown. Here are the steps to complete the project:

1. Run `serializationdemo.SerializationApplication`, select yellow color, and press the Store button to store the current `MessagePanel` in beans.dat file.

2. Record the ID of the `MessagePanel` class using the serialver utility, and create a new `MessagePanel` class in the serializationdemo project, as shown in Listing 9.5 with the same ID as the old version's. This new class replaces the old `MessagePanel` in the same directory.

3. Compile the new class and restart `serializationdemo.SerializationApplication`. Press the Restore button in the frame. You will see a yellow background message panel with no message shown. This is because the `showing` property is not defined in the old version and becomes `false` when the object is loaded from the stream.

```
package serializationdemo;

import javax.swing.*;
import java.awt.*;

public class MessagePanel extends JPanel {
  // Specify the bean ID using the ID of the previous version
  static final long serialVersionUID = -8742739684817110253L;

  // Add a new property
  private boolean showing = true;

  private String message = "Welcome to Java"; // Message to display

  // (x, y) coordinates where the message is displayed
  private int xCoordinate = 20;
  private int yCoordinate = 20;

  // Indicating whether the message is displayed in the center
  private boolean centered;

  /** Default constructor */
  public MessagePanel() {
    repaint();
  }

  /** Construct with a message parameter */
  public MessagePanel(String message) {
    this.message = message;
    repaint();
  }

  public String getMessage() {
    return message;
  }

```

Listing 9.5 *The new MessagePanel.java*

```
  public void setMessage(String message) {
    this.message = message;
  }

  public int getXCoordinate() {
    return xCoordinate;
  }

  public void setXCoordinate(int x) {
    this.xCoordinate = x;
  }

  public int getYCoordinate() {
    return yCoordinate;
  }

  public void setYCoordinate(int y) {
    this.yCoordinate = y;
  }

  public boolean isCentered() {
    return centered;
  }

  public void setCentered(boolean centered) {
    this.centered = centered;
  }

  /** Display the message at specified location */
  public void paintComponent(Graphics g) {
    super.paintComponent(g);

    if (centered) {
      // Get font metrics for the font
      FontMetrics fm = g.getFontMetrics(getFont());

      // Find the center location to display
      int w = fm.stringWidth(message);  // Get the string width
      int h = fm.getAscent(); // Get the string height
      xCoordinate = (getSize().width - w) / 2;
      yCoordinate = (getSize().height + h) / 2;
    }

    g.drawString(message, xCoordinate, yCoordinate);
  }

  public Dimension getPreferredSize() {
    return new Dimension(200, 100);
  }

  public Dimension getMinimumSize() {
    return new Dimension(200, 100);
  }

  /** Move the message in the pane to the left */
  public void moveLeft() {
    if (getXCoordinate() > 10) {
      // Shift the message to the left
      setXCoordinate(getXCoordinate() - 10);
      repaint();
    }
  }
```

Listing 9.5 *continued*

continued

Example 9.6 Testing Bean Versioning

```

    /** Move the message in the panel to the right */
    public void moveRight() {
      if (getXCoordinate() < getSize().width - 20) {
        // Shift the message to the right
        setXCoordinate(getXCoordinate() + 10);
        repaint();
      }
    }

    /** The getter method for the showing property */
    public boolean isShowing() {
      return showing;
    }

    /** The setter method for the showing property */
    public void setShowing(boolean showing) {
      this.showing = showing;
      repaint();
    }
  }
```

Listing 9.5 *The new MessagePanel.java*

Example Review

There are two MessagePanel.java files. One is in the project messagepaneldemo, which was created in Example 2.1. The other is the new one created in this example, which is stored in the project serializationdemo. After this new file is created, the new `MessagePanel` class is used when running `serializationdemo.SerializationApplication`. The new `MessagePanel` is assigned the same ID as its previous version, so you can restore the `MessagePanel` beans that were saved with the previous version of `MessagePanel`.

Assigning the new class the same ID as its old version does not guarantee compatibility. To ensure that the new class is backward-compatible with the old version, do not delete a data field, change its declaration to `transient` or `static`, or change it to a different type.

Chapter Summary

This chapter addressed the issues of bean interoperability and compatibility. Bean persistence ensures that a bean can be restored to the same state as when it was saved. This feature makes beans useful in the Java and non-Java builder tools that require beans to be stored during design time. Bean versioning makes different versions of the beans compatible.

Review Questions

9.1 How do you declare a class so that its objects will be serializable?

9.2 How do you serialize an object, and how do you deserialize an object?

9.3 How do you serialize a component in Forte?

9.4 What is the `transient` modifier for?

9.5 How do you load a bean directly without using the `new` operator?

9.6 How do you use the `Beans.instantiate(. . .)` method to instantiate beans?

9.7 How do you install a bean into the ToolBox window in the BeanBox? How do you associate a source bean with a target bean in the BeanBox?

9.8 How do you customize serialization by implementing the `readObject` and `writeObject` methods? How do you customize serialization using the `Externalizable` interface? Is `Externalizable` a subinterface of `Serializable`?

9.9 How do you enable a new class to deserialize a bean that was serialized with the old version of the class? How do you create the *serialVersionUID*?

Programming Exercises

9.1 Create an application to register students, as shown in Figure 9.22. Student information is defined in a serializable class, as follows:

Figure 9.22 *The program gathers the name and address, and stores it in a file.*

```
// Student.java: Student class encapsulates student information
import java.io.*;

public class Student implements Serializable {
  private String name;
  private String street;
  private String city;
  private String state;
  private String zip;

  /** Default constructor */
  public Student() {
  }

  /** Construct a Student with specified name, street, city,
       state, and zip */
  public Student(String name, String street, String city,
    String state, String zip) {
    this.name = name;
    this.street = street;
    this.city = city;
    this.state = state;
    this.zip = zip;
  }
```

```
    public String getName() {
      return name;
    }

    public String getStreet() {
      return street;
    }

    public String getCity() {
      return city;
    }

    public String getState() {
      return state;
    }

    public String getZip() {
      return zip;
    }
  }
```

Your program stores student objects in a data file.

9.2 Use the Bean Box to customize Clock for London, and serialize it as London.ser. Customize it for New York, and serialize it as NewYork.ser. Create an applet that contains these two clocks using the `Beans.instantiate` method.

9.3 Modify Example 8.7, "Using Table Models," to save the table in a vector to a data file.

CHAPTER 10

Bound and Constraint Properties

Objectives

- To understand the concept of bound and constraint properties.
- To know the role of bound properties in implementing property editors in builder tools.
- To learn to implement bound and constraint properties.
- To create bound and constraint properties using Forte's Bean Pattern wizard.
- To use bound properties to simplify the implementation of model-view components.

10.1 Introduction

A *bound property* of a component is one for which a property notification service is provided when the property changes. Bound properties are very useful in the implementation of property editors for beans, and they notify the beans of changes of property values in the editor. *Constraint properties* allow the listener component to verify the property change to determine whether to accept or reject it.

10.2 Implementing Bound Properties

The implementation of bound properties is based on the JavaBeans event model. The event set `java.beans.PropertyChangeEvent` and `java.beans.PropertyChangeListener` is provided to facilitate bean communications through bound properties. When a change is detected, the source bean creates a `PropertyChangeEvent` and invokes the listener's `propertyChange` method defined in `PropertyChangeListener`.

The `PropertyChangeListener` interface is used to provide notification of changes in bound properties. In order to support bound properties, the source component must declare a variable of `PropertyChangeListener` and implement a pair of `PropertyChangeListener` registration methods. When a change in the bound property occurs in the source bean, a `PropertyChangeEvent` is constructed and passed to the `propertyChange` method implemented in the listener bean.

To construct a `PropertyChangeEvent`, use the constructor

```
PropertyChangeEvent(source, propertyName, oldValue, newValue)
```

In the listener handler, you can get the property name using the `getPropertyName()` method, and the old and new values of the bound property using the `getOldValue()` and `getNewValue()` methods from an instance of `PropertyChangeEvent`.

Example 10.1 Bean Communications Through Bound Properties

This example creates a property editor for the `Clock` component in Example 4.2, "Creating a `Clock` Component." This property editor can be used during runtime to change the properties of `Clock`, as shown in Figure 10.1. A change in a property in the editor is passed to the `Clock` bean through its bound property.

For simplicity, the property editor will contain only five representative properties from the `Clock` component: `hourHandColor`, `showingDigitalTime`, `timeZone`, `timeZoneOffset`, and `usingTimeZoneID`. Here are the steps to create the editor:

1. Create a new package named `boundconstraintpropertydemo`. Create a new panel named `ClockEditor` using the Forte Swing JPanel form wizard.
2. Drop a `JPanel` to the west of the form to create `jpLabels`, and drop a `JPanel` to the center of the form to create `jpProperties`.

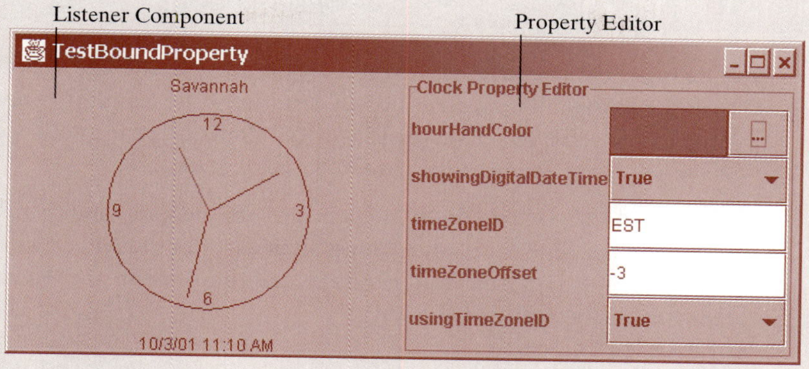

Figure 10.1 *You can set the property values in* `Clock` *from the property editor.*

3. Set the `layout` property of `jpLabels` to `GridLayout` with five rows. Drop a `JLabel` to `jpLabels` five times, and set the `text` properties of the labels to `hourHandColor`, `showingDigitalDateTime`, `timeZoneID`, `timeZoneOffset`, and `usingTimeZoneID`.

4. Set the `layout` property of `jpProperties` to `GridLayout` with five rows. Drop a `JPanel` to `jpProperties` to create `jpColor`. Set its `layout` to `BorderLayout` and its `border` to Line. Drop a `JButton` to the east of `jpColor` to create `jbtColor`. Drop a `JLabel` to the center of `jpColor` to create `jlblColor`. Set the line border for `jlblColor`. Set the `opaque` property of `jlblColor` to True. Set the `text` property of `jbtColor` to an ellipsis symbol (...).

5. Drop a `JComboBox` to `jpProperties` to create `jcboShowingDigitalDateTime`. Drop a `JTextField` twice into `jpProperties` to create `jtfTimeZoneID` and `jtfTimeZoneOffset`. Drop a `JComboBox` to `jpProperties` to create `jcboUsingTimeZoneID`.

6. Write the code to create an instance of `JColorChooser`, named `jColorChooser1`, as shown in Line 9 in Listing 10.1.

7. Now that you have created the UI for the property editor, you are ready to write the code to send the bound properties to the listener. Import `java.beans.*`, declare a listener to be `PropertyChangeListener`, and implement the registration methods `addPropertyChangeListener` and `removePropertyChangeListener`, as shown in Listing 10.1 (Lines 170–180). Add the `fire` method for firing property change event (Lines 182–187).

8. Double-click on `jbtColor` to generate the adapter and handler `jbtColorActionPerformed(ActionEvent e)` for the button. Implement the handler, as shown in Lines 150–168.

9. Add the items "True" and "False" into `jcboShowingDigitalDateTime` and `jcboUsingTimeZoneID` in the constructor (Lines 24–28).

continued

Example 10.1 continued

10. Double-click `jcboShowingDigitalDateTime` to generate the adapter and handler for handling the selection of True and False from the combo box. Implement the handler (Lines 135–148). Similarly, generate the code for handling the selection of the item in `jcboUsingTimeZone`.

11. Double-click `jtfTimeZoneID` to generate the adapter and handler for changing the time zone value, and implement it as shown in Listing 10.1 (Lines 127–133). You can generate and implement the handler for `jtfTimeZoneOffset` the same way.

```
1    package boundconstraintpropertydemo;
2
3    import java.awt.*;
4    import javax.swing.*;
5    import java.beans.*;
6    import java.awt.event.*;
7
8    public class ClockEditor extends javax.swing.JPanel {
9      private JColorChooser jColorChooser1 = new JColorChooser();
10
11     // The ClockEditor component is the source of PropertyChangeEvent
12     private PropertyChangeListener listener;
13
14     // Track the previous property values
15     private String oldShowingDigitalDateTime = new String();
16     private String oldUsingTimeZoneID = new String();
17     private String oldTimeZoneID = new String();
18     private int oldTimeZoneOffset = 0;
19
20     /** Creates new form ClockEditor */
21     public ClockEditor() {
22       initComponents();
23
24       // Initialize combo boxes
25       jcboShowingDigitalDateTime.addItem("True");
26       jcboShowingDigitalDateTime.addItem("False");
27       jcboUsingTimeZoneID.addItem("True");
28       jcboUsingTimeZoneID.addItem("False");
29     }
30
31     private void initComponents() {
32       jpLabels = new javax.swing.JPanel();
33       jLabel1 = new javax.swing.JLabel();
34       jLabel2 = new javax.swing.JLabel();
35       jLabel3 = new javax.swing.JLabel();
36       jLabel4 = new javax.swing.JLabel();
37       jLabel5 = new javax.swing.JLabel();
38       jpProperties = new javax.swing.JPanel();
39       jPanel3 = new javax.swing.JPanel();
40       jbtColor = new javax.swing.JButton();
41       jlblColor = new javax.swing.JLabel();
42       jcboShowingDigitalDateTime = new javax.swing.JComboBox();
43       jtfTimeZoneID = new javax.swing.JTextField();
44       jtfTimeZoneOffset = new javax.swing.JTextField();
45       jcboUsingTimeZoneID = new javax.swing.JComboBox();
46       setLayout(new java.awt.BorderLayout());
47       jpLabels.setLayout(new java.awt.GridLayout(5, 0));
```

Listing 10.1 *ClockEditor.java*

```
    jLabel1.setText("hourHandColor");
    jpLabels.add(jLabel1);
    jLabel2.setText("showingDigitalDateTime");
    jpLabels.add(jLabel2);
    jLabel3.setText("timeZoneID");
    jpLabels.add(jLabel3);
    jLabel4.setText("timeZoneOffset");
    jpLabels.add(jLabel4);
    jLabel5.setText("usingTimeZoneID");
    jpLabels.add(jLabel5);
    add(jpLabels, java.awt.BorderLayout.WEST);
    jpProperties.setLayout(new java.awt.GridLayout(5, 0));
    jPanel3.setLayout(new java.awt.BorderLayout());
    jbtColor.setText(". . .");
    jbtColor.addActionListener(new java.awt.event.ActionListener() {
      public void actionPerformed(java.awt.event.ActionEvent evt) {
        jbtColorActionPerformed(evt);
      }
    });
    jPanel3.add(jbtColor, java.awt.BorderLayout.EAST);
    jlblColor.setBorder(new javax.swing.border.LineBorder(
      java.awt.Color.black));
    jlblColor.setOpaque(true);
    jPanel3.add(jlblColor, java.awt.BorderLayout.CENTER);
    jpProperties.add(jPanel3);
    jcboShowingDigitalDateTime.addActionListener(
      new java.awt.event.ActionListener() {
      public void actionPerformed(java.awt.event.ActionEvent evt) {
        jcboShowingDigitalDateTimeActionPerformed(evt);
      }
    });
    jpProperties.add(jcboShowingDigitalDateTime);
    jtfTimeZoneID.addActionListener(
      new java.awt.event.ActionListener() {
      public void actionPerformed(java.awt.event.ActionEvent evt) {
        jtfTimeZoneIDActionPerformed(evt);
      }
    });
    jpProperties.add(jtfTimeZoneID);
    jtfTimeZoneOffset.addActionListener(
      new java.awt.event.ActionListener() {
      public void actionPerformed(java.awt.event.ActionEvent evt) {
        jtfTimeZoneOffsetActionPerformed(evt);
      }
    });
    jpProperties.add(jtfTimeZoneOffset);
    jcboUsingTimeZoneID.addActionListener(
      new java.awt.event.ActionListener() {
      public void actionPerformed(java.awt.event.ActionEvent evt) {
        jcboUsingTimeZoneIDActionPerformed(evt);
      }
    });
    jpProperties.add(jcboUsingTimeZoneID);
    add(jpProperties, java.awt.BorderLayout.CENTER);
  }

  private void jcboUsingTimeZoneIDActionPerformed(
    java.awt.event.ActionEvent evt) {
    if (!(oldUsingTimeZoneID.equals
      (jcboUsingTimeZoneID.getSelectedItem()))) {
```

Listing 10.1 *continued*

continued

Example 10.1 continued

```
      if (jcboUsingTimeZoneID.getSelectedItem().equals("True"))
        fire("usingTimeZoneID", new Boolean(true));
      else
        fire("usingTimeZoneID", new Boolean(false));
      oldUsingTimeZoneID =
        (String)jcboUsingTimeZoneID.getSelectedItem();
    }
  }

  private void jtfTimeZoneOffsetActionPerformed(
    java.awt.event.ActionEvent evt) {
    int newTimeZoneOffset =
      new Integer(jtfTimeZoneOffset.getText().trim()).intValue();
    if (!(oldTimeZoneOffset == newTimeZoneOffset)) {
      fire("timeZoneOffset", new Integer(newTimeZoneOffset));
      oldTimeZoneOffset = newTimeZoneOffset;
    }
  }

  private void jtfTimeZoneIDActionPerformed(
    java.awt.event.ActionEvent evt) {
    if (!(oldTimeZoneID.equals(jtfTimeZoneID.getText().trim()))) {
      fire("timeZoneID", jtfTimeZoneID.getText().trim());
      oldTimeZoneID = jtfTimeZoneID.getText().trim();
    }
  }

  private void jcboShowingDigitalDateTimeActionPerformed(
    java.awt.event.ActionEvent evt) {
    if (!(oldShowingDigitalDateTime.equals
      (jcboShowingDigitalDateTime.getSelectedItem()))) {
      if (jcboShowingDigitalDateTime.getSelectedItem().equals(
        "True"))
        fire("showingDigitalDateTime", new Boolean(true));
      else
        fire("showingDigitalDateTime", new Boolean(false));

      oldShowingDigitalDateTime =
      (String)jcboShowingDigitalDateTime.getSelectedItem();
    }
  }

  private void jbtColorActionPerformed(
    java.awt.event.ActionEvent evt) {
    Color oldColor = jlblColor.getBackground();
    jColorChooser1.setColor(oldColor);

    Color selectedColor =
    JColorChooser.showDialog(this, "Choose Color",
    jlblColor.getBackground());

    if ((selectedColor != null) &&
      !(oldColor.equals(selectedColor))) {
      jlblColor.setBackground(selectedColor);
      fire("hourHandColor", selectedColor);
      oldColor = jlblColor.getBackground();
    }

```

Listing 10.1 *continued*

```
        if (selectedColor != null)
          jlblColor.setBackground(selectedColor);
      }

      /** Add property change listener */
      public void addPropertyChangeListener(PropertyChangeListener l) {
        if (listener == null)
          listener = l;
      }

      /** Remove property change listener */
      public void removePropertyChangeListener(
      PropertyChangeListener l) {
        listener = null;
      }

      /** Fire property change event */
      private void fire(String propertyName, Object newValue) {
        if (listener != null)
          listener.propertyChange(
            new PropertyChangeEvent(this, propertyName, null, newValue));
      }

      // Variables declaration - do not modify
      private javax.swing.JPanel jpLabels;
      private javax.swing.JLabel jLabel1;
      private javax.swing.JLabel jLabel2;
      private javax.swing.JLabel jLabel3;
      private javax.swing.JLabel jLabel4;
      private javax.swing.JLabel jLabel5;
      private javax.swing.JPanel jpProperties;
      private javax.swing.JPanel jPanel3;
      private javax.swing.JButton jbtColor;
      private javax.swing.JLabel jlblColor;
      private javax.swing.JComboBox jcboShowingDigitalDateTime;
      private javax.swing.JTextField jtfTimeZoneID;
      private javax.swing.JTextField jtfTimeZoneOffset;
      private javax.swing.JComboBox jcboUsingTimeZoneID;
      // End of variables declaration
    }
```

Listing 10.1 *continued*

Any beans that implement the `PropertyChangeListener` can be listeners for the `ClockEditor` component. As shown in Listing 10.2, the component `ClockBoundPropertyListener`, derived from `Clock`, listens for changes in the bound properties `handHourColor`, `showingDigitalDateTime`, `TimeZoneID`, `TimeZoneOffset`, and `usingTimeZoneID`.

```
package boundconstraintpropertydemo;

import clockdemo.Clock;
import java.awt.*;
import java.beans.*;

public class ClockBoundPropertyListener
  extends Clock implements PropertyChangeListener {
  public ClockBoundPropertyListener() {
  }

```

Listing 10.2 *ClockBoundPropertyListener.java*

continued

Example 10.1 continued

```
    public void propertyChange(PropertyChangeEvent e) {
      if (e.getPropertyName().equals("hourHandColor"))
        setHourHandColor((Color)e.getNewValue());

      if (e.getPropertyName().equals("showingDigitalDateTime"))
        setShowingDigitalDateTime(
          ((Boolean)e.getNewValue()).booleanValue());

      if (e.getPropertyName().equals("timeZoneID"))
        setTimeZoneID((String)e.getNewValue());

      if (e.getPropertyName().equals("timeZoneOffset"))
        setTimeZoneOffset(
          ((Integer)e.getNewValue()).intValue());

      if (e.getPropertyName().equals("usingTimeZoneID"))
        setUsingTimeZoneID(((Boolean)e.getNewValue()).booleanValue());
    }
  }
```

Listing 10.2 *continued*

Follow the steps below to create a test program to hook the listener bean with the source bean and see how they interact.

1. Create a frame named `TestBoundProperty` using the Forte Swing JFrame form wizard. Set the `layout` of the frame to `GridLayout` with two columns (due to a bug in Forte, you need to set the `row` property to 0).

2. Drop a `ClockBoundPropertyListener` and a `ClockEditor` from the component palette to the frame to create instances renamed `clock` and `editor`. Set the border title of editor to "Clock Property Editor."

3. In the inspector of `editor`, double-click the value field of `propertyChange` in the Events tab to generate the adapter and handler for bound property change. Implement the `editorPropertyChange` method, as shown in Listing 10.3 (Lines 33–36), to notify bound property changes to `clock`. The `clock` object becomes a listener for `editor`.

4. Run `TestBoundProperty` to test the project, as shown in Figure 10.1. Click the ellipsis button to bring up the dialog box for choosing color. Choose True in the value field of `showingDigitalDateTime` to display date and time. Type a time zone ID (i.e., CST) and press return to set the time zone for the clock. Type a numeric value (i.e., -6) for setting a new time with the specified offset to GMT with `usingTimeZoneID` set to False.

```
1    package boundconstraintpropertydemo;
2
3    public class TestBoundProperty extends javax.swing.JFrame {
4      /** Creates new form TestBoundProperty */
5      public TestBoundProperty() {
6        initComponents();
7      }
8
```

Listing 10.3 *TestBoundProperty.java*

```
    private void initComponents() {
      clock = new ClockBoundPropertyListener();
      editor = new boundconstraintpropertydemo.ClockEditor();
      getContentPane().setLayout(new java.awt.GridLayout(0, 2));
      setTitle("TestBoundProperty");
      addWindowListener(new java.awt.event.WindowAdapter() {
        public void windowClosing(java.awt.event.WindowEvent evt) {
          exitForm(evt);
        }
      });
      getContentPane().add(clock);
      editor.setBorder(new javax.swing.border.TitledBorder(
        "Clock Property Editor"));
      editor.addPropertyChangeListener(
        new java.beans.PropertyChangeListener() {
        public void propertyChange(
          java.beans.PropertyChangeEvent evt) {
          editorPropertyChange(evt);
        }
      });
      getContentPane().add(editor);
      pack();
    }

    private void editorPropertyChange(
      java.beans.PropertyChangeEvent evt) {
      clock.propertyChange(evt);
    }

    /** Exit the Application */
    private void exitForm(java.awt.event.WindowEvent evt) {
      System.exit(0);
    }

    public static void main(String args[]) {
      new TestBoundProperty().show();
    }

    // Variables declaration - do not modify
    private ClockBoundPropertyListener clock;
    private ClockEditor editor;
    // End of variables declaration
  }
```

Listing 10.3 *continued*

Example Review

The implementation of this project and the relationship of the classes in the project are shown in Figure 10.2.

The use of `PropertyChangeEvent` is usually associated with a bound property of the bean. Theoretically, however, it could be used with no relation to any property of the bean.

A `PropertyChangeEvent` is fired in `editor` when changes occur in the bound property. The bean fires the `PropertyChangeEvent` only when the new value of the property is different from its old value.

continued

Example 10.1 continued

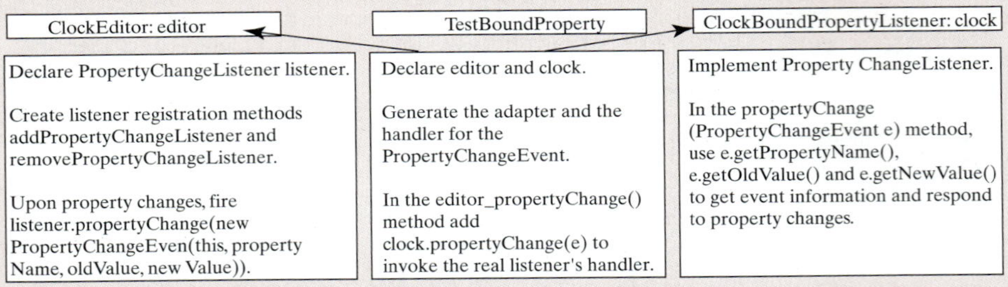

Figure 10.2 *Changes in bound properties in* `editor` *are notified to* `clock` *through the adapter created in* `TestBoundProperty`.

The `ClockEditor` class uses unicasting for simplicity. It can be modified to enable multicasting. When adapters are used in tools like Forte, the effect of multicasting can be easily achieved for unicasting source components. For example, if you have two clocks (say `clock1` and `clock2`) in the applet, you could simply write the code in the `editorPropertyChange` method like this to invoke the handlers from `clock1` and `clock2`:

```
void editorPropertyChange(PropertyChangeEvent e) {
  clock1.propertyChange(e);
  clock2.propertyChange(e);
}
```

However, this approach is not equivalent to multicasting. For instance, if an exception is raised in the course of executing `clock1.propertyChange(e)`, `clock2` will not have a chance to respond to the `PropertyChangeEvent`.

NOTE

The constructor of `PropertyChangeEvent` is

```
PropertyChangeEvent(Object source, string propertyName,
  Object oldValue, Object newValue);
```

If the property is of the primitive data type, its value has to be wrapped using the wrapper class in order to pass it the `PropertyChangeEvent`.

10.3 The *PropertyChangeSupport* Class

Java also provides a utility class called `java.beans.PropertyChangeSupport` that can be used to simplify creating source components with bound properties. You can either inherit from this class or use an instance of the class as a member field of your bean and delegate various kinds of work to it. To use it for supporting bound properties in the `ClockEditor` class, follow the steps below.

1. Declare an instance of `PropertyChangeSupport`, or its subclass. For example,

```
private PropertyChangeSupport changes =
  new PropertyChangeSupport(this);
```

2. To report a bound property update to any registered listener, invoke the `firePropertyChange` method:

```
changes.firePropertyChange(
  "color", null, jColorChooser1.getColor());
```

3. The `firePropertyChange` method automatically checks whether the new value is the same as the old value and fires the event only when they are different.

4. Implement the registration methods:

```
public void addPropertyChangeListener(PropertyChangeListener l) {
  changes.addPropertyChangeListener(l);
}

public void removePropertyChangeListener
  (PropertyChangeListener l) {
  changes.removePropertyChangeListener(l);
}
```

NOTE

Contrary to many support classes in Java, `PropertyChangeSupport` does not implement `PropertyChangeListener`. You create an instance of `PropertyChangeSupport` for the source bean using its constructor, `PropertyChangeSupport(sourceBean)`, and this instance handles property changes in the source bean.

You will see examples of using `PropertyChangeSupport` in the next section.

10.4 Using Forte's Bean Pattern Wizard to Create Bound Properties

You can use Forte's Bean Pattern wizard to create a bound property and generate the necessary code for handling it. Forte uses the `PropertyChangeSupport` class to support bound properties. The following example demonstrates the use of the Bean Pattern wizard to create bound properties.

Example 10.2 Using BeansExpress to Create Bound Properties

This example rewrites ClockEditor.java, as presented in Example 10.1, using the Bean Pattern wizard.

Here are the steps to complete the project.

1. In the `boundconstraintpropertydemo` package, create a new panel named `ClockEditorUsingSupportClass` using the Forte Swing JPanel wizard.

2. Repeat Steps 2, 3, 4, 5, and 6 in the example for creating `ClockEditor` to create the same UI for `ClockEditorUsingSupportClass`.

continued

Example 10.2 continued

3. In the Explorer, choose *New, Property* from the context menu of Beans Patterns of `ClockEditorUsingSupportClass` (Figure 10.3) to display the New Property Pattern dialog box, as shown in Figure 10.4.

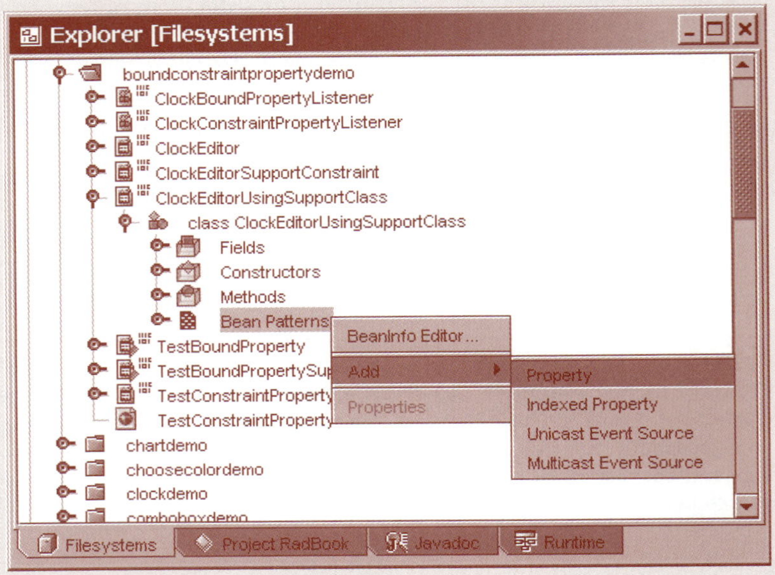

Figure 10.3 *You can start the Bean Pattern wizard from the Explorer.*

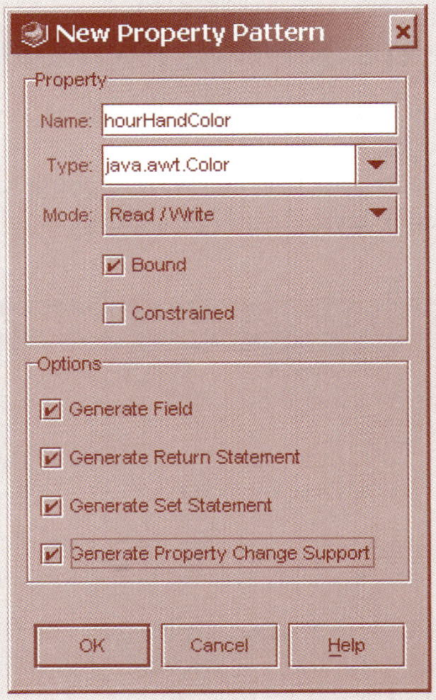

Figure 10.4 *You can create a bound property using the New Property Pattern dialog box.*

4. Type `hourHandColor` in the Name field, type `java.awt.Color` in the Type field, and check *Bound, Generate Field, Generate Return Statement, Generate Get Statement,* and *Generate Property Change Support.* Click *OK* to create the bound property `hourHandColor`. Forte automatically generates the code for this bound property and the property change listener.

5. Similarly, create the bound properties `showingDigitalDateTime (boolean)`, `timeZoneID (String)`, `timeZoneOffset (int)`, and `usingTimeZoneID (boolean)`.

6. In the Form Editor, generate the event handlers for `jbtColor`, `jcboShowingDigitalDateTime`, `jtfTimeZoneID`, `jtfTimeZoneOffset`, and `jcboUsingTimeZoneID`. Implement these handlers as shown in Listing 10.4.

7. Create a new program named TestBoundPropertySupportClass.java, which is the same as TestBoundProperty.java in Example 10.1, except that `ClockEditorUsingSupportClass` is used to replace `ClockEditor`.

8. Run the program. It should work the same as Example 10.1.

```
package boundconstraintpropertydemo;

import java.awt.*;
import javax.swing.*;
import java.beans.*;
import java.awt.event.*;

public class ClockEditorUsingSupportClass
  extends javax.swing.JPanel {
  /** Holds value of property hourHandColor. */
  private java.awt.Color hourHandColor;

  /** Utility field used by bound properties. */
  private java.beans.PropertyChangeSupport propertyChangeSupport =
  new java.beans.PropertyChangeSupport(this);

  /** Holds value of property showingDigitalDateTime. */
  private boolean showingDigitalDateTime;

  /** Holds value of property timeZoneID. */
  private String timeZoneID;

  /** Holds value of property timeZoneOffset. */
  private int timeZoneOffset;

  /** Holds value of property usingTimeZoneID. */
  private boolean usingTimeZoneID;

  private JColorChooser jColorChooser1 = new JColorChooser();

  /** Creates new form ClockEditorUsingSupportClass */
  public ClockEditorUsingSupportClass() {
    initComponents();

    // Initialize combo boxes
    jcboShowingDigitalDateTime.addItem("True");
    jcboShowingDigitalDateTime.addItem("False");
```

Listing 10.4 *ClockEditorUsingSupportClass.java*

continued

Example 10.2 continued

```
    jcboUsingTimeZoneID.addItem("True");
    jcboUsingTimeZoneID.addItem("False");
  }

  private void initComponents() {
    jpLabels = new javax.swing.JPanel();
    jLabel1 = new javax.swing.JLabel();
    jLabel2 = new javax.swing.JLabel();
    jLabel3 = new javax.swing.JLabel();
    jLabel4 = new javax.swing.JLabel();
    jLabel5 = new javax.swing.JLabel();
    jpProperties = new javax.swing.JPanel();
    jPanel3 = new javax.swing.JPanel();
    jbtColor = new javax.swing.JButton();
    jlblColor = new javax.swing.JLabel();
    jcboShowingDigitalDateTime = new javax.swing.JComboBox();
    jtfTimeZoneID = new javax.swing.JTextField();
    jtfTimeZoneOffset = new javax.swing.JTextField();
    jcboUsingTimeZoneID = new javax.swing.JComboBox();
    setLayout(new java.awt.BorderLayout());
    jpLabels.setLayout(new java.awt.GridLayout(5, 0));
    jLabel1.setText("hourHandColor");
    jpLabels.add(jLabel1);
    jLabel2.setText("showingDigitalDateTime");
    jpLabels.add(jLabel2);
    jLabel3.setText("timeZoneID");
    jpLabels.add(jLabel3);
    jLabel4.setText("timeZoneOffset");
    jpLabels.add(jLabel4);
    jLabel5.setText("usingTimeZoneID");
    jpLabels.add(jLabel5);
    add(jpLabels, java.awt.BorderLayout.WEST);
    jpProperties.setLayout(new java.awt.GridLayout(5, 0));
    jPanel3.setLayout(new java.awt.BorderLayout());
    jbtColor.setText("...");
    jbtColor.addActionListener(new java.awt.event.ActionListener() {
      public void actionPerformed(java.awt.event.ActionEvent evt) {
        jbtColorActionPerformed(evt);
      }
    });
    jPanel3.add(jbtColor, java.awt.BorderLayout.EAST);
    jlblColor.setBorder(new javax.swing.border.LineBorder(
      java.awt.Color.black));
    jlblColor.setOpaque(true);
    jPanel3.add(jlblColor, java.awt.BorderLayout.CENTER);
    jpProperties.add(jPanel3);
    jcboShowingDigitalDateTime.addActionListener(
      new java.awt.event.ActionListener() {
      public void actionPerformed(java.awt.event.ActionEvent evt) {
        jcboShowingDigitalDateTimeActionPerformed(evt);
      }
    });
    jpProperties.add(jcboShowingDigitalDateTime);
    jtfTimeZoneID.addActionListener(
      new java.awt.event.ActionListener() {
      public void actionPerformed(java.awt.event.ActionEvent evt) {
        jtfTimeZoneIDActionPerformed(evt);
      }
    });
```

Listing 10.4 *continued*

```
      jpProperties.add(jtfTimeZoneID);
      jtfTimeZoneOffset.addActionListener(
        new java.awt.event.ActionListener() {
        public void actionPerformed(java.awt.event.ActionEvent evt) {
          jtfTimeZoneOffsetActionPerformed(evt);
        }
      });
      jpProperties.add(jtfTimeZoneOffset);
      jcboUsingTimeZoneID.addActionListener(
        new java.awt.event.ActionListener() {
        public void actionPerformed(java.awt.event.ActionEvent evt) {
          jcboUsingTimeZoneIDActionPerformed(evt);
        }
      });
      jpProperties.add(jcboUsingTimeZoneID);
      add(jpProperties, java.awt.BorderLayout.CENTER);
    }

    private void jcboUsingTimeZoneIDActionPerformed(
      java.awt.event.ActionEvent evt) {
      if (jcboUsingTimeZoneID.getSelectedItem().equals("True"))
        setUsingTimeZoneID(true);
      else
        setUsingTimeZoneID(false);
    }

    private void jtfTimeZoneOffsetActionPerformed(
      java.awt.event.ActionEvent evt) {
      setTimeZoneOffset(
        new Integer(jtfTimeZoneOffset.getText().trim()).intValue());
    }

    private void jtfTimeZoneIDActionPerformed(
      java.awt.event.ActionEvent evt) {
      setTimeZoneID(jtfTimeZoneID.getText().trim());
    }

    private void jcboShowingDigitalDateTimeActionPerformed(
      java.awt.event.ActionEvent evt) {
      if (jcboShowingDigitalDateTime.getSelectedItem().equals("True"))
        setShowingDigitalDateTime(true);
      else
        setShowingDigitalDateTime(false);
    }

    private void jbtColorActionPerformed(
      java.awt.event.ActionEvent evt) {
      jColorChooser1.setColor(jlblColor.getBackground());

      Color selectedColor =
      JColorChooser.showDialog(this, "Choose Color",
      jlblColor.getBackground());

      if (selectedColor != null) {
        setHourHandColor(selectedColor);
        jlblColor.setBackground(selectedColor);
      }
    }

```

Listing 10.4 *continued*

continued

Example 10.2 continued

```
  /** Add a PropertyChangeListener to the listener list.
   * @param l The listener to add.
   */
  public void addPropertyChangeListener(
    java.beans.PropertyChangeListener l) {
    propertyChangeSupport.addPropertyChangeListener(l);
  }

  /** Removes a PropertyChangeListener from the listener list.
   * @param l The listener to remove.
   */
  public void removePropertyChangeListener(
    java.beans.PropertyChangeListener l) {
    propertyChangeSupport.removePropertyChangeListener(l);
  }

  /** Getter for property hourHandColor.
   * @return Value of property hourHandColor.
   */
  public java.awt.Color getHourHandColor() {
    return hourHandColor;
  }

  /** Setter for property hourHandColor.
   * @param hourHandColor New value of property hourHandColor.
   */
  public void setHourHandColor(java.awt.Color hourHandColor) {
    java.awt.Color oldHourHandColor = this.hourHandColor;
    this.hourHandColor = hourHandColor;
    propertyChangeSupport.firePropertyChange("hourHandColor",
    oldHourHandColor, hourHandColor);
  }
  /** Getter for property showingDigitalDateTime.
   * @return Value of property showingDigitalDateTime.
   */
  public boolean isShowingDigitalDateTime() {
    return showingDigitalDateTime;
  }

  /** Setter for property showingDigitalDateTime.
   * @param showingDigitalDateTime New value of
   * property showingDigitalDateTime.
   */
  public void setShowingDigitalDateTime(
    boolean showingDigitalDateTime) {
    boolean oldShowingDigitalDateTime = this.showingDigitalDateTime;
    this.showingDigitalDateTime = showingDigitalDateTime;
    propertyChangeSupport.firePropertyChange(
      "showingDigitalDateTime",
    new Boolean(oldShowingDigitalDateTime),
    new Boolean(showingDigitalDateTime));
  }

  /** Getter for property timeZoneID.
   * @return Value of property timeZoneID.
   */
  public String getTimeZoneID() {
    return timeZoneID;
  }

```

Listing 10.4 *continued*

```
  /** Setter for property timeZoneID.
   * @param timeZoneID New value of property timeZoneID.
   */
  public void setTimeZoneID(String timeZoneID) {
    String oldTimeZoneID = this.timeZoneID;
    this.timeZoneID = timeZoneID;
    propertyChangeSupport.firePropertyChange("timeZoneID",
      oldTimeZoneID, timeZoneID);
  }

  /** Getter for property timeZoneOffset.
   * @return Value of property timeZoneOffset.
   */
  public int getTimeZoneOffset() {
    return timeZoneOffset;
  }

  /** Setter for property timeZoneOffset.
   * @param timeZoneOffset New value of property timeZoneOffset.
   */
  public void setTimeZoneOffset(int timeZoneOffset) {
    int oldTimeZoneOffset = this.timeZoneOffset;
    this.timeZoneOffset = timeZoneOffset;
    propertyChangeSupport.firePropertyChange("timeZoneOffset",
    new Integer(oldTimeZoneOffset), new Integer(timeZoneOffset));
  }

  /** Getter for property usingTimeZoneID.
   * @return Value of property usingTimeZoneID.
   */
  public boolean isUsingTimeZoneID() {
    return usingTimeZoneID;
  }

  /** Setter for property usingTimeZoneID.
   * @param usingTimeZoneID New value of property usingTimeZoneID.
   */
  public void setUsingTimeZoneID(boolean usingTimeZoneID) {
    boolean oldUsingTimeZoneID = this.usingTimeZoneID;
    this.usingTimeZoneID = usingTimeZoneID;
    propertyChangeSupport.firePropertyChange("usingTimeZoneID",
      new Boolean(oldUsingTimeZoneID), new Boolean(usingTimeZoneID));
  }

  // Variables declaration - do not modify
  private javax.swing.JPanel jpLabels;
  private javax.swing.JLabel jLabel1;
  private javax.swing.JLabel jLabel2;
  private javax.swing.JLabel jLabel3;
  private javax.swing.JLabel jLabel4;
  private javax.swing.JLabel jLabel5;
  private javax.swing.JPanel jpProperties;
  private javax.swing.JPanel jPanel3;
  private javax.swing.JButton jbtColor;
  private javax.swing.JLabel jlblColor;
  private javax.swing.JComboBox jcboShowingDigitalDateTime;
  private javax.swing.JTextField jtfTimeZoneID;
  private javax.swing.JTextField jtfTimeZoneOffset;
  private javax.swing.JComboBox jcboUsingTimeZoneID;
  // End of variables declaration
}
```

Listing 10.4 *continued*

10.5 Implementing Constraint Properties

When a constraint property changes, the source bean creates an instance of `PropertyChangeEvent` and invokes the `vetoableChange` method. If the listener rejects the change, it throws a `PropertyVetoException`. The source bean then catches this exception and reverts to the old value.

Often the bound property and the constraint property are used together to verify and update the property in a so-called *two-phase approach*. The constraint property is used first to check whether the change is valid. If it is, the bound property is used to actually commit the change; if it is invalid, no change is made.

As in the case of the `PropertyChangeSupport` class, JavaBeans provides `java.beans.VetoableChangeSupport` to simplify the implementation of the constraint properties. The use of `VetoableChangeSupport` is similar to the use of the `PropertyChangeSupport` class.

Example 10.3 Using Constraint Properties

This example modifies Example 10.2 to allow the listener (clock) to reject any values of `timeZoneOffset` not in the range between -12 and 12. The example creates a new editor bean component, `ClockEditorSupportConstraint`, that generates constraint property changes, and a new clock component, `ClockConstraintPropertyListener`, to listen for constraint property changes. Since `ClockEditorSupportConstraint` extends `ClockEditor`, and `ClockConstraintPropertyListener` extends `ClockBoundPropertyListener`, these two new classes need to reference superclass data members and override some handlers. For convenience, this example will be created in the project boundconstraintpropertydemo.

Follow the steps below to complete the project.

1. Reopen the boundconstraintpropertydemo package and create `ClockEditorSupportConstraint` using the Forte Swing JPanel form wizard. Create the same UI interface as in `ClockEditorUsingSupportClass` in Example 10.2. Use the Bean Pattern wizard to create the bound property for `hourHandColor`, `showingDigitalDateTime`, `timeZoneID`, and `timeZoneOffset` the same way as in `ClockEditorUsingSupportClass`. Use the Bean Pattern wizard to create bound and constraint properties for `usingTimeZoneID`, as shown in Figure 10.5. The following code is automatically generated:

   ➤ An instance of `VetoableChangeSupport` is created as follows (Lines 11–12 in Listing 10.5):

   ```
   private java.beans.VetoableChangeSupport vetoableChangeSupport =
     new java.beans.VetoableChangeSupport(this);
   ```

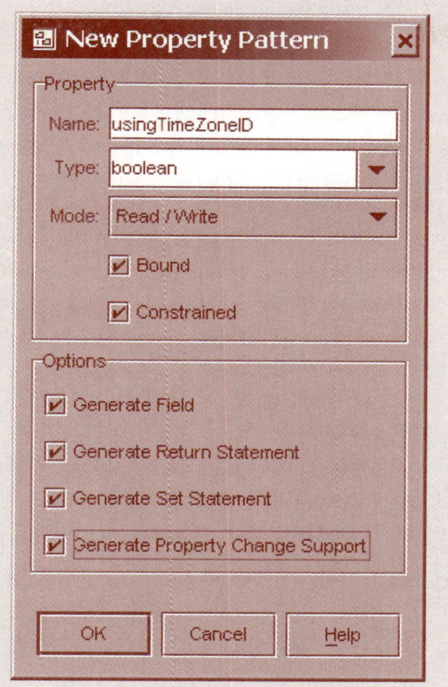

Figure 10.5 *You can create bound properties and constraint properties using the New Property Pattern dialog box.*

- Registration methods for `VetoableChangeListener` are created as follows (Lines 181–195 in Listing 10.5):

```
public void addVetoableChangeListener(
  java.beans.VetoableChangeListener l) {
  vetoableChangeSupport.addVetoableChangeListener(l);
}

public void removeVetoableChangeListener(
  java.beans.VetoableChangeListener l) {
  vetoableChangeSupport.removeVetoableChangeListener(l);
}
```

- Accessor methods for the `usingTimeZoneID` property are created as follows (Lines 265–280 in Listing 10.5):

```
public boolean isUsingTimeZoneID() {
  return usingTimeZoneID;
}

public void setUsingTimeZoneID(boolean usingTimeZoneID) {
  boolean oldUsingTimeZoneID = this.usingTimeZoneID;
  this.usingTimeZoneID = usingTimeZoneID;
  propertyChangeSupport.firePropertyChange("usingTimeZoneID",
    new Boolean(oldUsingTimeZoneID),
    new Boolean(usingTimeZoneID));
}
```

continued

Example 10.3 continued

2. Create `ClockConstraintPropertyListener`, which extends `ClockBoundPropertyListener` and implements `VetoableChangeListener` with the capability of handling constraint property changes, as shown in Listing 10.6. Compile and install it in the component palette.

3. Create a new applet named TestConstraintProperty.java using the Forte Swing JApplet form wizard. Drop a `ClockConstraintPropertyListener` to the west of the applet, and a `ClockEditorSupportConstraint` to the center of the applet, and change their names to `clock` and `editor`, respectively.

4. In the Events page of `editor`, double-click on the value field of `propertyChange` to generate the adapter and handler for bound property change. Double-click on the value field of `vetoableChange` to generate the adapter and handler for constraint property change. Implement these two handlers as shown in Listing 10.7 (Lines 34–42).

5. Run "TestConstraintProperty" to test the project. Point the mouse at the clock and click the right mouse button to display the property editor. Select False in `usingTimeZoneID` field, type 10 in the `timeZoneOffset` field, and press the ENTER key. You will see that the hour hand moves. Enter 13 in the `timeZoneOffset` field and press the ENTER key. You will see that nothing happens, because this value is rejected by the listener.

```
package boundconstraintpropertydemo;

import java.awt.*;
import javax.swing.*;
import java.beans.*;
import java.awt.event.*;

public class ClockEditorSupportConstraint
  extends javax.swing.JPanel {
  /** Utility field used by constrained properties. */
  private java.beans.VetoableChangeSupport vetoableChangeSupport =
    new java.beans.VetoableChangeSupport(this);

  /** Holds value of property hourHandColor. */
  private java.awt.Color hourHandColor;

  /** Utility field used by bound properties. */
  private java.beans.PropertyChangeSupport propertyChangeSupport =
    new java.beans.PropertyChangeSupport(this);

  /** Holds value of property showingDigitalDateTime. */
  private boolean showingDigitalDateTime;

  /** Holds value of property timeZoneID. */
  private String timeZoneID;

  /** Holds value of property timeZoneOffset. */
  private int timeZoneOffset;

```

Listing 10.5 *ClockEditorSupportConstraint.java*

```
  /** Holds value of property usingTimeZoneID. */
  private boolean usingTimeZoneID;

  private JColorChooser jColorChooser1 = new JColorChooser();

  /** Creates new form ClockEditorSupportConstraint */
  public ClockEditorSupportConstraint() {
    initComponents();

    // Initialize combo boxes
    jcboShowingDigitalDateTime.addItem("True");
    jcboShowingDigitalDateTime.addItem("False");
    jcboUsingTimeZoneID.addItem("True");
    jcboUsingTimeZoneID.addItem("False");
  }

  private void initComponents() {
    jpLabels = new javax.swing.JPanel();
    jLabel1 = new javax.swing.JLabel();
    jLabel2 = new javax.swing.JLabel();
    jLabel3 = new javax.swing.JLabel();
    jLabel4 = new javax.swing.JLabel();
    jLabel5 = new javax.swing.JLabel();
    jpProperties = new javax.swing.JPanel();
    jPanel3 = new javax.swing.JPanel();
    jbtColor = new javax.swing.JButton();
    jlblColor = new javax.swing.JLabel();
    jcboShowingDigitalDateTime = new javax.swing.JComboBox();
    jtfTimeZoneID = new javax.swing.JTextField();
    jtfTimeZoneOffset = new javax.swing.JTextField();
    jcboUsingTimeZoneID = new javax.swing.JComboBox();
    setLayout(new java.awt.BorderLayout());
    jpLabels.setLayout(new java.awt.GridLayout(5, 0));
    jLabel1.setText("hourHandColor");
    jpLabels.add(jLabel1);
    jLabel2.setText("showingDigitalDateTime");
    jpLabels.add(jLabel2);
    jLabel3.setText("timeZoneID");
    jpLabels.add(jLabel3);
    jLabel4.setText("timeZoneOffset");
    jpLabels.add(jLabel4);
    jLabel5.setText("usingTimeZoneID");
    jpLabels.add(jLabel5);
    add(jpLabels, java.awt.BorderLayout.WEST);
    jpProperties.setLayout(new java.awt.GridLayout(5, 0));
    jPanel3.setLayout(new java.awt.BorderLayout());
    jbtColor.setText("...");
    jbtColor.addActionListener(new java.awt.event.ActionListener() {
      public void actionPerformed(java.awt.event.ActionEvent evt) {
        jbtColorActionPerformed(evt);
      }
    });
    jPanel3.add(jbtColor, java.awt.BorderLayout.EAST);
    jlblColor.setBorder(
      new javax.swing.border.LineBorder(java.awt.Color.black));
    jlblColor.setOpaque(true);
    jPanel3.add(jlblColor, java.awt.BorderLayout.CENTER);
    jpProperties.add(jPanel3);
    jcboShowingDigitalDateTime.addActionListener(
      new java.awt.event.ActionListener() {
```

Listing 10.5 *continued*

continued

Example 10.3 continued

```
        public void actionPerformed(java.awt.event.ActionEvent evt) {
          jcboShowingDigitalDateTimeActionPerformed(evt);
        }
      });
      jpProperties.add(jcboShowingDigitalDateTime);
      jtfTimeZoneID.addActionListener(
        new java.awt.event.ActionListener() {
        public void actionPerformed(java.awt.event.ActionEvent evt) {
          jtfTimeZoneIDActionPerformed(evt);
        }
      });
      jpProperties.add(jtfTimeZoneID);
        jtfTimeZoneOffset.addActionListener(
          new java.awt.event.ActionListener() {
          public void actionPerformed(java.awt.event.ActionEvent evt) {
            jtfTimeZoneOffsetActionPerformed(evt);
          }
        });
      jpProperties.add(jtfTimeZoneOffset);
      jcboUsingTimeZoneID.addActionListener(
        new java.awt.event.ActionListener() {
        public void actionPerformed(java.awt.event.ActionEvent evt) {
          jcboUsingTimeZoneIDActionPerformed(evt);
        }
      });
      jpProperties.add(jcboUsingTimeZoneID);
      add(jpProperties, java.awt.BorderLayout.CENTER);
    }

    private void jcboUsingTimeZoneIDActionPerformed(
      java.awt.event.ActionEvent evt) {
      if (jcboUsingTimeZoneID.getSelectedItem().equals("True"))
        setUsingTimeZoneID(true);
      else
        setUsingTimeZoneID(false);
    }

    private void jtfTimeZoneOffsetActionPerformed(
      java.awt.event.ActionEvent evt) {
      try {
        setTimeZoneOffset(
          new Integer(jtfTimeZoneOffset.getText().trim()).intValue());
      }
      catch (PropertyVetoException ex) {
        jtfTimeZoneOffset.setText(
          new Integer(getTimeZoneOffset()).toString());
      }
    }

    private void jtfTimeZoneIDActionPerformed(
      java.awt.event.ActionEvent evt) {
      setTimeZoneID(jtfTimeZoneID.getText().trim());
    }

    private void jcboShowingDigitalDateTimeActionPerformed(
      java.awt.event.ActionEvent evt) {
      if (jcboShowingDigitalDateTime.getSelectedItem().equals("True"))
        setShowingDigitalDateTime(true);
```

Listing 10.5 *continued*

```
      else
        setShowingDigitalDateTime(false);
    }

    private void jbtColorActionPerformed(
      java.awt.event.ActionEvent evt) {
      jColorChooser1.setColor(jlblColor.getBackground());
      Color selectedColor =
        JColorChooser.showDialog(this, "Choose Color",
        jlblColor.getBackground());

      if (selectedColor != null) {
        setHourHandColor(selectedColor);
        jlblColor.setBackground(selectedColor);
      }
    }

    /** Add a PropertyChangeListener to the listener list.
     * @param l The listener to add.
     */
    public void addPropertyChangeListener(
      java.beans.PropertyChangeListener l) {
      propertyChangeSupport.addPropertyChangeListener(l);
    }

    /** Removes a PropertyChangeListener from the listener list.
     * @param l The listener to remove.
     */
    public void removePropertyChangeListener(
      java.beans.PropertyChangeListener l) {
      propertyChangeSupport.removePropertyChangeListener(l);
    }

    /** Add a VetoableChangeListener to the listener list.
     * @param l The listener to add.
     */
    public void addVetoableChangeListener(
      java.beans.VetoableChangeListener l) {
      vetoableChangeSupport.addVetoableChangeListener(l);
    }

    /** Removes a VetoableChangeListener from the listener list.
     * @param l The listener to remove.
     */
    public void removeVetoableChangeListener(
      java.beans.VetoableChangeListener l) {
      vetoableChangeSupport.removeVetoableChangeListener(l);
    }

    /** Getter for property hourHandColor.
     * @return Value of property hourHandColor.
     */
    public java.awt.Color getHourHandColor() {
      return hourHandColor;
    }

    /** Setter for property hourHandColor.
     * @param hourHandColor New value of property hourHandColor.
     */
```

Listing 10.5 *continued*

continued

Example 10.3 continued

```
    public void setHourHandColor(java.awt.Color hourHandColor) {
      java.awt.Color oldHourHandColor = this.hourHandColor;
      this.hourHandColor = hourHandColor;
      propertyChangeSupport.firePropertyChange("hourHandColor",
        oldHourHandColor, hourHandColor);
    }

    /** Getter for property showingDigitalDateTime.
     * @return Value of property showingDigitalDateTime.
     */
    public boolean isShowingDigitalDateTime() {
      return showingDigitalDateTime;
    }

    public void setShowingDigitalDateTime(
      boolean showingDigitalDateTime) {
      boolean oldShowingDigitalDateTime = this.showingDigitalDateTime;
      this.showingDigitalDateTime = showingDigitalDateTime;
      propertyChangeSupport.firePropertyChange(
        "showingDigitalDateTime",
        new Boolean(oldShowingDigitalDateTime),
        new Boolean(showingDigitalDateTime));
    }

    /** Getter for property timeZoneID.
     * @return Value of property timeZoneID.
     */
    public String getTimeZoneID() {
      return timeZoneID;
    }

    /** Setter for property timeZoneID.
     * @param timeZoneID New value of property timeZoneID.
     */
    public void setTimeZoneID(String timeZoneID) {
      String oldTimeZoneID = this.timeZoneID;
      this.timeZoneID = timeZoneID;
      propertyChangeSupport.firePropertyChange(
        "timeZoneID", oldTimeZoneID, timeZoneID);
    }

    /** Getter for property timeZoneOffset.
     * @return Value of property timeZoneOffset.
     */
    public int getTimeZoneOffset() {
      return timeZoneOffset;
    }

    public void setTimeZoneOffset(int timeZoneOffset)
        throws java.beans.PropertyVetoException {
      int oldTimeZoneOffset = this.timeZoneOffset;
      vetoableChangeSupport.fireVetoableChange("timeZoneOffset",
        new Integer(oldTimeZoneOffset), new Integer(timeZoneOffset));
      this.timeZoneOffset = timeZoneOffset;
      propertyChangeSupport.firePropertyChange("timeZoneOffset",
        new Integer(oldTimeZoneOffset), new Integer(timeZoneOffset));
    }

```

Listing 10.5 *continued*

```
  /** Getter for property usingTimeZoneID.
   * @return Value of property usingTimeZoneID.
   */
  public boolean isUsingTimeZoneID() {
    return usingTimeZoneID;
  }

  /** Setter for property usingTimeZoneID.
   * @param usingTimeZoneID New value of property usingTimeZoneID.
   */
  public void setUsingTimeZoneID(boolean usingTimeZoneID) {
    boolean oldUsingTimeZoneID = this.usingTimeZoneID;
    this.usingTimeZoneID = usingTimeZoneID;
    propertyChangeSupport.firePropertyChange("usingTimeZoneID",
      new Boolean(oldUsingTimeZoneID), new Boolean(usingTimeZoneID));
  }

  // Variables declaration - do not modify
  private javax.swing.JPanel jpLabels;
  private javax.swing.JLabel jLabel1;
  private javax.swing.JLabel jLabel2;
  private javax.swing.JLabel jLabel3;
  private javax.swing.JLabel jLabel4;
  private javax.swing.JLabel jLabel5;
  private javax.swing.JPanel jpProperties;
  private javax.swing.JPanel jPanel3;
  private javax.swing.JButton jbtColor;
  private javax.swing.JLabel jlblColor;
  private javax.swing.JComboBox jcboShowingDigitalDateTime;
  private javax.swing.JTextField jtfTimeZoneID;
  private javax.swing.JTextField jtfTimeZoneOffset;
  private javax.swing.JComboBox jcboUsingTimeZoneID;
  // End of variables declaration
}
```

Listing 10.5 *continued*

```
package boundconstraintpropertydemo;

import java.awt.*;
import java.beans.*;

public class ClockConstraintPropertyListener
  extends ClockBoundPropertyListener
  implements VetoableChangeListener {
  public ClockConstraintPropertyListener() {
  }

  public void vetoableChange(PropertyChangeEvent e)
    throws PropertyVetoException {
    if (e.getPropertyName() == "timeZoneOffset") {
      int timeZoneOffset = ((Integer)e.getNewValue()).intValue();
      if (timeZoneOffset > 12 || timeZoneOffset < -12)
        throw new PropertyVetoException("Invalid timeZoneOffset", e);
    }
  }
}
```

Listing 10.6 *ClockConstraintPropertyListener.java*

continued

Example 10.3 continued

```
package boundconstraintpropertydemo;

public class TestConstraintProperty extends javax.swing.JApplet {
  public TestConstraintProperty() {
    initComponents();
  }

  private void initComponents() {
    editor = new boundconstraintpropertydemo.
      ClockEditorSupportConstraint();
    clock = new boundconstraintpropertydemo.
      ClockConstraintPropertyListener();

    editor.addPropertyChangeListener(
      new java.beans.PropertyChangeListener() {
      public void propertyChange(
        java.beans.PropertyChangeEvent evt) {
        editorPropertyChange(evt);
      }
    });

    editor.addVetoableChangeListener(
      new java.beans.VetoableChangeListener() {
      public void vetoableChange(java.beans.PropertyChangeEvent evt)
      throws java.beans.PropertyVetoException {
        editorVetoableChange(evt);
      }
    });

    getContentPane().add(editor, java.awt.BorderLayout.CENTER);
    getContentPane().add(clock, java.awt.BorderLayout.WEST);
  }

  private void editorVetoableChange(java.beans.PropertyChangeEvent
    evt) throws java.beans.PropertyVetoException {
    clock.vetoableChange(evt);
  }

  private void editorPropertyChange(
    java.beans.PropertyChangeEvent evt) {
    clock.propertyChange(evt);
  }

  // Variables declaration - do not modify
  private boundconstraintpropertydemo.
    ClockEditorSupportConstraint editor;
  private boundconstraintpropertydemo.
    ClockConstraintPropertyListener clock;
  // End of variables declaration
}
```

Listing 10.7 *TestConstraintProperty.java*

Example Review

The implementation of the project and the relationship of the classes in the project are shown in Figure 10.6.

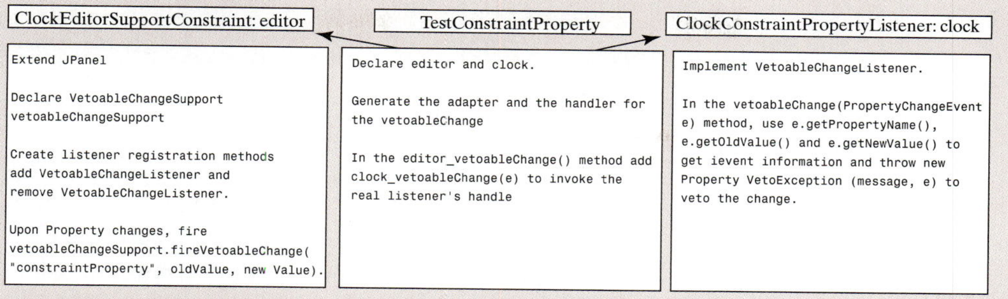

Figure 10.6 *Changes of constraint properties in* `editor` *are notified to* `clock` *through the adapter created in* `TestConstraintProperty`.

Note that Java does not have a class named `VetoableChangeEvent`. Both `VetoChangeListener` and `PropertyChangeListener` listen for `PropertyChangeEvent`.

When invoking `firePropertyChange` in `ClockEditorSupportConstraint`, all three parameters (`propertyName`, `oldValue`, and `newValue`) must be given, and they must be non-null. Like the `firePropertyChange` method, the `fireVetoableChange` method does not fire `PropertyChangeEvent` if the new value is the same as the old value, which reduces the danger of infinite loops when methods are cross-connected in classes.

When `fireVetoableChange`, invoked from the `setTimeZoneOffset` method (Line 258) in the `ClockEditorSupportConstraint` class, throws a `PropertyVetoException`, the other statements in this method are skipped. In consequence, the property is not changed in the clock. Furthermore, `timeZoneOffset` is reset to the previous value in the catch clause.

Just as you used Forte's Bean Pattern Wizard to create bound properties, you can use it to create constraint properties and generate the code needed to carry out the task of handling constraint properties.

10.6 Implementing Model-View Components Using Bound and Constraint Properties

Bound properties are ideal for implementing model-view components. In Example 4.4, "Developing Model-View Components," you created a model, named `CircleModel`, which notifies the listeners of its property changes through an `ActionEvent`. The notification is implemented in the property's set method using the `fireActionPerformed` method. Instead of firing an `ActionEvent` with every property change, you can simply make it either a bound or a constraint property. Using bound and constraint properties simplifies the task of creating the model and the views.

The following example demonstrates how to create model-view components using bound properties.

Example 10.4 Implementing Model-View Components Using Bound Properties

This example rewrites Example 4.4 to create a new circle model, circle editor, and circle view, named `CircleModelUsingBoundProperties`, `CircleEditorUsingBoundProperties`, and `CircleViewUsingBoundProperties`, respectively. The `CircleEditorUsingBoundProperties` class is like a property editor that enables you to change the properties of the circle. The `CircleViewBoundProperties` class displays the circle visually and enables you to increase or decrease the radius with a mouse click on the left or right button. Both `CircleEditorUsingBoundProperties` and `CircleViewUsingBoundProperties` are views that use the data stored in `CircleModelUsingBoundProperties`. A sample run of the test program that uses these three components is shown in Figure 10.7.

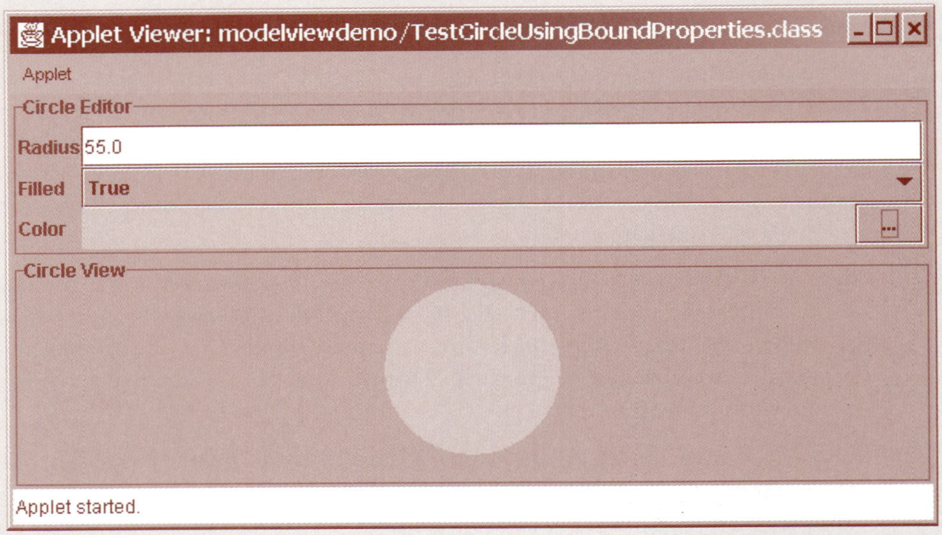

Figure 10.7 *You can change the circle's properties from the circle editor and increase or decrease the circle's radius by clicking the left or right button.*

The following are the steps to create `CircleModelUsingBoundProperties`.

1. In the modelviewdemo package, create `CircleModelUsingBoundProperties` using the Forte Class wizard.

2. Use the Bean Pattern wizard to add three bound properties, `color`, `filled`, and `radius`, with type `java.awt.Color`, `boolean`, and `double`, respectively. For each property, check the options *Bound, Generate Field, Generate Return Statement, Generate Set Statement,* and *Generate property Change Support,* as shown in Figure 10.8. `CircleModelUsingBoundProperties` is generated, as shown in Listing 10.8.

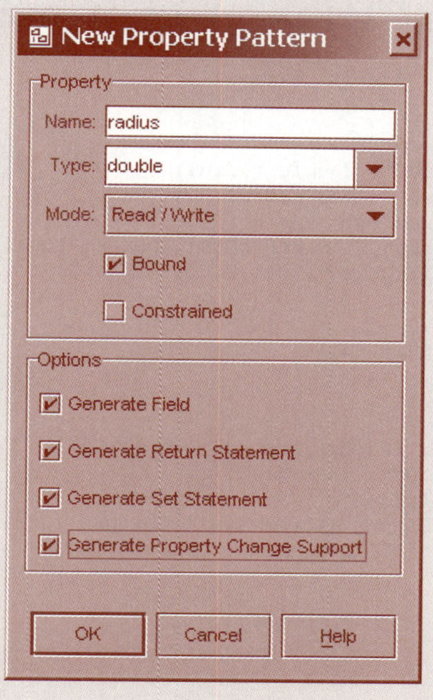

Figure 10.8 *You can create bound properties from the New Property Pattern's dialog box.*

```
package modelviewdemo;

public class CircleModelUsingBoundProperties {
  /** Holds value of property radius. */
  private double radius;

  /** Utility field used by bound properties. */
  private java.beans.PropertyChangeSupport propertyChangeSupport =
    new java.beans.PropertyChangeSupport(this);

  /** Holds value of property filled. */
  private boolean filled;

  /** Holds value of property color. */
  private java.awt.Color color;

  /** Creates new CircleModelUsingBoundProperties */
  public CircleModelUsingBoundProperties() {
  }

  public void addPropertyChangeListener(
    java.beans.PropertyChangeListener l) {
    propertyChangeSupport.addPropertyChangeListener(l);
  }

  public void removePropertyChangeListener(
    java.beans.PropertyChangeListener l) {
    propertyChangeSupport.removePropertyChangeListener(l);
  }

```

Listing 10.8 *CircleModelUsingBoundProperties.java*

continued

Example 10.4 continued

```
31    public double getRadius() {
32      return radius;
33    }
34
35    public void setRadius(double radius) {
36      double oldRadius = this.radius;
37      this.radius = radius;
38      propertyChangeSupport.firePropertyChange("radius",
39        new Double(oldRadius), new Double(radius));
40    }
41
42    public boolean isFilled() {
43      return filled;
44    }
45
46    public void setFilled(boolean filled) {
47      boolean oldFilled = this.filled;
48      this.filled = filled;
49      propertyChangeSupport.firePropertyChange("filled",
50        new Boolean(oldFilled), new Boolean(filled));
51    }
52
53    public java.awt.Color getColor() {
54      return color;
55    }
56
57    public void setColor(java.awt.Color color) {
58      java.awt.Color oldColor = this.color;
59      this.color = color;
60      propertyChangeSupport.firePropertyChange(
61        "color", oldColor, color);
62    }
63  }
```

Listing 10.8 *continued*

The following are the steps to create `CircleEditorUsingBoundProperties`.

1. Create `CircleEditorUsingBoundProperties`, which extends `JPanel` using the Forte Swing JPanel form wizard.

2. Drop a `JPanel` to the west of the panel to create `jpLabels`, and drop a `JPanel` to the center of the applet to create `jpProperties`.

3. Set the `layout` of `jpLabels` to `GridLayout` with three rows. Drop a `JLabel` three times to jpLabels to create labels "Radius," "Filled," and "Color." Set the `layout` of `jpProperties` to `GridLayout` with three rows. Drop a `JTextField`, a `JComboBox`, and a `JPanel` into `jpProperties` to create `jtfRadius`, `jcboFilled`, and `jpColor`. Set the `layout` of `jpColor` to `BorderLayout`. Drop a `JButton` and `JLabel` into the east and center of `jpColor` to create `jbtColor` and `jlblColor`. Set the button's text to the ellipses (. . .).

4. Write the code to create `jColorChooser1`, an instance of `JColorChooser` (Line 9).

5. Add a property named `model` with type `CircleModelUsingBoundProperties` using the Bean Pattern wizard. Modify the `setModel` method to register `model` and initialize value in the editor, as shown in Listing 10.9 (Lines 104–108).

6. Double-click `jtfRadius` to generate the code for handling text input. Double-click `jcbFilled` to generate the code for handling the selection of combo box values. Double-click `jbtColor` to generate the code for handling the button action. Implement these event handlers as shown in Listing 10.9 (Lines 101–109).

7. Add items True and False in the `jcbFilled` combo box (Lines 16–18).

8. Implement the `PropertyChangeListener` interface and its handler, `propertyChange`, to update the values in the editor (Lines 111–131).

```
1    package modelviewdemo;
2
3    import javax.swing.*;
4    import java.beans.*;
5    import java.awt.*;
6
7    public class CircleEditorUsingBoundProperties
8      extends javax.swing.JPanel implements PropertyChangeListener {
9      JColorChooser jColorChooser = new JColorChooser();
10     CircleModelUsingBoundProperties model;
11
12     /** Creates new form CircleEditorUsingBoundProperties */
13     public CircleEditorUsingBoundProperties() {
14       initComponents();
15
16       // Add items True and False in the combo box
17       jcboFilled.addItem("True");
18       jcboFilled.addItem("False");
19     }
20
21     private void initComponents() {
22       jpLabels = new javax.swing.JPanel();
23       jLabel1 = new javax.swing.JLabel();
24       jLabel2 = new javax.swing.JLabel();
25       jLabel3 = new javax.swing.JLabel();
26       jpProperties = new javax.swing.JPanel();
27       jtfRadius = new javax.swing.JTextField();
28       jcboFilled = new javax.swing.JComboBox();
29       jpColor = new javax.swing.JPanel();
30       jbtColor = new javax.swing.JButton();
31       jlblColor = new javax.swing.JLabel();
32       setLayout(new java.awt.BorderLayout());
33       jpLabels.setLayout(new java.awt.GridLayout(3, 0));
34       jLabel1.setText("Radius");
35       jpLabels.add(jLabel1);
36       jLabel2.setText("Filled");
37       jpLabels.add(jLabel2);
38       jLabel3.setText("Color");
39       jpLabels.add(jLabel3);
40       add(jpLabels, java.awt.BorderLayout.WEST);
```

Listing 10.9 *CircleEditorUsingBoundProperties.java*

continued

Example 10.4 continued

```
      jpProperties.setLayout(new java.awt.GridLayout(3, 0));
      jtfRadius.addActionListener(new java.awt.event.ActionListener() {
        public void actionPerformed(java.awt.event.ActionEvent evt) {
          jtfRadiusActionPerformed(evt);
        }
      });
      jpProperties.add(jtfRadius);
      jcboFilled.addActionListener(
        new java.awt.event.ActionListener() {
        public void actionPerformed(java.awt.event.ActionEvent evt) {
          jcboFilledActionPerformed(evt);
        }
      });
      jpProperties.add(jcboFilled);
      jpColor.setLayout(new java.awt.BorderLayout());
      jbtColor.setText("...");
      jbtColor.addActionListener(new java.awt.event.ActionListener() {
        public void actionPerformed(java.awt.event.ActionEvent evt) {
          jbtColorActionPerformed(evt);
        }
      });
      jpColor.add(jbtColor, java.awt.BorderLayout.EAST);
      jlblColor.setOpaque(true);
      jpColor.add(jlblColor, java.awt.BorderLayout.CENTER);
      jpProperties.add(jpColor);
      add(jpProperties, java.awt.BorderLayout.CENTER);
    }

    private void jbtColorActionPerformed(
      java.awt.event.ActionEvent evt) {
      Color selectedColor =
        JColorChooser.showDialog(this, "Choose Color",
          jlblColor.getBackground());

      if (selectedColor != null) {
        model.setColor(selectedColor);
        jlblColor.setBackground(selectedColor);
      }
    }

    private void jcboFilledActionPerformed(
      java.awt.event.ActionEvent evt) {
      if (((String)jcboFilled.getSelectedItem()).equals("True")) {
        if (model != null) model.setFilled(true);
      }
      else {
        if (model != null) model.setFilled(false);
      }
    }

    private void jtfRadiusActionPerformed(
      java.awt.event.ActionEvent evt) {
      model.setRadius(
        new Double(jtfRadius.getText()).doubleValue());
    }

    public CircleModelUsingBoundProperties getModel() {
      return model;
    }

```

Listing 10.9 *continued*

```
    public void setModel(CircleModelUsingBoundProperties model) {
      this.model = model;

      // Register listener
      if (model != null) {
        model.addPropertyChangeListener(this);
        updateEditor();
      }
    }

    public void propertyChange(PropertyChangeEvent e) {
      // TODO: implement this java.beans.PropertyChangeListener method;
      updateEditor();
    }

    /** Update property values in the editor */
    private void updateEditor() {
      // Update radius
      jtfRadius.setText(new Double(model.getRadius()).toString());

      // Update filled
      if (model.isFilled()) {
        jcboFilled.setSelectedIndex(0);
      }
      else {
        jcboFilled.setSelectedIndex(1);
      }

      // Update color
      jlblColor.setBackground(model.getColor());
    }

    // Variables declaration - do not modify
    private javax.swing.JPanel jpLabels;
    private javax.swing.JLabel jLabel1;
    private javax.swing.JLabel jLabel2;
    private javax.swing.JLabel jLabel3;
    private javax.swing.JPanel jpProperties;
    private javax.swing.JTextField jtfRadius;
    private javax.swing.JComboBox jcboFilled;
    private javax.swing.JPanel jpColor;
    private javax.swing.JButton jbtColor;
    private javax.swing.JLabel jlblColor;
    // End of variables declaration
}
```

Listing 10.9 *continued*

The following are the steps to create `CircleViewUsingBoundProperties`.

1. Create `CircleViewUsingBoundProperties` using the Forte Swing JPanel form wizard.

2. Add a property named `model` with type `CircleModelUsingBoundProperties` using the Bean Pattern wizard. Modify the `setModel` method to register `model` and initialize value in the view, as shown in Listing 10.10 (Lines 43–45).

continued

Example 10.4 continued

3. Implement the `PropertyChangeListener`, and implement the handler `propertyChange` to repaint the circle in the view (Line 37).

4. In the Events tab of the component inspector for the panel, double-click the `mouseClicked` value field to generate the handler `formMouseClicked`. Implement it as shown in Listing 10.10 (Lines 26–33).

5. Override the `paintComponent` method to draw the circle on the panel (Lines 52–72).

```
1    package modelviewdemo;
2
3    import javax.swing.*;
4    import java.beans.*;
5    import java.awt.*;
6
7    public class CircleViewUsingBoundProperties
8    extends JPanel implements PropertyChangeListener {
9      /** Holds value of property model. */
10     private CircleModelUsingBoundProperties model;
11
12     /** Creates new form CircleViewUsingBoundProperties */
13     public CircleViewUsingBoundProperties() {
14       initComponents();
15     }
16
17     private void initComponents() {
18       setLayout(new java.awt.BorderLayout());
19       addMouseListener(new java.awt.event.MouseAdapter() {
20         public void mouseClicked(java.awt.event.MouseEvent evt) {
21           formMouseClicked(evt);
22         }
23       });
24     }
25
26     private void formMouseClicked(java.awt.event.MouseEvent evt) {
27       if (model == null) return;
28
29       if (evt.isMetaDown())
30         model.setRadius(model.getRadius() - 5);
31       else
32         model.setRadius(model.getRadius() + 5);
33     }
34
35     public void propertyChange(PropertyChangeEvent evt) {
36       // TODO: implement this java.beans.PropertyChangeListener method;
37       repaint();
38     }
39
40     public void setModel(CircleModelUsingBoundProperties newModel) {
41       model = newModel;
42
43       // Register listener
44       if (model != null)
45         model.addPropertyChangeListener(this);
46     }
47
```

Listing 10.10 *CircleViewUsingBoundProperties.java*

```
    public CircleModelUsingBoundProperties getModel() {
      return model;
    }

    /** Paint the circle */
    public void paintComponent(Graphics g) {
      super.paintComponent(g);

      if (model == null) return;

      g.setColor(model.getColor());

      int xCenter = getSize().width / 2;
      int yCenter = getSize().height / 2;
      int radius = (int)model.getRadius();

      if (model.isFilled()) {
        g.fillOval(xCenter - radius, yCenter - radius,
          2 * radius, 2 * radius);
      }
      else {
        g.drawOval(xCenter - radius, yCenter - radius,
          2 * radius, 2 * radius);
      }
    }
  }
```

Listing 10.10 *continued*

Finally, let us put the model and views together to create a test program, as follows:

1. Create an applet named `TestCircleUsingBoundProperties` using the Forte Swing JApplet form wizard.
2. Drop a `CircleEditorUsingBoundProperties` to the north of the applet to create `editor`. Drop a `CircleViewUsingBoundProperties` to the center of the applet to create `view`. Set the border title of `editor` to Circle Editor, and the border title of `view` to Circle View.
3. Drop a `CircleModelUsingBoundProperties` to the form to create `circleModel`. Set the `model` property of `editor` and `view` to `circleModel` from the property editor for `model`, as shown in Figure 10.9.

The generated code for `TestCircleUsingBoundProperties` is shown in Listing 10.11.

```
package modelviewdemo;

public class TestCircleUsingBoundProperties
  extends javax.swing.JApplet {
  /** Creates new form TestCircleUsingBoundProperties */
  public TestCircleUsingBoundProperties() {
    initComponents();
  }

  private void initComponents() {
    circleModel = new modelviewdemo.
      CircleModelUsingBoundProperties();
```

Listing 10.11 *TestCircleUsingBoundProperties.java*

continued

Example 10.4 continued

```
        editor = new modelviewdemo.CircleEditorUsingBoundProperties();
        view = new modelviewdemo.CircleViewUsingBoundProperties();
        editor.setBorder(
          new javax.swing.border.TitledBorder("Circle Editor"));
        editor.setModel(circleModel);
        getContentPane().add(editor, java.awt.BorderLayout.NORTH);
        view.setBorder(
          new javax.swing.border.TitledBorder("Circle View"));
        view.setModel(circleModel);
        getContentPane().add(view, java.awt.BorderLayout.CENTER);
      }

      // Variables declaration - do not modify
      private modelviewdemo.CircleModelUsingBoundProperties circleModel;
      private modelviewdemo.CircleEditorUsingBoundProperties editor;
      private modelviewdemo.CircleViewUsingBoundProperties view;
      // End of variables declaration
    }
```

Listing 10.11 *continued*

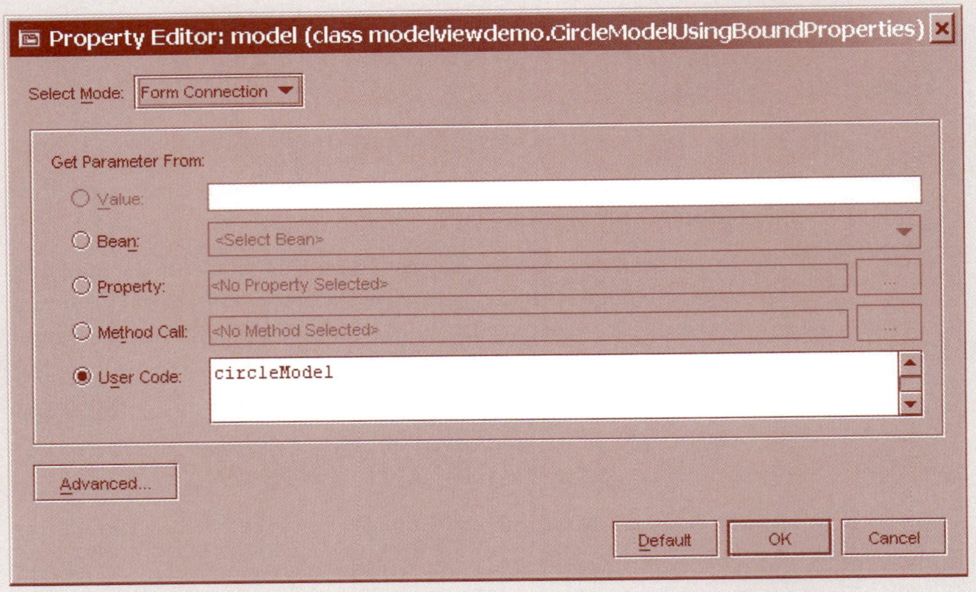

Figure 10.9 *You can set the model property for* `circleEditor` *and* `circleView` *in the property editor for* `model`.

Example Review

Through the `model` property, the objects `editor`, `view`, and `circleModel` are glued together. The property values of these objects are synchronized. A change in a property value in one object is immediately changed in the other objects.

The properties `radius`, `filled`, and `color` are defined as bound properties in the `CircleModelUsingBoundProperties` model. The editor and view are the listeners of these properties. Whenever there is a change in one of these properties, the listeners of the model are notified to update the property values through `circleModel`.

`CircleEditorUsingBoundProperties` and `CircleViewUsingBoundProperties` are both views for the data model `CircleModelUsingBoundProperties`.

`CircleEditorUsingBoundProperties` allows you to edit circle properties `radius`, `filled`, and `color`. `CircleViewUsingBoundProperties` allows you to increase the radius with a right mouse click and decrease the radius with a left mouse click.

Chapter Summary

Bound and constraint properties provide a mechanism that notifies the listener beans of changes to the properties of one bean. Constraint properties allow the listener beans to veto the change. Bound and constraint properties are useful in developing beans that are related through mutual properties.

Review Questions

10.1 Does a bound property or a constraint property use a special data type for declaration? How do you declare a bound property? How do you declare a constraint property?

10.2 Is `PropertyChangeSupport` a subclass of `PropertyChangeListener`? What are the differences between using `PropertyChangeSupport` and `PropertyChangeListener`?

Programming Exercises

10.1 Rewrite Exercise 4.4 using bound properties.

10.2 Rewrite Exercise 4.5 using bound properties.

CHAPTER 11

BEAN INTROSPECTION AND CUSTOMIZATION

Objectives

- To use a bean information class to control the properties and events of the component to be exposed in builder tools.
- To analyze beans using the `java.beans.Introspector` class.
- To develop and deploy custom property editors.
- To create custom property editors and generate `BeanInfo` classes using the Bean Pattern wizard.
- To create GUI custom property editors.
- To create customizers for editing a group of related properties.

11.1 Introduction

If your component follows the standard design patterns, the builder tool can automatically recognize the properties and events it supports through introspection of a bean during design time. You can then use the property editors from the component inspector to view and modify the bean's properties. You can also inspect the events and let the builder tool generate event listener adapters for them. The design patterns provide a simple framework that allows you to develop components that support introspection. You are not limited to using the standard patterns, however. You can choose to provide your own bean information class to describe the properties and events to be exposed, and it would supersede the standard design patterns for the properties and events.

In this chapter, you will learn how to use `BeanInfo` classes to describe beans to a builder tool, create custom editors for editing individual properties, and use customizers for editing a group of related properties.

11.2 Creating *BeanInfo* Classes

To specify component information, you need to create a class that describes your component, thereby allowing you to hide or expose properties and events, give them aliases for design purposes, and give them brief descriptions that will be visible in design tools. This class is referred to as the *bean information* class (or `BeanInfo`) for the component. The bean information class causes specified properties and events of a component to appear in the component inspector.

The bean information class can be outlined as follows:

```
public class MyClassBeanInfo implements BeanInfo {
  public BeanDescriptor getBeanDescriptor() {
    // TODO: implement this java.beans.BeanInfo method;
  }

  public EventSetDescriptor[] getEventSetDescriptors() {
    // TODO: implement this java.beans.BeanInfo method;
  }

  public int getDefaultEventIndex() {
    // TODO: implement this java.beans.BeanInfo method;
  }

  public PropertyDescriptor[] getPropertyDescriptors() {
    // TODO: implement this java.beans.BeanInfo method;
  }

  public int getDefaultPropertyIndex() {
    // TODO: implement this java.beans.BeanInfo method;
  }

  public MethodDescriptor[] getMethodDescriptors() {
    // TODO: implement this java.beans.BeanInfo method;
  }
```

```
    public BeanInfo[] getAdditionalBeanInfo() {
      // TODO: implement this java.beans.BeanInfo method;
    }

    public Image getIcon(int iconKind) {
      // TODO: implement this java.beans.BeanInfo method;
    }
  }
```

Place the bean information class in the same package with the component. By default, the bean information class should be named `<Component>BeanInfo`, which directly implements the `java.beans.BeanInfo` interface or extends the `java.beans.SimpleBeanInfo` class. The `BeanInfo` interface provides methods for learning about properties and events, and for specifying bean image icons. You can create a custom bean information class by directly implementing the `BeanInfo` interface, but it is easier to extend the `SimpleBeanInfo` class. `SimpleBeanInfo` is a support class that itself implements the `BeanInfo` interface. All the methods in `SimpleBeanInfo` return `null`. You can override these methods to provide explicit information on the properties, events, and methods of the beans.

You need to provide your own `BeanInfo` classes if—

- You have existing classes that don't follow the naming patterns for properties or events. These classes were developed before JavaBeans API was introduced.
- You don't want to give the user of your bean access to every public property at design time.
- You wish to use a particular custom editor with some property that might otherwise be assigned a default editor.

A `BeanInfo` class contains the following methods to describe bean properties, events, and other useful information to the builder tool.

- The `getPropertyDescriptors` method describes properties and returns an array of objects of the `PropertyDescriptor` class.
- The `getEventSetDescriptors` method describes event sets and returns an array of objects of the `EventSetDescriptor` class.
- The `getIcon` method describes an icon that can be used to represent the bean in the builder tool.
- The `getBeanDescriptor` method describes the customizer for the bean. The customizer is introduced in Section 11.7, "Creating Component Customizers."

To provide property information, you need to override `getPropertyDescriptors` with the code to instantiate an array of `PropertyDescriptor` objects containing information on each property of the component you want the builder tool to access.

To provide event information, you need to override `getEventSetDescriptors` with the code to instantiate an array of `EventSetDescriptor` objects containing information on each event set your bean may generate.

11.2.1 The *PropertyDescriptor* Class

A `PropertyDescriptor` object describes a property, its accessor methods, and the custom editor for the property to the builder tool. Suppose you developed the `Circle` class before the JavaBeans standards were introduced. The property `radius` of `Circle` is read and written using the methods `readRadius` and `writeRadius`, rather than the standard names `getRadius` and `setRadius`. To describe `radius` as a bean property to the builder tool, construct a `PropertyDescriptor` object, as follows:

```
new PropertyDescriptor("radius", Circle.class, "readRadius",
  "writeRadius");
```

This object describes the `radius` property in the `Circle` class with the get and set methods `readRadius` and `writeRadius`. If the accessor methods conform to the design patterns, you could simply construct a property descriptor using this constructor:

```
new PropertyDescriptor("radius", Circle.class);
```

The following instance methods of the `PropertyDescriptor` objects are useful to get property information and set custom property editors.

- `public Class getPropertyType()`

  Returns the data type of the property. The `java.lang.Class` class encapsulates the class information, including the class name, data members, methods, and superclass.

- `public Method getReadMethod()`

  Returns the method that is used to read the property if the method is defined in the component; otherwise, it returns `null`. The `java.lang.reflect.Method` class encapsulates the method information, including the method name, return type, and parameter profile.

- `public Class getPropertyEditorClass()`

  Returns a custom editor class that has been registered for this property. The custom editor class is registered using the `setPropertyEditorClass` method, as follows:

- `public void setPropertyEditorClass(Class propertyEditorClass)`

  Usually a default property editor is used. However, if for some reason you want to associate a certain property editor with a given property, you can do it with this method. You will learn how to customize editors in Section 11.4, "Customizing Property Editors."

11.2.2 The *EventSetDescriptor* Class

An `EventSetDescriptor` describes a group of events fired by the Java bean. The events in a given group are all delivered as method calls on a single event listener interface, and an event listener object can be registered via a call on a registration method supplied by the event source.

Suppose your `Circle` component fires `SmallRadiusEvent` when radius is less than 10. The listener interface of the event is `SRListener`, and two methods, `radiusChanging` and `radiusChanged`, are defined in the interface. You may create an `EventSetDescriptor` object to describe the event set to the builder tool:

```
new EventSetDesriptor(Circle.class, "SmallRadiusEvent", "SRListener",
  {"radiusChanging", "radiusChanged"},
  "addRadiusListener", "removeRadiusListener");
```

The `EventSetDescriptor` provides instance methods to get the event set information, such as the listener type (`getListenerType`) and listener registration methods (`getListenerMethods`).

11.2.3 The *MethodDescriptor* Class

A `MethodDescriptor` describes a specific method of external access from other components that is supported by a Java bean. The `MethodDescriptor` class provides the `getMethod` method for getting the method that this `MethodDescriptor` encapsulates, and the `getParameterDescriptor` method for getting the `ParameterDescriptor` for each of this `MethodDescriptor`'s method's parameters.

NOTE

Some builder tools (not Forte) allow you to inspect all the public methods; you can provide custom information on the methods by overriding the `getMethodDescriptors()` method with the code to instantiate an array of `MethodDescriptor` objects containing information on the public methods in the component.

11.2.4 Specifying Image Icons

By overriding the `getIcon()` method, whose signature is shown below, you can specify an image icon to graphically represent a bean in the component palette of a builder tool.

```
public Image getIcon(int iconKind)
```

Four types of icons are represented in the following constants:

- **`ICON_COLOR_16x16`:** A 16 x 16-pixel color icon.
- **`ICON_MONO_16x16`:** A 16 x 16-pixel monochrome icon.
- **`ICON_COLOR_32x32`:** A 32 x 32-pixel color icon.
- **`ICON_MONO_32x32`:** A 32 x 32-pixel monochrome icon.

The `iconKind` parameter is determined by the builder tool that displays the bean icon. You override the `getIcon` method with the code that loads the image based on `iconKind`. To load, use the `loadImage` method provided in the `SimpleBeanInfo` class. This method returns `null` if loading fails.

Example 11.1 Using the BeanInfo Class

This example demonstrates how to develop and use the `BeanInfo` class for a bean component. First, a new component named `Circle` will be created with a property field `radius`, whose accessor methods are deliberately named `readRadius` and `writeRadius`, neither of which follows the standard design pattern. `Circle` also has a property named `filled`, with standard accessor methods, `isFilled` and `setFilled`. Second, you will create the `CircleBeanInfo` class to describe the properties and events.

Follow the steps below to complete the project.

1. Create a new package named `beaninfodemo` under radft, and create a new class named `Circle`, as shown in Listing 11.1.

```
package beaninfodemo;

import javax.swing.*;
import java.awt.*;

public class Circle extends JPanel {
  private int radius = 30;
  private boolean filled;

  public Circle() {
  }

  public int readRadius() {
    return radius;
  }

  public void writeRadius(int radius) {
    this.radius = radius;
  }

  public boolean isFilled() {
    return filled;
  }

  public void setFilled(boolean filled) {
    this.filled = filled;
  }

  public void paintComponent(Graphics g) {
    super.paintComponent(g);

    int xCenter = getSize().width / 2;
    int yCenter = getSize().height / 2;

    if (filled)
      g.fillOval(xCenter - radius, yCenter - radius,
        2 * radius, 2 * radius);
    else
      g.drawOval(xCenter - radius, yCenter - radius,
        2 * radius, 2 * radius);
  }
}
```

Listing 11.1 *Circle.java*

2. Suppose you want the properties `radius` and `filled`, and the mouse event to be exposed to the builder tool, and you also want to provide two color icons (circle16.gif and circle32.gif) for the builder tool to use. Create `CircleBeanInfo`, as shown in Listing 11.2.

```
package beaninfodemo;

import java.beans.*;
import java.awt.event.MouseListener;
import java.awt.Image;

public class CircleBeanInfo extends SimpleBeanInfo {
  public PropertyDescriptor[] getPropertyDescriptors() {
    try {
      PropertyDescriptor pdsRadius = new PropertyDescriptor
        ("radius", Circle.class, "readRadius", "writeRadius");
      PropertyDescriptor pdsFilled = new PropertyDescriptor
        ("filled", Circle.class);
      PropertyDescriptor[] pds = {pdsRadius, pdsFilled};
      return pds;
    }
    catch (IntrospectionException e) {
      return null;
    }
  }

  public EventSetDescriptor[] getEventSetDescriptors() {
    try {
      String[] methodNames = {"mouseClicked", "mouseEntered",
        "mouseExited", "mousePressed", "mouseReleased"};
      EventSetDescriptor esMouseEvent = new EventSetDescriptor
        (Circle.class, "MouseEvent", MouseListener.class,
          methodNames, "addMouseListener", "removeMouseListener");
      EventSetDescriptor[] es = {esMouseEvent};
      return es;
    }
    catch (IntrospectionException e) {
      return null;
    }
  }

  public Image getIcon(int iconKind) {
    if (iconKind == BeanInfo.ICON_COLOR_16x16)
      return loadImage("circle16.gif");
    else if (iconKind == BeanInfo.ICON_COLOR_32x32)
      return loadImage("circle32.gif");
    return null;
  }
}
```

Listing 11.2 *CircleBeanInfo.java*

3. Install `Circle` in the component palette. Create TestCircle.java using the Swing JApplet Form wizard.

4. In the Form Editor of TestCircle.java, drop a `Circle` bean to the frame. You will see the properties `radius` and `filled` in the component inspector shown in Figure 11.1, and the `MouseEvent` handlers on the Event page of the inspector shown in Figure 11.2.

continued

Example 11.1 continued

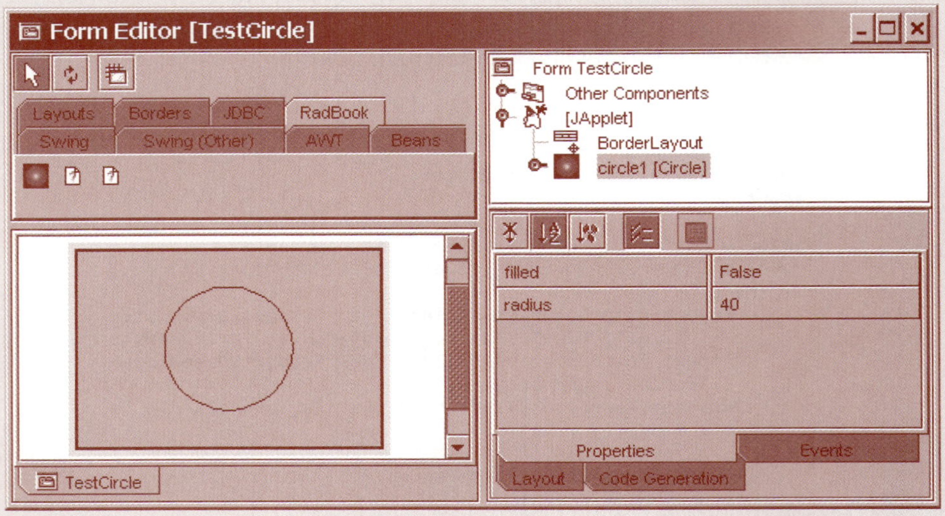

Figure 11.1 *The properties described in the* `CircleBeanInfo` *class are shown on the Properties page of the component inspector.*

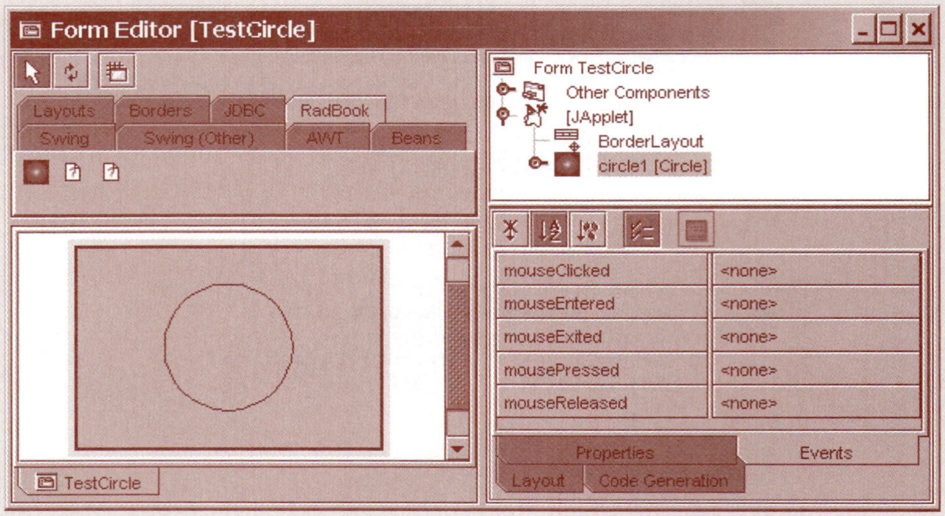

Figure 11.2 *The event listener methods described in the* `CircleBeanInfo` *classes are shown on the Events page of the component inspector.*

Example Review

The `PropertyDescriptor` object `pdsRadius`, shown below, describes property `radius` and its accessor methods, `readRadius` and `writeRadius`.

```
PropertyDescriptor pdsRadius = new PropertyDescriptor
  ("radius", Circle.class, "readRadius", "writeRadius");
```

The `PropertyDescriptor` object `pdsFilled`, shown below, indicates that the property `filled` uses its default accessor methods.

```
PropertyDescriptor pdsFilled =
  new PropertyDescriptor("filled", Circle.class);
```

The `EventSetDescriptor` object `esMouseEvent`, shown below, describes the mouse event source, mouse event name, mouse event listener, mouse event handlers, and mouse event registration methods, where `methodNames` is an array of strings containing all the handlers.

```
EventSetDescriptor esMouseEvent = new EventSetDescriptor
  (Circle.class, "MouseEvent", MouseListener.class,
   methodNames, "addMouseListener", "removeMouseListener");
```

Since the constructors for `PropertyDescriptor` and `EventSetDescriptor` may throw `IntrospectionException`, the `try/catch` block is necessary to wrap the code that invokes the constructors.

If you don't override `getPropertyDescriptors()`, the builder tool will obtain the bean properties through automatic analysis based on the design patterns. If `getPropertyDescriptors()` is overridden, only the properties described in the method are accessible in the inspector. The same principle applies to the `getEventSetDescriptors()` method.

The `CircleBeanInfo` provides two color icons for the bean. If the builder tool does not support color icons, a builder tool default icon will be used.

TIP

You may create a template of a bean info class using the BeanInfo wizard by choosing *New, Beans, BeanInfo* from the context menu of the package node in the Explorer, as shown in Figure 11.3.

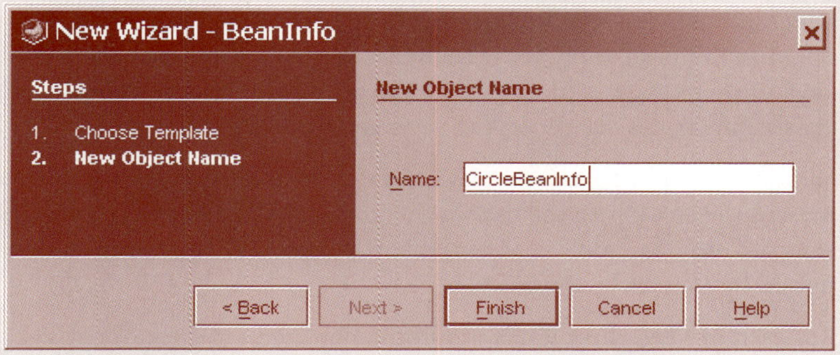

Figure 11.3 *The BeanInfo wizard can be used to create the* `BeanInfo` *class.*

continued

Example 11.1 continued

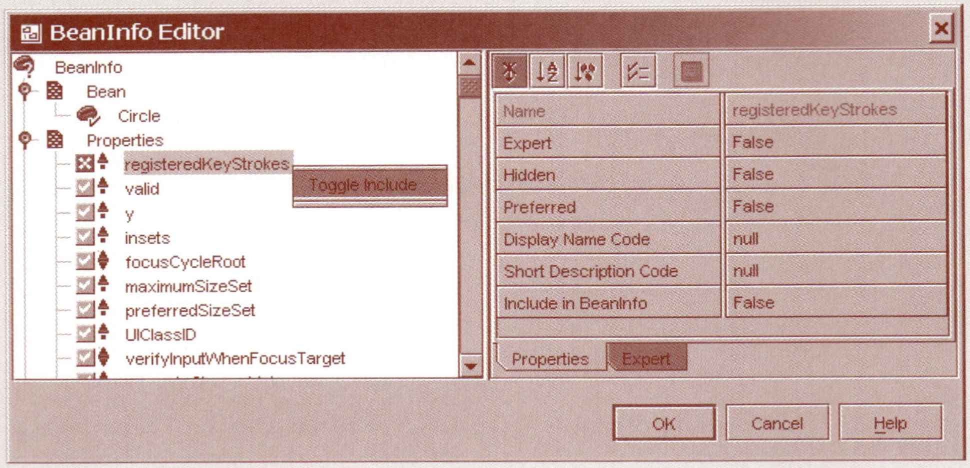

Figure 11.4 *The BeanInfo Editor can be used to edit the* `BeanInfo` *class.*

You can then use the BeanInfo Editor to edit the BeanInfo class, as shown in Figure 11.4, which can be displayed by choosing BeanInfo Editor from the context menu of the Bean Patterns node of the class in the Explorer. Click *Toggle Include* to include or exclude property from the BeanInfo class. Set the property description in the Properties tab and in the Expert tab.

11.3 Inspecting Bean Components

To programmatically discover which properties and events are exposed during *runtime* in a bean, you can use the `java.beans.Introspector` class to analyze the bean. This class uses the Java Reflection API to expose the properties, events, and methods that the bean supports. The Reflection API comprises the `Class` class in the `java.lang` package and the `Constructor`, `Field`, `Member`, `Method`, and `Modifier` classes in the `java.lang.reflect` package.

All the builder tools use the `java.beans.Introspector` class to analyze beans and present the analysis to the user in the inspector. The `Introspector` class provides a standard way for tools to learn about the properties, events, and methods supported by a target Java bean.

For each of these three kinds of information, the `Introspector` will separately analyze the bean's class and superclasses, looking for explicit or implicit information, and will use this information to build a `BeanInfo` object that comprehensively describes the target bean.

If the component's `BeanInfo` class exists, the non-null return values of the `getPropertyDescriptors`, `getEventSetDescriptors`, and `getMethodDescriptors` provide the information on the properties, event sets, and methods. If the return value is null or the component's `BeanInfo` class does not exist, the `Introspector` uses standard design patterns to analyze the bean.

To use the `Introspector` class programmatically, simply use the static method `getBeanInfo(beanClass)` in the `Introspector` class to create an object of the `BeanInfo` interface. You can then use the `BeanInfo` object's `getPropertyDescriptors()`, `getEventSetDescriptors()`, and `getMethodDescriptors()` methods to get properties, event sets, and methods.

Example 11.2 Analyzing Components

The program enables you to enter a fully qualified class name and select the type of information (properties, events, and methods). The information is displayed in a text area, as shown in Figure 11.5.

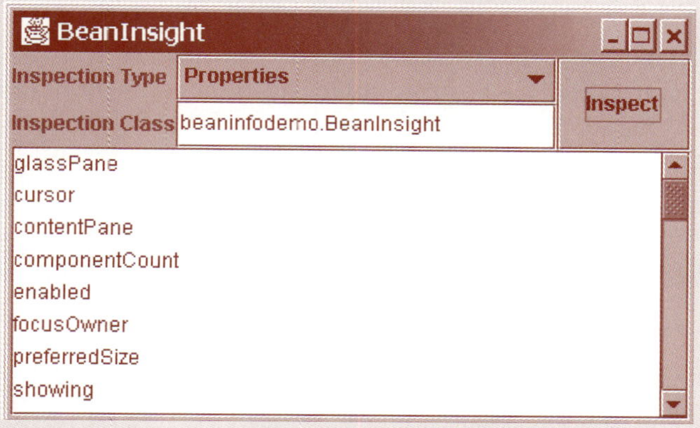

Figure 11.5 *The program lets you specify a class and choose the type of information for introspection.*

Follow the steps below to build the project.

1. In the beaninfodemo package, create BeanInsight.java using the Swing JFrame form wizard.
2. Drop a `JPanel` into the north of the frame to create `jpInspect`. Drop a `JScrollPane` to the center of the frame, and drop a `JTextArea` into the scroll pane to create `jta`.
3. Set the `layout` of `jpInspect` to `BorderLayout`. Drop a `JPanel` to the west of `jpInspect` to create `jpLabels`, drop a `JPanel` to the center of `jpInspect` to create `jpSelections`, and drop a `JButton` to the east of `jpInspect` to create `jbtInspect`.

continued

Example 11.2 continued

4. Set the `layout` of `jpLabels` to `GridLayout` with two rows, and drop a `JLabel` twice into `jpLabels` to create labels with `text` "Inspection Type" and "Inspection Class."

5. Set the `layout` of `jpSelections` to `GridLayout` with two rows. Drop a `JComboBox` into it to create `jcboTypes`, and drop a `JTextField` into it to create `jtfClass`.

6. Insert the code in the constructor to add the items into the combo box, as shown in Lines 13–15 in Listing 11.3.

```
jcboTypes.addItem("Properties");
jcboTypes.addItem("Events");
jcboTypes.addItem("Methods");
```

7. Double-click `jcboTypes` to generate the code for handling selection of inspection types. Implement the handler as shown in Listing 11.3.

8. Double-click `jbtInspect` to generate the code for inspecting the bean. Implement the handler as shown in Listing 11.3 (Line 112).

9. Hand-code the `introspectBean()` method to introspect the selected information from the component (Lines 82–108). Run BeanInsight-Application.java to test the program.

```
1   package beaninfodemo;
2
3   import java.beans.*;
4
5   public class BeanInsight extends javax.swing.JFrame {
6     // Declare introspection type
7     private String introspectionType = "Properties";
8
9     /** Creates new form BeanInsight */
10    public BeanInsight() {
11      initComponents();
12
13      jcboTypes.addItem("Properties");
14      jcboTypes.addItem("Events");
15      jcboTypes.addItem("Methods");
16    }
17
18    private void initComponents() {
19      jpInspect = new javax.swing.JPanel();
20      jpLabels = new javax.swing.JPanel();
21      jLabel2 = new javax.swing.JLabel();
22      jLabel3 = new javax.swing.JLabel();
23      jpSelections = new javax.swing.JPanel();
24      jcboTypes = new javax.swing.JComboBox();
25      jtfClass = new javax.swing.JTextField();
26      jbtInspect = new javax.swing.JButton();
27      jScrollPane1 = new javax.swing.JScrollPane();
28      jta = new javax.swing.JTextArea();
29
```

Listing 11.3 *BeanInsightFrame.java*

```
      setTitle("BeanInsight");
      addWindowListener(new java.awt.event.WindowAdapter() {
        public void windowClosing(java.awt.event.WindowEvent evt) {
          exitForm(evt);
        }
      });

      jpInspect.setLayout(new java.awt.BorderLayout());
      jpLabels.setLayout(new java.awt.GridLayout(2, 0));
      jLabel2.setText("Inspection Type");
      jpLabels.add(jLabel2);
      jLabel3.setText("Inspection Class");
      jpLabels.add(jLabel3);
      jpInspect.add(jpLabels, java.awt.BorderLayout.WEST);
      jpSelections.setLayout(new java.awt.GridLayout(2, 0));

      jcboTypes.addActionListener(new java.awt.event.ActionListener() {
        public void actionPerformed(java.awt.event.ActionEvent evt) {
          jcboTypesActionPerformed(evt);
        }
      });

      jpSelections.add(jcboTypes);
      jpSelections.add(jtfClass);
      jpInspect.add(jpSelections, java.awt.BorderLayout.CENTER);
      jbtInspect.setText("Inspect");

      jbtInspect.addActionListener(
        new java.awt.event.ActionListener() {
        public void actionPerformed(java.awt.event.ActionEvent evt) {
          jbtInspectActionPerformed(evt);
        }
      });

      jpInspect.add(jbtInspect, java.awt.BorderLayout.EAST);
      getContentPane().add(jpInspect, java.awt.BorderLayout.NORTH);
      jScrollPane1.setViewportView(jta);
      getContentPane().add(jScrollPane1,
        java.awt.BorderLayout.CENTER);
      pack();
    }

    private void jbtInspectActionPerformed(
      java.awt.event.ActionEvent evt) {
      try {
        introspectBean(Class.forName(jtfClass.getText()));
      }
      catch (ClassNotFoundException ex) {
        System.out.println("class not found");
      }
    }

    /** Invoked from the button action to introspect a bean */
    public void introspectBean(Class beanClass) {
      try {
        BeanInfo bi = Introspector.getBeanInfo(beanClass);
        if (introspectionType.equals("Properties")) {
          PropertyDescriptor[] pd = bi.getPropertyDescriptors();
          jta.setText(null);
```

Listing 11.3 *continued*

continued

Example 11.2 continued

```
          for (int i=0; i<pd.length; i++)
            jta.append(pd[i].getName() + "\n");
        }
        else if (introspectionType.equals("Events")) {
          EventSetDescriptor[] ed = bi.getEventSetDescriptors();
          jta.setText(null);
          for (int i=0; i<ed.length; i++)
            jta.append(ed[i].getName() + "\n");
        }
        else if (introspectionType.equals("Methods")) {
          MethodDescriptor[] md = bi.getMethodDescriptors();
          jta.setText(null);
          for (int i=0; i<md.length; i++)
            jta.append(md[i].getName() + "\n");
        }
      }
      catch (IntrospectionException ex) {
        System.out.println("Error during introspection");
      }
    }

    private void jcboTypesActionPerformed(
      java.awt.event.ActionEvent evt) {
      introspectionType = (String)jcboTypes.getSelectedItem();
    }

    /** Exit the Application */
    private void exitForm(java.awt.event.WindowEvent evt) {
      System.exit(0);
    }

    /**
     * @param args the command line arguments
     */
    public static void main(String args[]) {
      new BeanInsight().show();
    }

     // Variables declaration - do not modify
    private javax.swing.JPanel jpInspect;
    private javax.swing.JPanel jpLabels;
    private javax.swing.JLabel jLabel2;
    private javax.swing.JLabel jLabel3;
    private javax.swing.JPanel jpSelections;
    private javax.swing.JComboBox jcboTypes;
    private javax.swing.JTextField jtfClass;
    private javax.swing.JButton jbtInspect;
    private javax.swing.JScrollPane jScrollPane1;
    private javax.swing.JTextArea jta;
    // End of variables declaration
    }
  }
```

Listing 11.3 *continued*

Example Review

The `getBeanInfo(beanClass)` method is static and may throw `IntrospectionException`. The `Introspector` class also provides another overloaded method, `getBeanInfo(beanClass, stopClass)`, to let you introspect a Java bean and learn all about its properties, events, and methods in the class/superclass chain up to the `stopClass`.

You need to provide a fully qualified class name in the text field for introspection. For example, enter `beaninsightdemo.BeanInsight` for introspection of `BeanInsight.class`.

11.4 Customizing Property Editors

Forte provides standard editors for the properties of primitive data types, arrays of strings, and several commonly used object types, such as `Color` and `Font`. You can, however, create your own property editors to complement or customize property editing.

To create your own property editor and enable the inspector to use it to edit the property, you must—

- Create a property editor class that directly implements the `java.beans.PropertyEditor` interface or extends the `java.beans.PropertyEditorSupport` class.
- Specify that the custom editor for the property in the `BeanInfo` class is to supersede the standard editor for the property.

The `PropertyEditor` interface, shown in Figure 11.6, provides several ways to update and display property values. How property values are displayed and edited depends on which methods of the `PropertyEditor` interface you implement.

```
PropertyEditor
-----------------------------------------------------------------------
getAsText(): String
getCustomEditor(): Component
getJavaInitializationString(): String
getTags(): String[]
getValue(): Object
isPaintable(): boolean
paintValue(gfx: Graphics, box: java.awt.Rectangle): void
setAsText(text: String): void
setValue(Object value): void
supportsCustomEditor(): boolean
addPropertyChangeListener(listener: PropertyChangeListener): void
removePropertyChangeListener(listener: PropertyChangeListener): void
```

Figure 11.6 *The* `PropertyEditor` *interface provides support for the component inspector to allow users to edit a property value of a given type.*

11.4.1 Displaying Property Values

The builder tool invokes one of the following three methods in the `PropertyEditor` to display a property value:

- `public String getAsText()`

  Returns the property value as a string to be displayed in the component inspector.

- `public String[] getTags()`

  Returns a list of allowed property values to be displayed as a drop-down menu in the component inspector.

- `public void paintValue()`

  Paints a representation of the value into the value field of the property in the component inspector. You need to return `true` in the `isPaintable()` method to enable the `paintValue()` method. An example of using the `paintValue()` method is the `Color` property value, in which a small rectangle for color is displayed along with a description of the color.

11.4.2 Editing Property Values

The builder tool invokes one of the following two methods in the `PropertyEditor` to edit a property value:

- `public void setAsText(String text) throws IllegalArgumentException`

  Can be used to retrieve the value as text from the component inspector, parse the text to an appropriate value, and then invoke the `setValue` method to set the value in `PropertyEditor`. This method may throw `java.lang.IllegalArgumentException` if the `text` is badly formatted or if this kind of property cannot be expressed as text.

- `public Component getCustomEditor()`

  Returns a GUI component that serves as a custom editor for the property. Examples of such editors are the color editor and font editor in Forte.

11.4.3 Creating Property Editors

Each property editor must implement the `getJavaInitializationString()` method, which returns a string representation of the property value for use by the builder tool to generate the code for the property change. For example, if you change the `message` property for a `MessagePanel` bean in the component inspector to "Welcome to HTML," Forte generates the code `setMessage("Welcome to HTML")` in the `initComponents()` method. "Welcome to HTML" is returned by invoking the `getJavaInitializationString()` method.

Each property editor must maintain a list of event listeners that are interested in changes to the property value. When the user changes a value in the component inspector through the `setAsText` method or through a GUI editor, it must send a

PropertyChangeEvent to all registered listeners. The PropertyEditor class defines the standard event registration and removal methods addPropertyChangeListener and removePropertyChangeListener.

The PropertyEditorSupport class is often used to create custom editors. This support class implements all of the methods in the PropertyEditor interface. As an example, this is how the getAsText and setAsText methods are implemented:

```
public String getAsText() {
  return ("" + value); // Return a string
}

public void setAsText(String text)
  throws java.lang.IllegalArgumentException {
  if (value instanceof String) {
    setValue(text);
    return;
  }
  throw new java.lang.IllegalArgumentException(text);
}
```

The PropertyEditorSupport also notifies the property changes in the setValue method. This is how the setValue method is implemented:

```
public void setValue(Object value) {
  this.value = value;
  firePropertyChange();
}
```

The variable value is defined in the PropertyEditorSupport class to hold the property. The setValue method fires the PropertyChangeEvent to the builder tool so that it can respond to the property change and display the new property in the component inspector by invoking the getAsText method.

Example 11.3 Providing Custom Property Editors

This example creates a class named Student that describes student information, containing student full name, age, and gender. The full name, consisting of the first name, the middle name, and the last name, is edited using Forte's standard string editor. The example creates an editor for the age property to restrict the age to the range between 0 and 150, inclusively. For the gender property, the example provides an editor that lets the user choose Male and Female from a combo box.

The Student class with properties fullName, age, and gender is created using the Swing JPanel form wizard, and its source code is given in Listing 11.4. The properties are displayed in the text fields in a panel.

```
package beaninfodemo;

public class Student extends javax.swing.JPanel {
  // Sample student properties
  private String firstName = "Jim";
```

Listing 11.4 *Student.java*

Example 11.3 continued

```
  private String middleName = "A";
  private String lastName = "Richard";
  private int age = 19;
  private String gender = "male";

  /** Creates new form Student */
  public Student() {
      initComponents();
  }

  public String getFullName() {
    return firstName + "," + middleName + "," + lastName;
  }

  public void setFullName(String fullname) {
    java.util.StringTokenizer st =
      new java.util.StringTokenizer(fullname, ",");
    try {
      firstName = st.nextToken();
      middleName = st.nextToken();
      lastName = st.nextToken();
    }
    catch (Exception e) {
      System.out.println("Names are not formed right");
    }

    jtfName.setText(firstName + " " + middleName + " " + lastName);
  }

  public int getAge() {
    return age;
  }

  public void setAge(int age) {
    this.age = age;
    jtfAge.setText(new Integer(age).toString());
  }

  public String getGender() {
    return gender;
  }

  public void setGender(String gender) {
    this.gender = gender;
    jtfGender.setText(gender);
  }

  private void initComponents() {
    jPanel1 = new javax.swing.JPanel();
    jLabel1 = new javax.swing.JLabel();
    jLabel2 = new javax.swing.JLabel();
    jLabel4 = new javax.swing.JLabel();
    jPanel2 = new javax.swing.JPanel();
    jtfName = new javax.swing.JTextField();
    jtfAge = new javax.swing.JTextField();
    jtfGender = new javax.swing.JTextField();

```

Listing 11.4 *continued*

```
      setLayout(new java.awt.BorderLayout());
      jPanel1.setLayout(new java.awt.GridLayout(3, 0));
      jLabel1.setText("Name");
      jPanel1.add(jLabel1);
      jLabel2.setText("Age");
      jPanel1.add(jLabel2);
      jLabel4.setText("Gender");
      jPanel1.add(jLabel4);
      add(jPanel1, java.awt.BorderLayout.WEST);
      jPanel2.setLayout(new java.awt.GridLayout(3, 0));
      jPanel2.add(jtfName);
      jPanel2.add(jtfAge);
      jPanel2.add(jtfGender);
      add(jPanel2, java.awt.BorderLayout.CENTER);
    }

    // Variables declaration - do not modify
    private javax.swing.JPanel jPanel1;
    private javax.swing.JLabel jLabel1;
    private javax.swing.JLabel jLabel2;
    private javax.swing.JLabel jLabel4;
    private javax.swing.JPanel jPanel2;
    private javax.swing.JTextField jtfName;
    private javax.swing.JTextField jtfAge;
    private javax.swing.JTextField jtfGender;
    // End of variables declaration
  }
```

Listing 11.4 *continued*

The editor `AgeEditor` for editing the `age` property shown in Listing 11.5 restricts the user to enter an integer between 0 and 150 for `age`.

```
package beaninfodemo;
import java.beans.PropertyEditorSupport;

public class AgeEditor extends PropertyEditorSupport {
  /** Override this method from PropertyEditorSupport */
  public String getAsText() {
    return getValue().toString();
  }

  /** Override this method from PropertyEditorSupport */
  public void setAsText(String text)
    throws IllegalArgumentException {
    Integer val = new Integer(text);
    if (val.intValue()<= 0)
      throw new IllegalArgumentException(
        "Age may not be negative or zero");
    else if (val.intValue() >= 150)
      throw
        new IllegalArgumentException(
          "Age may not be greater than or equal to 150");
    setValue(val);
  }

  /** Override this method from PropertyEditorSupport */
  public String getJavaInitializationString() {
    return getAsText();
  }
}
```

Listing 11.5 *AgeEditor.java*

Example 11.3 continued

The editor `GenderEditor` for editing the `gender` property (see Listing 11.6) lets the user choose the value "Male" or "Female" from a combo box.

```
package beaninfodemo;

import java.beans.PropertyEditorSupport;

public class GenderEditor extends PropertyEditorSupport {
  /** Override this method from PropertyEditorSupport */
  public String[] getTags() {
    String[] choices = {"Male", "Female"};
    return choices;
  }

  /** Override this method from PropertyEditorSupport */
  public String getJavaInitializationString() {
    return "\"" + getValue().toString() + "\"";
  }
}
```

Listing 11.6 *GenderEditor.java*

As can be seen in Listing 11.7, you need to provide a `BeanInfo` class `StudentBeanInfo` to describe the custom editor to the builder tool.

```
package beaninfodemo;

import java.beans.*;

public class StudentBeanInfo extends SimpleBeanInfo {
  /** Override this method from PropertyEditorSupport */
  public PropertyDescriptor[] getPropertyDescriptors() {
    try {
      PropertyDescriptor pdsFullName = new PropertyDescriptor
        ("fullName", Student.class);
      PropertyDescriptor pdsAge = new PropertyDescriptor
        ("age", Student.class);
      pdsAge.setPropertyEditorClass(AgeEditor.class);
      PropertyDescriptor pdsGender = new PropertyDescriptor
        ("gender", Student.class);
      pdsGender.setPropertyEditorClass(GenderEditor.class);
      PropertyDescriptor[] pds = {pdsFullName, pdsAge, pdsGender};
      return pds;
    }
    catch (IntrospectionException e) {
      return null;
    }
  }
}
```

Listing 11.7 *StudentBeanInfo.java*

Follow the steps below to complete the example.

1. In the beaninfodemo package, create an applet TestSimplePropertyEditor.java using the Swing JApplet form wizard.

2. Create and compile `Student`, `AgeEditor`, `GenderEditor`, and `StudentBeanInfo`, and install `Student` in the component palette.

3. Drop a `Student` bean to the center of the applet to create `student1`.
4. With `student1` selected, test edit the `age` property by entering integers in and out of the permissible age range, and test edit the property by choosing Male or Female from a combo box, as shown in Figure 11.7.

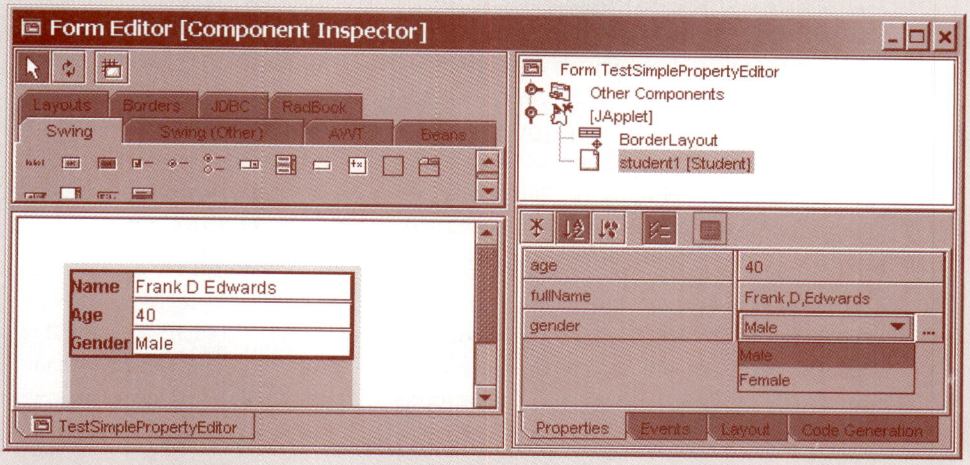

Figure 11.7 *The built-in property is used for editing* `fullName`, *and the custom property editors* `AgeEditor` *and* `GenderEditor` *are used for editing* `age` *and* `gender`.

Example Review

The `fullName` property is a string consisting of `firstName`, `middleName`, and `lastName` separated by commas, such as "Frank,D,Edwards." Adhere to this pattern when modifying the property. The property editor does not validate a change. For example, if you change the value of `fullName` to " Frank D Edwards," Forte would generate the following incorrect code in the `initComponents()` method:

```
student1.setFullName("Frank D Edwards");
```

The `AgeEditor` can validate changes in the value of the `age` property. If you enter a value that is not within the permissible range, the property editor rejects it and generates no code. To understand how this editor works, let us examine it at the component inspector. When the user presses the RETURN key with the mouse pointed at the value column of the `age` property, the builder tool invokes the property editor's `setAsText` method, which reads the value as text from the component inspector and validates the value. If the value is valid, the `setValue` method sets the value as an `Integer` object; otherwise, an `IllegalArgumentException` is raised and the change is aborted. In the case of a valid change, the builder tool invokes the `getAsText` method to get the `Integer` object and converts it into text for display on the component inspector. Finally, a builder tool generates the following code to reflect the change by invoking the `getJavaInitializationString` method:

```
student1.setAge(ageEditor.getJavaInitializationString());
```

continued

Example 11.3 continued

Here, `ageEditor` is an instance of `AgeEditor`.

The `GenderEditor` is an enumeration-type editor that allows the user to choose a value from a drop-down choice list, thus eliminating the necessity of data validation. When the user double-clicks the value column of the `gender` property, the component inspector displays a list of values by invoking the property editor's `getTags` method, which predefines a list of values for the user to choose. Upon choosing a value from the choice menu, a builder tool invokes `getAsText` to get the value and present it to the component inspector. Finally, the builder tool generates the code for setting `gender` property programmatically in the source code by invoking the `getJavaInitializationString` method, which returns the text of the selected value enclosed by double-quote symbols.

The builder tool does not recognize the custom editors unless they are described in the `BeanInfo` class. The custom editor should be stored in the same directory with the `BeanInfo` class. The `setPropertyEditor(editorClassName)` of a `PropertyDescriptor` object sets the editor for the property. The following statements in `StudentBeanInfo` set the property editors for the properties `age` and `gender`:

```
pdsAge.setPropertyEditorClass(AgeEditor.class);
pdsGender.setPropertyEditorClass(GenderEditor.class);
```

11.5 The *FeatureDescriptor* Class

The `FeatureDescriptor` class is the common base class for the bean descriptor classes, such as `PropertyDescriptor`, `EventSetDescriptor`, and `MethodDescriptor`. The following methods of the `FeatureDescriptor` class are often used to set and retrieve common information for any of the introspection descriptors in the `BeanInfo` class.

- `public void setHidden(boolean hidden)`

  Specifies whether the property is hidden. By default it is not hidden. A hidden property is not displayed in the builder tool.

- `public void setDisplayName(String displayName)`

  Sets a display name for this feature. For example, you can use it to set a display name for a property descriptor. This name is displayed as a tool tip in the inspector.

- `public void setValue(String attributeName, Object value)`

  Associates a named attribute with this feature. You can use it to associate string values to an enumeration property.

Example 11.4 Creating the `TimeZoneIDEditor` and the `BeanInfo` Class for the `Clock` Component

The `Clock` component in Example 4.2, "Creating a Clock Component," contains a `timeZoneID` property. In this example, you will create a drop-down menu for the `timeZoneID` property so that the user can select a `timeZoneID` from a list of available IDs. In the clockdemo package, create a property editor named `TimeZoneIDEditor`, as shown in Listing 11.8. Create a `BeanInfo` class named `ClockBeanInfo` for the `Clock` class, as shown in Listing 11.9.

```
package clockdemo;

import java.beans.*;
import java.util.TimeZone;

public class TimeZoneIDEditor extends PropertyEditorSupport {
  public TimeZoneIDEditor() {
  }

  /** Override this method from PropertyEditorSupport */
  public String[] getTags() {
    return TimeZone.getAvailableIDs();
  }

  /** Override this method from PropertyEditorSupport */
  public String getJavaInitializationString() {
    return "\"" + getAsText() + "\"";
  }

  public void setAsText(String text)
    throws IllegalArgumentException {
    setValue(text);
  }
}
```

Listing 11.8 *TimeZoneIDEditor.java*

```
package clockdemo;

import java.beans.*;

public class ClockBeanInfo extends SimpleBeanInfo {
  Class beanClass = Clock.class;

  public ClockBeanInfo() {
  }

  /** Specify the customizer (to be introduced in Example 11.6 */
  public BeanDescriptor getBeanDescriptor() {
    return new BeanDescriptor(Clock.class, ClockCustomizer.class);
  }

  public PropertyDescriptor[] getPropertyDescriptors() {
    try {
      PropertyDescriptor _dateStyle = new PropertyDescriptor
        ("dateStyle", beanClass, "getDateStyle", "setDateStyle");
```

Listing 11.9 *ClockBeanInfo.java*

continued

Example 11.4 continued

```
        PropertyDescriptor _digitalDateTimeColor =
          new PropertyDescriptor("digitalDateTimeColor", beanClass,
            "getDigitalDateTimeColor", "setDigitalDateTimeColor");
        PropertyDescriptor _header = new PropertyDescriptor
          ("header", beanClass, "getHeader", "setHeader");
        PropertyDescriptor _headerColor = new PropertyDescriptor
          ("headerColor", beanClass, "getHeaderColor",
          "setHeaderColor");
        PropertyDescriptor _hourHandColor = new PropertyDescriptor
          ("hourHandColor", beanClass,
           "getHourHandColor", "setHourHandColor");
        PropertyDescriptor _minuteHandColor = new PropertyDescriptor
          ("minuteHandColor", beanClass,
           "getMinuteHandColor", "setMinuteHandColor");
        PropertyDescriptor _preferredSize = new PropertyDescriptor
          ("preferredSize", beanClass, "getPreferredSize", null);
        PropertyDescriptor _running = new PropertyDescriptor
          ("running", beanClass, "isRunning", "setRunning");
        _running.setDisplayName("Enable the clock to run");
        PropertyDescriptor _secondHandColor = new PropertyDescriptor
          ("secondHandColor", beanClass,
           "getSecondHandColor", "setSecondHandColor");
        PropertyDescriptor _showingDigitalDateTime =
          new PropertyDescriptor("showingDigitalDateTime", beanClass,
           "isShowingDigitalDateTime", "setShowingDigitalDateTime");
        PropertyDescriptor _showingHeader = new PropertyDescriptor
          ("showingHeader", beanClass,
           "isShowingHeader", "setShowingHeader");
        PropertyDescriptor _timeStyle =
          new PropertyDescriptor("timeStyle",
            beanClass, "getTimeStyle", "setTimeStyle");
        PropertyDescriptor _timeZoneID = new PropertyDescriptor
          ("timeZoneID", beanClass, "getTimeZoneID", "setTimeZoneID");
        _timeZoneID.setPropertyEditorClass(
          clockdemo.TimeZoneIDEditor.class);
        PropertyDescriptor _timeZoneOffset = new PropertyDescriptor
          ("timeZoneOffset", beanClass,
           "getTimeZoneOffset", "setTimeZoneOffset");
        PropertyDescriptor _usingTimeZoneID = new PropertyDescriptor
          ("usingTimeZoneID", beanClass, "isUsingTimeZoneID",
          "setUsingTimeZoneID");

        // Set the enumeration values in the timeStyle property
        _timeStyle.setValue("enumerationValues", new Object[] {
          "FULL - 0", new Integer(0), "0",
          "LONG - 1", new Integer(1), "1",
          "MEDIUM - 2", new Integer(2), "2",
          "SHORT - 3", new Integer(3), "3",
        });

        // Set the enumeration values in the dateStyle property
        _dateStyle.setValue("enumerationValues", new Object[] {
          "FULL - 0", new Integer(0), "0",
          "LONG - 1", new Integer(1), "1",
          "MEDIUM - 2", new Integer(2), "2",
          "SHORT - 3", new Integer(3), "3",
        });

```

Listing 11.9 *continued*

```
78          PropertyDescriptor[] pds = new PropertyDescriptor[] {
79            _dateStyle,
80            _digitalDateTimeColor,
81            _header,
82            _headerColor,
83            _hourHandColor,
84            _minuteHandColor,
85            _preferredSize,
86            _running,
87            _secondHandColor,
88            _showingDigitalDateTime,
89            _showingHeader,
90            _timeStyle,
91            _timeZoneID,
92            _timeZoneOffset,
93            _usingTimeZoneID,};
94          return pds;
95        }
96        catch(IntrospectionException ex) {
97          ex.printStackTrace();
98          return null;
99        }
100     }
101
102     /** Expose PME( Properties, Methods, and Events in the superclass */
103     public BeanInfo[] getAdditionalBeanInfo() {
104       Class superclass = beanClass.getSuperclass();
105       try {
106         BeanInfo superBeanInfo = Introspector.getBeanInfo(superclass);
107         return new BeanInfo[] { superBeanInfo };
108       }
109       catch(IntrospectionException ex) {
110         ex.printStackTrace();
111         return null;
112       }
113     }
114   }
```

Listing 11.9 *continued*

Example Review

The `getTags()` method (Lines 11–13) in the TimeZoneIDEditor property editor class returns a list of available time zone IDs, which can be obtained using the `TimeZone.getAvailableIDs()` method. These IDs are displayed in a drop-down choice menu in the component inspector.

The `getAdditionalBeanInfo()` method (Lines 103–114) in the `BeanInfo` interface allows a `BeanInfo` object to return an arbitrary collection of other `BeanInfo` objects that provide additional information on the current bean. In this example, it returns the `BeanInfo` object of its superclass. If there are conflicts or overlaps between the information provided by different `BeanInfo` objects, then the current `BeanInfo` takes precedence over the `getAdditionalBeanInfo` objects, and later elements in the array take precedence over earlier ones.

continued

Example 11.4 continued

The `setDisplayName` method (Line 38) of a `PropertyDescriptor` object sets a display name for property. You can see the name in the component inspector, as shown in Figure 11.8. The `setDisplayName` method is defined in the `FeatureDescriptor` class.

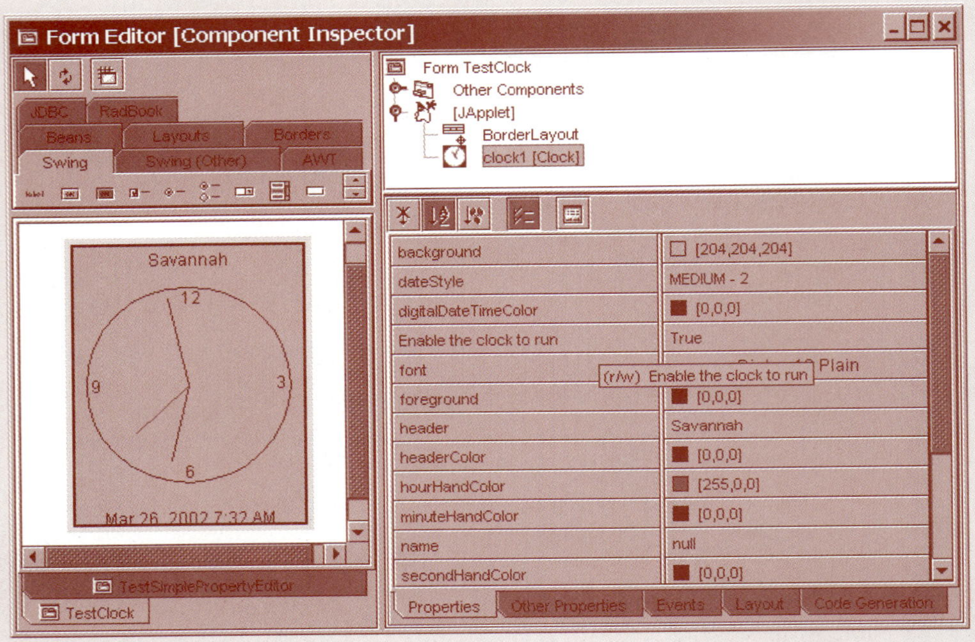

Figure 11.8 *The name "Enable the clock to run" is displayed in the component inspector for the running property.*

You can use the `setValue` method (Lines 62–76) in the `FeatureDescriptor` class to associate a property value with a string representing the value in the component inspector. For example, you can associate the `dateStyle` property values with strings using the following statement:

```
_dateStyle.setValue("enumerationValues",
  new Object[] {
   "FULL - 0", new Integer(0), "0",
   "LONG - 1", new Integer(1), "1",
   "MEDIUM - 2", new Integer(2), "2",
   "SHORT - 3", new Integer(3), "3",
  });
```

You will see strings "FULL - 0," "LONG - 1," "MEDIUM - 2," and "SHORT - 3" in the value field of `dateStyle` as a drop-down choice menu, as shown in Figure 11.9.

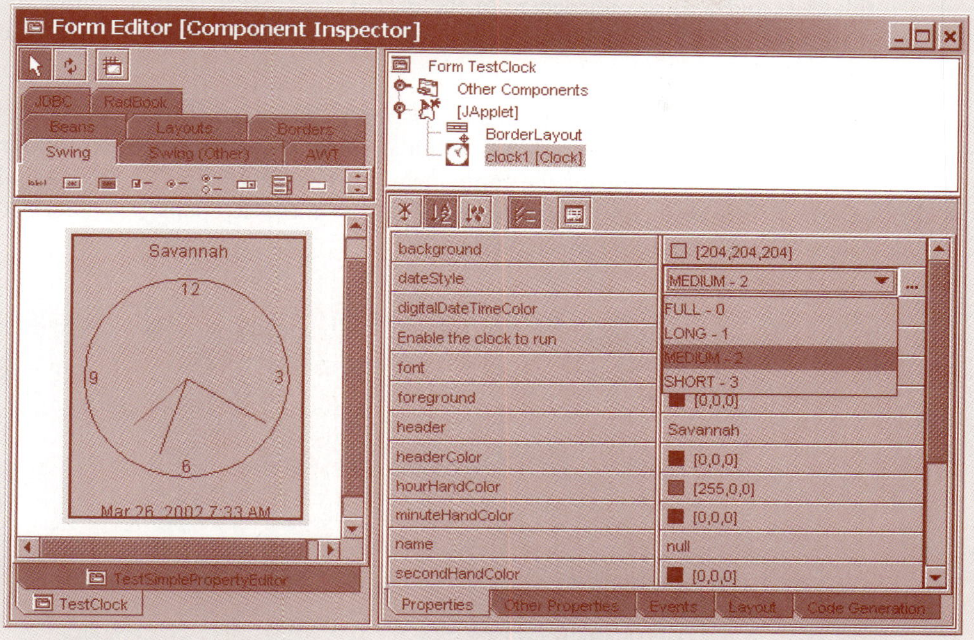

Figure 11.9 *The* `dateStyle` *property values (0, 1, 2, 3) are represented by strings in a drop-down choice menu.*

11.6 Creating GUI Custom Editors

While standard editors, customized simple editors, or enumeration-type editors will meet most of your needs, there are situations in which you might want to use more specialized and sophisticated editors. For example, the `Color` editor allows you to choose colors visually for a property of the `Color` type. The property with advanced editors appears in the component inspector with an ellipsis at the right of the value column when the property is selected. The editor pops up a GUI component when the user clicks the ellipsis. Therefore, the advanced editor is also referred to as a *popup property editor* or GUI property editor.

To create a GUI property editor like the `Color` editor, override the methods `supportsCustomEditor()` and `getCustomEditor()` in addition to other methods in the `PropertyEditorSupport` class that you may need to use.

By default, `supportsCustomEditor()` returns `false`. To use a GUI editor, this method must return `true` to enable a builder tool to invoke the `getCustomEditor()` method to start the GUI editor.

By default, `getCustomEditor()` returns `null`. You need to implement `getCustomEditor()` to return a `Component` as the GUI editor. You need to create a class that extends `Component` or a subclass of `Component` so that you can create an object of this class and have it returned from the `getCustomEditor()` method. Forte automatically creates a standard dialog box to hold the object, as in the `Color` editor shown in Figure 11.10.

The dialog window has four buttons: "Advanced," "Default," "OK," and "Cancel." "Advanced" opens the Advanced Code Initialization dialog that enables you to initialize the property value for the component, as shown in Figure 11.11. "Default" sets the default value for the component. "OK" signifies acceptance of the selected value. "Cancel" voids the selected value.

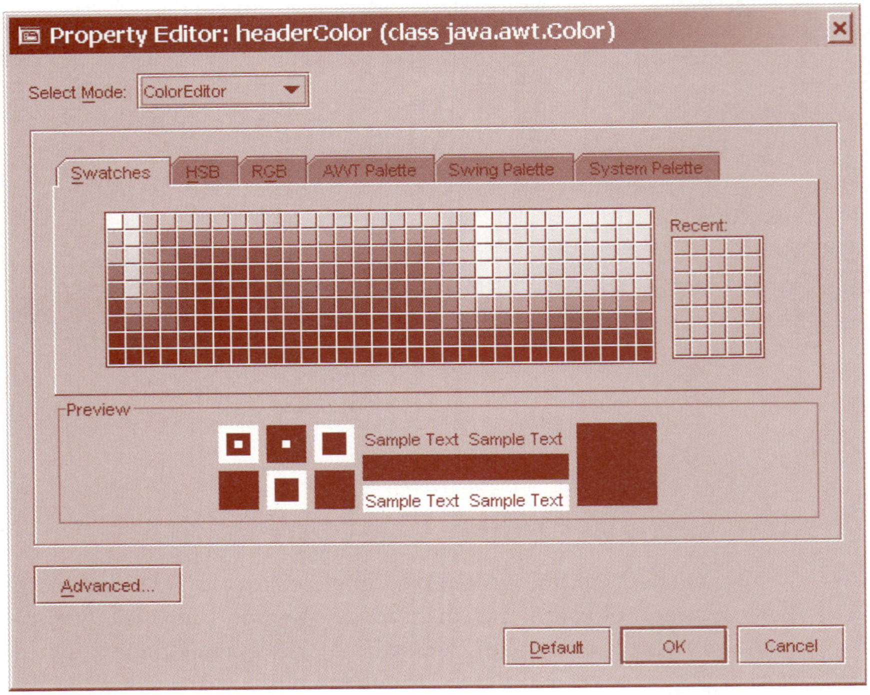

Figure 11.10 *The editor is placed in the dialog box created by Forte.*

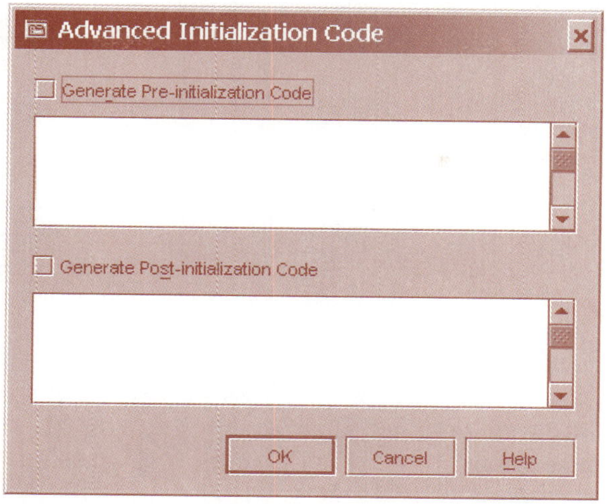

Figure 11.11 *The Advanced Initialization Code dialog box enables you to initialize the properties for the component.*

Example 11.5 Creating GUI Property Editors

This example creates an editor for selecting an image file. The editor enables the user to browse a set of eight images and select one of them. A sample run of the property editor is shown in Figure 11.12.

The example involves the following classes:

`ImageViewer`: This is the component for displaying an image. It was developed in Example 4.1, "Creating an Image Viewer." The component contains five properties: `image`, `imageFilename`, `stretched`, `xCoordinate`, and `yCoordinate`. The `image` property specifies the image to be displayed. The `imageFilename` property specifies the filename for the image to be displayed. You can set images using either the `image` property or the `imageFilename` property. The `stretched` property indicates whether the image is stretched to fill in the entire viewing area. The `xCoordinate` and `yCoordinate` properties specify the upper-left corner of the image.

`ImageFilenameEditor`: This is the property editor for `imageFilename`. It extends `PropertyEditorSupport` and contains an object of `ImageFilenameGUIEditor` as the GUI editor. The complete code of this class is shown in Listing 11.10.

`ImageFilenameGUIEditor`: This is the GUI component for choosing `imageFilename`. It extends `JPanel` and implements `MouseListener`. It displays eight images for selection using the mouse. An instance of this class is returned from the `getCustomEditor()` method. A builder tool invokes `getCustomEditor()` to get the GUI editor and display it from the component inspector. The complete code of this class is shown in Listing 11.11.

continued

Example 11.5 continued

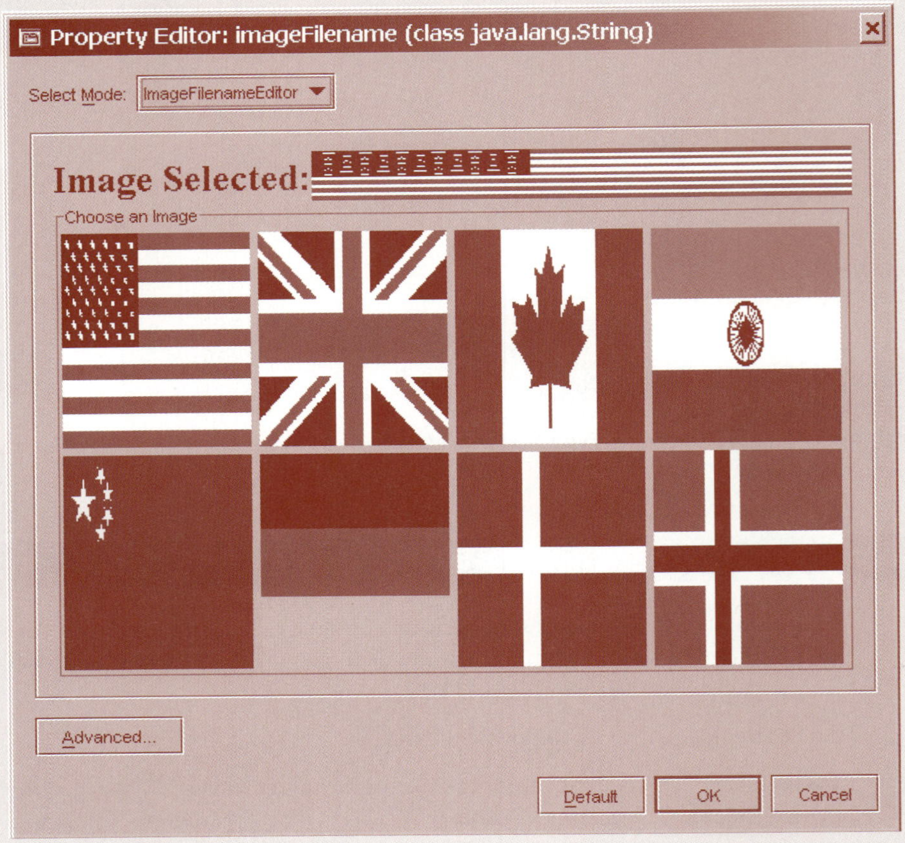

Figure 11.12 *The user selects an image by pointing the mouse, double-clicking on the image, and pressing OK.*

`ImageViewerBeanInfo`: This is the `BeanInfo` class for `ImageViewer`. It describes all the properties of the `ImageViewer` class and the GUI property editor for `imageFilename` to the builder tool. The complete code of this class is shown in Listing 11.12.

`TestImageViewer`: This is for testing the `ImageViewer` class and its supporting classes: `ImageFilenameEditor`, `ImageFilenameGUIEditor`, and `ImageViewerBeanInfo`.

```
package guipropertyeditordemo;

import java.awt.*;
import java.beans.*;

public class ImageFilenameEditor extends PropertyEditorSupport {
  private String imageFilename = "";
```

Listing 11.10 *ImageFilenameEditor.java*

```
  private ImageFilenameGUIEditor guiEditor;

  /** Override this method from PropertyEditorSupport */
  public void setAsText(String text) {
    setValue(text);
  }

  /** Override this method from PropertyEditorSupport */
  public void setValue(Object o) {
    imageFilename = (String)o;
    if (guiEditor != null)
         guiEditor.imageFilename = imageFilename;

    firePropertyChange();
  }

  /** Override this method from PropertyEditorSupport */
  public Object getValue() {
    if (guiEditor != null)
      this.imageFilename = guiEditor.imageFilename;

    return imageFilename;
  }

  /** Override this method from PropertyEditorSupport */
  public String getAsText() {
    return imageFilename;
  }

  /** Override this method from PropertyEditorSupport */
  public boolean supportsCustomEditor() {
    return true;
  }

  /** Override this method from PropertyEditorSupport */
  public Component getCustomEditor() {
    if (guiEditor == null)
      guiEditor =  new ImageFilenameGUIEditor(imageFilename);
    return guiEditor;
  }

  /** Override this method from PropertyEditorSupport */
  public String getJavaInitializationString() {
    return "\"" + getAsText() + "\"";
  }
}
```

Listing 11.10 *continued*

```
package guipropertyeditordemo;

import java.awt.*;
import java.awt.event.*;
import javax.swing.*;
import javax.swing.border.*;

public class ImageFilenameGUIEditor extends JPanel
  implements MouseListener {
  private ImageViewer selectedImageViewer = new ImageViewer();
  String imageFilename = "";

```

Listing 11.11 *ImageFilenameGUIEditor.java*

continued

Example 11.5 continued

```
  public ImageFilenameGUIEditor(String imageFilename) {
    // Create panel p for holding images for selection
    JPanel p = new JPanel();
    p.setLayout(new GridLayout(2, 4, 5, 5));
    p.setBorder(new TitledBorder("Choose an Image"));

    // Place images in the panel p
    ImageViewer[] imageViewers = new ImageViewer[8];
    for (int i = 0; i < 8; i++) {
      imageViewers[i] = new ImageViewer();
      imageViewers[i].addMouseListener(this);
      p.add(imageViewers[i]);
    }

    imageViewers[0].setImageFilename("/image/us.gif");
    imageViewers[1].setImageFilename("/image/uk.gif");
    imageViewers[2].setImageFilename("/image/ca.gif");
    imageViewers[3].setImageFilename("/image/india.gif");
    imageViewers[4].setImageFilename("/image/china.gif");
    imageViewers[5].setImageFilename("/image/germany.gif");
    imageViewers[6].setImageFilename("/image/denmark.gif");
    imageViewers[7].setImageFilename("/image/norway.gif");

    // Panel p1 for organizing the selected image
    JPanel p1 = new JPanel();
    p1.setLayout(new BorderLayout());

    // Create a label
    JLabel jlbl;
    p1.add(jlbl = new JLabel("Image Selected:"), BorderLayout.WEST);
    jlbl.setFont(new Font("TimesRoman", Font.BOLD, 24));

    // Create selectedImageViewer
    selectedImageViewer.setBackground(Color.yellow);
    selectedImageViewer.setImageFilename(imageFilename);
    p1.add(selectedImageViewer, BorderLayout.CENTER);

    // Place p and p1 in the main panel
    this.setLayout(new BorderLayout());
    this.add(p1, BorderLayout.NORTH);
    this.add(p, BorderLayout.CENTER);
  }

  /** Override this method from JPanel */
  public Dimension getPreferredSize() {
    return new Dimension(350, 150);
  }

  public void mouseClicked(MouseEvent e) {
    ImageViewer imageViewer = (ImageViewer)e.getComponent();
    imageFilename = imageViewer.getImageFilename();
    selectedImageViewer.setImageFilename(imageFilename);
  }

  public void mousePressed(MouseEvent e) {
  }

```

Listing 11.11 *continued*

```
    public void mouseReleased(MouseEvent e) {
    }

    public void mouseEntered(MouseEvent e) {
    }

    public void mouseExited(MouseEvent e) {
    }
  }
```

Listing 11.11 *continued*

```
package guipropertyeditordemo;

import java.beans.*;

public class ImageViewerBeanInfo extends SimpleBeanInfo {
  Class beanClass = ImageViewer.class;

  public ImageViewerBeanInfo() {
  }

  public PropertyDescriptor[] getPropertyDescriptors() {
    try {
      PropertyDescriptor _image = new PropertyDescriptor("image",
        beanClass, "getImage", "setImage");
      PropertyDescriptor _imageFilename = new PropertyDescriptor(
        "imageFilename", beanClass, "getImageFilename",
        "setImageFilename");
      _imageFilename.setPropertyEditorClass(
        ImageFilenameEditor.class);
      PropertyDescriptor _stretched = new PropertyDescriptor(
        "stretched", beanClass, "isStretched", "setStretched");
      PropertyDescriptor _XCoordinate = new PropertyDescriptor(
        "XCoordinate", beanClass, "getXCoordinate",
        "setXCoordinate");
      PropertyDescriptor _YCoordinate = new PropertyDescriptor(
        "YCoordinate", beanClass, "getYCoordinate",
          "setYCoordinate");
      PropertyDescriptor[] pds = new PropertyDescriptor[] {
          _image,
          _imageFilename,
          _stretched,
          _XCoordinate,
          _YCoordinate};
      return pds;
    }
    catch(IntrospectionException ex) {
      ex.printStackTrace();
      return null;
    }
  }

  public BeanInfo[] getAdditionalBeanInfo() {
    Class superclass = beanClass.getSuperclass();
    try {
      BeanInfo superBeanInfo = Introspector.getBeanInfo(superclass);
      return new BeanInfo[] { superBeanInfo };
    }
```

Listing 11.12 *ImageViewerBeanInfo.java*

continued

Example 11.5 continued

```
        catch(IntrospectionException ex) {
          ex.printStackTrace();
          return null;
        }
      }
    }
```

Listing 11.12 *continued*

Follow the steps below to complete the example.

1. Create a new package named guipropertyeditordemo.
2. Create and compile `ImageViewer`, `ImageFilenameEditor`, `ImageFilenameGUIEditor`, and `ImageViewerBeanInfo`, and install `ImageViewer` in the component palette.
3. Create TestImageViewer.java using the Swing JApplet form wizard. Drop a `JTabbedPane` from the Swing tab to the applet to create `jTabbedPane1`.
4. Drop an *ImageViewer* from the component palette four times into `jTabbedPane1` to create `imageViewer1`, `imageViewer2`, `imageViewer3`, and `imageViewer4`.
5. In the Layout tab of `imageViewer1` in the component inspector, set Tab Title to US, as shown in Figure 11.13. Double-click the ellipsis button in the value field of the *imageFilename* property to display the editor for *imageFilename*, as shown in Figure 11.12. Double-click the first image icon and then press OK; you will see the new image displayed in `imageViewer1` and `imageViewer1.setImageFilename("/image/us.gif")` inserted in the `initComponents` method. The filename /image/us.gif now appears in the imageFilename, as shown in Figure 11.14.

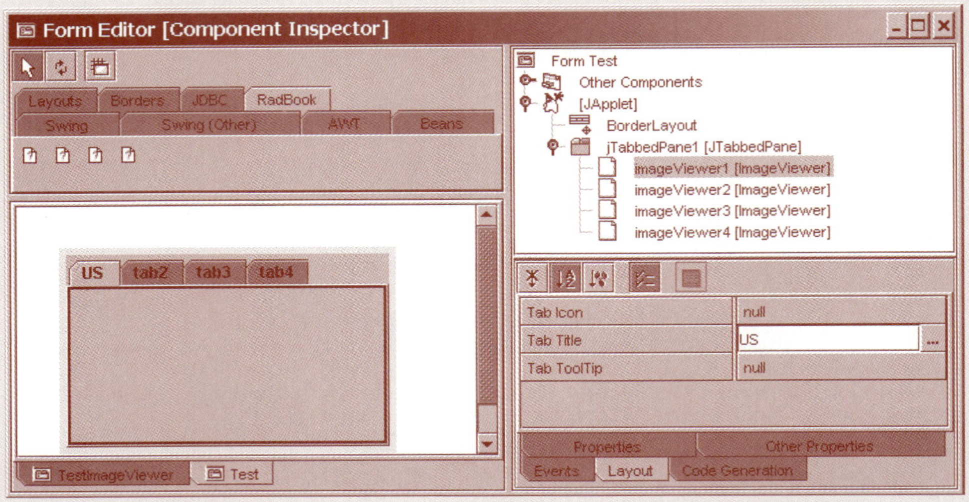

Figure 11.13 *You can set the tab title for the component inside a* `JTablePane` *in the Layout tab of the component inspector.*

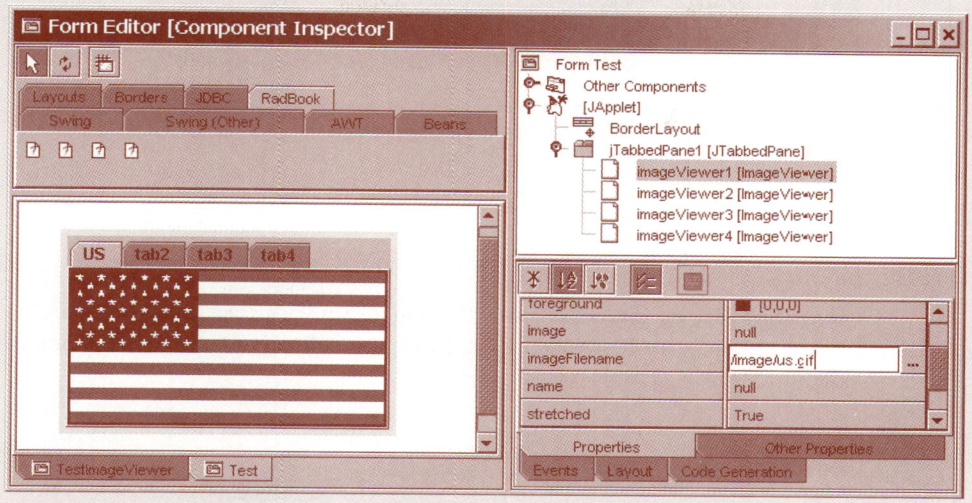

Figure 11.14 *The* `imageFilename` *is selected from a GUI property editor, which is shown in Figure 11.12.*

6. Repeat Step 5 for `imageViewer2`, `imageViewer3`, and `imageViewer4`; choose an image from the editor.

7. Run the program. Select four tabs in the tab set panel to see the images. The complete code for TestImageViewer.java is shown in Listing 11.13.

```
package guipropertyeditordemo;

public class TestImageViewer extends javax.swing.JApplet {
  /** Creates new form TestImageViewer */
  public TestImageViewer() {
    initComponents();
  }

  private void initComponents() {
    jTabbedPane1 = new javax.swing.JTabbedPane();
    imageViewer1 = new guipropertyeditordemo.ImageViewer();
    imageViewer2 = new guipropertyeditordemo.ImageViewer();
    imageViewer3 = new guipropertyeditordemo.ImageViewer();
    imageViewer4 = new guipropertyeditordemo.ImageViewer();
    imageViewer1.setImageFilename("/image/us.gif");
    jTabbedPane1.addTab("US", imageViewer1);
    imageViewer2.setImageFilename("/image/uk.gif");
    jTabbedPane1.addTab("UK", imageViewer2);
    imageViewer3.setImageFilename("/image/ca.gif");
    jTabbedPane1.addTab("Canada", imageViewer3);
    imageViewer4.setImageFilename("/image/india.gif");
    jTabbedPane1.addTab("India", imageViewer4);
    getContentPane().add(jTabbedPane1, java.awt.BorderLayout.CENTER);
  }

  // Variables declaration - do not modify
  private javax.swing.JTabbedPane jTabbedPane1;
```

Listing 11.13 *TestImageViewer.java*

continued

Example 11.5 continued

```
        private guipropertyeditordemo.ImageViewer imageViewer1;
        private guipropertyeditordemo.ImageViewer imageViewer2;
        private guipropertyeditordemo.ImageViewer imageViewer3;
        private guipropertyeditordemo.ImageViewer imageViewer4;
        // End of variables declaration
    }
```

Listing 11.13 *continued*

Example Review

The `ImageFilenameEditor` class, extending `PropertyEditorSupport`, facilitates intercommunication between the GUI property editor and the builder tool, as shown in Figure 11.15.

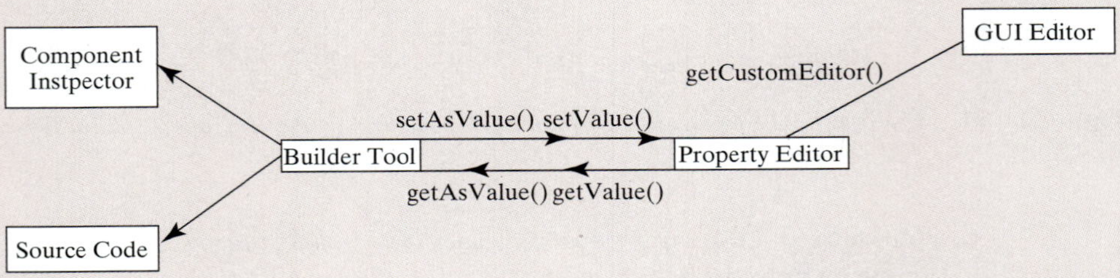

Figure 11.15 *The user selects an image from the GUI editor; the builder tool displays the image file name on the component inspector and updates the source code for setting the image in* `initComponents`.

Since `supportsCustomEditor()` (Line 39 in Listing 11.10) returns `true`, the GUI property editor `guiEditor` (an instance of `ImageFilenameGUIEditor`) is used for editing `guiEditor.imageFilename`, which lets the user choose an image graphically and sets the corresponding file name for the image in `guiEditor.imageFilename`.

The `getValue()` method (Lines 24–30) returns the `imageFilename` value chosen from the `guiEditor` instance, and `getAsText()` (Lines 32–35) returns `imageFilename` as a string. The `setAsText()` method (Lines 10–13) invokes `setValue()` to set `imageFilename` from the component inspector to `guiEditor. imageFilename`.

The `ImageViewerBeanInfo` class describes the `imageFilename` property of the `ImageViewer` class and specifies its custom editor `ImageFilenameEditor`.

`TestImageViewer` uses a `JTabbedPane` to hold four instances of `ImageViewer`. The `ImageFilenameEditor`, `ImageFilenameGUIEditor`, and `ImageViewerBeanInfo` classes are used only during design time and are not needed at runtime.

Note
The images are not displayed in the form or in the GUI property the first time because of a bug in Forte. To see the images, restart Forte.

NOTE
Forte requires that a property be a noncontainer in order for a GUI custom editor to work correctly. Since `ImageViewer` extends `Component`, it is not a subclass of `Container`. If `ImageViewer` were a subclass of `Container`, the GUI editor would not be displayed.

NOTE
Since `ImageViewer` and its bean info class, `ImageViewerBeanInfo`, must be in the same folder, the `ImageViewer` that was used in Example 4.1 was copied into the guipropertyeditordemo package.

11.7 Creating Component Customizers

Bean properties can be edited with default property editors, custom property editors, or GUI property editors. Property editors enable you to edit single property values in the component inspector, so that all the properties are edited independently. Some properties, however, are related. The value of one property may affect the selection of values for other properties. For example, the `Clock` component contains the properties `showingDigitalDateTime`, `dateStyle`, and `timeStyle`. These three properties are related. You do not have to set `dateStyle` and `timeStyle` if `showingDigitalDateTime` is false. It would be nice to disable the selection of `dateStyle` and `timeStyle` when `showingDigitalDateTime` is false. This feature cannot be implemented by property editors, but it can be done with customizers.

A *customizer* is a GUI component that makes it possible to edit all the properties in a group of properties at once. You can implement the rules of editing in a customizer to edit the properties interactively. A customizer is usually a panel displayed in a dialog box created by the builder tool. A customizer is not limited to just one window. You can create many wizard-like dialog boxes to collect information from the user and edit the properties based on the user's responses.

A customizer must implement the `Customizer` interface. The `Customizer` interface contains the following three methods:

- `public abstract void setObject(Object bean)`

  Passes the bean to be customized to the customizer, so that it can find the state of the bean, update the bean, and interact with the bean. The builder tool starts a customizer by invoking this method.

- `public abstract void addPropertyChangeListener(PropertyChangeListener listener)`

  Registers a listener for the `PropertyChange` event. When a builder tool starts a customizer, it creates an instance of the customizer and registers a listener to listen for property changes by invoking this method. Whenever a property is changed, the customizer should fire a `PropertyChange` event to notify the builder tool so that it can update the bean accordingly.

- `public abstract void removePropertyChangeListener(PropertyChangeListener listener)`

  Removes a listener for the `PropertyChange` event.

By convention, the name of a customizer should be the same as the name of the component it customizes, with "Customizer" appended to it. For example, if your component is named `Clock`, the customizer should be named `ClockCustomizer`. Following this naming convention, a customizer can be automatically recognized by builder tools without the need to create a `BeanInfo` class. If a `BeanInfo` class is used to describe a component, you have to specify the name of the customizer in the `getBeanDescriptor()` method. For example, since you created `ClockBeanInfo` for the `Clock` class, you must implement the `getBeanDescriptor()` method in the `ClockBeanInfo` class, as follows:

```
public BeanDescriptor getBeanDescriptor() {
  return new BeanDescriptor(Clock.class, ClockCustomizer.class);
}
```

Finally, how does a user start a customizer? It depends on the builder tool. In Forte, you start the customizer as follows:

1. Select the bean in the component tree or in the form.
2. In the context menu of the component, choose *Customize* to display the Customizer dialog box. (If the bean does not have a customizer, its context menu does not contain the Customize command.)

Example 11.6 Creating a Customizer for the `Clock` Component

In this example, a customizer is created to set values for properties `showingDigitalDateTime`, `dateStyle`, and `timeStyle` in the `Clock` component, as shown in Figure 11.16.

Follow the steps below to complete the example.

1. In the clockdemo package, create `ClockCustomizer` using the Swing JPanel form wizard that implements `java.bean.Customizer` and `java.awt.event.ItemListener`.
2. Set the `layout` of `ClockCustomizer` to `BorderLayout`. Drop a `JCheckBox` to the south of `ClockCustomizer` to create `jCheckBox1`. Set `jCheckBox1`'s horizontal alignment to CENTER.
3. Drop a `JPanel` to the center of `ClockCustomizer` to create `jPanel1` with `GridLayout` that has one row and two columns. Drop a `JPanel` twice into `jPanel1` to create `jPanel2` and `jPanel3`. Rename `jPanel2` to `jpDateStyle`, `jPanel3` to `jpTimeStyle`. In the inspector for `jpDateStyle`, click the ellipsis

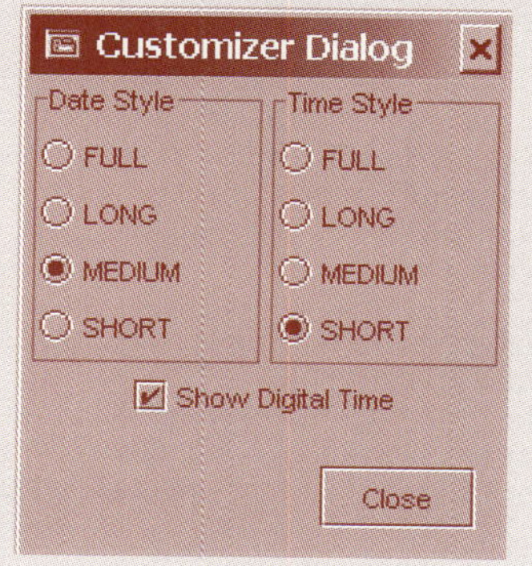

Figure 11.16 *This customizer enables you to set values for properties that specify whether and how to display a digital date and time in a clock.*

button in the value field of the `border` property to display the GUI property editor for border. Choose titledBorder and set the Title property to Date Style. Similarly, create a border titled "Time Style" for `jpTimeStyle`.

4. Set the `layout` of `jpDateStyle` to `GridLayout` with four rows. Drop a `JRadioButton` four times to `jpDateStyle` to create `jRadioButton1`, `jRadioButton2`, `jRadioButton3`, and `jRadioButton4`. Set the `text` property of the buttons to `FULL`, `LONG`, `MEDIUM`, and `SHORT`, respectively. Similarly, add four instances of `JRadioButton` named `jRadioButton5`, `jRadioButton6`, `jRadioButton7`, and `jRadioButton8` with text FULL, LONG, MEDIUM, and SHORT into the `jpTimeStyle` panel of the `GridLayout` of four rows.

5. Drop a `ButtonGroup` twice into the form to create `jButtonGroup1` and `jButtonGroup2`. Set the `buttonGroup` property of `jRadioButton1`, `jRadioButton2`, `jRadioButton3`, and `jRadioButton4` to `jButtonGroup1`, and set the `buttonGroup` property of `jRadioButton5`, `jRadioButton6`, `jRadioButton7`, and `jRadioButton8` to `jButtonGroup2`.

6. Declare and create an instance of `PropertyChangeSupport`, and implement the methods `setObject`, `addPropertyChangeListener`, and `removePropertyChangeListener` (from the `Customizer` interface), as shown in Listing 11.14 (Lines 77–134).

7. Register the customizer (`this`) as the listener for all the radio buttons and the check box (Lines 89–98). Implement the `itemStateChanged` handler (from the `ItemListener` interface) to process the change in the state of the check box and eight radio buttons, as shown in Listing 11.14 (Lines 136–203).

```
1    package clockdemo;
2
3    import java.beans.*;
4    import java.awt.event.*;
5    import javax.swing.*;
6
```

Listing 11.14 *ClockCustomizer.java*

continued

Example 11.6 continued

```
public class ClockCustomizer extends java.awt.Panel implements
  java.beans.Customizer, java.awt.event.ItemListener {
  // Declare a variable for notifying property change
  PropertyChangeSupport pcs = null;
  // Declare a variable for Clock
  Clock clock = null;

  /** Creates new form ClockCustomizer */
  public ClockCustomizer() {
    // Delete the code for invoking initComponents here.
    // initComponents() should be invoked from setObject(),
    // because setObject() must be called before initComponents.
  }

  private void initComponents() {
    buttonGroup1 = new javax.swing.ButtonGroup();
    buttonGroup2 = new javax.swing.ButtonGroup();
    jCheckBox1 = new javax.swing.JCheckBox();
    jPanel1 = new javax.swing.JPanel();
    jpDateStyle = new javax.swing.JPanel();
    jRadioButton1 = new javax.swing.JRadioButton();
    jRadioButton2 = new javax.swing.JRadioButton();
    jRadioButton3 = new javax.swing.JRadioButton();
    jRadioButton4 = new javax.swing.JRadioButton();
    jpTimeStyle = new javax.swing.JPanel();
    jRadioButton5 = new javax.swing.JRadioButton();
    jRadioButton6 = new javax.swing.JRadioButton();
    jRadioButton7 = new javax.swing.JRadioButton();
    jRadioButton8 = new javax.swing.JRadioButton();
    setLayout(new java.awt.BorderLayout());
    jCheckBox1.setText("jCheckBox1");
    jCheckBox1.setHorizontalAlignment(
      javax.swing.SwingConstants.CENTER);
    add(jCheckBox1, java.awt.BorderLayout.SOUTH);
    jPanel1.setLayout(new java.awt.GridLayout(1, 0));
    jpDateStyle.setLayout(new java.awt.GridLayout(4, 0));
    jpDateStyle.setBorder(
      new javax.swing.border.TitledBorder("Date Style"));
    jRadioButton1.setText("FULL");
    buttonGroup1.add(jRadioButton1);
    jpDateStyle.add(jRadioButton1);
    jRadioButton2.setText("LONG");
    buttonGroup1.add(jRadioButton2);
    jpDateStyle.add(jRadioButton2);
    jRadioButton3.setText("MEDIUM");
    buttonGroup1.add(jRadioButton3);
    jpDateStyle.add(jRadioButton3);
    jRadioButton4.setText("SHORT");
    buttonGroup1.add(jRadioButton4);
    jpDateStyle.add(jRadioButton4);
    jPanel1.add(jpDateStyle);
    jpTimeStyle.setLayout(new java.awt.GridLayout(4, 0));
    jpTimeStyle.setBorder(
      new javax.swing.border.TitledBorder("Time Style"));
    jRadioButton5.setText("FULL");
    buttonGroup2.add(jRadioButton5);
    jpTimeStyle.add(jRadioButton5);
    jRadioButton6.setText("LONG");
    buttonGroup2.add(jRadioButton6);
```

Listing 11.14 *continued*

```
    jpTimeStyle.add(jRadioButton6);
    jRadioButton7.setText("MEDIUM");
    buttonGroup2.add(jRadioButton7);
    jpTimeStyle.add(jRadioButton7);
    jRadioButton8.setText("SHORT");
    buttonGroup2.add(jRadioButton8);
    jpTimeStyle.add(jRadioButton8);
    jPanel1.add(jpTimeStyle);
    add(jPanel1, java.awt.BorderLayout.CENTER);
  }

  public void setObject(Object bean) {
    // TODO: implement this java.beans.Customizer method;
    // initComponents is fired from here instead of the constructor
    // because it is assumed in the Beans Spec that setObject() is
    //called first.
    try {
      initComponents();
    }
    catch (Exception e) {
      e.printStackTrace();
    }

    // Register listeners
    jRadioButton1.addItemListener(this);
    jRadioButton2.addItemListener(this);
    jRadioButton3.addItemListener(this);
    jRadioButton4.addItemListener(this);
    jRadioButton5.addItemListener(this);
    jRadioButton6.addItemListener(this);
    jRadioButton7.addItemListener(this);
    jRadioButton8.addItemListener(this);
    jCheckBox1.addItemListener(this);

    if(bean instanceof Clock) {
      clock = (Clock)bean;

      jCheckBox1.setSelected(clock.isShowingDigitalDateTime());

      switch (clock.getDateStyle()) {
        case 0: jRadioButton1.setSelected(true); break;
        case 1: jRadioButton2.setSelected(true); break;
        case 2: jRadioButton3.setSelected(true); break;
        case 3: jRadioButton4.setSelected(true); break;
      }

      switch (clock.getTimeStyle()) {
        case 0: jRadioButton5.setSelected(true); break;
        case 1: jRadioButton6.setSelected(true); break;
        case 2: jRadioButton7.setSelected(true); break;
        case 3: jRadioButton8.setSelected(true); break;
      }
    }
  }

  /** Required by implementation of Customizer Interface */
  public void addPropertyChangeListener(
    PropertyChangeListener parm1) {
```

Listing 11.14 *continued*

continued

Example 11.6 continued

```
      if (pcs == null)
        pcs = new PropertyChangeSupport(this);
      pcs.addPropertyChangeListener(parm1);
  }

  /** Required by implementation of Customizer Interface */
  public void removePropertyChangeListener
    (PropertyChangeListener parm1) {
    if (pcs != null)
      pcs.removePropertyChangeListener(parm1);
  }

  public void itemStateChanged(ItemEvent e) {
    if (e.getSource() instanceof JCheckBox) {
      if (clock != null)
        clock.setShowingDigitalDateTime(jCheckBox1.isSelected());
      if (pcs != null)
        pcs.firePropertyChange("showingDigitalDateTime",
          new Boolean(!jCheckBox1.isSelected()),
          new Boolean(jCheckBox1.isSelected()));

      // Enable radio buttons for date style and time style
      // if showingDigitalDateTime is checked
      if (jCheckBox1.isSelected()) {
        jRadioButton1.setEnabled(true);
        jRadioButton2.setEnabled(true);
        jRadioButton3.setEnabled(true);
        jRadioButton4.setEnabled(true);
        jRadioButton5.setEnabled(true);
        jRadioButton6.setEnabled(true);
        jRadioButton7.setEnabled(true);
        jRadioButton8.setEnabled(true);
      }
      else {
        jRadioButton1.setEnabled(false);
        jRadioButton2.setEnabled(false);
        jRadioButton3.setEnabled(false);
        jRadioButton4.setEnabled(false);
        jRadioButton5.setEnabled(false);
        jRadioButton6.setEnabled(false);
        jRadioButton7.setEnabled(false);
        jRadioButton8.setEnabled(false);
      }
    }
    else { // A radio button is changed
      int currentDateStyle = clock.getDateStyle();
      int newDateStyle = currentDateStyle;

      if (jRadioButton1.isSelected())
        newDateStyle = 0;
      else if (jRadioButton2.isSelected())
        newDateStyle = 1;
      else if (jRadioButton3.isSelected())
        newDateStyle = 2;
      else if (jRadioButton4.isSelected())
        newDateStyle = 3;

```

Listing 11.14 *continued*

```
181          clock.setDateStyle(newDateStyle);
182          if (pcs != null)
183            pcs.firePropertyChange("dateStyle",
184              new Integer(currentDateStyle), new Integer(newDateStyle));
185
186          int currentTimeStyle = clock.getTimeStyle();
187          int newTimeStyle = currentTimeStyle;
188
189          if (jRadioButton5.isSelected())
190            newTimeStyle = 0;
191          else if (jRadioButton6.isSelected())
192            newTimeStyle = 1;
193          else if (jRadioButton7.isSelected())
194            newTimeStyle = 2;
195          else if (jRadioButton8.isSelected())
196            newTimeStyle = 3;
197
198          clock.setTimeStyle(newTimeStyle);
199          if (pcs != null)
200            pcs.firePropertyChange("timeStyle",
201              new Integer(currentTimeStyle), new Integer(newTimeStyle));
202        }
203      }
204
205      // Variables declaration - do not modify
206      private javax.swing.ButtonGroup buttonGroup1;
207      private javax.swing.ButtonGroup buttonGroup2;
208      private javax.swing.JCheckBox jCheckBox1;
209      private javax.swing.JPanel jPanel1;
210      private javax.swing.JPanel jpDateStyle;
211      private javax.swing.JRadioButton jRadioButton1;
212      private javax.swing.JRadioButton jRadioButton2;
213      private javax.swing.JRadioButton jRadioButton3;
214      private javax.swing.JRadioButton jRadioButton4;
215      private javax.swing.JPanel jpTimeStyle;
216      private javax.swing.JRadioButton jRadioButton5;
217      private javax.swing.JRadioButton jRadioButton6;
218      private javax.swing.JRadioButton jRadioButton7;
219      private javax.swing.JRadioButton jRadioButton8;
220      // End of variables declaration
221    }
```

Listing 11.14 *continued*

Example Review

`ClockCustomizer` implements the `Customizer` interface. The `setObject` method is invoked first by the builder tool when the customizer starts. For this reason, the statement for invoking the `initComponents()` statement is moved from the constructor to the `setObject()` method (Lines 89–118), so that you can initialize the customizer to display the current state of the clock passed from the builder tool. The implementation of `addPropertyChangeListener` and `removePropertyChangeListener` involves registering and unregistering the listener with an instance of `PropertyChangeSupport` named `pcs`.

You could use the Form Editor to generate nine `ItemEvent` adapters for the check box and eight radio buttons. However, a more efficient way in this example is to use a single centralized adapter to handle all the item events from the check box and the radio buttons, as shown in Lines 136–203.

continued

Example 11.6 continued

When a check box is unchecked, all the radio buttons are disabled, since there is no need to set date style or time style when the date and time are not displayed. Whenever a property is changed, the builder tool is notified by invoking `pcs.firePropertyChange("propertyName", oldValue, newValue)`. The builder tool updates the bean property by generating a statement in the `initComponents` method code using the property's set method. To ensure that a change takes effect during design, you need to invoke the property's set method in the customizer. For instance, the following code

```
clock.setShowingDigitalDateTime(jCheckBox1.isSelected());
```

updates `clock`'s `showingDigitalDateTime` property in the Form Editor.

The customizer is contained in a dialog box created by Forte. The dialog box contains a Close button. You can close the customizer by clicking it.

Chapter Summary

This chapter introduced the JavaBeans API that a builder tool can use to discover the properties, methods, and events of a bean so that it can be manipulated visually during design time. You learned how to create custom property editors, GUI property editors, and customizers for editing bean properties.

Review Questions

11.1 Are the `BeanInfo` class, the property editor class, and the customizer class necessary at runtime?

11.2 How do you expose properties whose get and set methods do not follow standard naming patterns?

11.3 How do you expose events whose registration and removal methods do not follow standard naming patterns?

11.4 How do you programmatically inspect bean properties and events at runtime?

11.5 Describe the methods `getAsText`, `setAsText`, `getValue`, `setValue`, and `getTags` in the `PropertyEditor` interface.

11.6 Describe the implementation of the `PropertyEditorSupport` class. How are the methods `getAsText`, `setAsText`, `getValue`, `setValue`, and `getTags` implemented in the `PropertyEditorSupport` class?

11.7 How do you create a custom property editor to display property values in a choice menu in the component inspector?

11.8 How do you specify a custom property editor in the `BeanInfo` class?

11.9 Describe the role of the methods `setDisplayName` and `setValue` in the `FeatureDescriptor` class.

11.10 How do you create a property editor in Forte? How do you generate a `BeanInfo` class in Forte?

11.11 How should the methods `getCustomEditor` and `supportsCustomEditor` be implemented to create a GUI property editor? How do you start a GUI property editor in the component inspector? How is a GUI property displayed?

11.12 Describe the methods `setObject`, `addPropertyChangeListener`, and `removePropertyChangeListener` in the `Customizer` interface. How do you start a customizer? How is a customizer displayed? How do you specify a customizer in the `BeanInfo` class?

Programming Exercises

11.1 The `CalendarPanel` class in Exercise 4.6 contains a `month` property and a `year` property. Both properties are `int` values. Create a property editor for the `month` property to display locale-sensitive month names in a choice menu, as shown in Figure 11.17, and create a property editor for the `year` property to display and validate `year` to ensure that `year` is non-negative.

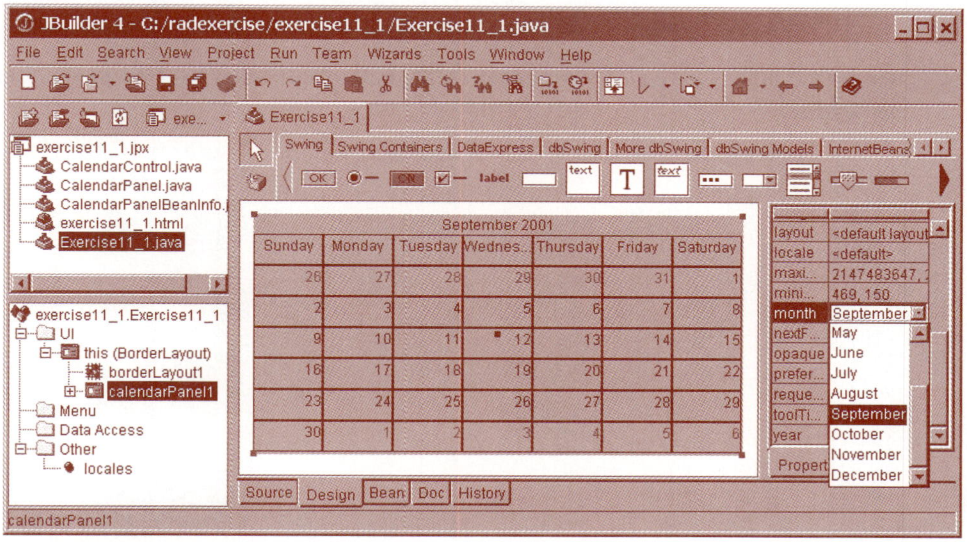

Figure 11.17 *The* `month` *property is displayed in a choice menu of month names.*

11.2 Create a GUI property editor for selecting colors just like the one used in Forte.

11.3 The Student class in Example 11.3 contains a property named `fullName`, which consists of first name, middle name, and last name. The entire full name must be edited at one time in the component inspector. Create a customizer for the Student class to enable the user to edit first name, middle name, and last name separately. The customizer is shown in Figure 11.18. The name labels are placed in a `JPanel` named `labelPanel` of `GridLayout`, and the text fields are placed in a `JPanel` named `textPanel` of `GridLayout`. `labelPanel` and `textPanel` are placed in a `JPanel` of `BorderLayout`, with `labelPanel` on the east and `textPanel` in the center. The Apply button applies the change to the bean, and the Revert button restores the original names in the bean.

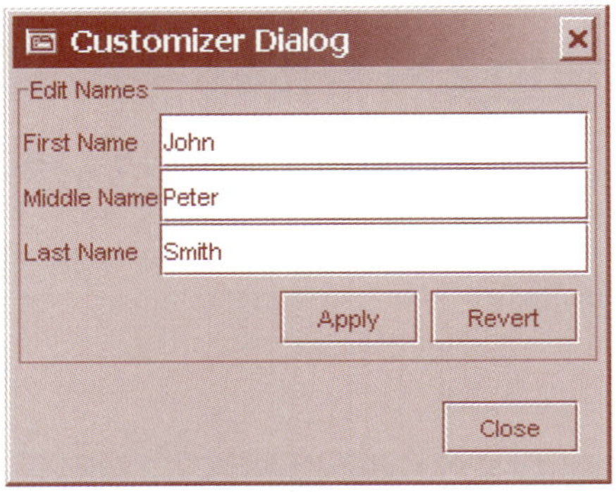

Figure 11.18 *The* `StudentCustomizer` *enables you to edit first name, middle name, and last name separately.*

PART IV

Java Database Programming

This part of the book discusses how to use Java to develop database projects. You will learn JDBC interfaces and classes, create and process SQL statements, and obtain database metadata. You will also learn to use Forte's database explorer to connect and browse databases, and Forte JDBC form wizard to rapidly develop Java database projects.

CHAPTER 12

Introduction to Java Database Programming

Objectives

- To learn the architecture of JDBC.
- To know the four types of JDBC drivers.
- To use JDBC drivers.
- To be able to write simple JDBC programs.
- To use Forte's database explorer.

12.1 Introduction

JDBC is a Java API that provides Java programmers with a uniform interface for accessing and manipulating a wide range of relational databases. Before JDBC, database clients were typically developed using Microsoft Visual Basic, Borland Delphi, and other development tools provided by database vendors, such as PowerBuilder by Sybase and Oracle Developer 2000 by Oracle. These are excellent rapid application development tools, but the programs developed with them can only run on certain platforms. With JDBC, you can write database programs that run on any platform that has a Java Virtual Machine with an appropriate JDBC driver.

The relationships between Java programs, JDBC API, JDBC drivers, and relational databases are shown in Figure 12.1. The JDBC API is a set of Java interfaces and classes used to write Java programs for accessing and manipulating relational databases. Since a JDBC driver serves as the interface to facilitate communications between JDBC and a proprietary database, JDBC drivers are database-specific. You need Oracle JDBC drivers to access an Oracle database, and Sybase JDBC drivers to access a Sybase database. Even for the same vendor, the drivers may be different for different versions of a database. For instance, the JDBC driver for Oracle 8 and 9 is different from the one for Oracle 7. A JDBC-ODBC bridge driver is included in JDK to support Java programs that access databases through ODBC drivers. ODBC, introduced before Java, defines a protocol for accessing relational databases.

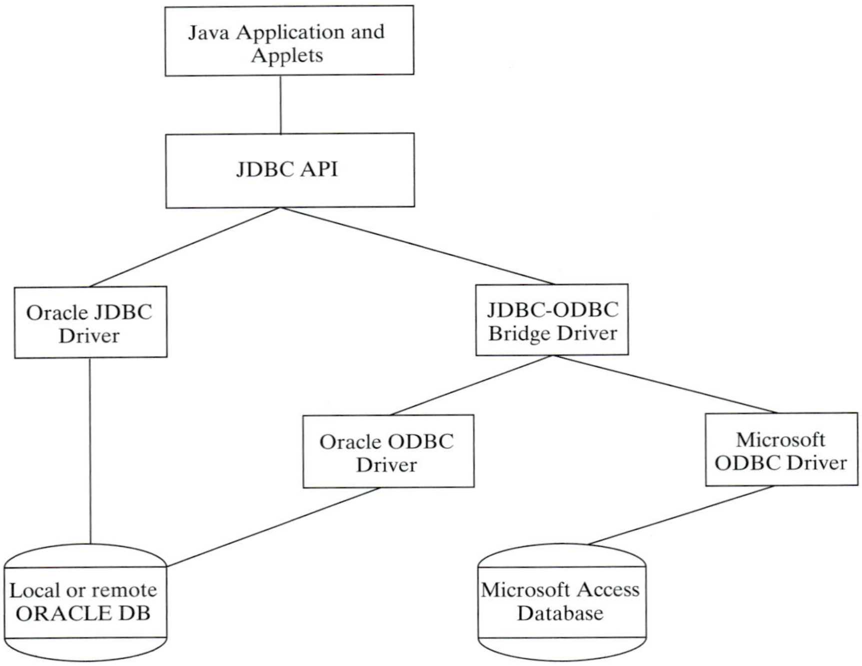

Figure 12.1 *Java programs access and manipulate databases through JDBC drivers.*

NOTE
JDBC is the trademarked name of a Java API that supports Java programs to access relational databases. JDBC is not an acronym, but it is often thought to stand for Java Database Connectivity.

12.2 Overview of the JDBC API

The JDBC API is a Java application program interface to generic SQL databases that enables Java developers to develop DBMS-independent applications using a uniform interface.

The JDBC API consists of classes and interfaces for establishing connections with databases, sending SQL statements to databases, processing the results of the SQL statements, and obtaining database metadata. The JDBC interfaces and classes can be classified by type as drivers, connections, statements, result sets, metadata, processing supports, and exceptions, as shown in Table 12.1.

NOTE
The initial design of JDBC API was based on JDK 1.02, known as *JDBC 1*. When JDBC 1 was released, many important Java technologies, such as JavaBeans and Java Internationalization, had not yet been developed. With the release of JDK 1.2 of Java 2, JavaSoft added new features and enhancements to JDBC 1. The new JDBC product is known as *JDBC 2*. JDBC 1 is compatible with Java 2. Any application developed with JDBC 1 will continue to work under JDK 1.2. However, you will need JDBC 2 drivers to use the new features in JDBC 2. The JDBC-ODBC driver, which is bundled with JDK 1.3, does not support all features of JDBC 2. If you run a program that uses the unsupported new features, an exception indicating that the operations are not supported will occur.

The interfaces define a framework for generic SQL database access. The JDBC driver vendors provide implementation for these interfaces. The relationship of these interfaces and classes is shown in Figure 12.2. A JDBC application loads an appropriate driver using the `Driver` interface, connects to the database using the `Connection` interface, creates and executes SQL statements using the `Statement` interface, and processes the result using the `ResultSet` interface if the statements return results. Note that some statements, such as SQL data definition statements and SQL data modification statements, do not return results.

12.2.1 The *Driver* Interface

The `Driver` interface is database-specific. The JDBC vendor should implement this interface and provide proprietary database information to enable Java programs to communicate with the database.

An appropriate driver must be loaded before your application can connect to a database. The driver can be loaded using the following statement:

```
Class.forName("TheDriverName")
```

TABLE 12.1 JDBC Classes

Type	*Class/Interface*
Driver management	`java.sql.Driver (Interface)`
	`java.sql.DriverPropertyInfo`
	`java.sql.DriverManager`
Establishing connections	`java.sql.Connection (Interface)`
Processing statements	`java.sql.Statement (Interface)`
	`java.sql.PreparedStatement (Interface)`
	`java.sql.CallableStatement (Interface)`
Handling result sets	`java.sql.ResultSet (Interface)`
Metadata	`java.sql.DatabaseMetaData (Interface)`
	`java.sql.ResultSetMetaData (Interface)`
Exceptions	`java.sql.SQLException`
	`java.sql.SQLWarning`
	`java.sql.DataTruncation`
	`java.sql.BatchUpdateException (JDBC 2)`
Support classes	`java.sql.Date`
	`java.sql.Time`
	`java.sql.TimeStamp`
	`java.sql.Types`
	`java.sql.Blob (JDBC 2)`
	`java.sql.Clob (JDBC 2)`
	`java.sql.Array (JDBC 2)`
	`java.sql.SQLInput (JDBC 2)`
	`java.sql.SQLOutput (JDBC 2)`
	`java.sql.Ref (JDBC 2)`
	`java.sql.Struct (JDBC 2)`

This statement attempts to locate, load, and link the driver class. If it succeeds, it returns an anonymous `Class` object representing the driver class. You don't need to return an explicit driver reference, because each newly loaded driver is capable of registering itself with the `DriverManager`.

The driver is anonymous; you don't need to reference it explicitly to make a database connection. After the driver is registered, the `DriverManager` can use it to make database connections. If the driver is not found, the method throws a `ClassNotFoundException`.

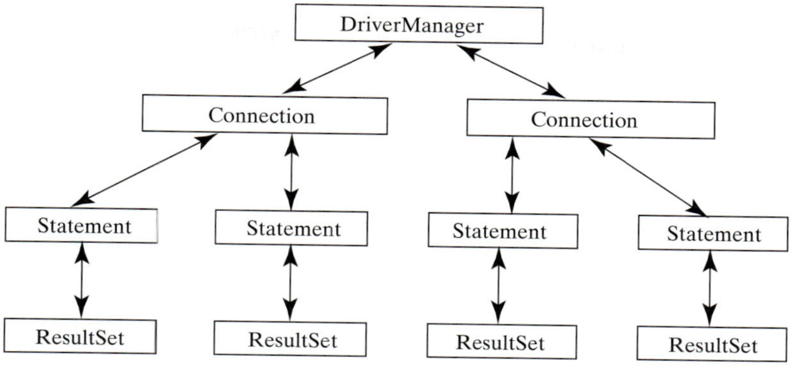

Figure 12.2 *JDBC classes enable Java programs to connect to the database, send SQL statements, and process results.*

12.2.2 The *DriverManager* Class

The `DriverManager` class, a layer of JDBC working between the driver and the user, is responsible for registering and managing the drivers. It serves as a ringmaster to keep track of all the registered drivers, establishing a connection between the database and an appropriate driver.

All the methods in `DriverManager` are static. A programmer can use its `getConnection()` method to get a connection to the database, which returns an object of `Connection`. For example, the following statement connects the database at the specified `url` with `username` and `password`:

```
Connection connection =
  DriverManager.getConnection(url, username, password);
```

Database URL will be introduced in Section 12.5.1.

12.2.3 The *DriverPropertyInfo* Class

The `DriverPropertyInfo` class is used by advanced programmers to manage specific properties of a `Driver` instance. It should be used only by developers who need to interact with a driver to discover and supply properties for connections.

12.2.4 The *Connection* Interface

A `Connection` instance represents a session with a specific database. In the context of a `Connection` instance, SQL statements are sent to the database for execution, and the results of the execution, if any, are returned. Think of a connection as a pipeline through which database transactions travel back and forth between your program and the database.

A `Connection` instance can be used to create various `Statement` objects for executing SQL statements and stored procedures using the `createStatement` method. You can also use it to set transaction properties for the connection. By default the `Connection` instance automatically commits changes after executing each statement. If auto-commit has been disabled, an explicit commit must be done or database changes will not be saved.

You can use the `getMetaData()` method to get an object of `DataBaseMetaData` that describes the connected database information on the tables, views, supported SQL grammar, stored procedures, and capabilities of this connection. Chapter 13, "Advanced Java Database Programming," gives an in-depth look at retrieving metadata.

12.2.5 The *Statement, PreparedStatement,* and *CallableStatement* Interfaces

The `Statement`, `PreparedStatement`, and `CallableStatement` interfaces are related in a hierarchical relationship. `CallableStatement` inherits `PreparedStatement`, which inherits `Statement`. These interfaces are used for sending SQL statements to the database for execution on a given connection. A `Statement` object is used to execute a static SQL statement; a `PreparedStatement` object is used to execute a precompiled SQL statement with or without IN parameters; and a `CallableStatement` object is used to execute a call to a stored procedure in the database.

The `executeQuery` method of the object is used if the statement is an SQL SELECT query, and the `executeUpdate` method is used if the statement is an SQL INSERT, UPDATE, or DELETE and also an SQL DDL (Data Definition Language) statement like `CREATE TABLE`, `CREATE VIEW`, `DROP TABLE`, or `DROP VIEW`.

The `executeQuery` method returns the query result in a `ResultSet` object. Only one `ResultSet` per `Statement` can be open at any single point in time. Therefore, if the reading of one `ResultSet` is interleaved with the reading of another, each must have been generated by a different statement. All statement-execute methods implicitly close a statement's current `ResultSet` if an open one exists.

When executing a stored procedure, the execution may return multiple result sets. The `execute` method should be used to execute the SQL statement in this case. You can then use `getResultSet` or `getUpdateCount` to retrieve the result, and `getMoreResults` to move to the next result set.

12.2.6 The *ResultSet* Interface

A `ResultSet` provides access to a table of data generated by executing a query statement.

A `ResultSet` maintains a cursor pointing to its current row of data. The current row can be set using the cursor movement methods, such as `absolute`, `first`, `last`, `next`, and `previous`. Initially the cursor is positioned before the first row. The `next` method moves the cursor to the next row. The first call to `next` makes the first row the current row, the second call makes the second row the current row, and so on.

Various get methods are provided to retrieve column values for the current row. You can retrieve values by using either the index number of the column or the name of the column. For example, to retrieve a column of the `String` type, you may use `rs.getString("ColumnName")`, where `rs` is an object of `ResultSet`.

The column values within a row can be accessed in any order.

12.2.7 The *SQL Exception* Classes

The JDBC methods may raise the `SQLException`, `SQLWarning`, `DataTruncation`, and `BatchUpdateException` exceptions. `SQLException` is the root of all the exceptions in the JDBC.

The `SQLException` class provides information on a database access error. The `SQLWarning` exception, a subclass of `SQLException`, provides information on a database access warning. A warning is silently chained to the object whose method caused it to be reported. An `SQLWarning` exception may be ignored in order to allow the normal course of the execution to proceed. A `DataTruncation` exception, a subclass of `SQLWarning`, is raised when JDBC unexpectedly truncates a data value. A `BatchUpdateException` exception, a subclass of `SQLException`, is raised if exceptions occur during a batch operation.

12.2.8 The *DatabaseMetaData* Interface

The `DatabaseMetaData` interface enables you to obtain information about the database, such as tables, views, columns, primary keys, and foreign keys.

Many of these methods return the information in `ResultSet`. You can use the normal `ResultSet` methods, such as `getString` and `getInt`, to retrieve the data from these result sets. If a given form of metadata is not available, these methods should throw an `SQLException`. For example, to find all the catalogs in the database, you can use the `getCatalogs` method to return a list of catalogs in an object of `ResultSet`, then retrieve all the catalogs from the result set.

12.2.9 The *ResultSetMetaData* Interface

The `ResultSetMetaData` interface provides various methods for getting information about a `ResultSet` object. You can use a `ResultSetMetaData` object to get the number of columns and find out about the types and properties of the columns in a `ResultSet`.

12.2.10 The JDBC Support Classes

JDBC provides many support classes. The `Date`, `Time`, and `TimeStamp` classes are for accepting and processing SQL DATE, TIME, and TIMESTAMP values. All these classes extend the `java.util.Date` class.

The `Types` class contains a list of predefined constants for identifying SQL types that can be used in JDBC, such as `INTEGER`, `FLOAT`, `DOUBLE`, `VARCHAR`, `BLOB`, `CLOB`, and so on. No methods are defined in this class.

The `Blob`, `Clob`, `Array`, `Ref`, `Struct`, `SQLInput`, and `SQLOutput` are new support classes introduced in JDBC 2. The `Blob` class represents an SQL BLOB type for storing a binary large object, such as an image. The `Clob` class represents an SQL CLOB type for storing a character large object, such as a text document. The `Array` class represents an SQL ARRAY type for storing a sequence of values. The `Ref` class is a reference to an SQL structured type value in the database. The `Struct` class maps to an SQL structured type. The `SQLInput` and `SQLOutput` classes provide a mechanism for mapping structured SQL types to Java objects.

12.3 Developing JDBC Applications

The JDBC interfaces and classes are the building blocks in the development of Java database programs. A typical Java program takes the following steps to access the database, as shown in Figure 12.2.

1. Load drivers.

   JDBC allows multiple drivers to be loaded in one program. A program can load a JDBC driver at any time. For example, `MyDriver` is loaded with the following statement:

   ```
   Class.forName("MyDriver");
   ```

   The statement loads the driver. The driver is automatically registered with the driver manager. You may use the static method `registerDriver` in the `DriverManager` class to explicitly register a driver with the driver manager. For example, this statement registers `MyDriver`:

   ```
   DriverManager.registerDriver(new MyDriver());
   ```

2. Establish connections.

   Once the driver is loaded and registered, the `DriverManager` is able to choose an appropriate one from a list of registered drivers to fulfill the connection to the database. You simply invoke `DriverManager.getConnection()` to establish a session with the database. In the unusual situation where more than one driver is suitable for a connection to a given database and you have a preference as to which should be chosen, the `connect` method in a `Driver` object can be invoked directly to use the preferred driver to connect to the database.

3. Create statements.

   You can create three types of statements for executing SQL: `Statement`, `PreparedStatement`, or `CallableStatement`. The `Statement` class is used to execute static SQL. The `PreparedStatement` and `CallableStatement` classes are used to construct dynamic SQL.

4. Execute statements.

   Statements can be executed using the `executeQuery`, `executeUpdate`, or `execute` method. The result of the query is returned in `ResultSet`.

5. Process `ResultSet`.

   The `ResultSet` maintains a table whose current row can be retrieved. The initial row position is `null`. The methods, such as `absolute`, `first`, `last`, `next`, and `previous`, can be used to set the row position. The various get methods are used to retrieve values from a current row.

Here is a simple example (see Listing 12.1) of connecting to a database, executing a simple query, and processing the query result.

```
package jdbcdemo;

import java.sql.*;

public class SimpleJdbc {
  public static void main(String[] args)
    throws SQLException, ClassNotFoundException {
    // Load the JDBC driver
    Class.forName("sun.jdbc.odbc.JdbcOdbcDriver");
    System.out.println("Driver loaded");

    // Establish a connection
    Connection connection = DriverManager.getConnection
      ("jdbc:odbc:LiangBookDB_MDB", "", "" );
    System.out.println("Database connected");

    // Create a statement
    Statement stmt = connection.createStatement();

    // Select the columns from the Student table
    ResultSet rset = stmt.executeQuery
      ("select firstName, mi, lastName from Student");

    // Iterate through the result and print the student names
    while (rset.next())
      System.out.println(rset.getString(1) + " " + rset.getString(2)
        + ". " + rset.getString(3));
  }
}
```

Listing 12.1 *SimpleJDBC.java*

The statement

```
Class.forName("sun.jdbc.odbc.JdbcOdbcDriver")
```

loads the `JdbcOdbcDriver` for connecting to an ODBC data source, such as Microsoft Access Database. In Example 12.1, you will learn how to set up the ODBC data source to test this program.

The statement

```
Connection connection = DriverManager.getConnection
  ("jdbc:odbc:LiangBookDB_MDB", "", "");
```

creates a `Connection` object `connection`, which represents a logical session for sending SQL statements and getting query results back from the database. You can create an instance of `Statement` for executing static queries as used in the example, create `PreparedStatement` for precompiled SQL statements, or create `CallableStatement` for executing stored procedures. Their applications are discussed in Chapter 13, "Advanced Java Database Programming."

The statement

```
ResultSet rset = stmt.executeQuery
  ("select firstName, mi, lastName from Student");
```

executes the query and returns the result in a `ResultSet` object, which can be perceived as a table of three columns consisting of firstName, mi, and lastName. The `getString(1)`, `getString(2)`, and `getString(3)` methods retrieve the column values for firstName, mi, and lastName, respectively. Alternatively, you can use `getString("firstName")`, `getString("mi")`, and `getString("lastName")` to retrieve the same three column values.

The first execution of the `next()` method sets the current row to the first row in the result set, and subsequent invocation of the `next()` method sets the current row to the second, third, and so on, to the last row.

Note

The MS Access database (LiangBookDB_MDB.mdb) in the book was created using Microsoft Access 2000. This database cannot be used with MS Access 97. If you use MS Access 97 or 95, please create your own database.

12.4 JDBC Drivers

A JDBC driver is a software component that works between JDBC and the database. The driver is responsible for accepting SQL statements, sending them to the database system, and returning the execution results to JDBC. The driver is specific to each database. For instance, to enable JDBC to connect to the Oracle database, you need a JDBC driver that works specifically for Oracle. Even among Oracle databases, the drivers are different for various versions of Oracle DBMS.

There are many JDBC drivers now available on the market. They can be classified into the four types listed in Table 12.2.

TABLE 12.2 JDBC Driver Types

Types of drivers	*Description*
Type 1: JDBC-ODBC Bridge	Provides access through ODBC drivers
Type 2: Native-API	Provides access through native database API
Type 3: Middle-tier	Provides access through a middle-tier server
Type 4: Native-protocol	Provides access through a network protocol used by DBMS

12.4.1 Type 1: JDBC-ODBC Bridge Driver

ODBC (Open DataBase Connectivity) is an API for accessing relational databases. It was originally designed to enable database clients on PCs to access databases on a server by Microsoft. It became a popular industry standard API for connecting to the relational databases for the client on all types of platforms. Since ODBC is widely available, it makes sense to provide a driver that accesses the database through ODBC drivers. Such a driver is referred to as a *JDBC-ODBC bridge driver.*

A JDBC-ODBC driver is bundled with JDK 1.4. This driver bridges JDBC with ODBC by mapping the JDBC calls into ODBC calls; the ODBC calls interact with the database, as shown in Figure 12.3.

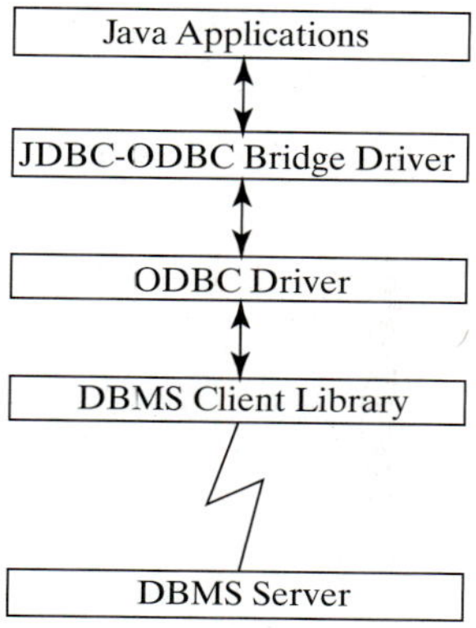

Figure 12.3 *The JDBC-ODBC bridge driver maps JDBC calls to ODBC calls.*

The JDBC-ODBC bridge driver provides convenient access to every existing system, since most database systems already have ODBC drivers. However, the driver is slow and is not suitable for applets. The ODBC drivers are specific to the database. For example, you need an Oracle ODBC driver to access Oracle databases. The JDBC application using the JDBC-ODBC bridge driver requires that the ODBC driver and the client database library must be loaded on the client machine. This approach is obviously not efficient, because it requires the JDBC driver to talk to the database via an ODBC driver. Since the ODBC driver is written in C, it cannot be downloaded and used by applets.

12.4.2 Type 2: Native-API Driver

The native-API driver converts JDBC calls into native database calls and communicates directly with the database server, as shown in Figure 12.4.

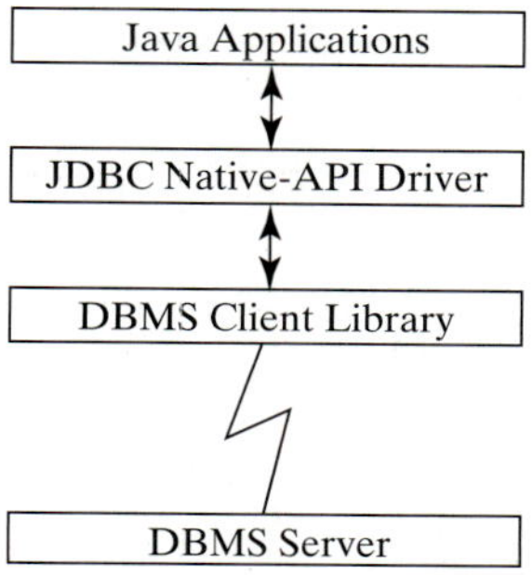

Figure 12.4 *The JDBC native-API driver maps JDBC calls to native API calls.*

Native-API drivers are usually provided by database vendors. For example, Oracle provides a native-API driver that maps JDBC with the Oracle Call Interface. Like the bridge driver, this driver requires some binary code for the native database API to be loaded on the client machine. But it is more efficient than the JDBC-ODBC bridge approach, since it allows you to talk to the database directly.

12.4.3 Type 3: Middle-Tier Driver

The middle-tier driver converts JDBC calls into a DBMS-independent network protocol and sends them to a middle-tier server. The server then translates the calls to a DBMS-specific protocol for Oracle, Sybase, DB2, InterBase, or some other DBMS, as shown in Figure 12.5.

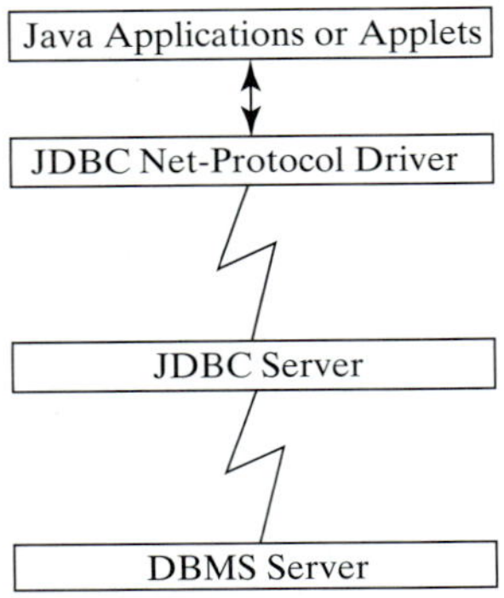

Figure 12.5 *The middle-tier driver maps JDBC calls to a DBMS-independent middle-tier server that communicates with a proprietary DBMS.*

The middle-tier JDBC server connects to Java applications or applets with a database server. Borland's InterClient and Symantec's dbAnyWhere are middle-tier servers based on this kind of architecture. The middle-tier server can reside on a machine different from the client and the DBMS server.

The middle-tier driver is a pure Java JDBC driver that enables platform-independent client/server development for the Internet. The advantage of a pure Java driver, as opposed to a native-code driver, is that you can deploy applets without having to manually load platform-specific JDBC drivers on each client system. Since the Web servers automatically download the driver's classes along with the applets, there is no need to manage local native database libraries, and this simplifies administration and maintenance of customer applications. As part of a Java applet, the driver can be dynamically updated, further reducing the cost of application deployment and maintenance.

12.4.4 Type 4: Native-Protocol Driver

The native-protocol driver converts JDBC calls into a network protocol used by a DBMS and communicates with the DBMS directly, as shown in Figure 12.6.

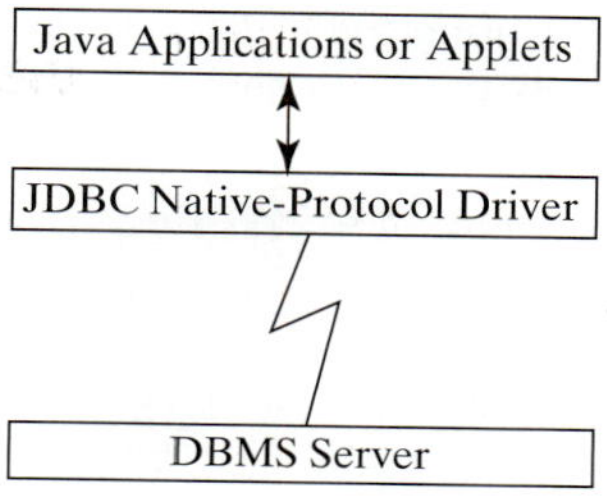

Figure 12.6 *The native-protocol driver facilitates communications between Java applications and applets with a DBMS server.*

Like the middle-tier driver, the native-protocol driver does not require any database-specific binary code to be loaded on the client. The native-protocol driver, however, is more flexible than the middle-tier driver, because it eliminates the middle-tier JDBC server.

Note

The JDBC-ODBC driver and the native-API driver use native methods, which makes them platform-specific. They are not suitable for Java applets intended to be downloaded into browsers running on universal platforms. Middle-tier drivers are preferred for use with multi-tier architecture where connectors are used to link clients with database servers. Native-protocol drivers are ideal for direct access to the database. Both middle-tier and native-protocol drivers are written in 100% pure Java; thus they are suitable for Java applets.

12.5 Connecting to Databases Using JDBC Drivers

A number of JDBC drivers have already been developed. Many of them can be downloaded from vendors for thirty or more days of evaluation. Information for locating the drivers can be obtained from the following URL:

```
http://industry.java.sun.com/products/jdbc/drivers
```

This section provides examples of the use of JDBC drivers. Specifically, you will use the Sun JDBC-ODBC driver, the Oracle JDBC OCI driver (native-API), and the Oracle thin-client driver (native-protocol).

Note

A driver is not just a member of a single class. In fact a JDBC driver is a set of classes that provide mappings between JDBC and a specific database. The driver must include classes that implement the eight interfaces in the `java.sql` package: `Driver`, `Connection`, `Statement`, `PreparedStatement`, `CallableStatement`, `ResultSet`, `DatabaseMetaData`, and `ResultSetMetaData`. For example, the `oracle.jdbc.drive.OracleStatement` class implements `java.sql.Statement`. Figure 12.7 lists all the classes in the Oracle 8i and 9i JDBC Thin driver bundled in the classes12.zip file using the WinZip utility. These classes are used by JDBC, but not directly by JDBC programmers.

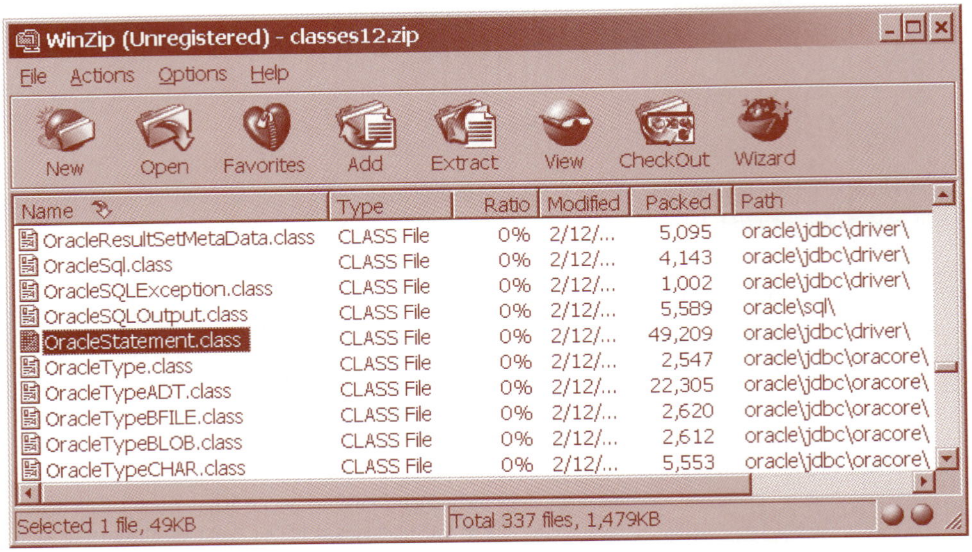

Figure 12.7 *A JDBC driver contains classes that enable JDBC to interact with a specific database.*

12.5.1 JDBC URL Naming Conventions

How does a Java program find its database? It finds the database by using its JDBC URL. A JDBC URL provides a way for the appropriate driver to identify the database. The standard syntax of a URL is:

```
jdbc:<subprotocol>:<datasource>
```

The first part of the syntax is always `jdbc`. The second part is the `subprotocol` specified by the driver vendor. For example, the `subprotocol` for Sun drivers is always sun, and the `subprotocol` for Oracle drivers is always oracle. The `datasource` consists of the database name and the host machine where the database resides. Information needed to access the data source, such as the user's login name and password, may be included in `datasource` or may be supplied separately.

The `subprotocol` is used by the `DriverManager` class to associate an appropriate driver with the database. When the `DriverManager` class presents the `subprotocol` of the URL to its list of registered drivers, the driver that matches the protocol is used to establish a connection to the database specified in the data source. The `subprotocol` name is defined by the vendor, but it must be registered with JavaSoft to avoid naming conflicts. JavaSoft acts as an informal registry for JDBC `subprotocol` names.

The `subprotocol odbc` is reserved for JDBC-ODBC bridge drivers. For example, the URL to access an ODBC data source "MyDataSource" through a JDBC-ODBC driver is:

```
jdbc:odbc:MyDataSource
```

In this example, the `subprotocol` is `odbc`, and the data source is the ODBC data source "MyDataSource."

The subprotocol may consist of several words. For example, the subprotocol `oracle:oci8` is reserved for accessing the Oracle 8 database through native Oracle OCI (Oracle Call Interface), and `oracle:thin` is reserved for accessing Oracle 8i and 9i using the Type 4 native-protocol driver.

The JDBC URL provides an indirection in the data source. You may use a logical host or database name that is dynamically translated to an actual name by a network naming system. For example, the URL to access a remote Oracle database using the Oracle JDBC Thin driver may look like:

```
jdbc:oracle:thin:scott/tiger@liang.armstrong.edu:1521:test
```

This URL indicates that the Oracle database with the ID oracle runs at port 1521 on `liang.armstrong.edu`. The user name is **scott** and the password is **tiger**.

12.5.2 Using the JDBC-ODBC Driver

To use the JDBC-ODBC driver to access databases in Java, two drivers must be installed on the client machine: a universal JDBC-ODBC bridge driver and a vendor-specific ODBC driver. The JDBC-ODBC driver comes with Java 2 SDK 1.2 or higher, or any Java development tool that supports JDK 1.2, or higher. The ODBC driver is not included in JDK and is usually provided by database vendors. The example chosen to demonstrate the JDBC-ODBC approach in this section is the Microsoft ODBC driver for the MS Access database on Windows, since it is bundled with Microsoft Office Suite and easily available to many readers. This section uses the ODBC driver on Windows 2000.

NOTE
Using the JDBC-ODBC approach, the database is not necessarily on the same machine with the client. For example, you may use an Oracle ODBC driver to access a remote Oracle database.

Example 12.1 Using the JDBC-ODBC Bridge Driver

This example develops a Java program that creates a table named Student in an MS Access database. Each record consists of student firstName, mi, and lastName. Your program inserts two records into Student and then displays all the records on the console.

Follow the steps below to complete the project.

continued

Example 12.1 continued

1. Install an MS ODBC driver for MS Access if necessary.

   By default the ODBC driver is installed on Windows 2000. If not, install MS Access to get the proper ODBC driver on your system. Upon successful installation, you should see the icon Data Sources (ODBC) in the Administrative Tools subwindow under the control panel for Windows 2000. For Windows 98 and NT, you should see a "32-bit ODBC" icon appearing on the control panel.

2. Set up a Data Source as the database for storing the Student table.

   2.1. From the Windows Start button, choose *Setting, Control Panel* to bring up the Control Panel dialog box.

   2.2. Double-click Administrative Tools, and then double-click Data Sources (ODBC) to display the "ODBC Data Source Administrator," as shown in Figure 12.8.

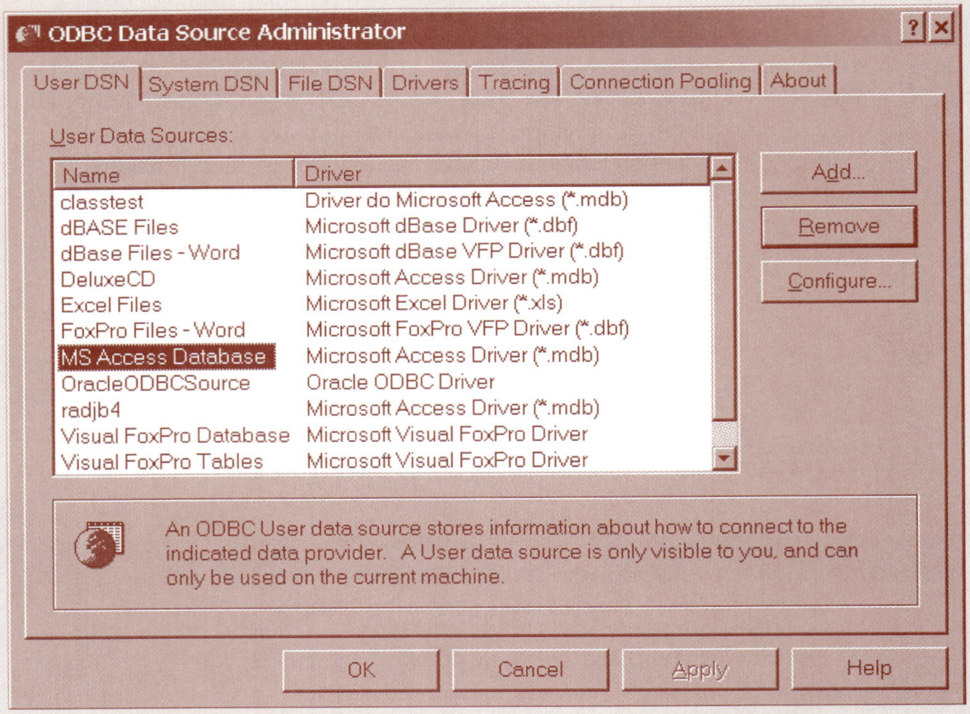

Figure 12.8 *The ODBC Data Source Administrator is the main dialog box to manage the data source and the drivers.*

   2.3. Click *Add* to bring up the "Create New Data Source" dialog box, as shown in Figure 12.9.

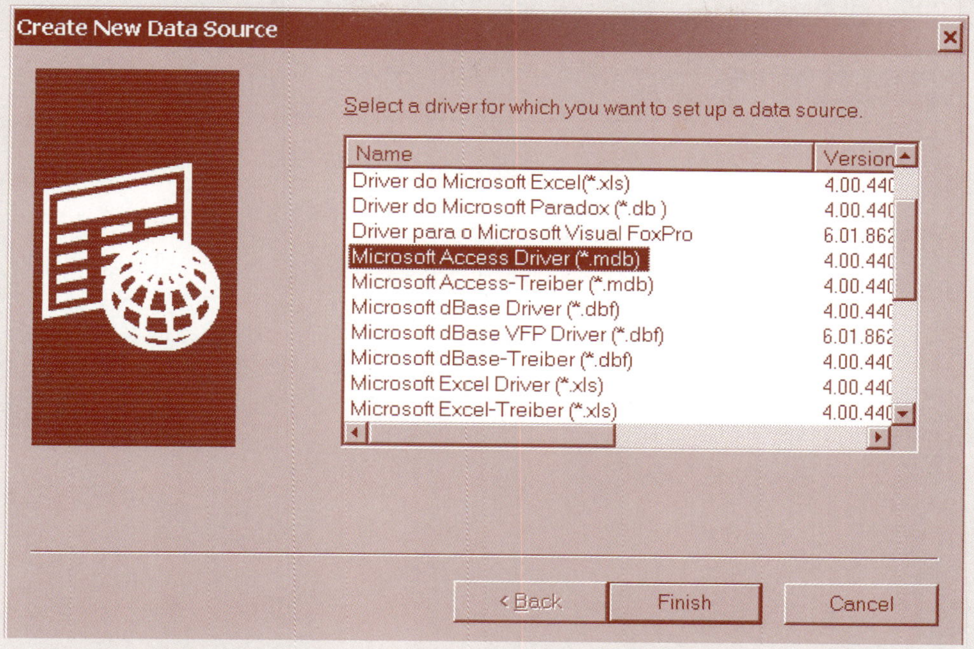

Figure 12.9 *Select a proper driver for the data source in the "Create New Data Source" window.*

2.4. Select *Microsoft Access Driver* and press *Finish* to bring up the "ODBC Microsoft Access Setup" dialog window, as shown in Figure 12.10. Type "LiangBookDB_MDB" in the Data Source Name field, and type "Liang Book MS Access database" in the Description field. Press *Select* to bring up the "Select Database" dialog window, as shown in Figure 12.11.

2.5. Since LiangBookDB_MDB.mdb has already been created, select LiangBookDB_MDB.mdb from the directory **c:\radft**. Press *OK* to close the Select Database dialog window, click *OK* to close the ODBC Microsoft Access Setup window, and click *OK* to close the ODBC Data Source Administrator window.

3. Create a new package named jdbcdemo and create a class named `TestJdbcOdbc` (see Listing 12.2) to create a Student table, insert two records, and retrieve the records from the database.

continued

Example 12.1 continued

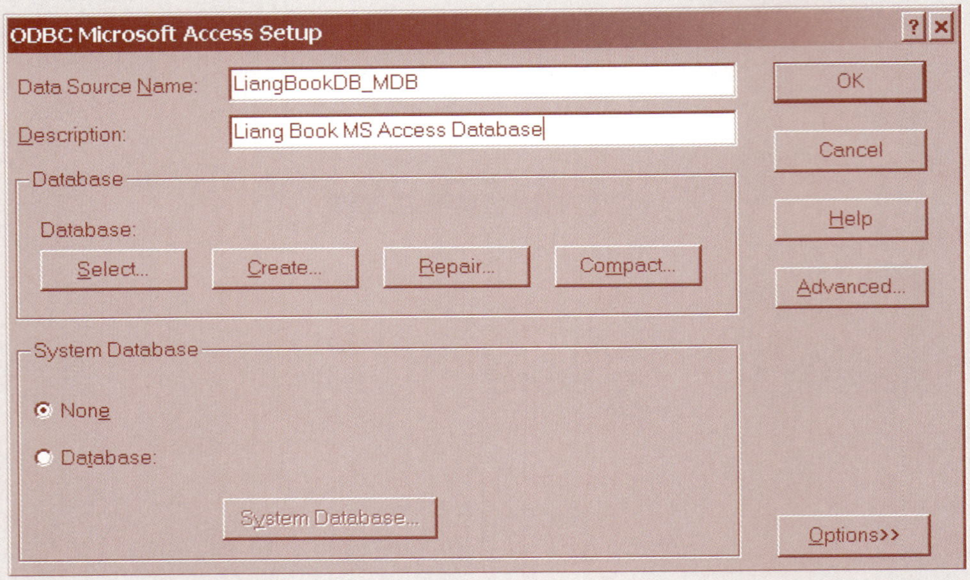

Figure 12.10 *Specify the Data Source Name to associate it with a database in the "ODBC Microsoft Access Setup" window.*

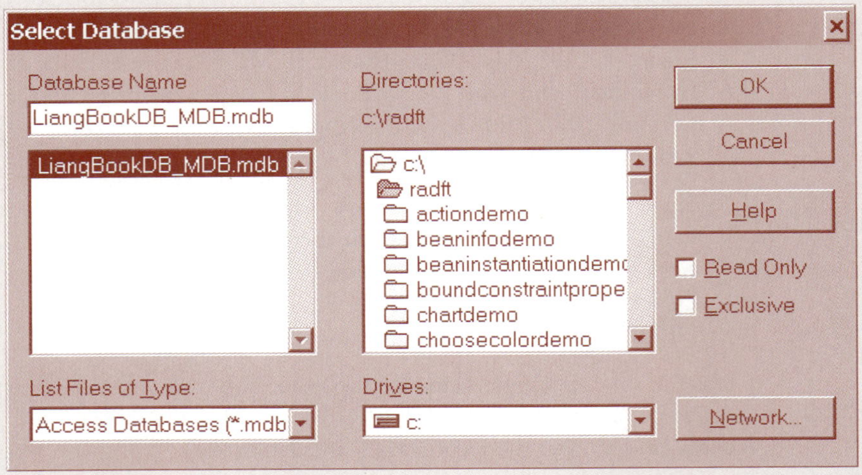

Figure 12.11 *Specify the physical database file name that corresponds to the data source name in the "Select Database" window.*

```
package jdbcdemo;

import java.sql.*;

public class TestJdbcOdbc {
  public static void main(String[] args)
    throws SQLException, ClassNotFoundException {
    // Load the JDBC-ODBC bridge driver
    Class.forName("sun.jdbc.odbc.JdbcOdbcDriver");
    System.out.println("Driver sun.jdbc.odbc.JdbcOdbcDriverloaded");

    // Establish connection
    Connection connection = DriverManager.getConnection
      ("jdbc:odbc:LiangBookDB_MDB", "", "");
    System.out.println("Database LiangBookDB_MDB connected");

    // Create a statement
    Statement stmt = connection.createStatement();

    try {
      // Create the Student TABLE
      stmt.executeUpdate(
        "create table Student(firstName varchar(20), "
        + "mi varchar(1), lastName varchar(20))");

      // Insert two records into the Student TABLE
      stmt.executeUpdate(
        "insert into Student values ('John', 'F', 'Smith')");
      stmt.executeUpdate(
        "insert into Student values ('Wade', 'E', 'Bush')");
    }
    catch (SQLException ex) {
      System.out.println("Table Student already exists");
    }

    // Select the column student from the Student table
    ResultSet rset = stmt.executeQuery
      ("select firstName, mi, lastName from Student");

    // Iterate through the result and print the student names
    while (rset.next())
      System.out.println(rset.getString(1) + " " +
        rset.getString(2) + ". " + rset.getString(3));

    // Close the connection
    connection.close();
  }
}
```

Listing 12.2 *TestJdbcOdbc.java*

4. Compile and test the program. A sample run of the program is shown in Figure 12.12.

Example Review

Java does not run on 16-bit platforms. You must use a 32-bit ODBC driver, not a 16-bit ODBC driver. The program was tested using MS Access 2000. It should also work with MS Access 97.

continued

Example 12.1 continued

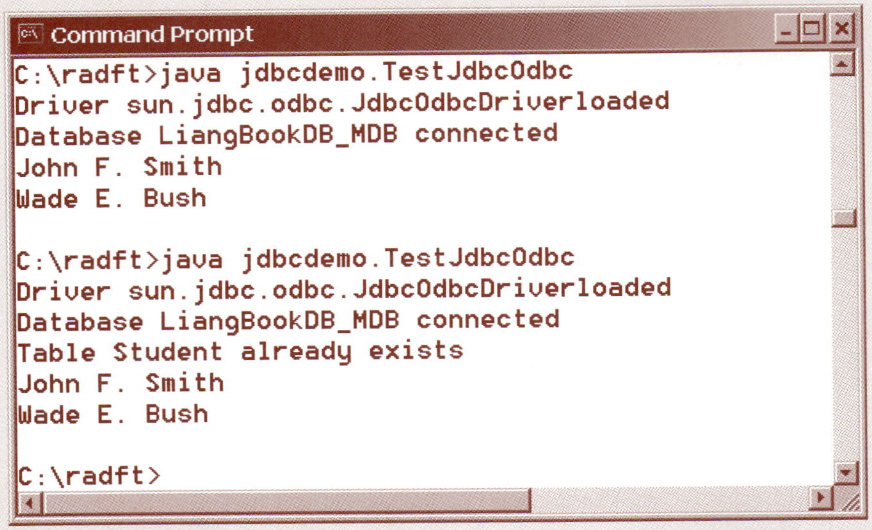

Figure 12.12 *The Java program accesses an MS Access data source through the JDBC-ODBC bridge driver.*

The URL of a data source for a JDBC-ODBC connection is `jdbc:odbc:ODBC-Source-Name`. So `jdbc:odbc:LiangBookDB_MDB` is the URL used in the statement (Lines 13–14)

```
Connection connection = DriverManager.getConnection
  ("jdbc:odbc:LiangBookDB_MDB", "", "" );
```

to establish a connection to the data source LiangBookDB_MDB.

The program creates the Student table, inserts two records, and displays the records in the table. The SQL statements are passed as string arguments.

TIP

The statement `connection.close()` (Line 46) closes the connection, but it is not necessary in this example because the connection is automatically closed upon exiting the program. However, I recommend that you use this statement whenever a connection is no longer needed. Closing it will release the resource associated with the connection.

NOTE

When executing this example using MS Access 97, close MS Access, because only one active session is allowed on MS Access 97. Access Windows 2000 running on Windows 2000 does not have this restriction.

12.5.3 Using the Native-Protocol Driver

A native-protocol driver translates JDBC calls into network protocol used by a DBMS and communicates with the DBMS directly. Since some part of the network protocol for facilitating database communications is vendor-specific, a driver of this kind is usually provided by the vendor. The driver is written in 100% pure Java to implement high-level network communication to the server. Since the native-protocol driver, unlike the native-API driver, does not require that any database-specific binary code be loaded on the client, it is suitable for deploying Java applets.

Oracle, the most popular database, is used by many large corporations. In this section, you will learn how to use the Oracle JDBC Thin driver to develop Java applets for accessing remote Oracle databases. Oracle's JDBC Thin driver is a native-protocol driver that provides an implementation of the Oracle high-level communications protocol known as TNS (Transparent Network Substrate). This driver can access local or remote servers of Oracle 8i or higher from a client on any platform.

Note
The Oracle JDBC OCI drivers for Oracle 7 and Oracle 8 or higher are different. You have to use the driver that matches the database.

Example 12.2 Using the Oracle JDBC Thin Driver

This example develops a Java applet that connects to a remote Oracle 8i or 9i server using an Oracle JDBC Thin driver. After the connection is established, the program obtains the system time from the server and displays it on the applet.

Follow the steps below to complete the project.

1. If you have already installed Oracle 8i or 9i, it is likely that you have the JDBC driver installed in \jdbc\lib of your Oracle installation directory. If not, join Oracle Tech Network to download it. It is also bundled with Personal Oracle 8i or 9i.

2. In the jdbcdemo package, create an applet named `TestOraJdbcThin` that connects to the test database on liang.armstrong.edu, obtains the current system time from the server, and displays it on the applet. The program is given in Listing 12.3.

3. Copy ORACLE_HOME\jdbc\lib\classes12.zip to FORTE_HOME\lib\ext. Restart Forte.

4. Compile TestOraJdbcThin.java and run the program. A sample run of the program is shown in Figure 12.13.

continued

Example 12.2 continued

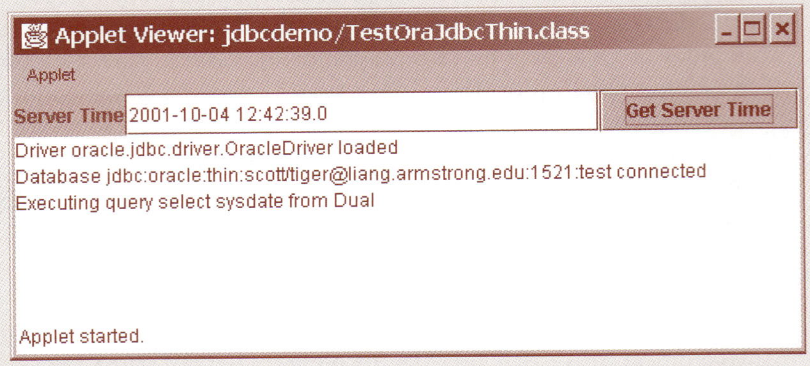

Figure 12.13 *Using the Oracle JDBC Thin driver, the Java applet accesses a remote database and obtains the time from the server.*

```
package jdbcdemo;

import java.awt.*;
import java.awt.event.*;
import java.applet.*;
import javax.swing.*;
import java.sql.*;

public class TestOraJdbcThin extends JApplet {
  // SQL Statement
  Statement stmt;

  boolean isStandalone = false;
  JPanel jPanel1 = new JPanel();
  JTextArea jtaOutput = new JTextArea();
  BorderLayout borderLayout1 = new BorderLayout();
  JLabel jLabel1 = new JLabel();
  JTextField jtfTime = new JTextField();
  JButton jbtGetTime = new JButton();

  /** Initialize the applet */
  public void init() {
    try {
      jbInit();
    }
    catch(Exception e) {
      e.printStackTrace();
    }
  }

  /** Component initialization */
  private void jbInit() throws Exception {
    this.setSize(new Dimension(399, 166));
    jPanel1.setLayout(borderLayout1);
    jLabel1.setText("Server Time");
    jbtGetTime.setText("Get Server Time");
```

Listing 12.3 *TestOraJdbcThin.java*

```
    jbtGetTime.addActionListener(
      new java.awt.event.ActionListener() {
      public void actionPerformed(ActionEvent e) {
        jbtGetTime_actionPerformed(e);
      }
    });
    this.getContentPane().add(jPanel1, BorderLayout.NORTH);
    jPanel1.add(jLabel1, BorderLayout.WEST);
    jPanel1.add(jtfTime, BorderLayout.CENTER);
    jPanel1.add(jbtGetTime, BorderLayout.EAST);
    this.getContentPane().add(jtaOutput, BorderLayout.CENTER);

    // Initialized JDBC
    initializeJDBC();
  }

  private void initializeJDBC() {
    try {
      // Load the Oracle JDBC Thin driver
      Class.forName("oracle.jdbc.driver.OracleDriver");
      jtaOutput.append("Driver oracle.jdbc.driver.OracleDriver" +
        " loaded"+'\n');

      // Connect to the sample database
      Connection connection = DriverManager.getConnection
        ("jdbc:oracle:thin:@liang.armstrong.edu:1521:test",
         "scott", "tiger");
      jtaOutput.append("Database jdbc:oracle:thin:scott/tiger" +
        "@liang.armstrong.edu:1521:test connected"+'\n');

      // Create a Statement
      stmt = connection.createStatement();
    }
    catch (Exception ex) {
      jtaOutput.append(ex.getMessage() + '\n');
    }
  }

  void jbtGetTime_actionPerformed(ActionEvent e) {
    String query = "select sysdate from Dual";

    if (e.getSource() instanceof JButton) {
      try {
        // Execute the query
        jtaOutput.append("Executing query " + query + "\n");
        ResultSet rset = stmt.executeQuery(query);

        // Display the time
        while (rset.next())
          jtfTime.setText(rset.getString(1));
      }
      catch (Exception ex) {
        jtaOutput.append(ex.getMessage() + '\n');
      }
    }
  }
}
```

Listing 12.3 *continued*

continued

Example 12.2 continued

Example Review

The Oracle JDBC Thin connection URL is `jdbc:oracle:thin:@hostname:port:sid`. So the following statement (Lines 61–63)

```
Connection conn = DriverManager.getConnection
  ("jdbc:oracle:thin:@liang.armstrong.edu:1521:test",
   "scott", "tiger");
```

establishes a connection to the remote database on liang.armstrong.edu using username **scott** and password **tiger** to the database with a system id test whose listener is at port 1521.

You can test the applet using the appletviewer utility, as shown in Figure 12.13. If this applet is deployed on the server where the database is located, any client on the Internet can run it from a Web browser. Since the client may not have the Oracle Thin driver, you should make the driver available along with the applet in one archive file. This archive file can be created as follows:

1. Copy ORACLE_HOME\jdbc\lib\classes12.zip to TestOraJdbcThin.zip.
2. Add TestOraJdbcThin.class into TestOraJdbcThin.zip using the WinZip utility.
3. Add TestOraJdbcThin$1.class into TestOraJdbcThin.zip using the WinZip utility. TestOraJdbcThin$1.class is for the anonymous inner event adapter class for listening to the button action.

You need to deploy TestOraJdbcThin.zip and TestOraJdbcThin.html on the server. TestOraJdbcThin.html should use the applet tag with a reference to the Zip file, as follows:

```
<applet
  code="jdbcdemo/TestOraJdbcThin"
  archive="TestOraJdbcThin.zip"
  width=500
  height=200
>
</applet>
```

NOTE
To access the database from an applet, it is necessary, because of security restrictions, for the applet to be downloaded from the server where the Oracle database is located. Hence, you have to deploy the applet on the server.

NOTE
Do not use a semicolon (;) to end the Oracle SQL command. The semicolon does not work with the Oracle JDBC drivers, but it does work with the other drivers used in the book.

NOTE
To run this program standalone as an application, add a main method. Add ORACLE_HOME\jdbc\lib\classes12.zip in the classpath if you want to run the program standalone from the DOS prompt.

12.5.4 Using the Native-API Driver

A native-API driver translates JDBC calls directly into calls on the DBMS-specific client API. Thus, you must install the JDBC driver as well as the DBMS client-side library. Major enterprise database vendors like Oracle, Sybase, and IBM already provide native support of database connectivity for development tools like Visual Basic and Borland Delphi, among many others, through their proprietary client API. The support extended by these companies enables JDBC to talk directly to the client API through the native-API driver.

This section demonstrates how to develop a Java application that accesses a remote Oracle database via the Oracle JDBC OCI driver. Oracle's JDBC OCI driver is a native-API driver that provides an implementation of the JDBC interfaces on top of the OCI (Oracle Call Interface) to interact with an Oracle database. This driver can access a local or remote Oracle database from a client on Windows.

Example 12.3 Using the Oracle JDBC OCI Driver

This example develops a Java program that gets the system time from a remote database. The server is accessible on the Internet with the host name liang.armstrong.edu (IP address 130.254.204.33). An Oracle database is running on the server. You can access the database using username **scott** and password **tiger**.

Follow the steps below to set up the client on Windows.

1. Install Oracle client if necessary. Oracle client includes SQL*Net and all other dependent files required to support connecting the JDBC OCI driver to the Oracle server. SQL*NET is an Oracle proprietary product that supports network service to the server from the client.
2. Install the Oracle 8i or 9i JDBC driver if necessary. The Oracle 8 JDBC OCI driver and JDBC Thin driver are bundled in the same files classes12.zip.
3. Add the Oracle TNS alias name for the sample database in the \network\admin\tnsname.ora file as follows, so that the program can access the Oracle test database for this book.

continued

Example 12.3 continued

```
liang =
  (description =
    (address_list =
      (address =
        (protocol = TCP)
        (host = liang.armstrong.edu)
        (port = 1521)
      )
    )
    (connect_data =
      (sid = test)
    )
  )
```

4. In the jdbcdemo package, create a class name TestOraJdbcOci8, as shown in Listing 12.4.

5. To run the program from the DOS prompt, add ORACLE_HOME\jdbc\lib in the path, and add ORACLE_HOME\jdbc\lib\classes12.zip in the classpath. Since you have already copied ORACLE_HOME\jdbc\lib\classes12.zip to FORTE_HOME\lib\ext in the preceding example, you can also run this program from Forte.

```
package jdbcdemo;

import java.sql.*;

public class TestOraJdbcOci8 {
  public static void main(String[] args)
    throws SQLException, ClassNotFoundException {
    // Load the Oracle JDBC driver
    Class.forName ("oracle.jdbc.driver.OracleDriver");
    System.out.println("Driver loaded");

    // Connect to the sample database
    Connection connection = DriverManager.getConnection
      ("jdbc:oracle:oci8:@liang", "scott", "tiger");
    System.out.println("Database connected");

    // Create a Statement
    Statement stmt = connection.createStatement();

    // Select the date and time from the server
    ResultSet rset = stmt.executeQuery("select sysdate from Dual");

    // Show the system date and time
    while (rset.next())
      System.out.println(rset.getString(1));
  }
}
```

Listing 12.4 *TestOraJdbcOCI8.java*

6. Compile and run the program. A sample run of the program is shown in Figure 12.14.

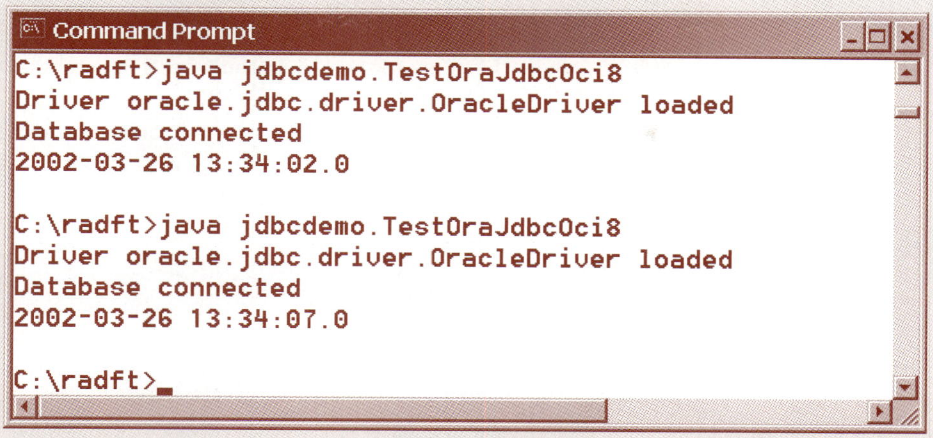

Figure 12.14 *Using an Oracle 8 JDBC OCI driver, the Java program accesses a remote database and obtains the time from the server.*

Example Review

The Oracle 8 JDBC OCI connection url is jdbc:oracle:oci8@tnsname. So the following statement (Lines 13–14)

```
Connection connection = DriverManager.getConnection
  ("jdbc:oracle:oci8:@liang", "scott", "tiger");
```

establishes a connection to the remote database on the host liang.armstrong.edu through the TNS alias name liang using username **scott** and password **tiger**.

The SQL statement "select sysdate from Dual" is specific to Oracle, which returns the current system date and time on the database server.

The success of this example depends on a sequence of steps, each of which must be done exactly right to avoid frustrating errors. Here is a list of things to check:

- Check whether you can log on to the database using **sqlplus scott/tiger@liang**. If this fails, check whether you have created the right alias in the tnsname.ora file for the database server.
- If you get a `ClassNotFoundException`, you probably did not set ORACLE_HOME\jdbc\lib\classes12.zip in the classpath.
- If you get an error indicating that ocijdbc8.dll file was not found when running this program from the DOS prompt, it is because you did not add \jdbc\bin in the path.

12.6 A Universal SQL Client

You have learned how to use various drivers to connect to the database, create statements for executing SQL statements, and process the results from SQL queries. This section presents a bean component for connecting to databases, and a useful utility for processing interactive SQL commands.

Example 12.4 Creating a Connection Dialog Component

This example develops a dialog bean component that connects to a database, as shown in Figure 12.15. The user enters or selects a JDBC driver, a database URL, a username, and a password, and clicks the Connect button to connect to the database. Once connected, an instance of the `Connection` interface can be obtained from the `getConnection` method in the dialog bean.

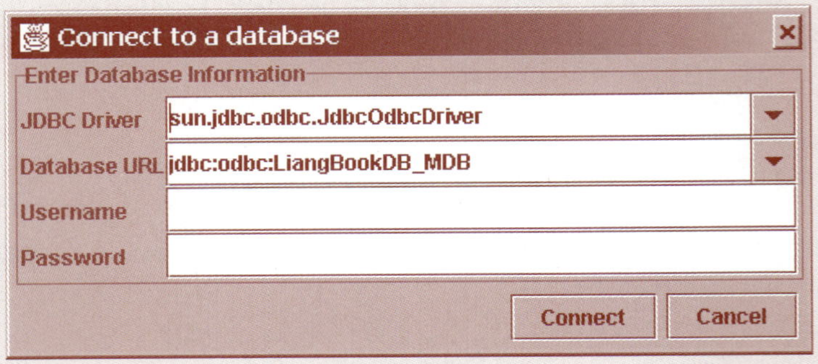

Figure 12.15 *The Connect to a Database dialog box enables you to connect to any JDBC data source.*

Here are the steps to create this component.

1. In the jdbcdemo package, create a dialog class named `DBConnectDialog` using the Forte Dialog form wizard.

2. Set the `modal` property of the dialog to `true`, and the `title` to "Connect to a database." Drop a `JPanel` to the south of `panel1` to create `jPanel1`, and drop a `JPanel` to the center of `panel1` to create `jPanel2`.

3. In `jPanel2`, set the `layout` to `BorderLayout`, and set a border with the title "Enter Database Information."

4. Drop a `JPanel` to the west of `jPanel2` to create `jPanel3`, and drop a `JPanel` to the center of `jPanel2` to create `jPanel4`. Set the `layout` of both `jPanel3` and `jPanel4` to `GridLayout`, with the `row` property set to 4 and the `column` property set to 1.

5. Drop a `JLabel` four times to `jPanel3`, and set the `text` of the labels to "JDBC Driver," "Database URL," "Username," and "Password." Drop a `JComboBox` twice to `jPanel4`, and rename the combo boxes `jcboDriver`, and `jcboURL`. Set the `editable` property of the combo boxes to `true` so as to allow the user to type in a driver name and URL in addition to selecting them from the combo boxes. Drop a `JTextField` to `jPanel4` and rename the object `jtfUsername`. Drop a `JPasswordField` to `jPanel4` and rename the object `jpfPassword`.

6. Set the `layout` of `jPanel1` to `FlowLayout` with right alignment. Drop a `JButton` twice to create buttons Connect and Cancel, and rename the buttons `jbtConnect` and `jbtCancel`.

7. Add a property named `connection` of the `java.sql.Connection` type with a get method. This field stores the connection to the database once a connected session is established.

8. Use the `addItem` method to add JDBC driver classes and database URLs to `jcboDriver` and `jcboURL`. Generate and implement the handlers for the Connect and Cancel buttons, as shown in Listing 12.5 (Lines 102–128).

```
1   package jdbcdemo;
2
3   import java.sql.*;
4
5   public class DBConnectDialog extends javax.swing.JDialog {
6     private java.sql.Connection connection;
7
8     /** Creates new form DBConnectDialog */
9     public DBConnectDialog() {
10      this(null, true);
11    }
12
13    /** Creates new form DBConnectDialog */
14    public DBConnectDialog(java.awt.Frame parent, boolean modal) {
15      super(parent, modal);
16      initComponents();
17
18      // Add items to the combo boxes
19      jcboDriver.addItem("sun.jdbc.odbc.JdbcOdbcDriver");
20      jcboURL.addItem("jdbc:odbc:LiangBookDB_MDB");
21      jcboDriver.addItem("oracle.jdbc.driver.OracleDriver");
22      jcboURL.addItem
23        ("jdbc:oracle:thin:@liang.armstrong.edu:1521:test");
24      // Oracle Type 2 JDBC Connection
25      jcboURL.addItem("jdbc:oracle:oci8:@liang");
26      // Pointbase driver and url
27      jcboDriver.addItem("com.pointbase.jdbc.jdbcUniversalDriver");
28      jcboURL.addItem
29        ("jdbc:pointbase://localhost:9092/sample");
30      // Interbase driver and url
31      jcboDriver.addItem("interbase.interclient.Driver");
32      jcboURL.addItem
33        ("jdbc:interbase://localhost/C:/LiangBook/LiangBookDB.gdb");
34      // Username and password for Oracle scott/tiger
35    }
36
37    private void initComponents() {
38      jPanel1 = new javax.swing.JPanel();
39      jbtConnect = new javax.swing.JButton();
40      jbtCancel = new javax.swing.JButton();
41      jPanel2 = new javax.swing.JPanel();
42      jPanel3 = new javax.swing.JPanel();
43      jLabel1 = new javax.swing.JLabel();
44      jLabel2 = new javax.swing.JLabel();
45      jLabel3 = new javax.swing.JLabel();
46      jLabel4 = new javax.swing.JLabel();
47      jPanel4 = new javax.swing.JPanel();
48      jcboDriver = new javax.swing.JComboBox();
49      jcboURL = new javax.swing.JComboBox();
50      jtfUsername = new javax.swing.JTextField();
```

Listing 12.5 *DBConnectDialog.java*

continued

Example 12.4 continued

```
    jpfPassword = new javax.swing.JPasswordField();
    setTitle("Connect to a database");
    setModal(true);
    addWindowListener(new java.awt.event.WindowAdapter() {
      public void windowClosing(java.awt.event.WindowEvent evt) {
        closeDialog(evt);
      }
    });
    jPanel1.setLayout(
      new java.awt.FlowLayout(java.awt.FlowLayout.RIGHT));
    jbtConnect.setText("Connect");
    jbtConnect.addActionListener(
      new java.awt.event.ActionListener() {
      public void actionPerformed(java.awt.event.ActionEvent evt) {
        jbtConnectActionPerformed(evt);
      }
    });
    jPanel1.add(jbtConnect);
    jbtCancel.setText("Cancel");
    jbtCancel.addActionListener(new java.awt.event.ActionListener() {
      public void actionPerformed(java.awt.event.ActionEvent evt) {
        jbtCancelActionPerformed(evt);
      }
    });
    jPanel1.add(jbtCancel);
    getContentPane().add(jPanel1, java.awt.BorderLayout.SOUTH);
    jPanel2.setLayout(new java.awt.BorderLayout());
    jPanel2.setBorder(new javax.swing.border.TitledBorder(
      "Enter database information"));
    jPanel3.setLayout(new java.awt.GridLayout(4, 0));
    jLabel1.setText("JDBC Driver");
    jPanel3.add(jLabel1);
    jLabel2.setText("Database URL");
    jPanel3.add(jLabel2);
    jLabel3.setText("Username");
    jPanel3.add(jLabel3);
    jLabel4.setText("Password");
    jPanel3.add(jLabel4);
    jPanel2.add(jPanel3, java.awt.BorderLayout.WEST);
    jPanel4.setLayout(new java.awt.GridLayout(4, 0));
    jcboDriver.setEditable(true);
    jPanel4.add(jcboDriver);
    jcboURL.setEditable(true);
    jPanel4.add(jcboURL);
    jPanel4.add(jtfUsername);
    jPanel4.add(jpfPassword);
    jPanel2.add(jPanel4, java.awt.BorderLayout.CENTER);
    getContentPane().add(jPanel2, java.awt.BorderLayout.CENTER);
    pack();
  }

  private void jbtCancelActionPerformed(
    java.awt.event.ActionEvent evt) {
    // Close the dialog box
    setVisible(false);
  }

  private void jbtConnectActionPerformed(
    java.awt.event.ActionEvent evt) {
```

Listing 12.5 *continued*

```
110        // Get database information from the user input
111        String driver = (String)jcboDriver.getSelectedItem();
112        String url = (String)jcboURL.getSelectedItem();
113        String username = jtfUsername.getText().trim();
114        String password = new String(jpfPassword.getPassword());
115
116        // Connection to the database
117        try {
118          Class.forName(driver);
119          System.out.println("Driver " + driver + "loaded\n");
120          connection = DriverManager.getConnection(
121          url, username, password);
122          System.out.println("Connected to " + url + '\n');
123          setVisible(false);
124        }
125        catch (java.lang.Exception ex) {
126          ex.printStackTrace();
127        }
128      }
129
130      /** Closes the dialog */
131      private void closeDialog(java.awt.event.WindowEvent evt) {
132        setVisible(false);
133        dispose();
134      }
135
136      /** Return connection */
137      public java.sql.Connection getConnection() {
138        return connection;
139      }
140
141      // Variables declaration - do not modify
142      private javax.swing.JPanel jPanel1;
143      private javax.swing.JButton jbtConnect;
144      private javax.swing.JButton jbtCancel;
145      private javax.swing.JPanel jPanel2;
146      private javax.swing.JPanel jPanel3;
147      private javax.swing.JLabel jLabel1;
148      private javax.swing.JLabel jLabel2;
149      private javax.swing.JLabel jLabel3;
150      private javax.swing.JLabel jLabel4;
151      private javax.swing.JPanel jPanel4;
152      private javax.swing.JComboBox jcboDriver;
153      private javax.swing.JComboBox jcboURL;
154      private javax.swing.JTextField jtfUsername;
155      private javax.swing.JPasswordField jpfPassword;
156      // End of variables declaration
157    }
```

Listing 12.5 *continued*

Example Review

An example of the use of this dialog component will be given in the next example.

The `modal` property of the dialog box is set to `true` (Line 10) to ensure that the Connect to Database dialog is dealt with before performing other tasks.

You can choose a JDBC driver (or a database URL) from the combo box or enter a driver class (or a database URL) in the combo box.

Once a connection is established, the `getConnection` method returns the `Connection` object. If the return value is null, there is no active connection.

Example 12.5 Creating an Interactive SQL Client

This example creates a Java applet for submitting and executing SQL commands interactively, as shown in Figure 12.16. The client can connect to any JDBC data source, and submit SQL SELECT commands and non-SELECT commands for execution. The execution result is displayed for the SELECT queries, and the execution status is displayed for the non-SELECT commands.

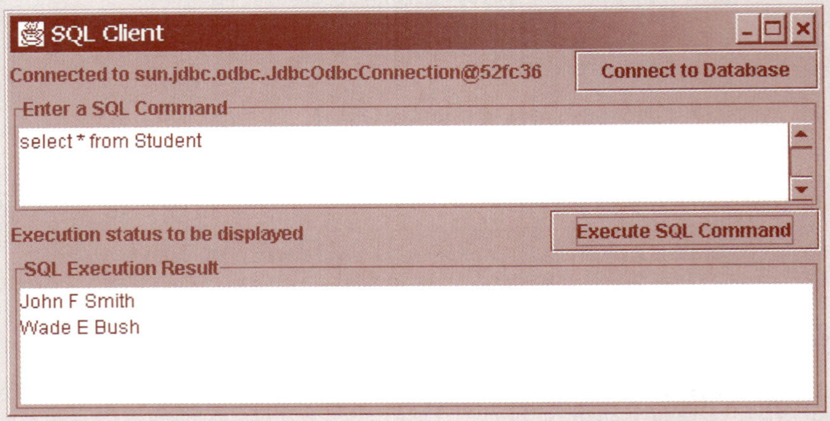

Figure 12.16 *You can connect to any JDBC data source and execute SQL commands interactively.*

Here are the steps to create this applet.

1. In the jdbcdemo package, create a new applet named SQLClient.java using the Forte Swing JApplet form wizard.

2. Drop a `JPanel` to the north of the applet to create `jPanel1`, and drop a `JScrollPane` to the center of the applet to create `jScrollPane1`.

3. In `jPanel1`, set the `layout` to `BorderLayout`. Drop a `JPanel` to the north of `jPanel1` to create `jPanel2`. Drop a `JPanel` to the south of `jPanel1` to create `jPanel3`. Drop a `JScrollPane` to the center of `jPanel1` to create `jScroll-Pane2`.

4. In `jPanel2`, set the `layout` to `BorderLayout`. Drop a `JButton` to the east of `jPanel2` and rename the button `jbtConnect`. Set the `text` of the button to Connect. Drop a `JLabel` to the center of `jPanel2` and rename the label `jlblConnectionStatus`.

5. In `jScrollPane2`, set its border title to "Enter an SQL Command." Drop a `JTextArea` into `jScrollPane2` to create `jtaSQLCommand`.

6. In `jPanel3`, set the `layout` to `BorderLayout`. Drop a `JButton` to the east of `jPanel3` and rename the button `jbtExecuteSQL`. Set the `text` of the button to "Execute SQL Command." Drop a `JLabel` to the center of `jPanel3` and rename the label `jlblExecutionStatus`.

7. In `jScrollPane1`, set its border title to "SQL Execution Result." Drop a `JTextArea` into `jScrollPane1` to create `jtaSQLResult`.

8. Create an instance of `DBConnectDialog` named `dBConnectDialog1`, as shown in Line 12 in Listing 12.6.

9. Generate and implement the handlers for the Connect button and the Execute SQL Command button, as shown in Listing 12.6 (Lines 65–89).

```
1  package jdbcdemo;
2
3  import java.sql.*;
4
5  public class SQLClient extends javax.swing.JApplet {
6    // Connection to the database
7    Connection connection;
8
9    // Statement to execute SQL commands
10   Statement statement;
11
12   DBConnectDialog dBConnectDialog1 = new DBConnectDialog();
13
14   /** Creates new form SQLClient */
15   public SQLClient() {
16     initComponents();
17   }
18
19   private void initComponents() {
20     jPanel1 = new javax.swing.JPanel();
21     jPanel2 = new javax.swing.JPanel();
22     jlblConnectionStatus = new javax.swing.JLabel();
23     jbtConnect = new javax.swing.JButton();
24     jScrollPane2 = new javax.swing.JScrollPane();
25     jtaSQLCommand = new javax.swing.JTextArea();
26     jPanel3 = new javax.swing.JPanel();
27     jbtExecuteSQL = new javax.swing.JButton();
28     jlblExecutionStatus = new javax.swing.JLabel();
29     jScrollPane1 = new javax.swing.JScrollPane();
30     jtaSQLResult = new javax.swing.JTextArea();
31     jPanel1.setLayout(new java.awt.BorderLayout());
32     jPanel2.setLayout(new java.awt.BorderLayout());
33     jPanel2.add(jlblConnectionStatus, java.awt.BorderLayout.CENTER);
34     jbtConnect.setText("Connect");
35     jbtConnect.addActionListener(
36       new java.awt.event.ActionListener() {
37       public void actionPerformed(java.awt.event.ActionEvent evt) {
38         jbtConnectActionPerformed(evt);
39       }
40     });
41     jPanel2.add(jbtConnect, java.awt.BorderLayout.EAST);
42     jPanel1.add(jPanel2, java.awt.BorderLayout.NORTH);
43     jScrollPane2.setBorder(new javax.swing.border.TitledBorder(
44       "Enter an SQL Command"));
45     jScrollPane2.setViewportView(jtaSQLCommand);
46     jPanel1.add(jScrollPane2, java.awt.BorderLayout.CENTER);
47     jPanel3.setLayout(new java.awt.BorderLayout());
48     jbtExecuteSQL.setText("Execute SQL Command");
49     jbtExecuteSQL.addActionListener(
50       new java.awt.event.ActionListener() {
```

Listing 12.6 *SQLClient.java*

continued

Example 12.5 continued

```
      public void actionPerformed(java.awt.event.ActionEvent evt) {
        jbtExecuteSQLActionPerformed(evt);
      }
    });
    jPanel3.add(jbtExecuteSQL, java.awt.BorderLayout.EAST);
    jPanel3.add(jlblExecutionStatus, java.awt.BorderLayout.CENTER);
    jPanel1.add(jPanel3, java.awt.BorderLayout.SOUTH);
    getContentPane().add(jPanel1, java.awt.BorderLayout.NORTH);
    jScrollPane1.setBorder(new javax.swing.border.TitledBorder(
      "SQL Execution Result"));
    jScrollPane1.setViewportView(jtaSQLResult);
    getContentPane().add(jScrollPane1, java.awt.BorderLayout.CENTER);
  }

  private void jbtExecuteSQLActionPerformed(
    java.awt.event.ActionEvent evt) {
    if (connection == null) {
      jtaSQLResult.setText("Please connect to a database first");
      return;
    }
    else {
      String sqlCommand = jtaSQLCommand.getText().trim();
      if (sqlCommand.toUpperCase().startsWith("SELECT")) {
        processSQLSelect(sqlCommand);
      }
      else {
        processSQLNonSelect(sqlCommand);
      }
    }
  }

  private void jbtConnectActionPerformed(
    java.awt.event.ActionEvent evt) {
    dBConnectDialog1.setVisible(true);
    connection = dBConnectDialog1.getConnection();
    if (connection != null) {
      jlblConnectionStatus.setText("Connected to " + connection);
    }
  }

  /** Execute SQL SELECT commands */
  private void processSQLSelect(String sqlCommand) {
    try {
      // Get a new statement for the current connection
      statement = connection.createStatement();

      // Execute a SELECT SQL command
      ResultSet resultSet = statement.executeQuery(sqlCommand);

      // Find the number of columns in the result set
      int columnCount = resultSet.getMetaData().getColumnCount();
      String row = "";

      while (resultSet.next()) {
        for (int i = 1; i <= columnCount; i++) {
          row += resultSet.getString(i) + " ";
        }

```

Listing 12.6 *continued*

```
            jtaSQLResult.append(row + '\n');

            // Reset row to empty
            row = "";
          }
        }
        catch (SQLException ex) {
          jlblExecutionStatus.setText(ex.toString());
        }
      }

      /** Execute SQL DDL, and modification commands */
      private void processSQLNonSelect(String sqlCommand) {
        try {
          // Get a new statement for the current connection
          statement = connection.createStatement();

          // Execute a non-SELECT SQL command
          statement.executeUpdate(sqlCommand);

          jlblExecutionStatus.setText("SQL command executed");
        }
        catch (SQLException ex) {
          jlblExecutionStatus.setText(ex.toString());
        }
      }

      /** Main method */
      public static void main(String[] args) {
        SQLClient applet = new SQLClient();
        javax.swing.JFrame frame = new javax.swing.JFrame();
        frame.setDefaultCloseOperation(javax.swing.JFrame.EXIT_ON_CLOSE);
        frame.setTitle("SQLClient");
        frame.getContentPane().add(applet, java.awt.BorderLayout.CENTER);
        frame.setSize(400,320);
        java.awt.Dimension d =
        java.awt.Toolkit.getDefaultToolkit().getScreenSize();
        frame.setLocation((d.width - frame.getSize().width) / 2,
        (d.height - frame.getSize().height) / 2);
        frame.setVisible(true);
      }

      // Variables declaration - do not modify
      private javax.swing.JPanel jPanel1;
      private javax.swing.JPanel jPanel2;
      private javax.swing.JLabel jlblConnectionStatus;
      private javax.swing.JButton jbtConnect;
      private javax.swing.JScrollPane jScrollPane2;
      private javax.swing.JTextArea jtaSQLCommand;
      private javax.swing.JPanel jPanel3;
      private javax.swing.JButton jbtExecuteSQL;
      private javax.swing.JLabel jlblExecutionStatus;
      private javax.swing.JScrollPane jScrollPane1;
      private javax.swing.JTextArea jtaSQLResult;
      // End of variables declaration
    }
```

Listing 12.6 *continued*

continued

Example 12.5 continued

Example Review

The Connect button displays the dialog box for connecting to a database. You can retrieve the connection from the `getConnection` method in `dBConnect-Dialog1`.

The Execute SQL Command button gets the SQL command from the text area (`jtaSQLCommand`), and determines whether the command is a SELECT query or a DDL or data modification statement. If the command is a SELECT query, the `executeQuery` method is invoked to obtain the query result. The result is displayed in the text area (`jtaSQLResult`). If the command is a non-SELECT query, the `executeUpdate` method is invoked to execute the SQL command. The result of execution is displayed in the label (`jlblExecutionStatus`).

The `getMetaData` method in the `ResultSet` interface is used to obtain an instance of `ResultSetMetaData`. `ResultSetMetaData` can be used to find the metadata information on the result set, including the number of columns in the result set. `ResultSetMetaData` will be further discussed in Chapter 13, "Advanced Java Database Programming." In Exercise 13.3, you will modify this program to display the query result in a table.

If you connect to an Oracle database, do not use a semicolon at the end of the SQL command.

12.7 Database Explorer

You can use Forte's database explorer to browse a set of databases, and its associated tables, views, and stored procedures, in addition to database metadata. You can also use it to add drivers, test drivers, execute SQL statements, and migrate database schemas across different databases. To use the database explorer, choose the Runtime tab in the Explorer, as shown in Figure 12.17.

The Databases node contains the subnodes Adaptors and Drivers. You can create an adaptor and use it to replace missing metadata. The Drivers node contains all drivers. You can add a new driver by choosing Add Driver from the context menu of the Drivers node. Once a driver is added, you can test it by choosing Test Driver from the context menu of a driver, as shown in Figure 12.17. The or icon indicates that the driver file is not present. You need to copy the driver file into FORTE_HOME/lib/ext and restart Forte.

12.7.1 Add Connection Nodes

To explore the database, you need to first add a connection node by choosing Add Connection from the context menu of the Databases node (Figure 12.18) to display the New Database Connection dialog box, as shown in Figure 12.19. Select a driver name from the Name field. Enter database URL, user name, and password

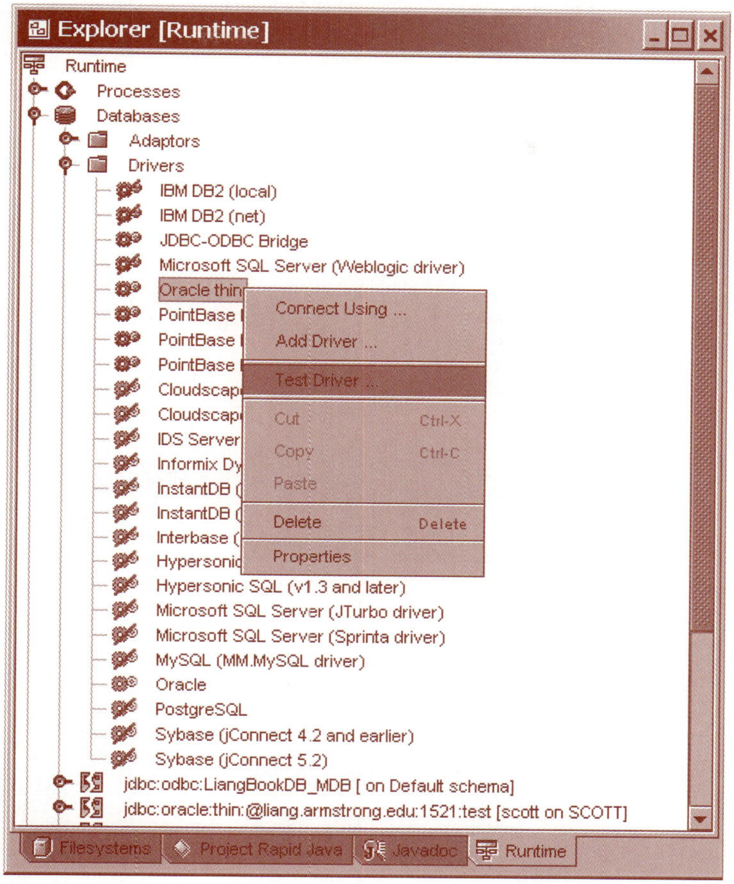

Figure 12.17 *The Database Explorer enables you to explore databases from Forte.*

to connect to a database. You will see a Connection Node for the database under the Databases node in the Explorer.

NOTE

If you use MS Access database, the user name and password are optional.

12.7.2 Browsing Tables, Views, and Procedures

To explore database contents and metadata, you need to first connect to the database by choosing Connect from the context menu of the Connection Node, as shown in Figure 12.20.

Once the database is connected, you can view metadata information by choosing Properties from the context menu of the Databases node, as shown in Figure 12.21. You can also browse tables, views, and procedures in the database from the Connection node, as shown in Figure 12.22.

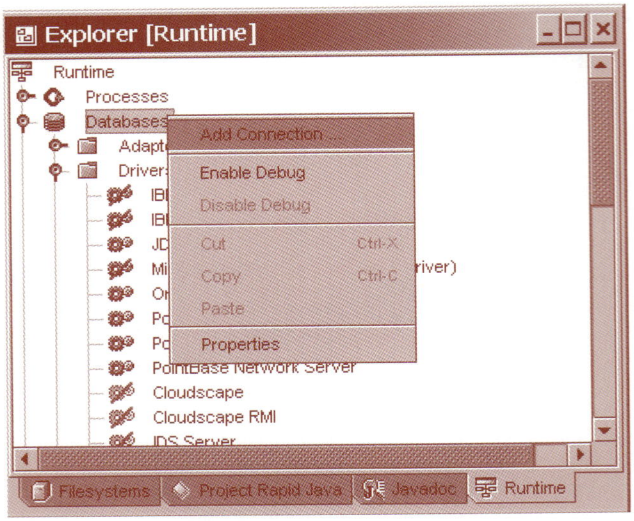

Figure 12.18 *You can add a connection node to explore the database from the context menu of the Databases node.*

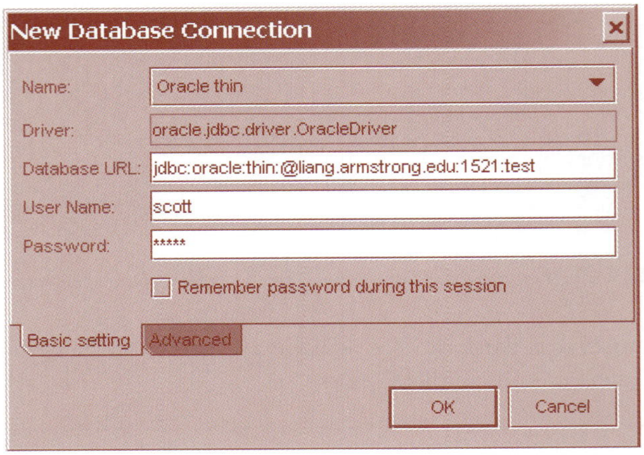

Figure 12.19 *You need to specify a driver, database URL, user name, and password to connect to a database.*

You can create or delete a new table, add or delete a column, view table data, execute SQL commands, and migrate table schemas by using the commands in the context menu of the table, as shown in Figure 12.22.

To view data in a table, choose View Data from the context menu of the table. The data is displayed in the Command Editor window, as shown in Figure 12.23. You can also type in SQL commands and display the execution results in this window.

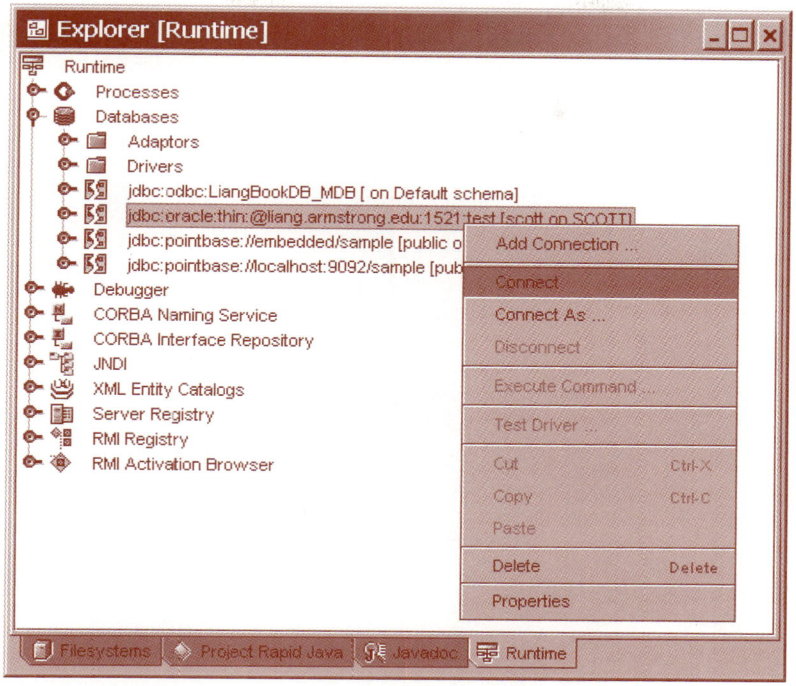

Figure 12.20 *You need to specify a driver, database URL, user name, and password to connect to a database.*

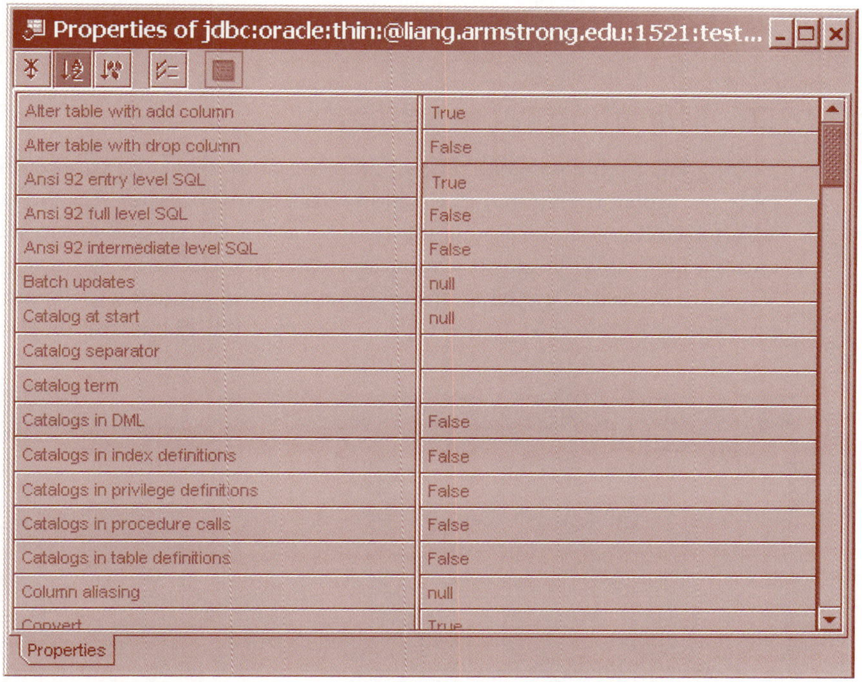

Figure 12.21 *The database metadata information is displayed in the Properties window.*

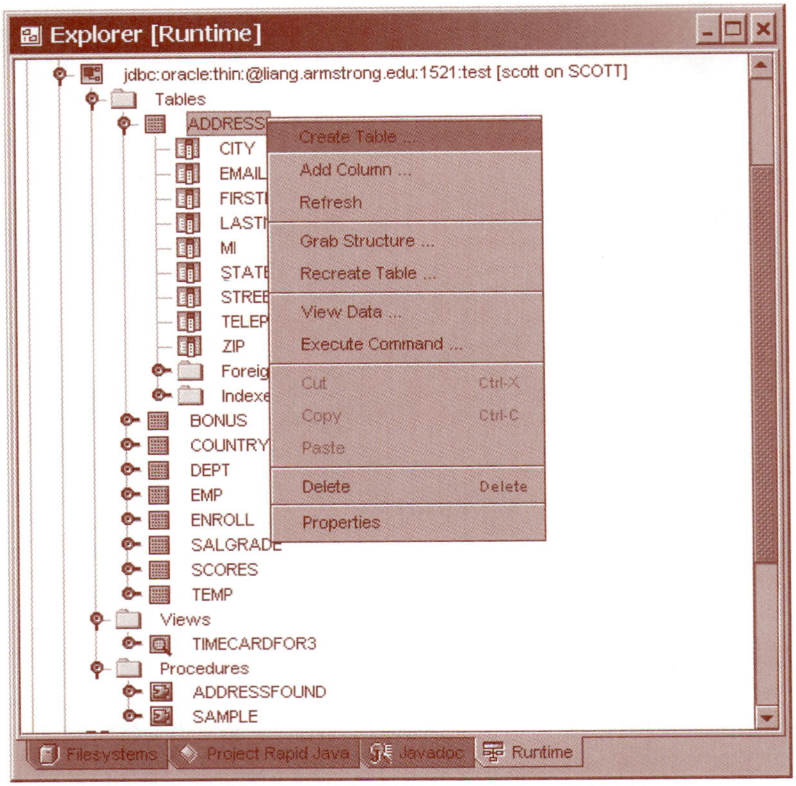

Figure 12.22 *You can browse tables, views and procedures in the database from the Connection node.*

12.7.3 Migrating Table Schemas

To migrate a table schema, choose Grab Structure from the context menu of the table to display the Grab Table window, as shown in Figure 12.24. Save the file. This file contains the structural information about the table. You can use the file to create a new table. To do so, choose Recreate Table from the context menu of the Tables node to display the Recreate Table window, as shown in Figure 12.25. Select the .grab file and choose Open to display the Name the table window, as

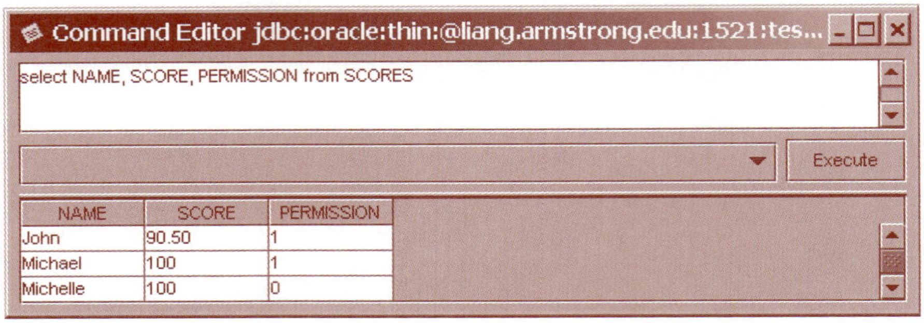

Figure 12.23 *You can browse tables, views and procedures in the database from the Connection node.*

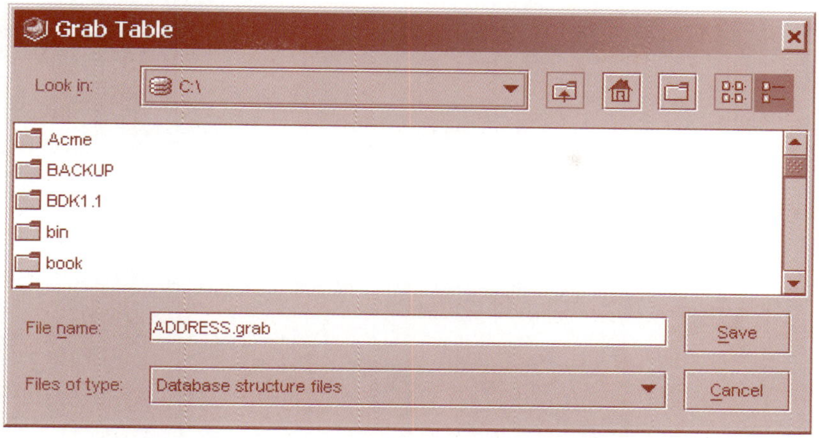

Figure 12.24 *You can save the data base schema in a .grab file and use it to create a new table.*

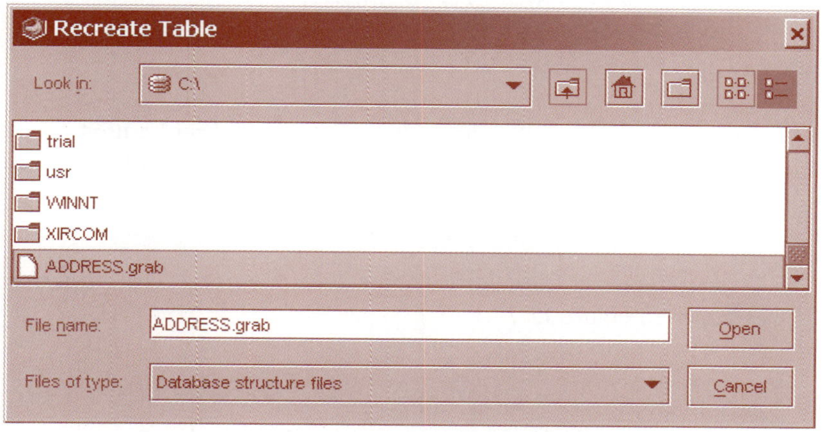

Figure 12.25 *You can recreate a table from a .grab file.*

shown in Figure 12.26. The create table statement is automatically generated to recreate the table. You can edit the script if necessary. Click OK from the Name the table window to generate the table.

12.8 PointBase Database (Optional)

PointBase is an object-relational database developed by PointBase Inc. using Java. It is SQL92 compliant and requires no administration. The entire database is stored in one file, so it is easy to transport. You can use PointBase databases through the PointBase type 4 JDBC driver locally or remotely.

PointBase has three versions: network version, embedded version, and mobile version. The *network version* can be used to serve multiple users across the network. The *embedded version* is suitable for applications running on desktop computers

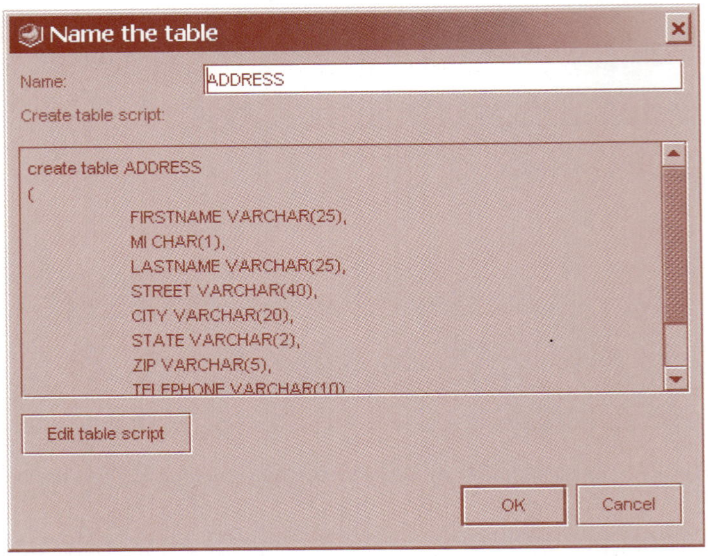

Figure 12.26 *You can recreate a table from a .grab file.*

that require local access only. The *mobile version* can be used on mobile devices such as a cell phone. The network version is bundled with Forte for evaluation use.

12.8.1 Using PointBase in Forte

To start the server from Forte, choose *Tools, PointBase Network Server, Start Server,* as shown in Figure 12.27.

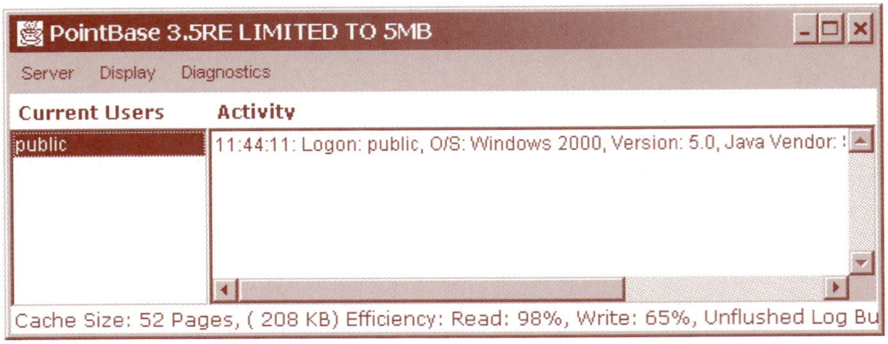

Figure 12.27 *PointBase database can be started from Forte.*

A connection node for accessing the PointBase server from a local host in Forte was pre-created. To add a new connection node, choose *Add Connection* from the context menu of the Databases node to display the Add New Connection window, as shown in Figure 12.28. Enter the host name, port number, the database name, user name, and password to connect to the database. The default database name is sample. You can use user name public and password public to logon to the database.

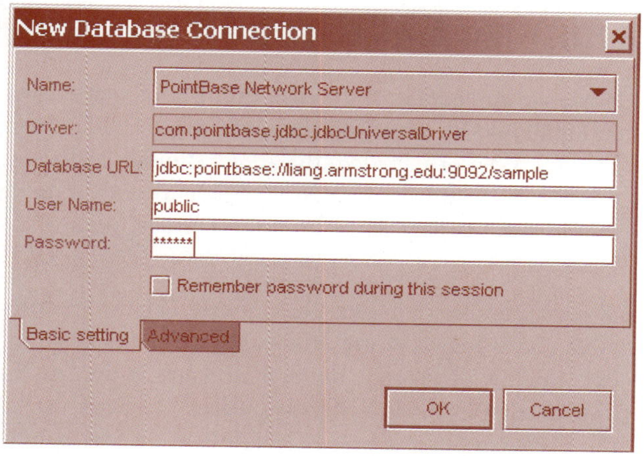

Figure 12.28 *You can add a new connection for the PointBase server.*

> **NOTE**
> The database server's default port name is 9092. To use a different port, you can start the database server from the DOS prompt. From the DOS prompt, you can specify a port name.

Chapter Summary

This chapter introduced JDBC, which is the Java API for accessing relational databases. You learned how to write a simple JDBC program by loading the driver, connecting to the database, creating statements, executing statements, and processing statements. The chapter gave step-by-step instructions for working with several representative JDBC drivers. It also provided a database connection dialog bean component and a universal interactive SQL client.

Review Questions

12.1 Describe the following JDBC interfaces: `Driver`, `Connection`, `Statement`, `ResultSet`.

12.2 How do you load a JDBC driver?

12.3 How do you create a JDBC connection? What is the syntax for a JDBC URL?

12.4 How do you create an instance of `Statement`? How do you execute a statement? Does every execution of the statement return a ResultSet?

12.5 How do you retrieve values in a `ResultSet`?

12.6 What are the four types of JDBC drivers? Which types of drivers require the DBMS client library? Which types of drivers can be downloaded and maintained on the server side?

Programming Exercises

12.1 Write an applet that shows the number of visits made to a Web page. The count should be stored on the server side in a database table. Every time the page is visited or reloaded, the applet should send a request to the server, and the server should increase the count and send it to the applet. The applet should then display the count in a message, such as You are visitor number: 1000.

12.2 Write an applet that gets stock quotes. The stock information is stored in a table consisting of six fields: stock symbol, stock share value, the high of the day, the low of the day, the highest value in the last fifty-two weeks, and the lowest value in the last fifty-two weeks. To get a stock quote, the user enters the stock symbol and presses ENTER in the text field for the stock symbol to display the stock information.

12.3 Write a Java applet that views, inserts, and updates staff information stored in a database, as shown in Figure 12.29. The Staff table is created as follows:

```
create table Staff
(
  id char(9) not null,
  lastName varchar(15),
  firstName varchar(15),
  mi char(1),
  address varchar(20),
  city varchar(20),
  state char(2),
  telephone char(10),
  email varchar(40),
  primary key (id)
);
```

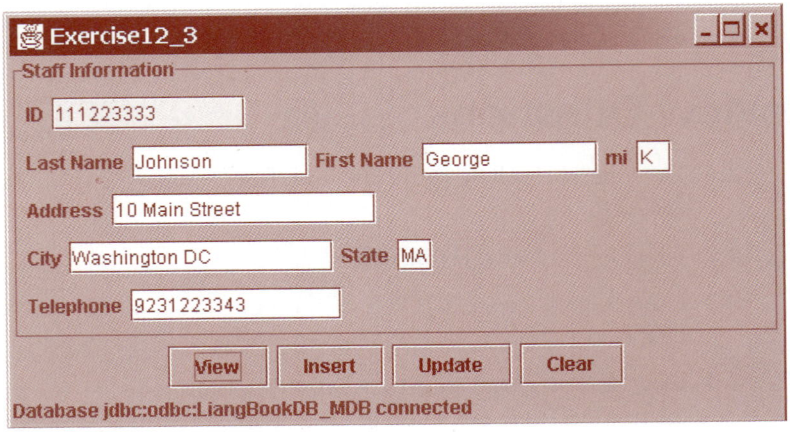

Figure 12.29 *The applet lets you view, insert, and update staff information.*

12.4 Modify Example 12.5 to add a File menu with a menu item named Connect to connect a database using the `DBConnectDialog` component, as shown in Figure 12.30.

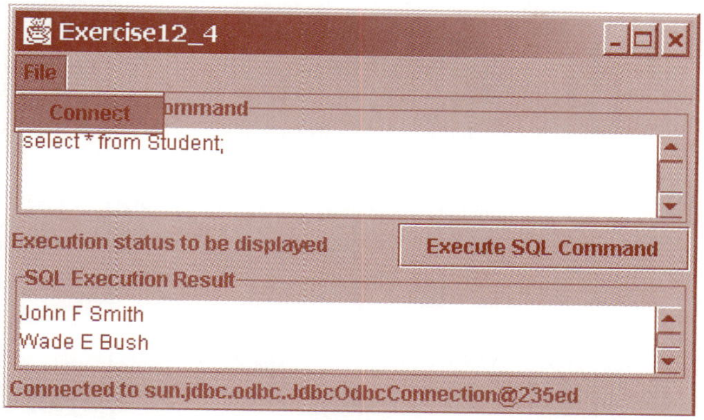

Figure 12.30 *The Connect menu item connects to a database using the* `DBConnectDialog` *component.*

12.5 Rewrite Exercise 4.8 to display the number of employees in each department in a pie chart and a bar chart, as shown in Figure 12.31. The number of employees for each department can be obtained dynamically from the database tables Department and Employee. The Department table has three columns: deptno, deptname, and deptchair. The Employee table has four columns: empno, name, office, and deptno. The number of employees in each department can be obtained using the following SQL statement:

```
select deptname, count(*)
from Department, Employee
where department.deptno = employee.deptno
group by deptname;
```

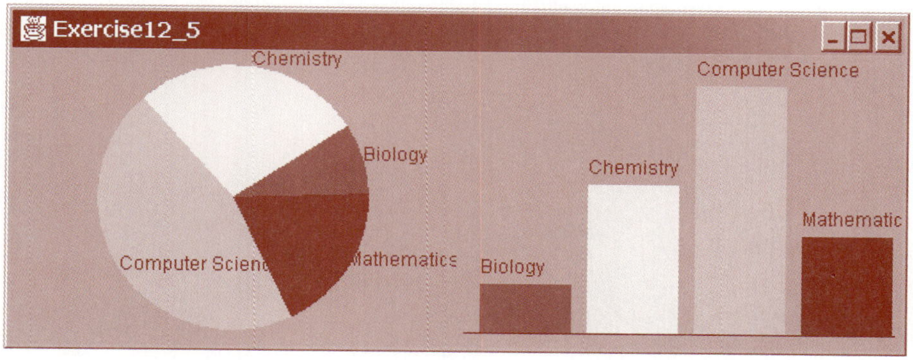

Figure 12.31 *The PieChart and BarChart display the query data obtained from the data module.*

The `PieChart` component and the `BarChart` component were created in Exercise 4.8.

CHAPTER 13

Advanced Java Database Programming

Objectives

- To handle transactions in the `Connection` interface.
- To explore database metadata using the `DatabaseMetaData` and `ResultSetMetaData` interfaces.
- To create and execute statements using the `Statement`, `PreparedStatement`, and `CallableStatement` interfaces.
- To process updateable and scrollable result sets.
- To store and retrieve images in JDBC.

13.1 Introduction

Chapter 12, "Introduction to Java Database Programming," presented an overview of the JDBC concept and examples of the use of various drivers to connect to databases. JDBC is a comprehensive approach to the development of platform-independent Java database applications. This chapter gives an in-depth look at transaction processing in the `Connection` interface, retrieving metadata in the `DatabaseMetaData` interface and result set metadata in the `ResultSetMetaData` interface, creating and executing static statements, dynamic statements and callable statements, processing scrollable and updateable result sets, and storing and retrieving images from the database.

13.2 Handling Transactions in the *Connection* Interface

The `Connection` interface establishes a connection to a database. Within the context of a connection, SQL statements are executed and results are returned. A connection also provides access to database metadata information that describes database tables, supported SQL grammar, stored procedures, the capabilities of the database, and so on. This information is obtained by invoking the `getMetaData` method from a `Connection` object. Database metadata will be introduced in Section 13.3, "Getting Database MetaData."

The `Connection` interface handles transactions and specifies how they are processed. By default, a new connection is in auto-commit mode, and all its SQL statements are executed and committed as individual transactions. The commit occurs when the statement completes or the next execute occurs, whichever comes first. In the case of statements returning a result set, the statement completes when the last row of the result set has been retrieved or the result set has been closed. If a single statement returns multiple results, the commit occurs when all the results have been retrieved.

You can use the `setAutoCommit(false)` method to disable auto-commit, so that all SQL statements are grouped into one transaction that is terminated by a call to either the `commit` or the `rollback` method. By default, new connections are in auto-commit mode. Table 13.1 lists all the methods in the `Connection` interface.

TABLE 13.1 Methods Defined in the `Connection` Interface

Method	*Description*
`void clearWarnings()`	Clears all warnings reported for this connection.
`void close()`	Closes this connection and releases its associated resource.
`void commit()`	Saves all changes made since the previous commit/rollback.
`Statement createStatement()`	Creates a statement to execute static SQL commands.

TABLE 13.1 continued

Method	*Description*
`Statement createStatement(int resultSetType, int resultSetConcurrency)`	Creates a statement that executes static SQL commands with a specified result set type and currency mode.
`boolean getAutoCommit()`	Gets current auto-commit mode.
`String getCatalog()`	Gets the catalog for the connection.
`DatabaseMetaData getMetaData()`	Gets the database metadata catalog.
`int getTransactionIsolation()`	Gets the connection's current transaction isolation level.
`Map getTypeMap()`	Gets the type map object associated with this connection. (JDBC 2)
`SQLWarning getWarnings()`	Gets the first warning on this connection.
`boolean isClosed()`	Returns `true` if the connection is closed.
`boolean isReadOnly()`	Returns `true` if the connection is in read-only mode.
`String nativeSQL(String sql)`	Converts the given SQL statement into the system's native SQL grammar.
`CallableStatement prepareCall(String sql)`	Creates a statement to execute stored procedures.
`CallableStatement prepareCall(String sql, int resultSetType, int resultSetConcurrency)`	Creates a statement to execute stored procedures with specified result set type and concurrency mode. (JDBC 2)
`PreparedStatement prepareStatement(String sql)`	Creates a statement to execute dynamic SQL statements.
`PreparedStatement prepareStatement(String sql, int resultSetType, int resultSetConcurrency)`	Creates a statement to execute dynamic SQL statements with specified result set and concurrency mode. (JDBC 2)
`void rollback()`	Rolls back all changes made since the previous commit/rollback.
`void setAutoCommit(boolean autoCommit)`	Specifies an auto-commit mode.
`void setCatalog(String catalog)`	Sets a catalog name for this connection.
`void setReadOnly(boolean readOnly)`	Sets read-only `true` or `false` for this connection.
`void setTransactionIsolation(int level)`	Sets a new transaction level.
`void setTypeMap(Map map)`	Installs the given type map as the type map for this connection. The type map will be used for the custom mapping of SQL-structured types and distinct types. (JDBC 2)

13.3 Getting Database MetaData

Database *metadata* is information that describes the database itself. JDBC provides the `DatabaseMetaData` interface for obtaining database-wide information and the `ResultSetMetaData` interface for obtaining information on the specific `ResultSet`.

The `DatabaseMetaData` interface provides more than a hundred methods for getting database metadata concerning the database as a whole. These methods can be divided into three groups: for retrieving general information, for finding database capabilities, and for getting object descriptions. The *general information* includes the URL, username, product name, product version, driver name, driver version, available functions, available data types, and so on. Information on *database capabilities* includes such matters as whether the database supports the GROUP BY operator, the ALTER TABLE command with add column option, and entry-level or full ANSI92 SQL grammar. Examples of *database objects* are tables, views, and procedures.

13.3.1 Obtaining General Database Information

The methods for obtaining general information usually return a string or an integer, except that the method for retrieving available data types returns a `ResultSet`. Most methods of this type do not have parameters. Table 13.2 lists some of the methods for retrieving database information.

13.3.2 Finding Database Capabilities

The methods for finding database capabilities return a `boolean` value indicating whether the database possesses a certain capability. Most methods of this type do not have parameters and are named with prefix *supports*. Table 13.3 lists some of the methods for finding database capabilities.

13.3.3 Getting Database Objects

The methods that get database objects shown in Table 13.4 return lists of information in `ResultSets`. You can use the normal `ResultSet` methods, such as `getString` and `getInt`, to retrieve data from these `ResultSets`. If a given form of metadata is not available, these methods should throw an `SQLException`.

Many of these methods take arguments that are string patterns. Within a pattern string, "%" means a match with any substring of 0 or more characters, and "_" means a match with any one character. Only metadata entries matching the search pattern are returned. If a search pattern argument is set to a `null` reference, it means that the argument's criteria should be dropped from the search.

13.3.4 Retrieving Tables

The `getTables` method is used to find tables in a database. For example, you can use the following method to obtain all the user-defined tables in the database:

```
DatabaseMetaData dbMetaData = connection.getMetaData();
ResultSet rsTables = dbMetaData.getTables(null, null, null,
  new String[] {"TABLE"});
```

TABLE 13.2 Some Methods for Retrieving General Information in the `DatabaseMetaData` Interface

Method name	*Description*
`getURL`	Gets the URL of the database.
`getUserName`	Gets the username of the currently connected user.
`getDataBaseProductName`	Gets the name of the database product.
`getDataBaseProductVersion`	Gets the version of the database product.
`getDriverName`	Gets the JDBC driver name for connecting to the database.
`getDriverVersion`	Gets the JDBC driver version.
`getNumericFunctions`	Gets a list of comma-separated numeric functions.
`getStringFunctions`	Gets a list of comma-separated string functions.
`getSystemFunctions`	Gets a list of comma-separated system functions.
`getTimeDateFunctions`	Gets a list of comma-separated time and date functions.
`getMaxConnections`	Gets the maximum number of active connections to the database.
`getMaxCursorNameLength`	Gets the maximum cursor name length.
`getMaxSchemaNameLength`	Gets the maximum schema name length.
`getMaxRowLength`	Gets the maximum length of a single row.
`getMaxStatementLength`	Gets the maximum length of an SQL statement.
`getMaxTableNameLength`	Gets the maximum length of a table name.
`getTypeInfo`	Returns a `ResultSet` of all the SQL types supported by this database.

The parameters of `getTables` are `catalog` (`String`), `schemaPattern` (`String`), `tableNamePattern` (`String`), and `tableTypes` (`String[]`). The parameter `tableTypes` is an array of `String`. Each string specifies a table type. Typical types are "TABLE," "VIEW," "SYSTEM TABLE," "GLOBAL TEMPORARY," "LOCAL TEMPORARY," "ALIAS," and "SYNONYM." The arguments for `catalog`, `schemaPattern`, and `tableNamePattern` are null in the statement, so all the tables are returned with or without a catalog or a schema. The returned table information is in the `ResultSet`, which has the following five columns:

Column Name	*Value*
`TABLE_CAT`	A `String` object for the table catalog.
`TABLE_SCHEM`	A `String` object for the table schema.
`TABLE_NAME`	A `String` object for the table name.
`TABLE_TYPE`	A `String` object for the table type.
`REMARKS`	A `String` object describing the table.

TABLE 13.3 Some Methods for Finding Database Capabilities in the `DatabaseMetaData` Interface

Method name	*Description*
`allProceduresAreCallable`	Returns `true` if all the procedures returned by `getProcedures` (in Table 13.4) can be called by the current user.
`allTablesAreSelectable`	Returns `true` if all the tables returned by `getTables` (in Table 13.4) can be selected by the current user.
`isReadOnly`	Returns `true` if the database is in read-only mode.
`supportsAlterTableWithAddColumn`	Returns `true` if "ALTER TABLE" with add column is supported.
`supportsAlterTableWithDropColumn`	Returns `true` if "ALTER TABLE" with drop column is supported.
`supportsANSI92EntryLevelSQL`	Returns `true` if the ANSI92 entry-level SQL grammar is supported. All DBC-compliant drivers must return `true`.
`supportsANSI92FullSQL`	Returns `true` if the ANSI full-SQL grammar is supported.
`supportsANSI92IntermediateSQL`	Returns `true` if the ANSI92 intermediate-SQL grammar is supported.
`supportsBatchUpdates`	Returns `true` if batch update is supported. (JDBC 2)
`supportsFullOuterJoins`	Returns `true` if full-nested outer join is supported.
`supportsGroupBy`	Returns `true` if some form of "GROUP BY" clause is supported.
`supportsGroupByBeyondSelect`	Returns `true` if a "GROUP BY" clause can add columns not in the select, provided it specifies all the columns in the select.
`supportsIntegrityEnhancementFacility`	Returns `true` if the SQL Integrity Enhancement Facility is supported.
`storesLowerCaseIdentifiers`	Returns `true` if the database treats mixed-case unquoted SQL identifiers as case-insensitive and stores them in lower-case.
`storesLowerCaseQuotedIdentifiers`	Returns `true` if the database treats mixed-case quoted SQL identifiers as case-insensitive and stores them in lower-case.

TABLE 13.3 continued

Method name	*Description*
`storesMixedCaseIdentifiers`	Returns `true` if the database treats mixed-case unquoted SQL identifiers as case-insensitive and stores them in mixed-case.
`supportsMultipleTransactions`	Returns `true` if multiple transactions are allowed.
`supportsOrderUnrelated`	Returns `true` if an "ORDER BY" clause can use columns not in the select.
`supportsOuterJoin`	Returns `true` if some form of outer join is supported.
`supportsPositionDelete`	Returns `true` if positioned DELETE is supported.
`supportsPositionUpdate`	Returns `true` if positioned UPDATE is supported.
`supportsResultSetType(int type)`	Returns `true` if the given type is supported in the result set. (JDBC 2)
`supportsResultSetConcurrency(int type, int concurrency)`	Returns `true` if the database supports the concurrency type in combination with the given result set type. (JDBC 2)
`supportsUnion`	Returns `true` if SQL UNION is supported.
`supportsUnionALL`	Returns `true` if SQL UNION ALL is supported.
`useLocalFiles`	Returns `true` if the database stores tables in a local file.
`useLocalFilesPerTable`	Returns `true` if the database uses a file for each table.

You can now print the table name using the following loop:

```
while (rsTables.next())
  System.out.println(rsTables.getString("TABLE_NAME"));
```

13.3.5 Retrieving Column Names

To find all the column names for a specified table, use the `getColumns` method. For example, you can use the following method to obtain all the columns in the table Address:

```
ResultSet rsColumns = dbMetaData.getTables(null, null,
  "Address", null);
```

TABLE 13.4 Some Methods for Getting Database Objects in the DatabaseMetaData Interface

Method name	*Parameter*	*Description*
getCatalogs	()	Gets catalog names in this database.
getColumns	(String catalog, String schemaPattern, String tableNamePattern, String columnNamePattern)	Gets a description of columns.
getColumnPrivileges	(String catalog, String schemaPattern, String tableNamePattern, String columnNamePattern)	Gets a description of the access rights of a table's columns.
getExportedKeys	(String catalog, String schema, String table)	Gets a description of the primary key columns that are referenced by a table's foreign key columns.
getImportedKeys	(String catalog, String schema, String table)	Gets a description of the primary key columns referenced by a table's foreign key columns.
getIndexInfo	(String catalog, String schema, String table, boolean unique, boolean approximate)	Gets a description of a table's indices and statistics.
getPrimaryKeys	(String catalog, String schema, String table)	Gets the primary key in a table.
getProcedures	(String catalog, String schemaPattern, String procedureNamePattern)	Gets a description of stored procedures.
getProcedureColumns	(String catalog, String schemaPattern, String procedureNamePattern, String columnNamePattern)	Gets a description of a catalog's stored procedure parameters and result columns.
getSchemas	()	Gets all the schemas in this database.
getTables	(String catalog, String schemaPattern String tableNamePattern, String[] tableTypes)	Gets a description of tables.

TABLE 13.4 continued

Method name	*Parameter*	*Description*
`getTableTypes`	`()`	Gets table types available in the database. Typical types are "TABLE," "VIEW," "SYSTEM TABLE," "GLOBAL TEMPORARY," "LOCAL TEMPORARY," "ALIAS," and "SYNONYM."
`getTablePrivileges`	`(String catalog, String schemaPattern, String tableNamePattern)`	Gets a description of the access rights for each table available in a catalog.

The parameters of `getColumns` are `catalog` (`String`), `schemaPattern` (`String`), `tableNamePattern` (`String`), and `tableTypes`. The arguments for `catalog`, `schemaPattern`, and `tableTypes` are null in the statement, so all the column names in the table Address are returned with or without a catalog or a schema. The returned column information is in the `ResultSet`, which contains eighteen columns. The columns shown below are often used:

Column Name	*Value*
TABLE_CAT	A `String` object for the table catalog.
TABLE_SCHEM	A `String` object for the schema of the table that contains the column.
TABLE_NAME	A `String` object for the table name that contains the column.
COLUMN_NAME	A `String` object for the column name.
TYPE_NAME	A `String` object specifying the SQL type for the column.
COLUMN_SIZE	The maximum size of characters in the case of character or date types, or the precision of NUMERIC OR DECIMAL types.

You can now print all the columns and their information:

```
// Get column count
int columnCount = rsColumns.getMetaData().getColumnCount();

// Store rows to rowData
while (rsColumns.next()) {
  for (int i = 0; i < columnCount; i++) {
    System.out.print(rsColumns.getObject(i + 1) + "  ");
    System.out.println();
  }
```

13.3.6 The *ResultSetMetaData* Interface

The `ResultSetMetaData` interface describes information pertaining to the result set. A `ResultSetMetaData` object can be used to find out about the types and properties of the columns in a `ResultSet`. The methods in `ResultSetMetaData` have a single `int` parameter representing the column, except that the `getColumnCount` method has no parameters. All these methods return `int`, `boolean`, or `String`. The `ResultSetMetaData` interface has fewer methods than the `DatabaseMetaData` interface. Table 13.5 lists all the methods defined in `ResultSetMetaData`.

For more detailed information about the methods defined in the `DatabaseMetaData` and `ResultSetMetaDate` interfaces, please consult the JDBC API documentation.

NOTE

An `SQLException` will be thrown if a driver does not support a metadata method. In the case of methods that return a `ResultSet`, either a `ResultSet` (which may be empty) is returned or an `SQLException` is thrown.

TABLE 13.5 Methods in the `ResultSetMetaData` Interface

Method name	*Description*
`getCatalogName(int column)`	Gets the catalog name of the table of the column.
`getColumnClassName(int column)`	Gets the class name (a string) of the column.
`getColumnCount()`	Gets the number of columns in the `ResultSet`.
`getColumnDisplaySize(int column)`	Gets the column's maximum width in characters.
`getColumnLabel(int column)`	Gets the column's title for use in printouts and displays.
`getColumnName(int column)`	Gets the column's name.
`getColumnType(int column)`	Gets the column's type in `int`, listed in `java.sql.Types`.
`getColumnTypeName(int column)`	Gets the column's type in `String`.
`getPrecision(int column)`	Gets the column's decimal precision.
`getScale(int column)`	Gets the column's number of digits to right of the decimal point.
`getSchemaName(int column)`	Gets the schema name of the table of the column.
`getTableName(int column)`	Gets the table name of the column.
`isAutoIncrement(int column)`	Is the column automatically numbered, thus read-only?
`isCaseSensitive(int column)`	Is the column case-sensitive?

TABLE 13.5 continued

Method name	*Description*
`isCashValue(int column)`	Is the column a monetary value?
`isDefinitelyWritable(int column)`	Will a write on the column definitely succeed?
`isNullable(int column)`	Does the column accept `null`?
`isReadOnly(int column)`	Is the column read-only?
`isSearchable(int column)`	Can the column be used in a where clause?
`isSigned(int column)`	Is the column a signed number?
`isWritable(int column)`	Is it possible for a write on the column to succeed?

Example 13.1 Exploring Databases

In this example, you will develop a useful utility that discovers database information. A sample run of the utility is shown in Figure 13.1. The utility contains the Connection menu with the Connect to Database command. Clicking this command displays a dialog box, as shown in Figure 13.2, which lets you specify a database to connect. Once a database is connected, its structural information is displayed in a tree. You can navigate the database, the table types, tables, and columns from the tree. The metadata for the database, tables, and columns are displayed in the content pane.

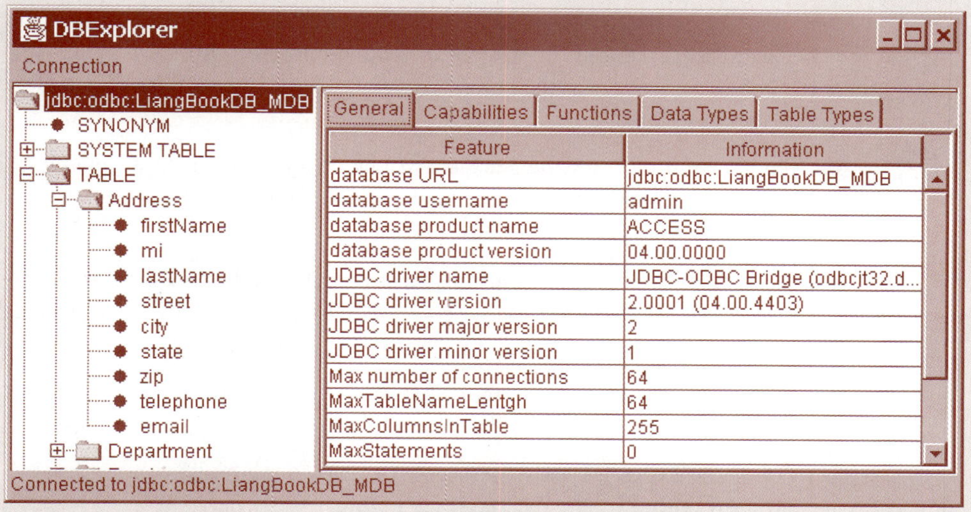

Figure 13.1 *The* `DBExplorer` *utility explores database information.*

continued

Example 13.1 continued

Figure 13.2 *You can specify a database to connect in the Connect to a database dialog box.*

The utility consists of four classes: `DBExplorer` (see Listing 13.1), `DBConnectDialog` (created in Example 12.4, "Creating a Connection Dialog Component"), `DBInfoPanel` (see Listing 13.2), and `TableInfoPanel` (see Listing 13.3). `DBExplorer` displays the main interface with the menu, a split pane, and a status label. The split pane holds a tree on the left and a content pane on the right. The status label displays the database-connection information. `DBConnectDialog` is a subclass of `JDialog` for gathering the connection information of the database and establishing connections. Once a database is connected, its URL is displayed as the root of the tree. The table types are the children of the root, the tables are the children of the table types, and the columns are the children of the tables.

When you select the root, an instance of `DBInfoPanel` with the connection for the database is placed in the right-hand section of the split pane. The `DBInfoPanel` class contains five tabs: General, Capabilities, Functions, Data Types, and Table Types.

- The General tab uses the `showGeneralInfo()` method to show general information about the database, such as the database URL, current user name, and the JDBC driver name (see Figure 13.1).
- The Capabilities tab uses the `showCapability()` method to show the database capabilities, such as whether the database uses local files, uses local file per table, supports group by, and so on (see Figure 13.3).
- The Functions tab uses the `showFunctions()` method to show the standard functions supported by the database (see Figure 13.4).
- The Data Types tab uses the `showDataTypes()` method to show the data types supported by the database (see Figure 13.5).
- The Table Types tab uses the `showTableTypes()` method to show the table types supported by the database (see Figure 13.6).

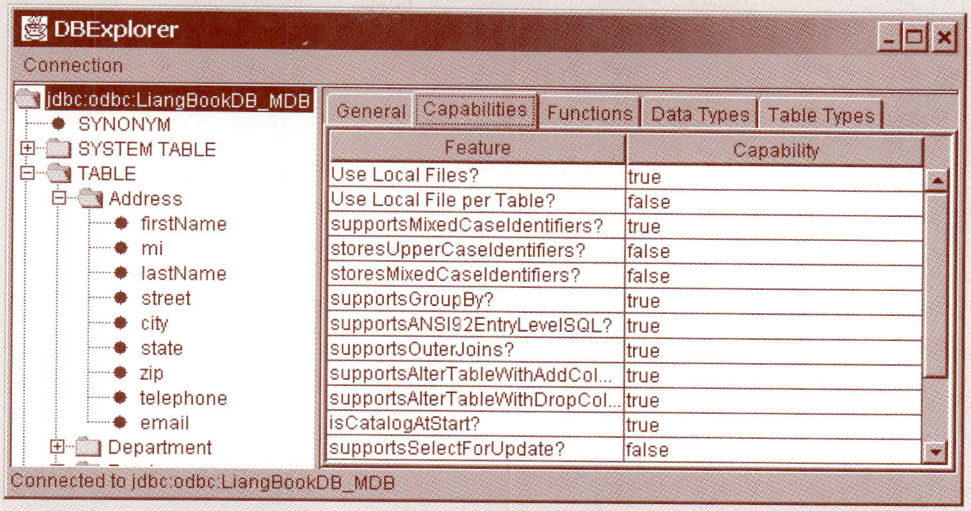

Figure 13.3 *The Capabilities tab displays the database capabilities.*

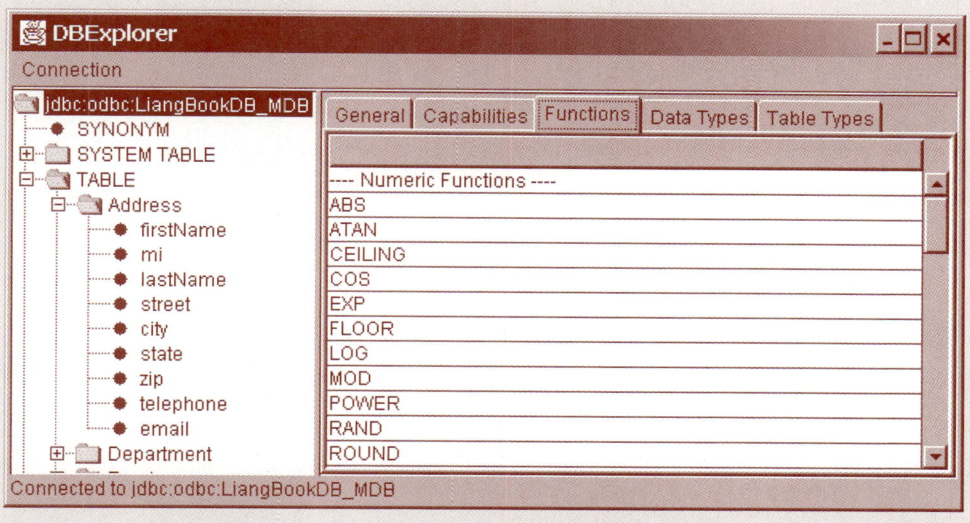

Figure 13.4 *The Functions tab displays the functions supported in the database.*

When you select a table, an instance of `TableInfoPanel` is placed in the right section of the split pane. You need to set connection and table name in this instance in order to display the table data and table definition. The `TableInfoPanel` class contains two tabs: Data and Definition.

- The Data tab uses the `showData()` method to display the table data (see Figure 13.7).

continued

Example 13.1 continued

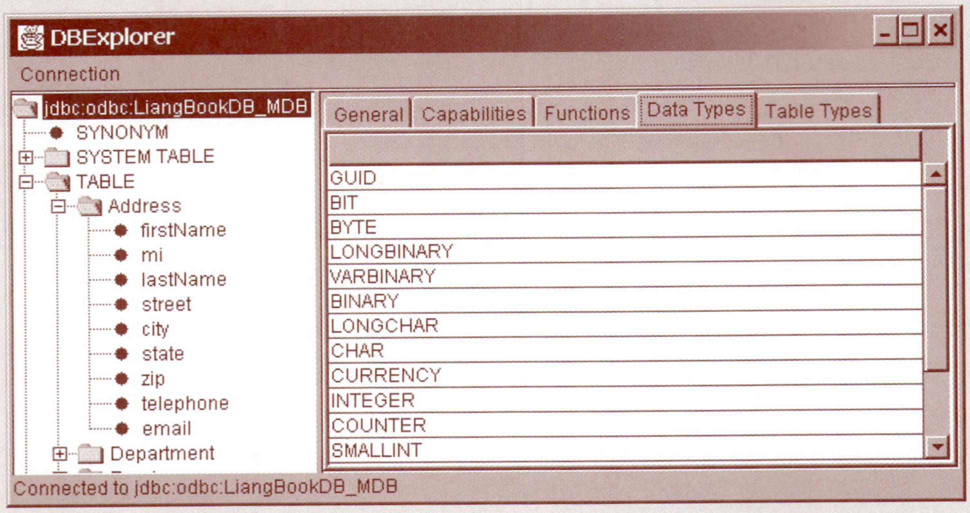

Figure 13.5 *The Data Types tab displays the data types supported in the database.*

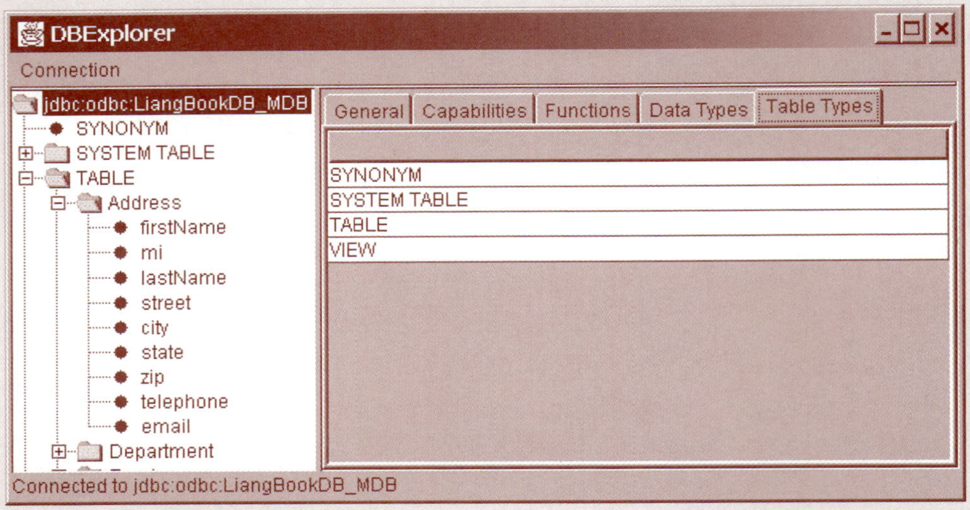

Figure 13.6 *The Table Types tab displays the table types available in the database.*

- The Definition tab uses the `showTableDef()` method to display the column name, column name type, and column size (see Figure 13.8).

Here are the steps to complete the project.

1. In the jdbcdemo package, create an applet named `DBExplorer` using the Forte Swing JApplet form wizard, create a JavaBeans component named

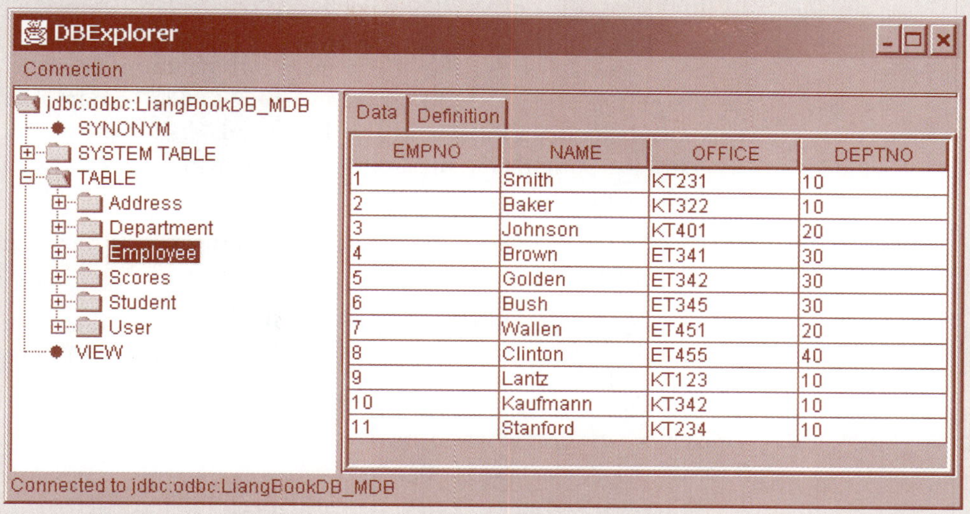

Figure 13.7 *The Data tab displays the contents for the specified table.*

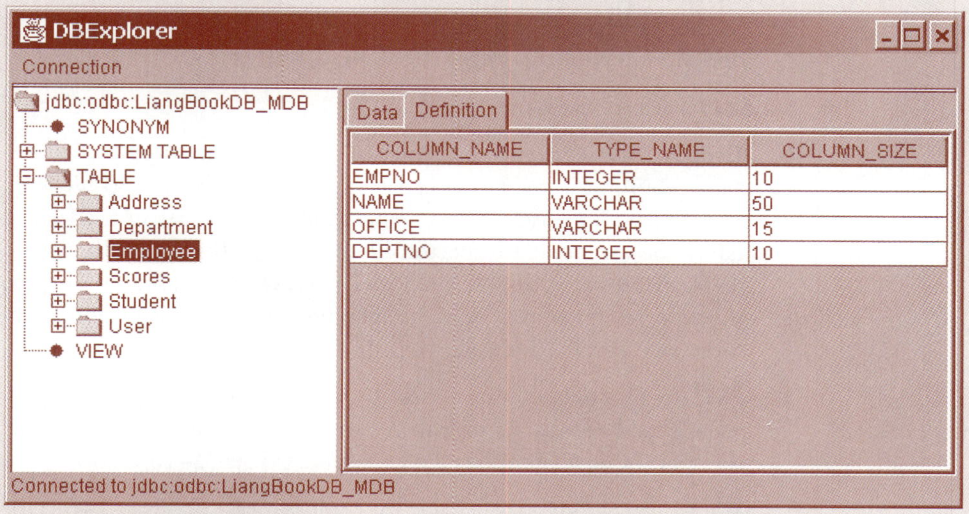

Figure 13.8 *The Definition tab displays column name, type, and size for the specified table.*

`DBInfoPanel` that extends `JPanel` using the Forte JPanel form wizard, and create a JavaBeans component named `TableInfoPanel` that extends `JPanel` using the Forte JPanel form wizard.

2. Build `DBExplorer` as follows:

 2.1. Drop a `JLabel` to the south of the applet to create `jlblStatus`. Drop a `JSplitPane` from the Swing (Other) page to the center of the applet (this) to create `jSplitPane1`. Drop a `JTree` to the left of `jSplitPane1` to create `jTree1`.

continued

Example 13.1 continued

2.2. Drop a `JMenuBar` from the Swing page to the form to create `jMenuBar1` and `jMenu1`. Set the text of the menu to Connection. Add two menu items, "Connect to Database" and "Exit," and add a separator between them. Rename the menu item components to `jmiConnect` and `jmiExit`.

2.3. Write the code to create instances for `DBConnectDialog`, as shown in Listing 13.1 (Line 20).

2.4. Generate and implement the code for handling the action events for menu items (Connect to Database and Exit), as shown in Listing 13.1 (Lines 99–120).

2.5. Implement the `updateTree()` method to build the tree, as shown in Listing 13.1 (Lines 122–154).

2.6. Create an instance of `DBInfoPanel` and `TableInfoPanel` (Lines 22–23). These components will be created in Steps 3 and 4.

2.7. Generate the `valueChanged` handler to `jTree1`, and implement the method to handle the selection event for the root and the table nodes, as shown in Listing 13.1 (Lines 72–97).

3. Build `DBInfoPanel` as follows:

3.1. Drop a `JTabbedPane` to the center of the panel, and drop a `JScrollPane` five times into the tabbed pane. Set the tab titles to General, Capabilities, Functions, Data Types, and Table Types in the Layout tab of the component inspector. Drop a `JTable` to each scroll pane to create `jTable1`, `jTable2`, `jTable3`, `jTable4`, and `jTable5`. In the model property editor for each table, press the Default button to remove the sample table data.

3.2. Declare five default table models named `model1`, `model2`, `model3`, `model4`, and `model5`, as shown in Listing 13.2 (Lines 8–13), and set them in the `model` property for each table (Lines 22–26).

3.3. Write the code to create a `connection` property of type `java.sql.Connection` with a set method. Implement the `setConnection` method to invoke the method `showMetaData`, which then invokes the methods `showGeneralInfo`, `showCapability`, `showFunctions`, `showDataTypes`, and `showTableTypes` to fill in database metadata information in the appropriate tables, as shown in Listing 13.2 (Lines 55–199).

4. Build `TableInfoPanel` as follows:

4.1. Drop a `JTabbedPane` to the center of the panel, and drop a `JScrollPane` twice into the tabbed pane. Set the tab titles to Data and Definition. Drop a `JTable` to each scroll pane to create `jTable1` and `jTable2`. In the model property editor for each table, press the Default button to remove the sample table data.

4.2. Declare two default table models named `model1` and `model2`, and set them in the `model` property for each table, as shown in Listing 13.3 (Lines 19–20).

4.3. Implement the `setConnectionAndTable` method to set a database connection and a table name in `TableInfoPanel`.

4.4. Write the code to add a property named `connection` of type `java.sql.Connection` with a set method. Implement the `setConnection` method to invoke the methods `showData` and `showTableDef` to display data and table definition in the respective panel.

```
package jdbcdemo;

import javax.swing.tree.*;
import javax.swing.*;
import javax.swing.event.*;
import java.sql.*;

public class DBExplorer extends javax.swing.JApplet {
  // Create tree root
  DefaultMutableTreeNode root = new DefaultMutableTreeNode(
    "No database connected");

  // Create the tree model
  DefaultTreeModel treeModel = new DefaultTreeModel(root);

  // Database connection and meta data for the connection
  Connection connection;
  DatabaseMetaData dbMetaData;

  DBConnectDialog dBConnectDialog1 = new DBConnectDialog();

  DBInfoPanel dBInfoPanel1 = new DBInfoPanel();
  TableInfoPanel tableContentPanel1 = new TableInfoPanel();

  /** Creates new form DBExplorer */
  public DBExplorer() {
    initComponents();

    jTree1.setModel(treeModel);
  }

  private void initComponents() {
    jMenuBar1 = new javax.swing.JMenuBar();
    jMenu1 = new javax.swing.JMenu();
    jmiConnect = new javax.swing.JMenuItem();
    jSeparator1 = new javax.swing.JSeparator();
    jmiExit = new javax.swing.JMenuItem();
    jSplitPane1 = new javax.swing.JSplitPane();
    jTree1 = new javax.swing.JTree();
    jlblStatus = new javax.swing.JLabel();
```

Listing 13.1 *DBExplorer.java*

continued

Example 13.1 continued

```
      jMenu1.setText("Connection");
      jmiConnect.setText("Connect to Database");
      jmiConnect.addActionListener(
        new java.awt.event.ActionListener() {
        public void actionPerformed(java.awt.event.ActionEvent evt) {
          jmiConnectActionPerformed(evt);
        }
      });
      jMenu1.add(jmiConnect);
      jMenu1.add(jSeparator1);
      jmiExit.setText("Exit");
      jmiExit.addActionListener(new java.awt.event.ActionListener() {
        public void actionPerformed(java.awt.event.ActionEvent evt) {
          jmiExitActionPerformed(evt);
        }
      });
      jMenu1.add(jmiExit);
      jMenuBar1.add(jMenu1);
      jTree1.addTreeSelectionListener(
        new javax.swing.event.TreeSelectionListener() {
        public void valueChanged(
          javax.swing.event.TreeSelectionEvent evt) {
          jTree1ValueChanged(evt);
        }
      });
      jSplitPane1.setLeftComponent(jTree1);
      getContentPane().add(jSplitPane1, java.awt.BorderLayout.CENTER);
      getContentPane().add(jlblStatus, java.awt.BorderLayout.SOUTH);
      setJMenuBar(jMenuBar1);
    }

    private void jTree1ValueChanged(
      javax.swing.event.TreeSelectionEvent evt) {
      TreePath path = jTree1.getSelectionPath();
      if (path == null) return;

      String tableName = null;

      switch (path.getPathCount()) {
        case 1:
          dBInfoPanel1.setConnection(connection);
          jSplitPane1.setDividerLocation(0.2);
          jSplitPane1.add(dBInfoPanel1, JSplitPane.RIGHT);
          break;
        case 3:
          tableName = (String)(((DefaultMutableTreeNode)
          (path.getPathComponent(2))).getUserObject());
          tableContentPanel1.setConnectionAndTable(
            connection, tableName);
          jSplitPane1.setDividerLocation(0.2);
          jSplitPane1.add(tableContentPanel1, JSplitPane.RIGHT);
          break;
        default:
          jSplitPane1.remove(dBInfoPanel1);
          jSplitPane1.remove(tableContentPanel1);
      }
    }

```

Listing 13.1 *continued*

```
    private void jmiExitActionPerformed(
      java.awt.event.ActionEvent evt) {
      System.exit(0);
    }

    private void jmiConnectActionPerformed(
      java.awt.event.ActionEvent evt) {
      dBConnectDialog1.setVisible(true);

      try {
        connection = dBConnectDialog1.getConnection();
        if (connection != null) {
          dbMetaData = dBConnectDialog1.getConnection().getMetaData();
          jlblStatus.setText("Connected to " + dbMetaData.getURL());
          updateTree();
          jSplitPane1.add(jTree1, JSplitPane.LEFT);
        }
      }
      catch (SQLException ex) {
        jlblStatus.setText(ex.getMessage());
      }
    }

    private void updateTree() throws SQLException {
      root.setUserObject(dbMetaData.getURL());

      ResultSet rsTableTypes = dbMetaData.getTableTypes();

      while (rsTableTypes.next()) {
        String tableType = rsTableTypes.getString("TABLE_TYPE");

        // Add table names to the tree node under database
        DefaultMutableTreeNode tableTypeNode =
          new DefaultMutableTreeNode(tableType);
        root.add(tableTypeNode);

        ResultSet rsTables = dbMetaData.getTables(null, null, null,
          new String[] {tableType});

        while (rsTables.next()) {
          String tableName = rsTables.getString("TABLE_NAME");
          // Add table names to the tree node under database
          DefaultMutableTreeNode tableNode =
            new DefaultMutableTreeNode(tableName);
          tableTypeNode.add(tableNode);

          ResultSet rsColumns = dbMetaData.getColumns(
            null, null, tableName, null);

          // Add column names to the table
          while (rsColumns.next()) {
            tableNode.add(new DefaultMutableTreeNode
              (rsColumns.getString("COLUMN_NAME")));
          }
        }
      }
    }

```

Listing 13.1 *continued*

continued

Example 13.1 continued

```
    /** Main method */
    public static void main(String[] args) {
      DBExplorer applet = new DBExplorer();
      javax.swing.JFrame frame = new javax.swing.JFrame();
      frame.setDefaultCloseOperation(javax.swing.JFrame.EXIT_ON_CLOSE);
      frame.setTitle("DBExplorer");
      frame.getContentPane().add(applet, java.awt.BorderLayout.CENTER);
      frame.setSize(400,320);
      java.awt.Dimension d =
        java.awt.Toolkit.getDefaultToolkit().getScreenSize();
      frame.setLocation((d.width - frame.getSize().width) / 2,
        (d.height - frame.getSize().height) / 2);
      frame.setVisible(true);
    }

    // Variables declaration - do not modify
    private javax.swing.JMenuBar jMenuBar1;
    private javax.swing.JMenu jMenu1;
    private javax.swing.JMenuItem jmiConnect;
    private javax.swing.JSeparator jSeparator1;
    private javax.swing.JMenuItem jmiExit;
    private javax.swing.JSplitPane jSplitPane1;
    private javax.swing.JTree jTree1;
    private javax.swing.JLabel jlblStatus;
    // End of variables declaration
  }
```

Listing 13.1 *continued*

```
package jdbcdemo;

import javax.swing.table.*;
import java.util.*;
import java.sql.*;

public class DBInfoPanel extends javax.swing.JPanel {
  // Table models for the five tables
  DefaultTableModel model1 = new DefaultTableModel();
  DefaultTableModel model2 = new DefaultTableModel();
  DefaultTableModel model3 = new DefaultTableModel();
  DefaultTableModel model4 = new DefaultTableModel();
  DefaultTableModel model5 = new DefaultTableModel();

  private java.sql.Connection connection;
  DatabaseMetaData dbMetaData;

  /** Creates new form DBInfoPanel */
  public DBInfoPanel() {
    initComponents();

    jTable1.setModel(model1);
    jTable2.setModel(model2);
    jTable3.setModel(model3);
    jTable4.setModel(model4);
    jTable5.setModel(model5);
  }

```

Listing 13.2 *DBInfoPanel.java*

```
  private void initComponents() {
    jTabbedPane1 = new javax.swing.JTabbedPane();
    jScrollPane1 = new javax.swing.JScrollPane();
    jTable1 = new javax.swing.JTable();
    jScrollPane2 = new javax.swing.JScrollPane();
    jTable2 = new javax.swing.JTable();
    jScrollPane3 = new javax.swing.JScrollPane();
    jTable3 = new javax.swing.JTable();
    jScrollPane4 = new javax.swing.JScrollPane();
    jTable4 = new javax.swing.JTable();
    jScrollPane5 = new javax.swing.JScrollPane();
    jTable5 = new javax.swing.JTable();
    setLayout(new java.awt.BorderLayout());
    jScrollPane1.setViewportView(jTable1);
    jTabbedPane1.addTab("General", jScrollPane1);
    jScrollPane2.setViewportView(jTable2);
    jTabbedPane1.addTab("Capabilities", jScrollPane2);
    jScrollPane3.setViewportView(jTable3);
    jTabbedPane1.addTab("Functions", jScrollPane3);
    jScrollPane4.setViewportView(jTable4);
    jTabbedPane1.addTab("Data Types", jScrollPane4);
    jScrollPane5.setViewportView(jTable5);
    jTabbedPane1.addTab("Table Types", jScrollPane5);
    add(jTabbedPane1, java.awt.BorderLayout.CENTER);
  }

  public void setConnection(java.sql.Connection newConnection) {
    connection = newConnection;

    try {
      showMetaData();
    }
    catch (SQLException ex) {
      ex.printStackTrace();
    }
  }

  /** Show database meta data */
  private void showMetaData() throws SQLException {
    dbMetaData = connection.getMetaData();
    showGeneralInfo();
    showCapability();
    showFunctions();
    showDataTypes();
    showTableTypes();
  }

  /** Find general database information */
  private void  showGeneralInfo() throws SQLException {
    Object[][] data = new Object[][] {
      {"database URL", dbMetaData.getURL()},
      {"database username", dbMetaData.getUserName()},
      {"database product name", dbMetaData.getDatabaseProductName()},
      {"database product version",
        dbMetaData.getDatabaseProductVersion()},
      {"JDBC driver name", dbMetaData.getDriverName()},
      {"JDBC driver version", dbMetaData.getDriverVersion()},
      {"JDBC driver major version",
       new Integer( dbMetaData.getDriverMajorVersion()) },
```

Listing 13.2 *continued*

continued

Example 13.1 continued

```
        {"JDBC driver minor version",
         new Integer(dbMetaData.getDriverMinorVersion())},
        {"Max number of connections",
         new Integer(dbMetaData.getMaxConnections())},
        {"MaxTableNameLength",
         new Integer(dbMetaData.getMaxTableNameLength())},
        {"MaxColumnsInTable",
         new Integer(dbMetaData.getMaxColumnsInTable())},
        {"MaxStatements",
         new Integer(dbMetaData.getMaxStatements())},
        {"MaxColumnsInSelect",
         new Integer(dbMetaData.getMaxColumnsInSelect())},
        {"getSchemaTerm", dbMetaData.getSchemaTerm()},
        {"getProcedureTerm", dbMetaData.getProcedureTerm()},
        {"getCatalogTerm", dbMetaData.getCatalogTerm()}};

      Object[] columnNames = new Object[]{"Feature", "Information"};

      // Set new data to the table model
      model1.setDataVector(data, columnNames);
    }

    /** Find database capability */
    private void showCapability() throws SQLException {
      Object[][] data2 = new Object[][] {
        {"Use Local Files?",
         new Boolean(dbMetaData.usesLocalFiles())},
        {"Use Local File per Table?",
         new Boolean(dbMetaData.usesLocalFilePerTable())},
        {"supportsMixedCaseIdentifiers?",
         new Boolean(dbMetaData.supportsMixedCaseIdentifiers())},
        {"storesUpperCaseIdentifiers?",
         new Boolean(dbMetaData.storesUpperCaseIdentifiers())},
        {"storesMixedCaseIdentifiers?",
         new Boolean(dbMetaData.storesMixedCaseIdentifiers())},
        {"supportsGroupBy?",
         new Boolean(dbMetaData.supportsGroupBy())},
        {"supportsANSI92EntryLevelSQL?",
         new Boolean(dbMetaData.supportsANSI92EntryLevelSQL())},
        {"supportsOuterJoins?",
         new Boolean(dbMetaData.supportsOuterJoins())},
        {"supportsAlterTableWithAddColumn?",
         new Boolean(dbMetaData.supportsAlterTableWithAddColumn())},
        {"supportsAlterTableWithDropColumn?",
         new Boolean(dbMetaData.supportsAlterTableWithDropColumn())},
        {"isCatalogAtStart?",
         new Boolean(dbMetaData.isCatalogAtStart())},
        {"supportsSelectForUpdate?",
         new Boolean(dbMetaData.supportsSelectForUpdate())},
        {"supportsStoredProcedures?",
         new Boolean(dbMetaData.supportsStoredProcedures())},
        {"supportsUnion?",
         new Boolean(dbMetaData.supportsUnion())},
        {"supportsTransactions?",
         new Boolean(dbMetaData.supportsTransactions())},
        {"supportsDataDefinitionAndDataManipulationTransactions? ",
         new Boolean(dbMetaData.
         supportsDataDefinitionAndDataManipulationTransactions())}};

```

Listing 13.2 *continued*

```
    Object[] columnNames2 = new Object[]{"Feature", "Capability"};
    model2.setDataVector(data2, columnNames2);
  }

  /** Find functions available in the database */
  private void showFunctions() throws SQLException {
    model3.setColumnCount(1); // Set column count
    jTable3.removeAll(); // Clear the table

    model3.setColumnIdentifiers(new Object[]{" "}); // No column name
    model3.addRow(new Object[]{"-- Numeric Functions --"});
    addFunctions(dbMetaData.getNumericFunctions());
    model3.addRow(new Object[]{" "});
    model3.addRow(new Object[]{"-- String Functions --"});
    addFunctions(dbMetaData.getStringFunctions());
    model3.addRow(new Object[]{" "});
    model3.addRow(new Object[]{"-- System Functions --"});
    addFunctions(dbMetaData.getSystemFunctions());
    model3.addRow(new Object[]{" "});
    model3.addRow(new Object[]{"-- Date and Time Functions --"});
    addFunctions(dbMetaData.getTimeDateFunctions());
  }

  private void addFunctions(String s) {
    StringTokenizer st = new StringTokenizer(s, ",");

    while (st.hasMoreTokens())
      model3.addRow(new Object[]{st.nextToken()});
  }

  /** Show available data types */
  private void showDataTypes() throws SQLException {
    model4.setColumnCount(1); // Set column count
    model4.setColumnIdentifiers(new Object[]{" "}); // No column name

    jTable4.removeAll(); // Clear the table

    ResultSet rs = dbMetaData.getTypeInfo();
    while (rs.next())
      model4.addRow(new Object[]{rs.getString("TYPE_NAME")});
  }

  /** Show available table types */
  private void showTableTypes() throws SQLException {
    model5.setColumnCount(1); // Set column count
    model5.setColumnIdentifiers(new Object[]{" "}); // No column name

    jTable5.removeAll(); // Clear the table

    ResultSet rs = dbMetaData.getTableTypes();
    while (rs.next())
      model5.addRow(new Object[]{rs.getString("TABLE_TYPE")});
  }

  // Variables declaration - do not modify
  private javax.swing.JTabbedPane jTabbedPane1;
  private javax.swing.JScrollPane jScrollPane1;
  private javax.swing.JTable jTable1;
  private javax.swing.JScrollPane jScrollPane2;
  private javax.swing.JTable jTable2;
```

Listing 13.2 *continued*

continued

Example 13.1 continued

```
    private javax.swing.JScrollPane jScrollPane3;
    private javax.swing.JTable jTable3;
    private javax.swing.JScrollPane jScrollPane4;
    private javax.swing.JTable jTable4;
    private javax.swing.JScrollPane jScrollPane5;
    private javax.swing.JTable jTable5;
    // End of variables declaration
  }
```

Listing 13.2 *continued*

```
package jdbcdemo;

import javax.swing.table.*;
import java.util.*;
import java.sql.*;

public class TableInfoPanel extends javax.swing.JPanel {
  // Create data model for jtbData and jtbDef
  DefaultTableModel model1 = new DefaultTableModel();
  DefaultTableModel model2 = new DefaultTableModel();

  private java.sql.Connection connection;
  private String tableName;

  /** Creates new form TableInfoPanel */
  public TableInfoPanel() {
    initComponents();

    jTable1.setModel(model1);
    jTable2.setModel(model2);
  }

  private void initComponents() {
    jTabbedPane1 = new javax.swing.JTabbedPane();
    jScrollPane1 = new javax.swing.JScrollPane();
    jTable1 = new javax.swing.JTable();
    jScrollPane2 = new javax.swing.JScrollPane();
    jTable2 = new javax.swing.JTable();
    setLayout(new java.awt.BorderLayout());
    jScrollPane1.setViewportView(jTable1);
    jTabbedPane1.addTab("Data", jScrollPane1);
    jScrollPane2.setViewportView(jTable2);
    jTabbedPane1.addTab("Definition", jScrollPane2);
    add(jTabbedPane1, java.awt.BorderLayout.CENTER);
  }

  public void setConnectionAndTable(Connection newConnection,
    String newTableName) {
    connection = newConnection;
    tableName = newTableName;
    showData();
    showTableDef();
  }

  private void showData() {
    try {
      Statement statement = connection.createStatement();

```

Listing 13.3 *TableInfoPanel.java*

```
      // Vector to store rows
      Vector rowData = new Vector();

      ResultSet rs = statement.executeQuery(
        "select * from " + tableName + ";");

      // Get column count
      int columnCount = rs.getMetaData().getColumnCount();

      // Store rows to rowData
      while (rs.next()) {
        Vector singleRow = new Vector();
        for (int i = 0; i < columnCount; i++)
          // Store cells to a row
          singleRow.addElement(rs.getObject(i + 1));
        rowData.addElement(singleRow);
      }

      // Vector to store column names
      Vector columnNames = new Vector();

      // Column name result set
      ResultSet rsColumns = connection.getMetaData().getColumns(
        null, null, tableName, null);

      // Add column names to the table
      while (rsColumns.next()) {
        columnNames.addElement(rsColumns.getString("COLUMN_NAME"));
      }

      // Set new data to the table model
      model1.setDataVector(rowData, columnNames);
    }
    catch (Exception ex) {
      ex.printStackTrace();
    }
  }

  private void showTableDef() {
    try {
      // Vector to store rows
      Vector rowData = new Vector();

      // Column name result set
      ResultSet rsColumns = connection.getMetaData().getColumns(
        null, null, tableName, null);

      // Store rows to rowData
      while (rsColumns.next()) {
        Vector singleRow = new Vector();
        // Store cells to a row
        singleRow.addElement(rsColumns.getObject("COLUMN_NAME"));
        singleRow.addElement(rsColumns.getObject("TYPE_NAME"));
        singleRow.addElement(rsColumns.getObject("COLUMN_SIZE"));
        rowData.addElement(singleRow);
      }

      // Vector to store column names
      Vector columnNames = new Vector();
      columnNames.addElement("COLUMN_NAME");
```

Listing 13.3 *continued*

continued

Example 13.1 continued

```
        columnNames.addElement("TYPE_NAME");
        columnNames.addElement("COLUMN_SIZE");

        // Set new data to the table model
        model2.setDataVector(rowData, columnNames);
      }
      catch (Exception ex) {
        ex.printStackTrace();
      }
    }

    // Variables declaration - do not modify
    private javax.swing.JTabbedPane jTabbedPane1;
    private javax.swing.JScrollPane jScrollPane1;
    private javax.swing.JTable jTable1;
    private javax.swing.JScrollPane jScrollPane2;
    private javax.swing.JTable jTable2;
    // End of variables declaration
  }
```

Listing 13.3 *continued*

Example Review

The variable `connection` encapsulates all the work in the `DBConnectDialog` class. An instance of `DBConnectDialog` is created in `DBExplorer`, and the dialog box is displayed when the Connect to Database menu command is issued. The program attempts to establish a connection when the OK button is clicked in the dialog box. This variable is non-null if a connection to the database is established. The classes `DBConnectDialog`, `DBExplorer`, `DBInfoPanel`, and `TableInfoPanel` are related through the `connection` variable.

Once connected, the database structural information is displayed in the tree. The `updateTree()` method (Lines 122–155) in `DBExplorer` builds the tree. The database URL is shown as the root. The second level of the tree contains the table types supported by the database. The third level of the tree displays the tables. The fourth level of the tree displays the columns of the tables.

Each node is an instance of `DefaultMutableTreeNode`. When you select a tree node, a `TreeSelectionEvent` occurs. The `jTree1_valueChanged` handler responds to the selection of a node. How do you know whether a root or a table node is selected? The solution is to get the selected path and use the `getPathCount` method of the path to determine the level of the selected node. If the root is selected, the `getPathCount()` method returns 1. If a table node is selected, the `getPathCount()` method returns 3.

When the root is selected, an instance of `DBInfoPanel` is placed into the right section of `jSplitPane1` after setting the database connection in the instance. When a table node is selected, the table name is retrieved through the `getPathComponent` method on the path. The table name and the database connection are set to the instance of `DBInfoPanel`, which is then placed into the right section of `jSplitPane1`. If a selected node is not the root or a table node, the content displayed in the split pane is removed.

The `setConnectionAndTable` method (Lines 37–43) in the `TableInfoPanel` class sets a database connection and a table name. You could break this into two methods, one to set the connection, and the other to set the table name. However, the combined method is more appropriate because table data and definition cannot be obtained until both the connection property and the table name property are set.

13.4 Processing Statements

Once a connection to a particular database is established, it can be used to send SQL statements from your program to the database. JDBC provides the `Statement`, `PreparedStatement`, and `CallableStatement` interfaces to facilitate sending statements to a database for execution and receiving execution results from the database, as shown in Figure 13.9.

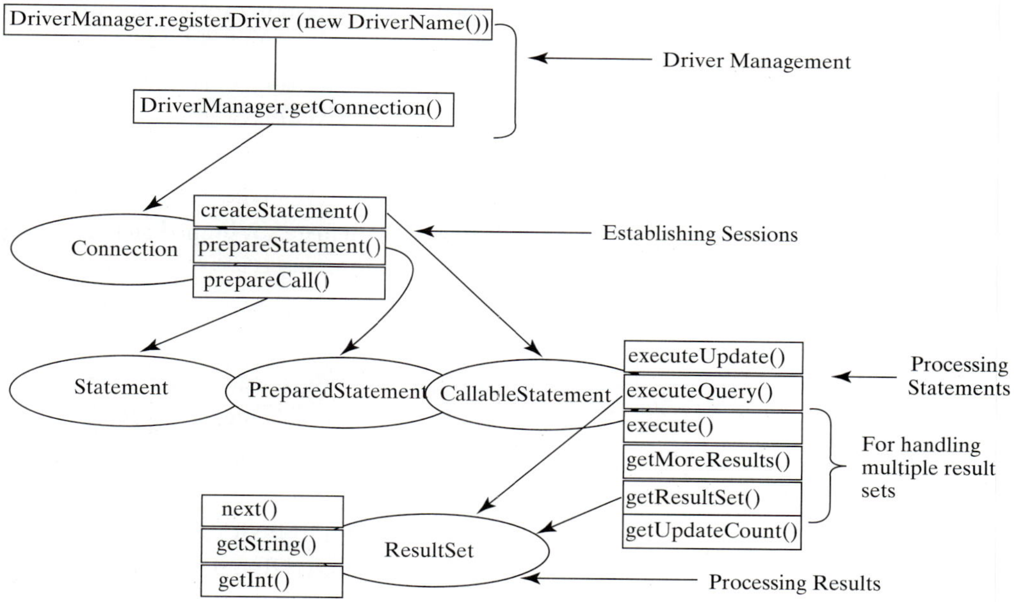

Figure 13.9 *JDBC classes enable Java programs to connect to the database, send SQL statements, and process results.*

`Statement` interface is used to execute static SQL statements that contain no parameters. The `PreparedStatement`, extending `Statement`, is used to execute a precompiled SQL statement with or without IN parameters. The `CallableStatement`, extending `PreparedStatement`, is used to execute a call to a database-stored procedure.

If a `Connection` object can be envisioned as a cable linking your program to a database, an object of `Statement` or its subclass can be viewed as a cart that takes the

SQL statements for execution by the database and brings the result back to the program. A `Statement` object is created using the `createStatement()` method in the `Connection` interface. For example, the following code creates a `Statement stmt` on a particular `Connection connection`:

```
Connection connection = DriverManager.getConnection
  ("jdbc:odbc:LiangBookDB_MDB", "", "" );
Statement stmt = connection.createStatement();
```

The `Statement` interface provides many methods, listed in Table 13.6, to execute various types of SQL statements, get execution results and information, and control the executions.

TABLE 13.6 `Statement` Methods

Method name	*Description*
`void addBatch(String sql)`	Adds an SQL command to the current batch of commands for the statement. (JDBC 2)
`void cancel()`	Called by one thread to cancel a statement being executed by another thread.
`void clearBatch()`	Clears the current batch of commands for the statement. (JDBC 2)
`void clearWarnings()`	Clears the warnings for the current SQL statement.
`void close()`	Closes the statement for immediately releasing the associated resource.
`boolean execute(String sql)`	Executes an SQL statement that may return multiple result sets.
`int[] executeBatch()`	Executes all the SQL commands in the current batch for the statement. (JDBC 2)
`ResultSet executeQuery(String sql)`	Executes an SQL statement that returns a single result set.
`int executeUpdate(String sql)`	Executes an SQL INSERT, UPDATE, DELETE, or SQL DDL statement.
`Connection getConnection()`	Gets the connection object that produced this `Statement` object. (JDBC 2)
`int getFetchDirection()`	Gets the direction for fetching rows in a table. (JDBC 2)
`int getFetchSize()`	Gets the number of rows to be fetched. (JDBC 2)

TABLE 13.6 continued

Method name	*Description*
`int getMaxFieldSize()`	Gets a maximum size for all the columns a result set can have.
`int getMaxRows()`	Gets the maximum number of rows a result set can contain.
`boolean getMoreResults()`	Moves to the next result set. Used for SQL statements that return multiple results.
`int getQueryTimeout()`	Gets the number of seconds the driver will wait for a statement to execute.
`ResultSet getResultSet()`	Returns a `ResultSet` for the current result.
`int getResultSetConcurrency()`	Returns the result set concurrency. (JDBC 2)
`int getResultSetType()`	Returns the result set type. (JDBC 2)
`int getUpdateCount()`	Returns current result as an update count.
	Used for SQL INSERT, UPDATE, and DELETE statements.
`SQLWarning getWarnings()`	Returns an `SQLWarning` for the current statement.
`void setCursorName(String name)`	Sets the cursor name for subsequent use in SQL positioned update/delete statements.
`void setEscapeProcessing (boolean enable)`	Sets true or false on escape processing for the statement.
`void setFetchDirection(int direction)`	Sets the direction in which rows will be fetched. (JDBC 2)
`void setFetchSize(int rows)`	Sets the number of rows to be fetched. (JDBC 2)
`void setMaxFieldSize(int max)`	Sets the maximum size for a column in a result set.
`void setMaxRows(int max)`	Sets the maximum number of rows in a result set.
`void setQueryTimeout(int seconds)`	Sets the maximum time for a driver to wait for a statement to execute.

13.4.1 The *execute, executeQuery,* and *executeUpdate Methods*

The methods for executing SQL statements are `execute`, `executeQuery`, and `executeUpdate`, each of which accepts a string containing an SQL statement as an argument. This string is passed to the database for execution. The `execute` method should be used if the execution produces multiple result sets, multiple update counts, or a combination of result sets and update counts. The `executeQuery` method should be used if the execution produces a single result set, such as the SQL select statement. The `executeUpdate` method should be used if the statement results in a single update count or no update count, such as an SQL INSERT, DELETE, UPDATE, or DDL statement.

The `executeQuery` method returns a `ResultSet` object. The `executeUpdate` returns an update count, that is, an `int` value for the number of rows affected by the SQL statements. This value is the number of rows inserted, deleted, or updated for successful execution of an SQL INSERT, DELETE, or UPDATE statement. This value is 0 for an SQL DDL statement.

The `execute` method returns a `boolean` value. The value is `true` if the first result is a `ResultSet`, false if it returns an update count or there are no more results. The `getResultSet()` and `getUpdateCount()` are called to process the result produced by the `execute` method. The `getResultSet()` method is used to get the current result set. If the current result is an update count or there are no more results, `getResultSet()` returns `null`. The `getUpdateCount()` method returns the current result as an update count; if the result is a `ResultSet` or there are no more results, -1 is returned. When `getUpdateCount()` returns -1, this means that the result is a `ResultSet` or that there are no more results. To determine what -1 really means, you can call `getResultSet()`. If `getResultSet()` returns `null` and `getUpdateCount()` returns -1, there are no more results.

After the current result, whether a `ResultSet` or an update count, you need to call `getMoreResults()` to move to a statement's next result. This method returns a `boolean` value, which returns `true` if the result is a `ResultSet`; `false` if it is an update count or there are no more results. If `getMoreResults()` returns `false` and `getUpdateCount()` returns -1, there are no more results.

Example 13.2 Using `Statement` to Execute Static SQL Statements

In this example, you will write a program that creates an address book for viewing addresses and inserting new addresses. The addresses are stored in an Address table consisting of the following fields: firstName, mi, lastName, street, city, state, zip, telephone, and email, defined in the following statement:

```
create table Address
(
  firstname varchar(25),
  mi char(1),
  lastname varchar(25),
  street varchar(40),
  city varchar(20),
  state varchar(2),
  zip varchar(5),
  telephone varchar(10),
  email varchar(30)
)
```

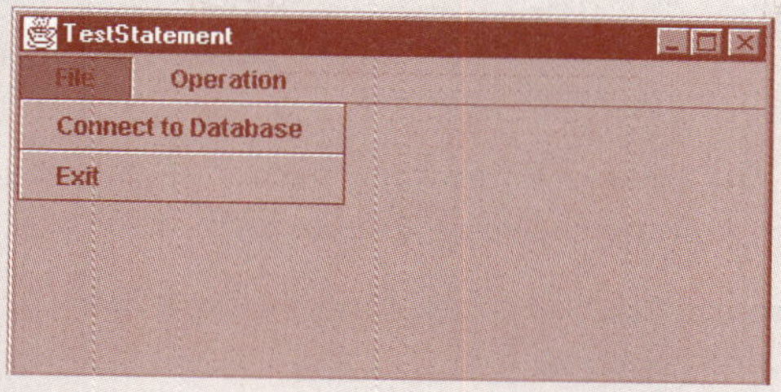

Figure 13.10 *You may connect to a JDBC-compliant database and test static SQL statements in this program.*

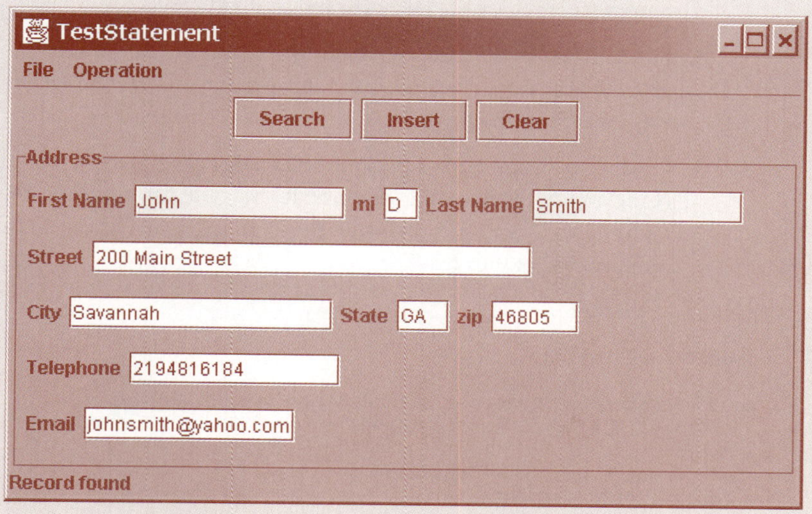

Figure 13.11 *Static SQL statements are used in this program to retrieve and modify database information.*

The program contains two menus: File and Operation. The File menu contains the menu items "Connect to Database" and "Exit," as shown in Figure 13.10. The Operation menu contains a single menu item, "Using Static SQL Statements." Choosing "Connect to Database" brings up a dialog box, as shown in Figure 13.2, to let you connect to a database. After your program is connected to the database, you may choose "Using Static SQL Statements" to view and insert an address, as shown in Figure 13.11. To view an address, enter the first name and the last name, then click the Search button. The Insert button inserts a new address in the database. The Clear button clears all the fields.

The project can be divided into two steps: creating the applet with menus, and creating the panel for processing the address. The panel is placed onto the applet when the "Using Static SQL Statements" menu is selected after connecting to a particular database.

continued

Example 13.2 continued

1. Creating the applet with menus

   1.1. In the jdbcdemo package, create an applet named `TestStatement` using the Forte Swing JApplet form wizard.

   1.2. Drop a `JMenuBar` to the form to create `jMenubar1` and `jMenu1`. Set the text of `jMenu1` to File.

   1.3. Add the menu items "Connect to Database," a separator, and "Exit" in the File menu. Create the Operation menu and add the menu item "Using Static SQL Statements" to it. Change the menu item names to `jmiConnect`, `jmiExit`, and `jmiStaticSQL`.

   1.4. Drop a `DBConnectDialog` from the component palette to create `dBConnectDialog1`. Set its `modal` property to True. `DBConnectDialog` was created in Example 12.4.

   1.5. Create an instance of DBConnectDialog, as shown in Listing 13.4 (Line 17). Generate and implement the code for handling the menu commands "Connect to Database," "Exit," and "Using Static SQL Statements" (Lines 64–77).

```
1   package jdbcdemo;
2
3   import java.awt.*;
4
5   public class TestStatement extends javax.swing.JApplet {
6     DBConnectDialog dBConnectDialog1 = new DBConnectDialog();
7
8     /** Creates new form TestStatement */
9     public TestStatement() {
10      initComponents();
11    }
12
13    private void initComponents() {
14      jMenuBar1 = new javax.swing.JMenuBar();
15      jMenu1 = new javax.swing.JMenu();
16      jmiConnect = new javax.swing.JMenuItem();
17      jSeparator1 = new javax.swing.JSeparator();
18      jmiExit = new javax.swing.JMenuItem();
19      jMenu2 = new javax.swing.JMenu();
20      jmiStaticSQL = new javax.swing.JMenuItem();
21      jMenu1.setText("File");
22      jmiConnect.setText("Connect to Database");
23      jmiConnect.addActionListener(
24        new java.awt.event.ActionListener() {
25          public void actionPerformed(java.awt.event.ActionEvent evt) {
26            jmiConnectActionPerformed(evt);
27          }
28        });
29      jMenu1.add(jmiConnect);
30      jMenu1.add(jSeparator1);
31      jmiExit.setText("Exit");
32      jmiExit.addActionListener(new java.awt.event.ActionListener() {
```

Listing 13.4 *TestStatement.java*

```
          public void actionPerformed(java.awt.event.ActionEvent evt) {
            jmiExitActionPerformed(evt);
          }
        });
        jMenu1.add(jmiExit);
        jMenuBar1.add(jMenu1);
        jMenu2.setText("Operation");
        jmiStaticSQL.setText("Using Static SQL Statements");
        jmiStaticSQL.addActionListener(
          new java.awt.event.ActionListener() {
          public void actionPerformed(java.awt.event.ActionEvent evt) {
            jmiStaticSQLActionPerformed(evt);
          }
        });
        jMenu2.add(jmiStaticSQL);
        jMenuBar1.add(jMenu2);
        setJMenuBar(jMenuBar1);
      }

      private void jmiExitActionPerformed(
        java.awt.event.ActionEvent evt) {
        System.exit(0);
      }

      private void jmiStaticSQLActionPerformed(
        java.awt.event.ActionEvent evt) {
          addAddressPanel(new AddressPanel(
          dBConnectDialog1.getConnection()));
        }

      private void jmiConnectActionPerformed(
        java.awt.event.ActionEvent evt) {
        dBConnectDialog1.setVisible(true);
      }

      /** Add an address panel to the center of applet */
      void addAddressPanel(AddressPanel addressPanel) {
        if (dBConnectDialog1.getConnection() != null) {
          // Remove UI components from the applet
          this.getContentPane().removeAll();

          // Add AddressPanel panel to the applet
          this.getContentPane().add(addressPanel,
          BorderLayout.CENTER);

          this.validate();
        }
        else
          System.out.println("Database not connected");
      }

      // Variables declaration - do not modify
      private javax.swing.JMenuBar jMenuBar1;
      private javax.swing.JMenu jMenu1;
      private javax.swing.JMenuItem jmiConnect;
      private javax.swing.JSeparator jSeparator1;
      private javax.swing.JMenuItem jmiExit;
      private javax.swing.JMenu jMenu2;
      private javax.swing.JMenuItem jmiStaticSQL;
      // End of variables declaration
    }
```

Listing 13.4 *continued*

continued

Example 13.2 continued

2. Creating the `AddressPanel` panel

   2.1. Create `AddressPanel`, which inherits `JPanel`, using the Forte Swing JPanel form wizard.

   2.2. Drop a `JLabel` to the south of `AddressPanel` to create `jlblStatus`.

   2.3. Drop a `JPanel` to the north of `AddressPanel` to create `jpButtons`. Drop a `JButton` three times into `jpButton` to create the Search, Insert, and Clear buttons. Rename them `jbtSearch`, `jbtInsert`, and `jbtClear`.

   2.4. Drop a `JPanel` to the center of `AddressPanel` to create `jpAddress`. Set its `layout` to `GridLayout`, with `row` set to 5 and `column` set to 1. Drop a `JPanel` five times to `jpAddress`, and drop appropriate labels and text fields for displaying address into these panels. Set the `text` property of the labels to "First Name," "MI," "Last Name," "Street," "City," "State," "Zip," "Telephone," and "Email." Rename the text fields `jtfFirstName`, `jtfMi`, `jtfLastName`, `jtfStreet`, `jtfCity`, `jtfState`, `jtfZip`, `jtfTelephone`, and `jtfEmail`. Set an appropriate value in the `column` property of each text field.

   2.5. Create a variable `connection` of the `java.sql.Connection` type in `AddressPanel`, and create a new constructor with a parameter of the `Connection` type, as shown in Listing 13.5.

   2.6. Generate and implement the code for handling the three buttons, as shown in Listing 13.5.

```
package jdbcdemo;

import java.sql.*;

public class AddressPanel extends javax.swing.JPanel {
  // Database connection passed from DBConnectDialog
  Connection connection;

  /** Construct an AddressPanel with a specified connection */
  public AddressPanel(Connection connection) {
    this();
    this.connection = connection;
    jlblStatus.setText("Using static SQL statements");
  }

  /** Creates new form AddressPanel */
  public AddressPanel() {
    initComponents();
  }

  private void initComponents() {
    jlblStatus = new javax.swing.JLabel();
    jpButtons = new javax.swing.JPanel();
```

Listing 13.5 *AddressPanel.java*

```
      jbtSearch = new javax.swing.JButton();
      jbtInsert = new javax.swing.JButton();
      jbtClear = new javax.swing.JButton();
      jpAddress = new javax.swing.JPanel();
      jPanel3 = new javax.swing.JPanel();
      jLabel2 = new javax.swing.JLabel();
      jtfFirstName = new javax.swing.JTextField();
      jLabel3 = new javax.swing.JLabel();
      jtfMi = new javax.swing.JTextField();
      jLabel4 = new javax.swing.JLabel();
      jtfLastName = new javax.swing.JTextField();
      jPanel4 = new javax.swing.JPanel();
      jLabel5 = new javax.swing.JLabel();
      jtfStreet = new javax.swing.JTextField();
      jPanel5 = new javax.swing.JPanel();
      jLabel6 = new javax.swing.JLabel();
      jtfCity = new javax.swing.JTextField();
      jLabel7 = new javax.swing.JLabel();
      jtfState = new javax.swing.JTextField();
      jLabel8 = new javax.swing.JLabel();
      jtfZip = new javax.swing.JTextField();
      jPanel6 = new javax.swing.JPanel();
      jLabel9 = new javax.swing.JLabel();
      jtfTelephone = new javax.swing.JTextField();
      jPanel7 = new javax.swing.JPanel();
      jLabel10 = new javax.swing.JLabel();
      jtfEmail = new javax.swing.JTextField();
      setLayout(new java.awt.BorderLayout());
      add(jlblStatus, java.awt.BorderLayout.SOUTH);
      jbtSearch.setText("Search");
      jbtSearch.addActionListener(new java.awt.event.ActionListener() {
        public void actionPerformed(java.awt.event.ActionEvent evt) {
          jbtSearchActionPerformed(evt);
        }
      });
      jpButtons.add(jbtSearch);
      jbtInsert.setText("Insert");
      jbtInsert.addActionListener(new java.awt.event.ActionListener() {
        public void actionPerformed(java.awt.event.ActionEvent evt) {
          jbtInsertActionPerformed(evt);
        }
      });
      jpButtons.add(jbtInsert);
      jbtClear.setText("Clear");
      jbtClear.addActionListener(new java.awt.event.ActionListener() {
        public void actionPerformed(java.awt.event.ActionEvent evt) {
          jbtClearActionPerformed(evt);
        }
      });
      jpButtons.add(jbtClear);
      add(jpButtons, java.awt.BorderLayout.NORTH);
      jpAddress.setLayout(new java.awt.GridLayout(5, 0));
      jpAddress.setBorder(
        new javax.swing.border.TitledBorder("Address"));
      jPanel3.setLayout(
        new java.awt.FlowLayout(java.awt.FlowLayout.LEFT));
      jLabel2.setText("First Name");
      jPanel3.add(jLabel2);
      jtfFirstName.setColumns(10);
      jPanel3.add(jtfFirstName);
```

Listing 13.5 *continued*

continued

Example 13.2 continued

```
        jLabel3.setText("MI");
        jPanel3.add(jLabel3);
        jtfMi.setColumns(1);
        jPanel3.add(jtfMi);
        jLabel4.setText("Last Name");
        jPanel3.add(jLabel4);
        jtfLastName.setColumns(15);
        jPanel3.add(jtfLastName);
        jpAddress.add(jPanel3);
        jPanel4.setLayout(
          new java.awt.FlowLayout(java.awt.FlowLayout.LEFT));
        jLabel5.setText("Street");
        jPanel4.add(jLabel5);
        jtfStreet.setColumns(37);
        jPanel4.add(jtfStreet);
        jpAddress.add(jPanel4);
        jPanel5.setLayout(
          new java.awt.FlowLayout(java.awt.FlowLayout.LEFT));
        jLabel6.setText("City");
        jtfCity.setColumns(10);
        jPanel5.add(jtfCity);
        jLabel7.setText("State");
        jPanel5.add(jLabel7);
        jtfState.setColumns(2);
        jPanel5.add(jtfState);
        jLabel8.setText("ZIP");
        jPanel5.add(jLabel8);
        jtfZip.setColumns(5);
        jPanel5.add(jtfZip);
        jpAddress.add(jPanel5);
        jPanel6.setLayout(
          new java.awt.FlowLayout(java.awt.FlowLayout.LEFT));
        jLabel9.setText("Telephone");
        jPanel6.add(jLabel9);
        jtfTelephone.setColumns(12);
        jPanel6.add(jtfTelephone);
        jpAddress.add(jPanel6);
        jPanel7.setLayout(
          new java.awt.FlowLayout(java.awt.FlowLayout.LEFT));
        jLabel10.setText("Email");
        jPanel7.add(jLabel10);
        jtfEmail.setColumns(20);
        jPanel7.add(jtfEmail);
        jpAddress.add(jPanel7);
        add(jpAddress, java.awt.BorderLayout.CENTER);
      }

      private void jbtClearActionPerformed(
        java.awt.event.ActionEvent evt) {
        clear();
      }

      private void jbtInsertActionPerformed(
        java.awt.event.ActionEvent evt) {
        insert();
      }

```

Listing 13.5 *continued*

```
    private void jbtSearchActionPerformed(
      java.awt.event.ActionEvent evt) {
      select();
    }

    protected void select() {
      String query = "select * from Address where " +
      "firstName = " +
      "'" + jtfFirstName.getText().trim() + "'" +
      " and lastName = " +
      "'" + jtfLastName.getText().trim() + "'";

      try {
        Statement stmt = connection.createStatement();
        ResultSet rs = stmt.executeQuery(query);

        if (rs.next()) {
          jtfMi.setText(rs.getString(2));
          jtfStreet.setText(rs.getString(4));
          jtfCity.setText(rs.getString(5));
          jtfState.setText(rs.getString(6));
          jtfZip.setText(rs.getString(7));
          jtfTelephone.setText(rs.getString(8));
          jtfEmail.setText(rs.getString(9));

          jlblStatus.setText("Record found");
        }
        else {
          jlblStatus.setText("Record not found");
        }
      }
      catch (SQLException ex) {
        jlblStatus.setText(ex.getMessage());
      }
    }

    protected void insert() {
      String sqlInsert = "insert into Address values (" +
        "'" + jtfFirstName.getText().trim() + "'" + "," +
        "'" + jtfMi.getText().trim() + "'" + "," +
        "'" + jtfLastName.getText().trim() + "'" + "," +
        "'" + jtfStreet.getText().trim() + "'" + "," +
        "'" + jtfCity.getText().trim() + "'" + "," +
        "'" + jtfState.getText().trim() + "'" + "," +
        "'" + jtfZip.getText().trim() + "'" + "," +
        "'" + jtfTelephone.getText().trim() + "'" + "," +
        "'" + jtfEmail.getText().trim()+ "'" + ")";

      try {
        Statement stmt = connection.createStatement();
        int t = stmt.executeUpdate(sqlInsert);
        jlblStatus.setText("Insertion succeeded");
      }
      catch (SQLException ex) {
        jlblStatus.setText(ex.getMessage());
      }
    }

    protected void clear() {
      jtfFirstName.setText(null);
```

Listing 13.5 *continued*

continued

Example 13.2 continued

```
      jtfMi.setText(null);
      jtfLastName.setText(null);
      jtfStreet.setText(null);
      jtfCity.setText(null);
      jtfState.setText(null);
      jtfZip.setText(null);
      jtfTelephone.setText(null);
      jtfEmail.setText(null);
    }

    /** Set status */
    public void setStatus(String msg) {
      jlblStatus.setText(msg);
    }

    /** Return firstnmae */
    public String getFirstName() {
      return jtfFirstName.getText().trim();
    }

    /** Set firstnmae */
    public void setFirstName(String s) {
      jtfFirstName.setText(s);
    }

    /** Return lastnmae */
    public String getMi() {
      return jtfMi.getText().trim();
    }

    /** Set mi */
    public void setMi(String s) {
      jtfMi.setText(s);
    }

    /** Return lastnmae */
    public String getLastName() {
      return jtfLastName.getText().trim();
    }

    /** Set lastnmae */
    public void setLastName(String s) {
      jtfLastName.setText(s);
    }

    /** Return street */
    public String getStreet() {
      return jtfStreet.getText().trim();
    }

    /** Set street */
    public void setStreet(String s) {
      jtfStreet.setText(s);
    }

    /** Return city */
    public String getCity() {
      return jtfCity.getText().trim();
    }

```

Listing 13.5 *continued*

```
  /** Set city */
  public void setCity(String s) {
    jtfCity.setText(s);
  }

  /** Return zip */
  public String getZip() {
    return jtfZip.getText().trim();
  }

  /** Set zip */
  public void setZip(String s) {
    jtfZip.setText(s);
  }

  /** Return state */
  public String getState() {
    return jtfState.getText().trim();
  }

  /** Set state */
  public void setState(String s) {
    jtfState.setText(s);
  }

  /** Return telephone */
  public String getTelephone() {
    return jtfTelephone.getText().trim();
  }

  /** Set telephone */
  public void setTelephone(String s) {
    jtfTelephone.setText(s);
  }

  /** Return email */
  public String getEmail() {
    return jtfEmail.getText().trim();
  }

  /** Set email */
  public void setEmail(String s) {
    jtfEmail.setText(s);
  }

  // Variables declaration - do not modify
  private javax.swing.JLabel jlblStatus;
  private javax.swing.JPanel jpButtons;
  private javax.swing.JButton jbtSearch;
  private javax.swing.JButton jbtInsert;
  private javax.swing.JButton jbtClear;
  private javax.swing.JPanel jpAddress;
  private javax.swing.JPanel jPanel3;
  private javax.swing.JLabel jLabel2;
  private javax.swing.JTextField jtfFirstName;
  private javax.swing.JLabel jLabel3;
  private javax.swing.JTextField jtfMi;
  private javax.swing.JLabel jLabel4;
  private javax.swing.JTextField jtfLastName;
  private javax.swing.JPanel jPanel4;
```

Listing 13.5 *continued*

continued

Example 13.2 continued

```
    private javax.swing.JLabel jLabel5;
    private javax.swing.JTextField jtfStreet;
    private javax.swing.JPanel jPanel5;
    private javax.swing.JLabel jLabel6;
    private javax.swing.JTextField jtfCity;
    private javax.swing.JLabel jLabel7;
    private javax.swing.JTextField jtfState;
    private javax.swing.JLabel jLabel8;
    private javax.swing.JTextField jtfZip;
    private javax.swing.JPanel jPanel6;
    private javax.swing.JLabel jLabel9;
    private javax.swing.JTextField jtfTelephone;
    private javax.swing.JPanel jPanel7;
    private javax.swing.JLabel jLabel10;
    private javax.swing.JTextField jtfEmail;
    // End of variables declaration
}
```

Listing 13.5 *AddressPanel.java*

Example Review

You click the Connect to Database menu command to create an instance of `DBConnectDialog` and display the dialog box for establishing a database connection. After a connection to a database is established, you can click the Using Static SQL Statements menu command to display the `AddressPanel` panel. The constructor of `AddressPanel` has a parameter of the `Connection` type. The `dBconnectDialog1.getConnection()` is passed to the constructor of `AddressPanel` to create an instance of `AddressPanel`.

Static SQL statements are constructed to perform SQL select and SQL INSERT operations. An SQL `Statement` instance `stmt` is created to execute the static SQL statements. `stmt.executeQuery(sqlSelect)` executes an SQL select statement in the string `sqlSelect`, which returns a `ResultSet`; `stmt.executeUpdate(sqlInsert)` executes an SQL INSERT statement. In the example, only the first record in the `ResultSet` is displayed on the `AddressPanel` panel.

13.5 Batch Processing

In all the preceding examples, SQL commands are submitted to the database for execution one at a time. This is inefficient for processing a large number of updates. For example, suppose you wanted to insert a thousand rows into a table. Submitting one INSERT command at a time would take nearly a thousand times longer than submitting all the INSERT commands in a batch at once. To improve performance, JDBC 2 introduced the batch update for processing nonselect SQL commands. A batch update consists of a sequence of nonselect SQL commands. These commands are collected in a batch and submitted to the database all together.

To use the batch update, you add nonselect commands to a batch using the `addBatch` method in the `Statement` interface. After all the SQL commands are added to the batch, use the `executeBatch` method to submit the batch to the database for execution.

For example, the following code adds a create table command, two insert statements in a batch, and executes the batch.

```
Statement stmt = conn.createStatement();

// Add SQL commands to the batch
stmt.addBatch("CREATE TABLE T (C1 NUMBER, C2 VARCHAR(15))");
stmt.addBatch("insert into TABLE T values " +
  "(100, \'Smith\')");
stmt.addBatch("insert into TABLE T values " +
  "(200, \'Jones\')");

// Execute the batch
int count[] = stmt.executeBatch();
```

The `executeBatch` method returns an array of counts, each of which counts the number of the rows affected by the SQL command. The first count returns 0 because it is a DDL command. The rest of the commands return 1 because only one row is affected.

Example 13.3 Copying Text Files to Tables

In this example, you will write a program that gets data from a text file and copies the data to a table, as shown in Figure 13.12. The text file consists of the lines, each of which corresponds to a row in the table. The fields in a row are separated by commas. The string values in a row are enclosed in single quotes. You can view the text file by clicking the View File button and copy the text to the table by clicking the Copy button. The table must already be defined in the database.

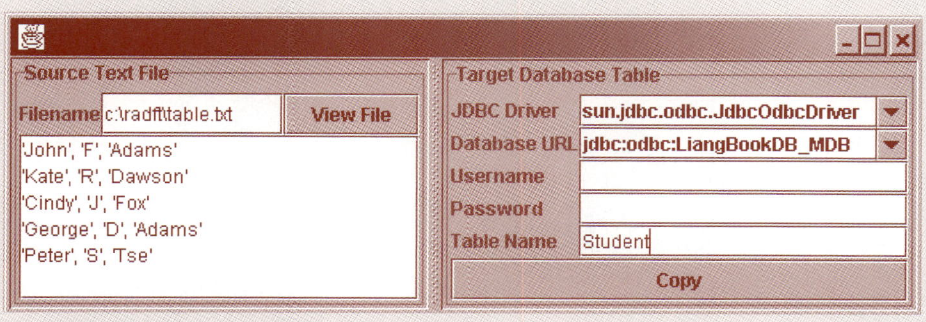

Figure 13.12 *The Copy File to Table utility copies text files to database tables.*

Here are the steps to create the project:

1. In the jdbcdemo package, create a new frame named `CopyFileToTable` using the Forte Swing JFrame form wizard.

continued

Example 13.3 continued

2. Drop a `JLabel` to the south of the applet, and rename it `jlblStatus`, and drop a `JSplitPane` to the center of the applet to create `jSplitPane1`.

3. Drop a `JPanel` to the left pane of `jSplitPane1` to create `jPanel1` and `jPanel2`. Set the border title of `jPanel1` and `jPanel2` to "Source Text File" and "Target Database Table," respectively. Set the `layout` of `jPanel1` and `jPanel2` to `BorderLayout`.

4. Drop a `JPanel` to the north of `jPanel1` to create `jPanel3`. Drop a `JScroll-Pane` to the center of the `jPanel1`. Drop a `JTextArea` into the scroll pane, and rename it `jtaFile`.

5. Set the `layout` of `jPanel3` to `BorderLayout`. Drop a `JLabel`, a `JButton`, and a `JTextField` to the west, east, and center of `jPanel3`. Rename the text field `jtfFilename`, and the button `jbtViewFile`. Set the text of the label to Filename, and the button to View File.

6. Drop a `JButton` to the south of the `jPanel2`, rename it `jbtCopy`, and set its `text` to Copy. Drop a `JPanel` twice to the west and center of `jPanel2` to create `jPanel4` and `jPanel5`. Set their `layout` to GridLayout with five rows and two columns.

7. Drop a `JLabel` five times to `jPanel4` and set their `text` to "JDBC Driver," "Database URL," "Username," "Password," and "Table Name." Drop a `JcomboBox` twice to `jPanel5` to create `jcboDriver` and `jcboURL`. Set their `editable` to True. Drop a `JTextField`, a `JPasswordField`, and a `JTextField` to create `jtfUsername`, `jtfPassword`, and `jtfTableName`.

8. Use the `addItem` method to add JDBC driver classes, and database URLs to `jcboDriver` and `jcboURL`, as shown in Listing 13.6 (Lines 11–18). Generate and implement the code for handling the buttons View File and Copy.

```
1  package jdbcdemo;
2
3  import java.io.*;
4  import java.sql.*;
5
6  public class CopyFileToTable extends javax.swing.JFrame {
7    /** Creates new form CopyFileToTable */
8    public CopyFileToTable() {
9      initComponents();
10
11     // Add items to the combo boxes
12     jcboDriver.addItem("sun.jdbc.odbc.JdbcOdbcDriver");
13     jcboDriver.addItem("interbase.interclient.Driver");
14     jcboDriver.addItem("oracle.jdbc.driver.OracleDriver");
15     jcboURL.addItem("jdbc:odbc:LiangBookDB_MDB");
16     jcboURL.addItem(
17       "jdbc:interbase://localhost/C:/LiangBook/LiangBookDB.gdb");
```

Listing 13.6 *CopyFileToTable.java*

```
      jcboURL.addItem("jdbc:oracle:thin:@sesrv00.ipfw.edu:1521:test");

      // Interbase login SYSDBA/masterkey and Oracle login scott/tiger
    }

    private void initComponents() {
      jlblStatus = new javax.swing.JLabel();
      jSplitPane1 = new javax.swing.JSplitPane();
      jPanel1 = new javax.swing.JPanel();
      jPanel3 = new javax.swing.JPanel();
      jLabel2 = new javax.swing.JLabel();
      jbtViewFile = new javax.swing.JButton();
      jtfFilename = new javax.swing.JTextField();
      jScrollPane1 = new javax.swing.JScrollPane();
      jtaFile = new javax.swing.JTextArea();
      jPanel2 = new javax.swing.JPanel();
      jbtCopy = new javax.swing.JButton();
      jPanel4 = new javax.swing.JPanel();
      jLabel3 = new javax.swing.JLabel();
      jLabel4 = new javax.swing.JLabel();
      jLabel5 = new javax.swing.JLabel();
      jLabel6 = new javax.swing.JLabel();
      jLabel7 = new javax.swing.JLabel();
      jPanel5 = new javax.swing.JPanel();
      jcboDriver = new javax.swing.JComboBox();
      jcboURL = new javax.swing.JComboBox();
      jtfUsername = new javax.swing.JTextField();
      jtfPassword = new javax.swing.JPasswordField();
      jtfTableName = new javax.swing.JTextField();
      addWindowListener(new java.awt.event.WindowAdapter() {
        public void windowClosing(java.awt.event.WindowEvent evt) {
          exitForm(evt);
        }
      });
      getContentPane().add(jlblStatus, java.awt.BorderLayout.SOUTH);
      jPanel1.setLayout(new java.awt.BorderLayout());
      jPanel1.setBorder(new javax.swing.border.TitledBorder(
        "Source Text File"));
      jPanel3.setLayout(new java.awt.BorderLayout());
      jLabel2.setText("Filename");
      jPanel3.add(jLabel2, java.awt.BorderLayout.WEST);
      jbtViewFile.setText("View File");
      jbtViewFile.addActionListener(
        new java.awt.event.ActionListener() {
        public void actionPerformed(java.awt.event.ActionEvent evt) {
          jbtViewFileActionPerformed(evt);
        }
      });
      jPanel3.add(jbtViewFile, java.awt.BorderLayout.EAST);
      jPanel3.add(jtfFilename, java.awt.BorderLayout.CENTER);
      jPanel1.add(jPanel3, java.awt.BorderLayout.NORTH);
      jScrollPane1.setViewportView(jtaFile);
      jPanel1.add(jScrollPane1, java.awt.BorderLayout.CENTER);
      jSplitPane1.setLeftComponent(jPanel1);
      jPanel2.setLayout(new java.awt.BorderLayout());
      jPanel2.setBorder(new javax.swing.border.TitledBorder(
        "Target Database Table"));
      jbtCopy.setText("Copy");
```

Listing 13.6 *continued*

continued

Example 13.3 continued

```
    jbtCopy.addActionListener(new java.awt.event.ActionListener() {
      public void actionPerformed(java.awt.event.ActionEvent evt) {
        jbtCopyActionPerformed(evt);
      }
    });
    jPanel2.add(jbtCopy, java.awt.BorderLayout.SOUTH);
    jPanel4.setLayout(new java.awt.GridLayout(5, 0));
    jLabel3.setText("JDBC Driver");
    jPanel4.add(jLabel3);
    jLabel4.setText("Database URL");
    jPanel4.add(jLabel4);
    jLabel5.setText("Username");
    jPanel4.add(jLabel5);
    jLabel6.setText("Password");
    jPanel4.add(jLabel6);
    jLabel7.setText("Table Name");
    jPanel4.add(jLabel7);
    jPanel2.add(jPanel4, java.awt.BorderLayout.WEST);
    jPanel5.setLayout(new java.awt.GridLayout(5, 0));
    jcboDriver.setEditable(true);
    jPanel5.add(jcboDriver);
    jcboURL.setEditable(true);
    jPanel5.add(jcboURL);
    jPanel5.add(jtfUsername);
    jPanel5.add(jtfPassword);
    jPanel5.add(jtfTableName);
    jPanel2.add(jPanel5, java.awt.BorderLayout.CENTER);
    jSplitPane1.setRightComponent(jPanel2);
    getContentPane().add(jSplitPane1, java.awt.BorderLayout.CENTER);
    pack();
  }

  private void jbtCopyActionPerformed(
    java.awt.event.ActionEvent evt) {
    try {
      copyFile();
    }
    catch (Exception ex) {
      jlblStatus.setText(ex.toString());
    }
  }

  private void jbtViewFileActionPerformed(
    java.awt.event.ActionEvent evt) {
    showFile();
  }

  /** Display the file in the text area */
  private void showFile() {
    // Use a BufferedReader to read text from the file
    BufferedReader infile = null;

    // Get file name from the text field
    String filename = jtfFilename.getText().trim();

    String inLine;

```

Listing 13.6 *continued*

```
      try {
        // Create a buffered stream
        infile = new BufferedReader(new FileReader(filename));

        // Read a line and append the line to the text area
        while ((inLine = infile.readLine()) != null) {
          jtaFile.append(inLine + '\n');
        }
      }
      catch (FileNotFoundException ex) {
        System.out.println("File not found: " + filename);
      }
      catch (IOException ex) {
        System.out.println(ex.getMessage());
      }
      finally {
        try {
          if (infile != null) infile.close();
        }
        catch (IOException ex) {
          System.out.println(ex.getMessage());
        }
      }
    }

    /** Exit the Application */
    private void exitForm(java.awt.event.WindowEvent evt) {
      System.exit(0);
    }

    /**
     * @param args the command line arguments
     */
    public static void main(String args[]) {
      new CopyFileToTable().show();
    }

    private void copyFile() throws Exception {
      // Load the JDBC driver
      System.out.println((String)jcboDriver.getSelectedItem());
      Class.forName(((String)jcboDriver.getSelectedItem()).trim());
      System.out.println("Driver loaded");

      // Establish a connection
      Connection conn = DriverManager.getConnection
        (((String)jcboURL.getSelectedItem()).trim(),
      jtfUsername.getText().trim(),
      jtfPassword.getText().trim());
      System.out.println("Database connected");

      // Read each line from the text file and insert it to the table
      insertRows(conn);
    }

    private void insertRows(Connection connection) {
      // Build the INSERT statement
      String sqlInsert = "insert into " + jtfTableName.getText()
      + " values (";

```

Listing 13.6 *continued*

continued

Example 13.3 continued

```
      // Use a BufferedReader to read text from the file
      BufferedReader infile = null;

      // Get file name from the text field
      String filename = jtfFilename.getText().trim();

      String inLine;

      try {
        // Create a buffered stream
        infile = new BufferedReader(new FileReader(filename));

        // Create a statement
        Statement statement = connection.createStatement();

        System.out.println("Driver major version? " +
        connection.getMetaData().getDriverMajorVersion());

        // Determine if the supportsBatchUpdates method supported in
        // DatabaseMetaData
        boolean batchUpdatesSupported = false;

        try {
          if (connection.getMetaData().supportsBatchUpdates()) {
            batchUpdatesSupported = true;
            System.out.println("batch updates supported");
          }
          else {
            System.out.println("The driver is of JDBC 2 type, but " +
            "does not support batch updates");
          }
        }
        catch (Exception ex) {
          System.out.println("The driver does not support JDBC 2");
        }

        // Determine if the driver is capable of batch updates
        if (batchUpdatesSupported) {
          // Read a line and add the insert table command to the batch
          while ((inLine = infile.readLine()) != null) {
            statement.addBatch(sqlInsert + inLine + ")");
          }

          statement.executeBatch();

          jlblStatus.setText("Batch updates completed");
        }
        else {
          // Read a line and execute insert table command
          while ((inLine = infile.readLine()) != null) {
            statement.executeUpdate(sqlInsert + inLine + ")");
          }

          jlblStatus.setText("Single row update completed");
        }
      }
      catch (SQLException ex) {
        System.out.println(ex);
      }
```

Listing 13.6 *continued*

```
        catch (FileNotFoundException ex) {
          System.out.println("File not found: " + filename);
        }
        catch (IOException ex) {
          System.out.println(ex.getMessage());
        }
        finally {
          try {
            if (infile != null) infile.close();
          }
          catch (IOException ex) {
            System.out.println(ex.getMessage());
          }
        }
      }

      // Variables declaration - do not modify
      private javax.swing.JLabel jlblStatus;
      private javax.swing.JSplitPane jSplitPane1;
      private javax.swing.JPanel jPanel1;
      private javax.swing.JPanel jPanel3;
      private javax.swing.JLabel jLabel2;
      private javax.swing.JButton jbtViewFile;
      private javax.swing.JTextField jtfFilename;
      private javax.swing.JScrollPane jScrollPane1;
      private javax.swing.JTextArea jtaFile;
      private javax.swing.JPanel jPanel2;
      private javax.swing.JButton jbtCopy;
      private javax.swing.JPanel jPanel4;
      private javax.swing.JLabel jLabel3;
      private javax.swing.JLabel jLabel4;
      private javax.swing.JLabel jLabel5;
      private javax.swing.JLabel jLabel6;
      private javax.swing.JLabel jLabel7;
      private javax.swing.JPanel jPanel5;
      private javax.swing.JComboBox jcboDriver;
      private javax.swing.JComboBox jcboURL;
      private javax.swing.JTextField jtfUsername;
      private javax.swing.JPasswordField jtfPassword;
      private javax.swing.JTextField jtfTableName;
      // End of variables declaration
    }
```

Listing 13.6 *continued*

Example Review

The `insertRows` method uses the batch updates to submit SQL INSERT commands to the database for execution, if the driver supports batch updates. Not all JDBC drivers support JDBC 2. Even if a driver supports JDBC 2, it may not support every feature of JDBC 2. The `DatabaseMetaData` interface does not have a method to verify whether the driver supports JDBC 2. To find out whether the driver supports JDBC 2, invoke the `supportsBatchUpdates` method in the `DatabaseMetaData` interface. If the driver does not support JDBC 2, a `java.lang.UnsupportedOperationException` would occur. If the driver supports JDBC 2, but does not support batch updates, invoking `supportsBatchUpdates` will return false.

continued

Example 13.3 continued

The JDBC-ODBC driver in JDK 1.2 does not support JDBC 2, but the JDBC-ODBC driver in JDK 1.3 or higher does. The Oracle Thin driver for Oracle 8i supports JDBC 2.

The tables are already created in the database. The file format and contents must match the database table specification. Otherwise, the SQL INSERT command would fail.

In Exercise 13.4, you will write a program to insert a thousand records to a database and compare the performance with and without batch updates.

13.6 *PreparedStatement*

The `PreparedStatement` interface is designed to execute dynamic SQL statements and SQL-stored procedures with IN parameters. These SQL statements and stored procedures are precompiled for efficient use when repeatedly executed.

A `PreparedStatement` object is created using the `preparedStatement` method in the `Connection` interface. For example, the following code creates a `PreparedStatement` `pstmt` on a particular `Connection` `connection` for an SQL INSERT statement.

```
Statement pstmt = connection.prepareStatement
  ("insert into Address (firstName, mi, lastName) " +
   "values (?, ?, ?)");
```

This INSERT statement has three question marks as placeholders for parameters representing values for firstName, mi, and lastName in a record of the Address table.

As a subclass of `Statement`, the `PreparedStatement` interface inherits all the methods defined in `Statement`. Additionally, it provides the methods for setting parameters in the object of `PreparedStatement`. These methods are used to set the values for the parameters before executing statements or procedures. In general, the set methods have the following name and signature:

```
setX(int parameterIndex, X value);
```

where *X* is the type of the parameter, and `parameterIndex` is the index of the parameter in the statement. For example, the method `setString(int parameterIndex, String value)` sets a `String` value to the specified parameter. Table 13.7 contains a complete list of the methods in `PreparedStatement`.

The following statements pass parameters "Jack," "A," "Ryan" to the placeholder (?) for firstName, mi, and lastName in the `PreparedStatement` `pstmt`.

```
pstmt.setString(1, "Jack");
pstmt.setString(2, "A");
pstmt.setString(3, "Ryan");
```

TABLE 13.7 `PreparedStatement` Methods

Method name	*Description*
`clearParameters`	Clears all the parameters in the statement.
`execute`	Executes a prepared statement that may return multiple result sets.
`executeQuery`	Executes a prepared statement that returns a single result set.
`executeUpdate`	Executes a prepared INSERT, UPDATE, DELETE, or SQL DDL statement.
`setAsciiStream`	Sets a parameter to an ASCII stream.
`setBigDecimal`	Sets a parameter to a `java.lang.BigDecimal` value.
`setBinaryStream`	Sets a parameter to a binary stream.
`setBoolean`	Sets a parameter to a Java `boolean` value.
`setByte`	Sets a parameter to a Java `byte` value.
`setBytes`	Sets a parameter to a Java array of `byte` values.
`setDate`	Sets a parameter to a `java.sql.Date` value.
`setDouble`	Sets a parameter to a Java `double` value.
`setFloat`	Sets a parameter to a Java `float` value.
`setInt`	Sets a parameter to a Java `int` value.
`setLong`	Sets a parameter to a Java `long` value.
`setNull`	Sets a parameter to an SQL NULL value.
`setObject`	Sets a parameter to a Java object.
`setShort`	Sets a parameter to a Java `short` value.
`setString`	Sets a parameter to a Java `String` value.
`setTime`	Sets a parameter to a `java.sql.Time` value.
`setTimestamp`	Sets a parameter to a `java.sql.Timestamp` value.
`setUnicodeStream`	Sets a parameter to a Unicode stream.

After setting parameters, you can execute the prepared statement by invoking `execute()`, `executeQuery()`, or `executeUpdate()`, depending on the type of SQL statement. The `execute()`, `executeQuery()`, and `executeUpdate()` methods are similar to the ones defined in the `Statement` interface except that they have no parameters, since the SQL statements are already specified in the `preparedStatement` method when the object of `PreparedStatement` is created.

Example 13.4 Using `PreparedStatement` to Execute Dynamic SQL Statements

In this example, you will use dynamic SQL statements to select addresses and insert new addresses. A new menu, "Using Dynamic SQL Statements," will be added to the applet from the preceding example. This new menu will bring up the same user interface as the menu "Using Static SQL Statements" with identical functions, but the dynamic SQL statements will be used to implement the SELECT and INSERT operations.

The example consists of two new classes: `TestPreparedStatement` and `AddressPanelUsingDynamicSQL`. `TestPreparedStatement` adds a new menu item, "Using Dynamic SQL," to the preceding example, and `AddressPanelUsingDynamicSQL` extends `AddressPanel` and uses the dynamic statements to override the `select()` and `insert()` methods.

Follow the steps below to complete the project.

1. From the DOS prompt, copy TestStatement.java to TestPreparedStatement.java and copy TestStatement.form to TestPreparedStatement.form in c:\radft\jdbcdemo.

2. In the Source Editor for TestPreparedStatement.java, replace TestStatement with TestPreparedStatement.

3. In the Form Editor of `TestPreparedStatement`, add a menu item "Using Dynamic SQL Statements" in the Operation menu, and change the menu item's name to `jmiDynamicSQL`. Implement the menu item handler, as follows:

```
void jmiDynamicSQLActionPerformed(ActionEvent e) {
  addAddressPanel(
    new AddressPanelUsingDynamicSQL(
          dBConnectDialog1.getConnection()));
}
```

4. Create a new class `AddressPanelUsingDynamicSQL` that extends `AddressPanel` and implements the `select()` and `insert()` methods using dynamic SQL statements, as shown in Listing 13.7.

5. Run `TestPreparedStatement` to test the program. The main frame is shown in Figure 13.13. When selecting "Using Dynamic SQL Statements," the same user interface as shown in Figure 13.11 appears in the frame for searching and inserting addresses.

NOTE

Since `TestPreparedStatement` is almost identical to `TestStatement` except that it added a new menu and the menu handler `jmiDynamicSQLActionPerformed`, the source code for `TestPreparedStatement` is not listed in the text. Please refer to the CD-ROM to review the source code.

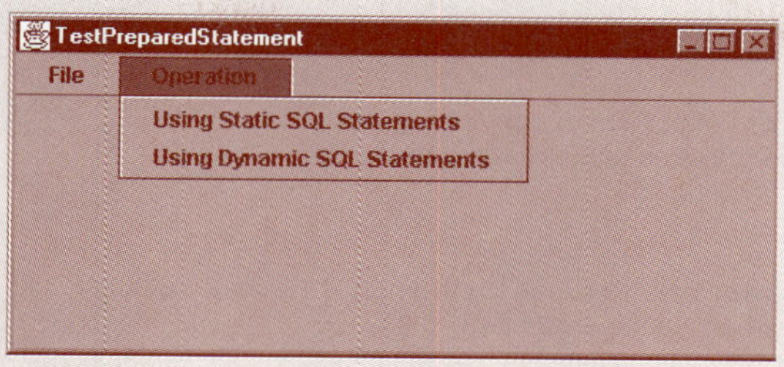

Figure 13.13 *The menu "Using Dynamic SQL Statements" was added to* `TestPreparedStatement`.

```
package package jdbcdemo;

import java.sql.*;

public class AddressPanelUsingDynamicSQL extends AddressPanel {
  PreparedStatement pstmt1;
  PreparedStatement pstmt2;

  public AddressPanelUsingDynamicSQL(Connection connection) {
    super(connection);

    // Create prepared SQL statements
    try {
      pstmt1 = connection.prepareStatement("select * from Address " +
        "where firstName = ? AND lastName = ?");
      pstmt2 = connection.prepareStatement("insert into Address " +
        "values (?, ?, ?, ?, ?, ?, ?, ?, ?)");
    }
    catch (SQLException ex) {
      setStatus(ex.getMessage());
    }

    setStatus("Using dynamic SQL statements");
  }

  /** Override this method from AddressPanel */
  protected void select() {
    try {
      pstmt1.setString(1, getFirstName());
      pstmt1.setString(2, getLastName());
      ResultSet rs = pstmt1.executeQuery();

      if (rs.next()) {
        setMi(rs.getString(2));
        setStreet(rs.getString(4));
        setCity(rs.getString(5));
        setState(rs.getString(6));
        setZip(rs.getString(7));
        setTelephone(rs.getString(8));
        setEmail(rs.getString(9));
        setStatus("Dynamic SQL selection succeeded");
      }
      else {
        setStatus("no record found");
      }
```

Listing 13.7 *AddressPanelUsingDynamicSQL.java*

continued

Example 13.4 continued

```
  }
  catch (SQLException ex) {
   setStatus(ex.getMessage());
  }
 }

 /** Override this method from AddressPanel */
 protected void insert() {
  try {
   pstmt2.setString(1, getFirstName());
   pstmt2.setString(2, getMi());
   pstmt2.setString(3, getLastName());
   pstmt2.setString(4, getStreet());
   pstmt2.setString(5, getCity());
   pstmt2.setString(6, getState());
   pstmt2.setString(7, getZip());
   pstmt2.setString(8, getTelephone());
   pstmt2.setString(9, getZip());

   pstmt2.executeUpdate();

   setStatus("Dynamic SQL Insertion succeeded");
  }
  catch (SQLException ex) {
   setStatus(ex.getMessage());
  }
 }
}
```

Listing 13.7 *continued*

Example Review

`AddressPanelUsingDynamicSQL` extends `AddressPanel` created in Example 13.2. The `select()` and `insert()` methods in `AddressPanel` were overridden to accommodate using the prepared statements `pstmt1` and `pstmt2`, where `pstmt1` can be used to select records from the Address table, and `pstmt2` can be used to insert records into Address table in the database.

The `addAddressPanel` method in `TestPreparedStatement` is the same as in `TestStatement` that enables you to add an instance of `AddressPanel` to the center of the applet's content pane. First, all the components in the applet's content pane were removed, using the `removeAll()` method. Then the menu bar and the `AddressPanel` instance were added to the applet. You may use the `remove()` method to remove a specified component from a container, if you assign a name for an instance of `AddressPanel` rather than use an anonymous instance.

`PreparedStatement` is more efficient than `Statement` in the project for viewing and inserting new records because the SQL statements are precompiled and reused without recompiling. Please refer to Exercise 13.1 for performance evaluations of using static SQL statements and dynamic SQL statements.

CAUTION

The methods `select` and `insert` are `protected` in `TestStatement`. To override them in the subclass `TestPreparedStatement`, the visibility must remain `protected` or increase to `pubic`.

13.7 *CallableStatement*

The `CallableStatement` interface is designed to execute SQL-stored procedures with OUT or IN OUT parameters. An OUT parameter returns a value after the procedure is completed, but it contains no value when the procedure is called. An IN OUT parameter contains a value passed to the procedure when it is called, and returns a new value after it is completed. For example, the following procedure in Oracle PL/SQL has IN parameter p1, OUT parameter p2, and IN OUT parameter p3.

```
create or replace procedure sample
  (p1 in varchar, p2 out number, p3 in out integer) is
begin
  --doing something
  null;
end sample;
/
```

NOTE

The syntax of stored procedures is vendor-specific. Oracle PL/SQL is used for demonstrations of stored procedures in this book. PL/SQL is a procedural language extension of SQL. It is a fully functional programming language whose syntax is very similar to Ada. In Oracle 8i, you can write stored procedures using Java. For more information, see the companion Web site at **www.prenhall.com/liang/radft.html**.

A `CallableStatement` object can be created using the `prepareCall(String call)` method in the `Connection` interface. For example, the following code creates a `CallableStatement cstmt` on `Connection connection` for procedure `sample`.

```
CallableStatement cstmt = connection.prepareCall(
  "{call sample(?, ?, ?)}");
```

`{call sample(?, ?, . . .)}` is referred to as the *SQL escape syntax*, which signals the driver that the code within it should be handled differently. The driver parses the escape syntax and translates it into code that the database understands. For this case, sample is an Oracle PL/SQL procedure. The call is translated to a string `"begin sample(?, ?, ?); end"` and passed to an Oracle database for execution.

You can call procedures as well as functions. The syntax to create an SQL callable statement for a function is:

```
{? = call FunctionName(?, ?, . . .)}
```

`CallableStatement` inherits `PreparedStatement`. Additionally, the `CallableStatement` interface provides methods for registering OUT parameters and for getting values from OUT parameters. These methods are listed in Table 13.8.

TABLE 13.8 `CallableStatement` **Methods**

Method name	*Description*
`getBigDecimal`	Gets an OUT parameter as a `java.math.BigDecimal` object.
`getBoolean`	Gets a `boolean` from an OUT parameter.
`getByte`	Gets a `byte` from an OUT parameter.
`getBytes`	Gets an OUT parameter as an array of `byte` values.
`getDate`	Gets an OUT parameter as a `java.sql.Date` object.
`getDouble`	Gets a `double` from an OUT parameter.
`getFloat`	Gets a `float` from an OUT parameter.
`getInt`	Gets an `int` from an OUT parameter.
`getLong`	Gets a `long` from an OUT parameter.
`getObject`	Gets an OUT parameter as a Java `Object`.
`getShort`	Gets a `short` from an OUT parameter.
`getString`	Gets a `string` from an OUT parameter.
`getTime`	Gets an OUT parameter as `java.sql.Time` object.
`getTimeStamp`	Gets an OUT parameter as `java.sql.TimeStamp` object.
`registerOutParameter`	Registers an OUT parameter's data type.
`wasNull`	Returns null if an OUT parameter is SQL NULL.

Before calling an SQL procedure, you need to use appropriate set methods to pass values to IN and IN OUT parameters, and use `registerOutParameter` to register OUT and IN OUT parameters. For example, before calling procedure sample, the following statements pass values to parameters `p1` (IN) and `p3` (IN OUT) and register parameters `p2` (OUT) and `p3` (IN OUT):

```
cstmt.setString(1, "dummy");
cstmt.setLong(3, 1);
cstmt.registerOutParameter(2, java.sql.Types.DOUBLE);
cstmt.registerOutParameter(3, java.sql.Types.INTEGER);
```

You may use `execute()` or `executeUpdate()` to execute the procedure depending on the type of SQL statement, then use get methods to retrieve values from the OUT parameters. For example, the next statements retrieve the values from parameters `p2` and `p3`.

```
double d = cstmt.getDouble(2);
int i = cstmt.getInt(3);
```

Example 13.5 Using `CallableStatement` to Execute SQL Stored Procedures

In this example, you will use an SQL stored function to check whether an address is already in the database before inserting a new address. The example is a continuation of Example 13.4. You will add a new menu, "Using Callable Statements," to demonstrate the use of stored procedures.

The following Oracle PL/SQL function returns the number of records in the table that match the specified firstName and lastName in the table Address.

```
create or replace function addressFound
  (first varchar2, last varchar2)
  -- Do not name firstName and lastName. 6/4/00 YDL
  return number is
  numberOfSelectedRows number := 0;
begin

  select count(*) into numberOfSelectedRows
  from Address
  where Address.firstName = first and
    Address.lastName = last;

  return numberOfSelectedRows;
end addressFound;
/
```

Suppose table Address and function `addressFound` are already created in the database. The example consists of two new classes: `TestCallableStatement` and `AddressPanelUsingStoredProc`. `TestCallableStatement` adds a new menu item, "Using Callable Statements," to the preceding example; `AddressPanelUsingStoredProc` extends `AddressPanelUsingDynamicSQL` and overrides the `insert()` method to check whether an address for the given first name and last name is already in the database. If so, nothing is done; if not, the superclass's `insert()` method is invoked to insert a new record.

To see the development in action, follow the steps below:

1. Copy TestPreparedStatement.java to TestCallableStatement.java and copy TestPreparedStatement.form to TestCallableStatement.form in c:\radft\jdbedemo.

2. In the Source Editor for TestCallableStatement.java, replace TestPreparedStatement with TestCallableStatement.

3. Add a new menu item, "Using Callable Statements," in the Operation menu. Change the menu name to `jmiStoredProc`. Generate and implement the code for handling the menu command, as follows:

```
void jmiStoredProcActionPerformed(ActionEvent e) {
  addAddressPanel(
    new AddressPanelUsingStoredProc(
      dBConnectDialog1.getConnection()));
}
```

continued

Example 13.5 Using `CallableStatement` to Execute SQL Stored Procedures

4. Create the class `AddressPanelUsingStoredProc`, which extends `AddressPanelUsingDynamicSQL` with additional features that check whether an address already exists before executing the insertion, as shown in Listing 13.8.

5. Run TestCallableStatement.java to test the program. The main frame is shown in Figure 13.14. When "Using Stored Procedures" is selected, the same user interface as shown in Figure 13.11 appears in the frame for searching and inserting addresses.

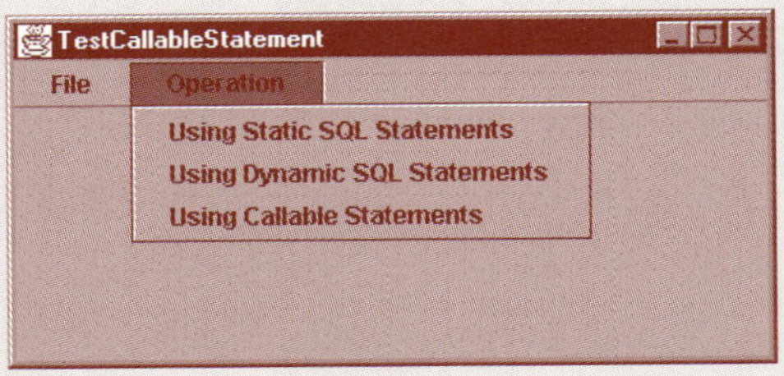

Figure 13.14 *The menu "Using Callable Statements" was added to* `TestCallableStatement`.

```
package jdbcdemo;

import java.sql.*;

public class AddressPanelUsingStoredProc
  extends AddressPanelUsingDynamicSQL {
  CallableStatement cstmt;

  public AddressPanelUsingStoredProc(Connection connection) {
    super(connection);

    try {
      // Create a callable statement
      cstmt = connection.prepareCall
        ("{ ? = call AddressFound(?, ?)}");
    }
    catch (SQLException ex) {
      setStatus(ex.getMessage());
    }

    setStatus("Using stored SQL procedures");
  }

  protected void insert() {
    try {
      if (addressFound() == 1)
        setStatus("Address already exist");
      else
        super.insert();
    }
    catch (SQLException ex) {
      setStatus(ex.getMessage());
    }
  }

```

Listing 13.8 *AddressPanelUsingStoredProc.java*

```
    /**Return true if an address matching the given firstname and
     * lastname is already in the database */
    int addressFound() throws SQLException {
      cstmt.setString(2, getFirstName());
      cstmt.setString(3, getLastName());
      cstmt.registerOutParameter(1, Types.INTEGER);
      cstmt.execute();
      return cstmt.getInt(1);
    }
  }
```

Listing 13.8 *continued*

Example Review

Since the syntax and capabilities of stored procedures vary among vendors, JDBC's escape syntax for invoking procedures is translated into vendor-specific code for invoking procedures. To see whether the database supports stored procedures, call `supportsStoredProcedures()` in the `DatabaseMetaData` interface.

Use `PreparedStatement` or `CallableStatement` to process stored procedures with IN parameters. You must use `CallableStatement` to process stored procedures with OUT parameters. Before executing a stored procedure with the OUT parameter, you must use `registerOutParameter()` to register the OUT parameter with a data type specified in `java.sql.Types`.

CAUTION

Putting a semicolon (;) at the end of the escape syntax for invoking stored procedures is a common mistake. It causes a runtime error in Oracle drivers.

13.8 Scrollable and Updateable Result Set

The result sets used in the preceding examples are read sequentially. A result set maintains a cursor pointing to its current row of data. Initially the cursor is positioned before the first row. The `next` method moves the cursor forward to the next row. This is known as *sequential forward reading*. It is the only way of processing the rows in a result set that is supported by JDBC 1.

With JDBC 2, you can scroll the rows both forward and backward and move the cursor to a desired location using the `first`, `last`, `next`, `previous`, `absolute`, or `relative` method. Additionally, you can insert, delete, or update a row in the result set and have the changes automatically reflected in the database.

To obtain a scrollable or updateable result set, you must first create a statement with an appropriate type and concurrency mode. For a static statement, use

```
Statement statement = connection.createStatement
  (int resultSetType, int resultSetConcurrency);
```

For a prepared statement, use

```
PreparedStatement statement = connection.prepareStatement
  (String sql, int resultSetType, int resultSetConcurrency);
```

For a callable statement, use

```
CallableStatement statement = connection.prepareCall
  (String sql, int resultSetType, int resultSetConcurrency);
```

The possible values of `resultSetType` are the constants defined in the `ResultSet`:

- `TYPE_FORWARD_ONLY`: The result set is accessed forward sequentially.
- `TYPE_SCROLL_INSENSITIVE`: The result set is scrollable, but not sensitive to changes in the database.
- `TYPE_SCROLL_SENSITIVE`: The result set is scrollable and sensitive to changes made by others. Use this type if you want the result set to be scrollable and updateable.

The possible values of `resultSetConcurrency` are the constants defined in the `ResultSet`:

- `CONCUR_READ_ONLY`: The result set cannot be used to update the database.
- `CONCUR_UPDATABLE`: The result set can be used to update the database.

NOTE
In English, "updatable" should be "spelled updateable." But it is spelled `CONCUR_UPDATABLE` in Java.

For example, if you want the result set to be scrollable and updateable, you can create a static statement:

```
Statement statement = connection.createStatement
  (ResultSet.TYPE_SCROLL_INSENSITIVE, ResultSet.CONCUR_UPDATABLE)
```

You use the `executeQuery` method in a `Statement` object to execute an SQL query that returns a result set as follows:

```
ResultSet resultSet = statement.executeQuery(query);
```

The methods `first`, `next`, `previous`, and `last` are used to move the cursor to the first row, next row, previous row, and last row; and the `getXxx(int columnIndex)` or `getXxx(String columnName)` method is used to retrieve the value of a specified field at the current row. The methods `insertRow`, `deleteRow`, and `updateRow` can also be used to insert, delete, and update the current row. Before applying `insertRow` or `updateRow`, you need to use the method `update(int columnIndex, Xxx value)` or `update(String columnName, Xxx value)` to write a new value to the field at the current row.

The methods for manipulating a result set are shown in Table 13.9.

TABLE 13.9 `ResultSet` Methods

Method name	*Description*
`boolean absolute(int row)`	Moves the cursor to the specified row.
`boolean afterLast()`	Moves the cursor to the end of the result set, just after the last row
`void beforeFirst()`	Moves the cursor to the front of the result set, just before the first row.
`void cancelRowUpdates()`	Cancels the updates made to a row.
`void clearWarnings()`	After this call, `getWarnings` returns null until a new warning is reported for this result set.
`void close()`	Closes result set and releases its resource.
`void deleteRow()`	Deletes the row from the result set in the underlying database.
`int findColumn(String columnName)`	Finds the column index for the column name.
`boolean first()`	Moves the cursor to the first row.
`getXxx(String columnName)`	Various get methods to get the cell value for the column specified by column name at the current row.
`getXxx(int columnIndex)`	Various get methods to get the cell value for the column specified by column index at the current row.
`ResultSetMetaData getMetaData()`	Gets `ResultSetMetaData` for the result set.
`SQLWarning getWarnings()`	Gets SQL warning from the result set.
`void insertRow()`	Inserts the contents of the row to the result set and its underlying database.
`boolean isAfterLast()`	Returns true if the cursor is after the last row.
`boolean isBeforeFirst()`	Returns true if the cursor is before the first row.
`boolean isFirst()`	Returns true if the cursor is at the first row.
`boolean isLast()`	Returns true if the cursor is at the last row.
`boolean last()`	Moves the cursor to the last row.
`void moveToCurrentRow()`	Moves the cursor to the current cursor position after inserting or deleting a row.
`void moveToInsertRow()`	Moves the cursor to the inserted row.
`boolean next()`	Moves the cursor to the next row.
`boolean previous()`	Moves the cursor to the previous row.
`void refreshRow()`	Refreshes the current row with its most recent value in the database.

TABLE 13.9 continued

Method name	*Description*
`boolean relative(int rows)`	Moves the cursor a relative number of the rows.
`boolean rowDeleted()`	Indicates whether a row has been deleted.
`boolean rowInserted()`	Indicates whether a row has been inserted.
`boolean rowUpdated()`	Indicates whether a row has been updated.
`boolean updateRow()`	Updates the underlying database with the new contents of the current row.
`void updateXxx(String columnName, Xxx value)`	Updates the value for the column with the specified column name at the current row.
`void updateXxx(int columnIndex, Xxx value)`	Updates the value for the column with the specified index at the current row.
`boolean wasNull()`	Indicates whether the last column read had a value of SQL NULL.

Example 13.6 Scrolling and Updating Tables

In this example, you will develop a useful utility that displays all the rows of a database table in a `JTable` and uses a scrollable and updateable result set to navigate the table and modify its contents.

As shown in Figure 13.15, you enter or select a JDBC Driver and Database, enter a username and a password, and specify a table name to connect the database and display the table contents in the `JTable`. You can then use the buttons First, Next, Prior, and Last to move the cursor to the first row, next row, previous row, and last row in the table, and use the buttons Insert, Delete, and Update to modify the table contents. When clicking the Insert button, a dialog box is displayed to receive input, as shown in Figure 13.16.

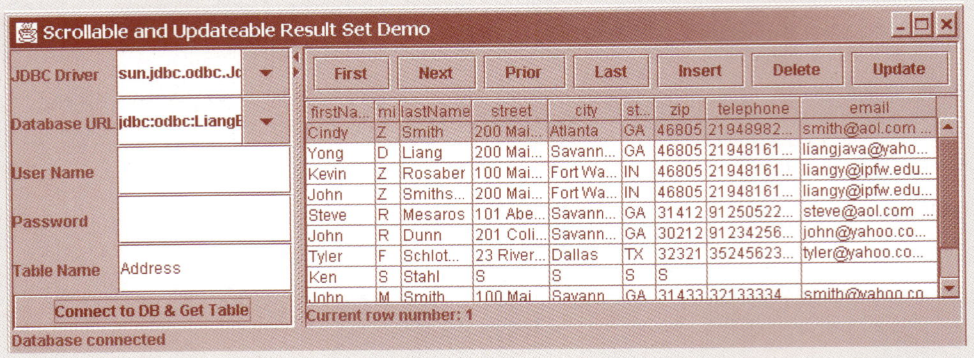

Figure 13.15 *The program enables you to navigate and modify the table.*

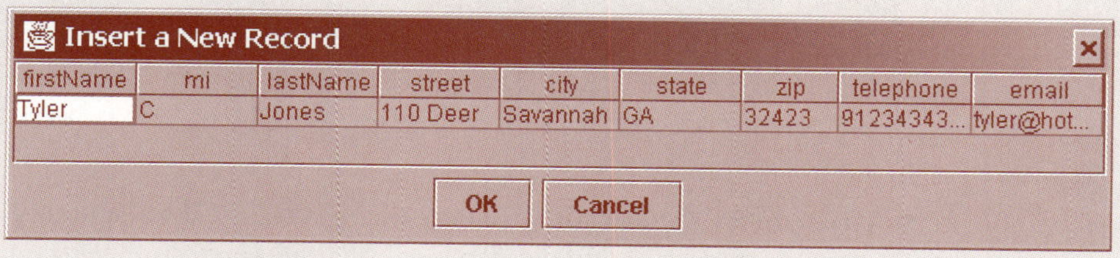

Figure 13.16 *The Insert a New Record dialog box lets the user enter a new record.*

The status bar at the bottom of the window shows the current row in the result set and the `JTable`. The cursor in the result set and the row in the `JTable` are synchronized. You can move the cursor by using the navigation buttons or by selecting a row in the `JTable`.

The example consists of three classes: `TestTableEditor` (see Listing 13.9), `TableEditor` (see Listing 13.10), and `NewRecordDialog` (see Listing 13.11). `TestTableEditor` is the main class that enables the user to enter the database connection information and a table name. Once the database is connected, the table contents are displayed in an instance of `TableEditor`. The `TableEditor` class is a JavaBeans component that can be used to browse a table and modify a table. An instance of `NewRecordDialog` is displayed to let you enter a new record when you click the Insert button in `TableEditor`.

Follow the steps below to create this project.

1. In the jdbcdemo package, create a new frame named `TestTableEditor` using the Forte Swing JFrame form wizard, create a new JavaBeans component named `TableEditor` that extends `JPanel` using the Forte Swing JPanel wizard, and create a new dialog component named `NewRecordDialog` using the Forte Swing JDialog form wizard.

2. Build `TestTableEditor` as follows:

   2.1. Drop a `JLabel` to the south of the applet and rename it `jlblStatus`, and drop a `JSplitPane` to the center of the applet to create `jSplitPane1`.

   2.2. Drop a `JPanel` to the left of `jSplitPane1` to create `jPanel1`, and set the `layout` of `jPanel1` to `BorderLayout`. Drop a `JButton` to the south of `jPanel1` to create `jbtConnect` with the text "Connect to DB & Get Table." Drop a `JPanel` to the west of `jPanel1` to create `jPanel2`, and drop a `JPanel` to the center of `jPanel1` to create `jPanel3`. Set the layout of `jPanel2` and `jPanel3` to `GridLayout` with five rows. Panel `jPanel2` holds the labels for "JDBC Driver," "Database URL," "Username," "Password," and "Table Name." Panel `jPanel3` holds combo boxes and text fields for storing and entering information. These panels can be created in the same way as in Example 13.3.

continued

Example 13.6 continued

2.3. Build TableEditor in Step 3. Compile TableEditor.java, install it in the component palette, and drop it to the right of `jSplitPane1` to create `tableEditor1`.

2.4. Generate the handler for "Connect to DB & Get Table," and implement it to connect to the database. Set the connection and table name to `tableEditor1`, as shown in Listing 13.9 (Lines 87–90).

3. Build `TableEditor` as follows:

3.1. Drop a `JPanel` to the north of the form, a `JLabel` to the south of the form, and a `JScrollPane` to the center of the form to create `jPanel1`, `jScrollPane1`, and `jlblStatus`.

3.2. Drop a `JButton` seven times into `jPanel1` to create buttons with the texts First, Next, Prior, Last, Insert, Delete, and Update. Rename the buttons `jbtFirst`, `jbtNext`, `jbtPrior`, `jbtLast`, `jbtInsert`, `jbtDelete`, and `jbtUpdate`.

3.3. Drop a `JTable` into the `jScrollPane1` to create `jTable1`. In the `model` property editor of `jTable1`, press Default to remove the sample data model. Create a table model named `tableModel`, and set it to the `model` property of `jTable1`. Create a list selection model named `listSelectionModel` (Lines 28–30), and set it to the `selectionModel` of `jTable1`, as shown in Listing 13.10 (Line 46).

3.4. Write the code to implement the buttons. Declare variables for JDBC `Connection`, `Statement`, and `ResultSet`. Declare the variable `rowVectors` to store the row data of `JTable`. Declare the variable `columnHeaderVector` to store the column names in `JTable`. Declare the variable `columnCount` to store the number of columns in `JTable`.

3.5. Create the method `setConnectionAndTable` to set a database connection and a table name for the component. Create the method `showTable()` to initialize the Swing table.

3.6. Generate the handler for the navigation buttons First, Next, Prior, and Last, implement these buttons to move the cursor in the result set, and set the corresponding row in `jTable1`.

3.7. Create a listener for the `valueChanged` event for processing a list selection change event in `listSelectModel`. Implement the handler to set the cursor of the result set to the row selected in the table.

3.8. Generate the handler for the buttons Insert, Delete, and Update, and implement these buttons to modify the database. To insert a record to the database, you use a dialog box to obtain the new record.

4. Build `NewRecordDialog` as follows:

   4.1. Set the `title` property to "Insert a New Record," and the `modal` property to `true`. Drop a `JPanel` to the south of `panel1` to create `jPanel1`. Drop a `JButton` twice to the panel to create `jbtOK` and `jbtCancel` with `text` properties OK and Cancel. Drop a `JScrollPane` to the center of `panel1`, and drop a `JTable` to the scroll pane to create `jTable1`. In the property editor of the `model` in `jTable1`, click the Default button to remove the sample table model.

   4.2. Add a new property named `newRecord` of the `Vector` type with a getter method, as shown in Listing 13.11 (Line 9).

   4.3. Declare the variable `tableModel` as the model for `jTable1`. Set the `model` property of `jTable1` to `tableModel` (Line 16).

   4.4. Generate and implement the handlers for the OK and Cancel buttons.

```
package jdbcdemo;

import java.sql.*;
import java.util.*;

public class TestTableEditor extends javax.swing.JFrame {
  /** Creates new form TestTableEditor */
  public TestTableEditor() {
    initComponents();

    // Add items to the combo boxes
    jcboURL.addItem("jdbc:odbc:LiangBookDB_MDB");
    jcboURL.addItem(
      "jdbc:oracle:thin:@liang.armstrong.edu:1521:test");
    jcboURL.addItem
      ("jdbc:borland:dslocal:C:\\radft\\LiangBookDB.jds");
    jcboURL.addItem
      ("jdbc:interbase://localhost/C:/radft/LiangBookDB.gdb");
    jcboDriver.addItem("sun.jdbc.odbc.JdbcOdbcDriver");
    jcboDriver.addItem("oracle.jdbc.driver.OracleDriver");
    jcboDriver.addItem(
      "com.borland.datastore.jdbc.DataStoreDriver");
    jcboDriver.addItem("interbase.interclient.Driver");
  }

  private void initComponents() {
    jlblStatus = new javax.swing.JLabel();
    jSplitPane1 = new javax.swing.JSplitPane();
    jPanel1 = new javax.swing.JPanel();
    jbtConnect = new javax.swing.JButton();
    jPanel2 = new javax.swing.JPanel();
    jLabel1 = new javax.swing.JLabel();
    jLabel2 = new javax.swing.JLabel();
    jLabel3 = new javax.swing.JLabel();
    jLabel4 = new javax.swing.JLabel();
    jLabel5 = new javax.swing.JLabel();
```

Listing 13.9 *TestTableEditor.java*

continued

Example 13.6 continued

```
      jPanel3 = new javax.swing.JPanel();
      jcboDriver = new javax.swing.JComboBox();
      jcboURL = new javax.swing.JComboBox();
      jtfUserName = new javax.swing.JTextField();
      jpfPassword = new javax.swing.JPasswordField();
      jtfTableName = new javax.swing.JTextField();
      tableEditor1 = new jdbcdemo.TableEditor();
      addWindowListener(new java.awt.event.WindowAdapter() {
        public void windowClosing(java.awt.event.WindowEvent evt) {
          exitForm(evt);
        }
      });
      getContentPane().add(jlblStatus, java.awt.BorderLayout.SOUTH);
      jPanel1.setLayout(new java.awt.BorderLayout());
      jbtConnect.setText("Connect to DB & Get Table");
      jbtConnect.addActionListener(
        new java.awt.event.ActionListener() {
        public void actionPerformed(java.awt.event.ActionEvent evt) {
          jbtConnectActionPerformed(evt);
        }
      });
      jPanel1.add(jbtConnect, java.awt.BorderLayout.SOUTH);
      jPanel2.setLayout(new java.awt.GridLayout(5, 0));
      jLabel1.setText("JDBC Driver");
      jPanel2.add(jLabel1);
      jLabel2.setText("Database URL");
      jPanel2.add(jLabel2);
      jLabel3.setText("Username");
      jPanel2.add(jLabel3);
      jLabel4.setText("Password");
      jPanel2.add(jLabel4);
      jLabel5.setText("Table Name");
      jPanel2.add(jLabel5);
      jPanel1.add(jPanel2, java.awt.BorderLayout.WEST);
      jPanel3.setLayout(new java.awt.GridLayout(5, 0));
      jPanel3.add(jcboDriver);
      jPanel3.add(jcboURL);
      jPanel3.add(jtfUserName);
      jPanel3.add(jpfPassword);
      jPanel3.add(jtfTableName);
      jPanel1.add(jPanel3, java.awt.BorderLayout.CENTER);
      jSplitPane1.setLeftComponent(jPanel1);
      jSplitPane1.setRightComponent(tableEditor1);
      getContentPane().add(jSplitPane1, java.awt.BorderLayout.CENTER);
      pack();
    }

    private void jbtConnectActionPerformed(
      java.awt.event.ActionEvent evt) {
      try {
        // Connect to the database
        Connection connection = getConnection();
        tableEditor1.setConnectionAndTable(connection,
          jtfTableName.getText().trim());
      }
      catch (Exception ex) {
        jlblStatus.setText(ex.toString());
      }
    }

```

Listing 13.9 *continued*

```
    /** Exit the Application */
    private void exitForm(java.awt.event.WindowEvent evt) {
      System.exit(0);
    }

    /**
     * @param args the command line arguments
     */
    public static void main(String args[]) {
      new TestTableEditor().show();
    }

    /** Connect to a database */
    private Connection getConnection() throws Exception {
      // Load the JDBC driver
      System.out.println((String)jcboDriver.getSelectedItem());
      Class.forName(((String)jcboDriver.getSelectedItem()).trim());
      System.out.println("Driver loaded");

      // Establish a connection
      Connection connection = DriverManager.getConnection
        (((String)jcboURL.getSelectedItem()).trim(),
      jtfUserName.getText().trim(), jpfPassword.getText().trim());
      System.out.println("Database connected");
      jlblStatus.setText("Database connected");

      return connection;
    }

    // Variables declaration - do not modify
    private javax.swing.JLabel jlblStatus;
    private javax.swing.JSplitPane jSplitPane1;
    private javax.swing.JPanel jPanel1;
    private javax.swing.JButton jbtConnect;
    private javax.swing.JPanel jPanel2;
    private javax.swing.JLabel jLabel1;
    private javax.swing.JLabel jLabel2;
    private javax.swing.JLabel jLabel3;
    private javax.swing.JLabel jLabel4;
    private javax.swing.JLabel jLabel5;
    private javax.swing.JPanel jPanel3;
    private javax.swing.JComboBox jcboDriver;
    private javax.swing.JComboBox jcboURL;
    private javax.swing.JTextField jtfUserName;
    private javax.swing.JPasswordField jpfPassword;
    private javax.swing.JTextField jtfTableName;
    private jdbcdemo.TableEditor tableEditor1;
    // End of variables declaration
}
```

Listing 13.9 *continued*

```
package jdbcdemo;

import java.util.*;
import java.sql.*;
import javax.swing.table.*;
import javax.swing.event.*;
import javax.swing.*;

```

Listing 13.10 *TableEditor.java*

continued

Example 13.6 continued

```
public class TableEditor extends javax.swing.JPanel {
  // Dialog box for inserting a new record
  NewRecordDialog newRecordDialog1 = new NewRecordDialog();

  // JDBC Connection
  Connection connection;

  // Table name
  String tableName;

  // JDBC Statement
  Statement statement;

  // Result set for the table
  ResultSet resultSet;

  // Table model
  DefaultTableModel tableModel = new DefaultTableModel();

  // Table selection model
  DefaultListSelectionModel listSelectionModel =
    new DefaultListSelectionModel();

  // New row vector
  Vector rowVectors = new Vector();

  // columnHeaderVector to hold column names
  Vector columnHeaderVector = new Vector();

  // Column count
  int columnCount;

  /** Creates new form TableEditor */
  public TableEditor() {
    initComponents();

    jTable1.setModel(tableModel);
    jTable1.setSelectionModel(listSelectionModel);

    listSelectionModel.addListSelectionListener(
    new javax.swing.event.ListSelectionListener() {
      public void valueChanged(ListSelectionEvent e) {
        listSelectionModel_valueChanged(e);
      }
    });
  }

  private void initComponents() {
    jPanel1 = new javax.swing.JPanel();
    jbtFirst = new javax.swing.JButton();
    jbtNext = new javax.swing.JButton();
    jbtPrior = new javax.swing.JButton();
    jbtLast = new javax.swing.JButton();
    jbtInsert = new javax.swing.JButton();
    jbtDelete = new javax.swing.JButton();
    jbtUpdate = new javax.swing.JButton();
    jlblStatus = new javax.swing.JLabel();
    jScrollPane1 = new javax.swing.JScrollPane();
```

Listing 13.10 *continued*

```
      jTable1 = new javax.swing.JTable();
      setLayout(new java.awt.BorderLayout());
      jbtFirst.setText("First");
      jbtFirst.addActionListener(new java.awt.event.ActionListener() {
        public void actionPerformed(java.awt.event.ActionEvent evt) {
          jbtFirstActionPerformed(evt);
        }
      });
      jPanel1.add(jbtFirst);
      jbtNext.setText("Next");
      jbtNext.addActionListener(new java.awt.event.ActionListener() {
        public void actionPerformed(java.awt.event.ActionEvent evt) {
          jbtNextActionPerformed(evt);
        }
      });
      jPanel1.add(jbtNext);
      jbtPrior.setText("Prior");
      jbtPrior.addActionListener(new java.awt.event.ActionListener() {
        public void actionPerformed(java.awt.event.ActionEvent evt) {
          jbtPriorActionPerformed(evt);
        }
      });
      jPanel1.add(jbtPrior);
      jbtLast.setText("Last");
      jbtLast.addActionListener(new java.awt.event.ActionListener() {
        public void actionPerformed(java.awt.event.ActionEvent evt) {
          jbtLastActionPerformed(evt);
        }
      });
      jPanel1.add(jbtLast);
      jbtInsert.setText("Insert");
      jbtInsert.addActionListener(new java.awt.event.ActionListener() {
        public void actionPerformed(java.awt.event.ActionEvent evt) {
          jbtInsertActionPerformed(evt);
        }
      });
      jPanel1.add(jbtInsert);
      jbtDelete.setText("Delete");
      jbtDelete.addActionListener(new java.awt.event.ActionListener() {
        public void actionPerformed(java.awt.event.ActionEvent evt) {
          jbtDeleteActionPerformed(evt);
        }
      });
      jPanel1.add(jbtDelete);
      jbtUpdate.setText("Update");
      jbtUpdate.addActionListener(new java.awt.event.ActionListener() {
        public void actionPerformed(java.awt.event.ActionEvent evt) {
          jbtUpdateActionPerformed(evt);
        }
      });
      jPanel1.add(jbtUpdate);
      add(jPanel1, java.awt.BorderLayout.NORTH);
      add(jlblStatus, java.awt.BorderLayout.SOUTH);
      jScrollPane1.setViewportView(jTable1);
      add(jScrollPane1, java.awt.BorderLayout.CENTER);
    }

    private void jbtDeleteActionPerformed(
      java.awt.event.ActionEvent evt) {
```

Listing 13.10 *continued*

continued

Example 13.6 continued

```
      try {
        // Delete the record from the database
        resultSet.deleteRow();
        refreshResultSet();

        // Remove the row in the table
        tableModel.removeRow(
        listSelectionModel.getLeadSelectionIndex());
      }
      catch (Exception ex) {
        jlblStatus.setText(ex.toString());
      }
    }

    private void jbtInsertActionPerformed(
      java.awt.event.ActionEvent evt) {
      // Display the dialog box
      newRecordDialog1.displayTable(columnHeaderVector);
      Vector newRecord = newRecordDialog1.getNewRecord();

      if (newRecord == null) return;

      // Insert the record to the Swing table
      tableModel.addRow(newRecord);

      // Insert the record to the database table
      try {
        for (int i=1; i<=columnCount; i++) {
          resultSet.updateObject(i, newRecord.elementAt(i-1));
        }

        resultSet.insertRow();
        refreshResultSet();
      }
      catch (Exception ex) {
        jlblStatus.setText(ex.toString());
      }
    }

    private void jbtNextActionPerformed(
      java.awt.event.ActionEvent evt) {
      moveCursor("next");
    }

    private void jbtPriorActionPerformed(
      java.awt.event.ActionEvent evt) {
      moveCursor("previous");
    }

    private void jbtLastActionPerformed(
      java.awt.event.ActionEvent evt) {
      moveCursor("last");
    }

    private void jbtFirstActionPerformed(
      java.awt.event.ActionEvent evt) {
      moveCursor("first");
    }

```

Listing 13.10 *continued*

```
    /** Set cursor in the table and set the row number in the status */
    private void setTableCursor() throws Exception {
      int row = resultSet.getRow();
      listSelectionModel.setSelectionInterval(row-1, row-1);
      jlblStatus.setText("Current row number: " + row);
    }

    private void jbtUpdateActionPerformed(
      java.awt.event.ActionEvent evt) {
      try {
        // Get the current row
        int row = jTable1.getSelectedRow();

        // Gather data from the UI and update the database fields
        for (int i = 1;
          i <= resultSet.getMetaData().getColumnCount(); i++) {
          resultSet.updateObject(i, tableModel.getValueAt(row, i - 1));
        }

        // Invoke the update method in the result set
        resultSet.updateRow();
        refreshResultSet();
      }
      catch (Exception ex) {
        jlblStatus.setText(ex.toString());
      }
    }

    /** Move cursor to the next record */
    private void moveCursor(String whereToMove) {
      try {
        if (whereToMove.equals("first"))
          resultSet.first();
        else if (whereToMove.equals("next"))
          resultSet.next();
        else if (whereToMove.equals("previous"))
          resultSet.previous();
        else if (whereToMove.equals("last"))
          resultSet.last();
        setTableCursor();
      }
      catch (Exception ex) {
        jlblStatus.setText(ex.toString());
      }
    }

    /** Refresh the result set */
    private void refreshResultSet() {
      try {
        resultSet = statement.executeQuery(
          "SELECT * FROM " + tableName);
        // Set the cursor to the first record in the table
        moveCursor("first");
      }
      catch (SQLException ex) {
        ex.printStackTrace();
      }
    }

```

Listing 13.10 *continued*

continued

Example 13.6 continued

```
  /** Set database connection and table name in the TableEditor */
  public void setConnectionAndTable(Connection newConnection,
  String newTableName) {
    connection = newConnection;
    tableName = newTableName;
    try {
      statement = connection.createStatement(ResultSet.
        TYPE_SCROLL_SENSITIVE, ResultSet.CONCUR_UPDATABLE);
      showTable();
      moveCursor("first");
    }
    catch (SQLException ex) {
      ex.printStackTrace();
    }
  }

  /** Display database table to a Swing table */
  private void showTable() throws SQLException {
    // Clear vectors to store data for a new table
    rowVectors.clear();
    columnHeaderVector.clear();

    // Obtain table contents
    resultSet = statement.executeQuery(
      "select * from " + tableName + ";");

    // Get column count
    columnCount = resultSet.getMetaData().getColumnCount();

    // Store rows to rowVectors
    while (resultSet.next()) {
      Vector singleRow = new Vector();
      for (int i = 0; i < columnCount; i++)
        // Store cells to a row
        singleRow.addElement(resultSet.getObject(i+1));
      rowVectors.addElement(singleRow);
    }

    // Get column name and add to columnHeaderVector
    ResultSet rsColumns = connection.getMetaData().getColumns(
      null, null, tableName, null);
    while (rsColumns.next()) {
      columnHeaderVector.addElement(
        rsColumns.getString("COLUMN_NAME"));
    }

    // Set new data to the table model
    tableModel.setDataVector(rowVectors, columnHeaderVector);
  }

  /** Handle the selection in the table */
  void listSelectionModel_valueChanged(ListSelectionEvent e) {
    int selectedRow = jTable1.getSelectedRow();

    try {
      resultSet.absolute(selectedRow+1);
      setTableCursor();
    }
```

Listing 13.10 *continued*

```
      catch (Exception ex) {
        jlblStatus.setText(ex.toString());
      }
    }

    // Variables declaration - do not modify
    private javax.swing.JPanel jPanel1;
    private javax.swing.JButton jbtFirst;
    private javax.swing.JButton jbtNext;
    private javax.swing.JButton jbtPrior;
    private javax.swing.JButton jbtLast;
    private javax.swing.JButton jbtInsert;
    private javax.swing.JButton jbtDelete;
    private javax.swing.JButton jbtUpdate;
    private javax.swing.JLabel jlblStatus;
    private javax.swing.JScrollPane jScrollPane1;
    private javax.swing.JTable jTable1;
    // End of variables declaration
}
```

Listing 13.10 *continued*

```
package jdbcdemo;

import java.util.*;
import java.awt.*;
import javax.swing.table.*;

public class NewRecordDialog extends javax.swing.JDialog {
  private Vector newRecord;

  // Table model
  DefaultTableModel tableModel = new DefaultTableModel();

  public NewRecordDialog(java.awt.Frame parent, boolean modal) {
    super(parent, modal);
    initComponents();
    jTable1.setModel(tableModel);
  }

  public NewRecordDialog() {
    this(null, true);
  }

  private void initComponents() {
    jPanel1 = new javax.swing.JPanel();
    jbtOK = new javax.swing.JButton();
    jbtCancel = new javax.swing.JButton();
    jScrollPane1 = new javax.swing.JScrollPane();
    jTable1 = new javax.swing.JTable();
    setTitle("Insert a New Record");
    setModal(true);
    addWindowListener(new java.awt.event.WindowAdapter() {
      public void windowClosing(java.awt.event.WindowEvent evt) {
        closeDialog(evt);
      }
    });
    jbtOK.setText("OK");
```

Listing 13.11 *NewRecordDialog.java*

continued

Example 13.6 continued

```
      jbtOK.addActionListener(new java.awt.event.ActionListener() {
        public void actionPerformed(java.awt.event.ActionEvent evt) {
          jbtOKActionPerformed(evt);
        }
      });
      jPanel1.add(jbtOK);
      jbtCancel.setText("Cancel");
      jbtCancel.addActionListener(new java.awt.event.ActionListener() {
        public void actionPerformed(java.awt.event.ActionEvent evt) {
          jbtCancelActionPerformed(evt);
        }
      });
      jPanel1.add(jbtCancel);
      getContentPane().add(jPanel1, java.awt.BorderLayout.SOUTH);
      jScrollPane1.setViewportView(jTable1);
      getContentPane().add(jScrollPane1, java.awt.BorderLayout.CENTER);
      pack();
    }

    private void jbtCancelActionPerformed(
      java.awt.event.ActionEvent evt) {
      newRecord = null;
      setVisible(false);
    }

    public java.util.Vector getNewRecord() {
      return newRecord;
    }
    /** Display the table */
    void displayTable(Vector columnHeaderVector) {
      this.setSize(new Dimension(400, 100));

      tableModel.setDataVector(new Vector(), columnHeaderVector);

      // Must create a new vector for a new record
      newRecord = new Vector();
      tableModel.addRow(newRecord);
      setVisible(true);
    }

    private void jbtOKActionPerformed(java.awt.event.ActionEvent evt) {
      setVisible(false);
    }

    public java.util.Vector getNewRecord() {
      return newRecord;
    }

    /** Closes the dialog */
      private void closeDialog(java.awt.event.WindowEvent evt) {
        setVisible(false);
        dispose();
      }

    /**
     * @param args the command line arguments
     */
```

Listing 13.11 *continued*

```
    public static void main(String args[]) {
      new NewRecordDialog(new javax.swing.JFrame(), true).show();
    }

    // Variables declaration - do not modify
    private javax.swing.JPanel jPanel1;
    private javax.swing.JButton jbtOK;
    private javax.swing.JButton jbtCancel;
    private javax.swing.JScrollPane jScrollPane1;
    private javax.swing.JTable jTable1;
    // End of variables declaration
  }
```

Listing 13.11 *continued*

Example Review

The key class in this example is `TableEditor`, which can be used to navigate and modify the table contents. To use it, simply create an instance of `TableEditor`, set the database connection and the table name in the instance, and place it in a graphical user interface. The `setConnectionAndTableName` method involves creating a statement, obtaining a result set, and displaying the result set in the Swing table. The statement is created with the arguments `TYPE_SCROLL_SENSITIVE` and `CONCUR_UPDATABLE` for obtaining scrollable and updateable result sets.

The `showTable()` method is responsible for transferring data from the database table to the Swing table. The column names and column count are obtained using the `ResultSetMetaData` interface. An instance of the `ResultSetMetaData` interface is obtained using the `getMetaData` method for the result set. Each record from the result set is copied to a row vector. The row vector is added to another vector that stores all the rows for the table model (`tableModel`) for the `JTable`.

The handling of the navigation buttons First, Next, Prior, and Last is simply to invoke the methods `first`, `next`, `previous`, and `last` to move the cursor in the result set and, at the same time, set the selected row in the Swing table.

The handling of the Insert button involves displaying the "Insert a New Record" dialog box (`newRecordDialog1`) for receiving the new record. Once the record is entered, clicking the OK button dismisses the dialog box. The new record is obtained by invoking the `newRecordDialog1.getNewRecord()` method. To insert the new record into the database, use the `updateXxx` method to update the fields and then use the `insertRow` method to insert the record to the database table. To insert the new record to the Swing table, use the `addRow` method to add the vector to the table model (`tableModel`). Finally, you need to refresh the result set by re-executing the query. Theoretically, you should not have to refresh the result set. The driver should automatically reflect the changes in the database to the result set. However, none of the drivers I have tested supports this.

continued

Example 13.6 continued

To implement the Delete button, invoke the `deleteRow` method in the result set to remove the record from the database, and use the `removeElementAt` method in the `Vector` class to remove the record from `rowVectors`.

To implement the Update button, invoke the `updateXxx` method in the result set, and then invoke the `updateRow` method to update the result set.

To implement the handler for list selection events on `jTable1`, set the cursor in the result set to match the row selected in `jTable1`.

NOTE

To ensure the effect of editing a field in the table, you need to press the Enter key or move the cursor to other fields.

NOTE

I have tested the program using several drivers. The only driver that completely supports this program is the JDBC-ODBC driver in JDK 1.4. The Oracle driver bundled with Oracle Enterprise Server 8i supports the read-only scrollable result set but not the updateable scrollable result set. Thus you cannot modify the result set. You can use `supportsResultSetType(int type)` and `supportsResultSetConcurrency(int type, int concurrency)` in the `DatabaseMetaData` interface to find out which result type and currency modes are supported by the JDBC driver. But even if a driver supports the scrollable and updateable result set, a result set for a complex query might not be able to perform an update. For example, the result set for a query that involves several tables is likely not to support update operations.

13.9 Storing and Retrieving Images in JDBC

The question of how to store and retrieve images from a database is frequently asked. Images are stored in binary in a table cell. The data type for the cell is BLOB (Binary Large OBject), which is a new SQL type in SQL3 for storing binary data. Another new SQL3 type is CLOB (Character Large OBject) for storing a large text in the character format. JDBC 2 introduced the interfaces `java.sql.Blob` and `java.sql.Clob` to support mapping for these new SQL types. JBDC 2 also added new methods, such as `getBlob`, `setBinaryStream`, `getClob`, `setBlob`, and `setClob`, in the interfaces `ResultSet`, `PreparedStatement`, and `CallableStatement` to access SQL BLOB, and CLOB values.

To store an image into a cell in a table, the corresponding column for the cell must be of the BLOB type. For example, the following SQL statement creates a table whose type for the flag column is BLOB.

```
create table Country(name varchar(30), flag blob,
  description varchar(500));
```

In the preceding statement, the `description` column is limited to 500 characters. The upper limit for the VARCHAR type is 32,672 bytes. For a large character field, you can use the CLOB type, which can store up to two GB characters.

To insert a record with images to a table, define a prepared statement like this one:

```
PreparedStatement pstmt = connection.prepareStatement(
  "insert into Country values(?, ?, ?)");
```

Images are usually stored in files. You may first get an instance of `InputStream` for an image file and then use the `setBinaryStream` method to associate the input stream with a cell in the table, as follows:

```
// Store image to the table cell
File file = new File(imageFilenames[i]);
InputStream inputImage = new FileInputStream(file);
pstmt.setBinaryStream(2, inputImage, (int)(file.length()));
```

To retrieve an image from a table, use the `getBlob` method, as shown below:

```
// Store image to the table cell
Blob blob = rs.getBlob(1);
ImageIcon imageIcon = new ImageIcon(
  blob.getBytes(1, (int)blob.length()));
```

Example 13.7 Storing and Retrieving Images in JDBC

In this example, you will create a table, populate it with data, including images, and retrieve and display images. The table is named Country. Each record in the table consists of three fields: name, flag, and description. Flag is an image field. The program first creates the table and stores data to it. Then the program retrieves the country names from the table and adds them to a combo box. When the user selects a name from the combo box, the country's flag and description are displayed, as shown in Figure 13.17.

Figure 13.17 *The program enables you to retrieve data, including images, from a table and displays them.*

continued

Example 13.7 continued

The example consists of two classes: `DescriptionPanel` (see Listing 13.12) and `StoreAndRetrieveImage` (see Listing 13.13). `DescriptionPanel` is a component for displaying a country (name, flag, and description). `StoreAndRetrieveImage` is the main class that initializes the table and creates the user interface using a `DescriptionPanel` and a combo box.

Follow the steps below to create this project.

1. In the jdbcdemo package, create a new frame named `StoreAndRetrieveImage` using the Forte Swing JFrame form wizard and create a new JavaBeans component named `DescriptionPanel` that extends `JPanel` using the Forte Swing JPanel form wizard.
2. Build `DescriptionPanel` as follows:
   - 2.1. Drop a `JSplitPane` from the Swing (Other) tab to the center of the panel to create `jSplitPane1`, and drop a `JPanel` to the left of the split pane to create `jPanel1` and a `JScrollPane` to the right of the split pane.
   - 2.2. Set the layout of `jPanel1` to `BorderLayout`. Drop a `JLabel` to the south of `jPanel1` to create `jLabel1`, and drop an `ImageViewer` (created in Example 4.1) to the center of `jPanel1` to create `imageViewer1`. Drop a `JTextArea` to the scroll pane to create `jTextArea1`.
   - 2.3. Create the properties `name`, `imageIcon`, and `description` using the Bean Pattern wizard. The set methods in these properties display the properties in `imageViewer1`, `jLabel1`, and `jTextArea1`, as shown in Listing 13.12 (Lines 32, 41, 50).
3. Build `StoreAndRetrieveImage` as follows:
   - 3.1. Drop a `JComboBox` to the north of the form to create `jComboBox1`, and drop a `DescriptionPanel` to the center of the applet to create `descriptionPanel1`.
   - 3.2. In the event tab of the component inspector for `jComboBox1`, press Enter in the value field of `itemStateChanged` to generate a handler for the `ItemEvent`. Implement the handler to retrieve data from the database and display them in `descriptionPanel1`, as shown in Listing 13.13 (Lines 51–54).
   - 3.3. Implement the code for connecting the database, for creating the table, for populating data, including images, into the table, for retrieving data, and for displaying data, as shown in Listing 13.13 (Lines 21–29).

```
package jdbcdemo;

public class DescriptionPanel extends javax.swing.JPanel {
  private String name;
  private String description;
  private javax.swing.ImageIcon imageIcon;

  /** Creates new form DescriptionPane */
  public DescriptionPanel() {
    initComponents();
  }

  private void initComponents() {
    jSplitPane1 = new javax.swing.JSplitPane();
    jPanel1 = new javax.swing.JPanel();
    jLabel1 = new javax.swing.JLabel();
    imageViewer1 = new guipropertyeditordemo.ImageViewer();
    jScrollPane1 = new javax.swing.JScrollPane();
    jTextArea1 = new javax.swing.JTextArea();
    setLayout(new java.awt.BorderLayout());
    jPanel1.setLayout(new java.awt.BorderLayout());
    jPanel1.add(jLabel1, java.awt.BorderLayout.SOUTH);
    jPanel1.add(imageViewer1, java.awt.BorderLayout.CENTER);
    jSplitPane1.setLeftComponent(jPanel1);
    jScrollPane1.setViewportView(jTextArea1);
    jSplitPane1.setRightComponent(jScrollPane1);
    add(jSplitPane1, java.awt.BorderLayout.CENTER);
  }

  public void setName(String newName) {
    name = newName;
    jLabel1.setText(name);
  }

  public String getName() {
    return name;
  }

  public void setDescription(String newDescription) {
    description = newDescription;
    jTextArea1.setText(description);
  }

  public String getDescription() {
    return description;
  }

  public void setImageIcon(javax.swing.ImageIcon newImageIcon) {
    imageIcon = newImageIcon;
    imageViewer1.setImage(imageIcon.getImage());
  }

  public javax.swing.ImageIcon getImageIcon() {
    return imageIcon;
  }

  // Variables declaration - do not modify
  private javax.swing.JSplitPane jSplitPane1;
  private javax.swing.JPanel jPanel1;
  private javax.swing.JLabel jLabel1;
```

Listing 13.12 *DescriptionPanel.java*

continued

Example 13.7 continued

```
  private guipropertyeditordemo.ImageViewer imageViewer1;
  private javax.swing.JScrollPane jScrollPane1;
  private javax.swing.JTextArea jTextArea1;
  // End of variables declaration
}
```

Listing 13.12 *continued*

```
package jdbcdemo;

import java.sql.*;
import java.io.*;
import javax.swing.*;

public class StoreAndRetrieveImage extends javax.swing.JFrame {
  // Connection to the database
  Connection connection;

  // Statement for static SQL statements
  Statement stmt;

  // Prepared statement
  PreparedStatement pstmt = null;

  /** Creates new form StoreAndRetrieveImage */
  public StoreAndRetrieveImage() {
    initComponents();

    try {
      connectDB(); // Connect to DB
      storeDataToTable(); //Store data to the table (including image)
      fillDataInComboBox(); // Fill in combo box
      retrieveFlagInfo((String)(jComboBox1.getSelectedItem()));
    }
    catch (Exception ex) {
      ex.printStackTrace();
    }
  }

  private void initComponents() {
    jComboBox1 = new javax.swing.JComboBox();
    descriptionPanel1 = new jdbcdemo.DescriptionPanel();
    addWindowListener(new java.awt.event.WindowAdapter() {
      public void windowClosing(java.awt.event.WindowEvent evt) {
        exitForm(evt);
      }
    });
    jComboBox1.addItemListener(new java.awt.event.ItemListener() {
      public void itemStateChanged(java.awt.event.ItemEvent evt) {
        jComboBox1ItemStateChanged(evt);
      }
    });
    getContentPane().add(jComboBox1, java.awt.BorderLayout.NORTH);
    getContentPane().add(descriptionPanel1,
      java.awt.BorderLayout.CENTER);
    pack();
  }

```

Listing 13.13 *StoreAndRetrieveImage.java*

```
  private void jComboBox1ItemStateChanged(
    java.awt.event.ItemEvent evt) {
    retrieveFlagInfo((String)(evt.getItem()));
  }

  /** Exit the Application */
  private void exitForm(java.awt.event.WindowEvent evt) {
    System.exit(0);
  }

  public static void main(String args[]) {
    new StoreAndRetrieveImage().show();
  }

  private void connectDB() throws Exception {
    // Load the driver
    Class.forName("oracle.jdbc.driver.OracleDriver");
    System.out.println("Driver loaded");

    // Establish connection
    connection = DriverManager.getConnection
      ("jdbc:oracle:thin:@liang.armstrong.edu:1521:test",
      "scott", "tiger");
    System.out.println("Database connected");

    // Create a statement for static SQL
    stmt = connection.createStatement();

    // Create a prepared statement to retrieve flag and description
    pstmt = connection.prepareStatement("select flag, description " +
      "from Country where name = ?");
  }

  private void storeDataToTable() {
    String[] countries = {"Canada", "UK", "USA", "Germany",
      "Indian", "China"};

    String[] imageFilenames = {"c:\\radft\\image\\ca.gif",
      "c:\\radft\\image\\uk.gif", "c:\\radft\\image\\us.gif",
      "c:\\radft\\image\\germany.gif", "c:\\radft\\image\\india.gif",
      "c:\\radft\\image\\china.gif"};

    String[] descriptions = {"A text to describe Canadian " +
      "flag is omitted", "British flag ...", "American flag ...",
      "German flag ...", "Indian flag ...", "Chinese flag ..."};

    try {
      stmt.executeUpdate("drop table Country" );
      System.out.println("Table Country removed.");
    }
    catch (Exception ex) {
      System.out.println(ex);
    }

    try {
      // Create the Country table
      stmt.executeUpdate("create table Country(" +
        "name varchar(30) not null, " +
```

Listing 13.13 *continued*

continued

Example 13.7 continued

```
        "flag blob, description varchar(1000), " +
        "primary key(name))");
      System.out.println("Table Country created");

      // Create a prepared statement to insert records
      PreparedStatement pstmt = connection.prepareStatement(
        "insert into Country values(?, ?, ?)");

      // Store all predefined records
      for (int i = 0; i < countries.length; i++) {
        pstmt.setString(1, countries[i]);

        // Store image to the table cell
        File file = new File(imageFilenames[i]);
        InputStream inputImage = new FileInputStream(file);
        pstmt.setBinaryStream(2, inputImage, (int)(file.length()));

        pstmt.setString(3, descriptions[i]);
        pstmt.executeUpdate();
      }

      System.out.println("Table Country populated");
    }
    catch (Exception ex) {
      ex.printStackTrace();
    }
  }

  private void fillDataInComboBox() throws Exception {
    ResultSet rs = stmt.executeQuery("select name from Country");
    while (rs.next()) {
      jComboBox1.addItem(rs.getString(1));
    }
  }

  private void retrieveFlagInfo(String name) {
    try {
      pstmt.setString(1, name);
      ResultSet rs = pstmt.executeQuery();
      if (rs.next()) {
        Blob blob = rs.getBlob(1);
        ImageIcon imageIcon = new ImageIcon(
        blob.getBytes(1, (int)blob.length()));
        descriptionPanel1.setImageIcon(imageIcon);
        descriptionPanel1.setName(name);
        String description = rs.getString(2);
        descriptionPanel1.setDescription(description);
      }
    }
    catch (Exception ex) {
      System.err.println(ex);
    }
  }

  // Variables declaration - do not modify
  private javax.swing.JComboBox jComboBox1;
  private jdbcdemo.DescriptionPanel descriptionPanel1;
  // End of variables declaration
}
```

Listing 13.13 *continued*

Example Review

Not all databases and their drivers support the SQL BLOB type. This example was tested using the Oracle type-4 driver on Oracle 8i. The example does not work on Microsoft Access and PointBase database.

The `storeDataToTable` method first drops the Country table if it exists, creates the Country table, and populates the table with data. The `fillDataInComboBox` method retrieves the country names and adds them to the combo box. The `retrieveFlagInfo(name)` method retrieves the flag and description for the specified country name.

Chapter Summary

This chapter gave an in-depth look at metadata, statements, result sets, and connections. You learned how to use the `DatabaseMetaData` interface to obtain database-wide information and the `ResultSetMetaData` interface to obtain metadata information on a specific `ResultSet`. You learned how to create and process statements using static SQL statements, prepared SQL statements, and callable SQL statements. You learned how to process batch updates, and how to process scrollable and updateable result sets. You learned how to use the methods in the `Connection` interface for processing transactions. You also learned how to store and retrieve images using JDBC.

Review Questions

13.1 How do you set auto-commit to true?

13.2 Describe the methods for retrieving general information in the `DatabaseMetaData` interface.

13.3 Describe the methods for finding database capabilities in the `DatabaseMetaData` interface.

13.4 Describe the methods for getting database objects in the `DatabaseMetaData` interface.

13.5 How do you create an instance of `DatabaseMetaData`?

13.6 What is `ResultSetMetaData` for? Describe the methods in `ResultSetMetaData`. How do you create an instance of `ResultSetMetaData`?

13.7 Describe static statements, prepared statements, and callable statements and their interrelationships. How do you create instances of `Statement`, `PreparedStatement`, and `CallableStatement`? How do you execute these statements?

Programming Exercises

13.1 Write a program to insert one hundred records into a table using static SQL statements, and another inserting the same hundred records into a table using dynamic SQL statements. Compare the two.

13.2 Modify Example 13.5 to create three tabs, "Static SQL," "Dynamic SQL," and "Callable SQL," instead of using menus.

13.3 Modify Example 12.5 to use a table to display the result set, as shown in Figure 13.18. Use `ResultSetMetaData` to obtain the column names, and use `DatabaseMetaData` to display the database URL and the username, once the connection is established.

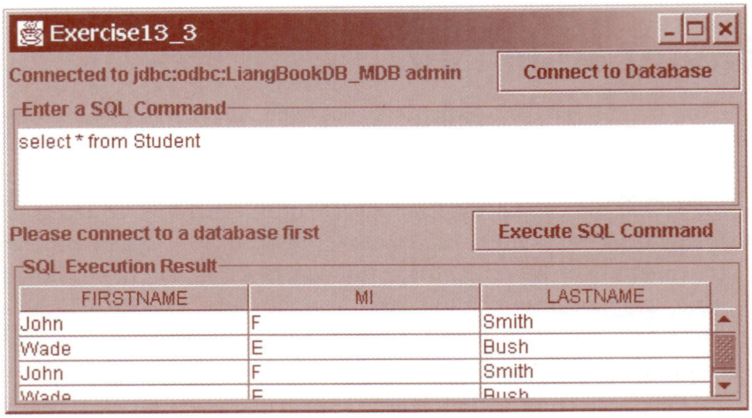

Figure 13.18 *The result set from the SQL select command is displayed in a table.*

13.4 Write a program to insert one thousand records to a database and compare the performance with and without batch updates, as shown in Figure 13.19. Suppose the table is defined as follows:

```
create table Temp(num1 number, num2 number, num3 number)
```

Use the `Math.random()` method to generate random numbers for each record. Test this program with a local database and a remote database.

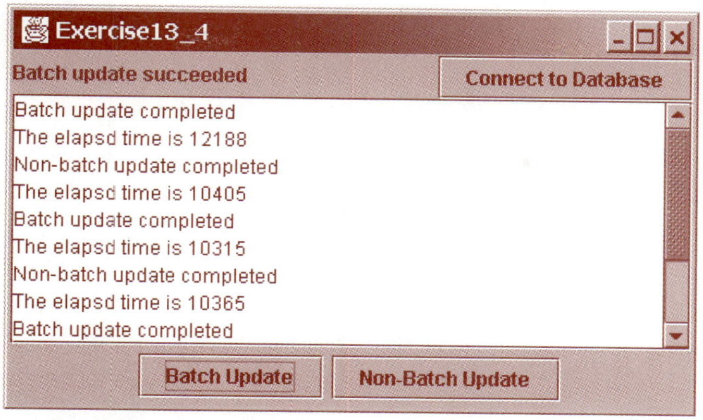

Figure 13.19 *The program demonstrates the performance improvements that result from using the batch updates.*

13.5 Write a program to use the buttons First, Next, Prior, Last, Insert, Delete, and Update display, and modify a single record in the Address table, as shown in Figure 13.20.

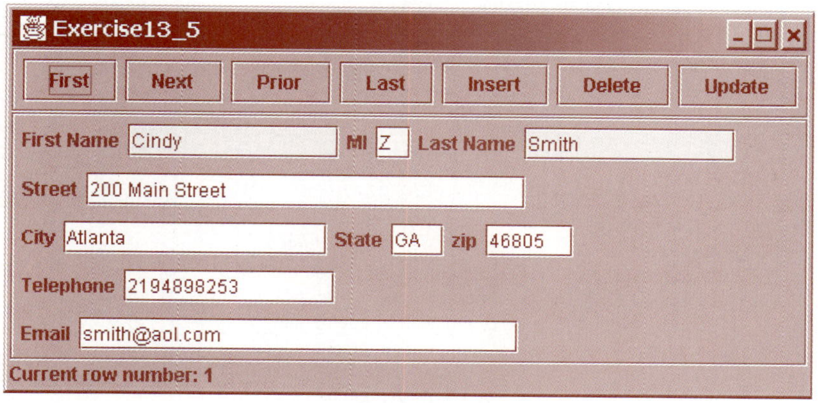

Figure 13.20 *You can use the buttons to display and modify a single record in the Address table.*

13.6 Modify Example 13.6 to display all the tables in the database for the specified user in a tree, as shown in Figure 13.21. You can choose a table from the tree instead of typing a table name in the text field, as in Example 13.6. Connect to the database using the `DBConnectDialog` class from a menu command in the Connection menu.

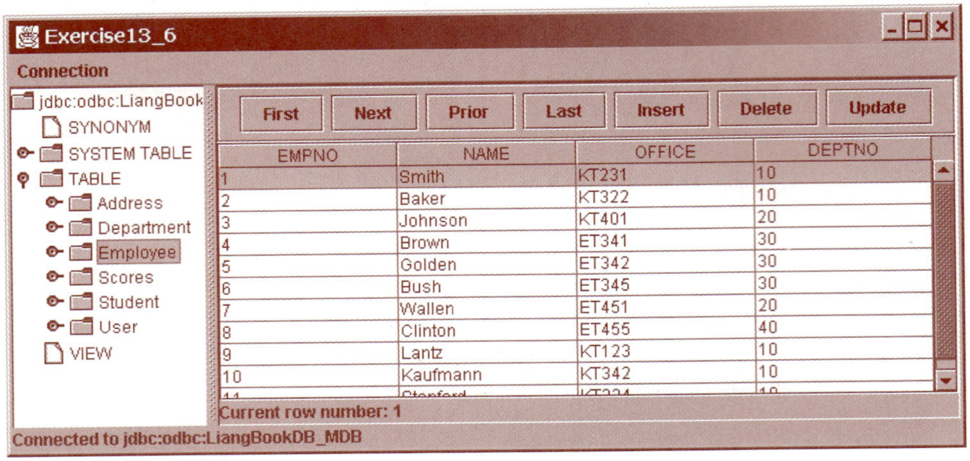

Figure 13.21 *You can choose a table from a tree.*

13.7 Improve Example 13.1 as follows:

1. Display the true/false value in the Capabilities tab in a check box, as shown in Figure 13.22.

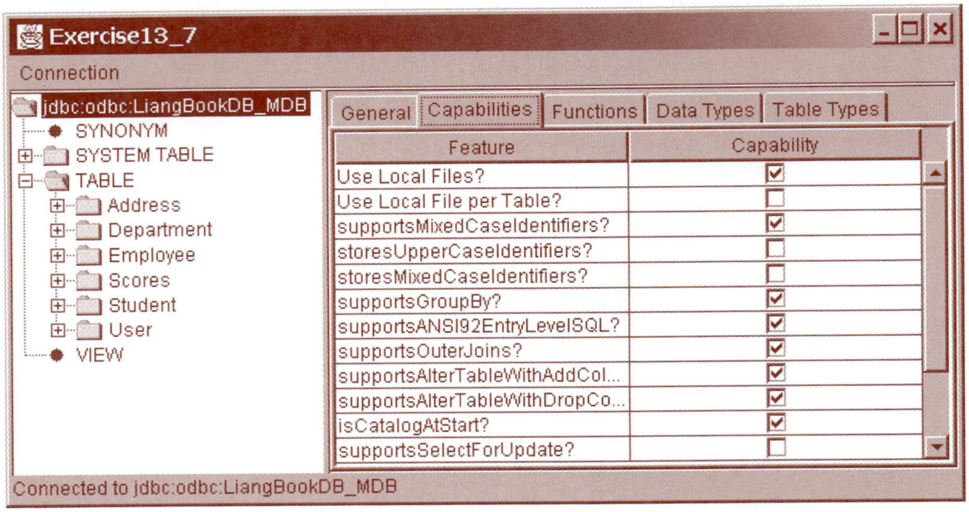

Figure 13.22 *The true/false value is displayed in a check box.*

2. Display functions in four tabs: Numeric, String, System, and Date and Time, as shown in Figure 13.23.

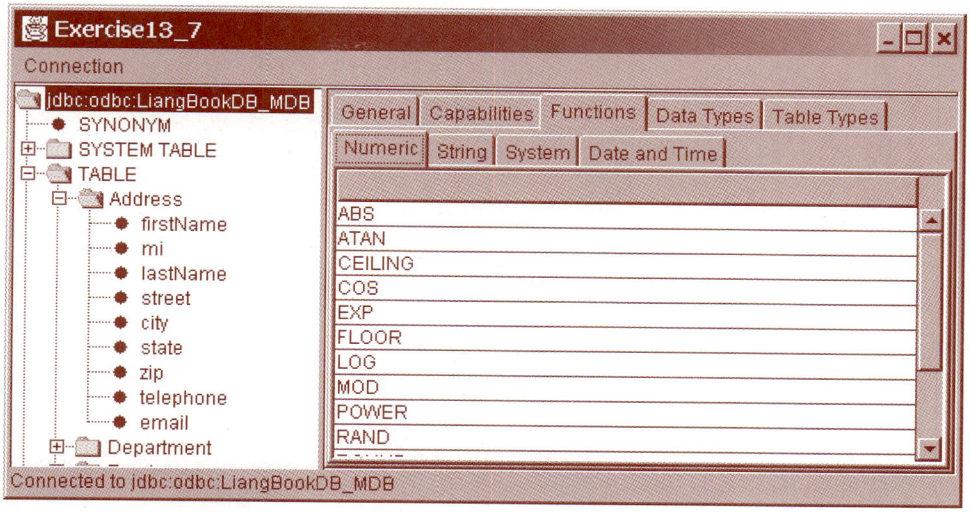

Figure 13.23 *The functions are displayed in groups using tabbed panes.*

3. Enable `DBExplorer` to display multiple connections, as shown in Figure 13.24.

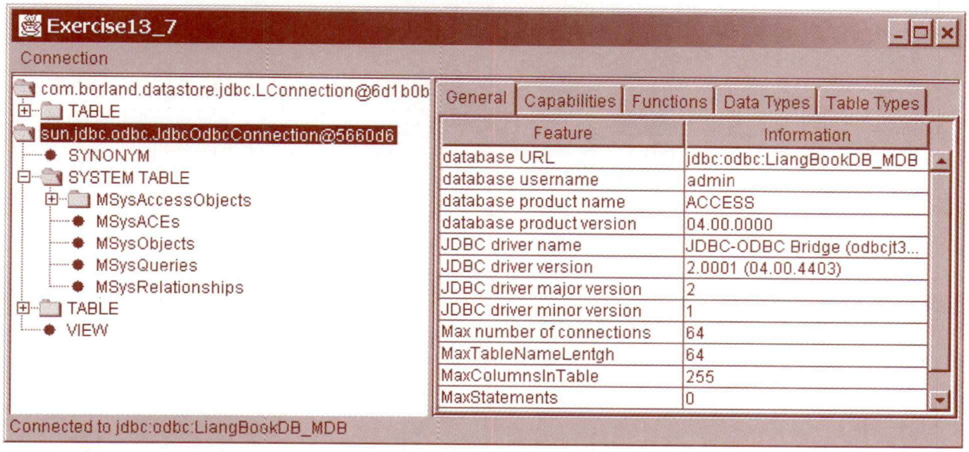

Figure 13.24 *Multiple connections are displayed in* `DBExplorer`.

4. Add a menu command Disconnect that removes a selected database connection from the tree, as shown in Figure 13.25.

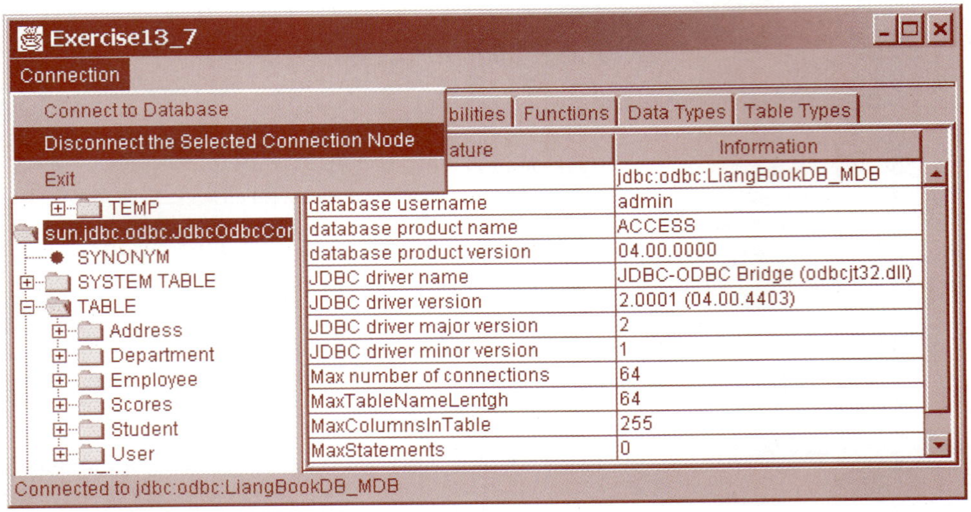

Figure 13.25 *You can remove a connection from* `DBExplorer`.

13.8 Write a program that uses `JTable` to display the Country table created in Example 13.7, as shown in Figure 13.26.

Figure 13.26 *The Country table is displayed in a* `JTable` *instance.*

PART V

Enterprise Java Programming

The final part of the book introduces server-side Java programming. You will learn how to use Java servlets and JSP to generate dynamic contents from Web servers and how to use remote method invocation to develop distributed applications.

CHAPTER 14

SERVLETS

Objectives

- To understand the concept of servlets.
- To become familiar with the HTML forms.
- To know the servlets API.
- To develop servlets to access databases.
- To use hidden fields, cookies, and `HttpSession` to track sessions.
- To send images from servlets.

14.1 Introduction

Servlet technology is primarily designed for use with the HTTP protocol of the Web. *Servlets* are Java programs that run on a Web server. Java servlets can be used to process client requests or produce dynamic Web pages. For example, you can write servlets to generate dynamic Web pages that display stock quotes or process client registration forms and store registration data in a database. This chapter introduces the concept of Java servlets. You will learn how to write Java servlets and run them from Forte.

14.2 HTML and Common Gateway Interface

Java servlets run in the Web environment. To understand Java servlets, let us review HTML and Common Gateway Interface (CGI).

14.2.1 Static Web Contents

You create Web pages using HTML. Your Web pages are stored as files on the Web server. The files are usually stored in the /htdocs on Unix, as shown in Figure 14.1. A user types a URL for the file from a Web browser. The browser contacts the Web server and requests the file. The server finds the file and returns it to the browser. The browser then displays the file to the user. This works fine for static information that does not change regardless of who requests it or when it is requested. Static information is stored in HTML files. The information in the files can be updated, but at any given time every request for the same document returns exactly the same result.

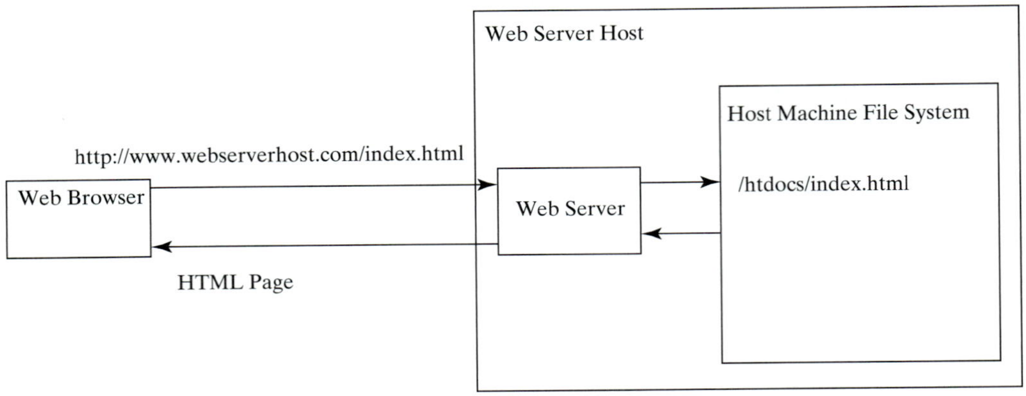

Figure 14.1 *A Web browser requests a static HTML page from a Web server.*

14.2.2 Dynamic Web Contents and Common Gateway Interface

Not all information, however, is static in nature. Stock quotes are updated every minute. Election vote counts are updated constantly on Election Day. Weather reports are frequently updated. The balance in a customer's bank account is updated whenever a transaction takes place. To view up-to-date information on the Web, the HTML pages for displaying this information must be generated dynamically. Dynamic Web pages are generated by Web servers. The Web server needs to run certain programs to process user requests from Web browsers in order to produce a customized response.

The *Common Gateway Interface*, or *CGI*, was proposed to generate dynamic Web content. The interface provides a standard framework for Web servers to interact with external programs, known as *CGI programs*. As shown in Figure 14.2, the Web server receives a request from a Web browser and passes it to the CGI program. The CGI program processes the request and generates a response at runtime. CGI programs can be written in any language, but the *Perl* language is the most popular choice. CGI programs are typically stored in the /cgi-bin directory. Here is a pseudocode example of a CGI program for displaying a customer's bank account balance.

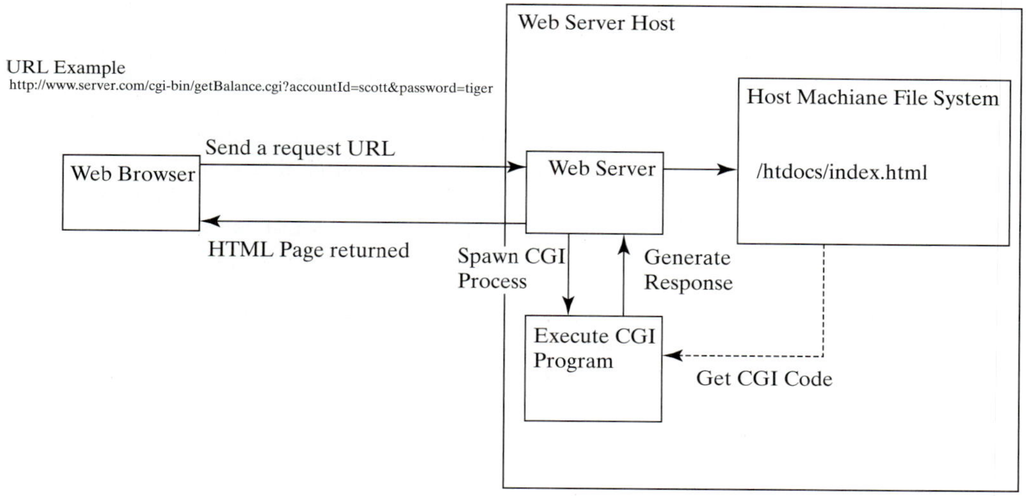

Figure 14.2 *A Web browser requests a dynamic HTML page from a Web server.*

1. Obtain account ID and password.
2. Verify account ID and password. If it fails, generate an HTML page to report incorrect account ID and password, and exit.
3. Retrieve account balance from the database; generate an HTML page to display the account ID and balance.

14.3 The GET and POST Methods

The two most common HTTP requests, also known as *methods*, are GET and POST. The Web browser issues a request using a URL or an HTML form to trigger the Web server to execute a CGI program. When issuing a CGI request directly from a URL, the GET method is used. This URL is known as *a query string*. The URL query string consists of the location of the CGI program, parameters, and their values. For example, the following URL causes the CGI program `getBalance` to be invoked on the server side.

```
http://www.webserverhost.com/cgi-bin/
  getBalance.cgi?accountId=scott+smith&password=tiger
```

The **?** symbol separates the program from the parameters. The parameter name and value are associated using the **=** symbol. Parameter pairs are separated using the **&** symbol. The **+** symbol denotes a space character.

When issuing a request from an HTML form, either a GET method or a POST method can be used. The form explicitly specifies which of the two is used. If the GET method is used, the data in the form are appended to the request string as if it were submitted using a URL. If the POST method is used, the data in the form are packaged as part of the request file. The server program obtains the data by reading the file.

Note

The GET and POST methods both send requests to the Web server. The POST method always triggers the execution of the corresponding CGI program. The GET method may not cause the CGI program to be executed if the previous same request is cached in the Web browser. Web browsers often cache Web pages so that the same request can be quickly responded to without contacting the Web server. The browser checks the request sent through the GET method as a URL query string. If the results for the exact same URL are cached on disk, then the previous Web pages for the URL might be displayed. To ensure that a new Web page is always displayed, use the POST method. For example, use a POST method if the request will actually update the database. If your request is not time-sensitive, such as finding the address of a student in the database, use the GET method to speed up the performance.

14.3.1 HTML Forms

HTML forms enable you to submit data to the Web server in a convenient form. As shown in Figure 14.3, the form can contain text fields, text area, check boxes, combo boxes, lists, radio buttons, and buttons.

The HTML code for creating the form in Figure 14.3 is shown in Listing 14.1.

```
<html>
<head>
<title>Student Registration Form</title>
</head>
```

Listing 14.1 *An HTML Form Demo*

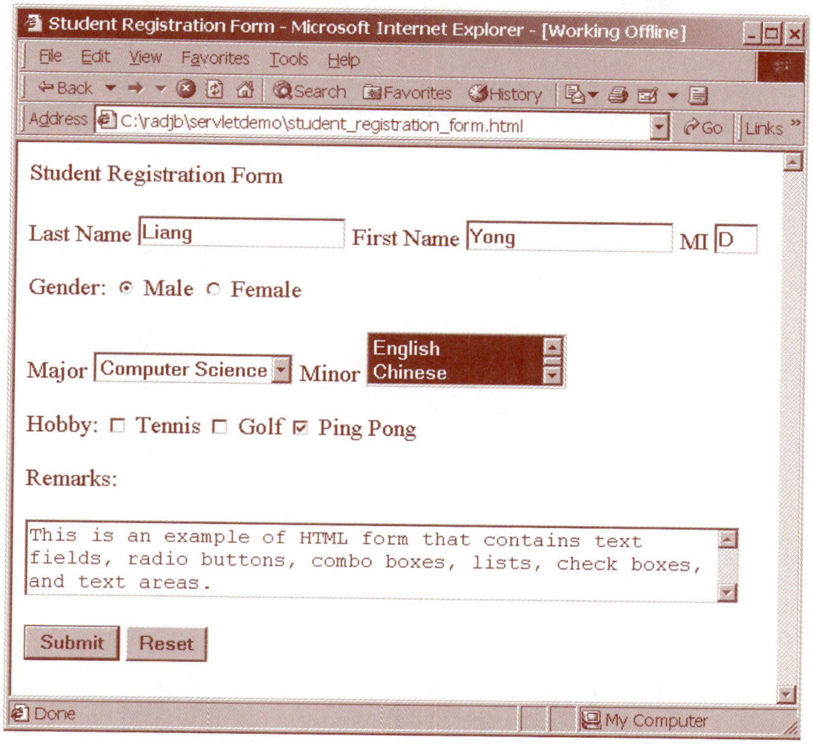

Figure 14.3 *This is an example of an HTML form that contains text fields, radio buttons, combo boxes, lists, check boxes, text areas, and buttons.*

```
<body>
Student Registration Form

<form action="http://www.webserverhost.com/cgi-bin/register"
  method="POST">
  Last Name <input type="text" name="lastName" size="20">
  First Name <input type="text" name="firstName" size="20">
  MI <input type="text" name="mi" size="1">
  <p>Gender: <input type="radio" name="gender"
              value="male" checked> Male
           <input type="radio" name="gender"
              value="Female"> Female</p>
  <p>Major <select name="major" size="1">
            <option>Computer Science
            <option>Mathematics
            <option>English
            <option>Chinese
         </select>
  Minor <select name="minor" size="2" multiple>
            <option>Computer Science
            <option>Mathematics
            <option>English
            <option>Chinese
       </select></p>
  <p>Hobby:
    <input type="checkbox" name="tennis"> Tennis
```

Listing 14.1 *continued*

```
      <input type="checkbox" name="golf"> Golf
      <input type="checkbox" name="pingPong" checked> Ping Pong</p>
    <p>Remarks:</p>
    <p><textarea name="remarks" rows="3" cols="56"></textarea></p>
    <p><input type="submit" value="Submit">
      <input type="reset" value="Reset"></p>
  </form>
  </body>
```

Listing 14.1 *continued*

The following HTML tags are used to construct HTML forms:

- **<form> . . . </form>** defines a form body. The attributes for the <form> tag are **action** and **method**. The action attribute specifies the CGI program to be executed on the Web server when the form is submitted. The method attribute is either **GET** or **POST**.
- **<input>** defines an input field. The attributes for this tag are **type**, **name**, **value**, **checked**, **size**, and **maxlength**. The type attribute specifies the input type. Possible types are **text** for a one-line text field, **radio** for radio button, and **checkbox** for check box. The name attribute gives a formal name for the attribute. This name is used by the CGI program to retrieve its associated value. The names of radio buttons in a group must be identical. The value attribute specifies a default value for a text field and text area. The checked attribute indicates whether a radio button or a check box is initially checked. The size attribute specifies the size of a text field, and the maxlength attribute specifies the maximum length of a text field.
- **<select> . . . </select>** defines a combo box or a list. The attributes for this tag are **name**, **size**, and **multiple**. The size attribute specifies the number of rows visible in the list. The multiple attribute specifies that multiple values can be selected from a list. Set size to 1 and do not use a multiple for a combo box.
- **<option>** defines a selection list within **<select> . . . </select>** tags.
- **<textarea> . . . </textarea>** defines a text area. The attributes are **name**, **rows**, and **cols.** The **rows** and **cols** attributes specify the number of rows and columns in a text area.

14.4 From CGI to Java Servlets

CGI provides a relatively simple approach for creating dynamic Web applications that accept a user request, process it on the server side, and return responses to the Web browser. But CGI is very slow when handling a large number of requests simultaneously, because the Web server spawns a process for executing each CGI program. Each process has its own runtime environment that contains and runs the CGI program. It is not difficult to imagine what will happen when many CGI programs are executed simultaneously. System resource would be quickly exhausted, potentially causing the server to crash.

Several new approaches have been developed to remedy the performance problem of CGI programs. Java servlets are one successful technology for this purpose. Java servlets are Java programs that function like CGI programs. They are executed upon request from a Web browser. All the servlets run inside a *servlet container*, also referred to as a *servlet server* or a *servlet engine*. A servlet container is a single process that runs in a Java Virtual Machine. The JVM creates a thread to handle each servlet. Java threads have much less overhead than full-brown processes. All the threads share the same memory allocated to the JVM. Since the JVM persists beyond the life-cycle of a single servlet execution, servlets can share objects already created in the JVM. For example, if multiple servlets access the same database, they can share the connection object. Servlets are much more efficient than CGI.

Servlets have other benefits that are inherent in Java. Since servlets are Java programs, they are object-oriented, portable, and platform-independent. Since you know Java, you can develop servlets immediately with the support of Java API for accessing databases, and network resources.

14.5 Creating and Running Servlets from Forte

To run Java servlets, you need a servlet container. Many servlet containers are available. *Tomcat*, developed by Apache (`www.apache.org`), is a standard reference implementation for Java servlet 2.2 and Java Server Pages 1.1. It is free. It can be used standalone as a Web server or be plugged into a Web server like Apache, Netscape Enterprise Server, or Microsoft Internet Information Server. Tomcat has been integrated with Forte. This section demonstrates how to create and run a Java servlet from Forte.

14.5.1 Setting a Default Web Server

You can install and set Web servers in Forte. Tomcat is bundled with Forte. To set Tomcat as the default Web server, choose *Set As Default* in the context menu of the *Tomcat 4.0* node under the *Default Servers* node of the *Server Registry* in the Runtime tab of the Explorer, as shown in Figure 14.4.

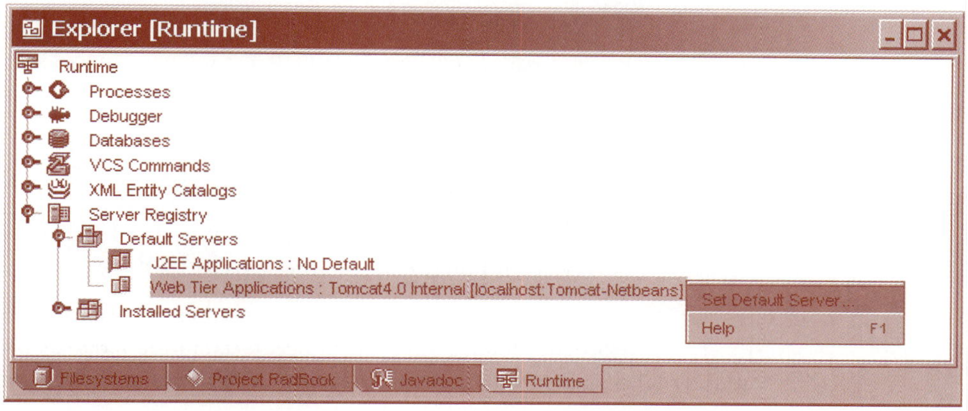

Figure 14.4 *You can set Tomcat as the default Web server in Forte.*

14.5.2 Creating a Web Module

To run servlets in Forte, you have to first create a Web module that holds the servlets and configuration files. Here are the steps to create a Web Module.

1. In the context menu of the *c:\radft* node in the Explorer, choose *New, JSP & Servlet*, and *Web Module* to display the Choose Target panel, as shown in Figure 14.5.

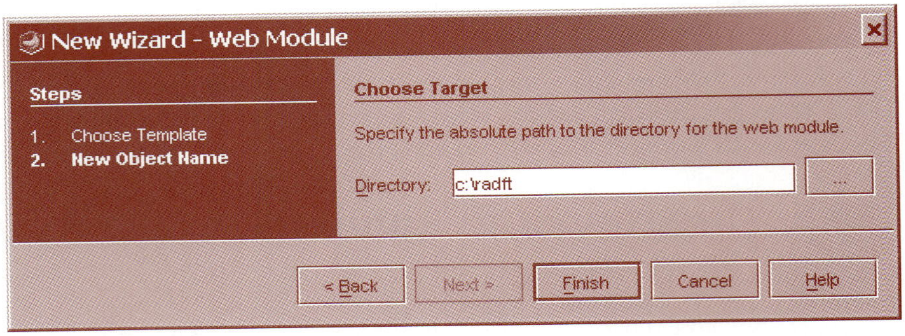

Figure 14.5 *The Web Module wizard enables you to create a Web module for servlets and JSP.*

2. Enter `c:\radft` in the Directory field and click *Finish*. You will see the Information dialog box (Figure 14.6) to indicate that the directory c:\radft is already mounted so you don't need to mount it again. Click *OK* to generate the Web module.

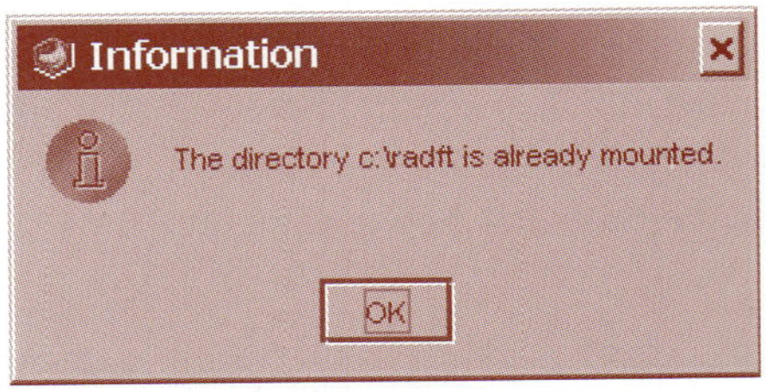

Figure 14.6 *The Information dialog box indicates that the directory for the Web module is already mounted.*

14.5.3 Setting Properties for Running Servlets

You need to specify whether to use internal or external Web browsers and which browser to use to run servlets in Forte. Here are the steps to set these properties:

1. Choose *Tools, Options* to display the Options window, as shown in Figure 14.7. In the properties for JSP & Servlets Settings, choose *External Browser*. The internal Swing HTML browser has limited features and does not sup-

port cookies. So you should choose an external browser, such as Internet Explorer or Netscape.

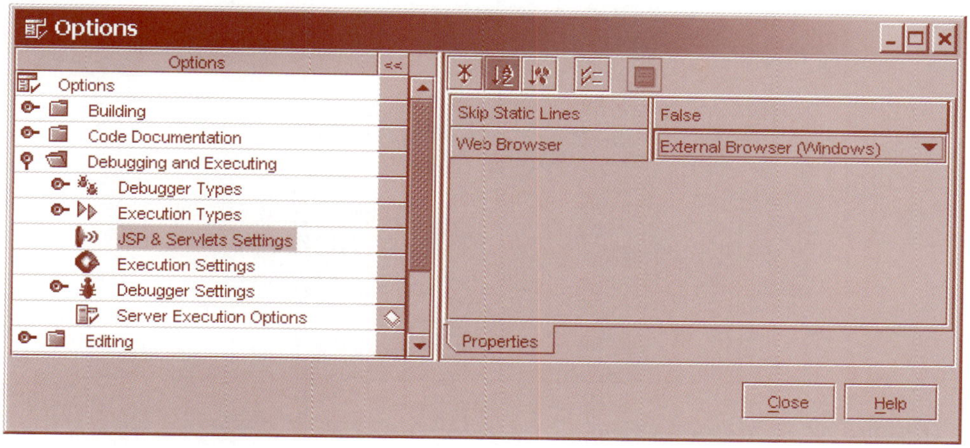

Figure 14.7 *You can choose whether to use an external browser or an internal browser in the Options window.*

2. To specify an external browser, in the Options window, expand *IDE Configuration*, *Server and External Tool Settings*, and *Web Browsers (Windows)*, select a browser in the DDE Server field, as shown in Figure 14.8.

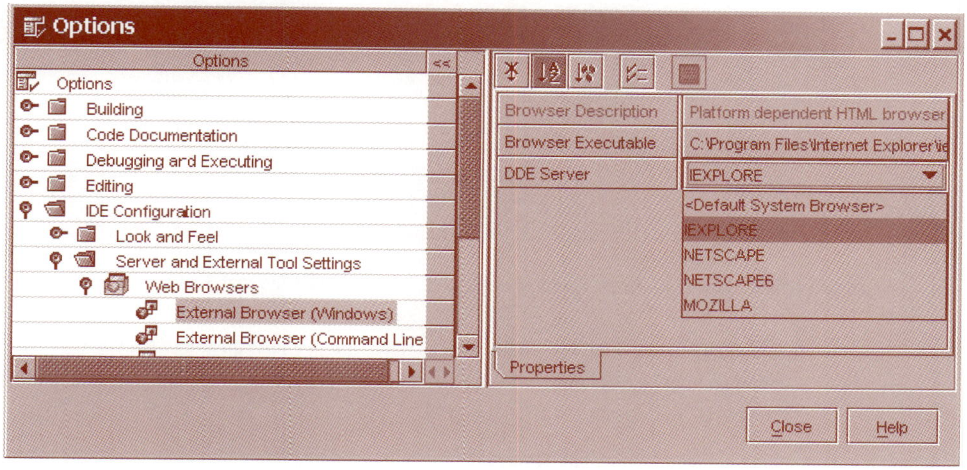

Figure 14.8 *You can specify an external browser, such as Internet Explorer or Netscape, in the Options window.*

NOTE

When you select a node in the left pane of the Options window, it may take a little while to display the properties in the right pane.

14.5.4 Creating Your First Servlet

1. In the context menu of *c:\radft* in the Explorer, choose *New, Java Package* to display the Java Package wizard as shown in Figure 14.9. Type `servletdemo` in the Name field and click *Finish* to create the servletdemo package.

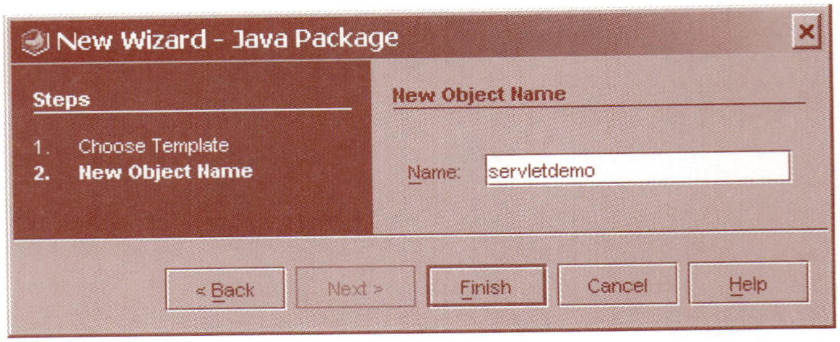

Figure 14.9 *The servletdemo package will hold all examples in this chapter.*

2. In the context menu of *servletdemo* in the Explorer, choose *New, JSP & Servlets, Servlet* to display the Forte Servlet wizard, as shown in Figure 14.10. Enter FirstServlet in the Name field, and click *Finish* to generate First-Servlet.java.

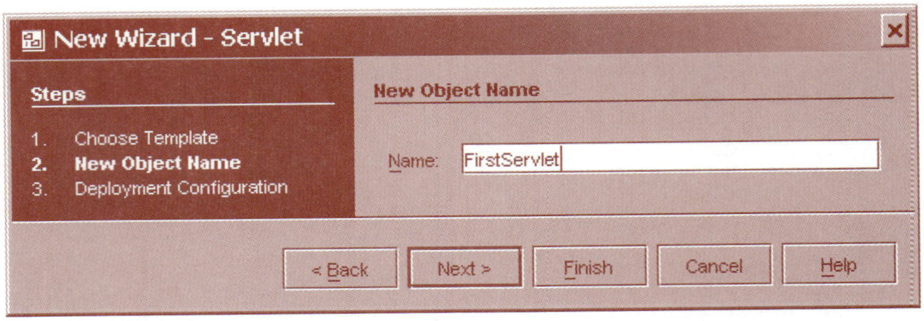

Figure 14.10 *You can create a servlet using the Forte's Servlet wizard.*

3. Uncomment the code in the `processRequest` method and add `out.println("Hello, Java Servlets");` in the `processRequest` method, as shown in Listing 14.2 (Line 34).

```
1     package servletdemo;
2
3     import javax.servlet.*;
4     import javax.servlet.http.*;
5
6     public class FirstServlet extends HttpServlet {
7       /** Initialize the servlet.
8        */
9       public void init(ServletConfig config) throws ServletException {
10        super.init(config);
11      }
12
```

Listing 14.2 *FirstServlet.java*

```
  /** Destroy the servlet.
   */
  public void destroy() {
  }

  /** Processes requests for both HTTP <code>GET</code> and
   * <code>POST</code> methods.
   * @param request servlet request
   * @param response servlet response
   */
  protected void processRequest(HttpServletRequest request,
    HttpServletResponse response)
  throws ServletException, java.io.IOException {
    response.setContentType("text/html");
    java.io.PrintWriter out = response.getWriter();
    // output your page here
    out.println("<html>");
    out.println("<head>");
    out.println("<title>Servlet</title>");
    out.println("</head>");
    out.println("<body>");
    out.println("Hello, Java Servlets");
    out.println("</body>");
    out.println("</html>");
    out.close();
  }

  /** Handle the HTTP <code>GET</code> method.
   * @param request servlet request
   * @param response servlet response
   */
  protected void doGet(HttpServletRequest request,
    HttpServletResponse response)
  throws ServletException, java.io.IOException {
    processRequest(request, response);
  }

  /** Handle the HTTP <code>POST</code> method.
   * @param request servlet request
   * @param response servlet response
   */
  protected void doPost(HttpServletRequest request,
    HttpServletResponse response)
  throws ServletException, java.io.IOException {
    processRequest(request, response);
  }

  /** Return a short description of the servlet.
   */
  public String getServletInfo() {
    return "Short description";
  }
}
```

Listing 14.2 *continued*

14.5.5 Compiling and Running the Servlet

When you created a Web module in Section 14.5.2, "Creating a Web Module" (see Figure 14.5), the WEB-INF directory was created under c:\radft. The WEB-INF directory holds the files that are used by Tomcat server at runtime. For the servlet to run correctly, you need to place the class files into the WEB-INF\classes directory. Due to a bug in Forte 4, you have to set the target class path to c:\radft\servletdemo\WEB-INF\classes for the compiled class files to be placed in the WEB-INF\classes directory. To do so, first mount the directory c:\radft\WEB-INF\classes in the Explorer, as shown in Figure 14.11, then set the path in the Target property of the External Compilation, as shown in Figure 14.12.

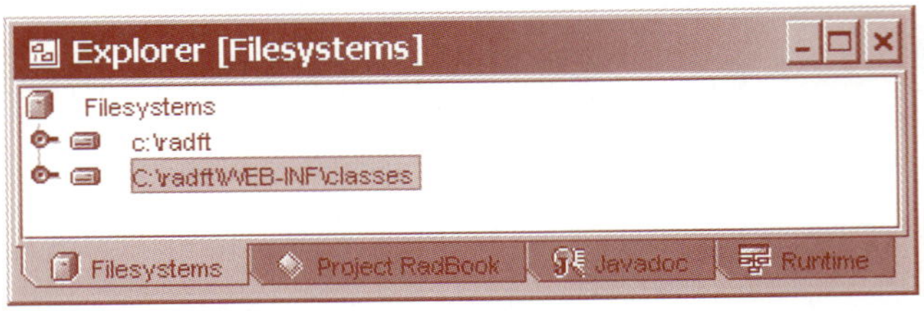

Figure 14.11 *You have to mount c:\radft\WEB-INF\classes to enable it to be a target directory in Forte.*

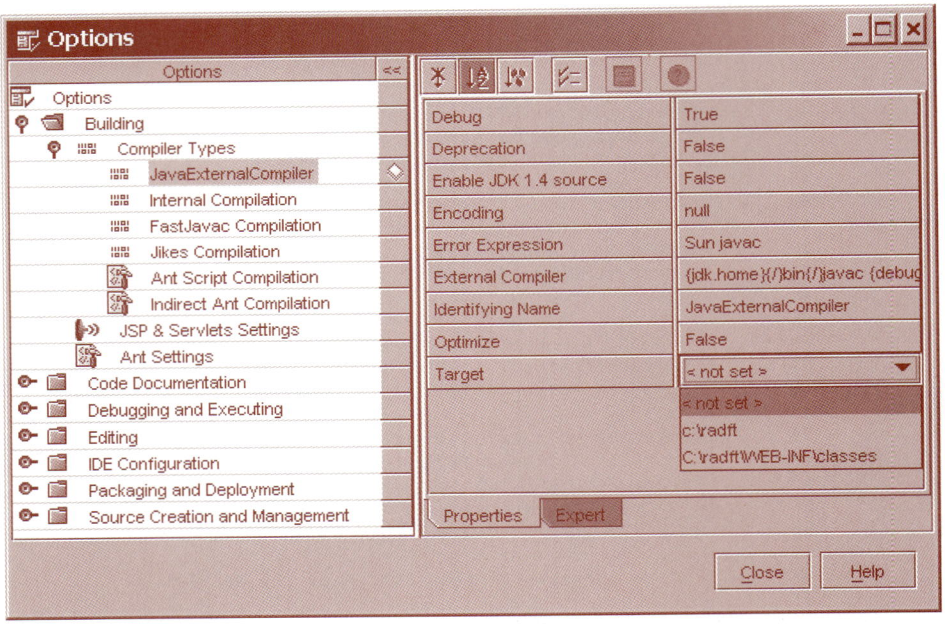

Figure 14.12 *You need to set the servlet target class path in the Target for the External Compilation.*

To run the servlet, choose *Compile* in the context menu of FirstServlet. The compiled class FirstServlet.class is now stored in c:\radft\WEB-INF\classes\servletdemo.

To run the servlet, choose *Execute* in the context menu of FirstServlet under c:\radft\servletdemo. The external Web browser is started to display the servlet output, as shown in Figure 14.13.

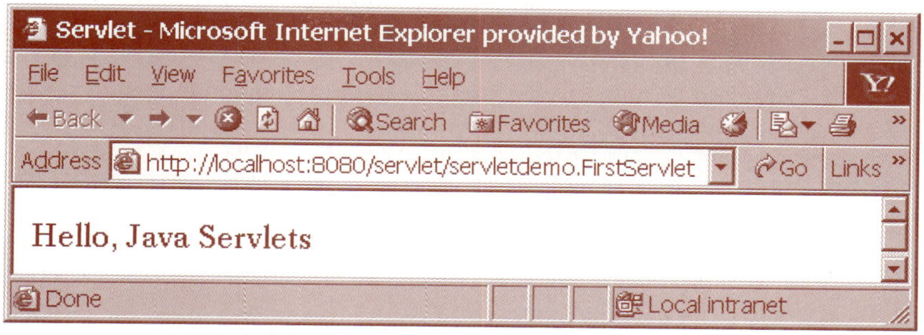

Figure 14.13 *A Web browser is started to display the servlet output.*

NOTE

The context menu of a servlet has the *Execute* and *Execute (Force Reload)* commands. If your servlet is modified, use the *Execute (Force Reload)* command to force reload of the servlet.

TIP

Due to an error in Forte, the *c:\radft\WEB-INF\classes* node may disappear from the Explorer. If so, you need to remount it and reset it to the target class path as shown in Figure 14.12.

TIP

When you run the servlet for the first time, the external Web browser is started. If the servlet output is not displayed, close the browser and rerun the servlet from Forte.

NOTE

By default, Tomcat server starts at port 8080. You can set a different port in the Tomcat Properties window, as shown in Figure 14.14. To display the property window, expand *Tomcat 4.0* under *Installed Servers* node in the Runtime tab of the Explorer. Choose *Properties* in the context menu of the *localhost* node under the *Internal* node.

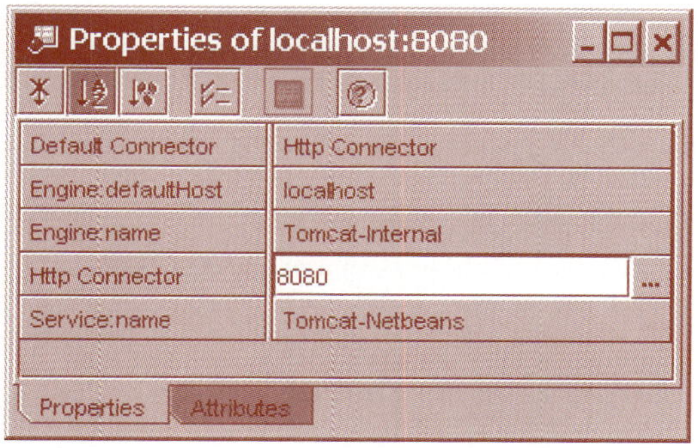

Figure 14.14 *You can set an HTTP port for Tomcat Web server.*

NOTE
You can use the servlet from anywhere on the Internet if you started Tomcat in Forte on a host machine on the Internet. Suppose the host name is liang.armstrong.edu; use the URL `http://liang.armstrong.edu:8080/servlet/servletdemo.FirstServlet` to test the servlet.

14.6 The Servlet API

You have to know the servlet API in order to understand the source code in Listing 14.2. The servlet API provides the interfaces and classes that support servlets. These interfaces and classes are grouped into two packages, `javax.servlet` and `javax.servlet.http`, as shown in Figure 14.15. The `javax.servlet` package provides basic interfaces, and the `javax.servlet.http` package provides classes and interfaces derived from them, which provide specific means for servicing HTTP requests.

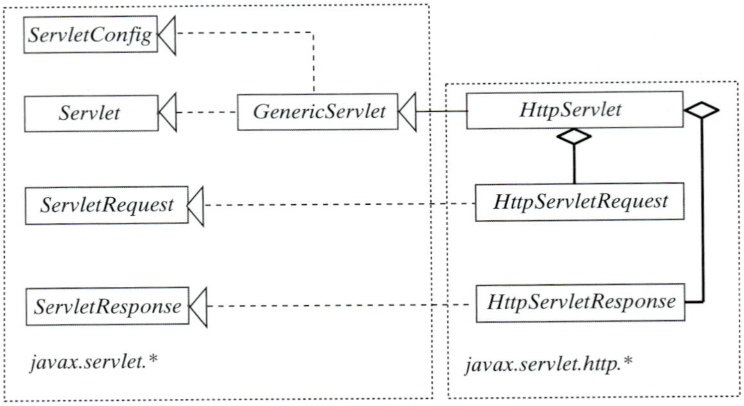

Figure 14.15 *The servlet API contains interfaces and classes that you use to develop and run servlets.*

14.6.1 The *Servlet* Interface

The `Servlet` interface defines the methods that all servlets must implement. The methods are listed below:

```
/** Invoked for every servlet constructed */
public void init(ServletConfig p0) throws ServletException;

/** Invoked to respond to incoming requests */
public void service(ServletRequest p0, ServletResponse p1)
  throws ServletException, IOException;

/** Invoked to release resource by the servlet */
public void destroy();

/** Return information about the servlet */
public String getServletInfo();

/** Return configuration objects of the servlet */
public ServletConfig getServletConfig();
```

The `init`, `service`, and `destroy` methods are known as *life-cycle methods* and are called in the following sequence:

1. The `init` method is called when the servlet is first created, and is not called again as long as the servlet is not destroyed. This resembles the applet's `init` method, which is invoked when the applet is created, and is not invoked again as long as the applet is not destroyed.

2. The `service` method is invoked each time the server receives a request for the servlet. The server spawns a new thread and invokes `service`.

3. The `destroy` method is invoked once all the threads in the servlet's `service` method have exited or after a timeout period has passed. This method releases resources for the servlet.

14.6.2 The *GenericServlet* Class, *ServletConfig* Interface, and *HttpServlet* Class

The `GenericServlet` class defines a generic, protocol-independent servlet. It implements `Servlet` and `ServletConfig`. `ServletConfig` is an interface that defines four methods (`getInitParameter`, `getInitParameterNames`, `getServletContext`, and `getServletName`) for passing information to a servlet during initialization. All the methods in `Servlet` and `ServletConfig` are implemented in `GenericServlet` except `service`. Therefore, `GenericServlet` is an abstract class.

The `HttpServlet` class defines a servlet for the HTTP protocol. It extends `GenericServlet` and implements the `service` method. The `service` method is implemented as a dispatcher of HTTP requests. The HTTP requests are processed in the following methods:

- **`doGet`** is invoked to respond to a GET request.
- **`doPost`** is invoked to respond to a POST request.
- **`doDelete`** is invoked to respond to a DELETE request. Such a request is normally used to delete a file on the server from the server.
- **`doPut`** is invoked to respond to a PUT request. Such a request is normally used to send a file to the server.
- **`doOptions`** is invoked to respond to an OPTIONS request. This returns information about the server, such as which HTTP methods it supports.
- **`doTrace`** is invoked to respond to a TRACE request. Such a request is normally used for debugging. This method returns an HTML page that contains appropriate trace information.

All these methods have the same signature:

```
protected void doXxx(HttpServletRequest req, HttpServletResponse resp)
  throws ServletException, java.io.IOException
```

The `HttpServlet` class provides default implementation for these methods. You need to override `doGet`, `doPost`, `doDelete`, and `doPut` if you want the servlet to process a GET request, POST request, DELETE request, or PUT request. By default, nothing will be done. Normally, you should not override the `doOptions` method unless the servlet implements new HTTP methods beyond those implemented by HTTP 1.1. Nor is there any need to override the `doTrace` method.

NOTE

GET and POST requests are often used. DELETE, PUT, OPTIONS, and TRACE are not frequently used. For information about using these requests from a Web browser, please refer to HTTP 1.1 specification from **www.cis.ohio-state.edu/htbin/rfc/rfc2068.html**.

NOTE

Although the methods in `HttpServlet` are all nonabstract, `HttpServlet` is defined as an abstract class. Thus you cannot create a servlet directly from `HttpServlet`. Instead you have to define your servlet by extending `HttpServlet`.

14.6.3 The *ServletRequest* Interface and *HttpServletRequest* Interface

Every `doXxx` method in the `HttpServlet` class has an argument of the `HttpServletRequest` type, which is an object that contains HTTP request information, including parameter name and values, attributes, and an input stream. `HttpServletRequest` is a subinterface of `ServletRequest`. `ServletRequest` defines a more general interface to provide information for all kinds of clients.

Listed below are some frequently used methods in the `ServletRequest` interface.

- `public String getParameter(java.lang.String name)`

  Returns the value of a request parameter as a String, or null if the parameter does not exist. Request parameters are extra information sent with the request. For HTTP servlets, parameters are contained in the query string or posted from data. Only use this method when you are sure that the parameter has only one value. If it might have more than one value, use `getParameterValues`.

- `public String[] getParameterValues(String name)`

  Returns an array of `String` objects containing all the values of the given request parameter, or null if the parameter does not exist.

- `public java.lang.String getRemoteAddr()`

  Returns the Internet Protocol (IP) address of the client that sent the request.

- `public String getRemoteHost()`

  Returns the fully qualified name of the client that sent the request, or the IP address of the client if the name cannot be determined.

In addition, the `HttpServletRequest` interface contains these commonly used methods:

- `public String getHeader(String name)`

  Returns the value of the specified request header as a String. If the request did not include a header of the specified name, this method returns null. Since the header name is case-insensitive, you can use this method with any request header.

- `public String getMethod()`

  Returns the name of the HTTP method with which this request was made; for example, GET, POST, DELETE, PUT, OPTIONS, or TRACE.

- `public String getQueryString()`

  Returns the query string that is contained in the request URL after the path. This method returns null if the URL does not have a query string.

- `public Cookie[] getCookies()`

  Returns an array containing all of the `Cookie` objects the client sent with the request. This method returns null if no cookies were sent. Using cookies is introduced in Section 14.9.2, "Session Tracking Using Cookies."

- `public HttpSession getSession(boolean create)`

  `getSession(true)` returns the current session associated with this request. If the request does not have a session, it creates one. `getSession(false)` returns the current session associated with the request. If the request does not have a session, it returns `null`. The `getSession` method is used in session tracking, which is introduced in Section 14.9.3, "Session Tracking Using the Servlet API."

14.6.4 The *ServletResponse* Interface and *HttpServletResponse* Interface

Every `doXxx` method in the `HttpServlet` class has an argument of the `HttpServletResponse` type, which is an object that assists a servlet in sending a response to the client. `HttpServletResponse` is a subinterface of `ServletResponse`. `ServletRequest` defines a more general interface for sending output to the client.

Here are some frequently used methods in the `ServletResponse` interface:

- `public PrintWriter getWriter() throws IOException`

  Returns a `PrintWriter` object that can send character text to the client. The character encoding used is the one specified in the `charset` property of the `setContentType(String)` method, which must be called before calling this method for the `charset` to take effect.

- `public void setContentType(String type)`

  Sets the content type of the response being sent to the client. Before writing a response to the client, this method must be called to set the MIME type of the HTTP response. The MIME type helps the browser determine how to display the data. When you are writing HTML to the client, the type should be set to "text/html." For plain text, use "text/plain." For sending a gif image to the browser, use "image/gif."

`HttpServletResponse` extends the `ServletResponse` interface to provide HTTP-specific functionality in sending a response. For example, it has the `addCookie` method to send an HTTP cookie to the browser. Cookies are introduced in Section 14.9.2, "Session Tracking Using Cookies."

14.7 Creating Servlets

Servlets are the opposite of Java applets. Java applets run from a Web browser on the client side. To write Java programs, you define classes. To write a Java applet, you define a class that extends the `Applet` class. The Web browser runs and controls the execution of the applet through the methods defined in the `Applet` class. Similarly, to write a Java servlet, you define a class that extends the `HttpServlet` class. The servlet container runs and controls the execution of the servlet through the methods defined in the `HttpServlet` class. Like a Java applet, a servlet does not have a main method. A servlet depends on the servlet server to call the methods. Every servlet has a structure like the one shown in Listing 14.4.

```
import javax.servlet.*;
import javax.servlet.http.*;
import java.io.*;
import java.util.*;

public class MyServlet extends HttpServlet {
  /** Called by the servlet engine to initialize servlet */
  public void init(ServletConfig p0) throws ServletException {
    super.init(p0);
    ...
  }

  /** Process the HTTP Get request */
  public void doGet(HttpServletRequest request, HttpServletResponse
    response) throws ServletException, IOException {
    ...
  }

  /** Process the HTTP Post request */
  public void doPost(HttpServletRequest request, HttpServletResponse
    response) throws ServletException, IOException {
    ...
  }

  /** Called by the servlet engine to release resource */
  public void destroy() {
    ...
  }

  // Other methods if necessary
}
```

Listing 14.4 *Servlet Outline*

The servlet engine controls the servlets using `init`, `doGet`, `doPost`, `destroy`, and other methods. By default, the `doGet` and `doPost` methods do nothing. To handle a GET request, you need to override the `doGet` method; to handle a POST request, you need to override the `doPost` method.

Example 14.1 Obtaining Current Time from the Server

This example gives a simple Java servlet that generates a dynamic Web page for displaying current time to the browser. The servlet program is shown in Listing 14.5. A sample run is shown in Figure 14.16.

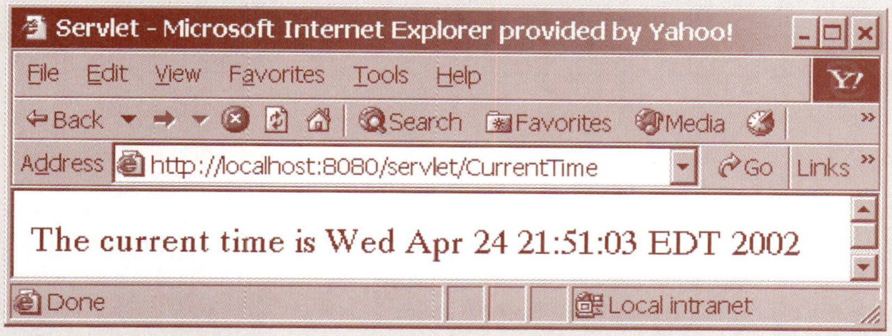

Figure 14.16 *Servlet CurrentTime displays the current time.*

```
package servletdemo;

import javax.servlet.*;
import javax.servlet.http.*;
import java.io.*;
import java.util.*;

public class CurrentTime extends HttpServlet {
  /** Process the HTTP Get request */
  public void doGet(HttpServletRequest request, HttpServletResponse
    response) throws ServletException, IOException {
    response.setContentType("text/html");
    PrintWriter out = response.getWriter();
    out.println("<p>The current time is " + new Date());
    out.close(); // Close stream
  }
}
```

Listing 14.5 *CurrentTime.java*

Example Review

The `HttpServlet` class has a `doGet` method. Since the `doGet` method is invoked when the browser issues a request to the servlet using the GET method, your servlet class should override the `doGet` method to respond to the GET request. In this case, you write the code to display the current time.

continued

Example 14.1 continued

Servlets return responses to the browser through an `HttpServletResponse` object. Since the `setContentType("text/html")` method (Line 12) sets the MIME type to "text/html," the browser will display the response in HTML. The `getWriter` method returns a `PrintWriter` stream (`out`) for sending HTML back to the client.

Note

The URL query string uses the GET method to issue a request to the servlet. The current time may not be current if the Web page for displaying the current time is cached. To ensure that a new current time is displayed, refresh the page in the browser. In the next example, you will write a new servlet that uses the POST method to obtain the current time.

Example 14.2 Obtaining Current Time Based on Locale and Time Zone

This example creates a servlet that processes the GET and POST requests. The GET request generates a form that contains a combo box for locale and a combo box for time zone, as shown in Figure 14.17. The user can choose a locale and a time zone from this form to submit a POST request to obtain current time based on the locale and time zone, as shown in Figure 14.18. The servlet program is shown in Listing 14.6.

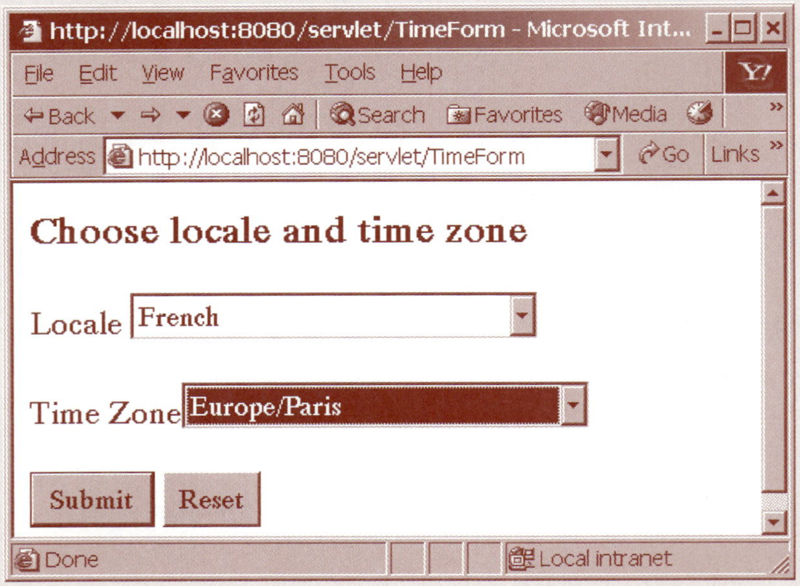

Figure 14.17 *The GET method in the* `TimeForm` *servlet displays a form.*

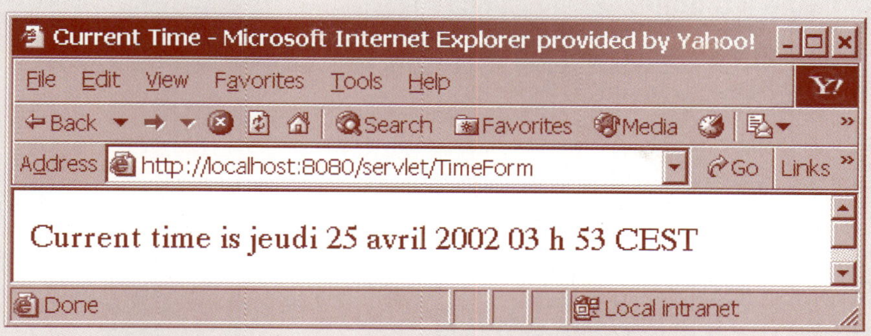

Figure 14.18 *The POST method in the* `TimeForm` *servlet displays the time based on locale and time zone.*

```
package servletdemo;

import javax.servlet.*;
import javax.servlet.http.*;
import java.io.*;
import java.util.*;
import java.text.*;

public class TimeForm extends HttpServlet {
  private static final String CONTENT_TYPE = "text/html";
  Locale[] allLocale = Locale.getAvailableLocales();
  String[] allTimeZone = TimeZone.getAvailableIDs();

  /** Process the HTTP Get request */
  public void doGet(HttpServletRequest request, HttpServletResponse
    response) throws ServletException, IOException {
    response.setContentType(CONTENT_TYPE);
    PrintWriter out = response.getWriter();
    out.println("<h3>Choose locale and time zone</h3>");
    out.println("<form method=\"post\" " +
      "action=servletdemo.TimeForm>");
    out.println("Locale <select size=\"1\" name=\"locale\">");

    // Fill in all locales
    for (int i = 0; i < allLocale.length; i++) {
      out.println("<option value=\"" + i +"\">" +
        allLocale[i].getDisplayName() + "</option>");
    }
    out.println("</select>");

    // Fill in all time zones
    out.println("<p>Time Zone<select size=\"1\" name=\"timezone\">");
    for (int i = 0; i < allTimeZone.length; i++) {
      out.println("<option value=\"" + allTimeZone[i] +"\">" +
        allTimeZone[i] + "</option>");
    }
    out.println("</select>");

    out.println("<p><input type=\"submit\"" +
      " value=\"Submit\" name=\"B1\">");
```

Listing 14.6 *TimeForm.java*

continued

Example 14.2 continued

```
      out.println("<input type=\"reset\" value=\"Reset\"></p>");
      out.println("</form>");
      out.close(); // Close stream
    }

    /** Process the HTTP Post request */
    public void doPost(HttpServletRequest request, HttpServletResponse
      response) throws ServletException, IOException {
      response.setContentType(CONTENT_TYPE);
      PrintWriter out = response.getWriter();
      out.println("<html>");
      int localeIndex = Integer.parseInt(
        request.getParameter("locale"));
      String timeZoneID = request.getParameter("timezone");
      out.println("<head><title>Current Time</title></head>");
      out.println("<body>");
      Calendar calendar =
        new GregorianCalendar(allLocale[localeIndex]);
      TimeZone timeZone = TimeZone.getTimeZone(timeZoneID);
      DateFormat dateFormat = DateFormat.getDateTimeInstance(
        DateFormat.FULL, DateFormat.FULL, allLocale[localeIndex]);
      dateFormat.setTimeZone(timeZone);
      out.println("Current time is " +
        dateFormat.format(calendar.getTime()) + "</p>");
      out.println("</body></html>");
      out.close(); // Close stream
    }
  }
```

Listing 14.6 *continued*

Example Review

When you use the URL `http://localhost:8080/servlet/servletdemo.TimeForm`, the servlet TimeForm's `doGet` method is invoked to generate the time form dynamically. The method of the form is POST, and the action invokes the same servlet, `TimeForm`. When the form is submitted to the server, the `doPost` method is invoked to process the request.

The variables `allLocale` and `allTimeZone`, respectively, hold all available locales and time zone ids. The names of the locales are displayed in the locale list. The values for the locales are the indexes of the locales in the array `allLocale`. The time zone ids are strings. They are displayed in the time zone list. They are also the values for the list. The index of the locale and the time zone are passed to the servlet as parameters. The `doPost` method obtains the values of the parameters and finds the current time based on the locale and time zone.

14.8 Database Programming Using Servlets

Many dynamic Web applications use databases to store and manage data. Servlets can connect to any relational database via JDBC. In Part IV, "Java Database Programming," you learned how to create Java programs to access and manipulate relational databases via JDBC. Connecting a servlet to a database is no different from connecting a Java application or applet to a database. If you know Java servlets and

JDBC, you can combine them to develop interesting and practical Web-based interactive projects. The following example demonstrates how to connect to a database from a servlet.

Example 14.3 Registering a Student in a Database

This example creates a servlet that processes a registration form. The client enters data in an HTML form and submits it to the server, as shown in Figure 14.19. The result of the submission is shown in Figure 14.20. The server collects the data from the form and stores them in a database. The HTML file is shown in Listing 14.7, and the servlet is shown in Listing 14.8.

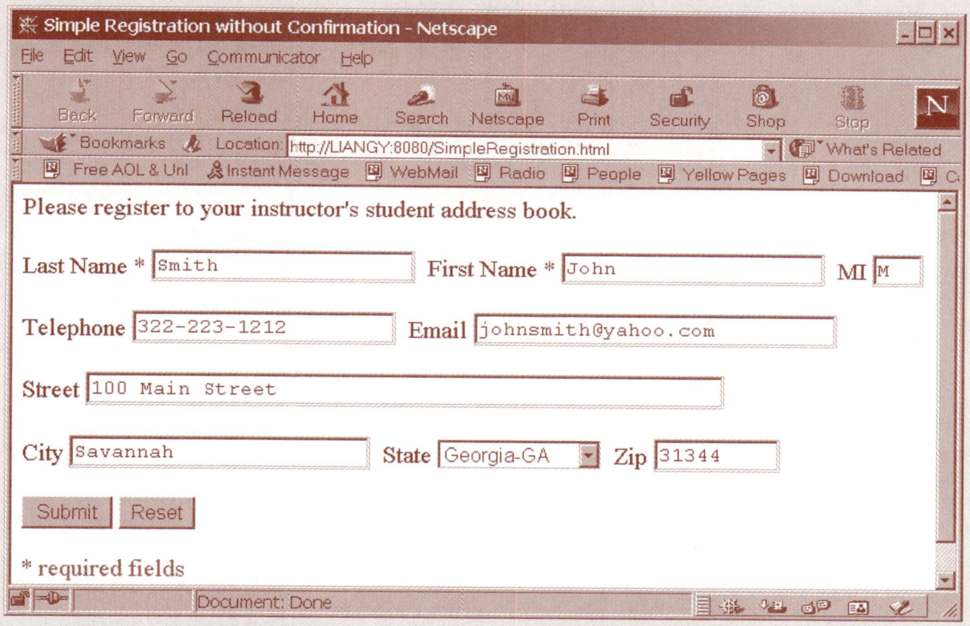

Figure 14.19 *The HTML form enables the user to enter student information.*

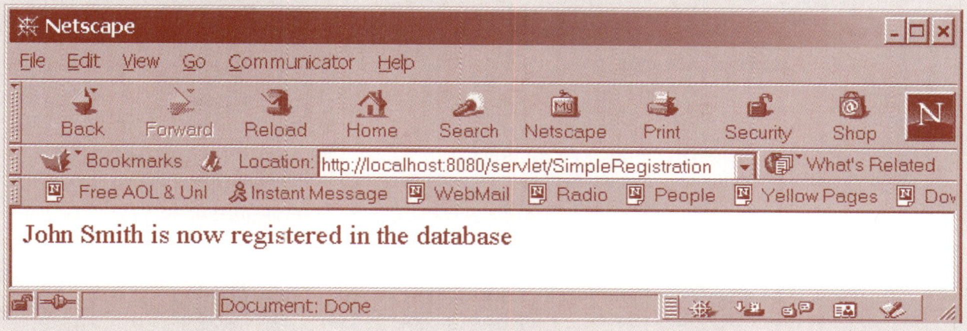

Figure 14.20 *The servlet processes the form and stores data in a database.*

continued

Example 14.3 continued

```
<html>
<head>
<title>Simple Registration without Confirmation</title>
</head>
<body>
Please register to your instructor's student address book.</font>

<form method="post" action=
  "/servlet/sevletdemo.SimpleRegistration">
<p>Last Name <font color="#FF0000">*</font>
    <input type="text" name="lastName"> 
   First Name <font color="#FF0000">*</font>
    <input type="text" name="firstName"> 
   MI <input type="text" name="mi" size="3"></p>
<p>Telephone <input type="text" name="telephone" size="20"> 
   Email <input type="text" name="email" size="28"> </p>
<p>Street <input type="text" name="street" size="50"></p>
<p>City <input type="text" name="city" size="23"> 
   State <select size="1" name="state">
          <option value="GA">Georgia-GA</option>
          <option value="OK">Oklahoma-OK</option>
          <option value="IN">Indiana-IN</option>
         </select> 
   Zip <input type="text" name="zip" size="9"></p>
<p><input type="submit" name="Submit" value="Submit">
   <input type="reset" value="Reset"></p>
</form>
<p><font color="#FF0000">* required fields</font></p>
</body>
</html>
```

Listing 14.7 *SimpleRegistration.shtml*

```
package servletdemo;

import javax.servlet.*;
import javax.servlet.http.*;
import java.io.*;
import java.sql.*;

public class SimpleRegistration extends HttpServlet {
  // Use a prepared statement to store a student into the database
  private PreparedStatement pstmt;

  /** Initialize global variables */
  public void init(ServletConfig config) throws ServletException {
    super.init(config);
    initializeJdbc();
  }

  /** Process the HTTP Post request */
  public void doPost(HttpServletRequest request, HttpServletResponse
    response) throws ServletException, IOException {
    response.setContentType("text/html");
    PrintWriter out = response.getWriter();

    // Obtain parameters from the client
    String lastName = request.getParameter("lastName");
    String firstName = request.getParameter("firstName");
```

Listing 14.8 *SimpleRegistration.java*

```
      String mi = request.getParameter("mi");
      String phone = request.getParameter("telephone");
      String email = request.getParameter("email");
      String address = request.getParameter("street");
      String city = request.getParameter("city");
      String state = request.getParameter("state");
      String zip = request.getParameter("zip");

      if (lastName.length() == 0 || firstName.length() == 0) {
        out.println("Last Name and First Name are required");
        return; // End the method
      }

      try {
        storeStudent(lastName, firstName, mi, phone, email, address,
          city, state, zip);

        out.println(firstName + " " + lastName +
          " is now registered in the database");

        out.close(); // Close stream
      }
      catch(Exception ex) {
        out.println("Error: " + ex.getMessage());
        return; // End the method
      }
    }

    /** Initialize database connection */
    private void initializeJdbc() {
      try {
        // Declare driver and connection string
        String driver = "sun.jdbc.odbc.JdbcOdbcDriver";
        String connectionString = "jdbc:odbc:LiangBookDB_MDB";
        /* For Oracle
        String driver = "oracle.jdbc.driver.OracleDriver";
        String connectionString =
        "jdbc:oracle:thin:scott/tiger@liang.armstrong.edu:1521:oracle";
        */
        // Load the Oracle JDBC Thin driver
        Class.forName(driver);

        // Connect to the sample database
        Connection conn = DriverManager.getConnection
          (connectionString);

        // Create a Statement
        pstmt = conn.prepareStatement("insert into Address " +
          "(lastName, firstName, mi, telephone, email, street, city, "
           + "state, zip) values (?, ?, ?, ?, ?, ?, ?, ?, ?)");
      }
      catch (Exception ex) {
        System.out.println(ex);
      }
    }

    /** Store a student record to the database */
    private void storeStudent(String lastName, String firstName,
      String mi, String phone, String email, String address,
      String city, String state, String zip) throws SQLException {
```

Listing 14.8 *continued*

continued

Example 14.3 continued

```
        pstmt.setString(1, lastName);
        pstmt.setString(2, firstName);
        pstmt.setString(3, mi);
        pstmt.setString(4, phone);
        pstmt.setString(5, email);
        pstmt.setString(6, address);
        pstmt.setString(7, city);
        pstmt.setString(8, state);
        pstmt.setString(9, zip);
        pstmt.executeUpdate();
      }
    }
```

Listing 14.8 *continued*

Example Review

The `init` method is executed once the servlet starts. After the servlet has started, the servlet can be invoked many times as long as it is alive in the servlet container. Load the driver, and connect to the database from the servlet's `init` method. If a prepared statement or a callable statement is used, it should also be created in the `init` method. In this example, a prepared statement is desirable, because the servlet always uses the same insert statement with different values.

A servlet can connect to any relational database via JDBC. The `initializeJdbc` method in this example loads a JDBC-ODBC bridge driver. Use of the Oracle Thin driver is commented in the code. Once connected, it creates a prepared statement for inserting a student record into the database. The Access database and the Oracle database are the same as were used in Part IV, "Java Database Programming." To use the MS Access database, the ODBC data source LiangBookDB_MDB must be created. Please refer to Chapter 12, "Introduction to Java Database Programming," to create an ODBC data source. To use Oracle database, you must have the Oracle JDBC Thin driver in the library of the project.

Last name and first name are required fields. If either of them is empty, the servlet sends an error message to the client. Otherwise, the servlet stores the data in the database using the prepared statement.

NOTE

If a parameter `param` is not passed to the servlet, the `request.getParameter(param)` method returns `null`. If an empty value of the parameter is passed to the servlet, the `request.getParameter(param)` method returns a string with empty value. In this case, the length of the string is 0.

NOTE

The example uses the JDBC-ODBC driver to access MS Access database. If you use an Oracle database, you need to add the Oracle driver to the Tomcat server classpath in the External Execution Process field. To do so, in the

Runtime tab of the Explorer, expand *Server Registry, Installed Servers, Tomcat 4.0*, and choose Properties in the context menu of the *Internal* node to display the Properties of Internal dialog box. Insert `;e:\oracle9i\jdbc\lib\classes12.jar` (the Oracle driver on my machine) after `{tomcat_filesystems}` in the External Execution Process field, as shown in Figure 14.21.

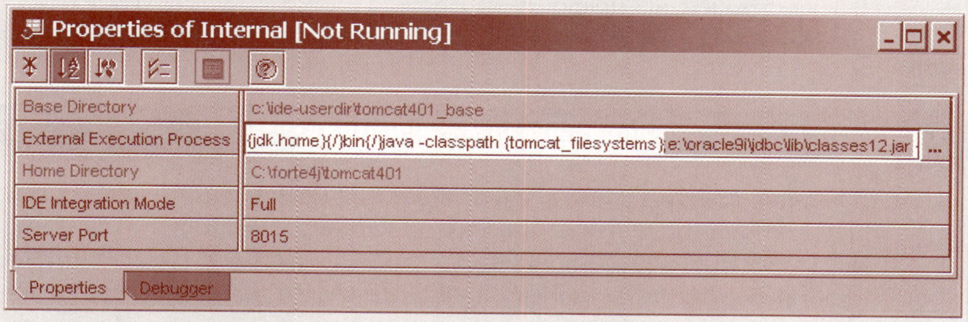

Figure 14.21 *Configuring Oracle driver in the External Execution Process is necessary for Tomcat server to locate the JDBC driver at runtime.*

14.9 Session Tracking

Web servers use Hyper-Text Transport Protocol (HTTP). HTTP is a stateless protocol. An HTTP Web server cannot associate requests from a client, and therefore treats each request independently. This protocol works fine for simple Web browsing, where each request typically results in an HTML file or a text file being sent back to the client. Such simple requests are isolated. However, the requests in interactive Web applications are often related. Consider the two requests in the following scenario:

Request 1: A client sends registration data to the server; the server then returns the data to the user for confirmation.

Request 2: The client confirms the data by resubmitting them.

In Request 2, the data submitted in Request 1 were sent back to the server. These two requests are related in a session. A *session* can be defined as a series of related interactions between a single client and a Web server over a period of time. Tracking data among requests in a session is known as *session tracking*.

This section introduces three techniques for session tracking: *using hidden values, using cookies*, and *using the session tracking tools from servlet API.*

14.9.1 Session Tracking Using Hidden Values

You can track a session by passing data from the servlet to the client as hidden value in a dynamically generated HTML form by including a field like the one shown below:

```
<input type="hidden" name="lastName" value="Smith">
```

The next request will submit the data back to the servlet. The servlet retrieves this hidden value just like any other parameter value using the `getParameter` method.

Example 14.4 Using Hidden Values in the Registration Form

This example creates a servlet that processes a registration form. The client submits the form using the GET method, as shown in Figure 14.19. The server collects the data in the form, displays them to the client, and asks the client for confirmation, as shown in Figure 14.22. The client confirms the data by submitting the request with the hidden values using the POST method. Finally, the servlet writes the data to a database.

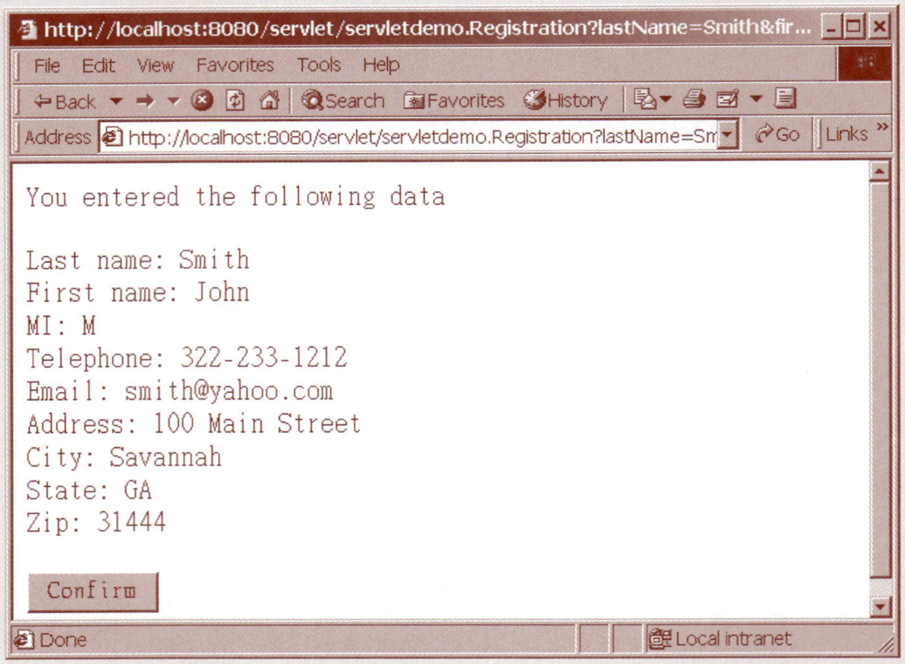

Figure 14.22 *The servlet asks the client for confirmation of the input.*

The HTML file is shown in Listing 14.9, which is the same as Listing 14.7, except that the method for the request is GET and the servlet program is named Registration. The servlet program is shown in Listing 14.10.

```
<html>
<head>
<title>Registration Using Hidden Data for Session Tracking</title>
</head>
<body>
Please register to your instructor's student address book.</font>

<form method="get"
  action="/servlet/servletdemo.Registration">
<p>Last Name <font color="#FF0000">*</font>
    <input type="text" name="lastName"> 
   First Name <font color="#FF0000">*</font>
    <input type="text" name="firstName"> 
   MI <input type="text" name="mi" size="3"></p>
<p>Telephone <input type="text" name="telephone" size="20"> 
   Email <input type="text" name="email" size="28"> </p>
<p>Street <input type="text" name="street" size="50"></p>
<p>City <input type="text" name="city" size="23"> 
   State <select size="1" name="state">
          <option value="GA">Georgia-GA</option>
          <option value="OK">Oklahoma-OK</option>
          <option value="IN">Indiana-IN</option>
         </select> 
   Zip <input type="text" name="zip" size="9"></p>
<p><input type="submit" name="Submit" value="Submit">
   <input type="reset" value="Reset"></p>
</form>
<p><font color="#FF0000">* required fields</font></p>
</body>
</html>
```

Listing 14.9 *Registration.shtml*

```
package servletdemo;

import javax.servlet.*;
import javax.servlet.http.*;
import java.io.*;
import java.sql.*;

public class Registration extends HttpServlet {
  // Use a prepared statement to store a student into the database
  private PreparedStatement pstmt;

  /** Initialize global variables */
  public void init(ServletConfig config) throws ServletException {
    super.init(config);
    initializeJdbc();
  }

  /** Process the HTTP Get request */
  public void doGet(HttpServletRequest request, HttpServletResponse
    response) throws ServletException, IOException {
    response.setContentType("text/html");
    PrintWriter out = response.getWriter();

    // Obtain data from the form
    String lastName = request.getParameter("lastName");
    String firstName = request.getParameter("firstName");
```

Listing 14.10 *Registration.java*

continued

Example 14.4 continued

```
      String mi = request.getParameter("mi");
      String telephone = request.getParameter("telephone");
      String email = request.getParameter("email");
      String street = request.getParameter("street");
      String city = request.getParameter("city");
      String state = request.getParameter("state");
      String zip = request.getParameter("zip");

      if (lastName.length() == 0 || firstName.length() == 0) {
        out.println("Last Name and First Name are required");
        return; // End the method
      }

      // Ask for confirmation
      out.println("You entered the following data");
      out.println("<p>Last name: " + lastName);
      out.println("<br>First name: " + firstName);
      out.println("<br>MI: " + mi);
      out.println("<br>Telephone: " + telephone);
      out.println("<br>Email: " + email);
      out.println("<br>Address: " + street);
      out.println("<br>City: " + city);
      out.println("<br>State: " + state);
      out.println("<br>Zip: " + zip);

      // Set the action for processing the answers
      out.println("<p><form method=\"post\" " +
        "action=servletdemo.Registration>");
      // Set hidden values
      out.println("<p><input type=\"hidden\" " +
        "value=" + lastName + " name=\"lastName\">");
      out.println("<p><input type=\"hidden\" " +
        "value=" + firstName + " name=\"firstName\">");
      out.println("<p><input type=\"hidden\" " +
        "value=" + mi + " name=\"mi\">");
      out.println("<p><input type=\"hidden\" " +
        "value=" + telephone + " name=\"telephone\">");
      out.println("<p><input type=\"hidden\" " +
        "value=" + email + " name=\"email\">");
      out.println("<p><input type=\"hidden\" " +
        "value=" + street + " name=\"street\">");
      out.println("<p><input type=\"hidden\" " +
        "value=" + city + " name=\"city\">");
      out.println("<p><input type=\"hidden\" " +
        "value=" + state + " name=\"state\">");
      out.println("<p><input type=\"hidden\" " +
        "value=" + zip + " name=\"zip\">");
      out.println("<p><input type=\"submit\"" +
        " value=\"Confirm\" name=\"B1\">");
      out.println("</form>");
    }

    /** Process the HTTP Post request */
    public void doPost(HttpServletRequest request, HttpServletResponse
      response) throws ServletException, IOException {
      response.setContentType("text/html");
      PrintWriter out = response.getWriter();

```

Listing 14.10 *continued*

```
    try {
      String lastName = request.getParameter("lastName");
      String firstName = request.getParameter("firstName");
      String mi = request.getParameter("mi");
      String telephone = request.getParameter("telephone");
      String email = request.getParameter("email");
      String street = request.getParameter("street");
      String city = request.getParameter("city");
      String state = request.getParameter("state");
      String zip = request.getParameter("zip");

      storeStudent(lastName, firstName, mi, telephone, email,
        street, city, state, zip);

      out.println(firstName + " " + lastName +
        " is now registered in the database");
    }
    catch(Exception ex) {
      out.println("Error: " + ex.getMessage());
      return; // End the method
    }
  }

  /** Initialize database connection */
  private void initializeJdbc() {
    try {
      // Declare driver and connection string
      String driver = "sun.jdbc.odbc.JdbcOdbcDriver";
      String connectionString = "jdbc:odbc:LiangBookDB_MDB";
      /* For Oracle
      String driver = "oracle.jdbc.driver.OracleDriver";
      String connectionString =
      "jdbc:oracle:thin:scott/tiger@liang.armstrong.edu:1521:oracle";
      */
      // Load the Oracle JDBC Thin driver
      Class.forName(driver);

      // Connect to the sample database
      Connection conn = DriverManager.getConnection
        (connectionString);

      // Create a Statement
      pstmt = conn.prepareStatement("insert into Address " +
        "(lastName, firstName, mi, telephone, email, street, city, "
        + "state, zip) values (?, ?, ?, ?, ?, ?, ?, ?, ?)");

    }
    catch (Exception ex) {
      System.out.println(ex);
    }
  }

  /** Store a student record to the database */
  private void storeStudent(String lastName, String firstName,
    String mi, String phone, String email, String address,
    String city, String state, String zip) throws SQLException {
    pstmt.setString(1, lastName);
    pstmt.setString(2, firstName);
    pstmt.setString(3, mi);
    pstmt.setString(4, phone);
```

Listing 14.10 *continued*

continued

Example 14.4 continued

```
        pstmt.setString(5, email);
        pstmt.setString(6, address);
        pstmt.setString(7, city);
        pstmt.setString(8, state);
        pstmt.setString(9, zip);
        pstmt.executeUpdate();
      }
    }
```

Listing 14.10 *continued*

Example Review

The servlet processes the GET request by generating an HTML page that displays the client's input and asks for the client's confirmation. The input data are hidden values in the newly generated forms. So the data will be sent back in the confirmation request. The confirmation request uses the POST method. The servlet retrieves the hidden values and stores them in the database.

Since the first request does not write anything to the database, it is appropriate to use the GET method. Since the second request results in an update to the database, the POST method must be used.

NOTE
The hidden values could also be sent from the URL query string if the next request uses the GET method.

14.9.2 Session Tracking Using Cookies

You can track sessions using cookies, which are small text files that store sets of name-value pairs on the disk in the client's computer. Cookies are sent from the server through the instructions in the header of the HTTP response. The instructions tell the browser to create a cookie with a given name and its associated value. If the browser already has a cookie with the key name, the value will be updated. The browser will then send the cookie with any request submitted to the same server. Cookies can have expiration dates set, after which they will not be sent to the server.

To create a cookie in the servlet, use the following constructor:

```
public Cookie(String name, String value)
```

The frequently used methods in the `Cookie` class are listed below:

- `public String getName()`

  Returns the name of the cookie.

- `public void setMaxAge(int expiry)`

  Specifies an integer that specifies how long (in seconds) the cookie will persist. By default, this value is –1, which implies that the cookie persists until the browser exits. If you set this value to 0, the cookie is deleted. Use `getMaxAge` to obtain this value.

- `public void setValue(String newValue)`

  Assigns a new value in the cookie after the cookie is created. Use `getValue` to obtain this value.

- `public void setDomain(String pattern)`

  Sets the Internet domain, such as prenhall.com. By default, the cookie is sent to the server that originally created it. Use `getDomain` to obtain the domain.

- `public void setSecure(boolean flag)`

  Sets `true` if a secure protocol should be used for the cookie. Use `getSecure` to obtain this value.

- `public void setPath(String uri)`

  Specifies a target directory under which the servlet can receive the cookie. Use `getPath` to obtain the path.

- `public void setComment(String purpose)`

  Sets a comment to describe the cookie. Use `getComment` to obtain the comment.

- `public void setVersion(int v)`

  Sets the version of the cookie protocol that this cookie complies with. Version 0 complies with the original Netscape cookie. Use `getVersion` to obtain the version.

To send a cookie to the browser, use the `addCookie` method in the `HTTPServletResponse` class, as shown below:

```
response.addCookie(cookie);
```

where `response` is an instance of `HTTPServletResponse`.

Example 14.5 Using Cookies in the Registration Form

This example accomplishes the same task as Example 14.4. Instead of using hidden values for session tracking, it uses cookies. The new HTML file named RegistrationWithCookie.shtml can be found in the companion CD-ROM; it is the same as the one in Listing 14.9, except that the servlet is named RegistrationWithCookie. The servlet is shown in Listing 14.11.

```
package servletdemo;

import javax.servlet.*;
import javax.servlet.http.*;
```

Listing 14.11 *RegistrationWithCookie.java*

continued

Example 14.5 continued

```
import java.io.*;
import java.sql.*;

public class RegistrationWithCookie extends HttpServlet {
  private static final String CONTENT_TYPE = "text/html";
  // Use a prepared statement to store a student into the database
  private PreparedStatement pstmt;

  /** Initialize global variables */
  public void init(ServletConfig config) throws ServletException {
    super.init(config);
    initializeJdbc();
  }

  /** Process the HTTP Get request */
  public void doGet(HttpServletRequest request, HttpServletResponse
    response) throws ServletException, IOException {
    response.setContentType("text/html");
    PrintWriter out = response.getWriter();

    // Obtain data from the form
    String lastName = request.getParameter("lastName");
    String firstName = request.getParameter("firstName");
    String mi = request.getParameter("mi");
    String telephone = request.getParameter("telephone");
    String email = request.getParameter("email");
    String street = request.getParameter("street");
    String city = request.getParameter("city");
    String state = request.getParameter("state");
    String zip = request.getParameter("zip");

    // Create cookies and send cookies to browsers
    Cookie cookieLastName = new Cookie("lastName", lastName);
    // cookieLastName.setMaxAge(1000);
    response.addCookie(cookieLastName);
    Cookie cookieFirstName = new Cookie("firstName", firstName);
    response.addCookie(cookieFirstName);
    // cookieFirstName.setMaxAge(0);
    Cookie cookieMi = new Cookie("mi", mi);
    response.addCookie(cookieMi);
    Cookie cookieTelephone = new Cookie("telephone", telephone);
    response.addCookie(cookieTelephone);
    Cookie cookieEmail = new Cookie("email", email);
    response.addCookie(cookieEmail);
    Cookie cookieStreet = new Cookie("street", street);
    response.addCookie(cookieStreet);
    Cookie cookieCity = new Cookie("city", city);
    response.addCookie(cookieCity);
    Cookie cookieState = new Cookie("state", state);
    response.addCookie(cookieState);
    Cookie cookieZip = new Cookie("zip", zip);
    response.addCookie(cookieZip);

    System.out.println("MaxAge? " + cookieLastName.getMaxAge());
    System.out.println("MaxAge fir? " + cookieFirstName.getMaxAge());

    if (lastName.length() == 0 || firstName.length() == 0) {
      out.println("Last Name and First Name are required");
```

Listing 14.11 *continued*

```
        return; // End the method
      }

      // Ask for confirmation
      out.println("You entered the following data");
      out.println("<p>Last name: " + lastName);
      out.println("<br>First name: " + firstName);
      out.println("<br>MI: " + mi);
      out.println("<br>Telephone: " + telephone);
      out.println("<br>Email: " + email);
      out.println("<br>Street: " + street);
      out.println("<br>City: " + city);
      out.println("<br>State: " + state);
      out.println("<br>Zip: " + zip);

      // Set the action for processing the answers
      out.println("<p><form method=\"post\" action=" +
        "servletdemo.RegistrationWithCookie>");
      out.println("<p><input type=\"submit\"" +
        " value=\"Confirm\" name=\"B1\">");
      out.println("</form>");
      out.close(); // Close stream
    }

    /** Process the HTTP Post request */
    public void doPost(HttpServletRequest request, HttpServletResponse
      response) throws ServletException, IOException {
      response.setContentType(CONTENT_TYPE);
      PrintWriter out = response.getWriter();

      String lastName = "";
      String firstName = "";
      String mi = "";
      String telephone = "";
      String email = "";
      String street = "";
      String city = "";
      String state = "";
      String zip = "";

      // Read the cookies
      Cookie[] cookies = request.getCookies();

      // Get cookie values
      for (int i = 0; i < cookies.length; i++) {
        if (cookies[i].getName().equals("lastName"))
          lastName = cookies[i].getValue();
        else if (cookies[i].getName().equals("firstName"))
          firstName = cookies[i].getValue();
        else if (cookies[i].getName().equals("mi"))
          mi = cookies[i].getValue();
        else if (cookies[i].getName().equals("telephone"))
          telephone = cookies[i].getValue();
        else if (cookies[i].getName().equals("email"))
          email = cookies[i].getValue();
        else if (cookies[i].getName().equals("street"))
          street = cookies[i].getValue();
        else if (cookies[i].getName().equals("city"))
          city = cookies[i].getValue();
```

Listing 14.11 *continued*

continued

Example 14.5 continued

```
      else if (cookies[i].getName().equals("state"))
        state = cookies[i].getValue();
      else if (cookies[i].getName().equals("zip"))
        zip = cookies[i].getValue();
    }

    try {
      storeStudent(lastName, firstName, mi, telephone, email, street,
        city, state, zip);

      out.println(firstName + " " + lastName +
        " is now registered in the database");

      out.close(); // Close stream
    }
    catch(Exception ex) {
      out.println("Error: " + ex.getMessage());
      return; // End the method
    }
  }

  /** Initialize database connection */
  private void initializeJdbc() {
    try {
      // Declare driver and connection string
      String driver = "sun.jdbc.odbc.JdbcOdbcDriver";
      String connectionString = "jdbc:odbc:LiangBookDB_MDB";
      // For Oracle
      // String driver = "oracle.jdbc.driver.OracleDriver";
      // String connectionString = "jdbc:oracle:thin:scott/
      //   tiger@liang.armstrong.edu:1521:oracle";

      // Load the Oracle JDBC Thin driver
      Class.forName(driver);
      System.out.println("Driver " + driver + " loaded");

      // Connect to the sample database
      Connection conn = DriverManager.getConnection
        (connectionString);
      System.out.println("Database " + connectionString +
        " connected");

      // Create a Statement
      pstmt = conn.prepareStatement("insert into Address " +
        "(lastName, firstName, mi, telephone, email, street, city, "
        + "state, zip) values (?, ?, ?, ?, ?, ?, ?, ?, ?)");
    }
    catch (Exception ex) {
      System.out.println(ex);
    }
  }

  /** Store a student record to the database */
  private void storeStudent(String lastName, String firstName,
    String mi, String telephone, String email, String street,
    String city, String state, String zip) throws SQLException {
    pstmt.setString(1, lastName);
    pstmt.setString(2, firstName);
    pstmt.setString(3, mi);
```

Listing 14.11 *continued*

```
181          pstmt.setString(4, telephone);
182          pstmt.setString(5, email);
183          pstmt.setString(6, street);
184          pstmt.setString(7, city);
185          pstmt.setString(8, state);
186          pstmt.setString(9, zip);
187          pstmt.executeUpdate();
188      }
189    }
```

Listing 14.11 *continued*

Example Review

You have to create a cookie for each value you want to track, using the `Cookie` class's only constructor, which defines a cookie's name and value, as shown below (Line 37):

```
Cookie cookieLastName = new Cookie("lastName", lastName);
```

To send the cookie to the browser, use a statement like this one (Line 39):

```
response.addCookie(cookieLastName);
```

If a cookie with the same name already exists in the browser, its value is updated; otherwise, a new cookie is created.

Cookies are automatically sent to the Web server with each request from the client. The servlet retrieves all the cookies into an array using the `getCookies` method (Line 104).

```
Cookie[] cookies = request.getCookies();
```

To obtain the name of the cookie, use the `getName` method (Line 108):

```
String name = cookies[i].getName();
```

The cookie's value can be obtained using the `getValue` method (Line 109):

```
String value = cookies[i].getValue();
```

Cookies are stored as strings just like form parameters and hidden values. If a cookie represents a numeric value, you have to convert it into an integer or a double, using the `parseInt` method in the `Integer` class or the `parseDouble` method in the `Double` class.

By default, a newly created cookie persists until the browser exits. However, you can set the expiration date, using the `setMaxAge` method, to allow a cookie to stay in the browser for up to 2,147,483,647 seconds (approximately 24,855 days).

14.9.3 Session Tracking Using the Servlet API

You have now learned both session tracking using hidden values and session tracking using cookies. These two session-tracking methods have problems. They send data to the browser either as hidden values or as cookies. The data are not secure, and anybody with knowledge of computers can obtain them. The hidden data are in HTML form, which can be viewed from the browser. Cookies are stored in the Cache directory of the browser. Because of security concerns, some browsers do not accept cookies. The client can turn the cookies off and limit their number. Another problem is that hidden data and cookies pass data as strings. You cannot pass objects using these two methods. To address these problems, Java servlet API provides a session-tracking tool that enables tracking of a large set of data. The data can be stored as objects and are secure because they are kept on the server side.

To use the Java servlet API for session tracking, first create a session object using the `getSession` method in the `HttpServletRequest` interface:

```
HttpSession session = request.getSession(true);
```

This obtains the session or creates a new session if the client does not have a session on the server.

The `HttpSession` class provides the following methods for reading and storing data to the session, and for manipulating the session:

- `public Object getAttribute(String name)`

  Returns the object bound with the specified name in this session, or `null` if no object is bound under the name.

- `public void setAttribute(String name, Object value)`

  Binds an object to this session, using the specified name. If an object of the same name is already bound to the session, the object is replaced.

- `public String getId()`

  Returns a string containing the unique identifier assigned to this session. The identifier is assigned by the servlet container and is implementation-dependent.

- `public long getLastAccessedTime()`

  Returns the last time the client sent a request associated with this session as the number of milliseconds since midnight January 1, 1970 GMT.

- `public void invalidate()`

  Invalidates this session.

- `public boolean isNew()`

  Returns true if the session was just created in the current request.

- `public void removeAttribute(String name)`

  Removes the object bound with the specified name from this session. If the session does not have an object bound with the specified name, this method does nothing.

- `public void setMaxInactiveInterval(int interval)`

  Specifies the time, in seconds, between client requests before the servlet container will invalidate this session. A negative time indicates that the session will never time-out. Use `getMaxInactiveInterval` to retrieve this value.

NOTE

HTTP is stateless. So how does the server associate a session with multiple requests from the same client? This is handled behind the scenes by the servlet container and is transparent to the servlet programmer.

Example 14.6 Using `HttpSession` in the Registration form

This example accomplishes the same task as Examples 14.4 and 14.5. Instead of using hidden values or cookies for session tracking, it uses servlet HttpSession. The new HTML file, named RegistrationWithHttpSession.shtml, can be found in the companion CD-ROM; it is the same as the one in Listing 14.9, except that the servlet is named RegistrationWithHttpSession. The servlet is shown in Listing 14.12.

```
package servletdemo;

import javax.servlet.*;
import javax.servlet.http.*;
import java.io.*;
import java.sql.*;
import java.util.*;

public class RegistrationWithHttpSession extends HttpServlet {
  // Use a prepared statement to store a student into the database
  private PreparedStatement pstmt;

  /** Initialize global variables */
  public void init(ServletConfig config) throws ServletException {
    super.init(config);
    initializeJdbc();
  }

  /** Process the HTTP Get request */
  public void doGet(HttpServletRequest request, HttpServletResponse
    response) throws ServletException, IOException {
    // Set response type and output stream to the browser
    response.setContentType("text/html");
    PrintWriter out = response.getWriter();

    // Obtain data from the form
    String lastName = request.getParameter("lastName");
    String firstName = request.getParameter("firstName");
    String mi = request.getParameter("mi");
    String telephone = request.getParameter("telephone");
    String email = request.getParameter("email");
    String street = request.getParameter("street");
    String city = request.getParameter("city");
```

Listing 14.12 *RegistrationWithHttpSession.java*

continued

Example 14.6 continued

```
    String state = request.getParameter("state");
    String zip = request.getParameter("zip");

    if (lastName.length() == 0 || firstName.length() == 0) {
      out.println("Last Name and First Name are required");
      return; // End the method
    }

    // Create a Student object
    Student student = new Student(lastName, firstName,
      mi, telephone, email, street, city, state, zip);

    // Get an HttpSession or create one if it does not exist
    HttpSession httpSession = request.getSession(true);

    // Store student object to the session
    httpSession.setAttribute("student", student);

    // Ask for confirmation
    out.println("You entered the following data");
    out.println("<p>Last name: " + lastName);
    out.println("<p>First name: " + firstName);
    out.println("<p>MI: " + mi);
    out.println("<p>Telephone: " + telephone);
    out.println("<p>Email: " + email);
    out.println("<p>Address: " + street);
    out.println("<p>City: " + city);
    out.println("<p>State: " + state);
    out.println("<p>Zip: " + zip);

    // Set the action for processing the answers
    out.println("<p><form method=\"post\" action=" +
      "servletdemo.RegistrationWithHttpSession>");
    out.println("<p><input type=\"submit\"" +
      " value=\"Confirm\" name=\"B1\">");
    out.println("</form>");

    out.close(); // Close stream
  }

  /** Process the HTTP Post request */
  public void doPost(HttpServletRequest request, HttpServletResponse
    response) throws ServletException, IOException {
    // Set response type and output stream to the browser
    response.setContentType("text/html");
    PrintWriter out = response.getWriter();

    // Obtain the HttpSession
    HttpSession httpSession = request.getSession(true);

    // Get the Student object in the HttpSession
    Student student = (Student)(httpSession.getAttribute("student"));

    try {
      storeStudent(student);

      out.println(student.firstName + " " + student.lastName +
        " is now registered in the database");
      out.close(); // Close stream
    }
```

Listing 14.12 *continued*

```
      catch(Exception ex) {
        out.println("Error: " + ex.getMessage());
        return; // End the method
      }
    }

    /** Initialize database connection */
    private void initializeJdbc() {
      try {
        // Declare driver and connection string
        String driver = "sun.jdbc.odbc.JdbcOdbcDriver";
        String connectionString = "jdbc:odbc:LiangBookDB_MDB";

        // Load the Oracle JDBC Thin driver
        Class.forName(driver);
        System.out.println("Driver " + driver + " loaded");

        // Connect to the sample database
        Connection conn = DriverManager.getConnection
          (connectionString);
        System.out.println("Database " + connectionString +
          " connected");

        // Create a Statement
        pstmt = conn.prepareStatement("insert into Address " +
          "(lastName, firstName, mi, telephone, email, street, city, "
          + "state, zip) values (?, ?, ?, ?, ?, ?, ?, ?, ?)");
      }
      catch (Exception ex) {
        System.out.println(ex);
      }
    }

    /** Store a student record to the database */
    private void storeStudent(Student student) throws SQLException {
      pstmt.setString(1, student.getLastName());
      pstmt.setString(2, student.getFirstName());
      pstmt.setString(3, student.getMi());
      pstmt.setString(4, student.getTelephone());
      pstmt.setString(5, student.getEmail());
      pstmt.setString(6, student.getAddress());
      pstmt.setString(7, student.getCity());
      pstmt.setString(8, student.getState());
      pstmt.setString(9, student.getZip());
      pstmt.executeUpdate();
    }

    class Student {
      private String lastName = "";
      private String firstName = "";
      private String mi = "";
      private String telephone = "";
      private String email = "";
      private String street = "";
      private String city = "";
      private String state = "";
      private String zip = "";

      Student(String lastName, String firstName,
        String mi, String telephone, String email, String street,
```

Listing 14.12 *continued*

continued

Example 14.6 continued

```
154        String city, String state, String zip) {
155        this.lastName = lastName;
156        this.firstName = firstName;
157        this.mi = mi;
158        this.telephone = telephone;
159        this.email = email;
160        this.street = street;
161        this.city = city;
162        this.state = state;
163        this.zip = zip;
164      }
165
166      public String getLastName() {
167        return lastName;
168      }
169
170      public String getFirstName() {
171        return firstName;
172      }
173
174      public String getMi() {
175        return mi;
176      }
177
178      public String getTelephone() {
179        return telephone;
180      }
181
182      public String getEmail() {
183        return email;
184      }
185
186      public String getAddress() {
187        return street;
188      }
189
190      public String getCity() {
191        return city;
192      }
193
194      public String getState() {
195        return state;
196      }
197
198      public String getZip() {
199        return zip;
200      }
201    }
202  }
```

Listing 14.12 *continued*

Example Review

The statement (Line 47)

```
HttpSession httpSession = request.getSession(true);
```

obtains a session, or creates a new session if the session does not exist.

Since objects can be stored in `HttpSession`, this program defines a `Student` class (Lines 141–201). A `Student` object is created and is stored in the session using the `setAttribute` method, which binds the object with a name like the one shown below (Line 50):

```
httpSession.setAttribute("student", student);
```

To retrieve the object, use the following statement (Line 85):

```
Student student =  (Student)(httpSession.getAttribute("student"));
```

There is only one session between a client and a servlet. You can store any number of objects in a session. By default, a session stays alive as long as the servlet is not destroyed. You can explicitly set the session active time using the `setMaxInactiveInterval` method.

14.10 Sending Images from Servlets

So far you have learned how to write Java servlets that generate dynamic HTML text. Java servlets are not limited to sending text to a browser. They can return images in GIF, JPEG, or PNG format. This section demonstrates how to return images in GIF format.

To send contents as a GIF image, the content type must be set to image/gif, as below:

```
response.setContentType("image/gif");
```

In the preceding examples, you used a `PrintWriter` object to return HTML text. Since images are binary data, you have to use a binary output stream:

```
OutputStream out = response.getOutputStream();
```

You can then create an instance of the `Image` class filled with content. Before the image is sent to a browser, it must be encoded into a format acceptable to the browser. Image encoders are not part of Java API, but several free encoders are available. One of them is the `GifEncoder` class from Acme (**http://www.acme.com/java/software/Acme.JPM.Encoders.GifEncoder.html**), which is included in the book's CD-ROM in \radft\acme.zip.

Use the following statement to encode and send the image to the browser:

```
new GifEncoder(image, out, true).encode();
```

Example 14.7 Getting Images from Servlets

This example creates a servlet that dynamically generates the flag of a country, as shown in Figure 14.23. The servlet is given in Listing 14.13.

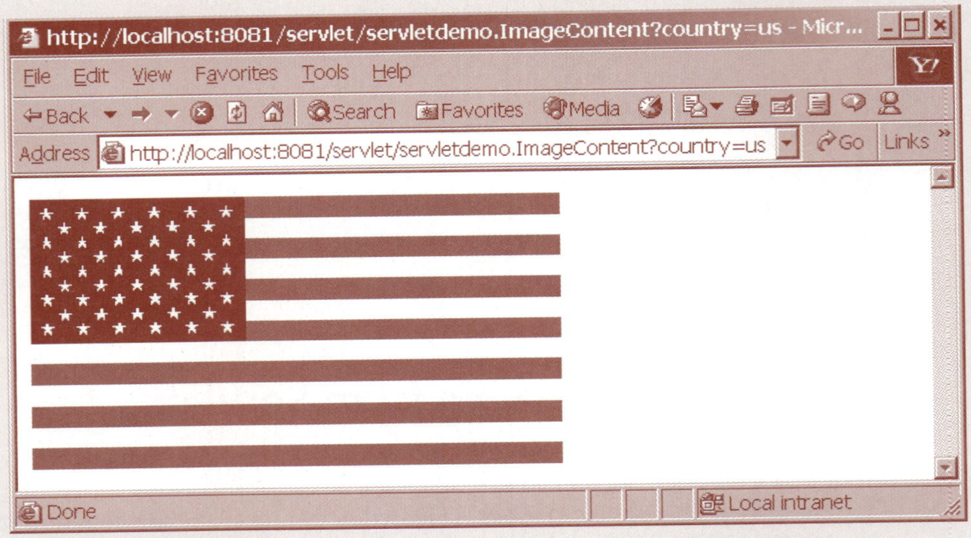

Figure 14.23 *The servlet returns an image of the country flag.*

```
package servletdemo;

import javax.servlet.*;
import javax.servlet.http.*;
import java.io.*;
import java.util.*;
import java.awt.Image;
import javax.swing.ImageIcon;
import Acme.JPM.Encoders.GifEncoder;

public class ImageContent extends HttpServlet {
  /** Process the HTTP Get request */
  public void doGet(HttpServletRequest request, HttpServletResponse
    response) throws ServletException, IOException {
    response.setContentType("image/gif");
    OutputStream out = response.getOutputStream();

    // Obtain an image icon
    ImageIcon imageIcon = new ImageIcon("c:\\radft\\image\\" +
      request.getParameter("country") + ".gif");

    // Obtain image from image icon
    Image image = imageIcon.getImage(); // Get the image

    // Encode the image and send to the output stream
    new GifEncoder(image, out, true).encode();

    out.close(); // Close stream
  }
}
```

Listing 14.13 *ImageContent.java*

Example Review

Before you start the Tomcat server from Forte, make sure that acme.zip is mounted in the Explorer to enable ImageContent.java to be compiled. To mount it, choose *Mount JAR* from the context menu of the *FileSystems* node to display the Mount JAR File dialog box and mount acme.zip. You also need to add c:\radft\acme.zip in the External Execution Process field as shown in Figure 14.21.

The content type of the response is image/gif, and the output stream is binary. The image is sent to the browser as binary data. The `GifEncoder` class is used to encode the image into content understood by the browser. The content is sent to the `OutputStream` object `out`.

You need to test this servlet from a browser using the URL **`http://localhost:8080/servlet/ImageContent?country=ca`**.

14.10.1 Creating Images from Drawings

The preceding example creates an image from a GIF file. You can also create an image from a drawing and send it to the browser, as is demonstrated in the next example.

Example 14.8 Creating Images by Drawing

This example creates a servlet that displays a clock to show the current time, as shown in Figure 14.24. The servlet is given in Listing 14.14.

```
package servletdemo;

import javax.servlet.*;
import javax.servlet.http.*;
import java.io.*;
import java.util.*;
import java.text.*;
import java.awt.*;
import java.awt.image.BufferedImage;
import javax.swing.*;
import Acme.JPM.Encoders.GifEncoder;

public class ImageContentWithDrawing extends HttpServlet {
  /** Initialize global variables */
  private final static int width = 300;
  private final static int height = 300;

  /** Process the HTTP Get request */
  public void doGet(HttpServletRequest request, HttpServletResponse
    response) throws ServletException, IOException {
    response.setContentType("image/gif");
    OutputStream out = response.getOutputStream();

```

Listing 14.14 *ImageContentWithDrawing.java*

continued

Example 14.8 continued

```
      // Create image
      Image image = new BufferedImage(width, height,
        BufferedImage.TYPE_INT_ARGB);

      // Get Graphics context of the image
      Graphics g = image.getGraphics();

      drawClock(g); // Draw a clock on graphics

      // Encode the image and send to the output stream
      new GifEncoder(image, out, true).encode();

      out.close(); // Close stream
    }

    private void drawClock(Graphics g) {
      // Initialize clock parameters
      int clockRadius =
        (int)(Math.min(width, height) * 0.7 * 0.5);
      int xCenter = (width) / 2;
      int yCenter = (height) / 2;

      // Draw circle
      g.setColor(Color.black);
      g.drawOval(xCenter - clockRadius,yCenter - clockRadius,
        2 * clockRadius, 2 * clockRadius);
      g.drawString("12", xCenter - 5, yCenter - clockRadius + 12);
      g.drawString("9", xCenter - clockRadius + 3, yCenter + 5);
      g.drawString("3", xCenter + clockRadius - 10, yCenter + 3);
      g.drawString("6", xCenter - 3, yCenter + clockRadius - 3);

      // Get current time using GregorianCalendar
      TimeZone timeZone = TimeZone.getDefault();
      GregorianCalendar cal = new GregorianCalendar(timeZone);

      // Draw second hand
      int second = (int)cal.get(GregorianCalendar.SECOND);
      int sLength = (int)(clockRadius * 0.9);
      int xSecond = (int)(xCenter + sLength * Math.sin(second *
        (2 * Math.PI / 60)));
      int ySecond = (int)(yCenter - sLength * Math.cos(second *
        (2 * Math.PI / 60)));
      g.setColor(Color.red);
      g.drawLine(xCenter, yCenter, xSecond, ySecond);

      // Draw minute hand
      int minute = (int)cal.get(GregorianCalendar.MINUTE);
      int mLength = (int)(clockRadius * 0.75);
      int xMinute = (int)(xCenter + mLength * Math.sin(minute *
        (2 * Math.PI / 60)));
      int yMinute = (int)(yCenter - mLength * Math.cos(minute *
        (2 * Math.PI / 60)));
      g.setColor(Color.blue);
      g.drawLine(xCenter, yCenter, xMinute, yMinute);

      // Draw hour hand
      int hour = (int)cal.get(GregorianCalendar.HOUR_OF_DAY);
      int hLength = (int)(clockRadius*0.6);
      int xHour = (int)(xCenter + hLength * Math.sin((hour + minute
```

Listing 14.14 *continued*

```
83              / 60.0) * (2 * Math.PI / 12)));
84            int yHour = (int)(yCenter - hLength * Math.cos((hour + minute
85              / 60.0) * (2 * Math.PI / 12)));
86            g.setColor(Color.green);
87            g.drawLine(xCenter, yCenter, xHour, yHour);
88
89            // Set display format in specified style, locale and timezone
90            DateFormat formatter = DateFormat.getDateTimeInstance
91              (DateFormat.MEDIUM, DateFormat.LONG);
92
93            // Display current date
94            g.setColor(Color.red);
95            String today = formatter.format(cal.getTime());
96            FontMetrics fm = g.getFontMetrics();
97            g.drawString(today, (width -
98              fm.stringWidth(today)) / 2, yCenter + clockRadius + 30);
99          }
100       }
```

Listing 14.14 *continued*

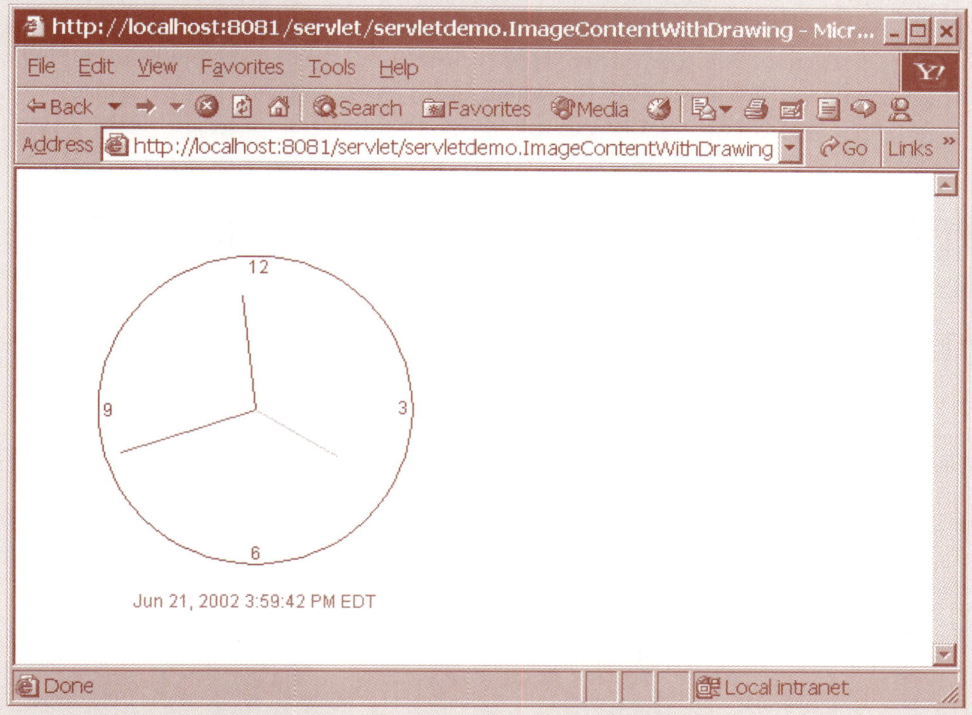

Figure 14.24 *The servlet returns a clock that displays the current time.*

Example Review

The program creates an image with the specified width, height, and image type, using the `BufferedImage` class (Lines 25–26):

```
Image image = new BufferedImage(width, height,
  BufferedImage.TYPE_INT_ARGB);
```

continued

Example 14.8 continued

To draw things on the image, you need to get its graphics context using the `getGraphics` method:

```
Graphics g = image.getGraphics();
```

You can use various drawing methods in the `Graphics` class to draw simple shapes, or you can use Java 2D to draw more sophisticated graphics. This example uses simple drawing methods to draw a clock that displays the current time.

14.10.2 Sending Images and Text Together

The servlets in the two preceding examples return images. Often images are mixed with text. In this case, you have to set the content type to “image/gif” before sending images, and set the content type to “text/html” before sending the text. However, the content type cannot be changed in one request. To circumvent this restriction, you may embed a get request for displaying the image in the HTML content. When the HTML content is displayed, a separate get request for retrieving the image is then sent to the server. Thus text and image are obtained through two separate get requests.

Example 14.9 Mixing Images and Texts

This example creates a servlet that dynamically generates the flag of a country and a text that describes the flag, as shown in Figure 14.25. The servlet is given in Listing 14.15.

```
package servletdemo;

import javax.servlet.*;
import javax.servlet.http.*;
import java.io.*;
import java.util.*;
import java.awt.*;
import javax.swing.*;
import Acme.JPM.Encoders.GifEncoder;

public class MixedContent extends HttpServlet {
  /** Process the HTTP Get request */
  public void doGet(HttpServletRequest request, HttpServletResponse
    response) throws ServletException, IOException {
    response.setContentType("text/html");
    PrintWriter out = response.getWriter();

    String country = request.getParameter("country");

    out.println("<img src = \"/servlet/servletdemo.ImageContent" +
      "?country=" + country + "\" align=left>");

```

Listing 14.15 *MixedContent.java*

```
      // Read description from a file and send it to the browser
      BufferedReader in = new BufferedReader(new FileReader(
        "c:\\radft\\servletdemo\\" + country + ".txt"));

      // Text line from the text file for flag description
      String line;

      // Read a line from the text file and send it to the browser
      while ((line = in.readLine()) != null) {
        out.println(line);
      }

      out.close();
    }
  }
```

Listing 14.15 *continued*

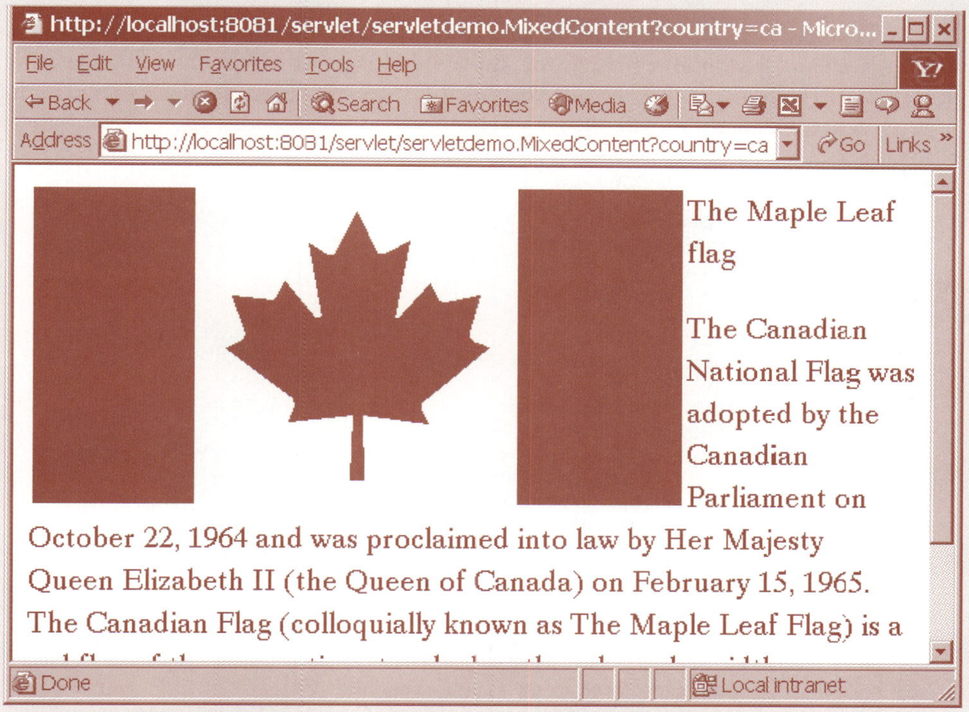

Figure 14.25 *The servlet returns an image along with the text.*

Example Review

When you test the servlet using the URL **`http://localhost:8080/servlet/MixedContent?country=ca`**, it generates an HTML file with the image tag

```
<img src = "/servlet/ImageContent?country=ca" align=left>
```

followed by the text from the file ca.txt.

continued

Example 14.9 continued

The HTML file is rendered by the browser. When the browser sees the image tag, it sends the request to the server. The servlet `ImageContent` created in Example 14.7 is invoked to retrieve the image file ca.gif. Thus the first get request dynamically prepared the second request. The content type for the first request is "text/html," and the second is "image/gif."

The first request invoked the servlet `MixedContent`, and the second request invoked the servlet `ImageContent`. Sometimes, it is convenient for both requests to invoke the same servlet. To do so, you can add a hidden value in the image tag to differentiate this request from the other. For example, use the following URL for the image tag:

```
<img src = "/servlet/MixedContentNew?country=ca&img=1">
```

Your servlet `doGet` method can check whether the hidden value is present in the request. If so, the request is for displaying image, otherwise, it is for rendering text. Here is the source code (Listing 14.16) that processes the two requests in one GET method.

```
package servletdemo;

import javax.servlet.*;
import javax.servlet.http.*;
import java.io.*;
import java.util.*;
import java.awt.*;
import javax.swing.*;
import Acme.JPM.Encoders.GifEncoder;

public class MixedContentNew extends HttpServlet {
  /** Process the HTTP Get request */
  public void doGet(HttpServletRequest request, HttpServletResponse
    response) throws ServletException, IOException {
    if (request.getParameter("img") != null) {
      response.setContentType("image/gif");
      OutputStream out = response.getOutputStream();

      // Obtain an image icon
      ImageIcon imageIcon = new ImageIcon("c:\\radft\\image\\" +
        request.getParameter("country") + ".gif");

      // Obtain image from image icon
      Image image = imageIcon.getImage(); // Get the image

      // Encode the image and send to the output stream
      new GifEncoder(image, out, true).encode();

      out.close(); // Close stream
    }
    else {
      response.setContentType("text/html");
      PrintWriter out = response.getWriter();

      String country = request.getParameter("country");

```

Listing 14.16 *MixedContentNew.java*

```
            out.println("<img src = \"" + request.getRequestURI() +
              "?country=" + country + "&img=1\" align=left>");

            // Read description from a file and send it to the browser
            BufferedReader in = new BufferedReader(new FileReader(
              "c:\\radft\\servletdemo\\" + country + ".txt"));

            // Text line from the text file for flag description
            String line;

            // Read a line from the text file and send it to the browser
            while ((line = in.readLine()) != null) {
              out.println(line);
            }

            out.close();
          }
        }
      }
```

Listing 14.16 *continued*

14.10.3 Getting Images from Components

The preceding examples obtained images from drawings. Occasionally, the drawings already exist in a component. This section demonstrates how to obtain images from components.

Example 14.10 Getting Images from Components

In Example 14.8, you created an image of a clock by drawing the clock on a `Graphics` object. You wrote the code to draw a clock. The code is the same as in the `Clock` component presented in Example 4.2, "The `Clock` Component." This example reuses the `Clock` component to create a clock image in a servlet, as shown in Listing 14.17.

```
package servletdemo;

import javax.servlet.*;
import javax.servlet.http.*;
import javax.swing.*;
import java.io.*;
import java.awt.*;
import java.awt.image.BufferedImage;
import Acme.JPM.Encoders.GifEncoder;
import clockdemo.Clock;

public class ImageContentFromComponent extends HttpServlet {
  /** Initialize global variables */
  private final static int width = 300;
  private final static int height = 300;

```

Listing 14.17 *ImageContentFromComponent.java*

continued

Example 14.10 continued

```
    // Create image
    private Image image = new BufferedImage(width, height,
      BufferedImage.TYPE_INT_ARGB);

    // Get Graphics context of the image
    private Graphics g = image.getGraphics();

    // Create clock
    private Clock clock = new Clock();

    // Create a frame to provide graphics environment for rendering
    // the clock
    private JFrame frame = new JFrame();

    /** Initialize global variables */
    public void init(ServletConfig config) throws ServletException {
      super.init(config);
      frame.setSize(width, height); // Set the frame size
      frame.getContentPane().add(clock); // Add clock to the frame
    }

    /** Process the HTTP Get request */
    public void doGet(HttpServletRequest request, HttpServletResponse
      response) throws ServletException, IOException {
      response.setContentType("image/gif");
      OutputStream out = response.getOutputStream();

      frame.setVisible(true);
      g.setColor(Color.white);
      g.fillRect(0, 0, width, height);
      clock.paint(g);
      frame.setVisible(false);

      // Encode the image and send to the output stream
      new GifEncoder(image, out, true).encode();

      out.close(); // Close stream
    }
  }
```

Listing 14.17 *continued*

Example Review

This example displays the same clock as shown in Figure 14.24. Instead of writing the code to draw the clock, the example reuses the `Clock` component to draw the clock on a component. The image of the clock is then obtained through the `Graphics` object. The method `clock.paint(g)` invokes the `paint` method in the `Clock` component and draws the clock on `g`.

The `Clock` object is put into a frame. Why is a frame necessary in this example? There are two reasons. First, the `paint` method in the `Clock` component uses the `getWidth()` and `getHeight()` methods to obtain the component's width and height in order to draw a clock. Second, the `paint` method uses the `getLocale` method. In order to determine its locale, the clock must be placed in a frame or an applet.

Chapter Summary

This chapter introduced the creation of dynamic Web pages using Java servlets in Forte. You learned how to write HTML forms with the GET and POST methods. You wrote Java servlets that extended the `HttpServlet` class. Java servlets respond to GET requests with the `doGet` method and to POST requests with the `doPost` method.

The chapter introduced the Servlets API. You learned how to develop servlets with database applications. Three session-tracking techniques were introduced. You learned how to track sessions using HTML hidden values, HTML cookies, and `HttpSession` objects. Finally, you learned how to generate images from servlets.

Review Questions

14.1 What are the differences between CGI and servlets?

14.2 What is the difference between the GET and POST methods in an HTML form?

14.3 Can you submit a GET request directly from a URL? Can you submit a POST request directly from a URL?

14.4 What is wrong in the following URL for submitting a GET request to the servlet FindScore on host liang at port 8080 with parameters name?

```
http://liang:8080/servlet/FindScore?name="P Yates"
```

14.5 How do you set a default Web server in Forte? Why is it necessary to create a Web module in Forte? How do you choose an external Web browser to run servlets in Forte?

14.6 Where should you set the target of the servlet .class files?

14.7 When you run Tomcat from Forte, which port does it use? What happens if the port is already in use?

14.8 Describe the life-cycle of a servlet.

14.9 What would be displayed if you changed the content type to "html/plain" in Example 14.1?

14.10 What is session tracking? What are three techniques for session tracking?

14.11 What output stream should you use to send images to the browser?

14.12 How do you deal with dynamic contents with images and text?

Programming Exercises

14.1 Write a servlet that displays the number of visits on the servlet. Also display the client's host name, IP address, and request URL, as shown in Figure 14.26. This information can be obtained using the appropriate GET methods in the `HttpServletRequest` class.

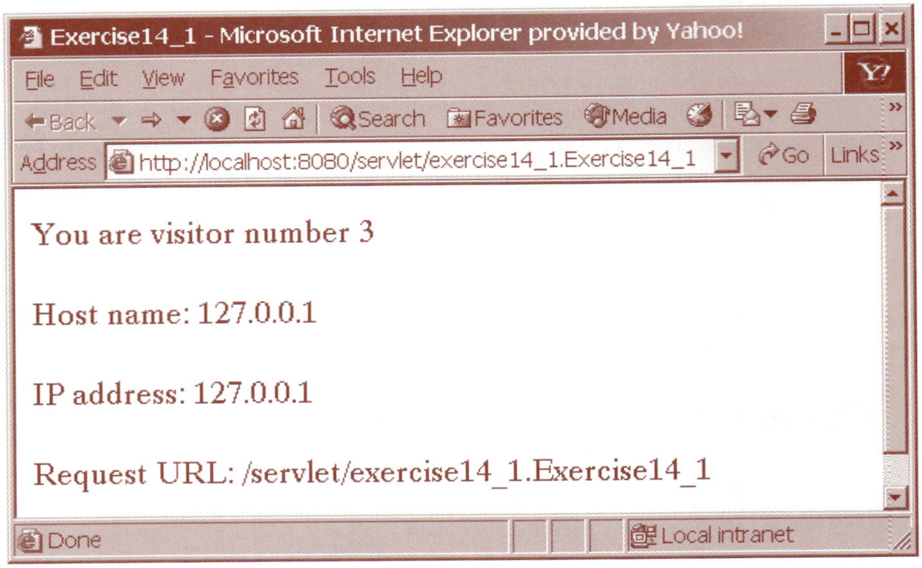

Figure 14.26 *The servlet displays the number of visits, client's host name, IP address, and request URL.*

(Can you modify the servlet to display the number of visits made by a client identified by the client's IP address? Hint: Use `Map` to store a pair of IP addresses and visit counts. For the first visit, an entry is created in the map. For subsequent visits, the visit count is updated.)

14.2 Write a servlet that displays the student name and the current score, given the ssn and class ID. For each class, a text file is used to store the student name, ssn, and current score. The file is named after the class id with .txt extension. For instance, if the class id were csci1301, the file name would be csci1301.txt. Suppose each line consists of student name, ssn, and score. These three items are separated by the # sign. Create an HTML form that enables the user to enter the ssn and class ID, as shown in Figure 14.27. Upon clicking the Submit button, the result is displayed, as shown in Figure 14.28. If the ssn or the class ID does not match, report an error.

14.3 Rewrite the preceding servlet. Assume that for each class, a table is used to store the student name, ssn, and score. The table name is the same as the class ID. For instance, if the class id were csci1301, the table name would be csci1301.

14.4 Write a servlet that stores the following cookies in a browser, and set their max age for two days.

Cookie 1: name is "color" and value is red.

Cookie 2: name is "radius" and value is 5.5.

Cookie 3: name is "count" and value is 2.

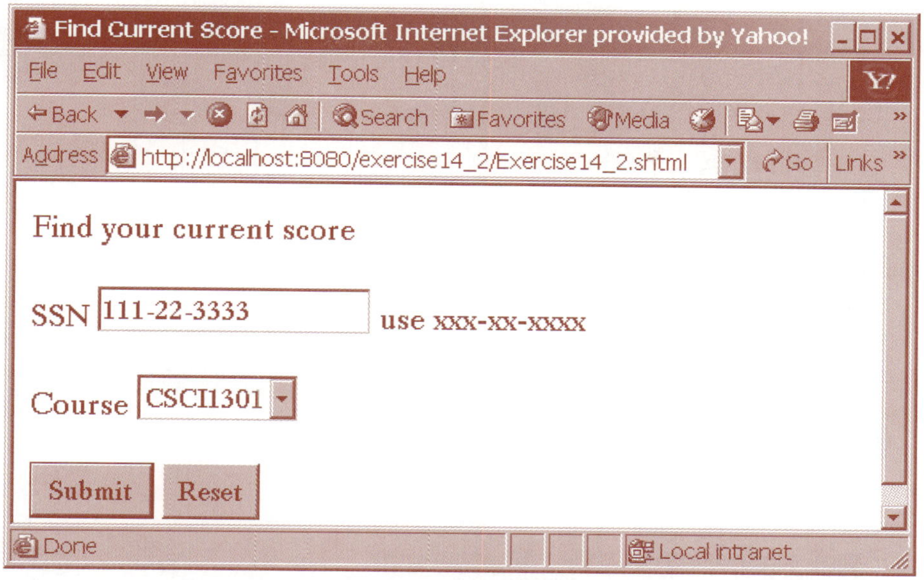

Figure 14.27 *The HTML form accepts the ssn and class ID from the user.*

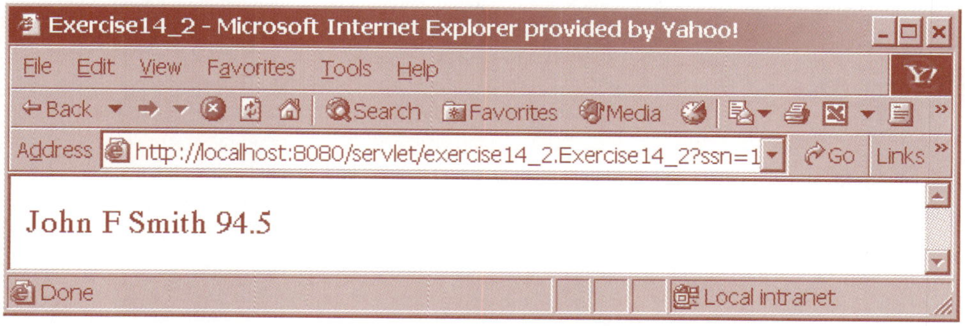

Figure 14.28 *The student name and score for the given ssn and class ID are displayed.*

14.5 Write a servlet that displays all the cookies on the client. The client types the URL of the servlet from the browser to display all the cookies stored on the browser. See Figure 14.29.

14.6 Write a servlet that enables the user to change the password from an HTML form, as shown in Figure 14.30. Suppose that the user information is stored in a database table named User with three columns: username, password, and name, where name is the real name of the user. The servlet performs the following tasks:

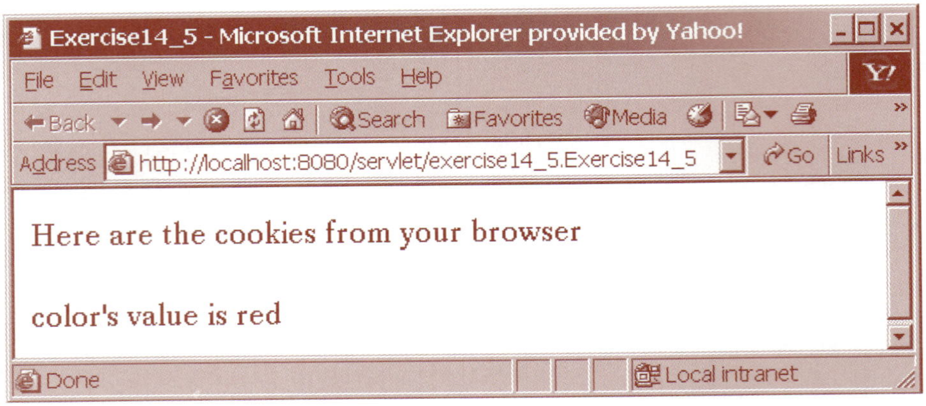

Figure 14.29 *All the cookies on the client are displayed in the browser.*

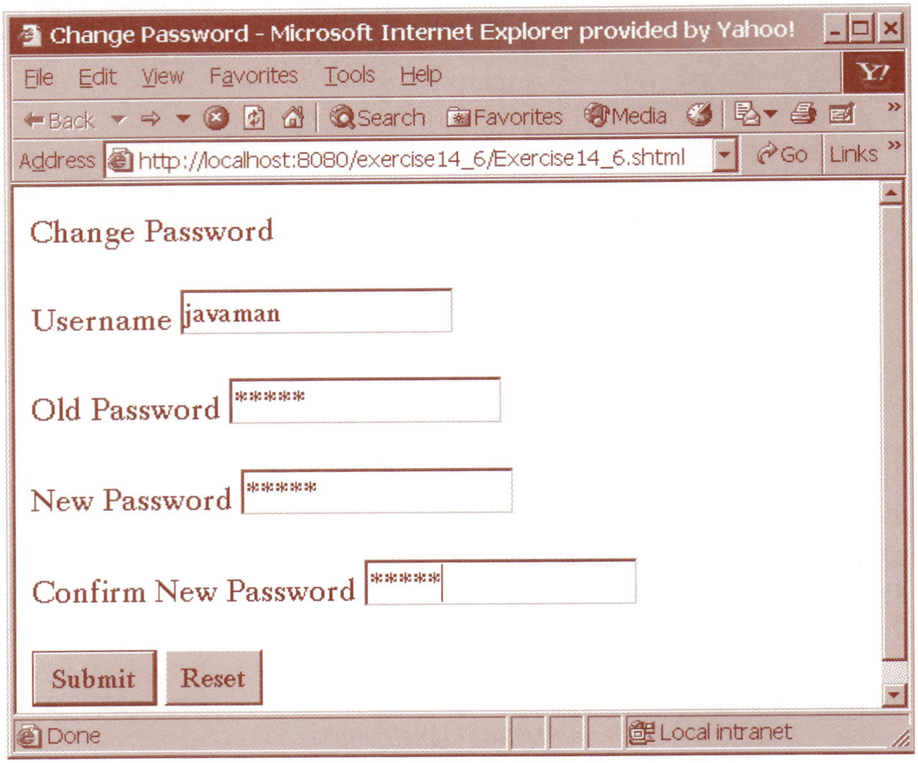

Figure 14.30 *The user enters the username and the old password and sets a new password.*

a. Verify that the username and old password are in the table. If not, report the error and redisplay the HTML form.

b. Verify that the new password and the confirmed password are the same. If not, report this error and redisplay the HTML form.

c. If the user information is entered correctly, update the password and report the status of the update to the user, as shown in Figure 14.31.

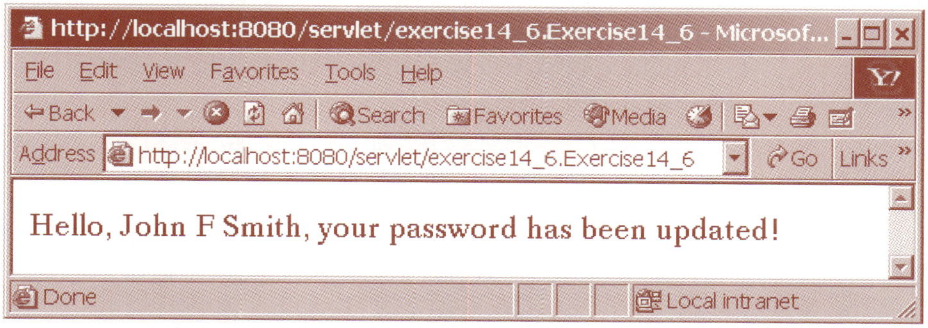

Figure 14.31 *The servlet reports the status of the update to the user.*

14.7 Write a servlet that displays a bar chart on the number of employees in each department from a database, as shown in Figure 14.32. The number of employees in each department can be obtained dynamically from the database tables Department and Employee. The Department table has three columns:

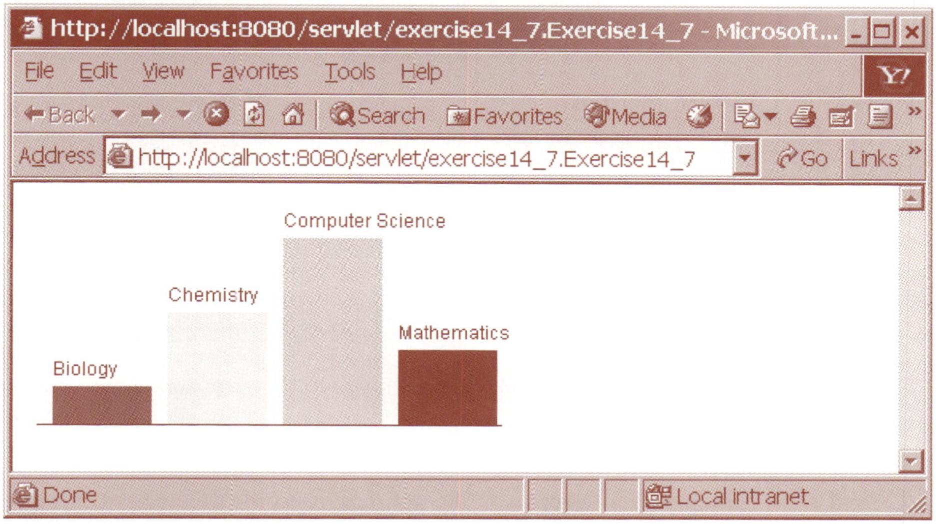

Figure 14.32 *The servlet sends a bar chart to display the number of employees for each department in the database.*

deptno, deptname, and deptchair. The Employee table has four columns: empno, name, office, and deptno. The number of employees in each department can be obtained using the following SQL statement:

```
select deptname, count(*)
from department, employee
where department.deptno = employee.deptno
group by deptname;
```

Write the code to draw the bar chart on a `Graphics` object.

14.8 Rewrite Exercise 14.7 using the `BarChart` component and the `ChartModel` from Exercise 4.8 so that you can reuse the code in the `BarChart` component to display the bar chart.

14.9 Write a servlet that displays the current calendar, as shown in Figure 14.33. The current calendar user interface can be obtained from the `CalendarPanel` component in Exercise 4.6.

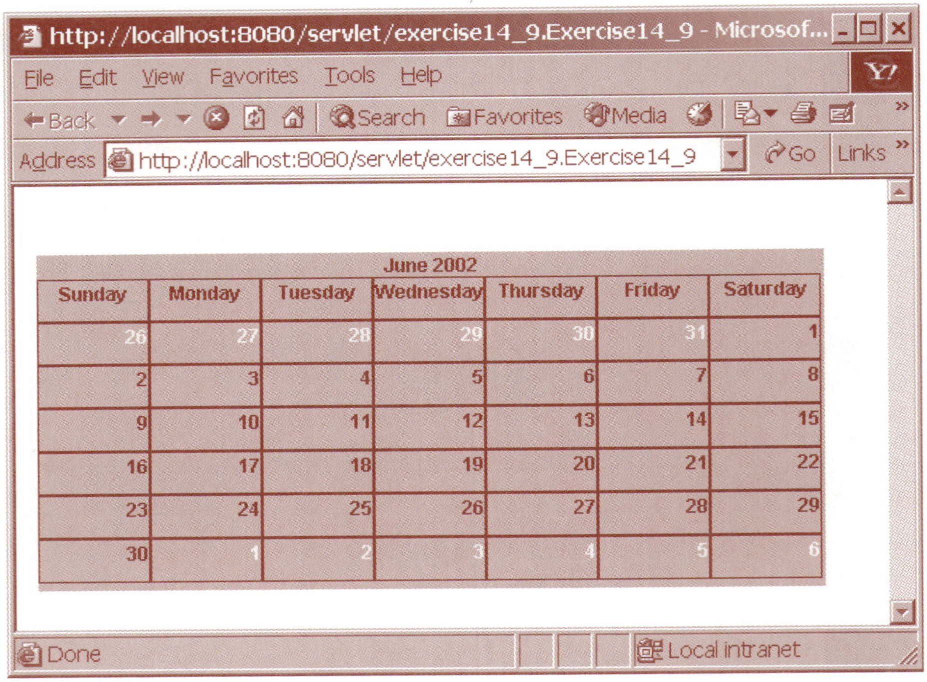

Figure 14.33 *The servlet uses the CalendarPanel component to create a user interface that displays the calendar and sends the image to the client.*

14.10 Develop an interactive online test that meets the following requirements:

a. The test consists of multiple-choice questions. Each test is stored in a text file, as follows:

```
1. Question 1
a. Choice-a
b. Choice-b
c. Choice-c
d. Choice-d
e. Choice-e

# (Question separator)
2. Question 2
a. Choice-a
b. Choice-b
c. Choice-c
d. Choice-d
e. Choice-e

# (Question separator)
More questions

& End of the questions. Answers begins
1.d
2.c
More answers
```

b. The user starts the test from a URL that consists of the servlet name and the parameter to specify a test, as shown in Figure 14.34.

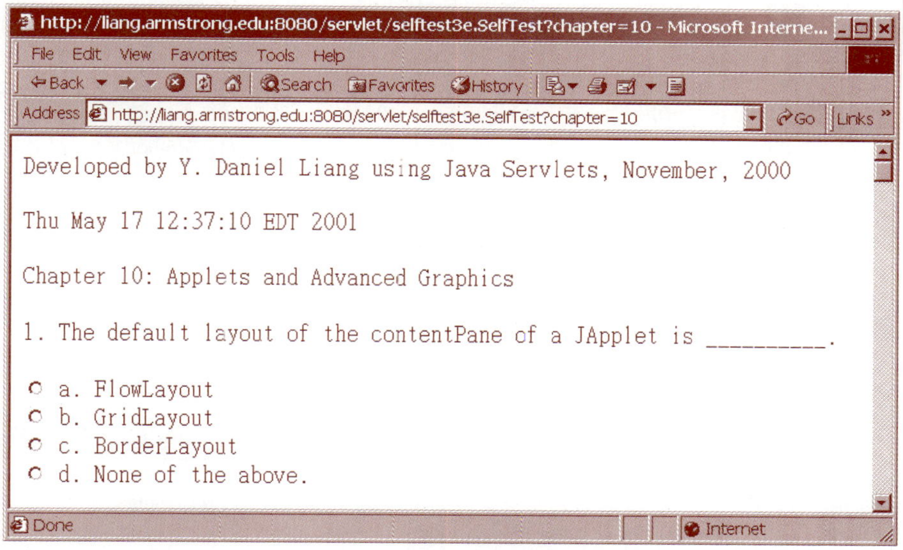

Figure 14.34 *The servlet dynamically generates the test.*

c. Upon submitting the test, the servlet grades it and sends the result back to the client. The servlet also generates a chart to show the number of correct answers, incorrect answers, and unanswered questions, as shown in Figure 14.35. (Please refer to **www.cs.armstrong.edu/liang/introft.html** and click Multiple Choice to see a live demo of this exercise. The source code for the servlet is at **http://liang.armstrong.edu:8082/selftestft/SelfTest.java**.

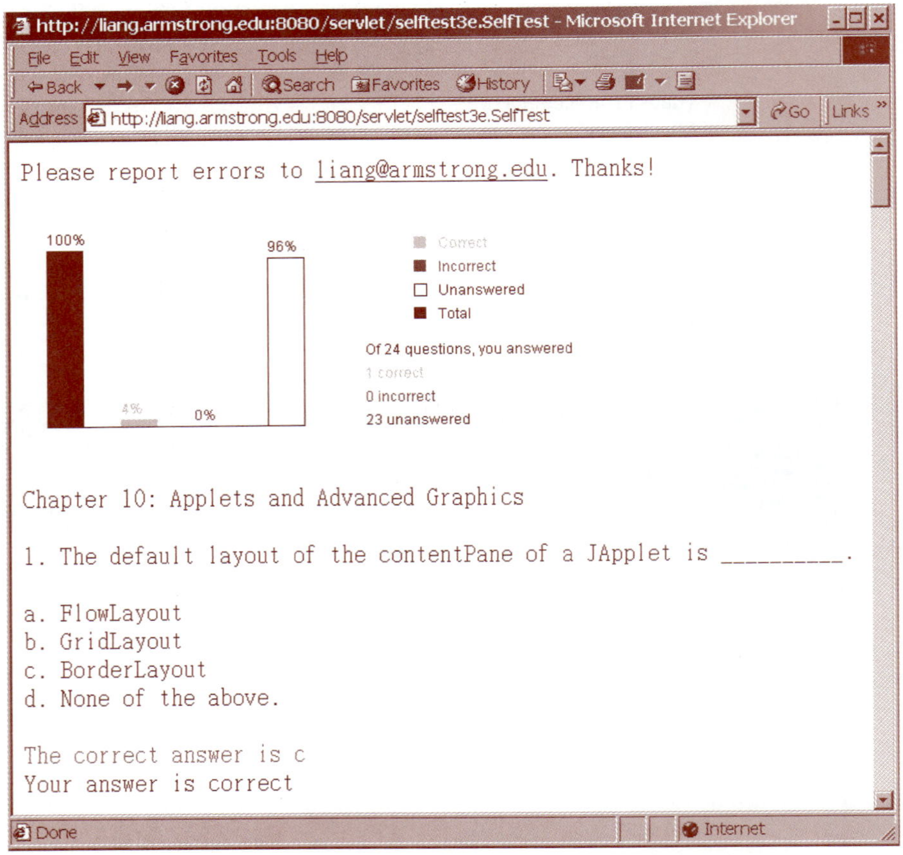

Figure 14.35 *The servlet grades the test and sends the result back to the client.*

CHAPTER 15

JavaServer Pages

Objectives

- To understand how a JSP page is processed.
- To know how to use JSP constructs.
- To become familiar with JSP predefined variables and JSP directives.
- To use JavaBeans components in JSP.
- To access database using JSP.
- To know how to forward requests from JSP.

15.1 Introduction

Servlets can be used to generate dynamic Web contents. One drawback, however, is that you have to embed HTML tags and text inside Java source code. A Web page usually contains both static and dynamic contents. Using servlets, you have to modify the Java source code and recompile it if changes are made to the static HTML text. If you have a lot of static HTML code mixed with some dynamic code in a servlet, the code is difficult to read and maintain, since the regular HTML code is part of the Java source code. JavaServer Pages (JSP) technology was introduced to remedy this drawback. JSP enables you to write regular static HTML code in the normal way and embed Java code to produce dynamic contents.

15.2 A Simple JSP Page

JSP provides an easy way to create dynamic Web pages and simplify the task of building Web application. A JavaServer page is like a regular HTML page with special tags, known as *JSP tags*, which enable the Web server to generate dynamic contents. You can create a Web page with static HTML and enclose the code for generating dynamic contents in the JSP tags. Here is an example of a simple JSP page.

```
<HTML>
<HEAD>
<TITLE>
CurrentTime
</TITLE>
</HEAD>
<BODY>
Current time is <%= new java.util.Date() %>
</BODY>
</HTML>
```

Listing 15.1 *CurrentTime.jsp*

As shown in Listing 15.1, the dynamic content is enclosed in the tag that begins with `<%=` and ends with `%>`. The current time is returned as a string by invoking the `toString` method of the `java.util.Date` class.

15.3 How Is a JSP Page Processed?

A JSP page must first be processed by a Web server before it can be displayed in a Web browser. The Web server must support JSP, and the JSP page must be stored in a file with a .jsp extension. The Web server translates the .jsp file into a Java servlet, compiles the servlet, and executes it. The result of the execution is sent to the browser for display. Figure 15.1 shows how a JSP page is processed by a Web server.

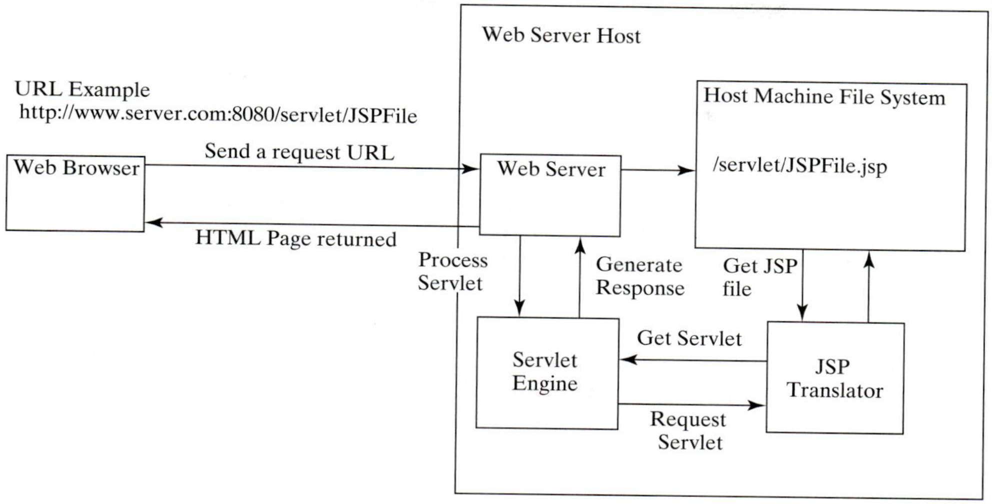

Figure 15.1 *A JSP page is translated into a servlet.*

Note

A JSP page is translated into a servlet when the page is requested for the first time. It is not retranslated if the page is not modified. To ensure that the first-time real user does not get a delay, the JSP developers may test the page after it is installed.

15.4 JSP Constructs

There are three main types of JSP constructs: scripting constructs, directives, and actions. *Scripting* elements enable you to specify Java code that will become part of the resultant servlet. *Directives* enable you to control the overall structure of the resultant servlet. *Actions* enable you to control the behaviors of the JSP engine.

15.5 Scripting Constructs

There are three types of scripting constructs that can be used to insert Java code into the resultant servlet: expressions, scriptlets, and declarations.

A JSP *expression* is used to insert a Java expression directly into the output. It has the following form:

```
<%= Java-expression %>
```

The expression is evaluated, converted into a string, and sent to the output stream of the servlet.

A JSP *scriptlet* enables you to insert a Java statement into the servlet's `jspService` method, which is invoked by the `service` method. A JSP scriptlet has the following form:

```
<% Java statement %>
```

A JSP *declaration* is for declaring methods or fields into the servlet. It has the following form:

```
<%! Java method or field declaration %>
```

HTML comments have the following form:

```
<!-- HTML Comment -->
```

If you don't want the comment to appear in the resultant HTML file, use the following comment in JSP:

```
<%-- JSP Comment --%>
```

Example 15.1 Computing Factorials

This example creates a JavaServer page that displays factorials for numbers from 0 to 10. Figure 15.2 shows a sample run of the JavaServer page.

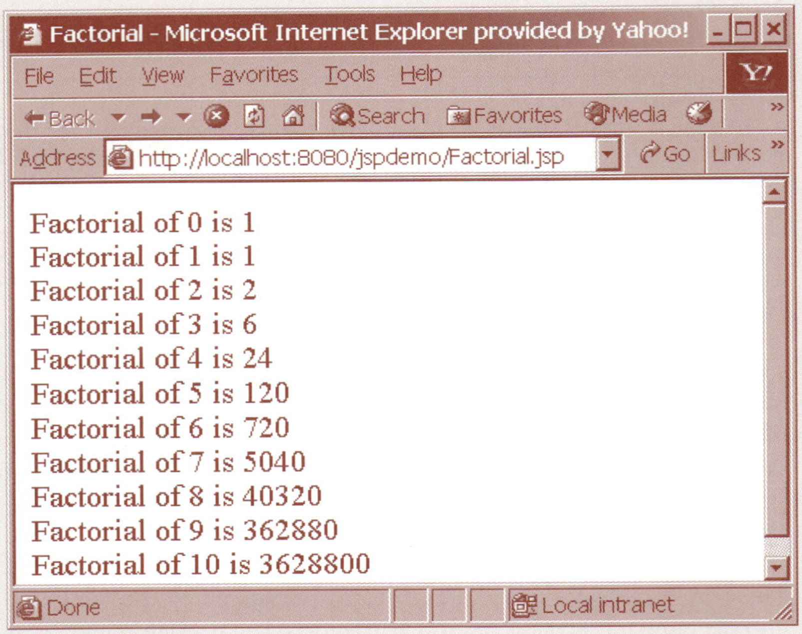

Figure 15.2 *JavaServer page is displayed on a Web browser.*

Here are the steps to complete the example.

1. Assume that a Web module was already created in the preceding chapter. To learn how to create a Web module, see Section 14.5.2, "Creating a Web Module." In the context menu of *c:\radfi* in the Explorer, choose *New, Java Package* to display the Java Package wizard, as shown in Figure

15.3. Type `jspdemo` in the Name field and click Finish to create the jspdemo package.

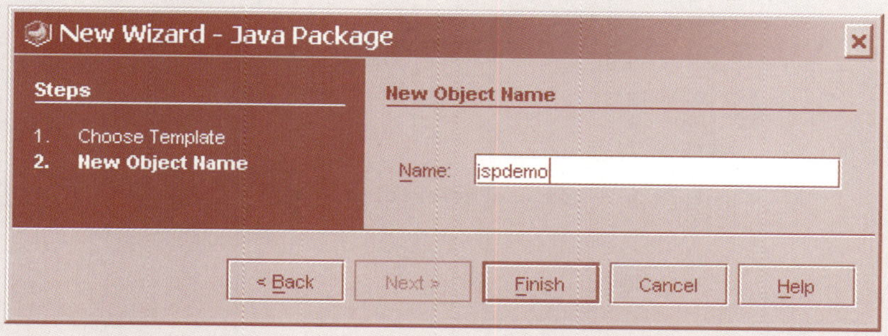

Figure 15.3 *The jspdemo package will hold all examples in this chapter.*

2. Create a JSP as follows:

   2.1. In the context menu of the *jspdemo* node, choose *New, JSP & Servlet, JSP* to display the JSP wizard, as shown in Figure 15.4.

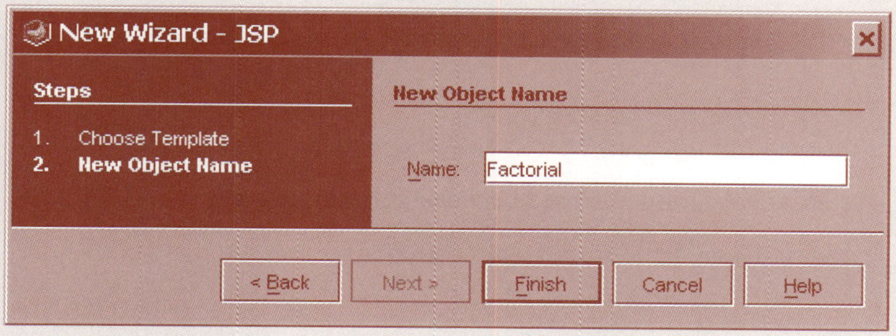

Figure 15.4 *You use the JSP wizard to create a JSP file.*

   2.2. Type `Factorial` in the Name field, and click *Finish* to generate the template.

   2.3. Enter the code for Factorial.jsp, as shown in Listing 15.2.

3. Run Factorial.jsp by choosing *Execute (Force Reload)* from the context menu of Factorial.jsp in the Explorer.

```
<HTML>
<HEAD>
<TITLE>
Factorial
</TITLE>
</HEAD>
<BODY>

```

Listing 15.2 *Factorial.jsp*

continued

Example 15.1 continued

```
<%  for (int i = 0; i <= 10; i++) { %>
Factorial of <%= i %> is
<%= computeFactorial(i) %> <br>
<%  } %>

<%! private long computeFactorial(int n) {
      if (n == 0)
        return 1;
      else
        return n * computeFactorial(n - 1);
    }
%>

</BODY>
</HTML>
```

Listing 15.2 *continued*

Example Review

The JSP scriptlet enclosed between `<%` and `%>`, such as

```
for (int i = 0; i <= 10; i++) {,
```

is inserted directly into the servlet's `jspService` method.

The JSP expression enclosed between `<%=` and `%>`, such as

```
<%= i %>,
```

is inserted into the output stream of the servlet.

The JSP declaration enclosed between `<%!` and `%>`, such as

```
<%! private long computeFactorial(int n) {
     ...
}
%>
```

defines methods or fields in the servlet.

15.6 Predefined Variables

You can use variables in JSP. For convenience, JSP provides eight predefined variables from the servlet environment that can be used with JSP expressions and scriptlets. These variables are also known as *JSP implicit objects*.

- **`request`** represents the client's request, which is an instance of `HttpServletRequest`. You can use it to access request parameters, HTTP headers such as cookies, hostname, etc.
- **`response`** represents the servlet's response, which is an instance of `HttpServletResponse`.
- **`out`** represents the output stream, which is an instance of `PrintWriter`.
- **`session`** represents the `HttpSession` object associated with the request.

- **`application`** represents the `ServletContext` object, which can be obtained from `getServletConfig().getContext()` in the servlet. Servlets and JSP pages can store persistent data in the `ServletContext` object rather than in instance variables. The difference between `session` and `application` is that session is tied to one client, but `application` is for all clients to share persistent data.
- **`config`** represents the `ServletConfig` object for the page.
- **`pageContext`** represents the `PageContext` object. `PageContext` is a new class introduced in JSP to give a central point of access to many page attributes.
- **`page`** is an alternative to `this`.

NOTE
Like Java, JSP is case-sensitive.

Example 15.2 Using Predefined Variables

This example prompts the user to enter username and password, as shown in Figure 15.5. If the password is the reverse of the username, login is successful, as shown in Figure 15.6.

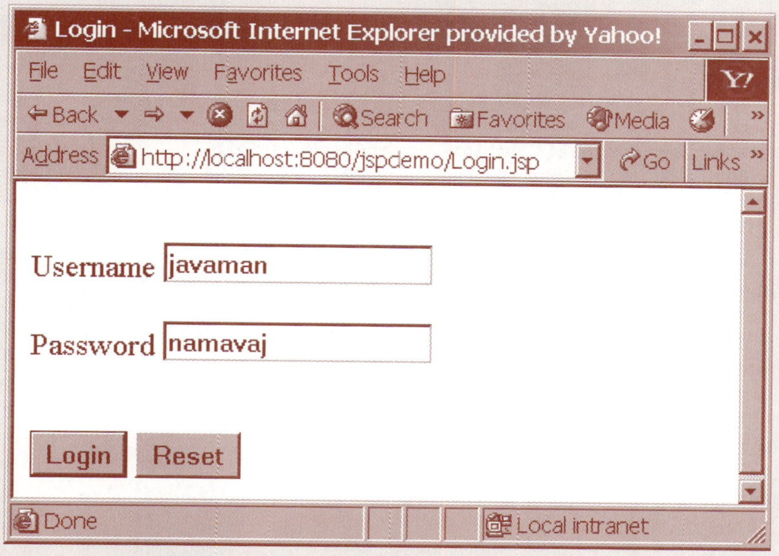

Figure 15.5 *You enter the username and password to login.*

The example uses two JSP files named Login.jsp (in Listing 15.3) and LoginCheck.jsp (in Listing 15.4).

continued

Example 15.2 continued

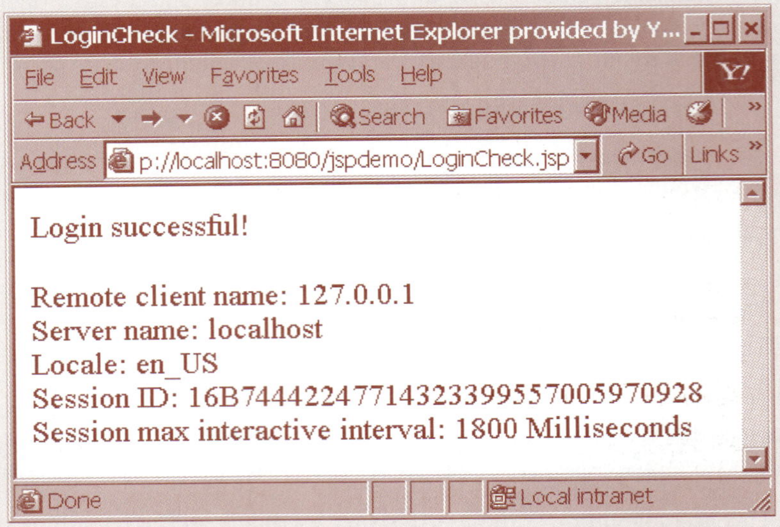

Figure 15.6 *Login successful is displayed if the username is the reverse of the password.*

```
<HTML>
<HEAD>
<TITLE>
Login
</TITLE>
</HEAD>
<BODY>
<FORM method="post" action="LoginCheck.jsp">
<BR>Username  <INPUT NAME="username"><BR>
<BR>Password  <INPUT NAME="password"><BR><BR><BR>
<INPUT TYPE="SUBMIT" NAME="Submit" VALUE="Login">
<INPUT TYPE="RESET" VALUE="Reset">
</FORM>
</BODY>
</HTML>
```

Listing 15.3 *Login.jsp*

```
<HTML>
<HEAD>
<TITLE>
LoginCheck
</TITLE>
</HEAD>
<BODY>
<%  String username = request.getParameter("username");
    String password = request.getParameter("password");

    StringBuffer sbuf = new StringBuffer(username);

    if (sbuf.reverse().toString().equals(password)) {%>
      Login successful!<p>
```

Listing 15.4 *LoginCheck.jsp*

```
      <% } else { %>
        Login failed!<p>
      <% } %>

    Remote client name: <%= request.getRemoteHost() %><BR>
    Server name: <%= request.getServerName() %><BR>
    Locale: <%= request.getLocale() %><BR>
    Session ID: <%= session.getId() %><BR>
    Session max interactive interval:
      <%= session.getMaxInactiveInterval() %> Milliseconds
    </BODY>
    </HTML>
```

Listing 15.4 *continued*

Example Review

Login.jsp is displayed first to prompt the user to enter the username and password. Since this file does not contain any JSP elements, it could be named with an .html extension as a regular HTML file.

LoginCheck.jsp is invoked upon clicking the Submit button in Login.jsp. LoginCheck.jsp obtains the parameters username and password using the predefined variable `request`. It uses JSP scriptlets to check whether the username is the reverse of the password.

NOTE

For an `if` statement in a JSP scriplet, you should use braces to group statements, even for a single statement.

15.7 JSP Directives

A JSP directive is a statement that gives the JSP engine information about the JSP page. For example, if your JSP page uses a Java class from a package other than the `java.lang` package, you have to use a directive to import this package. The general syntax for a JSP directive is as follows:

```
<%@ directive attribute="value" %>, or
<%@ directive attribute1="value1"
              attribute2="value2"
              ...
              attributen="vlauen" %>
```

Three possible directives are the following:

- **page** lets you provide information for the page, such as importing classes and setting up content type. The page directive can appear anywhere in the JSP file.

- **include** lets you insert a file to the servlet when the page is translated to a servlet. The `include` directive must be placed where you want the file to be inserted.
- **tablib** lets you define custom tags.

The following are useful attributes for the `page` directive:

- **import** specifies one or more packages to be imported for this page. For example, the directive `<%@ page import="java.util.*, java.text.*" %>` imports `java.util.*` and `java.text.*`.
- **contentType** specifies the MIME type for the JSP resultant page. By default, the content type is `text/html` for JSP. The default content type for servlets is `text/plain`.
- **session** specifies a `boolean` value to indicate whether the page is part of the session. By default, `session` is `true`.
- **buffer** specifies the output stream buffer size. By default, it is 8KB. For example, the directive `<%@ page buffer="10KB" %>` specifies that the output buffer size is 10KB. The directive `<%@ page buffer="none" %>` specifies that buffer is not used.
- **autoFlush** specifies a `boolean` value to indicate whether the output buffer should be automatically flushed when it is full or whether an exception should be raised when the buffer overflows. By default, this attribute is `true`. In this case, the buffer attribute cannot be `none`.
- **isThreadSafe** specifies a `boolean` value to indicate whether the page can be accessed simultaneously without data corruption. By default, it is `true`. If it is set to false, the JSP page will be translated to a servlet that implements the `SingleThreadModel` interface.
- **errorPage** specifies a JSP page that is processed when an exception occurs in the current page. For example, the directive `<%@ page errorPage="HandleError.jsp" %>` specifies that HandleError.jsp is processed when an exception occurs.
- **isErrorPage** specifies a `boolean` value to indicate whether the page can be used as an error page. By default, this attribute is `false`.

Example 15.3 Using Directives

This example prompts the user to enter an integer (see Figure 15.7) and displays the factorial for the integer (see Figure 15.8). If a noninteger value is entered by mistake, an error page is displayed, as shown in Figure 15.9.

The example uses three JSP files named FactorialInput.jsp (in Listing 15.5), ComputeFactorial.jsp (in Listing 15.6), and FactorialInputError.jsp (Listing 15.7).

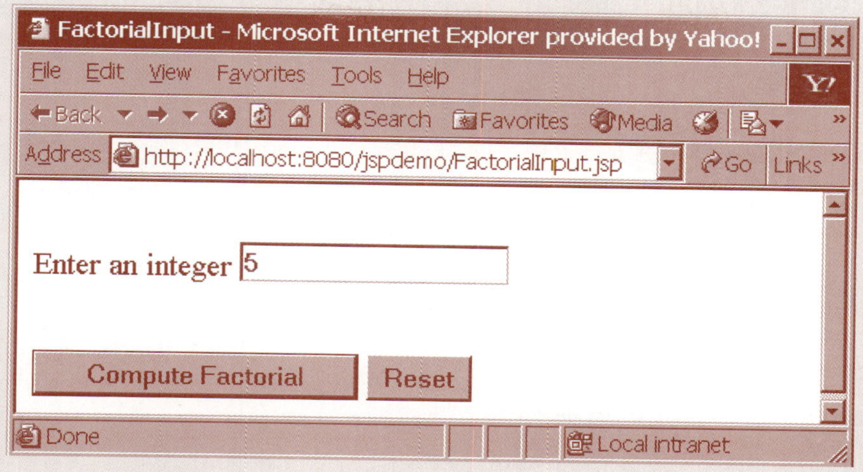

Figure 15.7 *You enter an integer to obtain its factorial.*

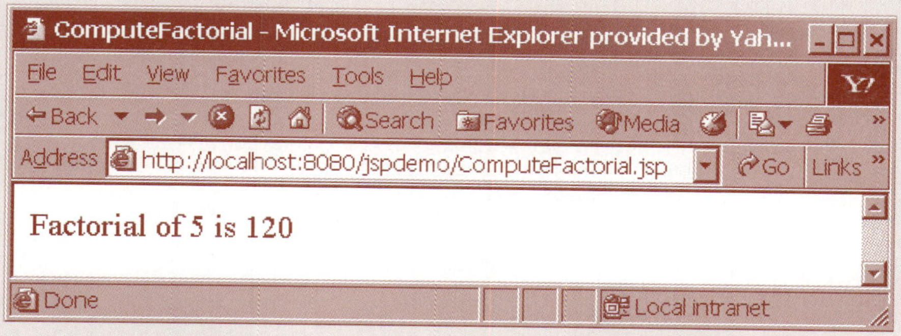

Figure 15.8 *The factorial of the integer is displayed.*

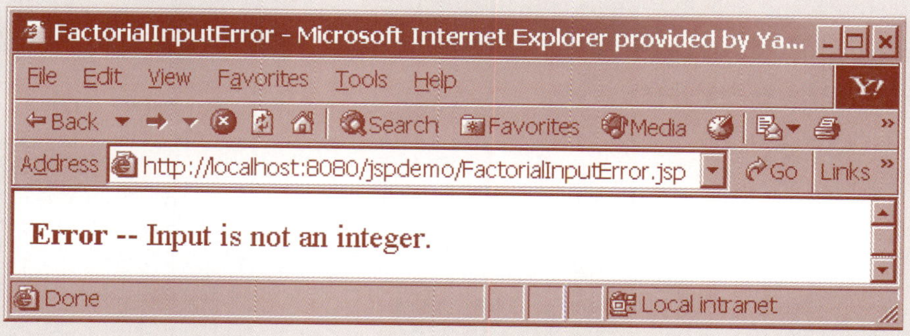

Figure 15.9 *An error page is displayed when an exception occurs.*

continued

Example 15.3 continued

```
<HTML>
<HEAD>
<TITLE>
FactorialInput
</TITLE>
</HEAD>
<BODY>
<FORM method="post" action="ComputeFactorial.jsp">
<BR>Enter an integer  <INPUT NAME="number"><BR><BR><BR>
<INPUT TYPE="SUBMIT" NAME="Submit" VALUE="Compute Factorial">
<INPUT TYPE="RESET" VALUE="Reset">
</FORM>
</BODY>
</HTML>
```

Listing 15.5 *FactorialInput.jsp*

```
<HTML>
<HEAD>
<TITLE>
ComputeFactorial
</TITLE>
</HEAD>
<BODY>
<%@ page import ="java.text.*" %>
<%@ page errorPage = "FactorialInputError.jsp" %>

<%  NumberFormat format = NumberFormat.getNumberInstance();
    int number = Integer.parseInt(request.getParameter("number")); %>
Factorial of <%= number %> is
<%= format.format(computeFactorial(number)) %> <br>

<%! private long computeFactorial(int n) {
      if (n == 0)
        return 1;
      else
        return n*computeFactorial(n-1);
    }
%>
</BODY>
</HTML>
```

Listing 15.6 *ComputeFactorial.jsp*

```
<HTML>
<HEAD>
<TITLE>
FactorialInputError
</TITLE>
</HEAD>
<BODY>
<%@ page isErrorPage = "true" %>

<b>Error</b> -- Input is not an integer.

</BODY>
</HTML>
```

Listing 15.7 *FactorialInputError.jsp*

Example Review

FactorialInput.jsp is displayed first to prompt the user to enter an integer. If the user enters an integer, its factorial is displayed; otherwise, the error page is displayed.

The directive `<%@ page import ="java.text.*" %>` imports the `java.text` package because the `NumberFormat` class is in this package. The directive `<%@ page errorPage = "FactorialInputError.jsp" %>` specifies that FactorialInputError.jsp is processed when an exception in ComputeFactorial.jsp occurs. The directive `<%@ page isErrorPage = "true" %>` denotes that FactorialInputError.jsp can be used as an error page.

15.8 Using JavaBeans in JSP

You used the `computeFactorial` method to compute the factorial in Examples 15.1 and 15.3. You defined the `computeFactorial` method in both examples. You could have defined the method in a class and shared it in both examples. Normally you create an instance of a class in each program and use it in that program. This is for sharing the class, not the object. JSP allows you to share the object of a class among different pages.

To enable an object to be shared, its class must be a JavaBeans component. A class is a JavaBeans component if it has the following three features:

- The class is public.
- The class has a public constructor with no arguments.
- The class is serializable.

To create an instance for a JavaBeans component, use the following syntax:

```
<jsp:useBean id="objectName" scope="scopeAttribute"
  class="ClassName" />
```

This syntax is equivalent to

```
<% ClassName objectName = new ClassName() %>
```

except that the scope attribute specifies the scope of the object. Listed below are four possible values for the scope attribute:

- **`page`** is the default scope, which specifies that the object is bound to the page. The object is stored in the `PageContext` object for the duration of the current page. It can be retrieved using the predefined `pageContext` variable.
- **`application`** specifies that the object is bound to the application. The object is stored in the `ServletContext` object for the duration of the current application. It can be retrieved using the `getServletContext()` method via the predefined `application` variable.

- **`session`** specifies that the object is bound to the client's session. It is stored in the `HttpSession` object so that it can be retrieved using the `getValue(objectName)` method via the predefined `session` variable.
- **`request`** specifies that the object is bound to the client's request. It is stored in the `ServletRequest` object so that it can be retrieved using the `getAttribute(objectName)` method via the predefined `request` variable.

When `<jsp:useBean id="objectName" scope="scopeAttribute" class="ClassName" />` is processed, the JSP engine first searches for the object of the class with the same id and scope. If found, the preexisting bean is used; otherwise, a new bean is created.

Another syntax for creating a bean is the following:

```
<jsp:useBean id="objectName" scope="scopeAttribute"
   class="ClassName" >
statements
</jsp:useBean>
```

The statements are executed when the bean is created. If a bean with the same id and className already exists, the statements are not executed.

15.8.1 Getting and Setting Properties

By convention, A JavaBeans component provides the get and set methods for reading and modifying its private properties. You can get the property in JSP using the following syntax:

```
<jsp:getProperty name="beanId" property="sample" />
```

This is equivalent to

```
<%= beanId.getSample() %>
```

You can set the property in JSP using the following syntax:

```
<jsp:setProperty name="beanId" property="sample"
  value="test1" />
```

This is equivalent to

```
<% beanId.setSample("test1"); %>
```

15.8.2 Associating Properties with Input Parameters

Often properties are associated with input parameters. Suppose you want to get the value of the input parameter named `score` and set it to the JavaBeans property named `score`. You may write the following code:

```
<% double score = Double.parseDouble(
     request.getParameter("score")); %>
<jsp:setProperty name="beanId" property="score"
  value="<%= score %>" />
```

This is cumbersome. JSP provides a convenient syntax that can be used to simplify it:

```
<jsp:setProperty name="beanId" property="score"
  param="score" />
```

Instead of using the `value` attribute, you use the `param` attribute to name an input parameter. The value of this parameter is set to the property.

NOTE

Simple type conversion is performed automatically when a bean property is associated with an input parameter. A string input parameter is converted to an appropriate primitive data type or a wrapper class for a primitive type. For example, if the bean property is of the `int` type, the value of the parameter will be converted to the `int` type. If the bean property is of the Integer type, the value of the parameter will be converted to the `Integer` type.

Often the bean property and the parameter have the same name. You can use the following convenient statement to associate all the bean properties in `beanId` with the parameters that match the property names.

```
<jsp:setProperty name="beanId" property="*" />
```

Example 15.4 Using JavaBeans in JSP

This example creates a JavaBeans component named FactorialBean (see Listing 15.8) and uses it to compute the factorial of an input number in a JSP page named FactorialBean.jsp (see Listing 15.9). Figure 15.10 is a sample run of the page.

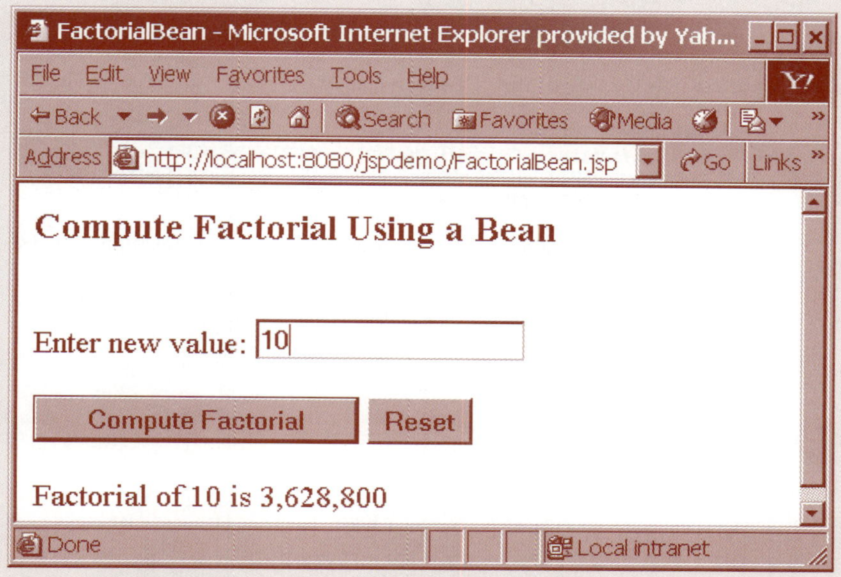

Figure 15.10 *The factorial of an input integer is computed using a method in the* `FactorialBean`.

continued

Example 15.4 continued

```
package jspdemo;

public class FactorialBean {
  private int number;

  /** Return number property */
  public int getNumber() {
    return number;
  }

  /** Set number property */
  public void setNumber(int newValue) {
    number = newValue;
  }

  /** Obtain factorial */
  public long getFactorial() {
    long factorial = 1;
    for (int i = 1; i <= number; i++)
      factorial *= i;
    return factorial;
  }
}
```

Listing 15.8 *FactorialBean.java*

```
1  <HTML>
2  <HEAD>
3  <jsp:useBean id="factorialBeanId" class="jspdemo.FactorialBean" >
4  </jsp:useBean>
5  <jsp:setProperty name="factorialBeanId" property="*" />
6  <TITLE>
7  FactorialBean
8  </TITLE>
9  </HEAD>
10 <BODY>
11 <H3>
12 Compute Factorial Using a Bean
13 </H3>
14 <FORM method="post">
15 <BR>Enter new value:  <INPUT NAME="number"><BR><BR>
16 <INPUT TYPE="SUBMIT" NAME="Submit" VALUE="Compute Factorial">
17 <INPUT TYPE="RESET" VALUE="Reset">
18 <P>Factorial of
19 <jsp:getProperty name="factorialBeanId" property="number" /> is
20 <%@ page import="java.text.*" %>
21 <% NumberFormat format = NumberFormat.getNumberInstance(); %>
22 <%= format.format(factorialBeanId.getFactorial()) %>
23 </FORM>
24 </BODY>
25 </HTML>
```

Listing 15.9 *FactorialBean.jsp*

Example Review

The `jsp:useBean` tag (Line 3) creates a bean `factorialBeanId` of the `FactorialBean` class. The `<jsp:setProperty name="factorialBeanId" property="*" />` associates all the bean properties with the input parameters that have the same name. In this case, the bean property number is associated with the input parameter number. When you click the Compute Factorial button, JSP automatically converts the input value for number from string into int and sets it to factorialBean before other statements are executed.

The <jsp:getProperty name="factorialBeanId" property="number" /> tag is equivalent to <%= factorialBeanId.getNumber() %>. The method factorialBeanId.getFactorial() returns the factorial for the number in factorialBeanId.

NOTE

As in the preceding chapter, please make sure the target class path is set to c:\radft\WEB-INF\classes, as shown in Figure 14.12. The compiled FactorialBean class is placed in c:\radft\WEB-INF\classes\jspdemo\.

Example 15.5 Testing Bean Scopes

This example creates a JavaBeans component named CountBean (see Listing 15.10) and uses it to count the number of visits to a page (see Listing 15.11). Figure 15.11 is a sample run of the page.

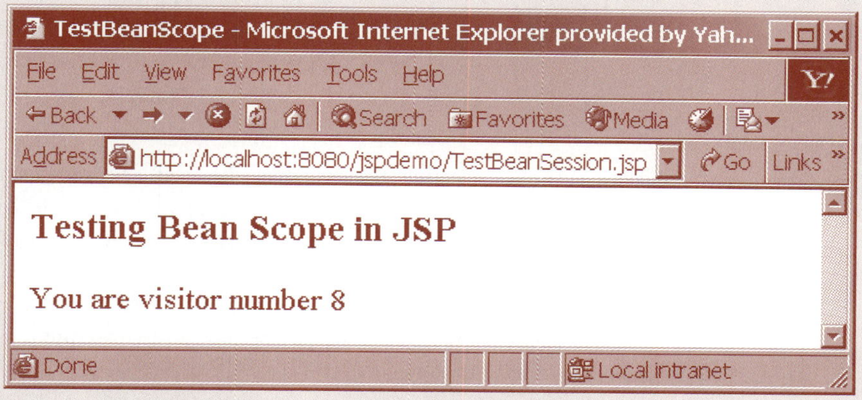

Figure 15.11 *The number of visits to the page is increased when the page is visited.*

```
package jspdemo;

public class CountBean {
  private int count = 0;

  /** Return count property */
  public int getCount() {
    return count;
  }

```

Listing 15.10 *CountBean.java*

continued

Example 15.5 continued

```
    /** Set count property */
    public void setCount(int count) {
      this.count = count;
    }

    /** Increase count */
    public void increaseCount() {
      count++;
    }
  }
```

Listing 15.10 *continued*

```
1   <HTML>
2   <HEAD>
3   <jsp:useBean id="countBeanId" scope="application"
4     class="jspdemo.CountBean" >
5   </jsp:useBean>
6   <jsp:setProperty name="countBeanId" property="*" />
7   <TITLE>TestBeanScope</TITLE>
8   </HEAD>
9   <BODY>
10  <H3>
11  Testing Bean Scope in JSP
12  </H3>
13  <% countBeanId.increaseCount(); %>
14  You are visitor number
15  <jsp:getProperty name="countBeanId" property="count" />
16  </FORM>
17  </BODY>
18  </HTML>
```

Listing 15.11 *TestBeanSession.jsp*

Example Review

The `scope` attribute (Line 3) specifies the scope of the bean. `scope="application"` specifies that the bean is alive in the JSP engine and available for all clients to access. The bean can be shared by any client with the directive `<jsp:useBean id="countBeanId" scope="application" class="CountBean" >`. Every client accessing TestBeanSession.jsp causes the count to increase by 1. The first client causes `countBeanId` object to be created, and subsequent access to `TestBeanSession` uses the same object.

If `scope="application"` is changed to `scope="page"`, the scope of the bean is limited to the page, and any other page cannot access this bean. The page will always display count 1. If `scope="application"` is changed to `scope="session"`, the scope of the bean is limited to the session from the same browser. The count will increase if the page is requested from the same browser.

15.9 Forwarding Requests from JavaServer Pages

Web applications developed using JSP generally consist of many pages linked together. JSP provides a forwarding tag in the following syntax that can be used to forward a page to another page.

```
<jsp:forward page="destination" />
```

Example 15.6 Browsing Database Tables

This example creates a JSP database application that browses tables. When you start the application, the first page prompts the user to enter the JDBC driver, url, username, and password for a database, as shown in Figure 15.1.2. After you login to the database, you can select a table to browse, as shown in Figure 15.13. Upon clicking the Browse Table Content button, the table content is displayed, as shown in Figure 15.14.

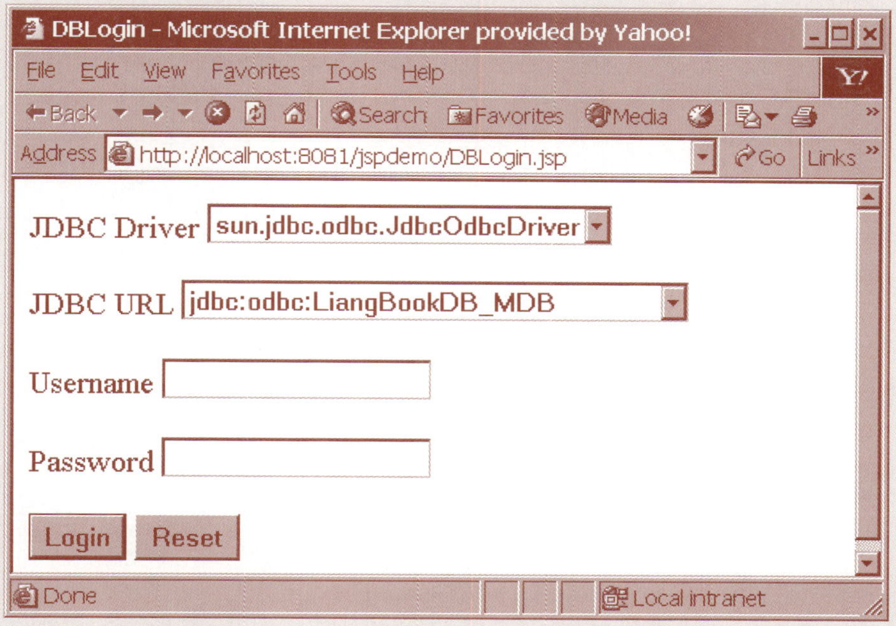

Figure 15.12 *To access a database, you need to provide the JDBC driver, url, username, and password.*

The example consists of the following files: DBBean.java (in Listing 15.12), DBLogin.jsp (in Listing 15.13), DBLoginInitialization.jsp (in Listing 15.14), Table.jsp (in Listing 15.15), and BrowseTable.jsp (in Listing 15.16).

continued

Example 15.6 continued

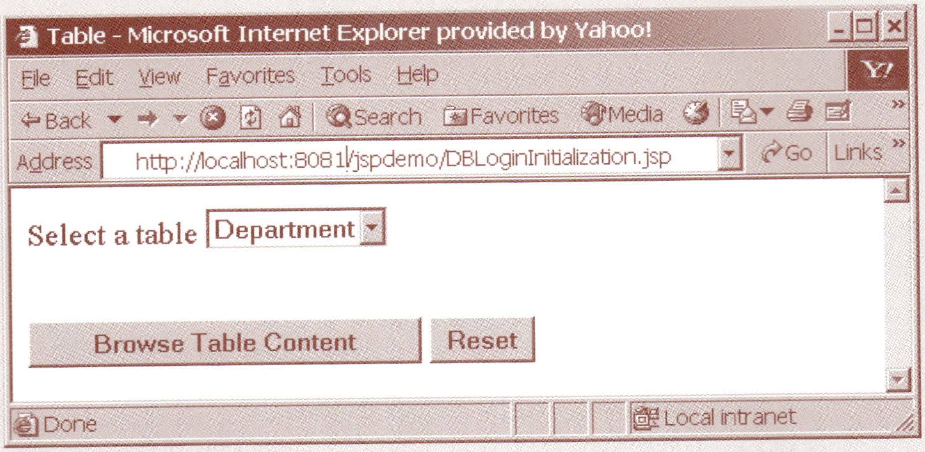

Figure 15.13 *You can select a table to browse from this page.*

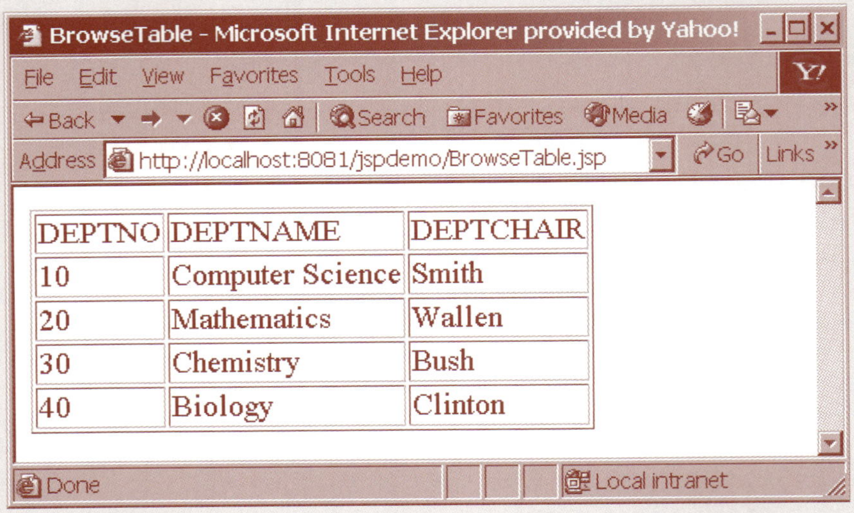

Figure 15.14 *The contents of the selected table are displayed.*

```
package jspdemo;

import java.sql.*;

public class DBBean {
  private Connection connection = null;
  private String username;
```

Listing 15.12 *DBBean.java*

```
  private String password;
  private String driver;
  private String url;

  public DBBean() {
  }

  /** Initialize database connection */
  public void initializeJdbc() {
    try {
      System.out.println("Driver is " + driver);
      Class.forName(driver);

      // Connect to the sample database
      connection = DriverManager.getConnection(url, username,
        password);
    }
    catch (Exception ex) {
      ex.printStackTrace();
    }
  }

  public String[] getTables() {
    String[] tables = null;

    try {
      DatabaseMetaData dbMetaData = connection.getMetaData();
      ResultSet rsTables = dbMetaData.getTables(null, null, null,
        new String[] {"TABLE"});

      int size = 0;
      while (rsTables.next()) size++;

      rsTables = dbMetaData.getTables(null, null, null,
        new String[] {"TABLE"});

      tables = new String[size];
      int i = 0;
      while (rsTables.next())
        tables[i++] = rsTables.getString("TABLE_NAME");
    }
    catch (Exception ex) {
      ex.printStackTrace();
    }

    return tables;
  }

  /** Return connection property */
  public Connection getConnection() {
    return connection;
  }

  public void setUsername(String newUsername) {
    username = newUsername;
  }

  public String getUsername() {
    return username;
  }

```

Listing 15.12 *continued*

continued

Example 15.6 continued

```
    public void setPassword(String newPassword) {
      password = newPassword;
    }

    public String getPassword() {
      return password;
    }

    public void setDriver(String newDriver) {
      driver = newDriver;
    }

    public String getDriver() {
      return driver;
    }

    public void setUrl(String newUrl) {
      url = newUrl;
    }

    public String getUrl() {
      return url;
    }
  }
```

Listing 15.12 *continued*

```
<HTML>
<HEAD>
<TITLE>
DBLogin
</TITLE>
</HEAD>
<BODY>
<FORM method="post" action="DBLoginInitialization.jsp">
JDBC Driver
  <select name="driver" size="1">
    <option>sun.jdbc.odbc.JdbcOdbcDriver
    <option>oracle.jdbc.driver.OracleDriver
  </select><BR>
<BR>JDBC URL
  <select name="url" size="1">
    <option>jdbc:odbc:LiangBookDB_MDB
    <option>jdbc:oracle:thin:@liang.armstrong.edu:1521:test
  </select><BR>
<BR>Username <INPUT NAME="username"><BR>
<BR>Password <INPUT NAME="password"><BR><BR>
<INPUT TYPE="SUBMIT" NAME="Submit" VALUE="Login">
<INPUT TYPE="RESET" VALUE="Reset">
</FORM>
</BODY>
</HTML>
```

Listing 15.13 *DBLogin.jsp*

```
<HTML>
<HEAD>
<jsp:useBean id="dBBeanId" scope="session"
  class="jspdemo.DBBean">
</jsp:useBean>
```

Listing 15.14 *DBLoginInitialization.jsp*

```
<jsp:setProperty name="dBBeanId" property="*" />
<TITLE>DBLoginInitialization</TITLE>
</HEAD>
<BODY>

<%-- Connect to the database --%>
<% dBBeanId.initializeJdbc(); %>

<% if (dBBeanId.getConnection() == null) { %>
     Error: Login failed. Try again.
<% }
   else {%>
     <jsp:forward page="Table.jsp" />
<% } %>
</BODY>
</HTML>
```

Listing 15.14 *continued*

```
<HTML>
<HEAD>
<jsp:useBean id="dBBeanId" scope="session"
  class="jspdemo.DBBean">
</jsp:useBean>
<TITLE>Table</TITLE>
</HEAD>
<BODY>
<% String[] tables = dBBeanId.getTables();
   if (tables == null) { %>
     No tables
<% }
   else { %>
     <FORM method="post" action="BrowseTable.jsp">
     Select a table <select name="tablename" size="1">
     <% for (int i = 0; i < tables.length; i++) { %>
       <option><%= tables[i] %>
<%   }
   } %>
</select><BR><BR><BR>
<INPUT TYPE="SUBMIT" NAME="Submit" VALUE="Browse Table Content">
<INPUT TYPE="RESET" VALUE="Reset">
</FORM>
</BODY>
</HTML>
```

Listing 15.15 *Table.jsp*

```
<HTML>
<HEAD>
<jsp:useBean id="dBBeanId" scope="session"
  class="jspdemo.DBBean" >
</jsp:useBean>
<%@ page import="java.sql.*" %>
<TITLE>BrowseTable</TITLE>
</HEAD>
<BODY>

<%String tableName = request.getParameter("tablename");

```

Listing 15.16 *BrowseTable.jsp*

continued

Example 15.6 continued

```
    ResultSet rsColumns = dBBeanId.getConnection().getMetaData().
      getColumns(null, null, tableName, null);
  %>
    <table border="1">
      <tr>
  <%  // Add column names to the table
    while (rsColumns.next()) { %>
        <td> <%= rsColumns.getString("COLUMN_NAME") %> </td>
  <%} %>
    </tr>

  <%
    Statement statement = dBBeanId.getConnection().createStatement();
    ResultSet rs = statement.executeQuery(
      "select * from " + tableName + ";");

    // Get column count
    int columnCount = rs.getMetaData().getColumnCount();

    // Store rows to rowData
    while (rs.next()) {
      out.println("<tr>");
      for (int i = 0; i < columnCount; i++) { %>
        <td> <%= rs.getObject(i+1) %> </td>
  <%  }
      out.println("</tr>");
    } %>
  </table>
  </BODY>
  </HTML>
```

Listing 15.16 *continued*

Example Review

You start the application from DBLogin.jsp. This page prompts the user to enter a JDBC driver, url, username, and password to login to a database. A list of accessible drivers and urls are provided in the selection list. You must make sure that these databases are accessible from the JSP server and that their drivers are installed on the server side in the Explorer.

When you click the Login button, DBLoginInitialization.jsp is invoked. When this page is processed for the first time, an instance of `DBBean` named `dBBeanId` is created. The input parameters `driver`, `url`, `username`, and `password` are passed to the bean properties. The `initializeJdbc` method loads the driver and establishes a connection to the database. If login fails, the `connection` property is `null`. In this case, an error message is displayed. If login succeeds, control is forwarded to Table.jsp.

Table.jsp shares `dBBeanId` with DBLoginInitialization.jsp in the same session, so it can access `connection` through `dBBeanId` and obtain tables in the database using the database metadata. The table names are displayed in a selection box in a form. When the user selects a table name and clicks the Browse Table Content button, BrowseTable.jsp is processed.

BrowseTable.jsp shares `dBBeanId` with Table.jsp and DBLoginInitialization.jsp in the same session. It retrieves the table contents for the selected table from Table.jsp.

Note
If you use an Oracle database, please see Figure 14.21 on how to set the Oracle driver in the execution classpath for Tomcat server.

Chapter Summary

This chapter introduced to embed Java code in HTML to produce dynamic contents. You learned the relationship and differences between Java servlets and JSP. You learned that a Web server processes JSP by translating it to a servlet. You learned to use JSP constructs (scripting constructs, directives, and actions), JSP predefined variables, and JSP directives to create JSP pages. You also learned to use JavaBeans in JSP and forward requests from JSP.

Review Questions

15.1 What is the file name extension of a JavaServer page? How is a JSP page processed?

15.2 What are a JSP expression, a JSP scriptlet, and a JSP declaration? How do you write these constructs in JSP?

15.3 Describe the predefined variables in JSP.

15.4 Describe the JSP directives and attributes for the `page` directive.

15.5 You can create an object in a JSP scriptlet. What is the difference between an object created using the `new` operator and a bean created using the `<jsp: useBean . . . >` tag?

15.6 What is the `scope` attribute for? Describe four scope attributes.

15.7 Describe how a `<jsp:useBean . . . >` statement is processed by the JSP engine.

15.8 How do you write a statement to forward requests to another JSP page?

Programming Exercises

15.1 Write a JavaServer page to display a table that contains factorials for the numbers from 0 to 10, as shown in Figure 15.15.

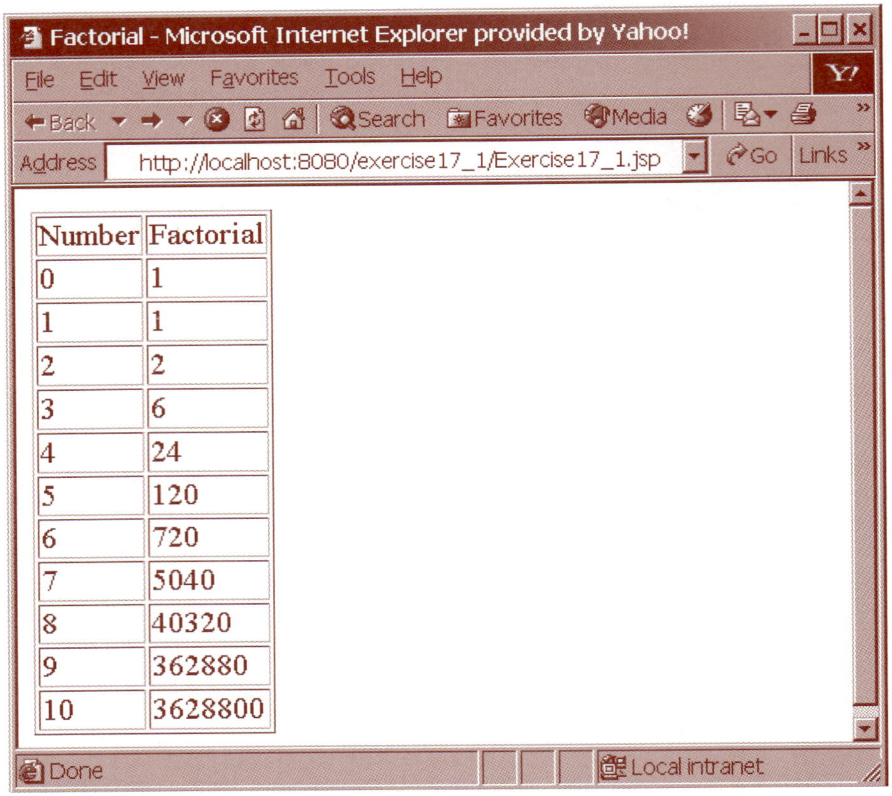

Figure 15.15 *The JSP page displays factorials for the numbers from 0 to 10 in a table.*

15.2 Rewrite Exercise 14.2 using JSP.

CHAPTER 16

REMOTE METHOD INVOCATIONS

Objectives

- To know how RMI works.
- To learn the process of developing RMI applications.
- To know the differences between RMI and socket-level programming.
- To develop three-tier applications using RMI.
- To use callbacks to develop interactive applications.

16.1 Introduction

The Java language is superior for developing reusable software components, and the JavaBeans technology enables you to create Java applications by using a builder tool to assemble JavaBeans components during design time. Remote Method Invocation (RMI) technology provides a framework for building distributed Java systems. Using RMI, a Java object on one system can invoke a method in an object on another system on the network. A *distributed Java system* can be defined as a collection of cooperative distributed objects on the network. This chapter introduces RMI basics. You will learn how to use RMI to create useful distributed applications.

> **NOTE**
> Forte 4 CE does not support RMI. You have to use Forte 4 Enterprise Edition for this chapter.

16.2 RMI Basics

RMI is the Java Distributed Object Model for facilitating communications among distributed objects. RMI is a higher-level API built on top of sockets. Socket-level programming allows you to pass data through sockets among computers. RMI enables you not only to pass data among objects on different systems, but also to invoke methods in a remote object.

RMI is similar to Remote Procedure Calls (RPC) in the sense that both RMI and RPC enable you to invoke methods, but there are some important differences. With RPC, you call a standalone procedure. With RMI, you invoke a method within a specific object. RMI can be viewed as object-oriented RPC.

In many ways, RMI is an evolution of the client/server architecture. A *client* is a component that issues requests for services, and a *server* is a component that delivers the requested services. Like the client/server architecture, RMI maintains the notion of clients and servers, but the RMI approach is more flexible than the client/server paradigm.

- An RMI component can act as both a client and a server, depending on the scenario in question.
- An RMI system can pass functionality from a server to a client, and vice versa. A client/server system typically only passes data back and forth between server and client.

16.2.1 How Does RMI Work?

For an object to be invoked remotely, it must be defined in a Java interface accessible to both the server and the client. Furthermore, the interface must extend the `java.rmi.Remote` interface. Like the `java.io.Serializable` interface, `java.rmi.Re-`

`mote` is a marker interface that contains no constants or methods. It is only used to identify remote objects. The implementation of the remote object interface, referred to as *server implementation*, resides on the server machine and is registered with the RMI registry, as shown in Figure 16.1. A client looks through the RMI registry for the remote object. Once it is located, it can be used in the same way as a local object.

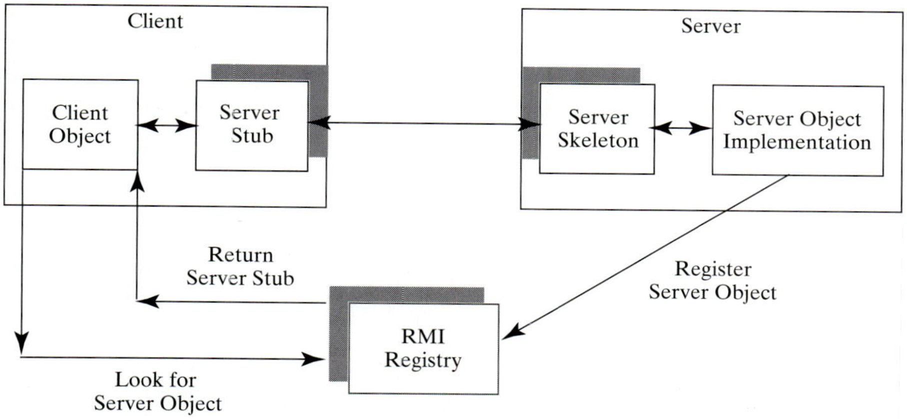

Figure 16.1 *Java RMI uses a registry to provide naming services for remote objects, and uses the stub and skeleton to facilitate communications between client and server.*

Obviously, invoking methods in a remote object on a server is very different from invoking methods in a local object on a client, since the remote object is in a different address space on a separate machine. The following steps are usually involved in invoking a remote method:

1. The client sends method parameters to the server.
2. The server receives the method parameters and executes the method.
3. The server sends the result back to the client.
4. The client receives the result.

Implementing this service is complicated, but the good news is that RMI provides a mechanism that liberates you from writing the tedious code for handling parameter passing and invoking remote methods. The basic idea is to use two helper classes known as *stub* and *skeleton* for handling communications between client and server, as shown in Figure 16.1.

The stub and the skeleton can be automatically generated from the server implementation using an RMI utility called `rmic`. The *stub* resides on the client machine. It contains all the reference information the client needs to know about the server object. When a client invokes a method on a server object, it actually invokes a method that is encapsulated in the stub. The stub is responsible for sending parameters to the server, and for receiving the result from the server and returning it to the client.

The *skeleton* communicates with the stub on the server side. The skeleton receives parameters from the client, passes them to the server for execution, and returns the result to the stub.

16.2.2 Passing Parameters

When a client invokes a remote method with parameters, passing the parameters is handled by the stub and the skeleton. Let us consider three types of parameters:

- **Primitive data types**, such as `char`, `int`, `double`, or `boolean`, are passed by value like a local call.
- **Local object types**, such as `java.lang.String`, are also passed by value, but this is completely different from passing an object parameter in a local call. In a local call, an object parameter's reference is passed, which corresponds to the memory address of the object. In a remote call, there is no way to pass the object reference because the address on one machine is meaningless to a different Java VM. Any object can be used as a parameter in a remote call as long as it is serializable. The stub serializes the object parameter and sends it in a stream across the network. The skeleton deserializes the stream into an object.
- **Remote object types** are passed differently from local objects. When a client invokes a remote method with a parameter of a remote object type, the stub of the remote object is passed. The server receives the stub and manipulates the parameter through it. See Example 16.4, "Developing a TicTacToe Game with RMI," for details.

16.3 Developing RMI Applications

Now that you have a basic understanding of RMI, you are ready to write simple RMI applications. The steps in developing an RMI application are shown in Figure 16.2.

The following example demonstrates the development of an RMI application through these steps.

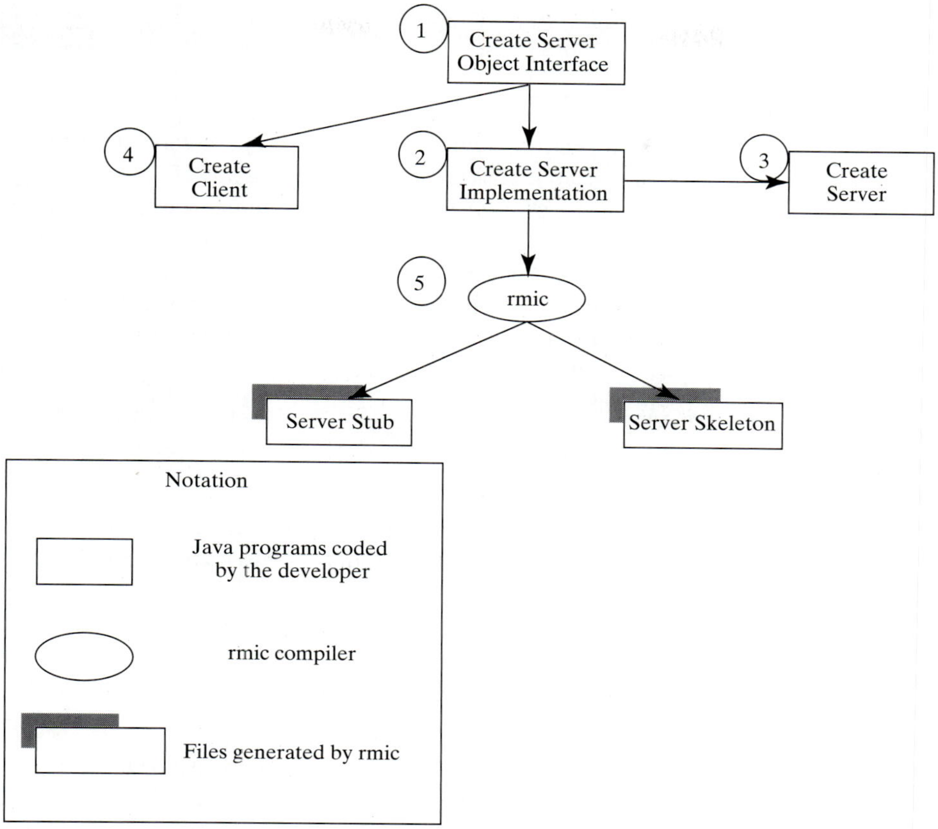

Figure 16.2 *The steps in developing RMI applications.*

Example 16.1 Retrieving Student Scores from an RMI Server

This example creates a client that retrieves student scores from an RMI server. The client, shown in Figure 16.3, displays the score for the specified name.

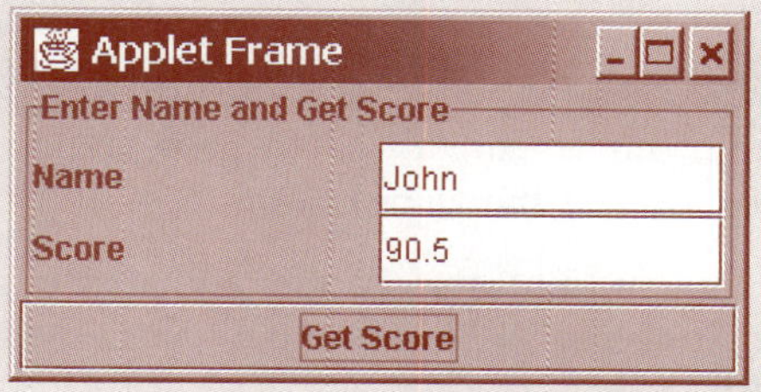

Figure 16.3 *You can get the score by entering a student name and clicking the Get Score button.*

continued

Example 16.1 continued

Here are the steps to complete this example:

1. Create a new package named `rmidemo`. From the context menu of the rmidemo node, choose *New, RMI, UnicastRemoteObject* to display the RMI wizard. Type `Student` in the Interface Name field, and click *Next* to display the Add New Remote Methods panel. Click *Next* to skip to display the Implementation Panel, and type `StudentImpl` in the Implementation Name field. Click *Finish* to create the templates for the remote interface `Student` and its implementation, `StudentImpl`. `StudentImpl` contains a main method to start the server.

2. Implement the server interface `Student`, as shown in Listing 16.1. The interface tells the client how to invoke the server's `findScore` method to retrieve a student score.

3. Implement `StudentImpl`, as shown in Listing 16.2. The `findScore` method returns the score for a specified student. This method returns -1 if the score is not found.

4. Now turn your attention to developing the client.

   4.1. Create an applet named `StudentClient` using the Forte Swing JApplet form wizard.

   4.2. Create the user interface. Drop a JButton to the south of the applet to create `jbtGetScore`. Drop a `JPanel` to the center of the applet to create `jPanel1`, and change the panel's `layout` to `GridLayout` to create `gridLayout1`. Select `gridLayout1` in the component tree, and set `columns` and `rows` to 2. Drop a `JLabel`, a `JTextField`, a `JLabel`, and a `JTextField` to the applet, and rename them to `jlblName`, `jtfName`, `jlblScore`, and `jtfScore`. Set the `text` property of `jlblName` to "Name," and the `text` property of `jlblScore` to "Score."

   4.3. Create the method `initializeRMI` for locating the `Student` server, as shown in Listing 16.3. Add the code to invoke this method from the constructor.

   4.4. Double-click `jbtGetScore` in the form to generate the handler for the button. Implement this handler for finding and displaying the student's score, as shown in Listing 16.3.

5. Compile StudentImpl.java. Forte automatically generates the stubs StudentImpl_Stub.class and StudentImpl_Skel.class.

6. Follow the steps below to run this example.

   6.1. Run `StudentImpl` to start the server. This action does the following: (1) It automatically starts the RMI registry if it is not started. (2) It starts the server. You will see a server process displayed from the

Runtime tab in the Explorer, as shown in Figure 16.4. (3) The server object is registered with the RMI registry, which is displayed in the Output window (Figure 16.5) from the print statement in Line 75 in Listing 16.2.

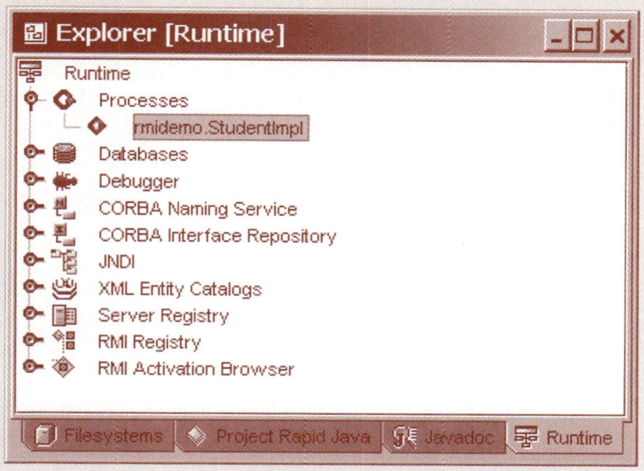

Figure 16.4 *From the Runtime tab, you can see that the server object is registered with the registry.*

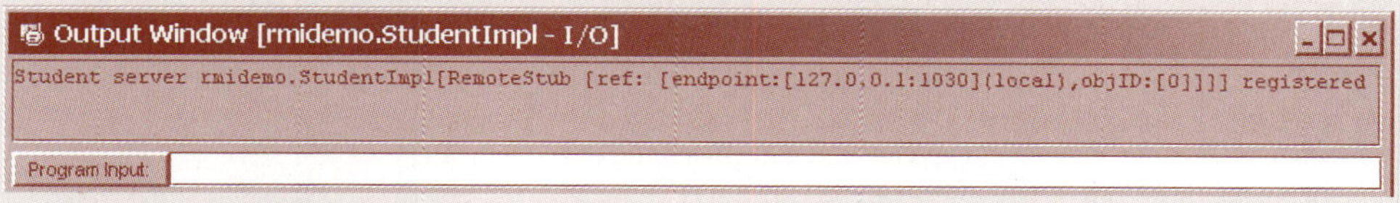

Figure 16.5 *From the Output window, you can display a message to show that the server object is registered with the RMI registry.*

6.2. Run `StudentClient` as an application. A sample run of the application is shown in Figure 16.3.

6.3. Run rmidemo.StudentClient.html from the appletviewer. A sample run is shown in Figure 16.6.

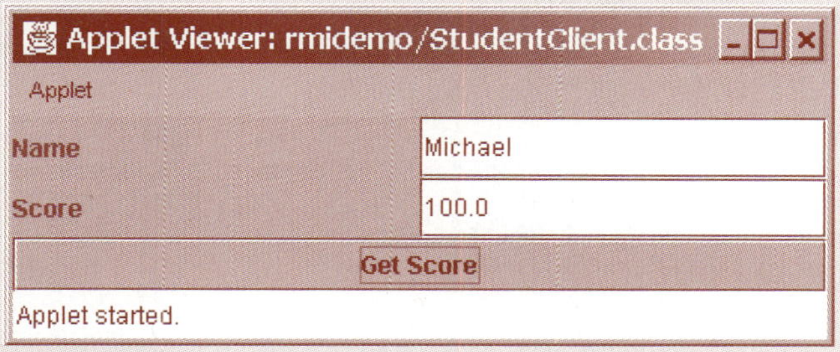

Figure 16.6 *You can run* `StudentClient` *as an applet.*

continued

Example 16.1 continued

```
// Student.java: Student server interface
package rmidemo;

import java.rmi.*;

public interface Student extends Remote {
  /**
   * Return the score for specified the name
   * @param   name   the student name
   * @return  an double score or -1 if the student
   *     is not found
   */
  public double findScore(String name) throws RemoteException;
}
```

Listing 16.1 *Student.java*

```
// StudentImpl.java: implementation for Student.java
package rmidemo;

import java.rmi.*;
import java.rmi.server.*;
import java.rmi.registry.*;
import java.net.MalformedURLException;
import java.util.*;

public class StudentImpl extends UnicastRemoteObject implements Student {
  // Stores scores in a map indexed by name
  private HashMap scores = new HashMap();

  /** Constructor */
  public StudentImpl() throws RemoteException {
    initializeStudent();
  }

  /** Initialize student information */
  protected void initializeStudent() {
    scores.put("John", new Double(90.5));
    scores.put("Michael", new Double(100));
    scores.put("Michelle", new Double(98.5));
  }

  /** Implement the findScore method from the Student interface */
  public double findScore(String name) throws RemoteException {
    Double d = (Double)scores.get(name);

    if (d == null) {
      System.out.println("Student " + name + " is not found ");
      return -1;
    }
    else {
      System.out.println("Student " + name + "\'s score is "
        + d.doubleValue());
      return d.doubleValue();
    }
  }

  /** Register StudentImpl object with the RMI registry.
```

Listing 16.2 *StudentImpl.java*

```
   * @param name - name identifying the service in the RMI registry
   * @param create - create local registry if necessary
   * @throw RemoteException if cannot be exported or bound to RMI
   *    registry
   * @throw MalformedURLException if name cannot be used to
   *    construct a valid URL
   * @throw IllegalArgumentException if null passed as name
   */
  public static void registerToRegistry(String name, Remote obj,
    boolean create) throws RemoteException, MalformedURLException{

    if (name == null) throw new IllegalArgumentException(
      "registration name can not be null");

    try {
      Naming.rebind(name, obj);
    } catch (RemoteException ex){
      if (create) {
        Registry r =
          LocateRegistry.createRegistry(Registry.REGISTRY_PORT);
        r.rebind(name, obj);
      } else throw ex;
    }
  }

  /** Main method.
   */
  public static void main(String[] args) {
    System.setSecurityManager(new RMISecurityManager());

    try {
      StudentImpl obj = new StudentImpl();
      registerToRegistry("StudentImpl", obj, true);
      System.out.println("Student server " + obj + " registered");
    } catch (RemoteException ex) {
      ex.printStackTrace();
    } catch (MalformedURLException ex) {
      ex.printStackTrace();
    }
  }
}
```

Listing 16.2 *continued*

```
// StudentClient.java: Student RMI Client
package rmidemo;

import java.rmi.*;
import javax.swing.*;
import java.awt.*;

public class StudentClient extends javax.swing.JApplet {
  // Declare a Student instance
  Student student;

  boolean isStandalone;

  /** Creates new form StudentClient */
```

Listing 16.3 *StudentClient.java*

continued

Example 16.1 continued

```
  public void init() {
    initComponents();

    // Initialize RMI
    initializeRMI();
  }

  private void initComponents() {
    jbtGetScore = new javax.swing.JButton();
    jPanel1 = new javax.swing.JPanel();
    jlblName = new javax.swing.JLabel();
    jtfName = new javax.swing.JTextField();
    jlblScore = new javax.swing.JLabel();
    jtfScore = new javax.swing.JTextField();
    jbtGetScore.setText("Get Score");
    jbtGetScore.addActionListener(
      new java.awt.event.ActionListener() {
      public void actionPerformed(java.awt.event.ActionEvent evt) {
        jbtGetScoreActionPerformed(evt);
      }
    });
    getContentPane().add(jbtGetScore, java.awt.BorderLayout.SOUTH);
    jPanel1.setLayout(new java.awt.GridLayout(2, 2));
    jlblName.setText("Name");
    jPanel1.add(jlblName);
    jPanel1.add(jtfName);
    jlblScore.setText("Score");
    jPanel1.add(jlblScore);
    jPanel1.add(jtfScore);
    getContentPane().add(jPanel1, java.awt.BorderLayout.CENTER);
  }

  private void jbtGetScoreActionPerformed(
    java.awt.event.ActionEvent evt) {
    try {
      // Get student score
      double score = student.findScore(jtfName.getText().trim());

      // Display the result
      if (score < 0)
        jtfScore.setText("Not found");
      else
        jtfScore.setText(new Double(score).toString());
    }
    catch(Exception ex) {
      System.out.println(ex);
    }
  }

  /** Initialize RMI */
  protected void initializeRMI() {
    String url;

    if (isStandalone) {
      // System.setSecurityManager(new RMISecurityManager());

      url = "rmi:///";
      // Use rmi://hostname/ if the server is located on hostname,
```

Listing 16.3 *continued*

```
      // i.e. rmi://liang.armstrong.edu/
    }
    else {
      // Initialize RMI for an applet
      url = getCodeBase().getHost();
      if (url.equals("default")) url = "";
      url = "rmi://" + url + "/";
    }

    try {
      student = (Student)Naming.lookup(url + "StudentImpl");
      System.out.println("Server object " + student + " found");
    }
    catch(Exception ex) {
      System.out.println(ex);
    }
  }

  /** Main method */
  public static void main(String[] args) {
    StudentClient applet = new StudentClient();
    applet.isStandalone = true;
    JFrame frame = new JFrame();
    frame.setTitle("StudentClient");
    frame.getContentPane().add(applet, BorderLayout.CENTER);
    frame.setSize(250, 150);
    applet.init();
    Dimension d = Toolkit.getDefaultToolkit().getScreenSize();
    frame.setLocation((d.width - frame.getSize().width) / 2,
    (d.height - frame.getSize().height) / 2);
    frame.setVisible(true);
    frame.setDefaultCloseOperation(3);
  }

  // Variables declaration - do not modify
  private javax.swing.JButton jbtGetScore;
  private javax.swing.JPanel jPanel1;
  private javax.swing.JLabel jlblName;
  private javax.swing.JTextField jtfName;
  private javax.swing.JLabel jlblScore;
  private javax.swing.JTextField jtfScore;
  // End of variables declaration
}
```

Listing 16.3 *continued*

Example Review

Any object that can be used remotely must be defined in an interface that extends the `java.rmi.Remote` interface (Line 6 in Listing 16.1). The `Student` interface, extending `Remote`, defines the `findScore` method that can be remotely invoked by a client to find a student's score. Each method in this interface must declare that it may throw a `java.rmi.RemoteException` (Line 13). So your client code that invokes this method must be prepared to catch this exception in a try-catch block.

On the server side, the `StudentImpl` class (Listing 16.2) implements the `Student` interface. This class must also extend the `java.rmi.server.RemoteServer` class or its subclass. `RemoteServer` is an abstract class that defines the methods needed to create and export remote objects. Often its subclass

continued

Example 16.1 continued

`java.rmi.server.UnicastRemoteObject`is used (Line 10 in Listing 16.2). This subclass implements all the abstract methods defined in `RemoteServer`.

`StudentImpl` implements the `findScore` method (Lines 26–39) defined in the `Student` interface. For simplicity, three students, John, Michael, and Michelle, and their corresponding scores are stored in an instance of `java.util.HashMap` named `scores`. `HashMap` is a concrete class of the `Map` interface in the Java Collections Framework, which makes it possible to search and retrieve a value using a key. Both values and keys are of `Object` type. The `findScore` method returns the score if the name is in the hash map, and returns -1 if the name is not found.

`StudentImpl` contains a main method, which is responsible for starting the server. It performs the following tasks:

1. Installing an RMI security manager to control the classes that are dynamically loaded with the following code (Line 70):

   ```
   System.setSecurityManager(new RMISecurityManager());
   ```

2. Invoking the `registerToRegistry("StudentImpl", obj, true)` method (Line 74) to register the server object named `StudentImpl` in the RMI registry. The code to register is:

   ```
   Naming.rebind("StudentImpl", obj);
   ```

`java.rmi.Naming` provides the bootstrap mechanism for locating remote objects. The server registers with the service, and the client retrieves the stub of the remote object through the service. The static `bind` method binds the name to a specified remote object. You can also use the `rebind` method to rebind the name to a new object and replace any existing binding associated with the name.

`StudentClient` invokes the `findScore` method on the server to find the score for a specified student. The key method in `StudentClient` is the `initializeRMI` method (Lines 64–89), which is responsible for locating the server stub. The stub is specified in an RMI URL using the usual host name, port, and server name:

rmi://hostname:port/servername

where *hostname* is the host name of the RMI registry (defaults to current host), *port* is the port number of the RMI registry (defaults to the registry port number), and *servername* is the name for a remote object, such as "Student Server" in this example.

The `initializeRMI()` method treats standalone applications differently from applets. The hostname should be the name where the applet is downloaded. It can be obtained using the `Applet`'s `getCodeBase().getHost()`. For standalone applications, the hostname should be specified explicitly.

The `Naming.lookup()` method (Line 83) returns the remote object for the specified RMI URL. Once a remote object is found, it can be used just like a local object. The stub and the skeleton are used behind the scenes to make the remote method invocation work.

If you run the client and the server on separate machines, you need to start RMIRegistry and run `StudentServer` on the server machine before running `StudentClient` on the client machine. To run `StudentClient` standalone, you need to deploy Student.class, StudentImpl_Stub.class, and StudentClient.class on the client machine, and place Student.class, StudentImpl.class, StudentImpl_Skel.class, and StudentServer.class on the server machine. To run `StudentClient` from a Web browser, you need to place Student.class, StudentImpl.class, StudentImpl_Stub.class, StudentImpl_Skel.class, StudentClient.class, and StudentClient.html on the server machine.

CAUTION

If you modify the remote object implementation class, you must regenerate stub and skeleton classes. You need to restart the server class to reload the skeleton to the RMI registry. In some old versions of rmiregistry, you may have to restart rmiregistry.

16.4 RMI vs. Socket-Level Programming

Example 16.1 involves many files, but the stub and the skeleton were automatically generated by the `rmic` utility. These programs are easy to develop once you understand RMI. To demonstrate the power and elegance of the RMI concept, this section rewrites Example 16.1 using socket-level programming so that you can compare RMI programming with socket-level programming.

Example 16.2 Retrieving Student Scores from a Server Using Socket-Level Programming

This example rewrites Example 16.1 using socket-level programming. The purpose is to highlight the differences between RMI and socket-level programming and to demonstrate the superiority of RMI for client/sever applications. If you are not familiar with socket-level programming, please refer to Chapter 18, "Networking," in my *Introduction to Java Programming with Sun ONE Studio 4.*

Here are the steps to complete the example.

1. Create a new project named socketprogrammingdemo.jpr.
2. Create the server class named `SocketStudentServer`, as shown in Listing 16.4.

continued

Example 16.2 continued

3. Create the client class named `SocketStudentClient`, as shown in Listing 16.5.
4. Start SocketStudentServer and then start SocketStudentClient. SocketStudentClient runs like StudentClient, as shown in Figure 16.6.

```
// SocketStudentServer.java
package socketprogrammingdemo;

import java.io.*;
import java.net.*;
import java.util.*;

public class SocketStudentServer {
  private HashMap scores = new HashMap();

  /** Constructor */
  public SocketStudentServer() {
    // Initialize scores hashtable
    initializeStudent();

    try {
      // Create a server socket
      ServerSocket serverSocket = new ServerSocket(8000);

      // Server the clients
      while (true) {
        // Listen for a new connection request
        Socket connectToClient = serverSocket.accept();
        System.out.println(
          "Starting a new server thread for a new client");

        // Create a new thread for the connection
        ThreadHandler thread = new ThreadHandler(connectToClient);

        // Start the new thread
        thread.start();
      }
    }
    catch(IOException ex) {
      System.err.println(ex);
    }
  }

  public static void main(String[] args) {
    // Initialize SocketStudentServer
    new SocketStudentServer();
  }

  /** Initialize student information */
  protected void initializeStudent() {
    scores.put("John", new Double(90.5));
    scores.put("Michael", new Double(100));
    scores.put("Michelle", new Double(98.5));
  }

```

Listing 16.4 *SocketStudentServer.java*

```
    /** Get student score. Return -1 if score is not found */
    public double findScore(String name) {
      Double d = (Double)scores.get(name);

      if (d == null) {
        System.out.println("Student " + name + " is not found ");
        return -1;
      }
      else {
        System.out.println("Student " + name + "\'s score is "
          + d.doubleValue());
        return d.doubleValue();
      }
    }

    /** The server for handling a client, an inner class */
    class ThreadHandler extends Thread {
      private Socket connectToClient; // A connected socket

      public ThreadHandler(Socket socket) {
        connectToClient = socket;
      }

      public void run() {
        try {
          // Create data input and print streams
          BufferedReader isFromClient = new BufferedReader(
            new InputStreamReader(connectToClient.getInputStream()));
          PrintWriter osToClient =
            new PrintWriter(connectToClient.getOutputStream(), true);

          // Continuously serve the client
          while (true) {
            // Receive student name from the client in string
            String name = isFromClient.readLine();
            System.out.println(
              "Student name received from client is " + name);

            // Find score
            double score = findScore(name);

            // Send score back to the client
            osToClient.println(score);
          }
        }
        catch(IOException ex) {
          System.err.println(ex);
        }
      }
    } // End of the inner class
  }
```

Listing 16.4 *continued*

```
// SocketStudentClient.java: Student Client
package socketprogrammingdemo;

import javax.swing.*;
import java.awt.*;
import java.awt.event.*;
```

Listing 16.5 *SocketStudentClient.java*

continued

Example 16.2 continued

```
import javax.swing.border.*;
import java.io.*;
import java.net.*;
import java.util.*;

public class SocketStudentClient extends JApplet {
  // Declare I/O streams
  protected BufferedReader isFromServer;
  protected PrintWriter osToServer;

  boolean isStandalone = false;

  public void initialize() {
    try {
      // Create a socket to connect to the server
      Socket connectToServer = new Socket("localhost", 8000);

      // Create a buffered input stream to receive data
      // from the server
      isFromServer = new BufferedReader(
        new InputStreamReader(connectToServer.getInputStream()));

      // Create a buffered output stream to send data to the server
      osToServer =
        new PrintWriter(connectToServer.getOutputStream(), true);
    }
    catch (IOException ex) {
      System.err.println(ex);
    }
  }

  /** Creates component */
  public SocketStudentClient() {
    initComponents();

    initialize();
  }

  private void initComponents() {
    jbtGetScore = new javax.swing.JButton();
    jPanel1 = new javax.swing.JPanel();
    jlblName = new javax.swing.JLabel();
    jtfName = new javax.swing.JTextField();
    jlblScore = new javax.swing.JLabel();
    jtfScore = new javax.swing.JTextField();
    jbtGetScore.setText("Get Score");
    jbtGetScore.addActionListener(
      new java.awt.event.ActionListener() {
      public void actionPerformed(java.awt.event.ActionEvent evt) {
        jbtGetScoreActionPerformed(evt);
      }
    });
    getContentPane().add(jbtGetScore, java.awt.BorderLayout.SOUTH);
    jPanel1.setLayout(new java.awt.GridLayout(2, 2));
    jlblName.setText("Name");
    jPanel1.add(jlblName);
    jPanel1.add(jtfName);
    jlblScore.setText("Score");
    jPanel1.add(jlblScore);
    jPanel1.add(jtfScore);
```

Listing 16.5 *continued*

```
    getContentPane().add(jPanel1, java.awt.BorderLayout.CENTER);
  }

  /** Main method */
  public static void main(String[] args) {
    SocketStudentClient applet = new SocketStudentClient();
    applet.isStandalone = true;
    JFrame frame = new JFrame();
    frame.setTitle("SocketStudentClient");
    frame.getContentPane().add(applet, BorderLayout.CENTER);
    applet.init();
    applet.start();
    frame.setSize(250, 150);
    Dimension d = Toolkit.getDefaultToolkit().getScreenSize();
    frame.setLocation((d.width - frame.getSize().width) / 2,
      (d.height - frame.getSize().height) / 2);
    frame.setVisible(true);
    frame.setDefaultCloseOperation(3);
  }

  void jbtGetScoreActionPerformed(ActionEvent e) {
    try {
      // Send student name to the server
      osToServer.println(jtfName.getText().trim());

      // Get score from the server as a string
      StringTokenizer st = new StringTokenizer(
        isFromServer.readLine());

      // Convert string to double
      double score = new Double(
        st.nextToken()).doubleValue();

      // Display the result
      if (score < 0)
        jtfScore.setText("Not found");
      else
        jtfScore.setText(new Double(score).toString());
    }
    catch (IOException ex) {
      System.err.println(ex);
    }
  }

  private JLabel jlblName = new JLabel();
  private JTextField jtfName = new JTextField();
  private JButton jbtGetScore = new JButton();
  private JTextField jtfScore = new JTextField();
  private JPanel jPanel1 = new JPanel();
  private GridLayout gridLayout1 = new GridLayout();
  private BorderLayout borderLayout1 = new BorderLayout();
  private TitledBorder titledBorder1;
  private JLabel jlblScore = new JLabel();
}
```

Listing 16.5 *continued*

Example Review

The server class `SocketStudentServer` does the following things:

1. It initializes the scores in the hash map (Lines 44–49), which is the same as in Example 16.1.

continued

Example 16.2 continued

2. It creates an instance of `java.net.ServerSocket` named `serverSocket` (Line 18), which is the base for listening to incoming connection requests from clients. The server socket is associated with a specific port. In this case, port 8000 is the server socket.

3. It creates an instance of `java.net.Socket` for connecting to a client (Line 23), and starts a new server for handling the client on a separate thread. Since this server (`ThreadHandler`) is an inner class, `scores` and the `findScore()` method defined in `SocketStudentServer` are directly accessible in this class. `ThreadHandler` continuously reads a name from the client, finds the score, and sends it to the client.

The client class `SocketStudentClient` is similar to `StudentClient` in Example 16.1 except that it communicates with the server through socket I/O, as follows:

1. Create an instance of `java.net.Socket` for connecting with the server at port 8000 (Line 22). Instantiate the I/O streams for sending and receiving data from the server (Lines 26–31).

2. In the handler for the button Get Student Score, write the code to send the name to the server and receive the score from the server (Lines 88–108).

A comparison of Examples 16.1 and 16.2 clearly shows the advantages of using RMI against using socket-level programming.

- RMI enables you to program at a higher level of abstraction. It hides the details of socket server, socket, connection, and sending or receiving data. It even implements a multithreading server under the hood, whereas with socket-level programming you have to explicitly implement threads for handling multiple clients.

- RMI applications are scalable and easy to maintain. You can change the RMI server or move it to another machine without modifying the client program except for resetting the URL to locate the server. (To avoid resetting the URL, you can modify the client to pass the URL as a command-line parameter.) In socket-level programming, a client operation to send data requires a server operation to read it. The implementation of client and server at the socket-level is tightly synchronized.

- RMI clients can directly invoke the server method, whereas socket-level programming is limited to passing values.

As you can see, socket-level programming is very primitive. Avoid using it to develop client/server applications. As an analogy, socket-level programming is like programming in assembly language, while RMI programming is like programming in a high-level language.

16.5 Developing Three-Tier Applications Using RMI

Three-tier applications have gained considerable attention in recent years, largely because of the demand for more scalable and load-balanced systems to replace traditional two-tier client/server database systems. A centralized database system not only handles data access but also processes the business rules on data. Thus, a centralized database is usually heavily loaded because it requires extensive data manipulation and processing. In some situations, data processing is handled by the client and business rules are stored on the client side. It is preferable to use a middle tier as a buffer between a client and the database. The middle tier can be used to apply business logic and rules, and to process data to reduce the load on the database.

A three-tier architecture does more than just reduce the processing load on the server. It also provides access to multiple network sites. This is especially useful to Java applets that need to access multiple databases on different servers, since an applet can only connect with the server from which it is downloaded.

The following example demonstrates the use of RMI to create three-tier applications.

Example 16.3 Retrieving Student Scores on a Database Using RMI

This example rewrites Example 16.1 to find scores stored in a database rather than a hash map. In addition, the system is capable of blocking a client from accessing a student who has not given the university permission to publish his/her score. An RMI component is developed to serve as a middle tier between client and database; it sends a search request to the database, processes the result, and returns an appropriate value to the client.

For simplicity, this example reuses the `Student` interface and `StudentClient` class from Example 16.1 with no modifications. Here are the steps to complete the project.

1. In the rmidemo package created in Example 16.1, choose *New, RMI, UnicastRemoteServer (group)* to display the New From Template wizard. Type `Student3Tier` in the Name field and click *Finish*. The wizard generates an interface in Student3Tier.java and its implementation, Student3TierImpl.java. Since you will reuse the `Student` interface, delete Student3Tier.java.

2. Modify Student3TierImpl.java to implement the `Student` interface for accessing a JDBC data source, as shown in Listing 16.7 (Lines 22, 32). This implementation retrieves a record from the Scores table, processes the retrieved information, and sends the result back to the client.

continued

Example 16.3 continued

3. In the main method, register the server object using StudentImpl, the same name as in Example 16.1, so that you can use StudentClient, created in Example 16.1, to test the server.

4. Compile Student3TierImpl to generate the stub and skeleton for Student3TierImpl.

5. Run `Student3TierServer` to start the server. Terminate rmidemo.StudentImpl if it is currently running. You can terminate it from the context menu of the process in the Runtime tab.

6. Run `StudentClient` to find student scores.

```
// Student3TierImpl.java: implementation for Student.java
// for accessing JDBC source
package rmidemo;

import java.rmi.*;
import java.rmi.server.*;
import java.rmi.registry.*;
import java.net.MalformedURLException;
import java.sql.*;

public class Student3TierImpl extends UnicastRemoteObject
  implements Student {
  // Use prepared statement for querying DB
  private PreparedStatement pstmt;

  /** Constructs Student3TierImpl object and exports it on
   * default port.
   */
  public Student3TierImpl() throws RemoteException {
    super();

    initializeDB();
  }

  /** Constructs Student3TierImpl object and exports it on
   * specified port.
   * @param port The port for exporting
   */
  public Student3TierImpl(int port) throws RemoteException {
    super(port);

    initializeDB();
  }

  /** Register Student3TierImpl object with the RMI registry.
   * @param name - name identifying the service in the RMI registry
   * @param create - create local registry if necessary
   * @throw RemoteException if cannot be exported or bound to
   *   RMI registry
   * @throw MalformedURLException if name cannot be used to construct
   *   a valid URL
   * @throw IllegalArgumentException if null passed as name
   */
```

Listing 16.7 *Student3TierImpl.java*

```
  public static void registerToRegistry(String name, Remote obj,
    boolean create) throws RemoteException, MalformedURLException{

    if (name == null) throw new IllegalArgumentException(
      "registration name can not be null");

    try {
      Naming.rebind(name, obj);
    } catch (RemoteException ex){
      if (create) {
        Registry r = LocateRegistry.createRegistry(
          Registry.REGISTRY_PORT);
        r.rebind(name, obj);
      } else throw ex;
    }
  }

  /** Main method.
   */
  public static void main(String[] args) {
    System.setSecurityManager(new RMISecurityManager());

    try {
      Student3TierImpl obj = new Student3TierImpl();
      // Register the server with the name StudentImpl,
      // which is the same as in Example 16.1 so it can be used
      // by Example 16.1.
      registerToRegistry("StudentImpl", obj, true);
      System.out.println("Server " + obj + " registered");
    } catch (RemoteException ex) {
      ex.printStackTrace();
    } catch (MalformedURLException ex) {
      ex.printStackTrace();
    }
  }

  /** Load JDBC driver, establish connection and create statement */
  protected void initializeDB() {
    try {
      // Load the JDBC driver
      // Class.forName("oracle.jdbc.driver.OracleDriver");
      Class.forName("sun.jdbc.odbc.JdbcOdbcDriver");
      System.out.println("Driver registered");

      // Establish connection
      /*Connection conn = DriverManager.getConnection
        ("jdbc:oracle:thin:@drake.armstrong.edu:1521:test",
          "scott", "tiger");  */
      Connection conn = DriverManager.getConnection
        ("jdbc:odbc:LiangBookDB_MDB", "", "" );
      System.out.println("Database connected");

      // Create the Scores table and initialize it if necessary
      initializeTable(conn);

      // Create a prepared statement for querying DB
      pstmt = conn.prepareStatement(
        "select * from Scores where name = ?");
    }
```

Listing 16.7 *continued*

continued

Example 16.3 continued

```
    catch (Exception ex) {
      System.out.println(ex);
    }
  }

  /** Create the Scores table and initialize it if necessary */
  private void initializeTable(Connection conn) {
    try {
      // Create a statement
      Statement stmt = conn.createStatement();

      // stmt.executeUpdate("DROP TABLE Scores");

      // Create the table,
      // if already exists, an exception would be raised
      stmt.executeUpdate(
        "create table Scores" +
        "(name varchar(20), score number, permission number)");

      // Insert three records into the Scores TABLE
      stmt.executeUpdate(
        "insert into Scores values ('John', 90.5, 1)");
      stmt.executeUpdate(
        "insert into Scores values ('Michael', 100, 1)");
      stmt.executeUpdate(
        "insert into Scores values ('Michelle', 100, 0)");
    }
    catch (SQLException ex) {
      System.out.println(ex);
    }
  }

  /** Return the score for specified the name
   * Return -1 if score is not found.
   */
  public double findScore(String name) throws RemoteException {
    double score = -1;
    try {
      // Set the specified name in the prepared statement
      pstmt.setString(1, name);

      // Execute the prepared statement
      ResultSet rs = pstmt.executeQuery();

      // Retrieve the score
      if (rs.next()) {
        if (rs.getBoolean(3))
          score = rs.getDouble(2);
      }
    }
    catch (SQLException ex) {
      System.out.println(ex);
    }

    System.out.println(name + "\'s score is " + score);
    return score;
  }
}
```

Listing 16.7 *continued*

Example Review

This example is similar to Example 16.1 except that the `Student3TierImpl` class finds the score from a JDBC data source instead from a hash map.

The table named Scores consists of three columns, name, score, and permission, where permission indicates whether the student has given permission to show his/her score. Since SQL does not support a `boolean` type, permission is defined as a number whose value of 1 indicates `true` and 0 indicates `false`.

The `initializeDB()` method (Lines 80–106) loads the appropriate JDBC driver, establishes connections with the database, initializes the table if necessary, and creates a prepared statement for processing the query. If the table does not exist, the `initializeTable()` method creates a table and initializes it with three records.

The `findScore` method sets the name in the prepared statement, executes the statement, processes the result, and returns the score for a student whose permission is `true`.

16.6 RMI Callbacks

In a traditional client/server system, a client sends a request to a server, and the server processes the request and returns the result to the client. The server cannot invoke the methods on a client. One of the important benefits of RMI is that it supports *callbacks*, which enable the server to invoke the methods on the client. With the RMI callback feature, you can develop interactive distributed applications.

The following example demonstrates the use of the RMI callback feature to develop an interactive TicTacToe game.

Example 16.4 Developing a TicTacToe Game with RMI

This example creates a distributed application for playing TicTacToe. In a TicTacToe game, two players alternate turns by marking an available cell in a 3 x 3 grid with their token (X or O). One player is X, and the other is O. When one player places three tokens in a row on the grid (whether horizontally, vertically, or diagonally), the game is over and that player has won. A draw (no winner) occurs when all the spaces on the grid have been filled with tokens and a win has not been achieved by either player. Figures 16.7 and 16.8 are representative sample runs of the example.

All the examples you have seen so far in this chapter have simple behaviors that are easy to model with classes. The behavior of the TicTacToe game is somewhat complex. To create the classes to model the game, you need to study and understand it and distribute the process appropriately between client and server.

continued

Example 16.4 continued

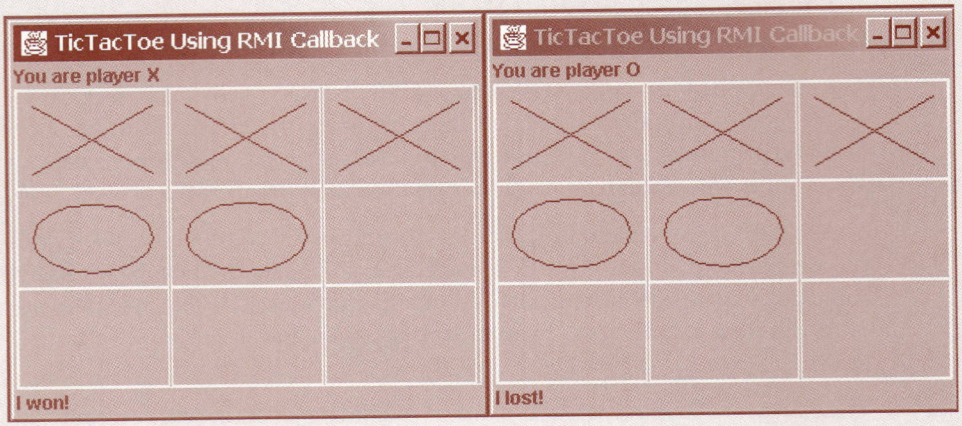

Figure 16.7 *This sample shows that player X has won.*

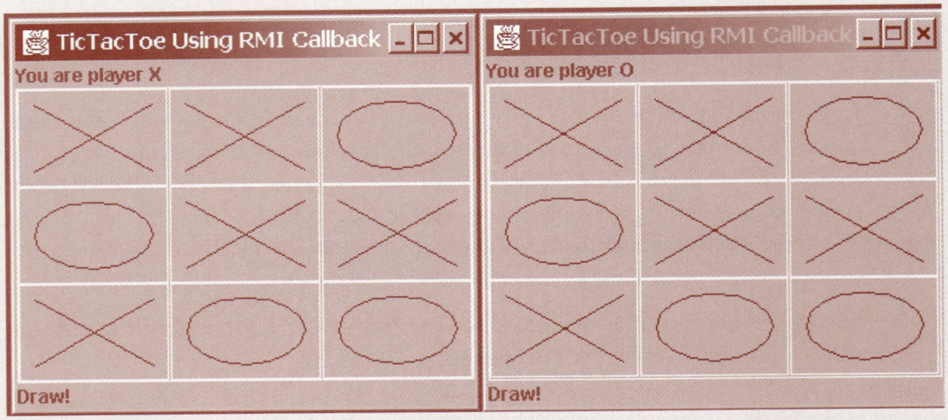

Figure 16.8 *This sample shows a draw with no winner.*

Clearly the client should be responsible for handling user interactions, and the server should coordinate with the client. Specifically, the client should register with the server, and the server can take two and only two players. Once a client makes a move, it should notify the server; the server then notifies the move to the other player. The server should determine the status of the game, that is, whether the game has been won or drawn, and should notify the players. The server should also coordinate the turns, that is, which client has the turn at a given time. The ideal approach for notifying a player is to invoke a method in the client that sets appropriate properties in the client or sends messages to a player. Figure 16.9 illustrates the relationship between clients and server.

All the calls a client makes can be encapsulated in one remote interface named `TicTacToe` (Listing 16.9), and all the calls the server invokes can be defined in another interface named `CallBack` (Listing 16.10).

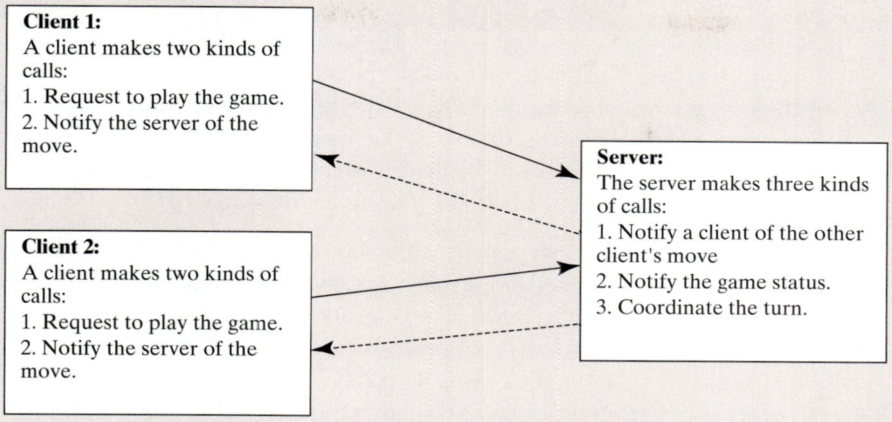

Figure 16.9 *The server coordinates the activities with the clients.*

```
// TicTacToe.java: TicTacToe RMI interface, invoked by clients
package rmitictactoedemo;

import java.rmi.*;

public interface TicTacToe extends Remote {
  /**
   * Connect to the TicTacToe server and return the token.
   * If the returned token is ' ', the client is not connected to
   * the server
   */
  public char connect(CallBack client) throws RemoteException;

  /** A client invokes this method to notify the server of its move*/
  public void myMove(int row, int column, char token)
    throws RemoteException;
}
```

Listing 16.9 *TicTacToe.java*

```
// CallBack.java: CallBack RMI interface, invoked by the server
package rmitictactoedemo;

import java.rmi.*;

public interface CallBack extends Remote {
  /** The server notifies the client for taking a turn */
  public void takeTurn(boolean turn) throws RemoteException;

  /** The server sends a message to be displayed by the client */
  public void notify(java.lang.String message)
    throws RemoteException;

  /** The server notifies a client of the other player's move */
  public void mark(int row, int column, char token)
    throws RemoteException;
}
```

Listing 16.10 *CallBack.java*

continued

Example 16.4 continued

What does a client need to do? The client interacts with the player. Assume that all the cells are initially empty, and that the first player takes the X token and the second player takes the O token. To mark a cell, the player points the mouse to the cell and clicks it. If the cell is empty, the token (X or O) is displayed. If the cell is already filled, the player's action is ignored.

From the preceding description, it is obvious that a cell is a GUI object that handles mouse-click events and displays tokens. The candidate for such an object could be a button or a canvas. Canvases are more flexible than buttons. The token (X or O) can be drawn on a canvas in any size, but it only can be displayed as a label on a button. `Canvas` is an AWT component, its Swing counterpart is `JPanel`. Therefore, a `JPanel` is used to model a cell in this example.

Let `Cell` be a subclass of `JPanel`. You can declare a 3 x 3 grid to be an array `Cell[][] cell = new Cell[3][3]` for modeling the game. How do you know the state of a cell (marked or not)? You can use a property named `marked` of the `boolean` type in the `Cell` class. How do you know whether the player has a turn? You can use a property named `myTurn` of `boolean`. This property (initially `false`) can be set by the server through a callback.

The `Cell` class is responsible for drawing the token when an empty cell is clicked, so you need to write the code for listening to the `MouseEvent` and for painting the shape for tokens X and O. To determine which shape to draw, introduce a variable named `marker` of the `char` type. Since this variable is shared by all the cells in a client, it is preferable to declare it in the client and to declare the `Cell` class as an inner class of the client so that this variable will be accessible to all the cells.

Now let us turn our attention to the server side. What does the server need to do? The server needs to implement the `TicTacToe` interface and notify the clients of the game status. The server has to record the moves in the cells and check the status every time a player makes a move. The status information can be kept in a 3 x 3 array of `char`. You can implement a method named `isFull()` to check whether the board is full and a method named `isWon(token)` to check whether a specific player has won.

Once a client is connected to the server, the server notifies the client which token to use; that is, X for the first client, and O for the second. Once a client notifies the server of its move, the server checks the game status and notifies the clients.

Now the most critical question is how the server notifies a client. You know that a client invokes a server method by creating a server stub on the client side. A server cannot directly invoke a client, because the client is not declared as a remote object. The `CallBack` interface was created to facilitate the server's callback to the client. In the implementation of `CallBack`, an instance of the client is passed as a parameter in the constructor of `CallBack`. The client creates an instance of `CallBack` and passes its stub to the server, using a remote method named `connect()` defined in the server. The server then invokes the client's method through a `CallBack` instance. The triangular relationship of client, `CallBack` implementation, and server is shown in Figure 16.10.

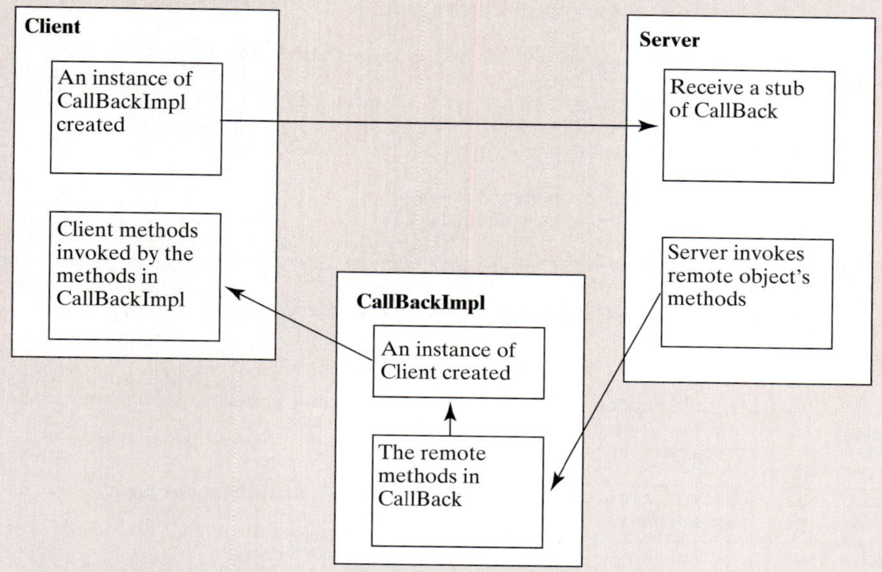

Figure 16.10 *The server receives a* `CallBack` *stub from the client and invokes the remote methods defined in the* `CallBack` *interface, which can invoke the methods defined in the client.*

Here are the steps to complete the example.

1. Create a new package named rmitictactoe.
2. Create TicTacToe.java and TicTacToeImpl.java using the UnicastRemoteServer (group) wizard. Complete these two classes, as shown in Listings 16.9 and 16.11.
3. Create CallBack.java and CallBackImpl.java using the UnicastRemoteServer (group) wizard. Complete these two classes, as shown in Listings 16.10 and 16.12. Remove the main method from CallBackImple.java.
4. Compile TicTacToeImpl.java and CallBackImpl.java to generate the stubs and the skeletons for `TicTacToeImpl` and `CallBackImpl`.
5. Create `TicTacToeClient` for interacting with a player and communicating with the server, as shown in Listing 16.13.
6. Run TicTacToeImple to start an RMI registry and start `TicTacToeServer`. Start `TicTacToeClient` twice to create two players to play the game.

continued

Example 16.4 continued

```
// TicTacToeImpl.java: The TicTacToe RMI Server Implementation
package rmitictactoedemo;

import java.rmi.*;
import java.rmi.server.*;
import java.rmi.registry.*;
import java.net.MalformedURLException;

public class TicTacToeImpl extends UnicastRemoteObject
  implements TicTacToe {
  // Declare two players, used to call players back
  CallBack player1 = null;
  CallBack player2 = null;

  // board records players' moves
  char[][] board = new char[3][3];

  /** Constructs TicTacToeImpl object and exports it on default port.
   */
  public TicTacToeImpl() throws RemoteException {
    super();
  }

  /** Constructs TicTacToeImpl object and exports it on specified
   * port.
   * @param port The port for exporting
   */
  public TicTacToeImpl(int port) throws RemoteException {
    super(port);
  }

  /**
   * Connect to the TicTacToe server and return the token.
   * If the returned token is ' ', the client is not connected to
   * the server
   */
  public char connect(CallBack client) throws RemoteException {
    if (player1 == null) {
      // player1 (first player) registered
      player1 = client;
      player1.notify("Wait for a second player to join");
      return 'X';
    }
    else if (player2 == null) {
      // player2 (second player) registered
      player2 = client;
      player2.notify("Wait for the first player to move");
      player2.takeTurn(false);
      player1.notify("It is my turn (X token)");
      player1.takeTurn(true);
      return 'O';
    }
    else {
      // Already two players
      client.notify("Two players are already in the game");
      return ' ';
    }
  }

```

Listing 16.11 *TicTacToeImpl.java*

```
  /** A client invokes this method to notify the server of its move*/
  public void myMove(int row, int column, char token)
  throws RemoteException {
    // Set token to the specified cell
    board[row][column] = token;

    // Notify the other player of the move
    if (token == 'X')
      player2.mark(row, column, 'X');
    else
      player1.mark(row, column, 'O');

    // Check if the player with this token wins
    if (isWon(token)) {
      if (token == 'X') {
        player1.notify("I won!");
        player2.notify("I lost!");
        player1.takeTurn(false);
      }
      else {
        player2.notify("I won!");
        player1.notify("I lost!");
        player2.takeTurn(false);
      }
    }
    else if (isFull()) {
      player1.notify("Draw!");
      player2.notify("Draw!");
    }
    else if (token == 'X') {
      player1.notify("Wait for the second player to move");
      player1.takeTurn(false);
      player2.notify("It is my turn, (O token)");
      player2.takeTurn(true);
    }
    else if (token == 'O') {
      player2.notify("Wait for the first player to move");
      player2.takeTurn(false);
      player1.notify("It is my turn, (X token)");
      player1.takeTurn(true);
    }
  }

  /** Check if a player with the specified token wins */
  public boolean isWon(char token) {
    for (int i=0; i<3; i++)
      if ((board[i][0] == token)
      && (board[i][1] == token)
      && (board[i][2] == token))
        return true;

    for (int j=0; j<3; j++)
      if ((board[0][j] == token)
      && (board[1][j] == token)
      && (board[2][j] == token))
        return true;

    if ((board[0][0] == token)
    && (board[1][1] == token)
```

Listing 16.11 *continued*

continued

Example 16.4 continued

```
        && (board[2][2] == token))
          return true;

        if ((board[0][2] == token)
        && (board[1][1] == token)
        && (board[2][0] == token))
          return true;

        return false;
      }

      /** Check if the board is full */
      public boolean isFull() {
        for (int i=0; i<3; i++)
          for (int j=0; j<3; j++)
            if (board[i][j] == '\u0000')
              return false;

        return true;
      }

      public static void registerToRegistry(String name, Remote obj,
        boolean create) throws RemoteException, MalformedURLException{
        if (name == null) throw new IllegalArgumentException(
          "registration name can not be null");

        try {
          Naming.rebind(name, obj);
        } catch (RemoteException ex){
          if (create) {
            Registry r =
              LocateRegistry.createRegistry(Registry.REGISTRY_PORT);
            r.rebind(name, obj);
          } else throw ex;
        }
      }

      public static void main(String[] args) {
        System.setSecurityManager(new RMISecurityManager());

        try {
          TicTacToeImpl obj = new TicTacToeImpl();
          registerToRegistry("TicTacToeImpl", obj, true);
          System.out.println("Server " + obj + " started");
        } catch (RemoteException ex) {
          ex.printStackTrace();
        } catch (MalformedURLException ex) {
          ex.printStackTrace();
        }
      }
    }
```

Listing 16.11 *continued*

```
// CallBackImpl.java: The CallBack RMI interface implementation
package rmitictactoedemo;

import java.rmi.*;
import java.rmi.server.*;

```

Listing 16.12 *CallBackImpl.java*

```
public class CallBackImpl extends UnicastRemoteObject
  implements CallBack {
  // The client will be called by the server through callback
  TicTacToeClient thisClient;

  /** Constructor */
  CallBackImpl(Object client) throws RemoteException {
    thisClient = (TicTacToeClient)client;
  }

  /** The server notifies the client for taking a turn */
  public void takeTurn(boolean turn) throws RemoteException {
    thisClient.setMyTurn(turn);
  }

  /** The server sends a message to be displayed by the client */
  public void notify(java.lang.String message)
    throws RemoteException {
    thisClient.setMessage(message);
  }

  /** The server notifies a client of the other player's move */
  public void mark(int row, int column, char token)
    throws RemoteException {
    thisClient.mark(row, column, token);
  }
}
```

Listing 16.12 *continued*

```
// TicTacToeClient.java: TicTacToeClient applet
package rmitictactoedemo;

import java.rmi.*;
import java.awt.*;
import java.awt.event.*;
import java.applet.*;
import javax.swing.*;
import javax.swing.border.*;

public class TicTacToeClient extends JApplet {
  // marker is used to indicate the token type
  char marker;

  // myTurn indicates whether the player can move now
  private boolean myTurn = false;

  // Each cell can be empty or marked as 'O' or 'X'
  private Cell[][] cell;

  // ticTacToe is the game server for coordinating with the players
  TicTacToe ticTacToe;

  // Border for cells and panel
  Border lineBorder =
    BorderFactory.createLineBorder(Color.yellow, 1);

  boolean isStandalone = false;

```

Listing 16.13 *TicTacToeClient.java*

continued

Example 16.4 continued

```
  /** Initialize the applet */
  public void init() {
    initComponents();

    // Create cells and place cells in the panel
    cell = new Cell[3][3];
    for (int i = 0; i < 3; i++)
      for (int j = 0; j < 3; j++)
        jPanel1.add(cell[i][j] = new Cell(i, j));

    // Initialize the CORBA environment
    try {
      initializeRMI();
    }
    catch (Exception ex) {
      ex.printStackTrace();
    }
  }

  /** Component and RMI initialization */
  private void initComponents() {
    // Create user interface
    this.setSize(400, 300);
    jPanel1.setLayout(gridLayout1);
    gridLayout1.setRows(3);
    gridLayout1.setHgap(1);
    gridLayout1.setColumns(3);
    jlblIdentification.setText("jLabel1");
    this.getContentPane().add(jlblStatus, BorderLayout.SOUTH);
    this.getContentPane().add(jPanel1, BorderLayout.CENTER);
    this.getContentPane().add(jlblIdentification,
      BorderLayout.NORTH);
    jPanel1.setBorder(lineBorder);
  }

  /** Initialize RMI */
  protected boolean initializeRMI() throws Exception {
    String url;

    if (isStandalone) {
      // Initialize RMI for a standalone application
      // System.setSecurityManager(new RMISecurityManager());
      url = "rmi:///";
      // Use rmi://hostname/ if the server is located on hostname,
      // i.e. rmi://liangy.liangy.edu/
    }
    else {
      // Initialize RMI for an applet
      url = getCodeBase().getHost();
      if (url.equals("default")) url = "";
      url = "rmi://" + url + "/";
    }

    ticTacToe = (TicTacToe)Naming.lookup(url + "TicTacToeImpl");
    System.out.println("Server found");

    // Create callback for use by the server to control the client
    CallBackImpl callBackControl = new CallBackImpl(this);

```

Listing 16.13 *continued*

```
    if (
      (marker = ticTacToe.connect((CallBack)callBackControl)) != ' ')
    {
      System.out.println("connected as " + marker + " player.");
      jlblIdentification.setText("You are player " + marker);
      return true;
    }
    else {
      System.out.println("already two players connected as ");
      return false;
    }
  }

  /** Set variable myTurn to true or false */
  void setMyTurn(boolean myTurn) {
    this.myTurn = myTurn;
  }

  /** Set message on the status label */
  public void setMessage(String message) {
    jlblStatus.setText(message);
  }

  /** Mark the specified cell using the token */
  void mark(int row, int column, char token) {
    cell[row][column].setToken(token);
  }

  /** Inner class Cell for modeling a cell on the TicTacToe board */
  public class Cell extends JPanel implements MouseListener {
    // marked indicates whether the cell has been used
    private boolean marked = false;

    // row and column indicate where the cell appears on the board
    int row, column;

    // The token for the cell
    private char token;

    /** Construct a cell */
    public Cell(int row, int column) {
      this.row = row;
      this.column = column;
      addMouseListener(this);
      setBorder(lineBorder);
    }

    /** Set token on a cell (mark a cell) */
    public void setToken(char c) {
      token = c;
      marked = true;
      repaint();
    }

    /** Paint the cell to draw a shape for the token */
    public void paintComponent(Graphics g) {
      super.paintComponent(g);

      // Draw the border
      g.drawRect(0, 0, getSize().width, getSize().height);

```

Listing 16.13 *continued*

continued

Example 16.4 continued

```
      if (token == 'X') {
        g.drawLine(10, 10, getSize().width - 10,
          getSize().height - 10);
        g.drawLine(getSize().width - 10, 10, 10,
          getSize().height - 10);
      }
      else if (token == 'O') {
        g.drawOval(10, 10, getSize().width - 20,
          getSize().height - 20);
      }
    }

    public void mouseClicked(MouseEvent e) {
      // TODO: implement this java.awt.event.MouseListener method;
      if (myTurn && !marked) {
        // Mark the cell
        setToken(marker);

        // Notify the server of the move
        try {
          ticTacToe.myMove(row, column, marker);
        }
        catch (RemoteException ex) {
          System.out.println(ex);
        }
      }
    }

    public void mousePressed(MouseEvent e) {
      // TODO: implement this java.awt.event.MouseListener method;
    }

    public void mouseReleased(MouseEvent e) {
      // TODO: implement this java.awt.event.MouseListener method;
    }

    public void mouseEntered(MouseEvent e) {
      // TODO: implement this java.awt.event.MouseListener method;
    }

    public void mouseExited(MouseEvent e) {
      // TODO: implement this java.awt.event.MouseListener method;
    }
  }

  /** Main method */
  public static void main(String[] args) {
    // Omitted for brevity
  }

  private JLabel jlblStatus = new JLabel();
  private JPanel jPanel1 = new JPanel();
  private GridLayout gridLayout1 = new GridLayout();
  private JLabel jlblIdentification = new JLabel();
}
```

Listing 16.13 *continued*

Example Review

The `TicTacToe` interface in Listing 16.9 defines two remote methods, `connect(CallBack client)` and `myMove(int row, int column, char token)`. The `connect` method plays two roles: one is to pass a `CallBack` stub to the server, and the other is to let the server assign a token for the player. The `myMove` method notifies the server that the player has made a specific move.

The `CallBack` interface in Listing 16.10 defines three remote methods, `takeTurn(boolean turn)`, `notify(String message)`, and `mark(int row, int column, char token)`. The `takeTurn` method sets the client's `myTurn` property to `true` or `false`. The `notify` method displays a message on the client's status label. The `mark` method marks the client's cell with the token at the specified location.

`TicTacToeImpl` in Listing 16.11 is a server implementation for coordinating with the clients and managing the game. The variables `player1` and `player2` are instances of `CallBack`, each of which corresponds to a client, passed from a client when the client invokes the `connect` method. The variable `board` records the moves by the two players. This information is needed to determine the game status. When a client invokes the `connect` method, the server assigns a token X for the first player and O for the second player, and only two players are accepted by the server. You can modify the program to accept additional clients as observers. See Exercise 16.4 for more details.

Once two players are in the game, the server coordinates the turns between them. When a client invokes the `myMove` method, the server records the move and notifies the other player by marking the other player's cell. It then checks to see whether the player wins or whether the board is full. If neither conditions applies and therefore the game continues, the server gives a turn to the other player.

The `CallBackImpl` in Listing 16.12 implements the `CallBack` interface. It creates an instance of `TicTacToeClient` through its constructor. The `CallBackImpl` relays the server request to the client by invoking the client's methods. When the server invokes the `takeTurn` method, `CallBackImpl` invokes the client's `setMyTurn()` method to set the property `myTurn` in the client. When the server invokes the `notify()` method, `CallBackImpl` invokes the client's `setMessage()` method to set the message on the client's status label. When the server invokes the `mark` method, `CallBackImpl` invokes the client's `mark` method to mark the specified cell.

`TicTacToeClient` can run as a standalone application or as an applet. The `initializeRMI` method is responsible for creating the url for running as a standalone application or as an applet, for locating the `TicTacToe` server stub, for creating the `CallBack` server object, and for connecting the client with the server.

continued

Example 16.4 continued

Interestingly, obtaining the `TicTacToe` stub for the client is different from obtaining the `CallBack` stub for the server. The `TicTacToe` stub is obtained by invoking the `lookup()` method through the RMI registry, and the `CallBack` stub is passed to the server through the `connect` method in the `TicTacToe` stub. It is a common practice to obtain the first stub with the `lookup` method, but to pass the subsequent stubs as parameters through remote method invocations.

Since the variables `myTurn` and `marker` are defined in `TicTacToeClient`, the `Cell` class is defined as an inner class within `TicTacToeClient` in order to enable all the cells in the client to access them. Exercise 16.4 suggests alternative approaches that implement the Cell as a non-inner class.

Chapter Summary

RMI is a high-level Java API for building distributed applications using distributed objects. The key idea of RMI is its use of stubs and skeletons to facilitate communications between objects. The stub and skeleton are automatically generated, which relieves programmers of tedious socket-level network programming. For an object to be used remotely, it must be defined in an interface that extends the `java.rmi.Remote` interface. In an RMI application, the initial remote object must be registered with the RMI registry on the server side and be obtained using the `lookup` method through the registry on the client side. Subsequent use of stubs of other remote objects may be passed as parameters through remote method invocations. RMI is especially useful for developing scalable and load-balanced multi-tier distributed applications.

Review Questions

16.1 How do you define an interface for a remote object?

16.2 Describe the roles of the stub and the skeleton.

16.3 How do you generate the stub and the skeleton?

16.4 What is the RMI registry for? How do you create an RMI registry?

16.5 How do you register a remote object with the RMI registry?

16.6 How does a client locate a remote object stub through the RMI registry?

16.7 What can you do if you encounter a security violation?

16.8 Describe how parameters are passed in RMI.

16.9 What is the problem if the `connect` method in the `TicTacToe` interface is defined as

```
public boolean connect(CallBack client, char token) throws RemoteException;
```

or as

```
public boolean connect(CallBack client, Character token) throws
RemoteException;
```

16.10 What is callback? How does callback work in RMI?

Programming Exercises

16.1 Modify Example 16.1 to limit the number of concurrent clients to ten.

16.2 Write an applet to show the number of visits made to a Web page. The count should be stored on the server side in a file. The applet should send a request to the server every time the page is visited or reloaded, and the server should increase the count and send it to the applet. The applet should then display the count in a message, such as *You are visitor number: 1000*. The server can read or write to the file using a random file access stream.

16.3 Use the three-tier approach to modify Example 13.2, "Using Statements to Execute Static SQL Statements," as follows:

- Create an applet client to manipulate student information, as shown in Figure 13.11.
- Create a remote object interface with methods for retrieving, inserting, and updating student information, and an object implementation for the interface.

16.4 Modify Example 16.4 as follows:

- Allow a client to connect to the server as an observer to watch the game.
- Rewrite the `Cell` class as a non-inner class.

INDEX

J

END USER LICENSE AGREEMENTS

Terms and conditions of the license & export for Java™ 2 SDK, Standard Edition 1.4.0

Sun Microsystems, Inc.

BINARY CODE LICENSE AGREEMENT

READ THE TERMS OF THIS AGREEMENT AND ANY PROVIDED SUPPLEMENTAL LICENSE TERMS (COLLECTIVELY "AGREEMENT") CAREFULLY BEFORE OPENING THE SOFTWARE MEDIA PACKAGE. BY OPENING THE SOFTWARE MEDIA PACKAGE, YOU AGREE TO THE TERMS OF THIS AGREEMENT. IF YOU ARE ACCESSING THE SOFTWARE ELECTRONICALLY, INDICATE YOUR ACCEPTANCE OF THESE TERMS BY SELECTING THE "ACCEPT" BUTTON AT THE END OF THIS AGREEMENT. IF YOU DO NOT AGREE TO ALL THESE TERMS, PROMPTLY RETURN THE UNUSED SOFTWARE TO YOUR PLACE OF PURCHASE FOR A REFUND OR, IF THE SOFTWARE IS ACCESSED ELECTRONICALLY, SELECT THE "DECLINE" BUTTON AT THE END OF THIS AGREEMENT.

1. LICENSE TO USE. Sun grants you a non-exclusive and non-transferable license for the internal use only of the accompanying software and documentation and any error corrections provided by Sun (collectively "Software"), by the number of users and the class of computer hardware for which the corresponding fee has been paid.

2. RESTRICTIONS. Software is confidential and copyrighted. Title to Software and all associated intellectual property rights is retained by Sun and/or its licensors. Except as specifically authorized in any Supplemental License Terms, you may not make copies of Software, other than a single copy of Software for archival purposes. Unless enforcement is prohibited by applicable law, you may not modify, decompile, or reverse engineer Software. You acknowledge that Software is not designed, licensed or intended for use in the design, construction, operation or maintenance of any nuclear facility. Sun disclaims any express or implied warranty of fitness for such uses. No right, title or interest in or to any trademark, service mark, logo or trade name of Sun or its licensors is granted under this Agreement.

3. LIMITED WARRANTY. Sun warrants to you that for a period of ninety (90) days from the date of purchase, as evidenced by a copy of the receipt, the media on which Software is furnished (if any) will be free of defects in materials and workmanship under normal use. Except for the foregoing, Software is provided "AS IS". Your exclusive remedy and Sun's entire liability under this limited warranty will be at Sun's option to replace Software media or refund the fee paid for Software.

4. DISCLAIMER OF WARRANTY. UNLESS SPECIFIED IN THIS AGREEMENT, ALL EXPRESS OR IMPLIED CONDITIONS, REPRESENTATIONS AND WARRANTIES, INCLUDING ANY IMPLIED WARRANTY OF MERCHANTABILITY, FITNESS FOR A PARTICULAR PURPOSE OR NON-INFRINGEMENT ARE DISCLAIMED, EXCEPT TO THE EXTENT THAT THESE DISCLAIMERS ARE HELD TO BE LEGALLY INVALID.

5. LIMITATION OF LIABILITY. TO THE EXTENT NOT PROHIBITED BY LAW, IN NO EVENT WILL SUN OR ITS LICENSORS BE LIABLE FOR ANY LOST REVENUE, PROFIT OR DATA, OR FOR SPECIAL, INDIRECT, CONSEQUENTIAL, INCIDENTAL OR PUNITIVE DAMAGES, HOWEVER CAUSED REGARDLESS OF THE THEORY OF LIABILITY, ARISING OUT OF OR RELATED TO THE USE OF OR INABILITY TO USE SOFTWARE, EVEN IF SUN HAS BEEN ADVISED OF THE POSSIBILITY OF SUCH DAMAGES. In no event will Sun's liability to you, whether in contract, tort (including negligence), or otherwise, exceed the amount paid by you for Software under this Agreement. The foregoing limitations will apply even if the above stated warranty fails of its essential purpose.

6. Termination. This Agreement is effective until terminated. You may terminate this Agreement at any time by destroying all copies of Software. This Agreement will terminate immediately without notice from Sun if you fail to comply with any provision of this Agreement. Upon Termination, you must destroy all copies of Software.

7. Export Regulations. All Software and technical data delivered under this Agreement are subject to US export control laws and may be subject to export or import regulations in other countries. You agree to comply strictly with all such laws and regulations and acknowledge that you have the responsibility to obtain such licenses to export, re-export, or import as may be required after delivery to you.

8. U.S. Government Restricted Rights. If Software is being acquired by or on behalf of the U.S. Government or by a U.S. Government prime contractor or subcontractor (at any tier), then the Government's rights in Software and accompanying documentation will be only as set forth in this Agreement; this is in accordance with 48 CFR 227.7201 through 227.7202-4 (for Department of Defense (DOD) acquisitions) and with 48 CFR 2.101 and 12.212 (for non-DOD acquisitions).

9. Governing Law. Any action related to this Agreement will be governed by California law and controlling U.S. federal law. No choice of law rules of any jurisdiction will apply.

10. Severability. If any provision of this Agreement is held to be unenforceable, this Agreement will remain in effect with the provision omitted, unless omission would frustrate the intent of the parties, in which case this Agreement will immediately terminate.

11. Integration. This Agreement is the entire agreement between you and Sun relating to its subject matter. It supersedes all prior or contemporaneous oral or written communications, proposals, representations and warranties and prevails over any conflicting or additional terms of any quote, order, acknowledgment, or other communication between the parties relating to its subject matter during the term of this Agreement. No modification of this Agreement will be binding, unless in writing and signed by an authorized representative of each party.

JAVA™ 2 SOFTWARE DEVELOPMENT KIT (J2SDK), STANDARD EDITION, VERSION 1.4.X SUPPLEMENTAL LICENSE TERMS

These supplemental license terms ("Supplemental Terms") add to or modify the terms of the Binary Code License Agreement (collectively, the "Agreement"). Capitalized terms not defined in these Supplemental Terms shall have the same meanings ascribed to them in the Agreement. These Supplemental Terms shall supersede any inconsistent or conflicting terms in the Agreement, or in any license contained within the Software.

1. Software Internal Use and Development License Grant. Subject to the terms and conditions of this Agreement, including, but not limited to Section 4 (Java Technology Restrictions) of these Supplemental Terms, Sun grants you a non-exclusive, non-transferable, limited license to reproduce internally and use internally the binary form of the Software complete and unmodified for the sole purpose of designing, developing and testing your Java applets and applications intended to run on the Java platform ("Programs").

2. License to Distribute Software. Subject to the terms and conditions of this Agreement, including, but not limited to Section 4 (Java Technology Restrictions) of these Supplemental Terms, Sun grants you a non-exclusive, non-transferable, limited license to reproduce and distribute the Software, provided that (i) you distribute the Software complete and unmodified (unless otherwise specified in the applicable README file) and only bundled as part of, and for the sole purpose of running, your Programs, (ii) the Programs add significant and primary functionality to the Software, (iii) you do not distribute additional software intended to replace any component(s) of the Software (unless otherwise specified in the applicable README file), (iv) you do not remove or alter any proprietary legends or notices contained in the Software, (v) you only distribute the Software subject to a license agreement that protects Sun's interests consistent with the terms contained in this Agreement, and (vi) you agree to defend and indemnify Sun and its licensors from and against any damages, costs, liabilities, settlement amounts and/or expenses (including attorneys' fees) incurred in connection with any claim, lawsuit or action by any third party that arises or results from the use or distribution of any and all Programs and/or Software. (vi) include the following statement as part of product documentation (whether hard copy or electronic), as a part of a copyright page or proprietary rights notice page, in an "About" box or in any other form reasonably designed to make the statement visible to users of the Software: "This product includes code licensed from RSA Security, Inc.", and (vii) include the statement, "Some portions licensed from IBM are available at http://oss.software.ibm.com/icu4j/".

3. License to Distribute Redistributables. Subject to the terms and conditions of this Agreement, including but not limited to Section 4 (Java Technology Restrictions) of these Supplemental Terms, Sun grants you a non-exclusive, non-transferable, limited license to reproduce and distribute those files specifically identified as redistributable in the Software "README" file ("Redistributables") provided that: (i) you distribute the Redistributables complete and unmodified (unless otherwise specified in the applicable README file), and only bundled as part of Programs, (ii) you do not distribute additional software intended to supersede any component(s) of the Redistributables (unless otherwise specified in the applicable README file), (iii) you do not remove or alter any proprietary legends or notices contained in or on the Redistributables, (iv) you only distribute the Redistributables pursuant to a license agreement that protects Sun's interests consistent with the terms contained in the Agreement, (v) you agree to defend and indemnify Sun and its licensors from and against any damages, costs, liabilities, settlement amounts and/or expenses (including attorneys' fees) incurred in connection with any claim, lawsuit or action by any third party that arises or results from the use or distribution of any and all Programs and/or Software, (vi) include the following statement as part of product documentation (whether hard copy or electronic), as a part of a copyright page or proprietary rights notice page, in an "About" box or in any other form reasonably designed to make the statement visible to users of the Software: "This product includes code licensed from RSA Security, Inc.", and (vii) include the statement, "Some portions licensed from IBM are available at http://oss.software.ibm.com/icu4j/".

4. Java Technology Restrictions. You may not modify the Java Platform Interface ("JPI", identified as classes contained within the "java" package or any subpackages of the "java" package), by creating additional classes within the JPI or otherwise causing the addition to or modification of the classes in the JPI. In the event that you create an additional class and associated API(s) which (i) extends the functionality of the Java platform, and (ii) is exposed to third party software developers for the purpose of developing additional software which invokes such additional API, you must promptly publish broadly an accurate specification for such API for free use by all developers. You may not create, or authorize your licensees to create, additional classes, interfaces, or subpackages that are in any way identified as "java", "javax", "sun" or similar convention as specified by Sun in any naming convention designation.

5. Notice of Automatic Software Updates from Sun. You acknowledge that the Software may automatically download, install, and execute applets, applications, software extensions, and updated versions of the Software from Sun ("Software Updates"), which may require you to accept updated terms and conditions for installation. If additional terms and conditions are not presented on installation, the Software Updates will be considered part of the Software and subject to the terms and conditions of the Agreement.

6. Notice of Automatic Downloads. You acknowledge that, by your use of the Software and/or by requesting services that require use of the Software, the Software may automatically download, install, and execute software applications from sources other than Sun ("Other Software"). Sun makes no representations of a relationship of any kind to licensors of Other Software. TO THE EXTENT NOT PROHIBITED BY LAW, IN NO EVENT WILL SUN OR ITS LICENSORS BE LIABLE FOR ANY LOST REVENUE, PROFIT OR DATA, OR FOR SPECIAL, INDIRECT, CONSEQUENTIAL, INCIDENTAL OR PUNITIVE DAMAGES, HOWEVER CAUSED REGARDLESS OF THE THEORY OF LIABILITY, ARISING OUT OF OR RELATED TO THE USE OF OR INABILITY TO USE OTHER SOFTWARE, EVEN IF SUN HAS BEEN ADVISED OF THE POSSIBILITY OF SUCH DAMAGES.

7. Trademarks and Logos. You acknowledge and agree as between you and Sun that Sun owns the SUN, SOLARIS, JAVA, JINI, FORTE, and iPLANET trademarks and all SUN, SOLARIS, JAVA, JINI, FORTE, and iPLANET-related trademarks, service marks, logos and other brand designations ("Sun Marks"), and you agree to comply with the Sun Trademark and Logo Usage Requirements currently located at http://www.sun.com/policies/trademarks. Any use you make of the Sun Marks inures to Sun's benefit.

8. Source Code. Software may contain source code that is provided solely for reference purposes pursuant to the terms of this Agreement. Source code may not be redistributed unless expressly provided for in this Agreement.

9. Termination for Infringement. Either party may terminate this Agreement immediately should any Software become, or in either party's opinion be likely to become, the subject of a claim of infringement of any intellectual property right.

For inquiries please contact: Sun Microsystems, Inc. 901 San Antonio Road, Palo Alto, California 94303 (LFI#109998/Form ID#011801)

Sun(TM) ONE Studio 4, Community Edition License

Sun Microsystems, Inc. Binary Code License Agreement

READ THE TERMS OF THIS AGREEMENT AND ANY PROVIDED SUPPLEMENTAL LICENSE TERMS (COLLECTIVELY "AGREEMENT") CAREFULLY BEFORE OPENING THE SOFTWARE MEDIA PACKAGE. BY OPENING THE SOFTWARE MEDIA PACKAGE, YOU AGREE TO THE TERMS OF THIS AGREEMENT. IF YOU ARE ACCESSING THE SOFTWARE ELECTRONICALLY, INDICATE YOUR ACCEPTANCE OF THESE TERMS BY SELECTING THE "ACCEPT" BUTTON AT THE END OF THIS AGREEMENT. IF YOU DO NOT AGREE TO ALL THESE TERMS, PROMPTLY RETURN THE UNUSED SOFTWARE TO YOUR PLACE OF PURCHASE FOR A REFUND OR, IF THE SOFTWARE IS ACCESSED ELECTRONICALLY, SELECT THE "DECLINE" BUTTON AT THE END OF THIS AGREEMENT.

1. LICENSE TO USE. Sun grants you a non-exclusive and non-transferable license for the internal use only of the accompanying software and documentation and any error corrections provided by Sun (collectively "Software"), by the number of users and the class of computer hardware for which the corresponding fee has been paid.

2. RESTRICTIONS. Software is confidential and copyrighted. Title to Software and all associated intellectual property rights is retained by Sun and/or its licensors. Except as specifically authorized in any Supplemental License Terms, you may not make copies of Software, other than a single copy of Software for archival purposes. Unless enforcement is prohibited by

applicable law, you may not modify, decompile, or reverse engineer Software. You acknowledge that Software is not designed, licensed or intended for use in the design, construction, operation or maintenance of any nuclear facility. Sun disclaims any express or implied warranty of fitness for such uses. No right, title or interest in or to any trademark, service mark, logo or trade name of Sun or its licensors is granted under this Agreement.

3. LIMITED WARRANTY. Sun warrants to you that for a period of ninety (90) days from the date of purchase, as evidenced by a copy of the receipt, the media on which Software is furnished (if any) will be free of defects in materials and workmanship under normal use. Except for the foregoing, Software is provided "AS IS". Your exclusive remedy and Sun's entire liability under this limited warranty will be at Sun's option to replace Software media or refund the fee paid for Software.

4. DISCLAIMER OF WARRANTY. UNLESS SPECIFIED IN THIS AGREEMENT, ALL EXPRESS OR IMPLIED CONDITIONS, REPRESENTATIONS AND WARRANTIES, INCLUDING ANY IMPLIED WARRANTY OF MERCHANTABILITY, FITNESS FOR A PARTICULAR PURPOSE OR NON-INFRINGEMENT ARE DISCLAIMED, EXCEPT TO THE EXTENT THAT THESE DISCLAIMERS ARE HELD TO BE LEGALLY INVALID.

5. LIMITATION OF LIABILITY. TO THE EXTENT NOT PROHIBITED BY LAW, IN NO EVENT WILL SUN OR ITS LICENSORS BE LIABLE FOR ANY LOST REVENUE, PROFIT OR DATA, OR FOR SPECIAL, INDIRECT, CONSEQUENTIAL, INCIDENTAL OR PUNITIVE DAMAGES, HOWEVER CAUSED REGARDLESS OF THE THEORY OF LIABILITY, ARISING OUT OF OR RELATED TO THE USE OF OR INABILITY TO USE SOFTWARE, EVEN IF SUN HAS BEEN ADVISED OF THE POSSIBILITY OF SUCH DAMAGES. In no event will Sun's liability to you, whether in contract, tort (including negligence), or otherwise, exceed the amount paid by you for Software under this Agreement. The foregoing limitations will apply even if the above stated warranty fails of its essential purpose.

6. Termination. This Agreement is effective until terminated. You may terminate this Agreement at any time by destroying all copies of Software. This Agreement will terminate immediately without notice from Sun if you fail to comply with any provision of this Agreement. Upon Termination, you must destroy all copies of Software.

7. Export Regulations. All Software and technical data delivered under this Agreement are subject to US export control laws and may be subject to export or import regulations in other countries. You agree to comply strictly with all such laws and regulations and acknowledge that you have the responsibility to obtain such licenses to export, re-export, or import as may be required after delivery to you.

8. U.S. Government Restricted Rights. If Software is being acquired by or on behalf of the U.S. Government or by a U.S. Government prime contractor or subcontractor (at any tier), then the Government's rights in Software and accompanying documentation will be only as set forth in this Agreement; this is in accordance with 48 CFR 227.7201 through 227.7202-4 (for Department of Defense (DOD) acquisitions) and with 48 CFR 2.101 and 12.212 (for non-DOD acquisitions).

9. Governing Law. Any action related to this Agreement will be governed by California law and controlling U.S. federal law. No choice of law rules of any jurisdiction will apply.

10. Severability. If any provision of this Agreement is held to be unenforceable, this Agreement will remain in effect with the provision omitted, unless omission would frustrate the intent of the parties, in which case this Agreement will immediately terminate.

11. Integration. This Agreement is the entire agreement between you and Sun relating to its subject matter. It supersedes all prior or contemporaneous oral or written communications, proposals, representations and warranties and prevails over any conflicting or additional terms of any quote, order, acknowledgment, or other communication between the parties relating to its subject matter during the term of this Agreement. No modification of this Agreement will be binding, unless in writing and signed by an authorized representative of each party.

FORTE™ FOR JAVA™ 4, COMMUNITY EDITION

SUPPLEMENTAL LICENSE TERMS

These supplemental license terms ("Supplemental Terms") add to or modify the terms of the Binary Code License Agreement (collectively, the "Agreement"). Capitalized terms not defined in these Supplemental Terms shall have the same meanings ascribed to them in the Agreement. These Supplemental Terms shall supersede any inconsistent or conflicting terms in the Agreement, or in any license contained within the Software.

1. Software Internal Use and Development License Grant. Subject to the terms and conditions of this Agreement, including, but not limited to Section 4 (Java Technology Restrictions) of these Supplemental Terms, Sun grants you a non-exclusive,

non-transferable, limited license to reproduce internally and use internally the binary form of the Software complete and unmodified for the sole purpose of designing, developing and testing your applets and applications ("Programs"). To the extent that you are designing, developing and testing Java applets and applications for a particular version of the Java platform, any executable output generated by a compiler that is contained in the Software must (a) only be compiled from source code that conforms to the corresponding version of the OEM Java Language Specification; (b) be in the class file format defined by the corresponding version of the OEM Java Virtual Machine Specification; and (c) execute properly on a reference runtime, as specified by Sun, associated with such version of the Java platform.

2. License to Distribute Software. Subject to the terms and conditions of this Agreement, including, but not limited to Section 4 (Java Technology Restrictions) of these Supplemental Terms, Sun grants you a non-exclusive, non-transferable, limited license to reproduce and distribute the Software in binary code form only, provided that (i) you distribute the Software complete and unmodified, (ii) you do not distribute additional software intended to replace any component(s) of the Software, (iii) if you are distributing Java applets and applications for a particular version of the Java platform, any executable output generated by a compiler that is contained in the Software must (a) only be compiled from source code that conforms to the corresponding version of the OEM Java Language Specification; (b) be in the class file format defined by the corresponding version of the OEM Java Virtual Machine Specification; and (c) execute properly on a reference runtime, as specified by Sun, associated with such version of the Java platform, (iv) you do not remove or alter any proprietary legends or notices contained in the Software, (v) you only distribute the Software subject to a license agreement that protects Sun's interests consistent with the terms contained in this Agreement, and (vi) you agree to defend and indemnify Sun and its licensors from and against any damages, costs, liabilities, settlement amounts and/or expenses (including attorneys' fees) incurred in connection with any claim, lawsuit or action by any third party that arises or results from the use or distribution of any and all Programs and/or Software.

3. License to Distribute Redistributables. Subject to the terms and conditions of this Agreement, including but not limited to Section 4 (Java Technology Restrictions) of these Supplemental Terms, Sun grants you a non-exclusive, non-transferable, limited license to reproduce and distribute the binary form of those files specifically identified as redistributable in the Software "RELEASE NOTES" file ("Redistributables") provided that: (i) you distribute the Redistributables complete and unmodified (unless otherwise specified in the applicable RELEASE NOTES file), and only bundled as part of Programs, (ii) you do not distribute additional software intended to supersede any component(s) of the Redistributables, (iii) you do not remove or alter any proprietary legends or notices contained in or on the Redistributables, (iv) if you are distributing Java applets and applications for a particular version of the Java platform, any executable output generated by a compiler that is contained in the Software must (a) only be compiled from source code that conforms to the corresponding version of the OEM Java Language Specification; (b) be in the class file format defined by the corresponding version of the OEM Java Virtual Machine Specification; and (c) execute properly on a reference runtime, as specified by Sun, associated with such version of the Java platform, (v) you only distribute the Redistributables pursuant to a license agreement that protects Sun's interests consistent with the terms contained in the Agreement, and (v) you agree to defend and indemnify Sun and its licensors from and against any damages, costs, liabilities, settlement amounts and/or expenses (including attorneys' fees) incurred in connection with any claim, lawsuit or action by any third party that arises or results from the use or distribution of any and all Programs and/or Software.

4. Java Technology Restrictions. You may not modify the Java Platform Interface ("JPI", identified as classes contained within the "java" package or any subpackages of the "java" package), by creating additional classes within the JPI or otherwise causing the addition to or modification of the classes in the JPI. In the event that you create an additional class and associated API(s) which (i) extends the functionality of the Java platform, and (ii) is exposed to third party software developers for the purpose of developing additional software which invokes such additional API, you must promptly publish broadly an accurate specification for such API for free use by all developers. You may not create, or authorize your licensees to create, additional classes, interfaces, or subpackages that are in any way identified as "java", "javax", "sun" or similar convention as specified by Sun in any naming convention designation.

5. Java Runtime Availability. Refer to the appropriate version of the Java Runtime Environment binary code license (currently located at http://www.java.sun.com/jdk/index.html) for the availability of runtime code which may be distributed with Java applets and applications.

6. Trademarks and Logos. You acknowledge and agree as between you and Sun that Sun owns the SUN, SOLARIS, JAVA, JINI, FORTE, and iPLANET trademarks and all SUN, SOLARIS, JAVA, JINI, FORTE, and iPLANET-related trademarks, service marks, logos and other brand designations ("Sun Marks"), and you agree to comply with the Sun Trademark and Logo Usage Requirements currently located at http://www.sun.com/policies/trademarks. Any use you make of the Sun Marks inures to Sun's benefit.

7. Source Code. Software may contain source code that is provided solely for reference purposes pursuant to the terms of this Agreement. Source code may not be redistributed unless expressly provided for in this Agreement.

8. Termination for Infringement. Either party may terminate this Agreement immediately should any Software become, or in either party's opinion be likely to become, the subject of a claim of infringement of any intellectual property right.

For inquiries please contact: Sun Microsystems, Inc. 4150 Network Circle, Santa Clara, California 95054. (LFI#112968/Form ID#011801)

PEARSON EDUCATION LICENSE AGREEMENT AND LIMITED WARRANTY

READ THE FOLLOWING TERMS AND CONDITIONS CAREFULLY BEFORE OPENING THIS DISK PACKAGE. THIS LEGAL DOCUMENT IS AN AGREEMENT BETWEEN YOU AND PEARSON EDUCATION, INC. (THE "COMPANY"). BY OPENING THIS SEALED DISK PACKAGE, YOU ARE AGREEING TO BE BOUND BY THESE TERMS AND CONDITIONS. IF YOU DO NOT AGREE WITH THESE TERMS AND CONDITIONS, DO NOT OPEN THE DISK PACKAGE. PROMPTLY RETURN THE UNOPENED DISK PACKAGE AND ALL ACCOMPANYING ITEMS TO THE PLACE YOU OBTAINED THEM FOR A FULL REFUND OF ANY SUMS YOU HAVE PAID.

1. GRANT OF LICENSE: In consideration of your payment of the license fee, which is part of the price you paid for this product, and your agreement to abide by the terms and conditions of this Agreement, the Company grants to you a nonexclusive right to use and display the copy of the enclosed software program (hereinafter the "SOFTWARE") on a single computer (i.e., with a single CPU) at a single location so long as you comply with the terms of this Agreement. The Company reserves all rights not expressly granted to you under this Agreement.

2. OWNERSHIP OF SOFTWARE: You own only the magnetic or physical media (the enclosed disks) on which the SOFTWARE is recorded or fixed, but the Company retains all the rights, title, and ownership to the SOFTWARE recorded on the original disk copy(ies) and all subsequent copies of the SOFTWARE, regardless of the form or media on which the original or other copies may exist. This license is not a sale of the original SOFTWARE or any copy to you.

3. COPY RESTRICTIONS: This SOFTWARE and the accompanying printed materials and user manual (the "Documentation") are the subject of copyright. You may not copy the Documentation or the SOFTWARE, except that you may make a single copy of the SOFTWARE for backup or archival purposes only. You may be held legally responsible for any copying or copyright infringement which is caused or encouraged by your failure to abide by the terms of this restriction.

4. USE RESTRICTIONS: You may not network the SOFTWARE or otherwise use it on more than one computer or computer terminal at the same time. You may physically transfer the SOFTWARE from one computer to another provided that the SOFTWARE is used on only one computer at a time. You may not distribute copies of the SOFTWARE or Documentation to others. You may not reverse engineer, disassemble, decompile, modify, adapt, translate, or create derivative works based on the SOFTWARE or the Documentation without the prior written consent of the Company.

5. TRANSFER RESTRICTIONS: The enclosed SOFTWARE is licensed only to you and may not be transferred to any one else without the prior written consent of the Company. Any unauthorized transfer of the SOFTWARE shall result in the immediate termination of this Agreement.

6. TERMINATION: This license is effective until terminated. This license will terminate automatically without notice from the Company and become null and void if you fail to comply with any provisions or limitations of this license. Upon termination, you shall destroy the Documentation and all copies of the SOFTWARE. All provisions of this Agreement as to warranties, limitation of liability, remedies or damages, and our ownership rights shall survive termination.

7. MISCELLANEOUS: This Agreement shall be construed in accordance with the laws of the United States of America and the State of New York and shall benefit the Company, its affiliates, and assignees.

8. LIMITED WARRANTY AND DISCLAIMER OF WARRANTY: The Company warrants that the SOFTWARE, when properly used in accordance with the Documentation, will operate in substantial conformity with the description of the SOFTWARE set forth in the Documentation. The Company does not warrant that the SOFTWARE will meet your requirements or that the operation of the SOFTWARE will be uninterrupted or error-free. The Company warrants that the media on which the SOFTWARE is delivered shall be free from defects in materials and workmanship under normal use for a period of thirty (30) days from the date of your purchase. Your only remedy and the Company's only obligation under these limited warranties is, at the Company's option, return of the warranted item for a refund of any amounts paid by you or replacement of the item. Any replacement of SOFTWARE or media under the warranties shall not extend the original warranty period. The limited warranty set forth above shall not apply to any SOFTWARE which the Company determines

in good faith has been subject to misuse, neglect, improper installation, repair, alteration, or damage by you. EXCEPT FOR THE EXPRESSED WARRANTIES SET FORTH ABOVE, THE COMPANY DISCLAIMS ALL WARRANTIES, EXPRESS OR IMPLIED, INCLUDING WITHOUT LIMITATION, THE IMPLIED WARRANTIES OF MERCHANTABILITY AND FITNESS FOR A PARTICULAR PURPOSE. EXCEPT FOR THE EXPRESS WARRANTY SET FORTH ABOVE, THE COMPANY DOES NOT WARRANT, GUARANTEE, OR MAKE ANY REPRESENTATION REGARDING THE USE OR THE RESULTS OF THE USE OF THE SOFTWARE IN TERMS OF ITS CORRECTNESS, ACCURACY, RELIABILITY, CURRENTNESS, OR OTHERWISE.

IN NO EVENT, SHALL THE COMPANY OR ITS EMPLOYEES, AGENTS, SUPPLIERS, OR CONTRACTORS BE LIABLE FOR ANY INCIDENTAL, INDIRECT, SPECIAL, OR CONSEQUENTIAL DAMAGES ARISING OUT OF OR IN CONNECTION WITH THE LICENSE GRANTED UNDER THIS AGREEMENT, OR FOR LOSS OF USE, LOSS OF DATA, LOSS OF INCOME OR PROFIT, OR OTHER LOSSES, SUSTAINED AS A RESULT OF INJURY TO ANY PERSON, OR LOSS OF OR DAMAGE TO PROPERTY, OR CLAIMS OF THIRD PARTIES, EVEN IF THE COMPANY OR AN AUTHORIZED REPRESENTATIVE OF THE COMPANY HAS BEEN ADVISED OF THE POSSIBILITY OF SUCH DAMAGES. IN NO EVENT SHALL LIABILITY OF THE COMPANY FOR DAMAGES WITH RESPECT TO THE SOFTWARE EXCEED THE AMOUNTS ACTUALLY PAID BY YOU, IF ANY, FOR THE SOFTWARE.

SOME JURISDICTIONS DO NOT ALLOW THE LIMITATION OF IMPLIED WARRANTIES OR LIABILITY FOR INCIDENTAL, INDIRECT, SPECIAL, OR CONSEQUENTIAL DAMAGES, SO THE ABOVE LIMITATIONS MAY NOT ALWAYS APPLY. THE WARRANTIES IN THIS AGREEMENT GIVE YOU SPECIFIC LEGAL RIGHTS AND YOU MAY ALSO HAVE OTHER RIGHTS WHICH VARY IN ACCORDANCE WITH LOCAL LAW.

ACKNOWLEDGMENT

YOU ACKNOWLEDGE THAT YOU HAVE READ THIS AGREEMENT, UNDERSTAND IT, AND AGREE TO BE BOUND BY ITS TERMS AND CONDITIONS. YOU ALSO AGREE THAT THIS AGREEMENT IS THE COMPLETE AND EXCLUSIVE STATEMENT OF THE AGREEMENT BETWEEN YOU AND THE COMPANY AND SUPERSEDES ALL PROPOSALS OR PRIOR AGREEMENTS, ORAL, OR WRITTEN, AND ANY OTHER COMMUNICATIONS BETWEEN YOU AND THE COMPANY OR ANY REPRESENTATIVE OF THE COMPANY RELATING TO THE SUBJECT MATTER OF THIS AGREEMENT.

Should you have any questions concerning this Agreement or if you wish to contact the Company for any reason, please contact in writing at the address below.

Robin Short
Pearson Education
One Lake Street
Upper Saddle River, New Jersey 07458